W9-DBO-057

Summary

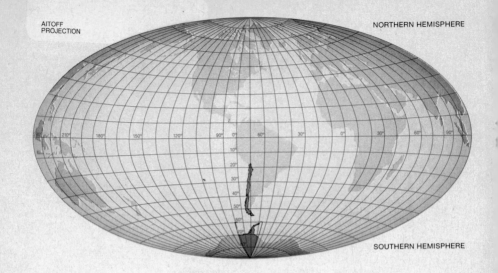

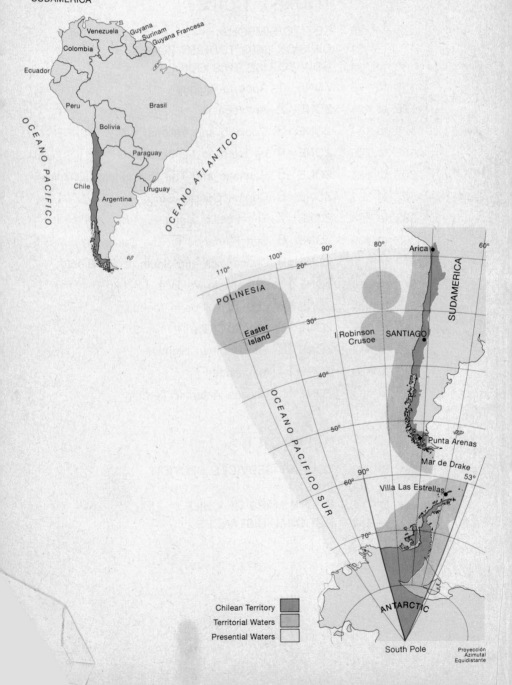

SUDAMERICA

Venezuela
Guyana
Surinam
Guyana Francesa
Colombia
Ecuador
Peru
Brasil
Bolivia
Paraguay
Chile
Uruguay
Argentina

OCEANO PACIFICO

OCEANO ATLANTICO

POLINESIA
Easter Island

Robinson Crusoe

SUDAMERICA
Arica
SANTIAGO

OCEANO PACIFICO SUR

Punta Arenas
Mar de Drake
53°
Villa Las Estrellas

ANTARCTIC

South Pole

Chilean Territory
Territorial Waters
Presential Waters

Proyección
Azimutal
Equidistante

INTRODUCTION

GEOGRAPHICAL FEATURES OF CHILE

POSITION AND AREA the territory of Chile is present in three continents: South America, Oceania and Antarctica, situated in the extreme south of the Southern Hemisphere surrounding a large portion of the South Pacific Ocean, and controlling the only oceanic passes joining the Atlantic and Pacific oceans: Straits of Magellan and Drake Passage.

In South America the contours of Chile form a large and narrow strip sited on the west coast of the South American cone. The average width of the country is 180 km (the same distance between Rome and Naples) and the total length is over 4,300 km. As regards meridians it is the longest country with a length equivalent to more than 1/10 of the Earth's perimeter, this being equal to the distance between Lisbon and Moscow, or between Singapore and Tokyo.
Area of Chilean territory within South America is 746,767 square kilometers, and is seventh in size of the Latin American countries; however, it is larger than any European country, with the exception of Rusia. Its area is similar to that of France, Belgium, Holland and Portugal added together, and double the area of Japan.
The most southern city in the world is located at the extreme south of the country, Puerto Williams, and 100 km further south the South American continent ends in Cape Horn. Chile is the country nearest to the Antarctic continent that is at 900 km distance.

In The Antartic the Chilean Antarctic territory is a triangle lying between meridians 53° W and 90° W, extending to the South Pole. This a natural elongation of the Chilean territory in South America.
It has a surface of 1,250,000 square kilometers, inhabited by 15 research bases, both Chilean and of other nations, in addition to the small settlement of Villa Las Estrellas for the civilian population.

In Oceanía Chile is present in the region with Easter Island, a small Polynesian island of volcanic origin that has an area of 180 square kilometers, comparable to the surface of Liechtenstein in Europe.
Placed in the center of the Pacific Ocean, this is the most isolated point on the globe, given that the nearest inhabited land is over 2,500 km distant. The people from Easter Island call it «Te Pito Te Henua», meaning the navel of world.

GEOGRAPHY practically 100% of the population of Chile lives in the South American continent and the most significant activities of the country are developed here. The geography of the country is intricate and of extraordinary variety. In the north the Atacama desert -the most arid in the world; to the west, lies the great Pacific Ocean; to the east the boundary is the Andes Mountain Range, with heights of up to 7,000 m above sea level, and to the south, the Drake Sea and Antarctica.
This unusual geographical isolation has given its people and history special characteristics, generating an interesting evolution of native flora and fauna, and liberating the country from the majority of plagues that affect agriculture and livestock in other regions of the world.
The surface of Chile has three clearly defined features: the Andean Mountains, the Coast Mountain Range and the depressions or valleys enclosed by these ranges.

The Andes Mountains this range runs from north to south over more than 4,000 km, ending in the south at Cape Horn where it disappears in the Drake Sea to reappear in the Chilean Antarctic region. The height of these mountains decreases towards the south, from above 6,000 m above sea level to 1,500 m in the Magellan Straits. The Andes command the Chilean scenery as the high snow caps are always visible in the background. The Andes Mountains were formed 80 million years ago, in a process where the sea bed was thrust up owing to the pressure caused by the Nazca block in the Pacific Ocean producing an elevation above the American continental plate. This elevation also generated a deep oceanic trench parallel to the

TOPOGRAPHY

Arica
Iquique
Calama
Antofagasta
Easter Island
Copiapó
La Serena
Valparaíso
SANTIAGO
Is R Crusoe
Talca
Concepción
Temuco
Valdivia
Osorno
Puerto Montt
Castro
Chaitén
Coihaique
Cochrane
Puerto Natales
Punta Arenas
Puerto Williams

19°
32°
43°
56°

CHILEAN ANTARCTIC TERRITORY
Is Diego Ramirez
90° — 60° — 53°

Andes Mountain Range
Longitudinal Valleys
Coastal Range

3

coastline of 200 km in length (Atacama rift of more than 7,000 m depth and Ojos del Salado volcano rift of 5,893 m).

The Andes presents diverse features throughout its length.

In the North it is high with a plateau called «Altiplano» 3,500 m high.

A series of active and extinct volcanoes rise over the flat land reaching over 6,000 m. The Altiplano generated human population of the Aymara natives that lived in the rich oases of the high plateau, feeding their herds of Llamas and Alpacas (South American cameloids) with the rough grass of the pastures.

In the Central Region opposite Santiago, the mountains reach 5,000 m height with the heaviest snowfall in winter. The major ski centers are situated in this region, and in summer mountain climbing and trekking activities are practiced here as the area has the best access from populated centers.

In the Southern Central Region between Temuco and Puerto Montt, extreme changes in temperature occurred over 10,000 years ago making the glaciers existing in the the the Andes disappear, generating a chain of lakes at the foot of the snow capped mountains that reach a height of 2,600 m approximately.

In Patagonia to the south of Puerto Montt, the effect of the ocean, the glaciers and large expanses of ice still in movement dismembered the Andean Range into numerous islands that form the West Patagonia Archipelago. The high peaks of ice average close to 2,000 m height. At lower altitudes wet forestland is found and glaciers fall directly in the sea.

The Coast Mountain Range is an uninterrupted chain of 3,000 km in length. Lying close to the ocean coastline, with heights of under 2,000 m, sufficiently compact and elevated to prevent the action of ocean winds affecting the lands beyond.The origin of this range is prior to the formation of the Andes, hilltops are rounded, eroded by time, of a light brown soil indicated the predominating presence of clay. To the north the range is desertic and on slopes facing the coast over 120 varieties of native Chilean cactii grow. In the center and up to Puerto Montt the mountains are covered with plantations of forest species, the basis of the country's cellulose industry.

Longitudinal Depressions are the extense flatlands found between both mountain ranges. To the north the Atacama desert and the Tamarugal Pampa, both desertlands. In the center and southern central regions the fertile agricultural valleys appear. In Patagonia this depression emerges to the east of the Andes mountains forming steppes where cattle can graze. In general terms, the greatest part of the country's population inhabits these valleys.

The Volcanoes a distinctive surface element with over 600 volcanoes throughout the Andes Mountains, 47 of which are considered active, representing nearly 10% of all the active volcanoes on the planet. 80% of Chile is mountain land and the major part are of volcanic origin. Volcanoes rise over the entire length of the territory, continuing in the Antarctic Region. Easter Island is also of volcanic origin. Many of them have extraordinarily beautiful outlines crowned with perfect cones.

In the northern desertland, the impressive Licancabur 5,930 m high guards over the San Pedro oasis and the vast Atacama salt lake; close by is Llullaillaco volcano of 6,723 m height, sanctuary and ritual site of the Atacama culture. This sequence culminates with the Copiapó volcano and its neighbour Ojos del Salado of 6,893 m, the highest active volcano in the world.

In the south and Patagonia the perfect silhouettes of volcanoes covered in snow, reflect their shapes in lakes and in the sea; their outstanding beauty attracts thousands of tourists every year.

WEATHER CONDITIONS the enormous variety of climates in the country is due mainly to four factors that are: the latitude, the action of the sea, the surface contours and the east winds.

Latitude in the South American continent Chile is situated between parallel 18° S and 56° S. This practically straight expanse along 38° latitude is equivalent in the northern hemisphere to the latitude crossing from Senegal in Africa to Denmark in Europe; and on the coast of Asia, to latitudes between Vietnam and the end of the Kamchatka peninsula.

In Chile temperatures descend gradually towards the south, but climate is neither as warm nor as cold as in countries indicated as comparisons in the northern hemisphere. This is due to the

CLIMATIC INFLUENCES

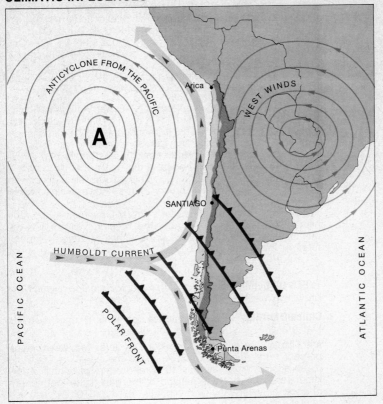

moderating effect of the Pacific ocean bordering the entire western coast.

Effect of the sea there are three actions caused by the ocean, that modify the climate generally:

Pacific Ocean Anticyclone is an atmospheric high pressure area located in the ocean facing the north and the center of Chile. Its winds rotate anticlockwise and are warm and dry. They are the reason why there is no rainfall in the north of the country, producing stable weather, desertic or semi-arid conditions. The anticyclone or high pressure center moves to the south in the summer spreading its influence to the area of the city of Concepción; in winter this center moves north, level with the city of La Serena. This displacement allows other oceanic winds to act.

Polar Front is a mass of cold air issuing from the South Pole, that comes into contact with the warm air over the ocean, causing rainfall on the continent. Its advance is slowed down by the Anticyclone: in summer the Polar Front enters from Concepción to the south, and in winter, this front rises to La Serena in the north, causing rain in winter and dry weather in summer in this region.

Humboldt Current an oceanic current originated by cold waters emerging from the sea bed (12° C to 15° C) and extending across 100 km, running along the length of the coast northwards. This has an influence on the general climate that makes temperatures drop, especially on the coast, where morning fog is produced, called «camanchaca». Arica in Chile and Río de Janeiro in Brazil are close to the same parallel; Río has a tropical climate, due to the Humboldt Current.

Surface the presence of mountains all the length of Chile is another factor controlling the climate. The **Coast Mountain Range** prevents the marine damp air to enter the inland valleys, where the temperature during the day is higher than on the coast, and also colder at night.

The **Andes Mountains** of great height, are a barrier for bad weather fronts that come from the Pacific Ocean, making them lose all the humidity, and is deposited in the form of snow on the mountains instead.

As a consequence of this surface, Chile has climates of drastic contrasts across its width -from the sea to the Andes- and slight changes throughout its length, where the weather differs at approximately every 1,000 km. In fact, between Arica on the

TYPES OF CLIMATE

coast (18° C annual mean temperature and 0 mm rainfall) and Visviri in the Andes (2° C annual mean temperature and 285 mm rainfall) there is a violent contrast in climate in only 140 km distance; and between Arica and Caldera at 1,000 km to the south, the annual mean temperature drops only by 2° C and rainfall increases to 27 mm. Another example of the contrast of sea and mountains is that opposite Santiago, it is possible to ski in the Andes and to travel 160 km to the coast and bathe in the sea on the same day in Springtime.

East Winds in the central region of South America, Chaco, when the sun is over the Tropic of Capricorn in December, the highest degree of radiation is reached with the consequent evaporation of humidity that on condensating at a certain height, falls as rain. The winds from the east impel part of this humid mass against the Andes in the north of Chile, where it precipitates as snow and rain. This occurs in the summer months of January and February and is known as the **Altiplano Winter**.

This water and snow gives life to the small oases in the foot-hills of the northern Andes, but the water never reaches the ocean because of the porous volcanic soil and high temperatures in the desert.

TYPES OF CLIMATE according to meteorological definitions, the prevailing weather conditions in Chile are the following:

Chilean territory in South America presents 3 main climates that are arid, temperate and cold weather.

Arid Climate there are two versions of this, the **desertic** type present from Arica to La Serena. On the coast of Arica the mean annual temperature is 18° C and 0 mm of rainfall. A few kilometers inland, in the flatland of the desert the thermal difference between day and night is 35° and 0° C, with extremely dry air; This produces rock bursts and in the vast salt lakes the creaking sounds of salt crystals can be heard at night.

From La Serena to the north of Santiago, the arid climate is similar to **warm steppes**, with a slight decrease of temperature and occasional winter rains that allow the existence of vegetation consisting mainly of low bushes.

Temperate Climate all the remaining territory, excepting the Patagonia and high Andes, is catalogued as temperate climate in all its various forms.

From Santiago to Concepción **mediterranean climate** prevails, with a dry summer season, rainfall ranging from 340 mm and 1,200 mm, and mean average temperatures between 14° C and 15° C. This type of climate exists only in four points of the world: Mediterranean coast; California coast; Cape of Good Hope and the South East coast of Australia. The largest crops of fruit and vineyards of Chile are cultivated in this region and the four most populated cities are also located here.

To the south of the city of Concepción, temperatures decrease gradually and the rainfall increases exceeding 2,500 mm. This is **rainy temperate** climate and continues on to Puerto Montt. Further south, to parallel 47° S, the climate is **maritime temperate**, with more abundant rains and moderate temperatures because of the marine influence; high volcanoes close to the coast are covered with eternal snow. San Valentín glacier is in this region from which portions of ice fall into the sea; it is nearest to the equator.

To the south of parallel 47° S the ocean border is covered with wet forestland and has a **temperate cold** climate, with rainfall of between 4,000 and 7,000 mm. The sea is cold due to the great number of icebergs present.

Cold Climate only two variations of this climate are experienced in Chile. **Steppe** type cold climate in prairies east of the Patagonian Andes, in Coyhaique and Punta Arenas. Mean temperature in winter can drop to 2.5° C below, but rise in summer to 11° and 12° C. Rainfall does not exceed 350 mm, given that the humidity carried by the Polar Fronts, precipitates before, in the Andes mountains, in the form of snow.

The high peaks of the Andes have a cold climate of the **icy altitude** type, with abundant snow and very low temperatures. This harsh weather improves in summer, to the extent of keeping the level of eternal snow only.

The Antarctic Region of Chile has cold **polar** type climate, with temperatures below zero all year. In the Bernardo O'Higgins

Base the mean annual temperature is 3.6° C below zero; in the warmest month -January- the average only reaches 1.4° C. Rains are very scarce but abundant snow falls.

The Oceanic Region of Chile
the two most important islands are the Pacific Ocean are Easter Island and Robinson Crusoe Island.

Easter Island has a warm subtropical type of climate with rains all year (1,149 mm) but more frequently during the months of June to August. The temperature is even during all the year with an average of 20.4° C.

Robinson Crusoe Island forms part of the small archipelago of Juan Fernández. Temperate mediterranean type climate, with rains distributed throughout the year (922 mm), but heavier in winter. The annual mean temperature is 14° C. This has made it possible for a moist forest to exist, with a large number of species.

POPULATION
the population of Chile according to the census taken in 1982 is 11,329,737 inhabitants, with a growth of 2%. Estimates show that by 1990 the population was over 13 million people.
Undoubtedly this is a reduced population in a vast territory; compared to Japan, South American Chile has double the area and a population ten times lower.

The population is not distributed evenly. Nearly 50% of the population of the country lives in the region of Santiago and Valparaíso and in an area equivalent to one third of the territory, with a density of 254 inhabitants per square km. Regions in the extreme north and south of Chile are practically uninhabited: in the desertland of the north, from Arica to Copiapó, 7% of the population of Chile lives with a density of 3.2% inhabitants per square km. In the extreme south, Aisén to Magallanes, 1.8% of the population lives with a density of under 1 inhabitant per square km.
Easter Island has 2,000 inhabitants in an area of 180 square km, with a density of 11 inhabitants per square km.

THE PEOPLE
there is much less racial diversity in Chile than in most of the countries of Latin America. The people are essentially homogeneous, the result of the mixing of Spanish and Indian blood during over four centuries of history, that has practically finished the original native population.

Certain ethnic minorities exist concentrated in small areas of the territory, such as the **Aymaras** in the Altiplano in the north of Chile, the Easter Islanders (2,000 inhabitants) of **Polynesian** origins and, the most important, the **Mapuche** indians (approximately 300,000 inhabitants) concentrated around Temuco, between Bíobío and Toltén rivers.
Between 1850 and 1890 the country received an immigration from Europe that did not exceed 32,000 people, a figure very much lower than the millions of immigrants received by Argentina, Uruguay and Brazil during the same period. Of those arriving at that time, 28% were of Spanish origins, 22% were Italian, 13% were German, 9% from Switzerland and 6% British. They settled mainly in the south, between Temuco and Puerto Montt, occupying the uninhabited forests and also land that was owned before by the Mapuche tribes.
The influence of this immigration, specially from Germany, is not in proportion to the reduced number of immigrants. Their hardworking people that farmed virgin land has given a characteristic seal to the rural and urban scenery of the south of Chile, between Valdivia and Puerto Montt.

Between 1890 and the beginning of World War One, Chile received a new immigrant contingent, from Serbia and Croatia who arrived in Tierra del Fuego seeking gold, and also British people who came out to the new sheep farms in Magallanes. Immigrants from Palestine, Syria and Lebanon also arrived and settled in various points of Chile.

During the Second World War, Chile opened its frontiers to a new immigration, principally to people affected by the war, such as Republicans from Spain and others from Central Europe.
In general, immigration has not been significant from an ethnic point of view, given that foreigners never reached a total of more than 4% of the entire population of the country.

POPULATION DISTRIBUTION

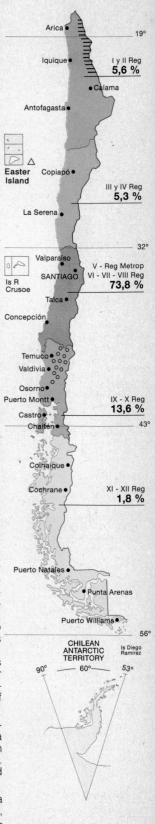

I y II Reg **5,6 %**

III y IV Reg **5,3 %**

V - Reg Metrop
VI - VII - VIII Reg **73,8 %**

IX - X Reg **13,6 %**

XI - XII Reg **1,8 %**

CHILEAN ANTARCTIC TERRITORY

≡ Aymaras
△ Easter Islanders
°o°o° Mapuches

POPULATION DENSITY

Arica •
19°

Iquique •

• Calama

Antofagasta •

Is de Pascua

Copiapó •

La Serena •

Valparaíso
32°

Is R Crusoe

SANTIAGO

Talca •

Concepción •

Temuco •
Valdivia •

Osorno •
Puerto Montt •

Castro •
Chaitén •
43°

Coihaique •

Cochrane •

Puerto Natales •

• Punta Arenas

Puerto Williams •
56°

TERRITORIO CHILENO ANTARTICO

Is Diego Ramirez

90°   60°   53°

less than 1 inhab/km²
less than 5 inhab/km²
less than 10 inhab/km²
less than 20 inhab/km²
less than 30 inhab/km²
less than 40 inhab/km²
less than 250 inhab/km²

Even though ethnically speaking the Chilean people are of mixed ancestry, in cultural aspects a strong Spanish-European culture is predominant, mainly Catholic and Rationalist. For this reason Chile, together with Argentina and Uruguay, is one of the most European minded countries in South America.

This is because the native population did not have a strong enough culture to counteract the cultural and religious influence of Spain. In addition there was no slavist current towards the country that could have contributed a black cultural bias issuing from Africa, as happened in other American countries.

The Chilean people are at present one of the most literate of the world, 98% of the population reads and writes. Also the life span expectancy is estimated at 70 years of age.

One of the most particular characteristics of the Chilean population is their high degree of urbanization. 81% of the population lives in towns and cities provided with public utility services, and thus Chile is considered as the most urbanized country of Latin American.

From a point of view of social composition, Chile has a very important middle class population, since the second half of the 20th Century. Also there is a large proportion of the population catalogued in the poverty group. However, Chile is not socially polarized as the differences between rich and poor are not abysmal, and the task of reverting this process in the short and medium term is a first priority subject of the current government, supported by all strains of political forces.

BASIC STRUCTURE   in spite of its difficult topography, Chile has complete subordinate services and facilities.

Roads   the country is linked from north to south by a spinal column of over 4,500 km in length from which transversal roads lead to the Andes Mountains and to the coast. This spine is named the **Panamerican Highway** with an extension of 3,078 km from the border with Perú in the north to Puerto Montt in the south. The **Austral Highway** continues southwards for over 1,000 km and ends in the impassable fields of Southern Ice, located between parallel 48o S and 51o S. Another main highway of 600 km joins Torres del Paine to Punta Arenas and Tierra del Fuego Island.

The crossing of the South Ice Fields, or to reach the extreme of Chile in Puerto Williams, can be done by ship navigating on the channels or by land circulating on roads in Argentina.

The road network in Chile consists of 80,000 km of roads, of which 10,500 km are first class paved roads. In addition, there are 32,000 km of unpaved secondary roads. The latter are mainly used in the summer months.

Railways   although Chile built the first railway of South America in 1848, and the country had a vast railway service owned by the State, a great part of it has been discontinued and what is left is destined mainly to the transport of cargo.

The most important passenger trains run from Santiago to Puerto Montt and intermediate cities. The railway going from Arica to Tacna in Perú and from Arica to La Paz in Bolivia also carries passengers.

Air Transport   because of the enormous distances separating Chile from the principal cities of the world and also due to the long internal distances, air transport has great importance. There are 5 airports of international dimensions and a network of air terminals in the main cities.

International Flights   the principal international airlines fly to Chile, besides the 2 national airlines. Over 850,000 passengers are transported a year, of which 300,000 travel on the Chilean airlines.

Domestic Flights   transport 700,000 passengers a year. Two principal airlines in addition to 5 other smaller lines that operate principally in Patagonia.

Surface Transport   is the most used means in the country and is served by more than 30 companies that provide modern buses. Daily service from Santiago to Arica in the north and to Punta Arenas in the south, stopping also in cities on the way. From each city buses depart daily to neighbouring rural towns, both to the Andes and to the coast.

Communications   a modern microwave network connects the country from Arica to Puerto Montt. Patagonia, Easter Island and the Antarctic are reached by satellite. Communications by

telephone, telex and fax are available in all the Chilean territory, with direct dialing and automatic systems for local and international calls.
From La Serena to Puerto Montt a cellular telephone system exists that allows communications from the most remote points with the rest of the country and from overseas.

Health there is a public health system attended by the State and private enterprises. There are a number of hospitals, clinics, first aid centers and medical consulting and outpatient services throughout the length of Chile, in due proportion to the population in need of medical attention.
There are fourteen medical areas, each one with one or more hospitals providing full attention. In addition there is a hospital in each important city. Even in the smallest villages a first aid center exists.
If the traveler goes on adventure tourism in remote points, there will be a hospital located at not more than 3 or 4 hours by car, at the most.

ECONOMY
during the decade of 1980 only 5 countries in Latin America showed economical growth. One of these was Chile. This is one of the reasons why it is considered as the most stable nation in South America and the most secure regarding investments, by the World Bank and the International Monetary Fund.

Economic growth in Chile was actually consolidated in the second half of the past decade after overcoming the world recession, not without difficulties, that occurred at the beginnig of the 1980's. From 1984 to 1988 the mean rate of growth in economy was situated at 5,5% per year, a level reached by developed countries. After a short period of adjustment, in 1991 the growth rate borders close to 6%.

Economic growth in Chile is based on ordered public finance, in the internal aspects, with a practically non-existent deficit and low inflation rates for Latin American standards, of 18% in 1991.
In the external aspects, economy has been stressed mainly on a strong impulse of exports. In 1970 Chile exported 7 relevant products, among these copper and alloys that represented 80% of total exports. In 1990, twenty years later, Chile was exporting 17 significant products, the more important being minerals, fresh fruit, fish-meal, cellulose, paper and wood, also copper and alloys.
The latter product represents 59% of current exports.
An aggressive policy has also been present in diversifying markets.
In 1970, 83.3% of exports went to Europe, U.S.A. and Japan. In 1990, 66.6% of exports were shipped to the mentioned markets and the rest to Brazil, Argentina, Taiwan, South Korea, China, Turkey, Arab Emirates and others.

A dynamic element in the economy has been the opening granted to foreign capital, that has found great advantages for investment in Chile. In the 1984-1989 period the country received an average of 1,000 million dollars as an annual average in foreign investment.

The present challenge of the Chilean economy is to ensure its stable growth and, at the same time, to redistribute the income this development generates in the social system.

Fruits and Vegetables fruit is the third item in importance exported from Chile and, however, probably the most acknowledged in the northern hemisphere.
Products are mainly grapes, apples, kiwis, plums, apricots, cherries, raspberries, strawberries, avocados, etc.; and among the vegetable exports the most important is asparragus.
Chile is the first fruit producer in the southern hemisphere, exporting over 120 million cases annually, that is equivalent to 5,600 million rations for human consumption... enough for one fruit for each inhabitant of the planet.

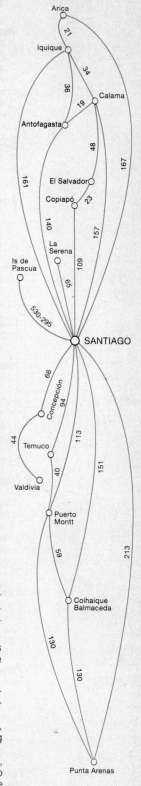

Arica
21
Iquique
34
36
19
Calama
Antofagasta
48
167
161
El Salvador
Copiapó 23
140
157
La Serena
Is de Pascua
601
65
530-295
SANTIAGO
66
Concepción 94
44
113
Temuco
40
151
Valdivia
Puerto Montt
59
213
Coihaique Balmaceda
130
130
Punta Arenas

Prices (US Dollars), January 1992

9

A FEW HISTORICAL FACTS

PRIMITIVE INHABITANTS the most acceptable hypothesis regarding the inhabitants of the American continent is the one supposing a migratory current originating from central Asia that crossed over to this continent by the Bering Strait, populating North and South America in a progressive advance towards the south, reaching Cape Horn finally. 13 thousand years ago the first man stepped on Chilean soil according to this theory.

People inhabiting Chile when the Spaniards arrived were the following from north to south:

Aymara shepherds and farmers occupying the Altiplano (see Zone I). Related to ethnic groups that developed the Tiwanaku empire in the valleys of the Titicaca lake in Bolivia, reaching maximum evolution towards 1300 A.D.

Atacameños and other settlers of the valleys, or from Arica to San Pedro de Atacama. They developed an autonomous system of seignory rule in valleys and oases, with defense fortresses called «Pukara». The cultural peak was reached between 1100 and 1470 A.D. at the time the Incas invaded the region.

Changos nomad fishermen that navigated the desertic coastline from Arica to Copiapó. Their vessels were made of inflated sea lion skins, and they traded dried fish for grain with the inhabitants of inland valleys.

Diaguitas farmers that inhabited the valleys from Copiapó to the north of Santiago (see Zones 3 and 4). They achieved a refined artistic expression in earthenware towards 1300 A.D.

Incas the Inca empire in Perú initiates the conquest of Chile in 1470, that extended to the south to the Maule river (see Zones 1, 2, 3, 4, 5, 6 and 8), occupying the territory of the Aymara, Atacameño, Diaguita and Picunche people. They built the **Inca Trail** that crossed the territory and established their «**Mitimaes**» (agricultural/military colonies) in all the populated centers. These Mitimaes were integrated by Peruvian people that were transplanted, who taught the native people new techniques in cultivation and irrigation, besides the new styles of ceramic articles.

Mapuches farmers recently become sedentary who on the arrival of the Spaniards did not present formed settlements, or villages. They constituted an ethnic and linguistic unit extending over 1,400 km, from the Choapa river in the north, to the Chiloé island in the south (see Zones 5, 8, 9, 10, 11 and 12). The northern group called themselves **Picunches**; the population inhabiting the region of Biobío and Toltén rivers were called **Mapuches** (people of the earth), and **Huilliches** were those living further south. The Mapuches were a warrior group that made Chile the most difficult country to conquer in America.

Canoeros nomad fishermen and collectors that navigated around the archipelago of West Patagonia in their canoes. Three linguistic groups are identified as: **Chonos**, who lived near Aisén (see Zone 13); **Qawasqar** who inhabited the region between Penas Gulf and the Straits of Magellan; and **Yamanas** who lived in land surrounding the Beagle Channel and Cape Horn (see Zone 14).

Patagones hunters and nomad collectors that covered the steppe flatlands to the east of the Andes, following the migration of fauna on pastures in summer and winter. They were very tall and due to the size of their footprints the name of Patagonia was given to this region (Pata meaning foot) (see Zone 14).

Two groups are identified, the **Aonikenk** who moved from the north to the Straits of Magellan and the **Selkman** who inhabited Tierra del Fuego (Land of Fire).

Polynesian radicated in Easter Island. When the island was declared Chilean territory in 1888, the population had been practically destroyed by disease and slavist incursions of previous travelers. Only 111 islanders survived.

There are very few facts regarding the density of this population when the Spaniards arrived. In the area of Santiago (Zones 5, 6 and 8), the first estimate practiced in 1543 states 25,000 inhabitants. In 1609 the Jesuit missionaries counted between 10,000 and 12,000 natives in the Chiloé island (Zone 12).

The highest population concentration was radicated in the Mapuche-Huilliche territory (Zones 9, 10 and 11). A realistic estimate of the total native population of Chile at the beginning of the Sixteenth Century states between 200,000 and 300,000 inhabitants.

Of the original population, in present days the Aymara population is still present as an ethnic minority, the Mapuche that are the most numerous, and those of Polynesian origin from Easter Island, that together are under 300,000 inhabitants.
The reason explaining the disappearance of the other ethnic groups and decrease of those existing today, is due mainly to three factors:
Diseases, measles, smallpox and typhoid introduced by conquerors decimated native populations in the Sixteenth and Seventeenth Centuries.
There were five massive epidemics that ended the lives of nearly all the original population.

Cross blood the fusion of Spanish and native races was a natural process that occurred during the period of the Conquest and Colony.
Spanish soldiers and settlers mated with native women, and the natives (Mapuches) considered the kidnapping of women of Spanish origin to be the greatest booty of their warrior actions. Pure races disappeared giving origin to a new people: the Chileans.

Migrations brutal working conditions in mines imposed by the Spanish conquerors, not only exterminated the native population but was the incentive for migrating to territory that was still free. In the Seventeenth Century the Aymara population emigrated from Bolivia and settled in the Chilean Altiplano to avoid working in the silver mines of Potosí. Towards the end of the Eighteenth Century and beginning of the Nineteenth Century, an important percentage of the Mapuche population emigrated to the pampas in Argentina to control the lucrative trading of wild cattle practiced in that region. In the last decades of the past century and beginning of this era, two groups of natives were extinguished that were absorbed by new industrial towns: Changos in the nitrate ports in the north and Qawasqar from Magallanes.

SPANISH CONQUEST 1536 - 1599 on October 21st. of 1520, 28 years after Columbus discovered America, Hernando de Magallanes, the navigator who tirelessly sought for a pass joining the Atlantic and Pacific oceans, discovers the Strait named after him and steps on Chilean soil for the first time.

In 1536 the conqueror Diego de Almagro and an army of Spaniards and natives to the south with the purpose of conquering Chile. He reaches the valley of Santiago, but is discouraged by the difficulties of traveling and absence of gold, returning to Perú. Six years later Pedro de Valdivia starts off from Perú to definitely conquer Chile. He is the founder of the city of Santiago in 1542, distributes land to his army, he divides the native population ordering them to work the land and mines of the conquerors. During the first 10 years his efforts are focused on bringing new settlers from Spain and Perú and consolidating the conquest of a territory of 1,100 km long, between La Serena in the north, founded in 1544, and Concepción in the south founded in 1550.

The following 50 years mark the greatest effort at expansion and conquest.
The Spaniards advance from Concepción to the south reaching Chiloé island.
This was the heart of Mapuche-Huilliche territory, with the greatest density of native population and lands and climate adequate for farming without requiring irrigation. Eight villages were founded and the larger part of the Spanish population settled in these lands.

The Mapuche people developed progressive belligerent attitudes, learning warrior strategies from the Spaniards and adopted the use of horses which they rode with great skill. In successive encounters they defeated the Spaniards.
Pedro de Valdivia died in 1553 in the battle of Tucapel. Finally the Mapuche rebellion of 1599 destroys all the Spanish forts south of Concepción and they expel the conquerors from this region. Said territory is reincorporated to Chile nearly three centuries later.

COLONIAL PERIOD 1600 - 1809 the Mapuche rebellion of 1599 marks the end of the Spanish conqueror period. Territory actually conquered is from Copiapó in the north to Concepción and the southshore of the Biobío river.
Further south, Chiloé island with its village called Castro founded in

1567, was kept as an isolated colony during the entire colonial period.

All the Spanish population expelled from the south by the Mapuche rebellion settles later from La Serena to Concepción. Farming and mining work is intensified in the region with exports of gold, tallow, leather and wheat. During the Seventeenth Century and up to the middle of the Eighteenth Century, the only urban centers existing in Chile were Santiago, the capital city and seat of the Government; La Serena and Concepción that were frontier cities.

The growing population of Spaniards born on American land and those of mixed ancestry (the major population), did not live in cities but instead close to the Haciendas where they worked.

From the middle of the Eighteenth Century and given the great increase of creole and mixed ancestry population growing apart from Spanish culture and religion, the Crown of Spain sponsored a policy for its American colonies consisting of the building of roads joining up the rural lands and also the creation of new villages with parishes and adjoining schools. In this period the founding of new cities flourishes in Chile and the present cities of Copiapó, Vallenar, Melipilla, Rancagua, San Fernando, Curicó, Talca and Linares were established among others.

Farmers and artisans were obliged to move to these new towns. Chile was a poor colony that always required contributions from the Spanish Crown to cover its main public expenses, the frontier army, and necessary reconstructions following frequent earthquakes.

From the middle to the end of the Eighteenth Century and coinciding with a certain prosperity of the country as a result of successful exports of wheat to Perú, the main public and religious buildings of Santiago were constructed, that survive to this day: The Government Palace, Royal Audience House, Casa Colorada, Merced and Santo Domingo churches, and the facade and towers of the Cathedral.

Arauco War is a singular confrontation in the history of America. The Spaniards called the Mapuches «Araucanos», a name that became popular after the publication of the poem **«La Araucana»**, the most famous epic poem of the Spanish language in the Sixteenth Century, written by Alonso de Ercilla, poet and soldier who participated in the conquest of Chile and where he relates the epic war against the Mapuches.

During two centuries of the colonial period the frontier was established on the shores of the Biobío river and a permanent professional army was based there, unique case in America; from where with various types of fortresses they defended themselves from warrior attacks from the Mapuches. This menace of war generated a constant lack of stability during the colonial period and the emerging Chilean nation was impoverished with the military efforts demanded. However the tough war was not permanent but only sporadic and with unexpected attacks. During the periods of peace trade was activated, the civilian aspects, the missionary efforts and cultural contacts were intensified. The frontier military forces continued active after the Independence of Chile was declared in 1882 when the Mapuche territory was finally occupied.

INDEPENDENCE 1810-1823 the first years of the Nineteenth century no signs were present to predict the prompt independence of Spanish colonies because of the empire's stern controlling unity and the loyalty of American local population to the King of Spain, however, certain anarchist examples impressed the educated younger groups in America: the French Revolution and the Declaration of Independence of United States.

In 1810 King Ferdinand VII was overtrown and Napoleon's troops occupied Spain. In Santiago a **Government Junta** was established to direct the Colony in the King's name. This was considered insubordination by the Viceroy of Perú, who was the hierarchical superior at the time, and who sen his troops to suffocate this conspiratory act in 1814. The young local people had organized and commanded the army and emigrated to Mendoza in Argentina, in order to prepare the resistance forces, with the support of this neighbouring nation that had already declared their independence from Spain.

In 1817, an army formed by Chileans and Argentines, commanded by General José de San Martín, crossed the border to Chile through seven different passes of the Andes Mountains with the purpose of confusing the King's troops. They defeated these troops in successive battles and **National Independence** was procalimed on September 18 th. of 1818.

Bernardo O'Higgins was then designated Supreme Director of the new nation. He was of mixed ancestry, had commanded the national army until 1814, later emigrated to Argentina and organized the Liberating Army with San Martín, fighting in the principal battles. His father, Ambrosio O'Higgins, an Irishman at the service of the Spanish Crown was Governor of Chile and later Viceroy of Perú. The Independence process continued in 1820 with the establishment of the navy and army that embarked towards Perú to contribute to their liberation. But it was only in 1826 that Chiloé Island was conquered. In the fort at Ancud in Chiloé the last Spanish flag to wave in South America was finally lowered.

CONSOLIDATION OF THE REPUBLIC 1823-1861 following a period of eight years of anarchy (1823-1831), with a series of governments and tentative constitutional efforts pertinent to a nation emerging to a life of independence and no prior political experience, a republican regime was first consolidated as undivided, presidential and authoritarian, that governed Chile during 30 years.

The period described was responsible for the political order that eliminated tyranny and despotism in the provinces and for creating a strong national unity. In economic aspects, ports were opened to international trade and foreign corporations were allowed to invest, principally English, German and French concerns that managed the import commercial affairs in the country.

In this period the silver mine in Chañarcillo was discovered (1832) that was the third largest silver mine in America and represented a fortune for Copiapó and the country's revenue. In the northern regions copper mines and foundries were operated transforming Chile in the principal exporte of copper of the world. In 1851 the railway joining Copiapó and Caldera was inaugurated, the first to be built in South America.

Regarding educational matters the University of Chile and the National School for Teachers were founded (1842), with the collaboration of a staff of European professors. In territorial aspects Bulnes Fort was established in the Straits of Magellan (1843), which later would be the city of Punta Arenas. In 1851 the city of Puerto Montt is founded and German immigration is promoted in the southern region between Valdivia and Puerto Montt.

LIBERAL REPUBLIC 1861-1891 during the second half of the century Chile achieves extraordinary prosperity situating the nation among the first in Latin America. This wealth was essentially from minerals mined in the northern desert in points such as Tamaya copper mine, Caracoles silver mine and also the recently discovered nitrate deposits. Significant economic interests at stake in the desert region began to generate a dangerous competition with neighbouring countries such as Perú and Bolivia, that eventually was the cause of the Pacific War (1879-1881). Chile arose from this conflict as the military power of South America, wealthy due to the possession of monopoly of nitrate, dominion of the Atacama desert and Tamarugal pampas with a new dominant social class enriched by working in mining, trade and banking concerns.

At this time the railway was built in the center and north of the country; also telegraph network, State schools in the principal cities and transformation of agricultural work in the central valley of Chile took place with the construction of irrigation canals. Large vineyards were planted that have given fame to Chilean wines.
In territorial aspects, the Mapuche territory lying to the south of BíoBío river was definitely occupied and part of these lands was handed over to a new immigration of European origin. In 1888 Easter Island was incorporated to the nation.

The new dominant social class acquired capitalist and liberal features. Their interests gradually clashed with the State's strong and presidentialist policies. They proposed greater power for parliament (executive power) that would allow them to impose their intentions of greater economic freedom. This feud culminated in the Revolution of 1891, a civil war in which President Balmaceda was overtrown.

PARLIAMENTARISM AND SOCIAL PROBLEMS 1891-1932 after the civil war of short duration was over a parliamentary regime was established where in the President was practically a decorative figure, contrary to Latin American political traditions. The dominant class conquered the entire political power and soon this caused a serious social, political and economic crisis in the country.

In the first years of the Twentieth century the situation of working classes, specially in mining works, became untenable due to very deteriorated living conditions. Violent battles broke out in 1905 and 1907 and as a consequence the first laws ruling social matters were passed, and in 1909 the first trade union was formed.
The governing class was outnumbered by a new and massive middle class that presented proposals for resolving prevailing social and political problems. With a greater understanding of requirements and ambitions of the working classes both opposing parties achieved an agreement regarding a common program that lead Arturo Alessandri Palma to the presidency (1920-1924).
Finally, in 1925 a new constitution was approved that abolished parliamentarism and strengthened the President's powers.

Nitrate was the first export product of Chile and also the main source of income for the State. In 1917, 3 million tons were exported, equivalent to 65% of nitrogenous fertilizers consumed in the world.
During the First World War (1914-1918), synthetic ammonium sulphate was invented in Germany, and this gradually displaced the use of nitrate, producing a crises in the industry and State revenue. The world crisis of 1929 added to this bringing the country to bankruptcy.

Between 1924 and 1932 a period of political turbulence was experienced with active participation of the new social entities: middle classes and worling classes.
In 1932 Chile returned to constitutional rule of law and Arturo Alessandri was re-elected as President of the Republic.

CONTEMPORARY HISTORICAL FACTS from 1938 onwards the country was governed by Presidents elected by political alliances of which center faction parties were the great participants and the left-wing parties acquired increasing power and relevance. The concept of the State as benefactor in social matters and in favour of development in economic affairs was established.
In social matters the people's needs were given greater attention through wide span policies; trade unions for workers and farmers were promoted, compulsory welfare systems were projected more accurately, health and pension schemes designed, and the State assumes the responsibility of free education. Budgets for State education and health received strong increment, and the construction of State hospitals throughout the country was initiated in addition to new educational buildings for all levels covering grade school to University studies.

In economic affairs the State becomes an enterprising entity, producer and promotional agent. The construction of the Panamerican highway that is the spinal column of rural roads is undertaken; ports and airports with mechanical facilities are built and a significant irrigation plan and hydraulic works in semi-desertic regions of the north is designed.
In urban aspects a plan for supplying drinking water to all villages and small towns is initiated, including sewer systems for larger towns and cities.

The State creates CORFO, an agency in charge of industrial development and promotion. With fiscal funds hydroelectric plants are built and electric power lines are extended to all the country; a basic steel mill for heavy industry, plants for extraction and refining of petroleum, microwave communications network are installed, among other services. All these works open the road to the modern industrialized basic facilities of the country.

During the decades of 1950 and 1960, world policy is essentially opposed to conflictive political issues: creation of NATO, Korean War, Warsaw Pact, Berlin Wall, Vietnam War, Cultural Revolution in China, etc. In Chile, as from 1964 on, political conclusive projects are also put in practice, such as global planning with the intention of remodelling society on an integral basis. These proposals were discriminating and confrontational and were fed by excessive idealization of society. The lack of compliance with expectations engendered, destruction of industrial and agricultural productive basic structures and bankruptcy of the State impelled the downfall of President Salvador Allende in 1973 and assumption of power by the Armed Forces headed by General Augusto Pinochet.

Pinochet ruled the contry for 16 years, thus becoming the governing power of longest duration in Chilean history. This was also the most prolongued period of a government not generated by popular election, as in its 170 years of independent life as a nation, Chile has had a long democratic tradition interrupted only by three dictaroship rules, that added total 10 years.

The economic pattern proposed by Pinochet's government consisted in making public finance healthy, eliminating fiscal deficit and opening the economy to free action in world markets. With this purpose the enormous State bureaucracy was eliminated, the majority of productive and service enterprises were privatized and the entering of foreign investment capitals was encouraged. This demanded a high social cost together with high unemployment levels that were partially subsidized by the State. However, in a short time and notwithstanding the world crisis of 1980, the country achieved a high degree of income, duplicating exports and reaching a balance of payments that was clearly positive. Products exported were diversified and purchasing markets were extended. The growth rate reached a sustained rythm of over 5% per year and unemployment dropped to its traditional level of 6%.

Policies proposed by Pinochet's government, although this may seem a pradox, also implied global planning of social matters, being confrontational and exclusive. This time though those excluded were the major political actors in the two previous governments. Supported by a strong political police, certain politicians suffered persecution, exile and frequent and harsh attempts against human rights. This, the same as propositions described above of a global nature demonstrated their profound inefficiency: in popular election called in 1989 by Pinochet himself to vote for the new governing authority and parliament members, a coalition of social and political groups previously excluded by his government triumphed by a clear margin.

In March of 1990 President Patricio Aylwin came into power. His government is characterized by abandoning «all or nothin at all» or «starting from zero» policies, returning instead to old democratic Chilean tradition. He has worked in favour of agreement of all political factions, normalized civilian-military relationships and maintained the economic growth rates.

His great social policy involves a better distribution of accumulated wealth to end with extreme poverty still suffered by part of the population in the short term.

CRONOLOGICAL ORDER VARIOUS FACTS

PRIMITIVE INHABITANTS

	13000	man arrives in Chile.
	6000	Chinchorro culture in Arica, hunter and collector tribe who developed mummification process in sand, the oldest known in the world.
building of Cheops pyramid in Egypt	2800	
	2000	beginning of domestication and pasturing of cameloids in the north of Chile, traces of cultivation.
Minos Palace in Crete	1500	
Amon Temple in Karnak Egypt	1300	
Nabucodonosor I, King of Babylon	1117	
Chavin culture on coast of Perú	800-200	
Yimmu Tenno, first Emperor of Japan	600	
Palace of Darius in Susa	500	
Pericles governs Athens	500-429	
Parthenon in Athens	447-432	
Venus by Milo	306	
Alexander the Great King of Macedonia	336-323	
	100	appearance of first settlements: Tulor in San Pedro de Atacama.
Spartacus leads slave rebellion	73-71	
Pont du Gard in Nimes, France	27-14	
BIRTH OF CHRIST	0	
Nero Roman Emperor	54-68	
Segovia Acqueduct, Spain	100	
	200	El Molle culture emerges, close to La Serena, first farming-pottery group in Chile, Mapuches start development.
Lucius Septimius Severus Arch in Rome	204	
	300	Diaguitas, farmer-pottery tribe, starts evolution of elaborate ceramic work.
height of Maya culture in Central America, Inca culture starts in Perú	300-450	
Japan dominates present Korea	363-662	
Christianity becomes Roman Empire religion	391	
Nazca culture in Perú	400-800	
San Vitale church in Ravenna, Italy	526	
Saint Sophia church in Istambul	532-537	
Mahomet, Prohet of Islam	570-632	
Buddhist official religion in Japan	592	
T'ang Dynasty in China	618-907	
Hara period in Japan	710-782	
Arabs enter Spain	711	
Mosque in Córdoba, Spain initiated	750	
Charlemagne crowned Emperor of Franks	800	
	900	Tiwanaku Empire influence in cultures of northern Chile.
Sung period in China	960-1280	
Saint Mark's church in Venice	1042-1071	
schism in Catholic Church, origin of Orthodox Church	1054	
Urban II summons First Crusade	1095	
	1100	Local princedom period in oases between Arica and Antofagasta; building of Pukaras.
founding of University of Paris	1150	
founding of Oxford University	1160	
building of Notre Dame in Paris started	1163-1235	
building of Tower of Pisa started	1174	
Kamakura Shogun in Japan	1192-1333	
Alhambra in Granada, Spain	1230-1354	
Cologne Cathedral, Germany	1248	
Palazzo Vecchio in Florence	1298	
	1300	Classical period of Diaguita culture reaches highest expression in earthenware.
Ashikaga Shogun in Japan	1338-1573	
Ca d'Oro Palace in Venice	1350	
height of Aztec culture, Mexico	1377	
height of Inca Empire in Perú	1400-1520	
Inca conquest of Ecuador	1400-1537	
height of Ming Dynasty in China	1450-1550	
Saint Peter's Church, Rome	1459	
	1470-1535	Inca Empire invades Chile reaching Maule river 250 km south of Santiago.
Botticelli paints «Primavera»	1475	

16

Arabs expelled from Spain after the conquest of Granada	1491	
Cristopher Columbus discovers America	1492	
Albrecht Durer draws self-potrait	1494	
Leonardo da Vinci paints Monalisa Pedro Alvarez Cabral discovers Brazil	1500	
Michael Angelo Buonarroti's David	1503	
Sistine Chapel fresco by Michael Angelo Buonarroti	1508-1512	
Juan de Solís discovers La Plata River in Argentina	1516	
Martin Luther publishes his 95 thesis	1517	
death of Niccolo Machiavelli	1527	
	1529	Hernao de Magalhaes discovers the Straits of Chile, named after him (Strait of Magellan).
Francisco Pizarro initiates conquest of Perú	1532	
founding of the Company of Jesus (Jesuit Order)	1534	

SPANISH CONQUEST

founding of Lima in Perú	1535	Diego de Almagro initiates reconaissance expedition in Chile.
Anglican faith begins in England	1536	
Juan de Salazar founds Asunción in Paraguay	1537	
Francisco de Orellana, first to cross continent navigating on Amazon River	1539	
	1541	Pedro de Valdivia embarks on expedition of conquest and is named Governer of Chile.
	1542	Capital city of Santiago is founded.
	1544	La Serena in founded.
Council of Trent	1545	
first Jesuit Mission in Japan	1549	
	1550	Concepción is founded.
height of Mogul period in India	1550-1650	
	1551-1561	founding of Imperial, Valdivia, Villarrica, Osorno, Angol, Cañete and Purén cities, south of Bío Bío river.
	1553	Battle of Tucapel, Mapuches commanded by Lautaro, defeat Spaniards, Pedro de Valdivia taken prisoner and killed.
	1561	first smallpox epidemic.
	1567	taking posession of Chiloé Island and founding of the city of Castro.
	1569	Alonso de Ercilla publishes «La Araucana», epic poem relating warrior events of Mapuche tribes.
	1570	city of Arica founded.
	1574	Robinson Crusoe Island discovered by navigator Juan Fernández.
	1578	English corsair Sir Francis Drake is the second navigator to cross Strait of Magellan and to sail round the world.
founding of Buenos Aires, Argentina	1580	founding of Putre near Arica.
	1582	first epidemic of measles, devastating population.
Sir Walter Raleigh founds the first British colony in North America	1584	founding of Nombre de Jesus and Rey Felipe in Strait of Magellan. Over 300 settlers die of famine.
	1587	English corsair Thomas Cavendish crosses Strait of Magellan and rescues one survivor of Spanish forts.
	1593	Jesuit Order is established in Chile
	1598	Battle of Curalaba; Mapuches commanded by Pelanteru defeat Spaniards and destroy all Spanish cities south of Bío Bío river.

COLONIAL PERIOD

	1605	Jesuit Luis de Valdivia initiates plan of pacification of Mapuches, «Defensive War», that fails to have prompt effects.
	1608	Jesuits are established in Chiloé and initiate their missionary work.
	1609	Royal Audience is established for the first time in Chile.
Jesuits found 30 missions in Paraguay	1609-1767	
William Shakespeare dies	1616	discovery of Cape Horn channel pass by Dutch navigators Jacob le Maire and Cornelius Schouten
	1620	founding of Belen inland from Arica.
founding of New York City by Dutch colonist	1624	
founding of Boston by English Puritans	1630	
	1633	Typhoid fever epidemic, attacks native population mainly.
all Japanese ports are closed to foreigners	1639	
Velázquez paints «Venus»	1642	
	1643	Dutch corsair Sebastian de Cordes, sets fire to the city of Castro, Chiloé Island, and remains in the bay of Valdivia for a short period.

	1645	second founding of Valdivia and building of a naval fort and frotresses in Niebla, Mancera and Corral. Jesuit, Alonso de Ovalle publishes «Historical Account of the Kingdom of Chile» in Rome.
	1647	Santiago destroyed by earthquake.
Peace in Westphalia, Spain acknowledges independence of Netherlands	**1648**	
	1655	Mapuches initiate another general rebellion.
Rembrandt paints selfportrait	**1659**	
	1665-1696	two small-pox epidemics.
Saint Paul's Cathedral in London	**1675-1710**	
Versailles Palace and Gardens Paul Revere's house in Boston	**1680**	
change of Dynasty in Spain, Bourbones replace Hapsburgs	**1700**	
	1704	Alexander Selkirk is abandoned for four years on Robinson Crusoe Island. Is inspiration of novel written by Daniel Defoe.
	1722	Easter Island is discovered on Easter Sunday by Jacob Roggeveen from Holland.
	1730	seismic movement devastates Santiago.
Fontana di Trevi in Rome	**1735**	
	1742-1744	founding of Copiapó, Rancagua, San Fernando, Curicó and Talca.
	1767	building of Cal y Canto bridge in Santiago initiated, the greatest engineering work completed during Colonial period.
Boston Tea-party mutiny	**1773**	
San Antonio Mission church, Texas	**1774**	Jesuit Order expelled from Chile and all America.
	1777	construction of «Moneda» Government Palace in Santiago, current Government seat.
Kent publishes «Criticism of Pure Race»	**1781**	
Watt invents steam engine	**1786**	
	1787	construction of towers and facade of Cathedral in Santiago.
Start of French Revolution	**1789**	
	1789-1794	foundation of Vallenar, Linares and Constitución.
death of Benjamin Franklin	**1790**	
	1795	construction of La Merced church in Santiago
	1796	Osorno founded again on the same spot of first foundation in 1558.
Goya paints «La Maja Desnuda»	**1797**	
Brandenburg Gate in Berlin	**1798**	
Santa Barbara Mission in California	**1800**	
Napoleon crowned Emperor of France	**1804**	
Napoleon invades Spain and unthrones Fernando VII	**1808**	Building of Santo Domingo Church and Royal Audience Palace in Santiago.

INDEPENDENCE

	1810	September 18, Mateo de Toro y Zambrano summons an open Town Council meeting in Santiago. A Government Junta is formed. This event is celebrated as National Independence Day.
	1811	inauguration of National Congress.
	1814	Spaniards reconquer control of Chile.
Victorious States of Napoleon redistribute European frontiers at Viena Congress	**1814-1815**	
Battle of Waterloo, defeat of Napoleon	**1815**	
	1817	Libertador Army, commanded by José de San Martín crosses the Andes Mountains and defeats Spanish troops in Chile.
	1817-1823	Bernardo O'Higgins designated Supreme Director.
	1818	Bernardo O'Higgins proclaims the Independence of Chile.
construction of Independence Hall in Philadelphia and White House in Washington	**1820**	

CONSOLIDATION OF THE REPUBLIC OF CHILE

	1826	Chiloé Island librated, last Spanish fortification in South America.
	1829	end of internal anarchic period and initiation of times of great political stability and economic progress.
	1830	first export of nitrate from the port of Iquique.
	1832	discovery of silver mine in Chañarcillo, Copiapó.
	1833	approval of authoritative and presidential Constitution, in force until 1891.
Arch of Triumph in Paris	**1836**	
	1837	Chile enters war against Perú-Bolivia confederation.
Houses of Parliament in London	**1840-1868**	
	1842	University of Chile founded in Santiago.
	1843	founding of Bulnes Fort in Straits of Magellan. Transferred to Punta Arenas in 1848.
Marx and Engels publish Communist Manifest	**1848**	

Process of unification of Italy	1850-1871	
World Exhibition of London	1851	inauguration of Caldera-Copiapó railway, first in South America.
	1852	Matías Cousiño begins works in coal mines in Lota. Discovery of copper mine named Tamaya, near La Serena
	1853	founding of Puerto Montt, German settlers in the region of Llanquihue Lake.
Japan opens frontiers to Western World	1854	
	1859	Copper foundries in Tongoy, Coquimbo and Huasco
	1860	Orelie Antoine I, French citizen living in among Mapuches self-procalimed as King of Araucanía and Patagonia.
President Abraham Lincoln and Civil War in United States	1861-1865	

LIBERAL REPUBLIC

	1863	founding of Antofagasta.
unification process of Germany	1866-1871	
Karl Marx publishes «Das Kapital»	1867	
Suez Canal is opened	1869	
	1872-1877	improvement works in Santiago: new avenues and transformation of Santa Lucía hill into a park, construction of natural History Museum and Cousiño Palace and Gardens.
L'Opera in Paris inaugurated	1874	founding of Viña del Mar.
Sacre Coeur church in Paris	1874-1900	
	1875	Inauguration of National Congress building in Santiago.
	1879	Chile confronts Bolivia and Perú in Pacific War. Ending with victory of Chile and annexing of Pampa del Tamarugal.
	1881	Chile and Argentina sign a boundary agreement granting Argentina sovereignty of Patagonia and Chile the Magellan Straits.
Japan and China declare war	1884-1885	
	1885	Occupation of Mapuche territory between Bío Bío and Toltén rivers. Founding of Temuco. Establishment of European settlers in region. English citizen Oliver North controls 60% of nitrate business.
	1888	Easter Island annexed to Chilean territory, founding of Catholic University in Santiago.
World Exhibition of Paris, inauguration of Eiffel Tower. «The Thinker» statue by Rodin	1889	

PARLIAMENTARISM AND SOCIAL PROBLEMS

publication of Rerum Novarum encyclical letter Paul Gaugin paints women from Tahiti	1891	civil war culminating with President J. M. Balmaceda's suicide. Parliament sessions initiated.
	1898	railway reaches the city of Temuco.
	1902	government of Chile grants first concession in the world of Antarctica to a fishing enterprise.
	1903-1907	strikes in Valparaíso, Santiago, Antofagasta and Iquique are repressed, leaving a balance o hundreds of dead.
inauguration of Trans Siberian railway	1904	
Japan and Russia declare war	1904-1905	
	1908-1910	urban remodelling of Santiago in commemoration of Independence Centennary: San Cristóbal Virgin, Beaux Arts Museum, access ornamental stairs in Santa Lucía Hill, squares and monuments.
	1909	founding of Workers Federation of Chile.
	1910	inauguration of Arica-La Paz (Bolivia) railway. new trans Andean railway joining Chile and Mendoza in Argentina.
	1912	Puerto Montt connected by railway to Santiago. Founding of Workers Socialist Party by L.E. Recabarren.
Opening of Panamá Canal	1914	Yelcho vessel of Chilean Navy rescues explorer Ernest Schackleton in Antarctica. First nitrate crisis. Naval Battle opposite Coronel between English and German Navy ships.
beginning of First World War	1914-1918	
	1915	Chuquicamata copper mine starts production, being the largest producer of the country. German cruiser «Dresden» is sunk by English ships in Robinson Crusoe Island.
Russian Revolution leading communists to the government	1917	
	1920	Compulsory Basic Education law passed.
Mussolini, Fascist government in Italy	1922	Communist Party in Chile founded by Recabarren.
Mustafa Kemal Ataturk, president of Turkey	1923-1938	
	1925	new Constitution of presidentialist trends; end of parliament period.
Hirohito Emperor of Japan Stalin assumes power in USSR	1926	
	1927	El Teniente starts production of copper mine, the second largest of Chile.
World financial crisis	1929	
	1929-1930	Chilean financial crisis.
Hitler takes power in Germany	1933	

CONTEMPORARY HISTORICAL FACTS

	1934	women acquire right to vote in municipal elections.
Spanish Civil War	1936-1939	
	1939	Chillán and Concepción destroyed by violent seismic movement. Chilean State creates CORFO Promotion and Development Corporation.
beginning of Second World War	1939-1945	
	1940	boundaries of Chilean Antarctic Territory are defined.

Japan attacks Pearl Harbour	1941	
	1942	Chile stops diplomatic relations with Germany and countries of axis, in response to pressure by United States.
	1944	Chilean State creates ENDESA, National Electricity Enterprise. inauguration of Pilmaiquén Hydroelectric plant of 35,040 KW capacity.
establishment of United Nations Hiroshima and Nagasaki destroyed by first atomic bombs	1945	Gabriela Mistral obtains Nobel Prize in literature.
	1946	Chile, Perú and Ecuador proclaim the thesis of 200 mile Patrimonial Ocean, today accepted by a great number of countries. first section of Panamerican Highway opened between Santiago and La Serena.
	1947	visit by President Gabriel González Videla to Antarctica, the first governor of the world to do so.
establishment of the State of Israel Mahatma Gandhi murdered in India	1948	inauguration of El Abanico hydroelectric plant 136,000 KW capacity.
	1949	women acquire right to vote in Presidential elections.
Konrad Adenauer governs Germany	1949-1963	
	1950	CAP Pacific Steel Company, owned by the State starts up activites.
Korean War	1950-1953	
	1952	opening of Technical State University.
Cuban Revolution	1959	inauguration of El Salvador copper mine, fifth in importance in Chile. Inauguration of Cipreses hydroelectric plant, 101,400 KW capacity.
	1960	violent seismic movements on land and sea devastate the south from Concepción to Chiloé Island.
erection of Berlin Wall	1961	
J.F. Kennedy, President of U.S.A.	1961-1963	
	1962	first television transmissions for World Cup Football Championship held in Chile.
beginning of Vietnam War	1964	Panamerican Highway completed between Arica and Puerto Montt.
	1965	nationalization of Chilean copper: the State acquires 50% of shares in companies owned by North Americans.
	1966	World Ski Championship held in Chile. Rapel hydroelectric power station, 350,000 KW.
	1967	Eduardo Frei's government starts an agrarian reform plan and trade union system for farmers.
Martin Luther king assassinated	1968	
Neil Armstrong walks on the Moon	1969	
	1970	Salvador Allende, Socialist-Marxist, is elected President of the Republic of Chile.
	1971	Allende's government nationalizes copper mines. Pablo Neruda obtains Nobel Prize in literature.
fuel and energy crisis	1973	Government coup, General Augusto Pinochet heads a Military Junta.
	1974	Inauguration of El Toro hydroelectric power plant, 400,000 KW capacity.
Francisco Franco dies in Spain	1975	
	1980	New Political Constitution is approved and made legal.
	1981	inauguration of Antuco hydroelectric power station, 300,000 KW.
	1982	Austral Highway starts construction.
	1984	Pope John Paul II is mediator in boundary conflict between Chile and Argentina.
Mijail Gorbachov governs USSR, introducing Perestroika and Glasnost	1985	This ends with a peace and friendship treaty.
	1987	Pope John Paul II visits Chile.
Berlin Wall falls	1989	Patricio Aylwin is elected President of the Republic of Chile.
Emperor Hirohito of Japan dies reunification of Germany	1990	Patricio Aylwin assumes as President. National Congress initiates activites in new building sited in Valparaíso.
USSR dismembered	1991	inauguration of La Escondida copper mine, the third largest in the country. Inauguration of Canutillar, 145,000 KW and Pehuenche, 500,000 KW hydroelectric power stations.

PRACTICAL INFORMATION

HOW TO GET TO CHILE

Verification of this information at the time of traveling is recommended given that itineraries are liable to seasonal changes, especially regarding international flights.

BY AIR all international flights arrive in Santiago, the capital of Chile, at «Comodoro Arturo Merino Benítez Airport, at 15 km distance from the center. Figures quoted in brackets indicate the number of flights per week.

From Europe Air France (6) from Paris; British Airways (3) from London one night stopover in Buenos Aires; Alitalia (2) from Milan; Lan Chile (2) from Madrid and Iberia (4) from Madrid; Lan Chile (1) and Lufthansa (3) from Frankfur; KLM (2) from Amsterdam; Swissair (3) from Zurich; Sabena (1) from Brussels; SAS (3) from Copenhague; Aeroflot (3) from Moscow.
South American airlines Aerolíneas Argentinas, Varig, Viasa, Avianca, also have flights from Europe to Santiago, Chile; stopping at respective capital cities Buenos Aires, Río de Janeiro, Caracas or Bogotá.

From Polynesia Lan Chile (2) from Tahití via Easter Island connecting with flights from Japan, Australia and New Zealand.

From Australia via South Pole and Buenos Aires, Aerolíneas Argentinas (1).

From North America Lan Chile (7), Ladeco (5) and American Airlines (3) from New York; American Airlines from Washington, Los Angeles and New Orleans; Ladeco (5) from Miami; AeroPerú (3) and American Airlines (11) from Miami.

From South America Lan Chile, Ladeco, Aerolíneas Argentinas, Varig, AeroPerú, Avianca, Air France, Iberia, KLM, Lufthansa and American Airlines (30) from Buenos Aires. Lan Chile, Ladeco, Varig, Aerolíneas Argentinas and Lufthansa (4) from Río de Janeiro. Lan Chile, Ladeco and Pluna (9) from Montevideo. Ladeco and Lapa (5) from Asunción, Lloyd Aéreo Boliviano (2) from La Paz.
Lan Chile, Ladeco, AeroPerú and Avianca (2) from Lima. Ladeco and Ecuatoriana (5) from Quito. Avianca (3) from Bogotá, Viasa (2) from Caracas.
During the summer months extra flights are implemented (January to March) by Lan Chile, Aerolíneas Argentinas and Tan connecting Neuquén in Argentina with Temuco in Chile; Bariloche in Argentina with Puerto Montt and Santiago in Chile.

BY RAILWAY connection only to Perú and Bolivia.

From Peru train from Tacna to Arica in Chile, 1 hour journey, departures Monday to Saturday at 12:00, 16:00 and 18:00 hours.

From Bolivia train from La Paz to Arica in Chile, 12 hour journey in electric coach train. Departures from Arica every Thursday at 17:00 hours. In summer (Jan to Mar) additional train at 9:00 hours.
Oruro Railway (connecting in La Paz) to Calama in Chile, First and Third class coaches.

BY BUS regular services in comfortable buses connecting Santiago, Chile, with neighbouring countries.

From Argentina direct routes to Santiago from Buenos Aires, Córdoba and Mendoza, crossing the Andes Mountains through international tunnel in Portillo pass. Direct journeys to Santiago and Puerto Montt from Bariloche in Argentina, crossing the Andes Mountains by Vicente Pérez Rosales pass.
Direct journeys to Calama and Antofagasta from Salta in Argentina (only Dec to Mar) crossing Andes Mountains by Sico pass.
In Patagonia, direct trips between Comodoro Rivadavia and Coihaique Alto; and between Río Gallegos and Punta Arenas crossing Monte Aymond pass.

From Peru from Lima to Santiago direct by Panamerican Highway.

From Ecuador direct service from Guayaquil to Santiago by Panamerican Highway.

From Brazil direct service to Santiago from Río de Janeiro and Sao Paulo, crossing Argentina and entering Chile by Mendoza and Portillo mountain-pass.

BY CAR a number of roads connect Chile with border countries, and are described in the different chapters of this Guide, where time-tables of attention in Customs are also given. This section only describes the most important routes.

From Peru by Chacalluta pass, north of Arica, by Panamerican Highway, completely paved. Distance of 2,080 km from border to Santiago. Description in Zone 1.

From Bolivia the best pass for crossing is Tambo Quemado that borders Chungará lake on the route to Arica; Santiago is 2,317 km distant from this pass, and Arica is 225 km away. Another good alternative is Cochane pass, unpaved but transitable road to Huara connecting with Panamerican Highway; 2,017 km to Santiago and 183 km to Huara. Description in Zone 1 of this edition. Ollague pass to Calama and Antofagasta, unpaved, good condition, infrequent traffic. Description in Zone 2.

From Argentina principal road through Portillo pass, completely paved road, tunnel on borderline; joins Mendoza to Los Andes in Chile. Periodic interruptions due to snow in winter months of July to September; 141 km to Santiago from border. Description in Zone 5.
Third important pass is Monte Aymond in Patagonia joining Río Gallegos in Argentina with Punta Arenas in Chile. Difficulties due to snow and ice in winter months of June to September. There are also 19 open passes such as Sico (Zone 2); San Francisco (Zone 3); Aguas Negras (Zone 4); Pehuenche (Zone B); Pino Hachado, Icalma, Mamuil Malal; Caririñe; Huahun (Zone 10). Futaleufú, Palena, Río Cisnes, Puerto Viejo; Coihaique Alto; Balmaceda; Puerto Ibáñez and Los Antiguos (Zone 13); and Cerro Castillo and Villa Dolores (Zone 14). All mentioned passes unpaved roads, transitable generally in summer from December to March.

BY LAKE FERRY BOAT probably the most spectacular means of crossing the Andes Mountains from Argentina. From Bariloche to Puerto Montt in Chile, 3 different tourist boats and three laps by bus, crossing the most majestic lakes, wet forests and volcanoes. Interconnected service all year, journey of 1 day, described in Zone 11 of this Guide.

WHEN TO GO in general Chileans are very fond of the sea side and spend hopidays of 3 weeks every year on the shores of the ocean and lakes. They prefer the warmer summer months (December to March), the most popular months being January and February (high season), during which time reservations in advance should be made for hotel accommodation. Chile is a country of climate and topography that changes considerably and December to March are the most favourable months for marine activities and sports on beaches, lakes and rivers. However, different regions of the country are preferable during other seasons.

Zones 1 and 2 from March to December: in summer it is also excellent but very much warmer in the desert and in the Altiplano frequent rainfalls and snow in January and February is usual.

Zones 3 and 4 all year: beaches from September to April and the desert in flower in September and October.

Zones 5; 8 and 9 all year in cities. Agricultural scenery is splendid from September to March. Mountain climbing activities from December to March. Ski Season from June to August.

Zone 6 the Central coastline and its beaches full of tourists in January and February. Temperate to warm and sunshine from September to March.

Zone 7 Easter Island all year. Robinson Crusoe Island from October to March.

Zones 10 and 11 from December to March with great concentration of tourists in January and February. Ski centers from July to October.

Zones 12; 13 and 14 best season from November to March.

Zone 15 Antarctica, tourist expeditions from November to March.

IMMIGRATION DOCUMENTS the essential document is a **Passport, Visas** are required only in the case of some countries (see below). Residents of bordering countries like Argentina, Brazil, Uruguay and Paraguay only require **Identity Card** to enter Chile as tourists.

National health certificates are not necessary.

For legal effects Chile considers 21 years old as being of full age. Foreigners under this age limit can enter freely when carrying a Passport.

If minors are accompanied by their parents and later depart alone, Chilean law demands a permit previously signed by both parents, signed before a Notary Public.

VISAS countries that do not require Visas for entering Chile are: Germany; Argentina; Australia; Austria; Belgium; Brazil; Canada; Colombia; Costa Rica; Denmark; Ecuador; El Salvador; Spain; U.S.A.; Finland; Greece; Honduras; India; Indonesia; Ireland; Iceland; Israel; Italy; Jamaica; Japan; Liechtenstein; Luxembourg; Morocco; Mexico; Netherlands; Paraguay; Portugal; United Kingdom; San Marino; Holy See; Singapore; Sweden; Switzerland; Surinam; Turkey; Tuvalu; Uruguay and Yugoslavia.

Tourists arriving from other countries must request a Tourist Visa before traveling at the Chilean Consulate in their country of origin or in any other country before embarking.

IMMIGRATION REQUIREMENTS in all bordering countries and at international airport of Santiago, every person entering -Chilean or foreign- must comply with three formalities performed promptly and successively. The are:

International Police checks immigration document -Passport or Identity Card- and stamps date of entry.

Livestock and Agricultural Service (SAG) checks thoroughly all hand luggage and suitcases. Every kind of perishable product of animal or vegetable origin is strictly prohibited from entry to Chile. Do not intent concealing this kind of item to avoid serious problems. It is preferable to declare these if present in luggage: alternatives are to consume them on the spot or discard them in bins for incineration. This is a necessary control that has allowed Chile to be free of plagues in agriculture and livestock.

Custom Swift and expedite revision. Articles allowed entry, free of custom duties are: personal effects -clothing, photographic cameras, video sets, etc, also a maximum of 500 cigarettes, 50 cigars, 500 grms. of tobacco, 2 and 1/2 liters of wine or liquor and reasonable quantity of perfume.

BUDGET PLANNING

Chile is a relatively cheap country, even as compared to neighbouring countries in South America. As a guideline for probable expenses we have listed average prices expressed in US Dollars.

Hotel rates for 2 people, including tax, double bedroom, high season from December to March. In first category hotels rates are reduced during low season.

★★★★★ US$ 180
★★★★ US$ 106
★★★ US$ 70

Camping varies according to facilities, beauty of scenery or exclusive sites. Rates fluctuate between US$ 6 to US$ 20 per day or campingsite for up to 6 persons.

Long Distance Conveyances there are three means of transport: Buses, Trains and Domestic Flights.

Long Distance Buses prices vary according to mileage and services provided. From Santiago to Arica US$ 38 to US$ 59. Santiago to Puerto Montt US$ 14 to US$ 20. Santiago to Punta Arenas US$ 89 to US$ 90

Trains from Santiago to Puerto Montt, second class US$ 18 round trip; in first class US$ 13; in Pullman or Sleeper US$ 22.

Domestic Flights from Santiago to Arica US$ 167; Santiago to Antofagasta US$ 140; Santiago to Calama US$ 157; Santiago to Temuco US$ 94. Santiago to Puerto Montt US$ 113. Santiago to Punta Arenas US$ 213.

Airport Tax on departure; International flights US$ 12.50; domestic flights US$ 3.50.

Urban Transport rates for buses, metro (underground) and «Colectivos» (taxis shared by 4 people on fixed routes) form US$ 0.30 and US$ 0.50.

Rent a Car small automobiles, average price per day US$ 20.- plus US$ 15 for insurance, plus US$ 0.25 per km, plus 18% VAT tax.
Large Automobiles, deluxe, average price per day US$ 45 plus US$ 15 insurance, plus 0.50 per km, plus 18% VAT tax.
All car rental agencies offer special prices on week-ends, full week, 10 day period, etc.

Gasoline, Petrol price for 1 liter of 93 octane gasoline = US$ 0.7.

Meals average price per person, including tax: Tips are extra and correspond to 10% of bill.

Restaurants of excellent quality, including 1 bottle of wine and cocktails or liqueurs = US$ 23.

Restaurant of average level, including 1 jug of wine and coffee = US$ 12. Majority of restaurants offer a fixed menu at lunchtime of US$ 6.

Fast Food, Pizzas, Hamburgers, Sandwiches = US$ 3.

Coffee and Beverages the price varies if consumed in a Cafeteria or Restaurant. Coffee US$ 0.50.- to US$ 1.50. Soft Drinks US$ 0.50 to US$ 2. Beer US$ 1. to US$ 3.

Cigarettes sold in 20 unit packets. Different brands vary from US$ 1. to US$ 1.50.

Camera Film average price for a roll of 35 mm colour film, 36 frames, 100 ASA = US$ 5. Developing of 36 photographs in colour, on paper, size 9 x 12 cm = US$ 9.

Public Phone Booths Local Calls cost US$ 0.07 for 3 minutes. **Long Distance Calls** in the country vary according to distance between US$ 0.70 and US$ 1 for 3 minutes. **Long Distance International Calls** US$ 2 first toll charge.

NATIONAL CURRENCY the monetary unit in Chile is the «Peso» and is expressed by $.
Coins is circulation are of $ 1 and $ 5, seldom used; $ 10, $ 50 and $ 100.
Bills in circulation are of $ 500; $ 1,000; $ 5,000 and $ 10,000; The latter is not recommended as it may be difficult to change in rural areas or purchases of low value.

MONEY EXCHANGE there are two exchange areas in operation, both official: Official Rate of Exchange and Free Rate of Exchange. There are no restrictions in Chile for purchasing or selling foreign currency.

Official Exchange Rate regulated by the Central Bank of Chile with daily variations of exchange rates, following inflation of previous month. Used mainly in commercial transactions.

Free Rate of Exchange regulated by offer and demand of foreign currency. Always slightly higher than the official rate and best recommended for tourists. Exchange is performed in authorized agencies that bear a sign announcing them as «Money Exchange» or «Casas de Cambio», or simply «Cambio»; at the entrance a board indicating exchange rates of the day is usually visible from the street. Never try to change money with street vendors; they will pay less and it is risky. In most Hotels foreign currency is recieved in payment of bills, but is converted at official rates of exchange.
Best free exchange rates are obtained in Money Exchange Agencies in Santiago downtown -principal offices are in Agustinas Street in Santiago. Also in Money Exchange Agencies in Arica, Iquique, Antofagasta, La Serena, Valparaíso, Viña del Mar, Concepción, Pucón, Temuco, Valdivia, Puerto Montt and Punta Arenas. In the rest of the country lower rates are paid and difficulties may be encountered in remote towns.
Free Exchange Rates are influenced by inflation, with has kept at an average of 1.5% a month over recent years.
This average fluctuation should be considered if your stay is prolongued. If at the end of your stay you have a surpluss of Chilean Pesos, exchange at in any Money Exchange Agency in the city or at the International Airport.

Banking Hours Monday to Friday from 9:00 to 14:00 hours.

Money Exchange Hours Monday to Friday from 9:00 to 13:00 and 15:00 to 18:00 hours.

CAMPING Chile has a great variety of Camping sites available, with good adjoining facilities. Also in the case of Adventure Tourism places of extreme beauty in remote places have been chosen.
For complete information consult **Camping Guide** published by Turistel.

CAR RENTAL The better known international firms are in Chile: Avis-Budget-Dollar-Hertz. Also very reliable local enterprises such as the Automobile Club of Chile and others. All of them have offices in the center of the larger cities of the country.
Advantages of renting a car are many: total freedom of movement, possibility of staying at any suitable place on the route and opportunity to stop when something of interest is encountered. Cars can be returned at the airport when the visit is over.

Requirements of Driver, to be over 25 years old, to carry an international driving license, passport and credit card.

Driving in Chile roads are good and speed limit is 100 km per hour, except in restricted areas indicated that must be complied with. Secondary roads are good generally, with a few not so good, attention and precaution in driving are recommended.
Highways are properly indicated and road signs are of the international format and colour.

CELLULAR TELEPHONES a wide network of 1,500 km covers the country from La Serena -in the north- to Punta Arenas -in the south- and from the Andes mountains to sea-side resorts on the ocean. This represents useful support in adventure tourism -fishing, trekking, skiing, mountain climbing- from faraway places it is possible to communicate with all Chile and the rest of the world. Cellular telephones can be rented by day, week-ends, weeks, etc. Main offices in Santiago and International Airport.
Different telephone companies provide services in Chile. CTC and Cidcom cover Santiago, the central coast and mountain areas. VTR and Telecom cover the northern region to La Serena and to the south to Puerto Montt.
CTC Apoquindo 7071 Huérfanos 540 11 de Septiembre 2155
Cidcom Lota 7071 ☎ 232 0031
VTR Enrique Foster Sur 24 ☎ 231 1785
Telecom Lota 2241 ☎ 232 0031

CIGARETTES to be found in all food markets, soda fountains and news stands. There are no specialized tobacconists. Over 25 brands of cigarettes of different prices and well know trade marks such as Lucky Strike, Pall Mall, Marlboro, Kent, Barklay and Viceroy are on sale, but are the more expensive. If going on a rural excursion, take a supply of cigarettes, as it is possible that only one or two cheaper brands will be on sale.

CLOTHING RECOMMENDED climate in Chile varies according to the Zone or region.
Zones 1, 2, 3 and 4 during winter and summer clothing should be light for daytime and warmer for the evening.
Zones 5, 6, 8 and 9 seasons of the year are very contrasting. In winter (June and August) warm clothing; Autumn and Spring (April, May, September and October) reasonably warm requiring heavier garments for the evening. Summer (December to March) very light clothes and little need for evening wraps.
Zone 7 easter Island, light clothing. Robinson Crusoe Island, light for day and warm clothes for evening wear. Windbreakers are recommended.
Zone 10, 11, 12 in summer (December to March) lighter clothes for daytime and warmer clothes for evenings; and in winter (June to November) very warm clothing and rainwear required.
Zones 13, 14 and 15 clothes must be warm in winter and summer, and windbreakers are needed.

CONSULATES AND EMBASSIES. Embassies of all countries with diplomatic relations are based in Chile. If any problem is encountered contact your consular representative first. Telephone call is advised to agree on an appointment, as each Embassy has its own office hours.
Consulate Addresses in Santiago:

Country	Adress	Phone
Argentina	Av Vicuña Mackenna 41	2228977
Bolivia	Av San Martín 279	2328180
Brazil	Enrique Mac Iver 225-15 fl	398867
Colombia	La Gioconda 4317	2288369
Ecuador	Av Providencia 197	2318945
Spain	Av Providencia 329-4 fl	40239
United States	Merced 230	6710139
Guatemala	Los Españoles 2155	2317367
Uruguay	Av Pedro de Valdivia 711	2238398
Venezuela	Bustos 2021-3 fl	2258681

CREDIT CARDS internationally used credit cards, American Express; Diners; Mastercard and Visa are accepted immediately in the majority of restaurants, shops and hotels. However, it is always advisable to carry a small amount of cash, for incidental expenses. Main offices in Santiago for these credit cards are:

American Express Agustinas 1360 ☎ 672 2156
Diners Av. Providencia-3 fl ☎ 2322629/232000
Mastercard Morandé 315-3 fl ☎ 6952023
Visa Morandé 315 ☎ 695 2023

CRUISER, SHIP EXCURSIONS different excursions available on lakes, rivers and the ocean. The most spectacular are those in the Patagonia Archipelago, navigating around thousands of solitary islands covered with wet forests and massive glaciers that fall to the sea. Points of departure are in Puerto Montt, Puerto Chacabuco and Punta Arenas. Complete information in Services Section at the end of this Guide.

DOMESTIC FLIGHTS all principal cities have airports and are operated by the Aeronautical Control, agency of the Chilean Air Force. Five airports have international dimensions, where the larger planes can land; Santiago, Antofagasta, Puerto Montt, Punta Arenas and Easter Island airports. Due to long distances in Chile, air transport is frequently used, specially when time is short. There are two national airlines: **Ladeco** and **Lan Chile**, both flying domestic and international routes. These offer foreign tourists a «Visit Pass» of 7 domestic flight programs with a duration of a total of 21 days, that allows visiting the most beautiful cities in Chile and Easter Island, at very favorable rates. Consult your travel agent. The Visit Pass, can only be bought overseas, in any travel agency.

For domestic flights, transport from airport to the center of town is included in the cost of the ticket. Confirm this service on buying your plane ticket. There are smaller airlines that operate in Puerto Montt, Coihaique and Punta Arenas. These flights allow access to very far and beautiful points such as Tierra del Fuego and Cape Horn. See description in Services Section.

DRUGSTORES, CHEMISTS in all cities of Chile drugstores are easily found, there is always one on night duty and on holidays. Your Hotel or tourist guide will indicate the nearest one.

Chemists stock farmaceutical products of the best known international laboratories and also of certified national laboratories. If seeking a certain medicine sold under a name not known in Chile, take the container to the drugstore and the chemist will indicate the equivalent prescription.

If going on Adventure Tourism programs, far from populated areas, take any medicine you need to have regularly in sufficient quantity as a precaution.

ELECTRIC POWER electricity in Chile is 220 Volts. Plugs have two or three openings. More important hotels supply adapting devices for appliances.

GASOLINE, PETROL automobile fuel of 85 and 93 octanes is sold, besides Diesel oil. Sales points are known as «Bombas de Bencina» (gas pumps) and are located on all main highways, in all cities and even in small villages, all of them indicated in maps contained in this Guide.

Gas pumps on highways and cities are open all day and night. In small towns only during the day.

On the main highways most service stations have rest rooms, minimarkets, etc., indicated as «Rutacentros», where, in addition to fuel, there is a cafeteria, bathrooms and hot showers; also facilities for changing small children and for preparing their bottle or food.

HOTELS Chile provides good accommodation, from 5 star hotels to rooms in private houses. This Guide, in Services Section, offers a list of the more suitable hotels in each region for enjoying your stay, as support information. Make reservations in advance during the high season, from January to February.

INTERNATIONAL AIRPORT Comodoro Arturo Merino Benítez airport, at 15 km from Santiago, point of arrival for all international flights.

In Air Terminal Money Exchange is available, various car rental agencies and Tourist Information Centers also operate.

Transport to the center of Santiago is expedite on buses departing every 15 minutes that take 1/2 an hour, US$ 1. Minibuses, door to door services, US$ 6. Also Taxi services.

LONG DISTANCE BUS SERVICE all the length of Chile is connected by a network of buses. From Santiago to Arica in the north and to Punta Arenas in the extreme south. All first class vehicles circulate at controlled speed limits.

Single or double decker buses; some with sleepers, other with pullman seats or regular seats. In many services the value of the fare includes meals served on the bus.

Prices of surface transport vary according to mielage and extra services provided. In general the fare is not expensive and it is the most used means of transport in the country. For further information see Section on Services.

MEDICAL ASSISTANCE to be absolutely safe, buy an insurance policy covering risks of sickness and accidents during your vacations. Hopefully you shall never need it, but in any case it is wise to be protected from all medical expenses.

In Chile an efficient line of Hospitals and Private Clinics exists throughout the country. If a Medical Doctor is needed request help at Hotel reception desk.

METRO only runs in the city of Santiago. Cost of fare is similar to that of urban buses. It is the most modern, swift and expedite urban transport system with clean ample stations that are worth visiting. Due to it being an underground train though, the city is not visible.

MUSEUMS TIMETABLES these are specialized in many subjects that in each case are specified in this Guide. Generally they are open to public from Tuesday to Sunday, and closed on Mondays.

NATIONAL HOLIDAYS all comercial offices and shops close on these set dates. Only Shopping Malls remain open, with the exception of May 1st. (Labour Day). January 1 - (New Year Day); Easter - (Friday, Saturday and Sunday) movable date between the last week in March and first fortnight of April); May 1 - (Labour Day); May 21 - (Naval Battle Anniversary); June 18 (Corpus Christi); June 29 - (Saint Peter and Saint Paul); August 15 - (Assumption of Our Lady); September 18 and 19 (Independence Day and Army Anniversary); October 12 (Cristopher Columbus Day); November 1 - (All Saints Day); December 8 - (Immaculate Conception); December 25 - (Christmas Day).

PHOTOGRAPHY this line of shops has signs with the word «FOTOS». The best known rolls of colour or black and white film are stocked at very convenient prices. In Santiago a wide selection of these items is found with less variety in provinces; take necessary supplies of film if visiting rural areas, mountains or desert locations.
Developing of films available in each province capital city that deliver in 24 hours. In Santiago it is possible to develop film in a few hours. Slides in colour take over 1 day.

POLICE There is one police force in Chile called **Carabineros de Chile**. A very well organized police force in charge of its Director General in Santiago. Policemen perform a number of functions such as Guards of Honour in the Presidential Palace in Santiago, police controls of cities and traffic in all points of the country, control of borderlines, control of highways, educational and social work. They are addressed as **Carabinero** and wear khaki-green uniforms. In the larger cities there is a women's police force that collaborates in general activities.
Patrol cars are black with a white roof. The Police Station is a **Comisaría** and all bear signs with their symbol in green and white.
Different to other South American countries, do not try to tip a Carabinero because this will lead to serious consequences.

POST OFFICES Every city, town and village has a Post Office service, open from Monday to Friday from 9 AM to 5 PM and on Saturdays from 9 A.M. to 12 noon. This is a very efficient service for national and international mail. An airmail letter from New York to Santiago takes 3 days.

RAILWAYS a complete railway network of several thousands of km crosses the country, but at present the transport of passengers by trains only operates in the region from Santiago to Puerto Montt.
The departure station in Santiago is «Estación Central» located in Alameda Bdo. O'Higgins 3322, connected to the Metro station under the same name. Reservations and purchase of tickets in the station ☎ 91682, and in « Escuela Militar» east terminal Metro station ☎ 2282983. Cost of fare is cheaper than the buses traveling long distances, in similar category. Trains of different speed and services run regularly. Express trains have sleeper carriages, pullman cars, diners (regular and expensive service) and wagons that transport vehicles (cars), the latter is very useful for long journeys as driving is relieved and the car is delivered immediately on disembarking at a given station.

SOFT BEVERAGES are found everywhere of international brands such as Coca-Cola, Fanta, Sprite, Pepsi-Cola, besides other local flavours. Also fruit pulp juices in bottles are in sale. Beer is of very good quality and there are different kinds on the market. Black beer is called «Malta».

TAXIS all over Chile taxi cabs are black with yellow tops, easily identified. All taxis in Santiago have a meter that marks the value of the run to be paid. During the night (from 9 P.M. on) double the value indicated is charged. No tips are expected. In other parts of the country taxis also have meters but their use is not so strict. It is preferable to agree on the value of the fare beforehand.

TELEPHONES BOOTHS all the country is interconnected by a telephone network supported by a central chain of microwave plants reaching 3,000 km distance. More remote points such as Coihaique, Punta Arenas, Easter Island and Antarctica are interconnected via satelite system the same as international communications. Telephones are automatic. Communications within and out of the country can be dialed direct (DDD) with a code number for each area of the country. International calls also have direct dialing systems (DDI), by first dialing 00, then the code of the country, followed by area code of city and finally telephone number where call is placed.

In each city and town there are local Telephone Centers called «Central de Llamadas». Open from 9 A.M. to 8 P.M. Larger cities have public phone booths in the street. These operate with coins of Ch$ 50 and Ch$ 100. Telephones that are **yellow** are for local calls and **blue** telephones are for national long distance calls (DDD); the **grey** telephones are for international long distance calls (DDI) and have instructions in Spanish and English attached.

TELEX national and international service attended by private enterprise, with offices in all principal cities and towns of Chile.

TIME DIFFERENCE Chile and the other capitals of the world have a time difference indicated in the chart below.
From the second half of October to the second half of March, clocks are set back 1 hour (summer time).

Santiago	New York	Tokyo	Rome	Buenos Aires
+ -0	-1 hr	-12 hr	+6 hr	+1 hr

TIPS by law the cost of services is included in the total bill issued by hotels and restaurants. However, the custom is to leave a tip, specially if good attention has been received. Taxi drivers do not expect to be tipped.

Hotel maid	Ch $ 1,000 to Ch $ 2,000 on leaving
Restaurant Waiter	10 % of bill total
Porter (luggage)	Ch $ 500 to Ch $ 1,000
Hairdresser	10 % of value paid
Room Service	10 % of order

TOURIST INFORMATION SERNATUR (National Tourism Service) has offices throughout Chile prepared to supply useful information to tourists. The head office in Santiago is located in Av. Providencia 1550, ☎ 6982151. Open from 9 AM to 6 P.M.
There is a tourist information center in the international airport of Santiago.

TRAVELER CHECKS accepted in Banks and Exchange Agencies, quick and safe procedures. The most used are issued by City Bank and American Express. Passports must be presented in these exchange transactions.
Loss of Traveler Checks, contact Police immediately. Then advise issuing Bank, giving identification and serial numbers of checks. Addresses in Santiago are:

American Express	Agustinas 1360 ☎ 6722156
City Bank	Av. Providencia 2653-3 fl ☎ 2324243

URBAN BUS ROUTES Santiago and the principal cities of Chile have an important number of urban buses running from 5 A.M. all day and til 1 A.M. at night.
On working days, during the rush hours of office and other workers, the buses are usually full, but the rest of the day it is a pleasure to travel in them besides being the best way to see a city. Value of the bus fare is cheap.
Taxi Colectivo is a new kind of urban transport means. These are taxis that run on a fixed route taking 4 passengers. They can be identified by a sign on the roof indicating destination. Value of fare is 30% higher than the urban bus. They are quicker, but less useful for the tourist.

WATER tap water is potable in all cities and towns of the country. It can be consumed with no risk. Mineral bottled water with or without gas is also available.

YOUTH HOSTELS if a member of the International Association of Youth Hostels lodging is available in one of the three open in the city of Santiago, or in other parts of Chile where there are thirteen hostels in the most attractive points for tourists.
For Further information contact Head Offices in Providencia 2594, suite 420-421 ☎ 233 3220, Santiago.

«Autorizada su circulación en cuanto a los mapas y citas que contiene esta obra, referente o relacionadas con los límites internacionales y Fronteras del Territorio Nacional por resolución N° 37 del 5 de Marzo de 1992 de la Dirección Nacional de Fronteras y Límites del Estado.
La edición y circulación de mapas y cartas geográficas u otros impresos y documentos que se refieren o relacionen con los Límites y Fronteras de Chile, no comprometen en modo alguno, al Estado de Chile de acuerdo con el art. 2° letra g del DFL N° 83 de 1979, del Ministerio de Relaciones Exteriores»

TRANSLATOR
Julio Saavedra

GASTRONOMICAL ADVISER
(Section The City of Santiago)
Alex González

PHOTOGRAPHIES

Bruhin, Daniel pag 394 • Cerda, Pablo pag 62 • Codelco Chile (Francisco Aguayo) pag 115 • Dominguez, Augusto pags 262, 265, 267, 535, 602 • Edwards, Hernán pag 152 • Fotobanco S A pags 56, 64, 263, 298, 416, 437, 530, 577, 583, 598 • Gedda, Manuel pags 75, 118, 345, 390, 391, 393, 501, 526, 580, 597, 636 • Haramoto, Charles pag 414 • Hacienda Los Lingues pag 407 • Hotel Cabo de Hornos pag 635 • Hotel Portillo pag 318 • Hotel Ralún pag 542 • Hotel Termas de Huife pag 495 • Huber, Alex pags 268, 599 • Jones, Michael pags 312, 341, 342, 343, 347, 352, 357, 360, 362, 365, 367, 371, 459, 572 • Kactus Foto pags 121, 193, 203, 324, 466, 488, 505, 538, 544, 611, 659 • López, Daniel pag 647 • Museo RP Gustavo Le Paige (M A Readi) pag 122 • Naviera Navimag pag 609 • Oyarzún, Gastón pags 72, 158, 322, 612 • Piwonka, Nicolás pags 100, 117 • Taller Valparaíso pags 144, 192, 356, 368, 545 • Turismo Terra Australis pag 643 • Valenzuela, Pablo pags 58, 74, 96, 119, 123, 126, 143, 195, 201, 260, 264, 271, 281, 304, 363, 373, 380, 392, 418, 419, 422, 438, 447, 487, 491, 499, 503, 628, 640, 646, 658 • Venturini, Pierino pag 159.

KEY TO SYMBOLS

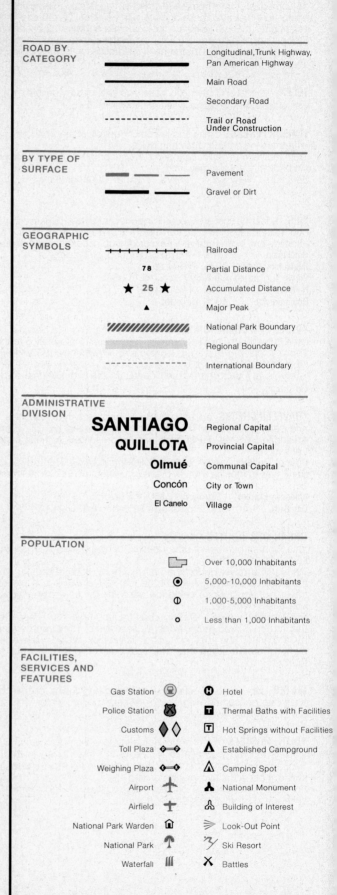

ROAD BY CATEGORY

Longitudinal, Trunk Highway, Pan American Highway

Main Road

Secondary Road

Trail or Road Under Construction

BY TYPE OF SURFACE

Pavement

Gravel or Dirt

GEOGRAPHIC SYMBOLS

Railroad

78   Partial Distance

★ 25 ★   Accumulated Distance

▲   Major Peak

National Park Boundary

Regional Boundary

International Boundary

ADMINISTRATIVE DIVISION

SANTIAGO   Regional Capital

QUILLOTA   Provincial Capital

Olmué   Communal Capital

Concón   City or Town

El Canelo   Village

POPULATION

Over 10,000 Inhabitants

5,000-10,000 Inhabitants

1,000-5,000 Inhabitants

Less than 1,000 Inhabitants

FACILITIES, SERVICES AND FEATURES

Gas Station   Hotel

Police Station   Thermal Baths with Facilities

Customs   Hot Springs without Facilities

Toll Plaza   Established Campground

Weighing Plaza   Camping Spot

Airport   National Monument

Airfield   Building of Interest

National Park Warden   Look-Out Point

National Park   Ski Resort

Waterfall   Battles

TOURIST GUIDE
Divided into Tourist Zones

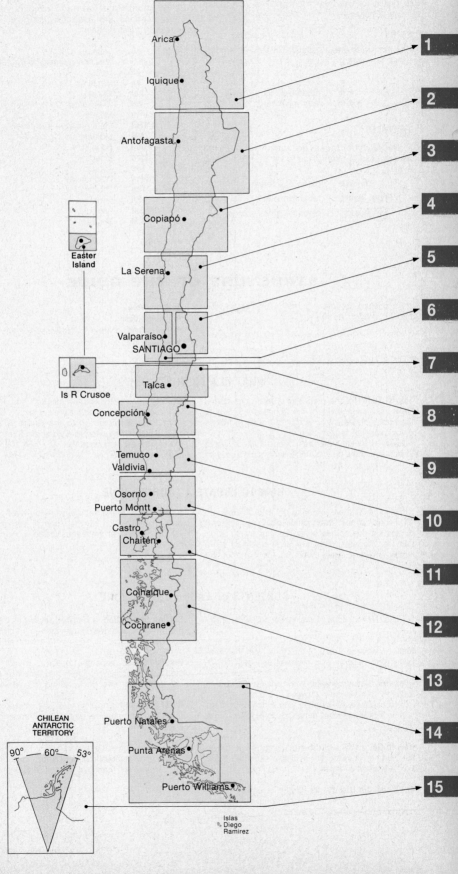

Arica

Iquique

Antofagasta

Copiapó

Easter Island

La Serena

Valparaíso

SANTIAGO

Is R Crusoe

Talca

Concepción

Temuco

Valdivia

Osorno

Puerto Montt

Castro

Chaitén

Coihaique

Cochrane

CHILEAN ANTARCTIC TERRITORY

90° — 60° — 53°

Puerto Natales

Punta Arenas

Puerto Williams

Islas Diego Ramírez

1
2
3
4
5
6
7
8
9
10
11
12
13
14
15

HOW TO USE THE GUIDE

SINGS AND ABBREVIATIONS USED:

This Guide uses different forms of terminology to quality or describe information of use to the tourist. These are :

STARS

Used to grade a tour's general interest. The guide makes no reference to tour of interest less than 1 ★.

★	interesting tour
★★	attractive tour
★★★	very interesting tour

TYPEFACES

Different type faces are used to rate the attractivness of each place to be a visited during a tour.

Trovolhue	place of interest
Playa Blanca	attractive place
VILLARRICA	place of great interest

ABBREVIATIONS

To shorten the text and simplify reading, abbreviations are used for words or names occuring most frequently.

°C	Degrees Celcius
Conaf	(National Forestry Corporation).
h	Hours
ha	Hectares
hol	Holiday
km	Kilometers
m	Meters
m/a/s/l	Meters above sea level
NM	Monumento Nacional
pop	population
Mon	Monday
Tue	Tuesday
Wed	Wednesday
Thu	Thursday
Fri	Friday
Sat	Saturday
Sun	Sunday

STRUCTURE OF THE GUIDE

As pointed out in the Summary on page 1, this booklet divided as follows:

- Presentation
- Practical Data
- Tourist Guide divided in 15 Zones
- Appendice

WHAT IS A TOURIST ZONE ?

Tourist Zone for the purposes of this travel guide, Chile has been divided into zones according to the radius covered in one day of travelling from a given place of tourist interest.

Each of these areas has been labelled Tourist Zone, and they do not necessarily coincide with the country's administrative division into Regions or Provinces. For instance, Chile's Region X extends from Valdivia southward to the Chiloé island. In this GUIDE, this territory is divided into three Tourist Zones, namely Temuco to Valdivia (Zone 10), Osorno to Puerto Montt (Zone 11) and Chiloé (Zone 12).

HOW TO LOCATE A TOURIST ZONE

On page 31 there is a map of Chile divided into 15 Tourist Zones, each delimited by a box and containing the names of its main cities. In addition, the Tourist Zones are also identified by a **number** on blue background on the edge of the page. Thus, you can always find which pages contain information on the Zone of your interest just by looking at the pages' edge.
For example:
Temuco to Valdivia is Zone **10**.

10

NUMBER OF ZONE

CONTENTS OF EACH TOURIST ZONE

Each Tourist Zone contains the following information:

Map an enlarged map of the Zone, with the complete road network and highway services.

Overview a double page summarizing the Zone's features, and a map showing the Zone divided into Sections, each labelled with a number. There is also a table of zonal distances to assist in planning a trip.

How to Get there a chart explaining how to get to the Zone or showing the available detours off the Pan-American highway.

The Land, Its History, Its People a survey of the Zone's most significant geographic, historical, cultural and economic features.

Section Description a detailed review of the Section's history and geological features, main sights, and the tours that can be made around the area.

Excursions an appendix to some Tourist Zones that are particularly suitable for trekking, hiking, excursions on horseback, rafting, mountain bike.

Rural Transport showing rural and interprovincial bus services, including destination, frequency and schedules.

Tips some Zones have particularly convenient or high-quality establishments dealing in handicrafts, gastronomy, or industrial goods. We point them out for you.

DIVISION BY SECTIONS

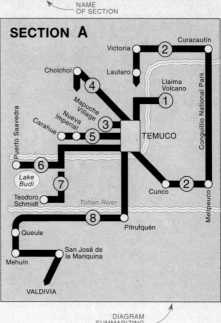

SECTION A   TEMUCO

LETTER
OF SECTION

NAME
OF SECTION

STRIP OF
IDENTIFICATION
OF SECTION

SECTION A

Curacautín

Victoria

2

Cholchol

Lautaro

4

Llaima
Volcano

Conguillio National Park

Puerto Saavedra

Mapuche
Village

Nueva
Imperial

1

Carahue

3

TEMUCO

5

6

Lake
Budi

7

Cunco

2

Melipeuco

Teodoro
Schmidt

Tolten River

8

Pitrufquén

Queule

San José de
la Mariquina

Mehuín

VALDIVIA

DIAGRAM
SUMMARIZING
THE TOUR

Each Tourist Zone is divided into several Sections, differing geographically or because of the existence of an important city which is the starting point for interesting trips.

At the beginning of each Section you will find a wide **Strip of Identification** across the whole page carrying the **letter** and **Name of Section**.

In the top right-hand corner of each page you will also find the corresponding **Name of Section** and **letter** in blue.

At the beginning of the description of each Section there is a **diagram summarizing the tours** to be described, the final destination of each tour and the corresponding number of their description. Thus, you can choose a tour and locate the corresponding text by its number.

TOURS OF A SECTION

Each tour is headed by a **Strip of Colour** which makes it easy to located on that page.

On the colour strip you first see the **Number of the Tour** which shows you where to find it on the diagram summarizing the tour. After this comes the **Name of the Tour** and lastly the **Stars** rating its degree of attractiveness.

The text in *italic typeface* provides practical information, such as distance to be covered, type of road surface, approximate duration of the journey, and services along the way.

The next in **Bold Typeface**, summarizes the tour's main features. It is followed by paragraphs **Normal Typeface** in describing the journey in detail from the departure point (km 0) to its destination.

Example:

NUMBER
OF TOUR

NAME
OF TOUR

ATTRACTIVE
OF TOUR

STRIP OF
COLOUR

2 **TO THE CONGUILLIO NATIONAL PARK ★★★**

a circuit of 251 km, allow at least one day. Cabins and campground at Conguillío. Take food. Gasoline at Melipeuco and Curacautín. This tour can also be combined with the circuit through Lonquimay and lake Icalma described under Section D of Zone 9.

A visit a wonderful National Park, among the best equipped in Chile.

There are several alternative routes leading to the park. We suggest to start from Temuco (km 0) through Las Hortensias and then Cunco (km 59); the town is described under Tour 11, Section B. Continue towards Melipeuco (km 91), to climb behind the Llaima volcano to the

ITALIC
TYPEFACE

BOLD
TYPEFACE

NORMAL
TYPEFACE

DRIVING BY THE PANAMERICAN HIGHWAY

Those who travel for the first time south of Santiago, hope to get at least as far as Puerto Montt or farther, to Quellón on the island of Chiloé.

Similarly, those who travel to the "Norte Grande" hope to reach Arica on one trip.

These tourists see the country from the Panamerican Highway, visiting cities on the way and planning one or two detours to see some highlight of nearby interest.

For these, the GUIDE gives a description of the Panamerican Highway, pointing out interesting and attractive the tours nearby.

To help find the description of the Panamerican Highway within the Tourist Zone, this has a **blue background**.

The traveller can easily follow the road map of the Panamerican Highway through the different Zones outlined in this Guide

Example:

PAN-AMERICAN HIGHWAY FROM PAILLACO TO PAILLACO ★★★ *the paved highway offers two alternatives: via Los lagos, with 191 km, and via Valdivia, with 211 km.*

The Pan-Am starts to run through a thoroughly southern landscape, with native forests, large rivers and towering, perfect-coned volcanoes.

South of Temuco (km 0; city description in Section A), the Pan-Am has a stretch of double-carriage highway and crosses the Cautín river, running through soft-rolling reddish land. On the left is a picturesque religious construction in a style introduced by the Bavarian Capuchin monks who preached the Gospel in the Araucanía.

At km 12 in the Metrenco Sanctuary with a restaurant and campground across the street.

At km 14 is the Quepe toll-only those heading

BACKGROUND
OF COLOUR

CITY MAPS

A **General Map** of each city, town and village is provided. For larger cities, a second, enlarged map shows the **Downtown Area**, where hotels, get-together points, museums, interesting buildings and telephone offices are concentrated.

All these places are identified by symbols, letters or numerals and are listed at the foot of the map. In some cases, the entry in the list is accompanied by an **asterisk** (*), indicating that this item is to be found not in the downtown blow-up, but in the **general city map**.

Visiting a City

The description of all bigger cities and towns includes a **What To See** section, describing the main sights, the square, pointing out the shopping streets, how to find them, and, where possible, a **look-out** point commanding a view over the city and its environs.

The circuit proposed for a city follows the streets marked with a white background and a darker outline. The names of such streets are shown both in the map and mentioned in the corresponding text.

Lastly, a **list of restaurants** is provided, indicating those having the best cuisine, those suitable for families with children, inexpensive restaurants or those offering quicker meals, the so-called get-together establishments, and sites suitable for a picnic.

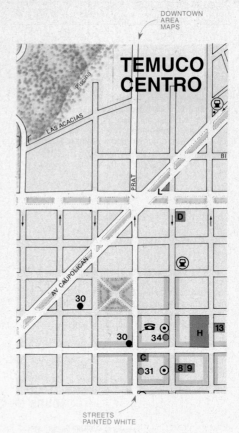

URBAN POPULATION

In the larger cities the number of inhabitants living within the **urban area** is indicated in accordance with the 1982 census.

This information will be brougth up to date with the 1992 census. In Chile there is a definite tendency to migrate from rural areas to the cities, which accounts for the increase in population density of urban centers compared to the rest of the country.

You will be surprised to find that the population figures on road signs differ greatly from those in this Guide. This is due to two factors:

a the figure on the road signs include an estimate of the population increase since the last census.

b the figure on the road signs indicates the total municipal population which inclues the **urban population** plus the **rural population** living nearby.

This Guide only takes into account the **urban population**, as that will give you a better idea of the size of the services offered in any city or town.

APPENDICE

The Services Section is at the end of this Guide, with information needed when touring the country.

- **Cost of Gasoline** varies throughout the country. The % of variation as compared to the price in Santiago is shown.
- **Price of Fares** are listed between Santiago and the main cities.

- **Lodgings** the principal hotels in cities and towns.
- **Car Rental** where cars can be hired and the different types available.
- **Pleasure Tours** companies affering this service and a list of proposed tours.
- **Excursions by Sea** with a description of the boats and the trips available.

Zone 1
ARICA-IQUIQUE

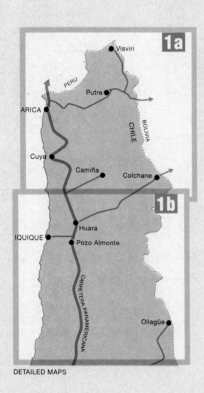

1a

Visviri

PERU

Putre

ARICA

CHILE

BOLIVIA

Cuya

Camiña

Colchane

1b

Huara

IQUIQUE

Pozo Almonte

CARRETERA PANAMERICANA

Ollagüe

DETAILED MAPS

1

Arica

Iquique

Antofagasta

Easter
Island

Copiapó

La Serena

Valparaíso

Is R
Crusoe

SANTIAGO

Talca

Concepción

Temuco

Valdivia

Osorno

Pto Montt

Castro

Chaitén

Coihaique

Cochrane

Puerto Natales

Punta Arenas

Puerto Williams

Is Diego
Ramirez

90°   60°   53°

CHILEAN
ANTARCTIC
TERRITORY

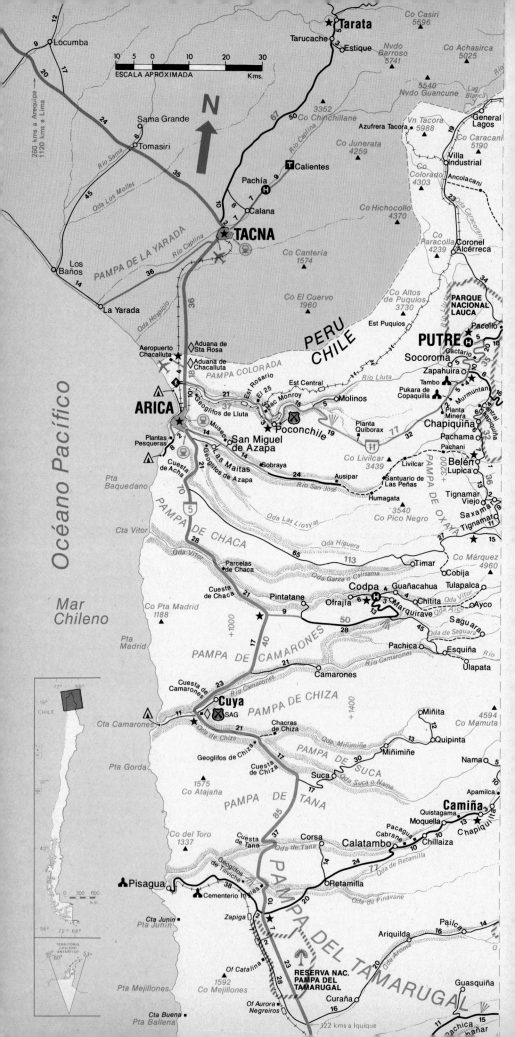

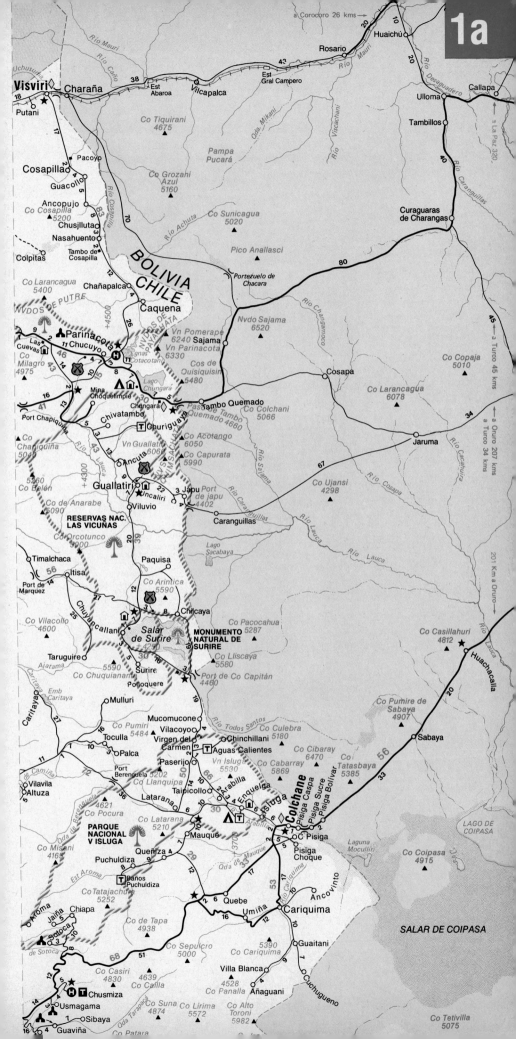

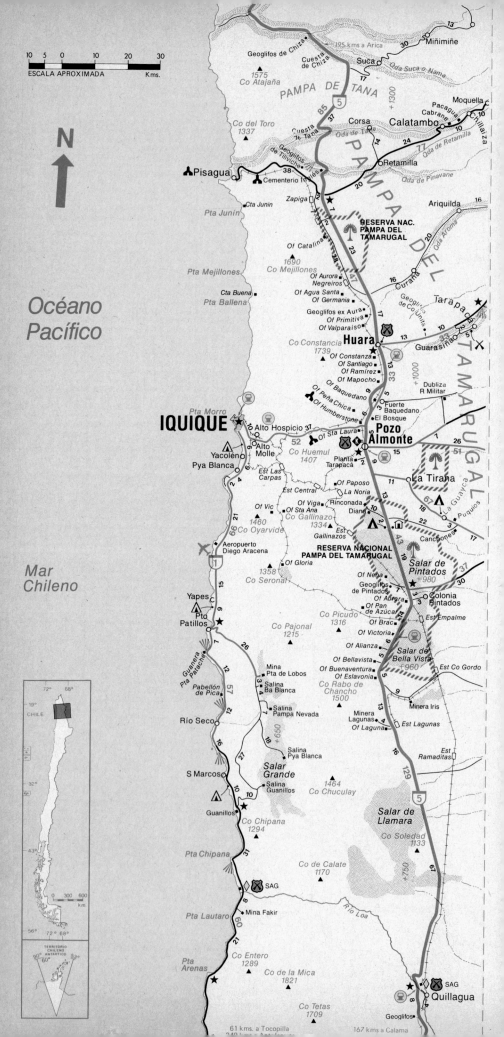

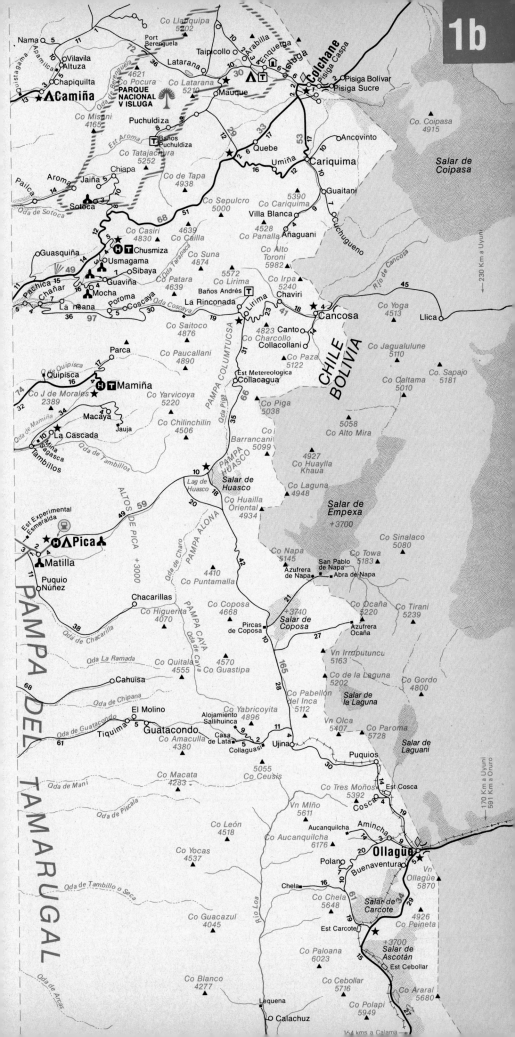

1b

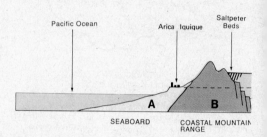

Pacific Ocean — Arica Iquique — Saltpeter Beds

A B

SEABOARD — COASTAL MOUNTAIN RANGE

OVERVIEW

Chile's fascinating Deep North stretches from Visviri in the north, at which point Chile, Perú and Bolivia meet, to the Loa river in the south.

Four distinct areas are clearly defined throughout its entire length: the **Seaboard**, where the two main cities are located; the Central Plain or **Pampa del Tamarugal**; the **Sierra** or Andean counterforts, a rugged area climbing up to the Andes (the Cordillera) and dotted with numerous beautiful oases; and the **High Plateau** (Altiplano), a flat expanse covering the upper reaches of the Andes, sparsely populated by scattered Aymara herdsmen.

The Pampa del Tamarugal shows a marked contrast from north to south, the former being often cleft by deep ravines (quebradas), the latter uninterruptedly flat. This Zone's geographical features prompt its subdivision into four areas, namely:

Section A Iquique including the coast, the Pampa del Tamarugal and the oases in the Sierra up to Zapiga in the north, where the first large ravine breaks the Pampa's evenness.

Section B High Plateau and Salt Flat covering the Andes Range inland from Iquique and including the least known and most beautiful spots, only accessible to the more adventure-minded.

Section C Arica with the splendid valleys of Azapa and Lluta, picturesque mountain villages and a possibility to hop across the border to visit Tacna in Perú.

Section D Nationals Parks accessible through the partly-paved international road to Bolivia. It includes the superb Lauca National Park with the high-altitude Chungará lake and many other remote and breathtakingly beautiful spots.

REGIONAL DISTANCES

Arica														
272	Camiña													
120	252	Cadpa												
425	307	405	Colchane											
324	206	304	101	Chusmiza										
471	353	451	413	311	Mounth to the Loa									
322	200	298	259	158	154	Iquique								
206	478	323	631	530	677	525	Lake Chungara							
353	231	329	290	188	280	125	559	Mamiña						
190	467	315	620	519	666	517	13	548	Parinacota					
346	224	322	283	181	273	119	485	137	476	Pica				
279	157	255	216	114	206	51	453	74	469	67	Pozo Almonte			
149	421	269	574	473	620	471	57	502	46	495	428	Putre		
451	329	427	388	286	378	223	625	246	641	166	172	600	Quillagua	
181	370	232	530	407	534	404	478	432	371	426	363	345	529	Surire Salt Flat

Zone 1
ARICA - IQUIQUE

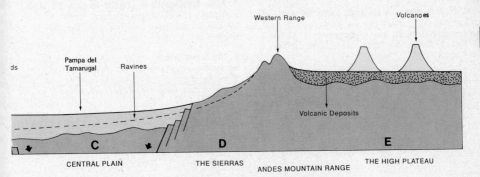

Volcano es

1

Western Range

Pampa del
Tamarugal   Ravines

Volcanic Deposits

C   D   E

CENTRAL PLAIN   THE SIERRAS   THE HIGH PLATEAU
ANDES MOUNTAIN RANGE

DIVISION BY SECTIONS

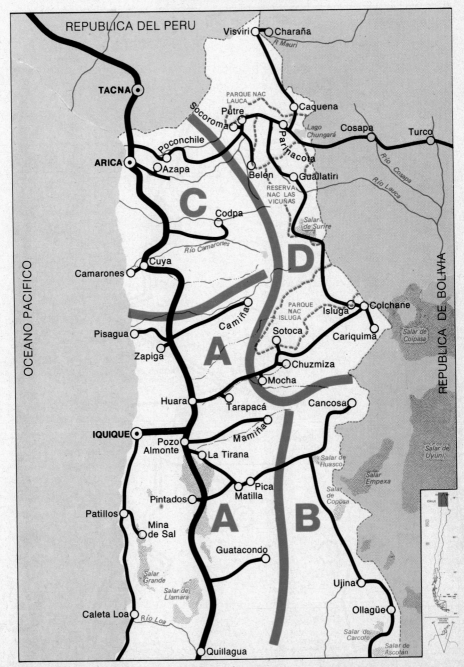

41

DETOURS OFF THE PAN-AMERICAN HIGHWAY

The sketch below shows the routes alternative to the Pan-American Highway for touring this Zone. Some are accessible to all vehicles, others preferably for vehicles travelling in convoys, and others solely for 4-wheel-drive off-roaders.

1 From Iquique to Antofagasta along the coast with half the road paved and the rest gravel. A beautiful way to return south, described in Section A, Tour 3 and in the Antofagasta Zone, Section B, Tour 4.

2 A visit to Pica the oasis nearest the Pan-American Highway. Good road. Described in Section A, Tour 4.

3 A tour of the National Parks a spectacular way to return from Arica to Iquique through the High Plateau. It is advisable to travel in a convoy of at least 2 vehicles. Described in Section D.

4 From Antofagasta to Iquique through the High Plateau a breathtaking expedition recommended for 2 or more 4-wheel-drive vehicles. Described in Section B.

5 The Grand Circuit a truly adventurous tour covering the entire High Plateau from Calama to Arica. Only recommendable for convoys of 2 or more 4-wheel-drive vehicles. Described in Sections B and D.

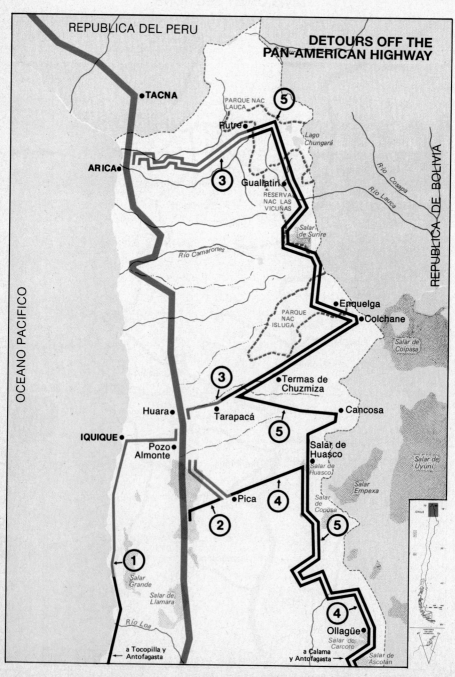

THE LAND, ITS HISTORY, ITS PEOPLE

DESCRIPTION this zone stretches from Visviri to the Loa river and is made up of five distinct geographic areas:

Coastal Mountain Range decreasing gradually both in altitude and width from Antofagasta northwards, until dying at the Morro de Arica, the massive headland towering above the city of Arica. Farther north the mountains flatten out until totally disappearing and the flat expanses westward of the Andes roll down directly to the sea.

Seaboard spawned by erosion of the western slopes of the Coastal Range. It is narrow from Iquique to the south, spanned lengthwise by a road, and nonexistent from Iquique to the Morro de Arica, where the cliffs plummet directly to the sea. This area harbors 80% of the population as well as both major cities.

Central Plain a flatland nestled between the Andes and Coastal mountain ranges, also known as the Pampa del Tamarugal. Varying in altitude from 1,000 to 1,200 meters above sea level and sloping gently from east to west, it originated from a local sinking of the earth crust which was subsequently filled up by erosion from the Andes.

The Pampa's alluvial material is porous and lets the water flowing down from the Andes seep through. This water accumulates into superficial water tables upon reaching the Coastal Range, made up of impervious granitic material, giving rise to **salt flats** as the underground water evaporates and deposits the salts on the surface. A similar origin have the **nitrate fields**, occurring at the point where the coastal granitic ground meets the porous pampa soil; they appear to have been formed by selective seepage flowing along such fissures.

Over 30,000 hectares of this area of superficial water tables have been planted with **Tamarugo**, a tree superbly adapted to saline soils and arid lands.

The pampa ends at the Azapa valley, in Arica, but, prior to that and starting at the **Quebrada (Ravine) de Tiliviche** (Zapiga and Pisagua), it is slashed four times by deep crosswise gorges. These odd gashes in the pampa were carved by streams which managed to flow all the way to the ocean over the top of the Coastal Range –here running low and narrow–, thanks to sedimentation having completely filled up the central depression until reaching the coastal mountain tops.

These four canyon like formations used to be the natural boundary for colonial territories and now for the present day provinces of Tarapacá and Arica. The chasms are so deep and wide that they made it impossible for the railroad to reach Arica.

The Sierra corresponds to the western slopes of the Andes, crisscrossed by a myriad ravines, some with water springs. Here are hundreds of small villages dating from pre Conquest times, growing crops on hillside terraces and supplying farm produce to the cities.

A different case is the **Pica oasis**, where the ravines at the Andean slopes were filled up by volcanic rock and ashes from eruptions in the High Plateau. The water flows through underground water tables and emerges at the foothills as springs.

The High Plateau (Altiplano) is a nearly flat table perched atop the Andes, with some very high volcanoes protruding here and there. It originated from volcanic deposits filling up the area and producing a high altitude treeless plain. East flowing streams and wet, spongy, grassy areas called bofedales support a varied fauna and large herds of camelids. Scattered on these vast expanses live a small number of herdsmen of Aymara origin. The municipal districts of Visviri, Putre and Colchane have recently been created to organize this population.

CLIMATE each of the above areas has its own climate:
The Coast receives no rainfall whatsoever, has a mean annual temperature of 18° C and 70% of cloudless afternoons a year (mornings are usually cloudy). It is somewhat humid.
The Pampa lying at about 1,000 1,200 meters altitude and out of reach of the moderating influence of the sea, shows a wide temperature oscillation between day and night (30° and 0° C in winter). It is one of the driest deserts in the world.

Somewhat higher up is the **Sierra** with a transition desert climate averaging 20° C in summer and 9° C in winter. Rain falls in summer, swelling the streams considerably.
The High Plateau with elevations ranging from 3,500 to 4,500 meters above sea level, is a high altitude steppe with summer rains and mean temperatures varying from 10° C to 5° C.

The classical desert climatic phenomena, such as the so called High Plateau or Bolivian winter (curiously occurring in summer) and the thick fog known as camanchaca are described in the Antofagasta section.

EARLY INHABITANTS the most complete collections of artifacts illustrating the cultural development of the pre Conquest period are found at the **Museo de Azapa**, in Arica, and the **Museo Regional**, in Iquique.

Three different ethnic groups inhabited this area since the earliest times: the Aymaras in the **High Plateau**, related to the race which brought about the Tiwanaku empire; the **Sierra** people, involved with the creators of the Inca empire; and the Changos at the **coast**.

These groups lacked a clearcut territorial base and, prompted by rigorous survival imperatives, occupied simultaneously all the three above geographic areas, without competing against one another. Thus, there were Aymara colonies growing coca at the Azapa valley, and Sierra people settlements at the High Plateau engaged in nomadic livestock raising. The coastal dwellers also used to go inland to raise their crops. The cultural periods, similar to those described under the Antofagasta section, are the

Archaic Period from the year 8000 to 1000 BC. The hunters gatherers of the **Chinchorro culture** stand out in Arica, with their mummification process in sand, the oldest in the world.

Formative Period 1000 BC to AD 300, marked the beginning of animal domestication and flock tending, together with incipient agriculture and coarse, rudimentary pottery and manipulation of locally mined metals. Textiles were decorated with geometric patterns.

Tiwanaku Period AD 300 to AD 1100. The empire established from the Titicaca lake basin in present day Bolivia extended its influence over vast areas of Chile. Trade between coast, Sierra and High Plateau grew more intense and new agricultural techniques were introduced, such as the use of terraces and irrigation canals. New designs and patterns were applied to pottery, such as black strokes over white or red backgrounds, and geometric volutes to textiles. They also introduced the use of hallucinogens into rites and ceremonies.

Regional Development Period AD 1100 to AD 1470. This was the period of autonomous territories at the High Plateau, the sierra and the coastal valley at Arica. Garments, ornaments and utensils showed an extraordinary development in the use of color. There are beautiful artifacts from this period, particularly headdresses or hats. The establishment of these autonomous territories accounts for the appearance of defensive pukaras or fortresses during this period.

Inca Period from AD 1470 to AD 1535. The Inca Empire originated in the Peruvian sierras and spread south through Chile up to the Maule river, where its southward drive was controlled by the fierce Mapuches (Araucanos). The Incas brought with them farming and military settlements and undertook the construction of expeditious roads known as Caminos del Inca. They also introduced many new styles in the decoration of baskets, pottery and textiles, as well as new types of uten-

Llama
(Lama glama)

Alpaca
(Lama pacos)

Guanaco
(Lama guanicoë)

Vicuña
(Vicugna vicugna)

sils, such as bowls and decorated jars and pitchers. This short period ended with the arrival of the first conquistadors, who produced a tremendous upheaval among native communities.

GEOGLYPHS these are archaeological manifestations falling under Rupestrian Art and consisting of figures drawn or «painted» on hillsides; their significant cultural value has earned them the status of National Monuments.

One of two techniques was used to produce such geoglyphs: either the darker rocks were used to design a sort of «**mosaic**» against the lighter ground; or the oxidized, darker surface was «**swept aside**», creating a lighter design over a dark background.

Geoglyphs were placed at highly visible spots, such as the slopes of isolated hills at the pampa, on the eastern slopes of the Coastal Range, such as at Pintados, and in the ravines crossing the pampa. Geoglyphs can be found from the Loa river northwards up to the Azapa valley in Arica and along the Peruvian coastal plains up to Nazca.

The pictures fall into different families, such as a **geometric family**, with circles, squares and rhombi, in addition to broken lines; **zoomorphic family**, depicting animals, mainly camelids, and also felines, birds and snakes; **anthropomorphic family**, with human figures sometimes bearing bow and arrows, staff, headdresses and other elements. Geoglyphs generally group figures belonging to more than one of these families.

Geoglyphs are estimated to date from the years AD 1000 to 1400, corresponding to the **Regional Development** Period, when intense social and cultural exchange was usual between the autonomous territories. Their purpose is thought to have been as «signposts» along herding routes between the Sierra and the coast, or to fulfill certain ritual or cult purposes.

THE CAMELIDS relatives of the camel, are the largest animals native to this zone. The Spaniards used to call the llama «sheep»; the llama was the only pack animal of the pre Hispanic Andean cultures. Camelids in general were particularly important for such cultures, but retained some significance during the colonial period, and continue to be a valuable resource for the present inhabitants of the High Plateau. They provide meat, hides and wool. There are four different species, which can be crossbred but at the second generation the predominant species returns in full.

Llama is the largest of the four species. It can be domesticated and is mainly used as a pack animal and as a source of meat. It yields about 4 kilos of wool –the thickest among camelids– every two years. Llamas are the least selective in terms of fodder, grazing usually at lower quality pastures.

Alpaca is somewhat smaller than llama, with a thick woolly coat covering even the eyes and ranging in color from pure white, through varying hues of brown and gray, to black. It yields 5 kilos of wool every two years; the wool is fine and silky and widely used for high quality knitted garments. Alpaca is the most selective in feeding, grazing solely at bofedales (swamps).

Vicuña is the smallest of the four species and cannot be domesticated. It lives in family groups of one male and up to five females, grazing equally at bofedales or other pastures. The female bears only one offspring a year. The demand for its wool –the finest animal fibre after silkworm's and used for the choicest textiles by native cultures– and its hide had all but wiped it out. It yields only about 300 grams of wool every 3 to 4 years. Now it is protected within the High Plateau national parks and reserves under administration by the Chilean Forest Service (Conaf). From 1,000 animals in 1973, they climbed to 16,400 in 1984 and by now have very nearly reached the maximum carrying capacity of the local pastures, estimated at around 26,000 vicuñas.

The future vicuña exploitation management plan aims at benefiting the High Plateau inhabitants without uprooting them from their physical and cultural milieu, following the excellent example of textile production at Lirima (see Section 2, Tour 2).

Guanaco with a short haired, light brown pelt and slightly larger than vicuña, is wild and difficult to tame. Some 1,000 individuals live in the frontier national parks.

SPANISH RULE started with the passage through these lands of conquistadors Diego de Almagro in 1536 and Pedro de Valdivia in 1540.

Administrative Division the Corregimiento de Arica was established in 1565, subordinate to the Perú Viceroyship and bordering in the south with the «Atacama Wilderness», at the Loa river. North-wards it stretched up to Tacna and eastwards up to Bolivia; its capital was Arica.

Two centuries later the southern chunk of this Corregimiento was separated to become the Corregimiento de Tarapacá, extending from Zapiga in the north to the Loa river in the south; its capital was the village of Tarapacá.

Early on Spaniards settled here running encomiendas de indios estates granted by the Spanish king with a number of Indians at the dis-posal of each assignee under a serfdom system. Gradually a Spanish population built up, remaining always a minority with respect to the aboriginal inhabitants. They homesteaded oases up in the sierras and the fertile valleys at the bottom of the ravines in the pampa. They tended to cluster at **Tacna**, **Belén**, **Putre**, **Tarapacá** and **Pica**, on account of their better climate and absence of malaria, the terrible illness that then swept the coastal lands.

In the seventeenth century the Corregimientos were divided into Repartimientos, each with a head town, Indian chieftain and Spanish administration. These were **Arica**, including the Azapa valley; **Codpa**, ruling all the «Indian settlements» in the Sierra and High Plateau; **Camiña**, with jurisdiction up to Isluga; **Tarapacá**, controlling the area downstream from the town of Tarapacá; **Sibaya**, ruling the townships upstream of Tarapacá; and **Pica**, extending up to Guatacondo.

The Catholic church set out promptly to spread the Gospel among the Indian communities, found-ing the first chapels. Once the administrative make up was in place, around 1620, curacies were es-tablished with a parish at the head town of each Repartimiento, subordinate to the Arequipa Archbishopric. Over 60 beautiful chapels and bel-fries still stand as witnesses to this missionary zeal.

Economic Development- barter trade was predomi-nant since pre Hispanic times. The discovery of silver mines in 1545 at Potosí, in the Bolivian high plateau, turned Arica into a bustling shipping and supply seaport, spawning an intense merchandise traffic between Arica and Potosí over the next one and a half centuries. The Spaniards, afraid of malaria existing at Arica, settled in **Putre** (1580) and **Belén** (1620).

The goods were transported by mule trains along the Lluta valley through Socoroma, Putre and the Chungará lake, or through the Azapa valley to Belén and Putre. Potosí became the largest city in the Western Hemisphere, with over 160,000 inhab-itants and generating a great demand for food for people and animals; it was supplied by the Azapa and Lluta valleys and the fertile ravines in the Si-erra.

During the 18th century a higher value crop started to be raised at the **Azapa**, **Codpa**, **Tarapacá** and **Pica** valleys: vineyards producing a much ap-preciated wine that found its way to Potosí through the old mule trails or through new ones running from Tarapacá through Isluga or from Pica through Cancosa.

Another resource generating wealth was the «mining» of the **guano beds** at the Iquique coast. This activity had been practiced by the natives since pre Hispanic times and was intensified by Spaniards bringing Indian serfs and black slaves.

By 1730 the **Huantajaya silver mine**, located some way up from Iquique, was reactivated and re-mained productive until the turn of the century. It came to have a population of over 3,000 and made some families in Pica and Tarapacá considerably rich.

COLONIAL CHURCHES they were erected from the

Tarapacá

✳ Matilla

✳ Caspana
Caspana

✳ Ayquina
✳ Ayquina

✳ Peine
✳ Peine

Socaire
Socaire

✳ Parinacota
✳ Parinacota

Guañacagua
Guañacagua

Guallatiri
Guallatiri

Caquena
Caquena

Dibujos a igual escala

0 1 2 3 4 5m

✳ Indica Monumento Nacional
✳ National Monument

46

early seventeenth century in lands within Indian settlements lacking urban layouts. They were built based on a spatial concept attempting to depict the oneness of the religious creed: a volume with a single nave and a single main entrance, enclosed by a wall delimiting the sacred space, where religious processions were performed. The origin of the present villages dates from a later time and in some the houses are clustered around the church, resembling the arrangement of Chiloé villages, some 3,000 km to the south.

The bell tower was added later, as an annex to the main church building and in a great variety of positions with respect to it. In some cases it was even placed outside the walled compound, as at Pachama, near Belén. This church belfry duality represents, for the High Plateau cultures, a man woman relationship.

The illustration shows belfries, drawn at the same scale, located at Regions I and II; they were subordinate to the Arequipa and Charcas archbishoprics, respectively. They evidence a strong dependence in style from the fact of whether there was a Spanish population residing at the place or not. The bell towers of **Matilla** (baroque) and **Tarapacá** (classical), both of careful proportions, were located at towns with a sizable Spanish population; the same holds for the bell tower at San Pedro de Atacama, but it dates from late last century. The villages of **Putre** and **Socoroma** were also Spanish centers on the route to Potosí, but their bell towers, with their classical solidity, reveal a strong Andean influence. Somewhat more refined is the bell tower at Toconao, also a town with a large Spanish community.

The remaining bell towers are located in marginal villages and therefore are strongly influenced by the local architecture. Outstanding are those at **Caspana** and **Ayquina** and, higher up in the High Plateau, **Parinacota** and **Guallatire**; the latter two show the influence of the so called «Andean Baroque» originated in Arequipa, Perú, with its most striking expression at the **Guañacagua** bell tower.

The walls surrounding the church compounds are also remarkably beautiful, crowned by cornices of all shapes and patterns and with richly ornamented stone portals in baroque style. In the churches themselves there is usually an impressive array of baroque statuary placed in polychrome wooden or stone altarpieces or niches.

The most interesting collections can be found at the Calama and Atacama Salt Flat area, at the Tarapacá ravine –with a magnificent baroque style– and at the High Plateau in Region I.

THE WAR OF THE PACIFIC from the creation of the Republic of Perú until 1878, this region enjoyed considerable prosperity derived from the discovery of nitrate fields and the exploitation of guano beds. The corresponding surge in activity and population gave a boost to agriculture at the oases, grapevines being then replaced by fruit tree orchards. Mining towns sprouted in the pampa and, most significantly, seaports were established at Iquique and Pisagua.

Chile declared the war against Perú on April 5, 1879 (see The Land, Its History, Its People, in Antofagasta). A short time before, between February 14 and March 23, Chilean troops had retaken all the territory from Parallel 24° S up to the Loa river, which had been previously occupied by Bolivia 50 years ago.

The bulk of the Chilean forces was stationed at Antofagasta, ready for the assault northwards. The strategy adopted was to always land somewhat farther north from the points to be taken, thus cutting off the enemy forces. But this entailed first gaining supremacy at sea.

The Naval Campaign started with the **blockade of Iquique** (April 5) by the Chilean vessels Esmeralda and Covadonga. The first sea battle took place off the coast of **Chipana** (April 12), when the Chilean gunship Magallanes ran into the Peruvian warships Unión and Pilcomayo, both larger and with more firepower; the latter withdrew.

Peruvian ships started then to stage surprise raids against Chilean cargo ships, sinking or capturing some, and bombing the seaports. They set out from their naval bases at Callao and Arica, where the bulk of the Peruvian fleet –the Huáscar, Independencia, Unión and Manco Cápac– had their bases. The Chilean fleet, by contrast, had no bases up in the north, and its major warships Blanco Encalada, Cochrane and O'Higgins sailed all the way up to Callao seeking to engage head on the Peruvian forces. On May 21, the Peruvian warships Huáscar and Independencia attacked the Chilean ships –Esmeralda and Covadonga– which had been blockading Iquique now for over six weeks. The ironclad Huáscar sank the wooden Esmeralda in the heroic **Iquique Sea Battle**, where Captain Arturo Prat and most of his men died. The Covadonga, by contrast, being light and small, managed to make the much larger Independencia run aground and subsequently surrender. This date is remembered by a holiday in Chile. One Perwian wariphs Huascar and Union were finally neutralized and defeated in the Angamos Sea Battle (October 8), Chilean troops prepared to attack.

The Land Campaign on November 2, Chilean troops landed at **Pisagua** and brought it under their control after a fierce battle. Next fell Iquique and some time later Tacna, at which point the Bolivian forces withdrew from the conflict. The only stronghold still remaining was Arica, with its fortress and naval base at the **Morro de Arica**, the large bluff towering above the town. It was conquered by the Chileans in 55 minutes in a legendary bayonet thrust. Thus ended, on June 7, 1880, the War of the Pacific in this zone.

The present international boundary with Perú is known as «Boundary of Concord», and was achieved through a treaty subscribed in 1929. It runs 10 km north of the railroad linking Arica to La Paz, Bolivia, with a detour to the north in order to leave the Tacora volcano and sulphur deposit within Chilean territory.

SALTPETER was a gigantic source of wealth for this region and the country as a whole. At one time it provided 51% of the total tax revenue. Only two saltpeter fields –known as oficinas– are still active: María Elena and Pedro de Valdivia, near Antofagasta. With only a tenth of the labor employed in the golden years, they produce nearly one third of the peak output of those times.

The Nitrate Fields they were known as **cantones salitreros**. They were not made up of a single vast unit, but of many beds surfacing in the proximity of coastal or midway hills. They took the form of thick hard layers of a grayish hue called caliche and covered by a thin earthen crust. They occurred from Zapiga in the north down to Lagunas, south of the Pintados salt flat. There were some 17 of them in this zone, with peculiar names such as **Nebraska**, **Kitchen**, **Bishop's Salt** and the like.

Farther south was the **Cantón Toco**, inland from Tocopilla; **Cantón Central**, between Antofagasta and Calama; **Cantón Aguas Blancas**, south of Antofagasta, and lastly **Cantón Taltal**, inland from the namesake seaport.

Each cantón had several nitrate beds, sometimes belonging to the same owner; those nearest the coast were the first to be mined. Later, railroads linked all saltpeter works.

HIGH PLATEAU BELL TOWERS

＊ S Pedro de Atacama   ＊ Toconao

＊ Isluga   Socoroma   Putre   ＊ Sotoca

Mining processes three main processes were employed. In the so called

Oficinas de Parada –«stopover» works– a small installation –the «office»– was set up at a particular spot, buying saltpeter from a number of independent laborers who extracted the stuff within a small radius around the «office» and crushed it with a sledge hammer. The «office» would then dissolve it in water using boilers heated up by direct fire; the resulting concentrated liquid mother liquor was then placed under the sun in crystallizing troughs. These were called «stopover works» because when the high grade nitrate –50% to 60% saltpeter content– was depleted at their current mining spot, they would move on and then again «stopover» somewhere else.

Oficinas de Máquinas these machine works appeared in 1853, when Pedro Gamboni introduced a system for dissolving saltpeter in steam heated troughs, making it possible to process material containing as little as 30% niter. This technique required stationary installations, such as boilers, serpentines, troughs and so on. This, in turn, called for a settled population, which meant building houses, offices, desalination plants, etc. Thus appeared the mining works known as «oficinas», easily spotted in the barren landscape by the huge waste dumps they generated.

In 1866, Gamboni patented a process for **extracting iodine** from a nitrous solution and in 1878, at the Oficina Agua Santa, Santiago Humberstone developed the **Shanks process**, which consisted of dissolving saltpeter in double bottomed steam heated troughs at lower temperatures than was then customary and treating mother liquor in such a manner as to make it possible to extract nitrate from material with as little as 13% nitrate content. This process was further improved with filters, vacuum application and other refinements, being employed until the oficinas were dismantled by 1945.

The Oficinas de Máquinas developed as well systems for hauling material from the mines to the processing plants, first using mule drawn wagons and later, by 1875, by means of their own internal railways.

Oficina Guggenheim it is the system used at the Pedro de Valdivia and María Elena mines, introduced around 1930. It involves basically the application, on the one hand, of large scale mining technologies such as hauling material with electrified railways, mechanized raw material extraction and crushing, and, on the other hand, saltpeter dissolution in gigantic troughs heated to lower temperatures over a longer period of time, and chemical processing to extract niter from material containing as little as 7% saltpeter. The combined output of these two outfits accounts for one third of the total output in Chile; their lower production costs enable them to still be in operation.

Market Development saltpeter mining started around 1810, the product being used for gunpowder production in Perú. In 1830 the first shipment left Iquique for Europe and the USA, to be used as a fertilizer. The output skyrocketed soon thereafter: by 1840 73,000 tons were extracted; by 1860, 320,000 tons; by 1870, half a million tons. Tarapacá was until then the only producing area, but was soon joined by Antofagasta. Output soared to 1 million tons by the turn of the century and peaked at 3 million tons/year in 1917. In 1875 the government of Perú expropriated all the Tarapacá nitrate mines, paying for them with Saltpeter Certificates. During the War of the British Pacific these certificates dropped to 10% of their face value, triggering the sharp nosed resident Briton John North into a buying frenzy financed by loans granted by Chilean banks, which left him as the owner of the lion's share of the certificates. He promptly registered these as assets into corporations established in London. By the turn of the century, English capitals controlled around 60% of the saltpeter industry and North came to be known as the Saltpeter King.

The saltpeter industry crisis started with the onset of World War I, when exports plummeted due to a drop in the availability of ships. It soon rebounded, however, fueled by the strong nitrate demand for war purposes in 1916 17, only to nosedive thereafter when synthetic nitrate entered the market. The very large world demand for nitrogenous fertilizers and the urge to meet gunpowder production needs during the war prompted some European nations, particularly Germany, to develop their own supplies based on synthetic ammonium sulfate. Their success was such that the synthetic version gradually elbowed the Chilean product out of the markets. In 1910, Chilean saltpeter met 65% of the world's nitrogenous fertilizer needs; by 1920 this share had dropped to 30%, and by 1930, to 10%. During the 1950s it accounted for a mere 3%.

To avert a wholesale folding of the saltpeter works, the state and the producers established Covensa in 1934, an organization under their joint management and entrusted with allocating production quotas and centralizing saltpeter marketing abroad. A number of companies failed nonetheless. In 1955 a Saltpeter Act granted producers tax breaks, duty exemptions and other facilities which also failed to stem the slide in output.

In 1969 a new company was established, the Sociedad Química y Minera de Chile, SOQUIMICH, with private and state capitals. It ran and still runs the María Elena and the Pedro de Valdivia plants and, after becoming a state company in 1971, also the few saltpeter works then still operating. It is now a prosperous, reprivatized company looking forward to a foreseen upswing in the saltpeter industry fueled by the high prices of iodine and a newly found world appetite for natural fertilizers.

Nitrate Railways between 1870 and 1903 a number of railroads were laid to serve the saltpeter works, hauling water, food, fuel and other supplies up to the various settlements and carrying their output down to the shipping ports. The major ones in Tarapacá were those running from **Iquique** to **La Noria**, and from **Pisagua** to **Zapiga**, established around 1870, and the one running from **Cantón Lagunas** to **Patillos**, established somewhat later. In 1882 control of the Iquique and Pisagua railways was acquired by the **Nitrate Railway Co**, based in London and controlled by John North, who had founded many saltpeter mining companies. The independent producers felt the pinch of running against a monopoly and two new railways were set up: from **Aguas Blancas** to **Caleta Buena** (1893) and from **Cantón Zapiga** to **Caleta Junín** (1894); both ended in aerial trams cars which plunged 600 meters from the clifftop to bring the cargo down to the shipping docks.

In Antofagasta railways linked the **port** and **Cantón Central** (1876), **Caleta Coloso** and **Cantón Aguas Blancas** (1903), **Tocopilla Cantón Toco** (1890), and **Taltal Cantón Taltal** (1883).

Three of these railways belonged to British interests, 4 were English Chilean joint ventures under British management; the Coloso railway, built by a Spanish company using German machinery, was under Chilean management. Each railway had its own repair and maintenance shops, mostly employing English engineers and English technology; this technology had a considerable influence on the saltpeter industry.

In 1923, the State built the «longino» railway from Pueblo Hundido (now Diego de Almagro) to Iquique, linking all the nitrate railroads with one another. The only railways still operating in the area are the Tocopilla railroad, serving María Elena and Pedro de Valdivia; the Antofagasta railroad, later extended up to La Paz, Bolivia, and the «longino».

The Men Behind Saltpeter hundreds of characters gave shape and flavor to the saltpeter epic life. The first exporters (1830) were the Chilean Santiago Zavala, and H García and F Bustos, Peruvians. The Englishman Jorge Smith (1856) and the German Juan Gildemeister (1870) brought innovations into the milling technology and good entrepreneurial drive.

In the early 1900s, HB Sloman set up saltpeter works at Toco, built a dam at the Loa river and erected the giant Chile Haus in Hamburg, Germany (1923), rated among the most important modern architectural undertakings of that time.

Pedro Gamboni born in Valparaíso in 1825, settled in Iquique in 1850 and, working at the pampa, developed and patented the «indirect heating» saltpeter dissolving system (1853), whose application was pioneered by the Sebastopol works. After 10 years of testing, in 1866 he patented a process for extracting iodine from the saltpeter «mother liquor». He was granted and exclusive 10 year franchise to extract iodine with this process by the Peruvian and Bolivian governments, making a fortune with his invention. He died in Iquique in 1895.

Santiago Humberstone arrived in Pisagua in 1875, at the age of 25. With a degree in chemical engineering earned in England, he obtained a job at the San Antonio works of the Campbell Outram Co, where he developed the foundations of the so called Shanks saltpeter dissolving process, pioneered at the Agua Santa works of this same company in 1878. He devised several improvements and set up the Tres Marías works, while running the Primitiva works of the north group. In 1892 he built the Huara railway, running from Agua Santa to Caleta Buena. He retired in 1925, after half a century dedicated to saltpeter. He died in Santiago in 1939.

John T North arrived in Chile in 1866, at the age of 24, to work as a railway technician at Carrizal Bajo and, later, Caldera. From 1868 to 1875 he worked in Iquique at the English railway maintenance shop, in addition to partaking in supplying operations for English nitrate companies. In 1875 he founded the Iquique Water Company, supplied by tankers bringing the water from Arica by sea and by a seawater desalination plant in Iquique, laying the foundation of his wealth and good credit. In the midst of war, in 1880 81, using funds loaned by the Banco de Valparaíso, he bought the depreciated saltpeter certificates issued by the Peruvian government. When Chile returned the nitrate fields to the corresponding certificate holders, North already controlled the Primitiva, Peruana, Ramírez, Buen Retiro, Jazpampa and Virginia saltpeter works.

In 1882 he returned to London and stayed there eight years, busily building an economic empire, founding companies which he then floated at the London Stock Exchange and controlling directly or indirectly 15 nitrate companies, 4 railway companies (Iquique, Pisagua, Patillos and Curanilahue Concepción, in southern Chile), the Tarapacá Waterworks (supplying Iquique with water from Pica), the Bank of Tarapacá and London, and the Nitrate Provisions Co, a distributor of food and imported goods in Tarapacá and Antofagasta.

Dubbed «Saltpeter King» and one of the most powerful and influential men in London banking circles, he used his railway monopoly to regulate nitrate prices and production volumes, thus making it possible for his saltpeter companies to generate profits of up to 25% annually. He lived ostentatiously and cultivated close ties with the most powerful European economic groups. When he died in London in 1896 he had sold most of his nitrate interests and had invested in silver and gold mines in Congo and Australia.

PRESENT DEVELOPMENT this zone has a population of 274,000, ninety percent of which living in Iquique and Arica. The remaining 10% live in nearly 100 villages or towns scattered throughout the pampa, Sierra and High Plateau.

In the past, the main source of wealth was the desert, with its saltpeter fields; now this role is played by the sea. Industrial fisheries account for a full 26% of the gross regional product. Iquique is the main fishing port in Chile, with some 35% of the total national catch (580,000 tons/year). Most of the catch (95%) of the 170 fishing vessels along these coasts is used for fishoil and fishmeal production; the rest is canned or frozen.

Manufacturing accounts for 5% of the gross regional product, with shipyards, machine shops and production of parts and implements for the fishing industry. Agriculture is one of the traditional activities in the region, with fruit production in the Azapa and Pica valleys, olive groves at Azapa, vegetables and alfalfa at sierra ravines and oases, man made tamarugo forests at the pampa and bofedales in the High Plateau, these last two supporting livestock farming operations.

Metal mining is carried out at the gold and silver mines of Choquelimpie (near Putre) and Challacollo; copper is mined at Sagasca, on the road to Tarapacá. The flagship of non metal mining is the sodium chloride (common salt) bed at Salar Grande, the largest in the world: 280 km² of nearly pure and crystalline salt (98%). Close to 600,000 tons are extracted every year.

The cities of Iquique and Arica are bustling urban centers –the former being a tax free zone– and enjoy an active cultural life fueled by both regional universities, Arturo Prat and Tarapacá.

SECTION A   IQUIQUE

This section includes the coastal area, the Pampa del Tamarugal and the Sierra oases, stretching from Zapiga in the north to Quillagua in the south.

It offers interesting constrasts between the central desert plain, the lush inland oases and lots of beaches strewn along a coastal road.

Iquique is an excellent «base camp» from which to set out on exploration tours. For those driving to Arica on the Pan-American Highway, a good alternative is to visit the mountain oases on the northbound leg, come down to Iquique on the return leg and continue south along the coastal road. The route offers the following options:

1° Straight from Quillagua to Arica 304 km with some steep stretches, takes about 5 hours.

2° A visit to Pica –a 61 km detour– staying there overnight.

3° A stay overnight in Pica then on to Mamiña and Tarapacá, sleeping at Chusmiza.

4° The Grand Tour making all the oases; start as described in 3 above, then continue to Camiña and stay at Codpa, arriving in Arica on the fourth day.

TOURS FROM IQUIQUE

1   PAN-AMERICAN HIGHWAY FROM QUILLAGUA TO ZAPIGA ★★★ *252 km on a very good road; gasoline at Quillagua, Victoria (112 km), Pozo*

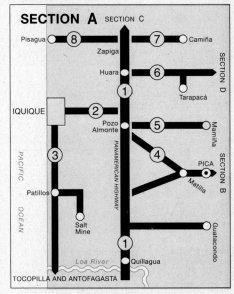

Almonte (172 km), Huara (205 km). Modest but good restaurants at Pozo Almonte and Huara. Nice campground at the forest of the Pampa del

Pintados, geoglyphs

Tamarugal National Reserve. The Zapiga-Arica stretch is described in Section C, Tour 1.
Drive or ride through the best section of the tamarugo forests growing in the middle of the desert, with possibilities of taking detours towards the mountains or the coast.

Quillagua (Km 0) is a border customs and sanitary checkpoint (description in Antofagasta Zone, Section B, Tour 1). North of the Loa starts the **Pampa del Tamarugal**, a vast sedimentary expanse falling gently to the west. The road runs near the Coastal Range. The Soledad Hill to the left is 1333 m high, but it looks low since the salt flat is at 750 m above sea level.

Starting at km 25, you can see the Llamara salt flat to the left. It is unusual because it lacks the typical rugged salty crust. Farther ahead the plain opens up towards the coast, and small green patches can be seen now and then; they are wild tamarugos, the tree indigenous to this area to which the plain owes its name.

At km 66 a gravel road branches off the Pan-American Highway to the right, a 66 kilometer road that goes up to **Guatacondo**, a small oasis at the bottom of a gorge graced by some crops growing on contour terraces. Located astride the ancient Inca Road from Arica to Quillagua, it used to produce fruit and flowers during the saltpeter heyday. Now it is being gradually deserted by its residents.

Back at the Pan-American Highway, at km 82 from Quillagua, the soil to the left of the road has been upturned: it is the **Lagunas Saltpeter Bed**. Work was started here in 1872 by the Peruvian firm Montero y Cía, which built its own railway linking it to the coast at Patillos. In 1881 the place was acquired by a Chilean family, who sold it in 1887 to John North. He then established the Lagunas Syndicate Ltd. It was the richest saltpeter bed in Tarapacá. All that is left now are waste dumps, the wreckage of living quarters and processing facilities, and cemeteries surrounded by fences. Most have been ransacked.

At km 95 is the Bellavista saltpeter field, with three large old abandoned nitrate works, Buenaventura, Bellavista, and Alianza. Some 30 km later comes

Oficina Victoria in the process of being dismantled. It was the last nitrate town with active works in Tarapacá, surviving until the late 1970s. It belonged to a group headed by Osvaldo de Castro which, pooling machinery and equipment from a number of nitrate works then shutting down their operations, managed to modernize five old works at the richest saltpeter beds.

At km 129 is the turn-off for Pica (detour described in Tour 4). We are now in the great **Pintados Salt Flat**, the largest in Tarapacá. To the right there is a farming community established by the state in 1945 as an experimental station; today it is run by small private farmers. To the left there is a round hillock: it is the last counterfort of the Coastal Range. Turn left to visit the

PINTADOS GEOGLYPHS (NM) drive 2 km in and then another 3 km and you will see one of the largest displays of ancient aboriginal art. Over 50,000

square meters of hillslopes are decorated by more than 400 figures depicting humans, animals, birds or abstract shapes, isolated or arranged into thematic groups. The place is highly visible from the pampa and is thought to have been a votive center. It was restored in 1981-82 by the Universidad de Tarapacá.

Somewhat farther ahead, at km 148, the highway plunges headlong into something seemingly out of place in this very dry desert: a green forest. It is the

PAMPA DEL TAMARUGAL NATIONAL RESERVE 23 hectares of man-made forests and 4,500 ha of natural forests under the management of the Chilean Forest Service (Conaf) since 1983. It contains an agricultural center, tree nurseries, park wardens and a good campground. Tamarugo (Prosopis tamarugo) is a multistemmed tree superbly adapted to saline soils. It used to cover large stretches of pampa, but started to be felled in times of Spanish domination and was nearly wiped out during the nitrate mining period, to be used as fuel. Its pods and foliage are good fodder for sheep and goats -even cattle- and its wood can be used for making furniture, flooring or fenceposts. In the 1920s, a saltpeter producer named Junoy succeeded in raising a 3,000 ha tamarugo plantation. In 1960, the State's Production Development Agency (Corfo) started a forest and livestock farming program at three separate locations (see map). The plots are now rented out to livestock farmers and support a stable livestock population thriving in the midst of the desert.

At the campground you can observe the nitrous crust and hear it cracking as the temperature changes.

Water is tapped in this area from underground water tables and piped some fifty kilometers down to Iquique. At km 172 is

Pozo Almonte a town of about 1,500 people owing its name («Almonte Well») to rich colonial landowners from Pica, who had an artesian well here. By 1875, with the arrival of the railway, it became a water supplier and a service and recreation town for the saltpeter operations. At the main street there are houses with long porches, some old-style general stores and a few picturesque restaurants (the best one is at the Shell gasoline station). In the square, next to the church, there is a beautiful parochial house. The place livens up considerably in the evening. The road to Mamiña starts here, described under Tour 5.

During the War of the Pacific, Peruvian and Bolivian troops were quartered here awaiting the Chilean onslaught. During the civil war in 1891, a bloody clash took place here between both contending factions, Congresistas and Balmacedistas.

Continuing, at km 177 is the **Iquique road intersection**, where the road running down to Iquique branches off (described under Tour 2). At the intersection itself you can see an old saltpeter cart and a water cart, with wheels 1.7 meters across. They used to be drawn by mules and hundreds of them were used at each nitrate works. There is also a small locomotive dating from 1876, pulling a saltpeter car.

Northwards of this point lies the core of the old saltpeter industry, with the De La Peña, Huara, Negreiros, Pampa Negra, del Rincón, Sal del Obispo and Zapiga fields and works. At km 183 the road makes a detour to bypass a large army outpost, **Fuerte Baquedano**, and runs through some old nitrate beds where the soil has been totally upturned. Ruined towns, ancient cemeteries and huge waste dumps can be seen here and there, sometimes right next to the road. At km 205 you cross

Huara a village of 500 inhabitants where the road to the town of Tarapacá starts off (it is worth a detour, described under Tour 6). Most houses in Huara are deserted and padlocked. Continue to the station and the beautiful, solitary **main street** that has an 8-m-wide covered sidewalk and an ancient drugstore –botica Libertad– with a valuable collection of porcelain medicine jars. It is unfortunately closed.

Across from the train station there is a **municipal**

swimming pool, good for taking a refreshing dip before continuing the drive through the desert. The picturesque –and opportune– Flor de Huara restaurant sits right next to the Pan-American Highway. Huara was the main entertainment and services center during the saltpeter times; founded around 1885, it once had a population of 7,000.

Farther ahead loom the waste dumps of the Valparaíso and the Primitiva works, owned by the Primitiva Nitrate Co, founded by North in 1886 and ran by Humberstone. At km 218, to the left of the road are the **Ex Aura geoglyphs**, with depictions of people, the sun and animals. Note that geoglyphs were always placed at slopes that would not be affected by material loosened up from erosion taking place farther above. At km 221, some 600 m to the left of the road, is the site of a bloody battle between Chilean and Peruvian forces during the War of the Pacific, the

Battle of Pampa Germania nearby are the large waste dumps of the old Oficina Germania and, beyond them, the ruins of the **Agua Santa** nitrate bed and works, the most important at the time. Agua Santa was owned by Campbell Outram Co and managed by S Humberstone; it was at this plant where he introduced his Shanks nitrate extraction process in 1878. To break North's railway monopoly, he had a railroad built from here to Caleta Buena in 1892.

Back on the Pan-American Highway, some way ahead there is another **tamarugo forest** straddling the road, planted by Corfo between 1968 and 1972. At km 244, a couple of kilometers to the left, is the site of the

Battle of Dolores fought during the War of the Pacific between Chilean troops and a Peruvian-Bolivian detachment.

Next along the highway to the north comes the **Zapiga saltpeter deposit**, the first one to be exploited in the early 1800s. Later, it was to become the core of John North's nitrate empire.

At km 252 is a road intersection, the road to the right leading to **Camiña**, described under Tour 7, and the one to left going to **Pisagua**, described under Tour 8.

A short distance to the left is the ghost town and train station of **Zapiga**, a major recreation center during the saltpeter times. Here ends the saltpeter district and the ruins of nitrate works.

For the continuation of the Pan-Am to Arica, see Section C, Tour 1.

2   A VISIT TO IQUIQUE ★★★

47 km from the Pan-Am Highway intersection.
This is the only access to the capital of Region I.

As you leave the Pan-Am Highway, km 0, an old nitrate town can be seen a bit farther ahead. It is

Oficina Humberstone (NM) founded in 1862 under a different name and renamed in the late 1930s, when the new living quarters were built –the only part surviving– using anhydrite-stuccoed boards for the walls and slag as insulation. Orderly laid out around the square –the only trees surviving are the tamarugos–, it has a theater with the seats still in place, a general store, administration buildings and a curious covered swimming pool, the walls of which are made of riveted steel plates.

The place can be visited only Saturdays and Sundays (the guide collects a modest fee). The processing plant is being dismantled; it ceased to operate in 1960.

A couple of kilometers ahead, to the left of the road, is the

Oficina Santa Laura (NM) only the processing plant remains, along with a slender smokestack, the administration building and the warehouse. If you manage to go into the warehouse (beware of the dogs; there is a caretaker at the place), you can see the nail and screw containers, numbered by size, as well as the remains of some other odds and bits of its installations. This is one of the oldest nitrate works, operating between 1890 and 1910; together with Humberstone and Chacabuco, in Antofagasta, is one of the handful which have not been thoroughly dismantled.

The road drops steadily down towards the coast until, at km 37, it takes a spectacular plunge down the face of a 600 m cliff. At the bottom is the Pacific Ocean and, squeezed on a narrow strip of flat land between cliff and sea, lies Iquique. This is the closest thing to an airplane landing you will experience without leaving the ground. As you start the descent, directly to the left is a gigantic sharp-crested sand dune known as «the Dragon» on account of its shape. At km 47 you arrive at

| IQUIQUE | a city of around 140,000 inhabitants and capital of Region I, which stretches from Arica to the Loa river. Placed in a narrow litoral platform and surrounded by a high coastal slope (faldeo) more than 600 m high.

It used to be the capital of the saltpeter industry; now it is a fishing center and the world's top fishmeal shipping port. Since 1975 it enjoys a tax-free status which boosted trade and spawned a significant number of exporting industries.

This new role has also brought about vigorous urban growth and remodelation, with special attention granted to the historical center; a long promenade along its superb beach has also been built. It has reoriented the city toward the sea; this promenade is the actual gathering place of the young.

The city of Iquique is recent. Its cove, however, is known since pre-Hispanic times for its guano deposits. During the colonial period, guano harvesting was greatly increased by a Spanish concessionaire using natives and slaves as laborers. The main deposits were located at Serrano island, Punta Patache, Patillos, and Pabellón de Pica.

By 1730, the silver mine of Huantajaya (located at the plateau above Iquique) was reactivated, reaching at one time a population of over 3,000. Ships from Chile and Perú arrived at Iquique with supplies for the mine and other villages, but the settlement of Iquique itself did not climb above 100 inhabitants during that entire century. Water was brought by ship either from Pisagua (somewhat brackish) or Arica.

In 1828 the government of Perú authorized the exporting of saltpeter. The first shipment was made in 1830 and signalled the start of urban growth.

In 1855 Iquique was made into a Major Port and ten years later it shipped some 320,000 tons of nitrate. Its population of 2,500 was made up mainly of the families of saltpeter workers, port laborers and miners.

By 1878 it had climbed to around 10,000 people, with many foreigners taking part in nitrate and railway businesses. By then it was already a provincial capital, and from this period date the Customs building, the clock tower in the main square, the street lighting and the railway running from the port to La Noria. John North was the owner of the Iquique Water Company, operating a desalination plant.

The War of the Pacific started in 1879. Off the shores of this port, the Chilean ship Esmeralda - blockading access to it together with the Covadonga- was sunk by the Peruvian ironclad Huáscar. The remains of Chilean captain Arturo Prat were buried at the local cemetery. Five months later Chilean troops landed at Pisagua, farther up north, and defeated the Peruvian-Bolivian army at Dolores, which subsequently retreated from Iquique. The town was then occupied by Chilean forces.

The period from 1880 to 1920 saw the heyday of saltpeter. It brought about an architectural transformation, witnesses of which are the Astoreca Palace, the Municipal Theater, the Spanish Club and large wooden, Victorian-style houses mainly at Baquedano street. Hundreds of clippers crowded the harbor of what then was Chile's main nitrate shipping port.

When the saltpeter activity started to wind down, fishing took its place. The first cannery was set up in 1935 and the first fishmeal plant in 1950. Today Iquique is a thriving city with flourishing trade, interesting architecture, good tourist facilities and excellent beaches.

What To See the Duty Free Zone **(Zofri)** is worth a

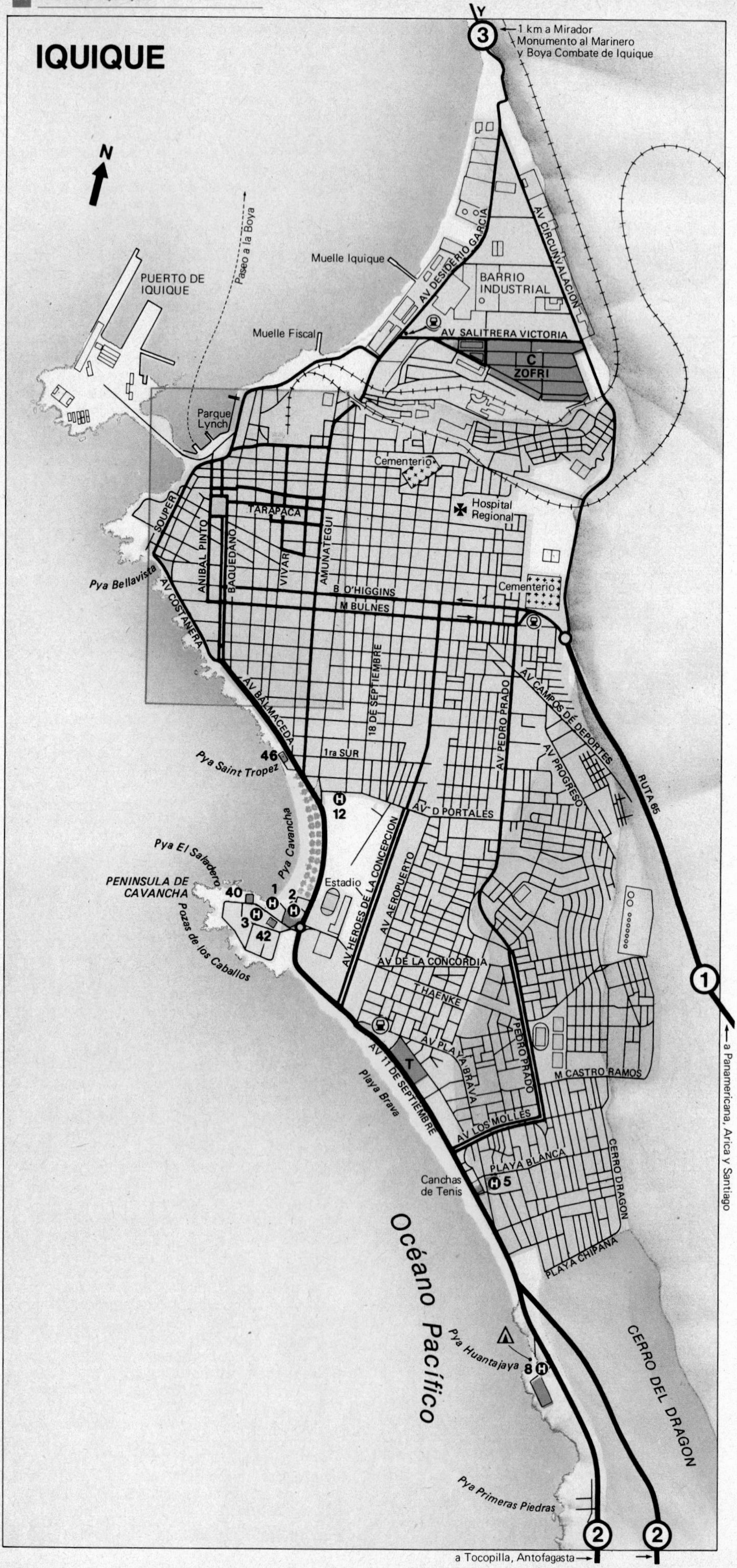

IQUIQUE

N

1

PUERTO DE
IQUIQUE

Paseo a la Boya

Muelle Iquique

Muelle Fiscal

AV CIRCUNVALACION-J

BARRIO
INDUSTRIAL

AV DESIDERIO GARCIA

1 km a Mirador
Monumento al Marinero
y Boya Combate de Iquique

3
Y

AV SALITRERA VICTORIA

C
ZOFRI

Parque
Lynch

Cementerio

Hospital
Regional

Cementerio

SOPER

ANIBAL PINTO

BAQUEDANO

VIVAR

TARAPACA

AMUNATEGUI

B O'HIGGINS

M BULNES

AV COSTANERA

Pya Bellavista

AV BALMACEDA

18 DE SEPTIEMBRE

1ra SUR

Pya Saint Tropez

46

Pya Cavancha

H
12

AV D PORTALES

AV PEDRO PRADO

AV CAMPOS DE DEPORTES

AV PROGRESO

RUTA 05

Pya El Salvador

PENINSULA DE
CAVANCHA

Pozas de los Caballos

40

1
H

2

3
H

42

Estadio

AV HEROES DE LA CONCEPCION

AV AEROPUERTO

AV DE LA CONCORDIA

1

a Panamericana, Arica y Santiago

T HAENKE

PEDRO PRADO

M CASTRO RAMOS

CERRO DRAGON

AV PLAYA BRAVA

Playa Brava

AV 11 DE SEPTIEMBRE

T

AV PLAYA BRAVA

AV LOS MOLLES

PLAYA BLANCA

Canchas
de Tenis

H 5

PLAYA CHIPANA

Océano Pacífico

Pya Huantajaya

8 H

CERRO DEL DRAGON

Pya Primeras Piedras

2

2

a Tocopilla, Antofagasta

1

Legend

- ☎ Telephone Center
- ★ Touristic Information
- ⊙ Café, Metting Point
- ◉ Gasoline Station
- ≫ Lookout Point
- ❋ ✚ Hospital
- **A** Regional Government (4A)
- **B** Town Hall (2C)
- **X** Cathedral (2B)
- ❋ **C** Duty–Free Zone (Zofri)
- **D** Bus Terminal (1B)
- **K** Taxis to Arica (3C)
- **E** Post Office (2B)
- **F** Regional Museum (3B)
- **G** Astoreca Museum (4B)
- **H** Naval Museum (2B)
- **J** Marketplace (3C)
- **L** Handicrafts (3B)
- **S** Clock Tower (2B)
- ❋ **Y** Monument to the Sailor

BUILDING OF INTEREST
- **M** Passenger Pier (1A)
- **N** Railway Station (NM), (1C)
- **P** Baquedano Ave (NM), (3B)
- **G** Astoreca Palace (NM), (4B)
- **L** Municipal Theatre (NM), (2B)
- **H** Customs House (NM), (2B)
- ❋ **T** Arturo Prat University
- **U** Santa María School (3C)

ACCOMODATIONS
- ❋ **1** Hs Cavancha
- ❋ **2** H Chucumata
- ❋ **3** H Atenas
- **4** H Arturo Prat (2A)
- ❋ **5** H Playa Brava
- **6** H Tamarugal (2B)
- **7** H Barros Arana (4C)
- ❋ **8** H Huantajaya
- **9** H Camino del Mar (4B)
- **10** H Inti-Llanka (3B)

- **11** H San Martín (2C)
- ❋ **12** H Eben Ezen
- **13** H Icaisa (4B)
- **14** H Major's (4A)
- **15** H Belén (3C)
- **16** H De la Plaza (2B)
- **17** H Durana (2B)
- **18** H Phoenix (2A)
- **19** Bh Wilson (3B)
- **20** Bh Colonial (4C)
- **21** Bh Catedral (2B)
- **22** Bh Vivar (5C)
- **23** Bh Nan-King (2C)
- **24** Bh Bolivar (2B)
- **25** Bh Danny (4C)
- **26** Bh Li -Ming (3C)
- **27** Bh Santa Ana (2C)
- ❋ ⚠ Campground

RESTAURANTS
- ❋ **40** El Sombrero

- **41** Club Español (2B)
- ❋ **42** Choris
- **43** Club de Yates (1A)
- **44** Yugolavensky Dom (2B)
- **45** Cantón Nebraska (2B)
- ❋ **46** Drive In Luquillo
- **47** D'Alfredo (2C)
- **48** Bavaria (3A)
- **J** Marketplace Eateries (3C)

TOURIST SERVICES
- **30** Viajes Inquitour (2B)
- **31** Viajes Mamiña (3C)
- **32** Viajes Lirima (3B)
- **36** Buses to Pica (3C)
- **33** Lan Chile (2A)
- **34** Ladeco (2B)
- **35** Hertz Rent a Cars (2A)

❋ See general map of Iquique

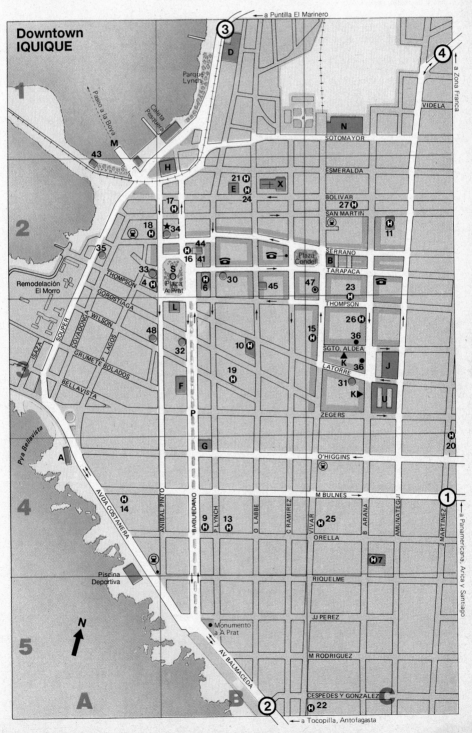

Downtown IQUIQUE

Iquique, Baquedano street

visit. You can get there by colectivo (shared taxis serving a fixed route) or, if you are driving, take Amunátegui to the north, through the underpass and then turn right at the first wide avenue.

ZOFRI is open Mon through Fri 10:00-13:00 h and 16:00-21:00 h; Sat 10:00-14:00 h. It is a large compound for assembling or storing duty-free imported products, most of which are then reexported both to neighboring countries and to the rest of Chile. Zofri storage and industrial areas are not accessible to the general public, but a large three-story building houses over 200 shops where visitors can buy electronic articles, photographic equipment, textiles, automobile parts and a lot more at convenient prices, free of import duties and tax on the value added. There are banks, telephone and telex offices, and restaurants. Any articles bought in a quantity larger than for personal consumption or use must pay import duties at the city airport, at the Pan-American customs checkpoint at Quillagua or at the Río Loa checkpoint on the coastal road.

If you are driving, you can continue to the north through the industrial area where the fish processing plants are located, then 2 km along the coast to

Puntilla del Marinero with a monument to the sailor located on a lookout over the rocks. A **buoy** some way from the shore marks the place where the Esmeralda was sunk. Two railways scar the cliff face behind: the saltpeter railroad and the state-built «longino» railway. The former zigzags down the cliff, forcing the train to go some stretches in reverse. The latter, by contrast, overshoots Iquique still some way up the cliff face and then goes into a tunnel, turning deep within the bowels of the hill back towards Iquique and emerging at a lower altitude.

Return to the city on the same road and once you pass Zofri, take your right to continue through the costanera. You will go through **Patricio Lynch Park** to stop at the dock and

HISTORICAL QUARTER at the northern end of Aníbal Pinto street. A quaint old covered passenger pier with benches offers a view to the harbor and its innumerable fishing vessels. Boats offer rides around the harbor. To one side is the

Customs building (NM) erected in 1871 as gate into the city and to house the offices of the Peruvian administration and the customs premises. The 2-story classical colonial building is crowned by an octagonal steeple and has an inner courtyard surrounded by galleries in two levels.

On its side is the **Naval Museum** (Tue through Sat, 09:30 -12:30 h and 14:30 -18:00 h; Sun 10:00 -18:00 h), containing exhibits which provide an insight into the Iquique Sea Battle and other historical occasions.

Continuing along Souper street and then **Costanera**, which runs along the seafront, you pass a **monument to Arturo Prat** and then come to Balmaceda avenue. Here starts a promenade running the entire length of the beach, with restaurants and

cafés, ending at

Cavancha Beach far the most frequented. The peninsula starting here contains a restaurant, hotels and a residential area.

Farther south along **Playa Brava** are new housing compounds, restaurants and the **Arturo Prat University**. At the end of the urban area starts the **Dragon Hill**, the gigantic sand dune resulting from the action of the wind against the cliff behind. This is good place for sand buggies.

To visit downtown, return by the costanera until the Arturo Prat Monument so that you can see

BAQUEDANO STREET AND MAIN SQUARE with gay colored timber houses built in American Georgian style between 1880 and 1920. They have long porches facing the sidewalk, with slender pillars and wooden balustrades, and nice door and window frames. The roofs, supported by pillars, are raised from the main body of the house in such a way as to permit air circulation to cool the inner rooms. Some wooden walls are lined by stuccoed Guayaquil cane. Two buildings stand out:

Regional Museum (Mon through Fri 09:00-13:00 h, 16:00-20:00 h; Sat and Sun 10:30-13:00 h), at 951 Baquedano in what formerly was the seat of the Court of Justice. Archaeological and ethnographic exhibits give an insight into the indigenous sierra and high plateau cultures, and ample historical exhibits document the saltpeter times.

Astoreca Palace an imposing mansion at the corner of Baquedano and O'Higgins (Tue-Fri 10:00-13:00 h and 16:00-20:00 h; Sat-Sun 10:00-13:00 h). Erected in 1904, it still has furniture dating from that period, and a collection of paintings and sea shells.

Baquedano leads to the **main square**, with old trees and palms surrounding the **Clock Tower** the symbol of the town. Built in 1877, it has a massive base with pointed arches and three levels supporting the ancient clock. Around the square are hotels, old clubs and stores. Two buildings are particularly interesting:

Municipal Theater (NM) inaugurated in 1890 as an opera theater. Over several decades, all renowned artists visiting Chile had to perform here. Erected during the saltpeter heyday, it stands as witness to the intense and refined cultural life attained at this desert outpost. Spacious and with two mezzanine levels, it was designed in Renaissance style by architect Bliederhauser and built in cane-covered, anhydrite-stuccoed wood.

It was restored with funds contributed by the municipal government and fishing companies and then reopened to the public.

Centro Español erected in 1904 for the resident Spanish community by Miguel Retornano, it was built in Moorish style with minutely carved wood. Note the polychrome stuccoes, and the series of large oil paintings depicting scenes of Don Quixote's life made by Spanish artist Vicente Tordecillas in 1908. The Spanish Club is a busy place with a good restaurant well worth a visit.

Continue the tour by car along Tarapacá street to Plaza Condell across from the Town Hall. Turn left at Vivar and continue on to the

Central Station (NM) beautiful group around the square; to the left is the **Railway Administration building (NM)**, now housing the Civil Court for Minors. To the right, the old station. Both buildings were erected in 1883, when J North acquired control of the nitrate railway, using Oregon pine in Georgian style, then commonly found in British colonies. Inside the station there is some rail equipment having the National Monument status: 143 cm gauge locomotive Nº 8 and a passenger car, belonging to the British railway but carrying Chilean national emblems, and 100 cm gauge locomotive Nº 1035 and a passenger car, belonging to the State railway.

Finally, you can walk to visit the active retail section; you can see at **Tarapacá** street **educational exhibits** in a kiosk at Plaza Condell; at **Vivar** street there is a well assorted **Market** and the modern Santa María School. Nearby is the marketplace, busy shopping streets, and a monolith in memory of a bloody labor conflict from 1907.

Return to the square by Thompson street among old buildings and good stores at side streets.

Where To Eat club de Yates, near the Historical Quarter; hotels at the Cavancha peninsula; the best cuisine is found at the four main hotels. Club Español is charming and offers the traditional northern drink at its best: pisco sour in Pica lemon juice. Pisco is a strong spirit distilled from grape juice, typical of Chile and Perú. Pica lemons are tiny, uniquely-tasting, and grown at the Pica oasis. Cantón Nebraska boasts a variety of 100 different sandwiches and brands of beer. Cheap eateries can be found at the marketplace. Picnic area at Playa Brava, to the South.

Transportation there are several car rental companies; the cars can be returned at the Arica airport. Shared taxis («colectivos») cover the route to Arica on a regular schedule. Big hotels and tourist agencies organize tours to Pica, Mamiña and Pica.

3 TO ANTOFAGASTA ON THE COASTAL ROAD

★★★   *437 km to Antofagasta, 249 km to Tocopilla and 154 km to the mouth of the Loa river, where customs and farm produce control checkpoints are located. The road is paved up to the Loa river; gasoline, food and lodging only at Tocopilla; camping sites on beaches along the way. A one-day trip, take enough gasoline and water.*
This is a good alternative to the Pan-Am highway to return south on the coastal road, stopping by at nice beaches and visiting interesting mining operations along the way.

Leave Iquique, km 0, taking the road south. At km 10 there is a police road control and, to the right, a fishery. At km 15 is Playa Blanca and a curious golf club, with «greens» of packed sand instead of grass. At km 19 is

Punta Gruesa off this point of the coast, on May 21 1879, the small Chilean corvette Covadonga

1

Iquique, Opera theater

avenged the sinking of its sister ship Esmeralda earlier that day at Iquique by making the Peruvian ironclad Independencia run aground and then surrender.

A string of small beaches follows: greenish, rocky **Los Verdes**, at km 30; **Las Pizarras**, at km 33, where the surf laps against stone slabs; at km 36, secluded **Seremeño Beach**; the white floaters mark the site of oyster fields.

From km 41 to km 46 is Los Cóndores Air Force Base and Diego Aracena airport, serving Iquique. To the right is a fairly wide seaboard and to the left the uninterruptedly even cliff face of the Coastal Range. A little farther ahead the hills are used as a firing range by fighter jets.

Some way beyond are some white rocks and lots of seabirds: here are the famous guano beds. At km 56, private **Yapes beach**, with a few houses and water brought by truck from Iquique. At km 64.

Chanavallita fishing cove and beach frequented by campers. There are some houses and a restaurant. Water is brought from Iquique. At km 68,

Puerto Patillos with a mechanized wharf to load ships with salt, mining installations and large mounds of salt. Near the shore are guano covered rocks. This port acquired importance during colonial times on account of its guano beds. In 1872 it became a major nitrate shipping port, with a railway linking it to Cantón Lagunas. Acquired by J North in 1887, it was shut down by the turn of the century in order to allow the Iquique railway to monopolize nitrate transportation. At present, the mechanized wharf is operated by the Punta de Lobos salt works. Here we recommend the following detour:

A VISIT TO SALAR GRANDE 53 km round trip on a

good paved road to an open pit salt mine, located at the world's largest sodium chloride (common salt) deposit.

1 km before Patillo take the road to the left, climbing the steep cliff all the way to the top of the Coastal Range. The **view** is magnificent. Farther below, the roadbed of the old nitrate railway can still be made out. The road traverses the Coastal Range; on the roadside you can see huge chunks of salt fallen from mine trucks. At km 25, behind some hillocks, is the vast expanse of **Salar Grande**, a huge salt flat flanked by Coastal Range mountains.

The road leads to several different salt mining installations. To the left is the **Punta de Lobos Salt Mine**. The gate warden authorizes visits to the mine any day of the week. A large open pit of very white walls, with spiral ramps where trucks circulate and the salt is extracted. This pit is almost depleted, and a new one is being dug 1 km beyond. Visitors are allowed at this second pit only on Sundays.

Back on the coastal road and continuing to the south, at km 68 is **Cáñamo beach**, with green-hued waves lapping on the shore. At km 75, **Punta Patache**, with active guano works. White guano is recent, while the highly-valued red one is a fossil, thousands of years old. There is a nice view from the promontory, from where guano extraction works dating from last century can be seen.

Next comes Punta Negra, surrounded by the wall of an old guano plant. At km 84 is **El Aguila beach**, good for bathing. It enjoys a Nature Sanctuary status as giant sea turtles lay their eggs here. Farther ahead is **Chanavaya beach**.

This bay ends at the massive headland of **Pabellón de Pica**, an old guano deposit «harvested» since pre-Hispanic times by natives of Pica, then intensely exploited during the colonial period and last century. A trail leads to the top of the steep promontory, rugged terrain. Between Pabellón de Pica and Río Seco is **Torrecilla Beach**, a nice, white-sanded beach. You can fish flounders and see the guano excavations.

Beyond is a wide bay with fishing vessels normally resting at anchor. At km 99 is **Río Seco**, a fishing village, old port and processing plant for salt brought from Salar Grande. The remnants of evaporation ponds, a ferry cable and a road climbing to the salt works can be seen. Farther on are some guano-covered rocks. At km 102 is the **Punta de Lobos** promontory, with two white islets favored by innumerable guanay, the guano-producing seabirds, and by a busy sea wolf colony.

The road winds through rocky outcrops and around promontories jutting into the sea, hemmed in by towering hills where perfectly-shaped **erosion cones** can be seen. At km 110 is **Chomache beach**

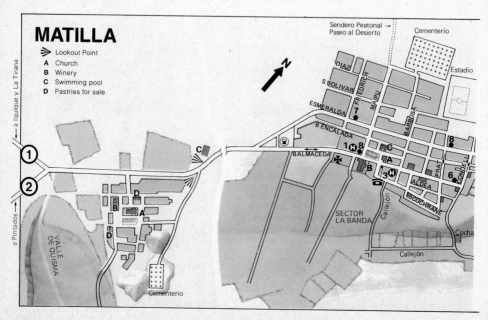

MATILLA

➢ Lookout Point
A Church
B Winery
C Swimming pool
D Pastries for sale

a Iquique y La Tirana

a Pintados

VALLE DE QUISMA

Cementerio

Sendero Peatonal →
Paseo al Desierto

Cementerio

DIAZ

Estadio

S BOLIVAR

FREDRICH

MAIPU

ESMERALDA

BARBOSA

7

B ENCALADA

BALMACEDA

A

PRAT

ALDEA

CONDELL

COCHRANE

SECTOR LA BANDA

Callejón

Cocha

Callejón

and, a little farther, **Peruana beach**, the best in this coast and excellent for bathing and camping. At km 125 is

Guanillos with the wreckage of an old salt processing plant, lodgings built in mud brick, a cemetery harking back to the long history of the place, a road climbing to Salar Grande and, erected on rocks, a huge concrete administration building, a veritable castle. It is all abandoned.

To the south is **Punta Blanca**, with a volcano-shaped guano deposit, and then **Chipana bay**, with a long beach, aptly named **Playa larga**, and a fishing village and a cemetery at its end. Some **cacti** grow on the hills, the only vegetation along this entire stretch of coast. At the end of the bay is **Punta Chipana**, a large promontory ending in a long, low tongue of land jutting into the sea.

A few miles off the coast took place the first sea battle of the War of the Pacific: the **Battle of Chipana**, on April 12, 1879, between the Chilean gunship Magallanes, under the command of J J Latorre, and the Peruvian corvettes Unión and Pilcomayo. The latter withdrew from the engagement.

Ahead is a straight stretch of road, at the end of which, through a deep cut in the Coastal Range, the Loa river runs into the ocean as a thin stream fringed by grass. It is Chile's longest river. At km 154 are the

Bridge, Customs and Agricultural Products Control Checkpoint cars brought into Region I from the rest of the country must be registered as leaving it, and articles bought at the Duty-Free Zone will be checked. Most perishable foodstuffs –fruit, vegetables and the like– will not be allowed through by the Agricultural Products Control agents.

The stretch to Tocopilla and Antofagasta is described in the Antofagasta Zone, Section B, Tour 4.

---

4 A VISIT TO PICA AND MATILLA ★★★

coming from the south, it is better to take the road to Pica at Pintados -not in top shape- and return to the Pan-American highway through La Tirana. 104 km from Pintados through Pica to Pozo Almonte, 87 km of which are paved. From Iquique to Pica it is 119 km, all paved. Gasoline, hotels and campground at Pica.

The first oasis, easily accessible from the Pan-American highway and having the best infrastructure.

From the Pan-Am highway at Pintados, km 0, take road to the right leading to Pica. Almost immediately comes the Agricultural Colony, with plots of land in what used to be an experimental station set up in 1945 by the Production Development Agency (Corfo). The road ascends gently and the trees from Pica and Matilla can be seen in the distance. From km 15 the road is paved and in fair shape. At km 30 is a bridge crossing the

stream flowing out of the Quisma ravine, then the junction with the road coming from Iquique. At km 33 is Matilla and at km 37 is

PICA an old Indian town dating from pre-Conquest times and located at the foothills of the Andes. Several springs surface here and water the oasis. Now the district's head town, it has a population of 1,245. It consists of 250 hectares of ravines covered by thick vegetation, citrus groves, and large mango and guava trees. The town, complete with church and square, is fringed by farming areas such as La Banda, Resbaladero and Miraflores, each having a **cocha** or pool where the water flowing up from the springs is stored for irrigation and bathing. People come here throughout the year to enjoy the climate and the water.

Pica was one of the stations of the Inca Road, and the Spanish conquistador Diego de Almagro passed through here and fought the natives. The Spaniards settled here in 1556 and by 1559 an «encomienda de indios» -estates granted by the Spanish king with a number of Indians at the disposal of each assignee under a serfdom system- had already been established.

The settlement kept growing until it clustered the largest proportion of Spaniards in the area. Social traditions were closely observed, partly to offset the isolation of the place. The main product of Pica was a much favored wine, sought after as far as Arequipa in Perú and Potosí in Bolivia. Later, in the early 1700s, the Huantajaya silver mine brought considerable wealth to some local families and a boost to the town.

The saltpeter boom at the pampa by the mid 1850s brought about changes in the area: the vineyards were replaced by fruit tree orchards, particularly citrus, and Pica became an exclusive spot for relaxation and recreation. From that period date most houses, stores and the church.

Water the quest for water has been Pica's eternal struggle. In addition to the springs emerging here, the Spaniards dug over 12 km of tunnels connecting wells, using a mining technique applied in Potosí, to tap seeping underground water and increase the volume available at Pica. It is the only one of its kind in America and is still in use; its breathing holes can be seen in the desert.

In 1887, the just-founded Tarapacá Waterworks Co acquired rights to the water and piped it down to Iquique. In 1912, the State set up a new plant tapping water at the Quisma ravine.

What To See walk along the main street past the square towards the cocha (pond) Resbaladero, located between lush orchards, and walk some 600 m beyond the cocha up the road to Salar de Huasco; from the top of the knoll you will have a **panoramic view** of the oasis. Walk back to the

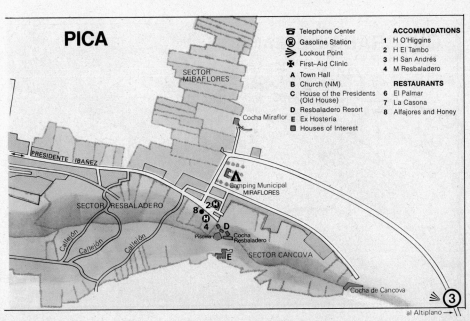

PICA

SECTOR MIRAFLORES

Cocha Miraflor

PRESIDENTE IBAÑEZ

SECTOR RESBALADERO

Camping Municipal MIRAFLORES

8 2

4 D

Piscina   Cocha Resbaladero

Callejón   Callejón   Callejón

E   SECTOR CANCOVA

Cocha de Cancova

al Altiplano

☎	Telephone Center
⛽	Gasoline Station
🔭	Lookout Point
✴	First–Aid Clinic
A	Town Hall
B	Church (NM)
C	House of the Presidents (Old House)
D	Resbaladero Resort
E	Ex Hosteria
■	Houses of Interest

ACCOMMODATIONS
1 H O'Higgins
2 H El Tambo
3 H San Andrés
4 M Resbaladero

RESTAURANTS
6 El Palmar
7 La Casona
8 Alfajores and Honey

1

Church of Matilla

Cocha Resbaladero a natural pool among the rocks used as a swimming pool. The water flows out of a deep cave.

In the town itself, the main street is the **Historical Quarter**, with nice old houses, some with long porches and intricate doors which leave an opening on the upper side to permit air circulation. Beautiful bouganvilles in unusual colors border the sidewalks. And the end of Balmaceda St. is a small hut built using guava tree trunks, joined with branches fastened with leather straps and stuccoed.

Most buildings are wooden, lined with Guayaquil cane and stuccoed with anhydrite, a type of gypsum. The same construction technique was used at the

SAN ANDRES CHURCH (NM) (mass Mar-Sep, Mon-Fri 19:30 h; Oct-Feb, Mon-Sat 20:00 h, Sun 11:00) towering over the square, with a high classical façade framed by pilasters, three doors with a circular top ornament and twin bell towers over the portico. The roof consists of two sections arranged as a cross, with a large dome at the point where both sections meet. Built from 1880 to 1886, it is the third church erected on this site; the two previous ones, dating from 1600 and 1768 respectively, were destroyed by earthquakes. The interior has three well-lit naves, with grooved columns supporting the great central dome. Paintings and a depiction of the **Last Supper** with life-sized figures decorate the walls.

Find the time to have a look at the orchards

walking along the **callejones** (back alleys; see map), so that you can see how the land is worked and subdivided.

Accommodations and Restaurants residencial. El Tambo is spotless, offers good accommodation, as well as other hotels shown on map. Adequate but poorly shaded municipal campground. During the off season, ask whether it is possible to stay at the former Hostería. Lunch at the restaurant at Cocha Resbaladero and other restaurants shown on map.

Heading back to the Pan-Am highway you will see the first drip-irrigated crops. 4 km ahead is

Matilla an old and formerly thriving oasis. It was settled in 1760 by the leading families of Pica. Its main product used to be wine, with sizable vineyards at the Quisma ravine. Always struggling to check the sand encroaching upon the crops, it finally collapsed in 1912 as the water from Quisma ravine was tapped to supply Iquique. There are some interesting buildings:

SAN ANTONIO CHURCH (NM) it presides over the village from its square, with a fine baroque bell tower built in stone, small slabs of borax and gypsum. Same as the foundations, the bell tower is from a previous church dating from the late 18th century and subsequently destroyed by an earthquake. The present one, wooden and built in 1887, has a neoclassical façade, with a vault arranged as a cross and stuccoed with clay. The altar and retable were kept from the previous church. Here is also a depiction of the **Last Supper** with life-sized figures. On one of its sides is the

Matilla Wine Press (NM) an open-air museum (Mon through Sun, 09:00-17:00 h) a winery dating from the early 1700s with all the equipment still in place, including a giant wine press and large earthen jars. It has been well preserved and the labels on displays are very illustrative.

Before leaving, taste the alfajores, pastries typical of this area, and take a stroll down to the **Quisma ravine** to see a superb mango plantation.

Back on the road to the Pan-Am highway, 3 km ahead and to the right is the

Esmeralda Experiment Station established by Corfo in 1945 with 8 hectares, it is now being reorganized into drip irrigation. This will bring the irrigated area from 5 to 6 times. It aims at raising fruit trees already adapted to the soil's salinity and graft them with new strains. The «specialty» are giantsized oranges, lemons, grapefruit and limes, and 8 varieties of mangoes, including some violet colored giants. Date palms are also grown here. Fruit can be bought at the local shop.

		ACCOMMODATIONS	
B Pre–Conquest Ruins		1 H Refugio del Salitre	6 H Tamarugal
C Mud Baths		4 H La Niña de Mis Ojos	2 H La Coruña
D Cocha de Ipla			3 Hs El Tambo

 Lookout Point
A Church (NM)

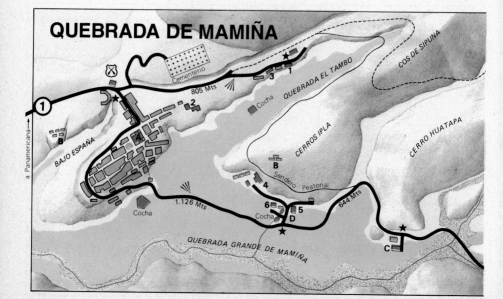

QUEBRADA DE MAMIÑA

1

Continuing to the Pan-Am highway, a 15 km stretch of pure desert is followed by a greenish area: it is the **Huayca area**, with the only natural forest in the entire pampa, where tamarugos and algarrobos -both members of the Prosopis family- grow along some cultivated patches. The oldest **algarrobo** in Chile stands out with its 4.85 cm girth and 27 meters in height; it is over 150 years old.

Next are some houses, stony ruins and strange rectangles on the ground, delimited by small earth ridges. They are called **canchones** (see description below), and can be seen all the way to

La Huayca a village organized by 1850, with a long main street flanked by stone houses and a small square shaded by old trees. The place looks like any common farming area in Chile, except that it is located in the middle of the desert. It used to have vast forests during the colonial period, the trees tapping the water of superficial water tables. By 1720 some silver mining works were set up in the area and tree felling started in order to obtain firewood. The saltpeter industry made demand for firewood increase manifold; many farmers settled here and started growing alfalfa in **canchones** to feed the thousands of mules used in mining operations. Lots of new houses -now in ruins- were built using chunks of the tough crust covering nitrate beds, squaring the sides and filling the gaps with clay. It was the village's golden age, with relatively large farms run by residents of Pica.

Canchones were the imaginative answer to the dramatic scarcity of water in the desert. The technique dates from pre-Hispanic times and is still used at sites where the water table is close to the surface. The soil's salty crust is removed, planting first melons and watermelons in the «uncorrupted» soil; later, alfalfa is planted. In about 5 years evaporation turns the upper salt layer salty once again and a new 10 cm layer is then removed, heaping it at the canchón's edge and thus starting a new 5 year cycle. A new aqueduct has been built which pipes water from these underground tables to Iquique, thereby slowly starving these canchones of their water supply.

Back on the road, at a signposted site there is another giant tree: a 23 m high **Tamarugo** with a 5 m girth and reportedly over 500 years old. Five kilometers ahead is

LA TIRANA a religious village in the desert, consisting of a rectangle of 10 by 20 dirt streets and adobe shacks covered up with cardboard and nearly all padlocked. The ghost town awakens between the 12th and 18th of July, peaking on the 16th: it is the **Virgen del Carmen** festivity, in honor of the Virgin.

Nearly 80,000 people crowd the small village, following a ritual procession through the streets

Mamiña, National Monument

which includes a Calvary and a Sanctuary, with gaily-clad dancing groups known as **Chinese confraternities**, wearing masks and attires original from the High Plateau. These confraternities come from throughout the north, from Arica down to Copiapó. Their official performance includes dancing routines and offers to the Virgin. Thousands of pilgrims come to settle mandas, or promises to make a sacrifice in return for a favor granted, often by performing punishing physical feats like walking on the knees over long distances.

The Sanctuary of La Tirana is located in the middle of the village, at a ceremonial square. There is a church and across from it a long 3-story house with galleries; it doubles as a **museum** and festivity organization center. Sun shelters, restaurants and cafés -open year-round- flank the square.

The church built using wooden boards lined with corrugated sheet iron, follows the model of the Matilla church. The vaults are arranged into a cross layout, with a dome going up at the intersection point. At the central altar is a statue of the **Virgin of Carmen** and on the lateral ones a **Virgin and the Woodman** and the **Lord of Miracles.** Masses on Sunday at 12:00 h and 20:00 h, Mondays at 19:00 h. A smaller festivity is held on January 5 and 6, coinciding with Epiphany.

Tradition tells that at this site, located on an old herding trail, was an inn ran by a beautiful but despotic woman, dubbed «the tyrant» («La Tirana»). A village took form here around 1839, with a chapel that took the present form as early as the 1870s.

The road runs now through empty desert and intersects the Pan-American highway 11 km later. Iquique is 61 km ahead.

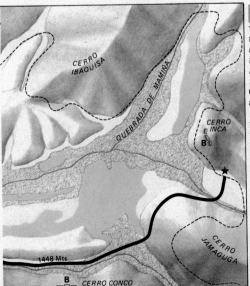

CERRO IBAQUISA

QUEBRADA DE MAMIÑA

CERRO INCA
B

CERRO JAMAGUGA

1448 Mts

B CERRO CONCO

Camino Tropero a Macaya →

5 A VISIT TO THE MAMIÑA HOT SPRINGS

★★★ *126 km from Iquique, 148 km round trip from Pozo Almonte, 30 km are paved. Gasoline at Pozo Almonte, good hotels in Mamiña. A one-day tour from Iquique, more relaxed if you stay at Mamiña overnight. Tours can be arranged at hotels and travel agencies in Iquique.*
Old hot spring oasis with a picturesque stone village, a church and Inca ruins.

From Pozo Almonte, km 0, the road runs through the desert 15 km until coming to an intersection; take the left road, the other one leads to the Sagasca mine. At km 22, another intersection with restricted access to **Dupliza**, a green oasis in the pampa. It used to be an experimental agricultural station, now it is a' military outpost.

Ahead is a mountain range parallel to the Andes. The road turns north and at km 55 arrives at the **Quispisca gorge**, running along the bottom of a deep dry dell –a short stretch, **Dupliza Hill**, with amazing views– climbing to a plain behind the hills and ascending further around smaller ravines. At km 74 is

MAMIÑA nestled in a ravine with water and crops. The slopes are clad in contour terraces where

1

formerly alfalfa was grown. Now they are abandoned. The village is 2,700 meters above the sea and has only 375 inhabitants. It is perched atop a rocky cliff, with irregular stone-paved streets and stone houses, some with carved doorframes and thatched or thatch-clay roofs. At one side of the small square is the

Church of Our Lady of the Rosary

built in 1632 as a viceparish subordinate to the Pica curacy. It boasts massive stone buttresses and well-made walls, and two thick towers (only such case in Andean architecture; the towers possibly date from later) crowned by blue-painted wooden belfries. The adjoining esplanade used to contain the cemetery, which was moved to the entrance of the town in 1865. The doorframe is of carved pink stone; inside, the nave is surprisingly high, with full 6 meters. The central altar is arranged into three levels, with vaulted niches and large images dating from colonial times. The lateral altars are made of stone and have small staircases on the sides. The choir is wooden and supported by wooden pillars with painted stone bases, and has an ancient organ. The large slate gate swings on hinges resting on stone, as was usual during the colonial period.

The village dates from pre-Conquest times. It was once a pukará -defensive fortress- and an Inca administrative center. One of its hot springs, says the legend, cured an Inca princess of an illness. During the saltpeter days it was a favored spot for relaxation, and from then dates the Hotel del Salitre.

The best thermal baths are the tubs at this hotel, with a powerful jet of scalding water, and the Del Chino mud baths. The latter are very primitive, but offer the unique chance of daubing oneself from head to toes with a black mud that sun-dries into a grayish hue. It is then removed in a dark pool of water (open 09:30-13:00 h). The best time to go into the pool is just after 13:00 h, paying a higher fee to the caretaker and having the pool to yourself; bring a towel with you. Later in the afternoon the wind rises and makes it somewhat less enjoyable.

You can walk or drive to different spots (see map), making a stay of more than one day a possibility to consider. There are 6 hotels, hostels and a campground.

6 A VISIT TO TARAPACA possible continue on to Chusmiza and Colchane at the boundary ★★★
60 km round trip from Huara at the Pan-Am highway, 46 of which are paved; gasoline at Huara. A two-hour drive, bring some food. 65 km from Tarapacá to Chusmiza, 155 km to Colchane, in the High Plateau. You can stay overnight at Chusmiza and visit some interesting villages in the vicinity. A visit to Colchane is more recommendable coming south from Arica, described in Section D, Tours 4 and 7.

A visit to the former Colonial Capital of this province. At Chusmiza there is a quaint thermal hotel, a good staging point for visiting Sotoca, Usmagama and other picturesque colonial villages.

At the road junction at Huara (km 0) there is a police road checkpoint. (A good tip for hitchhikers: on Friday afternoon cars go up to the Colchane open-air market, held every Saturday.) The paved road runs straight towards the mountains. This stretch is particularly suitable to observe the sedimentation process which spawned this pampa. The first section is flat and yellowish; then, the road climbs gently and the ground turns brown and is peppered with small stones; nearer the hills, where the slope is steeper, the soil is reddish (clay) and covered with large, round boulders, illustrating the erosion-triggered sedimentation process which loosened material from the hills.

Two odd sights along the road: an abandoned airstrip which uses part of the road at km 6, and the island-hill **Unita** at km 14. It is a perfect-shaped small cone with abstract geoglyphs where the most prominent is the «**Atacama Giant**», a man-like figure stretching over 86 meters, considered the largest anthropomorphic figure made in prehistoric times.

At km 23 take the road to the right, be sure to signalize, and at km 25 the plain is slashed by the deep gorge of the **Tarapacá ravine**, with watered orchards and some houses. The road descends and runs along the bottom of the gorge. At km 28, drive or walk 300 m to the side to visit the site of the

Tarapacá Battle

held on Nov 27, 1879. Chilean troops, after defeating the Peruvian-Bolivian forces stationed at Dolores (near Zapiga), crossed the Pampa to occupy this ravine. Here they ran into the bulk of the enemy armies and, after one day of fighting and with considerable casualties on both sides, the Chileans retreated to the pampa, the Peruvians to Arica through Camiña and Camarones, and the Bolivians to the High Plateau. There is a crypt containing the remains of Chilean soldiers and a bust of fallen commander Eleuterio Ramírez. At km 30 is

TARAPACA a humble village now almost totally decayed, with a glorious past and some valuable remains of the historical role it once played.

A Church	
B Bell Tower	D Old Arcades
C Square & Kiosk	E Former Convent

F Colonial Houses	H Manor House
G Old Government Building	∴ Ruins

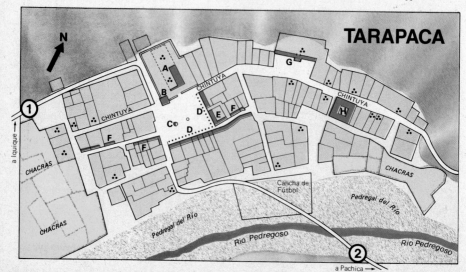

TARAPACA

In 1536 Diego de Almagro stopped here on his way back to Arequipa and Cuzco through the Inca road. Four years later, Pedro de Valdivia came from Cuzco with 20 soldiers; Inés de Suárez, awaited here the reinforcements coming from the High Plateau.

Soon thereafter these lands were allocated as encomiendas. Tarapacá's first active chapel was built in 1613 and a parish followed in 1685. In 1768 the Corregimiento de Tarapacá -a Spanish administrative division- was established here, with four subdivisions -the Repartimientos- each with a parish: Camiña, Sibaya (upstream of Tarapacá), Tarapacá, and Pica down to the Loa river. Tarapacá was the capital, with a governor and a council, known as Cabildo. This status lasted until 1855, when the local government moved to Iquique. Here lived the richest landowner in the entire Tarapacá province, Basilio de la Fuente; he died in 1774 and financed important public works in the valley.

What To See walk along the streets shown in the map. The **square** has no trees and is paved with flat stone slabs, flanked by houses with long wooden arcades in the front. In the center of the square is a simple kiosk and an old marble monolith in memory of the battle of 1879. To the north the square is flanked by the

Church and Bell Tower (NM) San Lorenzo church is built in mud bricks and dates from the late 17th century. It was refined in 1773 and later destroyed by a fire. Its walls remained, as well as some stone altar elements, the foot of some columns and the front and side gates. An outer wall used to enclose the area. The bell tower stood as an annex to the main building; it was the tallest in the entire north and its refined neoclassical style was devoid of Andean influence. Built in ashlar masonry and covered by yellow stucco, it was renovated recently.

A stone-paved street leads to the old **Government Palace**, of which only the esplanade and stone arches remain. A walk through the few other streets shows the river-pebble pavements, some stone doorframes, wooden doors with copper nails, steeply inclined roofs with skylights, the walls of an old convent and a large manor house.

Back on the road again, you can continue to the Chusmiza hot springs. You can sleep here and visit mountain villages which used to be part of the Repartimiento Colonial de Sebaya, with 4 beautiful churches (National Monuments). Cars must be tuned for high altitude conditions (3.000 mt). The gravel road climbs steadily and at km 37 another road branches off to the right, leading to **Pachita**; you are very near the edge of the deep Tarapacá ravine, and a 50 m walk brings you to a lookout

providing a **view** to the village down below, with its cultivated fields and a road climbing to the east in the direction of Lirima.

Resuming the drive to Chusmiza, the road ascends gently, commanding a view of the lands dropping away towards the coast and, ahead, the towering **Lirima peak**. At km 58 the road to Guasquiña branches off to the left and at km 73 another road branches off to the right, towards **Mocha**, **Guaviña** and Sibaya. Sibaya used to be the head town of the Sibaya Department during the colonial period. The barren, stony desert landscape starts to show patches of coirón, a type of bunch-grass, and two kinds of cacti, one of which bears a delicious fruit called rumba. At km 87 the road to **Usmagama** branches off to the right and at km 91 there is a road intersection. Follow the sign to Chusmiza, to the right. The road plunges into a deep ravine. At km 94 is the **Chusmiza plant**, a modern mineral water bottling establishment. First set up in 1927, it used to bring its output by mule train to the marketplaces of the saltpeter towns. Two kilometers ahead are the

CHUSMIZA HOT SPRINGS located 3,250 m above sea level, at the bottom of a rocky gulch. A thick stream of scalding crystal-clear water issues from a cavity. The hotel, long and narrow, seems to lean against the rock wall. Each room is equipped with a pool 3 m in length, 1 m wide and 1,5 m deep, which can be quickly filled up with the spring water. Service is good and the place is spotless. It is a good staging point for Tours 9, 10 and 11, described under Section D.

7 A VISIT TO CAMIÑA ★★★

154 km round trip from the Pan-Am highway intersection; gravel road. Considering its distance from Arica, Iquique and the Pan-Am highway, it is perhaps less strenuous if one stays at Camiña overnight, either at the campground or its unpretentious pensión. Take enough gasoline. A slow tour of about 4 hours, visiting villages and oases.
One of the most fertile ravines in Tarapacá, preserving the colonial traditions and in a nice mountainous setting.

From the Pan-Am intersection at Zapiga (km 0) the road climbs to the east. At km 17 it crosses the Retamilla ravine, with some houses and crops, and then continues through a yellowish desert. At km 44 it descends into the **Tana ravine**. Shallow and enclosed by smooth shoulders, it has a flat bottom some 300 meters across, checkered with crops growing in square patches.

The road runs along the bottom of the valley and through the village of Moquella at km 64, a nice stretch together with plain and green open

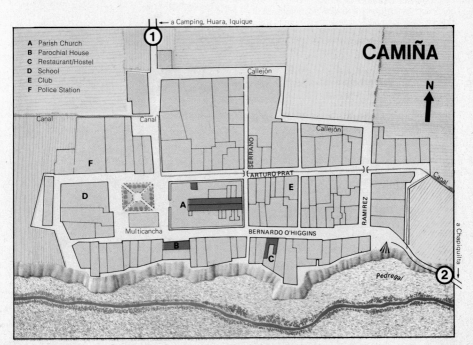

Camiña Valley

country. Eventually the valley grows wider and the crops seem better tended, until at km 77 is

CAMIÑA a village of 269 inhabitants, it dates from pre-Hispanic times, with a sizable native population. A chapel is active here since 1613; later it became the seat of one of the four parishes of Tarapacá, subordinate to the Arequipa Bishopric. It was the capital town of the Camiña Repartimiento during the colonial period, stretching from the Tana valley through Sotoca up to the border at Isluga. Although allocated as an encomienda, it never had any significant Spanish population.

Most houses are built of mud bricks -adobe- and the church has a nice portal dating from the eighteenth century. The municipal campground is adequate and well-shaded. The pensión offers food and lodging, including typical meals such as cazuelas, ears of corn with butter and spicy rabbit or chicken stew.

Chusmiza is perhaps the most beautiful of the north's oases. Wandering along the mountain trails you will find the site from where the most striking photographs of the north have been shot, with sand dunes rolling down to the green bottom of the ravine.

A road goes up the ravine until it intersects the one coming down from Enquelga, in the High Plateau, described in Section D, under Tour 6.

8 A VISIT TO PISAGUA ★

80 km round trip from the Pan-Am highway on a poorly maintained gravel road. No gas stations.
A visit to an old and formerly important saltpeter shipping port and the site of a major battle during the War of the Pacific. Now it is nearly deserted.

A road towards the coast branches off the Pan-Am highway at the Zapiga intersection. It runs across the Zapiga nitrate bed, the northernmost one and the first one to be exploited by 1810. Here lay the foundation of John North's saltpeter empire. The road approaches the Coastal Range and descends along the Tana ravine. The roadbeds of the 1874 nitrate railway can still be seen. At km 40 you arrive at

Pisagua a run-down village of 166 inhabitants. It once was the third largest nitrate shipping port. Located on a narrow seaboard, it has only 2 streets, running parallel to each other, and a seafront wall where saltpeter shipping operations took place. Its houses, typical of the saltpeter heyday, are wooden and have elaborate balconies and porches.

Two buildings have been granted National Monument status: the **Municipal Theater (MN)** erected in 1892 as an integral part of the market building, the opera building and the municipal offices, located in the second floor. Built of wood with grooved columns, balustrades, cornices and carved door and window frames. It is now empty. The other National Monument is the **Clock Tower (MN)** built in 1887 on a rocky cliff. The 12-m-tall solid, wooden four-sided structure has a balcony halfway up and is crowned by a six-sided roof supported by slender pillars. In its base lie the remains of soldiers fallen during the capture of Pisagua, on Nov 2, 1879. The bulk of the Chilean forces landed here after relentlessly shelling the Peruvian defenses. Once the beachhead was secured, the Chilean expeditionary force attacked and defeated the Peruvian-Bolivian army stationed farther inland.

Pisagua has now lost its municipal head town status and is nearly deserted.

SECTION B   HIGH PLATEAU

This area is a treat for all those looking for nearly unspoiled nature with a bit of adventure on the side. It is a beautiful, little-known area perched atop the Andes, dotted with volcanoes –some active– and salt flats and home to interesting wildlife.

Adventure takes the form of having practically no supporting infrastructure to count on, save for the occasional –and remote- police border station. The most suitable vehicles are 4-wheel-drive ones, travelling in groups. Recommendations for driving on roads running higher than 3,500 m altitude are given under Section B.

This is what some label «adventure tourism», calling for some degree of specialization and preparation. A detailed description of the tours is therefore not possible here. Nonetheless, a brief account of two possible tours is provided below.

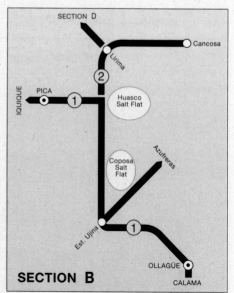

SECTION B

1 TO PICA THROUGH THE HUASCO SALT FLAT
★★★ *224 km from Ollagüe to Pica, with 60 additional km of detours. Last point for refuelling is Calama, 198 km from Ollagüe. The ascent from Pica is difficult in summertime.*
Adventure trip through a fairly unknown and desolate area, traversed by Royal couriers during colonial times. It was surveyed by mule in 1885 by Federico Philippi Jr on an exploratory mission to collect flora for the Natural History Museum in Santiago.

The leg from Calama to Ollagüe is described under the Antofagasta Zone, Section C, Tour 5.

Ollagüe located 3,700 m above sea level and at the foot of the Ollagüe salt flat is a border town living mainly from the nearby sulphur mine. There is a customs office and passport control checkpoint. Report your trip to the police.

The road leaves Ollagüe heading north through valleys and mountain passes and runs close to beautiful active volcanoes. A railway runs alongside the road; it was laid in the 1930s to serve the Collaguasi copper mine, later closed down due to flooding. At the **Uyuni railway station** sulphur is loaded from mines located in Bolivia, in the vicinity of the Empexa salt flat.

The Royal Road during the colonial period used to connect Pica to the Huasco salt flat and to Uyuni, to cross then into the Loa river basin through a mountain pass and then descend to Chiu Chiu and San Pedro de Atacama. It is likely that the Inca Road –traversed by conquistadors Diego de Almagro and Pedro de Valdivia– followed the same route.

Farther north the road skirts the **Coposa salt flat**, beyond which the vast expanses of the Huasco pampas spread out. These end at the great **Huasco salt flat**, a huge swampy lake teeming with waterfowl.

The road down from the salt flat to Pica skirts for a while the Quisma ravine, which ends at Matilla. This section of the road is prone to mud slides during the summer rainy season, making the drive up from Pica very difficult.

2   A VISIT TO LIRIMA AND CANCOSA ★★★

214 km round trip from the intersection at the Huasco salt flat to Cancosa. A poorly surfaced road leads from there on to the Tarapacá ravine and then on to the High Plateau, to make the grand tour from Antofagasta to Arica through the High Plateau. The Tarapacá-Arica stretch is described under Section D, Tour 6. Load fuel at Huara.
A tour along an old herding trail used for transporting the famed Pica wines to Potosí during the colonial period, stopping at two tiny villages.

Take the road heading north from the Huasco salt flat junction, running alongside the Collacagua stream. Two mountain passes and some *bofedales* –wet, spongy, grassy areas– later you arrive at **Lirima**, at km 64 from the intersection. It is a recent village, established some ten years ago by Aymara families. It is renowned for its splendid **woven carpets**, which they export directly to Europe.

The road to **Cancosa** (43 km) crosses a mountain range and runs through a wide pampa speckled with rich bofedales. The small village has a police station connected by radio to the outside world. In the past these grazing lands belonged to landowners based at Pica and were used to feed the mules employed in the mule-train traffic between Pica and Potosí.

Another road heads West from Lirima, arriving after 97 km to the village of **Pachica**, at the Tarapacá ravine. Huara is 33 km ahead, at the Pan-Am highway, where you can refuel before ascending to the High Plateau again through Colchane and Isluga and continuing to Arica. This route is described under Section D, Tour 4.

SECTION C   ARICA

This section covers the central plain and the coast from the Peruvian border to the Tiliviche ravine (Zapiga). The coastline is abrupt and inhospitable; there are no coastal roads and the only settled area in the coast is Arica.

The central plain, a natural continuation of the Pampa del Tamarugal, is slashed crosswise by four deep ravines, the largest of which, Camarones, requires 35 km to traverse it. There are some oases cultivated since pre-Conquest days and interesting examples of Spanish architecture dating from the colonial period.

Trips to Perú and Bolivia   From here it is also possible to visit neighboring Tacna, in Perú, and Bolivia. If travelling by car to Bolivia, get the necessary papers for the car at the local Automobile Club.

A train leaves for La Paz, Bolivia, on the 2nd and 4th Tuesday every month; another one, called Automotor Ferrobus, leaves Tuesdays and Saturdays at 09:00 h (US$ 49). On Tuesdays and Fridays, at 18:00 h, there are taxis to Visviri. From there you can cross the border and take the Bolivian buses leaving to La Paz on Wednesdays and Saturdays in the morning.

TOURS

1   PAN-AMERICAN HIGHWAY FROM ZAPIGA TO ARICA ★★★   *195 km on a good road; driving is made somewhat slow by the crossing of deep ravines. Gasoline at Huara (47 km before Zapiga) and at Arica. Iquique-Zapiga stretch described under Section A, Tour 1.*
The ravines give a different appearance to the pampa.

From the junction for Zapiga and Pisagua, km 0, the road continues on a flat pampa until at km 10 it starts descending into the first ravine, **Tiliviche**. It is a shallow ravine, with a bridge over the small stream at the bottom. Here is the Tiliviche farm, since 1855 in the hands of British interests in the saltpeter business. The old manor house has a

veranda in the ground floor and a balcony in the upper floor, in the style typical of British architecture in the Chilean north. The long distance from the Zapiga and Huara nitrate deposits to Iquique prompted resident Britons to establish here their

British Cemetery (NM)   on the northern slope of the ravine there is a perfect rectangle enclosed by a tall iron fence and shaded by tamarugo trees. Established in 1876, it contains over 100 graves, mainly of Britons but also of some Germans and Scandinavians. The main entrance is closed by a magnificent wrought-iron gate with an arch above it and the name of the place in metal letters. Some graves have wrought iron enclosures and crosses,

SECTION C

TACNA (PERU)

PUTRE

SECTION D

Poconchile

ARICA

Azapa

PACIFIC OCEAN

PANAMERICAN

Vitor Ravine

Codpa

Camarones Ravine

Cove Camarones

Cuya

Tana Ravine

Zapiga

Arica

other carved stone crosses; most have simple wooden crosses. Clean and well kept, it is a nostalgic reminder of the saltpeter days. To visit it, drive down from a point in the Pan-Am highway directly behind it; another option is to park past the bridge and walk.

The Pan-Am highway climbs out of the ravine and, at the top, there is a lookout commanding the best view of the **Tiliviche geoglyphs** on the distant southern slopes. They depict a group of llamas.

The road continues through the pampa until, at km 22, it plunges into another ravine, **Tana**, complete with stream and bridge at the bottom.

The pampa thereafter changes its name into **Pampa de Tana**, which is the natural prolongation of the Pampa de Tamarugal. At km 47 a dirt road branches off to the right, leading to the **Suca** oasis, which can be seen in the distance. The Andes Mountains loom in the distant background, their slopes cleft by deep gorges. A short distance ahead is the largest obstacle in the road, the

Chiza and Camarones Ravine it is a wide chasm in the pampa, steep and over 850 meters deep. The road needs 17 km to reach the bottom, a dry river bed. Near the **Chiza bridge** is the small **Chiza geoglyph**; being close to the road, it is easy to observe the technique used to create it. The road runs now 21 km along the dry river bed, arriving at km 85 to the **Cuya Customs Outpost and Agricultural Products Control**, located at the point where the Chiza ravine meets its sister, the Camarones ravine. A road starts here towards the coast, arriving after 11 km to the **Camarones fishing cove**, with a beach and nice cliffs. Another road branches off towards the fertile **Camarones valley**, checkered with small farms.

1 km past the control point a bridge spans the **Camarones stream** and the road then starts the 23-km climb up the face of a steep cliff, with a breathtaking **view** to the valley below, to reach the flat pampa once again. At km 108 you arrive at the **Pampa de Camarones**.

At km 125 a road branches off to the right, leading to Codpa. It is a nice oasis at the bottom of a steep ravine with an attractive hotel and nice surroundings described under Tour 5. It can be visited either on the way to Arica or on the return trip; watch your gasoline.

At km 128 the road crosses diagonally a new chasm, the **Chaca ravine**, next to the Vitor stream, surrounded by small farms. At km 159 is **Pampa de Chaca** and, at km 173, the road starts the descent of the Acha slopes to reach the seaboard at km 195. Here is

ARICA a provincial capital (pop 139, 017), a city of commercial and cultural exchange resulting from its proximity to Perú and Bolivia. It is the main shipping port for Bolivia and for the city of Tacna, Perú. Roads and railways link it to both countries.

Its markets, streets and hotels prove Arica's intense commercial traffic, especially in summer, when hundreds of tourists visit its magnificent beaches. The city, of old tradition and modern aspect, has very good facilities for travellers and it

is a center for amazing tours. Its present form started in 1953 when President Carlos Ibáñez gave Arica the status of a Duty Free port, attracting great numbers of tourist from the rest of the contry. In 1958 President Jorge Alessandri created the **Development Council**, unique in Chile for its autonomy in its decision-marking.

This council promoted Arica's urban renewal and the integration of the High-Plateau area. In 1964 a number of industrial companies set up plants here, including car assembly and electronics plants, to take advantage of the tax exemptions. Their products were aimed mostly at the Latin American market, under special clauses of the Latin American Free Trade Association. The population increased, new housing compounds were erected, parks with trees brought from abroad were created. The university, most modern hotels, the casino, seaport, airport and the stadium all date from this period.

The free market economic policy introduced in the 70s and 80s abolished Arica's tax exemptions and Free Port status. Its present strength derives from intense trade, traffic of goods from bordering countries, and the establishment of large fishing companies, with tens of fishing vessels filling the harbor.

Arica lies at the mouth of the Azapa valley, and is the only port in the desert area –including southern Perú– with water and vegetation. This accounted for its early settlement by native Indians. In 1565 the Perú Viceroyship established here the Corregimiento de Arica, a major administrative division stretching from Tacna to the Loa river. In 1570 the Spanish King granted it the status of a city. It is Chile's fifth oldest city.

In 1545 a fabulously rich silver mine was discovered at Potosí, in present-day Bolivia. Arica became the shipping and supply port for the mine, traffic between both locations being undertaken by mule train. Malaria prompted the resident Spaniards to flee to Putre, Belén and Tacna, located at a higher altitude and enjoying a better climate. In 1611 Potosí was the largest city in the Western Hemisphere, with 160,000 inhabitants, and Arica was a major producer of alfalfa for mule fodder.

With the establishment of the Viceroyship of Plata in 1776 (which included Bolivia), the Potosí traffic was rerouted to Buenos Aires. To make matters worse, in 1782 the Arequipa Governorship was created, depriving Arica of its administrative role.

A new boost for the town came with the birth of the Republic of Perú, bringing about the construction of the railway to Tacna in 1855 and, later, the government offices, the Customs house, the church and a marketplace. Arica was occupied by the Chilean Army in 1880. In 1913 the railway to La Paz was inaugurated, turning Arica once more into the main seaport serving Bolivia.

What To See a good starting point is to climb the **Morro** –the massive promontory towering over the city– for a **panoramic view** of the area. You can either drive or walk to the top (see map), where a square-like esplanade with a promenade at the edge of the cliff is located. Here is the

Arms Museum (Mon-Sun, 08:00-21:00 h), erected on the site of an old fortress. During the War of the Pacific, Chilean troops first occupied Arequipa and then Tacna. Arica was a strong Peruvian fortress, well defended against land and sea attacks. In the harbor was the Peruvian warship Manco Cápac, protected from the shore. The Chilean fleet was blocking access by sea, some way out; it suffered serious damage upon attempting to come closer. The fortress was under the command of Colonel Francisco Bolognesi, who refused to surrender in spite of being surrounded by sea and land. For the Chileans, there was no alternative but to attempt a frontal attack.

The Chilean troops came by train from Tacna to the Lluta valley, north of Arica, and fell upon the Azapa valley on the night of June 6, 1880. The objective was to take the Morro, which was defended by the **Ciudadela Fortress** on an eastern knoll (a monolith marks the place); the **Eastern Fort**, a bit to the south (the water tank is now there); the **Morro Gordo Fort**; several **batteries** of artillery at the esplanade; and by the **Morro Bajo Navy Base** –where the museum is now located–, which had four large guns and the ammunition depot.

The Chilean attack was commanded by José de San Martín and by Colonel Pedro Lagos, and was launched at daybreak on June 7th against the Ciudadela and Eastern forts. They were taken by knife. Commander San Martín was wounded and the surviving Peruvians retreated to the Morro proper. This quick success gave rise to considerable chaos and the Chilean troops, en masse, stormed the Morro against enemy fire, running across mine fields. In 55 minutes they wiped out all resistance, leaving behind some 1,500 casualties on both sides. Both commander San Martín and Peru's Bolognesi died, as well as most Peruvian officers.

Some broken guns can still be seen on the esplanade, together with some monuments to those fallen. The museum exhibits objects providing an insight into this battle.

A night visit to the Morro offers a sweeping view of the lit-up city and harbor.

Stroll down 21 de Mayo –the main shopping street– until you reach Av Costanera, with squares shaded by palm trees. On one side is the **Railway Station** - to Bolivia, erected in 1913 and still in operation. Across from it, at the **Aduana Square**, is a 1924-vintage **steam locomotive** built in Germany with toothed wheels used for part of the climb to Bolivia. On its side is the

Customs Building (NM) opened in 1874. A single-story building stuccoed in stripes and with cornices running the width of it, with a tympanum and a metallic awning above the entrance. Inside is a mezzanine accessible through a winding stair. The building and its storerooms –now torn down– were prefabricated at the **Gustave Eiffel et Cie.** workshops in Paris –the same of the Eiffel Tower– and erected on site on stone foundations. Each brick has the manufacturer's name stamped on one of its faces.

Go on to the **Plaza del Trabajador**. You will find a monument dedicated to those who died while building the port. Cross Plaza Colón and on the north side is the Roto Chileno square. On one of its sides is the

San Marco church (NM) (Services: Dec through March: Mo through Sat, 08:30 h and 20:30 h; Apr through Nov: Mon through Sat, 08:30 h and 20:00 h; Sun, 10:00 h, 12:00 h, and 20:00 h) erected on a wide esplanade overlooking the harbor. Gothic in style, it has a rectangular nave with two lateral chapels. Attached to the façade is a thick octagonal bell tower ending in a long spire. Inaugurated in 1876, it was also made at the **Gustave Eiffel et Cie.** workshops, prefabricated in iron and with walls and ceilings lined with stamped, molded iron plates. Only the door is made of wood (see the Guayacán church in Coquimbo).

At the foot of the Morro is the **Vicuña Mackenna square**, surrounded by tall Phoenix canariensis palms. This used to be the court of the magnificent Hotel Pacífico (1935-65), torn down due to corrosion in its structure.

Return, to your car and drive north one block on Máximo Lira, turn left to the

Fishing Terminal is located within the harbor section and has a good restaurant, commanding a view to the fishing vessels in the harbor and the swarms of seabirds surrounding them. At the harbor's northern end is the wharf built by the Chilean government for Peruvian shipping, under the terms of the treaty signed between both countries in 1929.

Driving north on the Costanera you will be able to see the nice shore and beaches. Leave Maximo Lira street and at the end of it make a right turn to the rotary to take General Velázquez. You arrive at a large park full of royal palms (Roystonea oleracea) brought from Brazil. Here is the

Arica Casino (open daily, 21:30-03:00 h), a large building with gambling rooms, a bar, a ball room, and shows.

Adjacent to it is an excellent hotel; beyond is the Velásquez Campus of the Universidad de Tarapacá. Farther ahead, beyond the underpass, starts the Costanera Luis Beretta, running for a

Arica, Azapa museum

stretch along the seashore.

To go down to the beach take the paved road to the left leading to a park containing a restaurant and crossing the railroad to Tacna. A gravel road runs along this enormous beach, which continues all the way to Perú.

Retracing this route back to the Morro you can go to Plaza Colón, accross from the San Marcos Church, and then continue south on the coastal drive, visiting the yachting club at the Alacrán peninsula, and the Laucho and Lisera beaches.

The evening is a good moment for strolling through

Downtown Arica with its narrow store-lined streets where old buildings coexist with newer ones, joined through short pedestrian streets such as Bolognesi and Sangra, and with an old market with iron pillars. Stop at the

Handicrafts Village (Pueblo Artesanal) (Tue-Sun 09:30-13:00 h and 15:30-19:30 h), with a folklore music club-café (Fri and Sat 21:30 h), a handicrafts exhibit room and workshops distributed among 12 white houses producing and selling knitted garments, ceramics and pottery, carved stones, ocarinas and other such items.

Accommodations the best hotel is the one on the seashore, with a swimming pool and access to the beach; downtown, the best one is El Paso hotel, with a swimming pool and a garden-courtyard. The Azapa Inn, set amid shady trees, and the modern Los Hibiscos Hotel are both located at the Azapa Valley, a short distance from the town. For those travelling on a budget there is a host of cheaper hotels, hostels and «residenciales» –ie boarding houses. The best site for camping and picnicking is at the mouth of the Lluta stream on Las Machas beach.

Where To Eat the best cuisine is found at the main hotels. Seafood and a good view at Acuario; restaurants El Fascinador and Las Rocas for those who like a beach setting; international cuisine at Casanova. Cheap eateries at fish shops (see map) and cocinerías in the market.

Transportation for those arriving by plane, cars can be rented and returned in Iquique. Tourist agencies organize daily tours to the Chungará lake, at the High Plateau, leaving at 7 AM and returning at 7 in the evening; they also offer tours to Tacna and the Azapa valley. Those arriving by car from Santiago and wishing to fly back can send the car by truck. Information at Transportes Progreso, Iquique, phone 424094; Arica, phone 231650; Santiago, phone 5520979.

TOURS FROM ARICA

2 **A DRIVE TO THE AZAPA VALLEY** ★★★
32 km round trip from Arica. Takes about 2 hours, having lunch on the way (see map). Shared taxis (colectivos) to the museum (until 22:00 h), leaving from the corner of Maipú and Lynch.
A visit to a fertile valley, with a good museum and interesting archeological sites.

Leave Arica through the road indicated in the map. The valley has small, lush cultivated plots flanking the road. A short way into the valley is the park surrounding the Azapa Inn and the El Parrón restaurant. The predominant plant species are Sevillian olive trees, producing the famed Azapa olives. There are also large banana plantations and lots of palms. At km 14, follow the sign to the left to visit the

SAN MIGUEL MUSEUM (summer, Mon-Sun 10:00-20:00 h; winter, Tue-Fri 11:00-18:00 h; Sat-Sun 13:00-18:00 h; entrance fee). Belonging to the Universidad de Tarapacá, it is the best archaeologi-

cal museum in this Zone. At the access courtyard there are petroglyphs and a bust of Max Uhle (1856-1944), a pioneer in anthropological research in the north. The museum contains a beautiful collection of fine Andean and coastal woven fabrics, baskets and pottery; Chinchorro mummies, the world's oldest, mummified using a peculiar sand technique. There is also a sixteenth-century olive press and a series of illustrative representations of the developmental stages of the Andean and coastal native cultures. Excellent literature on the subject is also for sale at the museum.

Back on the road, 2 km farther into the valley is the small **San Miguel de Azapa** village, with an

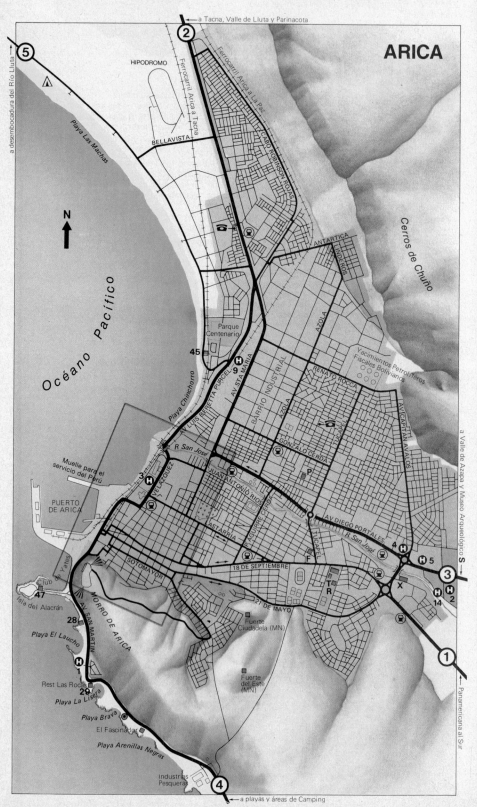

☎ Telephone Center
★ Touristic Information
⊙ Café, Meeting Point
Ⓖ Gasoline Station
⊙ Lookout Point
✠ Hospital (4C)
A Town Hall (4A)
B San Marco Church (NM), (4B)
W Post Office (4A)
C Bus Terminal (1C)
D Tacna Bus Terminal (1C)
E Taxis and Buses to Visviri (3A)
Y Taxis to Tacna (3B)
✳ F Buses to Putre and Belén
G Railway Station to Tacna (3A)
H Railway Station to La Paz (4A)
J Casino of Arica (3B)
K Central Marketplace (4B)
L Consulate of Perú (4C)
M Consulate of Bolivia (4B)
N Registry Office (3C)
✳ P International Police
Q Campus Velásquez U de T (2B)
✳ S San Miguel Museum (Azapa)

✳ R Campus Saucache
✳ T Anthropological Museum
U Saltpeter Museum (4B)
V Arms Museum (5A)
✳ X Handicraft Village

ACCOMMODATIONS

✳ 1 Hs Arica
✳ 2 Hs Azapa Inn
3 H El Paso (2B)
✳ 4 Hs Los Hibiscos
✳ 5 H Saint Gregory
6 H Central (4B)
7 H San Marcos (4B)
8 H King (4B)
9 H Marina Inn
10 H Aragón (4B)
11 H Tacora (4B)
12 H Diego de Almagro (4B)
13 H Lynch (4B)
✳ 14 M Saucache
15 H Savona (5B)
16 Bh El Hostal (4B)
17 Bh Leiva (4B)
18 Bh Velásquez (3B)
19 Bh Chungará (3B)
20 Bh Venecia (3B)
21 Bh Madrid (3B)
22 Bh Atenas (3B)
23 Bh Ibáñez (4B)
24 Bh Chillán (3B)
25 Bh Cantón (4C)
26 Bh Blanquita (4B)
27 Bh Sotomayor (4B)

RESTAURANTS

✳ 1 Hs Arica
✳ 2 Hs Azapa Inn
3 H El Paso (2B)
J Casino of Arica (3B)
40 Acuario (4A)
41 Casanova (4B)
42 Bavaria (3B)
43 Shun Sang (4C)
44 890 (4C)
✳ 45 Gallo Cojo
46 Fishing Market (4B)
✳ 47 Yacht Club
48 Honda (5A)
K Marketplace (4B)

TOURIST SERVICES

✳ 1 Euro Rent a Car
30 Jurasi Tour (4B)
31 Turismo Payachatas (4B)
32 Chungará Tour (4B)
33 Allen Rent a Car (4B)
34 Lan Chile (4A)
35 Ladeco (4B)
36 Aero Norte (4B)
37 Lloyd Aéreo Boliviano (4B)
38 Viva Rent a Car (4C)
39 Hertz Rent a Car (2B)

DISCOTHEQUE

J Casino of Arica (3B)
✳ 28 Infiernillo Discotheque
✳ 29 El Fascinador

INTERESTING BUILDINGS

B San Marco Church (NM),(4B)
Z Old Customs House (NM),(4A)
H Railway Station to La Paz (4A)
K Central Market (4B)

✳ See General Map of Arica

1

Downtown ARICA

ancient church and located some way up from the cultivated fields. Visit the **plant nursery**, containing subtropical species which can be acquired complete with a health certificate, so as to be allowed into the rest of the country by the officers at the agricultural products checkpoints (control SAG).

Take the road crossing the stream, almost across from the museum (see map), through the **Las Maitas** village; take the first road branching off to the left, running against the foot of the hillside. It will bring you to the

1

San Lorenzo Pukara (fortress)   climbing a short way on foot you can reach the top of the promontory, commanding a view of the valley. On this point are the ruins of a twelfth-century defensive fortress. You can return to the coast through this gravel road, which is the old road from Arica into the valley. After the **Alto Ramírez** inlet, four successive geoglyphs can be seen to the left of the road. This road ends at the Pan-Am highway, which brings you back to Arica.

3 A VISIT TO TACNA ★★★

108 km round trip, with delays at the customs checkpoints. Chilean nationals do not need a passport, but do require a special permit called «safeconduct», issued by the local Identification Bureau and stamped at the International Police office, Belén with Chapequiña street, Mon-Fri 08:30 -12:30 h and 15:00-19:00 h and Sat 08:30-12:30; it must then be okayed by the Peruvian Consulate. If you are driving, you must fill out 7 copies of the list of passengers (relación de pasajeros) travelling in the car; the corresponding forms can be bought at any bookstore. A train leaves Mon.-Sat. at 1200h, 1600h and 1800h, takes 1 hour (customs formalities are quicker). Shared taxis (colectivos) leave every 15 minutes from Chaca-buco and Baquedano streets, with slower customs formalities. Change Chilean pesos in Tacna.

Tacna, the first Peruvian city across the border, offers excellent handicrafts, particularly llama and alpaca-wool knitted garments.

Leave Arica, km 0, through the road north to Tacna (see map), running along the coastal plain. To the right are some hills, the last counterforts of the Andes; the Coastal Range dies at the Morro de Arica. Also to the right runs the Arica-La Paz railway, opened in 1913, and on the left the Arica-Tacna railway, opened in 1855; it is the third oldest in Chile, after the Caldera and the Valparaíso railroads. It belongs to Perú.

At km 10 is an intersection where the road to Bolivia branches off to the right; at km 14, the road to the Chacalluta airport branches off to the left. A short way ahead is the Chacalluta Customs Checkpoint, where the first inspection is carried out. At km 18 is the border and then the Peruvian Santa Rosa Customs Outpost (second slow inspection). Then comes a plain falling gently to the west. At km 54 is

TACNA   a busy border town somewhat smaller than Arica and with a totally different flavor. There are many good hotels. 386 km to the north is Arequipa, with very interesting colonial architecture.

4 A VISIT TO PUTRE AND CHUNGARA LAKE ★★★

149 km to Putre and 210 km to Chungará. 149 km are paved, the rest a gravel road with a short rough section. Gasoline at Arica and -with a hefty surcharge- at the largest general store in Putre (take a funnel and a canister). Cars must be tuned up for high altitude. Travel agencies operate daily tours to the area, returning on the same day. If you are driving, it is best to stay overnight at Putre. Watch your gasoline. A tip for hitchhikers: on certain days, taxis make the run to Visviri, to the weekly «Tripartite Open Air Market» held there. You might be able to hitch a ride. Otherwise, there is a relatively constant lorry traffic to Bolivia and to the High Plateau mines.

A tour to a major town in the High Plateau, from where you can make excursions to interesting High-Plateau locations, including ceremonial village of Parinacota and spectacular Chungara lake.

Leave Arica, km 0, on the road to Tacna. At km 10 take the international road heading East into the Lluta valley. The bottom of the valley is green and farmed; there are some experimental jojoba plantations, different from those at the Azapa valley because the water here is somewhat brackish. The Arica-La Paz railway runs alongside the road.

At km 14 and 16 are **geoglyphs** on the yellow slopes flanking the valley, depicting llamas and human figures. At km 30 and 34 are the farm houses of old haciendas; one of them, «La Pérgola de las Chilcas», is now a restaurant. At km 38 is

Poconchile   a village dating from pre-Inca times. It used to be a resting station in the route to the High Plateau and a way station during the construction of the Arica-La Paz railway. In the early 1900s, Dr. Juan Noé, working at the local clinic, managed to eradicate the last focus of malaria. There is a police control for those continuing on this international route. Across from the control outpost is the

San Gerónimo church   enclosed by a wall and containing a cemetery at the back. If you wish to visit it, ask for the key at the Curicó restaurant across the street. The first parish of the Corregimiento de Arica was established here in 1605. This church, built of mud bricks, dates from the seventeenth century. It was rebuilt last century, receiving in the process two wooden bell towers.

The road continues along the valley. At km 52 another road branches off to Molinos, 5 km away, with a small chapel at a tree-shaded spot. After the intersection the road starts to climb away from the Lluta valley. Three-fourths of the way up there

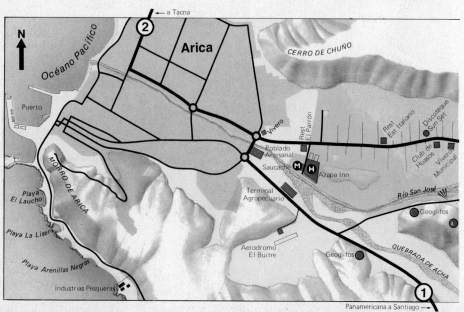

is a look-out commanding a **panoramic view** of the valley below. On the northern slopes of the valley you can see the sinuous railway which, from Estación Central to Estación Puquios, is racked to help the train climb the steep slope.

The road alternates between hills and plains and crosses a few dry river beds. Some mining works can be seen near the road. From km 80 to 90 some **candelabrum cacti** (Browningia candelaris) can be seen, with stems up to 4 m tall and many «arms» stretching upwards. At km 102 –the provincial boundary– the pavement ends. To the right is the **Pukará plant**, processing mineral from the Choquelimpie gold mine located farther inland. A short way ahead is the signpost for the

PUKARA DE COPAQUILLA (MN) one of the ancient defense fortresses set up by the native Indians. This one is located very close to the road, on a hilltop and surrounded by a double wall. Many other circular stone walls can be seen, possibly animal pens or defensive parapets. It dates from the twelfth century and was restored in 1979 by the Universidad de Tarapacá. From the top, the cultivated bottom of a 150 m deep gorge with sheer walls can be seen. The primitive settlement is located there.

The road runs now alongside a small stream with bofedales, the spongy, wet, grassy grounds typical of the High Plateau. At km 110 are the ruins of the modest **Tambo de Zapahuira (NM)** (a resting station), dating from Inca times. It is also a National Monument and is presently undergoing restoration. At km 114 is the **Zapahuira crossroads**; a village can

be seen to the left, among some eucalyptus. Here starts the road to Belén and other small villages on the old route from Arica to Potosí (described under Section D).

At km 124 a road branches off to Socoroma, also described under Section D. By now the road has become a mountain road, hugging the steep slopes and skirting deep gorges. At km 129 is an interesting collection of **High-Plateau cacti**, well worth a brief stop. There are trails and benches, overlooking the deep Socoroma ravine.

Not far ahead the landscape opens up and a wide valley can be seen under the massive, snow-capped **Putre Peaks**. At km 144 a road branches off to the valley below and to

PUTRE perched 3,500 m above sea level, the town offers a good hotel and interesting architectural manifestations from colonial days. It is the best place to acclimatize oneself to the considerable altitude and is a convenient staging point for excursions to the Chungará lake and other places. The town and its tours are described under Section D.

5 **A VISIT TO THE CODPA OASIS ★★★**

120 km south of Arica and 100 km round trip from the Pan-Am highway intersection. Only 16 km are paved; the rest is a gravel road. Adequate hotel. Watch your. gasoline.

The drive itself is part of the thrill, the road ending in a lovely oasis with one of the most noteworthy churches in the region.

The road descends gently from the Pan-Am in-

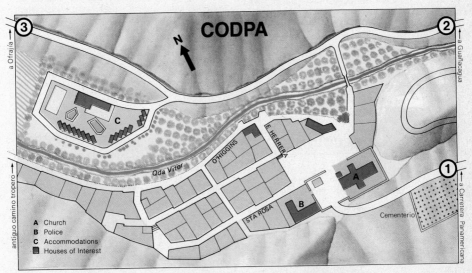

CODPA

A Church
B Police
C Accommodations
■ Houses of Interest

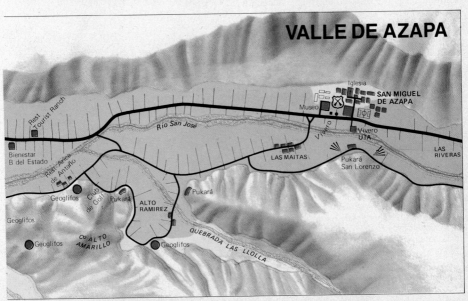

VALLE DE AZAPA

1

tersection, km 0, towards the East. In the distance looms the sharp peak of the **Chuquiananta** mountain. At km 8 asphalt gives way to gravel. This is desert at its pure, with boulders galore swept bare by the wind. The plain starts to ascend again; in the distant background the snowy peaks of the Andes march north, with volcanoes towering well above the 5,000-m snow line. At km 25 a deep gorge plunges to the right; at km 34 is a lookout over the reddish, barren canyon tumbling towards the Camarones stream. Some **Candelabrum Cacti** raise their arms here and there in splendid isolation. At km 37, a road branches off to Esquiña, deep in the sierras. At km 40 the road turns abruptly to the left and runs along the crest of a ridge, offering an awesome **view** to right and left.

At km 42 the road starts descending towards the Codpa ravine. Strange circular stone walls can be seen on the side, probably part of a **tambo** (resting station) along the Inca Road. At km 48 the real descent starts, the road just a narrow ledge carved on the face of a rocky cliff. At the bottom, km 50, is

CODPA a village nested in a narrow valley hemmed in by sheer rock walls, 1,800 m above sea level. It dates from pre-Conquest times; in 1668 it became the seat of a parish and the residence of the chieftain for the «Arica highlands», ruling the native tribes of Socoroma, Putre, Parinacota, Livilcar, Tignamar and other locations. With a temperate, friendly climate and pure water from the upper section of the Vitor stream, Codpa has also a notoriously fertile valley, albeit very narrow, suitable for all kinds of fruit trees, particularly guava. Its thick, fruity **pintatani wine** is renowned. Codpa has traditionally been one of the getaway spots for Arica residents; the Arica Development Council had a good hotel built here in 1973, now owned by a hotel chain.

At the cemetery, located at the entrance to the village, note the tombs with crosses on the ground and devoid of the typical mound. Some houses have interesting carved window sill railings and doorframes; many are empty after the harvesting

season. Visit the

San Martin de Tours church a major missionary center during colonial days. The present building used to be 7 m longer; it was trimmed near the turn of the century. It is built of adobe, with a carved-stone lateral portico. Inside, a large stone arch delimits two lateral chapels. At the far end is a two-tiered stone altarpiece with 6 niches. Among the statuary and religious paintings stands out a figure of St. Martin riding a donkey. There is also a polychrome wooden pulpit and two stone baptism basins. Ask for the keys at one of the sides.

The bridge over the stream is framed by two large guava trees. Beyond the bridge, on the northern banks, the road to the left leads to **Ofrajía**, a settlement 6 km farther downstream. To the right, the road runs some way up from the stream, above terraced plots covered by grapevines, fruit trees and lots of fig trees, along stony ground and cliffs until it reaches

GUAÑACAGUA a small village with huts huddled around two streets which act as a square of sorts. The huts have thick adobe walls, some are made of stone. Across the bridge and sitting all by itself is a beautiful stone church dating from the sixteenth century. Its portal was restored in 1904. It has a rectangular layout, with an attached sacristy and a presbytery, the latter vaulted behind. On the side facing the stream is an esplanade with shallow steps.

Its bell tower is perhaps the most beautiful in the entire north, built of carved stone, with carefully-chiseled cornices and capping. It is a remarkable example of Andean baroque architecture (see drawing under Zone's introduction). The church façade has encrusted stone slabs bearing the name of the donor and the amount contributed towards the renovation undertaken in 1904.

Four km beyond Guañacagua is **Chitita**, a tiny stone village located astride the old trail connecting Codpa to Putre and Belén. Its walled church has no bell tower and has a baroque carved-stone portal.

SECTION D   NATIONALS PARKS

This section comprises the western slopes of the Andes Mountains, also known as the Sierra, and the upper table-land known as High Plateau or Altiplano, ranging in altitude from 3,500 to 4,500 m above sea level.

Scattered throughout the sierra are quaint farming communities, growing their crops on terraces clinging to the slopes of narrow ravines. A disseminated Aymara population tends herds of llamas and other livestock at the High Plateau's bofedales. Picturesque, deserted ceremonial villages spring to life during religious festivities and carnivals.

Also located in the High Plateau are the superb Lauca and Isluga National Parks, the Surire Natural Monument and the Las Vicuñas National Reserve, all under the management of the Chilean Forest Service, Conaf.

The combined beauty of nearly unspoiled nature, lots of wildlife, high-altitude lakes and salt flats, snow-capped volcanoes and picturesque ceremonial villages makes this area one of Chile's most spectacular and a perfect setting for both adventure-tourism and eco-tourism.

Recommendations

1 Motor vehicles must be tuned for high-altitude conditions: the lower amount of oxygen available reduces motor power output considerably. The spark must be advanced; any garage in Arica can do the job in about 10 minutes. In cases of extreme loss of power, remove the air filter for a while.

2 Any expedition outside the international road to Bolivia must be reported beforehand to the police at the checkpoints. Within National Parks, report

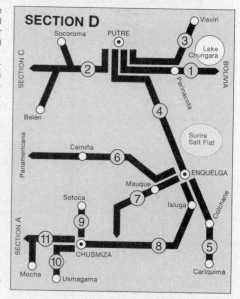

your intended destination to the park rangers. They are linked with one another by radio, and can provide useful information and advice.

3 Heavy rains in summer months (January-February) can make driving difficult outside the international road to Bolivia, the swelling of streams tur-ning certain fords impassable. Only four-wheel -drive, high-ground-clearance vehicles can do the trick.

4 Check road conditions with Carabineros (police) or Conaf in Arica (tel. 232856). Best seasons are March-April and September-December.

5 Remember that in many of these areas you will be pretty much on your own, so be sure to take enough gasoline, water and food. In winter, do not forget to put antifreezing fluid in the car's radiator.

6 Take warm clothing at any time of the year, including a parka, gloves, a ski cap and sunglasses. Ultraviolet radiation is strong; apply a suitable skin-protecting cream. Dry air parches the lips very quickly; take precautions.

7 Do not over-exert yourself at altitude; low oxygen availability strains your body enough as it is. Always walk or move about slowly.

8 Should your car break down, DO NOT leave the road or attempt to take shortcuts. Walk on the road itself.

9 Remember that water here boils at a lower temperature than at sea level; cooking takes much longer than normal.

Stretch Arica-Putre (149 km) described under Section C, Tour 4.

PUTRE capital of the Parinacota province, 588 inhabitants, located 3,500 m above the sea. Dating from pre-Hispanic times, Putre was given its present layout by 1580, when Spaniards settled here to provide services for the traffic between the Potosí silver mine and Arica. A new boom was ushered in 1643 by the Choquelimpie gold mine. It started to decline in 1825, as a result of Bolivian independence and the consequent rerouting of export traffic to seaports on the Antofagasta coast. The decline was made worse by an earthquake in 1868.

The oldest part of town is O'Higgins street, with a ditch running along its middle and spanned by stone bridges with benches.

Many houses still have carved-stone portals and window frames dating from the 17th century, when the town experienced its economic boom. Most buildings, however, date from last century and just kept the traditional colonial ornament style. The most interesting houses are shown on the map above. Climbing the Callejón you can have a good **view** of the whole town. At the entrance are **pens full of alpacas and llamas** selected for their size, wool quality and color. They are destined for export, and are a regrettable genetic drain depriving the High Plateau herds of their best individuals.

Around the **square** are the townhall, the church, the parochial house and the Hostería San Martín.

Church of Putre erected in 1670 to replace the previous one levelled by an earthquake. The old church, according to chroniclers, used to be lined in gold and silver. The stone façade, the choir and the outer enclosure date from a restoration undertaken in 1875. The bell tower dates from an earlier, unspecified date. The forecourt has a mosaic-patterned stone pavement. The nave is built in adobe, 33 m long and 6 m high, containing abundant colonial statuary, some of great value. The altar and retable are made of stone and date from 1895. The choir has a stone stair leading to it through the baptistery. Keys can be obtained from the janitor on Cochrane street.

The stone arches at the parochial house next to the church are the sole remnant from an old arcade surrounding the square.

Putre is a good place for acclimatizing to high altitude -for instance at the modern Las Vicuñas hotel- as well as a convenient staging point for the tours described below.

TOURS FROM PUTRE

1 TO PARINACOTA AND THE CHUNGARA LAKE
★★★ *121 km round trip on a gravel road with some rough stretches. The best time for starting is at the crack of dawn, as wildlife can then be best seen. A slow journey of some 6 hours. Take gasoline, water and food.*
A visit to the superb Lauca National Park and Biosphere Reserve.

Leave Putre, km 0, towards the international road to Bolivia. The intersection is at km 5; take the road climbing to the left, which traverses the western range of the Andes Mountains. At km 14 is the Pacollo military outpost, whence an unmade road branches off to the north. A little farther ahead is

☎ Public Phone   **D** Handicrafts Workshops
A Town Hall   **E** Conaf
B Church   **F** General Store

ACCOMMODATIONS
1 Hs Las Vicuñas
C Hs San Martín

■ Houses of Interest

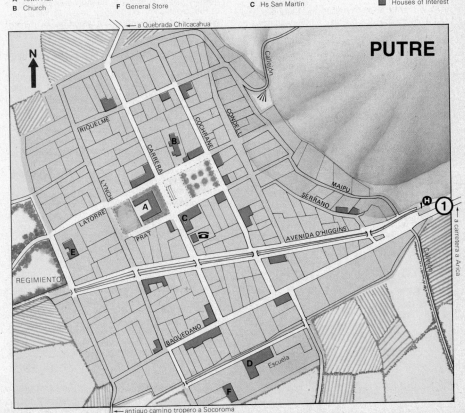

1

. Lake Chungará

the entrance to the **Lauca National Park**, beyond a mountain pass 4,400 m above the sea.

At km 24 and 4,300 m above sea level is **Conaf's Las Cuevas Ranger Outpost** with a radio link for emergencies. The road runs alongside the Taipicahue stream, with a narrow bofedal where vicuña flocks feed and romp in the morning hours. Shy and swift vizcachas -a sort of large hare with the tail of a fox- can be spotted, as well as large white-breasted geese with black-tipped wings called guayata.

At km 26 a road branches off to the right leading to Guallatire and Surire, described under Tour 4. The landscape is that of a **high-altitude steppe**. At km 27 is the so-called **drainage divide**, where the streams flowing west to the lower lands in Chile separate from those running east towards Bolivia, such as the Lauca river. Ahead is the magnificent

Parinacota Bofedal as described elsewhere, a bofedal –typical of the High Plateau– is wet spongy ground, rich in grass and, consequently, much favored by fauna. This one is interspersed by ponds swarming with waterfowl, particularly giant Taguas which build floating islands as nesting spots. Herds of llamas and alpacas graze in separate groups. In the background, the twin snow-capped Pomerape and Parinacota peaks tower above 6,000 m.

At km 37 a bridge crosses the **Lauca river**, running here southwards but later turning east towards Bolivia. On one side is a concrete canal built in the 1960s to tap water from this river and bring it through a tunnel down to a hydroelectric plant at Chapiquiña; it is then directed towards the San José river, which meanders through the length of the Azapa valley. Ahead is the **Chucuyo Police Checkpoint** (4,360 m), where all travellers must check in. Nearby is a pond with lots of taguas and long lava tongues delimiting the bofedal.

At km 41 is the village of **Chucuyo**, a relatively recent settlement which broke away from Parinacota. At km 42 a road branches off to the

left leading to **Parinacota**, which we recommend visiting on the return leg. You then cross long lava tongues, steadily climbing towards the east. Soon you can see, a bit farther below, the beautiful

Cotacotani Lagoons a myriad interconnected emerald-green ponds, surrounded by bofedales. This area illustrates the effect of water flow being blocked by volcanic eruptions. The Chungará lake was formed thus; its waters seep through and emerge farther down to spawn the Cotacotani ponds; these, in turn, seep through the ground to feed the Parinacota bofedal, which acts as the headwater of the Lauca river.

At km 54 you arrive at the upper lake. We recommend you to continue to the Conaf Ranger Station at km 57.

LAKE CHUNGARA at 4,500 m above sea level, this emerald-green lake is really breath-taking surrounded by a string of snow-capped peaks – Parinacota, Sajama, Quisiquisini, Quismachata a bit farther south and the smoking Guallatiri volcano–, some plummeting almost directly to its shores, the Chungará lake swarms with waterfowl –the place can get really loud– and at its shores romp other wildlife. The water is cold but not too cold for a quick dip. At the **Conaf Ranger Station** the park ranger can describe the features of this lake; he has a radio link to other locations and runs an established campground, frequented by those driving or bicycling their way to Bolivia. Customs and International Police control are located at the Chungará Outpost, 7 km farther up, and the international boundary is 3 km beyond.

Driving back from the Conaf station, km 0, note the water uptake installation at the western end of the lake. It was a failed attempt to tap this water to irrigate the Azapa valley, stopped by a public outcry. At km 8 the Cotacotani lagoons can be seen below. Look out here for a dirt road branching down to the right (there is no sign), leading to Parinacota and skirting the Cotacotani ponds. In the upper portion the roadbed is soft, but it gets firmer as it levels off at the bottom. It then runs alongside the ill-fated irrigation canal and at km 10 it reaches the Cotacotani shores. To the side you can see some **Yareta** (also spelled llareta), a light-green plant which envelops boulders, resembling a pillow. It is extraordinarily hard; each of the tiny upper «heads» is an individual plant, part of this closely-knit community. Most are hundreds of years old, and were all but wiped out by mining and nitrate works in the portion of the Andes mountains facing Calama: they happen to be an excellent fuel, with half the calorific power of bituminous coal.

The road skirts succesive ponds, all interconnected but separated from one another by volcanic slag. They are full of guayate geese, ducks and pink flamingoes. The latter are called parina in Aymara; «Parinacota» means «place of parinas». At km 14 is the mouth of the Lauca canal; 1 km farther the road leaves the ponds and runs alongside the Lauca river, among bofedales and large numbers of grazing alpacas. Llamas, less choosy when it comes to fodder, graze farther out at the coirón fields, a thatch-like bunch grass.

At km 18 the dirt road intersects a larger road leading to Visviri, to the right, and to Parinacota to the left, 1 km ahead.

VILLAGE OF PARINACOTA (NM) the whole village is a National Monument. Located 4,390 m above sea level, most of its 50 houses are padlocked. It is one of the High Plateau's ceremonial villages, resuscitating only during religious festivities and festivals. Its inhabitants spend the rest of the time tending their flocks in a nomadic fashion. The village dates from pre-Conquest times and was located on the herding trail from Arica to Potosí; hence the large pens located in the vicinity. The houses are built of stone using clay as mortar and have thatched roofs. Some have stone-slab roofing. They are huddled around the church. Don't miss the

Conaf Visitors Center with a good exhibition illustrating and explaining the features of this 137,000-

camino a Visviri y Caquena

②

PARINACOTA

Laguna

Bofedal de Parinacota

a carretera a Arica

①

N

A Church
B Shrines
C CONAF Warden House and Museum

hectare National Park established in 1970. It was later declared a Biosphere Reserve by UNESCO. Its main purpose is to protect its rich wildlife – nearly one third of Chile's bird fauna is found here. It is part of the natural range of guanacos, vizcachas and vicuñas. A relief model of the High-Plateau and satellite photos of the area provide an overall view of this region. Several stuffed birds complete the collection. Right behind is a pond swarming with waterfowl, with a path to walk around it. There are spartan sleeping accomodations –only four beds but plenty of floor space– with full kitchen facilities. Good for backpackers.

CHURCH OF PARINACOTA (NM)

enclosed by a clay-stuccoed stone wall with three arched doors and cappings on pink volcanic rock. A massive bell tower is attached to one of the wall's corners. The original church dates from the seventeenth century, rebuilt in 1789 in white-washed stone and with a thatched roof. Inside are 17th-century wall paintings and colonial statuary, the latter not in the best of shapes. Religious processions are held through the surrounding streets, where the shrines for placing statuary can be seen. The village and its church are among the most scenic in the north. Return to the International Highway (3 km) and go down to Putre.

2 TO VISVIRI, A TRINATIONAL MEETING POINT

★★★ 258 km round trip from Putre on a gravel road. Colectivo taxis from Arica on Tue. and Fri. to connect with bus from Charaña to La Paz. Advisable to plan the trip for those days. Take plenty of gasoline, food and water.

A trip through the best pastures and bofedales in the High Plateau, with pastoral villages on the way and ending at Chile's northernmost town.

Leave Putre, km 0, and head for Parinacota, km 46. From the village square a road leads to Caquena and Visviri. Beyond the mountain pass, at km 70, is the vast **bofedal de Caquena**, larger than the one at Parinacota and with hundreds of grazing llamas and alpacas. Renowned by its excellent pastures, it lies outside the boudaries of the Lauca National Park. At km 72 is

Caquena another ritual village. In addition to the padlocked houses, there is a police station, a school and administration buildings. Its walled church dates from the 16th century, restored in 1891. It is very interesting because of its patio enclosed by adobe walls, with a round top door and triangular openings all over its perimeter. The church has a simple stone door and a beautiful bell tower next to the wall of the patio.

The road continues alongside the Casopilla stream. At km 76 is another settlement, Chañapalca, also with a church complete with bell tower.

At km 90, small church in Nasahuento; at 93 is the hamlet of Chusjlluta across from the bofedal, with three large, round livestock pens and a small, isolated church enclosed by a wall nicely crowned by a diagonal stone arrangement.

The bofedal continues to the north, next to the

village of Ancopujo at km 101, then Guacollo at km 106, with a beautiful church and bell tower from the 16 th century. At 110 is **Cosapilla**, last village to be found at the bofedal. It is a longitudinal street with a church from the 17th century that has a large patio and 4 small altars for offerings, it also has an inside patio surrounded by a wall and a nice access with 2 round top doors.

The road leaves the bofedal and at km 127 arrives at

Visviri a frontier town with customs and international police controls. Travellers headed for Bolivia prefer to come here by colectivo taxi from Arica – it is cheaper– and then take the Bolivian bus across the border at Charaña, leaving early morning on Wednesday and Saturday. At Charaña there is a so-called **ghost market** (feria fantasma) where the fiery cocoroco –a 93° proof Bolivian spirit– is sold in tin cans. A little farther north a **tripartite market** is held at the point where Chile, Bolivia and Perú meet, gathering Aymara herdsmen from all three countries who come to trade their goods.

3 TO SOCOROMA AND BELEN ★★★

it is best to make these two villages on the return trip from Putre to Arica, leaving early. 223 km altogether, 74 more than driving directly to Arica. If you prefer to return to Putre, your distance will be 144 km. The road to Belén is difficult in January and February: the ford may be flooded. Check with Carabineros at Putre. Take gasoline, water and food.

Two charming towns with a colonial heritage derived from the old Arica-Potosí merchandise traffic.

Leave Putre, km 0, taking the international road towards Arica, described in Section C, Tour 4. You will see the **Cactario** at km 19 and a short distance ahead at km 24 take the signposted road to the right, which winds its way down the sides of a gorge. There is a dam where water from natural springs collects and is used for irrigating terraced crops. The road then levels off, passes a cemetery and arrives, at km 29, in

SOCOROMA

a pre-Columbian village occupied by Spaniards providing services for the Arica-Potosí mule traffic. Its chapel dates from 1560, and its colonial layout is nearly intact, with some stone-paved streets. The widest street was probably used to park the mounts of mule-train drivers. The houses indicated in the map have stone portals. At one end of the small square is the

Church of San Francisco erected on a man-made platform commanding a view of the crops raised on terraces descending to the bottom of the ravine.

The old adobe church was restored in 1883. Both size and style reflect a Spanish presence at the site. Doors and portal have carved stone frames, with signs and names of gospel chanters. There are four statues with silver crowns, Cuzco paintings and other objects harking back to the old glories, such as a strange eagle in polychrome wood used as a candle holder.

Back on the international road at km 34, continue in the direction of Arica. At km 44 is the Zapahuira junction; take the road to the left. This used to be the old muletrain route from Arica through the Azapa valley, Belén, Putre and to Potosí.

At km 52 is Murmuntani and then a ford which may become impassable in the rainy period (January-February). The road climbs to the Chapiquiña Hydroelectric Plant; the water comes through a tunnel from the Lauca river and, after doing its bit for energy generation, goes on to irrigate the Azapa valley. At km 57 is a police station.

The road winds through the mountains to arrive at km 63 to Chapiquiña, with an eighteenth-century church.

After some more mountainous stretches, at km 69 is

Pachama a pastoral village at the Quebrada San Andrés shaded by tall eucalyptus with lined, padlocked houses. It has a mud-brick church dating from the 17th century with very good polychrome frescoes on its inner walls and under the portal eave. The church has a broad external patio mine,

SOCOROMA

N

camino tropero a Putre

sendas de cultivo

a carretera a Arica

A Church
◻ Buildings of Interest
➤ Lookout Point

a cerros de pastoreo

Surire salt flat

piece. At the intersection of the Tignamar and Saxamar rivers are the ruins of 12th-century **Pukará de Saxamar** (NM).

4 TO ENQUELGA THROUGH THE NATIONAL PARKS ★★★

210 km from Putre to Enquelga, takes about 8 hours. The road has some soft, difficult stretches; the Lauca river fords can have up to 50 cm of water during the rainy period (January-February). It is advisable to travel in a 2-vehicle convoy, at the very least. Check road conditions beforehand with Conaf or Carabineros. Inform the Las Cuevas Park Ranger or the Conaf office at Putre of your trip.

Camping at Surire is highly recommendable: day-break at this superb salt lake is a unique experience. Enquelga can then be used as a staging point for other excursions, or you can continue to Chusmiza and stay at the hotel. Take enough gasoline for at least 500 km; next refuelling station is at Huara, 390 km from Putre if you don't make any detours.

A once-in-a-lifetime adventure trip through exceptionally beautiful national parks. It is one of the alternatives for going from Arica to Iquique.

Leave Putre (km 0) towards the international road and the **Las Cuevas Park Ranger Station** (described under Tour 1); inform the park ranger of your intended trip. Two km ahead take the road to the right leading to Guallatire. The **Guallatire** volcano looms in the distance. The road skirts the Miño ravine; on the roadside are odd pilar-like stone piles. At km 4 a road branches off to Chucuyo and some way ahead there is an abandoned stone crushing plant. At km 43 there is another intersection, this time leading to Chapiquiña. Next come the ruins of a village before crossing the bridge over the **Lauca** canal. Both the village and the stone crushing plant were used during the construction of this canal bringing water to the Azapa valley.

A short way ahead is a forking of the road; take the left road. At km 50 is the turn-off to the Camelid Experiment Station at Misitune. Then comes a **ford across the Lauca river**, the most difficult part of the road in the rainy period. Farther ahead is another forking: take the left road, as with the following forkings. You can see the **Choquelimpie open pit gold and silver mine** to the left. At km 55 starts the Las Vicuñas National Reserve. A road branches off to the left leading to Choquelimpie.

Note Choquelimpie is undergoing considerable expansion, and a new road is being open from the international road at the Zapahuira intersection through Murmutani and from there eastward to the

fenced by a beautiful wall crowned by diagonal adobe bricks and two vaulted, thatched doors; the bell tower has a dome.

Finally, continue going down another 7 km to the valley of Belén; at km 76 is

BELEN with 148 inhabitants and set 3,300 m above the sea, it was the only High-Plateau village founded by Spaniards, in 1625. Chosen for its good climate and its location astride the Arica-Potosí trail, it conserves its colonial layout with orderly streets, some of which are paved with stones and have a ditch in the middle. The mud-brick houses are joined by shared walls; the village is fringed by barren hills, grazing fields and lots of eucalyptus. At the three-tiered square are

Two churches the smallest –**Nuestra Señora de Belén**– is also the oldest, with a stepped bell tower as an annex; it dates from the village's foundation. The newer one –**Nuestra Señora del Carmen**– dates from the 18th century. Its **main entrance** is made of stone carved in baroque style, with spiral-shaped Salomonic columns, it has a stella above with images and the rest of the portico carved in stone, like the lateral door inlayed with stone in the thick adobe walls of the long nave (30 m). The statuary includes a remarkable Christ and more than 20 sacred images decorate its interior, highlighting the Virgen de la Silla and a nice fragment of a retable carved in polichrome wood.

Adventurous travellers can continue 14 km to **Tignamar Viejo**, now deserted. It has a church with a baroque portal and a polychrome stone altar-

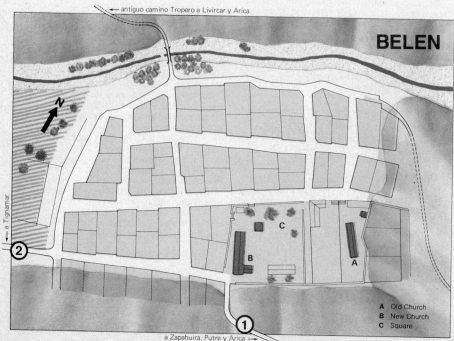

← antiguo camino Tropero a Livircar y Arica

BELEN

a Tignamar ←

② ←

① ←

a Zapahuira, Putre y Arica →

A Old Church
B New Church
C Square

Check with Carabineros if it is open to traffic, as it will be a better option.

Continuing to Enquelga, at km 60 is the turn-off to Chivatambo, at km 63 to Chiriguaya. At km 75 the road fords the nearly dry Chiriguaya stream. One km ahead is **Ancuta**, 6 houses, a chapel and a round pen for the camelids grazing in the nearby bofedal. Next comes a ford of the Ancuta stream -easy crossing- and to the left, at km 85 there is a detour to **Japu** that leads to

Guallatire a pre-Hispanic village with 50 dwellings in a plain facing the Guallatire volcano. Report your arrival at the local Conaf office and at Carabineros, so that they know you have made it this far. A wall-enclosed 17th-century church faces the volcano, it has a fine bell tower with cornered pinnacles; the whole whitewashed.

Continuing on the road you will see a silver smelter dating from the colonial period, at km 89. One km farther you ford the Ancuta stream again (20 cm water in summer) and then pass **Viluvio**, a small settlement. The road runs now alongside the river and its bofedal, where camelids graze and ñandúes –rheas, called suri in Aymara– sprint.

At km 96 you again ford the **Lauca river**, with up to 50 cm water in rainy summers; it can be rather difficult. The road has a stretch with cracks thereafter, and at km 112 is another cross-roads; take the right to Chilcaya and Surire.

At km 124, on the fringes of the salt flat, take the road branching off to the left and drive 3 km to report your arrival at the **Chilcaya police station** (km 127). Go back to the original road (km 129) and turn left at the junction. Ahead you will see a **borate plant** and, at km 137, the **Conaf Ranger Station**.

SURIRE SALT FLAT a strikingly white expanse with lakes and ponds perched 4,250 m above sea level, it owes its name to the suri or ñandú, otherwise known as rhea. By far the most striking sight are the myriad flamingoes –of the James flamingo, Andean flamingo, and Chilean flamingo varieties– feeding or flying about, along with geese and other waterfowl. The flat is flanked by the snowy mountains Lliscaya, Arintina and Pacocahua. A road runs around its entire perimeter, with some scattered settlements and natural hot springs at Pollogere. The best time to observe the wildlife is at dawn or dusk.

Surire was granted a Natural Monument status in 1983 in order to protect its rich wildlife. The Conaf ranger station is radio-linked with other areas. Camping is best at the foot of the salt flat, where the terrain affords some protection against wind and cold. **Important:** Travellers should make careful inquiries into the **stretch of road running alongside the Bolivian boundary** with Conaf Park Rangers before attempting to drive through that area.

To continue your trip to Enquelga from km 137, drive along the flat's southern edge through Chuyuncallani, a settlement where you can buy alpaca woollen garments. At km 141 the road climbs to the village of **Surire**.

At km 152 is the access to Pollogere, with geyser-like thermal springs. At km 160 is a cross-roads; the branch leading north goes to **Chilcaya**, the main village in the area; take from there the road to Bolivia through the Portezuelo de Cerro Capitán to arrive at the **boundary demarcation landmark** at km 164; turn right, **following always the most trafficked track**; at road forkings **always take the right branch** until km 170, where you meet a road leading into Bolivia. Turn right and at km 178 you cross the nearly dry **Mucomucone stream**; 1 km beyond is the **namesake village**, set in the great Parajaya pampa and bofedales, alive with camelids and rheas. In the background looms the scenic **Isluga volcano**. Then you cross the **Vilacoyo** village at km 183 and **Virgin of the Carmen** at km 185.

At km 188 there is a cross-roads (no singpost); the left branch leads to the Aguas Calientes thermal springs and the right one (a bad, unmade road) to Camiña. Straight ahead, at km 191, are the few huts of **Paserijo**. One km ahead cross a streamlet and walk a bit into the **Arabilla bofedal**, where **quinua** crops –a short plant producing a fruit like rice– are to be seen, together with **queñoa** shrubs up to 7 m tall; this is the world's highest-

Isluga Festival

growing tree-like plant. Its twisted wood has been used for making church roof beams.

At km 201, to the right, is the village of **Taipicollo** and, 2 km beyond, the new and old villages of **Arabilla**. At km 206 a bridge crosses the **Arabilla or Isluga river** and the Enquelga bofedal. The road has skirted the foot of the Isluga volcano to arrive at km 210 in

Enquelga a village of 90 stone dwellings orderly set at the foot of the bofedal, with vast potato and quinua crops. Its population is made up of catholic Aymaras possessing a rich heritage of High-Plateau traditions, such as communal land ownership and a cooperative arrangement for work; they are skillful producers of woollen goods. Their stone church is enclosed by a nice wall with pointed arched cappings and has a slender, sharp-pointed bell tower. Inside are polychrome wall paintings, votive writings on the walls and a stone altarpiece.

Here is also a **Conaf Ranger Station** and the Isluga National Park administration. Two km away is **Aguas Calientes**, natural thermal springs with their own pool and a campsite.

TOURS FROM ENQUELGA

If the road from Putre is impassable due to high water at the Lauca river, the alternative is to turn off the Pan American highway at Huara, driving through Tarapacá and Colchane to Enquelga, and from there to the Surire salt flat. The road from Huara to Colchane is an international route with frequent traffic, described under Tour 8.

5 **TO ISLUGA, COLCHANE AND CARIQUIMA** ★★★
2 km round trip from Enquelga; it takes about half a day.
A tour visiting three High Plateau villages illustrating the deep changes the Aymara population has undergone.

From Enquelga, Km 0, descend the hills, alongside a river a bofedal , crossing Aguas Calientes (recommended for camping); at km 6 is

ISLUGA a ritual village 3,800 m above sea level, typical of this herder culture where the people spend most of their time at ayllos or settlements around the bofedal tending their camelid flocks and come to the ritual village only during carnival time, the «fiesta patronal de Isluga», community feasts or burials. So used to be Parinacota, Caquena, Guallatire, and Cancosa; in all of these villages a school, an administrative center and stable population are now to be found. Only Isluga has kept its original character.

Isluga is also home to one of the most beautiful church compounds in the High Plateau. A whitewashed church, closed by a wall crowned by nice, thin arches made out of volcanic stone and two doors with a great circular arch above. The bell tower has two levels, it ends like a pyramid with carved doves as pinnacles. The church has one nave and thick buttresses in stairs to climb to the roof, which here exclusively is covered by clay tiles. There is a back window covered with an alabaster stone.

At the side of the church there is a vast space closed by a wall. It works as a plaza and the communities of Enquelga and Colchane meet here for rituals and games.

Drive 6 km farther down the plain to a sign-posted junction; 4 km to the left is

Colchane set 3,750 m above the sea. It is the municipal head town, and has a customs office, Carabineros station, radio link, general stores and electricity. It consists recently and consists of a sole street with houses huddled against the High-Plateau winds. Pickup trucks await Bolivian passengers to drive them down to Iquique.

Leave Colchane (km 16) on the same road back to the junction (km 20). Go on straight ahead to the next cross-roads, at km 25, with a signpost indicating Cariquima to the left. Take this road and, at km 45, you arrive at

Cariquima 3,850 m altitude. An old ritual village set at the foot of the snow-capped Cariquima mountain, it is now the nucleus of a major Pentecostal community, with services, a school, permanent residents, streets bearing names and electric power. Surprisingly, the traditional Aymara garments are not worn here. A dissident Catholic group moved out to found Lirima, well-known for its woven goods (see Section B, Tour 2).

A 5 km drive on the road to **Ancovinto** will give you a chance to see **giant cacti** (Trichocereus atacamensis) and a superb view to the great plain where the Isluga river empties, forming the Coipasa salt flat; in the background, the snowy Isluga volcano. Return by the same road to Enquelga.

If you want to continue to Chusmiza, go back to the junction at km 25 and take the road to the coast.

6 **TO THE PAN AMERICAN HIGHWAY THROUGH**
CAMIÑA ★★★ 180 km to the Pan American highway. There are 2 roads to Camiña, frequented by pickup trucks bringing vegetables to Colchane. Check road conditions with the Conaf wardens.
A chance to traverse the most scenic sierra valley.

Leave Enquelga, km 0, through the bridge over the Isluga river and take the road to Mauque, skirting the southern edge of the bofedal and the **Arabilla pond**, swarming with waterfowl. The road dives into a gorge and, at the junction at km 14, take the road to the right leading to Latarana. At km 22 is the small **Parinacota pond**, with camelids and waterfowl.

The road then climbs a steep, rough mountain side, reaching the **Berenguela pass** at km 40. It then descends to the **Alpajere plain**. At km 58 take the road leading to the coast. At km 79 is a farmed gorge and the Altuza village, and 7 km ahead the road runs along the ravine leading to Camiña (described under Section A, Tour 7).

7 **TO THE PAN AMERICAN HIGHWAY THROUGH**
MAUQUE ★★★ this route meets the international road at a distance 15 km shorter than through Isluga and Colchane, but it is recommendable only for 4-wheel-drive vehicles.
A shortcut through a scenic village and bofedal, with the possibility to stop by a geyser.

From Enquelga (km 0) cross the river bridge skirting the southern shore of the bofedal, next to **Laguna Arabilla**, and go into the canyon southbound. Go straight and at km 30 you arrive in

Mauque a 30-dwelling village with a typical walled church, bofedal and crops growing on hillsides. Strange vertical boulders state land ownership. On a higher location to the side is the Vilacollo pond.

At km 37 is a cross-roads. From here you can make a 42-km detour (there and back) to the right, climbing a rough, abandoned mountain road to **Baños de Puchuldiza**, with the ruins of an old sulphur mine, a Corfo camp kept by a guard and thermal ponds with water up to 85° C. There is a geyser which Corfo studied with the aim of tapping it as a source of energy.

At the cross-roads at km 37, take the road to the left running among boulders. It brings you to

the international road at km 45. Continuation to the coast described under Tour 8 below.

8 **TO THE PAN AMERICAN HIGHWAY THROUGH**
COLCHANE ★★★ international road suitable for any vehicle tuned for high-altitude conditions. It is 114 km from Enquelga to Chusmiza, 184 to Huara at the Pan Am highway. Takes about 5 hours.
The best road to return to the pampa.

Leave Enquelga (km 0) towards Isluga and continue to the junction at km 12. To the left is Colchane; take the road to the right. At km 17 is a new junction; take the road to the right. At km 41 you cross **Quebe**, in a gorge with sheer rock walls. At km 47 and 49 are the roads coming from **Enquelga via Mauque** (Tour 7). The road then descends into the Huanca gorge, where an inn offers food and drink in a very arid setting.

The road now zigzags its way up the western range of the Andes, to a pass at 4,450 m. From here you can see the plains dropping away below and the ocean, before winding your way down the mountains. At km 92 a road turns off to the right leading to Mocha. At km 114 is **Altos de Chusmiza**, with a basic inn. A road descends 5 km to the left to

CHUSMIZA HOT SPRINGS thermal baths with boiling waters at 3,250 m above sea level. Its hotel is excellent to rest and get used to the abrupt descent to the coast. Described under Section A, Tour 6.

TOURS FROM CHUSMIZA

9 **A VISIT TO SOTOCA** ★★★
56 km round trip from Chusmiza on a badly surfaced gravel road. Takes about half a day.
Pre-Conquest village with a baroque chapel declared a National Monument.

Leave Chusmiza towards the junction with the international road at km 5, turn East (right) climbing very curvy hills that take you to the Altiplano. At km 17 take road to the left and at km 25 take again road to the left. At km 28, after a short descent, is

Sotoca a village in the past subordinate to the Repartimiento de Camiña. It has crops growing on terraces and a walled chapel dating from the 17th century. Annexed to it is a thick stone bell tower with arched windows. The portal to the chapel is in carved stone. Inside is a polychrome, carved-wood altarpiece and statuary.

10 **A VISIT TO USMAGAMA** ★★★
24 km there and back from Chusmiza, with stretches in poor condition due to summer rains. Slow, it takes about half a day.
A scenic village with a National Monument church.

At the international road junction at km 5 from Chusmiza turn left towards the coast. Four km ahead take the road to the left, through Quebrada de Ocharaga. At km 12 is

Usmagama a Sierra village which at colonial times was part of the Repartimiento y Parroquia de Sibaya (a neighboring town), governing Tarapacá with several tributary villages. Its baroque-style **church (NM)** dates from the 17th century. Portal in chiseled white stone flanked by spiralling columns. Inside, a large altarpiece in wood and masonry and valuable statuary. It is worth a visit.

11 **RETURN TO IQUIQUE WITH DETOUR TO MOCHA AND GUAVIÑA** ★★★ 122 km to Huara, detours included, with 34 km paved. From Huara, 80 km to Iquique. Fuel at Huara. Takes ½ day. Leave early.
Another group of villages with baroque-andean- styled churches and better road access.

At the international road junction at km 5 from Chusmiza turn left towards the coast; the road descends gently across a plain with groups of cacti which disappear at km 83. Here is the turn-off to the left for Mocha. This section of the road is called «100 turns», and zigzags its way down to the dry bottom of **Infiernillo gorge**; it then climbs its southern slope to the top, to dive next into the **Tarapacá ravine**. You arrive at

Mocha a village with a 17th-century baroque **chapel (NM)**, with a chiselled-stone portal flanked by spiral columns that ends in pinnacles and a frame carved in stone.

Continue along the bottom of the ravine –narrow and with a small stream– to arrive at km 43 at

Guaviña another village with a small **church (NM)** dating from the 18th century, with an arched, carved-stone portal. Inside, a finely-carved altar-piece and valuable statuary probably of Cuzco origin.

Both churches were subordinate to the San Nicolás de Tolentino parish which existed since 1620 at **Sibaya**.

These were originally Indian villages, their residents working at the Huantajaya silver mine near Iquique. With their contributions and devotion they decorated these churches.

Return to the international road at km 63 and ontinue to the Pan American highway (stretch described under Section A, Tour 6).

PUBLIC TRANSPORTATION

The chart below shows intense interprovincial and international traffic along the Pan American highway. However, regular public transportation to the nearly one hundred oases in the Sierra and High Plateau is practically nonexistent.

The usual means of transport there are pickup trucks bringing farm produce to the bigger towns.

Scheduled transportation services are listed below from south to north:

To Pica daily buses and colectivo taxis from Iquique.

To Tarapacá daily bus from Huara; to Huara from Iquique, frequent buses headed for Arica.

Iquique-Arica multiple daily buses and colectivo taxis.

To Colchane trucks and pickup trucks leave Iquique Friday afternoon to arrive at Colchane Saturday morning. Pickup trucks bring farm produce to the market from Camiña on interior road. Daily colectivo taxis and pickup trucks bring people from Colchane to the Duty Free Zone in Iquique during the summer.

To Chungará Lake daily minibuses from Arica to Putre, Parinacota and the lake, organized by travel agencies in Arica.

To Belén twice-weekly buses from Arica.

To Putre thrice-weekly buses from Arica.

To Visviri colectivo taxis leave Arica around 1800h to connect with train leaving Charaña for La Paz; they return on the next day.

To Perú and Bolivia by railway and road, described under Section C.

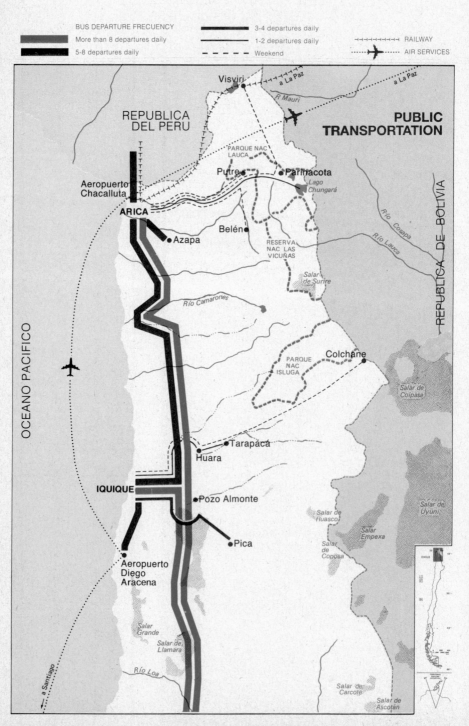

78

Zone 2
ANTOFAGASTA

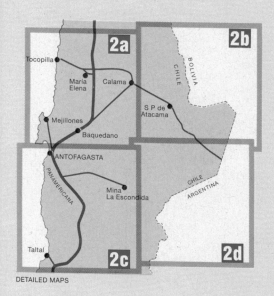

2a

Tocopilla
Maria Elena
Calama
Mejillones
Baquedano
S P de Atacama

2b

BOLIVIA
CHILE

2c

ANTOFAGASTA
PANAMERICANA
Mina La Escondida
Taltal

2d

CHILE
ARGENTINA

DETAILED MAPS

2

Arica

Iquique

Antofagasta

Copiapó

Easter Island

La Serena

Is R Crusoe

Valparaíso

SANTIAGO

Talca

Concepción

Temuco

Valdivia

Osorno

Pto Montt

Castro
Chaitén

Coihaique

Cochrane

Puerto Natales

Punta Arenas

Puerto Williams

Is Diego Ramirez

90°   60°   53°

CHILEAN ANTARCTIC TERRITORY

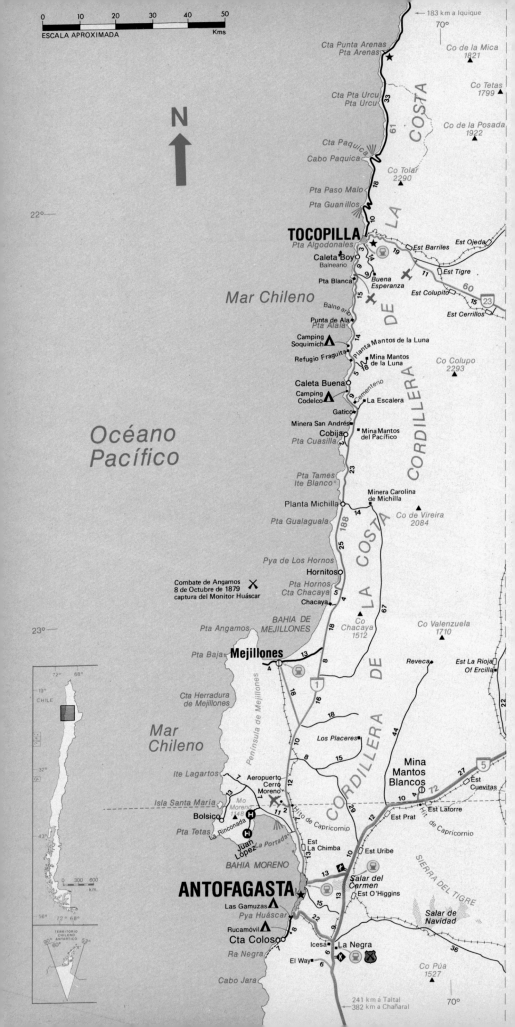

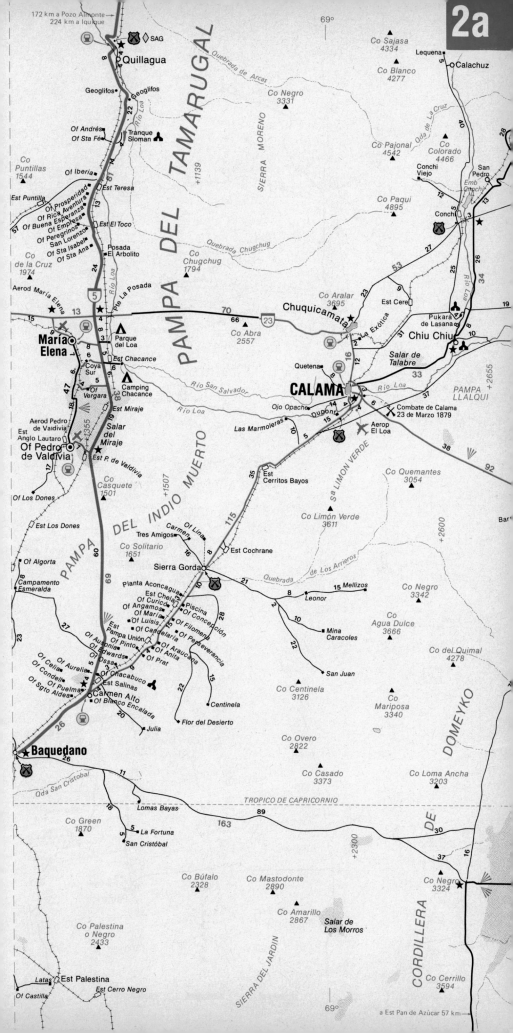

172 km a Pozo Almonte
224 km a Iquique

Quillagua
SAG

Co Sajasa
4334

Lequena
Calachuz

Geoglifos
Geoglifos

Co Negro
3331

Co Blanco
4277

Of Andrés
Of Sta Fé
Tranque Sloman

Co Pajonal
4542

Co Colorado
4466

Conchi Viejo

San Pedro
Emb Conchi

Co Puntillas
1544

Of Iberia

Est Puntilla

Est Teresa

Co Paqui
4895

Conchi

Of Prosperidad
Of Rica Aventura
Of Buena Esperanza
Of Empresa
Of Peregrinos
San Lorenzo
Of Sta Isabel
Of Sta Ana

Est El Toco

Quebrada Chugchug

Posada El Arbolito

Co Chugchug
1794

Pukará de Lasana

Chiu Chiu

Co de la Cruz
1974

Pte La Posada

Co Aralar
3695

Est Cere

Chuquicamata

La Exótica

Aerod María Elena

Co Abra
2557

Salar de Talabre

María Elena

Parque del Loa

Est Chacance

Quetena

CALAMA

Río Loa

PAMPA LLALQUI

Coya Sur

Camping Chacance

Río San Salvador

Ojo Opache

Combate de Calama
23 de Marzo 1879

Of Vergara

Est Miraje

Río Loa

Las Marmoleras

Dupont

Aerop El Loa

Aerod Pedro de Valdivia

Salar del Miraje

Est Anglo Lautaro

Of Pedro de Valdivia

Est P. de Valdivia

Est Cerritos Bayos

Co Quemantes
3054

Co Casquete
1501

Co Limón Verde
3611

Of Los Dones

Est Los Dones

Tres Amigos
Carmen
Of Linar

Est Cochrane

Co Negro
3342

Of Algorta

Co Solitario
1651

Sierra Gorda

Mellizos

Leonor

Co Agua Dulce
3666

Campamento Esmeralda

Planta Aconcagua
Of Chela
Of Curico
Of Angamos
Of María
Of Luisis
Of Candelaria
Of Pinto
Est Pampa Unión
Of Ausonia
Of Edwards
Of Ossa
Of Chacabuco

Piscina
Of Concepción
Of Filomena
Of Perseverancia
Of Araucana
Of Anita
Of Prat

Mina Caracoles

Co del Quimal
4278

Of Aurelia
Of Celia
Of Condell
Of Puelma
Of Sgto Aldea

Est Salinas
Carmen Alto
Of Blanco Encalada

Julia

San Juan

Co Centinela
3126

Centinela

Flor del Desierto

Co Mariposa
3340

Baquedano

Co Overo
2822

Co Casado
3373

Co Loma Ancha
3203

Qda San Cristóbal

TROPICO DE CAPRICORNIO

Lomas Bayas

La Fortuna

San Cristóbal

Co Green
1870

Co Búfalo
2328

Co Mastodonte
2890

Co Negro
3324

Co Amarillo
2867

Salar de Los Morros

Co Palestina o Negro
2433

Latas
Of Castilla

Est Palestina

Est Cerro Negro

Co Cerrillo
3594

a Est Pan de Azúcar 57 km

PAMPA DEL TAMARUGAL

SIERRA MORENO

PAMPA DEL INDIO MUERTO

Sa LIMON VERDE

CORDILLERA DE DOMEYKO

SIERRA DEL JARDIN

Quebrada de Arcas

Qda de La Cruz

Río Loa

Quebrada Chugchug

Quebrada de Los Arrieros

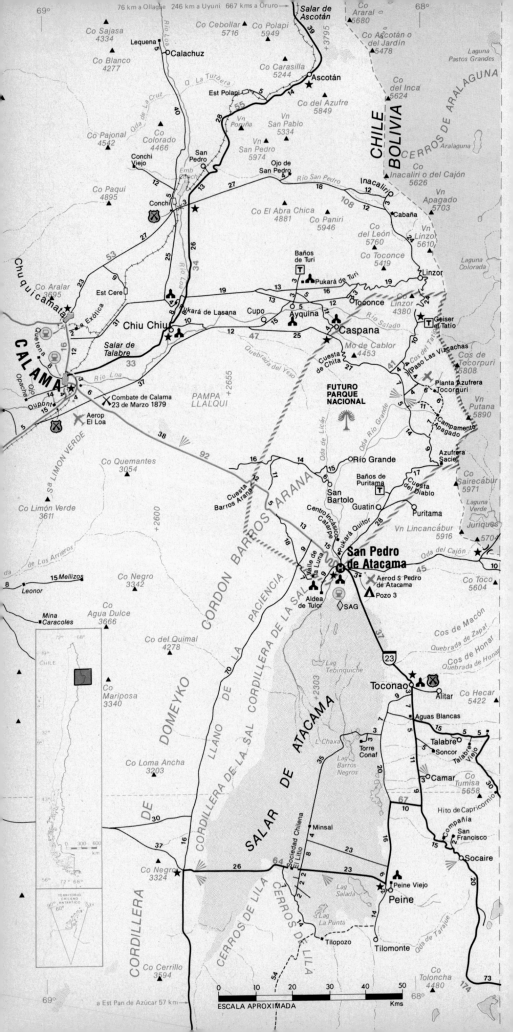

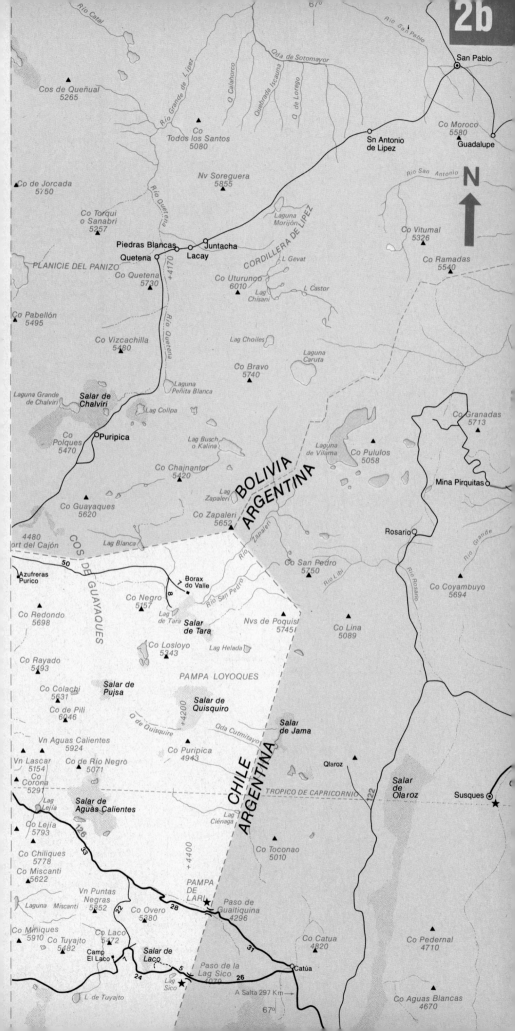

Río Catal

Río San Pablo

Río Grande de Lipez

O Calahorco

Quebrada Ascauna

Q de Lorego

Qda de Sotomayor

San Pablo

Cos de Queñual
5265

Co
Todos los Santos
5080

Sn Antonio
de Lipez

Co Moroco
5580

Guadalupe

Co de Jorcada
5750

Nv Soreguera
5855

Río San Antonio

Co Vitumal
5326

N

Río Quetena

Co Torqui
o Sanabri
5257

Laguna
Morijón

CORDILLERA DE LIPEZ

Co Ramadas
5540

Piedras Blancas
Quetena

Juntacha
Lacay

+4170+

L Gevat

PLANICIE DEL PANIZO

Co Quetena
5730

Co Uturunco
6010

L Castor

Lag
Chisani

Co Pabellón
5495

Río Quetena

Lag Choiles

Laguna
Caruta

Co Granadas
5713

Co Vizcachilla
5480

Co Bravo
5740

Laguna
Grande
de Chalviri

Laguna
Peñita Blanca

Salar de
Chalviri

Lag Collpa

Co
Polques
5470

Puripica

Lag Busch
o Kalina

Laguna
de Vilama

Co Pululos
5058

Mina Pirquitas

Co Chajnantor
5420

Co Guayaques
5620

Lag
Zapaleri

BOLIVIA
ARGENTINA

Co Zapaleri
5652

Río Zapaleri

Rosario

Río Grande

Lag Blanca

Co San Pedro
5750

Río L. Ibi.

Co Coyambuyo
5694

Río Rosario

4480
ort del Cajón

COS DE GUAYAQUES

50

Azufreras
Purico

Borax
do Valle

7

8

Río San Pedro

Co Negro
5157

Co Redondo
5698

Salar
de Tara

Nvs de Poquis
5745

Co Lina
5089

Lag
de Tara

Co Rayado
5493

Co Losloyo
5243

Lag Helada

Co Colachi
5631

Salar de
Pujsa

PAMPA LOYOQUES

Co de Pili
6046

Q de Quisquire

Salar de
Quisquiro

+4200

Oda Cutmitayo

Salar
de Jama

Vn Aguas Calientes
5924

Co Puripica
4943

Vn Lascar
5154

Co de Río Negro
5071

Qlaroz

Co
Corona
5291

Salar
de
Olaroz

Susques

Lag
Lejia

Salar de
Aguas Calientes

TROPICO DE CAPRICORNIO

122

CHILE
ARGENTINA

Lag
Ciénaga

Co Lejía
5793

126

Co Chiliques
5778

33

Co Miscanti
5622

+4400

Co Toconao
5010

Vn Puntas
Negras
5852

Laguna Miscanti

22

Co Overo
5280

28

PAMPA
DE LARI

Paso de
Guaitiquina
4296

Co Catua
4820

Co Pedernal
4710

Co Miniques
5910

Co Laco
5472

Co Tuyajto
5482

Camp
El Laco

31

Salar de
Laco

24

Lag Sico

5

Paso de la
Lag Sico
4079

Catúa

26

A Salta 297 Km

Co Aguas Blancas
4670

L de Tuyajto

67º

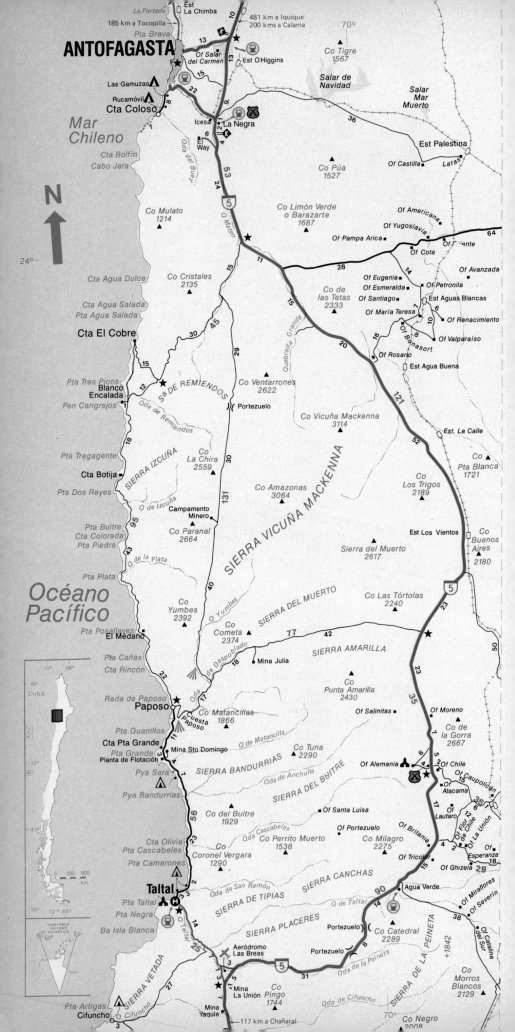

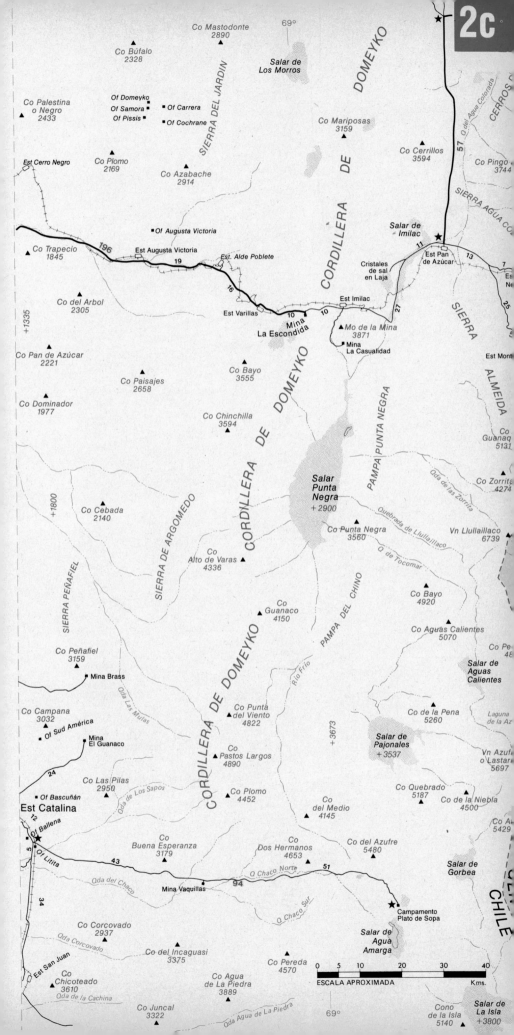

Co Mastodonte
2890

Co Búfalo
2328

Salar de
Los Morros

69°

CORDILLERA DE DOMEYKO

CERROS D...

Co Palestina
o Negro
2433

Of Domeyko
Of Samora   ■ Of Carrera
Of Pissis   ■ Of Cochrane

SIERRA DEL JARDIN

Co Mariposas
3159

Co Cerrillos
3594

Co Pingo
3744

57 Q. del Agua Colorada

SIERRA AGUA CO...

Co Plomo
2169

Co Azabache
2914

Est Cerro Negro

Of Augusta Victoria

Salar de
Imilac

Cristales
de sal
en Laja

Est Pan
de Azúcar

11

13

7

Co Trapecio
1845

196

Est Augusta Victoria

19

Est. Alde Poblete

Est Imilac

Est
Ne...

25

+1335

Co del Arbol
2305

16

Est Varillas   10   10

Mina
La Escondida

Mo de la Mina
3871

Mina
La Casualidad

27

SIERRA

ALMEIDA

Est Mont...

Co Pan de Azúcar
2221

Co Paisajes
2658

Co Bayo
3555

Co
Guanaq...
5131

Co Dominador
1977

Co Chinchilla
3594

CORDILLERA DE DOMEYKO

PAMPA PUNTA NEGRA

Salar
Punta
Negra
+2900

Qda de las Zorrita

Co Zorrita
4274

+1800+

Co Cebada
2140

SIERRA DE ARGOMEDO

Co
Alto de Varas
4336

Co Punta Negra
3560

Quebrada de Llullaillaco

Vn Llullaillaco
6739

Q. de Tocomar

SIERRA PEÑAFIEL

Co
Guanaco
4150

PAMPA DEL CHINO

Co Bayo
4920

Co Aguas Calientes
5070

Co Peñafiel
3159

Mina Brass

Qda Las Mulas

Río Frío

Salar de
Aguas
Calientes

Co Pe...
48...

Co Campana
3032

Of Sud América

Mina
El Guanaco

Co Punta
del Viento
4822

Co de la Pena
5260

Laguna
de la Az...

Salar de
Pajonales
+3537

Vn Azuf...
o Lastar...
5697

24

Co Las Pilas
2950

Qda de Los Sapos

Co
Pastos Largos
4890

Co Plomo
4452

Co Quebrado
5187

Co de la Niebla
4500

Of Bascuñán

Est Catalina

12

Of Ballena

Co
Buena Esperanza
3179

Co
Dos Hermanos
4653

Co
del Medio
4145

Co del Azufre
5480

Co A...
5429...

5

Of Litita

43

51

Salar de
Gorbea

CHILE

34

Oda del Chaco

Mina Vaquillas

94

Q Chaco Norte

Q Chaco Sur

Campamento
Plato de Sopa

Co Corcovado
2937

Oda Corcovado

Co del Incaguasi
3375

Co Pereda
4570

Salar de
Agua
Amarga

Est San Juan

Co
Chicoteado
3610

Oda de la Cachina

Co Agua
de La Piedra
3889

Co Juncal
3322

Oda Agua de La Piedra

69°

Cono
de la Isla
5140

Salar de
La Isla
+3800

0   5   10   20   30   40

ESCALA APROXIMADA   Kms.

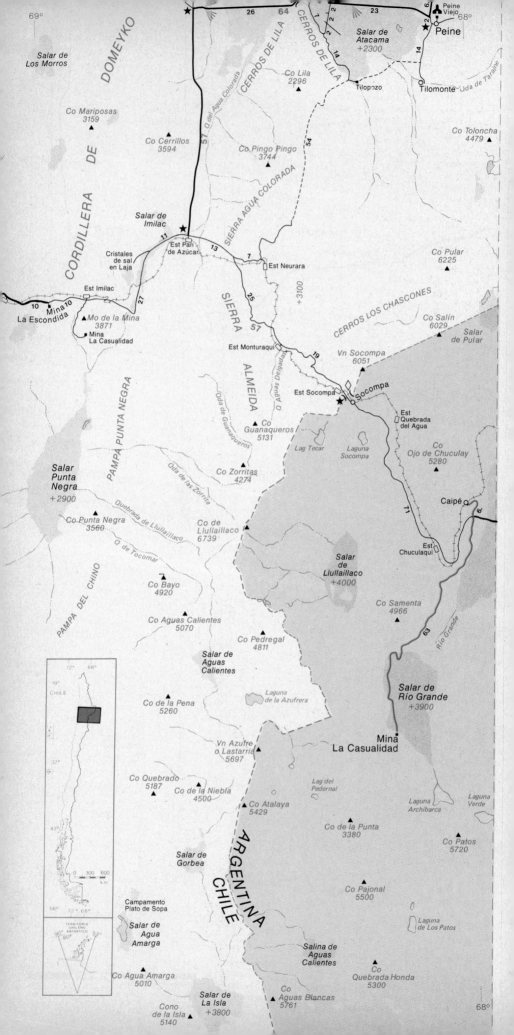

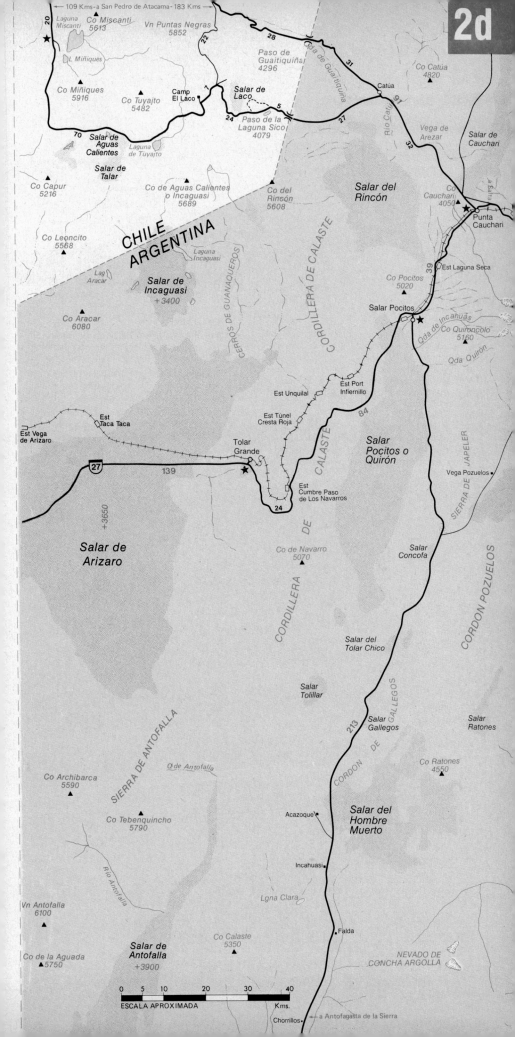

← 109 Kms-a San Pedro de Atacama- 183 Kms →

20

Laguna
Miscanti
★

Co Miscanti
5613

Vn Puntas Negras
5852

22

28

Qda de Guaitiquiña

31

Co Catúa
4820

Paso de
Guaitiquiñas
4296

Catúa

91

Rio Catúa

32

Vega de
Arezar

Salar de
Cauchari

Co Miñiques
5916

Co Tuyajto
5482

Camp
El Laco

1

Salar de
Laco

5

27

Salar del
Rincón

Co
Cauchari
4050
★

Punta
Cauchari

24

Paso de la
Laguna Sico
4079

39

Est Laguna Seca

70

Salar de
Aguas
Calientes

Laguna
de Tuyajto

Salar de
Talar

Co del
Rincón
5608

Co Pocitos
5020

Co Quironcolo
5160

Co Capur
5216

Co de Aguas Calientes
o Incaguasi
5689

Salar Pocitos

Qda de Incahuas

Qda Quirón

CHILE
ARGENTINA

Laguna
Incaguasi

CERROS DE GUANAQUEROS

CORDILLERA DE CALASTE

Est Port
Infiernillo

Co Leoncito
5568

Lag
Aracar

Salar de
Incaguasi
+3400

Est Unquilal

84

Salar
Pocitos o
Quirón

SIERRA DE JAPELER

Co Aracar
6080

Est Túnel
Cresta Roja

Vega Pozuelos

Est Vega
de Arizaro

Est Taca Taca

Tolar
Grande
★

Est
Cumbre Paso
de Los Navarros

Salar
Concofa

CORDILLERA

DE

CALASTE

CORDON POZUELOS

27

139

24

+3650

Salar de
Arizaro

Co de Navarro
5070

CORDILLERA

Salar del
Tolar Chico

Salar
Tolillar

CORDON DE GALLEGOS

Salar
Ratones

Co Archibarca
5590

Q de Antofalla

SIERRA DE ANTOFALLA

213

Salar
Gallegos

Co Ratones
4550

Co Tebenquincho
5790

Acazoque

Salar del
Hombre
Muerto

Rio Antofalla

Vn Antofalla
6100

Incahuasi

Co de la Aguada
5750

Salar de
Antofalla
+3900

Co Calaste
5350

Lgna Clara

Falda

NEVADO DE
CONCHA ARGOLLA

0   5   10   20   30   40

ESCALA APROXIMADA   Kms.

Chorrillos   → a Antofagasta de la Sierra

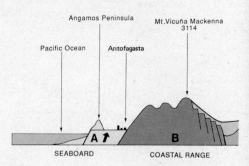

Angamos Peninsula Mt.Vicuña Mackenna 3114

Pacific Ocean   Antofagasta

A   B

SEABOARD   COASTAL RANGE

OVERVIEW

This Tourist Zone coincides with the territory of Chile's Region II, Antofagasta. It has a good road network providing access to all the interesting sights in the coastal area and the High Plateau. Antofagasta, Calama and San Pedro de Atacama have a complete tourist infrastructure, making them excellent jumping–off points for excursions throughout the Region.

In the higher reaches of this Zone is the great Atacama salt flat, with valuable relics of the old Indian cultures, superb scenery, and unusual geologic formations attracting a great deal of international visitors.

We have divided this Zone into four sectións, namely;

Section A Antofagasta and Taltal comprising these two cities, and the stretch of Pan–American highway and coastal road between the two.

Section B María Elena and Tocopilla an area of coast and desert with interesting mining operations and industrial archaeological sites.

Section C Calama the heart of the copper mining industry and a good jumping–off point for visiting historically interesting villages in the Loa river basin.

Section D Atacama Salt Flat the great depression where the Atacameño Indian culture developed, with lakes teeming with waterfowl, a grand scenery and some interesting new mining works.

REGIONAL DISTANCES

Antofagasta

213	Calama															
298	83	Caspana														
250	35	51	Chiu-Chiu													
229	16	100	49	Chuquicamata												
336	121	45	96	146	Geyser El Tatio											
205	102	186	135	86	231	María Elena										
60	273	349	298	281	394	207	Mejillones									
393	188	206	155	204	251	290	494	Ollagùe								
479	265	339	288	271	384	357	520	443	Paso de Guaitiquina							
426	180	280	229	212	325	298	461	384	173	Peine						
778	565	659	608	591	704	677	840	763	300	493	Salta (Argentina)					
320	105	176	125	108	221	·194	357	280	163	104	483	San Pedro de Atacama				
426	196	263	212	195	308	281	444	367	156	47	476	87	Socaire			
303	518	592	541	524	637	508	363	696	763	704	1083	600	687	Taltal		
359	144	213	162	145	258	231	394	317	126	67	446	37	50	637	Toconao	
188	159	250	199	150	295	69	138	354	425	362	724	258	345	545	295	Tocopilla

Zone 2
ANTOFAGASTA

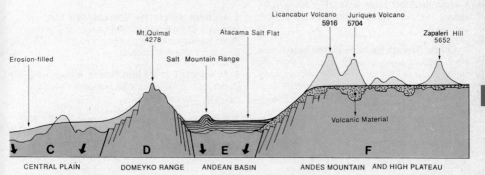

Erosion-filled • Mt.Quimal 4278 • Salt Mountain Range • Atacama Salt Flat • Licancabur Volcano 5916 • Juriques Volcano 5704 • Zapaleri Hill 5652 • Volcanic Material

C — CENTRAL PLAIN | D — DOMEYKO RANGE | E — ANDEAN BASIN | F — ANDES MOUNTAIN AND HIGH PLATEAU

DIVISION BY SECTIONS

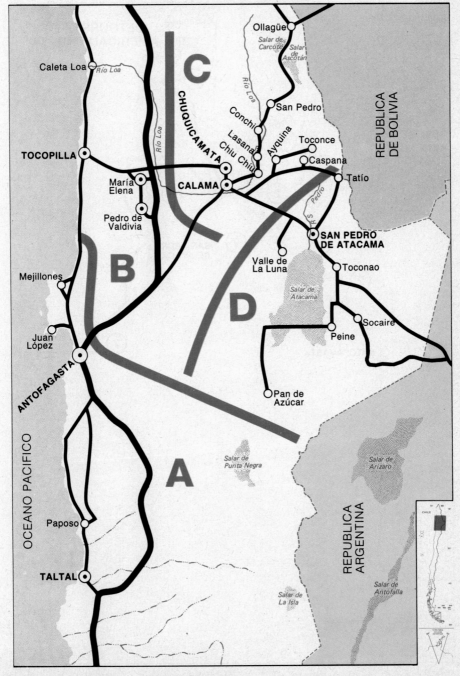

DETOURS OFF THE PAN-AMERICAN HIGHWAY

This Zone offers good alternative routes along the coast or through the highlands.

1 Along the Coast South to Taltal a little-known, solitary road with a long history, described under Section A.

2 A Circuit Through the Coast and the Desert from Antofagasta, a circuit providing a good insight into all the features of this Zone. The various tours making up this circuit are described under Sections B and C.

3 The Coastal Road from Iquique a long but fairly frequented road with beautiful beaches and interesting mine works. Described under Section B. The stretch from Iquique to the Loa river is described under Zone 1, Section A.

4 A Visit to Calama and Chuquicamata a good alternative route to the north, taking in Chile's largest copper mine. See Sections B and C.

5 A Circuit Around the Atacama Salt Flat an extension of the previous circuit, continuing to San Pedro de Atacama and returning through El Tatio. Described under Section D.

6 An Adventure on the High-Plateau a fascinating circuit only suitable for 4WD vehicles. See Zone 1, under Excursions.

7 Return Through Argentina another unusual alternative, offering the chance to see the eastern foot of the Andes visiting Salta, Tucumán, San Juan and Mendoza. See Section D.

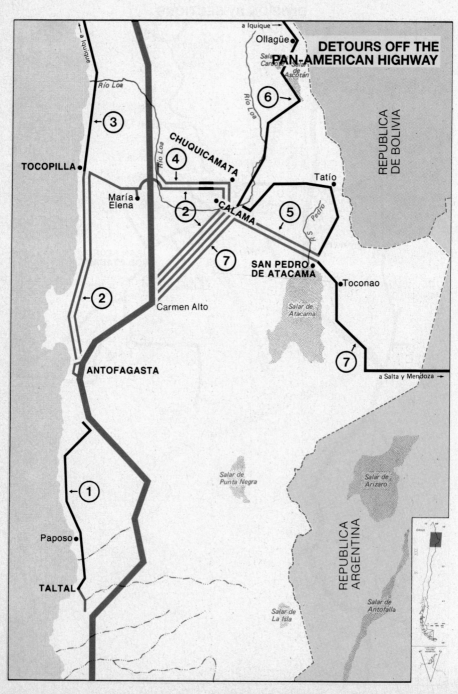

DETOURS OFF THE PAN-AMERICAN HIGHWAY

THE LAND, ITS HISTORY, ITS PEOPLE

DESCRIPTION this Zone covers an area of 125,306 square kilometers, Chile's second largest Region after the Antarctic Territory. Here is Chile's widest point, with 380 km from the Angamos peninsula to Mount Poquis. A short distance north, at mount Zapaleri, the borders of Chile, Argentina and Bolivia come together.

The Loa, the only water course reaching the ocean through the desert, is Chile's longest river, with 430 km. The Central Plain is known here as Atacama Desert, one of the world's driest deserts. The Andean peaks and volcanoes soar above 6,000 m, while the Coastal Range reaches here its highest point, Mount Vicuña Mackenna (3,114 m). To complete the singularities, here is also the world's largest open pit copper mine, Chuquicamata, the largest known lithium deposit –the Atacama salt flat–, the only active natural saltpeter mine –María Elena and Pedro de Valdivia, and the largest copper deposit, at La Escondida.

MORPHOLOGY there are five well-defined relief bands lying lengthwise, namely:

The Seaboard created by erosion of the Coastal Range, it is generally narrow and it disappears between Coloso and El Cobre, where the mountains plunge directly to the sea, leaving no room for roads. Between Antofagasta and Mejillones, in turn, the sea bottom has surged upwards and generated a wide plain.

The few spots with fresh water were originally inhabited by Chango Indians, and later became the seat of the first seaports, Tocopilla, Cobija, Paposo and Taltal. This area now concentrates the larger part of this Zone's population.

Coastal Range it is high, wide and marches parallel to the coast. Its western flank is steep and is undergoing strong erosion processes. Its eastern flank is rounded and does not rise as high above the surrounding terrain, as a result of a thick sediment layer in the Central Plain.

Central Plain a depression lying between the parallel Andes and Coastal mountain ranges, it has been filled up by sediment over the ages and varies in altitude from 1,200 and 2,000 m above sea level. It drops gently to the west and is known as **Atacama Desert**. It is extraordinarily dry.

Domeyko Range it is an arm of the Andes range, running parallel and to the west of it. The Andes fork into two arms opposite Copiapó (Domeyko and range). The Domeyko range disappears momentarily by Calama. When it reappears farther north, it has no name and skirts the upper course of the Loa river, running later along the border with Argentina. Its average altitude in this Zone is 3,500 m, but it does not receive much snow, thus contributing little to the Central Plain's water supply. It harbors the Chuquicamata copper mine and the giant La Escondida copper deposit.

The Andean Basin it lies between the Domeyko range. The former impedes water from flowing to the west. The water from the Andean snows accumulates here and, as a result of strong evaporation, it gives rise to the salt flats.

This basin stretches from Copiapó –with some interruptions– through the Atacama salt flat, Chiu Chiu, the Ascotán and Carcote salt flats, and then into Bolivia through the great Uyuni salt flat and lake Poopo.

The Atacama salt flat, Chile's largest, is also a great lithium, potassium and borax deposit. A scattered population engaged in agriculture and livestock farming dwells at the few areas having fresh water.

The Andes and the Puna this is a high–altitude area which suffered extremely active volcanism in the past. This volcanic activity filled up the depressions between the mountains with ash and slag, giving rise in time to a flat plain lying at an average altitude of about 4,000 meters, known as Puna. The water seeps into the porous ground here, washing away the salts and resurfacing much farther below, at the edge of the salt flats. It is a barren, uninhabited area containing rich sulfur deposits.

The Loa River this is the only river to reach the ocean through the desert, flowing through various gaps in the successive barriers rising in its course. After making a wide bow to the south, it empties into the ocean at the same latitude as its headwaters lie. It originates in the great upper Loa watershed. It appears that in the remote past, a geological barrier located near present-day Calama dammed the waters flowing west and created a great lake, a fact which would account for the flatness of the upper Loa valley. Eventually, a geological fault permitted the water to flow on to the ocean.

WHY IS THIS A DESERT? in all the western coasts of the Southern Hemisphere there are deserts between latitudes 10° and 25° south. This is due to the presence of **High Pressure Centers** in each ocean, lurking close to the coast and preventing the rain-bearing **low pressure fronts** from reaching the mainland.

The desert's dryness is made worse by the lack of rivers flowing across from the Andes due to the barrier represented by the Domeyko range.

Camanchaca is a thick coastal fog rolling in from the sea in the early morning hours, clearing away by midday. The high pressure prevents the strong sea evaporation from ascending, thus remaining in low-altitude strata. This fog does not produce rainfall, nor does it cross the Coastal Range to provide some moisture to the areas inland.

The High–Plateau Winter this is not really a winter; in fact, it occurs during the Southern Hemisphere's summer season. It is a climatic phenomenon affecting the higher areas of the Andes from Arica to Copiapó, from December to March. The most active months are January and February, with violent snow and hail storms. During the previous couple of months, the sun has steadily approached the Tropic of Capricorn, reaching the zenith on December 21. Solar radiation peaks during this period, provoking intense ascending evaporation in the Great Chaco region of Paraguay and Argentina, giving rise to rain fronts which are then pushed westwards by the Atlantic High Pressure Center.

EARLY INHABITANTS the coastal and the Andean basin dwellers were two different ethnic groups. The Central Plain and the puna were uninhabited, but strong trade traffic took place through the Central Plain between both aboriginal groups.

Changos they were nomadic coastal dwellers living in the area from Arica to Huasco, mostly in the vicinity of the scant places with fresh water, known as puquios. They were superb swimmers and great seamen, sailing in rafts made of inflated seawolf skins. They hunted seawolves and whales using harpoons; when they killed one, they would wait for the sea to wash it ashore. They also fished using hooks. They transported dry fish using llamas as pack animals towards the inland settlements, which they traded for coca and quínoa flour. Their main settlements in this Zone

2

91

were at Taltal, Paposo, Cobija and Tocopilla.

Atacameños they dwelled in the Andean basin from Chiu Chiu to the Atacama salt flat and towards the Argentinian sierras. They arrived in this area about 11,000 years ago, as hunters coming from the High Plateau. They dwelled in caves and rocky overhangs on the rivers, where they collected chañar fruit and developed some stone carving techniques. They were the seed of the splendid **Atacameño culture**.

Over a period of thousands of years, they mastered the taming of animals and a transhumant regime between valley pastures and puna meadows. Later they developed a selective gathering regime, and not long thereafter –about 3,000 years ago– they started to adopt a sedentary way of living, with rudimentary agriculture and the appearance of the first stable settlements. The **Túlor village**, from approximately 100 BC to AD 100, is perhaps the best example of their mature cultural development, including the mastery of ceramics, weaving, metallurgy and irrigation.

During the 10th century, the Atacama people received a strong influence from the High–Plateau **Tiawanaku** culture (lake Titicaca), expressed in the design of textiles and ceramics, in the use of carved wooden tablets and in the inhalation of hallucinogens.

The Atamaca culture reached its peak by the 12th century, with the establishment of complex villages and **local principalities**, the construction of defensive forts –known as **pukarás**– and a beautiful formal design in textiles, basketry and ceramics.

By 1450 the **Inca** influence spread southwards to this area from the sierras in Perú, bringing with it new technologies in metallurgy and ceramics, and entailing the area's absorption into an empire based in trade and using established roads (Inca Roads). The Inca administrative center for this region was at **Catarpe**, north of San Pedro de Atacama. Little over a century later, the Spanish conquerors swept into the area, bringing with them a whole new world and the demise of the Atacameño culture.

The **Archaeological Museum** at San Pedro de Atacama provides an excellent insight into the region's cultures and history.

Desert Trails when the Atacameño culture reached a certain degree of maturity by the first century after Christ, a growing barter trade started to take place between the coastal and the mountain dwellers, following natural paths. One of such natural paths was the Loa river. Cobija, on the coast, was reached through Chacance, and Tocopilla through Quillagua, both of which were Atacameño settlements on the banks of the Loa. Farther south, to reach Paposo and Taltal, the route traversed the southern portion of the Andean basin and then crossed the desert through small oases which still exist. There were three natural herding trails to the Altiplano, or high plateau; two of them are now roads: one leading through Ollagüe to Bolivia and the other, through Guaitiquina to Argentina. The third one ran through Socaire, in the Atacama salt flat, to Antofagasta de la Sierra in Argentina; this was the route followed by naturalist Federico Philippi in 1885.

The imperial concept of the Incas led them to build the **Inca Road**, a path running north-south with «way stations» known as **tambos** to provide lodging for the «chasquis» known as couriers travelling the Inca Road by foot, and for the herdsmen bringing their annual tributes. The road was three meters wide and lined with stones. It followed at times the old paths already existing in the area. From Pica it came down to Quillagua on the Loa and then to Chacance, Calama, Chiu Chiu and San Pedro de Atacama. It continued skirting the eastern edge of the Atacama salt flat, through the few

oases there, then to the Punta Negra salt flat to reach the Central Plain through El Salvador, Finca de Chañaral and Copiapó (see map). It was also followed by the Spanish conquerors to come into Chile. The water springs on the road were not very abundant, and Pedro de Valdivia, while at San Pedro de Atacama, sent his troops south in weekly parties, so as not to deplete the few water sources.

SPANISH DOMINATION the Atacameño culture and their territory entered the Western history in 1536, with the return of Diego de Almagro to Cuzco. Pedro de Valdivia was the next westerner to visit the area, in 1540. Soon thereafter, the Catholic Church and the Spanish administration started to operate in Atacameño territory, which came to be subordinate to the Charcas Bishopric and to the Corregimiento de Lipiez (Andean Sierra).

A mission was established at San Pedro de Atacama in 1557, which built a chapel; simultaneously, an encomienda was granted -an estate ran by a Spaniard with the natives subjected to a serfdom system. By 1600 there were curacies at San Pedro de Atacama and Chiu Chiu, and later an administrative center with corregidor –a kind of governor– and a cabildo or council were set up at San Pedro de Atacama (subordinate to Charcas and Lipes, both in High Perú). In 1776 the Charcas Archbishopric and the Lipes province broke away from the Perú Viceroyship and became part of the La Plata Viceroyship, with its capital at Buenos Aires. In 1793 the Viceroyship of Perú decreed that the border between Chile and Perú ran along the Loa river.

This Zone, then, belonged by the end of the colonial period to two administrative divisions of the Spanish Crown: the coast and the central plain –known then as the Atacama Wilderness– belonged to Chile up to the Loa river, and the Andean basin and the puna (the old territory of the Atacameño culture) belonged to the La Plata Viceroyship.

INDEPENDENCE at the end of the colonial period, the only urban centers were San Pedro de Atacama and Chiu Chiu; there were some scattered, tiny settlements in the Andean basin and in the central portion of the Loa river's course, such as Quillagua and Chacance. The rest was devoid of stable settlements. In 1825, when the Republic of Bolivia was founded, it declared **Cobija** as its Major Port on the Pacific and established the first settlement on the coast. It was soon followed by **Mejillones**, with guano beds which started to be worked by 1841; however, the village itself was not officially founded until 1866. **Tocopilla** was established in 1843 and became a Major Port in 1871; **Taltal** dates from 1858 and became an urban settlement in 1877. **Antofagasta** had a mining settlement in 1867, received official recognition in 1869 and became a municipal head town in 1872.

Two mining villages sprang up in the central plain: **Salinas**, a saltpeter center with a railroad connecting it to Antofagasta from 1873, and **Caracoles**, a silver mine. Both disappeared before the turn of the century.

With the saltpeter boom (1890–1925), over 80 mines sprang up in beds located in four different saltpeter fields in the central plain: **Taltal, Aguas Blancas, Central** and **Toco**, each oficina –as the nitrate mines were known– having a stable population of about 500. Now only two saltpeter towns survive: the **María Elena–Pedro de Valdivia** complex, established in 1930, and **Baquedano**, a service town on the railroad.

In the Andean basin, **Calama** flourished somewhat by 1865, as a way–station on the silver trail from Cobija to Potosí. In 1911 the first mining installations started to be built in **Chuquicamata**, a mining town springing up there shortly thereafter, which triggered explosive growth in Calama as a service and residence town. Of the colonial villages, the only ones still showing vitality are **San Pedro de Atacama**, **Toconao**, **Caspana** and **Peine**; the rest is undergoing a strong process of depopulation.

Establishment of Borders from the Conquest, the landlocked Corregimiento de Lipes (present–day Bolivia) received dry–fish supplies from the Cobija bay on the Pacific. When Lipes became part of the La Plata Viceroyship, a map of southern South America drawn by Cano and Olmedilla (1755) assigned to Lipes the coastal area from the Salado river in the south (Chañaral) to the Loa river in the north. However, the Viceroyship of Perú did not permit discontinuities in its territory, and stated that the Chile–Perú border lay along the Loa river.

Independence broke Spanish America into a number of countries, each claiming sovereignty over the territory delimited by its colonial boundaries. Chile, in her 1822 Constitution, defined the northern border as the «Atacama Desert». When the Republic of Bolivia came into being in 1825, Simón Bolívar sought an access to the Pacific for that country. First, he attempted unsuccessfully to be given the Peruvian city of Arica. He then commissioned a high–ranking officer, F Burdett O'Connor, to explore the coast in this area; O'Connor chose Cobija as a port for the nascent republic, and a trail was built from there to Potosí.

This amounted to a de facto occupation of Chilean territory, which at the time was not contested by Chile as a result of a deep political crisis then affecting the country. In 1842, Chile tacitly recognized latitude 23° South as the border, known as **Mejillones parallel**, and over the following 24 years Bolivia repeatedly demanded a border lying farther south.

During that period, Chilean explorers and industrialists surveyed the desert, discovering mines and setting up mining works along the coast up to the Loa river. The booming guano extraction operations gave rise to some friction with Bolivian authorities and, in 1863, an armed Chilean party occupied Mejillones.

On August 10, 1866, a treaty was signed between Chile and Bolivia establishing the borderline at parallel **24° South**, and agreeing to split equally between both countries the taxes generated by both existing and to–be–discovered guano and mining works between **latitudes 23° and 25° South**. Some difficulties in the application of the economic clauses of this treaty prompted the signing of a second treaty on August 6, 1874, establishing the Bolivian border at **parallel 24° South** and stating that the Chilean persons, industries and capitals established between **parallels 23° and 24° S** would not be levied higher taxes over a period of 25 years.

In the period between both treaties, Antofagasta was founded, saltpeter was discovered in the area, a railroad to Salinas was built and the rich Caracoles silver mine was discovered, all by Chilean explorers, capitals and businessmen. Eighty–five percent of the 8,500 inhabitants in the Antofagasta area were Chileans. In 1878, the Bolivian government raised the taxes on saltpeter exports, affecting the Compañía de Salitre y Ferrocarril de Antofagasta, a Chilean company based in Valparaíso, which refused to comply as this tax increase breached the 1874 treaty. The municipality of Antofagasta decided to bring the company to the auction block for unpaid debts. On February 14, 1879, one day before the auction, Chilean troops landed in Antofagasta and occupied it. The War of the Pacific had started.

WAR OF THE PACIFIC together with Antofagasta, Chilean forces occupied Mejillones, Salinas and the Caracoles mine, all located south of parallel 23, which Chile then claimed as the new border.

On March 1, 1879, Bolivia countered with a declaration of war. On march 20 and 21, Chilean troops landed in Cobija and Tocopilla and an expeditionary force set out from Caracoles to occupy Calama; the occupation was accomplished on the 23rd of that month. That was the only occasion in which Chilean and Bolivian troops came face to face in this Zone. On April 8 San Pedro de Atacama was occupied, and thereafter the puna area, Chile thus controlling the entire Bolivian territory south of parallel 23° S. This was an area of sierras and salt flats extending south to the pass of San Francisco, inland from Copiapó, and including the town of Antofagasta de la Sierra, now in Argentina.

On April 5, 1879, Chile declared war against Perú, as this country, by virtue of a secret pact with Bolivia, had refused to remain neutral in the conflict. The war then moved to present-day Region I. Bolivia withdrew from the conflict in May 1880 and signed a truce in 1884, acknowledging the new border with Chile. However, Bolivia secretly ceded to Argentina the territories of the puna of Atacama, which had fallen under Chilean control.

The present eastern boundary of this Zone, running from the Licancábur volcano through the Zapaleri and Socompa mountains to the pass of San Francisco, were drawn in 1899 by arbitrator W Y Buchanan, U S ambassador to Buenos Aires, who mediated in the Chilean–Argentine border dispute. Bolivia signed a peace treaty with Chile in 1904.

DESERT EXPLORERS a group of singular men surveyed the desert, their efforts laying the basis for Chile's later claim to this territory. All of them were natives to the Copiapó region or had been raised there, and were experienced in wandering through this most arid desert on prospecting journeys, and in setting up mining works far away from any inhabited places. They were a product of the «mining culture» developed during the two centuries of colonial rule.

During the 1830s, **Diego de Almeyda** explored the desert following numerous paths, discovering and installing mining works, one of which was at San Bartolo, on the edge of the Atacama salt flat. In 1854, at the age of 74, he travelled as a guide and companion to R A Philippi in an expedition commissioned by the government, which set out from Paposo to San Pedro de Atacama and returned following the Inca Road to Copiapó.

José Antonio Moreno was an admirer and disciple of Almeyda, who started his own surveys in 1832 and discovered important copper deposits near Copiapó, which brought him great wealth. In 1845 he started a colossal survey of the coast up to parallel 23° S, discovering copper deposits at Taltal, Paposo and El Cobre, exploiting them successfully. He settled with his family in this lonely area and later he discovered the Taltal saltpeter field. His mining works were the most outlying Chilean possession in the prickly border dispute with Bolivia.

José Santos Ossa settled at Cobija at the age of 19, in 1846. Over the following thirty years he surveyed the desert, finding fame, fortune and frequent close calls: once he was found in the desert close to death by starvation by an expedition headed by J A Moreno. A great businessman and miner, he had mines as far as Peine, in the Atacama salt flat. His greatest coup was the discovery and exploitation of the saltpeter field at the Carmen salt flat, which eventually gave rise to the city of Antofagasta.

José Díaz Gana arrived in 1860 and settled at Cobija and, later, Mejillones. Over the following ten years, he roamed the desert with a copper prospector, a herder, a laborer and a dog. In 1870 he came to a rock slide at Sierra Gorda; the rocks turned out to contain silver. He now needed to find the lode. He brought out of the Huasco jail a thieve, nicknamed El Cangalla, who was also a famous prospector for silver. He joined the group and, on March 24, 1870, they found the Caracoles silver deposit, which gave enormous wealth to the country over the following two decades.

THE QUEST FOR WATER around 80 percent of this Zone's population lives on the seaboard, an area lacking natural supplies of fresh water. Copper and saltpeter mining works, additionally, require great amounts of water both for their industrial processes and for the settlements established around the mines. During the 19th century, water was brought by tanker ships from Arica and Valparaíso. When the seaports in this area grew in size, coal–fired **seawater desalination plants** were set up. They were found at every port and were a good business for their owners. The one at Cobija was owned by José Santos Ossa.

A noteworthy development occurred in this connection. In 1872, Charles Wilson, a Scandinavia–born Englishman who had moved to Chile (he formed a family here and died by the turn of the century in Arica), built a **solar distillation plant** he had invented, now hailed internationally as the **world's first industrial application** of solar energy. It was located at Salinas, near Carmen Alto.

The drawings of this installation have been published in specialized journals (there is a photograph of it at the Museo Regional in Antofagasta). It consisted of caulked wooden crates, painted black and measuring 30 cm in height, covering almost one hectare of ground. They were sealed hermetically with a sloping glass. Brackish water was pumped from a well and made to run through the crates. Solar heat evaporated the water, which condensed on the glass and ran off through pipes to storage tanks. This drinking water supplied the neighboring settlements and the large mule trains hauling ore from Caracoles to the Salinas railway station.

The installation looked like a great greenhouse, and its performance has been figured as very close to the optimum achieved by present–day installations based on the same principle. It ceased to operate in 1914, when the Antofagasta–Bolivia railway got into the drinking water business and built a pipeline from the Andes –at Siloli Polapi– to Antofagasta. All that is left now is some broken glass near the Salinas railway station.

The growing demand for water for the coastal cities and towns, and for the mining operations and their new, water–intensive technologies, has transformed the landscape and altered the ecological balance at the extraction sites. Large pipelines run alongside every transverse road; on saline grounds, the pipelines are raised above the ground to prevent corrosion; otherwise, they are covered by earth. They tap the waters in the upper reaches of the Andes, depleting the supplies for the Andean farmers. This has brought about a gradual depopulation of the high Andes, most visibly at Vegas de Turi and at the foot of the San Pedro volcano.

Some positive correcting measures have been the diverting of the Salado river in 1951 –whose brackish water contaminated the Loa river– to be used for industrial purposes at Chuquicamata's new sulfur plant, and the construction of the Conchi dam in the 1970s to regulate the irrigation provided by the Loa. The Sloman dam dates from before (1911), at the lower Loa, destined originally for saltpeter works and now used for irrigating the Quillagua farms. Nowhere is this dramatic demand for water more evident that at the **Conchi bridge**, in the upper Loa, where six large–diameter pipelines converge, crossing the deep Loa canyon and heading down to the coastal cities and the mining operations.

Two of the important elements of this Zone, such as the history of saltpeter and the architectural relics –many of which have been granted a Natural Monument status– were described under Zone 1 (Arica and Iquique), as they are found throughout the Great North.

PRESENT DEVELOPMENT most of the population, as stated elsewhere, is concentrated on the coastal strip and in some copper or saltpeter mining towns. A very tiny proportion dwells in the rural areas. The capital, Antofagasta, is Chile's fourth largest urban center, after Santiago, Concepción–Talcahuano, and Valparaíso–Viña del Mar.

There are two universities, engaged in part in preserving this Zone's cultural heritage.

The main productive activity is mining, providing most of the employment and consuming most of the industrial products, services and commerce in the Region. It accounts for 50 percent of the gross regional product. Large investments have lately been made in the mining sector both to improve the mining processes and to increase output. Additionally, new mineral salts, such as lithium, borax, and phosphorus are starting to be exploited.

The next large player in the regional economy is fishing, with 20% of the gross regional product and 33 fishing companies. Four companies are engaged in fishmeal and fish–oil production; ten in frozen fish, seven in canned fish and two in smoked fish production. A further ten companies are engaged in algae farming in the Mejillones and Taltal areas.

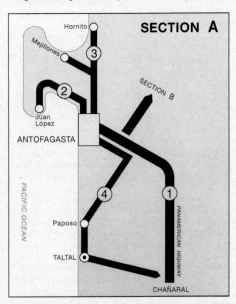

SECTION A   ANTOFAGASTA AND TALTAL

This section comprises the coastal area from Antofagasta to Taltal.

How to Get There if you are not driving, there are several bus services from Santiago (departures daily at 18:00 h), and daily services by airplane. In Antofagasta there are car rental services.

Another option is to come by car and return by plane, sending the car back by truck (eg, by Transportes Coloso).

Services Abroad the **railway** to Oruro and La Paz, Bolivia, starts now from Calama (dep Wednesdays), a bus providing a connection with the train. **Bus** to Salta through Guaitiquina

(Huaytiquina) pass with two weekly departures from Antofagasta, only November through March.

1 PAN-AMERICAN HIGHWAY FROM CHAÑARAL

TO ANTOFAGASTA ★★★ *a stretch of 420 km, paved. Traffic increases at night, preferred by truck drivers to avoid the heat of day in the desert. Gasoline at Agua Verde, 179 km from Chañaral, and La Negra, 397 km from Chañaral. Modest restaurant at Agua Verde. Accommodation at Taltal, a 25 km detour off the Pan-American highway.*

The Pan-American highway offers two detours in this section: through the Pan de Azúcar National Park (see Tour 6 from Chañaral) and along the coast via Taltal (see Tour 5 below).

The Pan-American highway out of Chañaral (km 0) runs through the Salado ravine, alongside the railway to El Salvador. At km 6, a trail branches off to the right to the famous former mine of Las Animas, which gave rise to Chañaral and had its own railway branch line. The ravine is flanked by the

Striped Hills a geological rarity, the only one of its kind in Chile, with yellowish slopes slashed vertically by wide stripes of black basalt. It is the only feature in an otherwise featureless desert.

At km 12 take the signposted road curving left; that is the Pan-American highway. The road straight ahead leads to El Salvador. The Pan-Am climbs out of a ravine up to km 19; a stretch of mountain road follows, beyond which is a gently sloping plain.

For the next 150 km, the Pan-Am runs along the center of the coastal Range, amid gently sloping plains and crossing transverse ravines. The railroad to the north is not visible from the Pan-Am because it runs along the Central Plain, farther east. The landscape is totally barren, not a plant in sight.

At km 45 the road from the Pan de Azúcar National Park meets the Pan-Am from the left (see Zone 4, Chañaral). At km 54, beyond a pass, the road descends into the Pan de Azúcar ravine to reach its dry bottom at km 59. Here is a place called **Las Bombas** («the pumps»), with some wells still active, providing water for some mining works. There is a restaurant.

A short way ahead to left hand is the **Las Bombas barium sulphate mine**. You might get permission to see the mine and its installations.

The road runs now along the stony bottom of the ravine, to start climbing out of it at km 65. An unsigned road branches off to the right to the once famous **Carrizalillo** copper mine (1863-1922). The ores from this mine were brought by mule-hauled railroad cars to Caleta Pan de Azúcar, where a smelter processed them to be shipped from the seaport operating at the site (see Land and History, Zone 3).

At km 70 is the **midpoint between Santiago and Arica** (km 1,040 of the Pan-American highway), and three km later, the border between Regions III and II. The road climbs gently to the north; a secondary road branches west to caleta Esmeralda, on the coast. At km 122 a road branches off to the left to

TALTAL a small seaport with a good hotel and beach, 25 km on a paved road. See Tour 4.

At km 122 the Pan-Am passes the Taltal airfield. At km 158 the road starts to wind its way across the Coastal Range, to start descending again at km 166, with a grand **view** of the Atacama desert's central plain. On the east marches the Domeyko range.

At km 179 is **Agua Verde**, a small, scattered, stony oasis, with a gasoline station and a restaurant. Lying in a ravine which ends at Taltal, the place

Antofagasta

has underground water tables which are tapped here and pumped to that city

Now the Pan-Am runs through a pampa formerly known as **Taltal Saltpeter District**, where once over 20 saltpeter works were in operation, all served by the former Taltal Railway Co since 1889. The most important ones were Flor de Chile, whose ruins are signposted at km 194, and, at km 211, hard by the road, the Chile (only waste dump remains) and Alemania mines; the latter operated until 1970 and was, unfortunately, dismantled in 1986. Signs indicate sites granted the Historical Monument status.

At km 265 the **Longino** railroad –built by the State around 1922 from Pueblo Hundido to Iquique– approaches the Pan-Am. At km 320, the ground has been upturned to the right: it is the **Aguas Blancas Saltpeter District**, with some 20 works served by a railroad from Coloso, south of Antofagasta. To the west soars the towering **Mount Vicuña Mackenna** (3,114 m), the highest peak in the entire Coastal Range.

At km 367, a signposted road branches west to Paposo (see Tour 5); at km 391, a paved road branches east to the El Way mine, which produces lime for a cement plant located at km 397.

La Negra is Antofagasta's industrial area. Here is a police control for vehicles, service stations and the cement factory Inacesa mentioned above, with a huge rotating drum where the ore is calcined. To the north, the modern facilities of Sociedad Chilena del Litio can be seen, where lithium concentrate brought by railroad from the Atacama salt flat is processed.

The Pan-American highway continues northward bypassing Antofagasta. A road branches west to Antofagasta, running along a ravine and flanked by two railroads: the nearest one on the left goes to Bolivia; the other one to Salta, Argentina. The latter was built in 1922 on the roadbed of the old railroad from the saltpeter mines to Coloso.

At km 420 is

ANTOFAGASTA (pop 185,000). The capital city of Region II, it lies on a long, narrow band squeezed between the Pacific and the Coastal Range slopes. The city has now a Costanera –the waterfront avenue– stretching along over 20 km of coast; it is Chile's longest.

Antofagasta is one of the biggest cities in Chile and the main city in the desert. It is a busy port, the terminal for the Bolivia railroad, and the shipping port for the copper produced in Chuquicamata. One of its first inhabitants were one Juan Chango López, a prospector who explored this section of coast since 1845, and who in 1866 settled with his family at La Chimba, a rocky area north of the present-day port. In 1872 he requested the Bolivian authorities to grant him a

La Portada beach

2

tract of land on the bay. Nothing else is known about him.

Cobija, 130 km north of here, was a Bolivian port and administrative center. The Chilean José Santos Ossa, a native of Huasco, lived there. He was one of the great desert explorers and a powerful businessman. In September 1866 he obtained an concession from the Bolivian government to exploit saltpeter fields in its territory; he only had to find them. In December of that same year he arrived at this bay, staying at Chango López's hut, whence he immediately set out on prospecting journeys into the desert. He soon found a saltpeter field at Carmen salt flat, inland from Antofagasta.

J Santos Ossa bought 300,000 m² on the Antofagasta bay (where the train station and Soquimich are located) and started to exploit his saltpeter bed, hauling the nitrate to the port. In 1868 Jorge Hicks, general manager of the Compañía de Salitre, drew a large anchor on the hillside to guide the ships, which survives to this day. His prospectors discovered the large nitrate fields at Salinas, on the way to Calama. In 1867, the first Bolivian officer came to Antofagasta to control shipments.

As the only holder of a concession to Bolivian saltpeter, Santos Ossa organized in 1868 the Compañía Exploradora del Desierto, in a partnership with Francisco Puelma, a lawyer, politician, diplomat and engineer, a disciple of Domeyko, adventurer and miner. In 1869 they sold half of their rights to Casa Gibbs, an English merchant house with branches in Valparaíso and Lima, who owned saltpeter fields in Perú. They sent an English manager and technicians from Tarapacá, reorganizing the operation under the name of Melibowrne Clark Co. They built a processing plant at Antofagasta, and an administration building, living quarters for the workers and a loading wharf. They started to export in 1872.

The company was granted a concession by the Bolivian government to build a 100 km railroad from Antofagasta to Salinas, forming the Antofagasta Nitrate and Railway Co, head-quartered in Valparaíso, by an equal-share partnership formed by Casa Gibbs, Agustín Edwards and F Puelma. Santos Ossa withdrew from the partnership to pursue other mining projects.

The port, meanwhile, had slowly grown and in 1869 received official acknowledgement, under the name of Peñablanca, from the Bolivian government. In 1870 the rich Caracoles silver deposit was discovered, the ores being hauled to the port by cart. By then it had 300 inhabitants; water was brought by tanker ship from Tocopilla and Arica.

In 1871 it was granted Major Port status and christened Antofagasta, a generic name under which at that time the Andean area opposite here was known, on account of the fact that its main city was called Antofagasta de la Sierra (now Argentine territory). In 1872 the municipality was established with nine councilmen elected by popular vote; six turned out to be Chilean, two German and one English. In 1878 the town and surrounding mining works had about 8,500 inhabitants, of which 6,554 were Chileans.

The city was occupied by Chilean troops on February 14, 1879, triggering the War of the Pacific. At the end of the conflict, the Antofagasta Railway and Nitrate Co was still the most powerful company in town. Its railroads linked it with Salinas (Central Saltpeter Field) since 1876, and in 1884 it obtained a concession from the Chilean government to continue building the railroad to Bolivia. That same year it also secured a contract with the Huanchaca mining company –Chilean capitals– to haul the silver ores from its mines at Pulcayo and Oruro, Bolivia, to the refinery in Antofagasta.

By 1900, the company split into two: the Nitrate Company and the Antofagasta and Bolivia Railway Co. The old railway station, the warehouses and the buildings now property of Soquimich all date from that period.

The city started to gather momentum. A large silver refinery was built to process the ores from Caracoles and, later, from Huanchaca. In 1903 the nitrate railway was finished from Caleta Coloso to Aguas Blancas, and in 1912 Anto-fagasta overtook Iquique as the first saltpeter shipping port. That same year, mining facilities started to be built at Chuquicamata, and ten years later the railway to Salta, Argentina, was inaugurated.

Now Antofagasta is the North's economic and cultural capital, and it is still dependent on the fortunes of mining.

What To See

HISTORICAL QUARTER (see map of downtown Anto-fagasta), a group of buildings erected in the plot of land acquired by J Santos Ossa. Saltpeter used to be loaded through several wharves now gone, in the Old Port. The only remaining Old Port facilities are the first dock and two lateral buildings.

Saltpeter Dock (NM) built in 1872 by Melibowrne Clark; saltpeter railroad cars unloaded here their cargo onto lateen-rigged vessels which would then transport it to ships waiting at anchor in the bay. On this dock landed also the 500 Chilean troops on Feb 14, 1879.

At the head of the dock are two interesting buildings:

Ex Coast Guard the one nearest the dock, was erected in 1910 to improve the access to the port as part of the Independence Centennial. Between both buildings there used to be a passenger pier. To the side is the building of the

Ex Port Authority (NM) dating from the same period as the above building. It now houses the **Regional Museum** (Apr–Oct, Tue–Sat 10:00–13:00 h and 15:30–18:30 h; Nov–Mar, Tue–Sat 10:00–13:00 h and 16:00–19:00 h ; Sun and Holidays 10:00 h and 13:00 h), containing a complete description of the town's and region's history from their earliest inhabitants to the saltpeter industry heyday.

Ex Customs House (NM) located behind the museum, at Balmaceda and Bolívar. It is an interesting example of the architecture prevailing during the desert-taming days. Two-storied, it has roofed galleries all around, accessible through external stairs. Built of Oregon pine, it had been originally erected in Mejillones, to house the Administration Office watching over Chilean mining interests, and moved to its present location in 1888. Nearby is a pier for the Yacht Club.

The FCAB Buildings erected by the old Antofagasta and Bolivia Railway Co, house now a private company operating modern railroad equipment which can be seen circulating through

Av Balmaceda to the port. Built around 1887, these buildings are part of a complex including the

Ex Railway Station (NM) (the upper story was added in 1900), with a passenger platform having a walkway in the upper floor. Built entirely of wood, it is lined with Guayaquil cane and stuccoed with lime (see description of this construction technique in Land and History, Zone 3). The remaining buildings housed the **engineer offices**. On Callejón San Martín are the **managers' houses**.

The Soquimich Offices were erected on land contributed by J Santos Ossa into the Compañía Exploradora del Desierto, which later became the Antofagasta Railway and Nitrate Co. In 1887, when the company started the construction of the railroad to Bolivia, it splits in two; the nitrate interests formed the Lautaro Nitrate Co, which merged with another firm in 1930 to form the Anglo Lautaro Nitrate Co, which was in turn acquired in 1968 by Sociedad Química y Minera de Chile, Soquimich. The buildings date from the same period as those of the railway station, one of the most interesting being the single–storied **Administration House**. The guard at the gate permits visitors to walk around the office building.

To end, visit on frontside the busy and picturesque **Fishing Terminal**, full of fishing vessels and with a market open to the public.

Following the **Costanera** 16 km to the north is La Portada, with good beaches and a restaurant. One of the beaches on the way to La Portada is called **El Trocadero**, with a stranded ship. At the end of the Costanera, at the point where the road turns inland, is **La Chimba**, the place where Chango López settled. The rocks there offer the best **panoramic view** of the city from the north. Follow the highway to the airport until a signposted road branching left, in 2 km of paved road leading to

LA PORTADA the road ends on a look–out platform above the cliff, with a restaurant and a superb view of the city to the south, the Angamos peninsula where is placed Mejillones to the north, and fantastic rock scenery. On an island a short distance from the shore is an erosion–carved arch–like rock formation which gives its name to the place, and is a symbol for the entire Region II. A path leads down the cliff to a good beach. On the cliff face you can see hundreds of horizontal layers of sand alternated with fossil shells. This used to be sea bottom, but it has been pushed up by tectonic movements. Back in town, the

Plaza Colón large old trees and interesting monuments donated by foreign communities residing in Antofagasta, for the commemoration of the Independence Centennial. Among these monuments are the

Clock Tower (NM) (British community), built with large ceramic blocks brought from England, and the **Bandstand** (Slavic community), with two levels, the lower one domed, and a monument to the Spanish Catholic Kings Ferdinand of Aragon and Isabella of Castille. Around the square are the administrative offices, the Cathedral church (ca 1920) and the recently built **Municipal Theater**.

The Pedestrian Zone is three blocks long, covering the main shopping, administrative and financial area. The

Plaza del Mercado (Market Square), on M A Matta, (see map) has tall palms and a monument donated by the German community, and the market on one side, which includes tropical fruits among its wares. On the side, a **Handicrafts Market** with High–Plateau textiles and other objects.

The **Central Campus** of the Universidad de Atacama is opposite the stadium, on Angamos street; farther ahead on the same street is the **campus of the Universidad del Norte**.

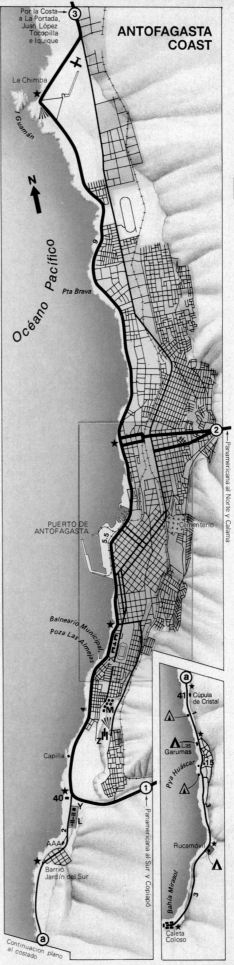

ANTOFAGASTA COAST

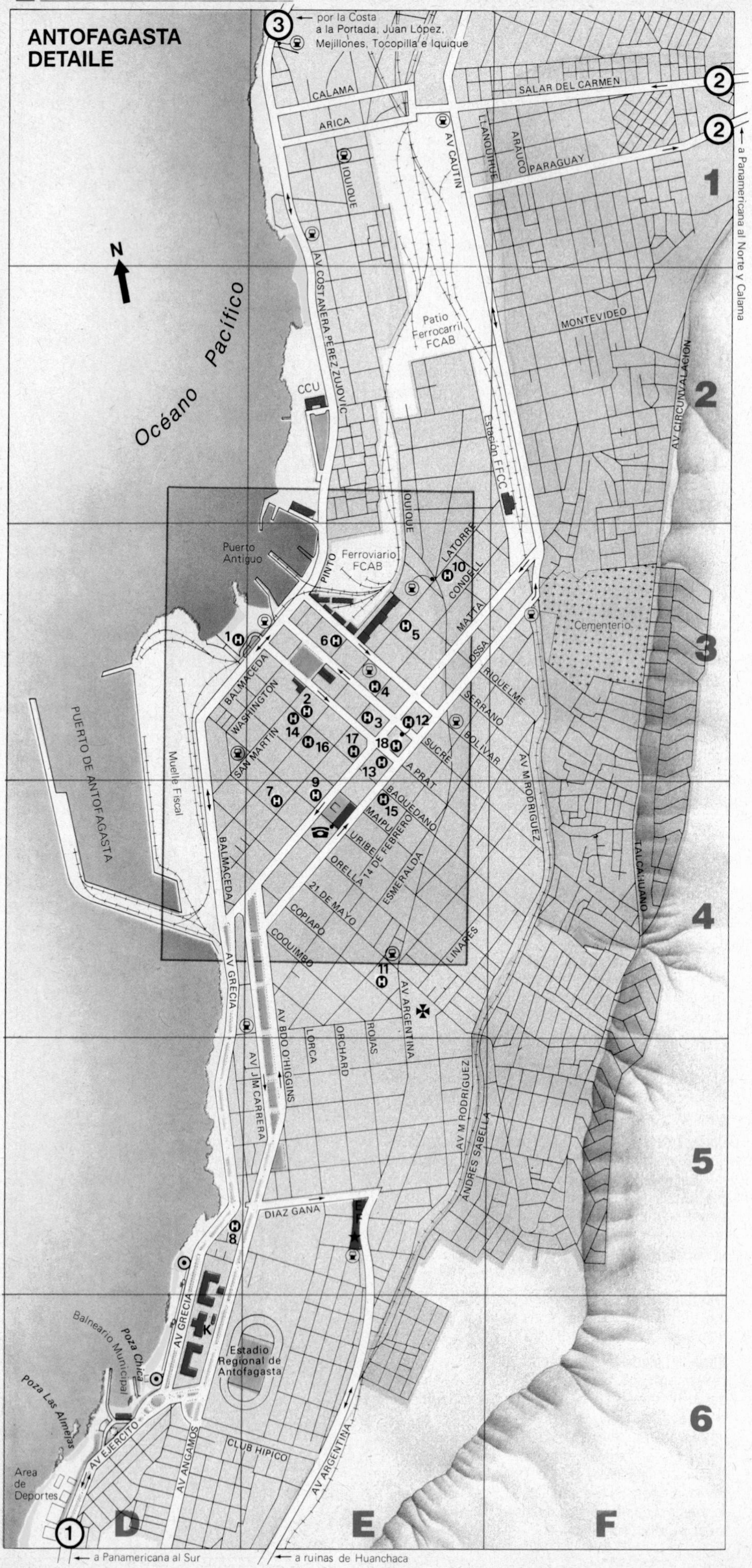

ANTOFAGASTA
DETAILE

3 → por la Costa
a la Portada, Juan López,
Mejillones, Tocopilla e Iquique

2
2

a Panamericana al Norte y Calama

1

CALAMA

ARICA

SALAR DEL CARMEN

IQUIQUE

AV CAUTIN

LLANQUIHUE

ARAUCO

PARAGUAY

N

Océano Pacífico

MONTEVIDEO

AV CIRCUNVALACION

2

AV COSTANERA PEREZ ZUJOVIC

CCU

Patio
Ferrocarril
FCAB

Estación FFCC

Puerto
Antiguo

Ferroviario
FCAB

PINTO

IQUIQUE

LATORRE

CONDELL

MATTA

10

3

Cementerio

BALMACEDA

WASHINGTON

SAN MARTIN

1

6

5

4

2

14

3

16

17

18

12

13

OSSA

RIQUELME

SERRANO

BOLIVAR

SUCRE

A PRAT

AV M RODRIGUEZ

TALCAHUANO

PUERTO DE ANTOFAGASTA

Muelle Fiscal

7

9

BAQUEDANO

MAIPU

15

URIBE

ORELLA 1ª DE FEBRERO

ESMERALDA

LINARES

4

BALMACEDA

21 DE MAYO

COPIAPO

COQUIMBO

11

AV ARGENTINA

AV GRECIA

AV BDO O'HIGGINS

AV JM CARRERA

LORCA

ORCHARD

ROJAS

AV M RODRIGUEZ

ANDRES SABELLA

5

DIAZ GANA

8

Balneario Municipal

Poza Chica

Poza Las Almejas

AV GRECIA

K

Estadio
Regional de
Antofagasta

AV ANGAMOS

CLUB HIPICO

AV ARGENTINA

6

Area
de
Deportes

AV EJERCITO

1

D

E

F

- ☎ Telephone Center
- ★ Touristic Information
- ⊙ Café, Meeting Point
- ⊠ Gasoline Station
- Lookout Point
- ✳✳ Hospital (4E)
- A Regional Government (3B)
- B Town Hall (3B)
- C Cathedral Church (2B)
- D Post Office (2B)
- ✳ E Bus Terminal (5E)
- ✳ F Bus Terminal for Salta, Calama &San Pedro de Atacama (5E)
- G Bus Terminal to the North, South & Calama (2C-5C)
- P Bus Terminal for Mejillones & Juan López (2C)
- H Central Market (4B)
- J Fish Market & Terminal (1B)
- ✳ K University of Antofagasta (6D)
- ✳✳ L University of Antofagasta (Campus Coloso)
- ✳✳ M Catholic University of the North

- N Regional Museum (2B)
- S Club Beach (2A)

INTERESTING BUILDINGS
- Q Ex Customs House (NM),(2B)
- N Ex Port Authority (NM),(2B)
- R Ex Coast Guard (NM),(2B)
- T Melbourne Clark Wharf (NM),(1B)
- V FCAB Offices and Platform (NM),(2B)
- U FCAB Employees Residence (2B)
- W E x Anglo Lautaro Building (1B)
- ■ Residences from 1920
- X Municipal Theater (2B)
- ✳✳ Y Square Of Francisco Vergara (NM)
- ✳✳ Z Huanchaca Ruins (NM)

ACCOMMMODATIONS
- 1 H Antofagasta (2A)
- 2 H Plaza (3B)
- 3 H Diego de Almagro (3B)
- 4 H Pieper (3B)
- 5 H San Marcos (2C)

- 6 H San Martín (2B)
- 7 H San Antonio (4B)
- ✳ 8 H Tatio (5D)
- 9 H Atenas (4B)
- 10 Hostal del Sol (1C)
- ✳ 11 H América (4E)
- 12 H Rawaye (3C)
- 13 H Paola (3C)
- 14 H Riojanita (3B)
- 15 H Rincón (4C)
- 16 H Latorre (3B)
- 17 H Astor (3B)
- 18 Bh El Cobre (3C)
- ✳✳ ▲ Campsite

RESTAURANTS
- 1 H Antofagasta (2A)
- 7 H San Antonio (4B)
- 30 El Arriero (3C)
- 31 Club de Yates (2A)
- 33 Club de La Unión (3B)
- 34 D'Alfredo (3B)
- 35 Carrillón (3C)

- 36 Apoquindo (3B)
- 37 Bavaria (4C)
- J Seafood Stalls (1B)
- H Market Food Stalls (4B)

DISCOTHEQUES
- ✳✳ 40 Popo's Discotheque
- ✳✳ 41 Cúpula de Cristal
- ✳✳ 43 Fandango

TOURIST SERVICES
- 20 Tatio Travel (3B)
- 21 National Rent a Car (2B)
- 22 Budget Rent a Car (3B)
- 23 Avis Rent a Car (2B)
- 23 Corsa Turismo (2B)
- 24 Hertz Rent a Car (2A)
- 26 Lan Chile (2A)
- 27 Ladeco (2B)

- ✳ See Antofagasta Close–Up
- ✳✳ See Antofagasta Coast Map

2

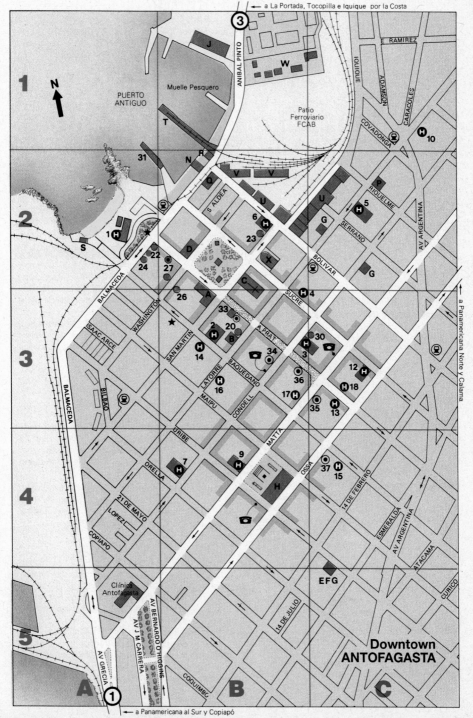

Downtown
ANTOFAGASTA

Antofagasta, Huanchaca ruins

2

Following **Av Argentina** (on the upper edge of town) to the south, there is a large esplanade with a **superb view** of the city. Below are the

Huanchaca Ruins (NM) a silver refinery erected ca. 1888 to process the ore from Caracoles, and later from Pulcayo and Oruro, Bolivia. It is a huge structure with several round furnaces built in brick masonry, the bricks imported from England. It is one of Antofagasta's most interesting buildings, but unfortunately not open to the public. Continue turning back along avenues Argentina and Club Hípico until reaching to sea, passing over the littoral until Caleta Coloso to

COSTANERA built on land reclaimed from the ocean, is the town's axis. It has an interesting waterfront, with beaches, restaurants, cafes, a sports center, etc. Its busiest section goes from the **Balneario** – opposite the horse racecourse– and the intersection of Av Grecia and Av Ejército, where the university students gather at night.

Following the Costanera to the south are several beaches and, on a hill, the **Huanchaca ruins** (good view from the end of street Dolores). Then, several military barracks and, beyond, the access to the Pan–American highway south. The Costanera continues south through several beaches. To the left is the

Campus Coloso of the Universidad de Antofagasta, still under completion. Inside is the

J F Vergara square (NM) (free access), a relic from the early days of mining; it was moved here from the Vergara saltpeter mine. Built entirely of wood, it has a roofed bandstand and four pavilions, one at each corner, to provide shade. The Vergara saltpeter works ceased to operate by 1938. A short way ahead on the Costanera is the

Jardín del Sur a residential quarter with plenty of gardens and flowers. Antofagasta, after all, is at the same latitude as Sao Paulo, Brazil, and the desert surrounding the city seems infertile only because of lack of water. As soon as water is made available, vegetation springs up eagerly.

The Costanera continues south skirting rocky areas and beaches that are frequented during the weekends. The best beach is **Balneario Huáscar**, with near campground. The reddish hills soon approach the waterfront to fall steeply into the ocean. Here is **Coloso bay**, with seafood restaurants and a good view of Antofagasta to the north.

Coloso was a major saltpeter loading port with its own railway (1903) bringing nitrate from the Aguas Blancas field. All that is left now is an esplanade with some ruins of the old village. Actually there is a terminal and shipping port for the new La Escondida copper mine.

Where To Eat best cuisine, good view and its own beach and swimming pool at Hotel Antofagasta. Club de Yates is good and has a view to the old harbor. For meat dishes, El Arriero. Quick dishes at the «get–together» cafes shown in map. Picnic at the beaches south of town.

TOURS FROM ANTOFAGASTA

2 TO JUAN LOPEZ BEACH ★★

a 62 km round trip from Antofagasta, with 26 km paved and the rest gravel. Hotel and restaurant. **A tour to the Mejillones peninsula and a good beach.**

Take the square of Antofagasta as your «km 0». Follow the Costanera towards the north; at its end, follow the signposted road to the airport and Mejillones, with several small industries, such as fishmeal storage compounds, poultry farms, vegetable cultivation in greenhouses, and, most surprising, a **golf club**. An inheritance of the old Britons, it has its hillocks and sand pits, lots of signs but no lawns or greens or trees.

At km 13, take signposted road to La Portada (left), running on top of a cliff, to end at a long beach which makes up the southern edge of the Mejillones peninsula. All of this area emerged from the sea bottom, pushed up by tectonic movements.

At km 24 the road starts to climb among rocks and reddish clay hillocks; the highest of these is **Cerro Moreno**, named after a great explorer of the desert.

At km 31 is

Balneario Juan López a group of houses on an arid stretch of coast, excellent for windsurfing. The residents buy drinking water from water trucks coming from Antofagasta. The beach is sheltered from the wind, with fine, dark sand, and the sea is relatively warm, placid. It is very popular in summer. There are other beaches within easy reach, and a modest, clean hotel with a restaurant specializing in seafood (good); good view to the beach. You may camp anywhere, but be sure to bring water. Following the road to Conchilla all the way to Bolsico, you may enjoy fine scenery and lots of birds, Humboldt penguins included.

3 TO MEJILLONES AND HORNITO BEACH ★★★

a round trip of 193 km from Antofagasta, with only 13 km graveled. Allow one day. Take food, water and a sunshade. Gasoline at Mejillones (60 km). **An excursion to the best beach, and to the historical port of Mejillones.**

Taking the square of Antofagasta as your km 0, follow the Costanera. At km 20 is the **Cerro Moreno Air Force Base**. A monolith indicates the point where you cross the **Tropic of Capricorn**.

At km 42 take the paved road branching left, to reach, at km 60,

MEJILLONES (pop 3,800). Facing the great bay, this small village lives from fishing. In 1853, the Chilean Navy steamer Janequeo brought a party of surveyors who charted the bay. They found 13 workers collecting guano for a company in Valparaíso; they used the cacti in the neighboring hills for fuel (R A Philippi).

Under the terms of the first border treaty with Bolivia, Chile ceded to Bolivia the territories lying north of latitude 24° south, Mejillones included. In 1866, the so–called Administrative Office was set up here to watch over the interests of Chilean mining operations.

After the War of the Pacific (1879), Mejillones returned to Chilean sovereignty, and the Administration Office building was disassembled and moved to Antofagasta, where it is now known as the ex Aduana. In 1895, the Antofagasta Railway Co finished its railroad to Bolivia and a branch line to Mejillones, as its terminal port, with wharves, **administrative buildings** and a large **machinery works** which built locomotives, railway cars, boilers and other machinery for domestic and foreign mining industry. It was the largest of its kind in South America and the second largest on the Pacific coast after another one in California. It ceased to operate in 1948. The well–preserved buildings are a good example of industrial architecture of that period. It is worth a visit.

Leave Mejillones (km 60) following the 13 km road to the highway. Follow now the paved road heading north. At km 95 is a detour to the left for

Hornito the best beach near Antofagasta, with good sand and relatively warm water. There are a few summer houses, but no restaurants or drinking water. Offshore from here there was a major sea battle on October 8, 1879, in which the Chilean ironclad ships Blanco and Cochrane, under the command of J J Latorre, cornered and brought the Peruvian ironclad Huáscar to surrender, after its captain, Miguel Grau, had been killed in the battle.

4 FROM ANTOFAGASTA TO TALTAL ALONG THE

COAST ★★★ *249 km via Blanco Encalada, Paposo, Taltal; a shorter option (240 km) is Pan–American highway–Paposo–Taltal. Both routes are about 40 km shorter than following only the Pan–American highway. The road is graveled, solitary, at times poor–surfaced but the most part is more or less well maintained by mining companies. Gasoline, hotel and food at Taltal. Take food and water.*

An excursion along the old route to the north, running at the foot of steep cliffs and skirting solitary beaches, excellent for wild camping. There are also interesting mining ruins as well as active mines.

Take the Pan–American highway out of Antofagasta heading south. At km 22 is La Negra; at km 53, a signposted gravel road branches west to Paposo. The road heads for the Coastal Range; at km 69 is a junction and a mine: the road branching right leads to Blanco Encalada and thence to Paposo (route described below). Continue straight, direct to Paposo; farther ahead (km 69) there is a multiple forking: take the road farthest left. It is the worst stretch, with a sandy roadbed, but it is not long. The Coastal Range is crested at km 98. To the left is **Mount Vicuña Mackenna**, the tallest in the Coastal Range.

The road continues straight, traversing three depressions resembling dry lake beds (km 98, 113, and 130). Some pirquineros (self–employed miners) can be seen working in the vicinity, and at km 127 there is a modest mining camp. At km 160, the road starts to run along the bottom of the Yumbes ravine, to meet at km 169 the Despoblado ravine, following this now down to the coast. Here are the ruins of the old mines of Santa Rosa, Gentil and La Fortuna, which brought some prominence to Paposo.

The Despoblado ravine has some vegetation of cacti and herbaceous plants, fed by some water springs, and a few scattered settlers. The water from this ravine does not reach the sea, but drops off some cliffs close to a pass in the Coastal Range, giving rise to an erosion cone below and some vegetation, particularly several kinds of cacti and other herbaceous plants, admired by R A Philippi and now frequently visited by specialists. The few samples of Berbis litoralis were found here.

At the top of the pass is a **statue of the Virgin** with beautiful mineral stones left by pirquineros as religious offerings; there is also a look–out with a superb **view** of the Pacific. At the foot of this cliff, at km 185, is

Paposo a small village which used to be a mining settlement, now living mostly by fishing. The place has several springs and pastures in the vicinity, but no potable water (it is brought daily from Taltal). Of old it was inhabited by Chango Indians. During the colonial period a Spaniard ran an encomienda here and called it Hacienda de Paposo. By 1800, Fray Andreu y Guerrero preached his mission among the Changos at this place and was named Missionary Bishop of Paposo. In 1850, the hacienda was acquired by the Gallo family of Copiapó. There was an administration house, a small chapel and natives working in copper mines.

In December 1853 it was visited by R A Philippi and D de Almeyda during their survey of the desert. They met here some natives of San Pedro de Atacama who came down to exchange flour and coca for dried fish. Under their guidance, the explorers crossed the desert to San Pedro de Atacama.

By 1858, Manuel Antonio Moreno, a legendary desert explorer and prospector, set up the seat of his mining empire in Paposo. He built his residence and a walled–in processing plant, a large shingled construction with walls lined with Guayaquil cane, still surviving. The property and the mines were inherited by his only daughter, Julia, who married Admiral J J Latorre, and later by his granddaughter, Marta Latorre, who married a Russian count who lived here until 1930.

ALTERNATIVE ROUTE TO PAPOSO VIA BLANCO

ENCALADA at the junction at km 69 from Antofagasta, take the road branching off to the right. For the next 30 km, the road winds among the Coastal Range mountains. At km 99 a road branches right to Caleta El Cobre (15 km), with a mine and a copper concentrate plant property of E Gordo and Cía; the mine was discovered in 1853 by M A Moreno –and is still active.

The road now runs along the bottom of a narrow ravine, to reach the coast at km 111 and then run along the coast for 83 km. The Coastal Range falls abruptly to the sea, with few but beautiful beaches. The road is very lonely. There are two deserted fishing coves, Botija at km 129, and Colorada at km 147. At

El Médano km 172, is the mouth of a ravine with a spring located next to a large sand dune. Up this ravine, between altitudes 1,300 m and 1,700 m above sea level, there is a religious center of the old Chango Indians, with red–hued rock paintings on a stretch of five kilometers. The climb from the coast is quite difficult and it takes not less than a whole day.

The seaboard widens by the next large bay, about 20 km ahead. This bay contains the village of Paposo (km 194).

FROM PAPOSO TO TALTAL take Paposo as your new km 0. The seaboard is here much wider. At km 11 is Punta Grande, a huge rock with round perforations, a geological rarity. Thirteen km to the east of here is the open–pit **Santo Domingo copper mine**, visible from the road. A short way ahead is the camp and ore mill of Gordo and Cía.

At km 18 starts the long Sara beach, with small rock outcrops interrupting it now and then, creating small, quiet beaches with sand, excellent for bathing with children. Very good for camping.

At km 32 is Bandurrias cape and the seaboard becomes squeezed between the cliffs and the ocean; the succession of beaches ends. The road runs among black rocks, with the twin promontories closing the Taltal bay straight ahead.

At km 39 is a small beach followed by a stretch of rocky coast up to km 50. Here starts the vast beach of Taltal, a place frequented by campers and summer tourists. A short way ahead is the old Enami plant, to reach at km 56

TALTAL (pop 7,714), a small, orderly village with a good hotel. It lives from mining and fishing, with an Enami copper concentrate plant which sends its output to the refineries at Ventanas and Paipote.

Founded as a city and seaport in 1858 by M A Moreno, it started to boom around 1876, with the opening of 21 nitrate mines at the Taltal saltpeter field, up in the pampa. The ores were brought by cart to the port.

When Chile ceded the territories north of latitude 24° South to Bolivia, this became Chile's most northerly outpost. The booming nitrate industry in Perú prompted some Chileans to explore the area for similar deposits; thus, M A Moreno discovered the Taltal saltpeter field in 1871, and Emeterio Moreno the one at Aguas Blancas.

To provide support for this new industry, the Chilean government ordered in 1877 the construction of this village. It also granted Blanco Encalada a Minor Port status for the loading of nitrate from the Aguas Blancas field.

In 1869, the London–based Taltal Railway Co finished the 150 km railroad linking Taltal with Cachinal de la Sierra, and with branch lines to all the nitrate mines in the area. It was sold to private interests in 1954, and dismantled in 1970 when the last of the nitrate mines, Alemania, ceased to operate.

During the saltpeter heyday, Taltal had a population of over 20,000, ranking as the third largest nitrate port.

What To See there is a good view from **Cerro La Virgen**. Along **Av Prat** are some old wooden houses, with the church and the Municipal Offices on the square; at the end of this street is the building formerly housing the Port Authority; from its balconies, President Pedro Aguirre Cerda addressed the crowds in 1939. The theater was built in 1921 and is still active. Up calle Torreblanca is also a good **view** of the town, the bay and the industrial

installations. Following the Costanera to the north are some old wharves and at its end, the

Railway Buildings a large industrial compound with many tracks, a wharf, a machinery shop, a locomotive shop and an administration building. All that is left now is a small 104–gauge locomotive granted the National Monument status.

On the side, a large house which used to house the **Head Office**. Next to it, the **Management Guest House** and the **General Manager's residence**, laid out as a U and with an arcaded gallery running along the face of the building.

Finally, the **Assistant Manager's residence**. They were all built by 1885 in Oregon pine walls lined with Guayaquil cane and stuccoed with mud, and are among the best examples of the period's architecture.

Tips banana and cinnamon ice cream at Capri, on the square, help to bear the midday heat. The best cuisine is at the Hostería, quicker dishes at the cafes shown in map. Picnic on the main beach and on beaches on the road to Paposo.

FROM TALTAL TO THE PAN-AMERICAN HIGHWAY

twenty–five kilometers, paved, the road ascending along the bottom of a ravine. At km 3 is a small palm–lined spring inhabited by Changos in the past. At km 13 a secondary road branches left, climbing on the roadbed of the old railway, along a pipeline bringing water from Agua Verde.

At km 14, a road branches right to

Cifuncho 30 km away on a gravel road. It is a cove and beach, among the finest in the North; frequented in summer. Very good for camping. Take water and food.

After the road climbs out of the ravine, the scenery is flat and arid. At km 25 is the Pan–American highway.

	Telephone Center					THE TALTAL RAILWAY Co
	Café, Meeting Point	A	Town Hall	E	Ex Government House	G Headquarters (NM)
	Gasoline Station	B	Church	F	Houses of Interest	H Manager's House (NM)
	Lookout Point	C	Museum		**ACCOMMODATIONS**	J Residence (NM)
		D	Theater	1	Hs de Taltal	K Locomotive (NM)

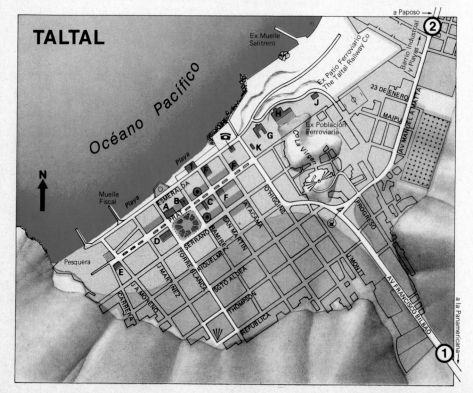

TALTAL

Océano Pacífico

SECTION B   NITRATES MINES AND TOCOPILLA

This section covers the Central Plain, known as Pampa del Tamarugal, up to the Loa river at Quillagua and, on the coast, from the mouth of the Loa river in the north to Antofagasta in the south. It includes interesting old and present mining works, and a fishing industry which accounts for 20% of the gross regional product.

TOURS

1   PAN-AMERICAN HIGHWAY FROM ANTO-
FAGASTA TO QUILLAGUA ★★★ *a 268 km stretch of paved highway, no mountain climbs. Gasoline at Carmen Alto and María Elena.*
The Pan-Am traverses the only active saltpeter field, with interesting ruins of the old nitrate days.

Take the access to the Pan-American highway heading north (see map) out of Antofagasta (km 0). The road crosses the Coastal Range to reach the **Carmen salt flat** at km 10, where J Santos Ossa discovered saltpeter in 1866; this discovery led, in time, to the establishment of Antofagasta. At km 13 is the Pan-American highway. The highway runs alongside the Antofagasta-Bolivia railroad, with several deserted stations. At km 45 are large waste rock dumps near the road: it is **Mantos Blancos**, a major copper mine. A short way ahead, next to the Latorre station, is a rock with a metal plate indicating the point at which the **Tropic of Capricorn** is crossed. This is the southernmost point reached by the sun during the summer; on December 21st, it shines from directly above this line, signalling the start of the summer period in the Southern Hemisphere.

At km 72 is

Baquedano a once famous village owing its fame to its lying astride the junction of the Longino – as the railway running from Pueblo Hundido to Iquique was popularly known– and the Antofagasta–Bolivia railway (FCAB). The **old railway station** has ticket offices on both sides: the northern side serves the privately–owned FCAB; on the southern, the state–owned railway. **Metal–ore cars** from Chuquicamata can be seen in the railway yard; they bring the ore to Antofagasta through the FCAB line or to Paipote through the state line. Note the old water towers for the locomotives, with a square metal tank. These towers can be seen at each station on the railway to Bolivia. Opposite the station is the

Railway Museum (free), housed in the former **Maintenance** and **Machine** Depot of the state railway. Exhibits include tools, workshops, the turntable and perfectly preserved locomotives and passenger cars. Recommended.

Back on the Pan–Am, the mounds alongside the road conceal the pipeline bringing water to Antofagasta. Soon the ground beside the road is seen to have been upturned: it is the Central Nitrate Field, the richest beds mined by the Lautaro Nitrate Co, with about 23 mines; its history is described by the signs next to the road. All that is left now are the waste dumps and, in some cases, the wreckage of the mining camps. At km 97 is one of these mines, called

Oficina Puelma (NM) the houses were built with stones extracted from the salt flat's crust. Only the walls and the cemetery remain.

At km 98 is Carmen Alto, where the highway to Calama branches east. There is a service station and a restaurant. Four km up the road to Calama from Carmen Alto is

Estación Salinas with only the old station building and two cemeteries remaining. It used to be a railhead, with a group of primitive houses serving

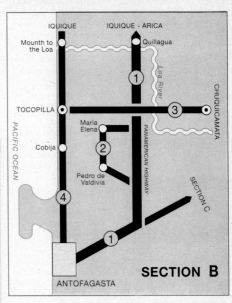

SECTION B

the «Stop–Over» nitrate works (see description under Land and History, Zone 1). The Chilean troops which occupied Caracoles in 1879 also stopped here.

Two hundred meters along the railway you will see a lot of broken glass. This is all that remains of the **solar distillation plant** designed and built by the Englishman Charles Wilson in 1872, to supply drinking water to Salinas and the animals pulling the ore carts from Caracoles. It operated until 1914, when FCAB finished laying a pipeline bringing water from the Andes to Antofagasta. The specialized literature hails this as the **world's first industrial utilization of solar energy.**

Oficina Chacabuco (NM) inaugurated in 1924, was the last and largest mine equipped with the Shanks system. It was built by the Lautaro Nitrate Co with an orderly layout and all the services, something quite unusual at the pampa in those days. The machinery has been partly dismantled, and the buildings are not very well preserved. Still, it is the best surviving relic in the Region. It is temporarily closed to public access.

The Pan–Am now runs through a large plain known as Indio Muerto. At km 167 the road starts the 30 km stretch traversing the Miraje nitrate field, which contains the **only nitrate mines still operative.** These mines have good restaurants, gasoline and a campsite. They deserve a detour, described as Tour 2.

At km 205 is the junction with the Chuqui–camata-Tocopilla road; four km east (right) is the **La Posada bridge** over the Loa river, a good spot for a picnic.

At km 220 is another nitrate field, called **Cantón Toco**, with over a dozen nitrate mines operating in the past. Signs placed before the few ruins and waste dumps provide a brief history of the place. The cemeteries –what is left of them– are most interesting. The main mines were **Prosperidad** and **Ricaventura**, with German capitals and a combined population of 1,800. At km 256 a signposted road branches east, leading in 4 km to the

Sloman Dam (NM) a 35 m high wall made of chiseled stone, damming the deep canyon of the Loa. Built in 1911 by Henry B. Sloman, a pioneer of the German saltpeter industry, its purpose was to provide electric power to the companies in his holding. The hydroelectric plant was dismantled in 1965. The dam, with its name spelled out in

103

large carved stones, now regulates irrigation at the Quillagua valley.

Thirty km ahead is the Quillagua Customs Outpost (km 286). On the way there, you will see two groups of **geoglyphs** (signposted) on isolated, small conical hills, depicting animals and people. They date from pre–Conquest times. Note also some weird white stripes visible on some road cuts; they are insoluble lime deposited on the pampa by geological sedimentation.

Quillagua then appears a small farming village at the bottom of the Loa river valley, with orchards and crops. The village has a church, an old railway station and a railroad bridge. It also dates from pre–Conquest times; it used to be one of the stations in the Inca Road, and was visited by Pedro de Valdivia in 1540. During the saltpeter heyday it was a place for summer vacations and resting. To visit it, take detour to the right, bringing you back to the Pan–Am some way ahead.

At km 286 a bridge spans the Loa to reach the **Quillagua Customs and SAG Control Post** this point acts as a border between Regions I and II. As Region I is a duty–free zone, all merchandise headed south of this point must be controlled. Vehicles headed north must register here (paying a small fee). **Keep the slip of paper accrediting this**; it will be required when you travel out of Region I. It is advisable to register all the accessories such as car stereo, photographic equipment, video cameras, etc, to avoid complications on the return trip.

The SAG control, in turn, **retains all fruits, plants and perishable foodstuffs which might introduce the fruit fly into the rest of Chile.**

2 VISITING THE NITRATE MINES ★★★
the detour is 16 km longer than taking the Pan–American highway. Paved road. Allow three hours.

MARIA ELENA Industrial Plant

The illustration depicts the industrial installations as seen from the look–out point described in the corresponding tour through María Elena, and shown in the corresponding map. The plant operates as follows:

10 Mills the nitrate ore arrives by rail from the mines. It is milled in successive steps into gravel size.

8 Leaching Troughs these are large, deep concrete troughs where the crushed nitrate ore is deposited. High-temperature water and steam is injected from the Leaching Plant (7). Nitrate is thus dissolved in the water, producing a liquid known as Mother Liquor.

At the bottom of the troughs there remains ster-

ile material which is removed by a huge moving crane known as Puente de Descarga. It loads the large trucks bringing this sterile material to the waste dump (2).

9 Filtering Plant the Mother Liquor from the troughs is processed at this plant. Strong solutions are piped to the Crystallization Plant (6); weak solutions are piped to the Coya Solar Plant.

6 Crystallization Plant the mother liquor is heated into crystallized Potassium Nitrate.

3 Granulation Tower crystallized nitrate, both that produced at María Elena and that from Coya, undergoes a fusion process in furnaces. The resulting liquid is dropped from the top of the 84 m-tall granulation tower. During the drop, the liquid solidifies into globular material known as Granulated Potassium Nitrate. The purpose of this proc-

MARIA ELENA
NITRATE MINE

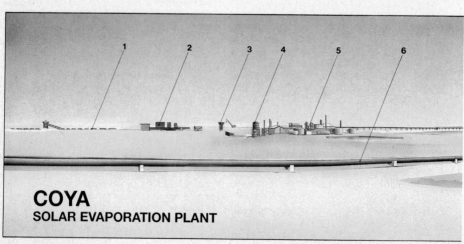

COYA
SOLAR EVAPORATION PLANT

Gasoline and restaurants at María Elena and Pedro de Valdivia, good campground on the banks of the Loa river.

A chance to see the last nitrate mines –and their towns– remaining in operation.

Take the signposted road branching west to Pedro de Valdivia, crossing the Longino railway. At km 9 is Pedro de Valdivia.

The history of the place starts in 1911, when Guggenheim Brothers (the same who in 1960 donated the Guggenheim Museum to New York, designed by Frank Lloyd Wright) bought Chuquicamata and started outfitting the world's largest copper mine, under the direction of Elias Anton Cappelens, a talented engineer who invented and developed mining technologies.

For over a decade, E A Cappelens studied the antiquated mining technology employed at the neighboring saltpeter industries (Central and Toco nitrate fields) and then designed a new process

to extract and refine nitrate. It was based on technology used in copper mining, and included large dissolving troughs operating at lower temperatures than was customary. This system was patented internationally as the **Guggenheim System**.

In 1924, Guggenheim Bros acquired from the Chilean state the lands containing the Miraje salt flat, establishing the María Elena mine in 1926 and Pedro de Valdivia in 1930. Both plants are gigantic when compared to the nitrate mines of that time, with a combined output of 1.22 million tons/year, exploiting at low cost ores with low nitrate content.

Guggenheim Bros and Lautaro Nitrate Co –the owner of the nitrate mines at the Central saltpeter field– merged in 1930, forming the Anglo Lautaro Nitrate Co. In 1950 the firm built the Coya plant, perfecting the solar evaporation technique, and in 1965 the company was acquired by Sociedad Química y Minera de Chile, Soquimich.

ess is to make a final product which will not absorb moisture too easily, thus preventing unwanted caking.

1, 4, 5 auxiliary buildings such as the Machinery Shop (1), Garage and Vehicle Maintenance (4) and Power Station (5).

COYA Solar Evaporation Plant

The illustration depicts the plant as seen from the look-out. It operates as follows:

7 and 8 Evaporation Ponds there are ten altogether. Weak mother liquor is piped into them from María Elena. Hot water is injected (6) to increase the strength of the solution. Solar radiation produces evaporation and precipitates the nitrate to the bottom, from where a machine

known as Elephant collects it. The ponds are like large concrete swimming pools. Coya has its own cement mixing facility (3).

5 Iodine Plant mother liquor having a certain strength is pumped from the evaporation ponds to a Iodine Plant to extract a byproduct known as laminated iodine. The liquor is then returned to the ponds.

2 Crystallization Plant the salts collected from the ponds are brought to this plant, where they are heated into crystallization. This process includes a cooling tower. The resulting product is crystallized potassium nitrate.

1 Loading Yard crystallized nitrate is brought as bulk cargo to the loading yard. There, a loader known as Loading Bird loads the material onto railway cars, which bring it to María Elena to process it into granulated potassium nitrate.

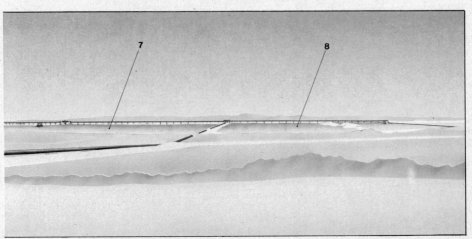

Pedro de Valdivia (pop 8,600). Visits authorized at the access gate. Beyond the gate is Av O'Higgins, lined with houses with roofed verandas facing the street, providing a welcoming shade. Around the **square** are the administration offices and white–collar office buildings. There is a complete service infrastructure, with quite a busy commerce. Not much is to be seen of the industrial installations, other than the large building housing the power generation plant, the smokestacks of the saltpeter furnaces and a tall white building, the granulator tower. For lunch, the Club Pedro de Valdivia is excellent.

Take now the 40 km paved road to María Elena, running through areas that have already been mined and alongside the railway to Tocopilla. At km 18, to the right, is the wreckage of the former **Oficina Vergara** (the square of which was moved to Antofagasta); the **Chinese community cemetery**, on the hill, has sadly been almost totally ransacked.

Six km ahead, take the road to the right to visit the

Coya Plant access is permitted to a **look–out point** commanding a view over the entire nitrate concentration plant, powered by the desert's strong solar radiation. Its technology is pretty modern. Experimental work was started in 1945 and the facility went on stream in 1954. A chart in these pages illustrates the process. On the right–hand side of the look–out is an interesting **cemetery** used both by Pedro de Valdivia and María Elena. The tombs have different styles, depending on how old they are. The newer ones have a little pavilion to provide shade. Seven km ahead is

MARIA ELENA (pop 7,700). The oldest of the two mining towns (1926), it was laid out·to resemble the Union Jack, and it was named after the wife of its first manager, A E Cappelens. Now it is the head of this municipality, but all the buildings and the ground are property of Soquimich. The industrial hours are three shifts. Business hours, Mon–Fri 07:30–12:00 h and 14:00–18:00 h; Sat 07:30 12:30 h. Shopping hours Mon–Sat 10:00–13:00 h and 16:00–21:00 h, Sun 09:00–13:00 h.

There is a church on the **square** (service Mon–Wed and Sat 19:30 h; Sun 8:30 h, 11:00 h and 19:30 h; summertime Sat and Sun 20:00 h) and a **Museum** (Mon–Sat 08:00–13:00 h and 14:00–20:00 h, Sun 10:00–13:00 h), providing an insight

☎	Public Phone	4	Mine Access	F	Police Station
⛽	Gasoline Station	△	Yerco Restaurant	G	Theater
⊙	Restaurant	⊙	Club Social Restaurant	H	Library
≫	Lookout Point	A	Town Hall	I	Supermarket
1	General Office	B	Museum	J	Market
2	Payroll Office	C	Parish Church	K	Open Air Market
3	Access to Industrial Plants	D	Freemason Temple	L	Hospital
		E	Railway Station	M	Polyclinic

N	Labor Union
P	Personnel Assistance
Q	General Management
R	Manager's House
S	Maria Elena Club
T	Cafeterias
W	Apartments for Unmarried Employees
Z	Schools

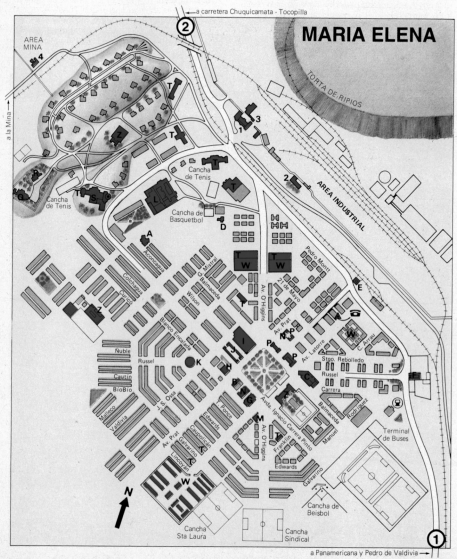

MARIA ELENA

into the pre–Conquest Indian cultures around the Loa river and, of course, into the saltpeter industry.

Following Av O'Higgins to the north you reach the employees residential quarter, with nice tree–shaded houses. There is also the interesting **compound housing the former manager**, with a small, shady park. Now the complex is a Guest House and a school. At the northern tip of the town there is a look-out point (see map), providing the best view over the industrial plant described in the illustration above.

For lunch, Club María Elena offers excellent service. There is also a restaurant next to the telephone company.

Drive one km back to Pedro de Valdivia, and take there the road branching east, leading in 8 km to the Pan–American highway. At the junction, a 3 km road branches east to the Loa river and the

Loa Park a shady spot with potable water, telephone and free camping lots.

3 **FROM CHUQUICAMATA TO TOCOPILLA ★★**
seventy km to the Pan–American highway from Chuquicamata, on a rough unpaved road, plus 73 paved km to Tocopilla.
The shortest way to continue north from Calama.

Take road branching west from Chuquicamata (km 0), which crosses a pass and then zigzags down to the Pampa del Tamarugal. After coming out of the mountain stretch, the road continues straight down the plain, with twin power lines marching parallel to the road; they bring electrical power to Chuquicamata from Tocopilla. At km 66, La Posada bridge over the Loa. At km 70, the junction with the Pan–Am. Straight ahead, at km 83, is the road branching to María Elena and, at km 113, the railway to Tocopilla.

The road dives into the Seca ravine and starts descending among the Coastal Range peaks. At km 143 is Tocopilla (description in Tour 4).

4 **THE COAST FROM THE MOUTH OF THE LOA**
TO ANTOFAGASTA ★★★ *278 km, with 120 paved but not continuous. Driving is slow. Gasoline, food and accommodation at Tocopilla, 90 km south of the mouth of the Loa river.*
A scenery providing relief from the evenness of the desert. This is the continuation of the coastal road described in Zone 1, Section A, Tour 3.

Take the bridge over the Loa as your km 0. This is one of the scant water courses reaching the ocean in the North. The Pejesapo beach, upon which the river empties into the ocean, is not suitable for swimming.

To the south the seaboard is narrow, with scant beaches and the hills plummeting directly to the sea. Perfect **erosion cones** can be seen now and then, some of them sliced through by the road. At km 8, opposite the Fakkir mine, is a nice beach, small and white–sanded, good for bathing. The bay is closed by a large promontory – **Punta Arena**– linked to the mainland by a narrow peninsula. At km 12 is another good beach. The road climbs thereafter, to run above the rocky coast.

At km 20 and 27, two further beaches. The few beaches south of the Loa have white sand, as they are not contaminated by the dark sands from the Andes, washed into the ocean by the Loa river. The sea here has a lot of seaweed.

At km 31 the road crosses the Punta Arenas peninsula. On the northern side of it is **Punta Arenas cove**, used by fishermen on a non–permanent basis; tents housing the fishermen families can be seen on the beach.

A new bay opens up, ending in the south on a cape –**Punta Urra**– with a large, hat–like hill at the tip. At km 42 is another white beach and, at km 44, Punta Urra. The next bay has as its southern limit the black Paquica cape. Small fishing vessels can be seen fishing offshore. The road runs a bit above the sea.

At km 62, the road starts to wind its way to a pass and then cross the cape over a cliff 300 m above the sea. Breathtaking **views**. At the foot of the cliff is the narrow, rocky caleta **Paquica**, where the fishing vessels normally spend the night at anchor.

At km 72 is Paso Malo, the road, now narrow and winding, running above a rocky cliff; careful driving is required. Ahead is Punta Guanillos, with a white, multi–crested islet, reached at km 75. Tocopilla can be seen in the distance. At km 84 is **Punta Mamilla**, with a **panoramic view** over Tocopilla. The road then runs straight, passing the fishing companies of Guayané, Tocopilla and Coloso, to reach, at km 90,

TOCOPILLA (pop 22,000), capital of the Tocopilla province. It is the terminal port of the nitrate railway, with a mechanized wharf, a large thermoelectric plant owned by Codelco and supplying Chuquicamata and the saltpeter mines, and sizable fishing industries.

The place was mainly a fishing cove until 1843, when a small copper refinery was installed here. The guano beds at Punta Paquica started to be exploited then as well. In 1870, the first nitrate shipments from Toco were loaded here, and in 1871 the Bolivian authorities granted it the status of a minor port.

In 1877, the French engineer Dominique Latrille designed the village under a commission of the Bolivian government. On march 22, 1879, the place was occupied by Chilean forces.

The village started to boom early this century, when the railroad from the Toco nitrate field was finished. In 1915, the thermo electrical power station was set up, and in 1929 Tocopilla became the number one saltpeter shipping port with the implementation of María Elena and, a short time later, Pedro de Valdivia.

What To See the waterfront street is **Arturo Prat**, where you can see a wooden church (service May-Nov, Mo–Fri 19:00 h, Sat 20:00 h; Dec–Apr, Mo–Sat 20:00 h, Sun and Holidays 12:00 and 20:00 h) and the old passenger station, and watch the port activity. The **Clock Tower**, made of wood, was originally at the María Elena square, but was donated to this port.

On one side was the **former Customs House** until it got burned. The **Balneario El Salitre** is the most popular beach, with a good view over the port, its many wharves and mechanized structures. The mechanized wharf with its massive arm and the nitrate silos opposite street San Martín (see map) are interesting. At the far end is the new dock built to unload coal for the power station.

Following Prat through the underpass, you can see the **power plant employee houses**, dating from 1912. A short way ahead is the large structure of the **power station**.

The road now runs among rocks to the curious **Camel Rock**, the town's symbol, followed by the popular **Covadonga beach**, with a restaurant, and a former tourist hotel built by the state, now housing a social club.

Accommodation and Food Hotel Vucina, on 21 de Mayo, is good. The best cuisine is at Club de la Unión. Caleta Boy has a good view as well. Chinese food at Jok San. Quick dishes at the «get-together» cafes shown on map. Seafood at the marketplace foodstalls. Picnic and seafood restaurants at Playa Punta Blanca, 8 km south.

ON TO ANTOFAGASTA taking now Tocopilla as your new km 0, Antofagasta is at km 188; 100 km are paved. At km 8 there is a police checkpoint,

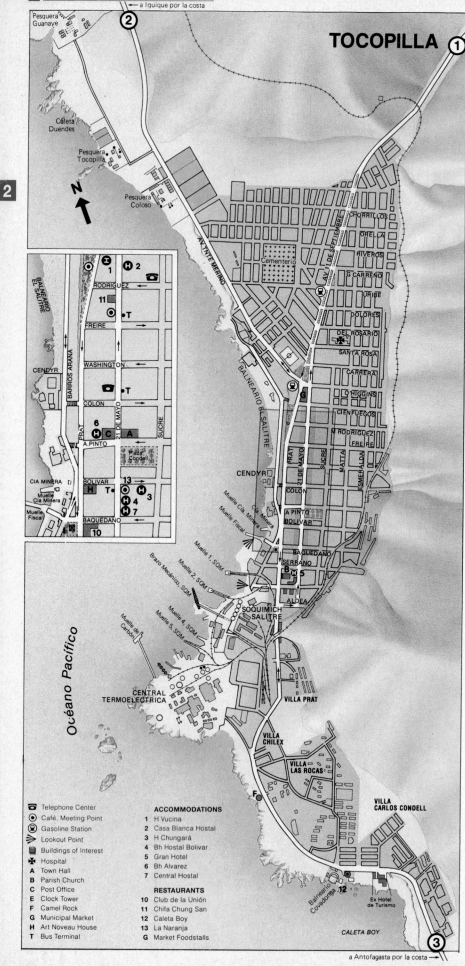

a Iquique por la costa

② ①

TOCOPILLA

a Panamericana, María Elena y Chuquicamata

Pesquera Guanaye

Caleta Duendes

Pesquera Tocopilla

Pesquera Coloso

N

CHORRILLOS
O'HELA
RIVEROS
G CARREÑO
URIBE
DOLORES
DEL ROSARIO
SANTA ROSA
CARRERA
O'HIGGINS
CIENFUEGOS
M RODRIGUEZ
FREIRE
MATTA
ESMERALDA

Cementerio

AV. 1 DE SEPTIEMBRE

AV. TNTE MERINO

BALNEARIO EL SALITRE

PRAT
21 DE MAYO
SUCRE
COLON
A PINTO
BOLIVAR
BAQUEDANO
SERRANO
ALDEA

CENDYR

Cia. Minera
Muelle Cia. Minera
Muelle Fiscal
Muelle 1, SQM
Muelle 2, SQM
Brazo Mecánico, SQM
Muelle 4, SQM
Muelle 5, SQM
Muelle del Carbón

SOQUIMICH SALITRE

B C 5

Océano Pacífico

CENTRAL TERMOELECTRICA

VILLA PRAT

VILLA CHILEX

VILLA LAS ROCAS

F

VILLA CARLOS CONDELL

Balneario Covadonga
12
Ex Hotel de Turismo

CALETA BOY

Inset map (upper left)

BALNEARIO EL SALITRE

1 H 2
RODRIGUEZ
11
T
FREIRE
WASHINGTON
T
COLON
6 H C A
21 DE MAYO
A. PINTO
Plaza Condell
BOLIVAR 13
H T
3
4 H
7
BAQUEDANO
10

CENDYR

CIA MINERA
Muelle Cia Minera
Muelle Fiscal

BARROS ARANA
PRAT
SUCRE

Legend

Symbols
- ☎ Telephone Center
- ◉ Café, Meeting Point
- Ⓖ Gasoline Station
- Lookout Point
- ▪ Buildings of Interest
- ✳ Hospital
- A Town Hall
- B Parish Church
- C Post Office
- E Clock Tower
- F Camel Rock
- G Municipal Market
- H Art Noveau House
- T Bus Terminal

ACCOMMODATIONS
1 H Vucina
2 Casa Blanca Hostal
3 H Chungará
4 Bh Hostal Bolivar
5 Gran Hotel
6 Bh Alvarez
7 Central Hostal

RESTAURANTS
10 Club de la Unión
11 Chifa Chung San
12 Caleta Boy
13 La Naranja
G Market Foodstalls

a Antofagasta por la costa →

③

2

followed by a fishing plant and, at km 10, **Punta Blanca beach**, with seafood restaurants. At km 24 is **Punta Atala**, with the best beach for bathing in the area, seafood restaurants and a discotheque. The seaboard widens gradually towards Mejillones, where it reaches its widest point. The Coastal Range peaks are still high, but they march now farther inland, leaving some space for beaches. There are several campgrounds and active mining works en route.

At km 41 are the **ruins of Gatico**, a water spring used by the native Changos, later a Bolivian fishing cove and, in 1907, home to a chapel moved from Cobija. It operated as a shipping port until 1930.

At km 60 are the ruins of

Cobija originally a Chango settlement, it had a water spring and a trail crossing the desert to Chacance, on the Loa river, whence it continued to Calama and to the High-Plateau. It was a major trading route for eastbound dried fish and westbound flour and coca leaves. Simón Bolívar, striving for a seaport for the nascent Republic of Bolivia, asked Perú to cede Arica, but was turned down.

In 1825 he commissioned the British colonel Francis Burdett O'Connor, one of his Chiefs of Staff, to survey the area and choose the best location for a seaport on the Atacama coast. He traversed the Indian trail and suggested Cobija as the port, on account of its water supply, a sheltered harbor and the trail. Bolívar, through a decree issued in Chuquisaca on December 25, 1825, declared Cobija as Bolivia's official seaport, christening it **Lamar**, after the Colombian founding father Francisco Lamar.

Soon the fishing cove became a seaport and

an elegant resort, some families from Sucre, Bolivia, building luxurious summer houses there. Even President Andrés Santa Cruz spent a summer here.

In 1846 the young José Santos Ossa came to settle here from Huasco, marrying Melchora Ruiz; she died here nine years later affected by yellow fever. Santos Ossa built in 1857 a desalination plant to supply potable water to the more than 1,000 inhabitants of the place, mostly Chileans. In addition to Santos Ossa, Cobija was also home to William Wheelwright, the builder of South America's first railroad from Copiapó to Caldera, Ramón Freire –exiled from Chile–, and the renowned naturalist D'Orbigny.

From Cobija set out the founders of Antofagasta, Mejillones and Tocopilla, and also the explorers of the desert and the discoverer of the Caracoles silver deposit in 1870, which brought a brief boom to the village.

Levelled by an earthquake in 1865 and by a tidal wave in 1877, Cobija did not survive the overwhelming impetus of Antofagasta. Its church was moved in 1907, and the village deserted. Lots of ruins still remain.

At km 82 is the hamlet of **Michilla**, with a restaurant·and a major ore leaching plant –and the only tire–repair shop between Tocopilla and Antofagasta. At km 95, the great peninsula and bay of Mejillones comes into view, with the large promontory of the **Angamos cape** at the tip.

The Hornito beach is at km 107, a fairly frequented beach (on weekends). The rest of the road to Antofagasta is described under Tour 3 above.

SECTION C   CALAMA

This Section covers the Loa river basin upstream of Calama, with its many pre-Conquest villages, as well as the Ascotán and Carcote salt flats, the natural access to the Bolivian High-Plateau.

How To Get There there are direct bus services to Calama from Santiago and Antofagasta, as well as regular air services from Santiago and Antofagasta to Calama's Loa Airport. Both Calama and Antofagasta have car rental agencies and tourist taxi services.
The train to Bolivia departs from Calama every Friday at 23:00 h.

1 ANTOFAGASTA TO CALAMA ★★★
a very good paved road, 213 km long. Gasoline at Carmen Alto (98 km). We recommend to leave at 08:00 h in order to accomplish tour 2 on the same day.
An excursion through the desert, the territory of the old Atacameño culture, and Chile's most important mining center.
Follow the Pan–American highway to the north up to Carmen Alto (km 98), a leg described under Tour 1 of Section B.
From **Carmen Alto** (km 0) the road traverses for 35 km the **Cantón Central** saltpeter field, the ground thoroughly upturned. There are over 20 waste dumps, cemeteries and the ruins of the settlements of old oficinas –mines– described on tablets placed close to the road.
At km 20 are the ruins of the **former Oficina Anita** mine, right beside the road, with buildings made using blocks of the crust covering the saltpeter fields, bound with mud as mortar. The main street has a square with dead trees and old shops still sporting their painted signs. The industrial installations were dismantled throughout this field by 1940 to meet the demand for scrap metal generated by World War II. The buildings were stripped

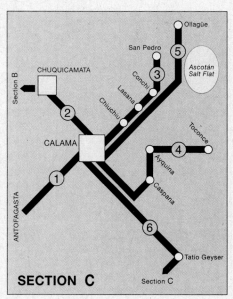

SECTION C

of all reusable materials, which were then employed in the coastal cities.
At km 37, on the right–hand side, there is a modest fenced–in oasis; it is a pool filled by the railway's drinking water pipeline. The place belonged to the former Concepción mine. It is a good spot for a pause. One km beyond the oasis is a waste dump of the Concepción mine, with a modest settlement at its foot. From the dump there is a panoramic view of the Cantón Central.
Sierra Gorda is at km 48, with a modest village and a police checkpoint. A 33 km dirt road

branches off southeast leading to the former Caracoles silver mine and the **ruins** of its attendant village. If you want to visit the place from here, check with the police about the road conditions.

Caracoles was discovered in Bolivian territory by José Díaz Gana on March 24, 1870. It was not a concentrated deposit like Chañarcillo, but a vast area peppered with silver outcrops. Exploited by Chilean capitals for over two decades, it gave rise to considerable wealth and to some of the biggest financial speculations ever seen in Chile. Díaz Gana erected the famous Moor–styled palace known by the name of its next owner, Concha Gazotte, in Santiago's Bernardo O'Higgins avenue. It was torn down in 1945. The village of Caracoles, with solid administration buildings and a huge collection of shanties, had an intense but short life. Occupied by Chilean troops immediately after Antofagasta (February 1879), José Victorino Lastarria wrote here his «Letters from the Desert».

Back on the highway to Calama, the road

climbs gently to **Cerritos Bayos**, a group of rocky, rounded hills. Beyond them is a vast **view** to the Loa river; to the north, you can see the ravine of the San Salvador tributary. At km 107 is a police checkpoint, opposite the Enex explosives factory, set up by DuPont to supply Chuquicamata and Chilean mines in general. At km 111 is a detour to the El Loa airport and four km ahead is

CALAMA (pop 90,000) capital of the El Loa province. Its lifeline is the neighboring Chuquicamata copper mine, for which it serves as residential and services center. It also has significant industry and commerce serving the sulfur and borax mines on the frontier and the nascent mining companies at the Atacama salt flat. Surrounded by irrigated agricultural lands, Calama is now the largest oasis in the entire Andean foothill area.

Located at a crossroads of the Inca Road, where the Cobija–High Perú and the Arequipa–Copiapó trails came together, Calama was a poor place with few inhabitants when Almagro and P

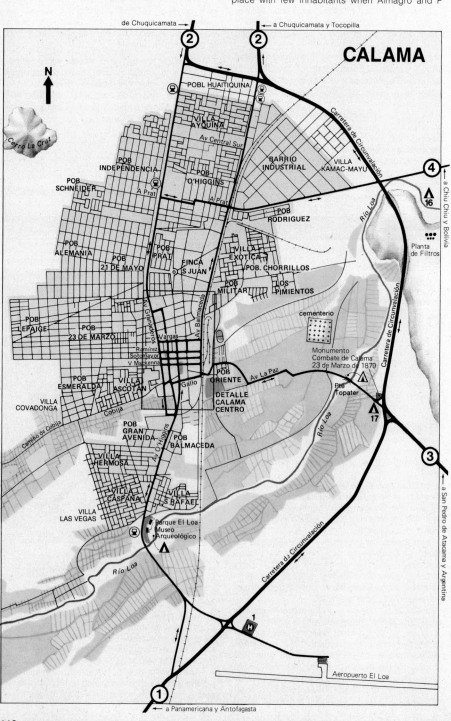

de Valdivia visited it. The pre–Conquest center was at Chiu Chiu (called Atacama la Chica), as the salty Salado river, which joined the Loa just down the slope from Chiu Chiu, polluted the entire water supply downstream, the lands alongside the river being able only to produce –at best– pastures for animals.

In 1833, Simón Bolívar established in Calama an administrative center and a station of the Cobija–Potosí post route. By 1865 it was the most important Bolivian administrative center in the area. It was occupied by Chilean troops on March 23, 1879, after the first battle with Bolivian forces in that war.

The railway reached Calama in 1886 and in 1888 it was granted Municipality status. In 1911 the first works started in Chuquicamata and from 1951 the water of the Salado river was diverted to Chuquicamata to be used for industrial processes, making the lands in Calama more fertile.

What To See the downtown area is small. The church has services daily at 20:00 h, Sun and holidays at 11:00 and 20:00 h. A couple of km from downtown on Av B O'Higgins is Parque Loa, with a museum, a zoo, an exhibition of High-Plateau life and a swimming pool. The best view of the orchards is through the old road to Cobija or along the access to the San Pedro de Atacama road (see general map).

Accommodation and Food best lodging at H Topotel; other good hotels listed in map's legend. There is a campground. The best cuisine is at H Topotel, Hostería Calama and Casona del 900. Quick meals at Bavaria, cheap at Feria Modelo (marketplace). Parque El Loa for a picnic.

TOURS FROM CALAMA

2 A VISIT TO CHUQUICAMATA ★★★

sixteen km from Calama. There are guided tours through the mining complex, Mon–Fri the year round. Take your ID and be at 10:00 h at Av J M Carrera, Sede Chuqui Ayuda a la Infancia Desvalida (see map); you can make a voluntary contribution for needy children. Industrial hours: three daily shifts. Business hours: Mon–Fri 08:00–12:00 h and 13:00–18:00 h; shopping hours, Mon–Fri 09:30–13:00 h and 14:00–21:00 h, Sat 09:30–13:30 h.
A visit to the world's largest open pit copper mine and its attendant city.

TOWN OF CHUQUICAMATA (pop 17,000) it is divided into two sections, known respectively as **Campamento Empleados** –the older section– and **Campamento Nuevo**, linked by Av Tocopilla. Campamento nuevo, with a modern layout and all the services, was built to replace the old residential area of Punta de Rieles, which had grown obsolete and was simply buried under the gigantic waste dump (110 m high). The land and the buildings are company property.

What To See access is through Av Brinkernoff. To the left is the cemetery, with a tree-lined avenue. Pepper trees and cypresses are the trees best adapted to this high (2,830 m), dry location.

Following Av Tocopilla you reach the new **Población de Supervisores** –the supervisors' quarter. At the end of Av Tocopilla is Gate 1, a major access to the mine. Farther up is the Campamento de Empleados –lit. Employees' Camp, ie, residential compound–, with a good view.

Where To Eat best are the Club de Empleados –White Collar Club– and the Club de Obreros –Blue Collar Club–, but are absolute full between 12:00 and 13:00 h. There are restaurants downtown, Arco Iris Center, and Michael y Carloncho.

CHUQUICAMATA MINE for a guided tour, be at 10:00 h (on the dot) at Gate 1 (Puerta 1). Visitors are taken around the mine by bus. The tour is free, but you can make a voluntary contribution for a social cause. It lasts about four hours.

The Company the mine was exploited as early as during the Inca days. In 1881 the first industrial facilities were set up. In 1911, Guggenheim Bros, a U S company, started the installation of modern facilities, the first pure copper ingot being produced on May 18, 1915. The company changed name several times over the years, such as Chile Copper Co, Anaconda Co and Chile Exploration Co

In 1969 the State of Chile acquired 50% of the mine and, on July 11, 1971, it acquired total control. It is now property of Codelco Chile, one of the world's 100 largest companies and the largest in metal mining. Its Chuquicamata division accounts for 47% of Chile's copper output, with over half a million tons of refined copper annually.

The Mine has two deposits exploited in open pit mines: **Chuqui** and **Sur**. There are two plants for processing the ore: **Minerales oxidados** for the Sur mine and **Minerales Sulfurados**. There are also an **electrolytic refinery**, a **copper smelter**, a **molybdenum extraction plant**, a **noble metals** plant and a **sulfuric acid** plant.

Power is supplied by a large coal-fired **electric power plant** at Tocopilla, with four 110–KV circuits spanning 140 km of desert. There are also dams

☎ Telephone Center	8 H Atenas
★ Touristic Information	9 H Hostal del Sol
◉ Café, Meeting Point	10 H Claris Loa
⊛ Gasoline Station	11 H Géminis
✠ Hospital	12 Bh John Keny
A Town Hall	13 Bh Internacional
B Post Office	15 Bh El Tatio
C FCAB Railway Station	⁕ 16 Cp Turistico El Paraíso
▲ Shared Taxis to Chuqui	⁕ 17 Cp Turistico El Palomar
TA Bus Terminal to Antofagasta	
TAP Bus Terminal to Antofagasta & San Pedro de Atacama	**RESTAURANTS**
	2 H Lican Antai
TAS Bus Terminal to Antofagasta & Salta	3 Hs Calama
	30 Casona del 900
D Market	31 Bavaria
E Open Air Market	32 Las Llaves del Rey
F Consulate of Bolivia	33 Chinese Food
ACCOMMODATIONS	**TOURIST SERVICES**
⁕ 1 H Topotel	1 Avis Rent a Car
2 H Lican Antai	20 Hertz Rent a Car
3 Hs Calama	21 Budget Rent a Car
4 H Alfa	22 American's Rent a Car
5 H Olimpo	23 Lan Chile
6 H Quitor	2 Ladeco
7 H Casablanca	4 Copper Tour
	24 Talikuna Excursiones

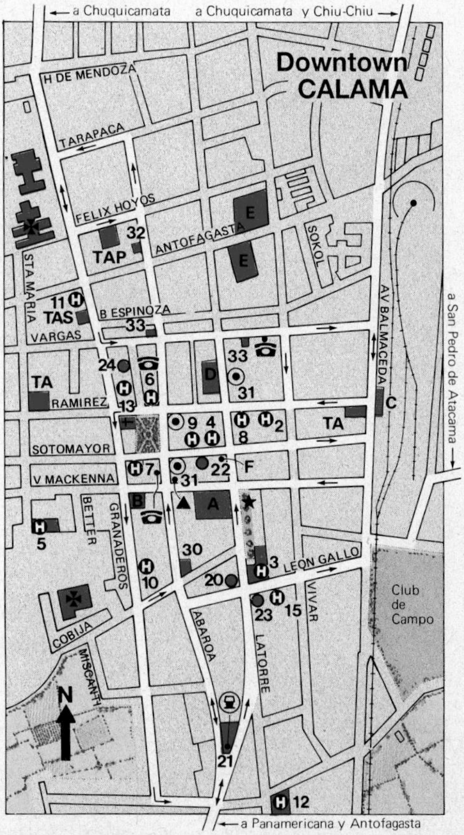

Downtown CALAMA

[map of Downtown Calama]

2

111

SULFUR PLANT, REFINERY AND SMELTER

The process follows the following steps:

1 Primary Milling ore with 1.64% copper content is brought by truck to the Milling Plant within the mine. The rocks are ground to the size of coarse gravel and brought by conveyor belt to the
2 Domed Heap enclosed to prevent dust from spreading. Another conveyor belt, located below the heap, brings the material to the
3 Secondary Mill where the coarse gravel is crushed to the size of small pebbles. The resulting material is then brought by an enclosed conveyor belt to the
4 Concentrate Plant this plant carries out two processes:
A Wet Milling the ground material is mixed with water in large, rotating horizontal cylinders. Inside are thousands of steel balls (known as ball mills) which, as the cylinders rotate, grind the pebbles to a fine powder. Mixed with water, this powder

becomes a paste which flows to the
B Flotation Cells hundreds of rectangular tanks which receive the paste and mix it with more water. Each tank has a powerful fan-like stirring device, and receives injections of air and chemicals. A thick foam is produced, which captures the copper particles and drifts to the surface, where it overflows into ducts. This foam is called **Collective Concentrate** and contains 36% copper and 1% molybdenum, silver, gold, sulfur, iron, etc. The sterile material settles at the tank's bottom, whence it is extracted into the
5 Waste Mud Canal flowing by gravity down to the dam in the desert.
6 Molybdenum Plant the Collective Concentrate is subjected to a further selective flotation process to extract its 1% molybdenum content. The final products of this plant are **Molybdenum sulfide, obtained from the concentrate,** and **Molybdenum Trioxide,** obtained by roasting the concentrate.
7 Settling Tanks these are large ponds where the foam settles; the superficial water is recycled into the Flotation Cells. The settled material is known as

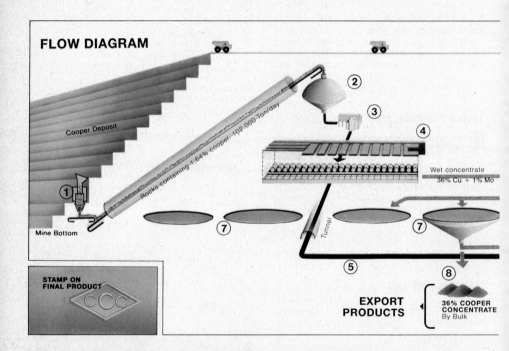

FLOW DIAGRAM

Cooper Deposit

Rocks containing 1.64% cooper. 102.000 Ton/day

Mine Bottom

Tunnel

Wet concentrate
36% Cu + 1% Mo

STAMP ON
FINAL PRODUCT
CCC

EXPORT
PRODUCTS

36% COOPER
CONCENTRATE
By Bulk

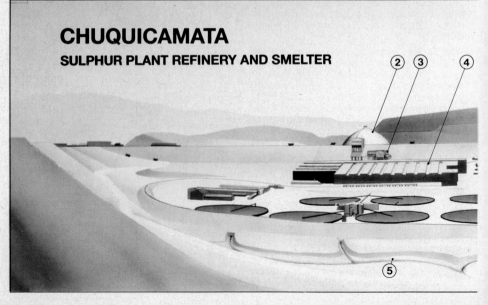

CHUQUICAMATA

SULPHUR PLANT REFINERY AND SMELTER

«wet concentrate» and has a 36% copper content. This concentrate is extracted from the bottom of the settling ponds and brought to the

8 Solar Drying Yards here, wet concentrate is sun-dried into Bulk Concentrate, which is shipped to domestic and foreign refineries.

9 Drying Plant most of the concentrate is brought to this plant, where it is heated into Dry Concentrate in furnaces. The resulting material is brought to the

10 Copper Refinery dry Concentrate has about 36% copper content, and is subjected to three successive fusion processes in a reverberatory furnace, a converter furnace and a refining furnace, respectively. The final product are plates of about 1m x 1m x 2 cm, known as Anodal or Blister Copper, with 99.3% copper content. These plates are brought to the

11 Electrolytic Refinery blister copper is subjected to electrolysis in tanks containing sulfuric acid, the resulting product being plates similar to the blister plates, known as **Electrolytic Cathodes**, with 99.8% copper content. Part of these plates are exported to factories producing wire.

The electrolytic process produces a residue known as Anodal Mud, which is brought to the

12 Noble Metals Plant here, the anodal mud is melted to yield 10-12-kg plates of Doré Metal, containing 98% silver and 1% gold.

13 Refining Furnaces most of the electrolytic cathodes are brought here for smelting, obtaining as final product ingots and bars with 99.98% copper content, suitable for the most demanding applications.

There are some complementary operations, such as:

14 Sulfuric Acid Plant it extracts the sulfur contained in the refinery smoke exhaust and transforms it into sulfuric acid, used in the electrolytic refining process.

15 Waste Dumps you can't miss them: they are the huge man-made hills surrounding the mine, containing the sterile material generated by the mining processes.

16 Oxygen Plant set somewhat apart from the rest of the installations, as oxygen is a very explosive gas. It produces the gas, which is injected into various stages of refining.

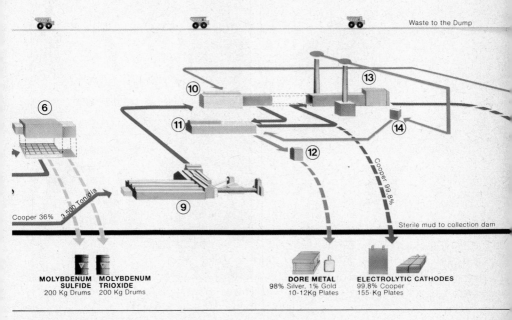

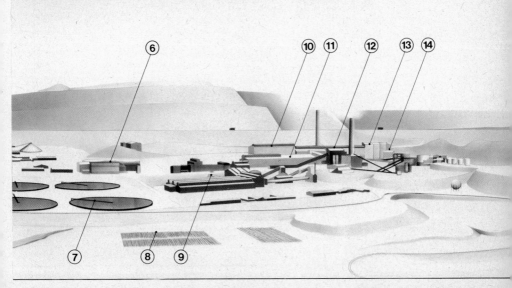

and six pipelines bringing drinking water and (brackish) industrial water from the mountains.

The Visit is altered according to the mining operations being performed at the time. They usually follow the pattern below:

Access through Gate 1 where you can admire the world's largest excavator, which was recently phased out. Once inside the mine's perimeter, the bus moves on the left lane; curiously enough, driving is English style in the mine: always on the left. The first stop is the

Chuqui Deposit the world's largest open pit, 4,000 m long, 2,000 m wide and 600 m deep. The huge «steps» are simultaneously exploitation ramps and access roads to the bottom. The ore has a 1.6% copper content. Copper is also found in «bags» surrounded by sterile material, which forces to remove 600,000 tons per day. One third of this is mineral-bearing rock, the rest waste rock. The latter is dumped in huge mounds called «cakes» (up to 120 m high), mushrooming all around.

Plaza Italia is a traffic hub at the pit's exit; it was named after a similarly-trafficked square in Santiago. Only that the traffic here is of the 156-strong fleet of giant trucks, each hauling up to 170-200 tons of material, the tires about 3 m in diameter and the driver perched some 5 m above the ground. Other trucks are permanently watering the ground to reduce tire wear –each tire costs more than a luxury car. Note the tall «masts» with a flag riding atop every pickup truck: it makes mammoth-truck drivers aware of their presence. The next stop is the **Sulfur Plant, Refinery and Smelter** perhaps the most interesting stop. Inaugurated in 1951, technical improvements have regularly been introduced, more than doubling its output since it became Chilean property. The accompanying illustrations describe their processes.

A	City	E	Chuqui Mine
B	Oxidized Minerals Plant	F	Italia Square
C	Sulfur Plant	G	Sur Mine
	Electrolytic Refinery	H	Waste Dump
	Smelter	--	Tourist Circuit
D	Supplies Purchasing & Storage		

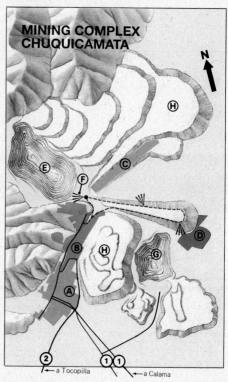

MINING COMPLEX CHUQUICAMATA

Waste material 298.000 Ton/day (15)

Waste dump

(16)

Cooper 99,98%

o dam in the desert, 99.000 Ton/day

(5)

ELECTROLITIC INGOTS
99,98% Cooper
20-Kg ingots
1,96-Ton bundles

ELECTROLITIC BARS
99,98% Cooper
120-Kg bars
1,8- Ton bundles

a Tocopilla   a Calama

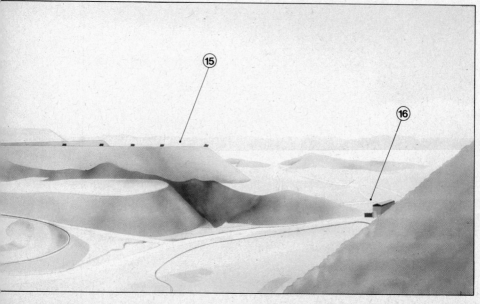

The tour continues over a huge waste dump to stop at a look–out point from where Calama can be seen far down below. At the foot of this dump is **The Supermarket** as the industrial depot is known, also known simply as «Km 6». It contains thousands of carefully arranged items outdoors, within a fenced area. On its side is the
South Mine inaugurated on September 27, 1967. Its pit has already reached about 1,5 km in diameter and 195 m in depth. Its copper content is 1.45%, and the mineral rocks are brought by a conveyor belt to the
Planta de Oxidos only seen from the outside during the tour. It is being modernized, as it is the same original plant which processed ore until 1950. Note the old railway cars from the trains which used to haul the superficial mineral rocks.

Chuquicamata mine

2

3 TO THE UPPER LOA BASIN ★★★
a round trip of 200 km on graveled roads. Allow

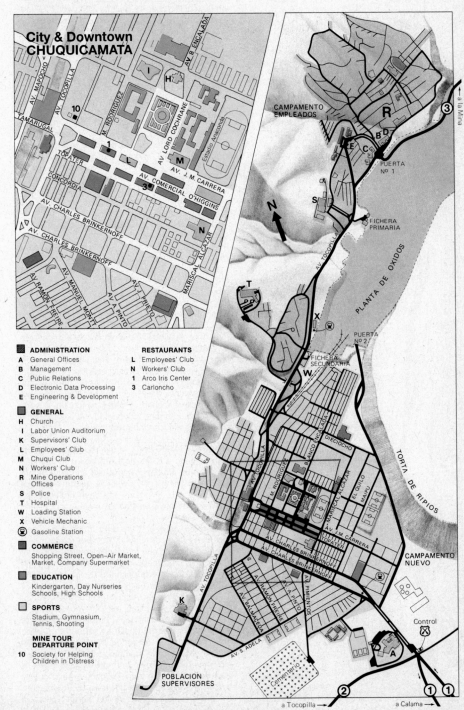

City & Downtown CHUQUICAMATA

ADMINISTRATION
A General Offices
B Management
C Public Relations
D Electronic Data Processing
E Engineering & Development

GENERAL
H Church
I Labor Union Auditorium
K Supervisors' Club
L Employees' Club
M Chuqui Club
N Workers' Club
R Mine Operations Offices
S Police
T Hospital
W Loading Station
X Vehicle Mechanic
⛽ Gasoline Station

COMMERCE
Shopping Street, Open–Air Market, Market, Company Supermarket

EDUCATION
Kindergarten, Day Nurseries Schools, High Schools

SPORTS
Stadium, Gymnasium, Tennis, Shooting

MINE TOUR DEPARTURE POINT
10 Society for Helping Children in Distress

RESTAURANTS
L Employees' Club
N Workers' Club
1 Arco Iris Center
3 Carloncho

115

a whole day for this; take food and water. Gasoline only at Calama.

An interesting circuit through an area with important archaeological relics, including the villages of Chiu Chiu and Lasana. Then a visit to Conchi to see water management in a desert environment and, lastly, a peek at the beautiful San Pedro and San Pablo volcanoes.

Follow the international road to Bolivia out of Calama (via Ollagüe, see map), which up to Chiu Chiu is in good condition. At km 20, on the right–hand side, there is a memorial to a hideous murder which shocked the nation several years ago. To the left is the nitrous Talabre pampa. At km 33 is

CHIU CHIU a village founded by Spaniards, located upstream of the confluence of the Salado and Loa rivers, at a place inhabited of old by the largest

✳ Chiu Chiu church

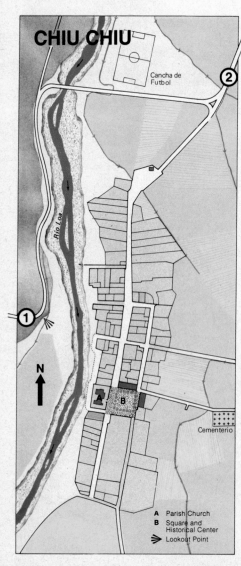

concentration of natives: here are the best lands in the area. The square was recently restored and it has the Region's most beautiful church (a copy of which can be seen at Calama's Parque Loa). The Inca Road used to run through here, and Diego de Almagro and Pedro de Valdivia stopped at the oasis.

The village's first Spanish name was Atacama la Chica, and it was subordinate to the Corre–gimiento de Lipes in High Perú. In 1611, the Archbishopric of Charcas (Sucre) set up a parish church here and the main mission at the Loa valley. When Cobija boomed as Bolivia's seaport –1830– there was a lot of traffic through Chiu Chiu, which had at one time 10,000 pack animals and was a busy supply post. The establishment of the railway by 1890 deprived it of this role, and many of its inhabitants were lured away by the nitrate and copper mines. Many of the irrigation canals were abandoned.

CHURCH OF SAN FRANCISCO (NM) (festivity of San Francisco, October 4). Built by 1675, with 120-cm-thick mud-brick walls, rafters made of chañar wood and tied with leather straps, the ceiling is made of cactus tablets lined with a thick layer of mud and straw. The cactus core is a woody ring, which can be flattened out when wet and cut into tablets. The doors are made of cedar lined with cactus tablets.

Its volume and massiveness are typical of the Atacameño culture. It contains a cemetery within its walled compound. The church has interesting statuary, including a crucifix with collapsible arms to transport it during processions, and a painting depicting Christ, painted on both faces of the canvas.

The external stone stair to the bell towers was added in 1965, to replace the original wooden one. The bell has an inscription in Dutch, but nothing is known of its origin.

Leave Chiu Chiu following the road heading north to Bolivia (see map), through alfalfa fields and vegetable patches. Soon you will reach a road fork, from which there is a good **view** over the valley and the Salado river; take the left branch, which runs alongside the Loa river; the other branch runs atop a cliff. From the junction is a singular sight: up to this point, the Loa runs along the bottom of a deep canyon carved in the rock; from this point downstream, the river runs through a flatland. This is as far as a thick layer of volcanic matter rolled down in the past, covering the valley upstream. The volcanic rock is whitish and soft, and is often used in construction.

The road runs on the river bank, through cultivated patches flanked by sheer cliffs. There are some **pictures** etched in rocks which have been numbered and are signposted. At km 41 is a modest hamlet, a bridge and the

PUKARA OF LASANA (NM) a fortress–village from the 12th century. It is the best–preserved Atacameño culture relic. Perched atop a cliff and with defensive walls facing east, it was the permanent place of habitation of chieftains and other high–ranking people, with an estimated permanent population of 800.

Restored between 1951 and 1953, it has narrow alleys flanked by octagonal and round rooms –look-out towers and granaries– made wholly of stone and presumably with wood-and-mud roofing, now gone. It was deserted by the time of the Spanish occupation. It is worth a visit.

The road crosses the river and climbs out of the ravine. As you climb the cliff you can see a tree–shaded swimming pool, property of Codelco. Beyond the crest of the cliff a vast barren pampa unfolds, with the Linzor volcano in the background. There is a pumping station and thick pipelines running down from the Salado river (industrial water) and from Toconce (drinking water). At the junction with the road to Bolivia, turn left and continue 26 km to the north. The road

[map labels: CHIU CHIU, Cancha de Futbol, Rio Loa, N, Cementerio, A Parish Church, B Square and Historical Center, ⇒ Lookout Point]

climbs gently towards the hills of Tatio and Paniri.

At km 67 from Calama there is a junction with a road flanked by pipelines coming down from **Incalari**, whence the first pipeline to Antofagasta started in 1914. The waters from Incalari now supply Chuquicamata, Calama and Tocopilla. At the junction, take the road to the left, following it for three km to the

Pukará of Lasana

2

CONCHI BRIDGE built in 1890 by the FCAB Bolivia Railway, it is contemporary of the Malleco bridge (in southern Chile) and about as high. Supported by seven pillars, it spans the deep canyon of the Loa river. Now it is only used for car traffic; the increasing weight of locomotives made it necessary to build a new, simpler bridge in 1945, a short way upstream.

The **struggle for water** is evident here. Urban and industrial water needs are met by tapping the mountain water sources, drying the grazing lands and depriving the scant Cordillera population of their livelihood, forcing them to migrate. From the cliff over the Loa you can see, towards the bridge, three large–diameter steel pipes which converge at one point and cross the deep canyon through a siphon; three further pipes span the canyon over the bridge.

On the far bank there is a military barrier and a short path down to the left to watch the bridge. Continue three km to the right from the barrier to the

Conchi Dam (you can drive over the dam wall). Built in the 1970s, it regulates irrigation along the upper the Loa river basin. It created a long, narrow lake in the middle of the desert, which has not yet given rise to vegetation on its shores to modify the landscape.

Back on the road to Bolivia heading north, a new pipeline (1986) runs alongside the road, raised above the ground on stone supports to prevent the ground's salinity from corroding the pipes. Continue a further 13 km until you see the abandoned **San Pedro railway station**, with a small, well-preserved cemetery and a few padlocked stone houses. Only one family lives here permanently; the rest come for the San Pedro festivity. Until 1955 it was a major yareta collection center; **yareta** (also spelled llareta) is a nearly prehistorical plant occurring at altitudes from 3,500 to 4,500 m; it is light-green and envelops boulders, resembling a pillow. It is extraordinarily hard; each of the tiny upper «heads» is an individual plant, part of a closely-knit community. Most are hundreds of years old, and were all but wiped out by mining and nitrate works: they happen to be an excellent fuel, with half the calorific power of bituminous coal.

Continue three km on the road, cross the San Pedro river and then eight further km to see the stately

San Pedro, San Pablo and Poruña volcanoes the first two soar above 6,000 m, their snowy summits showing large streaks of solidified lava flowing down the slope. The perfect–coned Poruña is a smaller volcano which emerged later on one of the sides.

Return to Calama retracing the road.

If you are travelling on a 2-car convoy, a suggested alternative is, instead of continuing north from the Conchi bridge, to take a good, solitary, pipeline-flanked road heading east to see the meadows and lake **Ojos del San Pedro** and skirt the massive San Pedro, San Pablo and Parini volcanoes, to visit **Inacaliri**, with a small village. It is a 114 km round trip from the junction.

4 TO VILLAGES ON THE LOA TRIBUTARIES

★★★ *the 211 km circuit runs on graveled roads built to serve the pipelines. Allow one day for this; take food and water. Gasoline only at Calama. This tour can also be made on the return trip from San Pedro de Atacama through the Tatio geysers, but only if you have a 4WD vehicle –and an adventurous nature (see Tour 6, Section D).*

A beautiful circuit visiting the villages of Caspana, Ayquina and Toconce, of pre-Conquest origin, and with buildings granted the National Monument status.

Take the road to San Pedro de Atacama out of Calama (km 0). At the small bridge spanning the Loa is a monument to the Calama battle of 1879.

At km 6 of the paved highway to San Pedro de Atacama take the graveled road branching left; it runs alongside pipelines bringing water to Antofagasta, and through flatland with some meadows on the Loa banks. To the left is the large, tree-filled oasis of Chiu Chiu. At km 43 is a short detour to the left, leading to a good spot for a picnic on the river bank. The river can be forded by car to visit Chiu Chiu.

At km 55 turn right and cross over the pipeline. The road heads for the Andean foothills. Some vegetation can be seen now, including Trichoreus atacamensis, a giant cactus species; it reaches up to 6 m in height, and tablets for construction can be made from its woody core. It is now nearly

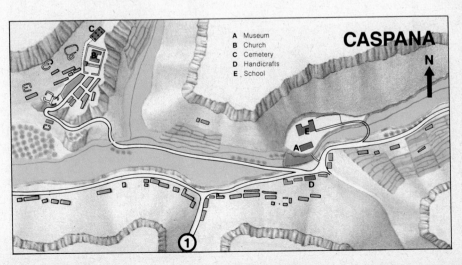

A   Museum
B   Church
C   Cemetery
D   Handicrafts
E   School

CASPANA

N

Caspana

2

extinct. This is the road to the Tatio geyser.

At km 80 follow the detour to the left leading to a walled-in cemetery (km 84); at the junction there, take the road branching right to

CASPANA a fertile valley at 2,900 m altitude, with fields terraced into the slopes and a small, quaint village with white-stone, mud-roofed houses. The community is quite well organized and produces flowers and vegetables for the Calama market. The local residents built a **footbridge** to an interesting **museum** dealing with the Atacameño culture. Opposite the museum is a crafts shop with alpaca–wool knitwear and cactus items. The village dates from pre–Conquest times. Upstream is the **Pueblo Nuevo** –the new village– and further terraced fields. Across the river is the **Pueblo Viejo** –the old village–, small and perched atop a steep cliff. It probably evolved from an ancient pukará, or fortress. It has two flagstone–paved streets lined with beautiful mud–roofed stone houses. At the end is the wall surrounding the church, with the cemetery walls beyond it. Above the village, some circular walls of old pens and grain silos are to be seen.

CHURCH OF SAN LUCAS (NM) (Festivity of the Candelaria on Feb 2). Surrounded by a large walled-in yard in two levels, it has a massive tower with a stair inside (illustration and description in Land and History, Zone 1). The church was erected in 1641 in chiseled stone, lined with cactus tablets and stuccoed with mud; it has a single nave and a lateral sacristy. Small reproductions in red volcanic stone of this church can be bought from the children who will instantly appear as you show

up at the place. They also have the key to the church.

Leave Caspana, km 84, on the same road up to the cemetery; take there road branching west (right). On the hills you can see thick layers of whitish volcanic stones, with some quarries to obtain construction rocks.

At km 89 the road descends to cross the Caspana river and then climbs up once more to start again descending into the Salado ravine, with a bridge at km 93.

A road branches here upstream to the reservoir storing water for Chuquicamata. Also to be seen is the metal siphon tapping water off the Caspana river. Beyond the bridge starts a new, gentle climb, with a good view of the Salado ravine. This road meets the larger road at km 97. Follow this road to the east (towards the Andes), running alongside another pipeline.

At km 106 is a pass, beyond which the roads descends towards the Toconce river, deep, squeezed by a canyon and commanding a **view** to terraced fields. Below is a filtering station for the water flowing to Chuquicamata. Ahead is a steep, zigzagging 2 climb ending at km 109. Here is

TOCONCE (3,200 m above sea level). A pre–Conquest village flanked by rocky cliffs, it has a police station, a wireless station and stone houses lying along the main irrigation canal. The village is surrounded by cultivated fields and has a magnificent view to the snowy Andean peaks. The **church** (festivity of St Santiago on July 25) is located on a small promontory; it is enclosed by a wall, it has no bell tower but it does boast four shrines for placing statuary during processions. It commands a superb **view** over fields terraced into steep slopes; many terraces have been abandoned.

Retrace now the road to the Caspana junction at km 121. Turn right there to see the **Vegas de Turi**, a meadowy area –now almost dry– where you can see some alpacas and llamas grazing. At km 129, on the right and on some black rocks 20 m above the meadow, is the

PUKARA OF TURI (NM) the largest fortress village in the Atacama Andean area. It was presumably an Inca administrative center for the region. Erected in the 12th century on a nearly flat platform, it has a square, straight streets and octago-

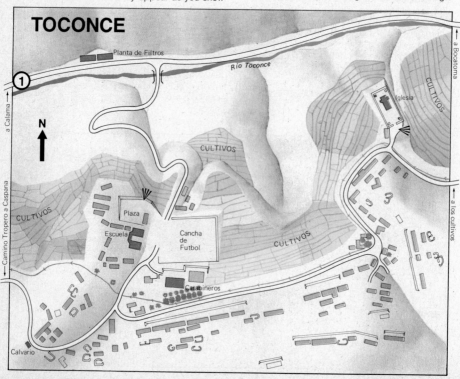

TOCONCE

nal houses. It was built on local hard volcanic stone, smaller stones filling the interstices. A group of round towers stand out, as well as a large walled court built of mud–brick.

Retrace the road back to the junction at Toconce; alternatively, you can continue to Lasana on the road running alongside the pipeline. At the Toconce junction, km 137, turn right. At km 142 is a signposted road branching left to

AYQUINA this is perhaps the most picturesque village in the region, built entirely of stone, with mud–straw roofs and no eaves. The houses are clustered around the church and sort of piled one on top of the other. The church lies on a lower platform stretching to a look–out on top of the cliff over the Salado canyon, with a superb view of the terraced fields below. The crops are irrigated with spring water, seeping down from the Vegas de Turi. The village is nearly deserted, most houses padlocked. Its inhabitants come only for the Festivity of the Virgin of Guadalupe, on September 8.

CHURCH OF OUR LADY OF GUADALUPE (festivity on Sept 8). Sitting at the end of a walled court, it is surrounded by large steps that also serve as seats. Its unusual bell tower has five stages and is made of red–stuccoed stone. See illustration in Land and History, Zone 1. The key is not available for visitors.

Return to the road (km 145) and continue to the west. At km 147 take road branching left (road to the right leads to Lasana) to descend into the Salado river and cross the bridge. At km 163 is the road to the left followed to reach Caspana. From here on, just retrace the road you followed from Calama. At km 202 is the paved highway to San Pedro de Atacama, and at km 211 is Calama.

5 TO THE HIGH-PLATEAU VIA OLLAGÜE ★★

it is a 414 km round trip from Calama, on a solitary, rough gravel road. Driving is slow; it is advisable to travel in a two–vehicle convoy. Take food, water, spare gasoline, warm clothing. Camping possible at the Ascotán salt flat.

A tour through the high Andean wilderness, with the beautiful Ascotán and Carcote salt flats, towering volcanoes and interesting mining operations.

Follow the road to Bolivia out of Calama (km 0), passing Chiu Chiu at km 33, Conchi bridge at km 67 and crossing the San Pedro river at km 85; this section of the road was described under Tour 3.

The road soon skirts the soaring **San Pedro** and **San Pablo** volcanoes, and then surrounds the foot of the smaller **Poruña volcano**, to climb to a pass on a volcanic ridge which closes the basin containing the salt flats. The railroad to Bolivia, built by 1890,

Ayquina

runs near the road.

At km 123 is the **Ascotán railway station** (3,960 m altitude), with the wreckage of a village. Here used to be a borax mine set up by English capitals around 1882. The ore was hauled by mule carts to Salinas, to be loaded there into the train. It ceased to operate by 1950.

This route was followed by naturalist Federico Philippi in 1885, by mule, on an exploratory journey to collect flora and fauna samples for the Natural History Museum of Santiago. He set out from Copiapó to the frontier, and followed the border to San Pedro de Atacama, Tatio, Inacarili, Ascotán, Ollagüe and farther north, to come down through Pica, inland from Iquique.

The road descends to the **Ascotán salt flat**, a white, flat expanse with ponds and mudflats full of flamingoes and flanked by towering mountains and volcanoes marching along the border. At the far end is the Ollagüe volcano, which erupted in 1885. At km 149 is the **Cebollar valley**, with a good spot for camping. The road climbs to a new pass and then descends into the **Carcote salt flat**, with the high peaks of Ollagüe and Aucanquilcha to the north. Ahead is a green meadow, the rest an arid desert. At km 198 is

OLLAGUE a frontier outpost 3,696 m above sea level. There are Customs and SAG checkpoints, a police station and a few residents. Climbing a further 9 km you can reach **Amincha**, a place with a water spring and the sulfur plant receiving the ore –by aerial tram– from Aucanquilcha, the world's highest mine, at an altitude of 5,580 m.

From Ollagüe, those seeking the adventurous paths –and driving a 4WD vehicle– can make an expedition from here through the Huasco salt flat to Pica. See Zone 1, Section B.

6 DESCENT FROM TATIO GEYSER TO CALAMA
★★★ *124 km, on a part gravel, part dirt road,*

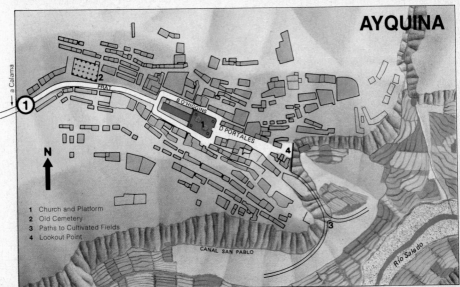

AYQUINA

a Calama

PRAT

R. O'HIGGINS

D PORTALES

N

CANAL SAN PABLO

Río Salado

1 Church and Platform
2 Old Cemetery
3 Paths to Cultivated Fields
4 Lookout Point

with a mountain stretch eroded by rain (check with the tourist taxi drivers at Calama or San Pedro de Atacama about its condition). The best is to ascend by San Pedro de Atacama and to descend by this route. It is more easy.

This is an option of descend from Tatio not coming back to San Pedro de Atacama. In addition it makes possible the Tour 4 in the descending road.

From Tatio, km 0, retrace the road followed to get here up to the road branching left to the airfield, at km 10. Go on straight to the next junction, at km 14; there turn right, crossing the Coya range and Cerro Negro. Ahead is **Morro de Cablor**, a large hill, which the road skirts on its western side through the **cuesta Chita**, a stretch of curvy descent normally very difficult after rain. To compensate, the views are extraordinary, with the Loa tributaries down below and towering mount Paniri in the background.

At km 41, almost unexpectedly, a road branches right to Caspana; follow this road if you prefer to make Tour 4. Otherwise, continue straight to Calama. The road from here is good, and is described under Tour 4.

SECTION D   ATACAMA SALT FLAT

This section comprises the territory lying in the great depression of the Atacama salt flat, a desert area with picturesque, scattered oases flanked by the towering Andes range.

The Atacama salt flat, Easter Island and the Antarctica are Chile's three areas ranked internationally as having «exceptional tourist interest». The Atacama salt flat derives its attraction from its important archaeological relics of the Atacameño culture, beautiful geologic formations and superb scenery.

How to Get There a paved highway provides good access by car. There are bus services mornings and afternoons from Calama (on Sunday they continue to Toconao); from Antofagasta, one Sunday bus only in summer. There are daily scheduled flights to Calama (except Saturday). Car rental companies and tourist taxis provide further transportation from there (see Tourist Services section at the end).

Best Season for Travelling autumn, winter and spring offer guaranteed sunshine and deep blue skies. Summer (Dec-Mar) is, however, the high season, although it coincides with the so-called «high-plateau winter», with heavy occasional downpours and cloudy days (See Land and History).

Appropriate Clothing days are hot the year round, nights warm in summer and cold in winter. Take a sweater and windbreaker in summer, parka and other appropriate garments for the winter nights. Also sunglasses, a hat, sun-blocking cream, lip protection, swimming gear.

Preparation of the Car low oxygen levels at altitude reduce engine power considerably. For Tours 5, 6, and 7, the spark must be advanced (a car mechanic in San Pedro de Atacama does the trick in ten minutes). In situations of extreme loss of power, remove the carburetor's air filter temporarily. The minimum car engine size for this area is 1,000 cc.

Travelling to Argentina immigration and customs are cleared at San Pedro de Atacama. The pass is open only from October through March. There are two regular bus services from Antofagasta to Salta (Argentina), which pass through San Pedro de Atacama at night on Wednesday and Saturday. Check itineraries with the Customs office.

1 FROM CALAMA TO THE ATACAMA SALT FLAT
★★★ *a 92 km stretch of paved road to San Pedro de Atacama. Gasoline at Calama and San Pedro de Atacama.*

The access road to Chile's largest salt flat, with San Pedro de Atacama, the largest settlement during pre-Conquest times and the administrative center for the region during the colonial period.

The road climbs gently from Calama to the Barros Arana range, the last arm of the Domeyko Range.

At km 47 a road branches left to Río Grande. The vehicles puff their way to the pass on the Barros Arana range, at km 53; 6 km later, another

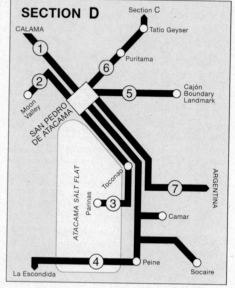

road branches left to Río Grande. This road is badly surfaced and it leads in 42 km to

Río Grande a small, quaint hamlet with stone houses and a church, lying on the fertile valleys of the Río Grande which flows to San Pedro de Atacama. Nearby is **San Bartolo**, a copper deposit already exploited by the Incas. In 1835, the industrialist and explorer Diego de Almeyda set up mining works here which remained active until 1920.

The road to San Pedro descends to cross the endless, desolate and aptly named Llano de la Paciencia –**Plain of Patience**–, which stretches to the right. Soon it climbs to cross the

CORDILLERA DE LA SAL (the «salt range»), a succession of weirdly shaped hills. Geologically, this is the pushed-up bottom of a former lake. The sediment layers, horizontal when they were at the lake bottom, have been pushed to a vertical position by folding of the earth's crust. Wind and rain then eroded the soft material into dinosaur-like shapes.

The highway crosses the Cordillera de la Sal and starts to descend to the Atacama salt flat. On the last descent, on the right, there is a rock outcrop affording the only **panoramic view** of the salt flat, the towering Licancábur volcano in the background and, below, all the ayllos or oases making up San Pedro de Atacama. It is worth a stop. At km 92 is the square of

SAN PEDRO DE ATACAMA (pop 905). The village is located 2,440 m above sea level and on the mouth of the largest river flowing into the salt flat.

It was the main center of Atacameño culture (see Land and History), with a defensive fortress at **Quitor** and the population distributed among 15 ayllos (a socio-economic grouping with kinship ties); the farmable land and the irrigation canals were allocated to the various **ayllos**.

By 1450 San Pedro de Atacama was conquered by the Incas, who set up a government and administration center at **Catarpe**. The place stepped into Spanish history when Diego de Almagro stopped here in 1536; Pedro de Valdivia did likewise in 1540. The latter was on his way to the south, and he waited here for a 25-troop reinforcement from High Perú.

It was christened **Atacama la Grande** and soon had a parish church subordinate to the Charcas Archbishopric, and the colonial administration subordinate to the Corregimiento de Lipes, with jurisdiction from Calama to the south.

Industrial development on the coast during the 19th century boosted San Pedro de Atacama's trading role: from 1830 to 1870, it controlled the mule and llama trains moving trade between Cobija, on the Pacific coast, and Salta, Argentina, where imported products brought this way were cheaper than through the Atlantic route. From 1870, its inhabitants flocked to the Caracoles silver mine, and the administrative center was moved to Calama. Between 1890 and 1925 there was intense livestock traffic from Argentina to the saltpeter mines.

Now, its few inhabitants are engaged in farming to supply the Calama market and in providing services to the sulfur mines and the new mineral

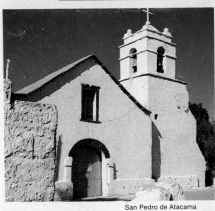

San Pedro de Atacama church

2

salt mines operating at the salt flat. It has a good hotel and tourist taxis (see Services and Prices).

What To See the village was built by the Spaniards. It is small, with narrow alleys. The houses are built of mud brick –the quarries are far– and stone is used only in the upper foundations. The orchards are surrounded by thick mud-brick walls crowned by branches to keep intruders out. There are three outstanding places to know:

CHURCH OF SAN PEDRO (NM) (services Sun 11:00 h; festivity of San Pedro on June 29). Facing a

☎ Telephone Center	E Police Station	5 Cb y Cs Takha Takha
⊕ Gasoline Station	F International Police	6 Compsite Hostal Puri
★ Touristic Information	T Tramaca Buses	7 Bh Pukará
✚ Hospital	**ACCOMMODATIONS**	**RESTAURANTS**
A Town Hall	1 Hs San Pedro de Atacama	1 Hs San Pedro de Atacama
B Church of San Pedro (NM)	2 Bh Chiloé	10 Bh Juanita
C Archaeological Museum	3 Bh La Florida	2 Bh Chiloé
D Pedro de Valdivia House	4 Bh Porvenir	4 Bh Porvenir

SHOPPING
20 Handicrafts
21 Supermarket
22 Groceries

TOURIST SERVICES
5 Excursiones Takha Takha
25 Turismo Ochoa

Golden mask, San Pedro museum

2

lovely square paved with stones and shaded by big pepper trees, it is one of the largest and most beautiful churches in the region. It is enclosed by a wall with three arched gates. It is a parish church since before 1641, but the present walls date from 1745; the tower was added by 1890. The roof is made of massive algarrobo rafters, and the ceiling is made of cactus tablets lined with mud and straw. The altar is made of carved stone, light streaming in through four thick-glassed windows. It has interesting statuary. The old church used to be near the museum; some foundations have been discovered.

ARCHAEOLOGICAL MUSEUM (Mon–Sun 08:00–12:00 h and 14:00–18:00 h, fee). At the entrance there is an Atacama cactus, bored-through stones and a statue of father Gustave Le Paige S I, its founder. He was a Belgian Jesuit missionary who took charge of the parish in 1955 and started an awesome collection of Andean archaeology, which he later donated to the Universidad del Norte. He died in 1980.

The museum, located in a modern building,

provides in 13 rooms an excellent insight into the evolution of the Atacameño culture, a culture that lasted 150 centuries. It displays beautiful objects selected from a collection of more than 300,000 archeological pieces. You can see the evolution of indigenous ceramics, mummies complete with clothing and hair (dating from pre-hispanic times), garments and ornaments and a collection of gold figures. It is well worth a visit.

The Inca House erroneously known as Pedro de Valdivia House, is the oldest building in town, with roofing made of thick logs covered with branches and lined with mud. It has trapezoidal door openings, typical of Inca architecture. The house is privately owned, but open for exhibition. Ask for the key at the next door to the south.

Accommodation and Food best is Hostería San Pedro, with a hotel and cabins in a park with a swimming pool. It also offers an information brochure on the area in English, German, French and Japanese. Cheaper and more modest is the Residencial Chiloé. There are several cheaper pensiones, and campgrounds at Pozo 3 and Takha Takha. Good food at the Hostería, also at restaurants Juanita and Chiloé. The Hostería also has a supermarket. For a picnic, Pozo 3.

SHORT TOURS

A lot of attractive tours, with a respective duration of no more than one hour, to:

PUKARA QUITOR (NM) follow the road passing the cemetery and then take the left branch, crossing irrigation canals and cultivated fields to reach the river bank in 4 km. Ahead is the Pukará (defensive fortress), with a clutch of buildings –restored in 1981– clinging to a steep slope; they are built of large stones, with smaller stones filling up the interstices. There is a perimeter defense wall and, on the back, the cliff above the river. A semicircular building sticks out in the center.

It dates from the 12th century and lost defensive importance with the Inca occupation. In 1540, Francisco de Aguirre, of the Pedro de Valdivia forces, attacked it with 30 mounted men. The fortress defenders surrendered.

A rather bad road continues along the river to the ayllo of Tabillos, with the ruins of the Inca administrative center of **Catarpe** up on the hill. Nearby is the **Chapel of San Isidro**, built in 1913 by Italian settler Lucas Cenzano and now maintained by his descendants.

TO THE AYLLO OF TULOR follow street O'Higgins to the west. Beyond the bridge, take the old road to Calama branching to the left. Then follow the route indicated in map. The ayllo of **Coyo** has lots of cultivated patches, the fences made of brea, a shrub that grows on the salt flat.

The **Tulor village** has two reconstructed round mud huts, where an archaeologist lives. To the left, buried under the sand which ruined the ayllo and the village, you will see a tightly clustered group of round houses. You walk at roof level. Tulor is the oldest relic of human habitation in the valley (ca 100 BC to AD 100), miraculously preserved by the very thing that doomed it: the shifting sand dunes.

THE AGRICULTURAL LANDS a 12 km circuit starting from street O'Higgins through the Domingo Atienza alley. High mud-brick walls line the alley, separating the ayllos of **Yaye** (right) and **Larache**, shaded by large trees. The golden vases which can now be seen in the museum were found here.

At km 1 you cross a wide street; straight ahead is the **ayllo of Sequitor**. Turn left through the **ayllo of Thecar**. The scenery opens up, and some cultivated patches can be seen struggling to survive amidst the sand. At km 4 is a road running south; follow this road to the right, heading to Solor –on the left– and, in the distance, **Cucuter**, ruined by

---

al Tatío y Baños de Puritama →

LOS AYLLOS DE SAN PEDRO DE ATACAMA

CATARPE

TAMBILLO

Centro Incásico Catarpe

Río San Pedro

Planta Azufrera Polan

VILAMA

N

Pukara Quitor

Planta Azufrera Purico

QUITOR

SAN PEDRO DE ATACAMA

a Calama

LARACHE

SOLCOR

POZO 3

Piscina Camping Parque

a Hito Cajó

①

YAYE 2

Escuela

TCHECAR

Canal

Canal

ALANA

SOLOR

Escuela

a Toconao y Argentina ↓

SEQUITOR

Canal

Canal

Canal R

Canal

②

Antiguo Camino a Calama →

COYO

Escuela

Canal

POCONCHE

CUCUTER

Aldea de Tulor

TULOR

Río San Pedro

BETER

---

sand. Continue 5 km and then turn left (unsigned) to Solor. The road crosses an irrigation canal and reaches the square, with a school containing a rocket and a metallic helicopter in the yard.

The **ayllo of Solor** is the most prosperous, with 95% of its farm land under cultivation. See map to return to San Pedro de Atacama.

TO POZO 3 a good place for bathing, 3 km from the town; entrance fee. See map. This place originated from a well bored by Corfo (Chile's Industrial Development Agency) in 1965; the 6 inch (15.2 cm) hole is over 200 m deep. A powerful water jet emerges from the depths.

It was acquired later by a smart local miner and entrepreneur, who built a swimming pool and set up a campground at the site. This is Chile's cleanest swimming pool, permanently fed by a warm spurt of pure water and emptied every night to irrigate the fields. The architecture of the place is unusual and ingenious. The molds used were metal plates from old water tanks of the FCAB railway, with their typical cross-pattern.

TOURS FROM SAN PEDRO DE ATACAMA

2 TO THE MOON VALLEY ★★★

a round trip of 62 km from San Pedro de Atacama, with 30 km of gravel road. Allow at least two hours. Best is to arrive there shortly before sunset: dusk at this place is trance-inducing. **An astoundingly beautiful geological formation.**

Follow the paved road to Calama, crossing the Cordillera de la Sal to descend onto the **Llano de la Paciencia**. At km 15 a road branches off to the left. Take this road and, at km 24, you will meet a road running diagonally. Turn left to follow this road to the foot of the hills, to climb the short **Las Salinas stretch.**

Right beyond the summit is a path to both sides (there is a salt mine to the right). You will see mounds with incrustations looking like broken glass: it is crystallized silica. At km 31 you reach the **Valle de la Luna** (Moon Valley), a small depression of saline ground, 500 m in diameter, containing a number of small, sharp-crested hills. The earth's crust has here been extensively modified by successive folding. As described under Tour 1 of this Section, this used to be a lake bottom, the sediment layers now standing vertically and eroded by wind and rain.

Retrace the road and, 2 km from the Valle de la Luna (look carefully), lives a miner in a hut among the rocks; he sells chunks of **gem salt**, a beautiful large-sized, absolutely clear crystal. It is mined locally and is formed by crystallization at high pressure and in absence of humidity.

3 TO TOCONAO AND THE FLAMINGOES ★★★

a round trip of 130 km, with some paved stretches. Allow one day; it is possible to bathe in Toconao. Take food, water, gasoline and swimming gear. **A visit to the salt flat and its flamingo colonies, and to a charming village and oasis with ponds suitable for bathing.**

Follow the signposted road to Toconao, running straight on a flat plain, with the **Licancábur volcano** looming in the distance. A perfect cone soaring to 5,916 m above sea level, its slopes plummet directly onto the salt flat in an awesome drop of 3,600 m (the salt flat is at 2,300 m altitude). A string of volcanoes stands at attention north and south of the great Licancábur. You are traversing the enormous

ATACAMA SALT FLAT a 3,000 –square– kilometer depression or basin where the waters from the San Pedro river and many other smaller streams flowing down from the Andes get trapped. It is Chile's largest salt flat, with a rugged salt crust peppered with desert dust. Under the white crust is a great lake -scattered ponds can be seen of briny water. This lake contains the world's largest

Moon valley

reserve of lithium, a sort of high-tech mineral salt, exploited now by Soc Chilena del Litio, in addition to borax, potassium and other salts mined by Minsal. It is a really giant valley, wider than the Santiago valley and endlessly long. Amazingly, you can see clear across the salt flat to the far end: the air is so dry, that visibility is nothing less than perfect, making it extraordinarily difficult to judge distances. From San Pedro de Atacama, for instance, you can see the dust raised by the trucks climbing the Licancábur slopes at dawn, over 30 km away.

This great salt flat used to fill the basin between the Andes and the Domeyko ranges. Later, tectonic pressures raised the **Cordillera de la Sal**. The Andes, in turn, contain several active volcanoes, like the Láscar, whose lava flows filled up the gap between the mountains until a high-altitude tableland (the High-Plateau) was formed. Some of this lava flowed into the salt flat, filling up all the crevices between the mountains to produce a homogeneous, gently-sloping drop from the high plateau to the salt flat.

This highly permeable volcanic material permits water from melting snow to seep through and emerge as springs at the piedmont, giving rise to oases where the villages of Toconao, Camar, Peine, Socaire and others are located.

The road continues straight, with some stretches paved. At km 29 is **Tambillos**, an old spring in the herding trail now supporting **tamarugo plantations** started by Corfo in 1965. This tree is superbly adapted to saline soils and very modest water availability, and produces nourishing pods year round. Its wood is suitable for furniture and other uses, and its flowers support bees. At km 37 is Toconao; check with the police about road conditions; you must report here your planned itinerary. Visit the village on the return leg.

Drive through Toconao up to km 40, to take the road branching right at that point, which descends to the salt flat. At km 56 (look out for it) is a detour to the right, leading in 3 km to the first pond. A further 3 km ahead is the fantastic

LAKE CHAXA its shores thickly encrusted with salt and its water with salt floating in the surface. It is lively with lizards and parinas, or **pink flamingoes**. The place is a flamingo breeding ground, protected and under Conaf administration.

Retrace the road to visit

TOCONAO (pop 446). Its fresh water allows this oasis to grow all kinds of fruits, although they are not offered for sale at the village. At the entrance there is a dam and two cultivated areas: the plain stretching toward the salt flat, with sunnier, more fertile ground, and the Jeria ravine, narrower and shadier, through which the stream flows. The fields are cultivated according to the traditional pre-hispanic pattern of irregularly-shaped small patches watered by a community irrigation system.

The village is small, built of whitish volcanic stone. The oldest alleys are those located on the western side. Ask for permission to visit the shady orchards. Local artisans make stone reproductions of Atacama churches. On the renovated square is the

CHURCH OF SAN LUCAS AND BELL TOWER (NM) (local festivity on October 18). Small and massive, it bears the typical Atacama features. Built in stone, it dates from earlier than 1744 and can be visited paying a fee to the caretaker. Separated from the church is the bell tower, built of chiseled stone using mud as mortar. Erected in 1750, it has three sections separated by cornices. It is one of Atacama's most beautiful churches (see illustration in Land and History, Zone 1).

Follow street Láscar two km beyond the poblacion Minsal (residential quarter for employees of the Minsal company) to the

Quarries where the whitish, soft volcanic rock is worked, called liparita. Toconao is the producer of this stone, used in constructions throughout the North. Note the bell-like sound produced by the stone when hit.

Walk down the path from the quarry to the

Jeria Gorge a long canyon through which flows the water feeding Toconao, with some ponds suitable for bathing, request permission from the local farmers. The northern cliffs are sheer, with birds nesting in the crevices of the rock face. The southern bank is not nearly as steep, and contains the fruit orchards, mostly quince and figs. The gorge makes a nice walk.

To return to San Pedro de Atacama, retrace the road.

4 A CIRCUIT AROUND THE SALT FLAT ★★★
a round trip of 401 km on a good but solitary road; advisable to make it in a group of two vehicles. Take food, water, gasoline and swimming gear. Leave early; it will take you the whole day.
An interesting circuit around the great salt flat, to end up taking a dip in the ponds of the Peine oasis.

Follow the road to Toconao; at Toconao (km 37) you must report your itinerary with the police, so that you may be assisted in case of problems, and then check with Conaf (see map) about the road conditions (there is more than one alternative).

Leave Toconao following the international road to the forking at km 40; take the right branch leading to the edge of the salt flat. (An alternative is to continue straight ahead and descend to the

salt flat shore farther ahead, but this road has some tricky sandy stretches.) The road runs on a flat plain, flanked by bunch grass and brea shrubs and with a great view to the cordillera peaks.

At km 76 you meet a road paved with salt blocks, climbing to the left and leading in 25 km to Socaire. Through here runs the international road through the **Pass of Laguna Sico**, at 4,079 m altitude somewhat lower than the 4,269 m Guaitiquina (or Huaytiquina) pass it replaced. Climbing 10 km you have a superb **panoramic view** of the salt flat, enormous and blue, with its edges white like surf. The road now runs along the slope to reach, at km 101,

Socaire rather than a village, this is a succession of cultivated terraces on a vast slope, with picturesque stone houses. At the far end is a small church with a stone tower. Local festivity (San Bartolomé) on August 24.

Socaire dates from pre-Conquest times and is supplied by several springs surging at the place. Its importance in the past was due to its location on the route to Antofagasta de la Sierra (Argentina) and as a supply post for the gold mines on the border. Federico Philippi passed through here on his plant-collection expedition of 1885.

Retrace the road, but now continue straight ahead from the junction at km 15 (where a road branches left). Nine km from this junction, a 3 km road branches east (right) to

Camar a small, quaint oasis with a church (local festivity June 13, San Antonio) and the best **view** over the salt flat.

Descend now to the edge of the salt flat; at km 150 (including the detours described) is the junction where you started climbing to Socaire and Camar. Turn left, the road is paved with salt blocks and at km 172 you will see the first trees of the Peine oasis to the left. Take here the road branching right (also paved with salt blocks) into the salt flat and leading to

Laguna Salada a small and isolated lake, fringed by large, white salt crust. Here you can see how the salt deposit is formed: small salt crystals float on the water surface and agglutinate into small floating plates. These plates crack as the salt crystallizes (crystallized salt is more voluminous

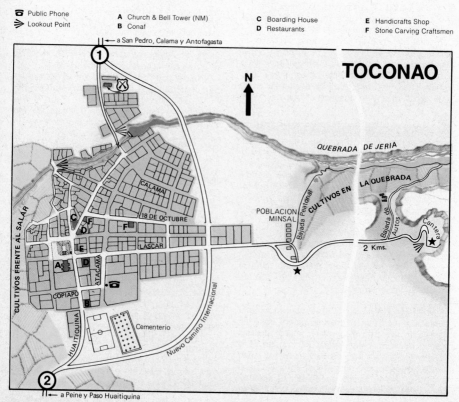

📞 Public Phone
⤢ Lookout Point

A Church & Bell Tower (NM)
B Conaf

C Boarding House
D Restaurants

E Handicrafts Shop
F Stone Carving Craftsmen

← a San Pedro, Calama y Antofagasta

TOCONAO

N

QUEBRADA DE JERIA

POBLACION MINSAL

CULTIVOS EN LA QUEBRADA

Cantera

2 Kms.

CULTIVOS FRENTE AL SALAR

CALAMA

18 DE OCTUBRE

LASCAR

COPIAPO

ATACAMA

HUAITIQUINA

Cementerio

Nuevo Camino Internacional

← a Peine y Paso Huaitiquina

than liquid salt). These cracks and fissures permit evaporation to continue, and as this happens more salt becomes crystallized. This, in turn, pushes up the plates, giving rise to the crust all over the salt flat.

From the lake there is a stunning view to the snowy volcanoes on the Andes, and to a vast erosion slide rolling to the salt flat. At its foot is the small **oasis of Tilomonte**.

Straight ahead, at km 195, is the checkpoint and buildings of **Soc Chilena del Litio**. No public access permitted. Take road branching left, with several trails branching to either side, leading to various mining works. At km 201 are the cliffs of the **Lila (Violet) Hills**, closing the salt flat. There is a junction: the road to the left leads to **Tilopozo**, the last oasis on the salt flat. Take the road to the right, running along the foot of the Lila Hills, to reach the salt-block-paved road again at km 208. This stretch of road is flanked by lithium mine works, pumping the salt flat's water and leaving it to evaporate in large ponds. The resulting concentrate is hauled by tanker trucks to the Pan de Azúcar railway station; there it is loaded into freight trains bringing it to La Negra (Antofagasta), where the processing plant is located.

To the west, the road crosses the foothills of the Lila Hills and then comes to the last piece of salt flat. Cross it to climb the last corner of the Cordillera de la Sal, at km 234, with a superb **view** of the salt flat with the Andes for a backdrop.

For those looking for more adventure, a 114 km round trip on a good gravel road (frequented by mine trucks) can be made to the **Pan de Azúcar railway station**, through interesting scenery and passing near the enormous **La Escondida** copper mine, undergoing initial exploitation by a foreign company. It is as important as Chuquicamata.

Retrace the route back to the road to Toconao, at km 298. Turn 2 km to the right to

PEINE an oasis inhabited since pre-Conquest times. It lies on a slope adjacent to a ravine where the cultivated fields are nestled. The village itself dates from the 17th century, and was moved to this location from Peine Viejo, on the northern bank.

The Inca Road, followed both by Diego de Almagro and Pedro de Valdivia, used to run through here. Around 1835 it was also visited by explorer and mining entrepreneur Diego de Almeyda and, in 1855, by R A Philippi, on his expedition from Paposo to San Pedro de Atacama. By 1858, José Santos Ossa was exploiting a silver mine in the vicinity.

What To See at the entrance of the village are some houses of the lithium company and then a long street lined with picturesque stone houses leading to the **Church of San Roque** (festivity on August 16). It was built ca. 1750, with a stone tower reconstructed in 1940 imitating the original tower. Opposite the church is a modest square

containing algarrobos, another valuable desert tree. A short way beyond is a pool where spring water is stored for irrigation. Below is the

Cocha de Peine a place where water from the main spring collects among rounded rocks, facing the desert. There are two pools storing the water for irrigation. Bathing is permitted (there is a small cabin for changing).

A path leads from the Cocha to the

Ruins of Peine Viejo (NM) this is one of the first archaeological sites to be granted the National Monument status, as early as 1951, together with La Moneda (the Government's palace) and the Church of San Francisco in Santiago. Only the church's walls and arched gate remain. It was an Atacameño village having wide streets, quite different from the pukarás. Built of stone using clay as mortar, the rooms are octagonal, while the grain silos are round. The chapel is estimated to date from the 16th century. It was deserted for unknown reasons by 1650. The locals can show you where the Inca road used to run through.

Retrace the road to return to San Pedro de Atacama (km 401).

5 TO THE LICANCABUR VOLCANO AND CAJON

BOUNDARY LANDMARK ★★★ *a round trip of 90 km on a gravel road, climbing to an altitude of 4,500 m. Better to make it on a week day, as then there is some truck traffic. The vehicle must be tuned for high-altitude. Leave early to avoid the heat. Take water, food and warm clothing. Allow at least half a day.*

A visit to the foot of the area's highest volcano, with lake Verde across the border.

Follow the road to Pozo 3 out of San Pedro de Atacama, after having reported your trip at the Customs office. Continue straight to the foot of the Licancábur volcano. The road then winds up its way among dry ravines to reach the edge of the volcano's cone, skirting it on its southern side: a stunning **view** of the entire salt flat. Best at dawn.

Behind the Licancábur is the **Juriques volcano**, the road running now across the Toco plain on the high plateau. The Cajón boundary landmark is reached at km 45. Ask the Bolivian control officers for permission to visit the emerald-green **Laguna Verde**, a major flamingo breeding ground, a short distance beyond the border.

If you wish to, you can climb 10 km to visit the **Purico sulfur mine**, on the Chilean side.

6 TO THE TATIO GEYSER ★★★

ninety-five km from San Pedro de Atacama to the geyser. Tatio is located at 4,300 m altitude. You may continue directly from there to Calama: however, the road for the climb down to Caspana is appalling at the best of times. The car must be

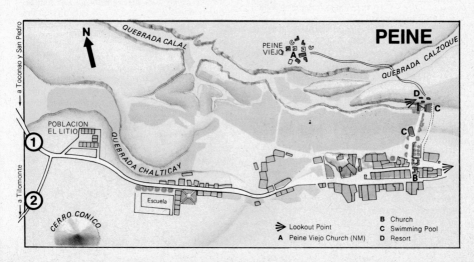

Tatío geisers

tuned for high altitude. Leave at 04:00 h (that's right: AM) to be ahead of the taxis climbing from San Pedro de Atacama (thus you may be assisted in case of problems). The geysers are most glorious at dawn. Another option is to go up in the afternoon and camp at the Corfo station at Tatio (you should ask for permission in advance). Take warm clothing and food. Do not attempt this excursion with snow or storm. Allow at least 2 hours for the climb.

A most attractive excursion to a site of unusual geologic interest.

See map of San Pedro de Atacama: take the road passing next to the cemetery, and then the road branching right at the junction. You will pass near the **Polán sulfur plant** and then cross the Vilama river, with its ayllo on its banks. At km 28 is a short detour to the left, leading to the

Puritama Baths a wide rock pool with a waterfall and a spring gushing forth warm water. The road now crosses a lava field and climbs the **Cuesta del Diablo**. At km 45 is the camp of the **Saciel sulfur mine**. The road climbs down to meet a signposted junction at km 54; to the right is the Campamento Volcán Apagado. Continue straight ahead to a new signposted junction at km 68, with another road branching off to the right for Campamento Volcán Apagado. Continue straight ahead towards a tributary of the Río Grande, and at km 73 there is yet another signposted junction. Here is **Loma Sánchez**, the highest point on the road (4,500 m).

Take the road branching right. The Tocopuri airfield is at km 77; turn left there. The **Putana volcano** soars in the background, superb with fumarolic activity at dawn. The road crosses the Las Vizcachas pass at 4,380 m altitude and reaches another junction at km 85. Turn right to the Campamento Corfo at km 91. A short distance beyond are the

TATIO GEYSERS a geothermic field flanked by soaring peaks. At dawn, powerful spurts of steam issue forth through various blowholes. The ponds of steaming water are encrusted with colorful mineral deposits. DO NOT GET TOO CLOSE TO THESE PONDS: the edges can collapse. The colors on the ground and the metal blue sky at dawn, framed by the rising steam columns, make a simply breathtaking sight.

Research to tap this energy for power generation was started in 1920 by Chuquicamata but later abandoned, and retaken by Corfo in 1968.

It is possible to descend directly to Calama, see Section C, Tour 6.

7 TO ARGENTINA THROUGH GUAITIQUINA
★★★ to Salta, 491 km, with gasoline at San Antonio de Los Cobres, 130 km from San Pedro de Atacama. The road is graveled, at times poorly surfaced. Vehicles must be tuned for high altitude; some passes are higher than 4,500 m above

sea level. It is advisable to travel in a group of two vehicles, or to start five hours ahead of the buses making the run on Wed and Sat. Otherwise, start in the late afternoon to avoid the heat of the day during the toughest part of the climb. Passport and Customs clearance at San Pedro de Atacama. You will need from 10 to 12 hours. During the summer there is also traffic of Argentinian cars.

A circuit crossing the High-Plateau to visit Salta, a busy and attractive city with important colonial monuments and subtropical vegetation, to return to Chile through excellent paved highways via Tucumán, San Juan and Mendoza.

Take the road to Toconao out of San Pedro de Atacama. At Toconao (km 37) is the last police outpost. Continue to the south up to **Aguas Blancas** at km 47, where a new oasis is in the process of being established, and take the road branching left. A gentle but steady climb starts, the road now running along the northern side of the Talabre ravine. At km 62 is the new Talabre village, and five km farther **Old Talabre**, nestled in a deep ravine; it was ruined a decade ago by a flash flood. Alongside the road, a stone-lined ditch covered by flagstones brings water (very cold) to Aguas Blancas. There is a spectacular **view** to the salt flat behind.

At km 72 is the modest hamlet of **Tumbré**, with stone houses and pens clustered at the foot of a huge rock; this is the last settlement this side of the border. The road continues climbing southwards to skirt the **Láscar volcano**; at km 90 is a monolith indicating the point where you cross the **Tropic of Capricorn**.

Now you are in the High Plateau proper. The ground appears to be sandy, but is in fact windswept volcanic rock. Wide rolling ground can be seen, but not a single stream: the water is absorbed immediately by the porous soil. The volcanoes look like small cones rearing up from this table land lying at 4,200 m altitude. Beyond a pass, at km 102, is

Lake Lejía small and lying on a totally barren depression. Its water is emerald-green and has mineral foam floating on the surface. In November, its shores come alive with huge flamingo colonies, which take to the air when someone approaches. Up to here, this is an interesting daytrip from San Pedro de Atacama.

The road climbs and dips across a plain with towering **mount Zapaleri** presiding on the north and several snow-capped volcanoes marching to the south. At km 135, a road branches right to the El Laco mine and, at km 163, is the border crossing, indicated by a sign. The road continues through the High Plateau to reach, at km 194, an oasis with a small picturesque Aymara hamlet called **Catúa**. Now it is an Argentine border outpost. At km 232, the road meets the Antofagasta-Salta railway, opposite the **Cauchari** salt flat.

Next are two rough, steep mountain stretches, to reach at km 302, **San Antonio de Los Cobres**, a pre-hispanic village at 3,770 m altitude and the most important in the sierra, with customs, border police, a TV relay station and a gasoline station. Its population is engaged in mining.

At km 324 is another mountain stretch. At km 342 the road descends into the **Toro Ravine**, along whose bed the road continues to Salta. On the side runs the Antofagasta-Salta railway, with many bridges and tunnels. At km 376, a tributary river comes from the left and the ravine widens out, but it is still hemmed in by sheer rock walls.

Then follows a stretch of 65 km along the bottom of a ravine, where the stream is forded 11 times; in winter, the fords inevitably are wiped out. At km 441 is a wide valley where the summer resort of **Campo Quijano** is located. Then, a 24 km stretch of paved road to reach **SALTA**, at km 457.

PUBLIC TRANSPORTATION

Antofagasta is served by interprovincial buses from Santiago and Arica. It is also a hub for regional traffic, with daily services to Tocopilla, María Elena, Pedro de Valdivia, and Taltal, in addition to several daily departures for Calama and Chuquicamata.

San Pedro de Atacama is served by two daily buses from Calama and one Sunday service from Antofagasta. Of the inland villages, only Toconao is served by regular bus services, with one departure on Sundays from Calama.

An excellent option is to travel by plane, with daily flights from Santiago and Arica to Anto–fagasta, and from Antofagasta to Calama. Both cities offer cars for hire, with or without a guide.

There are two weekly bus services from Antofagasta to Salta, Argentina, from October through March. There is also a weekly flight of Aerolíneas Argentinas from Antofagasta to Salta.

To Oruro, Bolivia, the Bolivian railway FCAB runs a weekly passenger service from Calama, coordinated with a bus from Antofagasta.

There are blue tourist taxis both at Antofagasta and Calama, offering rides to the inland villages, particularly San Pedro de Atacama.

2

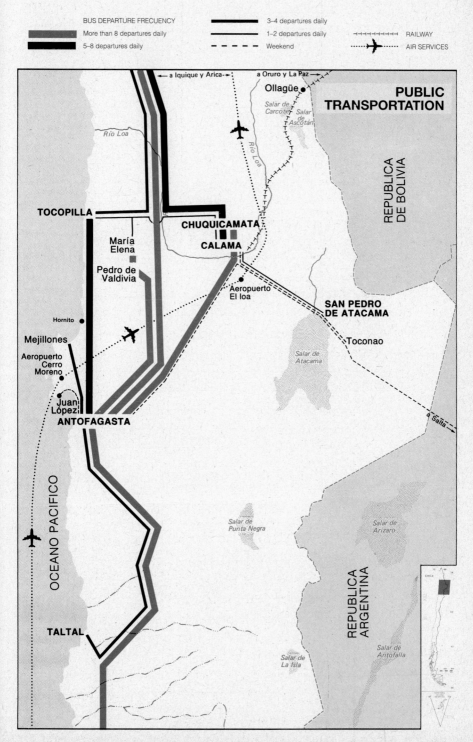

BUS DEPARTURE FRECUENCY

More than 8 departures daily
5–8 departures daily
3–4 departures daily
1–2 departures daily
Weekend

+++++++++ RAILWAY
··········✈ AIR SERVICES

PUBLIC TRANSPORTATION

a Iquique y Arica
a Oruro y La Paz
Ollagüe
Salar de Carcote
Salar de Ascotán
Río Loa
Río Loa

REPUBLICA DE BOLIVIA

TOCOPILLA
CHUQUICAMATA
María Elena
CALAMA
Pedro de Valdivia
Aeropuerto El loa
SAN PEDRO DE ATACAMA

Hornito
Toconao
Mejillones
Salar de Atacama
Aeropuerto Cerro Moreno
Juan López
ANTOFAGASTA
a Salta

OCEANO PACIFICO

Salar de Punta Negra
Salar de Arizaro

CHILE

TALTAL

REPUBLICA ARGENTINA

Salar de Antofalla

Salar de La Isla

Notes of This Zone

Zone 3
COPIAPO
and VALLENAR

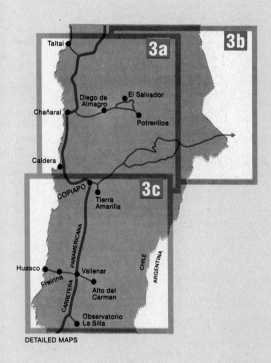

3a

Taltal

Diego de
Almagro

Chañaral

El Salvador

Potrerillos

Caldera

3b

3c

COPIAPO

Tierra
Amarilla

Huasco

Freirina

Vallenar

Alto del
Carmen

Observatorio
La Silla

PANAMERICANA

CARRETERA

CHILE

ARGENTINA

DETAILED MAPS

3

Arica

Iquique

Antofagasta

Easter
Island

Copiapó

La Serena

Is R
Crusoe

Valparaíso

SANTIAGO

Talca

Concepción

Temuco

Valdivia

Osorno

Pto Montt

Castro

Chaitén

Coihaique

Cochrane

Puerto Natales

Punta Arenas

Puerto Williams

Is Diego
Ramirez

90°   60°   53°

CHILEAN
ANTARCTIC
TERRITORY

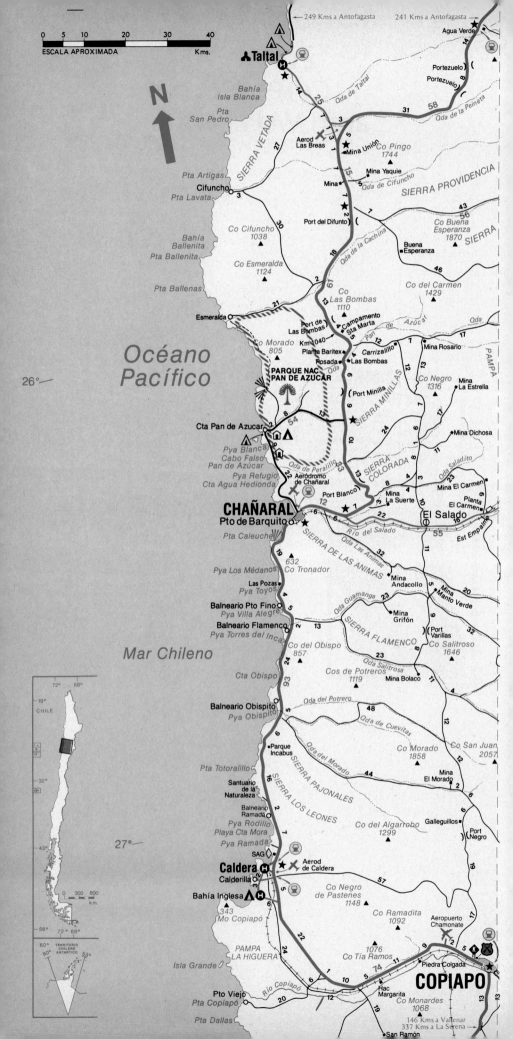

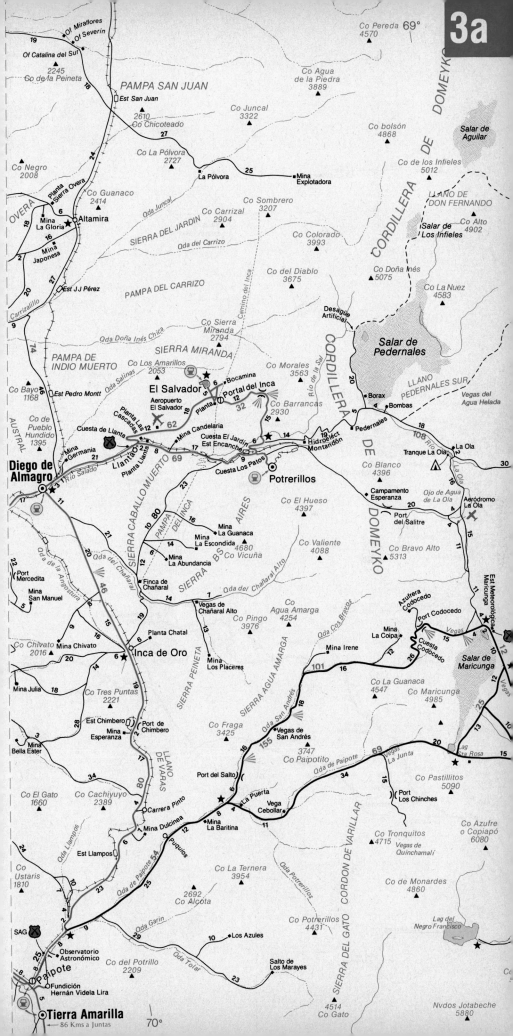

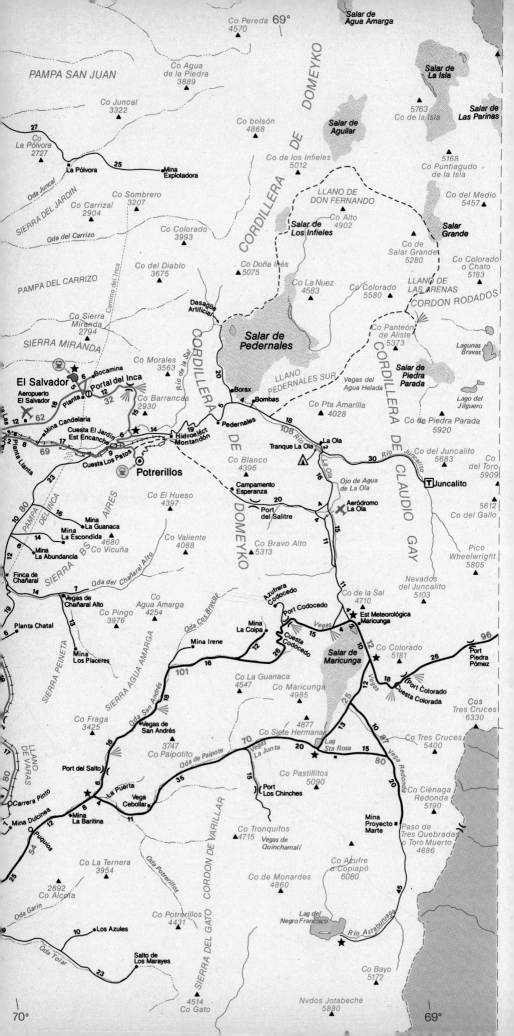

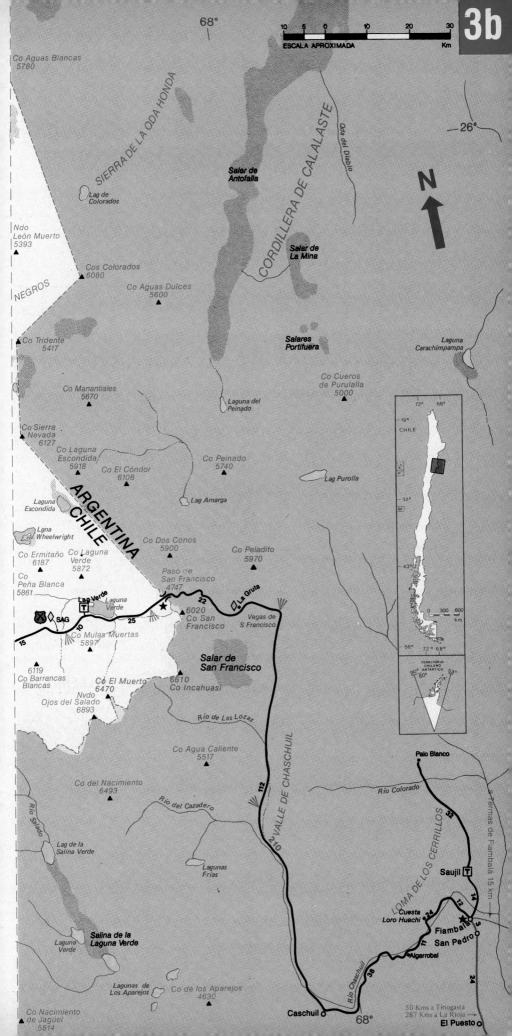

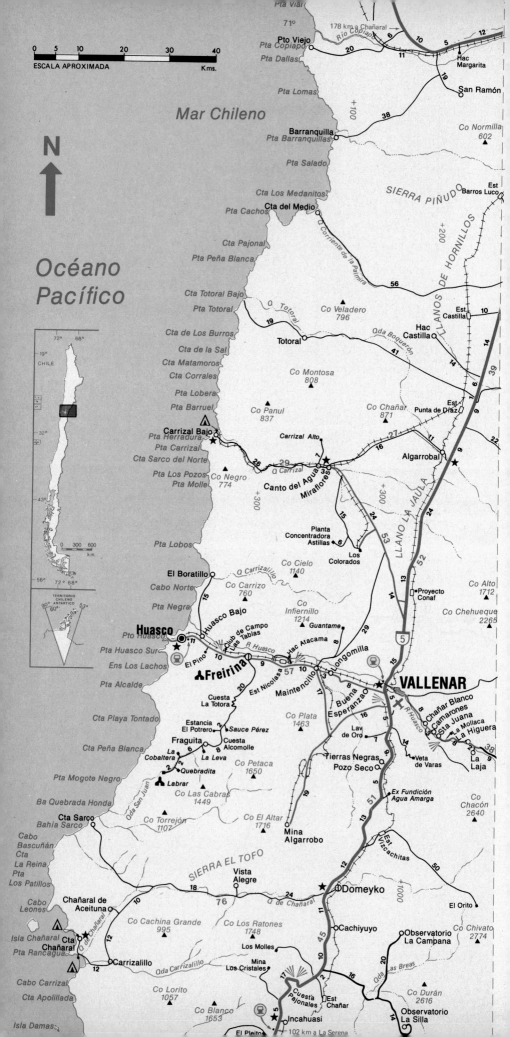

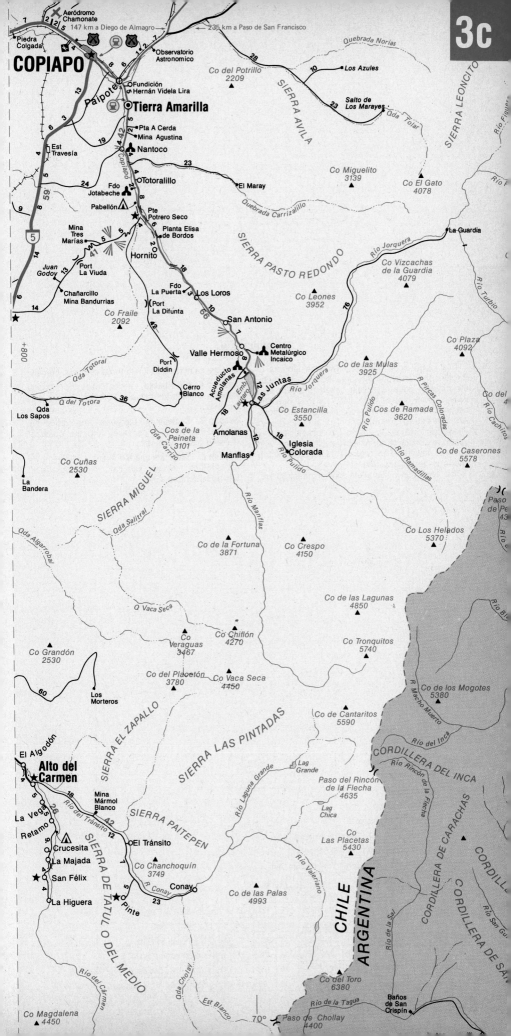

3

OVERVIEW

This tourist zone coincides with the territory of Region III (Atacama). An area rich in contrasts, the traveller goes from vast desert plains to lush valleys, from high-altitude salt flats to a beautiful national park preserving coastal fauna and flora. An interesting phenomenon is the so-called «flowering desert», triggered by occasional rainy years: the onset of spring carpets the desert with colorful flowers. The region's history of mining efforts is particularly rich.

The zone has a complete tourist infrastructure, and we have divided it into three sections, namely;

Section A   Río Huasco   it comprises the Huasco river basin, with the cities of Vallenar, Freirina and Huasco.

Section B   Copiapó and the Coast   the capital city of this Region, plus its valley and the coast of Caldera and Chañaral.

Section C   Salt Flats and the Andes   a little-known world of high-altitude salt flats, including the El Salvador copper mine.

REGIONAL DISTANCES

Alto del Carmen

258	Bahía Inglesa
262	5	Caldera
188	70	74	Copiapó
355	98	93	167	Chañaral
339	165	160	151	67	Diego de Almagro
401	227	222	213	129	62	El Salvador
296	178	182	108	275	251	313	Lautaro Dam
70	250	254	180	347	331	393	288	Freirina
97	277	281	207	374	358	420	315	27	Huasco
383	126	121	195	28	111	173	303	375	402	Pan de Azúcar National Park
349	231	235	286	328	387	449	386	341	368	356	San Francisco Pass
243	125	129	180	222	281	343	280	235	262	250	106	Maricunga Salt Flat
446	272	267	258	174	107	70	358	438	465	218	494	388	Pedernales Salt Flat
26	284	288	214	381	365	427	322	96	123	409	375	269	472	San Félix
38	220	224	150	317	301	365	258	32	57	345	436	330	408	64	Vallenar

Zone 3
COPIAPO and VALLENAR

DIVISION BY SECTIONS

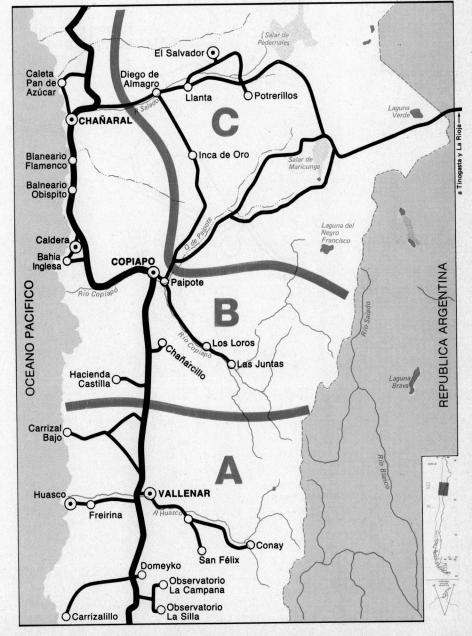

DETOURS OFF THE PAN-AMERICAN HIGHWAY

In this Zone we propose:

1 A Visit to Huasco ★★ a round trip of 114 km on a paved road, visiting an interesting port with a terminal for loading iron ore. Nice beach, Tour 3.

2 Through the Pan de Azúcar National Park ★★★ the detour is 9 km longer than driving directly on the Pan-American highway; good gravel road. Fine beaches, beautiful scenery, interesting fauna, Tour 6.

3 The Desert Route ★★★ fifty-one km longer than through the Pan-American highway, this detour is paved throughout. Interesting mine works, Tour 7, and, Tour 3.

4 The Salt Flat Route ★★★ this is what you would call travelling off the beaten track. Allow at least two days for this detour through fantastic, little-known high-Andean country, superb wildlife, Tours 1 & 2.

5 Return through Argentina ★★★ a very beautiful -albeit rough- road through rugged country, advisable for groups of two vehicles. Described under, Tour 1.

3

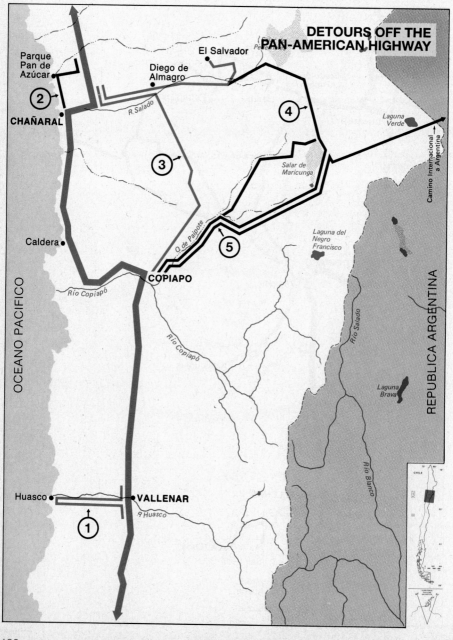

THE LAND, ITS HISTORY, ITS PEOPLE

DESCRIPTION this is a transitional zone between the northern deserts and the fertile heartland. The climate is temperate, warm in the coastal area and cold up in the mountains. Mean annual rainfall fluctuates between 30 mm in Copiapó and Vallenar, and 100 mm at the Andes mountains.

Four distinct topographical units can be made up: the well-defined **Seaboard,** which is particularly wide in the areas of Huasco and Caldera, where the best beaches are found. The **Coastal Range,** low and with rounded hills, marches the length of this zone close to the coast. The **Central Depression** runs smoothly between both mountain ranges, interrupted only by the transverse Copiapó valley. And the **Andes Mountains,** with Chile's highest peak, Ojos del Salado (6,893 m).

The Andes fork into two parallel ranges opposite Copiapó: **Domeyko** and **Claudio Gay,** a new depression lying between them. This basin has no outlet, thereby giving rise to salt flats, and it stretches northward -with some interruptions- up to the Atacama salt flat, where it veers into Bolivia with the Uyuni salt flat and lake Poopo, to end at lake Titicaca.

No other rivers flow to the ocean between the Loa river in the north and the Copiapó river, several hundred kilometers south. The snow from the Andes melts into the upper basin and stays there, impeded to flow westward by the Domeyko Range.

EARLY INHABITANTS different Indian tribes dwelled in the coastal strip and in the valleys.

Diaguitas they were a farming people dwelling in the valleys from La Ligua to Copiapó (see Land & History Zone 4).

Changos they were a semi-nomadic people dwelling on the coast from Arica to the Itata river and living of the sea. Few in numbers, they were superb swimmers and divers, sailing in rafts made of inflated seawolf skins. They disappeared late last century, absorbed by the new mining and port activity on the coast. R.A. Philippi, who surveyed these coasts in 1853, describes them as peaceful nomads living in small groups in the vicinity of the few coastal areas with fresh water, men separated from women and children, without making families.

Incas they conquered Chile up to the Maule river by 1470. To consolidate their conquest, they set up mitimaes -farming communities- in the valleys with settlers from Peru, who brought with them new farming and mining techniques. The Inca Metallurgical Center, located in the Copiapó valley and known as Viña del Cerro, is worth a visit.

SPANISH DOMINATION Diego de Almagro crossed into Chile through the pass of San Francisco and paused to rest at the Copiapó valley in March 1536. Some time later, Pedro de Valdivia came from the north following the Inca Road, which ran on the Andean foothills; at the Copiapó valley he took possession for the first time of the territory the Spanish Crown had assigned him. At the Huasco valley he gave seeds and foreign birds to the local chieftain. The fertile valleys were soon divided among the Spaniards, and the natives were subjected to a serfdom system known as encomienda. It consisted of unpaid labor which the natives performed as a «tribute» to the king of Spain. The choleric Francisco de Aguirre had his encomienda in La Serena and an estancia in Copiapó, to where he would withdraw when his temper became too hot. He set out from here several times across the Andes, eventually founding and governing Tucumán in Argentina.

The Catholic Church established a Franciscan convent in Copiapó in 1662, and a curacy at Huasco Bajo in 1667.

The first village founded was Copiapó, in 1744, followed by Santa Rosa de Huasco (Freirina) in 1752 and Vallenar in 1789, founded personally by Ambrosio O'Higgins. The seaports acquired stable populations when mining started to boom, in the early 1800s.

At the end of the colonial period, a permanent Spanish population dwelled in the agricultural valleys, engaged in farming and busily prospecting for gold and silver; some important deposits were found. They would be the forerunners of an industry which, drawing on their experience, boomed during the 19th century.

EXPLORATION OF THE DESERT Chile lacked thorough knowledge of its territory. The only people travelling the paths of the Atacama wilderness were the natives, both coastal and high-plateau dwellers, who knew the location of the scant water springs or puquios. It wasn't until 1853 that the government undertook to carry out a systematic survey of the desert.

Diego de Almeyda a native of Copiapó, had a late start in mining, but became a tireless explorer. He discovered the famous Las Animas copper deposit and founded Chañaral. He also surveyed in three different occasions up to the last corner of the Atacama salt flat, discovering and exploiting mines which brought considerable wealth to the region. He undertook his last excursion into the desert in 1853, at the age of 73, accompanying the expedition of R.A. Philippi. Together with José Santos Ossa and Manco Moreno (see biography in Antofagasta Zone), he formed the trio of legendary desert explorers and wealthy miners.

Rodulfo Armando Philippi (Rudolf Armin), a German naturalist who arrived in Chile in 1851, was commissioned by the government to carry out a geographic, mining and natural-history survey of the Atacama wilderness. He set out from Copiapó in November 1853, surveying the coast up to Taltal and Paposo, to cross the desert up to San Pedro de Atacama and return to Copiapó through the Inca Road in May 1854.

Francisco San Román a geographer and mining engineer native of Copiapó, was appointed by the government as director of the 1883 Desert Exploration Expedition, which undertook to make a cartographic survey of the territory. It was the best equipped expedition and worked during five consecutive summers; all the current geographic names stemmed from this expedition.

Federico Philippi a son of the naturalist, was commissioned by the government to prepare a botanic and zoologic description of the high plateau, collecting plants and animals which were then stuffed and placed at the Museum of Natural History. He set out from Copiapó in January 1885 and, riding a mule for 90 days through the upper basin between the Cordillera arms, he reached the Huasco salt flat, proceeding then down to Pica and then Iquique.

MINING gold was discovered at Capote in the early 1700s, and the Royal Mines of Santa Rosa were immediately set up; these mines provided the gold from which the doubloons circulating in Chile during that century were made. The first copper shipment was loaded at Chañaral in 1824. The main shipping ports and the mines they served are described below:

Chañaral in 1823, Diego de Almeyda discovered **Las Animas,** exploiting them for over half a century. In 1833, copper was struck at **El Salado** and little

3

139

later at **Carrizalillo**. Chañaral had by then three smelters. **Potrerillos**, the largest copper mine in this Zone, went on stream in 1927.

Huasco and Carrizal Bajo these two seaports were used for exporting copper from the rich mines of **Labrar, Fraguitas, El Sauce** and **Carrizal Alto**. By 1832, A. Edwards Ossandón (founder of the newspaper El Mercurio) started his fortune fitting out mines in the area, and the Walker brothers opened a mineral purchasing house at Vallenar. In 1820 there was a copper smelter at Labrar and later at El Sauce, Huasco and Carrizal Bajo. They were active until the turn of the century.

Caldera it was the shipping port for the ores from the Copiapó valley, mainly copper from the rich mines of **Amolanas, El Checo** and others, and of some silver mines such as **Tres Puntas**, until silver was struck at Chañarcillo.

Chañarcillo was discovered in 1832 by the prospector Juan Godoy. It was the third largest mine in America and a great source of wealth for the region and the whole country. Its owners were many Copiapó natives or people who had settled in this region, exploiting different holdings in the silver mountain. Foreign entrepreneurs -mainly Englishmen- did not participate actively at Chañarcillo; it was mostly a Chilean effort which brought about a new industrial, financial and political elite playing a major role in Chile's history.

A temporary town sprang up near the mine, becoming the Region's second largest settlement. The ore purification process required great quantities of energy and water, the ore being therefore hauled by mule to the Copiapó river. Between the city and Pabellón, a sizable industry fed from Chañarcillo took form, with twenty hydraulic mills and over 120 amalgamation troughs.

RAILWAYS mining was the driving force behind the construction of railway lines. In the desert, not only ore was hauled over long distances, but water as well. It is not surprising, therefore, that the first railway in South America was built here. All railway lines struck inland from a seaport, following a west-east course towards the mountains. Not until this century did the State build a railway running north-south and joining the various private lines. The seaport terminals had the necessary facilities for assembling, maintaining and repairing the rail equipment, which was supplied mostly by England or the United States.

Three private railways were built here, each belonging to a partnership formed by mine owners, the construction firms laying the railway, or the foreign suppliers. The main lines were:

Caldera-Copiapó inaugurated on December 25, 1851, was the first in South America. In 1854 branch lines from Pabellón to Chañarcillo and Paipote-Puquios were also inaugurated. By 1860, the railway was extended along the Copiapó valley up to San Antonio, in order to provide a more convenient outlet for the ore from Amolanas.

Carrizal Bajo the assembly shops were set up in 1866, to inaugurate the following year the line climbing the Carrizal ravine to the Carrizal Alto mine. Two branch lines were soon added, reaching into the central plain.

Chañaral the railway climbed through the El Salado ravine to the El Salado mine, inaugurated in 1871. A branch line was immediately built running south to the Las Animas mine and on through the central plain to Pueblo Hundido -now re-christened as Diego de Almagro. In 1925 the north-south branch from Pueblo Hundido to Puquios was finished, joining the Chañaral and Caldera railways.

Huasco this railroad reached Vallenar in 1892, and was built by a U.S. firm for the state railway company.

THE 1840-1865 PERIOD during this period, Copia-

pó concentrated Chile's new industrial, financial, mining, political, and intellectual elite. The owners of mining holdings at Chañarcillo and the processing plants at the Copiapó river were, among others, such familiar names in Chilean history as Goyenechea, Matta, Gallo, Cousiño, Ossa, Subercaseaux, Montt, Echeverría, and Carvallo.

In 1840, Agustín Edwards Ossandón moved from Vallenar to Copiapó to set up his Casa de Compra de Minerales, a sort of ore clearing house specializing as well in fitting out mines. When the Caldera railway partnership was formed in 1849, the shareholders were Agustín Edwards, Matías Cousiño, Tomás Gallo, Vicente Subercaseaux, Diego Carvallo, Blas and Gregorio Ossa, José M. Montt, J. Santos Cifuentes and William Wheelwright. This last partner was the one who built the railway.

Intellectual life in Copiapó was in full swing. A literary journal called El Copiapino and the works of José Joaquín Vallejo (pen name Jotabeche), an essayist, and of Guillermo Matta, a poet (both wealthy mining industrialists as well), achieved particularly high levels.

Two political events initiated in Copiapó had a profound impact throughout the country. In 1859, Pedro León Gallo took control of the city, setting in motion a liberal revolution against President Manuel Montt; it spread to the rest of the country but it was suppressed that same year. In 1863, Manuel Antonio Matta and P. León Gallo founded in Copiapó the Chilean Radical Party.

Europe exerted a strong cultural and social influence, attracting both intellectuals and businessmen. M.A. Matta studied philosophy and political science for five years at English and French universities. Francisco Echeverría, owner of the rich Constancia and Delirio silver lodes at Chañarcillo, travelled frequently to Paris, where he brushed with the Parisian rich and mighty. He had his wedding ceremony at the La Madeleine church with Teresa Blanco, a daughter of admiral Blanco Encalada; the main witnesses were no less than Emperor Napoleon III and Empress Eugenia. He returned to settle at Copiapó, where, years later, during the inauguration of a new ore processing plant at Totoralillo -opposite Jotabeche's hacienda-, his wife's Parisian dress got tangled up in rotating machinery and she was crushed to death.

Another noteworthy mine owner was Apolinario Soto, owner of rich silver lodes at Tres Puntas. He built the Italian-style Viña de Cristo villa, the most luxurious mansion in the entire Atacama province. Later, he built the beautiful neoclassical house and church of Nantoco.

By 1870, when the riches of Chañarcillo were near depletion, a good part of the fortunes it generated were inverted in other areas of the country, and the main characters emigrated to the new centers of economic and political activity, in Valparaíso and Santiago.

ARCHITECTONIC RELICS many buildings have survived from the silver mining heyday, and are described in the corresponding tours, particularly the churches, drawings of some of which accompany this text. The building tradition inherited from the Spaniards was rather primitive, consisting in the main of a wooden framework lined with branches and mud, and roofing of reeds and mud. Two developments brought new construction techniques and architectural styles:

Arrival of Foreign Carpenters and Builders Both the mines and the railways needed supporting infrastructure in the form of storage buildings, warehouses, workshops and railway stations. They could not be built using the traditional technology; therefore, British and U.S. specialists were brought to build these industrial installations, as well as new houses and churches in a marked English neoclassical style.

New Construction Materials the merchant ships plying the Pacific coast to California brought new construction materials from there. The main ones were **Oregon pine** sawnwood -a conifer which is neither a pine (it is pseudostuga) nor from Oregon, but from northern California-, an excellent timber. **Guayaquil cane** was a hollow bamboo of large diameter. It was sliced lengthwise and then flattened, the walls opening up but remaining connected through the nodes. The resulting material was a flat board about 50 cm wide and 9 m long. These two new materials permitted ingenious building solutions.

Construction Techniques all buildings were made of wooden walls. The Cathedral Church had a system of double walls 130 cm apart. This technique made it possible to reach great heights without need of intermediate strengthening devices. This church has withstood two massive earthquakes.

Most ingenious is the lining of the woodwork with Guayaquil cane boards. They were nailed horizontally on both faces of the wall, and then stuccoed with mud to a smooth finish. Hardly anyone could tell just by looking at them what the construction technique employed was, as the walls have no cracks; they seem to be works of masonry. This technique was developed locally, and made possible by the nearly total lack of rain.

Architectural Styles the houses show a predominant neoclassical style, with windows framed by wooden pilasters and pillared porticos. A special case is the Viña de Cristo villa, built in an Italian renaissance style, with elaborate balconies of imported wrought iron. The churches (see illustrations) have a marked English neoclassical influence, particularly evidenced by the position and preponderance of the bell tower over the central volume. The towers are interesting, made entirely of wood, with carefully worked pillars, columns and cornices.

PRESENT DEVELOPMENT four fields are dominant in the development of Region III:

Mining it is the most important activity, consisting mainly of copper and iron ore, and non-metallic products such as barium sulphate and

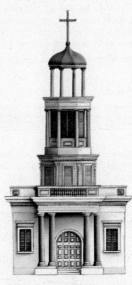

Piedra Colgada

Belén

✱ Nantoco

✱ National Monument

✱ Catedral

141

marble. An interesting local feature is that hundreds of small mining outfits account for a large share of the total output.

Copper the main mine is El Salvador, accounting for about 9% of the total output of Chile's so-called Large Mines. It has its own infrastructure including a concentration plant, a smelter at Potrerillos and a shipping port at Barquitos.

Iron over half of Chile's large iron ore mines are located in the Vallenar Province, with the Santa Fe, Algarrobo and Los Colorados mines. They belong to the Cía. Minera del Pacífico (CMP), with a pellet plant and mechanized ore loading at Huasco. At Caldera 2 there are also mechanized wharves for loading iron ore.

Barium Sulphate A non-metallic substance in great international demand, used primarily for lubricating oil drills. Annual output is about 250 thousand tons, extracted by small mining outfits at the Las Bombas, Chañarcillo and Domeyko areas.

Marble quarried at the El Tránsito valley in Vallenar; these are the only quarries in Chile producing marble for construction, the best varieties being white and red marble.

Agriculture although the area suitable for agricul-

ture does not exceed 42,000 hectares, the favorable climate more than makes up for the scantiness in area. The most significant plantations are vines and olive trees.

Vineyards state-of-the-art computerized drip irrigated farms produce table grapes and grape juice concentrate in the Copiapó valley upstream from the city. They produce the first grapes in the country, fetching good prices in the market. These are Chile's most expensive agricultural lands.

Olive Trees over 1,100 hectares of olive orchards stretch along the Huasco valley from Freirina to the coast, the largest extension of such plantations in Chile. They produce table olives and olive oil.

Fishing the main fishing ports are Caldera, Chañaral and Huasco. There are 10 large fishing companies at present.

Tourismo the reliable weather and natural beauty of its coast, desert and high-altitude salt flats have fueled a strong increase in tourist arrivals in this Region, with excellent hotels and other facilities throughout the Zone. Caldera and Huasco concentrate the largest number of summer tourists.

SECTION A   HUASCO

It stretches from the Los Choros ravine in the south to another ravine emptying into Carrizal Bajo in the north; it is slashed half way up by the Huasco river valley. Its capital city is Vallenar, a major agricultural center renowned for its olives. It is also the heart of Chile's iron ore mining. The Pan-American highway runs across a vast plain which, during the occasional «flowering desert», deserves a special visit.

There is nice scenery both in the mountain valleys and in the coast.

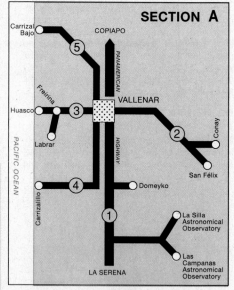

1 PAN-AMERICAN HIGHWAY FROM LA SERENA TO

VALLENAR ★★★ *198 km on a paved road, climbing two mountain ranges on long but not steep stretches. Best to fill up with gasoline at La Serena.Southern section of the Pan-Am described on Zone 4 Section C Tour 1.*

A foretaste of the desert, with interesting astronomical observatories and mining works in the vicinity.

At km 4 from La Serena there is a toll (to be paid by those headed south). To the right, the railway is blackened by iron ore dust.

At km 9 there is a police road control, and a road branching right to the **El Romeral iron mine**. It has an output of 4 million ton/year, hauled by its own railway line to the Guayacán port. Request permission to visit at P P Muñoz 675, La Serena.

Opposite the road control is the former cement factory of Juan Soldado. The limestone for the water fountains at the La Serena market is extracted from here.

At km 10 a road branches right to **Teatinos beach and cape** (described under La Serena Zone). Three km ahead is a straight climb known as Porotitos. The road runs close to the coast, but hidden from it. Some deep ravines are crossed and at km 31 is the **Juan Soldado bridge**, with a slender concrete arch. Five km farther, a last peek at the ocean, at the great Hornos bay. It won't be seen again until Caldera, almost 400 km farther north.

Caleta Hornos the Pan-American highway descends to Caleta Hornos at km 37: a few houses and trucker restaurants next to rock outcrops, a small beach and a dock. A vast beach stretches to the north.

The road then crosses a ravine and then turns inland. At km 41 a road branches left to Cruz Grande and Temblador beach (described in La Serena Zone). Ahead is a mountain range, the **Cuesta Buenos Aires,** climbed in 11 winding kilometers. Nice views.

Beyond the pass at the top a vast plain unfolds, flanked by tall hills. **This is the area, all the way to Copiapó, where the desert blooms in a sudden explosion of colors carpeting the entire plain after the occasional rainy winter (every three to ten years).** A road branches right at km 59 to La Higuera, a major mine last century, now a village. To the right, eucalyptus trees can be seen on the crest of a carved up sierra: here was the great **El Tofo** mine, once the world's largest iron ore mine, the mineral extracted in an open pit from 1914 to 1960; it was property of the U.S.'s Bethlehem Steel Co. The railway running from there to the Cruz Grande seaport was the first electrified railroad in South America. All that is left now are the ruins of the American quarter

3

at the summit, surrounded by eucalyptus. Here is also the **Camanchaca Project**, run by Conaf (the Chilean forest service). It harvests moisture from the heavy fogs rolling in nightly from the coast, using large towers supporting a dense web of threads. A road winds down to the sea: nice scenery and interesting wildlife.

At km 77 the road descends into the large Los Choros ravine and a dry river bed running to the west. A sizable underground river runs the length of the valley, which should support agriculture in this area -perhaps with drip irrigation- in the near future. A road branches off to some mines, to the Santa Dominga ore processing plant and to an experimental agricultural plot run by Conaf.

At km 80 is the village of **Los Choros,** with weird large-winged mills and small orchards, a chapel and an ore grinding project.

The road climbs out of the ravine; from km 89, the **Pozo Colorado** farm can be seen in the distance, like an island in the desert. At Pozo Colorado the road veers north, running alongside the railway.

At km 99 is a restaurant with gasoline supply at the foot of the huge waste dumps of the extinct **Santa Fe** iron ore mine.

Incahuasi is at km 103, at the end of the small, narrow ravine through which the old Inca Road used to run. Its name indicates that here was a house for the Inca.

At km 115 the road starts to zigzag up the Pajonales range; beyond the summit, at km 121, a large desert plain unfolds, the land becoming increasingly arid. At km 125 is an unsigned roundabout which is part of the road linking an iron ore mine and the railway station. This is part of the Santa Fe mining complex, one of the four large iron ore mines under exploitation. There is a restaurant and gasoline station at the roundabout.

| LA CAMPANA AND LA SILLA OBSERVATORIES | two mountain tops in the Cordillera are bedecked with telescope domes and related buildings: La Silla in the south and La Campana in the north. The former belongs to the Munich-based European Southern Observatory and the latter is administered by a U.S. institution. These two, together with the Tololo observatory inland from La Serena, are the most important observatories in the Southern Hemisphere. This location was selected on the basis of the remarkable lack of humidity and the record number of clear nights in a year. The road to both observatories branches off to the right at km 127. La Silla can be visited (request permission at Colina del Pino, casilla 601, T. 224680, La Serena).

Cachiyuyo at km 135, is an orderly village smack in the middle of the desert, with an afforestation project aiming at growing trees for firewood.

Domeyko (km 146) is an old mining town and railway station.

The road climbs to a pass and at km 170 it passes Agua Amarga and Pozo Seco, two humble groups of houses belonging to goat raising households. Stone walls surround some of them.

At km 190 is the irrigated plateau running along the Huasco river. A road branches left to the Algarrobo iron ore mine, the largest in the holdings of Cía. Minera del Pacífico. The road then starts to descend into the Huasco river valley, to reach a bridge at km 198. Here is a 2-km detour to the right leading to Vallenar.

| VALLENAR | (pop. 38,000), nestled at the bottom of the river valley amidst trees and palms and containing old, rambling houses, is the capital of the Huasco province. It is a busy farming and mining center. It was founded on Jan. 5, 1789, by orders of Governor Ambrosio O'Higgins, under

La Silla astronomical observatory

3

the name of San Ambrosio de Ballenary, in memory of his native town in Ireland. The governor, right after taking office at the age of 68, set out on a 6-month reconnaissance expedition, by horse and ship, of the northern territories up to Copiapó. On the return leg, he stopped at the Huasco valley and the Santa Rosa copper mines (Freirina). From quite early on during the colonial period the valley had been settled by Spaniards running encomiendas (see Land & History), mostly downstream all the way to the coast; there was a port at Huasco. To found Vallenar, O'Higgins chose personally the present location, at the midpoint between the coast and the Andean end of the valley.

In 1811, silver was struck at Agua Amarga (24 km south of Vallenar), and J.M. Carrera ordered the establishment of the Banco de Vallenar -the first bank in Chile- to «redeem silver pastes». In 1839, Alejandro and Guillermo Walker, who owned a mineral purchasing house (see map of Vallenar) issued the first private paper money; at their company, the young José Santos Ossa -later to become one of the region's great explorers- worked six years as an apprentice. Agustín Edwards Ossandón lived here 10 years, from 1832, starting the business of outfitting mines which would eventually make him rich.

An irrigation canal was built in 1823, the first of a large network now irrigating the vast fields around the city. In 1892 the railway from Huasco reached Vallenar. In 1959, the Cía. Minera del Pacífico started operations at their Santa Fe, Algarrobo and Los Colorados mines.

What To See Right beyond the bridge, to the left is the **steel building** of the Cía Minera del Pacífico. Turning right at Aldea is the **Museo del Huasco** (Tue-Fri 10.00-13.00h; 15.30-19.30h; Sat and Sun 10.00-13.00h.), exhibits include minerals and historical pictures. Across from it, at the Hostería, is a splendid sample of **Chilean palm**, the northernmost of its kind in Chile. At the **Vivero Municipal** -a tree nursery- there are old trees. A short way up the road to the inland valleys will give you a **panoramic view** of the city. Another **look-out** is up on the cliff following the street Verdaguer. At the main square there are some pavements and pedestals made of the local red marble.

Accommodation and Food Best hotel is Hostería de Vallenar, good cuisine. Good food at Club Social. Quick dishes at Bavaria, cheap meals at market food stalls. Picnic at the Vivero Municipal (grills and tables).

TOURS FROM VALLENAR

2 | TO THE INLAND VALLEYS | ★★★
a round trip of 212 km, with 190 km gravel road, slow. Fill up at Vallenar, food at San Félix. Allow one day.

Vallenar, desert blooms

A tour up a sinuous mountain valley, visiting villages where homemade pisco -a strong alcoholic beverage typical of Chile and Peru- is produced.

The road runs upstream from Vallenar (km 0) between arid hills and cultivated patches and fruit orchards. At km 11 the pavement gives way to gravel; the road is curvy and narrow.

The road crosses the river several times and sometimes it runs on ledges carved on the cliff face. Some settlements, vineyards and mining works are to be seen.

At km 15 is **Mollaca**, with a splendid view of the river gorge. The river carries a lot of water —for a desert. At km 25 is the hamlet of **La Laja**, with large avocado trees. At km 38 is the confluence

of the El Carmen and El Tránsito rivers, becoming then the Huasco river. The **El Carmen** river valley is predominantly agricultural, the original inhabitants being Spaniards running encomiendas. The **El Tránsito valley** has both farms and mines, including Chile's best marble quarries, ranging from pure white to the rare Vallenar red marble. The last scattered aborigines of the Huasco valley were relocated here.

One km into the El Carmen valley is

Alto del Carmen a small village with a church built in 1826 and restored on several occasions thereafter. Mass on Sat. at 2000h. The roofing is supported by logs, and the ceiling used to be of a colored fabric.

SAN FELIX the valley is intensely cultivated. At km 45 is **El Rosario**, a farm with large grapevines and two gold-mining works by the roadside. At km 64 is

the largest village in the valley, dates from the Conquest times. A church presides over the quaint, shady main square. Opposite is the Los Paltos restaurant.

Nearby is the **Horcón Quemado** pisco distillery (can be visited during working hours Mon.-Sat.; outside of working hours, ask at the adjacent house). Considered the best *pisco* in the North, it is produced using non-industrial techniques, with copper containers heated with firewood and having a peculiar refrigerating system. You may buy several varieties of pisco and other liquors.

Back downstream to **Alto del Carmen** (km 91), fol-

☎ Telephone Center	**A** Town Hall (1C)
★ Touristic Information	**B** Parish Church (2C)
◉ Café, Meeting Point	**C** Post Office (1C)
ⓖ Gasoline Station	**D** Bus Terminal (1C)
⮞ Lookout Point	**E** Railway Station (2C)
✳ Hospital (1D)	**F** Minera del Pacifico Company (2D)
	G Museum of Huasco (2D)

H Municipal Stadium (2D)	**3** H Ro-Del (2D)
J Swimming Pool (2D)	**4** H Cecil (2D)
K Rodeo Arena (3B)	
L Quinta Zlatar (1F)	**RESTAURANTS**
	1 Hs de Vallenar (2D)
ACCOMMODATIONS	**3** H Ro-Del (2D)
1 Hs Vallenar (2D)	**10** Club Social (2C)
2 H Real de Turismo (2C)	**13** Venecia (2C)

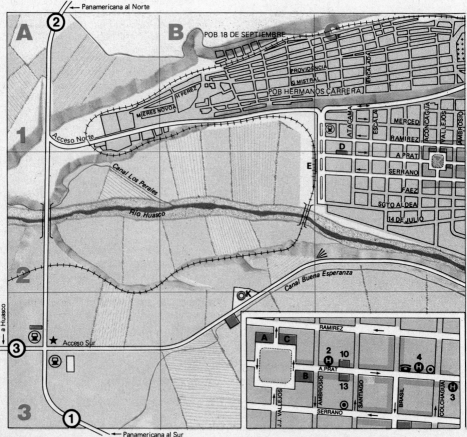

low now the El Tránsito valley, with several villages built in Indian architecture. At km 112 are the white marble quarries, 98% calcium carbonate.

Farther ahead you cross the Chanchoquín ravine, with a road branching left and 150 ha of plantations producing export-quality grapes and melons. Following the El Tránsito river upstream, you pass the **Chanchoquín** village, straddling the river, and at km 121 you reach **El Tránsito**, the largest village in the valley, with an old church on the square. Food at Pensión Santa Anita.

Continuing 7 km up the valley, you turn 5 km to the right, climbing out of the Pinte ravine, arid and with interesting geologic formations and marine fossils, to reach.

PINTE an oasis with a white church tower rearing above the greenery. The place is renowned for its loom-woven textiles, using wool dyed with roots.

To return to Vallenar, retrace the road. If you are adventure-minded and have a good vehicle, continue 40 km farther up the valley through Conay almost to the headwaters of the river, with sheer cliffs plunging over 100 m and some pods suitable for bathing.

3 ALONG THE VALLEY TO HUASCO ★★★

fifty-seven km one way, on a paved road. Gasoline at Huasco. Allow one day.

An excursion along the fertile Huasco valley, through the interesting town of Freirina and ending at the mining port and seaside resort of Huasco.

Leave Vallenar (km 0) heading for the Pan-American highway; at the junction south of the river, take the road heading west, towards the coast. The road

☎	Telephone Center	2	Church (NM)	4	El Uranio Restaurant		
1	Town Hall (NM)	3	Callejas House	5	Rearte Factory	6	Olives Factory

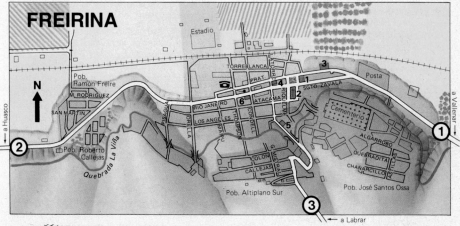

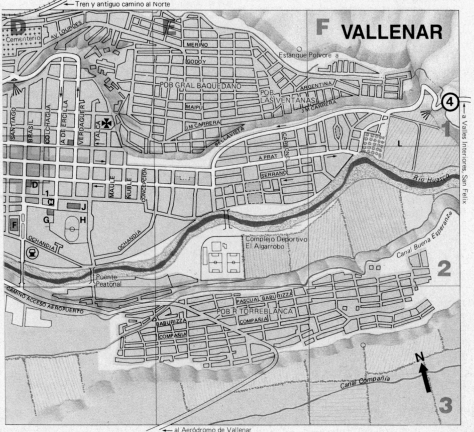

145

runs on a plateau above the valley; alfalfa fields can be seen on the plateaux at both sides of the valley. At Loncomilla and Buena Esperanza are the buildings of some old haciendas.

At km 17 is the busy **Maitencillo station,** a railway junction receiving and forwarding mineral shipments from the **Algarrobo mine** to the south, the **Los Colorados mine** to the north, and the Santa Fe mine, much farther south.

At km 25, on the northern bank, is the **Hacienda Atacama,** with a nice neoclassical house.

At km 27 are the first **olive orchards,** which will become a common site all the way to the coast. The dark-leaved, thick-stemmed trees grow both on the valley floor and the hillsides, and are sheltered by eucalyptus windbreaks. At km 36, almost unexpectedly, is

FREIRINA (pop. 3,500), a town with a rich tradition, the main town in the valley since colonial times. Founded as Santa Rosa de Huasco in 1752 and renamed Freirina in 1824, in honor of Ramón Freire, then Chile's highest authority, it has been a municipal head town since 1870.

Its importance was given by the mining industry. In 1699 prospectors struck gold at Capote, north of here; the mine's output supplied the gold used for most of the coins circulating during the colonial period. Between 1750 and 1790, copper was found at San Juan and **Labrar,** and later at **Fraguitas;** the mines were intensely exploited during the 19th century, when Chile was the world's number one copper producer. A new gold lode was found at Capote in 1923, giving a new boost to the town.

Freirina was an active center of merchants, entrepreneurs, mining engineers, and construction craftsmen, who left some interesting buildings, including some with shingled neoclassical façades and three that have been granted the National Monument status:

LOS PORTALES BUILDING (NM) a neoclassical building erected in 1870 as the seat of the government, now housing the municipal offices. It includes a central court and a high façade framed by nine circular arches ending in elaborate wooden columns.

CHURCH OF SANTA ROSA (NM) erected in 1869 with double Oregon-pine walls 40 cm apart, lined with Guayaquil cane and stuccoed with mud. The wooden tower ends up in a dome. Access to the three-nave interior is through three elaborate wooden doors. The church and the Los Portales building make up one side of the square, perhaps one of Chile's finest.

THE SMOKESTACKS OF LABRAR (NM) about 40 km south of Freirina is a copper smelter extinct since 1895. Two smokestacks survive, 18-m tall and made of brick brought from England, reinforced on the outside by metal bars. They are the only ones standing of the many which once dotted the North. The smelter's output was exported through the Peña Blanca port.

The (gravel) road to this place is lonely, climbing two ranges. The last inhabited place is Sauce Pérez. **Fraguita** and **Quebradita** were mining villages once boasting a square, post office, Registry Office, a school and a cemetery each, but they are now deserted. Right beyond these villages the two smokestacks rise in splendid solitude; a third one was knocked down to salvage the bricks.

At Freirina, the **Casa Callejas** is an art-nouveau house built in 1934.

A Tip superb olive oil can be found at Rearte (see map), where you can also watch the production process. Very good olives at the house of Mr Vega (nice house). Lunch at El Uranio. If you wish, you can order river shrimp (request in advance).

Back on the road to the coast, at km 39 is the Cía. Minera del Pacífico (CMP) country club. At km 45 is an olive oil factory (no sale to public). At km 48, next to the square of a village, is a road branching right to

Huasco Bajo the oldest native settlement in the valley. Pedro de Valdivia visited it when he arrived in Chile in 1540. In 1600 it was looted by Dutch pirate Oliver van Noort, who nevertheless praised the quality of its melons. The first church of the valley was also erected here, in 1667. Now it is a quaint hamlet with lush orchards. Restaurant Don Baucha is renowned, specializing in seafood.

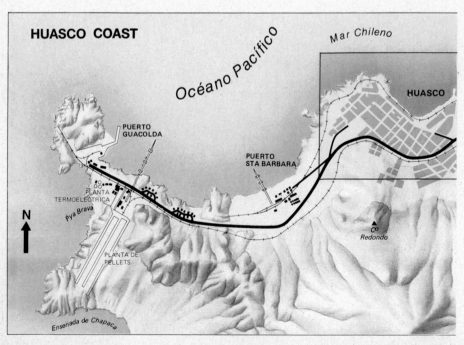

HUASCO COAST

Back on the main road, you will see the mouth of the valley on the sea, with large sand dunes, beaches and eucalyptus forests sheltering the olive orchards. At km 57 is

HUASCO (pop. 5,663), a seaport nestled on a bay flanked by tall hills. A port of call during the colonial period, it was occupied by Dutch pirate Oliver van Noort, who released here the Spaniards he had captured at Concepción, about a thousand kilometers to the south. In March 1681, Huasco fell prey to privateer Bartholomew Sharp.

During the 19th century, when the copper mining industry started to boom, it had a smelter and a railroad maintenance depot (1891), in addition to major trading houses and mining supplies companies, such as the one owned and ran by Agustín Edwards. The famous explorer José Santos Ossa was born here; he owed his prodigious swimming capacity to the teachings of the local Chango natives.

Huasco was levelled by an earthquake in 1922, most relics of the past gone forever. Now it is a busy mining port and seaside resort, with good accommodation at the Hostería, restaurants and nice beaches, such as **Playa Larga** at the town itself, and **Tres Playitas** and **Baratillo** farther north, accessible through a road starting from Huasco Bajo, across the river.

What To See walk along the Costanera, with a

☎ Telephone Center	**B** Church
⊙ Meeting Point	**C** Fishing Terminal
ⓖ Gasoline Station	**D** Bus Terminal
⋙ Lookout Point	**E** Post Office
A Town Hall	**F** Port Authority
	G Ex Customs House

H Agencia Maritima	
K Interesting House	

ACCOMMODATIONS
1 Hs de Huasco

RESTAURANTS
1 Hs de Huasco
5 Don Baucha
6 El Escorial
7 Las Delicias del Mar
8 Gratíssimo

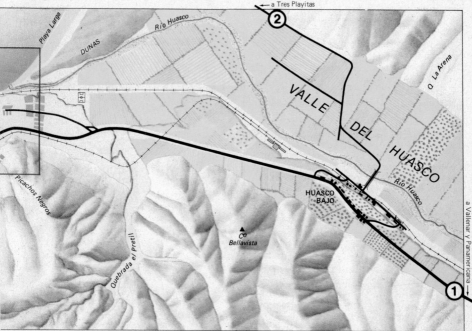

modern church an some old houses to the old port; good view from the fishing terminal. A short distance to the south is

GUACOLDA BAY with a scenery of barren hills and rocks covered by cacti and the ubiquitous black dust from the iron ore. There are two **mechanized wharves** property of CMP: the ageing **Las Rosas**, with a loading capacity of 1.5 million ton/year, and the new **Guacolda II**, with a capacity of 4 million ton/year. At the far end is the **Guacolda I** wharf, where material and implements for the pellet plant are unloaded.

4 TO THE DOLPHINS AT CHAÑARAL ISLAND ★★
a round trip of 254 km from Vallenar, with 102 km paved and the rest gravel. Gasoline at Vallenar. Allow one day for this. Camping at Chañaral bay. Take water and food.
An interesting excursion across the Coastal Range to a cultivated oasis next to the sea, and then by boat from a fishing cove to an islet with remarkable wildlife.

Leave Vallenar (km 0) following the Pan-American highway up to Domeyko (km 51). Take there the gravel road branching west, which soon crosses the Coastal Range through the gap formed by the Chañaral ravine. Deserted mining spots can be seen; at km 93 is a plain which rolls to the coast. At km 103 a road branches off to Chañaral de Aceitunas and at km 115 is **Carrizalillo**, a farming oasis with a chapel, a school and olive orchards. Continue to Carrizal bay, skirting the seashore towards the north to

Caleta Chañaral de Aceituna a small cove with a stony beach. Here you can hire a motor boat to take you, in one hour, to the **Chañaral island**, with a colony of 80 dolphins which romp and spring around the boat. It is a fascinating sight, particularly when you consider that dolphins are unknown in these waters. They appear to have been brought here by a stray warm current, taking a liking to the place and deciding to stay here.

5 TO THE COAST AT CARRIZAL BAJO ★★★
eighty-two km from Vallenar, 53 km of which are paved. Gasoline at Vallenar. Take food.
An excursion to a beautiful beach, popular in summer, and to an old mining port. It is an interesting detour for those wishing to continue to the North.

Leave Vallenar (km 0) following the Pan-American highway to the north. At km 15, take road branching left to the **Los Colorados** iron mine. At km 53 the road starts to cross the Coastal Range along the Carrizal ravine. In the past, a railway ran through here and at **Canto de Agua**, surrounded by small cultivated patches, there was a service town and railway station serving the famous **Carrizal Alto** copper mine, discovered by 1800. The road continues down the ravine to the coast, with many abandoned iron ore and copper mines, to reach at km 82

Carrizal Bajo with a nice, good beach next to the ruins of a mining port. It is very popular in summer among camping fans; buses run on holidays from Vallenar.

In the past here was a village of 1,000 people, with a church, customs office, hospital, post office, Registry, ore processing plants, maintenance depots and a wharf. In 1866, English railway technician John North came here to assemble the locomotives for the railway then being laid inland. He was to become the Saltpeter King.

Among botanists, Carrizal Bajo is renowned for its beautiful **Lion Paw** plant, a type of Alstroemeria with lovely flowers discovered by naturalist R.A. Philippi in 1873 and now listed as endangered. Do not disturb it. More recently, in 1986, Carrizal Bajo made the headlines as the site through which a huge arms shipment was smuggled into the country to arm terrorist movements.

For those wishing to continue to Copiapó, retrace the road up to the junction at km 29 from Carrizal Bajo, taking the road branching left which leads to the Algarrobal station on the Pan-American highway.

SECTION B   COPIAPO AND THE COAST

This section covers the entire basin of the Copiapó river, with the capital city of Region III, and the coast from Caldera and Bahía Inglesa in the south through Chañaral to the Pan de Azúcar National Park in the north.

The scenery offers some contrasts, and the main activities are farming, mining, and tourism. The climate is pleasant year round and the ocean water fairly warm in summer.

Copiapó, Caldera, Bahía Inglesa and Chañaral have good hotels and other tourist services.

1 PAN-AMERICAN HIGHWAY FROM VALLENAR TO
COPIAPO ★★★ *a 150-km stretch of good, paved road. Gasoline only at Vallenar and Copiapó.*
A nearly straight road running through a plain covered with cacti and shrubs. It is the «antechamber» to the real desert farther ahead. This is also «flowering desert» area after rainy winters.

The Pan-American highway climbs out of Vallenar and the Huasco valley to a plain stretching northward. At km 15 the road approaches the Coastal Range, and a road branches off to the left for Carrizal Bajo. At km 20 another road branches left to Carrizal Bajo. To the right is the volcano-looking Chehueque hill and next to the road, a Conaf trial plot to test algarrobo adaptation.

Vegetation here is mostly creeping plants and cacti; now and then, herds of donkeys can be seen browsing. At km 52 the road descends into

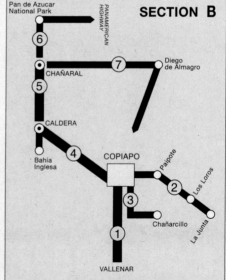

the dry bed of the Algarrobal ravine, about 3 km wide; here is the Algarrobal railway station, a junction where the railway to the Los Colorados iron ore mine starts, as well as another road to the coast.

At km 62 is the boundary of the Huasco province. At km 77 is a restaurant and a road branching left to **Estancia Castilla,** a large experimental farm in the midst of the desert, established two decades ago by a visionary entrepreneur.

At km 91 is a signposted turn-off to the right leading in 14 km to the Bandurrias mine, at the legendary **Chañarcillo** hill, America's second largest silver mine, discovered in 1832. It is an interesting excursion to be made in one hour (described under Tour 3).

At km 138, a long descent into the Copiapó valley starts, to reach the city at km 150.

COPIAPO (pop 70,000) is the capital of Region III, Atacama. It lies at the bottom of the Copiapó river valley and originally consisted of three different sections: the **San Francisco convent and church,** established in 1662 at the foot of La Cruz hill; the **Prat square,** the heart of the village founded in 1774; and the **San Fernando Indian village,** nowadays a group of orchards and cultivated plots lying to the east of the city.

The valley, called Copayapu by the native Diaguita indians, was intensely cultivated when Diego de Almagro arrived in 1536. Pedro de Valdivia took possession for the first time of the territory assigned him by the Spanish king in 1540.

The valley was soon occupied by Spaniards running encomiendas (see Land & History). The village was founded in 1744 to gather the scattered population and, in 1832, the herdsman and prospector Juan Godoy struck silver at the fabulous deposit of Chañarcillo, spurring an extraordinary boom which left some interesting architectonic works and the first railway in South America, running between Caldera and Copiapó.

This area has experienced a new boom in recent years, fueled particularly by fruit exports and new mining projects.

What To See Universidad de Atacama it is housed in a neoclassical building previously housing the Mining School founded in 1857. In one of the courtyards is the

Locomotora Copiapó the first train running in South America (Dec 25, 1851). Built by Norris Brothers of Philadelphia in 1850, it also has a luggage wagon and passenger cars with first, second and third classes. The cars in the different classes differ only in the type of seats and interior decoration. The coal car is missing. On one side is an old grinding stone for mineral ores, known as maray.

VIÑA DE CRISTO VILLA (NM) (see map), a palace built in 1860 by mining tycoon Apolinario Soto, owner of the Tres Puntas silver mine, was in its day the most luxurious mansion in Copiapó. Two lateral wings were torn down in 1958, and now the building houses the extension department of the Universidad de Atacama.

Following Av Copayapu to the east, running among orchards of the old village of **San Fernando** now gobbled up by Copiapó-, you reach **Paipote** in 5 km, an old, large copper smelter. Best seen from 500 m into the road to Diego de Almagro.

Santuario de la Candelaria (see map) it is a wide esplanade with a church built in 1800 and another one built in 1922. It originated as a place of worship of a 14-cm stone image resembling the Virgin, found in 1780 by herdsman Mariano Caro. The Fiesta de la Candelaria attracts now on the first Sunday in February over 5,000 gaily-clad religious dancers known as chinos, belonging to different confraternities; it is one of the major religious-folkloric festivities in Chile.

BELEN CHURCH (see map), built in 1856 by the Fraga family as a private chapel adjacent to their residence. Of beautiful proportions, it has a small garden in front and the furnishings and statuary were brought from France. Ask for permission to visit at the school adjacent to it.

Avenida Matta (see map), lined by shady trees, is the site of the first Spanish settlement in the valley. Here is the **Cripta de los Héroes,** in memory of the soldiers of the Atacama battalion fallen during the War of the Pacific. Across from it is the **Railroad Employee Residence** (NM), a neoclassical building erected in 1860 in wood with doric columns.

Farther down the avenue is a monument to **Manuel Antonio Matta** and, at the end of the avenue, a memorial to Diego de Almagro. Across from it is the statue of **Juan Godoy,** depicting a small man with strange shoes made of animal bladders, as was usual among poor prospectors at the time. A plate reads: «...discoverer of the Chañarcillo silver deposit on May 19th, 1832, the riches of which lifted Copiapó to the greatness it now enjoys...». It was financed by public contributions and commissioned in 1851 from Messenger Sands Manufacturers, Birmingham, England. It was first placed at the Plaza de Armas -the main square- and by 1870 moved -sort of demoted- to its present location.

On one side of the small square is the façade of the **Church of San Francisco** (mass Mon.-Sun. at 1900h), erected in late 1800. The interior was manufactured by Franciscan brethren. The church was built using the technique of wooden walls lined by stuccoed Guayaquil cane described under Land & History.

The **Railway Station** is a National Monument, built in wood in 1854 and restored in 1982. It contains a **Museum** (in summer, Mon-Sat 10.30-14.30h and 16.30-18.30h; sun 10.30-14.30h; off season, 09.30-13.30h and 15.30-18.30h.), with photographs and historical documents related to South America's first railroad.

The **Casa Matta** (NM) (see map) was the sprawling residence of the Matta-Goyenechea family, occupying an entire block. Here lived Guillermo Matta, the poet and industrialist, and his brother Manuel Antonio, the politician. The building was restored in 1982 in neoclassical style and now houses the **Regional Museum** (Tue.-Sat. 09.30h-12.45h and 15.30-19.00h, Sat until 18.30h., Sun and holidays, 10.00-13.00h), with historical exhibits.

Across from it is **House Maldini**. Originally it was the railway house at Caldera, and moved to this site by 1930.

PLAZA PRAT is the main square, or Plaza de Armas. In the old times it had no trees, but a beautiful wrought iron fence. At its center sat the statue of Juan Godoy. By 1880, the 84 trees were planted which today line it and shade it. In the center of it is a fountain and a marble statue, a French allegory of mining. It is traversed by 8-meter-wide alleys, and has four statues representing the four seasons.

Around the square are the buildings of the **Regional Government offices,** the old building housing the municipal offices, and the **Cathedral Church (NM)** (mass Mon-Sat 1900h, Sun. 0830, 1200 & 1930h). Built by the Englishman William Rogers in neoclassical style, it was inaugurated in 1851. Crowned by a large square wooden tower in three levels, the only of its type in Chile, its double wooden walls are separated by a 1.3-m gap, permitting one to walk between the walls. This gap is now used to hold the exhibits of the **Cathedral Museum.** The floor is paved with marble, and the front of the altar and the sacrarium are made of chiseled silver.

Also on the square is the **Mineralogical Museum** (see map) (Mon-Sat 09.00-13.00h and 15.00-

3

19.00h, Sun 10.00-15.00h). It is Chile's most complete and the second best in America, with excellent exhibits, including unusual ones such as meteorites found in the desert, and some ores and minerals only found at the Atacama desert.

Accommodations and Food Best lodging at Hostería Las Pircas, with a park and a swimming pool. Downtown, H. Diego de Almeyda and others shown in map.

Best cuisine at the above hotels. For meat dishes, the Bavaria. Quick dishes at the «meeting» cafes shown in map. Picnic at Parque El Pretil, by the river.

TOURS FROM COPIAPO

2 **THROUGH THE COPIAPO VALLEY** ★★★

a round trip of 216 km on a paved road. Gasoline at Copiapó and Tierra Amarilla. Food at Los Loros. Allow a whole day.

An excursion along a valley with a booming agroindustry and containing some national monuments.

Leave Copiapó (km 0) following the road to Paipote. The village of **Tierra Amarilla** is at km 14-15, with a pretty wooden gothic church.

The river now feeds the large agroindustries here, but in the past it powered ore mills and fed

other mineral processing installations. There used to be a railroad running upstream to San Antonio (see Tour 3). At km 24 are the

HOUSE AND CHURCH OF NANTOCO (NM) commissioned in 1870 by mining tycoon Apolinario Soto (the same of the Viña de Cristo Villa), is the valley's most architecturally interesting building. It includes a one-story manor house surrounded by a veranda supported by ten doric columns, and crowned by a lookout tower. Across from it a park spreads, with a church on one side. Only the church's façade and the bell tower -one of Atacama's most beautiful- remain.

Farther up the valley are large, drip-irrigated vine plantations; the water contains all the nutrients needed by the plant, the soil acting only as a mechanical support for it. The climate here makes the grapes ripen earlier than at any other location, fetching premium prices in foreign markets. Considerable investments have been made to make optimum use of this valley for export grape production, changing the landscape: there is a stark contrast between the arid hills and the green vines.

At km 34, on the right-hand side amid large shady trees, is the **house of Jotabeche** (José Joa-

---

☎ Telephone Center
★ Touristic Information
◉ Café, Meeting Point
Ⓖ Gasoline Station
✚ Hospital
A Regional Government Building (2C)
B Town Hall (3C)
T Bus Terminal (3C)
C Cathedral Church (NM) (3C)
D Mineralogical Museum (2D)
E Regional Museum (3A)
✳ F Railroad Museum
✳ G Locomotive 'La Copiapó' (NM)

ACCOMMODATIONS
1 Hs Las Pircas (4A)
2 H Diego de Almeyda (3C)
3 Hs Pan de Azúcar (4A)
4 H Montecatini (2C)
5 H Palace (3C)
✳ 6 H Archi Hotel
7 H San Francisco de la Selva (2B)
8 H Derby (3B)
9 Bh Plaza (3C)
10 Bh Chañarcillo (3C)

11 Bh Rodriguez (2B)
12 Bh Cristi (2B,2C)
13 Bh Torres (3B)
14 H La Casona (3A)
15 H Montecatini (3B)
16 H Flamenco (3B)
17 H España (2B)
18 Apart H Camasquil (2A)
19 H Inglés (3B)

RESTAURANTS
1 Hs Las Pircas (4A)
3 H Hs Pan de Azúcar (4A)
2 H Diego de Almeyda (3C)
20 A Chau (3C)
21 Bavaria (2B)
22 Pollo Stop (3C)
23 Rincón de la Papa (3B)
24 Galería (2C)
25 Hao Hwa (3C)
26 La Pizza de Tito (2C)
✳ 27 Corona del Inca
28 Restaurantes Populares (3C)

TOURIST SERVICES
2 Turismo Cristóbal (3C)

2 Lan Chile (3C)
32 Ladeco (2B)
33 Avis Rent a Car (3B)
34 Hertz Rent a Car (3C,4A)
35 Galerías Rent a Car (3B)
36 Rodaggio Rent a Car (3C)

BUILDINGS OF INTEREST
✳ G University of Atacama
✳ H Palacio Viña de Cristo (NM)
✳ F Railways Station (NM)
J Railways Employees' Residence (NM),(3A)
K Church of San Francisco (NM),(4A)
L House Gallo (3A)
M Church Belén (NM),(2B)
C Cathedral (NM) (3C)
B Municipal Building (NM),(3C)
N House Toro Lorca (NM),(3C)
✳ P La Candelaria Sanctuary

DISCOTHEQUES
✳ 40 Salón Top Top
✳ 41 Boite El Cortijo
✳ 42 La Carreta

✳ See location in general map of Copiapó

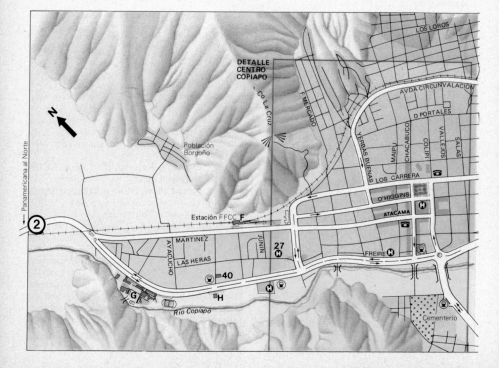

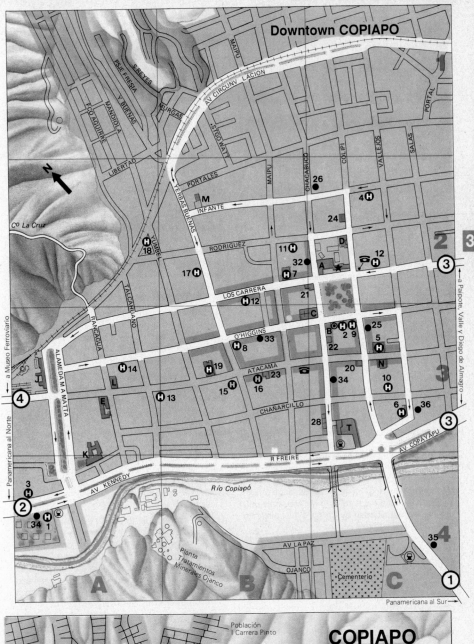

Downtown COPIAPO

COPIAPO

Copiapó, Inca Metallurgical Center

quín Vallejo), a mining entrepreneur, politician and essayist who lived and died here (1858).

At km 38 are the ruins of **Pabellón,** the point from where the branch railway to Chañarcillo started. Opposite, a basic **campground.**

At km 42 is a signposted road (very badly surfaced, bumpy) branching right to Cerro Blanco, following the roadbed of the Chañarcillo railroad.

At km 48, on the left, the ancient mine of **Elisa de Bordo** can be seen, the houses of which were reached by cable ferry. The road runs through a narrow gap from km 50 to 56; at Fundo La Puerta, to the right on the river bank, you may request permission to cross the river and see some petroglyphs. At km 71 is

Los Loros a mountain hamlet with temperate climate and dry air. The houses belonged to the emplo-yees of the former railroad. At the turn of the century, here was the exclusive sanatorium of Dr. Wolman -now in ruins- treating people affected by tuberculosis and «visited» by Santiago's high society. Opposite these ruins is Mr. Herrera's outdoor restaurant, shaded by Chile's oldest pimiento tree, with a 7-m girdle.

At km 81 is the village of **San Antonio.** It used to be the terminal for the railway from Copiapó.

At the eastern end of the valley, at km 88, there is a signposted detour to the left, leading in 500 m to the

INCA METALLURGICAL CENTER (NM) it commands a superb view, located atop a hill at the end of the valley. Here were 32 smelter braziers and the houses accommodating the workers of this ore processing center, dating from the Inca times. The place was very well chosen: here the wind, squeezed between the walls of the valley, gathers speed and provides a rich oxygen supply to the braziers. It was restored in 1982.

At km 96 is a signposted detour to Las Juntas. Take the dirt road branching right leading to **Embalse Lautaro.** Some 600 m beyond the Amolanas bridge (km 97), take short detour to the left to reach the

Amolanas Aqueduct (NM) Located at the foot of the Lautaro dam, this old aqueduct -made of stone and mortar, with 13 arches and 85 m in length- brought river water to a 16-m drop which powered an ore processing mill. It was built in 1890 by Spanish masons for the Amolanas mine, property of A. Edwards. It stopped operating in 1928 and is the only one of its kind in Chile. The building on the side used to house the plant's administration.

Go back 600 m to the first junction and turn left to see the wall of the **Lautaro dam,** erected in 1920, the only dam in this river. Drive to the other side of the dam to return to the original paved road, which continues a further 12 km to the Manflas river.

To return to Copiapó, retrace the road.

3 TO CHAÑARCILLO ★★★

a round trip of 146 km from Copiapó, 118 km paved and 28 km gravel. Better to make it either on the way to Copiapó or on the return trip. Take food and water. **A visit to a former mine of legendary wealth and the ruins of the Juan Godoy village.**

Take the Pan-American highway out of Copiapó (km 0) to the south. At km 59 is a signposted junction; a road branches right to Estación Castilla and another one branches left to Mina Bandurrias. Take the road to Mina Bandurrias.

At km 73 is

CHAÑARCILLO one of the richest silver mines ever. Unfortunately, much of the ruins was destroyed when the tips were reworked. On a road to the left you can see the ruins of the former village of Juan Godoy and, to the right, on a hillock, what is left of the cemetery. The mine was discovered in 1832 by prospector Juan Godoy. It was the world's third richest and a gigantic source of wealth for the entire country over three decades.

The mine had several owners, each burrowing into the mountain seeking the richer lodes. The neighboring hills suffered a similar fate. Some of the richest lodes, such as Delirios, had nearly pure silver. It was depleted by 1875.

The Juan Godoy village at the foot of the hill, grew up to be the province's second largest, overtaking Vallenar, Freirina and Caldera in population. It pea-ked in 1860 with some 14,000 people. A poet visiting it in 1846 said that its founders surely did not overexert themselves designing the place, and that the amazing general disorder fitted well into its crazy layout. Rich textiles and expensive wines were found alongside drinking joints and flophouses, billiard rooms and chicken sheds. All that is left now are some stone foundations and a ransacked cemetery.

Exploitation In order to extract the silver, the mineral ore had to be amalgamated, a process requiring a great deal of water and energy. The ore was hauled by mule train to Pabellón, on the Copiapó river, until 1854, when the railroad linking both sites was finished. Between Pabellón and Copiapó over 20 ore processing plants were soon set up, powered by the river's hydraulic energy.

Return to Copiapó retracing the same road. The road shown in the map connecting Chañarcillo and Pabellón is only passable in a high-clearance, 4WD vehicle, solitary, laborious driving; you can make it in about 3 hours.

4 PAN-AMERICAN HIGHWAY FROM COPIAPO TO CALDERA ★★★ *74 km, paved, gasoline at Caldera.* **Following part of the Copiapó valley downstream, then a piece of desert to Region III's main seaside resort.**

The road runs west through vine plantations and large fruit packing houses. The vine plantations soon peter out, though, as the breeze blowing in from the sea is not particularly suitable for grapevines. The land is given over to vegetable crops and grazing. At km 16 there is a short detour to the left leading to

Piedra Colgada Church (see illustration in Land & History). Small, with a three-arched portico and a wooden tower. The construction technique employed here is typical of the Atacama churches: wooden walls lined with Guayaquil cane and stuccoed with mud.

The road turns away from the river and the landscape becomes desert. At km 42 a road branches left leading to **Puerto Viejo,** with a long beach near the river mouth. This was Copiapó's port until Caldera was founded. The pipeline running alongside the road brings drinking water from Copiapó to Caldera and Chañaral.

At km 66 is the turn-off for Bahía Inglesa. There is a good view of the coast -with the bays of Caldera, Calderilla and Bahía Inglesa- from the crest of a little rise farther ahead. At km 71 a road branches off to the Calderilla mechanized wharf; at km 74 is the access to

CALDERA AND BAHIA INGLESA the main seaside resort in Region III is also a mining and fishing port. It consists of a string of three bays connected by paved roads, each with nice beaches and fairly warm ocean water. Caldera is waking up to its tourist potential, with good facilities and accommodations.

Caldera was a port of call since colonial times, but achieved city status only in 1850, when the railroad to Copiapó was built.

By 1870 it had climbed to be Chile's second most important port, after Valparaíso, and had a smelter, a sea water desalination plant and five docks for loading minerals. On April 23, 1891, the insurgent fleet seeking to topple President Balmaceda was attacked at the Caldera bay, one of the insurgent ships being sunk in the harbor. The fallen sailors were buried at the Caldera cemetery, the first non-catholic cemetery in Chile.

What To See On the access road (Av. Almeyda) is the **cemetery**. The **Church of San Vicente**, on the square, was erected in 1862 by English carpenters brought for the construction of the railroad installations.

One of the interesting houses is **Mackenzie**, with a tile-paved veranda overlooking the street. Other interesting houses are indicated in the map. The Costanera Guillermo Wheelwright (named after the constructor of the Caldera railroad) is the busier area during the tourist season, with outdoor cafes, hotels, and a beach. The former **Railway Station (NM)** erected in 1850, has a passenger platform and three roofed cargo platforms, the huge gates of which would be locked at night to protect the merchandise.

There is a **fishing terminal** and a **passenger pier,** with boats for hire to make a tour around the bay. On the Costanera, one of the interesting houses is that of **Siggelknow**, a local historian. At the end of the Costanera are several older houses, with galleries on the second floor and roofs with long alerce shingles; they were moved from Puerto Viejo by William Wheelwright himself.

Following Av. Prat you come to the **Yachting Club**, with a good view over the harbor; beyond it is the **mechanized wharf** for loading iron ore. The best view over the area is from **Anfiteatro del Mar** (see route in map), with a wooden lighthouse, the oldest still in operation.

Back in town, at Av. Canal Beagle you will see the **Gruta del Padre Negro**, a site where pilgrims come, built by a priest known as «Black Father»; wall paintings.

One kilometer into the road south from Caldera to Bahía Inglesa, a dirt road branches right leading to the **Calderilla bay**, with **fishing industries**, a nice **beach**, a modern **mechanized wharf** for loading iron ore and several algae farms. Back on the paved road, a short way to the south is

Bahía Inglesa a small resort with a haphazard layout, a motel-campground with facilities and the best beaches in Region III.

Accommodation and Food best lodgings at Portal del Inca, Caldera, with cabins and apartments; at Bahía Inglesa, Condominio Los Jardines and the Motel-Camping Bahía Inglesa (cabins and campground); Hostería Puerta del Sol is centrally located and has good views. Best cuisine at Portal del Inca and Club de Yates; in Bahía Inglesa there is a small restaurant. Quick dishes at cafes shown

in map; picnic at Las Machas beach.

Some short excursions to neighboring beaches:
Caleta El Cisne a nice beach 10 km from Bahía Inglesa, with an island a short distance from the shore. Grand surf and golden sand.
Playa Brava right north of Caldera, is popular on weekends.
Ramada and Rodillo beaches, on the road to Chañaral, are described below.

5 PAN-AMERICAN HIGHWAY FROM CALDERA TO CHAÑARAL ★★★ *a paved coastal stretch of 93 km; gasoline at Caldera and Chañaral.*
A beautiful stretch of coast with many beaches and some incipient seaside resorts. The ocean will not be seen again from the Pan-American highway until Arica, over one thousand kilometers farther north.

One km north of Caldera is a fruit and vegetable control outpost: no perishable foodstuffs -ie, farming produce- can be brought into the south (this is because the rest of Chile is remarkably free of agricultural pests and diseases, and they want to keep it that way).

At km 4 is **Ramadas beach**, wide and with white sands; very good on a calm day. Four km later is the access to **Rodillo beach**, with pounding surf, nice scenery and a restaurant offering seafood.

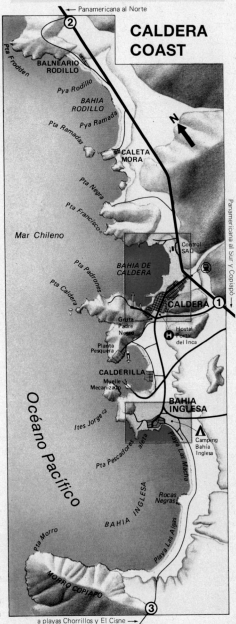

CALDERA COAST

← Panamericana al Norte
Pta Frodden
BALNEARIO RODILLO
Pya Rodillo
BAHIA RODILLO
Pta Ramadas
Pya Ramada
N
CALETA MORA
Pta Negra
Pta Francisco
Mar Chileno
Control SAG
Pta Padrones
BAHIA DE CALDERA
Pta Caldera
CALDERA
Gruta Padre Negro
Hostal Portal del Inca
Planta Pesquera
CALDERILLA
Muelle Mecanizado
BAHIA INGLESA
Océano Pacífico
Ites Jorge
Camping Bahía Inglesa
Pta Pescadores
Playa Las Macha
Rocas Negras
BAHIA INGLESA
Pta Morro
Playa Las Algas
MORRO COPIAPO
← a playas Chorrillos y El Cisne →
Panamericana al Sur y Copiapó

153

☎ Telephone Center
★ Touristic Information
◉ Café, Meeting Point
⛽ Gasoline Station
⇒ Lookout Point
✱ Hospital
A Town Hall
B Casa de la Cultura

C Church, Parochial House
D House Mackenzie
E House Tornini
F Ex Customs House
G Ex Railway Station (NM)
H House Sayago
K Seafood Stalls
L Anfiteatro del Mar

M Gruta Padre Negro
N Laic Cemetery
J Houses of Interest

ACCOMMODATIONS
1 H & M Portal del Inca
2 Hs Puerta del Sol
3 H Pucará
4 H Costanera

5 Bh El Quisco
6 Bh Los Andes
7 Bh Palermo
8 M Los Pinos

RESTAURANTS
1 H & M Portal del Inca
20 Yacht Club
R Other Restaurants

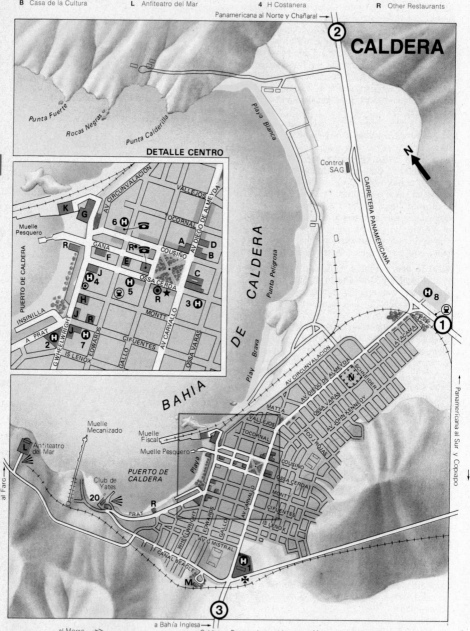

CALDERA

DETALLE CENTRO

BAHIA DE CALDERA

PUERTO DE CALDERA

R Restaurante El Corral

HOSPEDAJES
1 M Umbral de Bahía Inglesa
2 Cab y Cp de Bahía Inglesa
3 Cab Los Jardines de Ba Inglesa
4 M Villa Alegre

BAHIA INGLESA

BAHIA INGLESA

At km 10 there is a signpost indicating a place of geological interest. (Be careful if you are driving, as the roadbed is very soft and sandy.) Here are rocks of **orbicular granite**, with strange round or square incrustations. There are also small beaches, good for bathing.

Over the next twenty kilometers, the road runs among attractive rock formations. A pipeline runs alongside the road bringing drinking water from Copiapó to Chañaral. The **Parque Incabus**, on the right-hand side of the road, is a curious memorial to those killed in a tragic road accident many years ago. At km 37 is the wide, placid **Obispito beach**, with a few houses.

Next is the Obispo bay, without good beaches, at the foot of mount Obispo; with 857 m, it is the highest hill in this stretch of coast.

Playa Flamenco at km 63, is a long beach with a restaurant and an oyster farm at the fishing cove. The farm produces a Japanese variety of oysters, large-sized and of very smooth flavor. They are offered for sale here. At the northern end of the bay are the so-called «ponds», a good place for bathing among the rocks. Ahead is **Villa Alegre**, at km 68, a small, deep cove with a wind-sheltered beach, followed by a string of smaller beaches.

After km 84, the road runs on a cliff over the ocean to reach, at km 91,

Barquitos a copper-loading port squeezed between the rocky hills behind and the sea. It belongs to Codelco Chile, the state copper mining corporation. It was built in 1916 by the U.S. Andes Copper Mining Co., with a railway, a dock, a power generation plant (now shut down) and a residence area, to load the output of the Potrerillos copper mine. Now it loads the mineral from the El Salvador mine through a modern, recently built mechanized wharf. The administration house is up on the hill, surrounded by palm trees and araucarias, a conifer only found in southern South America. Two kilometers ahead is the access to

CHAÑARAL (pop. 10,626). A service town for the area's mines, it has gasoline stations, accommodations and restaurants, an airfield and vehicles for hire. The main attractions are good beaches, mines and the Pan de Azúcar National Park.

In 1824, the explorer Diego de Almeyda discovered the Las Animas mineral deposit and exported through Chañaral the first copper shipment in the history of the Republic. In 1833, he founded the village and two years later the large mineral deposit of El Salado was discovered.

The place boomed in the 1860s. A. Edwards & Co. set up a smelter at the site where the Hostería is now located (the Hostería was built using slag blocks from the old smelter). In 1861 an Anglican church was erected for the English residents, and four years later, a Catholic church. A railroad to Diego de Almagro and El Salado and Las Animas mine was finished in 1871. One year later, the large smelter of Cía. de Minas went on stream, followed in 1903 by another one called La Francesa. They all stopped operating around 1931.

The main sources of income for the town now are the Pan-American highway -it is a usual stop for meals of the long-haul bus services- and the El Salvador mine.

The Chañaral beach used to be very small. Over a period of 63 years, the outflow of the ore purification process at Potrerillos, and later El Salvador -both located over 100 km inland-, was dumped at the Salado river which tumbled down the slopes to empty into the sea here, silting the port and creating the enormous beach existing now; the old pier is buried under the sand. A canal was then dug to divert the outflow farther north. All along the river, private miners set up improvised settling tanks to salvage copper from the water.

When ecology became a household word, Chañaralians became concerned about the effects of this pollution on their coast -there is no marine fauna near the coast to speak of- and took El Salvador to the courts. They won. In 1988, a verdict of the Supreme Court ordered El Salvador to take appropriate action to keep the contaminants from reaching the sea. In 1990, the mine finished a large dam in the desert to contain and settle the toxic flows.

Accommodation and Food Hostería Chañaral is best. Good cuisine and view at El Trauco. Cheaper meals at the restaurants catering to the bus lines; quick meals at the café on the square. The Hostería offers cars for hire, with or without driver.

6 TO THE PAN DE AZUCAR NATIONAL PARK

★★★ *round trip from Chañaral, 62 km; good dirt road, which continues across the park to reach the Pan-American highway. If you are planning to continue to the north, this road is only 9 km longer than the direct route. Gasoline at Chañaral; take food.*
Beautiful coastal scenery, interesting vegetation and the best place for free-lance camping.

Take the road to the airfield (see map) and follow the signposted road veering left. It runs across a flat expanse of sandy terrain to the northern tip of the bay. There is a concrete canal which used to carry El Salvador's mineral outflow.

At km 12 is Bahía Hedionda («Smelly Bay»), where the outflow canal emptied into the ocean. Beyond is **Refugio beach,** white and enormous, created by silting provoked by the mine's outflow. It is undergoing a process of natural decontamination.

At km 22 is the entrance to the park. The road skirts the aptly-named **Blanca beach**, the most beautiful, also created by silting. The surrounding hills have some vegetation, and on the plains some strange cluster-cacti can be seen, resembling a pile of iron balls from the distance. At km 26 is **Pan de Azúcar island** a short distance from the shore, home to 3,000 Humboldt penguins and rich birdlife, sea otters and seawolves. Detours lead to the shore, where you can see stones with fine quartz veins. At the end of the bay is a promontory, at the foot of which there is a small beach, good for camping.

Skirting this peak at km 31 is

Caleta Pan de Azúcar a fishing settlement with 20 houses -some looking sort of temporary-, water tanks (water brought from Chañaral), a sheltered beach and the Park Administration house with a campsite nearby. This used to be a loading port for the output of the Carrizalillo mines, acquired by M. Cousiño by 1863. The place was shelled by the Peruvian battle ship Unión in 1879, and in 1922 a tidal wave swept the installations away. The dock, cranes and wagons are under the water, to the delight of divers.

PAN DE AZUCAR NATIONAL PARK (43,754 ha). Created in 1986 and administered by Conaf, the park has fine beaches, grand scenery, and a flora consisting mostly of a variety of cacti and other desert plants nourished by the thick camanchaca fogs rolling in nightly from the sea. The woody plants used to be harvested for firewood for Chañaral. Foxes and guanacos are easy to spot in the wilderness. From the upper part of the park there are very good views; good hiking country. There are paths and some jeep tracks (you will need a guide).

You may continue from here to the north, just following the same road you took to get here; it crosses the Coastal Range and meets the Pan-American highway in 23 km. The small white monoliths visible from the road indicate mining claims.

7 TO COPIAPO THROUGH DIEGO DE ALMAGRO

★★★ *a paved road, 218 km to Copiapó. Gasoline and modest restaurants at Diego de Almagro.*
An alternative route to return south through the heart of the mining district. It is 51 km longer than taking the Pan-American highway.

Take the Pan-American highway out of Chañaral to the north. At km 12 a paved road branches east to El Salvador. The road runs upstream the valley of the Salado river; a railroad runs parallel to it. At km 34 is **El Salado**, the seat of the old namesake copper mine. At km 46 are the remains of the ancient Santa Fe iron ore mine. At km 52 is **Estación Empalme**, a railway station where the longitudinal railroad built by the state in 1912 meets the railway climbing from Chañaral.

At km 67 is **Diego de Almagro** (pop. 7,000), a mining town formerly called Pueblo Hundido, meaning «sunken town».

Diego de Almagro is the head town of the municipal district where El Salvador and Potrerillos are located. In the past, it was the terminal point for the longitudinal railroad built by the state from La Calera to the north, joining all the transverse railroads then existing. By 1922, another railroad was built from the Pueblo Hundido to Iquique, completing the northern branch of the state's railroad.

☎ Telephone Center
★ Touristic Information
◉ Café, Meeting Point
🅖 Gasoline Station
⋙ Lookout Point
✠ Hospital

A Town Hall
B Provincial Government
C Parish Church
D Anglican Church
E Bus Terminal
F D de Almeyda Monument

G Ex Edwards Smelter
H Ex La Francesa Smelter
K House Molina

ACCOMMODATIONS
1 Hs Chañaral
2 H Mini

3 H Jiménez
4 H La Marina

RESTAURANTS
1 Hs Chañaral
10 El Trauco
11 Bus–catering Restaurants

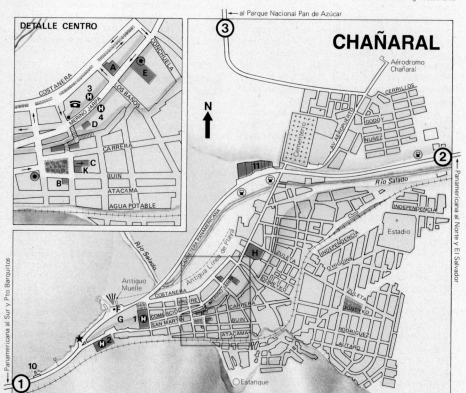

SECTION C   SALT FLAT AND THE ANDES

As described under Land & History, here the Andes Mountain range forks into two ranges, the cordilleras of Domeyko and Claudio Gay, separated by a depression. This basin has no outlet, thus giving rise to salt flats such as Maricunga and Pedernales.

Up from the Claudio Gay range is a large flatland, with the Ojos del Salado rearing up from it to claim the title of Chile's tallest mountain. A beautiful lake, Laguna Verde, sits at the foot of the mountain.

On the Cordillera de Domeyko are the important mining centers of El Salvador and Potrerillos.

The mountain area of this region is little known and very beautiful, with high-altitude lakes swarming with waterfowl, particularly flamingos.

It is accessible only from October through March, weather permitting. With bad weather, the roads to the salt flats are better from El Salvador.

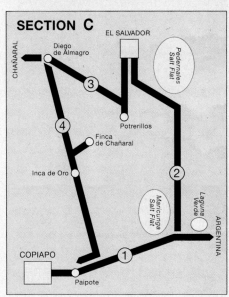

SECTION C

1 INTERNATIONAL ROAD TO ARGENTINA ★★★

it is 286 km to the border at Laguna Verde, and 253 km from there to Tinogasta, Argentina. The Chilean side of the road is graveled, poorly surfaced and narrow, best with a 4WD vehicle but also passable in normal cars. Driving is slow. Take water food. Gasoline only at Copiapó. Leave early: it is 6 hours to the border, 5 more to Tinogasta. There is no money exchange at Tinogasta: take Argentinian money from Chile. Argentine immigration control at La Gruta, 22 km beyond the border. The road on the Argentinian side is graveled, good. At Fiambalá starts a 70-km stretch of paved road to Tinogasta.

An interesting excursion through salt flats and high mountains, with the beautiful Laguna Verde at the foot of Chile's highest peak.

Recommendations 1. The road is open from October through March, when the weather is more favorable. Before departure, check with Vialidad in Copiapó or the tourist office about road conditions. **2.** Take food and water for more than one day. **3.** It is advisable to travel in a group of two vehicles. **4.** File your itinerary with the police at Teresita (Paipote Police Control Station) and check in with the police at Maricunga upon arrival (this way they can know if you had difficulties). **5.** Tune the car for high altitude, advancing the spark; you will be driving at altitudes of up to 4,700 m. In case of extreme loss of power, remove the carburetor's air filter. **6.** Take warm clothing: it is windy during the day and very cold at night. **7** In case of car breakdown, it is best to wait in the car for other traffic to come by.

Take the road to Paipote out of Copiapó (km 0), turning off at the signposted paved road to Diego de Almagro. At km 16 is the Teresita police station **(report your itinerary)**. A short way ahead you can see the domes of the Los Cóndores astronomical observatory. At km 25, the gravel road to Argentina branches east, running through the bottom of the Paipote ravine and climbing after a while along the bed of a dry river; this section can be affected by landslides in summer. Between km 59 and 60 are the ruins and cemetery of

Puquios a small, once thriving mining village which was the terminal of a railroad from Copiapó since 1854. The naturalist R.A. Philippi ended here his expedition from San Pedro de Atacama that year. The geographical survey headed by F.J. San Román, which christened the peaks and ranges in the area, set out from here in 1883. Two years later, the son of naturalist Philippi started his own colossal expedition from this place: by mule to the Maricunga salt flat, up in the high-plateau, and thence through the high-plateau all the way to Iquique.

The road climbs up the San Andrés ravine at km 79, narrow and with some vegetation, to cross the rocky gap known as **Portezuelo del Salto**, at km 85. Beyond the pass are some highland meadows, with livestock grazing, flanked by hills of interesting colors.

At km 101 are the **San Andrés meadows**, with a few huts, the only inhabited place along the road. Note a yellowish stripe on the hillsides: it is light, porous volcanic rock, easy to carve and used in buildings. Near the road you can see some boulders of this material that have rolled down the slope.

As the road climbs to the Domeyko range, some guanaco herds can be seen on the meadows.

The ravine ends at km 152 and the road winds up the **Codocedo** range, with an abandoned sulfur plant, to reach the pass at km 161 (4,500 m above sea level). There is a superb **view** over the salt flat depression, the **Claudio Gay range** and **Mount Ojos del Salado,** the world's highest active volcano, with 6,893 m.

The road then descends gently to reach the salt flat and the police station at km 182 (3,700 m above the sea).

Note a better road has been opened, leading to Mina Proyecto Marte. It branches off to the right 20 km beyond Puquios, following the Paipote ravine, climbing to the Pastillitos pass and descending to **lake Santa Rosa**, at the southern end of the Maricunga salt flat. From here you can continue through the Cuesta Colorada to Laguna Verde; the border control is right next to Laguna Verde.

MARICUNGA SALT FLAT large, white, solitary and with ponds swarming with flamingoes in a fantastic setting of snowy peaks. This is Chile's southernmost salt flat, and perhaps one of the most beautiful. This is the point where the Andes range forks into the parallel ranges of Domeyko and Claudio Gay, with the depression lying between them which creates the salt flats. The string of salt flats continues northward to the Atacama salt flat and then into Bolivia, with the Uyuni salt flat and lake Poopo.

From here you can continue to the north, to the Pedernales salt flat and El Salvador (Tour 2), or to Laguna Verde on the border.

From the police station (km 182) the road heads

Ojos del Salado, volcano

3

south skirting the salt flat. A road branches right at km 192 leading to the prospecting camp of Anglo American Corporation and to lake Negro Francisco (a flamingo breeding colony). On the main road, at km 197 the road turns left into a ravine with water and grass, heading for the Claudio Gay range.

At km 204 the road starts zigzagging up the Cuesta Colorado, to reach the pass at km 210; superb **views** of the salt flat and the towering mount Copiapó.

Beyond the pass is a vast plain -the altiplano or high plateau- known here as **Pampa de Piedra Pómez**, with towering volcanoes and snow-capped peaks, the most impressing of which are the **Ojos del Salado** and the **Nevado El Muerto**. At km 265, is

LAGUNA VERDE an emerald-green lake lying on a plain flanked by snow-capped volcanoes. Note the colors on the stripes encircling the lakeshore: they are due to successive lava and volcanic ash deposits. This lake, scenically, is perhaps more beautiful than lake Chungará, but it lacks the rich wildlife swarming in and around Chungará.

Diego de Almagro came into Chile in March 1536 through the pass of San Francisco, 21 km ahead, suffering great losses among his troops, Indians and pack animals, snatched by the bitter cold at night.

The stretch of road to the border is interesting only for those wishing to continue to Argentina.

2 **THROUGH PEDERNALES TO EL SALVADOR**

★★★ *starting from the Maricunga police station, it is 146 km to El Salvador on a gravel road, well maintained by mining companies. No gasoline or supplies. Wireless at Maricunga, La Ola and Montandón. La Ola is suitable for camping.*

A visit to the beautiful Pedernales salt flat and El Salvador, an unusual town and Chile's fourth largest copper mine.

Drive 2 km from the Maricunga police station to the west, taking there the signposted road to the right for Chañaral. The road runs through the salt flat basin. At km 12 you top a small rise and descend gently through a dry river bed to reach a forking of the road at km 17. Both branches lead to La Ola (see map); we recommend the left branch.

The mountain ranges start marching away from each other. A short way ahead a road branches off to the left for the **Esperanza** silver mine, owned by Anglo American. At km 28 is the **La Ola airstrip** (no facilities). At km 32 the road reaches another road running east-west. To the left is the **Esperanza mine**, to the right, La Ola and El Salvador.

Following the road to the right, you soon descend into a ravine with yellowish meadows and a stream, with mount **Doña Inés** towering at the northern end of the Pedernales flat.

At km 52, the road crosses the La Ola river, and a short way ahead it is joined by the road

descending from **Termas de Juncal** (a thermal spring). At km 52 is the **La Ola dam,** with a few houses, a wireless and a site suitable for camping. This is the reservoir of drinking water for El Salvador.

The road runs through the Pedernales plain, with the salt flat in the distance. At km 72 is a **pumping station**, on the edge of the salt flat, operated by the El Salvador mine.

PEDERNALES SALT FLAT a large, white expanse flanked by snow-capped peaks. Take a road skirting the edge of the salt flat to visit the former **borax mine**, established by British capitals in 1914, and to see the **ponds with flamingoes.** This road continues to the tunnel dug by the El Salvador mine to tap the area's water and bring it to the Salado river, which in turn carried the outflow from the ore purification process to the Chañaral bay. This detour provides the finest views of this salt flat.

Back on the road to Chañaral, at km 81 is the Domeyko range, which the road traverses climbing a 2-km stretch and then descending through an interminable succession of curves. At km 98 is the **Montandón hydroelectric plant**, property of El Salvador, with a few houses and a wireless. The road then continues straight to a junction at km 114; here is the paved, signposted highway to El Salvador. At km 146 is

EL SALVADOR (pop. 21,000, altitude 2,300 m). An unusual town, inaugurated (Nov. 18, 1959) but not founded, and built entirely by the U.S. firm Andes Copper Mining Co., a subsidiary of Anaconda, as a residential and services center for its new El Salvador mine and the old Potrerillos complex.

Well laid-out as an amphitheater on the hillsides, the town has wide avenues converging to the square, the commercial and administrative center. The houses are mostly alike, of two kinds: for blue-collar and white-collar workers, including the American personnel. It has a complete infrastructure, with a large hospital and a big school with all facilities, an airport with regular air services and much more. It is much neater-looking than the typical Chilean mining towns of the North.

Its orderly layout has led some to believe - wrongly- that it was designed by the Brazilian architect Oscar Niemeyer, who designed Brasilia, Brazil's capital.

As a town designed to serve the mine and under a central administration, it left no space for some of the providers of minor services in urban life, such as plumbers, shoemakers, artisans, tailors, and others, who set up their own satellite village called **Portal del Inca** (po. 2,000). To say that the urban contrast is stark is an understatement.

Drive or walk up to **the Gruta** on the hill for a panoramic **view** of the city and the mine, and Portal del Inca.

The Mine the mine entrance is called Túnel 2600, as it is located at that altitude above the sea level. This is an underground mine; you can see how the crest of the mountain has collapsed inward as the mountain is progressively hollowed.

The mountain is called Indio Muerto, with copper ore outcrops recorded since the Inca times. It was also recorded by both R.A. Philippi, in 1854, and Diego de Almeyda. The original mine was located at Potrerillos, but it soon showed signs of depletion. The company started prospecting in this area in 1951, but only in 1954 struck the core of the Indio Muerto deposit, with such an enormous potential as to justify the investment. This mine saved the whole project; thence the name «El Salvador.» The mine went on stream in 1959, minutes before the town was officially inaugurated.

El Salvador became a state company in 1970. Now it is part of the Codelco holding -the state copper mining corporation- and accounts for 9% of the Great Mines' output, with over 100,000 tons of refined copper annually.

Accommodation and Food Hotel Camino del Inca is excellent. Hostería El Salvador is good and mini Hotel Pucará. Food at hotels and local clubs.

Tips The **blue taxis** outside the Hotel Camino del Inca; take passengers to the salt flats. Arrange the price beforehand. The **Club de Exploradores del Desierto** -Desert Explorers Club-, formed by mine personnel fond of exploring the remotest corners of the desert in 4WD vehicles, can provide good advice and information for those loving adventure tourism. They meet at the hotel. If you need a guide, call Mr. Piero Venturini in advance. T. 052-47-2223, El Salvador. There are buses and colectivo (shared) **taxis** to Potrerillos.

Rally in salt flat of Pedernales

3 TO DIEGO DE ALMAGRO ★★★

the direct road is 62 km long, the one we recommend is 101 km; both are paved. Gasoline at El Salvador and Diego de Almagro.
A chance to see the impressive technological effort to enable the exploitation of the copper deposits in this area.

Take the road out of El Salvador to **Potrerillos**, passing **Portal del Inca**, from where you can see the train convoys emerging from the mountain to the Concentrate Plant. The road climbs gently to a pass at km 17, descending then towards the south.

At km 27 is the **widow's rock**, said to moan at night, and a short distance ahead the **Riachuelo de la Sal**, a stream with salt crusts on the banks, carrying water from the Pedernales salt flat

☎ Telephones	C Club Social	K Christian Union Church	T Tennis
⋙ Lookout Point	D Hospital	L Jehova Witness Church	U Soccer
⊙ Gasoline Station	E Central Administration	M Pentecostal Church	6 Club Pampa
1 Post Office	F House of the Board	N High School	**ACCOMMODATIONS**
2 Bus Terminal	G Catholic Church	Q Annex School	4 H Camino del Inca
A Shops	H Evangelic Church	R Elementary School	5 Hs El Salvador
B Inca Cinema	J Baptist Church	S Basketball	7 Mini Hotel Pucará

through a man-made drain. It is used at the mine for industrial processes.

At km 32, on the edge of the deep **Asiento canyon,** is a crossroads. Take the road to the right. Ahead, a spectacular view of

Potrerillos on the southern side of the canyon and perched atop a hill. It is a town, mine and smelter started in 1918, which went on stream in 1922 and was depleted by 1959. Few people live here now, working in the smelter and the refinery processing the concentrate from El Salvador. Waste rocks from the old mine roll down the slopes around Potrerillos, and the road and railroad wind their way out of the canyon. There is a modest hotel and a bus service from El Salvador.

The El Hueso gold mine, property of Codelco, is located on mount El Hueso and reached through a road from Potrerillos.

The road climbs down into the canyon, reaching the bottom at km 38. There is a pond, with grass and some animals grazing, in stark contrast with the aridity of the surrounding hills. A road branches off here to Potrerillos (11 km). The road runs now along the bottom of the valley, with the railroad on one side. There are several abandoned train stations. Note the roofed booths with crank-activated Western Electric telephones, still in operation.

Just beyond the third abandoned railroad station and before meeting the Río de la Sal (at km 55), you can see a path zigzagging up the left-hand cliff: it is the **Inca Road**, the only place where you can see it so clearly.

At km 70 is

Llanta a train station, ore mill, a large pipeline plunging down the slope bringing the copper concentrate from El Salvador, and large **solar drying ponds** for wet concentrate (see description above). The ore is brought by train from here to the Potrerillos smelter.

At km 72 is the **Las Cascadas plant,** reclaiming copper from the waste water. At km 74 is the other road -also paved- leading more directly to El Salvador. A short way ahead is the Llanta village and **railway maintenance depot,** built early this century. The landscape opens up and at km 101 is Diego de Almagro, described under, Tour 7.

4 **TO COPIAPO THROUGH THE DESERT** ★★★

a paved road, 151 km to Copiapó. Gasoline at D de Almagro and Copiapó. Beverages at Inca de Oro village.
A desertic landscape with an impressive view to the Andes and the Coastal Range. A possibility to visit a genuine oasis.

Taking Diego de Almagro as your km O, follow now the road heading south. The air is so dry in the neighboring Cachiyuyo plain, that from km 26

CONCENTRATE PLANT

The ore is hauled out of the mine by an underground railroad running at the mine's lowest level. Gravity is one of the most assiduous workers in the whole process: the cars, for example, are loaded by gravity. The train emerges at the same level as the Concentrate Plant.

The rocks contain only 1% copper. The process starts with a **Primary Milling**, where the rocks are ground to the size of coarse gravel (not shown in diagram above). A conveyor belt brings the resulting material to the

1 Domed Heap enclosed to prevent dust from spread-

ing. Another conveyor belt, located below the heap, brings the material to the

2 Secondary Mill where the stones are crushed to the size of small pebbles. The resulting material is then brought by an enclosed conveyor belt to the

3 Fine Ore Storage Plant Gravity brings the material to the next building down the slope, called

4 Wet Mill The ground material is mixed with water in large, rotating horizontal cylinders. Inside are thousands of steel balls which, as the cylinders rotate, grind the pebbles to a fine powder. Mixed with water, this powder becomes a paste which flows (by gravity) to the

EL SALVADOR
CONCENTRATE PLANT

you can see the village of Inca de Oro, a score of km ahead. To the east looms the Buenos Aires range, with Mt. Vicuña as its tallest peak.

Inca de Oro at km 46, is modest mining village and mineral loading station inhabited mostly by self-employed miners. Some strike it rich, just to squander their wealth over a short period of time, slumping back to poverty. Others mine enough everyday just to keep going. On the western side of town there is an odd walled-in house, belonging to a miner who did keep hted the North. The smelter's output was exported through the Peña Blanca port.

The (gravel) road to this place is lonely, climbing two rangesilometer before Inca de Oro, a dirt road branches east, leading in 19 km to

Finca de Chañaral a small oasis with trees and crops, where water emerges as if from nowhere. It is the only oasis between Copiapó and the Atacama salt flat. Inhabited since ancient times (old paintings on the rock walls), this was one of the stations of the Inca Road. Pedro de Valdivia was here, and naturist R.A. Phillippi stopped here on his return from San Pedro de Atacama. At that time, the place was owned by J. Waddington, a financier from Valparaíso with mining interests in the area, and produced fodder for pack animals. Now it is in state hands and is the source of water for Diego de Almagro and Inca de Oro.

Back on the road to Copiapó (km 46), the road runs across the vast Humito plain, to climb the Chimbero pass at km 65. The Varas plains drop away to the south, with the smoke from the Paipote smelter in the distance.

The plain ends at km 88; here are the ruins of **Carrera Pinto**, a formerly major mining town.

The road now descends into the Paipote depression, the road to Argentina branching east at km 126.

At km 135 is the **Teresita police station** and SAG control post:'no perishable foodstuffs are allowed south of here. Copiapó is at km 151.

5 Flotation Plant with hundreds of tanks holding about 1 cubic meter each; they receive the paste and mix it with more water. Each tank has a fan-like stirring device, and injection of air and chemicals. This produces a foam which captures the copper particles and drifts to the surface, where it overflows into ducts bringing it to the

6 Settling Tanks large ponds where the foam settles; the superficial water is recycled into the Flotation Plant. The settled material is known as «wet concentrate» and has a 36% copper content. This concentrate is extracted from the bottom of the settling ponds and brought by pipeline (by force of gravity, of course) down to Llanta, almost 40 km distant.

There it is sun-dried and then transported to Potrerillos for refining.

At the bottom of the flotation tanks (5) a sterile material known simply as «mud» settles. It is also gravity-piped to Llanta, where it used to be dumped into the Río Salado, which empties into the ocean. Now, forced by a court verdict, El Salvador built a dam to store this water and settle the contaminant materials.

7 Lime Plant and Silos Lime is one of the chemicals needed for the flotation plant.

8 Molybdenum Plant Wet concentrate contains about 1% molybdenum, which is extracted in this plant using a selective flotation process.

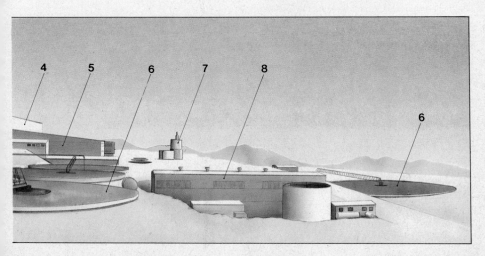

EXCURSIONS

This is Chile's best region for 4WD excursions. You can rove around the depression between the Domeyko and Claudio Gay ranges, including more than ten salt flats, or along the coast, with large sandy areas and few inhabited coves. Both areas have few roads and are, consequently, among the least known in Chile. There are no forests, so driving is easy. Additionally, the old mining works left a lot of tracks which are still passable.

Two institutions promote this activity: **Sernatur,** Chile's tourist board (tel. 052-212838, Copiapó), which organizes a **Coastal Raid** in the first week of February every year, and the **Club de Exploradores del Desierto**, which organizes the **Mountain Raid** (three days during the first half of December). It can be contacted at the Hotel Camino del Inca, El Salvador (Av. El Tofo 337, casilla 7, T. 2311). This club was organized by employees of the mine, who know the area very well and delight in riding their 4WD's to the remotest corners.

Coastal Raid

starts from Copiapó towards the coast, driving southwards along the coast to Huasco. It takes three days, usually with a group of some 50 vehicles. Each year a different route is followed.

All excursions on the high cordillera start from El Salvador. Follow the recommendations listed in Tour 1.

Skirting the edge of the Pedernles salt flat

this excursion is described in Tour 2, starting from the pumping station (Las Bombas) along the western edge of the flat to the drainage tunnel. The Club de Exploradores can provide more information.

To Termas de Juncal

from the Pedernales-Maricunga road, just beyond the La Ola dam (see Tour 2), a road branches east to the thermal springs (30 km), running alongside the Juncalito river. The springs are rock ponds in a setting of snowy peaks towering above 5,500 m. For both excursions, camping is possible at La Ola. More information from Club de Exploradores.

To Laguna del Negro Francisco

this excursion can be complementary to the two above. From the Maricunga police station at the northern tip of the Maricunga salt flat, take the road to Argentina, skirting the salt flat, and then the road branching right to **Lake Santa Rosa**; this lake swarms with waterfowl. The road runs along the Ciénaga Redonda ravine, where the Proyecto Marte mine is located, and then skirts the foothills of the Copiapó volcano (6,080 m), at which summit is an Inca altar. The road descends alongside the Astaburuaga brook to reach, at km 108 from the Maricunga police station, the

Lake Negro Francisco located in a large basin, which is a continuation of the depression containing the Maricunga and Pedernales salt flats, only that the Copiapó volcano decided to rear up in the middle interrupting the plain. The lake is habitat of giant taguas, wild ducks, Andean goose and large flocks of flamingoes. Small herds of guanaco can also be seen. Request updated information from the Club de Exploradores.

The Five-Salt-Flat Raid

an excursion of 390 km, lasting two days, starting from El Salvador. First stop is the Pedernales salt flat, skirting its western shore to continue northward to **Los Infieles salt flat**, then **Del Aguila** salt flat, across **Grande salt flat** and, finally, the **Piedra Parada** salt flat. Turning west, the southern shore of the Pedernales is reached, and from there back to El Salvador. The approximate route is shown as a dotted line in main map.

PUBLIC TRANSPORTATION

The main cities in this Zone are located on the Pan-American highway, and are served by interprovincial bus services from Santiago.

There are regular air services to Copiapó and El Salvador. Both cities offer cars for hire and tourist taxis.

In addition to the frequencies shown in the chart below, the following remarks can be made:

To Huasco and Freirina many daily buses and colectivo (shared) taxis from Vallenar, services are increased in summer.

To San Félix Two daily buses from Vallenar.

To Carrizal Bajo on Saturday and Sundeay buses from Vallenar to the beaches.

To Los Loros and Las Juntas daily buses from Copiapó.

To Caldera: Buses with increased services in summer.

To Bahía Inglesa there are also colectivo (shared) taxis. In summer, also direct bus service to/from Copiapó.

To El Salvador daily direct buses from Santiago and Antofagasta via Chañaral. To Copiapó, direct services via Diego de Almagro and Inca de Oro.

To Potrerillos colectivo taxis from El Salvador.

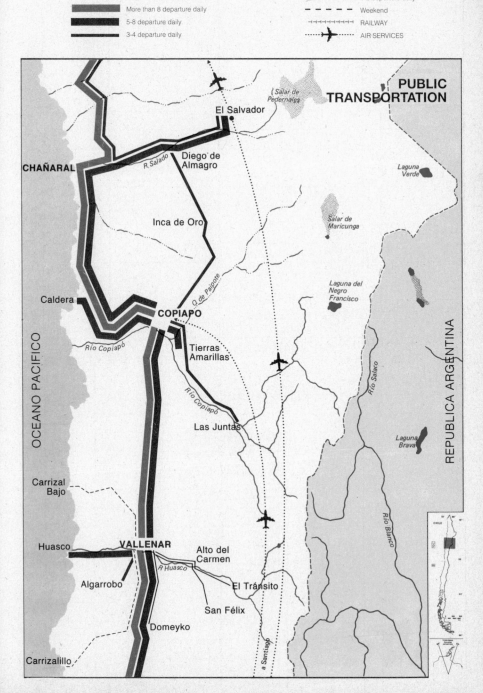

BUS DEPARTURE FREQUENCY
More than 8 departure daily
5-8 departure daily
3-4 departure daily
1-2 departure daily
Weekend
RAILWAY
AIR SERVICES

3

Zone 4
LA SERENA to LA LIGUA

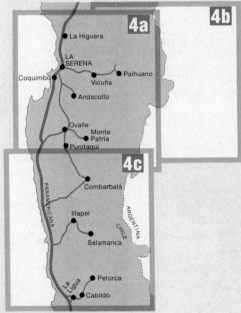

4a

La Higuera

LA SERENA

Coquimbo
Vicuña
Paihuano

Andacollo

Ovalle
Monte
Patria
Punitaqui

4b

4c

PANAMERICANA

Combarbalá

Illapel

Salamanca

ARGENTINA
CHILE

La Ligua
Petorca
Cabildo

DETAILED MAPS

Arica

Iquique

Antofagasta

4

Copiapó

Easter
Island

La Serena

Valparaíso

Is R
Crusoe

SANTIAGO

Talca

Concepción

Temuco

Valdivia

Osorno

Pto Montt

Castro
Chaitén

Coihaique

Cochrane

Puerto Natales

Punta Arenas

Puerto Williams

Is Diego
Ramirez

90°   60°   53°

CHILEAN
ANTARCTIC
TERRITORY

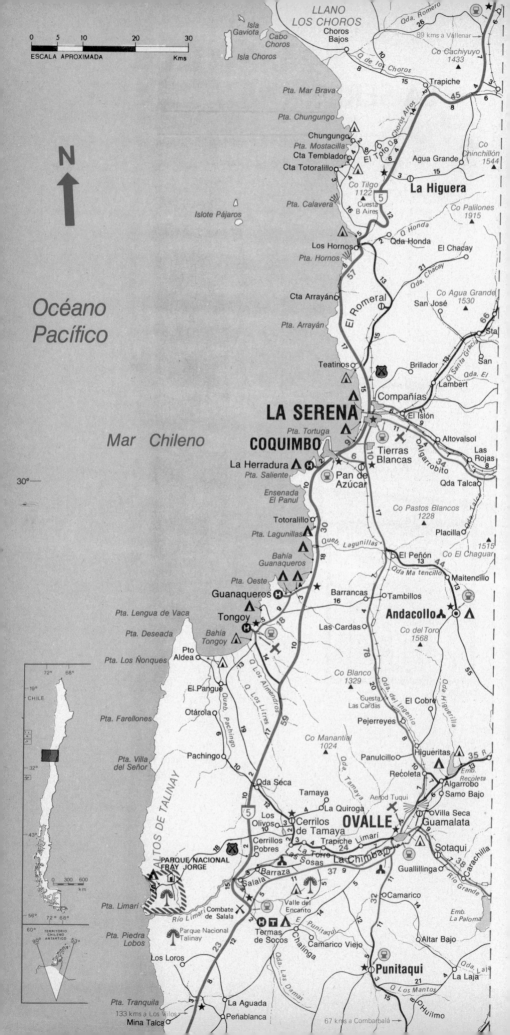

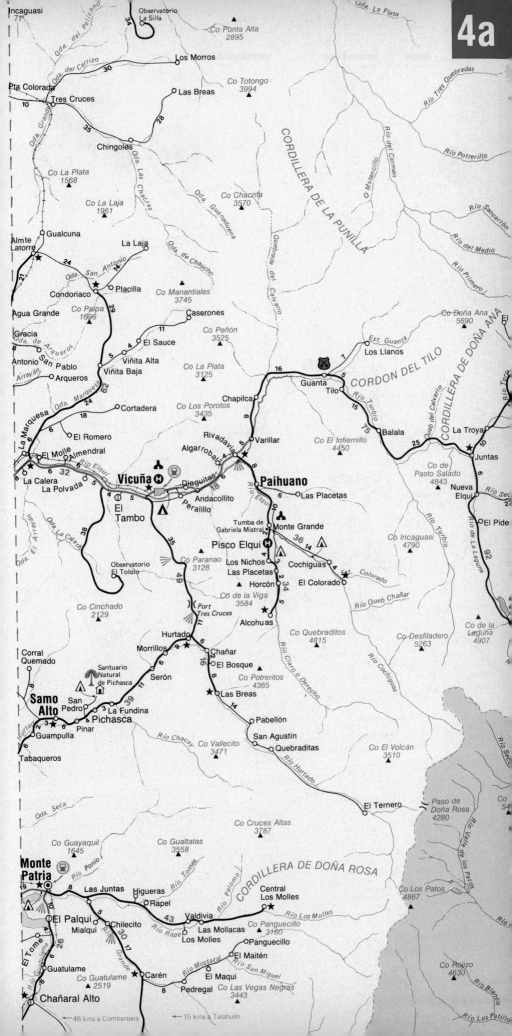

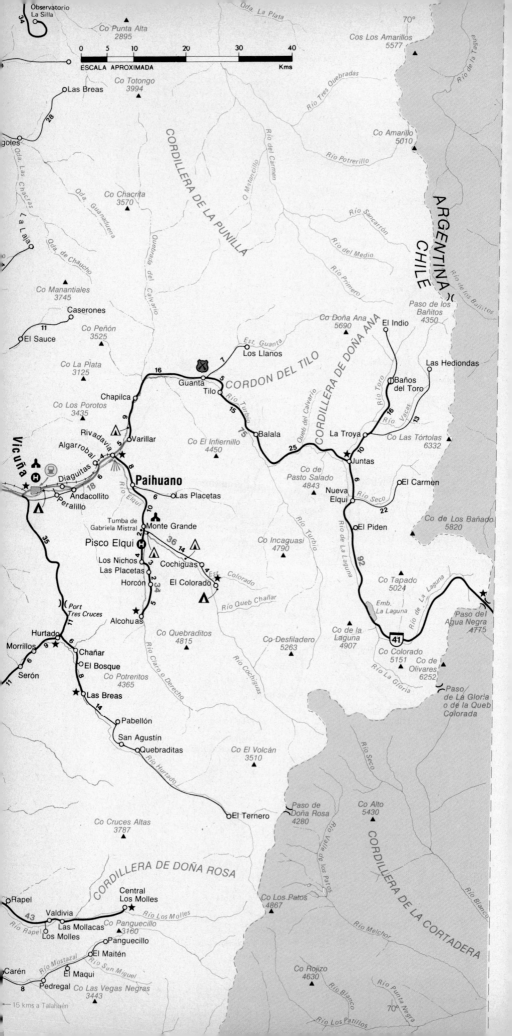

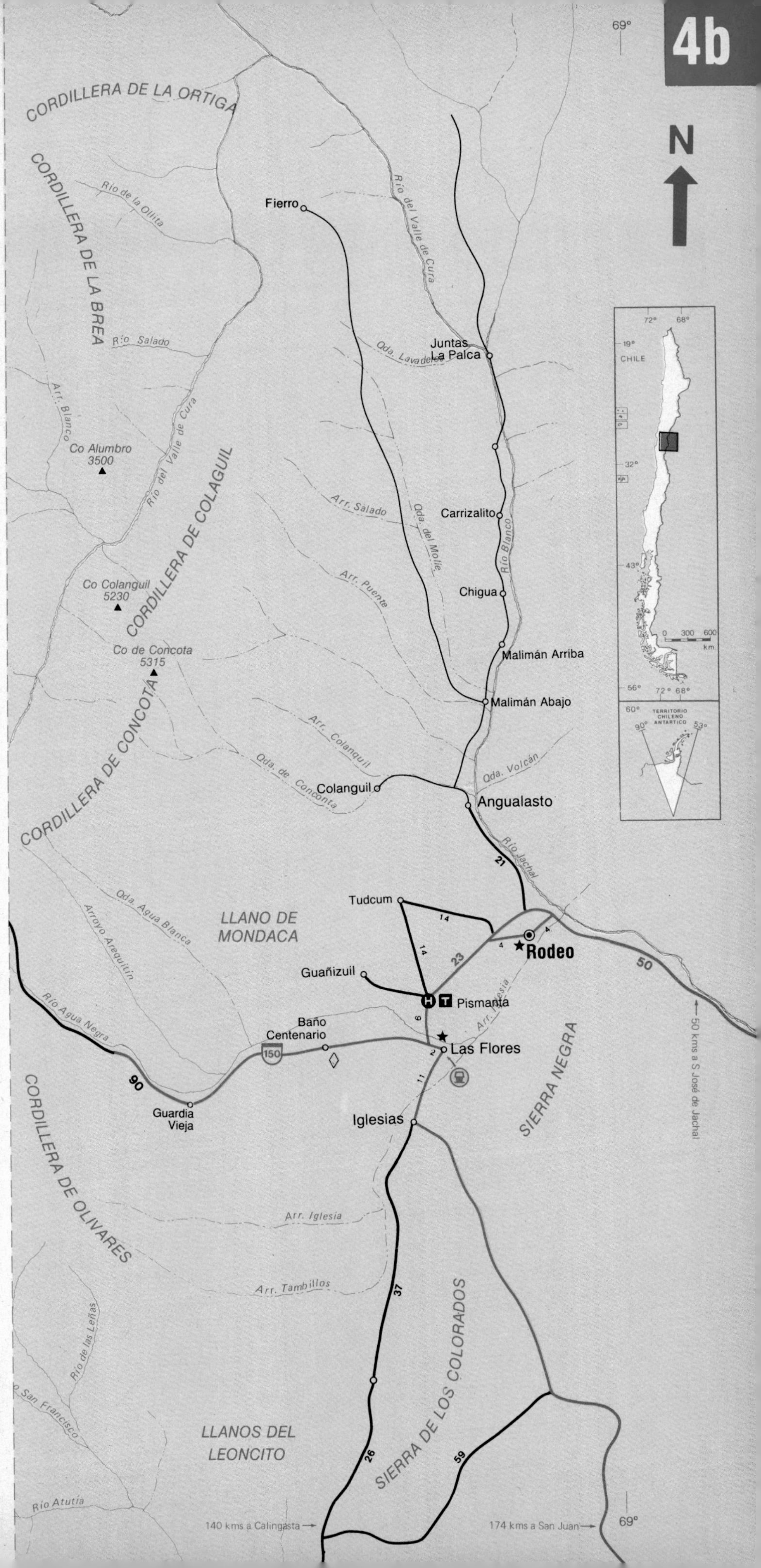

N

CORDILLERA DE LA ORTIGA

CORDILLERA DE LA BREA

Río de la Ollita

Fierro

Río Salado

Arr. Blanco

Río del Valle de Cura

Co Alumbro
3500 ▲

CORDILLERA DE COLAGUIL

Arr. Salado

Arr. Puente

Co Colanguil
5230 ▲

CORDILLERA DE CONCOTA

Co de Concota
5315 ▲

Arr. Colanguil

Qda. de Conconta

Colanguil

Río del Valle de Cura

Qda. Lavadero

Juntas
La Palca

Qda. del Molle

Carrizalito

Río Blanco

Chigua

Malimán Arriba

Malimán Abajo

Qda. Volcán

Angualasto

Río Jáchal

21

CHILE
19°
32°
43°
56°
72° 68°
72° 68°
0 300 600
km

60°
90°
TERRITORIO
CHILENO
ANTARTICO
53°

LLANO DE
MONDACA

Qda. Agua Blanca

Arroyo Arequitín

Río Agua Negra

Tudcum

14

14 23

Rodeo

4

50

50 kms a S José de Jáchal

Guañizuil

9 Pismanta

Arr. Pismanta

Baño
Centenario

150

11

Las Flores

SIERRA NEGRA

90

Guardia
Vieja

CORDILLERA DE OLIVARES

Iglesias

Arr. Iglesia

Arr. Tambillos

37

SIERRA DE LOS COLORADOS

Río de las Leñas

Río San Francisco

LLANOS DEL
LEONCITO

Río Atutía

26

SIERRA DE LOS COLORADOS

59

69°

140 kms a Calingasta →

174 kms a San Juan →

69°

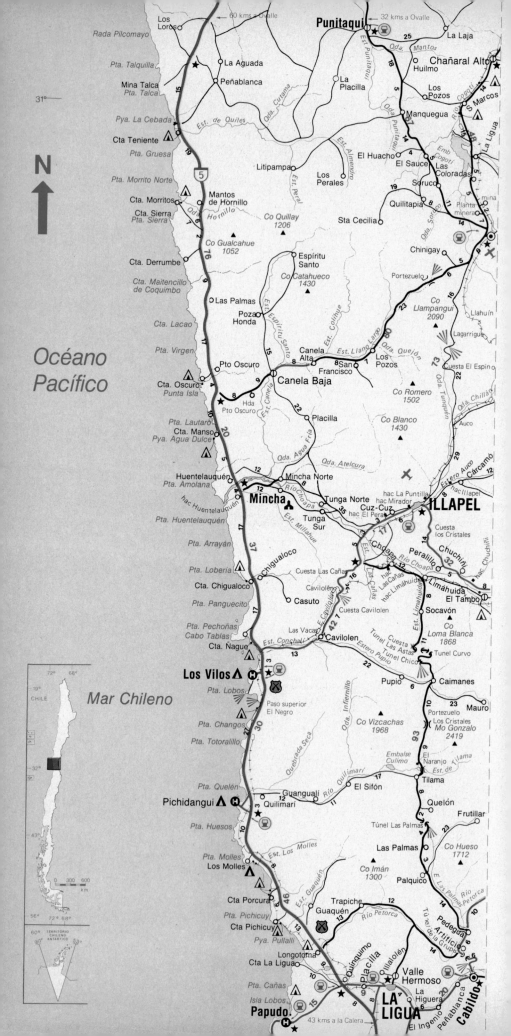

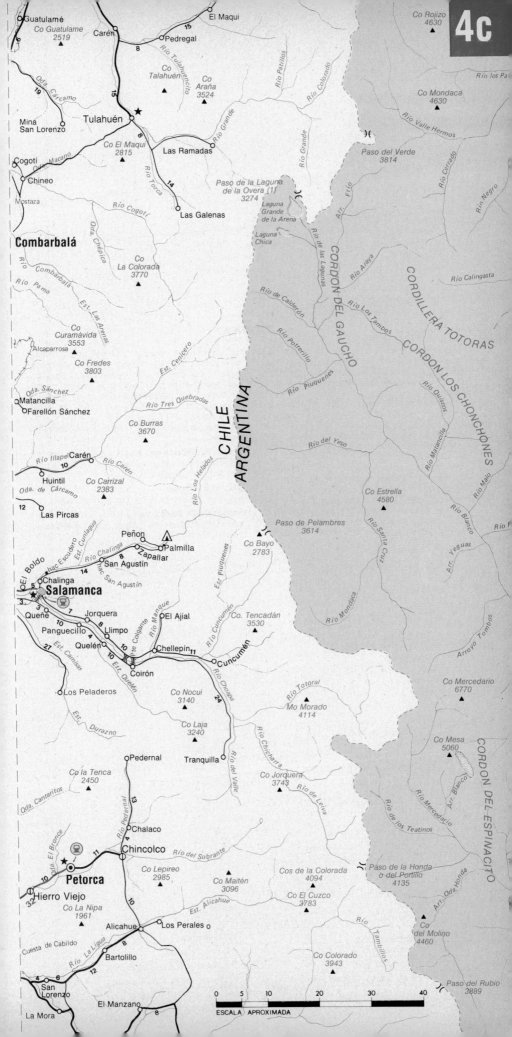

OVERVIEW

This Zone covers the area between the La Ligua river to the South and the Los Choros ravine, just North of La Serena, thus comprising the entire Region IV and the inland valleys of the Petorca province.

The inland landscape is doubly attractive, the semi-desert vegetation standing in stark contrast with the lush irrigated valleys. The ranges and ridges play a significant role, inevitably lying across the roads and forcing them to wind their way up the slopes.

The coastal strip is a world in itself, with wide, sheltered bays, calm, blue-green seawater and white-sanded beaches.

The climate on the coastal area is warm and mostly sunny, the one exception being La Serena, where cloudy mornings seem to be the rule (it normally clears up in the afternoon). Inland, it is hot and the air very clear. Climate and scenery have teamed up here to make of this a year-round busy Tourist Zone. Tourist infrastructure offers accommodations ranging from hotels through motels to campgrounds, as well as a wide variety of restaurants along the coast, in the big cities and in the inland valleys.

We have divided this Zone into three Sections, namely;

Section A Petorca and Illapel with busy seaside resorts and the valleys of the upper La Ligua river and the Choapa river basin.

Section B Ovalle with beautiful, well-cultivated mountain meadows in the Limarí river basin.

Section C La Serena with a lovely coastline, pleasant Metropolitan La Serena and picturesque inland valleys.

REGIONAL DISTANCES

Andacollo

186	Combarbalá														
50	183	Coquimbo													
82	110	79	Embalse Recoleta												
342	73	307	266	Illapel											
54	187	9	83	316	La Serena										
280	137	245	204	59	254	Los Vilos									
85	137	122	52	290	126	231	Monte Patria								
87	99	84	14	255	88	193	38	Ovalle							
116	144	113	30	300	117	238	83	45	Pichasca						
310	167	275	234	89	284	30	261	223	268	Pichidangui					
154	291	113	187	420	104	358	230	192	221	388	Pisco Elqui				
119	67	116	43	140	120	215	70	32	77	255	224	Punitaqui			
98	196	48	111	272	57	216	135	97	141	246	161	129	Tongoy		
107	109	104	34	246	107	183	58	20	65	213	212	47	87	Valle del Encanto	
120	253	75	144	382	66	320	192	154	88	350	38	186	123	173	Tocopilla

Zone 4
LA SERENA to LA LIGUA

DIVISION BY SECTIONS

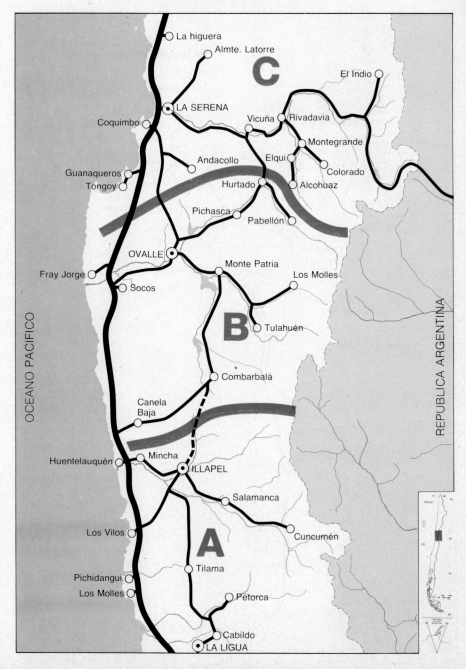

DETOURS OFF THE PAN-AMERICAN HIGHWAY

First-time travellers in this Zone would do well to travel along the coast following the Pan-American highway. For those who have already done the Pan-Am we suggest some detours below, which head North through the little-known inland portions of this Zone.

1 The Old Northbound Road ★★★ this route was used first by the Incas, then as a horse-trail during the colonial period. Later on it became the first highway to the North, before the Pan-Am was built. It slices through the landscape showing clearly the transition into ever more barren hills and increasingly green irrigated valleys. It is worth it. See Sections A & B.

2 Through Illapel ★★★ a 59-km detour, 23 km longer than the direct route from Los Vilos to Huentelauquén, offering a chance to see the Choapa valley, its capital city -Illapel- and the old village of Mincha. See Section A.

3 Into the Limarí Valley ★★★ the first leg of this detour brings you to Ovalle on a good gravel road, passing interesting mining works, the large Cogotí and Paloma dams, and some of the most fertile valleys in the North. Beyond Ovalle the road veers into the Cordillera until it reaches the Elqui river valley at Vicuña, heading west to reach La Serena «from behind». It is spectacular. See Section B.

4 To La Serena Via Ovalle ★★★ a paved detour starting at Socos, passing Ovalle and continuing to La Serena. It is 36 km longer than the direct route along the Pan-Am. See Sections B & C.

5 Through the Seaside Resorts ★★★ a short detour along the coast, visiting the busiest seaside resorts in this area, with beautiful beaches and bays. It is almost a must. See Section C.

4

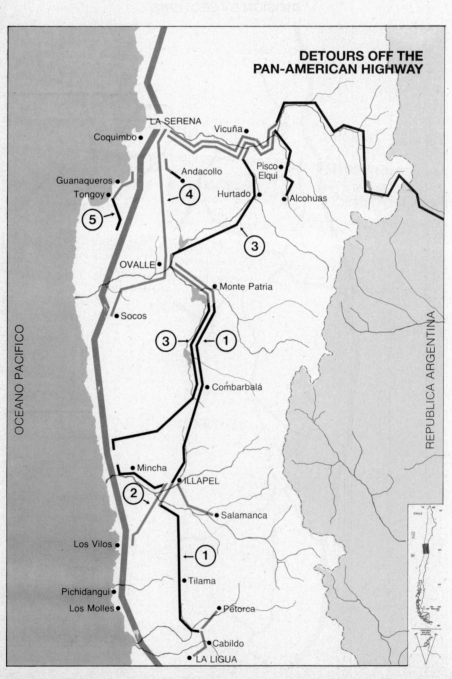

DETOURS OFF THE PAN-AMERICAN HIGHWAY

THE LAND, ITS HISTORY, ITS PEOPLE

DESCRIPTION one of the main features of this Zone is that the Andes and the Coastal mountain ranges are joined by spurs which make it all but impossible to tell where one range ends and the other one starts. Westward-flowing rivers run along the transverse valleys lying between these mountain spurs, such as the La Ligua, Choapa, Limarí -the largest- and Elqui rivers.

To cross from one valley to the next one must climb up and down these ridges, except along the coastal strip, which is relatively flat as it is raised sea bottom. This, in turn, gives rise to good bays and harbors, such as Pichidangui, Los Vilos, Tongoy and Coquimbo. The one exception is the coastline between Huentelauquén and Socos, where the mountains plunge almost directly into the sea, hindering road construction considerably.

The climate is transitional between desert and heartland. Mean temperature in the coastal strip is 14.4° C, with no frost, frequent morning fogs and 80% air humidity; it is quite temperate and stable. Further inland, mean temperature climbs to 16.5° C, the air extremely dry and transparent.

These climatic features, coupled with a winter-only rainfall regime, account for a native plant cover of semi-desert makeup, cacti and thorny bushes predominating; they are superbly adapted to withstand the long dry season. Solely at those sites where fogs shed their moisture there are some forests, such as at Talinay, Punta del Viento and Fray Jorge, with vegetation more reminiscent of Chile's South.

These very features -air dryness, heat and abundant sunlight- make these lands extraordinarily fruitful when provided with water through irrigation canals or drip-irrigation systems, making it possible to raise such exotic fruits as papaya, cherimoya and, during the colonial period, cotton and tobacco.

EARLY INHABITANTS the transverse valleys, with their rivers flowing year-round, and the sheltered bays invited human habitation since quite early on. On the coast dwelled the Changos, a tribe of fishermen and gatherers. Inland, tribes of various origins engaged first in hunting, later on in farming. Based upon archaeological evidence, they have been divided into five periods:

Paleo Indian hunters coming from the North, part of the first wave of human settlers in the Americas. Re-mains dating back 12 thousand years unearthed in the area of Los Vilos (see tours from that town) revealed coexistence of these people with extinct fauna including mastodons, mylodon (a type of ground sloth), etc.

Archaic hunters moving between the coast and the Andes and even into the Argentine plains. The oldest remains, unearthed at San Pedro Viejo (see excursion along the Hurtado river), are dated at 8,000 BC. By 2,500 BC these hunters became acquainted with agriculture, becoming then a hunter-gatherer people but still with transhumant customs.

El Molle by the beginning of the Christian era the first agro-pottery culture started to take form, related to other Indian cultures in northern Argentina. They were semi-permanently settled, and were acquainted with metallurgy, ceramics and the taming of animals. The first uncovering of remains from this culture took place at El Molle, in the Elqui valley. This cultural group either disappeared or moved elsewhere around AD 900.

Diaguitas these native Indians were engaged in agriculture, pottery and mastered complex techniques in agriculture, metallurgy and, particularly, surprisingly beautiful ceramics. Originally from beyond the Andes, these people moved into Chile around AD 900 and settled a district stretching from Copiapó to the Choapa valley, and later into the Aconcagua valley.

Incas the Inca empire thrust into Chile in 1470, establishing mitimaes -farming settlements- along the way, with settlers coming from present-day Peru. They introduced improved irrigation techniques and new styles in ceramics. The mitimaes at the Elqui valley were Altovalsol and Marquesa; at the Limarí valley, Guamalata, Chimba and Sotaquí; at the Choapa valley, Cuz Cuz and Chalinga; and at the La Ligua valley, present-day Cabildo.

DIAGUITA CERAMICS a surprisingly fine product with domestic as well as ritual purposes, ranked among the most beautiful ceramics in the American continent. Four stages can be made out in the evolution of its forms and style of ornamentation:

Las Animas (souls of the dead): a transition stage, with geometric patterns consisting of stripes forming stairs and crosses. It started around AD 900.

Diaguitas I a red background with white and black geometric patterns. The dishes became somewhat more extended, profusely ornamented both inside and outside. Human forms appeared. It started ca. AD 1100.

Diaguitas II a period considered classic on account of its stylistic development. The dishes acquired a curved bottom and straight walls. The so-called «duck-jars» appeared, shaped like an animal, asymmetric and with handles. An enormous variety in the styles of ornamentation, including incisions and applications in relief, was introduced. Anthropomorphic figures were used more profusely. It started ca. AD 1,300.

Diaguitas III as from 1470, Diaguita culture was influenced by the Inca invaders, who introduced new forms, such as bowls, jars with upper handles and animal shapes. New figures were used in ornamentation, such as triangles and checkerboard patterns. The best collections of ceramics from this period -Chile's pride- are to be found at the Museo Antropológico of La Serena and at the Museo Antropológico of Ovalle, with unique pieces of singular beauty.

SPANISH DOMINATION right after the foundation of Santiago in 1542, Pedro de Valdivia planned the dominion of his territory on the basis of two cities from North to South: La Serena (founded 1544 and founded anew in 1549) and Concepción (1550).

Francisco de Aguirre, appointed Lieutenant Governor of the district from Choapa to Atacama and responsible for maintaining the road open to Peru, founded La Serena anew after a war of attrition which depopulated the valleys. This made it necessary to import Mapuche labor from the South to man the alluvial gold washing works and the agriculture farms.

By 1600 all the lands in this zone had been allocated to the conquerors as a merced (land grant) and the Indians were subject to a serfdom system known as encomienda. The Catholic Church was active from the very beginning, building churches at the old Inca mitimaes and setting up convents at each valley, such as the Recoleta Franciscana in Ovalle, which had been erected at the site of the present-day Recoleta dam.

La Serena, from its foundation, exerted hegemony over Chile's North. Its families included the largest landowners in each of the transverse valleys. However, it always had a small population. It was the only city on the Northbound Route and it was the prime site for rest and recreation for those engaged in trade with Peru across the desert.

In similar fashion to the rest of colonial Chile, this district had no urban population other than La Serena; elsewhere there were only manor houses. In 1744 Manso de Velasco ordered the foundation of Copiapó and in 1752 y 1754, Ortiz de Rosas undertook the failed foundations of La Ligua and Illapel.

In 1788, just after taking office as Chile's Governor and at the age of 70, Ambrosio O'Higgins set out on a 3-month exploratory journey on horseback to Copiapó. He ordered the second founda-

FASE LAS ANIMAS

4

FASE DIAGUITAS I

FASE DIAGUITAS II

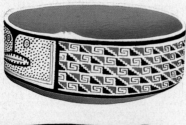

tion of La Ligua and, later, of Illapel at a different location; he also had founded Combarbalá and designed some urban and irrigation improvements for La Serena. He founded Vallenar and, lastly, introduced some improvements in the small village of Copiapó.

Chile attained her independence with an incipient urban network in the so-called Norte Chico (Little North). Over the first 50 years of the Republic, Coquimbo, Vicuña, Andacollo, Ovalle, Monte Patria, Punitaqui, Tongoy, Salamanca, Los Vilos and Cabildo were founded.

MINING copper, silver and gold were the main metals mined; this last one, coveted by the Incas for ritual purposes, was extracted at the Andacollo (queen-metal in Quechua), Illapel and Combarbalá mines. The Spanish conquerors, by contrast, sought gold for commercial purposes and continued to exploit these mines until the late 1600, when they were abandoned.

Copper starting in 1750, a worldwide demand for copper started to be felt to feed the armaments industry. Families from La Serena and new Spanish immigrants exploited old lodes and found new ones at Brillador and Higueras, north of La Serena; at Cerro Tamaya, Panulcillo, Andacollo and Combarbalá, at the Limarí valley; Illapel and Los Vilos, at the Choapa valley.

Ores with copper content ranging from 25% to 68% were mined (nowadays, the so-called Large-Scale Mining (Gran Minería) processes ores with as little as 2% copper content). The ore was smelted in «Catalonian furnaces», which resembled country ovens, fired directly with algarrobo (a Prosopis species), pepper tree and molle firewood; this technique wiped out the native forests in the region. When copper content dropped below 25%, the mine was abandoned, as no techniques were then available to refine such ore. The still-rich ore was then left lying on the surface or dumped in the waste dumps.

The Mines the large mine deposits, such as Cerro Tamaya, Andacollo, etc, were known of old. With the large demand for metals in the 19th century, a number of claims was raised by the new mining entrepreneurs (Tamaya had over 250 claims), and digging was started from different points in search of a lode. Each «holding» could be divided into 24 «bars» or shares.

The 19th Century Chilean Independence brought about the arrival of foreigners into the mining business and the introduction of new metallurgical techniques. It was the heyday for the Norte Chico, when the pioneers of Chile's industrialization gathered experience, making in the process some of the country's largest fortunes.

Silver Mines in 1825 silver was struck at Arqueros, north of La Serena, which brought considerable wealth to a number of La Serena residents, mainly Juan de Dios Carmona, Mariano Ariztía and Ramón Subercaseaux. Juan de Dios Carmona gave Subercaseaux six shares into one of his holdings, forming thus a most powerful mining partnership.

Copper Mines the sustained demand for copper and the development of new refining techniques gave a tremendous boost to this industry, propelling this district to be the world's leading copper producing area.

Between 1820 and 1830, work was started at the La Higuera and Brillador mines, just north of La Serena, and at Panulcillo and fabulous Tamaya, in Ovalle; this last mine accounted for one fourth of Chile's copper exports. By 1850 the mines of El Barco, Lambert, Campanilla and La Cubana went on stream in the La Serena district, as well as the La Laja mine in Ovalle, in addition to hundreds of smaller works scattered around the zone.

Furnaces and Refineries the introduction of a French technique of indirect fusion -reverberatory furnace-made it possible to exploit ores with low copper content. This type of furnace was introduced in 1821 by Charles Lambert, who built the first refinery in La Compañia (see tours from La Serena), concealing it behind an enclosing wall to preserve the secret. He made a fortune processing the waste rocks from old mines, in addition to ore from some mines he owned, such as Brillador, Lambert, Campanilla and La Cubana. Soon some refineries were set up on the coastal area: at Totoralillo to process ores from La Higuera, and El Barco, owned by Félix Vicuña; the Coquimbo refinery of Joaquín Edwards, and the Guayacán refinery -then the world's largest-, owned by José Tomás Urmeneta. At Tongoy, J T Urmeneta built another smelter to process the ore from Tamaya, which he owned.

The Present Century large-scale copper mining moved to other provinces in Chile. The only active mines are Condoriaco at the Elqui valley and Panulcillo, at Limarí, both mid-sized. The star performers are now other metals:

Gold Chile's largest mine of this metal is El Indio, at the Elqui valley; the Talca mine at the Ovalle coast, also large, has been active since colonial days.

Iron it was the hope which replaced copper. In 1912, the Bethlehem Steel Co set up at El Tofo what was then South America's largest iron-ore mine, with a shipping port at Cruz Grande. It was thoroughly mechanized and electrified. It became depleted by 1952, being replaced by El Romeral, which feeds the Huachipato steel mill and supplies the export market. Its mechanized shipping port is at Guayacán.

THE PIONEERS the wealthy miners native to this zone, such as J de D Carmona, M Ariztía, C Lambert, A Edwards, J T Urmeneta and R Subercaseaux, were also major entrepreneurs who were soon to play a significant role in Chile's industrialization, taking part in the construction of railways, in coal mining, building of canals and irrigating the Maipo, Limache and Quillota valleys, in addition to being engaged in banking and the export business. These new activities eventually prompted them to move to Santiago and Valparaíso.

Charles Lambert born in Alsace in 1793, he studied engineering at Paris and arrived at Coquimbo in 1818 with the novel technique of the reverberatory furnace. He set up a refinery at La Compañía (see tours from La Serena) and acquired at dirt-cheap prices the waste dumps of old mines, which he reprocessed to enormous profits. He was a singular character: his refinery was completely surrounded by a wall to prevent the secret from leaking; its buildings were made of molded slag blocks. In 1825 he lent money to the government to finance the Chiloé campaign. In 1836 he hired in Europe, on behalf of the Chilean government, the Pole Ignacio Domeyko. He enlarged his holdings with the acquisition of the El Brillador mine from J de D Carmona, and set up a works with state-of-the-art techniques in the construction of roads, adits, and tunnels 600 m below the surface, with a steam plant within the mine.

He felt vexed when the government commandeered one of his ships during the Revolution of 1850 and decided to move out of the country, leaving his interests under the management of capable administrators. He died in London in 1876, leaving a fortune of over £50 million. He was ranked as South America's richest man.

José Tomás Urmeneta he was born in 1808 to a Spanish couple engaged in copper trading. He studied in England and the United States and, upon his return, he took over the management of an hacienda owned by his brother-in-law, Mariano Ariztía, at Sotaquí and Guallillinga in the area of Ovalle. In 1833 he filed the Mollaca claim to part of the Tamaya hill. After 18 years of tireless digging -he even came to live with his family at the mine's entrance-, he struck a fabulous 2-m-wide bronze lode with 60% copper content in 1852. This was the initial stuff for his colossal fortune. In 1859 he inaugurated the railroad from Tongoy to Tamaya and a large refinery in the port. That same year, his refinery at Guayacán went on stream, then the world's largest copper smelter. A short time before that, he had acquired the non-irrigated fields of Limache and financed the construction of the Waddington canal to irrigate his French-strain vineyards. He promoted the industrial production of sugar from sugar beet, as well as the production of silk and textiles. He also introduced eucalyptus, telegraph, and gas. He founded the Casa de Orates (an institution to house the mentally insane) and supported the Firefighter Corps (traditionally in Chile made up solely of volunteers).

He was the president of the Southbound Railway up to San Fernando. In 1866 he started coal mining

FASE DIAGUITAS II

FASE DIAGUITAS III

4

activities at Lebu, and five years later he was a candidate to the Presidency of the Republic. He died of a heart attack in 1878, at Limache. His sons-in-law, Maximiliano Errázuriz and Adolfo Eastman, were his partners and heirs.

ROADS AND RAILROADS the first road was the Inca road, which reached the Elqui valley at La Marquesa, crossed over to the Limarí valley, at the site of present-day Recoleta dam, and descended to Sotaquí, turning inland to Combarbalá and then, after ascending four ridges, reached Cabildo, where it forked into branches leading to Argentina, the Mapocho valley and Quillota.

During the colonial period it was known as the Inland Road; the other route was known as the Coastal Road. The latter stretched from La Serena to Barraza and Socos, then turned inland to Canela and Mincha, and continued thence to Huentelauquén and southwards to Catapilco, crossed the El Melón ridge and reached Quillota.

The first «Royal Roads» crossed the valleys to the shipping ports. Then, during the Republic, the Inland Road was upgraded and remained as the only road connection to the North until the Pan-American highway was built, in the late 1950s.

In 1864 the railway from Tongoy to Tamaya was finished; it was extended in 1872 to Ovalle and had a branch line to Panulcillo. The railroad from Coquimbo to La Serena was finished in 1865; in 1888 this line reached Vicuña and Rivadavia. At the turn of the century trains were running between Illapel and Los Vilos, and between Calera and Cabildo.

In 1912 the construction of the trunk railway line to the North was started, linking the existing railroads with one another. The trunk line followed the route of the old Inland Road through Cabildo, Illapel, Combarbalá, Monte Patria, Ovalle and La Serena. The Cabildo-Illapel stretch was abandoned by 1940 -the five ridges it ascended required the use of racked lines- and was rerouted along the coast via Quínquimo, Pichidangui, and Los Vilos. It now operates by sections and carries cargo only.

AGRICULTURE it employs about a third of the Zone's labor force. With over 100,000 ha under irrigation and blessed by a favorable climate, its produce ripens quite early, reaching both domestic and international markets ahead of that from any other region and thereby fetches fat prices.

Hefty investments in vines, fruit for export and new agroindustries have been made in the district since 1981, in a process still under way aiming at bringing under productive use the many hectares supplied by irrigation canals but not yet farmed.

Irrigation the heart of this agricultural expansion is the Limarí valley, with the Region's largest irrigated area. It is supplied by the gigantic irrigation complex -South America's largest- made up of the Recoleta, Cogotí and Paloma dams and a canal network exceeding 1,500 km in length. Started in 1929 and completed with the Paloma dam in 1968, it reached its maximum water storage capacity in 1984; its full potential is yet to be realized.

Pisco this spirit is produced from grapes of the strains Rosada Pastilla, Blanca Italia and varieties of Moscatel, grown in high-altitude inland valleys, with warm temperatures and strong sunlight. The juice from the pressed grapes is distilled in firewood-heated stills; the resulting product is a concentrated aguardiente of around 60 to 70 degrees, with a pleasant taste and aroma resulting from the highly-mineralized soil the grapes grow on. The art of distillation has been refined over more than three centuries, since the colonial period. The resulting liquor is left to ripen in wooden casks over periods from six months to two years. Then it is mixed and finally diluted in pure water to reach the market in the commercial strengths of Tradicional 30°, Especial 35°, Reservado 40° and Gran Pisco, 43°.

THE SKY the air in the inland valleys is remarkably dry and clear, features that are quite dear to astronomy. Unsurprisingly, this area is the prime astronomical observation center in the Southern Hemisphere. It offers astronomical visibility conditions during at least 300 photometric nights a year, against 216 for the great Monte Palomar observatory in the USA and 56 at the Argentine El Plata observatory.

El Tololo Inter-American Observatory located in the Elqui valley, 88 km East of La Serena and at 2,200 m altitude, it is a spectacular complex started in 1960. It was run by the National Optical Astronomical Observatory (NOAO), an association of universities from the USA and the Universidad de Chile. It operates the world's second-largest telescope, with a 400-cm mirror, in addition to a further seven telescopes of various sizes.

La Silla Observatory located 150 km North of La Serena and at 2,440 m altitude, it belongs to the European Southern Observatory (ESO), financed by seven European countries. It is a vast complex made up of 12 domes and their telescopes, the Southern Hemisphere's most modern radio telescope (only four of its kind in the world), and 15 further support and accommodation buildings.

Las Campanas Observatory located 156 km North of La Serena and at 2,510 m altitude, it is run by the Carnegie Institution of Washington (USA) and operates four high-powered telescopes.

These three observatories constitute the world's largest concentration of astronomical observation facilities. They all have administrative offices in La Serena. For visits, see description of La Serena.

SECTION A   PETORCA AND ILLAPEL

1 **PAN-AMERICAN HIGHWAY FROM QUINQUIMO TO HUENTELAUQUEN** ★★★ *A stretch of 113 km; gasoline at Quínquimo, Pichidangui, Los Vilos and Huentelauquén. The section of Pan-Am from Santiago to Quínquimo is described under the Central Chile volume.*

A portion of the Pan-Am skirting the coast and passing beautiful beaches and seaside resorts.

The Quínquimo road junction lies 154 km North of Santiago and 96 km from Viña del Mar; here the Pan-Am is joined by the coastal road from Papudo, another road branching off to La Ligua. There is a gas station and a host of vendors selling local pastries («dulces de La Ligua»).

A few meters into the road to Papudo a dirt road branches right, running along the La Ligua river for ten km to

Caleta La Ligua a fishing cove located on the southern shore of the river mouth overlooking the vast Longotoma beach, with fine sand and good surf, ideal for a picnic. Camping is not permitted.

One km north of Quínquimo, the Pan-Am crosses a valley and a bridge spanning the small La Ligua river. To the right, some tall palms are to be seen in a park: they are the only remains of the Pullalli hacienda. The estate has a singular history: it was received as a land grant by the daughter of a companion of Pedro de Valdivia in the late 16th century. Her descendants established in 1703 Chile's first entailed estate, these lands remaining thereby undivided over almost four centuries in the hands of 17 generations of the same family, until 1971. At this hacienda were introduced the first eucalyptus in Chile, in 1884.

At km 9 the Pan-Am descends into the small Longotoma river valley, a tributary of the La Ligua river, with cultivated fields and the village of **Longotoma**, reached following a road branching off 50 meters before the police control outpost. It is a good spot for getting supplies for those headed for the

Longotoma or Pullalli beach the dirt road from Longotoma leads to large sand dunes where the car must be left, to continue one km on foot through private orchards; the owners charge a small passage fee.

It is a wind-swept, 6-km-long beach with fine white sand and pounding surf, stretching north from the mouth of the La Ligua river to cape Guallarauco at the Pichicuy cove. Camping is permitted on the beach or in the private fields.

The Pan-Am continues along the valley, passing large plant nurseries producing carnations for export. It then climbs out of the valley to peek for the first time at the distant sea.

At km 19 a dirt road branches left for

PICHICUY a picturesque fishing cove at the northern tip of the Longotoma beach, yellow-sanded and beautiful. In season, it is an extremely popular spot for down-market vacationers, with hundreds of buses parked in front of the beach and a sea of makeshift tents covering the sand. Off season, the place is deserted and much more attractive.

Continuing on the Pan-Am, among eucalyptus forests and non-irrigated farmland, at km 27 are the beaches of

Ballena and Porcura a long beach with a rocky outcrop dividing it and closed to the North by the Los Molles fishing cove. The Pan-Am skirts the beach. At its southern end, before the **Ballena Bridge**, the beach is accessible through a gate where a passage fee is charged; it has the best spot for camping. Almost at the far end, beyond **Chivato Bridge,** at km 33, is the **Quebrada El Chivato** campground. At km 34 a road branches left to

LOS MOLLES a seaside resort lying on a peninsula which juts into sea at this long beach's northern tip. It is an old fishing cove which gradually evolved into a resort of scattered summer houses, streets yet to be well defined, some residenciales and several restaurants.

Its main attractiveness lies in a very interesting marine and terrestrial ecosystem within walking distance, surveyed and studied by numerous Chilean and foreign research teams. Skirting the peninsula to the North of the fishing cove, in a striking stretch of coastline, are veritable **rock gardens**; strange formations can be seen at the bottom of the cliffs, such at the **Los Bolones** beach (climb down carefully and only when the tide is low) or at the renowned **Puquén**, a blowhole with a roaring sound produced naturally in underwater caves. You will also see natural caves, pools and islets teeming with marine fauna -sea lions included- and lots of birds. It is worth a visit.

The highway continues North across a wide peninsula graced by scenic rock outcrops and a plant cover typical to Los Molles. It then skirts the **Silla del Gobernador** (Governor's Seat), with 695-m tall Coastal Range's tallest peak falling directly to the sea. It can be seen from Valparaíso right before a storm, with its characteristic twin peaks resembling

a saddle. A short way ahead, at km 44, there is a gas station and a road branching left, which leads in 2 km to

PICHIDANGUI a seaside resort with an excellent crescent-shaped, sheltered, white-sand beach. It is popular in summer, good for watersports and with interesting excursions to nearby spots. It has good hotels, horses for hire, a good campground and varied restaurants.

The sights include the waterfront avenue, the harbor and, to the west, the rocky shore, an islet and a church overlooking the ocean.

The main excursions from Pichidangui are along the beach to the mouth of the river, with horses offered for hire, and to the large **La Quintrala cave**, carved by sea erosion and located at the beach's northern end. Also worth a visit is the neighboring village of **Quilimarí**, with its old **church** erected purposefully on the hillside in order to keep the river banks free for farming. A road leads from there to the Tilama dam, to return through Caimanes and Los Vilos.

Back on the Pan-Am, a further 4 km will bring you to a road junction with a branch leading right to the village of **Quilimarí**, described above, and another one heading left for the beach. At km 48 is the

QUILIMARI BRIDGE spanning the namesake low-volume river at a great height, supported by five pillars. Beyond the bridge there is a good view to the inland valley, the Silla del Gobernador and the wide bay and beach of Pichidangui.

To the side is the railway bridge ending on the old railway station where, in the past, the trains stopped over during the long, three-day journey to Iquique, for lunch on an outdoor counter.

The highway continues across a wide peninsula, the sea shimmering far to the left among rock formations. There is the **San Andrés urban development**, with nice views over cliffs. At km 61 is

Ensenada Totoralillo a small bay lined with black rocks and peppered with islets, the sea breaking into foam against them. It is a good spot for stopping over and eating at what might be the best restaurant in the entire Pan-American highway. A path leads to the stony beach. Across the peninsula is the **Bahía Azul** development. At km 67 is the rock-lined **El Negro bay**, with good surf. At its southern tip is the **Cascabeles fishing cove,** with a stony but sheltered beach and an access road. It is good for camping and looking for agates on the beach.

At km 76 is the junction for Los Vilos, the midpoint between Santiago and La Serena (232 km). The Hostería Copec offers seafood and ceviche, a tasty dish of fish cooked in lemon juice. Opposite Copec is a tourist office, open in season and also selling handicrafts. If you wish to take a bit longer for lunch and enjoy a better view, we suggest you to drive into

LOS VILOS (pop 9,000), a port and seaside resort offering all services. There are many fantastic versions regarding the origin of its name, but in fact it is derived from vilu, the Mapuche word for snake. In 1855 is was granted the status of a major port for shipping the province's mineral ore and farming produce. The old pier and some derricks still remain. The booming activities are now tourism and fishing. You will find all provisions and services like hardware, garages, stores, etc. It is very popular in summer, with a number of hotels, motels, campsites, restaurants, dancing establishments and two nice beaches: the **Principal** at the fishing cove and **Las Conchas** to the South. At both there is a large supply of seafood.

Drive or walk down the main street, continuing then along the Costanera -the waterfront street, quite busy in summer- to the **Muelle** (the pier) and, finally, to **Las Conchas** cove.

Good seafood and fine views at restaurants La Caleta, Bellavista, Internacional and the renowned Bahía. For cheaper, faster meals, try the seafood stalls at the fishing cove.

If you are staying longer than one day at Los Vilos, the following excursions can be recommended:

SECTION A

179

A Boat Tour fishermen offer boats for hire for a ride around the bay.

Isla de los Huevos an islet off the cove, frequented by tourists. Hire a boat at the cove.

Isla de Los Lobos five km south on a dirt road sandy in some stretches- is **Punta de Lobos**. From a promontory you can see, some 200 m off the shore, an islet with a population of over 1,400 seawolves frolicking in their natural habitat. Binoculars come in handy. It is a good spot for a picnic.

Quebrada de Quereo two km south of Los Vilos, on the coastal plain, there is a depression which in the past was a small lake. Remains of prehistoric animals and 14,000-year-old archaeological objects have been unearthed. It is known internationally in archaeological circles and the object of some important research.

Continuing North along the Pan-American highway from Los Vilos (km 76 from Quínquimo), the highway passes the road junction for Illapel (described in next tour). The Pan-Am follows the coastline, with the beautiful **Amarilla Beach**, ending at the **Conchalí brook**, at km 80. There is a gorgeous spot for camping, with fine sand and quiet sea water. Take water.

The Los Vilos bay ends to the North on the beautiful Ñagué beach, visible from the highway, with a sprawling, lonely mansion rearing above the beach. The beach is private.

The highway now continues along large fenced farms, with peculiar metal gates. Sizable investments are being made here into afforestation with forage shrubs to support sheep and goat flocks. **Atriplex** species -small, light green shrubs able to withstand prolonged drought and with a high fodder value- have been profusely and orderly planted, along with Acacia cianofila -with long, shiny, dark-green leaves- and other foreign species.

The highway leaves the coast for a while and reaches, at km 96,

Caleta Chigualoco a scenic beach with thundering surf. Access is through a dirt road branching left just before the bridge. The fine-sanded beach is suitable for camping; water is available from a well.

The Pan-Am then runs through rolling coastal country to reach, at km 111,

HUENTELAUQUEN two places at either bank of the Choapa river. On the southern bank is the farming complex of Hacienda Huentelauquén, with houses, churches, orchards and a kiosk selling papayas and a renowned local cheese.

The lush irrigated fields stand in stark contrast with the previous semi-arid landscape. The orchard-owners have 1-m-tall vine props which they also use as stands for drying fruit and legumes; in May, the vine props are buried under a yellow layer of corn left to dry.

On the northern bank, on a dry slope, is the old village of Huentelauquén, with a curious architecture. This is Chile's narrowest point, with a scant 80 km from the border to the sea. Camping is possible at the nice beaches of **Agua Dulce** and **Caleta Manso**, quite frequented in summer; they are located 5 km farther North along the Pan-Am, taking a dirt road branching left. We suggest a short visit to

MINCHA following a 24-km detour on a dirt road, upriver from Hacienda Huentelauquén, to return to the Pan-Am along the river's northern bank. Mincha lies on a fertile valley straddling the Choapa river, again in striking contrast with the arid surrounding hills. It was a Diaguita seat in the past, its name meaning «between hills».

The district of Mincha and Tunga was given as a land grant to Juan de Ahumada in the early 17th century. In 1704 it became the property of Bartolomé Rojo, who founded the village of Mincha; it eventually became the leading community in the province.

Its **church**, erected between 1760 and 1789, was granted the status of a National Monument in 1980. Its benefactor, Marcela Ahumada, who died in 1780, was embalmed and encased in a large piece of furniture made of canelo wood, long used as the altar. At present there is a new altar, and the body has been exhumed.

2 A VISIT TO ILLAPEL ★★

a 156-km round trip from the Pan-American highway, on a paved road.

Three km north of Los Vilos a road branches right (km 0) to Illapel, running along the Conchalí river bed; the land has seen little farming. At km 15 is the Pupio brook and valley, frequented for countryside outings from Los Vilos. The road becomes constricted and winds its way along the **Cavilolén** creek. At km 23 begins the beautiful cuesta Cavilolen Ridge of 5 kilometers with nice views to the inland valleys of Choapa and Illapel.

The descent of 6 kilometers is called cuesta Las Cañas (Las Cañas ridge). The railway crosses these hills through a tunnel of great extent. At km 39 there is a junction with a road leading to La Ligua. The Choapa river is spanned by the Confluencia bridge, at km 44. Three km beyond it a road branches west to Mincha, along the Illapel river.

Opposite the railway crossing, drive or walk 200 m to see the **Casas del Peral**, a rural building dating from ca. 1780, once part of the great Hacienda Choapa; it is laid around two inner courtyards: one for the daily chores, another for domestic activities.

Back on the highway, **Cuz Cuz** is at km 51, a village of Quechua origin and the main pre-Conquest population center in the district. A further five km will bring you to

ILLAPEL (pop 15,000), the provincial capital, a busy little town nestled in a valley hemmed in by

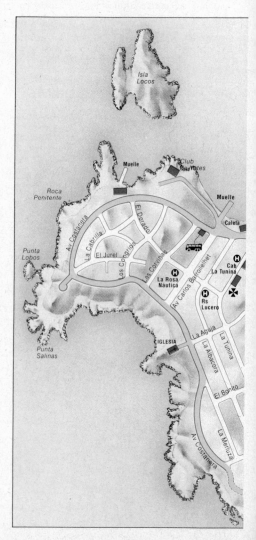

☎ Telephone
★ Touristic Information
⇗ Lookout Point
◉ Meeting Point
A Town Hall
B Parish
C Post Office
D Bus Terminal

RESTAURANTS
1 Hs Copec
2 Sta Emilia
3 Hs El Arrayán
4 Internacional
5 Bellavista
6 La Bahía
7 La Caleta
8 Seafood Stalls

ACCOMMODATIONS
9 M American
2 M Sta Emilia
10 M Hardy's
11 H Hs Lord Willow
5 H Bellavista
3 M Hs El Arrayán
12 M Choapa
13 M New Pacific
16 M El Pelusa

DISCOTHEQUES
14 La Terraza
15 Las Brisas

OF INTEREST
E Handicrafts

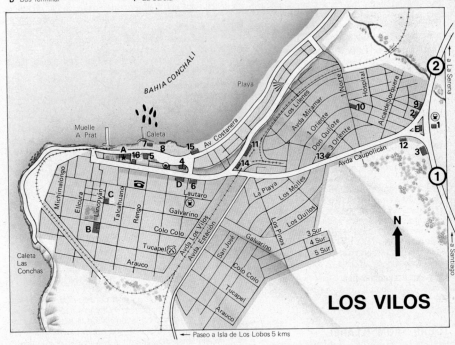

LOS VILOS

← Paseo a Isla de Los Lobos 5 kms

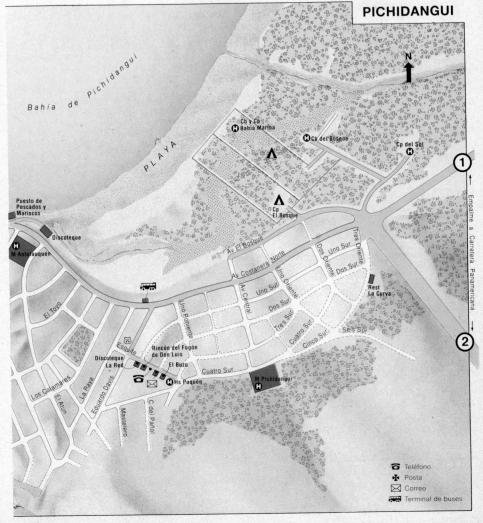

PICHIDANGUI

☎ Teléfono
✷ Posta
✉ Correo
🚌 Terminal de buses

hills and lying on the banks of the Illapel river. It was founded in 1752 at another location, but that early version was short-lived. In 1788 Ambrosio O'Higgins passed through the place on his survey journey to Copiapó, and he ordered the immediate reestablishment of the village to provide support to the scattered miners and farmers in the area.

Illapel saw its heyday last century, fueled by intense mining, cattle-raising and farming activity; its output was shipped through the port of Los Vilos using the railway laid up to Salamanca in 1888. Its mainstay is now agriculture.

What To See Visit the **Municipalidad**, a refurbished building in colonial style, and the **Casa de la Cultura**, with an interesting museum containing archaeological artifacts and ornamented with building elements from a colonial house.

The neighboring streets have interesting houses dating from last century (see map), one-storied, with stone foundations and mud-brick walls enclosing inner courts. Worth a look are the **House Villarroel** (ca. 1780, at the corner of O'Higgins and Recabarren), and **Correo Viejo** (Old Post Office, 18th century, on Independencia and Av Silva). Drive down Independencia to the west to the **Casas del Mirador**, a building from the late 18th century which is a good example of that period's rural construction; it originally had three bodies surrounding a large courtyard. Drive then across town and continue one km into the road to Combarbalá to see the **Casas de la Puntilla** (ca. 1780) in a nice setting and with solid, buttressed mud-brick walls. For the **grand view**, climb along Av Silva to Quillaicillo.

Food and Accommodation Hotel Domingo Ortiz de Rosas. Good food at Hostería Illapel and Tap Vital.

TOURS FROM ILLAPEL

3 | **TO SALAMANCA AND THE INLAND VALLEYS**
★★★ *A round trip of 128 km, with 33 km paved; the road is curvy but in good condition. Allow one day for this. Gasoline at Salamanca; take food.*
A visit to the most fertile section of the valley, with an interesting extension into mountain meadows.

Take exit labelled 2 in map of Illapel (km 0). At km 5 the road climbs out of the valley to descend soon into the neighboring Choapa valley and run for a while through an area covered by eucalyptus, pine, poplar and willow forests. At km 13 is the village of Peralillo and, at km 19, Chuchiñi. One km beyond the Quilmenco bridge a short road branches left to the **house of Hacienda Chuchiñi**, an interesting example of a rural mansion of 1900,

with a U-shaped building open towards the park and crowned by a small central tower. The valley becomes more tree-filled and, at km 32, is

SALAMANCA (pop 6,500). Founded in 1814 on land donated by the rich landowner Matilde Salamanca, it lies on a gentle slope at the foothills and is the last urban center in the valley. It is orderly laid-out and has a shady square in the middle. It is a peaceful village of hard-working people, lying in a fertile district. Its shopping streets -Bulnes and Salamanca- are open even on Sundays and holidays. The Cerro La Cruz offers you a sweeping view of the place. For camping and picnic, the **El Tambo resort** 3 km from town.

Continue the tour taking the gravel road out of Salamanca (km 32) leading to the valley and village of **Chalinga**, at km 34, an Indian village until the 18th century, with an interesting **church** dating from 1750.

Following the fertile mountain valley up to San Agustín, at km 46, you will reach the **Escudero Manor House** (ca. 1820), with a front court graced by palms and with 3 kilns for drying hot pepper and tobacco. The mud-brick house surrounds the other three sides of the yard. A short distance beyond the village are the **San Agustín houses** (1880), with a chapel and several sections cascading down the slope, surrounding a series of courtyards. It was the largest hacienda in the valley; now it is a rural school.

Those fond of angling for trout should continue to Zapallar (there is also a campsite). Total distance from San Agustín back to Salamanca is 48 km.

Drive across town and continue for 23 km into the northern bank of the Choapa river. The valley is intensely farmed, even on the hillsides, the fields delimited by stone or mud-brick walls. There are some small villages on the way, such as Jorquera at km 55 and Llimpo at km 62, and an impressive **suspension bridge** at km 71. A short distance downriver is a more modern version of recent construction.

Some 15 km upriver is **Cuncumén,** a good spot for those interested in hunting and fishing.

At km 62 you can cross the river to Coirón, to return following the south bank. The valley becomes more constricted, its bottom in stark contrast with the arid hills lining it. The winding, scenic road passes the hamlets of **Quelén Bajo** at km 71 and **Panguecillo** at km 75, both with small reed-roofed **sanctuaries**. At km 78 is the hamlet of Higuerilla with the Rosa Mística **church**.

At km 88 there is bridge into Salamanca. For bathing in the river or camping, continue 2 km

---

☎ Telephone Center	🚌 Bus Terminal	● Interesting Houses	**ACCOMMODATIONS**
Ⓖ Gasoline Station	A Town Hall	**RESTAURANTS**	1 H Dgo Ortiz.
✱ Hospital	B Church	3 Hs Illapel	2 H Alemán
✉ Post Office	C Culture House - Museum	5 Tap Vital	3 Hs Illapel
	D Entel – Chile		4 H Alameda

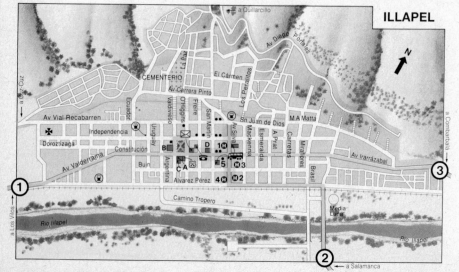

ILLAPEL

downriver to **El Tambo**, with a small lonely beach and a willow forest, and some low stone walls to delimit camping plots. El Tambo has an interesting modern **church**. A short way up the hill there is an old Indian cemetery, commanding a **sweeping view** over the area. Return via Salamanca, to reach Illapel on the paved road at km 128.

To Mincha on the Inner Road It is 40 km from Illapel, with 10 km paved up to the Mincha road junction. The dirt road is winding and has little traffic; drive carefully. On the way you will see fields terraced into the river and large fences designed with live cacti at the picturesque village of Tunga, with its houses made of clay and canes, and mud brick. Eleven km beyond Tunga is Mincha, described in Tour 1 above.

4 THE NORTHBOUND INLAND ROAD ★★

it is 73 km to Combarbalá on a gravel road, in some stretches narrow and poorly-surfaced, but passable. Frequented by mining trucks. Gasoline at Combarbalá. Allow three hours for the trip.

A chance to see what was the only route North before the Pan-Am was built (1950) and trafficked since the Colonial days.

Leave Illapel (km 0) heading for the Casa de la Puntilla at km 2, turning then North along the Tunquén valley. The railroad runs parallel to the road and the vegetation soon thins out, cacti and Acacia now prevailing.

At km 29, the valley is joined from the right by the Chillán ravine, and a road branches off to Farellón Sánchez. Here the railway turns away from the road and follows that valley towards the mining district. You will see **ore grinding mills** (trapiches) for gold extraction, which can be visited (see details under Andacollo description, Section C). The road becomes constricted at the Tunquén ravine until mount Lampanqui (2,090 m) starts to loom at the far end. This is part of the ridge separating the Limarí and Choapa river basins.

At km 51 starts a long climb called **Cuesta El Espino**, narrow and very curvy, devoid of protecting rails and with lots of mine-truck traffic. Here the land is much more arid, with a green-reddish hue afforded by its high copper content. You will see some pirquineros (self-employed miners) piling up mineral rock on the roadside; they will happily tell you about their work. The crest is reached at km 61, with a breathtaking **panoramic view** sweeping from the snowy peaks of the Andes on the East, to the arid plain of Combarbalá dropping away to the North. This is Chile's narrowest point, with some 80 km from the Argentine border to the Pacific coast, and the transverse spurs of Cordillera with their attendant valleys are plain to see. The descent is less curvy and shorter. The railway soon joins the road again.

At km 67 is the junction with the Combarbalá-Pan-American highway road. Turning right on this road you can see the **Cogotí dam** in the distance while crossing the dry bed of the Pama brook. Combarbalá is at km 73 (the stretch from Combarbalá to Illapel is described under Section B).

5 THE SOUTHBOUND INLAND ROAD ★★★

it is 176 km to La Ligua, including a 40-km round-trip detour to visit Petorca, with 86 km paved and 90 km graveled. The road is curvy, passable and with some traffic. Allow six hours for the journey. Gasoline at Petorca, Cabildo and La Ligua. Take food.

A journey following the route of the old Inca Road, used during the Colonial period and the only road North prior to the opening of the Pan-American highway, by 1950. The present road uses bridges and tunnels (narrow: single lane) built for the railroad in 1912; the railroad was rerouted following the coastline in 1940, as the three spurs of Cordillera to be crossed made it necessary to use a racked railway. It is an interesting journey along little known, old mining and farming communities.

Take exit labelled 1 in map of Illapel (km 0), the paved road to Los Vilos, crossing the Choapa river over the Confluencia bridge and continuing to km 14, where a signposted road branches left for Caimanes. This road is graveled and approaches the Choapa river. At km 20 are the **Casas de Lo Caña**, part of the old hacienda belonging to Matilde Salamanca. Built of mud brick by 1770, the

ground-floor walls and part of the storage rooms still remain. A short distance from here, by the river, are the **Casas de Limáhuida**, built by 1820 in another farm also owned by Matilde Salamanca; the houses are laid out as a U and have a covered veranda all around, and some palm trees presiding over them. There is a school.

The road then follows the Limáhuida creek, along green fields, until the hamlet of Socavón, at km 34. Beyond this point the land becomes more arid, the road hemmed in by the hills; the road starts ascending the Las Astas climb (from km 44), which crosses the ridge through three successive tunnels: **Las Astas, Curvo** and **Chico**, all narrow and humid. At the end is a view over the confluence of small irrigated valleys, to reach, at km 54,

Caimanes (pop 450), at the confluence of the Pupio and Rincón creeks. It is a picturesque hamlet with mud-brick houses, signposted alleys and a small square with a huge piece of **rock crystal** and an old **boiler** used in farm work. The village is engaged in small-scale mining, in quarrying quartz for glass factories, and in farming. Ask where you can buy chunks of rock crystal.

At km 63 is the **Los Cristales pass**, between soaring Mount Vizcachas and, to the right, Mount Gonzalo. This area is rich in quartz, quarried by the locals who pile up their output on the roadside. Three km later is a group of houses known as El Naranjo and then a cage-like metal bridge, followed by an identical bridge over the Quilimarí river at km 73. Here is Tilama, a modest hamlet in a small glen. A road starts here for Pichidangui; five km from here is the **Culimo dam**, a nice spot for a picnic, frequented by **anglers**; lisa -a river fish- is abundant.

Beyond Tilama the road starts to ascend again, at first gently and then more steeply, crossing the narrow Quelón pass and then the **Las Palmas tunnel** at km 83. A magnificent view opens up over a deep ravine along whose bottom the road will continue. The village of Las Palmas is at km 87, El Quisco at km 90 and the Petorca river valley, where the river is spanned by a 5-arched metal bridge, is at km 104.

On the south bank the road joins the La Ligua-Petorca paved highway. Take this road to the left, running along green fields flanked by cliffs, to reach, at km 124,

PETORCA (pop1,900), a rural village with lovingly tended fields, particularly those devoted to floriculture. The **Church** of Nuestra Señora de las Mercedes is interesting, with imagery and paintings brought by the Jesuits around 1620. The place produced a Chilean President, Manuel Montt, who was born here in 1808; his house is now a National Monument.

Drive back along the road to Cabildo; the junction with the road from the North is at km 144. Continue to Artificio; the long, single-laned **La Grupa tunnel** is at km 151. Beyond it, the road makes a spectacular descent into the La Ligua river valley, the creek spanned by two picturesque bridges, to reach at km 156

CABILDO (pop 8,600), with an orderly layout and a nice square with a beautiful parish **church**. The adjacent **Cerro La Cruz** is crowned by a huge cross made of rails.

The Inca Road followed the same route described above, crossing the La Grupa ridge. In Cabildo it forked into three branches: **to Argentina** following the La Ligua river upstream to Alicahue, mount El Cuzco and the Portillo pass, to reach the Argentine province of Cuyo; **to Quillota**, following the La Ligua river downstream, through the Catapilco valley and crossing the El Melón ridge; and **to the Santiago zone**, climbing through La Mora to descend to Putaendo, then through the Chacabuco range to the Mapocho river valley. An **Indian cemetery** can be visited climbing the road to Alicahue.

The paved highway runs along the river to reach La Ligua at km 176. The town is described in the Central Chile volume; see Central Coastline, Section A, Tour 4.

SECTION B   OVALLE

This Section covers the area of the Limarí basin and its tributaries, stretching between the Elqui river to the North and the Choapa river to the South. This vast and rich district is now the agricultural basket of Region IV, thanks to its privileged climate and to the availability of the widest-ranging irrigation infrastructure in South America.

Three large dams, hundreds of kilometers of irrigation canals, huge siphons carrying water from one side of a valley to the other, entire hillsides covered by drip-irrigated crops, astoundingly fruitful inland valleys and carefully tended mountain meadows are among the features of this district.

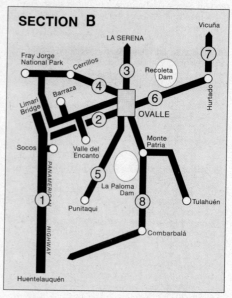

1 PAN-AMERICAN HIGHWAY FROM HUENTELAUQUEN TO THE LIMARI RIVER ★★★ *total distance of 101 km, paved. Gasoline at Socos.*

The road runs inland from the coast, the sea visible only on three occasions from the highway. The land is hilly, with spurs of Cordillera marching down to the ocean.

This leg starts at the northern bank of the Choapa river (km 0), just beyond Huentelauquén. At km 5 the sea can be seen and there is an access to

Agua Dulce Beach access is through an unsigned, open gate (an access fee is charged) followed by a dirt road leading to a small sheltered beach, with white sand and drinking water from a well. It is very popular in summer. Camping is permitted. A 2-km road branches right from the access road to **Caleta Manso**, a smaller, stony, wind-sheltered beach, with no surf and with a fishing hamlet. Camping is permitted.

Back on the Pan-Am, at km 15 there is a narrow valley where a road branches right to Combarbalá. Then, at km 19, there comes a place with small stands of eucalyptus and restaurants catering to truck drivers: it is **Puerto Oscuro**, an old mining spot where a dirt road branches off to the coast leading in 4 km to

Caleta Puerto Oscuro the dirt road follows a lush ravine, with a small dam at the beginning. The fishing cove was in the past a mining port; now it is a picturesque resort crossed by a brook, with a fine-sand beach and sea suitable for bathing. The beach is shaped like a triangle and is lined by cliffs. At the northern end there are summer houses **on stilts**; in the center there is a lagoon frequented by campers and, to the south, the fishing hamlet with a restaurant. The place livens up only in summer; in winter, even the fishermen emigrate.

The Pan-Am continues through rolling country, arid and barren in summer, with occasional huts occupied only in winter and spring by people tending goat flocks brought down to graze on the seasonal grasses. Odd cactus fences are to be seen, which are very effective for keeping goats from straying into fields that for them are off-limits. At km 36 is

Las Palmas canyon deep, narrow and dry, with a small plant for grinding and concentrating mineral ore. Three Chilean palms, each over 20 m tall, signal the northern limit of the range of this native species, once quite abundant and now endangered. At km 44 is the

Amolanas bridge with three arches and built in the 1950s, spanning a deep canyon. The highway continues on flat terrain which suggests the proximity of the sea. At km 63 is

El Teniente bridge from where the sea and the **El Teniente fishing cove** can be seen, encroached upon by a gigantic sand dune which a plantation of Hemofila arenaria heroically attempts to harness. The cove is accessible through a dirt road -sandy in stretches- branching off to the right before the bridge and which, skirting the brook, bypasses large dumps of mining waste until it reaches the beach. There are fishermen's huts, water from a well, fine sand, pounding surf and lots of rocks. Camping is permitted.

Crossing the El Teniente valley there are inns for trucks drivers. Two km later, in another valley,

a short road branches left to the **La Cebada** cove, with a narrow beach of fine sand and thundering surf; very popular in summer.

The highway then turns inland; the **Cerros de Talinay** ridge separates it from the coast.

At km 76 there is a truckers' inn and a road branching left to **Mina Talca**, the second-richest gold mine in this Zone. Some distance ahead, at km 96, is the Socos **gas station** and a road branching right to Ovalle (see below).

Opposite the gas station there is a memorial to the **Salala Battle,** held on Feb 11, 1817. It was a bloody surprise attack by Patriot forces which had crossed from Argentina; they marched along the valley and fell upon Spanish troops and civilians coming from La Serena, fleeing to Santiago along the coastal road.

TERMES DE SOCOS located 370 km North of Santiago and 2 km off the Pan-Am, the complex has thermal waters and a hotel, next to a creek flowing from Punitaqui and in a lush, shady setting. There is a good restaurant and a thermal pool, surrounded by old trees and interesting archaeological artifacts. The terraces are a good spot to stop for a meal. There is also a good **campsite** with amenities and a swimming pool; it is the best campsite in the district.

Continue on the Pan-Am skirting the Limarí river among osier-covered meadows. On the roadside there are several kiosks selling fresh **goat cheese** and **river shrimp** (the latter not available from December through April). This section ends at the bridge spanning the Limarí river at km 101.

2 DETOUR TO OVALLE ★★★

a 33-km stretch of paved highway running on flat terrain. It is also possible to continue North along the excellent interior highway to La Serena, which is 24 km longer than the Pan-Am.

This detour follows a nearly flat plateau slashed by the Limarí river (not visible from the road). The ground is a typical terrace filled up by sediment from an old lake bed, stretching widely on both sides of the river. To the North looms the famed mount Tamaya, while the Talinay ridge marches on the western horizon, gashed in the middle by the Limarí river.

It is surprising to find irrigated fields: they have been recently brought into production with the water supplied by new canals from the large **La Paloma dam.**

On the way there are two places of particular interest: Barraza (km 6) and Valle El Encanto (km 15), described under Tour 4.

184

The highway approaches Ovalle and descends to cross the river. Before starting the descent there is a sweeping view of

OVALLE (pop 67,000), capital of the Limarí province. It was founded by the Asamblea Provincial of La Serena on April 22, 1831, and christened after José Tomás Ovalle, then Vice-President of the Republic. From the Colonial times, the local landowners were related to and dependent upon La Serena, a feature which remained unchanged until this century.

At present, the inland valleys are the leading producers of vegetables, fruit and pisco in Region IV. Ovalle is the main supplier of farm produce for the Great North; its agricultural market is very important. It is also a busy road traffic hub, with buses linking it to the entire North; tickets are normally sold out. It is a busy, expanding city with good hotels. It deserves a visit.

What To See Av Vicuña Mackenna leads to the square, which is lined by century-old Phoenix palms and rows of jacaranda, and sporting an interesting **pavement** made of slag from an ore refinery. In the center there is a slender bronze fountain, cast at the Panulcillo mine and donated by José Tomás Urmeneta, the wealthy miner of Tamaya. On one of the sides is the **Parish Church**, with thick mud-brick walls and a single nave with an off-center vault.

Two blocks westward from the square on V Mackenna are the so-called «casas corridas», with quaint inner courtyards. The **Museum** is on Independencia 329 (Tue-Sat 09:00-13:00h & 15:00-19:00h; Sat until 18:00h, Sun 10:00-13:00h). It is small, but it contains the choicest **collection of Diaguita pottery**, with unique pieces well worth a visit.

Go up street Amalia Errázuriz (see map) to the look-out for a sweeping **view** over the city. Visit the **Feria Modelo de Ovalle** (see map) (Mon, Wed, Fri & Sat until 1600h), in the huge hangar-like structure which in the past housed the railway machinery shop. This is the largest, busiest farming fair in the entire North. Specialties include dried fruit, renowned fig cakes and tasty goat cheese from the mountain meadows.

Drive down Av. Romeral to the Northwest; three blocks beyond the VIP disco turn right on a dirt road, across the railway and then parallel to it to a rocky point, where a high bridge spans the Limarí river; another bridge does likewise below the first one, on the road to Monte Patria. Drive up this old road to Santiago, across the Camarico canal, for the best **panoramic view** over the city and its valley.

4

☎ Telephone Center	F Feria Modelo de Ovalle	5 H deFrance	23 VIP Discotheque
◉ Café, Meeting Point	G Railways Station	6 H Venecia	24 Comercial
★ Touristic Information	H Eastbound Buses	7 H Buenos Aires	25 Alamar
⛽ Gasoline Station	J Westbound Buses	8 H Roxy	26 Yun–Yun
≫ Lookout Point	K Rural Bus		27 Rancho Criollo
A Town Hall		**RESTAURANTS**	
B Post Office	**ACCOMMODATIONS**	1 H Turismo	**OF INTEREST**
C Archaeological Museum	1 H Turismo	20 Club Social	10 Tanneries
E Market	2 H American	21 Club Arabe	11 Dried Fruit
	3 H Quisco	22 Palmeira	12 Pasteleria Tosti (Pastries)
	4 Gran Hotel Ovalle	23 Casa Grande	13 Lapislázuli

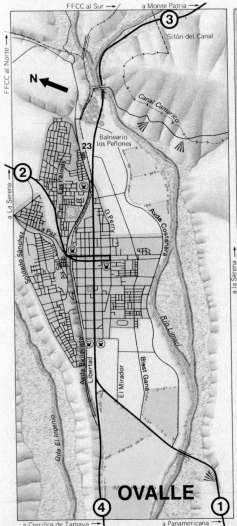

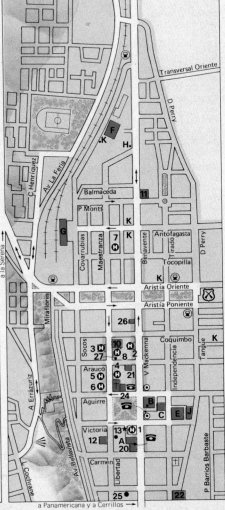

OVALLE

Where To Eat Quick meals and children friendly at get-together place shown in map. Good cuisine (including river shrimp in season) at Hotel Turismo and the Club Social. At night, the best is Disco-theque Casagrande Vip, with a grand view. The Tosti bakery and pastry shop is renowned.

TOURS FROM OVALLE

3 ROAD TO LA SERENA ★★★

an inland road of 88 km, paved and well laid. Described under Section C, starting from La Serena.

4 A CIRCUIT TO THE WEST ★★★

a 138-km circuit, with 50 km paved and 88 km graveled. Allow at least one day; camping at Termas de Socos. Gasoline at Socos.

A single circuit taking in all the places of interest to the West of Ovalle. For those not camping on the way, it is advisable to divide the circuit into several excursions from Ovalle.

Take exit 4 out of Ovalle (km 0). The road skirts the north bank of the Limarí river, among long stone walls and extensive vineyards. To the right is the creek of **Quebrada El Ingenio**, with little agriculture as its waters are polluted by waste from a mineral plant upriver.

At km 7 is **Hacienda Limarí**; only some massive mud-brick walls remain of what used to be the manor house of the district's largest hacienda, visited among others by Darwin and Domeyko.

Turn right at this point to cross the El Ingenio creek; soon there is a road branching left to the Villalón canal, the first large irrigation works (1928). Across the river you can see the high terrace upon which the paved road runs.

At km 13 the road passes the hacienda El Trapiche, with a **centuries-old building** now housing a school; it may be visited. The road runs through vast vineyards, and the roadbed of the old Cerrillos-Ovalle railway, built by J T Urmeneta, can still be made out. On the far bank is the San Julián chapel.

At km 17 is the village of **La Torre**, a long street with an interesting mud-brick **church** crowned by a balcony-girdled steeple, a style to be found repeatedly in Elqui valley churches.

At km 20 is the hamlet of **Las Sosas**, with rolling streets and high sidewalks lined with old, gaily-painted houses. At the square, take road to the right to climb out of the valley, among native pepper trees and capers. At the summit there is a road junction; continue straight ahead to reach, at km 25,

Cerrillos a village with all the services and laid out in the typical Spanish fashion, with regular blocks of equal length; the dirt streets are wide. It originated as an industrial and railway support center for J T Urmeneta's vast mining empire centered on the large Tamaya mine -in the high hill nearby-, once Chile's largest copper mine.

A railway to Tongoy was built in 1859 -one of the first in South America- and a large refinery was brought on stream. The railway climbed to the main mine, located on the eastern slope of the hill (it cannot be seen); there were two so-called placillas, with over 500 houses and several tunnels, such as **Socavón Lecaros**, sinking two km into the earth. All of this has been abandoned and access is not permitted.

The Quiroga and Tamaya mines, by contrast, can be visited. They date from later and tapped other lodes in the hill; they command a splendid view over the valley.

The railroad was dismantled in 1952 and only an old station remained at Cerrillos, adjacent to the police station. The present prosperity of the village rests upon the visionary works undertaken by Arturo Villalón S, who, with remarkable boldness, acquired 8,000 hectares of this non-irrigated plains, built in 1918 the San Antonio and Concepción dams and then the large Villalón canal, finished in 1928, and transformed the plain into today's fertile lands.

Retrace the road up to the **El Olivar** junction, turn-

ing 3 km into the vast olive tree plantation with a refining plant selling high-quality **pure olive oil** at a convenient price (Mon-Sat, business hours).

At km 26 a road branches right to Cerrillos Pobres, leading beyond it to the Pan-American highway at km 36. Right across the Pan-Am starts a dusty gravel road leading in 18 km to

FRAY JORGE NATIONAL PARK in which visits are restricted year-round to Sat, Sun & holidays 08:30-18:30h, with the purpose of minimizing fire hazards. Allow at least four hours. The road is curvy at the beginning and then fairly straight until the **Visitors' Center** run by Conaf. An entrance fee is charged and a detailed description of the excursions is provided. The road continues for 10 km to the summit; halfway up there is a well-equipped picnic area, but camping is not permitted. Beyond this point the road becomes quite bumpy; it is advisable to continue on foot.

At the summit of the Altos de Talinay, over 560 m above the sea, is a Valdivian-type relict Hydrophytic Forest, with canelos, olivillos and a large variety of ferns surviving in the heights since prehistoric times, nourished by thick fogs rolling in from the sea and condensing at this point. If you are lucky enough to catch a sunny day, you will marvel at the contrast between the aridity of the surrounding terrain and the luxuriance of the forest, which would by no means seem out of place at much more southerly locations.

Back on the paved road, at km 72, turn right, cross the police control post and then the bridge spanning the Limarí river, to reach the road junction for Ovalle at km 89. Follow this road to km 93 and take there the road branching left to

BARRAZA the gravel road descends for 3 km to a river bank where the old, quaint village of Barraza is located. During the Colonial period it was second only to La Serena in importance. Renamed Villa de San Antonio del Mar in 1818, it was left outside the new routes after Ovalle was founded in 1831.

Its **church** National Monument, was built of mud brick in 1681, but its tower dates from later. It has a beautiful side door and valuable records from the original period; a memorial plate hangs on the façade. Ask for the key at the convent next door. To complete the visit, follow the street upstream to the end; there, on a barren hillock, is the **cemetery**, commanding a view over the village and the valley. Retrace the road back to the highway, at km 99, and continue towards Ovalle until km 110, at the junction with the road to

VALLE DEL ENCANTO NATURAL MONUMENT (Mon-Sun 08:00-20:00 h; entrance fee is charged). The 5-km gravel access road descends into a ravine where the entrance control is located, manned by municipal wardens who offer their services as guides. There is a picnic area. The scenery is semi-arid, rocky and with a few trees. Described archaeologically in 1946, it was granted the National Monument status on account of the importance and large amount of remains of old cultures. Remains have been unearthed up of hunting peoples from 2,000 BC. The most visible stone artifacts are attributed to the Molle culture of ca. AD 700.

There are over **30 petroglyphs** depicting human and animal figures carved in bas-relief on rocks, and over 20 **"piedras tacitas"** (cupstones,) large boulders with multiple bored cavities presumably for placing food during ritual ceremonies. These objects are distributed among six large groups, all easy to visit. Valle del Encanto is the North's most important archaeological center of pre-Conquest cultures. It is well worth a visit, of at least two hours and it is interesting for children and adults alike.

To return, retrace the road. The highway is at km 120 and Ovalle at km 138.

5 TO PUNITAQUI ★★★

a round trip of 54 km, with 22 km paved. Allow half a day. Gasoline at Punitaqui.

Leave Ovalle following the road to Santiago. At km 2 take the signposted road to Punitaqui, which runs through the fertile fields of Camarico towards some hills closing this great plateau. Beyond

the hills the road descends into a new valley with a brook and at km 27 it reaches

Punitaqui (pop 1,800) its 3-km-long main street lined with façades painted in light colors, the village is located in a ravine close to the sharp-pointed Punitaqui peak (1,215 m); to the west loom the El Altar and La Laja mountains, where major copper mines were active last century.

The village owes its foundation to gold mining works in the vicinity. In 1785 rich lodes of mercury were struck; this metal was used for refining gold and silver through the amalgamation process. It was in great demand for the silver mines at Chañarcillo last century. In the vicinity is the Delirio mine, which still produces mercury.

A road to Combarbalá starts from here, a 67-km stretch of graveled, curvy, poorly-surfaced road running through lonely, dry country. Another option is described under Tour 8 below.

6 RECOLETA AND RIO HURTADO ★★★

a round trip of 157 km to Río Hurtado, on a flat but curvy gravel road. Allow 7 hours for the trip. Take food. There is a campsite on the way. Gasoline at Ovalle.
A scenic tour to the Recoleta dam, quaint villages in the small, fertile Río Hurtado valley, and the Pichasca Natural Monument. It is a good occasion to continue to Vicuña and reach La Serena from the east, a stretch of 126 km.

Take exit 2 out of Ovalle (km 0). At km 5 take gravel road branching right to Recoleta. A couple of hundred meters before that there is a grand **view** from the pass: towards the South you can see the confluence of the Hurtado and Grande rivers, the railroad bridge, the large siphon carrying the water of a canal across the ravine, and some vineyards; to the North is the deep El Ingenio ravine and the Panulcillo **ore grinding mill**, serving the famous mine located farther North.

The road runs across a vast plateau in which the fenced fields -with their hard grasses and shrubs- stand in stark contrast with those unfenced, grazed to barrenness by the goat flocks driven down to the lowlands late in the autumn. The Hurtado river runs at the bottom of a deep canyon next to the fertile valleys of **Guamalata** and **Samo Bajo**.

At km 10 a road branches left to Estación Recoleta. You are approaching now the village of Algarrobo at the edge of the plateau and, at km 14, is the

RECOLETA DAM which is crossed over the dam wall next to a forest planted fifty years ago. There is a small square, a boat ramp, a yacht club, and a picnic area in summer. Its faithful wind and good climate keep it busy as a watersports center throughout the year.

This is the oldest dam in the Zone, started in 1929 and finished in 1934. At the end there used to be the village of Recoleta, with a Franciscan convent from the 17th century. Now there is only a small cemetery visible on the hill.

The road skirts the lake's southern shore. At the beginning, where the mouth of the Hurtado river is located, is the **Bosque Hundido** (Sunken Forest), with old willows.

The road and the villages up to Samo Alto are located high up, on dry, rocky hills with unusual colors. Some tiny hamlets are passed, such as Eleuterio Ramírez, Tabaqueros and Guampulla, with new houses built using a strange mixture of timber and mud brick.

At km 30 the road crosses to the north bank and soon meets the road from Andacollo. At km 34 is

Samo Alto nestled in a wide section of the valley with the Andes for a backdrop. It was an old government seat of the Inca territory. Its small church is interesting. The road crosses to the south bank and winds its way at a lower area, along irrigation canals, through villages and fruitful orchards and fields. The valley is flanked by high, rocky, red and yellow hills.

At km 40 is **El Pinar**, with lots of fig tree and Acacia opuntia (tunas) groves. You will see the

typical rural construction of one story towards the street and two or more cascading down towards the river. At km 42 a road branches left, leading in 3 km to the

PICHASCA NATURAL MONUMENT (Mon-Sun 08:30-17:00 h; free). The road descends towards the river and crosses it, climbing beyond it to the village of **San Pedro**, where the province's oldest archaeological remains have been unearthed. The road climbs on a ledge to the crest of a hill, where the **Recepción** is located, manned by a park warden. There is a grand **view** over the cultivated valley, the neighboring village of Pichasca and the Andes in the background.

The road is lined with seats and steles built of large stone slabs of different colors; at km 45 it reaches a large **monolithic rock** where you must leave the car.

Climb the hill on foot, heading North; it is peppered with scattered **petrified tree trunks**, in which the wood structure can be clearly made out. The paths climbing down from the monolithic rock are worth a try. Allow at least 1 hours; it is worth a visit.

At km 48 you retake the highway to reach, at km 50,

Pichasca a quaint hamlet with a large mud-brick church painted blue and with the bell tower to a side, as is customary in this valley. In the distant past the place was called Inga Pichasca, when it was a seat of Peruvian population.

At the exit there is a police control outpost. The road continues very close to the river, passing **La Fundina** at km 54 and then running for a while on a ledge; it then descends to the river level and runs almost straight for 6 km through a willow forest. This detour was made when a rock slide blocked the road running among the hills. It climbs then to reach, at km 68,

Serón a pretty, well-cultivated valley with a picturesque village clinging to the hillside. It has nice, well-kept houses and a church. One km later is the

HACIENDA SERON the most beautiful manor house in the entire province. It is a long mud-brick house with one story facing the road and two stories cascading behind, with a balcony; the upper floor has the living quarters and the ground floor is storage room. It was named after an old castle in Sevilla, Spain. Opposite the house, across the road, is a simple church of stuccoed mud-brick walls, with a small central tower and a large main door made of American oak. Inside it has a nave of equal width and height, with a brick-paved floor. On the walls there are some tombs, the oldest dating from 1868. It was granted the status of vice-parish in 1972, but is now disused. Ask for the keys at the manor house.

At km 72 is **Morrillos**, next to a huge, jutting mass of rock. At km 74 the road crosses to the north bank and at km 77 is

Hurtado a quaint village of a single, 3-km-long winding street halfway up a slope, lined with houses with fruit orchards and lots of dahlias, chrysanthemums and geraniums. The place is renowned for its homemade marmalades, dried figs, quince jam and nuts. You can continue a further 16 km up the valley to Las Breas. In summer you can spot some **tricahue parrots**, a native species somewhat larger than choroy, with red chest and green feathers.

7 CONTINUATION TO VICUÑA ★★★

a 46-km stretch of fairly narrow, winding gravel road; do not attempt it after a snowfall. Allow two hours; watch your gasoline.
An excellent alternative to reach La Serena «from behind», i.e., from the East, travelling through mountainous scenery.

Just outside Hurtado, km 80, take road branching left, which climbs alongside a brook where you will see some old algarrobos with trunks exceeding 1 m in diameter. The summit, at **Alto 3 Cruces**, is reached at km 91. The climb takes some 40 minutes, and the **view** from the top is great: the Andes marching on the East and plains dropping gently away to the North, towards Vicuña.

4

The road runs on a lonely plateau and at km 105 you can see the **El Tololo Observatory** to the left, presiding over the landscape; it will accompany you for a good many kilometers. Then comes another long climb.

The road then descends after km 112 through a narrow ravine to the Elqui river and reaches Vicuña at km 126.

8 TO MONTE PATRIA, COMBARBALA AND SANTIAGO ★★★ *It is 194 km to the Pan-American highway at Puerto Oscuro, with 46 km paved and the rest graveled. A 90-km extension to Tulahuén. Gasoline at Monte Patria and Combarbalá. Allow 8 hours, leave early and take food. Stretch Puerto Oscuro-Santiago is 288 km.*

A journey through an intensely cultivated district, with the most fertile lands in the district, passing the La Paloma dam, scenic mountain valleys and the beautiful sierras of Combarbalá. For those spending a longer period at Ovalle, we suggest to divide this tour into two legs: first to Monte Patria and Tulahuén, then on to the South.

If you are planning to cover this route in a single leg, we suggest you make the trip in the direction described here, as the stretch Ovalle-Puerto Oscuro (Pan-American highway junction) will take you until evening, and then you can continue by night to Santiago. Take exit 3 out of Ovalle (km 0). The road skirts the Balneario Municipal Los Peñones (picnic area), crosses the bridge spanning the Limarí river under another road bridge soaring above. Soon comes the confluence of the Hurtado and Grande rivers and the long railroad bridge. At km 5 is the large metal siphon carrying water to the Camarico plains. Then the road crosses the Grande river and heads into the Sotaquí valley, where, at km 10, there are some tall palm trees, the remnants of the manor house of the 18th-century Hacienda Sotaquí, property of the Ariztía family. Right beyond this is the **Pisco Control distillery**, which can be visited during week days. Opposite it is the village of

SOTAQUI small and with a parish church founded prior to 1630, with jurisdiction over the curacies existing from Andacollo to Combarbalá. It was the most important inland urban center until the foundation of Ovalle, in 1831. The present church, erected in 1946, keeps the image of the **Niño Dios de Sotaquí**, with a festivity held on January 6th; it is the most impressive religious festivity in the entire province. On the ground at the entrance are the **tombstones** of the Ariztía family, the old owners of the Sotaquí and Guallillinga haciendas (the latter across the river), both managed by J T Urmeneta by 1831, before he struck it rich at the Tamaya mine.

Opposite the church, on the northwestern corner, there is a gate where you can buy delicious **marmalade** and fruit. Behind it there is an interesting fruit orchard with a nice house.

Continuing along the valley you will see some enormous constructions on the hillsides, resembling solar plates: they are greenhouses used for growing first fruits.

At km 18 is a cluster of dwellings called Carachilla and a road crossing the river to Guallillinga. Then the road crosses above another siphon carrying the water across the valley. The crops are raised on the land stretching below the canals, which are located way up on the hillside.

At km 22 a wide curve offers a view to the colossal wall, floodgates and spillway of the La Paloma dam. There is a small forest, an ideal spot for camping.

LA PALOMA DAM the edge of the wall is reached at km 26. A road runs along the top of the wall towards the gates and the spillway. It is Chile's largest irrigation dam and the second largest in South America, with a storage capacity of 750 million cubic meters and flooding an area of 3,000 ha. Its construction was finished in 1965, and in 1974 the water filled the gates and the trunk canal network was completed. The great lake reached its overflow level in 1984, making it necessary to open the spillway gates for the first time. Its shore has

been recently afforested with tree species. It is a magnificent sight.

The road follows the coastline and at km 30 a trail branches off to the water's edge. Soon you will see a host of anglers fishing for the abundant pejerrey argentino (season Nov-March). Then the valley into which the Grande river empties comes into view, with a large sandbank and hundreds of large birds resting: they are guairavos, nocturnal fishing birds. At km 34 is

Monte Patria at the access round-about there is a small forest used as a picnic area. The picturesque village lies on a slope and has an old mud-brick church of a single nave, with a small wooden tower sporting a painted clock forever saying it's 3 o'clock. The village's original name was Monte Rey and was changed with the advent of the Republic.

At the round-about starts a road heading south for Combarbalá, at 75 km, and another one for Tulahuén, 54 km inland.

DETOUR TO TULAHUEN ★★★ *a 90-km round trip on a winding road. Allow three hours.*

A visit to the scenic Grande river valley, set in a typically mountainous landscape.

Start at the round-about (km 0). Right next to it is the Monte Patria **pisco distillery**, which can be visited (prior permission by Pisco Control, head office at Rengifo 240, phone 224833, La Serena). Then the Ponio river is crossed to reach Las Juntas at km 8. There is a village at the confluence of the Rapel and Grande rivers. There starts a road along the river's north bank to **Rapel** -with a church from 1871- and the **Los Molles** hydroelectric power station, climbing a narrow valley.

At Las Juntas there is an old **manor house**, with the typical configuration of this area: a ground floor of mud brick and the upper floor made of timber, surrounded by a gallery-balcony.

Continuing to Tulahuén, the road crosses the Rapel river at km 9 and right beyond the bridge is the **Dos Ríos** hamlet, with high sidewalks made of stone and the remains of an old lead concentrating plant.

At km 13 is **Chilecito Bajo**, a narrow street hanging above the river, lined with houses, orchards and gardens. On the opposite bank is the picturesque village of **Mialqui**, with a significant agricultural infrastructure, a pretty church and a cemetery perched atop the hill. The family Prohens, now the pioneers in the farming of the Copiapó Valley, had their first vineyards here. The valley is not very wide and is intensely cultivated up to the altitude where the canals run. The road runs on a ledge above the river, is very curvy and each curve opens up a new perspective into the valley.

At km 15 is the village of Chilecito and at km 30 is

Carén a village of Diaguita roots located 920 m above sea level. It became a curacy in 1630 and has a pretty church which was upgraded to a parish church in 1823. It was second in importance to Sotaquí. The splendid house and park of Armando Salas, one km before the village, is worth a visit.

Leaving Carén (km 0) you reach Pulpica at km 1 (clay pottery). To the left is the only remaining algarrobo native forest in the zone. For the next 12 km the road climbs gently alongside the Grande river; the irrigation canals run farther below on the hillsides. The cultivated patches are somewhat smaller. This is comunero land, in which land ownership is shared by families, a system in practice since many generations ago.

At km 4 are the few houses of **Chañaral de Carén**, with an hostería and at km 10 are the **Llanos de Tulahuén;** at the point where the houses peter out on the right-hand side, a road leads left down to the river, where there is a petroglyph which sounds like a bell when hit. At km 12 is

TULAHUEN a picturesque village made of stone and mud brick, gaily painted with colors ranging from ocher to orange and red. The river water is warm, suitable for bathing. Here you can rest and buy dried fruit and goat cheese. To return, retrace the road.

A short detour to the right can be recommended for the best view over Tulahuén, at the Población El Chaguar. For lunch, the El Encuentro restaurant.

For those with more time, we suggest a 30-km excursion upriver towards Las Ramadas. You will see old ranch houses, petroglyphs, good spots for angling and camping and, up on the hills, the lapis lazuli mine, one of two of its kind in the world (the other one is in Afghanistan).

Here you can choose either of two alternatives: retrace the road or take the scenic inland road from Tulahuén to Combarbalá (54 km) and then continue to Puerto Oscuro on the Pan-American highway. This inland route is a dirt road with very little traffic; allow some three hours. Taking the square of Tulahuén as your km 0, at km 11 the road climbs some cliffs: drive carefully. At km 20 there is an ore grinding mill. At km 35, the Hacienda Cogotí, with large vineyards, then at km 39 the road crosses the Cogotí bridge; it is a good spot for a rest and a picnic under the trees or by the river. The road surface improves a bit and at km 54 you can see Combarbalá among the hills.

CONTINUATION OF THE JOURNEY TO COMBARBALA:
Continuing from the Monte Patria round-about (km 37) on the road to the South, you leave the shores of lake La Paloma. The road runs through barren country to reach another arm of the lake at the great valley of the Guatulame river.
The pavement ends at km 47, at

EL PALQUI with a grand view of this ample valley, covered with vines well up the hillsides; irrigation is provided by the Cogotí dam. This are the province's best soils and its grapes, thanks to the altitude and abundant sunlight, ripen earlier than those at any other place. The effort behind the establishment of these plantations is staggering, with vast fields watered by drip irrigation or under greenhouse-like structures, all fenced with carefully made stone walls. A high trunk canal, to the left, brings water from the neighboring Grande river valley.

The road reaches the village of **El Tomé** at km 51, on the river's far bank, set amid intensely culti-

vated fields. At km 57 is

Guatulame an old village on the river bank, with a tall mud-brick church of a single nave, erected ca. 1880. The road bypasses the place. Note the railway station made of brick and with massive diagonal timber poles. On the detour to the village vendors sell napales, square pieces made of woven cane and used as shades or screens in country houses; they also sell wickerwork objects made of willow.
At km 63 is

Chañaral Alto a picturesque, orderly village with high sidewalks and two-story mud-brick houses with balconies. There is a small square from 1907 and a mud-brick church, with a Greek-style portico and a tower lined with corrugated tin plates. The railway station is called San Lorenzo. The land is carefully cultivated, mostly using drip irrigation, easy to recognize for the dry, weedless soil. Greenhouses pepper the landscape.

At km 70 the intensive agriculture peters out and a stretch known as **Mal Paso** starts, the road winding its way through a gap between the mountains, where the Guatulame river hops on flat rocks forming pools and lapping on some beaches. It is the best spot for bathing or resting.
At km 77 there is a detour to

San Marcos the access road ducks under the railway bridge and dives into this mining village, with wide streets and square blocks. Unlike other villages in the mountains, this one lies on a valley used for farming. The houses are mostly 2-storied and have balconies; there are warehouses, large fig trees and a small church. The main street leads to a beach on the river bank, good for bathing and picnic.

The village saw its golden days when it was a loading station for the ores from Punitaqui.

Continuing the road veers away from the river, crossing some barren hills with cacti and occasional trees with naked trunks and high crowns, trimmed to this shape by goats. At km 87 the road descends into the dry Cogotí river valley and at km 89 it crosses the stream. A road branches right to the

COGOTI DAM access must be requested beforehand from the Asociación de Canalistas, Vicuña

4

☎	Telephone Center	**B**	Parish Church	
◉	Café, Meeting Point	**C**	Bus Terminal	
Ⓖ	Gasoline Station			**RESTAURANTS**
●	Carved-Stone Handicrafts	**ACCOMMODATIONS**		2 Club Social
A	Town Hall	**1**	M La Piscina	3 Imbiss
		4	H Chile	1 La Piscina
				5 El Parrón

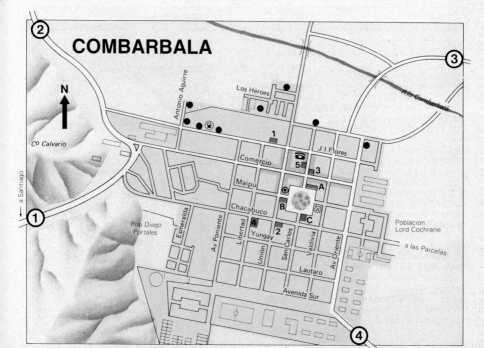

COMBARBALA

Mackenna 520, Ovalle. Started in 1929, restarted in 1935 and inaugurated in 1940, it has a storage capacity of 150 million cubic meters. Its shores are afforested and it is a good spot for an excursion.

Right next to the bridge is the village of **La Ligua**, renowned for its figs and dried peaches. Here starts a 9-km road to La Isla, where a shape resembling the **Virgin** can be seen on a rock. Festivity on the first Sunday in May. The road climbs from km 97 through the barren landscape; from the top there is a splendid view of the Cogotí dam. The place is called **Las Coloradas**, with a few houses scattered on the reddish soil, denuded by goats. The mud-brick dwellings are roofed with thatch and painted in a mustard color, using a local earth for dyeing.

Towards the Cordillera a large waste **dump** of surprising colors be seen: it is the La Mostaza open-pit silver mine. Near the mine there is a high, seven-arched railway bridge built in 1912.

At km 104 the road descends into the dry, stony Combarbalá river valley. In the midst of this barren landscape there is a vast drip-irrigated vineyard, using water from a well and producing export table grapes. At km 107 the road passes by the

Ore Grinding Mill of the Cerro Centinela Mining Co; it is the sector's largest facility of its kind. It can only be seen from the outside. It has a large ore yard with **3 grinding mills**. The ground material is conveyed to the triangular-shaped ore storage shed. Further conveyor belts carry the ore to the **fine milling** plant and then to the **flotation tanks**, where, using chemical and stirring methods, mineral and inert material are separated. The resulting product is stored in **concentrate tanks** and the waste is dumped at the **torta de relave**, the huge cake-like heap that can be seen from afar. The plant concentrates minerals both for silver and copper mines.

A short distance ahead a road branches right to Punitaqui and another waste dump from an old mining works. At km 112 is

COMBARBALA (pop 4,400), lying on an arid plain which stretches away towards the Cordillera. It is a small village with narrow, paved streets, and brick houses painted with local earth-dyes. There is a curious octagonal square decorated with Diaguita motifs in colored stones and a pretty mud-brick church, its façade graced by wooden Greek pillars. The village was founded in 1789 by Ambrosio O'Higgins to gather the scattered mining population; mining remains the place's mainstay to this day.

Its most attractive feature, however, are the carved objects using **combarbalita stone**, a semi-white stone similar to marble, with streaks in a wide range of colors; this is the only place in the world where this semiprecious stone occurs. It is interesting to see the more than 100 craftsmen cutting, boring and polishing these stones, always under water, creating the typical figures of churches, doves, eggs, ashtrays, etc. It is worth a visit. There is a motel with a swimming pool, and restaurants.

A good gravel road leads from Combarbalá (km 112) to the Pan-American highway. At km 117 a road branches left to Illapel, described under Section 1. Continuing towards Puerto Oscuro, the Pama creek is crossed at km 118; the road runs on a plain towards the Coastal Range, which is crested at km 126. The **view** is spectacular: down below is the arid plain of the Pama creek, with scattered houses of goat farmers and the massive wall of the Andes for a backdrop, its rocky peaks capped with snow. This is Chile's narrowest point, with a scant 80 km from the Argentine border to the Pacific coast. Along the crest of the range runs the water divide; from there, the water flows down to the Cogotí dam and thence to the Choapa river.

The road starts to descend near the mouth of Chile's first river having its source at the Coastal Range. It is the Llano Largo creek, a tributary of the Canela river, which in turn is a tributary of the Choapa.

The road winds its way down gently for the next 15 km until it reaches a stony plain with scant vegetation. It then fords the brook several times. A few scattered groups of houses are to be seen as the valley grows wider; at km 167 is **Canela Alta**, a quaint village with some more vegetation.

The road is paved for 8 km, running next to vegetable plots, to reach, at km 175,

Canela Baja an old, picturesque village with 3 streets lying parallel to the river, mud-brick houses -many of them painted blue- and old buildings on the main street. There is an hostería.

At the far edge of Canela the pavement ends and a bridge is crossed; the river veers South towards **Mincha**. The road crosses a vast dry plain -Hacienda Puerto Oscuro- with a beautiful olive grove and wide plowed expanses, to descend along a ravine to reach the Pan-American highway at km 194. From here, it is 288 km to Santiago.

SECTION C   LA SERENA

This is the main Section in this Zone and seat of Region IV's capital, La Serena. The city was founded in the early days of the Spanish Conquest, and ruled over all the lands and encomiendas (see Land & History) granted to the conquerors in the valleys of Copiapó, Huasco, Elqui, Limarí and Choapa. This old hegemony over the so-called Little North (Norte Chico) has now been elbowed away by the powerful agroindustries that have sprung up at the Copiapó and Limarí valleys.

This Section has a large number of good campgrounds, motels, and hotels, stemming from a tradition started with the very foundation of the city, as it was destined to be the rest and recreation spot for travellers plying the harsh desert route. Its gentle climate and beautiful beaches contribute to this tradition.

1 **PAN-AMERICAN HIGHWAY FROM THE LIMARI RIVER TO LA SERENA** ★★★ *a stretch of 118 km, paved, with detours to Tongoy and Guanaqueros. Gasoline at Tongoy and La Serena.*
A visit to the most important seaside resorts and beautiful bays in this coastline.

Crossing the bridge spanning the Limarí river (km 0), the Pan-Am climbs to the **Llano de Cerrillos**, with irrigated crops growing in the midst of the

SECTION C

desert landscape. The water comes from the Recoleta dam, and is carried by the Villalón canal. Towards the coast loom the Fray Jorge hills and to the East the majestic Mount Tamaya.

At km 7 there is a police road control post and at km 10 the road to the **Fray Jorge National Park** branches left (see Section B). At km 20 the road descends from the barren plain to Quebrada Seca, a ravine with some cultivated patches and a road branching left to Cerrillos. It soon climbs out of this ravine to the arid upland, with a **seashell mine**, which shows that these lands, unlike the former ones, belong to a **raised portion of the continental shelf** stretching North all the way to La Serena, at the Los Choros peninsula. At km 22 is the

First Detour to Tongoy unsigned. A 32-km dirt road, badly surfaced and suitable only for 4WD vehicles. This road follows the route of the old Tamaya railroad, passing through the coastal farm of **El Tangue** with some strange sheds for storing grass. A road branches off to the lonely beach of **Puerto Aldea**, a site with archaeological remains. The road continues to Tongoy behind the beach, but during the low tide, some cars drive on the sand to Puerto Aldea.

At km 39 is the second detour to Tongoy, 14 km long and difficult. Beyond the Quebrada Camarones and on a plain dropping gently away to the sea, at km 49, is the

Third Detour to Tongoy signposted. This is the most frequented road to the seaside resort, with a graveled stretch of 4 km through a shrubby plain and lots of shell-sand (conchuela) pits; it reaches a coastal paved road at km 53. Turn left until km 55, where a road branches right to

Playa Blanca the access road is 5 km long, at stretches sandy, and it leads to a small bay of placid, blue-greenish water and extremely white sand of **ground shells**. There is an excellent campground with a restaurant, quite frequented. An access fee to the beach is charged; toilets are available.

Continuing to Tongoy, at km 56 there is an open pit shell-sand mine, with deep roads dug to extract the petrified shells, which are sold to poultry farms as feed to strengthen eggshells. It is interesting and can be visited.

At km 61 you cross a brook and reach

TONGOY Region IV's largest seaside resort, lying on a small headland overlooking a vast bay surrounded by the Lengua de Vaca coastal range; to the south stretches the 14-km-long **Playa Grande** beach, and to the North the 4-km-long **Playa Socos**.

The name is Quechua in origin. In 1859 a port, a railway and a copper refinery were built here for the Tamaya copper mine, the world's largest. Nothing is left now, save for the curious layout of the streets around the square and the street names, such as Fundición Tamaya, Barnes (name of a metallurgical engineer), etc. It was one of the works of the powerful pioneer José Tomás Urmeneta.

Tongoy is very popular in summer, and has good accommodations, campsites, restaurants and entertainment at every level. It has a busy yacht harbor and a watersports area, in addition to splendid summer houses. Colectivo (shared) taxis shuttle between Tongoy and La Serena.

What To See Driving in through Av Fundición Norte you reach the Costanera, the waterfront street, lined with summer shops, with a **footbridge** leading to the best beach, **Socos** (camping not permitted; car access through the road beyond the bridge across the brook). This is the busiest part of town, with the best hotels and gathering points for the young.

Continue along the **Costanera** skirting the headland's coastline, with beautiful summer houses and the ground «paved» with white shell-sand. The tennis club is spectacular, the waves breaking just beyond the edge of the courts. Soon the great **Playa Grande** bay opens south, with the Fundación Chile facilities engaged in marine research. The Costanera passes then the church, the square and the school, where the **old residence** of José Domingo Silva is located.

191

Playa Blanca

Go next to the **fishing and yacht harbor**, full of vessels and busy day and night. Launches can be hired for a cruise along the coast. Go up street Marcelo Bachelet to the park and the **look-out** point for the grand view over Tongoy and the surrounding area.

Where to Eat Excellent cuisine at the Hotel Yachting Club and at Hostería Tongoy. Best view from the restaurant on Playa Grande. Quick meals and children-friendly atmosphere at the marisquerías (seafood stalls or restaurants).

Accommodations There is a range of hotels and residenciales along the beach. For camping, the best is Playa Blanca.

To continue to La Serena from Tongoy (km 61), take the paved road North up to km 75, to

GUANAQUEROS a small fishing cove with summer houses and a long, 8-km beach with fine sand and a placid sea; it is quite popular. The scenery is beautiful and its busy fishermen keep it well stocked with the **best fresh seafood** in the North. Specialties at seafood restaurants include high-depth machas (a mollusk), oysters and ostiones (a larger strain of oyster), steamed, Parmesan-style or al pilpil (with parsley).

There are several restaurants, motels and campsites. Summer tourist activity is intense, day and night, with lots of visitors dropping in from Tongoy

and La Serena to enjoy its seafood. The El Pequeño restaurant is renowned, with a terrace overlooking the sea.

Continuing along the paved road to the North, you meet the Pan-American highway at km 79. The Pan-Am follows the long Guanaqueros beach. At km 81 a 1-km dirt road branches left to **Las Mostazas**, an excellent beach with a good campsite open the year round.

At km 83 another road branches left, leading to

Morrillos a fashionable beach right below the highway, with a good restaurant and an excellent campsite open the year round.

At km 91, a road branches left for

Las Tacas a popular beach with a year-round camping site. At km 92, another road branches left, leading to

Totoralillo a 1.5-km-long beach with a fishing cove, where a parking fee is charged. It is a nice, frequented beach. Here is the modern Tiki-Tano tourist complex, with Polynesian-style cabins, a campsite and an excellent restaurant specialized in Tahitian cuisine.

At km 105 the road passes near the La Herradura Bay. The Pan-Am then widens out to four lanes, bypassing Coquimbo and reaching La Serena at km 118.

LA SERENA (pop 90,000) is the regional capital. Metropolitan La Serena, in turn, comprises La Serena, Coquimbo, Compañía and Tierras Blancas, and has a combined population of around 170,000. La Serena lies on a platform raised from the sea and made up of three distinct «terraces».

It is Chile's second oldest city, founded in 1544 to facilitate communications with Peru both by sea and overland, a vital link for supplying the new Reino de Chile. It was destroyed by the native Indians and rebuilt in 1549 by Francisco de Aguirre.

There are over 29 churches in La Serena, as a result of the fact that the religious orders had their convents here to take care of their personnel in transit. The city is pleasant, has excellent accommodations and is renowned for its pastries, beverages and liquors, which unfailingly delight travellers.

| ☎ | Telephone |
| A | Bus Terminal |

RESTAURANTS
6 La Picada
2 El Pequeño
1 La Bahía
3 Miramar
4 La Nave
5 La Ruca (kiosk)

9 Cheap Food

ACCOMMODATIONS
1 H La Bahía
7 Guanaqueros Compground
2 H El Pequeño

ENTERTAINMENT
8 El Suizo
2 El Pequeño Discotheque
10 La Coca Loca Discotheque

GUANAQUEROS

The city's layout and architecture bear the mark of three consecutive periods:

The Colonial Period, with the laying-out of square blocks around the main plaza. Only a few stone churches remain of this period, with beautiful façades, and a few mud-brick houses with elaborate stone portals.

The Mining Boom Period started in 1825 with the discovery of the rich Arqueros silver mine, and was fueled by an intense copper mining activity last century. It brought with it the most beautiful architectural buildings in town, with very interesting houses and churches in neoclassical style and an influence of American and Italian architecture (through architects Parker and Celli, respectively).

The Neocolonial Style Period was encouraged by President González Videla with the «Plan Serena», starting in 1948. The Avenida Francisco de Aguirre was refurbished and remodelled, the Pedro de Valdivia gardens were laid out and a look-out terrace was built at street Pedro P Muñoz. The so-called Spanish architectural style was promoted; the new public and private buildings had their façades built in a heavy version of the Californian colonial style. This stylistic imposition is still in force, although it is now applied with some flexibility, which in turn has led to the erection of some interesting, modern buildings downtown. The city dwellers have a strong urban awareness and a certain standard of living that an outsider cannot but notice.

Present-Day La Serena Considerable progress has been experienced since 1985, with the surge in fruit exports, gold mining, expansion of the astronomical observatories, etc, which have given rise to intense commercial activity and an improvement in the living standards. The opening of the **Avenida del Mar,** the waterfront avenue, has triggered a veritable explosion of tourist infrastructure at the site and the urban complex boasts now a hotel capacity comparable to that of Valparaíso, Viña del Mar, Reñaca and Concón combined. It is definitely on its way to Chile's major league in tourist destinations.

What To See Drive along Av Francisco de Aguirre, shaded by large trees and its central park graced by marble replicas of classical statues, as well as

La Serena

by sculptures by Chilean artists. The main shopping streets are Cordovez and Balmaceda. In the surroundings are to be seen

CHURCH OF SAN FRANCISCO with a small museum on the side through which you can go into the church and its sacristy. Erected between 1585 and 1627 in white stone brought from the heights of Peñuelas, in Coquimbo, its massive walls are one meter thick. The façade, in elaborate baroque style, is also of carved stone. It is undergoing reconstruction after the 1975 earthquake. The **Museo de Arte Religioso** (Jan-Feb, Mon-Fri 11:00-13:00h and 18:00-20:00h; Sat and Sun 11:00-13:00h; March-Dec, Sat and Sun 11:00-13:00h), small and containing mainly sacred objects, is located in the oldest part of the church, with beams in Mudéjar style. The funeral mask of Gabriela Mistral, Chile's Nobel laureate poetess, is held here; she was a third-sister of the order of San Francisco.

MUSEO ARQUEOLOGICO (Tue-Sat 0900-1300h & 1600-1900h; Sun 0900-1300h; in summer, Tue-Sat 0900-1400h & 1600-1930h; Sun 1000-1300h An entrance fee is charged). The building was erected in 1945, but the stone portal dates from 1820; it

4

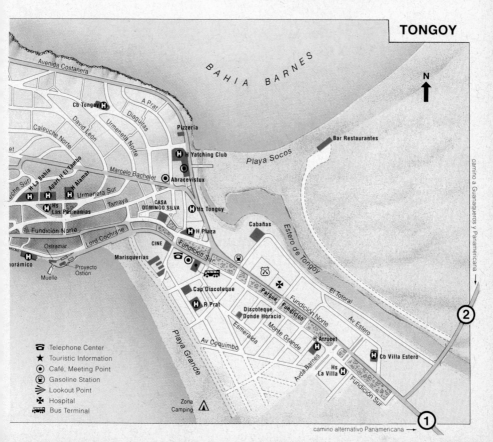

TONGOY

had been part of an old local residence. It contains the most complete collection of artifacts of pre-Spanish cultures of the so-called Little North, very well displayed. Noteworthy is its splendid collection of **Diaguita pottery**. It is well worth a visit.

LA RECOVA is a municipal market located in an arcaded building, with two central courtyards, good restaurants in the upper floor and the city's best **handicrafts market.** In orderly displays you will see a wide-ranging array of **non-industrial confectionery**, including candied papaya, papaya in its syrup and papaya beverages. There is also manjar blanco -a sort of blancmange made of sweetened condensed milk- in various forms and combinations. There are **handicrafts of carved stone** from Juan Soldado, ranging from water fountains to flower pots, as well as thousands of figures made of **combarbalita stone**, semiprecious ornaments made of **lapis lazuli**, ceramics sporting Diaguita motifs and lots of articles made of **alpaca wool** brought from Peru and Bolivia. It is interesting.

Adjacent to La Recova is the old Jesuit church, which later was taken over by the order of **St Augustin**.

Very damaged by the 1975 earthquake, it is undergoing restoration. The original stone construction dates from 1755, but significant modifications were introduced early this century. One block and a half from here along street Cienfuegos is **House Giliberto (NM)**, erected in 1895 in mud-brick and timber, two storied and with a massive look-out tower. It is an interesting example of the construction technique and style of those days, and is now used to lodge tourists during the summer season.

Drive up along street Vicente Zorrilla following the Alfalfares road up to the point shown in map There is

HOUSE ALFALFARES a splendid manor house of the old Hacienda Alfalfares, built by architect Celli around 1900 in Italian neoclassical style. Towards the river, its façade has large windows. It is very

⊙ Gasoline Station
⇘ Lookout Point

ACCOMMODATION
CbPeñuelas (2G)

Jardin del Mar 1 (2G)
M Canto del Agua (2G)
Apart H Mar Serena (2H)
M Hipocampo (2H)

Cb Las Añañucas (2H)
Cb Beach Pub (2H)
Jardin del Mar 2 (2H)
Les Mouëttes (2H)

Mar Ensueño (2J)
Hs La Serena (2J)
M Capilla del Mar (3G)
Cs El Frutillar (2G)

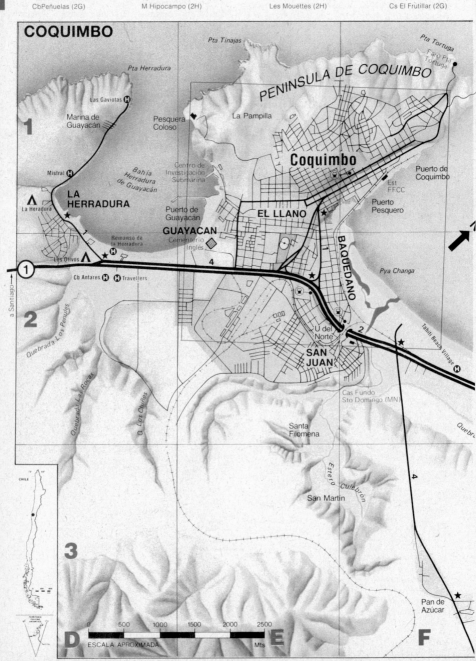

well preserved and still lived-in; it can only be seen from the outside. The façade can be seen from the Alfalfares road. The best view is from the look-out point at Plaza Los Héroes, opposite the cemetery.

Retrace the Alfalfares road and turn left at street Justo Donoso to visit the

CASA DE LA PROVIDENCIA (MN) an impressive neo-classical complex with a church and a large, 2-story house with an inner courtyard lined with galleries on both floors. It was built in 1890 for the Cunningham family and is now used by the La Providencia congregation. Ask whether it is possible to visit it.

Continue along the same street and turn at Novoa, skirting a park and military barracks, running atop a cliff over the Elqui river, to reach the

Los Héroes Cemetery and Square with a great view over the valley and the river. At the cemetery, established in 1856, you can see the grave of Presi-

La Serena, La Recova

M Villa Los Plátanos (2H)	Hostal Casa de Piedra (2G)	M Playa Casino (2G)	Remanso de la Herradura (2D)
M Niko's (2G)	Tahiti Beach Village (2F)	Cb Las Gaviotas (1D)	Antares (2D)
Cb Maroal (2G)	Cb Lonquimay (2G)	Mistral (1D)	Cb Quilacán (3J)
Hostal del Mar (2H)	M Los Refugios (2G)	Traveler's Motel (2D)	Cb Los Papagayos (3J)

4

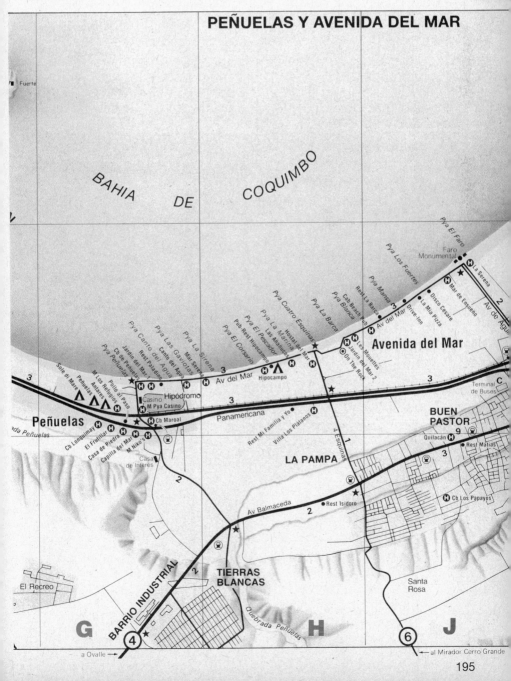

PEÑUELAS Y AVENIDA DEL MAR

dent González Videla and the mausoleums of old families native to La Serena, such as the Edwards, Ross, Vicuña and many others.

Drive down along the Av Colo Colo, lined with gardens and with a view towards the ocean. A genuine moai (Easter Island statue) is to be seen. Turn left on Larraín Alcalde and right on Amunátegui; at the corner is
House Carmona (NM) built between 1855 and 1860 for Juan de Dios Carmona, one of the lucky owners of the Arqueros silver mine. Its tower dates from the turn of the century.

One block from here on street Balmaceda is the **San Juan de Dios Chapel (NM)**, built late last century by Samuel Averell of mud-brick stuccoed to resemble stone, with a small pediment of alerce wood, a bell tower in two sections and a bulb-like dome. This Chapel is of delicate architecture.

You may continue along Balmaceda street, crossing Av. Francisco de Aguirre to come into downtown until street Prat.

Branch left, right here until to Plaza (the Square). Stop driving, park the car over around here and then continue on foot.

Downtown, on Prat street, opposite the Municipalidad, there are three old buildings, one of which contains the café **Rapsodia**, with La Serena's best pastries. On the square is the **Cathedral Church (NM)**, a stone building started in 1841 by French architect Jean Herbage; the bell tower dates from this century. On the opposite corner is the **Santo Domingo Church** complex, with a convent and a small square. Built of stone in 1673, the bell tower dates from the mid-19th century.

Opposite is **House González Videla**, built ca. 1890, a stuccoed two-story construction where the President lived from 1927 to 1977. It has been granted the status of a National Monument and contains a historical archive and a museum (Tue-Sat 0900-1300h & 1600-1900h; Sun 1000-1300h).

To round up the visit, drive to the **Balcón Sobre el Mar,** literally a «balcony above the sea», formed by

RESTAURANTS		
Paladino (2G)	La Barca (2J)	Mi Familia y Yo (2H)
Velamar (2G)	La Mia Pizza (2J)	Matías (3J)
Beach Pub (2H)	Carpa "On The Rock" (2H)	Isidoro (3H)
	Drive Inn (2J)	Pollo al Paso (2G)

DISCOTHEQUE
Disco Cesare (2J)

4

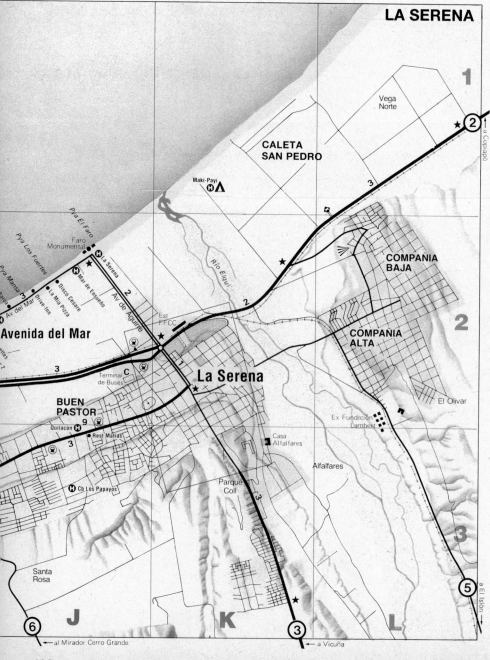

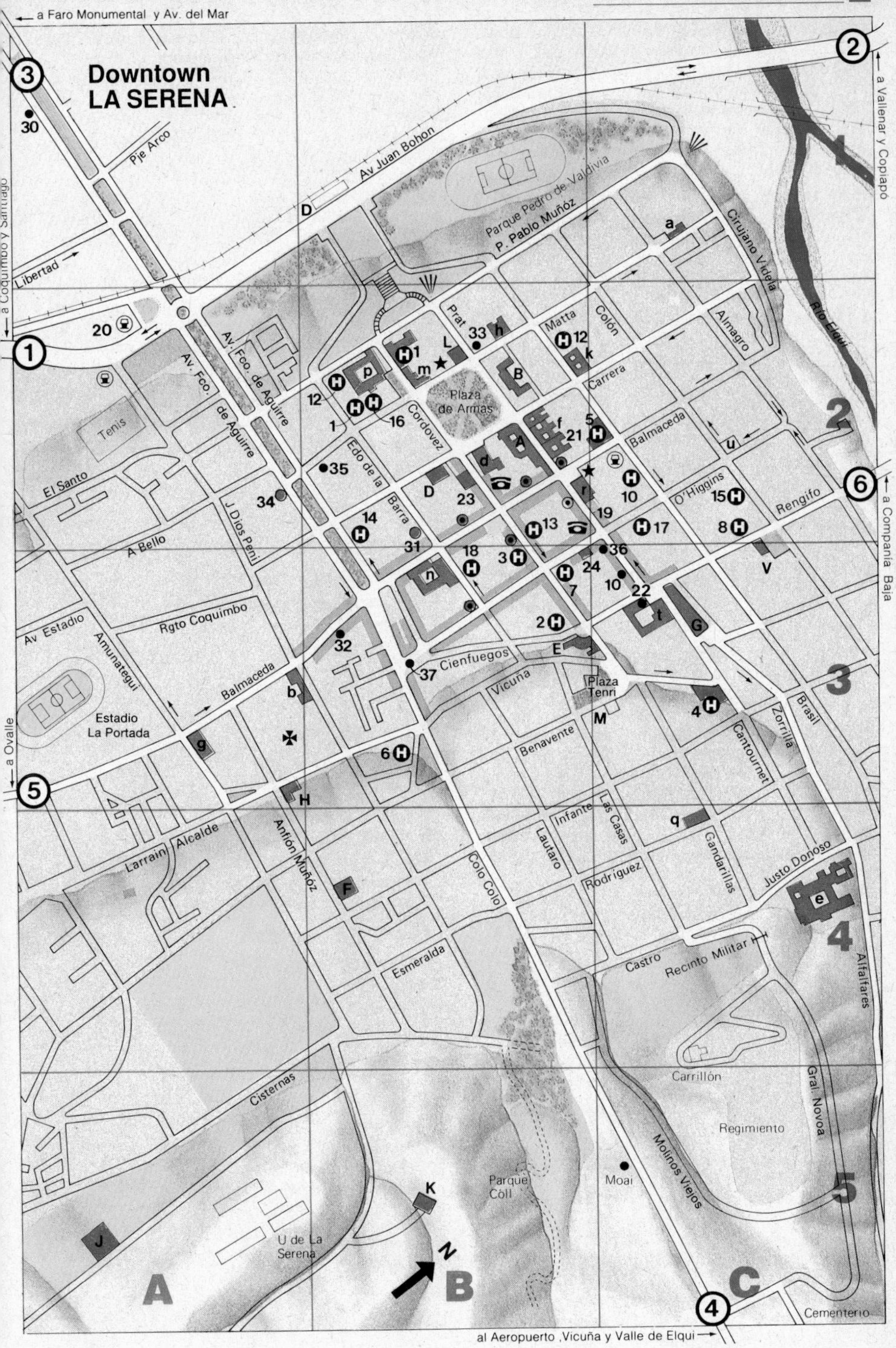

- ☎ Telephone Center
- ⦿ Café, Meeting Point
- Gasoline Station
- ★ Touristic Information
- Lookout Point
- ✠ Hospital (3A)

A Town Hall (2B)
B Government Building(2B)
✻ **C** Bus Terminal (2J)
D Handicrafts Market (2B)
E Archaeological Museum (3B)
F Mineralogical Museum (4B)
G La Recova Market (3C)
H Immigration (3B)
J Tololo Observatory Offices (5A)
K Las Campanas Observatory Offices (5B)
L Post Office (2B)
M Municipal Theater (3C)

BUILDINGS OF INTEREST

a Santa Inés Church (NM),(1C)
b Sn Juan de Dios Chapel (NM),(3A)
d Cathedral Church (NM), (2B)
e Casa de la Providencia (NM),(4C)
f House Piñera (NM), (2B)
g House Carmona (NM), (3A)
h House Herreros (NM), (2B)
k House Chadwic (NM), (2C)
m House González Videla (NM), (2B)
n Church & Museum Sn Francisco (3B)
p Sto Domingo Church (2B)
q Las Carmelitas Church (NM),(4C)
r La Merced Church (2C)
t San Agustín Church (3C)
u Sagrado Corazón Church (2C)
v House Giliberto (2C)
✻ House Alfalfares (3K)

ACCOMMODATIONS

1 H Francisco de Aguirre (2B)
2 H Mediterráneo (3B)
3 H Berlín (3B)
4 H Casablanca (3C)
5 H Pucará (2C)
6 H Los Balcones de Alcalá (3B)
7 Gran Hotel La Serena (3B)
8 H Los Balcones de Aragón (2C)
10 R Brasilia (2C)
11 H Pacífico (2B)
12 H Viña del Mar (2B)
13 H El Cobre (2B)
14 H Alameda (2B)
15 H El Escorial (2C)
16 R Chile (1C)
17 R El Loa (2C)
18 R Petit (3B)
✻ See in Map of Metropolitan La Serena further accommodations

RESTAURANTS

19 Domingo Domínguez (2C)
D Railway Station (1B)
G La Recova Marquet (3C)
20 Restaurant (2A)
21 Salón de Té Rapsodia (2B)
22 Pastelería Alvarez Carmona (3C)
23 Club Social La Serena (2B)
24 La Mía Pizza (3B)

TOURIST SERVICES

30 Hertz (1A)
31 Automóvil Club (2B)
32 Turismo Mistralia (3B) (Touristic Taxis)
33 Budget (2B)
34 Dollar (2A)
35 Rally (2B)
36 Daire (3C)
10 Gira Tour (3C)
1 Turismo Cristóbal (2B)
37 Colectivo taxis to Vicuña (3B)
✻ See location in map of Metropolitan La Serena

streets Pablo Muñoz & Cirujano Videla. Down below you will see the **Pedro de Valdivia park** with a mini-zoo and sports fields. Follow then Francisco de Aguirre all the way to the end, on the beach. There is a **lighthouse** at the place where the waterfront **Avenida del Mar** starts, running along several kilometers of beach with hotels, restaurants and playgrounds.

Where To Eat On the beach, Hostería La Serena, La Barca restaurant, Velamar and Beach Pub, and at Jardín del Mar (garden of the Sea), all with a view to the ocean. Best cuisine and fine service at the Casino and at Restaurante Paladinos, both at Av del Mar. A more typical atmosphere at the busy La Recova. Cheaper at the seafood eateries right across. Picnic at Gabriel Coll park. Meat and fish specialties at Mesón de Matías. Vegetarian food at Maracuyá and at Centro Naturista. Mai Fan Lan, excellent Chinese food. Bocaccio specializes in pizzas, as well as the Italian restaurants La Mia Pizza, Domingo Domínguez and Mi Familia y Yo.

Night Life The young gather at the Café La Creperie (O'Higgins 633) and the Salón de Té Bocaccio, at the corner of Prat and Balmaceda. For dancing, the Discothèque Cesare at Playa La Barca, and Casino de Peñuelas (the latter open Mon-Sun in summer, Tue-Sun in winter, with gambling rooms, bar and dining room-night club). Night life at Coquimbo: dancing at Galaxia, on the road to Cantera 2150, and El Castillo, at Regimiento Coquimbo 333.

Astronomical Observatories Visitors must request permission beforehand at the administrative offices in La Serena, which in the case of observatories **Tololo** and **Las Campanas** are located at Colina El Pino, near the Universidad de La Serena, and are open Mon-Fri 0800-1700h Tololo, telephone 225415, Casilla 603; Las Campanas, tel 224680, Casilla 601. Visiting times for Tololo are Sat 0900-1200h & 1300-1600h; for Las Campanas, Sat 1430-1730h. **La Silla Observatory** does not request a prior permission to visit; you need only show up at the gate control at 1300h. However, for groups of 10 people and up, permission must be requested in writing at least 20 days in advance at Casilla 567, La Serena (tel 224527).

SHORT EXCURSIONS

TO THE LAMBERT REFINERY see map of Metropolitan La Serena: Fundición Lambert is on the road to Exit 5. Leave La Serena along Cienfuegos street, crossing the new bridge to Compañía Baja. Right there branch right along the river (see map of Metropolitan La Serena) till reaching the ruins of the Refinery. Here was the core of the empire of pioneer Charles Lambert (see Land & History). The buildings were made of large blocks of molded black slag; several walls are still standing. This was a large industrial plant known as La Compañía, named after the Jesuits. The large **mud-brick house** up from the refinery ruins was Lambert's residence and a great park used to stretch upriver. Two hundred meters farther along the road, on a depression to the left and behind a fence, there is a stone **Gothic cross** with a tombstone bearing an engraved inscription of verses especially dedicated by the great poet Longfellow. It was a homage to Lambert's only son, who died in the Pacific Ocean while an officer of the British Royal Navy.

TO THE LOOK-OUT AT CERRO GRANDE: A 12-km climb with a splendid view on a clear day towards the coastline South to Tongoy, and inland towards the Elqui valley. Take food, as traffic is only uphill in the morning, only downhill in the afternoon.

Take Exit 6 (see map of Metropolitan La Serena). The road is narrow all the way to the summit (drive carefully), at 570 m altitude. It is worth it.

TOURS FROM LA SERENA

2 A VISIT TO COQUIMBO AND LA HERRADURA

★★★ *a short, 35-km tour. Allow at least three hours.*

An opportunity to visit the port city of Coquimbo, the old industrial area of Guayacán and the La Herradura beach.

Take the southbound Pan-American highway. At Balneario Peñuelas you cross the Coquimbo city limits. Right before the railroad overpass, to the left, are the houses of the **Santo Domingo farm,** now a National Monument.

COQUIMBO (pop 65,000), a city with two major ports, Guayacán and Coquimbo. Originally, these were two separate entities now forming a single urban center.

Coquimbo used since colonial times as a landing place for La Serena, the port and its buildings appeared as late as 1830. In 1846 the area was subdivided into lots and four years later it was granted the status of Major Port; in 1862 it became a municipality and its first mayor was Joaquín Edwards Ossandón. By 1854 there were already two copper refineries at the harbor, the Lambert one with 12 furnaces, and the Allison one with 8.

Guayacán a fishing cove used by native Indians until 1858, when the then world's largest copper refinery was built at the place, with 35 reverberatory furnaces and three 40-m-tall smokestacks made of brick, in addition to its own shipping port and living quarters for the workers and technicians, a significant proportion of whom was American or European. The creator was pioneer José Tomás Urmeneta, who was to be joined later by his sons-in-law Maximiliano Errázuriz and Adolfo Eastman as partners.

In 1862, a railway was finished between Coquimbo/Guayacán and La Serena and the mines in the Elqui valley. As recently as in early 1900 a road was built -Av Ossandón- to link both urban centers, until then quite separated from each other. The large number of foreigners residing in Coquimbo on a stable basis, engaged in trade, mining and mineral refining, lent a special character to the town, much different from La Serena. In 1865 the English Cemetery was established.

The peculiar architecture, still in evidence at Coquimbo, is the work of British and American carpenters who introduced an elaborate woodwork which lent their buildings a particular beauty and solidity. They rank among Chile's most interesting timber buildings.

What To See go into Coquimbo along Av J. Antonio Ríos until the intersection with Aldunate street. Branch left there along the street Henríquez and later branch right along street A. Pinto at the corner of Bilbao and Aníbal Pinto there is an interesting 3-story residence, with fine woodwork and protruding balconies. Street Pinto is at the edge of the hill, and stairs connect it to the streets lying on the hillside. Descent along Freire street to the

Plaza Prat beautiful esplanade overlooking the harbor and the waterfront section of the city, framed by interesting old buildings. Among these stands out **House Pablo Garriga** (1840), which belonged to the first owner of the port. It is a National Monument. Descend to

Costanera is the waterfront avenue, full of shipping flavor and small vessels. Here is the modern pyramidal building housing the Casa de la Cultura, which offers tourist information. Continue

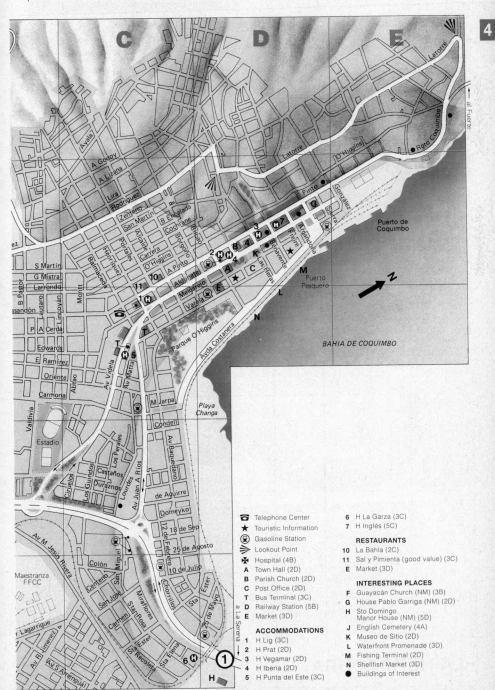

📞	Telephone Center
★	Touristic Information
⛽	Gasoline Station
	Lookout Point
✚	Hospital (4B)
A	Town Hall (2D)
B	Parish Church (2D)
C	Post Office (2D)
T	Bus Terminal (3C)
D	Railway Station (5B)
E	Market (3D)

ACCOMMODATIONS

1	H Lig (3C)
2	H Prat (2D)
3	H Vegamar (2D)
4	H Iberia (2D)
5	H Punta del Este (3C)
6	H La Garza (3C)
7	H Inglés (5C)

RESTAURANTS

10	La Bahía (2C)
11	Sal y Pimienta (good value) (3C)
E	Market (3D)

INTERESTING PLACES

F	Guayacán Church (NM) (3B)
G	House Pablo Garriga (NM) (2D)
H	Sto Domingo Manor House (NM) (5D)
J	English Cemetery (4A)
K	Museo de Sitio (2D)
L	Waterfront Promenade (3D)
M	Fishing Terminal (2D)
N	Shellfish Market (3D)
●	Buildings of Interest

along the Costanera to the Parque Centenario. Turn back to Plaza Prat until

Calle Aldunate that is the main shopping street, lined with interesting old buildings of two and three stories, such as those which housed the Pacific Steam Co, McAuliffe, the French Consulate, etc Stop at the

Plaza de Armas the leading gathering point in town, with a water fountain and serving as a stage for artistic performances. On one side is the San Pedro church (mass Mon-Fri 1930h; Sat 1930h and Sun & holidays 0830h, 1030h, 1215h & 1930h; in summer, Mon-Sat 2000h), started in 1857. In a small adjoining square is the Museo de Sitio, with excavations uncovering archaeological remains dating from ca. AD 900-1000, part of a cultural complex known as Las Animas. Continue along Aldunate till the end for

A Tour Around the Urban Center back on Pinto street, continue to its end. Beyond you will see strange rock formations and a large chalet which now houses a popular disco. At the tip of the cape starts a dirt road for the **Punta de Tortuga Lighthouse,** with a sweeping view towards La Serena. To visit, you must request permission in writing, at least one week in advance, to the Gobernación Marítima de Coquimbo (Av Costanera s/n, Coquimbo). Go up on street Latorre, which runs along the crest of the hill and offers a panoramic view over Coquimbo. Following streets Iquique and Rodríguez you reach

La Pampilla an unpaved esplanade among hills where a traditional festivity is held on September 20th. The surrounding area is peppered with pits where people have dug in search of fossil shells and the famed buried treasure of pirate Francis Drake. Continue along the road to Pesquera Coloso (see map) for the grand **view** over the Herradura bay at Guayacán. Return following streets Guacolda and Pedro Aguirre Cerda to the

Church of Guayacán on the square of the old refinery, flanked by old administrative buildings. The structure was acquired in Belgium in 1888 by Maximiliano Errázuriz and assembled at this place. The structure is metallic, lined inside and outside with stamped, bolted zinc plates. It has been granted a National Monument status. Mass Sundays and holidays at 1000h.
Continue along Los Rieles street and enter to the right to

English Cemetery. lying on a slope, it used to overlook the bay. Now it has been engulfed by the mechanized iron ore loading port and by fuel storage tanks. Ask the caretaker for permission to visit this nostalgic leftover with beautiful tombstones and crosses brought from Europe.
Take the Pan-Am heading South and in 2 km you will reach

LA HERRADURA an old fishing cove and seat of a copper smelter. Now it is a modern, busy seaside resort with excellent hotels, a campsite, country club and yacht club and harbor. We suggest a stroll along the entire Costanera (the waterfront street), from the beach to the exclusive Marina de Guayacán.

Where To Eat at **La Herradura** there are excellent restaurants. Good view from Hotel Bucanero and Restaurante Palafitos. Excellent traditional pastries at Pastelería Alvarez Carmona. At **Coquimbo**, Chinese food at Mai Lan Fan. Cheap meals at the Market.

3 THE BEACHES TO THE NORTH ★★★

a round trip of 161 km, with 110 km paved and the rest graveled. Gasoline at La Serena. Take food; otherwise, supplies can be bought at the fishing coves and at La Higuera. Allow a whole day; the alternative is to camp.
A circuit visiting beaches, fishing coves and interesting mining works, in addition to seeing the modern «harvesting» of camanchaca, the heavy fog rolling in nightly from the sea.

Leave La Serena (km 0) following the northbound Pan-American highway. At km 7 there is a police road control and a short distance beyond a road branches right to **Romeral**, a large iron ore mine linked by railway to the mechanized loading facilities at Guayacán. Continuing on the Pan-Am, take road branching left at km 10, leading to

Punta Teatinos a 2-km dirt road brings you to the northern tip of the great beach embracing the Coquimbo Bay. Fine sand, placid sea, a view over the bay. Near the beach there is a curious fig tree grove growing on the sand, watered by an underground spring.
Get back to the Pan-Am (km 14), which now runs on an arid plateau some distance from the coast. It climbs for a while to descend soon and then pass **Caleta Arrayán**, a modest group of houses on the shore, no beach. At km 40 there is a sweep-

◉ Meeting Point	**C** El Cocodrilo		**9** M La Herradura
⇛ Lookout Point	**D** Galpón del Tata	✳ **3** Condominio Las Gaviotas (1D)	**10** Hostal Las Golondrinas
A Tennis Court	**E** Pastries	✳ **4** Cb Antares (2D)	**14** Cs Los Olivos
		5 M Brisas del Mar	**15** Cs La Herradura
RESTAURANTS	**ACCOMMODATIONS**	✳ **6** Traveller's Motel (2D)	
1 H Bucaneros	**1** H Bucaneros	**7** H San Juan	✳ See location in map
B Yacht Club	**2** Complejo Turístico Mistral	**8** H La Herradura	Metropolitan La Serena

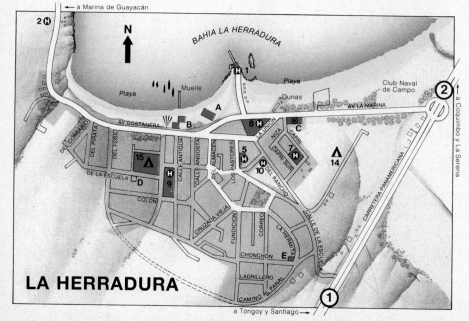

LA HERRADURA

ing view over the deep gulch of **Quebrada Honda**; the road descends to the bottom and reaches

Caleta Hornos a scattered village with a winding main street, a church and a school. It ends on a busy concrete pier and boat ramp. The beach is stony.

The road climbs out of Quebrada Honda, leaving the coastline for good. It won't see the Pacific again until Caldera, 380 km farther North. At the beginning of the **Buenos Aires range**, km 47, a sign-posted gravel road branches left, heading for a stretch of coast with high cliffs and a place called Yerbas Buenas (km 54), with the spectacular **Tilgos & Pájaros islets** a short distance off the shore.

At km 64 of the Pan-Am is the modest group of houses known as El Olivo; one km later, take the stony 3-km road branching left leading to Totoralillo, a beautiful 1-km beach in a sheltered cove, with sand and lots of slag. Lonely, devoid of water and with some seasonal fishermen. Since 1814 it was the shipping port for the large La Higuera copper mine. Some traces of the former port facilities are still to be found. To leave, follow the road from the northern tip of the beach (km 68), which climbs a slope and then reaches, at km 72, a road branching left leading in 2 km to

Playa El Temblador beautiful, white-sanded, open, with a calm sea and a fishing cove. Drive back to the junction and continue North. At km 78 another road branches left, leading to

CALETA CHUNGUNGO a small fishing village on a stony beach where camping is permitted. The place was named after a sea otter common in these waters. In the past, this was the shipping port for the El Tofo iron ore mine, started in 1914 by the Bethlehem Steel Co and active until the mine was depleted in 1954. It was one of the largest mines of its kind in the world, wholly mechanized, and its railway was the first electrified one in South America. There are some major buildings left from that period, such as the beautiful **pulpería**, a sort of company supermarket, the **thermoelectric power plant** and the storage tank.

A short stretch of road brings you to the **Cruz Grande** dock, a great wharf carved out of the rock and an amazing metal bridge running high up above the wharf. Large ships used to dock here to be loaded in a few hours directly from the railway cars running along the bridge. During its heyday, this bridge moved the largest tonnage in Chile. Access to Cruz Grande is restricted, but permission to visit is granted to anyone who requests it. The bridge is being dismantled since several years ago. It is worth a visit.

From Chungungo a road runs along the bottom of the ravine heading for the El Tofo mine (signposted). It climbs out of the ravine on a very curvy, breathtaking stretch with views towards the sea and the fishing coves. The astounding thing is the old railway, winding its way to the port. At km 92 is

EL TOFO the depleted open-pit iron ore mine. Now it looks like a gigantic demolition works. On the crest of the hill, next to small stands of eucalyptus, are the facilities of the **Proyecto Camanchaca**, with an installation for «harvesting» the thick camanchaca fogs rolling in nightly from the sea, in addition to a weather station and an experimental forest plot. Access is free, there is permanent attention by Conaf personnel. The devices for collecting moisture from fog are interesting: rectangular in shape, they look a bit like curtains made of fine threads; another kind is the so-called macrodiamond, donated by UNESCO. The water harvested is used for irrigating semi-desert areas.

A further 8 km will bring you to the Pan-American highway. The white dots atop some Andean peaks are the **La Silla** and **Las Campanas** observatories. The Pan-Am is reached at km 98 and 2 km south of this point is the village of

La Higuera a municipal head town with some 820 inhabitants. In 1844, the great La Higuera copper deposit was discovered, and later the El Tofo iron ore mine, both bringing great prosperity to the village. Lying on a slope, its houses are made of

El Tololo astronomical observatory

mud brick and it has a square with theaters and general stores. It is the nearest point for resupplying for those camping on the beaches. There is a **carnation nursery** at the El Trapiche hamlet on the highway. Retaking the Pan-Am at km 106, drive back southward to reach La Serena at km 161.

4

4   TO THE ELQUI RIVER VALLEY ★★★

a 227-km round trip with 152 km paved and the rest graveled. Allow a whole day, take food or buy it at Vicuña or Elqui. Gasoline at Vicuña. Take swimming gear; dress lightly.

An excursion into an enchanting, fruitful and tradition-rich valley.

Take exit labelled 3 in map of Metropolitan La Serena (4 in map of Downtown La Serena), passing the La Florida airport, vast cultivated fields and Cerro Grande towering to the right. At km 11 a road branches right to

Algarrobito a charming village with orchards enclosed by stone walls and old olive trees lining the streets. Its church, San José de Cutún, is built of mud brick and its bell tower is girdled by a balcony, in a fashion typical of this valley. On the square there is a wooden kiosk brought from the United States. The place is renowned for its homemade **manjar blanco**, in various combinations, its **candied fruit** and **marmalades**. It is worth a stop.

Back on the highway, on the valley's northern slope you will see the Loreto manor house, dating from last century. At km 15 is the ·turn-off for **Altovalsol**, with beautiful irrigated farmland across the river. It was an old seat of Peruvian settlers during the Inca dominion.

At km 23 a road branches left to **Las Rojas**, with a pretty mud-brick **church** built in 1892 on a platform rising in steps.

At km 33 on the highway you will start to see the vine plantations, accompanied by some papaya and cherimoya groves, sheltered from the wind by large plastic curtains. This area is warmer and lies somewhat higher, making fruit ripen much earlier.

At km 41 a road branches left for Condoriaco, a rich, distant copper mine. On the far bank is **La Marquesa**, with picturesque vineyards clinging to the slopes. At km 44 is

El Molle a quaint little village with an old mud-brick church and a square renowned for its shops and vendors selling fig and papaya jam. The first pre-Diaguita archaeological remains were unearthed here, belonging to the conveniently named **El Molle Culture.**

The highway runs now along the center of the valley. The old road to Vicuña wounds its way among the hills and passes the villages of Almendral and La Polvada, which lie now away from the highway. They can still be seen from the road, identifiable by their lush orchards and church towers. At km 59 is the turn-off for

Cerro Tololo Inter-American Observatory the Southern Hemisphere's largest astronomical observatory, with the world's second-largest reflecting telescope. Run by an association of universities, it is accessible through a very good 38-km gravel road.

Access is restricted; see note under La Serena description.

Back on the highway, at km 63 (4 km beyond the Tololo turn-off) a road branches right to

El Tambo, originally a resting station of the Inca road. The village clings to the hillside and is heavy with vines. Its streets are narrow and it has a tri-angular square with a giant molle -a native tree-and a singular mud-brick church. It epitomizes the urban structure of the valley's villages. A back road brings you back to the highway.

Continuing along the valley, at km 69 a road branches off to Peralillo and a road climbs to Hurtado and Ovalle, described under Section 2. A bridge over the Elqui river is crossed and at km 70 is

VICUÑA a small, picturesque town of 6,300 inhabitants. It was founded in 1821 by order of Bernardo O'Higgins. The order was carried out by Provincial Governor Joaquín Vicuña y Larraín, after whom it was christened. At present it is a municipal head town.

What To See At Sargento Aldea (see map) is Hostería Yunkai, with cabins and a swimming pool. On the same street, on the left, the Spanish-style façade of the Hostería Vicuña soon comes into view. Both offer the best accommodations in town.

The **square** -its old trees standing in stark contrast with the aridity of the surrounding hills- has been remodelled using stone motifs created by the School of Stonecutters of the Universidad de Chile.

Parish Church on the square, with a pretty wooden tower, erected in 1910. The mud-brick nave was built prior to 1860, with a beautiful polychrome vault and finely crafted wooden columns. Chilean poetess Gabriela Mistral was baptized at its baptismal font.

Bauer Tower is a strange wood-lined metal structure made to resemble a medieval tower with battlements. It was prefabricated in 1905 at Ulm, Germany, by order of Mayor Adolfo Bauer. The Town Hall is housed here and it has an interesting **Council Room**, with a portrait gallery. Then continue to

Museo Gabriela Mistral (Tue.-Sat 0900-1300h & 1500-1900h; Sun & holidays 1000-1300h; in summer Mon-Sat 0900-1900h, Sun 1000-1300h; for

location see map). Housed in a modern building designed by architect Oscar McClure and muralist Elías Castro, it contains the archives, library, paintings, awards and personal objects of Gabriela Mistral (1889-1957), bequeathed in her will to her native town. Adjacent to the entrance is the modest house where the poetess was born; it has been ideally reconstructed.

Climb the 1 km to **Cerro La Virgen** (see map) for the grand view of the town and valley; at the summit, the Virgen de los Rayos is venerated. At the foot of the hill is the **Balneario Municipal,** with a swimming pool, restaurant and the best campsite in the area.

You can also visit the **Pisco Capel distillery.** Tours Mon-Fri 0930-1130h & 1400-1700h; Sat 0930-1230h & 1400-1730h, January through March every 30 min and April-December every one hour. See map for location.

Where To Eat good cuisine at Hostería Vicuña and Hostería Yunkai. Also at the cheaper Club Social, housed in a charming old house with several inner courtyards. With children, best are Halley and the Balneario Municipal.

Leave Vicuña (km 70) following the road to Rivadavia, bypassing **Peralillo** at km 74, with a good church, and **Andacollito** at km 77. The fields are lovingly cultivated and surrounded by low stone walls. The valley grows narrower, the arid hills squeezing the road and the river. Here is the confluence of rivers Turbio and Elqui.

Along the Turbio river a road climbs to Argentina, described in next tour below.

THE ROAD TO ELQUI following the Elqui upriver there is a road winding its way along the hillsides, the intensively farmed valley bottom stretching below; the contrast between valley bottom and hillsides is striking. The air is dry and crystal-clear, the sky deep blue, setting off sharply the rocky contours of the hills. It is a 40-km round trip into the valley on a gravel road.

The road branches off the paved highway at km 89, signposted to Paihuano. It climbs the hill and runs through land where drip-irrigated vines thrive; the irrigation technique is given away by the weedless ground. On the hillsides there are a few modest dwellings, some manor houses and small pisco distilleries, all built on the hillsides to avoid

4

☎ Telephone Center
⊙ Café, Meeting Point
⊛ Gasoline Station
★ Touristic Information
A Parish Church

B Bauer Tower
C Gabriela Mistral Museum

RESTAURANTS
6 Social Club
5 Balneario Municipal

7 Halley
8 Continental

ACCOMMODATIONS
1 Hs Vicuña

2 Cb Yunkai
3 M Américo
4 H Yasna
5 Municipal Resort Campsite

using up the scant farmland.

At km 93 is **Paihuano,** a small village which is the municipal head town, its straight streets lined with pepper trees.

At km 103 is the hamlet of **Pueblo Hundido,** recognized for its face of Gabriela Mistral in ceramics on a rock. At km 106 is the manor house of **Las Palmas,** with a palm plantation and a truly enormous Ficus australis. Its construction is typical of this valley, with one floor at street level and two or more cascading towards the orchards and the river. You will also see caves dug into the hillside and sealed with a door: they are storerooms for grain and for cheese to ripen in.

There are two further spots of interest before reaching Monte Grande: **El Huerto** (signposted), where you can buy non-industrial perfumes made from wild mountain flowers, and **San Félix** (also signposted), with delicious dried fruit for sale at a charming, shady house surrounded by old farming implements. At km 107 is

Monte Grande

| MONTE GRANDE | a small village perched above the river, with an inn and a church with a tall, wooden bell tower. Here is the **School and Post-Office House** where Gabriela Mistral spent part of her childhood as a pupil of her sister, who was a teacher and the postmistress. Small-sized, it has a playground overlooking the river. Now it is a **museum,** very well preserved. Open 0930-1300h & 1500-1900h.

One kilometer farther up, on a rocky hillock overlooking the village and the valley, is **Gabriela Mistral's Grave** (1889-1957). The engraved inscription on the gravestone was taken from her testament: «It is my will that my body be buried at my beloved village of Monte Grande in the Elqui Valley.»

THE ROAD TO COCHIGUAZ at the foot of the grave there is a forking of the road. One branch climbs along the **Cochiguaz river.** The road is narrow, winding and runs atop cliffs up a valley part cultivated, part used as summer pastures. There are some quiet corners where self-contained communities live, engaged in meditation or spiritual retreat. Six km up from the road junction are the El Albaricoque cabins, well-equipped and comfortable. At El Colorado, 18 km up the valley, there is campsite with basic facilities.

From the forking at the foot of Gabriela Mistral's grave (km 107), another branch road climbs the Claro river valley, one of the most scenic sections. The vineyards climb the slopes to the top of the hills, the harvested grapes lowered via cable ferry. At km 109 is

| PISCO ELQUI | a charming small village perched atop a hill overlooking the valley, with winding streets and alleys inching their way up the hillside. In its center there is a small square with a **church** crowned by a tall steeple, visible from afar. The place has a long tradition as residential center for the valley's landowners. There are graceful houses and two pisco distilleries open to visitors. The Solar de Pisco Control (Mon-Sat 1000-1800h) is one of them. On the square there is a restaurant with a country house, a shady terrace, welcoming atmosphere for families. There is also the Hostal Don Juan, in a beautiful chalet built in 1910, where furniture from that period has been preserved. On its side there is a restaurant and a **handicrafts center.**

In the past the village was called Unión, but was renamed Pisco Elqui under a proposal of the then Member of Parliament González Videla, with the purpose of thwarting a Peruvian attempt to register internationally the exclusivity of the word «pisco».

Two kilometers further up the valley is the **Pisco Peralta** distillery, and a further 5 km are the village of **Los Nichos** and the **Pisco 3R** distillery, with an interesting storage room. Ask for permission to visit. Then comes **Las Placetas** and **Horcón,** two clusters of houses. On both sides of the road are small patches of vineyard. At the river crossing, some 6 km farther up, there is a good spot for camping or for a picnic under the willows growing on the river bank. Fourteen km up from the forking is **Alcohuaz,** with a church sporting a portico with four columns and a front garden with two large benches to sit

in the shade. Straight back to La Serena from here is 123 km.

5 TO ARGENTINA VIA AGUAS NEGRAS ★★

taking Vicuña as your km 0, it is 455 km to San Juan in Argentina. The next gas station is 319 km away. The road is very poorly surfaced. The pass is open during the summer season (November through April, weather permitting). It is advisable to leave early from Vicuña, as the pass is closed at 1800h on the Argentinian side. Tune the engine for high altitude (advance the spark), as the border lies at 4,765 m above sea level. See instructions for high altitude in Zone 1, Section D. Drive extremely carefully: the road is narrow, in bad condition and runs above cliffs. Bring Australes (Argentine currency) from La Serena to buy gasoline, as you won't find any place to change money until San Juan.

An option to cross into Argentina through an impressive -albeit very difficult- mountain road and visit San Juan, to return to Santiago via Mendoza.

Take Vicuña as your km 0. The first 25 km are paved, then gravel, rough. The scenery, however, is beautiful; the road passes through occasional valleys such as **Chapilca,** small and renowned for its beautiful hand-woven rugs; **Guanta,** and, at km 75, La Junta, with a road branching off (access restricted) to the **El Toro** and **El Indio** mines, where Chile's largest gold mine is located.

At km 93 is the Chilean **Customs outpost.** The road continues among rock formations of striking hues in the Cordillera, with an intensely blue sky above. At km 167 is the **La Laguna dam,** spectacular, the hand of man seems to have never touched the place.

At km 178 starts a tricky climb; in fact, the entire next 40 km should be driven with extreme caution. The border is reached at km 222 and 4,765 m above sea level. Starting at km 258 one of the lanes is paved with asphalt. Argentine police outpost (Gerdarmería) is at km 278. The road is paved on both lanes after km 291 and the **Argentine Customs** outpost is at km 314. Do not take any fruit with you: it will be confiscated.

At km 319 is Las Flores, with a gas station (called nafta in Argentina). At **Iglesia** take the road to San Juan, which you reach at km 452. Accommodations: Hotel Nogaró, on the square. To return to Chile, it is best to drive via **Mendoza,** 160 km from San Juan; from there to Portillo, Chile, it is 200 km, and a further 142 km to Santiago.

6 TO ANDACOLLO AND OVALLE ★★★

a total stretch of 138 km, with 52 km gravel and 86 km paved. Allow half a day. Gasoline at Andacollo.

An alternative to return South through the picturesque village of Andacollo.

Take Exit 4 in map of Metropolitan La Serena (5 in map of Downtown La Serena). You will pass Tierras Blancas, a new housing compound next to the busy modern industries of the Industrial Park, and then a vast stretch of farmland irrigated by the Bellavista canal, finished in the mid-18th century and which brought about the establishment of large haciendas. There are some interesting manor houses near the road, such as **House Vicuña** (1865), with several inner courts, a chapel, storerooms and a large so-called «chore yard» separating it from the road. It is on the left-hand side of the road and it can be visited: it is more or less deserted. Also **House Ripamonti**, large and built in Italian neo-classical style, one story with a central body and large lateral wings, set amid its own park. Then the desert starts.

At km 26 take the road branching left to Andacollo. The pavement ends at a place called **El Peñón** (km 27), with a few houses. The road (poorly surfaced, dusty) then heads into a barren sierra, with occasional dwellings of goat farmers and some goat pens with stone walls for fences. At km 39 is **Maitencillo**, a tiny cluster of dwellings; in the past it was an alluvial gold washing spot, some remains of which are still to be seen.

At km 42 the road starts a 6-km climb -gentle- which passes near a **grotto** with a water spring.

☎	Telephone Center	F	Post Office
◉	Café, Meeting Point	G	Bus Terminal
ⓖ	Gasoline Station		**RESTAURANTS**
✚	Hospital	1	Edo Restaurant
A	Basilica	2	Tirado Restaurant
B	Parish Church		**OF INTEREST**
C	Convent	3	Trapiche (ore grinding mill)
D	Town Hall	4	Non-industrial Trapiche
E	Museum		

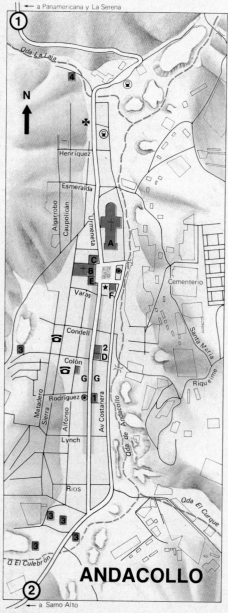

ANDACOLLO

From near the summit you can see, down below, the small **Olga mine**, with a grinding mill, concentrate tanks and a waste dump. The surrounding hills are crisscrossed by trails leading to small mining works.

At km 52 is

ANDACOLLO (pop 8,000), nestled amid barren hills, its houses tightly clustered at the bottom of a long ravine and around a 50-m-tall church. The village seems to be overhung with the waste material from a myriad mining works active one time or another around the place over the centuries. It looks as if a cataclysm had just shaken the whole place.

There is a good spot for camping at Parque de La Laja, with a swimming pool and toilets.

Andacollo is a Quechua word meaning «queen metal». Gold, silver and copper were being extracted here long before the Spaniards ever set foot in the district. In the 17th century the area was deserted, to be repopulated once more during the 18th century, undergoing ups and downs triggered by changes in metal prices. During the 19th century there was a significant boom in gold mining. This activity is carried on now by over a thousand pirquineros (self-employed miners) who bring their output to the grinding mills (trapiches) operating in the village.

Virgin and Sanctuary of Andacollo the 90-cm-tall image of the Virgen del Rosario was brought from Peru in 1676 and set in the old chapel. Its worship spread throughout the North, turning Andacollo into a major pilgrimage destination with what was then Chile's largest religious festivity.

Now there is a **Sanctuary** in the center of the village, formed by the Old Temple and the New Temple or Basilica, in addition to the convent, sacristy and museum, all around the square.

Old Temple erected in 1789 and now a National Monument. It has a single, narrow nave (7x40 m), where the Virgen del Rosario is worshiped, placed on a great altar of repoussé silver. This temple has been modified on several occasions: its two towers in 1855, the lateral chapel in 1925, the **dressing room** in 1938 (a room lined in black marble where the image's festivity garments are kept). Below this is the crypt, where the splendid gifts and donations brought for the Virgen de Andacollo are kept. Mass in winter Mon & Sat 10:00 & 19:00h. Sun 11:00h; in summer, Mon & Sat 1000 & 20:00h, Sun 11:00 & 20:00h Visiting times 09:00-12:00h & 15:00-18:00h; Sun 11:00-20:00h, save for the hours when a service is being held.

New Temple or Basilica inaugurated in 1893, it is also a National Monument. Designed by architect Eusebio Celli in neoclassical Italian style, it has five naves and a transept crowned by a 45-m-high dome. The façade has columns and two tall towers. Built of Oregon pine, its walls are filled with small mud bricks and lined with plates of galvanized iron. This colossal construction stands in striking contrast with the modest one-story dwellings surrounding it. It was designed to accommodate 1,000 pilgrims during the festivity days.

Festivity of the Virgen de Andacollo on the first Sunday of October the **Fiesta Chica** («small festivity») is held. The **Fiesta Grande** is held from the 23rd to the 27th of December, the main day being the 26th. Over 40,000 pilgrims stream to Andacollo from throughout the North, including the traditional gaily-clad dancing confraternities known as chinos, some with over two centuries in existence, with their peculiar banners, attires and dancing routines. It is one of the most picturesque religious ceremonies, with roots in the pre-Conquest past.

Trapiches are ore grinding mills. A number of them is to be found around the village. The operators usually welcome visitors; children offer themselves as self-fashioned guides to these for a small «retainer».

The trapiche is rented for the day. The miners bring their ore, which is first ground to the size of fine gravel, then fed by shovel into the trapiche. The mill is a round trough filled with water upon which two heavy wheels turn and grind the ore.

Gold is extracted by three different methods: **coarse gold** is left at the bottom when the trapiche is emptied. **Medium-sized gold** is recovered by placing copper plates covered with mercury on the trapiche walls; gold is alloyed through amalgamation on these plates and then scratched free. To recover **fine gold,** the ore is brought to flotation cells where it is concentrated by chemical processes.

The remaining material is dumped at a «torta», or «cake», which is then taken to a state-owned Enami refinery where residual gold can be extracted using more sophisticated techniques.

There are over 170 trapiches in operation; a great share of them is in Andacollo, as water is less abundant at other locations.

To continue the tour, retrace the 26-km road back to the paved highway to Ovalle. The road junction is reached at km 78; turn left (South).

At km 87 is the **Tambillos** mining works, which processes «ore cakes» from Andacollo.

The scenery is a barren desert, and the road runs along a wide valley flanked by sierras, with occasional oases with cultivated patches and some forest farms growing tamarugo, a Prosopis species superbly adapted to saline soils and scant water supply.

At km 97 the road climbs a stretch of mountain road called **Las Cardas**, reaching the summit after 5 km. The road then runs along a dry river bed lined with pepper trees.

At km 128 is **Lagunillas**, with some olive groves and irrigation canals. Here is the **Mistral** olive oil plant (open for visitors Mon-Sat 1000-1200h & 1500-1700h). A short distance beyond it is the turn-off for the **Recoleta Dam** (see Section B). Now the landscape turns lush green: you have reached the great fruitful valley stretching inland from Ovalle.

At km 134, from the summit of a hill, there is a **great view** over the rivers Hurtado and Grande, to the left, and the El Ingenio ravine to the right, with the Panulcillo mining complex.

Ovalle is at km 138.

4

PUBLIC TRANSPORTATION

A vast network of bus services link the main cities and towns with the large number of rural communities in the Elqui, Limarí, Hurtado, and Choapa river valleys, and even at the remotest corners in the mountains.

The chart below shows routes and frequencies for weekdays, each line a route and its thickness indicating the number of daily departures in one direction. The rule of thumb is that on Saturdays frequencies drop by half, while on Sunday there are usually no services. This is due to the fact that these services meet the needs of rural dwellers who come to buy or trade at the large markets of La Serena, Ovalle and Illapel.

Frequency low- frequency routes usually correspond to the pattern of an early morning departure from rural towns or villages to the main cities, returning the same day around 1600h to the rural town or village. In cases with more than one departure daily, the structure is the same, only that the buses start simultaneously from the city and the village to return in the afternoon.

Departure times the first batch of buses depart, in any route, between 0730 and 0830h; the second at 1030-1100h, and the third at 1630-1800h, at which time low-frequency buses return from the cities to the villages. There are no departures over lunchtime, with the exception of high-frequency routes; departures later than 2000h are rare. The time when you most certainly will find transportation out of a city is at 1630-1800h, and out of a village or town, early in the morning.

Seaside Resorts in season there are frequent bus and colectivo taxi services along the coast plying the route from La Serena-Coquimbo to La Herradura, Guanaqueros and Tongoy.

BUS DEPARTURE FREQUENCY

— More than 8 departures daily
— 5-8 departures daily
— 3-4 departures daily
— 1-2 departures daily

4

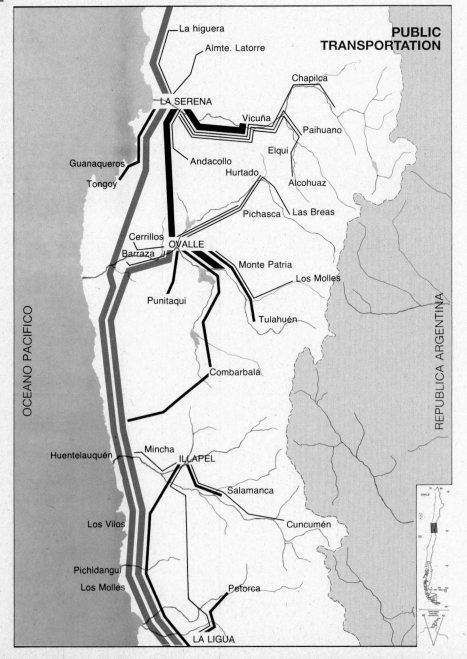

Zone 5
SANTIAGO and THE
SURROUNDING DISTRICT

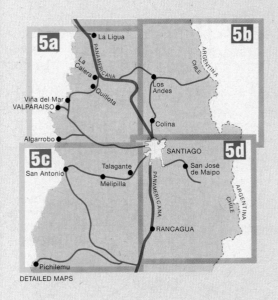

5a
La Ligua
PANAMERICANA
La Calera
Viña del Mar
VALPARAISO
Quillota
Algarrobo

5b
Los Andes
Colina
ARGENTINA
CHILE

SANTIAGO

5c
San Antonio
Talagante
Melipilla
PANAMERICANA

5d
San José de Maipo
ARGENTINA
CHILE

RANCAGUA
Pichilemu
DETAILED MAPS

Arica
Iquique
Antofagasta
Copiapó
Easter Island
La Serena
Is R Crusoe
Valparaiso
SANTIAGO
Talca
Concepción
Temuco
Valdivia
Osorno
Pto Montt
Castro
Chaitén
Coihaique
Cochrane
Puerto Natales
Punta Arenas
Puerto Williams
Is Diego Ramirez

5

90°   60°   53°

CHILEAN
ANTARCTIC
TERRITORY

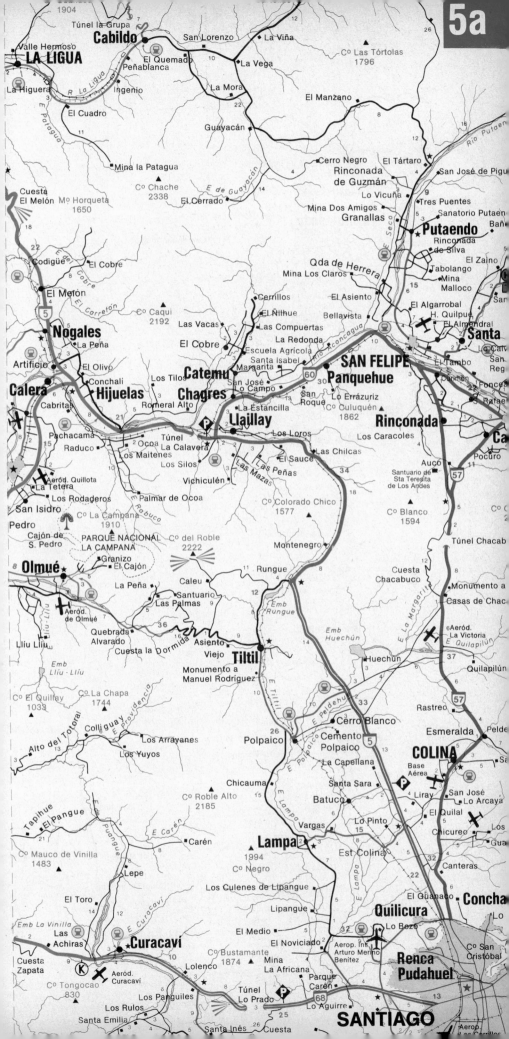

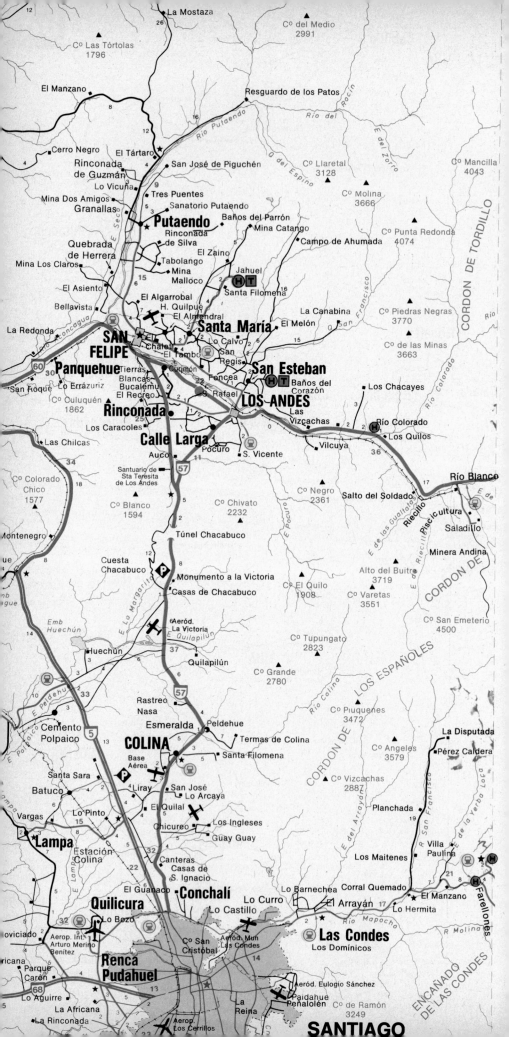

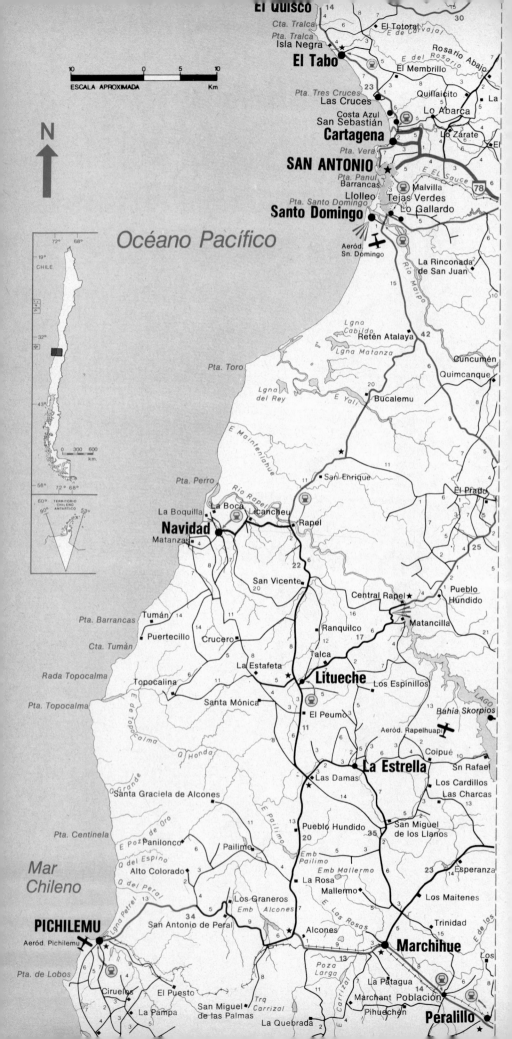

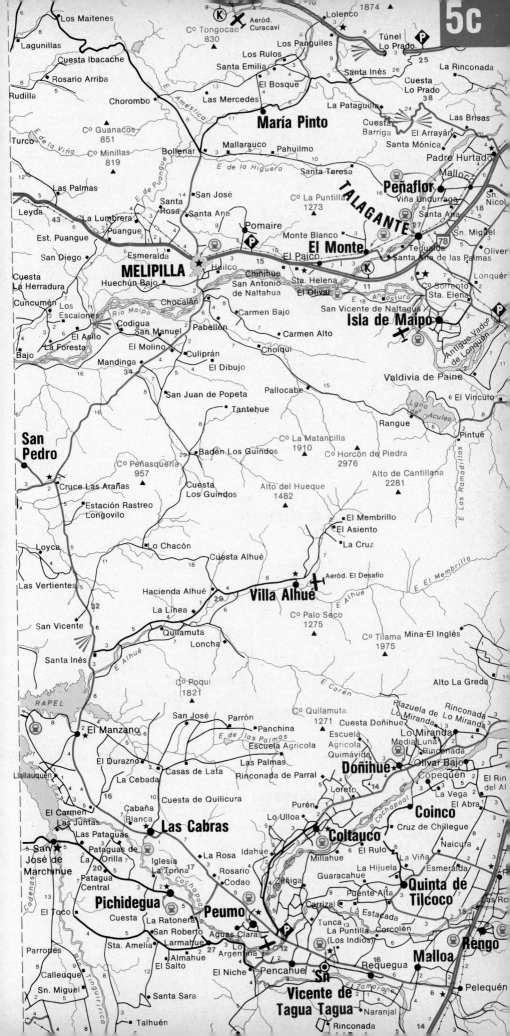

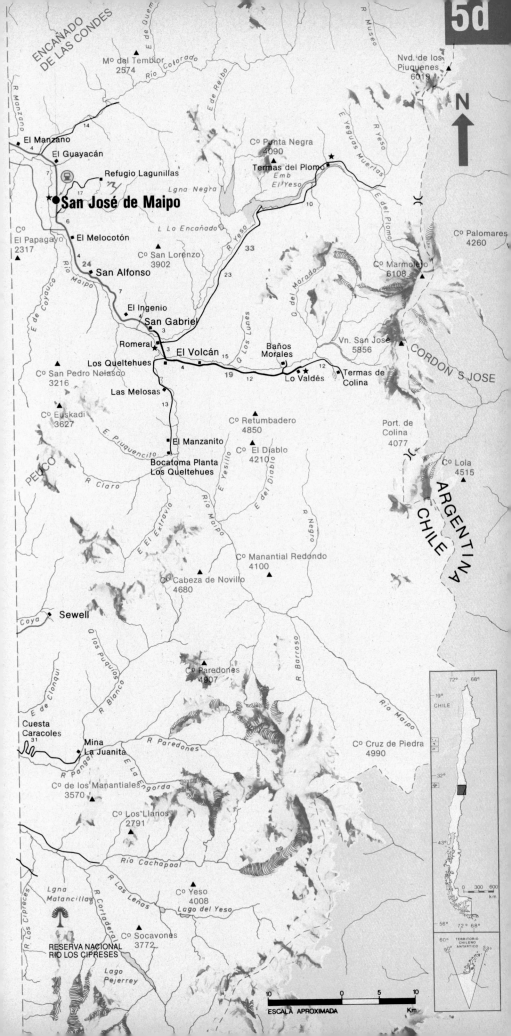

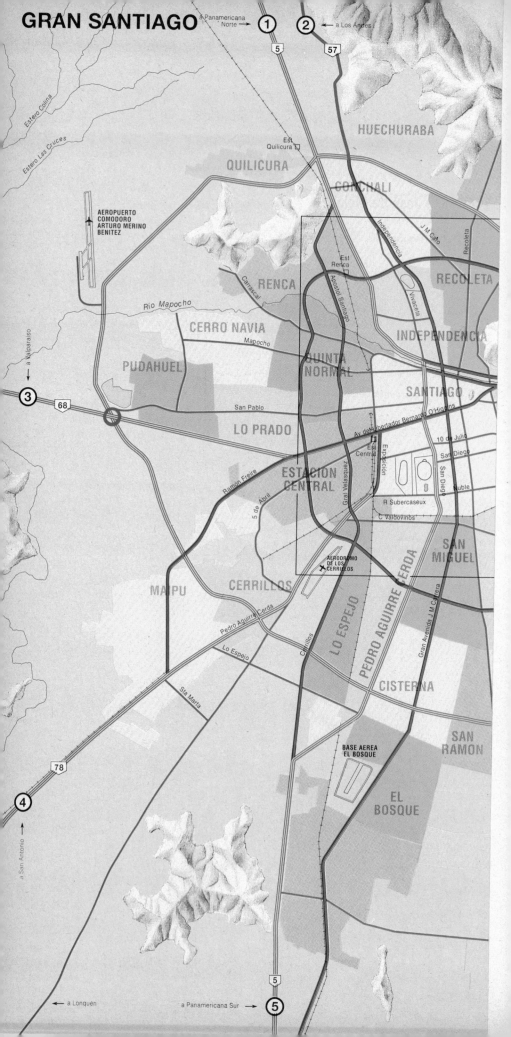

GRAN SANTIAGO

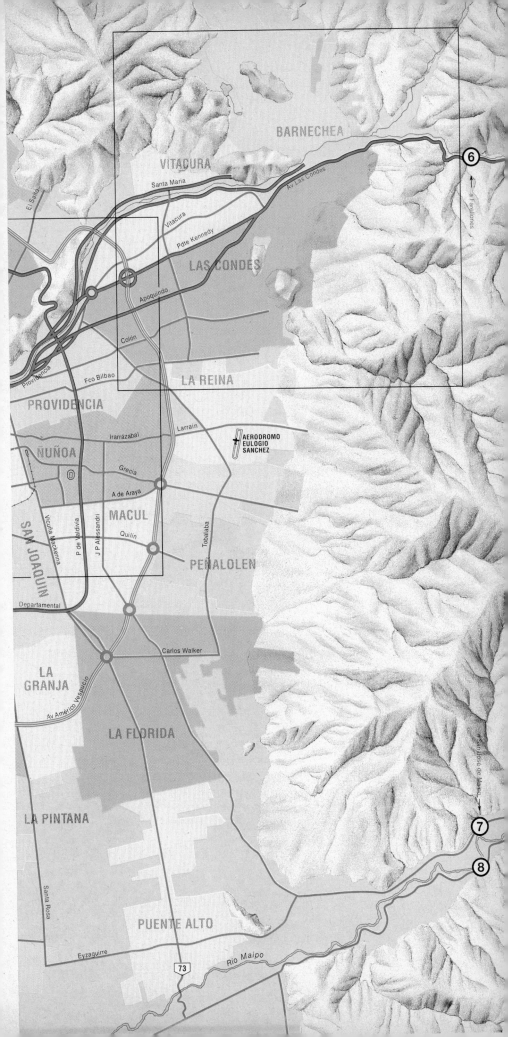

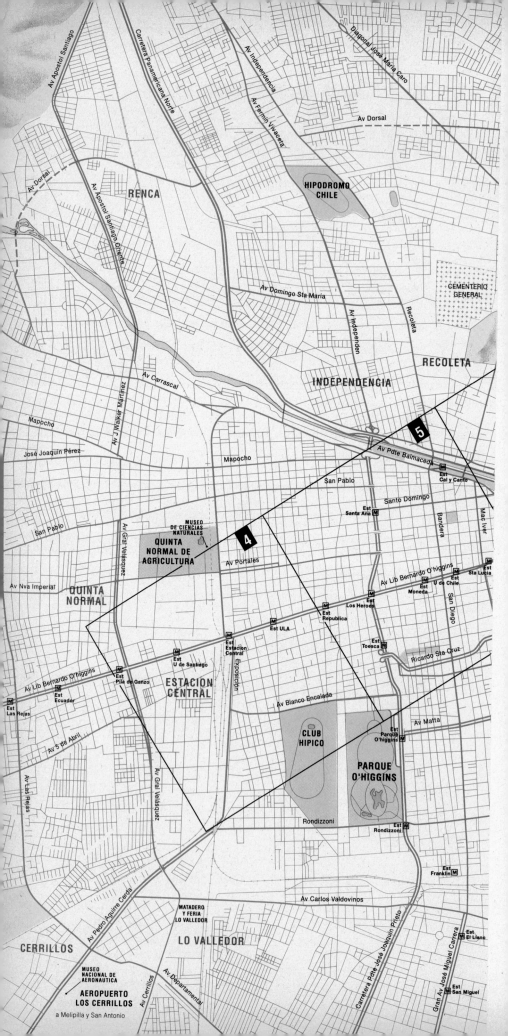

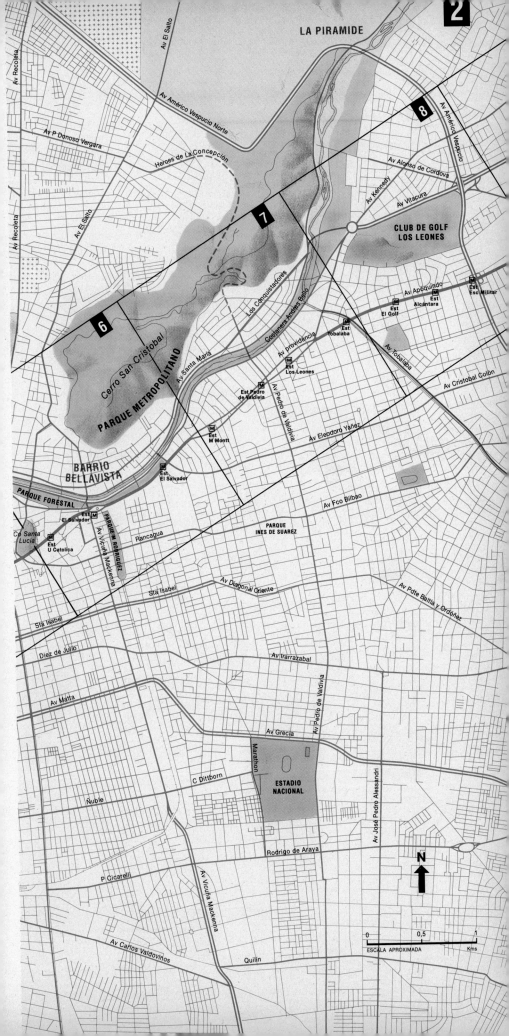

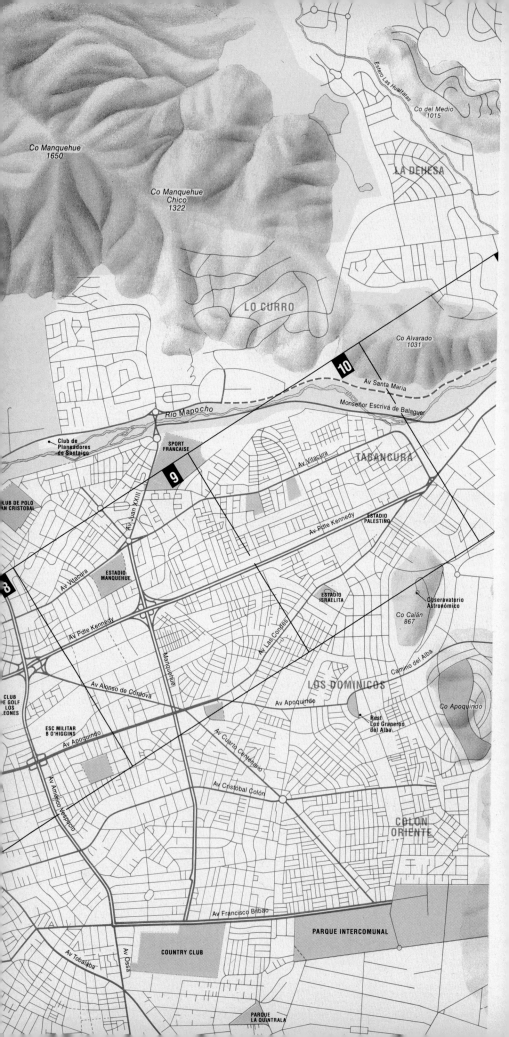

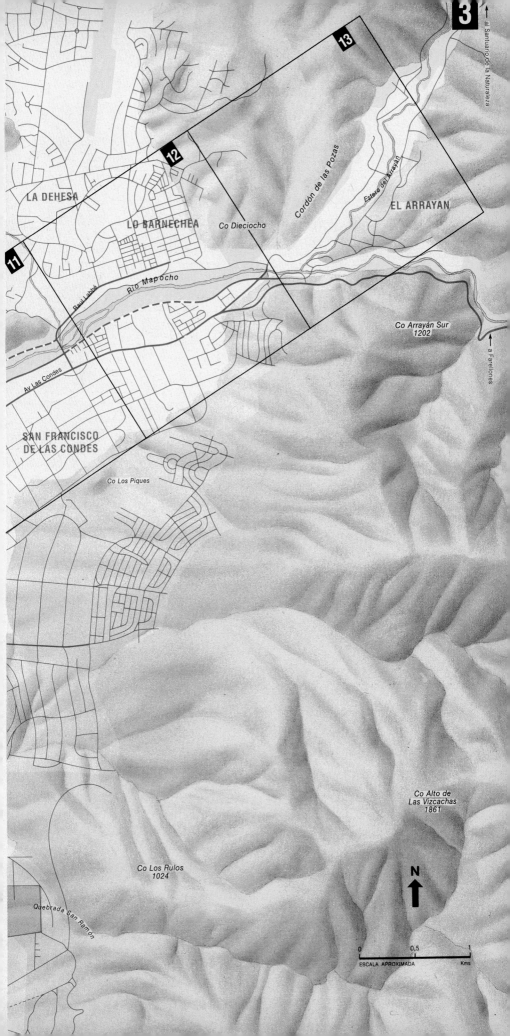

LA DEHESA

LO BARNECHEA

Co Dieciocho

Cordón de las Pozas

Estero del Arrayán

EL ARRAYAN

al Santuario de la Naturaleza

3

13

12

11

Paul Labbé

Río Mapocho

Co Arrayán Sur
1202

Av Las Condes

a Farellones

SAN FRANCISCO
DE LAS CONDES

Co Los Piques

Co Alto de
Las Vizcachas
1861

Co Los Rulos
1024

Quebrada San Ramón

N

0   0,5   1

ESCALA APROXIMADA   Kms

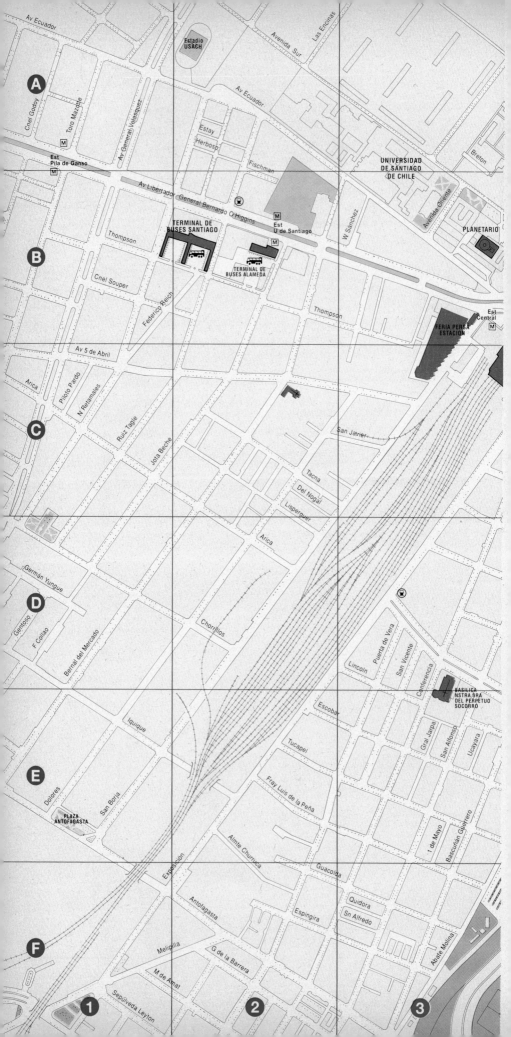

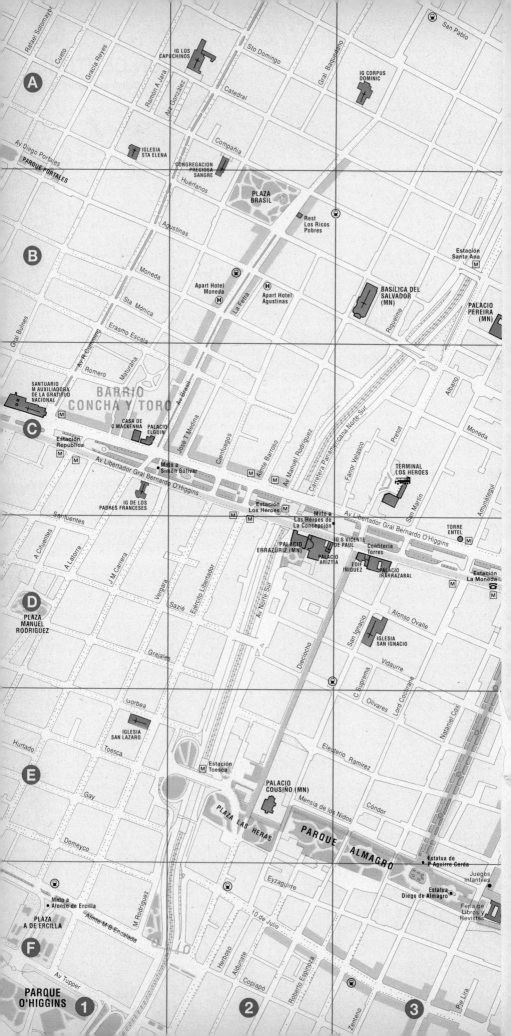

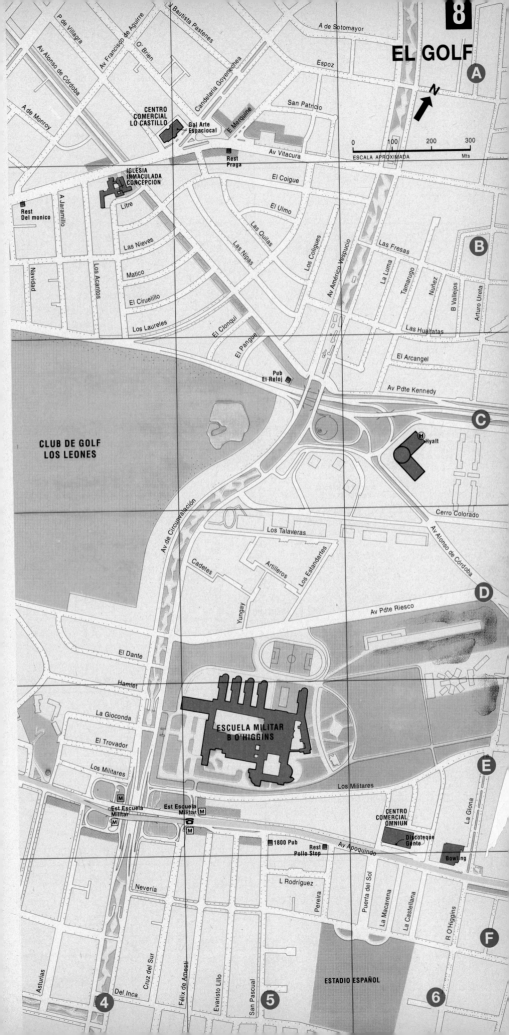

8

EL GOLF

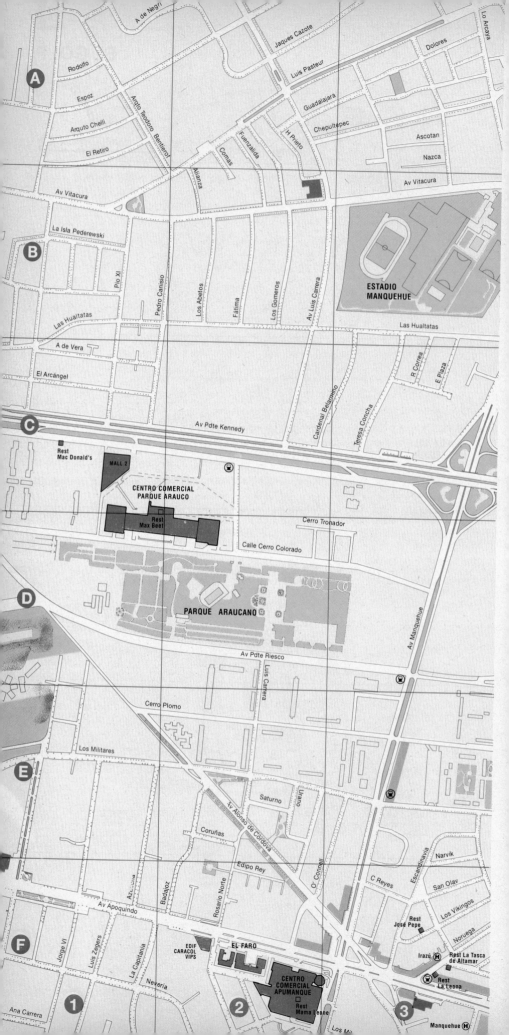

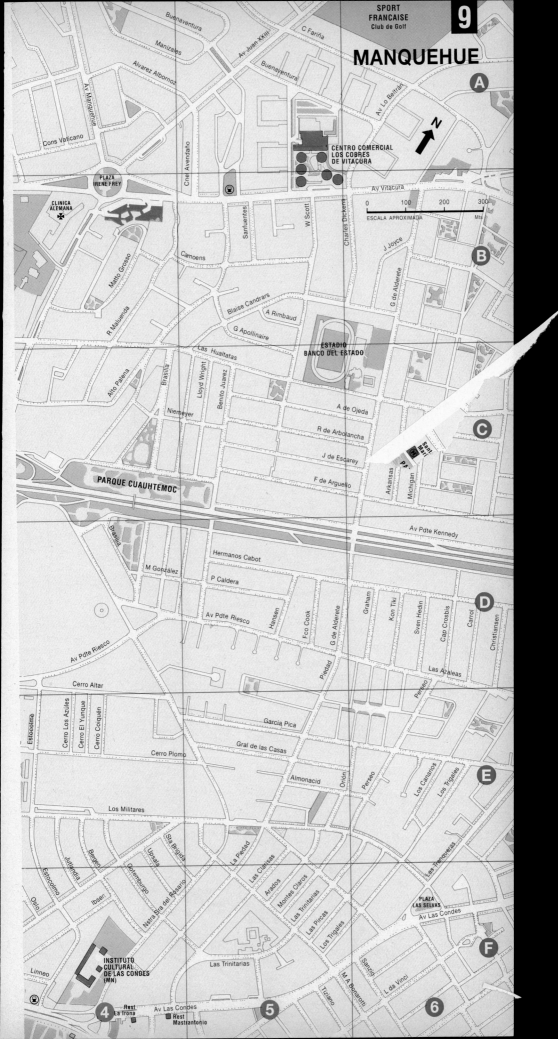

SPORT
FRANCAISE
Club de Golf

MANQUEHUE

A

Buenaventura

Manizales

Av Juan XXIII

C Fariña

Buenaventura

Alvarez Albornoz

Av Lo Beltrán

Cons Vaticano

Av Manquehue

Cne Avendaño

CENTRO COMERCIAL
LOS COBRES
DE VITACURA

N

PLAZA
IRENE FREY

CLINICA
ALEMANA

Santfuentes

W Scott

Charles Dickens

Av Vitacura

0   100   200   300
ESCALA APROXIMADA   Mts

Matto Grosso

Camoens

J Joyce

B

R Malvenda

Blaise Candrars

A Rimbaud

G de Alderete

Alto Palena

G Apollinaire

Las Hualtatas

ESTADIO
BANCO DEL ESTADO

Brasília

Lloyd Wright

Benito Juárez

Niemeyer

A de Ojeda

R de Arbolancha

J de Escarey

C

Santi
Mari

Arkansas

Michigan

F de Arguello

PARQUE CUAUHTEMOC

Brasília

Av Pdte Kennedy

Hermanos Cabot

M González

P Caldera

Hansen

Fco Cook

G de Alderete

Graham

Kon Tiki

Sven Hedin

Cap Crosbis

Carrol

Christiansen

D

Av Pdte Riesco

Piedad

Las Azaleas

Av Pdte Riesco

Cerro Altar

Pateo

Estocolmo

Cerro Los Azules

Cerro El Yunque

Cerro Coiquén

Cerro Plomo

García Pica

Gral de las Casas

Almonacid

Orión

Perseo

Los Canarios

Los Trigales

E

Los Militares

Jullandia

Estocolmo

Bergen

Gotemburgo

Upsala

Sta Brígida

Nstra Sra del Rosario

La Piedad

Las Clarisas

Arados

Montes Claros

Las Trinitarias

Las Pircas

Los Trigales

PLAZA
LAS SELVAS

Av Las Condes

Oslo

Ibsen

INSTITUTO
CULTURAL
DE LAS CONDES
(MN)

Las Trinitarias

Tiziano

M A Bonarotti

Sanzio

L da Vinci

F

Linneo

4

Rest
La Trona

Av Las Condes

Rest
Mastrantonio

5

6

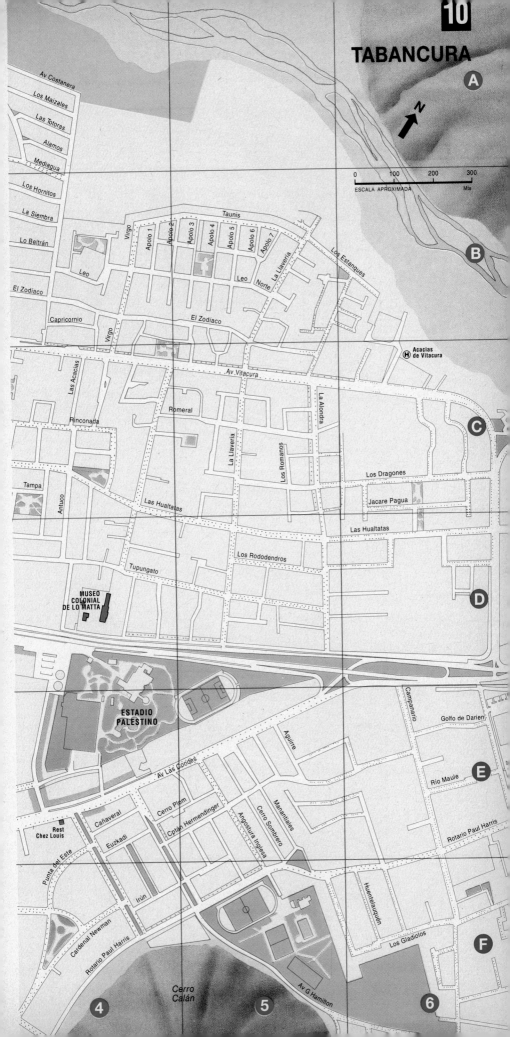

A

N

0   100   200   300
ESCALA APROXIMADA   Mts

Av Costanera
Los Maizales
Las Totoras
Alamos
Mediagua
Los Hornitos
La Siembra
Lo Beltrán
El Zodíaco
Capricornio

Taunis
Virgo
Apolo 1
Apolo 2
Apolo 3
Apolo 4
Apolo 5
Apolo 6
Apolo 7
Leo
Leo
Norte
La Llavería
El Zodíaco
Virgo

Los Estanques

B

Acacias
de Vitacura
H

Av. Vitacura

Las Acacias
Rinconada
Romeral
La Llavería
La Alondra
Los Romanos

C

Tampa
Antuco
Las Hualtatas
Los Dragones
Jacare Pagua

Los Hualtatas

Los Rododendros

Tupungato

MUSEO
COLONIAL
DE LO MATTA

D

ESTADIO
PALESTINO

Aguirre

Campanario
Golfo de Darien

Av Las Condes

E

Río Maule

Rest
Chez Louis
Cañaveral
Cerro Plom
Cptan Hermendinger
Angostura Inglesa
Cerro Sombrero
Manantiales

Rotario Paul Harris

Euzkadi
Punta del Este
Irún

Huentelauquén

Cardenal Newman
Rotario Paul Harris
Los Gladiolos

F

Cerro
Calán

Av G Hamilton

4   5   6

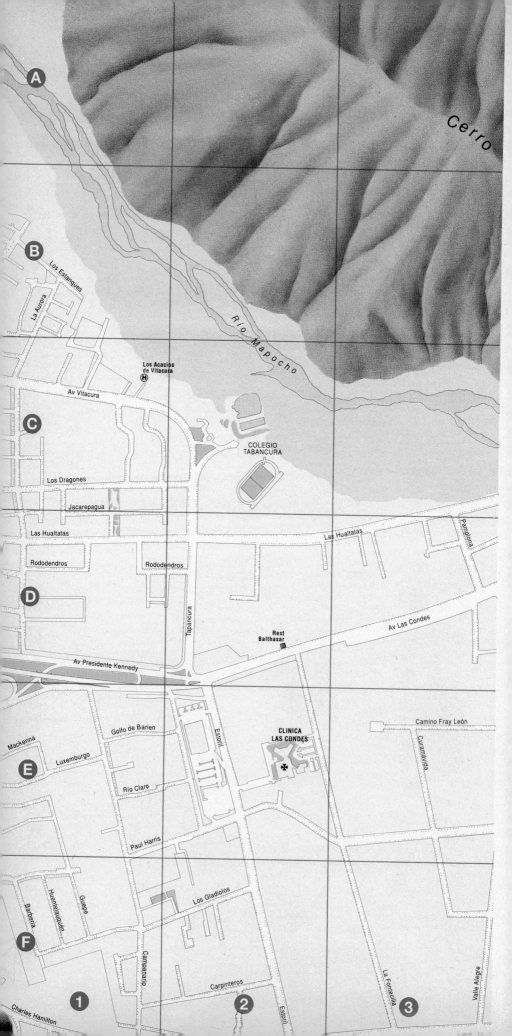

A

B

Los Estanques

La Aurora

Los Acacios
de Vitacura (H)

Av Vitacura

C

Los Dragones

Jacarepagua

Las Hualtatas

Las Hualtatas

Rododendros

Rododendros

D

Tapancura

Av Las Condes

Rest
Balthasar

Av Presidente Kennedy

Mackenna

Golfo de Barien

Luxemburgo

Estoril

CLINICA
LAS CONDES

Camino Fray León

Curanavida

E

Río Claro

*

Paul Harris

Barbería

Huemelauquen

Guape

Los Gladiolos

F

Campanario

Carpinteros

Estoril

La Fontecilla

Valle Alegre

1

2

3

Charles Hamilton

Río Mapocho

COLEGIO
TABANCURA

Cerro

Pamplona

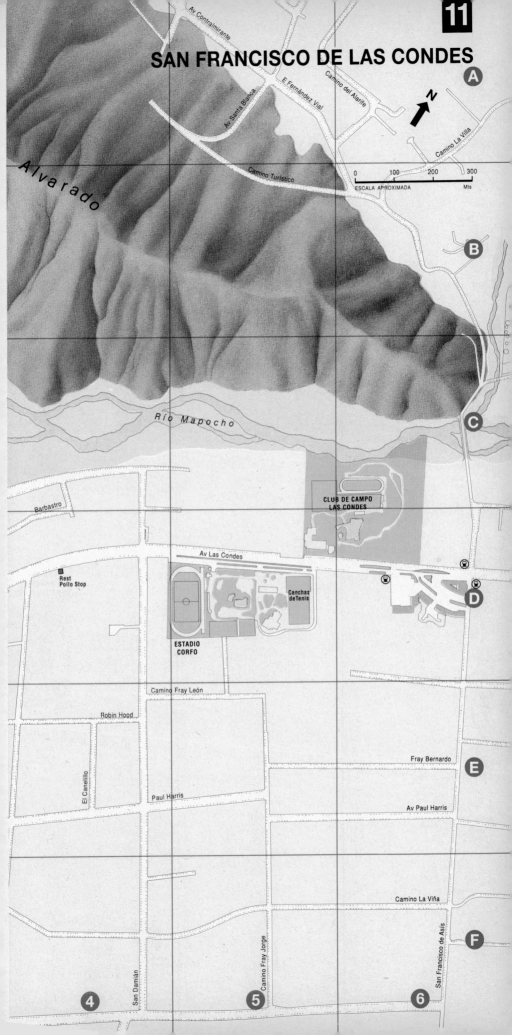

SAN FRANCISCO DE LAS CONDES

A

B

C

D

E

F

4

5

6

N

Av Contralmirante

E Fernández Vial

Camino del Alarife

Av Santa Blanca

Camino La Villa

Camino Turístico

0   100   200   300
ESCALA APROXIMADA   Mts

Alvarado

Río Mapocho

CLUB DE CAMPO
LAS CONDES

Barbastro

Av Las Condes

Rest
Pollo Stop

Canchas
de Tenis

ESTADIO
CORFO

Camino Fray León

Robin Hood

El Canelillo

Paul Harris

Fray Bernardo

Av Paul Harris

Camino La Viña

San Damián

Camino Fray Jorge

San Francisco de Asís

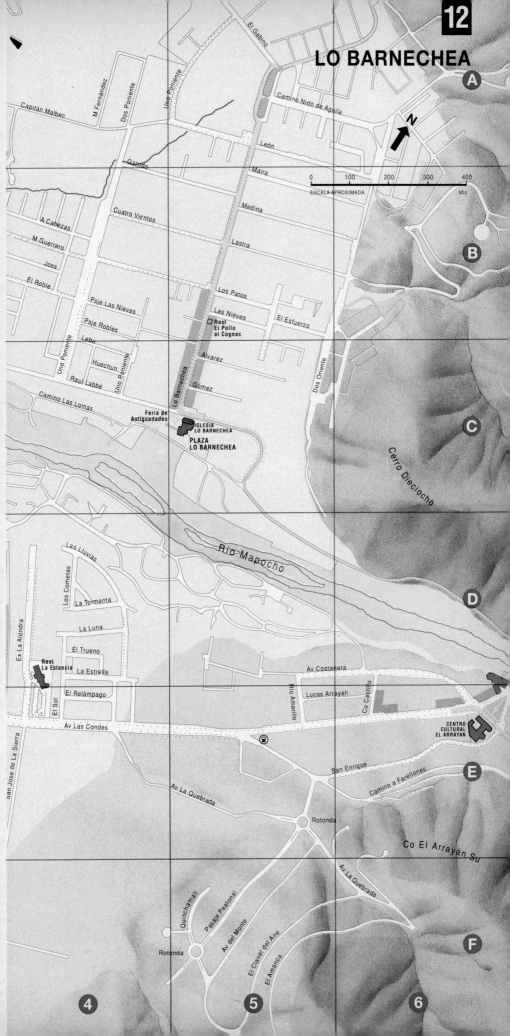

12

LO BARNECHEA

El Gabino

Camino Nido de Aguila

Capitán Malbec

M Fernández

Dos Poniente

Uno Poniente

León

Maira

Garrido

Medina

N

0   100   200   300   400
ESCALA APROXIMADA   Mts

Cuatro Vientos

Lastra

A Cabezas

M Guerrero

Joss

El Roble

Los Patos

Psje Las Nieves

Las Nieves

El Esfuerzo

Psje Robles

Rest
El Pollo
al Cognac

Lebu

Alvarez

Uno Poniente

Huechun

Uno Poniente

Dos Oriente

Raul Labbé

Gómez

Lo Barnechea

Camino Las Lomas

Feria de
Antigüedades

IGLESIA
LO BARNECHEA

PLAZA
LO BARNECHEA

C

Cerro Dieciocho

A

B

Río Mapocho

D

Las Lluvias

Los Cometas

La Tormenta

Ex La Alondra

La Luna

El Trueno

Rest
La Estancia

La Estrella

Av Costanera

El Relámpago

Lucas Arrayán

Co Castillo

El Sol

Río Amarillo

CENTRO
CULTURAL
EL ARRAYAN

Av Las Condes

San José de la Sierra

San Enrique

E

Av La Quebrada

Camino a Farellones

Rotonda

Co El Arrayán Su

Quinchamalí

Pasaje Peatonal

Av del Monte

Av La Quebrada

Rotonda

El Clavel del Aire

El Amanca

F

4

5

6

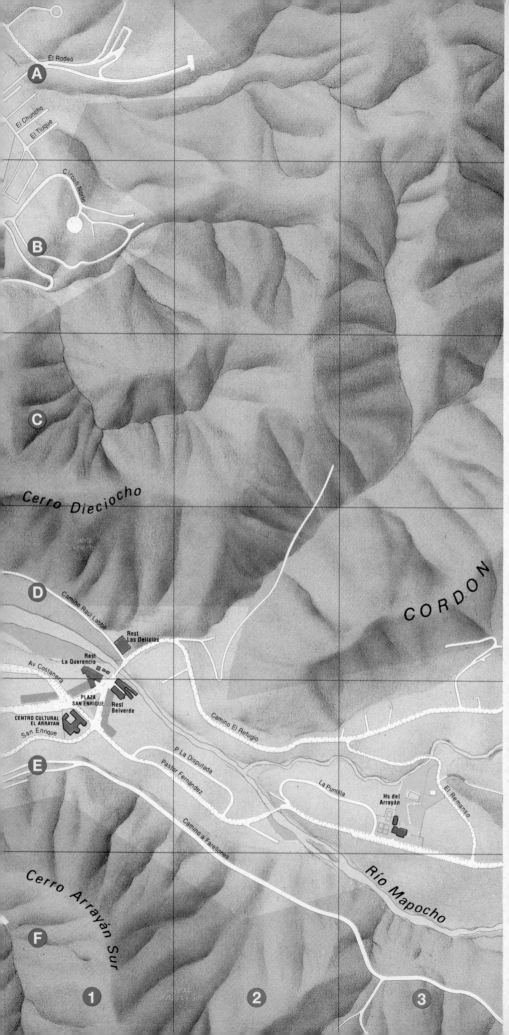

El Rodeo

A

El Chuncho

El Tiuque

C Uccrú Norte

B

Cerro Dieciocho

C

D

Camino Raúl Labbé

Rest
Las Delicias

Rest
La Querencia

Av Costanera

PLAZA
SAN ENRIQUE

Rest
Belverde

CENTRO CULTURAL
EL ARRAYÁN

San Enrique

C O R D O N

Camino El Refugio

E

P La Disputada

Pastor Fernández

La Puntilla

Hs del
Arrayán

El Remanso

Camino a Farellones

Cerro Arrayán Sur

Río Mapocho

F

1

2

3

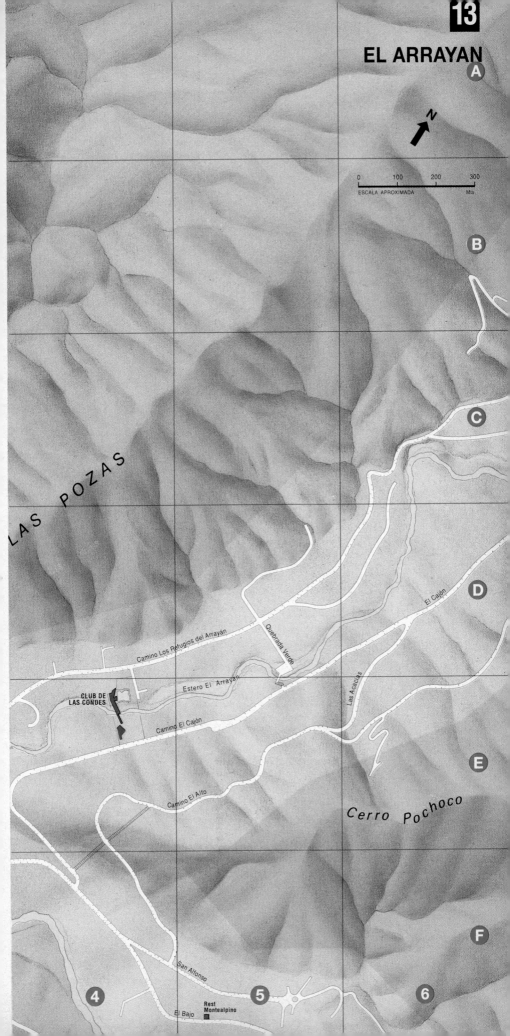

OVERVIEW

A little more than half of Chile's inhabitants live in Santiago and the surrounding district. Every weekend, thousands drive to the coast or the mountains, depending on the season. In the following pages we describe the many other attractions of this Zone and which, being relatively little known, offer a chance for an excursion without the ubiquitous traffic jams.

The territory covered by this Zone stretches between the Aconcagua valley to the North and Angostura de Pelequén to the South. Eastwards it extends into the Andes Mountains and westwards to the coastal lands including Puangue, lake Rapel and the villages of La Estrella and Litueche.

The area covered by this Zone corresponds to the radius of a one–day excursion by car. We have divided this Zone into ten sections, namely;

Section A   The City of Santiago with the main sights.

Section B   The Aconcagua Valley including the cities of Los Andes, San Felipe, and the inland valleys.

Section C   The Chacabuco Basin covering the great valley unfolding northward from Santiago up to the Chacabuco range.

Section D   Mountain District with the roads leading to ,Cajón del Maipo, Farellones, Portillo.

Section E   The Maipo Plains including Pirque, Calera de Tango and the surrounding area.

Section F   Rancagua Valley stretching southward from Angostura de Paine.

Section G   Cachapoal Valley with the little-known places near this river.

Section H   Mapocho Valley including the roads to the coast.

Section J   Coastal Lands including places and towns lying to the west of Santiago on the Coastal Range foothills.

REGIONAL DISTANCES

Doñihue	El Monte	El Volcán	Farellones	Lago Rapel	Laguna Aculeo	Los Andes	Melipilla	Portillo	Putaendo	Rancagua	San Felipe	Santiago	San Vicente de Tagua Tagua
114	El Monte												
160	107	El Volcán											
167	97	122	Farellones										
69	93	229	236	Lago Rapel									
82	50	121	124	146	Laguna Aculeo								
195	125	150	132	264	152	Los Andes							
133	19	126	116	112	69	144	Melipilla						
257	187	212	194	326	214	62	206	Portillo					
232	162	187	169	301	189	37	181	99	Putaendo				
23	121	138	144	92	59	172	110	234	209	Rancagua			
209	139	164	146	278	166	22	158	84	201	186	San Felipe		
110	45	70	52	179	72	80	64	142	109	87	94	Santiago	
40	168	185	191	53	106	219	157	281	248	47	233	134	San Vicente de Tagua Tagua

Zone 5
SANTIAGO and THE
SURROUNDING DISTRICT

DIVISION BY SECTIONS

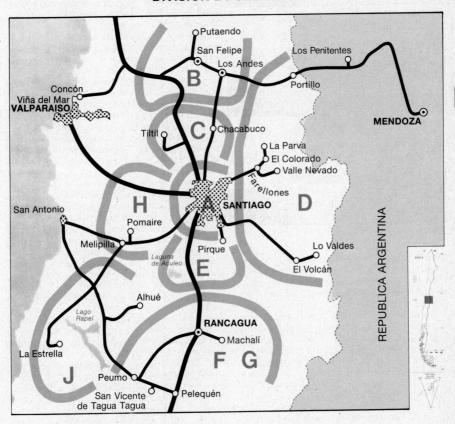

THE LAND, ITS HISTORY, ITS PEOPLE

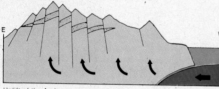

Original State

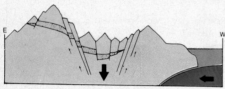

Uplift of the Andes

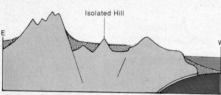

Sinking of the Central Depression

Isolated Hill

Silting of the Central Depression

DESCRIPTION the area covered by this Zone comprises part of the Aconcagua Valley, the Santiago basin and the Rancagua basin up to Angostura de Regolemu at Pelequén, as well as the Andes and the Coastal Ranges.

The Aconcagua Valley is, morphologically, the southernmost transverse valley and it marks the beginning of Central Chile; it consists of a watershed system slashing the country from the Andes to the Pacific. It is flanked by mountain spurs thrusting generally westwards from the Andes.

The Central Valley or Central Depression runs southwards flanked by the Andes and the Coastal Ranges; along the way it gives rise to a number of watersheds. The first such watershed or basin is the Santiago Basin, separated from the Aconcagua Valley by the Chacabuco range; it stretches southward up to Angostura de Paine («angostura» means «gap»; this is the name given to those points where the Central Depression is squeezed by spurs of mountain running westward from the Andes to meet the Coastal Range). Then comes the Rancagua Basin, stretching from Paine to the Regolemu gap at Pelequén. Both basins have tongues running westward, along which the rivers flow towards the sea; these valley tongues end at the coastal strip's softly rolling country.

The Cordillera of the Andes is slashed in this Zone by four large, deeply incised valleys known as cajones, each one with a river running along its bottom: Aconcagua, Mapocho, Maipo, and Cachapoal; these rivers have played a key role in shaping the Central Depression. The highest peaks in the Coastal Range, in turn, are Mount El Roble and Mount Cantillana, soaring over 2,000 m above sea level and plummeting directly to the Central Depression.

FORMATION OF THE LAND SEVERAL hundreds of million of years of tectonic, glacial, and volcanic interaction have been necessary to shape the land

as we see it today, in a process that is still under way. The tectonic process consists of a shifting and collision of the plates making up the earth's crust, whereby the Nazca plate (oceanic) is being subducted under the South American plate. This accounts for the fact the Easter Island gets one meter closer to the mainland every year. The enormous pressure generated by the collision of these two mammoth plates produces the earthquakes and volcanic activity which regularly affect this corner of the «Ring of Fire» around the Pacific Ocean. This pressure has also modified the crust's structure by producing a chain of very tall mountains, including the world's highest active volcano (Ojos del Salado, in Northern Chile), and the highest peak outside Asia (Mount Aconcagua, about a hundred km north of Santiago just beyond the Argentine border).

The Coastal Range existed already 100 million years ago. At the area now covered by the Andes Mountains there was a great depression flooded by seawater which was slowly being filled up by marine sediment. Eventually, a period of massively active tectonism started to lift up this marine depression, giving rise to the Cordillera of the Andes, uplifting in the process the old Coastal Range as well. Millions of years later, when the Ice Ages were approaching, a new surge in tectonic activity fractured the junction of these two ranges, sinking the ground and creating the central depression known as Central Valley. Once the two ranges and the intermediate valley had been formed, further processes took over the task of modelling the territory. A first ice age buried the mountains completely under ice masses whose glacier tongues descended into the intermediate depression, crushing and displacing rocks as they crept, and plugging the outlet of mountain valleys with walls known as moraines. While this process was in full swing, a period of strong volcanic activity spewed huge amounts of ash and provoked the melting of the ice and great mudslides, avalanches of a hot, liquid mass. These swept away all the material accumulated in the Andean ravines, mainly those of the Maipo and Cachapoal rivers, and filled up the Santiago and the Rancagua basin with thick sedimentary layers.

Only the loftiest peaks survived this filling up of the valley, known now as «island–hills»; they include the Chena, Tango, Santa Lucía, and San Cristóbal hills. The sedimentary layer was thicker near the Andes and thinner –and therefore lower in altitude– near the Coastal Range. This explains the difference in altitude at either side of the La Pirámide hill in Santiago, and between the Pudahuel and the Curacaví valleys, lying at either end of the Lo Prado Tunnel.

The second glaciation took place over 120,000 years ago, once again crushing the Cordillera's mother rock and carrying away material that had been softened in the previous glaciation. New moraine plugs were laid across the Andean ravines, still to be seen at the Mapocho river at La Ermita and Corral Quemado, a few kilometers upstream from El Arrayán. They are also to be seen at Los Queltehues, on the Maipo valley, and at the Yeso river, where the moraines dam the water of lake Negra. In the upper Aconcagua valley, the area of Portillo is a great moraine buildup which dammed the Laguna del Inca.

Circa 5,000 to 10,000 years ago, perhaps concurrently with the arrival of the first inhabitants into the country, a new, mighty volcanic activity took place, the resulting ashes covering the entire Andes mountains and the foothill area. Part of this massive amount of ash was washed away by rivers and rainwater run–off and deposited at the foot of the Coastal Range and beyond, filling up the depression and, in some cases, blocking the flow of rivers headed for the ocean. Thick ash layers are still to be seen at Pudahuel and Cerrillos de Maipú, in the Santiago area, and in the Cachapoal valley near Rancagua.

Today rivers are still modelling the topography, eroding away the moraine material remaining in the mountain valleys, removing loose material from the Andean slopes, eroding and depositing sediments on the central valley and, finally, dumping thousands of tons of sand into the sea.

EARLY INHABITANTS when the Spaniards arrived, the native population was mostly Mapuche, intermixed with tribes brought by the Incas from the Arequipa zone, Peru. Recent research has concluded that Mapuches were a single ethnic and linguistic entity scattered from the Choapa river in the North to Chiloé in the South. This 1,400–km–long territory contained markedly different areas in terms of climate, flora and fauna, thus giving rise to differing dialects and customs among its human inhabitants. The natives themselves called Picunches those of their number living in this area, Mapuches those living between the Biobío and Toltén rivers, and Huilliches those dwelling southward of the Toltén river. Around the mid–15th century the Inca empire thrust into Chile as far South as the Maule river, imposing military, economic and social dominion over the conquered area. Among their more outstanding works were the Inca Road, a 6–m–wide trail stretching from Peru down to the Cachapoal river, and their military outposts called pukara (one of which can still be seen on the Chena hill, just south of Santiago). They also established mitimaes –farming settlements– with settlers brought from Peru, who would pass on their language and agricultural techniques to the locals, and set up curacas –local government centers– at each valley, such as Vitacura, Talagante, Copequén, etc. During the Inca period the farmland was improved with irrigation canals and ditches, and hot pepper and maize were introduced as crops.

When the Spaniards arrived, native population in this area was sparse, well below the numbers found south of the Biobío river. The first Spanish chroniclers estimated the Indian population at not more than 25,000 individuals around 1543; fifteen years later they had dwindled to less than 9,000, decimated by work in the mines or simply because they fled to other territories. The natives had been promptly subject to the serfdom system known as encomienda, whereby they were forced to provide unpaid labor to the Spaniards; many of them were relocated to the far North as mining hands. Altogether, they fell under the encomiendas of 32 conqueror captains. The foremost encomendero in that period was Rodrigo de Quiroga who, together with his wife Inés de Suárez, had 1,500 natives in 5 encomiendas in 1546; 33 years later the number had fallen to 800 and, 160 years later, there were a scant 101 natives under encomiendas.

Prior to the Conquest, most natives had lived in scattered settlements not qualifying as villages or towns. The settlements in this area were Vitacura –the seat of the curaca–, Ñuñoa, Tobalaba, Macul, and Apoquindo. In the surrounding district were Lampa, Colina, Aculeo, Tango, Chada, Talagante, Chiñigüe, Mallarauco, Melipilla, Puangue, Pomaire and many others.

The native economy was geared at securing sustenance; in order to irrigate their crops, the Mapuches settled near rivers and streams. The lands in the Central Plain, nowadays rated as first class, were then virgin and uninhabited. They were not turned into productive uses until the 18th century, with a boom in livestock farming, and the 19th century, with the completion of large irrigation works. Camelid rearing (llamas) under the Mapuches did not go beyond meeting household needs; llamas were tended by herdsmen or placed in pens.

THE ORIGINAL LANDSCAPE barely 2% of the one million hectares of flatland in this zone is presumed to have been cultivated, with an additional 15% altered somewhat as a result of wildfire, firewood collection and browsing by livestock. Thus, over 80% of the total flatland area, in addition to the hilly areas, remained thoroughly untouched.

The Central Plain the plant cover included thick stands of trees growing on creek and river banks and in ravines, including such native species as boldos, peumos, arrayanes, canelos and maquis. Vegetation was somewhat sparser in sun-drenched open areas, where shrubby espinos (a type of acacia) and algarrobos (a Prosopis species) tended to predominate.

The rainfall pattern was then similar to today's, with four months of frequent rains, two months with occasional rains, and 6 months of drought. The fact that rain did not fall during the vegetative growth period (spring and summer) gave rise to a native plant cover made up of drought–resistance species having deep tap roots and very slow growth rates; they are still to be seen thriving at the Polpaico and Chacabuco valleys and at either end of the Lo Prado tunnel.

The Plain or Valley lands, covered by grasses and forbs in winter and dusty in summer, were devoid of human settlements. The colonial chroniclers described them as a plain where «highwaymen had their most readily available hideout and impunity.»

Ravines and South–Facing Slopes monopolized the tree cover, with fully–developed species reaching up to the very end of their life cycles. The most profuse species were peumo, maitén, boldo, quillay, litre and, on the coastal hills, avellano, lingue, the majestic belloto and the stately Chilean palm. This type of vegetation still occurs on many hills and in ravines, where the forests have regenerated; but the vast forests and large trees found by the conquerors can now only be found at a handful of places, such as the south–facing slopes of **Cuesta El Melón**, in the famous forests of the **Cantillana Hills**, at Aculeo, and in the **El Manzano ravine**, in the Cajón del Maipo (the Maipo river mountain valley). These trees were big enough to provide large timber pieces for beams and rafters for churches, warehouses and houses.

The Banks of the Great Rivers scenically, must have been at the time of the Conquest very similar to what we see there today, with a sparse riparian vegetation consisting mainly of maitén and a local variety of willow. The scenery has remained unchanged because the large rivers Aconcagua, Mapocho, Maipo, and Cachapoal have wide, stony riverbeds, whose banks are eroded by the increased water flow in spring, when melting snow swells the rivers; in summer, by contrast, the small amount of water runs deep and distant from the banks, contributing little to plant development on the adjacent lands.

Four factors played a determining role in transforming the original scenery during the colonial period: the introduction and proliferation of livestock of European origin, which pastured semi-wild in the central plain; the felling of trees to obtain timber both for urban construction and farm buildings, which depleted native forests on river banks; the use of charcoal and firewood as the sole fuels, obtained mostly from the espino (acacia) growing in the plains; and, lastly, the completion of the irrigation works in the valleys, which prompted the removal of the original plant cover.

LAND OWERSHIP the Spaniards established their seat at Santiago in 1541; the settlement remained the only urban center in the entire area comprised by this Zone for nearly two centuries. During the 16th century, the economy of this zone was based mainly on subsistence farming and gold mining. Plots of land were allocated on the best irrigated lands that had been worked by the natives, located in Vitacura, Tobalaba, Macul and Ñuñoa, and also along the Mapocho, downriver towards Talagante. The supply of labor for the demanding work at the mines was covered by the aforementioned encomiend, a serfdom system under which a group of Indians was placed under the command of a Spanish captain, forcing the natives to provide unpaid labor as a tribute to the Spanish Crown. An encomienda did not entail a right to land ownership, as that depended on another institution known as merced de tierra, literally, a land grant.

Since early on, in addition to a manor house

and a plot of land, Santiago residents were granted a merced de tierra in the valleys populated by natives, such as La Ligua, Aconcagua, Maipo and Cachapoal. These plots lacked clearcut boundaries and were not very much in demand, as most Spaniards moved farther south to Arauco, beyond the Biobío river. By 1600, however, a great Mapuche uprising forced the Spaniards to vacate their towns in the south and flee to central Chile, this area included. The newcomers needed access to land ownership to secure their livelihood. Thus, by 1650, all the land in this area had been allotted to both Spaniards and natives. Thereafter land ownership was acquired solely through inheritance or purchase.

The original size of farming properties varied depending on how close to Santiago they were located; the smaller ones had about 300 ha, the largest ones up to 1,500 ha of flatland in the valleys. The most coveted lands were those on the coast: these lands received more rainfall than the central valley lands, an important factor for non-irrigated crop production.

FARM PRODUCE the Indians grew mostly maize, potato and quínoa –an indigenous cereal–, and raised llamas. The Spanish conquerors introduced wheat and European fruit trees, which acclimatized readily, and cattle, horses, sheep, and pigs. Generally speaking, the farming potential output by 1600 exceeded largely the domestic needs of the scant population existing at the time. On the other hand, the increase in population in Peru and the development of silver mining at Potosí generated a large demand for farming products, which were supplied from Chile; these included mainly wheat, fat for candles and soap, leather for clothing and harnesses, jerked meat, and horses for hauling material in mining works.

Around 1700 a plague affected Peru's wheat seed stocks and wiped out the wheat output in that country for several decades. This catapulted Chile to the position of chief grain producer, exporting up to 10,000 tons of wheat yearly from the central zone, mainly produced in coastal farms.

THE HACIENDA the sustained demand from Perú for farming produce from this area made it necessary to introduce a much larger productive unit: the hacienda or fundo. The original size of the hacienda was increased through the acquisition of smaller plots and neighboring farms. The religious orders operating in the area ended up being the largest landowners, the Jesuit Order being the largest producer. By 1750 it owned, among others, the Graneros hacienda, with 14,000 ha of flatlands and 120,000 ha of hilly country; the 54,000-ha Bucalemu hacienda; the Calera de Tango hacienda, with 3,000 ha of flatlands, and the Chacabuco hacienda, with 29,000 ha.

The sheer size of these haciendas and their economic weight attracted the larger part of the population –mostly mestizos, ie, persons of mixed parentage– to them. Haciendas were largely self-sufficient, at any rate for the needs of the 17th- and 18th-century rural dwellers. They produced their own food, textiles and clothing, leather goods and candles and fruit, and had their own smithies and wine cellars and jerked-beef producers.

So came into being the Chilean rural society. Most mestizos were peones, or farm hands. But soon a new kind of farm worker appeared: the **inquilino** or tenant, paying rent for a small plot of land on the fringes of the hacienda and serving the purpose of protecting the owner's interests.

In the late 17th century and early 18th century, as a result of the large wheat exports, land ownership acquired a significant value. The chief landowners, headed by the Jesuits and by several families in this zone, became the country's foremost social group, veritable feudal rulers in their farms. They gave rise to the **mayorazgos** (see below). They also bought titles of nobility which the Court of Castilla offered for sale to finance the foundation of further cities in Chile.

The buildings at the hacienda were large enough to house hierarchically owners, laborers, workshops and warehouses; adjacent to them were the animal pens. No significant examples of these building complexes remain from the 17th century, but there are some good ones from the 18th century, such as the **Houses of Calera de Tango**, with a concentric layout surrounded by a protecting wall. The inner layout was based on a series of courtyards, with a chapel up front. These houses, built by the Jesuits, bear witness to the need of organizing the rural space in terms of the work to be done and providing the necessary protection against raids by highwaymen.

The architectonic characteristic of these haciendas changed after the mid–18th century, when the buildings started to be arranged into a linear pattern, preceded by the manor house and a chapel; these last two buildings were usually much larger that the remaining buildings. The new layout reached its peak with the manor houses and parks of the 19th century, many of which survive to this day and are described in these pages.

VILLAGES AND CITIES until the early 1700s, there were but seven cities in Chile; Santiago was the only urban center in this Zone. The rural population was clustered in the haciendas, posing major difficulties for religious indoctrination, education and, most paramount, for bringing the growing mestizo population into the embrace of Spanish traditions. Therefore, the Crown issued specific directives to the governors of Chile in the 18th century, in order that they undertake the foundation of towns and villages, both for Spaniards and natives. In this Zone this resulted in the foundation of **San Felipe** in 1740, **Melipilla** in 1742, **Rancagua** in 1743, **Alhué** in 1755, **Los Andes** in 1791, and also **Peumo** and **San José de Maipo**. The remaining cities and towns in this Zone were all founded after Chile attained independence.

For the natives, the authorities established the so-called «Indian towns» where they were forced to settle, encircled by plots of granted land. These were **Pomaire, Chillehue, Talagante, Lampa, Tiltil, Carrizal, Macul, Machalí** and many others. Most of these settlements were short-lived, as their lands were acquired by large landowners.

MAYORAZGOS AND VÍNCULOS the mayorazgo was the title holder to an entailed estate. It was legally established and regulated by the Spanish Crown and permitted persons of wealth to bequeath some of their properties to a given line of descendants, but without these descendants enjoying the right to encumber or alienate it, so as to transfer it undivided from one generation to the next. These properties were called **vínculo** («entailment»), as they were linked to a last will and testament; the inheritor was known as **mayorazgo** («first–male–born»), as he usually was the eldest son in each generation. The purpose behind this institution was to preserve the economic might of a family or of a title of nobility acquired from the Crown.

There were altogether twenty mayorazgos in Chile, and they were the basis of the social and economic power during the 18th and 19th centuries. The first one was established in 1703; the last one, in 1789, by Mateo de Toro y Zambrano, the Count of the Conquest. In the early days of the Republic mayorazgos were abolished by law by Bernardo O'Higgins. However, they did not cease to exist until late last century, when the vínculos were divided. It is noteworthy that of the twenty mayorazgos, 16 had their properties located in this region, and the remaining four in the immediate vicinity, such as Pullally (Papudo), La Ligua, Quillota, and Cunaco. Chile's central zone, therefore, concentrated the entire economic and social power at that time.

THE IRRIGATION CANALS last century a dramatic change in the physical aspect of agriculture took place in the central zone, spurred by the emergence of a new, large market for Chilean wheat in California and, later, in Australia. As a result,

If you want to make easier the program of a travel, it is advisable
to consult this synthesis of all the tours and traveled distances,
proposed by the Guide book. The graph provides for each circuit,
its interest, the duration, the distance of the travel and the facilities available.

	Characteristics				Facilities			
	INTEREST	DURATION (DAYS)	ROUND TRIP KILOMETERS	GRAVEL ROAD (KILOMETERS)	PICNIC	HOTELS	RESTAURANTS	CONDITIONS FOR BATHING
SECTION B THE ACONCAGUA VALLEY								
to Calle Larga, Los Andes and Curimón	★★★	1	180			•	•	
to San Felipe and The Aconcagua termal batths	★★★	1	240			•	•	•
to the Putaendo Valley	★★★	1	228				•	
to Llay Llay, Catemu and Panquehue	★★	1	223	10	•		•	•
SECTION C THE CHACABUCO BASIN								
to Colina, Peldehue and Chacabuco	★★★	1	120	14	•	•	•	•
to Tiltil, Rungue and Caleu	★★★	1	120	12	•	•	•	•
to Lampa, Chicauma and Polpaico	★★	1	100	15	•			
Circuit behind the InternationalAirport	★★	1/2	50	25	•		•	
SECTION D THE MOUNTAIN DISTRICT								
The Maipo Mountain Valley (Ríver Maipo)	★★★	1	180		•	•	•	•
Branch road to The Yeso Dam	★★	1	170	34	•	•	•	
to Farellones and Sky Resorts	★★★	1	82	46	•	•	•	•
to Portillo and the road to Argentina	★★★	1	290	65	•	•	•	•
SECTION E THE MAIPO PLAINS								
to Pirque, Río Clarillo and Environs	★★★	1	100	12	•		•	•
to Maipú and its Monuments	★★	1/2	20		•		•	
to Calera de Tango on the Royal road	★★★	1/2	77	33	•			
to Pukará de Chena	★★★	1/2	50	4	•			
to Buin, Maipo, Isla de Maipo and Naltagua	★★	1	110	52	•		•	
to Lake Aculeo	★★★	1	130		•	•	•	•
SECTION F RANCAGUA VALLEY								
to Rancagua on the Old Road	★★★	1	160	30	•	•	•	
to Machalí and Termas de Cauquenes	★★★	1	234	8	•	•	•	•
Extension to the Río Los Cipreces	★★★	1/2	270	44	•			•
to La Leonera and Hacienda la Compañía	★★★	1/2	170	30	•		•	•
SECTION G CACHAPOAL VALLEY								
to Lo Miranda, Doñihue and Coltauco	★★★	1	290	18	•	•	•	•
a Coinco, Quebrada de Tilcoco y Guacarhué	★★★	1	274	80	•		•	
to Pelequén, Malloa and San Vicente de Tagua Tagua	★★	1	260	6		•	•	
to Hacienda Los Lingues	★★★	1	260	10	•		•	
to Peumo and Palmar de Cocalán	★★★	1	394	32	•		•	•
to Pichidegua via the water wheels	★★★	1	335	44	•			
SECTION H MAPOCHO VALLEY AND MELIPILLA								
to Melipilla and Pomaire	★★★	1	160				•	
to Mallarauco and the Barriga Bridge	★★★	1	180	55	•			
to the Puangue Creek and Cuncumen	★★	1	184	38	•			
SECTOR J COSTINO								
to Villa Alhué	★	1	340	80	•			
to Central Rapel, Litueche, La Estrella and Marchihue	★★	2	300	95	•	•	•	•
to Rapel Lake	★★★	1	389	85	•	•	•	•

5

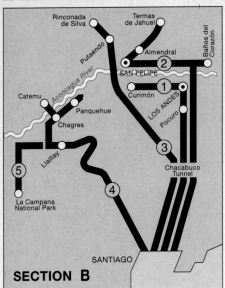

SECTION B

Only in the second half of the 19th century the land started to be fully exploited, fueled by investment in agriculture made by miners, nitrate tycoons, traders and financiers from Valparaíso, who introduced modern technologies, transforming both the rural landscape and traditions. The most significant development financed by these entrepreneurs, until then foreign to agricultural endeavors, was the construction of large irrigation canals which improved productivity and permitted the plantation of vineyards. In the 1920s, fruit production became an industry.

It is thus that this zone –unlike the other zones encircling the capital– owes its initial development not to Santiago but to Valparaíso. This dependence is clearly evidenced by the fact that the railway connecting Santiago and Valparaíso, financed by Valparaíso businessmen, was laid along the Aconcagua valley and not the Curacaví valley, although the latter route was much shorter. In the 1960s, however, the valley drifted steadily into the capital's area of influence as a result of the completion of the Chacabuco tunnel, which replaced the old colonial mountain road linking Santiago and the valley.

GASTRONOMY intense traffic between the countryside and the towns led to the establishment of many restaurants to cater to the travellers both along the way and in town.

They range from formal to quite simple, with the charm of little country inns. They are specialized in all varieties of pork dishes, as well as local wines and cider (chicha). Below we list the most frequented.

Traditional Restaurants good food and fine attention at **Hotel Plaza** (Los Andes), overlooking the square. **Baños del Corazón** is the best in the area, with excellent cuisine prepared by an Italian family; noteworthy are its sausages and hams. <u>**Termas de Jahuel**</u> is a hotel in a nice mountain setting, its restaurant overlooking the valley, very good food. **Club Social** (San Felipe) is located in a charming colonial house with several courtyards; good á la carte food. The **Shell** and the **Copec** gas stations on the Pan–American highway opposite Llayllay offer a varied, good menu, good service. Very frequented.

«Good–Value» Restaurants («Picadas») these are inexpensive, plain restaurants offering good, hearty fare, in this case also with the countryside charm. **La Ruca** (Rinconada) has a folkloric–tourist atmosphere, very frequented, good food. **Reinares** (San Felipe) keeps its countryside atmosphere in spite of being located downtown; excellent food. **La Palmera** (Putaendo) is perhaps the best of the picadas, with live music in summer and renowned for its canelita and the arrollado –strips of spicy pork arranged like a sausage– served slightly warm. **Piedras de Molino** (El Almendral) is a charming, inviting place, with traditional home–style dishes and an unusual appetizer consisting of chicha (cider) and charqui (jerked meat). **Bodegón Demetrio Mendoza** (El Almendral), with the Zone's best chicha produced by a household industry with a 150–year tradition. It has a large wine cave with huge earthen jars (worth a visit). **Heladería Olguín** (San Felipe) is one of those rare places where one can still eat excellent homemade ice–cream.

TOURS OF THE AREA

1 **TO CALLE LARGA, LOS ANDES AND CURIMON**

★★★ *a 180–km round trip from Santiago, paved road. Allow a whole day; any time of the year. For food, see Gastronomy above.*

A tour through farmland that is undergoing a remarkable boom in agribusinesses: you will see a number of new packing houses, fruit tree plantations and lots of traffic. You will also pass the new Claustro Carmelita monastery, where Sor Teresita de Los Andes is buried, as well as some old farm houses, and churches.

Leave Santiago on Route 57 heading for Los Andes. Beyond the Chacabuco tunnel the road descends into the green Aconcagua valley, leaving the arid landscape behind. The scenery displays pastures and cultivated fields until km 67.

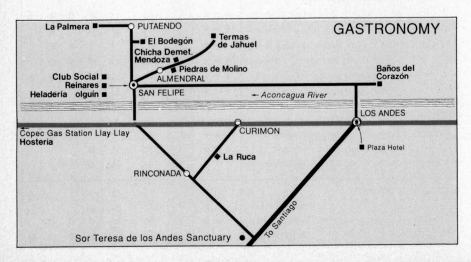

Here is a signposted detour to the left leading to the

Sor Teresa de Los Andes Sanctuary in a placid setting hemmed in by large hills. Here is the new Carmelita Cloister with the sanctuary for Sor Teresa, beatified in 1987 by Pope John Paul II during his visit to Chile. It has an enormous basilica containing the body of Chile's first saint. Many pilgrims come to the place throughout the year.

Get back to Route 57. At km 70 is Calle Larga, an aptly named one–street village straddling the road. At km 73 turn right into Pocuro street, a dirt road leading in a short distance to

POCURO an old, earthy Indian village. It has some nice colonial mud–brick houses with clay–tile roofs, several with arcaded verandas. Continuing on this same road you will reach the farmhouse where **President Aguirre Cerda** was born, now granted the status of National Monument and housing a farming school. If you want to visit it, ask for permission at the adjacent house. Get back to Route 57 to reach, at km 81,

LOS ANDES originally called Santa Rosa de Los Andes, it was founded by order of Ambrosio O'Higgins on July 31, 1791. Six years later there were 90 houses and 90 small farms and, in 1798, 849 inhabitants.

What To See you come into the city along **Av Sarmiento**, an avenue lined with plane trees. Turn right on O'Higgins to reach the square, the heart of the city, and then continue along Santa Rosa to Freire and then left on Rancagua to visit the **Cala** ceramics handicrafts, renowned for its hand–painted dishes, flower vases, pitchers, jars and other objects. You can see the artisans at work. It has a salesroom. Visits Mon through Sat –on the latter only until midday– and on Sunday prior arrangement (phone 421630 Los Andes).

On Av Sarmiento (see map) is the former **Convento de las Carmelitas Descalzas**, where Sor Teresa de Los Andes lived and died. On Esmeralda (see map) is the **Casa de los Villares**, a beautiful mansion erected in the 19th century as the manor house of a rich farm. Courtyards have been added to the central complex over the years; unlike the

---

☎ Telephone Center	**B** Archaeological Museum	**G** Railway Station
⊚ Gasoline Station	**C** Former Cloister Carmelita Convent	**H** Bus Terminal
⇒ Lookout Point		**R** Restaurant Donde El Guatón
✚ Hospital	**D** Cala Ceramics	**ACCOMMODATIONS**
A Town Hall	**E** Rodeo Arena (Medialuna)	**1** H Plaza
	F House Los Villares	

2 H Continental	
3 M Zava	
4 H Estación	
5 H Central	
6 H Valparaíso	

5

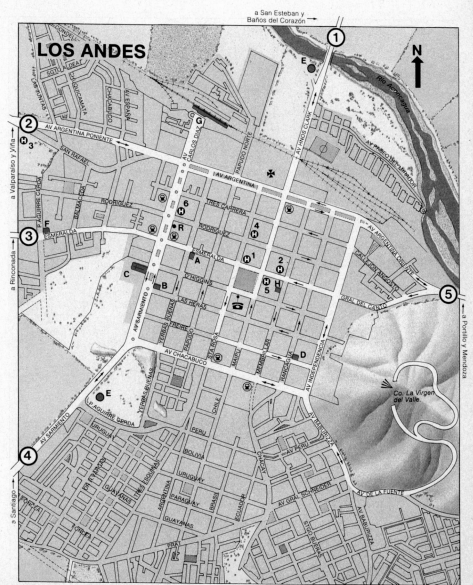

houses of that period, here the living quarters are upstairs.

Climb the **Cerro La Virgen** on foot or by car (see map) for the grand view over the city and the mountain range; from there you can see the flat–topped Mount La Mesa, an ancient Indian sanctuary.

Take exit 2 out of Los Andes (see map), which leads through lush fields to a tiny village called San Rafael, with rural houses on either side of the road offering local chicha for sale. At km 97 is the

SANTA ROSA DE VITERBO MONASTERY (NM)

at Curimón founded by the Franciscans. They came to Chile in 1553 upon a request submitted by Pedro de Valdivia to the King of Spain, Carlos I –better known as Charles V, Emperor of Germany–, with the purpose of preaching the Gospel to the locals. They founded on October 3rd of that year the first monastery of their order in Santiago and, in 1583, this one at Curimón.

The present buildings started to be erected ca 1700, and the monastery was finished in 1727. Of typical colonial style, it has a beautiful **courtyard** with corridors leading to the many rooms, **libraries** and the present–day **museum**. The museum was founded in 1966 and contains colonial paintings and statuary, wooden carvings, priestly vestments and important documents of the history of the Franciscan Order in Chile. In this monastery, Manso de Velasco signed the foundation act of San Felipe in 1740. The patriot soldiers coming into Chile across the Andes mountains rested here under the shade of the pepper trees, before marching on to the Chacabuco battle.

It can be visited Tue–Sun 09:30–12:30 h & 15:00–18:00 h The **church,** finished on October 4th, 1727, is large, with one–meter–thick mud–brick walls and enormous buttresses that have kept it standing through several violent earthquakes.

To round out the tour, continue along the secondary road to Rinconada, which eventually runs into Route 57.

2 TO SAN FELIPE AND THE ACONCAGUA THERMAL BATHS ★★★ *a 240–km round trip from*

5

☎ Telephone Center	**B** Post Office	**F** Bus Terminal and Municipal Market	**RESTAURANTS**
Ⓖ Gasoline Station	**C** Buen Pastor Monastery		**1** Reinares
Ⓒ Café, Meeting Point	**D** Social Club	**G** Railway Station	**2** Centro Arabe
A Town Hall	**E** Rodeo Arenas	**4** Hostel	**3** Helados Olguín

← a Putaendo

← a Hacienda Quilpué

N ↑

Abraham Ahumada

⑥

⑤

④

③

Av. Chacabuco

C Cordell

Estadio

Navarro

Salinas

Colinas

Prat

3

2

B

A

1

D

Merced

Av. Maipú

Freire

4

San Martín

Av. O'Higgins

Av. Yungay

Troncal

F

C

② ⑦

G **E**

Río Aconcagua

↕ a Valparaíso y Viña

SAN FELIPE

①

← a Santiago y Los Andes

Santiago on a paved road. Allow a whole day; any time of the year. For lunch, see Gastronomy above.

A circuit around a fruitful farming district with lots of vineyards, some historical villages, churches and thermal resorts.

Follow Route 57 to Los Andes (described in Tour 1 above), which you reach at km 77. Take then Exit 3 out of Los Andes to San Esteban, at km 81, where a road branches off to the right to Baños del Corazón. On the way you will pass the curiously-named village of **Cariño Botado** («Rejected Love»), so christened after the Liberating Army could not accept the village's hospitality as it passed through this area.

Baños del Corazón thermal resort reached at km 87. It lies 900 m above sea level, with good accommodations and a restaurant reputed for its good food, a swimming pool with spring water at 22° C and some entertainments. Its dry mountain air combines advantageously with the thermal waters to create a good healthy environment. It is worth a visit.

To continue to San Felipe, retrace the road up to San Esteban and take there the paved road running parallel to the Aconcagua river, passing vast vineyards and citrus plantations. There are several road junctions on the way. The **El Tambo** and **El Chalet** hamlets may be worth a visit. At km 105 is

SAN FELIPE EL REAL one of the valley's major cities, a meeting and supply point for the area's farmers. It was founded by Manso de Velasco on August 3rd, 1740, with the purpose of gathering the population scattered among the haciendas so that the youth could be taught «the Christian doctrine, reading and writing, and instructed in the letters in a social environment, and politics.»

What To See drive along Tocornal, which soon changes its name to Prat, to the splendid **square**, with huge, leafy trees and a fountain in the middle. Along the perimeter avenues **Yungay**, **Chacabuco** and **Maipú** (see map) some of the picturesque horse-drawn victorias are still to be seen rolling. These are, together with Av O'Higgins, the four avenues encompassing the typically-Spanish seven-by-seven-block grid. Small ditches run alongside every avenue and at given intervals are water fountains where pedestrians can drink. At Av Yungay is the **Buen Pastor Monastery**, a splendid construction dating from the 19th century, with an adjacent park.

Take exit 4 [...] San Felipe (see map). The Cordillera of the Andes provides a massive backdrop along the way to the charming village of

EL ALMENDRAL a good place for eating (see Gastronomy section above). Here is the **San Antonio del Almendral Monastery and Church (NM)**, built of mud-brick and timber. The bell tower was designed by Gustave Eiffel. The interior is interesting, with wooden pillars imitating marble and frescoes on the ceiling.

Continue towards the town of Santa María; the road climbs the mountains and passes the small village of Santa Filomena. The plant cover is mainly shrubs, mostly of the Acacia species, until you reach the excellent hotel of

Termas de Jahuel lying 1,180 m above sea level. Good accommodations and good food, also for non-staying visitors. It has a swimming pool fed by a spring where the water gushes up at 20° C, beautiful gardens and entertainments. There is a sweeping view over the valley and the village of Santa María.

Return to Santiago through Santa María, San Felipe and Rinconada to retake Route 57. Total

distance to Santiago is 103 km.

3 TO THE PUTAENDO VALLEY

a 228-km round trip from Santiago; allow a whole day. Any time of the year. Lunch at Rinconada de Silva or Restaurant La Palmera at Putaendo (see Gastronomy above).

A tour to a valley through which all parties invading central Chile had to pass. Good crochet needlework for sale.

Take Route 57 from Santiago to Los Andes. Beyond the Chacabuco tunnel, at km 68, take the signposted road branching left to Rinconada and San Felipe, running through vineyards and fruit plantations. You will pass the hamlet of **Rinconada**, with mud-brick houses lining the street. At km 90 is San Felipe (described in Tour 2 above). Take exit 6 out of that town (see map) heading for Putaendo. On the way you will pass

LAS COIMAS a quaint hamlet which had its hour of glory last century when rich silver and copper mines were in full production on the hills towering to the east. On February 7th, 1817, the first skirmish between royalist troops and the patriot army crossing into Chile through the Valle Hermoso pass took place here. At km 104 is

PUTAENDO the name is apparently derived from the Mapuche Phutaentu, meaning «place at the corner.» This was an old Indian town which attracted Spaniards to work on the gold mines discovered in the vicinity in the mid-18th century. Eventually a village sprung up and a church was built, called San Antonio. The village status was granted on March 20th, 1831, by the Aconcagua Assembly. Putaendo was the first village to which the patriot army headed by José de San Martín arrived in 1817.

Four centuries before that, during the Inca invasion headed by Túpac Yupanqui, in 1485 Huayna Cápac, a son of Yupanqui, descended from the Andean massif and pitched camp at Putaendo, bringing the Aconcagua valley into the Inca empire. The Diego de Almagro expedition also stopped here in 1536. The reason for so many «visitors» was that the Inca Road used to pass through here, the most expeditious route connecting the tribes disseminated throughout the La Ligua, Aconcagua and Mapocho valleys.

The village stretches from north to south; at the latter end is the square, shaded by large trees and with the **Church of San Antonio** on one side. Inside the church is a baroque statue of Christ from the 18th century. It can be visited getting permission from the casa parroquial adjacent to the church. Opposite, at Bulnes 55, are the famous crochet needlework artisans. Drive around the village to see the gaily-painted, continuous façades of the mud-brick houses.

Leave Putaendo following the signposted street leading north to Alicahue. Continue 7 km until you reach a signposted junction leading to Rinconada de Guzmanes. Here the scenery changes colors, from a lush green to ocher. The road soon crosses the Putaendo river and at km 10 it reaches the hacienda of

LO VICUÑA it was created in 1790 when the old Hacienda de Putaendo was divided. Between 1839 and 1880 the present church, the warehouses, corrals, general store, and the manor house were built. The manor house was reconstructed in 1915.

The layout is typical of a farm, with a large yard, and esplanade and the buildings arranged hierarchically starting with the warehouses, then the tenants houses and, lastly, the manor house, which, built in a different style, does not fit so smoothly

5

into the whole. You can see it from the outside, but ask for permission first.

Retrace the road up to two km beyond Putaendo. Take there the signposted road branching left to

RINCONADA DE SILVA the place was named after Pedro and María de Silva, a Castilian family who bought this land in 1605 from an old St Augustine monastery, and which they later bequeathed to their children. It is a picturesque place with an irregular layout, full of corners and colonial–style houses. During Easter Week, a Via Crucis ceremony is held here, ending at the hill's summit, at the foot of a large statue of Christ carved into a tree trunk about 50 years ago by a German called Peter Horn. The carvings depicting the 14 stations are remarkable. In addition, the hill offers a sweeping view over the valley. Here is also a very good traditional restaurant called El Bodegón.

Get back to the main road to retrace the highway back to Santiago.

4 TO LLAILLAY AND CATEMU

a round–trip of 223 km from Santiago, best in spring or autumn. For food, see Gastronomy above.

A tour through an area of rich contrasts, going from semi-arid to lush countryside.

Leave Santiago following the northbound Pan-American highway. The first stretch is flat. By 1960 these lands were arid plains covered with acacias and algarrobos. Later, deep wells were dug and water was pumped using electric pumps to irrigate the fields. That transformed the landscape. Along the way you can see the high-tension power lines which provide the energy for this irrigation system.

The road then climbs to the **El Tabón** plateau with a landscape that was typical of Chile's Central Valley 300 years ago: green with pastures in winter, dry in summer and speckled with acacias and algarrobos. Acacias are in full bloom in September and October.

At El Tabón you will see, on the right, the houses of **Los Azules del Tabón**, a construction from the 18th century that illustrates the rural architecture of that period: simple lines, colonnaded galleries encircling the house, which blends perfectly with the mountainous semi–desert scenery.

INTO THE LLAILLAY VALLEY the road then descends to Llay Llay, with mammoth boulders strewn on the side of the road, carried by glaciers thousands of years ago. Some hang precariously from the slopes, which are stud with many–armed cacti. The place is beautiful. To the right, you can see the railway track laboriously carved into the rocky hillside.

Below spreads the **Llaillay Valley**, covered with vineyards and fruit orchards. This area's productivity was enhanced by three irrigation canals built late last century and which, skirting the hillsides, bring water from the Aconcagua river.

The valley was owned in the past by the Letelier family; one of the descendants planted vineyards in the 1920s and built refrigerated storage rooms and packing houses, pioneering the now booming agribusiness. The Pan–American highway (built in 1945) runs along the middle of the valley. At km 88 is the signposted road branching right to

LLAY LLAY the village was spawned by a railway station and three copper smelters located at the place. In 1875 it was granted village status. The social center is the square, opposite the railway station. Until recently, it was renowned by its

white–clad ladies selling the delicious pastries and sandwiches that made the train stop worth it. Now its mainstay is agriculture and industry.

Continue the tour taking the road leading to Los Andes, which descends soon to the spacious Aconcagua Valley, covered by cultivated fields.

At km 93 is **Chagres**, a scattering of dwellings around the railway station and an industrial plant of the **Compañía Chilena de Tabacos**. You will see extensive tobacco plantations in the area, easy to spot for the plants' large leaves. Chagres was known in the past for its major **Copper Refinery**, which processed ores from the Central Zone's small–sized mines. The old buildings are still to be seen at the foot of the hill. A short distance beyond Chagres a road branches left leading in three km to the

CATEMU VALLEY an old Indian district. The name comes from Ca= «another», and temú, a native tree. The valley eventually became a large livestock–raising hacienda which, in the 18th century, was acquired by Francisco García–Huidobro, a trader and founder of the Mint (Casa de Moneda) in Santiago and owner of further large haciendas in Paine and El Principal de Pirque, where he set up an entailed estate.

At the head of the valley sits the village of **Catemu** lying atop small hills. Its origin can be traced to copper mining, with over 40 ore smelter furnaces operating in the area at one time. Now it is a farming center. A drive further along this road will show you farmland, mostly tobacco fields enclosed behind low stone walls. Three km into the valley from Catemu, on the right, are the houses of

LAS VARILLAS erected in one of the four farms into which the original 24,000–ha hacienda was divided last century. The housing complex was built in 1860 by Borja García Huidobro; the main building has two stories and a monumental neoclassical portico and colonial galleries. Lying on the hillside, the upper floor opens directly onto a garden. Now the complex houses the Salesian Agricultural School.

To continue the tour, go back to the highway leading to San Felipe (km 112) and follow this road. At km 124 is the village of **Panquehue,** where it is worth to take the road branching right to visit the

Hacienda Panquehue the road leads in 5 km to the great hacienda once owned by the Toro–Mazotte family. By 1870 it was bought by Maximiano Errázuriz, a powerful copper and coal mine owner, who had irrigation canals built and vineyards planted; these can still be seen on the hillsides. With 800 cuadras (a cuadra is about 83 m to a side), it was the world's largest privately–owned vineyard at that time, and its quality product made the Errázuriz Panquehue winery famous. You can visit the bodegas –the winery itself– and taste and buy wine. Opposite the bodegas are the manor houses and the fine park planted by Errázuriz.

To return, get back to the highway leading to San Felipe and take there Route 55 back to Santiago.

5 DETOUR TO LA CAMPANA NATIONAL PARK

★★★ 44 kms farther on the previous Llaillay and Catemu route (267 kms in all), or a total of 220 kms there and back straight from Santiago. Of these, 24 kms are unpaved; go for the day, in spring or summer, as in autumn the coconuts are harvested and in winter the rains make the roads difficult for driving. We recommend taking a picnic.

This side road leads to the fabulously beautiful Ocoa Palm Groves, one of the two surviving Chilean palm forests.

Leave Santiago by the northern Panamerican Highway reaching Llaillay at km.88, and keep on the highway going towards the coast for 10 kms more. This takes you a through the Los Andes crossroads, then through the toll gate to a short tunel known as «La Calavera», and then the Ocoa railway station, until you reach the **first bridge** over the Aconcagua river.

From this bridge, on a clear day, you get an imposing **view** of Mount Aconcagua, the peak in America, which you can see in all its majesty. This spectacular view will make you understand why Mount Aconcagua was considered sacred by the natives.

Shortly before reaching the **bridge**, a hardly noticeable gravelled road leads off to the left. If you take this road (0 km), you will reach the Ocoa Palm Groves 12 kms farther on. The road runs straight ahead, crossing the railway and a local street, then joins a farm avenue lined with **Taxodium distichum**, a beautiful and unusual conifer which sheds its leaves in winter. 2 kms farther on is the farm itself.

LOS MAITENES DE OCOA is made up of U–shape manor type houses, surrounded by tile roofed verandas, with a park over a hundred years old, beatifully laid out, in which Chilean palms grow and which can be seen through the farm fences. To the left are the **corrals**, **stables** and **storehouses**, even more ancient, built with adobe bricks and which have stood up through many violent earth-quakes. On the right at the edge of the park there is a small gothic style **chapel**, flanked by two groves of Chilean palm trees, which make a striking picture.

The road turns towards the right of the Los Maitenes manor houses, and 1 km farther ahead reaches the tip of a range of hills. This is know as the **Cerro de la Virgen**, beautifully forested with drought–resistant trees which form a small park, needing no irrigation, including a grove of graceful Trachycarpus palm, sone dark cork oaks (phellem), grey pines with long pine needles (pinus strobus), eucalyptus with pendulous branches beneath which are strewn flowering geraniums. It is well worth a short walk along these paths.

The road continues bordering the ip of this range and reaches the **Valley of the Palm Trees**. This valley is wide and entirely given over to farming, surrounded by the impressive hills of **La Campana** which form a sheer drop above it, and in to background the imposing Cerro **El Roble** is seen. Both are over 2,000 mts. in height and are seen from here in all their majesty.

Continue up the valley, along a well–marked road, as far as the entrance of the

LA CAMPANA NATIONAL PARK where the giant palm trees can now be seen growing in profusion beginning at the stream, forming groves among the rocky outcroppings, surrounded by bushes and huge organ pipe cacti. The road winds through wide palm tree trunks and shortly reaches a second, higher plateau from where thousands

Palm Grove in National Park La Campana

of palm trees can be seen growing next to the stream and up all the hillsides. Their typical sil-houettes crown the lonely moutain peaks as the Araucarias do in southern Chile. The road comes to an end at a peaceful spot next to the stream, which is an ideal place to bathe in its pools surrounded by the enormous 300–years–old palm trees which grow densely, one against the other. The scenery is magnificent and well worth the trip.

THE CHILEAN PALM TREE of the «Palmae» genus grows in hundreds of species, mainly in tropical and sub–tropical zones. The Chilean palm tree– Jubea spectabilis– is indigenous, and has trunk girth, growing in unusually southern latitudes.

It can be recognized by its branches which grow as a plume atop the smooth tree trunk. It grows slowly, bearing fruit only after 80 years. The small, round coconuts grow in large clusters and in winter are sold on the city streets.

These particular qualities, as well as their beauty, have led to their being taken to California and the Mediterranean, where they can be found in all the large parks. **Kew Gardens**, a famous botanical garden in **London**, boats a large glass conservatory know as the House of Palms.

Originally this palm tree grew profusely on the central Coastal Range and in the valleys near the sea. The delicious «**Miel de Palma**» (palm honey) is taken from the sap of these trees, but the only way of extracting it is by cutting down the tree. Palm honey, during the Colonial Period and also the last century became the main source of sugar, which practically exterminated the species, and the only surviving trees are found in a few of the valleys of this zone, and in the groves of **Ocoa** and of **Cocalán** near the Cachapoal river.

NB this palm tree valley is botanically considered a «forest relic»,the only one known in Chile, as well as a conservation sanctuary of this species, which has been preserved thanks to the care and replanting of palm trees during over a hundred years which was undertaken by different landown-ers.

When authorized to visit these parks, all pre-cautions should be respected, above to keep nature unpolluted by not discarding garbage and repairing damage caused by children.

To return to Santiago, travel the same road as far as the Panamerican Highway.

5

SECTION C   CHACABUCO BASIN

This Section comprises the valley stretching north of Santiago up to the Chacabuco range; the valley is flanked to the east by the Cordillera of the Andes and to the west by the Coastal Range. Here starts Chile's Central Valley, which stretches all the way to Puerto Montt, over 1,000 km further

South. This district has no rivers flowing through it. Therefore, over the years large efforts have been made to bring artificial irrigation into the area. At the turn of the century the Chacabuco canal was built, tapping water from the Acon-cagua river and bringing it to this valley through

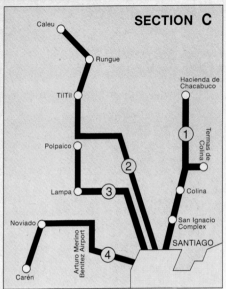

SECTION C

long tunnels bored through the mountains. However, as it is entitled only to the Aconcagua's surplus water, that canal cannot make a large contribution to agriculture here. Other canals take water from the Mapocho river and, skirting the slopes of the San Cristóbal hill –you can see them–. carry water northwards to the area of Colina, Lampa, etc.

Another oddity are the Batuco swamps, created by poor drainage in the middle of the valley and laboriously drained years ago. The construction of the northbound Pan–American highway in 1945 increased the value of these lands. The spread of electricity throughout the countryside made it possible to dig deep wells where electric pumps tap water from underground aquifers; this, added to the construction of the Rungue dam, which regulates the flow of the Tiltil river, has given a new face to the area, with vast irrigated farmland elbowing away the previous arid prairies covered by acacias and algarrobos.

This area contains several interesting relics from the large haciendas of the past. The main road

through this valley is known as «The Chile Route», as it was used by the Incas for their thrust southward into Chile in the 15th century, then by the Spanish conquerors and, later, by the Liberating Army. It connects the Mapocho and the Aconcagua valleys via Huechuraba, Colina and Chacabuco.

TOURS OF THE AREA

1 TO COLINA, PELDEHUE AND CHACABUCO

★★★ *a 120–km round trip on a paved road; allow half a day, or a whole day if planning a picnic or lunch at the inexpensive «El Solar de Araos» restaurant at Esmeralda.*
This circuit will show you historical sights, haciendas and churches, and a satellite–tracking station formerly operated by the NASA.

Take the northbound Pan–American highway out of Santiago up to the Quilicura road junction (with traffic lights; a new highway intersection is under construction). Take there the road branching right, which will bring you to Route 57 (signposted) to Los Andes. Turn left to follow this road, which runs between the Andes mountains and a scenic rural valley. At km 12, on the left, there is a church surrounded by palms, and the houses of

SAN IGNACIO DE HUECHURABA (NM) a beautiful complex dating from the 18th century which belonged to the Jesuits. It is located on the road which, since the Conquest, was the only route from the valley to the trans–Andean provinces of Mendoza and Cuyo, then part of Chile and lying now in Argentina. The chapel is crowned by a strange wooden tower. The place is now a venue for major auctions, advertised in the Santiago newspapers. Very well preserved, it is open for visitors every day.

At km 30 is

Colina a farming town with an unusual triangular, irregularly–shaped plaza where the locals converge to see and be seen. It used to be the seat of an Inca settlement with settlers brought from Peru; the governor was known as Coliruna, from whose name the village's name was derived. Continuing to Los Andes, to the right you will see a large Social Rehabilitation Center, a modern prison.

At km 35 the road passes the small village of **Esmeralda**, where the renowned «good–value» restaurant **El Sol de Araos** is located, specializing in Chilean dishes and roasted goat–kid. One km further along is **Peldehue**, a village straddling the highway and lined with tall poplars. The trees indicate that it evolved from a farm. A short distance east of the village, a rich gold mine was discovered in the 18th century –now depleted– which prompted the construction of the Dominican monastery of **Santa Catalina de Peldehue**; it served as a hospice until 1747. A little over one century later, in 1860, construction of the new church and of some houses was begun; the latter were built on the foundations of the old houses and have been extensively damaged by subsequent earthquakes.

Opposite the Peldehue church a dirt road branches right to **Termas de Colina**, at km 43. It has a hotel, a swimming pool and private bathing cabins. The season goes from September 18th until approximately April 30th. The thermal water emerging here contains a rich mixture of mineral salts, particularly recommended for rheum and other ailments, and therefore very popular in season.

Back on Route 57, at km 52 is the **Satellite Tracking Station**, which can be visited prior permission (Ph 698 1702, Santiago) on Mon–Thu between 08:00 h and 18:00 h. Beyond this sta-

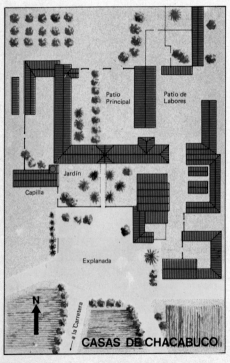

CASAS DE CHACABUCO

tion, the scenery abruptly changes into a semi–arid landscape, with sharp peaks towering close to the road and a superb backdrop of snowy Andean peaks. One km past an olive orchard a road branches right to the historical

HACIENDA DE CHACABUCO (NM) granted in 1599 by Pedro de Vizcarra to Pedro de la Barrera in recognition of his good services. Nearly a century later, in 1696, the Jesuits acquired the farm, which covered 28,869 hectares, and built the houses and the church around 1730. The access road, the church, the manor house, the tenant houses and other buildings have preserved the atmosphere of a large 18th century hacienda. In this manor house stayed San Martín, O'Higgins and their officers after the Battle of Chacabuco. Open everyday for visitors, it is not very well preserved.

Two km north of here along the highway is the **Monument to the Victory of Chacabuco**, rising at the site where the Royalist troops where defeated by the Liberating Army on Feb. 12, 1817, performing a decisive step towards Chile's independence. To return, retrace the road.

2 TO TILTIL, RUNGUE, AND CALEU

a 120–km round trip on a mostly paved road (12 km gravel); allow a whole day; best on a sunny spring day. Take food for a picnic.
A circuit through the countryside to a historical village and to the place where the guerrillero Manuel Rodríguez died.

Leave Santiago following the northbound Pan–American highway and take road branching left to Polpaico at km 33. Beyond Estación Polpaico take the road branching right to Tiltil. The road runs alongside the railway through a semi–arid landscape with lots of opuntia plantations. At km 48 is a **monument** on the place where Manuel Rodríguez, one of the most ingenious fighters for Chilean independence, died in 1818; his body was buried at the Tiltil church and later was moved to Santiago. The road runs a bit higher, passing lonely opuntia fields; this area is good for a picnic. At km 53 is

Tiltil a village nestled on a hillside, which sprang up when gold was struck in the vicinity. The name seems to be derived from the Mapuche word thiti, which means «many triles», ie, small tordos, a native thrush. In 1712 it had a stable population dwelling in houses clustered around the church, and five ore grinding mills to process the rocks from the neighboring gold mines. When the mines became depleted, the population dropped considerably.

Now it is a quiet, picturesque village with a nice square and a church from the early 18th century, where Manuel Rodríguez body was kept. The old road linking Santiago and Limache through the La Dormida ridge passes through here. Leaving Tiltil on the northbound gravel road, which climbs the slope, you will have a grand view of the village and the valley. The road runs through a narrow valley between the Coastal Range and a creek. This creek drains the **Rungue Dam**, which you will reach at km 61. A fee is charged to gain access to the shore, where you can bathe. Retracing the road a few meters, there is a road branching right, which climbs the mountain with great views of the valley and leads in 11 km to

CALEU a picturesque old «Indian village» of haphazard layout, nestled amidst the Coastal Range and with the towering Mount El Roble for a backdrop. A suspension cable railway leads from here to the television relay antenna atop the summit. A stroll through the village's quaint streets will set you back a hundred years. There are some small restaurants offering traditional Chilean dishes.

Retrace the road up to **Rungue**, a sleepy old

hamlet around a railway station. Follow the signs back to the Pan–American highway leading to Santiago.

3 TO LAMPA, CHICAUMA AND POLPAICO

a 100–km round trip, with 15 km graveled. Allow a whole day, preferably in spring or autumn. Take food.
A good tour if travelling with children; the solitary road runs through scenic land with small farms and old railway stations.

Take the northbound Pan–American highway and turn left at km 22 on the signposted road to Lampa, up to Estación Colina at km 26. It is a small village which thrived when lots of trains used to stop here. Now only occasionally a train calls at the station, and it is always a freight train. The place looks now quite forlorn. The paved road running west through a green plain leads to

Lampa at km 33, a town set between ravines and fruitful farmland. This was an old Indian settlement formed when gold was struck in the neighboring hillsides. Village status was granted in 1888. The place's mainstay is now vegetable production.

Continuing to Polpaico, the road is lonely and runs northward along a creek flowing through a narrow, green valley, skirting the Coastal Range foothills. There are good spots for a picnic, hiking or flying kites. Before Polpaico, at km 41, is the hamlet of **Chicauma**, an old farm now producing fruit and vegetables.

From km 48 the road is paved. A road branching right leads to the **Polpaico** railway station and then to the namesake village, which evolved from a mining and farming settlement; in the vicinity there were silver, copper and iron mines. Now it is the seat of a major cement mine; visits are not allowed. Continuing along this paved road you reach the Pan–American highway.

4 A CIRCUIT BEHIND THE INTERNATIONAL AIRPORT ★★ *a 50–km round trip, with half of it paved and the rest graveled. Allow half a day, best if sunny.*
A short circuit on a country road skirting the airport and, later, the Carén lake.

Take the northbound Pan–American highway – Route 5 in map- and at km 11 take road branching left towards Quilicura. A short stretch beyond the railway crossing turn left to follow the signposted road to the **Arturo Merino B Airport**. The road eventually reaches the airport perimeter fence and makes a sharp bend to the left. At this point, a gravel road branches right and skirts the length of the runway. 1 km further along is the renowned restaurant **Gran Parrillada de Pudahuel** – open every day, Sundays only half a day–, complete with children's playground, a large park and a sweeping view towards the airport.

Continue along this road, amid small cultivated fields and military areas. You will then cross the El Membrillo bridge spanning the Lampa creek and, a few meters farther along, a road branches north to Lampa and south to **El Noviciado**. Take the latter branch. El Noviciado evolved from a farm with a house for Probation of Novitiates, owned by the Jesuits until 1767. Now it is a modest farming village with small plots producing vegetables for local consumption and for the Santiago market. From the summit of the adjacent hill there is a splendid **view** towards Santiago and the Andes mountains. Leave Noviciado heading south on the road running alongside the Lampa creek, which eventually meets the Santiago–Viña del Mar highway. Turning right on this road, one km later you will reach the entrance to the **Carén lake and park**, on the right–hand side, managed by Digeder, the State's Sports Board. It is a good spot for watersports and for a picnic. An entrance fee is charged.

5

SECTION D   THE MOUNTAIN DISTRICT

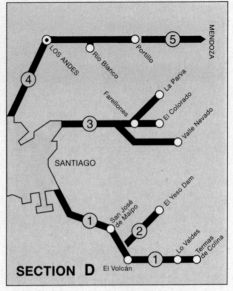

This Section comprises the entire Andean district lying East of Santiago, stretching from the Aconcagua valley in the North to the Maipo valley in the South. This segment of the Andes includes the tallest peak in the entire American continent, from Alaska to Cape Horn: Mount Aconcagua, soaring to just below 7,000 m above sea level (ca 21,000 ft). The Aconcagua, Mapocho and Maipo rivers all flow along deeply incised valleys they have carved into the Andean massif; roads run along these highly scenic valleys, leading to mountain resorts and ski centers.

The mountain scenery is solitary, rugged and at times overwhelming, with peaks capped by eternal snow towering directly above the road. It is semi–arid in the lower portions, and sterile and stony above the snow line. Unlike other mountain areas in countries with a longer history and larger population, the Chilean mountain area is still relatively free of human intervention. The villages there are recent and have evolved from mining operations, railroad construction or hydroelectric power complexes built in the area. The Indians only used the mountains as a passage towards the pampas stretching on the other side, and a few as religious shrines (eg Cerro El Plomo); there were no Indian settlements in the mountains and therefore, unlike the Central Valley, many names here are not Indian but Spanish in origin. The most populated and worked mountain valley is that of the Maipo river, with several small villages surrounded by fruit orchards, in full bloom in spring and beautifully hued in autumn.

The road that climbs highest is the one along the Aconcagua valley, which crosses into Argentina; next is the Mapocho valley road, which climbs to La Parva and Valle Nevado, both around 2,300 m above sea level (ca 6,900 ft). The road into the Maipo valley, in turn, reaches 1,845 m at Lo Valdés, although a branch road continues deeper into the mountains to the Yeso dam, at over 2,000 m altitude. Each of these roads goes through changing scenery, ranging from fruit orchards at the foothills –such as at Cajón del Maipo– to seasonal snow fields which, in summer, become mountain meadows where cattle graze – such as at Farellones and La Parva (in winter these are chic ski resorts)–, and lastly to the rocky, eternally snowy scenery of the deep Andes traversed by the upper reaches of the Aconcagua road.

TOURS OF THE AREA

1 THE MAIPO MOUNTAIN VALLEY (CAJON DEL MAIPO) ★★★ *a 180–km round trip, with 46 km of dirt road. Allow a whole day, best if sunny. Take food, or eat at any of the restaurants listed below.*

Tips for Accommodations Hostería San José (Las Vertientes); Posada El Canelo; Hotel Cabinas Millahue (Melocotón), Cabinas Cascada de las Animas (San Alfonso); Posada Los Ciervos (San Alfonso).

Tips for Lunch El Tucán, Chilean dishes (La Obra). Host San José, varied bill of fare (Las Vertientes). Parrilladas Argentinas, very good beef (El Canelo). Posada El Canelo, good Chilean food (El Canelo). Café Vienés (Guayacán). Hotel Millahue, tasty Chilean food (Melocotón). El Campito, inviting and offering good food (San José de Maipo). Refugio Alemán, good food and a breathtaking view (Lo Valdés).

Picnic Areas there is a large number of picnic areas (see map). Here we list the most outstanding: Picnic El Raco (La Obra), charming place, wooded, good facilities, swimming pool and a small lake with boats for hire. Picnic Peumos del

Canelo (El Canelo), attractive and well taken care of, with vast grassy areas shaded by local trees, excellent facilities, swimming pool. Picnic Fundo Estero del Manzano (El Manzano), a natural place with attractive mountain vegetation; hemmed in by towering peaks, it has access to the crystalline El Manzano creek; good facilities. Picnic Cascada de Las Animas (San Alfonso), an impressive setting upriver with a breathtaking view to the curiously striped peaks across the stream; shaded by a pine forest, it has good facilities and a swimming pool.

A tour into a scenic, deeply incised mountain valley carved by the Maipo river; it claws deep into the Andes and boasts a wide range of contrasts. The area is outstanding for hiking, climbing, bathing, picnic and rafting (see Rafting Excursions). It also has the incipient Lagunillas ski center, many restaurants, quaint villages and thermal springs.

Take Av Américo Vespucio Sur and at Rotonda Departamental follow the road to Las Vizcachas (see city maps) and then the road branching east into the Cajón del Maipo. Four hundred meters beyond the junction is **Centro Las Vizcachas**, a private club with good facilities and South America's largest swimming pool, with 3,000 square meters in area. Non-members have access to the casino (cafeteria), the drive–in movie, and the Las Vizcachas car racecourse, where Chile's most important car races (announced in the Santiago newspapers) are held.

Further along, at the **La Obra** area, you will see artisans carving stone near the road.

Three km from the junction, on the right, is the **Cavas de Maipo** winery. You can visit its wine vaults and taste its products on weekends. Strolling through its grapevine plantations and almond orchards one gets the feeling of being somewhere further south in the Central Valley. It is worth a visit.

The road continues into the valley, winding its way upriver. The white flags hanging outside many houses indicate that freshly–baked tortillas and bread are on offer, along with nuts, chicha (apple or grape cider) and honey.

As is to be expected, the air becomes progressively clearer as altitude (and distance from Santiago) increases. Seven km from the original junction you will pass the resort of **Las Vertientes**, with a few summer retreats, and the good Hostería San José, with cabins, a large swimming pool, a spacious restaurant and well-tended gardens.

Next comes a succession of restaurants, picnic

zones, some with swimming pool, children's playgrounds and places offering horses for hire, and then the village of <u>El Manzano</u>, evolved from an old railway station of the now extinct railroad running to El Volcán. Here is the **Estero El Manzano** picnic area (km 18); access is to the left, a fee is charged. It is a large farm with lush foothill vegetation hemmed in by towering, snowy mountains; in spring the snow line is very low. It is a good place for a picnic, the facilities located on the bank of the crystalline El Manzano creek, which gurgles among huge boulders forming some pools suitable for bathing.

Four km further, a road branches left into the El Colorado ravine; here is also the picturesque hamlet of **Guayacán**. Nearby is the signposted meeting point of Expediciones Altué, for rafting excursions down the Maipo river (see Rafting section). The vegetation becomes somewhat denser, signalling the proximity of the old town of

SAN JOSE DE MAIPO (km 25), lying on a flat area located 1,010 m above sea level, bounded on one side by the Maipo river. Silver lodes struck in the nearby hills promoted the foundation of the village in August 1791. The town was laid out by Ambrosio O'Higgins as a grid 27 blocks of 84 m per side, separated by nine streets and with a square in the middle. Many buildings have been made of mud-brick and thatch. The church was designed in colonial style and the square is the social center. The place has a healthy, pleasant mountain climate.

Beyond San José a road branches off to the **Lagunillas ski center**, an old winter resort with modern lifts, several shelters and small restaurants.

The valley becomes more constricted and the road is lined by peumos, boldos, aromos and poplars, with the river tumbling on the right. At km 27 is El Campito, a good restaurant. Three km further along, at the area called **El Toyo,** is a new bridge spanning the Maipo river, connecting with a road running along the other bank to Pirque.

At km 30 is the village of **Melocotón**, with lots of almond trees in full bloom in springtime. Here is the quiet Hotel Millahue. Continue to km 40, to

San Alfonso a placid village lying 1,109 m above the sea, with some summer houses. There is a nice view of curiously striped mountains. Here is the Cascada de Las Animas campground, with a picnic area, campsites, a beautiful swimming pool and four good cabins overlooking the striped hills.

By **San Gabriel** (km 47) the scenery has changed noticeably; the greenery has given way to ocher and brown. The air has a more mountainous tinge. The few houses of the place are located at the site of an old copper smelter, at 1,254 m altitude. Here ends the pavement and there is a police road control. Two km farther along a road branches left to the Yeso dam (described below). Crossing the bridge over the clear Volcán river you will reach the hamlet of **El Volcán**, at km 56 and 1,418 m altitude, hemmed in by steep mountains. The village was all but wiped out by a landslide. The scenery changes further, now with the grandeur and barrenness of high mountains. The road from here on is not in the best of shapes, but it is worth continuing through this area of hills of interesting colors to

LO VALDES at km 70. It is an oasis of sorts up in the mountains, with the greenery of trees and lawns. Here is the inviting Refugio Alemán, open year-round, offering accommodations and excellent lunch on the terrace, with a breathtaking view towards the snowy peaks and a natural pond where sunlight bounces off. Fossils of marine animals can be found in this area, bearing witness to the colossal tectonism that uplifted the Andes Mountains from below the sea millions of years ago.

In the vicinity are the thermal waters of **Baños**

Morales and, eleven km beyond Refugio Alemán, passing the police control, is **Baños de Colina**, natural thermal pools set like terraces into the slope, with water up to 60°C, open to the public from October. Bathing in these very hot pools, with the astounding Andean backdrop towering over a small valley far below, can be trance-inducing. Fascinating excursions by horse can be made from here to different small lakes high up in the mountains, and particularly to the glacier of the **El Morado National Park** (See Excursions by Horse).

To return, it is advisable to cross the Maipo river through the **El Toyo** bridge and drive down on the road on the left bank of the river, which is not as crowded. It runs through scenic hilly farmland. You can then either retake the original road by crossing the Maipo on the **Las Vertientes** bridge, or continue to the village of **Pirque**, two km farther along, and thence to Santiago.

2   BRANCH ROAD TO THE YESO DAM

a round trip of 170 km from Santiago, with 65 km of gravel road. Allow a whole day; any time of the year except winter. Take food or eat at any of the restaurants along the way.

A tour deep into the mountains, visiting a dam and the El Plomo thermal springs in a grand setting.

Follow the route described in Tour 1 above up to two kilometers beyond San Gabriel. Take there the signposted road branching left to Embalse El Yeso. The road runs first alongside the crystalline Yeso river to climb later among steep slopes. You will eventually reach a control outpost which grants permission to visit the place. One km farther along is the beautiful

EL YESO DAM a man-made dam to create a water reservoir. Its construction took ten years and was finished in 1964. The rich turquoise of its water stands in stark contrast with the mountain colors and the very near eternal snows.

3   TO FARELLONES AND SKI RESORTS

an 82-km round trip, paved. Allow a whole day; any time of the year. Take food or eat at the local restaurants. Mountain-bound traffic until 13:00 h; Santiago-bound traffic from 1500h onwards.

A tour to a string of ski resorts, driving on a newly paved road running along the narrow gorge of the Mapocho river and then climbing a series of more than 40 hairpin turns. The ride itself is worth the effort.

Take Av Kennedy (see map) heading east. Kennedy becomes Av Las Condes, which eventually forks into a left branch for **El Arrayán** and a right branch for Farellones. Take the right branch. There is a police control which, in winter, checks whether you have the mandatory equipment for driving on a mountain road: snow chains, a shovel, a piece of sackcloth, wooden wedges. If not, these items can be rented from the people offering them on the spot.

The first part of the road is moderately curvy and not too steep, but it nonetheless requires careful driving: there are some blind curves and the cliffs on the side of the road are sheer. The road first runs on the south side of the swift, noisy river, and then crosses to the other side through a high bridge.

At km 13, in a somewhat wider portion of the valley, is **La Ermita**, with a chapel sitting atop the crest of a hill. There is also a hydroelectric power plant feeding the La Disputada copper mine deep in the Andes. At km 19 is **Corral Quemado**, a tiny hamlet where in the past there was an ore smelter.

Beyond Corral Quemado the road forks: the left branch leads to the La Disputada mine (35 km), where visitors are not allowed. The right branch leads to Farellones. Now the real mountain road starts: the curves are so tight, that they are labelled by number. You zigzag up the steep slope in what becomes a test of your driving expertise. At km 26 a road branches left to the **Villa Paulina** valley, an excellent summer meadow, now a protected area administered by Conaf (Chile's Forest and Nature Protection Service) and superb for hiking. At km 28 is the **El Manzano** bridge, on a curve, and **Farellones** is a scant 7 km away –some 20 curves. At Curve 40 a road branches right leading in 14 km to the new –and expanding– **Valle Nevado** ski resort, with superb snow and lots of lifts, several hotels, restaurants and apartments.

Continuing to Farellones, the road crosses the village, the pioneer of skiing resorts near Santiago, and leads to **La Parva**, another excellent ski resort, and **Colorado**, with splendid slopes. See more details on these resorts under the Ski Excursions section.

This circuit has different attractions in different seasons.

In Autumn the scenery up to Corral Quemado has the contrast of yellowing leaves in the trees and hillsides turning green again, with eternal snows high up in the mountains.

Winter and Spring the high season, with Farellones, La Parva, Colorado and Valle Nevado turned into bustling resorts, the road full of traffic. These resorts offer the full range of services, from accommodations through restaurants to ski lessons and ski-gear rental. At La Parva and Valle Nevado there is snow until October.

Summer only recently people have come to the idea that the mountains can also be interesting when the snow is gone. Hiking excursions (see Excursions Section) and motocross rides attract a growing number of adepts, although it is true that these mountains –unlike the Alps, for instance– are pretty arid in summer.

4 PORTILLO AND THE ROAD TO ARGENTINA

★★★ *the Portillo ski resort is 61 km from Los Andes, 140 km from Santiago, and 192 km from Viña del Mar. The road is good, paved. Gasoline at Los Andes and Guardia Vieja (1.5 km beyond Río Blanco). There are several restaurants on the road. In winter the road can be blocked by snowstorms. Check with the Automóvil Club in Santiago (Ph 212 5702) or Viña del Mar (Ph 971815). There are police road controls at Los Andes and Guardia Vieja; at the latter point snow chains will be demanded if conditions require their use. They can be rented on the spot.*

Allow a whole day, best in sunny weather. Until December you can see snow near the road in the Portillo area. From January until the first snowfall, the snow line is much higher, but a cold wind blows permanently. For those travelling to Argentina, see Section 10 below.

A trip into the high Andes and to one of the world's renowned ski resorts.

<u>The Road to Argentina</u> follows the same route as the Inca Road, which later became a Colonial trail. By 1930 a highway was built –passable only in summer– which passed Portillo to climb to the Cristo Redentor monument at the border, and then descend to Argentina. The final version of this route was built and paved in the 1970s, and in 1980 the international tunnel was finished. Now there is an intense traffic of trucks, buses and cars to and from Argentina and Brazil.

Follow Route 57 from Santiago to Los Andes, which you reach at km 78. Take Los Andes as your new km 0. Take Exit 4 in Los Andes map, which runs along a fertile valley with grapevine plantations and leafy trees. At km 6 the road heads into the mountain section of the valley, with

a noticeable change in scenery. The predominating trees are now poplars, quillayes and walnut trees on the banks of the river, together with lots of shrubs and cacti. On the side runs the old trans–Andean railway, which now operates only up to the La Andina copper mine.

From km 17 to 19 is the small village of **Río Colorado**, with orchards, restaurants and hotels, such as Hotel Refugio El Colorado; Hostería La Gringa, with a certain charm and a garden; and Hotel Móvil. A short distance further along you will see the thick ducts carrying water to the **Los Quilos Hydroelectric Power Station**, built by the Sociedad Papelera de Puente Alto. There is a small chapel with mass service on Sunday at 19:00 h.

At km 24 a small valley opens up, with many trees and the Campo Lindo restaurant. On the slope, the railroad track is covered at stretches by snowsheds to protect it from being buried by avalanches or snow. You can also see the Chacabuco canal, which carries water through a tunnel from here to the valley stretching north of Santiago. The road then runs among arid, steep hills called **Los Azules**, where the blue–hued crushed stone is permanently sliding or rolling down toward the road. At km 28 is

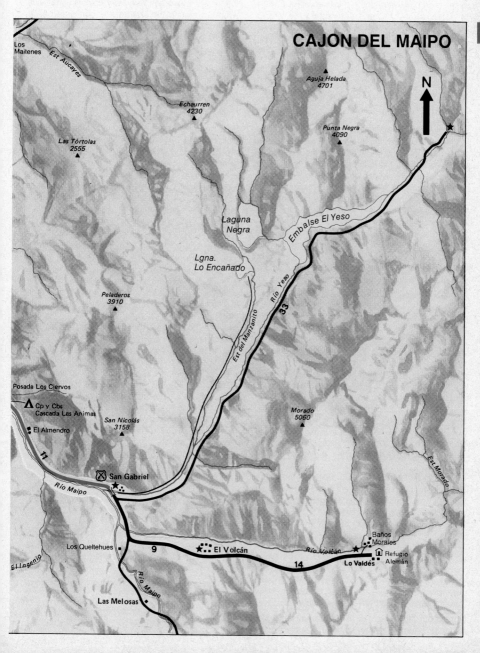

CAJON DEL MAIPO

5

Salto del Soldado a huge granitic mass which once blocked the river bed. It was sliced through by the river as if by a saw. A lake used to stretch behind the granitic plug; it is now gone. The story goes that a soldier gave his pursuers the slip by jumping across the abyss; thence the name. The railway climbing the slope on the other side dives into a tunnel bored through this granitic mammoth and emerges into a bridge spanning the abyss halfway up from the river to penetrate into another tunnel on the north side. The best view is from right above the abyss.

At km 30 is Hostería Luna, with cabins, a restaurant and a swimming pool. A short distance farther along are the locks and the inlet for the hydroelectric power station and the Chacabuco canal. At km 34 is

Río Blanco located 1,400 m above sea level. Here the valley widens out somewhat at the confluence of the Aconcagua and Blanco rivers. The scenery is attractive, with high-altitude vegetation and mountain houses enclosed by low stone walls. Here is the **Club de Campo** (Country Club) of the Minera Andina mining company, which receives public and has a good restaurant, a very good swimming pool and a golf course. On the side is the former Hotel Río Blanco, now military premises, and opposite it the old **railway station**. A road branches south to Minera Andina and the village of Saladillo. Just into this road there is a fish hatchery, one of the first of its kind in Chile. Then comes a control gate allowing passage only of vehicles going to the mine.

Continuing on the international road, you will soon pass the Guardia Vieja Mountain Regiment and, at km 38, a gasoline station and the **Guardia Vieja** compulsory road control, at 1,600 m above sea level. There is an hostería with a restaurant and cabins. In winter this area is above the snow line.

The road climbs gently along a valley hemmed in by mountains and devoid of trees. At km 42 there is a monolith in memory of the Guardia Vieja battle of Feb 2nd, 1818, between Spanish troops and a detachment of the Liberating Army that had crossed into Chile from Mendoza, Argentina. On the river bank there is a sheltered place for camping in summer. At km 50 is

Juncal (2,200 m above sea level), an old railway station, stone houses, a training ski lift of the Army's Mountain School, and the ruins of a house of the West Coast Cable Co., with the old underground cable connecting Santiago and Buenos Aires. The place has nothing remarkable to it, only that here starts the most spectacular segment of the road. The river valley stretches eastward into the mountains and the road turns away from it, climbing a steep slope which is a massive glacial moraine plug hemmed in by towering mountains. Up above you can see the opening («portillo») with a plateau where the ski resort and the lake are located. It is a 10-km zigzag stretch of 29 curves climbing 680 m from Juncal to Portillo. Half way up, the first **chairlifts** of the ski resort fly above the highway, which in turn passes a couple of tunnels over which the skiers swish down a very long ski run. The view is spectacular.

At km 60 the road reaches the crest of the zigzag stretch and passes underneath a railway bridge; to the left is the very steep slope of the Roca de Jack, where the world's speed record on skis was established. A short distance farther along, to the right, is the old hotel, now used by the Army's High Mountain School. At km 61 is

LAGUNA DEL INCA AND HOTEL PORTILLO (2,880 m above sea level). The hotel's parking lot is beyond the road-maintenance equipment shed and the old railway station. The hotel and the restaurant are open year-round; the dining room has a splendid view over the lake, nestled amid snowy mountains.

Laguna del Inca the lake is elongated, the water emerald green with the snowy Tres Hermanas

peaks for a backdrop, plummeting directly into the lake. A huge glacier tongue slid down through here in the past, and deposited the moraine plug which formed the lake. The highway climbs this moraine, and the hotel is located at its crest. The lake has no visible outlet (outlet is subterranean) and is frozen over in winter, superb for ice skating.

Hotel and Ski Center the area is good for hiking in summer, with paths around the lake and to the Plateau or other hills. Fabulous mule expeditions to the Cristo Redentor farther up, and to glaciers in the vicinity. In winter, it is one of South America's foremost ski centers, with excellent powder snow until well into the spring, good ski-lift infrastructure and varied, well-tended ski runs. The World Ski Championship was held here in 1966 – the only one held in South America until 1990 – and several times the world speed record on skis has been broken here; the last time in 1987, with 217 km/h.

A hotel was built across the road in 1940 (now owned by the Army) and the first Chilean competition skier team was formed, headed by the Errázuriz brothers and trained by Frenchman Emile Allais, a world champion, and Alfred Heusser, who trained children. Access was by railroad and for an entire decade there were no lifts. A hike up the slopes was organized every day with sealskins wrapped around the skis, for the one grand slide down the slopes. During that period all the runs were explored and christened, including vertigo-inducing Jack's Rock, named after US's Jack Hatton. The train was also used for excursions, riding it to the Caracoles station (tunnel) and then climbing to the Cristo Redentor to hike back down to the hotel, or skiing down to Juncal to get back to the hotel by train.

The present hotel started to operate in 1946, built by the State to attract international skiers. It was one story smaller, and it was connected to the train station (now in ruins) by a tunnel under the snow. The present owners have enlarged and modernized it, and offer all amenities, including cinema, sauna, discothèque and heated outdoor swimming pool. It also sponsors international ski events which have made it famous.

Trans-Andean Railway along the way you will have seen the railroad track running near the road, passing under many tunnels and sheds which keep it from being buried by snow or rock slides. At **Juncal** the railroad continues upriver to reappear above the zigzag section of the highway, which it crosses at Portillo. From there it continues to the nearly four-km-long tunnel crossing into Argentina. Now it operates only until Río Blanco, to serve the Minera Andina complex. The rest was discontinued in 1980.

It is an impressive work of engineering finished on April 5, 1910, under the direction of Americans John and Matthew Clark. The first locomotives were steam engines (one of which is to be seen at Santiago's Quinta Normal Railway Museum); the railway was electrified in the 1940s. The electric mountain **locomotives** had four unusual features: they were jointed in the middle to facilitate their negotiating of tight turns; they had a huge blade up front to clear the track from snow; they carried a large load of sand which they strewed on the ice-covered track to enhance traction, and along the centerline they had a toothed wheel to engage the portions of racked track, which you can see at Portillo and Los Libertadores customs complex.

One-and-a-half km farther up is the **Los Libertadores Customs Complex** and four km farther along the international tunnel. See description under Tour 5.

5 **A JOURNEY TO MENDOZA**

from Santiago, 341 km; from Viña del Mar, 394 km. The road is paved throughout. Motels and restaurants are indicated in the route description.

There are several gasoline stations in the Argentinian side, the first one at Las Cuevas, four km beyond the border. The leg from Santiago to the Chilean Customs outpost is described under Tour 4.

Schedules *the international tunnel is open 08:30–18:00 h from the third week in March to the second week in October. The rest of the year, 08:00-20:00 h, Chilean time. The customs outposts at both sides of the border operate according to the same schedule.*

Documents *most foreign visitors can enter Argentina without a visa; all need a valid passport. If driving, the car must be registered in the name of one of the travellers in the party; otherwise, a notarial permission from the car owner must be submitted.*

Fees per Person and per Vehicle *Mon–Fri no fees are paid at the Chilean customs. At the Argentinian customs, a charge of approx US$ 0.35 is made, payable in Chilean or Argentinian currency. On Sat & Sun, a fee of approx US$ 0.75 is charged by the Chilean customs, payable in Chilean pesos; at the Argentinian customs, approx US$ 1, payable only in australes.*

There is a further toll to be paid in Chile by Argentina–bounds car of appox US$ 1.5, in pesos; returning to Chile, a toll of approx US$ 0.50 is paid in Argentina, only in australes.

Facilities *at the Chilean customs outpost there is a money exchange booth and public telephones with direct dialing to the whole country. At the Argentinian customs there is only informal money exchange at the newstand. At both places there is a candy stall where you can shoot your remaining change.*

How Long It Takes *if travelling directly to Mendoza on a day without snow or ice, you will need about two hours from Santiago to the Customs outpost; from there to Mendoza, a further two–and–a–half hours, plus about fifteen minutes at each customs outpost –provided traffic is light.*

Recommendations *take a warm jacket, because even in summer a piercing wind blows in the heights. Leave Santiago no later than 7:30 in the morning, in order to reach the customs before the buses arrive: they slow down the process considerably, particularly on «long» weekends. The latest time advisable to start back from Mendoza is 14:30 Argentinian time. Declare at both customs valuable portables, such as video cameras or the like, to avoid problems bringing them back into the country.*

A journey across the lofty Andes to visit Mendoza, Argentina's fourth largest city and one of the most beautiful.

Overview the west and east slopes of the Cordillera of the Andes are very different from each other. Los Andes and Mendoza are at the foot of their respective sides of the Cordillera. The former is 822 m above sea level, the latter, 761 m. The highest point of the road betwen the two is on the border (international tunnel), with 3,185 m above sea level, located 69 km from Los Andes and 194 km from Mendoza. Therefore, the mountain stretch on the Argentinian side is nearly three times as long as that on the Chilean side. This means that the road on the Chilean side has a significantly steeper gradient, more curves and, therefore, slower–moving traffic, whereas the Argentinian portion has a gentle gradient, wide curves and faster traffic.

Another difference is rain– or snowfall, caused by the low–pressure fronts originated in the Pacific Ocean which sweep inland up to Uspallata, 90 km beyond the border into Argentina. Most of the moisture is shed on the Chilean side before crossing the wall of the Andes; into Argentina, precipitation rates are significantly lower. The Chilean side is thus a rocky massif whose slopes have been washed clean of any sediment, abrupt and heavily eroded; in the Argentinian side there are naked rock outcrops only at the mountain tops, the rest being gentle slopes where sedimentary deposits accumulate with beautifully contrasting colors. The respective mountain rivers, Acon–cagua and Mendoza, carry a similar volume of water, but the Chilean river follows a tortuous course, running at the bottom of a deeply incised canyon and noisily tumbling from rock to rock. The Argentinian river, by contrast, is wide, and meanders through a vast sedimentary deposit on the valley. These differences in scenery lend added attractiveness to the trip.

Los Libertadores Frontier Complex located 141 km from Santiago, 194 km from Viña del Mar, 63 km from Los Andes and 200 km from Mendoza, it is a vast concrete building with a large heated hall for the vehicles and passengers coming from Argentina (entry formalities take somewhat longer), and an outdoor esplanade for the Argentina–bound traffic (exit formalities are brief). The complex was rebuilt after being destroyed by an avalanche on August 3rd, 1984, which killed 14 employees and their relatives. It houses the premises of four bodies in charge of frontier traffic control: **Carabineros de Chile**, the police, controlling road traffic; **Policía Internacional**, immigration control; **Servicio de Aduanas**, the customs; and **Servicio Agrícola y Ganadero, SAG,** which controls the introduction of perishable foodstuffs (not allowed into Chile). The last two services are strict when entering into Chile. The intense truck traffic has outgrown the complex's capacity, and a larger facility is planned at a lower altitude.

At km 0, upon leaving the complex, there is a police barrier where the agents ascertain that all the formalities have been complied with. The highway heads then into a secondary valley. You can see the rails, rack and posts of the Trans–Andean railway, destroyed and twisted by the avalanche.

At km 4 is **Estación Caracoles**, where the customs complex was located in the past. On the southern slope you can see the zigzag of the old road to Argentina climbing to the crest, where the great **Cristo Redentor monument** is located, erected as a symbol of peaceful relations between the two countries; the monument is now inaccessible from the Chilean side.

At Caracoles, behind the buildings, is the mouth of the Trans–Andean railway tunnel; straight ahead is the mouth of the

International Road Tunnel located 3,185 m above the sea, its construction was started in 1971, suspended, reactivated in 1975, and finished in 1980. Of the total length of 3.9 km, 2.4 km were built by Chile and 1.5 km by Argentina. A line indicates where the border lies.

At km 7.9 you emerge from the tunnel; the mouth of the railway tunnel is to the right. From the north descends the Las Cuevas river valley, gathering the water flowing down from the soaring Mount Aconcagua (not visible). A short distance farther along is a toll, paid only by Chile-bound vehicles, and at km 10 is **Las Cuevas**, at 3,112 m altitude. It is a mountain village with stone buildings, a gasoline station and a Gerdarmería (Argentinian police) control. Here is the small **Casucha o Casa del Rey de Las Cuevas (NM)** («Las Cuevas King's House»); there are several of these along the route to Mendoza, built of brick between 1765 and 1770 by Ambrosio O'Higgins, engineer at Chile's service, as at that time the provinces of Mendoza, San Juan, and San Luis belonged to Chile. They were severed from Chile by royal decree of Carlos III on March 21, 1778, when the Buenos Aires Viceroyship was created.

At Las Cuevas you will see a strange building shaped like an arch; through the arch there used to pass the international road, which you can see zigzagging up the slope to the summit, where the **Cristo Redentor Monument** is located; it is a beautiful excursion with spectacular views (open only in summer).

From km 11 to km 16 the road traverses a glacial moraine (with a 400–m tunnel), then a short gorge; to the side, the railway is protected by a long snowshed. The valley extends ahead; here is the **Casa del Rey de los Paramillos (NM)**; The mountains are crowned by slender rocky pinnacles known as penitentes. The slopes, by contrast, are soft and boast beautiful blue, green and brown hues, caused by sediment that has never been washed away by water runoff.

At km 21 a gravel road branches left to the **Parque Provincial Aconcagua**. It is the only part of the highway from where the 6,959-m **Mount Aconcagua** can be seen, the highest peak from Alaska to Tierra del Fuego, and the world's tallest mountain outside the Himalaya mountain chain. Two km into this road is **Los Horcones valley**, with a small lake and the best view towards the Aconcagua; it is used by mountain climbers to reach the foot of the colossus.

Steel poles of up to 4 m in length line the road to indicate snow depth in winter, and low, square signs indicate the distance to Buenos Aires.

At km 22, on the left, is the modern building of the future **Los Horcones Customs Complex**. At km 25 is **Puente del Inca** (2,720 m), worth a stop. It is an attractive mountain village with a good hostería. To the left is the «bridge», an arch of rock spanning the Las Cuevas river and used by travellers in the old times; it has an impressive array of ocher hues on the edges. On its side a kiosk offers handicrafts made of ocher-hued clay, and glass pots containing earth of seven different colors. Nearby you can also see mule pens: this is an international center for summer trekking to the Aconcagua. The expeditions start from the Hostería Puente del Inca.

Two km further along, on the right, there is the small **Cementerio del Andinista** –it can be visited–, a cemetery for mountain climbers fallen while attempting to climb Mount Aconcagua. At km 31 is **Villa Los Penitentes** a ski and mountain resort established in 1985, with several hotels, an hostería, an apart-hotel, apartments, and a very good infrastructure of lifts and runs. There is a gasoline station and telephones. The hotels and the hostería are open year-round and the chair lifts operate on summer weekends, making for a good excursion with superb scenery from the heights. This is another center for trekking expeditions to Mount Aconcagua.

The valley grows wider, with hills sporting penitentes off to the right. At km 38 is the **Casa del Rey de los Puquios (NM)**. Soon the first trees are to be seen.

At km 41 is **Punta de Vacas** (2,325 m altitude), the present customs complex, ringed by rows of poplars and flanked by large esplanades to park vehicles. The formalities are brief, as here is no control equivalent to Chile's SAG (Chile is free of plant pests and diseases). The Las Cuevas and Las Vacas rivers join forces to form the **Mendoza river.**

The river canyon grows narrower and the road crosses it several times before reaching the village of **Polvareda** (2,050 m altitude). The higway runs on a ledge along a narrow, steep gorge plummeting to the river, and crosses several tunnels.

At km 70 the road emerges from the gorge. The valley grows wider again and the road runs level with the river; on the southern bank there is a huge wall of sediment, with layers of different hues, sliced clean by the stream. At km 89 the highway steers away from the Mendoza river and heads north into the great Uspallata river valley.

5

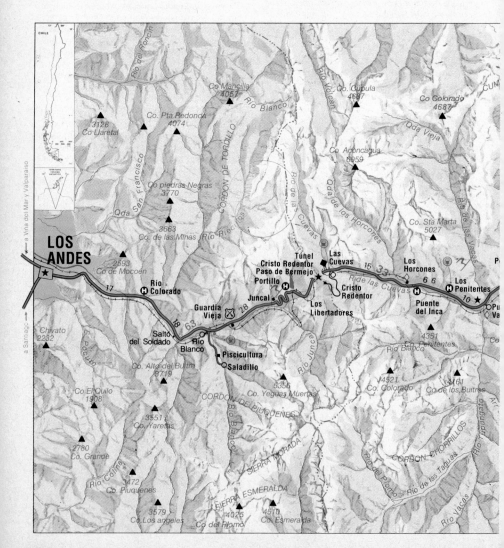

The eastern range of the Andes (the higher one) ends here and the western range starts, wide but much lower. At km 96 is

Uspallata
(1,900 m altitude). It is a summer village with several hotels, a good campsite at ACA, gasoline and a candy store, good to shoot your last australes before returning to Chile. There are beautiful rows of poplars, sporting their best colors in the autumn. This place is higher than Río Blanco in Chile, the last point where any afforestation has been carried out on the Chilean side.

At km 106 the road renews its friendship with the Mendoza river, crossing it over a bridge and running along its south bank. During the next 60 km, the highway traverses the eastern range along a narrow valley flanked by hills studded with cacti and shrubs. There are white and golden sands and reddish clay looking like petrified mud. The highway is narrower, curvy and has an old layout: drive carefully. It has not been modernized because construction of a planned dam on the Mendoza river will leave it under water; the new higway will follow a different route. At km 147 is

Potrerillos
a resort in the wide part of the valley, with vegetation, gasoline supply and, sitting on a small hill, the modern, state–owned **Hotel Potrerillos**, in Spanish style and with a nice view, gardens and a swimming pool. A 21–km paved road starts from here to the popular ski resort of **Vallecitos**.

At km 155 there is a campground on the river bank at a scenic spot. At km 158 is the water uptake for a hydroelectric power plant, and at km 161 is

Cacheuta
in a gap of the mountain valley. It is a popular resort with gasoline, restaurants, campsite and the famous **Termas de Cacheuta** hotel, once

the heart of Mendoza's social life. It has been modernized, with a thermal–water pool and individual cabins. It is worth a visit. A little distance ahead is the Cacheuta Hydroelectric Power Station, with a scenic conifer forest among the rocks. A short distance farther along, a narrow bridge spans the Mendoza river, the road running now along the north bank. At km 165 a rocky massif is the last spur of the eastern Andes, bored through by a curving tunnel. At its farther mouth, the unending pampa unfolds. From here on the highway is wide, modern and straight. Ahead you can see the fumes from a large oil refinery. At km 169 the road passes above the huge steel ducts feeding the Alvarez Condarco hydroelectric power station. Then come two traffic roundabouts, leading to the right to **Luján de Cuyo** (7 km), and then a further traffic circle leading right to the **Chacras de Coria** residential suburb. Continue always straight ahead. The pampa is here irrigated and covered by fruit orchards ringed by poplar windbreaks.

At km 192 you reach the outskirts of town at **La Puntilla**; the highway is lined by large trees and many popular parrilladas, ie grill restaurants where you can enjoy the superb Argentinian beef. Straight ahead you cross the railway at km 195; the road is now called **Avenida San Martín**. At km 200 you reach the downtown area of

MENDOZA the capital of the namesake province, with ca one million inhabitants in several boroughs making up **Greater Mendoza**. A bustling commercial, oil-processing, wine–producing and fruit–farming center, it is among the four most beautiful cities in Argentina, with the peculiar structure of an oasis amidst the unending arid pampa.

5

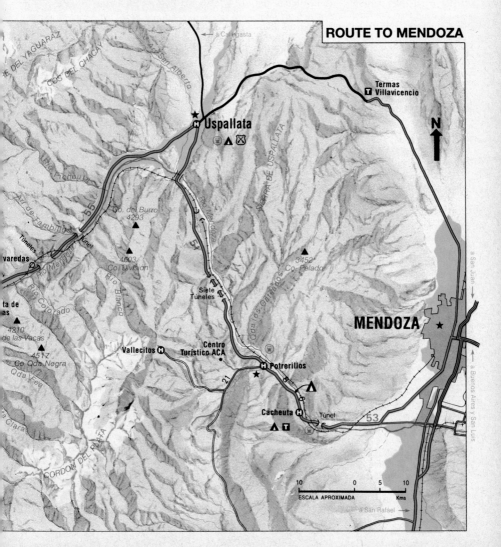

ROUTE TO MENDOZA

SECTION E   THE MAIPO PLAINS

This Section covers the great plain unfolding southward of Santiago, encircled by the Pirque hills to the East, the Angostura de Paine hills to the South, and the Aculeo hills and the Tango and Maipú rolling fields to the west. It is now an intensely farmed and thickly populated area. However, during the better part of the colonial period this was a semi–desert covered by scrub and where, according to a document from the 17th century «highwaymen have their most readily available hideout and impunity». In the early 18th century, a traveller described the area as a plain «of burning, dense dust raised by the South wind in that desert».

Agriculture started in the mid–18th century with the opening of an irrigation canal and other irrigation systems introduced by the Jesuits at their farm in Calera de Tango. Later on, the construction of the San Carlos Canal was started and by the turn of the century a large canal with 600 irrigation devices was opened at the El Principal de Pirque farm, part of the García–Huidobro entailed estate. By 1827 there were 1,500 hectares under irrigation. The real agricultural breakthrough did not take place until 1840, however, when wealthy mine owners from the North bought land in this district and had the vast network of irrigation canals laid out, which made it possible to plant the renowned Maipo Vineyards (see description under Excursions to the Vineyards). This zone became Chile's first breadbasket.

The main road through this district is the southbound Pan–American highway. A veritable «road market» has sprung up along the Pan–Am, offering everything from fruit to household animals, plants, pottery and basketry. A number of very good restaurants cater to the travellers, some of which are enough to justify a visit to the area.

The tours described below will give you a thorough insight into this district's present attractions and history.

GASTRONOMY AND OTHER SERVICES

Below we list some of the many services offered along the southbound Pan–American highway, indicating their specialty and the distance from San Bernardo (km 0).

Restaurants and Food Empanadas **Raquelita** at km 5; excellent, baked in clay ovens. **Parrilladas Donde La Cuca**, km 8, grilled Argentine beef; on Sundays with live music. **Mermeladas Caseras**, km 13, with renowned homemade marmalade made of selected fruit, great variety. **Aro Aro** restaurant at km 20, very good, specialized in Braserito de la Casa (grilled or barbecued meat) and Cazuela de Pava (turkey stew). Linfa 2 restaurant, at km 21, good Chinese food. **Las Carretas de Paine** restaurant, km 23, specialized in beef. **La Peña de Paine** restaurant, specialty Lomo a la Peña (stone–barbecued loin) with potatoes, eggs, vegetables and olives. **Buenos Aires de Paine** restaurant, km 24, very frequented and the oldest in the area; excellent grilled and barbecued meat. **La Pavoteca**, km 25, varied and inexpensive turkey dishes. **Bavaria** restaurant, km 25, very frequented, specialized in pork and sausages.

Plant Nurseries **San Juan**, km 5, a varied selection of fruit trees. **Lo Infante**, km 5, varied fruit trees, good prices. **San Francisco**, km 11, renowned, with an enormous variety of fruit trees and ornamental plants and trees. **Jardín Mónica**, km 12, large variety, hard by the road.

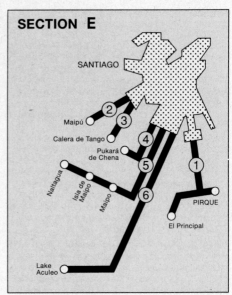

SECTION E

Handicrafts Pottery at km 11, with several stands and varied items.

TOURS OF THE AREA

1 PIRQUE AND ITS ENVIRONS ★★★

a 100–km round trip; allow half a day, in winter, autumn or spring, or a whole day if planning to picnic or eat lunch at La Vaquita Echá restaurant. A tour of the scenic Pirque valley and its old farms; it is very close to Santiago, in a mountain setting with much greenery.

Take Av Vicuña Mackenna heading for Puente Alto (see map), an industrial town at km 20 which became a suburb of Santiago. Continue straight through town to km 21, where a bridge spans the Maipo river; the river runs at the bottom of massive rocky cliffs. Before the arrival of the Spaniards, a suspension interwoven–liana bridge spanned the chasm. When the river swelled out, this was the only pass available to the South. The place was named after this «high bridge» (puente alto). It was replaced by an iron bridge in the mid–19th century.

Beyond the river, the Pirque Plains stretch to the right and, to the left, the Cajón de Pirque, or Pirque Mountain Valley. Until 1845 these were non–irrigated lands; that year they were acquired by Ramón Subercaseaux –a great mining entrepreneur from La Serena– who, using technology developed for mining operations, laid out an irrigation canal. This enabled the plantation of French vinestock as from 1853. When he died, the land was divided among his children.

The road winds and climbs alongside the mud-brick walls enclosing the

CONCHA Y TORO HOUSE AND PARK no visitors are allowed into this large complex, which can be seen only from the road; there are large residences, a large park, a chapel near the road and the wine vaults behind the houses. These buildings were part of the renowned vineyard and winery established by Melchor Concha y Toro in the lands inherited by his wife, Emiliana, daughter of Ramón Subercaseaux. The house –depicted in the label of some Concha y Toro wines– was built around 1875, when the park was laid out under the direction of French landscape architect Guillaume Renner.

Beyond the houses and the chapel the road comes to a T–junction. Turn right and you will reach the salesroom and **Viña Concha y Toro wine cellars** visitors allowed (see Excursions to the Maipo Vineyards).

Continuing on this road, at km 24 a road branches left to El Principal. Follow this road, which passes sleepy hamlets set in extensive pastures, with the Cordillera of the Andes marching on the left. The road then crosses the Clarillo creek and the pavement ends. A few meters farther along a signposted road branches left to El Principal. Follow this road, which runs near the Clarillo river and is lined with fruit orchards. Soon you will come to a signposted road branching right to

LO ARCAYA the road is lined by leafy trees and comes to an esplanade facing the manor house and the church of one of the farms created by the successive divisions of the El Principal hacienda. The buildings, whose construction was started in the mid–19th century, are made of mud–brick and have clay–tile roofs, and have six successive courtyards. The main building was crowned later by an octagonal steeple. The church was damaged by an earthquake. You may request permission to visit at the school opposite the church. Retrace the road to the junction and continue eastward until km 34, to the picturesque hamlet of

EL PRINCIPAL the houses were part of the large Hacienda El Principal. The farm was originally called Estancia del Principal de Córdova. In the early 18th century this farm was acquired by Francisco García–Huidobro, a businessman and founder of the Mint, and owner of other large haciendas at Catemu and Paine. By 1750 he set up an entailed estate at El Principal. His heirs built these houses in 1870. Now the church tower is still to be seen, together with the great manor house and the animal pens; the latter are in poor condition. They are a good sample of last century's farm construction; permission to visit can be obtained on site.

Retrace nine km of the route followed to get here until you reach the road running parallel to the Maipo river; follow this road heading east (towards the Andes). In about 5 km you will reach the renowned La Vaquita Echá restaurant, specialized in meat; it is an excellent place for lunch.

Continue straight alongside the river, where the road is constricted by the hills and a cliff plummeting to the river. You eventually pass the hamlet of La Puntilla, in a fine setting. Here is an excellent, inexpensive café (of those qualifying as picada) specialized in pastries; it is called Autopare. The road then crosses the river through the Coipo bridge and starts to climb away from the stream, through green scenery and many houses until **San Juan de Pirque**, a hamlet founded last century. The remarkable features here are the mountainous landscape and the houses set in their own parks; among these, outstanding is the

San Juan de Pirque Park enclosed by long, white–washed mud–brick walls. The park was planted by Alberto Mackenna in 1860; from this period are the stately Chilean palms, and the varied trees and shrubs covering an area of ten hectares. The road beyond the houses runs through beautiful mountain scenery, good for walking, and eventually it reaches a new stretch of road with bridges across the Maipo to Las Vertientes and to San José de Maipo.

Retracing the road, near the La Vaquita Echá restaurant a road branches left leading to a spec-

GASTRONOMY

TO SANTIAGO

Chena Old Houses — 0 — SAN BERNARDO

San Bernardo Handicraft — 2
Calera de Tango — 4

— 6 — Carozzi Nos Factory

Empanadas Raquelita — 7 — Italian Garden

San Juan Tree Nursery

Lo Infante Tree Nursery
Lo Herrera — 8

Panamerican Restaurant — 9
Mazapán Sta. Ana

Km from San Bernardo Junction

Parrilladas Donde la Cuca — 10
El Romeral — 11

Maipo River
Río Maipo

San Francisco Garden Tree Nursery — 13 — Manjar de Lúcuma
— Clay pottery

— 14 — Monica Garden

— Viña Sta. Rita

Homemade Marmalade — 15
San Francisco Tree Nursery — Parrillada La Campera

Las Delicias Fruit Tree
Sta Rosa Fruit Tree
Buin Garden
El Bosque Garden — La Sanchina Garden

BUIN — 16 — Alto Jahuel

— 18
Homemade Marmalade — 19
Villa Seca

California Tree Nursery
— 20 — LINDEROS

— 21
Parrilladas Aro-Aro
Fruit Stand

— 23
Linfa N°2 Restaurant

Fruit Stand
Motel Restaurant — 24
La Quintrala
— 25 — Las Carretas de Paine Restaurant
Peña de Paine Restaurant
Las Tranqueras de Paine Restaurant — 26 — Los Buenos Aires de Paine Restaurant
Pavoteca Restaurant — 27 — Handicraft
Empanadas's Factory — Bavaria Restaurant
Parrilladas — PAINE
El Cruce de Paine

TO THE SOUTH

tacular avenue shaded by gigantic plane trees and some tenant houses. The avenue ends up at a place called **Santa Rita**, with manor houses and a charming twin–towered chapel. To return to Santiago, retrace the road.

EXTENSION TO RIO CLARILLO ★★★

suitable for a picnic or as an extension of the previous tour. It is a 90-km round trip from Santiago and 15 km longer than Tour 1, if you drive straight to the Río Clarillo Reserve.

A tour to a scenic Conaf-managed National Reserve, excellent for a picnic outing –or camping– into mountain scenery and crystalline streams.

Follow the route described in Tour 1 above until El Principal. There, continue a further six km to the Reserve's access gate. An entrance fee is charged to the

RIO CLARILLO NATIONAL RESERVE spreading over 10,185 hectares of Andean foothills with a plant cover of cacti, bushes and trees which grows progressively thicker into the ravines of the crystalline Clarillo creek. The creek forms natural ponds suitable for bathing.

The place is also highly attractive in winter, the footpaths winding under snowed–in forests, and it has picnic areas and campgrounds with facilities. There is also an Environmental Information Center with a permanent exhibition of local flora and fauna. It is worth a visit.

2 TO MAIPU AND ITS MONUMENTS ★★

a 20-km round trip from downtown Santiago; for a half-day, any time of the year.

A visit to the monumental Maipú Votive Temple, venue of popular religious festivities and where Catholic visitors can attend the mass, and to a very interesting museum.

Take Av Libertador B O'Higgins heading west until you reach a forking in the outskirts of town (see city map); follow the Pajaritos branch leading to Maipú. The tree–lined road runs through farmed fields, housing compounds and industries for 8 km until Av Ramón Freire, where the

MONUMENT TO THE BATTLE OF MAIPU is located. It is a bronze statue on a large pedestal commemorating a battle fought here on April 5th, 1818. At that time there was no settled population in this area, only the plains and hills of Maipú. If you walk on

Maipú street up to the top of the rise, you will see the Chena and Tango hills rearing from the valley away to the South. At their foot is the **Lonquén ford,** used by the royalist army –headed by General Osorio– to approach Santiago from the South; the royalists stayed overnight at Calera de Tango on April 3rd, 1818. The patriot forces, commanded by generals O'Higgins and San Martín, took positions on the Maipú valley to block passage to the capital. From the surrounding hills, the patriot strategists directed the actions of April 5th which led to victory and to Chile's definitive independence.

Continue along the main street until you reach Av 5 de Abril, which leads to the

MAIPU VOTIVE TEMPLE a monumental building rising on the site where Bernardo O'Higgins made his public vow to consecrate the Virgin of the Carmen as Chile's patron saint and to erect a temple as a homage to her and as a token of gratefulness for the victory. The original temple, financed by public contributions, was destroyed over the years; only the walls remain inside the access esplanade. The present temple started to be built in 1944 and was opened to the public, still unfinished, in October 1974. It is open Mon–Sun 08:00–21:00 h. Masses are held Mon. through Fri at 18:30 h; Sat at 17:30 h; Sun. and religious holidays 10:00–14:00 h & 16:00–20:00 h.

MUSEO DEL CARMEN (Sat 16:00–20:00 h; Sun & holidays 11:00–14:00 h & 16:00–20:00 h). A large, important historical museum containing a rich collection of colonial furniture, religious statuary and images, historical documents, and a collection of old carriages, the most outstanding being Archbishop Ramón Valdivieso's coach, another one used by the French royalty and donated by the Cousiño family, and, most importantly, the one belonging to the Presidency of Chile and used until recently. This last coach was custom–made in France late last century and was rated as one of the most beautiful creations of French coachmakers, being exhibited at the Petit Palais before its delivery to Chile. The museum is worth a visit. Here is also the **Handicraft Gallery**, a sort of popular museum with articles donated by the faithful as thanksgiving (Mon–Sun, same hours as the church).

Religious Festivities the Votive Temple is a venue for several religious festivities, very colorful and popular, attractive for first–time visitors.

Fiesta de Cuasimodo held on the first Sunday after Easter week in memory of an old custom of taking the communion to the sick. It is a picturesque caravan on horseback or highly–ornamented bikes, headed by the priest carrying the chalice. You must arrive quite early at the temple if you want to see the caravan set out.

Fiesta del Huaso a colorful peasant–style celebration paying homage to the Virgen del Carmen, held on the first Sunday in September. It is a caravan of huasos –the Chilean peasant– on highly–decorated horses. Arrive early.

Fiesta de la Virgen del Carmen held on July 16th or on the first Sunday after that date. It is a popular festivity paying homage to the temple's patron saint; arrive early.

To return to Santiago take Av 5 de Abril and turn right on Av Ramón Freire. If you wish to have meat for lunch at a traditional restaurant, visit El Chancho con Chaleco, located on the same avenue. Ahead is Route 78, which leads to Santiago (left).

3 TO CALERA DE TANGO ON THE ROYAL ROAD

★★★ *a 77-km round trip with 33 km graveled.*

For half a day, any time of the year.

A tour along the old southbound Royal Road, passing old farms, including the largest and best preserved farm complex, built by the Jesuits in the 18th century.

Take the road to the Cerrillos Airport (see city map). Just beyond the airport, on the curve, a barely visible gravel road branches left: that is the Royal Road. During the colonial period it was one of the most trafficked roads to the South; it crossed the Maipo river through the Lonquén ford, and was the route followed by general Osorio and his royalist troops in their drive from the South heading for Maipú.

Taking this road, at km 9 is the **Club Alemán de Tenis**, with excellent tennis courts open to all devotees of this sport. Continuing south, the scenery is dominated by the Chena hills on one side and by a wide, green farmed valley on the other; large trees mark the entrance to the old farms. At km 15, on the right, are the houses of **San Ignacio**; from the road you can see the **Santa Filomena church**, donated over half a century ago by Filomena Eyzaguirre to the Mercedarios, a religious order. At km 20 is the road branching left for Calera de Tango. Follow this road until you reach the

CALERA DE TANGO HOUSES (NM) the farm was acquired by the Jesuit Order in 1685. Originally, the land was dry and of low fertility, suitable for raising cattle and non–irrigated wheat crops. There were also lime mines in the vicinity, which was roasted and sold as mortar for stone masonry. From 1740 to 1746 irrigation canals and ditches were built, enabling and introducing intensive agriculture in Chile.

Construction of the farm's buildings was started in 1741 and finished in 1761. The final product was a giant housing and farming complex sprawling over 24,000 square meters, with a church in the middle. It had seven colonnaded courtyards, including one for the offices, another one for the sleeping quarters, for the service, for workshops, ovens, for black slaves and for retirement.

When the Jesuit Order was expelled from Spanish America by order of King Carlos III in 1767, the monastery and the farm became state property and then were acquired by the Ruiz–Tagle family, who set up the property as an entailed estate. On April 3rd, 1818, this house provided lodging for general Osorio and his royalist forces on their way to the Battle of Maipú. Decades later, the Plenipotentiary Papal nuncio who would later become Pope Pio IX stayed here. When the Jesuits returned to Chile after the Republic had been established, the priest who had inherited the hacienda, Joaquín Ruiz–Tagle, bequeathed the houses again to the Jesuits, who refurbished them and introduced a number of modifications. The 1985 earthquake caused damage which was repaired with contributions from Sergio Ruiz–Tagle, a local farmer. Approximately half of the original buildings remain to this day, including the main façade, the church and some of the courtyards.

This complex, in addition to being the best–preserved sample of a large 18th–century hacienda, boasts also the title of having been the **birthplace of Chilean industry**. In 1711, the Jesuits brought two German coadjutor Brothers who were silversmiths by trade. Three years later a further 15 Brothers arrived and formed a school of architects, sculptors, turners, cabinetmakers, weavers, tailors, blacksmiths, apothecaries, and others. This visionary undertaking culminated with the arrival of 40 Bavarian Brothers among whom there were expert silversmiths, watchmakers, painters, sculptors, cabinetmakers, and farmers. The farmers were brought by German Jesuit father **Karl Haymhayssen**, who also contributed with a printing shop, tools

for a silversmith and assorted machinery for the above trades and for farming. The newcomers and their equipment were housed at the newly built Calera de Tango complex and their products changed colonial tastes and culture.

The talent of these craftsmen and artists can be seen at works preserved in Santiago's Cathedral Church, in whose sacristy there is a famous 17–m–long, 3–m–high carved wooden shelf. Here are also the main altar's **repoussé–silver pediment,** the giant **wrought–silver tabernacle**, the painting depicting the **Twelve Apostles** in the sacristy (by Brother José Ambrosi), and a clock –twin of the one presented to the Queen of Portugal– indicating, in addition to the time, the moon phases. The Bavarian monks' most remarkable work is a chiselled **Golden Chalice** with such tiny miniatures of Passion scenes, that the face expressions can only be seen with the aid of a magnifying glass.

Many other works were produced at Calera de Tango, either for export or to ornament religious buildings (see tour to Hacienda La Compañía at Graneros) or private properties. The expulsion of the Jesuits put an end to this school of artisans, and it was never reestablished. It did leave a legacy: the taste for the Bavarian–Baroque style. The Calera de Tango houses can be visited every day, prior permission (phone 859 4808).

Get back to the Royal Road heading for Lonquén. At km 22 you can see the **San Miguel de Tango hacienda** from the road, established late last century and set in a marvelous French–style park with iron and stone sculptures. The road continues straight among the Tango hills, flanked by green pastures, until it reaches a small hill called Sorrento, at which summit sits a manor house dating from late last century. This type of manor house resulted from the increase in cultivated area and the introduction of new farming techniques learned abroad by the farm owners during their frequent trips to other countries. These trips also brought about a taste for elegant furniture and a certain lavishness. As a result, some of the older, more traditional country residences were abandoned in search of locations with more independence and a better view; such is the case of the House of Sorrento Knoll, set in a vast park.

At the foot of the knoll a paved road branches left to the

5

Hacienda Calera de Tango
Originl name of each Section

1 Church	**6** Oven Yard
2 Office Courtyard	**7** Blacks' Yard
3 Sleeping-Quarter Yard	**8** Retreat Yard
4 Silversmith & Blacksmith Yard	**9** Festivity Courtyard
5 Workshop Yard	**10** Corral

CALERA DE TANGO

N

Planta del
Edificio en 1767 →

Santa Helena de Lonquén hacienda, the original location of the farm relinquished when the house was moved to Sorrento. It has old storage sheds built in the late 17th or early 18th centuries, a charming chapel and a picturesque, abandoned theater. Return by retracing the paved road and continuing about 7 km until you reach Route 78. Turn right to head for Santiago.

4 TO PUKARA DE CHENA ★★★

a 50-km round trip for a half-day, any time of the year; best if sunny.

A tour to an old Inca fortress, the only one of its kind preserved near Santiago; along the way you will see some old haciendas with beautiful parks.

Take the southbound Pan–American highway until km 13; follow then the signposted road branching right to Calera de Tango (the previous signposted branch road to the Pukará is not recommended). Two km into this road there is a good place (Pukará) for buying cheese. At km 17 take the dirt road branching right, leading in two km to

Hacienda San Agustín de Tango located on the slopes of the Chena hill. It is a beautiful construction from late last century, a manor house set in an old park that can be visited if authorized by the owner, who lives there. A short distance further along, where the road ends, is the entrance to

PUKARA DE CHENA an access fee is charged. It is a fortress and garrison built by the Incas who conquered Chile up to the Maule river. It is one of the late works of the Inca Empire, erected ca. 1480, sixty years before the Conquest and the foundation of Santiago by Pedro de Valdivia. Built of undressed stone and flanked by two defensive walls enclosing nine inner compounds, its ruins have been reconstructed with great accuracy; adjacent there is a museum dealing with the history of the place.

Strategically placed, the pukará commands a sweeping view of the valley and over the two fords of the Maipo river, the natural passes to the South. Now the Pan–American highway and the Lonquén road span the Maipo at those two sites. The view from the Pukará is wonderful during sunset.

Retrace the route back to the paved road and turn there right heading for Malloco. At Paradero 8 of this road there is a good spot for buying empanadas and homemade bread. A further nine km along this road, running through cropland punctuated by large trees, will bring you to the

Hacienda San Nicolás de Tango easy to spot for its huge mud-brick walls and the large trees of its park. New buildings have been added to this 18th-century construction, but always retaining the

original layout. It is private property: no visitors allowed. One km further along is Route 78 which leads to Santiago.

5 TO BUIN, MAIPO, ISLA DE MAIPO AND NALTAGUA ★★

a 110-km round trip with 52 km of gravel road. For half a day, winter or autumn. For food, see Gastronomy above.

A circuit through old, quaint villages to end up at the Naltagua orchards, of famously large trees.

Take the southbound Pan–American highway – Route 5– up to km 33, then follow the signposted road branching right to **Buin**, a village nestled in a plain and founded by decree on Feb. 14th, 1844, on lands donated by the owners of the neighboring farms, José Molina, Luis Goycolea, and Francisco Lefebvre. The place was named after the Buin River Battle in Peru, which ended with a Chilean victory on January 6th, 1879. At km 37 is

MAIPO a charming tree-shaded village with picturesque, gaily-painted mud-brick houses, many with front verandas joined with one another, giving rise to veritable covered sidewalks. The most attractive point is next to the post office, at the village's exit.

Take the dirt road heading south from Maipo, which has the Andes range marching on the left. At km 43 take the road branching right and at km 46, turn right once more at the junction. When you reach the paved road, follow it heading for

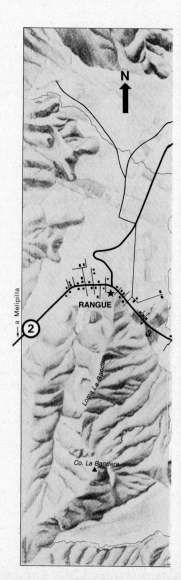

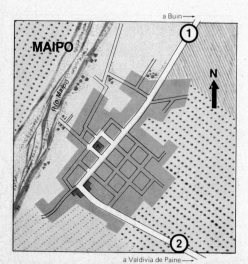

Talagante for 500 m and then turn left. The 8-km gravel stretch leads to

Valdivia de Paine (km 55). A picturesque place on the banks of the Maipo river, with large patches of forest, pretty houses and a dreamy pace to everything. Retrace the route to the main road and turn left. Two km later you will cross the Maipo on a railway bridge adapted also for road traffic; a toll is charged. The branch railway goes from Paine to Talagante and was built to transport the ores from the El Teniente copper mine to the shipping port of San Antonio, bypassing Santiago. The place is called **Vado de Lonquén** («Lonquén Ford»). Beyond the bridge, at km 69, the road ends at a paved highway; take this highway to the left to reach

Isla de Maipo a quaint village of haphazard layout and pretty houses located between arms of the Maipo river and its confluence with the Angostura creek. It was an old Indian settlement with fertile soils which promptly attracted Spanish settlers. It was granted village status in July 1902.

Three km into the paved road to Talagante you will cross another bridge spanning the Maipo. Here starts the

Naltagua District just beyond the bridge the road forks. The right branch leads to the renowned **Naltagua Orchards**, a very fertile area with a microclimate supporting fruit trees which grow to considerable size, including some huge avocado trees. The left branch runs along the slopes of the

hills next to a cliff flanking the Maipo river, with good views over the valley. The road then leaves the riverside and traverses a semi–arid stretch with native trees such as boldos, quillayes, etc. You eventually reach the gate to the **El Rosario de Naltagua** hacienda, where you can request permission to visit a wide tree–lined road where the peasants gather on sunny days to talk, do the laundry or rest, giving it a village–square atmosphere. Return to the Naltagua bridge and turn left on the paved road to reach, in 7 km, Route 78 back to Santiago.

6 TO LAKE ACULEO ★★★

a 130–km round trip of paved road. Allow one day. Take food or eat at any of the restaurants along the Pan–Am (see Gastronomy Section). If you just want to see the place, the best seasons are spring and autumn, as in summer it is exceedingly crowded. For watersports fans, summer is the season.

A varied circuit with «good–value» restaurants, picturesque roads and a scenic lake with watersports facilities, campgrounds, restaurants, motels, supplies and entertainment.

Take the southbound Pan–American highway to km 50; turn right at the signposted junction for Laguna de Aculeo. At km 51 is Champa, where the road is flanked by leafy, tall trees. At km 52, to the right, is the El Olivar Manso hacienda, with a fine, well–tended park. At km 57 is the tiny

5

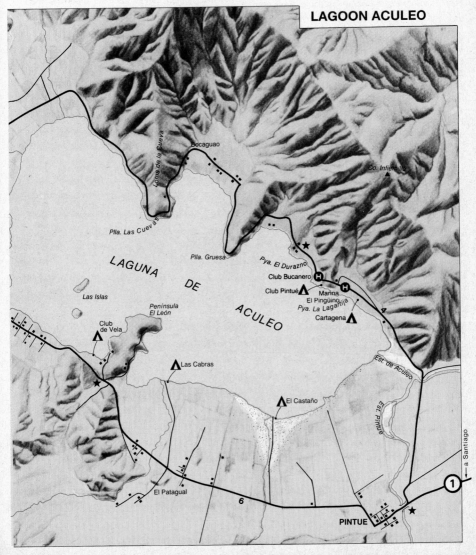

LAGOON ACULEO

lake Aculeo

particularly of fresh–water mackerel (pejerrey). Also carps, but this variety is not edible.

The lake is divided into two sections:

North Shore there are several clubs –some offering camping facilities– with restaurants, motels, launch moorings and piers. All have very good picnic facilities.

The North Shore clubs are: **Cartagena,** popular and very frequented; **Camping Club Pintué,** the best one on the lake, all amenities, excellent water-sports facilities, a restaurant, and a swimming pool. **Club Bucanero,** the oldest, good facilities, swimming pool. **Marina Los Pingüinos,** a private club, cabins. On this shore are also the summer houses.

South Shore a new road skirts the lake's entire southern shore, but in winter it is passable only in a four–wheel–drive vehicle. Otherwise, you have to get back to the main road, cross the bridge spanning the Pintué creek and pass the quaint **Pintué** hamlet at km 61. The hamlet evolved from the old Hacienda de Aculeo, originally covering 34,500 hectares. Here are the **Casas de Pintué**, a manor house complex built in stages; the storage rooms, stables and the corral all date from the late 18th century and the early 19th century, while the house and the chapel were built late last century. The complex is set in a fine, large park with a central fountain which can be seen from the road.

Farther along, the road is soon flanked by acacias, with the **Cantillana Hills** in the background. At their summit there are some impressive relict oak forests. This segment of the road runs distant from the lake, which cannot be seen from the road. Three–and–a–half km from Pintué is **Camping El Castaño**, in a lovely setting, spacious, quiet, with a good restaurant offering simple meals, and excellent picnic facilities. When the road approaches the shore again you will see the **Club de Velas Aculeo** in a sheltered natural bay with leafy vegetation; there are two lush islets a few meters off the shore.

The southern shore is particularly suitable for hiking or strolling. Continuing along the shore is the hamlet of Rangue; here starts the old road to Melipilla, now in an appalling condition.

hamlet of **El Vínculo**, evolved from a fundo –large farm– located a few meters further along on the left. The houses of El Vínculo were severely damaged by the 1985 earthquake. The peasant houses on either side of the road have verandas overlooking the road, with pictures –mostly of religious motifs– hanging on the street–facing walls. At km 65 take detour to the right, just before a bridge, to reach the northern shore of

5

LAKE ACULEO the name comes from the Mapuche expression Acuileufú, which means «the river arrived». The lake's size –4 km wide and 8 km long– varies somewhat according to the season of the year. The shores are swampy in some areas, and of low gradient, except at the sites where the hills jut into the lake. Since colonial times this lake has been an area for spending the summer; travellers used to come by ox–drawn cart to camp on the lake shore. The area has kept this resort atmosphere, stimulated particularly with the boom in watersports, such as windsurf, water ski and sailing: weather conditions here are particularly suitable. In the morning hours the water surface is very smooth, perfect for water ski; after midday wind blows from the coast through the cleft between the mountains, creating perfect conditions for windsurf and sailing. Fishing is very good,

SECTION F   RANCAGUA VALLEY

This Section covers the valley and mountain range stretching southward from Angostura de Paine up to the banks of the Cachapoal river. It is a farming district with its center at the city of Rancagua, capital of Region VI, a major commercial, farming and mining center, and seat of the headquarters of the giant El Teniente copper mine, located in the Andes mountains.

This area, like the Maipo plains described above, contained non–irrigated lands traversed by the modest streams of Codegua, Cadenas, and Machalí but, unlike the Maipo plains, it woke relatively early to agriculture. In 1595 a small farm was acquired by the Jesuits. This Order, through successive donations and purchases, came to own the entire valley plus 120,000 of mountainous area. This gigantic hacienda, called Graneros, introduced intensive agriculture in Chile, supported by a painstakingly laid–out irrigation canal and ditch network which irrigated a large portion of the valley.

Rancagua was founded in 1743, grouping a number of Spanish farmers. When the Jesuits were expelled from Chile in 1767, the great farm, whose headquarters were located at the present–day village of Compañía, was acquired from the Span-

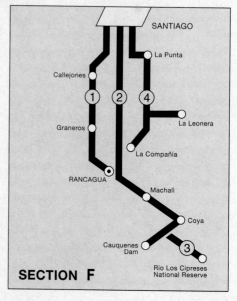

SECTION F

ish Crown by Mateo de Toro y Zambrano, the richest feudatory of the period. He turned this property into an entailed estate. The hacienda remained undivided until 1897, when it was partitioned into 11 fundos –large farms– which, in turn, have all been subsequently subdivided. The tours around this district include many beautiful testimonies of the old times.

TOURS OF THE AREA

1 TO RANCAGUA ON THE OLD ROAD ★★★

a round trip of 166 km, with 30 km of gravel road. For one day, best in spring or autumn. Take food or eat in Rancagua.

A circuit along the old Royal Road, which runs parallel to the Pan-American highway passing old farms with fine manor houses set in shady parks, to visit the bustling, prosperous city of Rancagua, with its monuments and churches.

Take the southbound Pan–American highway (also known as Route 5). Just beyond the Angostura toll plaza, at km 52, turn right to the town of **San Francisco de Mostazal**. The place was named after an old farm –Mostazal– located at the site and a small church built in 1858 called San Francisco; this church was the starting point for the village. The town has an orderly layout of square blocks centered around the train station. The road southward from San Francisco de Mostazal is graveled; at km 60 it reaches a signposted junction to Campo Escuela Callejones, of Guías y Scouts de Chile -Chilean Scouts and Girl-Guides-, which leads to the

PARK OF HACIENDA CALLEJONES, the beautiful houses and storage buildings were razed by the

1985 earthquake. The 10-ha park, in addition to its beauty, is unique in having been designed by the three great landscape architects who created most of Chile's parks. Its history dates back to 1880, when Guillaume Renner designed the original park on the basis of an existing group of trees. Then, in 1923, Frenchman Gachelin created the lawn esplanade and built the large water fountain in front of the houses. Lastly, Oscar Prager, in 1940, removed some trees and enlarged the lawn areas with the purpose of opening up the perspectives. Now the park is graced by wide sequoia avenues and a rich variety of conifers, among which a fine sample of blue–hued Atlantic cedar stands out. It belongs to the Catholic Scouts and Guides Association; access is permitted.

Return to the road and continue southward among tobacco, grapevine, and corn plantations. At km 63, on the right, is the fine

Parque de Graneros created in one of the 11 farms into which the great hacienda of Mateo de Toro y Zambrano was divided. One of his descendants, José Correa y Toro, devoted to botany, inherited these lands and commissioned Guillaume Renner to design a park in 1880. The manor houses are gone, but the park is still worth a visit, with its fine water fountains, sculptures, a large and varied collection of trees and beautiful flowers. A greenhouse inside the park offers flowers and plants for sale.

A few meters south of the park's exit a road branches left to **Graneros**, a village with a fine square and a railway station. The name comes from granaries existing here in the past, part of the vast Jesuit farm. It was granted village status on November 17th, 1899.

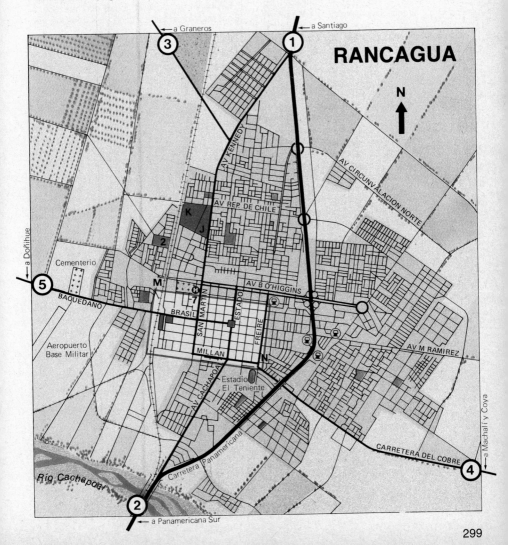

Get back to the main road and at km 71 you will see the **Santa Cristina** farm on the right, with a splendid park. One km further along is **La Moranina**, an old farm which, together with Santa Elena and Santa Cristina, was part of a single large farm until 1779. The houses, which include corrals, large courtyards and a small chapel, date from between 1820 and 1850. Now they house a Women's Rehabilitation Center; no visitors allowed. At km 74 is the Santa Elena farm, with an attractive manor house. Opposite, a road branches left to

RANCAGUA (pop 150,000) at km 78. A prosperous, bustling industrial and agricultural city. In the past it was a settlement of Picunche Indians and, later on, also of the Incas. The latter built a rope-and-wicker bridge across the Cachapoal river, which was later used by the Spanish conquerors. The last of the Picunche chieftains, Tomás Guaglén, ceded part of his territory for the future city, which was founded in 1743 by Governor Manso de Velasco under the name of Villa Santa Cruz de Triana. By 1745 there were forty houses and some grinding mills for the gold-bearing ores from the nearby Alhué range, which made a large contribution to the village's progress. Nearly one century later Rancagua became the stage for the dramatic Disaster of Rancagua, a battle in which patriot forces resisted two days in the center against the loyalist troops commanded by general Osorio, bringing about the levelling of nearly every building in the downtown area.

What To See Rancagua has a typically Spanish layout consisting of an eight-by-eight-block grid centered on the square, called **Los Héroes**. The square, however, is not typically Spanish, inasmuch as the streets originate not from the square's corners but from mid-block. It is a fine square, with large trees and benches full of rancagüinos whiling away their free hours. On one of the corners is the Provincial Government building, erected in 1930 and standing out for its beauty and size. There is also the beautiful

CHURCH OF LA MERCED (NM) at the corner of Estado and Cuevas. It was erected in the 18th century and it played a historical role during the Battle of Rancagua, during which the founding father Bernardo O'Higgins scrutinized in vain the horizon from the bell tower in search of reinforcements from Carrera. Adjoining the church is the parish house, with a large, beautiful front gate. Visits Mon. through Fri. Continuing along Estado, across Ibieta is a quaint corner with colonial buildings. In one of them actor Alejandro Flores created in 1954 the

Museo Regional de Rancagua (NM) (Tue–Fri 09:00–12:00 h and 14:30–18:30; Sat & Sun 09:00–13:00 h). It contains an interesting collection of colonial religious statuary and images, and preserves original ornaments and furniture of a typical 19th-century Rancagua house. The mud-brick building is very well preserved and is a good example of the area's traditional architecture. At the same corner, across from the museum we find the **Casa del Pilar de Esquina** (NM), which is at present being restoredA block farther south is the **Casa de la Cultura** (NM), where royalist general Mariano Osorio stayed on October 1st and 2nd, 1814. These three houses have been granted the status of National Monument.

This 8-by-8 downtown grid contains several other fine examples of colonial architecture. On the main street there are excellent confiterías, ie, cafés specialized in pastries. To return to Santiago, take the Pan-American highway.

2 TO MACHALI AND TERMAS DE CAUQUENES

★★★ *a 56-km round trip from Rancagua and a 234-km round trip from Santiago; 8 km graveled. Allow a whole day. Take food or eat at the Hotel Termas de Cauquenes.*

A tour along a modern, scenic road leading to Chile's second most important copper mine, passing interesting farms, a picturesque mining town in a spectacular mountain setting and, finally, a thermal resort visited since the old days by the high and mighty.

Take exit 2 out of Rancagua (see city map) until reaching, at km 7, the town of

MACHALI four kilometers before reaching this village is the beautiful **Hacienda La Sanchina**, a mud-brick and clay-tile construction dating from the early 19th century and bearing the typical features of the period: rectangular layout, arcaded verandas, and a chapel. Now the headquarters of the Educares University. A short distance further along is the picturesque village of Machalí, nestled on the foothills of the Andes in an area of lush vegetation. Of haphazard layout, it has lots of corners; its mud-brick houses have adjoining façades, each painted a different color. Machalí evolved from an old Indian settlement, a fact which accounts for its irregular layout. It was granted village status in 1899 and its main source of income are the taxes paid by the El Teniente mine, which lies in its commune.

What To See drive along Pisagua and turn left on San Juan (see map) to reach the **Plaza de Armas**, the inviting main square. On one side is the modern building housing the town hall. The **San Juan hill** is the village's recreational park and a good spot for a picnic. With a lush plant cover, it has a small lake with boats for hire and a eucalyptus forest with a good view over the valley.

Take exit 2 (see map) to follow the so-called **copper highway**, a road into the Andes built in 1967 to move the mine's residential quarters from Sewell to Rancagua, providing an adequate road connection to the mine.

The highway climbs a slope with several lookout points commanding spectacular views of the folded mountain scenery and the valley below. At

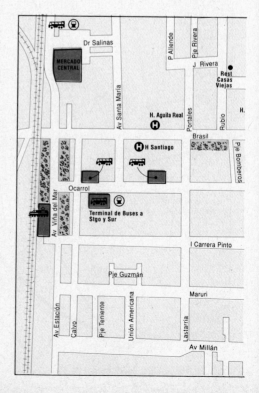

5

km 19 there is an access control outpost for the **El Teniente mine**. This is Chile's second most important copper mine and the world's largest underground mine. It is a giant complex comprising the mine and the concentrates plant at **Sewell**, the refinery with its soaring smokestack at **Caletones**, and the hydroelectric power station at **Coya**. The mine has been exploited since colonial times and in 1906 it was acquired by the American Braden Co, which transformed it into a great underground operation. Now it is property of Codelco and public visits are not allowed. The exception are specialists, who must request permission at Millán street in Rancagua, Oficina de Control de Pases de Codelco Chile, División El Teniente.

To the right of the control barrier continues the paved road to Coya. At km 24 there is a new control barrier. Here you must report your visit to Coya, a subsidiary town of El Teniente, with narrow streets and picturesque wooden houses. The Cachapoal river runs here at the bottom of a deep gorge with sheer cliffs; a suspension bridge spans the chasm.

Return to the access barrier and take the gravel road branching left. It leads to

HOTEL TERMAS DE CAUQUENES at km 28. Lying 766 m above sea level on a level space hacked away by volcanic eruptions on the south bank of the Cachapoal river, its thermal waters are known since 1646. Tradition tells that they were also used by the natives before the arrival of the Spaniards. The first owners of the place were the Jesuits, in the 18th century. During the early years after attaining Independence, Bernardo O'Higgins and José de San Martín enjoyed these waters on several occasions. They were also visited in 1834 by Charles Darwin, who commented on their excellence. In 1885 the construction of a large bathing establishment (the hotel) was undertaken, still in operation. Of remarkably beautiful architecture, the place deserves a visit, a stroll through its

well-kept park and, of course, a bath in its thermal waters. Its restaurant's cuisine and service are also renowned.

Return to Santiago taking the Pan–American highway.

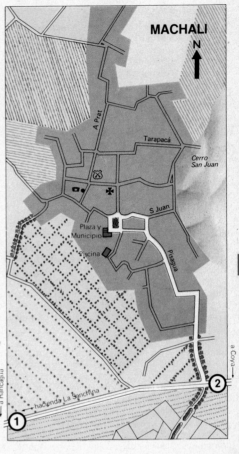

5

☎ Telephone Center	⊛ Gasoline Station	🚌 Bus Terminal	**M** Regional Bus Terminal
⊙ Café, Meeting Point	✉ Post Office	**J** Rodeo Arena	**2** Rest Centro Español
★ Touristic Information	🚂 Railway Station	**K** Sports Complex	**7** H Rancagua

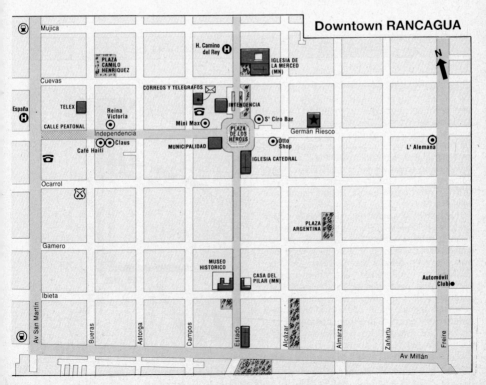

Downtown RANCAGUA

3 EXTENSION TO THE RIO LOS CIPRESES NATIONAL RESERVE ★★★

3 **EXTENSION TO THE RIO LOS CIPRESES NATIONAL RESERVE** ★★★ *a 44-km round trip extension on the previous tour on a gravel road. From the Coya–Termas de Cauquenes highway a road branches south leading in 5 km to the park's entrance. It then climbs for 17 km alongside the Los Cipreses river.*

Main Attractions an altitude native forest containing peumos and quillayes with some patches of cypress. There are swarms of tricahue parakeets that nest in hollows on the rocky faces. There are natural pools for bathing, picnic areas and an administration house. Farther in you will see impressing cliffs, petroglyphs, and waterfalls. Still further up are the cypress forests, with small herds of guanacos –a camelid similar to llama–, and the turquoise Agua de Vida lake, with mineral water. It is a beautiful place, not far from Santiago administrated by Conaf.

4 TO LA LEONERA AND HACIENDA LA COMPAÑIA ★★★

4 **TO LA LEONERA AND HACIENDA LA COMPAÑIA** ★★★ *a 170-km round trip, with 30 km of gravel road. Allow one day; for any time of the year. Take food or eat at the La Leonera restaurant.*
A circuit along an old southbound road running parallel to the Pan-American highway, with fine scenery and charming villages, to visit an hacienda which once was the Central Zone's largest and most important farm.

Take the southbound Pan-American highway and 8 km beyond the Angostura toll plaza take the paved road branching left to **La Punta** (km 72), a small, charming hamlet with a pretty church. From the side of the church a gravel road leads to **Hacienda La Punta**, with a beautiful house which can be seen from the road. It is a 10-km round trip among tobacco plantations and old trees.

Retrace the road heading for the Pan-Am. Two km beyond La Punta take the gravel road heading south which leads to **Codegua** (km 84). It was an Indian settlement whose name was derived from the words co, deuy and hue, meaning «place of rat water». Its mainstay is agriculture and has few houses. Continue 4 km south of this village to a signposted road branching left for La Leonera. At km 94 is

Hotel La Leonera this was an old fundo –large farm– with copper and silver mines in its sierra

section. Now it is a hotel in a scenic mountain setting on the bank of the Codegua creek. There is a restaurant, mini golf course, sauna, swimming pool, horses for rent and a shady park.

Retrace the road 6 km to retake the highway heading south. At km 107 is the old

HACIENDA DE LA COMPAÑIA DE GRANEROS donated to the Jesuits in 1595 by their former owners, captains Andrés de Torquemada and Agustín Briceño. The small hacienda, through successive donations and acquisitions, ballooned to a whopping 12,000 hectares of flatland and 120,000 hectares of hilly and mountainous land, stretching from the Argentine border in the east to the San Francisco de Mostazal hills in the west. Until the Jesuits were expelled from the Spanish possessions in 1767, this hacienda was the largest and most important agricultural, livestock and industrial complex in Central Chile. Its main areas of activity were livestock raising and slaughtering, the output being industrialized in large processing yards. There was also a wheat mill, tanneries, vineyards and wineries. The whole complex had the purpose of raising funds to enlarge the Gospel-preaching mission.

The original compound included imposing residential buildings, a church, sleeping quarters for the monks and servants, quarters for the «married blacks», storage buildings, granaries, mills and labor yards. All that remains now are one section of the service yard and the **chapel (NM)**. The latter, although refurbished on the outside, is now a parish; it used to house an altar to the Immaculate Conception built in 1763. The chapel can be visited everyday asking for the key at the parish house.

A 3-km paved road leads from La Compañía to the Pan-American highway.

SECTION G   CACHAPOAL VALLEY

The area covered by this Section is the cradle of the Chilean huaso traditions, and it stretches from Rancagua to Pelequén, a point at which the Central Depression is squeezed between a spur of the Andes reaching west and the Coastal Range. Westwards it extends up to the valleys and hills alongside the Cachapoal river, ending at the village of Las Cabras. There it borders on the territory covered by Section H of this Zone, Coastal Lands, whose center is at Lake Rapel.

This district is divided into two portions. One stretches southwest of Rancagua and is flanked by the Cachapoal and Claro rivers. Extensively settled and crisscrossed by a thick road network, its main centers are El Olivar, Doñihue, Lo Miranda, Guarcahue, and Quebrada de Tilcoco. The other portion is the southward extension of the Claro river valley up to Pelequén and the great opening of the valleys towards the coast, with urban centers at San Vicente de Tagua Tagua, Malloa, Peumo, Pichidegua, and Las Cabras.

These lands were inhabited by a relatively large

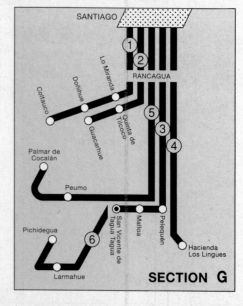

Indian population which, under the influence of the Incas in the 15th century, acquired mastery of advanced irrigation techniques. Their larger agricultural centers were located at points known as rinconadas, sheltered valleys, where irrigation using ditches can be best made use of. There were Indian settlements also south of San Vicente de Tagua Tagua, surrounding large marshy areas which were drained late last century.

The natives were subject to a serfdom system known as encomienda, whereby they were forced to provide unpaid labor to a Spanish conqueror – encomendero– as a tribute to the King of Spain. By 1613, land started to be granted to Spanish soldiers. The largest feudatory of that period was Juan de Quiroga, a soldier who was granted 8,000 hectares between the Cachapoal and the Tinguiririca rivers. He expanded his property through land purchases and exchanges until he had 30,000 hectares in the district of Pichidegua and Larmahue –nearly the whole area covered by this Section. In 1756 these lands were acquired by Pedro Gregorio Echeñique and around 1800 they started to be divided into smaller properties known as hijuelas.

During the second half of the 19th century large irrigation works were carried out. The most famous of these is the Larmahue canal, south of the Cachapoal, with interesting «water wheels», unique in Chile, which lift the water from the canal to the cultivated fields. The last canals to irrigate the more elevated portions of this valley –at Doñihue, Coltauco, and Peumo– were built in the 1920s and 1930s. This brought about a revolution in agriculture, with extensive plantings of fruit trees, such as oranges, lemons, avocados, and peaches, and grapevines. These lands are now extraordinarily fruitful and support some large agribusinesses, such as La Rosa de Sofruco and Viña Concha y Toro at the Peumo area, and others at Malloa, Peumo, Requínoa, and Rengo.

TOURS OF THE AREA

1 TO LO MIRANDA, DOÑIHUE, AND THE COLTAUCO AREA ★★★ *a round trip of about 290 km, with 18 km graveled. Allow a whole day; any time of the year, but best in springtime. Take food or eat in Rancagua; alternatively, stay overnight at San Vicente de Tagua Tagua.*

A circuit on a road running along the north bank of the Cachapoal river, with fine scenery and quaint towns, interesting handicrafts and lovely places for a picnic.

Take the southbound Pan-American highway to Rancagua, and take there Exit 5 (see Rancagua city map). One km into this road you will see a sign indicating **Vinos Santa Mónica** to the right; stop there if you want to taste some of their wines, or buy some at convenient prices. The road then approaches the stony bank of the river, which here runs wide. At km 13 turn right at the junction; at km 15 is

Lo Miranda the hamlet –named after its old owner, Pedro Miranda y Rueda– was in the past an Inca mitimae, and administrative Inca settlement. Later, in 1877, it was granted village status and now it is a small, charming farming hamlet with a square, few streets and old houses.

Two alternative excursions can be made from here: one is to head east from the square to visit **Rinconada de Lo Miranda**, two km along a picturesque dirt road lined with mud–brick houses with clay–tile roofs and brightly painted façades, ornamented with flower pots and small pictures hanging on the street–facing walls. The other option is to head west from the square to **Plazuela de Lo Miranda**; it is a three–km dirt road with a countryside reminiscent of the Chilean South. Get

back to the highway from Lo Miranda and continue until km 23; take the road branching right, indicated by a monolith, and turn right again at the next junction. This road leads to

Rinconada de Doñihue at km 25. Ask for directions to the Medialuna de Rinconada, next to which are the houses of the chamanteras, renowned weavers of huaso implements, displayed with pride at rodeos throughout Chile. They produce chamantos –a short jacket–, waistbands and belts in fine wool. Here you will also find lovely handicrafts of **carved stone,** including water fountains and the like.

Return to the first junction at km 27 and take the gravel road branching right, passing small villages where the popular chicha chacolí, a tasty cider, is sold. At km 30 is

DOÑIHUE an old Indian town where the Incas settled during their southward expansion; the name means «eyebrows» in Mapuche. In 1873 President Federico Errázuriz Zañartu granted it village status. It lies on the slopes of green hills surrounded by fertile pastures. Its excellent climate makes fruit ripen here earlier than at other locations. Its most remarkable activity is the manufacture of loom–woven textiles. Chilean huaso traditions have always been closely linked with Doñihue, as it is here where the chamantos and mantas (a short poncho), which are sine–qua–non parts of their apparel, are made. A chamanto can take three or four months to weave, with up to 8 hours a day dedicated to the task. The chamantos are graced by original designs including flowers, tassels or wheat spikes, grapevine leaves, horses, etc. They are reversible: the dark side to wear during the day, the light side for the night.

The area with the famous chamanteras is called Camarico. Take Emilio Cuevas street to the end, then left on a narrow, curving street, with a canal running on one side; the houses are accessible through small individual bridges. The other side of the street is lined with mud–brick houses with adjoined façades. On the doors hang little signs with the name of the weaving artisan who lives

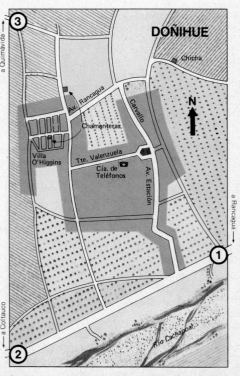

Quinta de Tilcoco

there. You can visit the houses to watch them at work and see their products. Outstanding for their tradition and expertise are Filomena Cantillana, at Emilio Cuevas 626; Marta Ortega at Los Claveles 542 (Mon–Sun 08:00–20:00 h), and Carmen Carrasco, Emilio Cuevas 693.

Before you leave Doñihue, an extension along the road to Quimávida may be recommended. Drive four km and turn right at the junction; one km ahead is the **Quimávida Agricultural School**. It is an old farm house with a very well–kept park containing an excellent tree collection; labels identify each species.

Retrace the road and leave Doñihue following the paved road to reach the highway again at km 40, heading west. The road passes the Viña Santa Luisa wine salesroom, and then turns away from the Cachapoal river to approach the mountain range. The pavement ends at km 51. The road continues through poplar forests and pastures delimited by rows of poplars. There are some small sawmills with old machinery reminiscent of those found in the deeper South. This ten–km stretch has many good spots for a picnic.

At km 63 the hills encroach upon the Cachapoal river; the road runs between the hills and the stream, with good picnic, camping and bathing spots. At km 70 the road crosses to the other bank through an adapted railway toll bridge. Take there the paved Peumo–Pelequén highway, which will bring you to the Pan–American highway and back to Santiago.

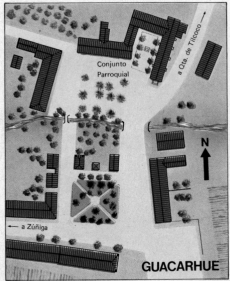

a Qta. de Tilcoco →

Conjunto
Parroquial

N ↑

← a Zúñiga

GUACARHUE

2 TO COINCO, QUINTA DE TILCOCO, AND GUACARHUE ★★★ a 274–km round trip from Santiago, with 80 km of gravel road. Allow a whole day; best in spring and autumn. Take food or eat at any of the highway restaurants near Rancagua.

A tour through scenic farmland, passing picturesque villages with old country houses, interesting churches and an enormous building that once was an Exercise House to bring the Gospel to the natives.

Take the southbound Pan–American highway through Rancagua; six km beyond the city turn right on the signposted road to El Olivar. The road ends at the Santa Julia farm; turn right to follow a road through orchards and old country houses to El Olivar Alto, at km 11, a picturesque village with the square as its heart. Turn right from the square to the church and parish house, a charming building from 1853 with clay–tile roof and pillars on the corner. It is well preserved.

Continuing west on the main road you will leave the village and pass El Olivar Bajo, a scattering of houses, at km 18. One km further along there is a junction; the road branching left leads to a small village called **Copequén**, evolved from an old farm. In the 16th century this was a Curaca seat –ie, the seat of the local Inca governor-, located at the site occupied now by the Cachantún mineral water bottling plant.

A short distance ahead starts the paved road to **Coinco**, at km 30, an old settlement called Coihuinco by some and which was granted village status in 1872. The entrance is beautiful, the road flanked by rows of stately poplars, surrounded by grapevine plantations and peasant houses. It has an attractive square with large, leafy trees; on one side is the building housing the Coinco Town Hall, a two-story colonial building. The quaint, curvy streets are lined by colorful houses with front gardens and well-kept sidewalks.

Leave the town on the paved road heading west; the pavement soon gives way to gravel. At km 37 is the small hamlet of Tres Puentes. At km 39 there is a junction marked by a cross; take the road branching left to Quinta de Tilcoco, passing Chillehue on the way, with attractive manor houses in European style. The road then runs higher up, with vast views over the valley. You eventually reach a T–junction; turn right to reach, at km 54, the town of

GUACARHUE the name comes from the Mapuche words Guaca and Rehue, meaning «district with many goods». It is a picturesque town, with attractive colonial buildings, many with adjoined verandas running the length of the block; very practical to watch the world go by, take shelter in case of rain or escape the basking sunlight. The **square** has a strange layout, with few trees and some old palms which continue on another street separated by a canal and a small orchard. Next to it is the **Church of Guacarhue**, a beautiful building from the 18th century designed by the famous Italian architect Toesca and rebuilt after the 1835 earthquake. It has two naves intersecting at right angles, with the altar at the intersection; in one nave sat the Spaniards and in the other, the Indians.

The large **parish house**, of colonial style, is also worth a visit. The whole town has an atmosphere reminiscent of times long gone.

Retrace the road to km 60, where the

QUINTA DE TILCOCO is located. The name comes from Co (water) and Thilco (a native shrub), meaning chilco tea. Following the main street you will reach the square; on one side are the manor houses and the park of the Cailloma farm. The park has a small lake and a wide assortment of trees. It was owned in the past by Daniel Ortúzar, who donated part of his lands to the Guacarhue parson, Tomás Argomedo, so that he could build his

CASA DE EJERCICIOS (Exercise House), aimed at teaching the Gospel to the local Indians and peasants. The huge complex was finished in 1880, the year the parson died; at its peak it had 14 courtyards. Opposite the Casa de Ejercicios there is a small hill called De la Virgen; climb to its summit for the grand view over the complex and the surrounding valley. The complex is open to visitors every day.

Leave the village following the gravel road which, in 11 km, reaches the paved road that, in turn, leads to the Pan–American highway and to Santiago.

3 SAN VICENTE DE TAGUA TAGUA ★★

a 260–km round trip from Santiago, with 6 km of gravel road. For one day or more; accommodations and food at San Vicente de Tagua Tagua. Good any time of the year.
A circuit through the countryside, passing villages with good handicrafts and visiting a prosperous city.

Take the southbound Pan–American highway. At km 104 you will see a large number of stands selling fresh fruit and hand–made brooms. Broom manufacture stemmed from the large curahuilla plantations, which provide the straw for the brooms; the seeds are sold in Santiago as birdseed.

At km 108 a road branches left for Pelequén, where the beautiful **Santa Rosa de Lima Church and Sanctuary** is located, venue for pilgrimage and festivities on August 30th. Santa Rosa (Saint Rose) was canonized in the 17th century, and was the first saint born in the American continent; she was declared Patron Saint of the Americas and the Philippines. Pelequén achieved certain notoriety as a railway station and farming produce depot. The name means «mud field».

Get back to the junction on the Pan–Am and cross to the west side to continue along the «Fruit Highway», built to bring the zone's fruit production to the shipping port at San Antonio.

Three km into this road you will see the San Alberto farm and its fine park.

A further three km will bring you to a junction where some old farming machinery stands as monument.

Take the right branch, leading in two km to the town of

MALLOA it was an old Indian settlement whose fertile lands and gold mines in the vicinity promptly attracted Spanish settlers. They erected a church in which the Foundation Act for San Fernando was issued in 1742, signed by Manso de Velasco. It was granted village status and named Villa de Malloa in 1873. Malloa means «site of white clay». The place has a haphazard layout, its long main street winding and lined with old houses with adjoined, colorful façades and tiled roofs. The street leads to the town's social center: the square and the church. Most people are employed by or work for the Malloa cannery.

Get back to the main road to San Vicente de Tagua Tagua, following it to the right. Soon it runs alongside the Zamorano creek. Nine km further along there is a detour to the left, which passes through the hamlet of **Requegua**. It consists of a three–km–long street running parallel to the highway and lined with attractive houses harking back to better times when it was a prosperous railway stop. The railway station is now disused. This road joins the highway again, which continues through fruit orchards, mainly oranges, to reach a signposted junction at km 137. Take the right branch leading to

Pueblo de Indios La Puntilla a hamlet lying on a hillside, with picturesque, modest houses. Its major attraction is its beautiful pottery, the locals' main occupation. Modelling the pieces is the woman's task, while the man collects the clay, prepares and kneads the mix and, finally, bakes the pieces. Most of the conveniently priced items are utilitarian in purpose, including frying pans, flower pots and bowls.

One km beyond Pueblo de Indios is the signposted junction with the road branching for

SAN VICENTE DE TAGUA TAGUA an old Indian settlement now evolved into a bustling city where people from the neighboring farms gather. The heart of the place is the main square. Each of its corners has trees of a given color of leaves and flowers, different from the other three corners. Some of the old buildings ringing it are very well preserved and feature balconies on the upper floor. Social life centers at Confitería El Portalón, a café on the square. San Vicente de Tagua Tagua is the head town of the Cachapoal valley and it is a good jumping–off point for visiting nearby

5

☎ Telephone Center	⊙ Café, Meeting Point
⛽ Gasoline Station	Ⓗ Hostel

R Restaurants
A Town Hall
B Church

C Post Office
D Rodeo Arena
E Swimming Pool

a Peumo y Lago Rapel

N

POBL MANUEL RODRIGUEZ
JOSE M CARRERA
WALKER
R 21 DE MAYO
AV ESPAÑA
PORTALES
AV ESPAÑA
RIESCO
PRAT
C
GONZALEZ
B A R
AV ARANGUIZ
GALLEGOS
TAGUA TAGUA
POBL MIGUEL BUSTAMANTE
H
POBL GERMAN RIESCO
AV PIO XII
E
AV LOS NARANJOS
AV O'HIGGINS
a Pencahue
a Pelequén y Santiago
Estero Zamorano
POBL ALBORADA

SAN VICENTE DE TAGUA TAGUA

places of historical interest. Accommodations at **Hostería San Vicente**. For lunch, the renowned **Requehue** restaurant, specialized in pork dishes.

Eight km south of San Vicente was **Lake Tagua Tagua** –drained in 1841– notable for its 31 square kilometers and its floating islets called chivines, described by Darwin in 1834. These islets were formed on the edges of the lake by accumulation of algae, grasses and other aquatic plants which interwove their roots and formed such compact masses that they could even support the weight of an animal. Wind eventually made them break away from the shore and drift around the lake surface. In the trench dug to drain the lake two mastodon skeletons were unearthed, proving that this prehistoric species had lived in Chile, as well as rests of bodies found over 11,400 years old. Now the lake bed can barely be made out, buried under a thick forest.

Retrace the road to return to Santiago, but check first the other excursions you can make from San Vicente de Tagua Tagua.

4 TO HACIENDA LOS LINGUES ★★★

an organized 260–km tour from Santiago, with 10 km of gravel road. You can either go in a tourist bus or on your own. Allow a whole day (Saturday or Sunday), any time of the year; lunch is included at the hacienda. Accommodation is also available. Reservations at any travel agent or at phone 235 2458, Santiago.

An interesting tour to a great hacienda of historical and architectural value. The building, of colonial style, has kept all the furnishings of the colonial period, is set in a well-kept park and has a thoroughbred horse farm.

Take the southbound Pan–American highway; two km beyond Pelequén a signposted road branches left to

HACIENDA LOS LINGUES the manor house was built in two stages: the nucleus dates from the late 17th and early 18th centuries, while the remaining wings were built 100 years later, preserving the original style. The construction materials included mud-brick, stone masonry, pink stone from Pelequén, oak, coligüe –a type of cane–, patagua –a type of wood–, and clay-tile roofs. Some of the doors were carved by Bavarian jesuits -the master cabinetmakers of the period– at Hacienda de Calera de Tango (see Section D). It also has a charming chapel. The manor house is set in a lovely park with large native trees, with manicured flower gardens in the inner courtyards.

The first owner of the hacienda was Melchor Jufré de Aguila, mayor of Santiago in 1599. He was granted the property by the King of Spain in recognition of his services as writer and chronicler. It was inherited by one of his daughters, who, in the mid 17th century, married Diego González Montero, Chile's governor, and since then it has remained in the hands of the same family.

The house has kept a large part of the original furnishings and appointments, including ornaments, fine silverware, glassware, game tables, lamps, Mapuche silver objects, Diaguita pottery, and fine French–style furniture. Visitors can roam through the salons and the arcaded galleries through which historical notables walked, such as Mateo de Toro y Zambrano, José Gregorio de Argomedo (a member of the first governing Junta), and many others.

The visit includes lunch in the wine vaults, made of thick stone masonry walls, where you can enjoy a typically Chilean meal prepared according to old recipes, accompanied by excellent wines and the typical Central-Chilean drinks for after dinner. Sometimes, folkloric music groups provide live music; with good

weather, lunch is held outdoors. In the afternoon the traditional taming of young bulls, horsemanship and the breaking of untamed horses is held at the medialuna –the rodeo arena–enjoying local drinks.

Here is also the renowned Aculeo thoroughbred horse farm, ranked among the best in the world. In addition to the fine horses, note the pink–flagstone work on the stable's floor; it sprawls over 3,500 square meters. Recently the owners set up a small pheasant, grouse and peacock farm. It also has a small lake, suitable for bathing or rowing.

Los Lingues is, additionally, a luxurious hotel with accommodations for 30 guests, associated to the exclusive international hotel chain Relais et Châteaux, with 372 establishments throughout the world, of which only four are in South America.

5 TO PEUMO AND LAKE RAPEL ★★★

an 88–km round trip from San Vicente de Tagua Tagua on a paved road. Best in autumn or spring. Allow a whole day. Lunch at Peumo or at the lake.

A circuit along the Cachapoal river, through farmland, old villages, and the Concha y Toro winery, to the Lake Rapel tourist center.

Take the «Fruit Highway» (see previous tour) out of San Vicente de Tagua Tagua heading west. The highway runs through avocado and lemon orchards and then crosses to the other bank through the adapted railway bridge (it is a toll bridge). At km 10 a road branches left to

PEUMO it was an old Indian settlement, whose native inhabitants started to dwindle after 1664, when these and the surrounding lands were granted to the Marquis of Villa Palma, of the Encalada family. Now it is a quaint village of haphazard layout and picturesque mud–brick houses with tiled roofs and well–kept front gardens. The **square** is shady and charming, ringed by trees popularly known as «cow feet» (Bahuinia sp) with strange leaves and large white flowers, resembling orchids, blooming in summer. On the square is the church, ornamented with inlaid wood designs; the tower and belfry are separated from the nave. A stroll through the village's meandering streets and its many corners will show you many charming peasant houses graced by lots of flowers. This love of flowers was introduced by a US–born mayoress a few decades ago.

Leaving Peumo, take the main highway heading west. Four km further along is the access gate to **Viña Concha y Toro**, on the right. The winery owns over 305 hectares of vineyards, Chile's largest one–piece grapevine plantation held by a single owner. You can visit the large, old wine vaults and the salesroom, both located on an avenue lined by huge evergreen oaks (Mon–Fri the whole day; Sat only until midday. If you are going on Sunday, check beforehand with phone 561579, Peumo).

Continuing on the main highway, at km 16 is the imposing house of Hacienda Codao, now housing a children's home. On the left side of the house a short dirt road branches north, skirting the farm's storage rooms and passing next to a small avenue lined by an unusual tree called Taxodium dischitum, a deciduous conifer –ie, it sheds its leaves in winter; its roots grow on the side of a canal and have strange protuberances. The road ends at the **Cerrito del Señor**, a small hill where a Via Crucis is held on Easter Week. Climbing the path to the summit you will have a panoramic **view** of the valley stretching beyond the river, including **Pichidegua**, the **La Torina** hills and the vast Concha y Toro grapevine plantations.

Get back to the main highway and continue westward. At km 20, on the right, is the large **La Rosa Sofruco** hacienda, now a major agribusiness, with an attractive manor house and a large park.

At km 27 is **Las Cabras**, a village evolved from a former 600–ha farm and a station of the Pelequén branch railway. Its layout is haphazard and it is the supply center for the Rapel district. From Las Cabras a poorly–surfaced road leads in 16 km to

PALMAR DE COCALAN it is not open to the public. Permission to visit is only granted for research or for ecological purposes, prior request at phone 555 2894, Santiago. The description below is for those having a visiting permit.

Take the signposted road heading north from Las Cabras to Cuesta de Quilicura. The road climbs a rise and passes a strange cemetery lying on the slopes. At the top of the three–km–long climb there is a grand **view** over Las Cabras and the typical rural scenery of Central Chile. On the other side of the ridge there is a scenic valley with unending corn plantations.

At km 37 a road branches right to **Cocalán**, a tiny hamlet evolved from a large old farm. A few palms can be seen, a foretaste of the forests to come.

At km 43 the road reaches an impressive relict forest with thousands of palms climbing the slopes, giving an exotic look to the place. It is an indigenous palm (Jubaea chilensis) featuring a thick smooth stem (the largest diameter of any palm tree); it is the world's most southerly palm. Of slow growth rate, the largest here are about 300–400 years old. From its stem a delicious syrup is obtained, known as miel de palma, or palm honey. The fruit –coquito– is much in demand. Until the colonial times there were lots of palms on the coastal areas of Chile's central valley; they were felled to obtain the syrup. The only palm groves remaining are those of Ocoa and Cocalán.

The present owners are carrying out a vast reforestation plan aimed at increasing fivefold the present number of palms.

Those not visiting the palm grove, continue from Las Cabras, km 27, towards the lake. At the village of El Carmen, km 34, take the road branching left to skirt the shore of a small peninsula, through **Llallauquén** to **Bahía Skorpio**. The lake is described under Section J, Coastal Lands.

6 TO PICHIDEGUA VIA THE WATER WHEELS

★★★ *a 65–km round trip from San Vicente de Tagua Tagua, with 44 km of gravel road. For half a day; best in spring, summer or autumn. Take food. From Santiago it is a 335–km round trip, with 44 km of gravel road; you will need a whole day.*

A circuit through scenic countryside, passing quaint water wheels still in operation, old farms, picturesque villages and an interesting church on the way.

Take exit 3 out of San Vicente de Tagua Tagua (see map). The road passes the village of **Pencahue** at km 5: a few farmhouses and a small church. Two km farther along is **Pencahue Central** and a further two km is Pencahue Alto; here, off to the right, is the old **Hacienda de Pencahue**, an attractive farm complex from the 19th century with houses, storage rooms and, the most interesting, a charming chapel at the end of a great avenue lined with maple trees. Try to get permission for a visit.

At km 11 pavement gives way to gravel. Beyond the bridge spanning an arm of the Cachapoal river is the hamlet of **El Niche,** ringed by orange orchards. Continue until you reach the Cachapoal river, whose water was tapped 60

years ago by a canal to irrigate the vast Larmahue hacienda. The road runs alongside the canal, where you will see the strange

WATER WHEELS they were designed to lift the water from the canal to the land to be irrigated. The wheels –primitive but efficient– are turned by the current; small buckets attached to the rim take water from the canal and lift it to a small duct in the upper part, from where it is conveyed to the fields.

This system is unique in Chile and it can be seen in operation from September through early winter along the entire road. Some are enormous; they merit a stop to watch their operation.

Continuing among orange orchards, colorful country houses and a pretty church, you will reach **Larmahue** at km 19, a village straddling the road with its houses graced by bougainvilleas in summer. At km 20 there is a road junction; the right branch leads to Pichidegua, the left one tops a rise into the Tinguiririca river valley. Three km into this road you reach **Almahue**, the road flanked by orange. The place evolved from a 4,500–ha irrigated farm; now it is a picturesque hamlet encircled by orange orchards. At km 26, off to the left, is the large **Santa Amelia** farm, with a chapel set in a French–style park with lawns and statues.

At km 30, on the right, is

FUNDO SAN ROBERTO good wine is sold in this farm. Here you can also see the buildings which in the past were the manor houses of the Larmahue farm; they are the oldest constructions in the valley. They include a small chapel, courtyards shaded by orange trees, storage rooms, and the residence. They are all in bad condition after the 1985 earthquake.

Leave Fundo San Roberto and turn right; climb **the Torina** ridge (now called El Alamo), with a good view from the crest. At km 35 take the road branching right, leading in 600 m to the old Hacienda La Torina, a private farm whose manor house and park are separated from the road by a big wall. A short distance farther along, to the left, is the **calle parroquial** and the beautiful **La Torina church**, formerly part of the farm. It was designed by the famous Italian architect Joachim Toesca, the same one who designed the Palacio La Moneda in Santiago.

A few meters ahead is **Viña Almahue**, a winery whose products you can buy at the wine vaults of Hacienda La Torina.

Turn left upon getting back to the main road. Eventually you will reach the village of **Pichidegua**, whose name comes from pichi –small– and a variation of deuy, country mouse. In the past it was an Indian village and now a single street lined by old, quaint houses; its square contains Chile's largest camphor tree.

Four km beyond Pichidegua the road reaches a bridge spanning the Cachapoal river and it joins then the paved road leading to San Vicente de Tagua Tagua and, thence, to the Pan–American highway.

5

SECTION **H**   MAPOCHO VALLEY

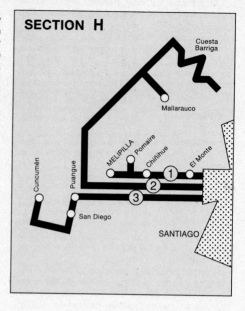

This Section covers the Mapocho valley downriver from Santiago up to the confluence with the Maipo river, and the district around this river up to the mouth of the Puangue creek. It also includes part of the Puangue valley up to María Pinto, bounded on the north by the Barriga ridge. In this area lies the four-lane highway to San Antonio. Alongside this highway, threading through the villages, runs the old road to the coast, which follows the route of the Royal Road, used since the Colonial days to go to Valparaíso via Melipilla. It was also known as the «Ladies' Route», as it was preferred by women, although it was longer, because it avoided the dreaded climbs of the Lo Prado and Zapata ridges.

Before the Spaniards arrived, this area had a sizable Indian population, with settlements at Talagante, El Monte, El Paico, Chiñihue, Pomaire, and Melipilla. The natives had settled this area so readily because, drawing on the irrigation techniques they had learned from the Incas in the 15th century, they needed places where the streams ran close to the hills. Thus, they could tap water from the stream and divert it through small ditches to their cropland.

When the Spaniards arrived, the natives were promptly subject to a serfdom system known as encomienda, whereby a Spaniard was granted a tract of land and the Indians provided the labor –unpaid, as a tribute to the King of Spain. Soon titles of ownership were also granted. However, unlike at the non-irrigated lands, being this valley fertile and populated, no vast farms –fundos– were formed, but many medium– and small–sized farms which exist to this day.

Late in the colonial period the great irrigation work known as «The King's Ditch» was built, now Canal de Puangue. The real agricultural boost, however, occurred in the mid–19th century, when major entrepreneurs invested in this area building large farm complexes, parks and the San José, El Paico, Chiñihue, San Diego and –the most costly– Mallarauco canals. This last canal was financed by a single farmer and took twenty years to reach completion.

The area is now bustling, the farmland in full production and the towns and villages starting to be shaken out of their sleepiness. The tours suggested below will provide you with an insight into this district's past and present.

GASTRONOMY

Along the road to Melipilla via Malloco, Talagante and El Monte (ie, not the four-lane highway) there is an old concentration of restaurants catering to the zone's farmers, specialized in beef and pork dishes. Some are formal and some offer the traditional country hospitality. We list here the best known: **Der Münchner** restaurant, just beyond Malloco, with excellent German food; famous are its grill including beef, sausages and Leberkäse, and their monumental once, the late–afternoon teatime so typical of Chile. A bit farther along, at Lo Chacón, signposted to the left is **Aravena** restaurant, rated as the best for pork dishes and cazuelas. Then comes **La Montina**, producer of sausages and the renowned Montina empanadas, which consist of dough–wrapped sausages. In Pomaire there are excellent restaurants (see Pomaire map); the best is **Los Naranjos**, with a collection of old gramophones. In Melipilla is **Parrilladas Argentinas,** more frequented and formal, with excellent food. Just beyond Melipilla is **El Descanso**, an inexpensive restaurant specializing in frog's legs and renowned for its good food.

TOURS OF THE AREA

1 TO MELIPILLA AND POMAIRE ★★★

a round trip of 160 km on a paved road. Allow a whole day, any time of the year. For food, see Gastronomy above.

A scenic tour through the countryside, visiting old towns with interesting churches and buildings, among which is the house of Javiera Carrera, one of Chile's historical figures. It also includes a visit to the pottery center at Pomaire and the town of Melipilla.

Take Route 78 out of Santiago until you reach the signposted road branching to Malloco. The branch road reaches the town of **Malloco** at km 18. Here you have the alternative of visiting Peñaflor or continuing on the old road to the coast. If going

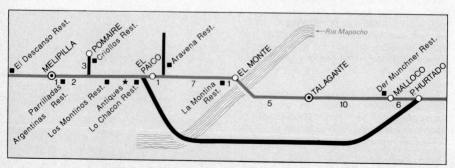

to Peñaflor, take Miraflores street, shaded by leafy tees: it was the old Malloco–Peñaflor road. At km 28 is

Peñaflor with a picturesque church and bustling commerce. Three blocks off the square is the large **Bata** shoe factory, employing 1,600 people. Leave Peñaflor following Av Vicuña Mackenna, which joins the old coastward road at km 47; turn left. You will pass **Der Münchner** restaurant along the way, with tennis courts and a skating rink, children's playgrounds and a mini zoo. Three km ahead is **Viña Undurraga,** with its old wine vaults and a fine park open to visitors (see Excursions to the Vineyards of Maipo). At km 43 is

Talagante a farming town evolved from an Indian settlement. The road goes through the town, passing the square on the way. Beyond the Tegualda resort near the highway you will reach

SANTA ANA DE LAS PALMAS a fine complex built in stages between the 17th and 18th centuries, which includes a manor house, a park–orchard, a chapel, cemetery, oratory, a guest house, storage rooms, stables, and a dairy. Santa Ana was founded as a Franciscan farm in 1579, thanks to a donation of Agueda Flores de Lisperguer, who lent these lands to the Franciscans in order for them to preach the Gospel to the natives. The houses were erected as a convent, but after some years they returned to the Lisperguers' ownership. A famous character in Chilean history, La Quintrala, was descended from them, and is said to have visited the place on several occasions.

The farm was then acquired by the Carrera family. It is well preserved and can be visited asking for permission at the site.

The road continues with the Mallarauco ridge to the right. At km 56 is

SAN FRANCISCO DEL MONTE a village evolved from the construction of the **Church of San Francisco (NM)** in 1690 by Franciscan father Andrés Corso. The church was rebuilt in 1796 and now enjoys the National Monument status. Adjacent to it is an attractive **parish house** in whose courtyard, goes the story, is the tunnel leading to the Casa de San Miguel del Monte, where the Carrera brothers and Manuel Rodríguez, heroes of Chile's struggle for Independence, met to plan their raids. It also has a small museum containing items –some of historical value– donated by local residents (open Mon through Sunday).

CASAS DE SAN MIGUEL DEL MONTE are located east of the square. Attractive 18th–century buildings which belonged to the Carrera Family and where Javiera Carrera lived, they used to have a beautiful park, one of the first in Chile, laid out and kept by Javiera. The place is still attractive, although the original line has not been maintained.

The houses are well preserved; one of the courtyards used to illustrate a currency note a couple of decades past. Open on Saturdays from 11:00 h; alternatively, you can arrange a visit with the administrator at Libertad 12.

Get back to the old coastward road; on the way you will pass the La Montina sausage producer and the Aravena restaurant, described above. Next comes the Paico zone, with no towns but only clusters of houses scattered in the countryside, with pastures, orchards and the parks of some private houses. At km 76, to the right and beyond the railway crossing, is

Santa Rosa de Chiñigüe a group of houses and parks built in 1890 by Claudio Vicuña, the most powerful and enterprising farmer of his period. He was also Minister of the Interior when President Balmaceda fell from power. Vicuña was of the opinion that a full–blooded farming entrepreneur couldn't but beautify the countryside with large works. True to his ideal, he had French landscape architect Guillaume Renner design parks for his three large farms, Bucalemu, Las Palmas, and Chiñigüe; they are now among Chile's finest parks. The Santa Rosa de Chiñigüe manor house sought to recreate the Renaissance model of Villa Palladiana, two–storied and with a classical tympanum and pillars. It was built at a period when the taste for art started to be felt in Chile, aroused by the frequent trips abroad of many influential people. This fondness for art also accounts for the paintings gracing the outer galleries. It has been poorly preserved. Ask for permission to visit at the gate.

Continuing on the highway, at km 80 is the road branching off to

POMAIRE the road runs through pastures and climbs a small hill, from where you can see a picturesque valley nestled at the foot of the Mallarauco range.

Pomaire is an old settlement of Indians presumably emigrated from Peru, given the analogy of the name with Quechua words. Traditions and customs have been preserved here in clay pottery, which the artisans classify into three categories: miniatures, handsomely made and with minute details, usually with peasant or religious motifs; decorative, somewhat larger and free regarding subject matter; and utilitarian, including pots, bowls, pans, tongs, flower pots, vases, etc.

Modelling is done by hand on a turntable. The finished wares are displayed at picturesque stands lining the town's main street. There are also many inexpensive restaurants specialized in pork and Chilean dishes (see map).

Get back to the highway. A short distance farther along is the excellent Parrilladas Argentinas restaurant. Then comes another Bata shoe factory

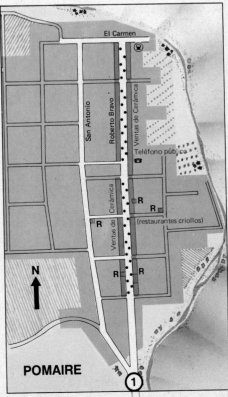

POMAIRE

a Carretera y Melipilla

and at km 90 is

MELIPILLA evolved in 1603 from an old Indian village into the seat of a textile factory supplying the army, it was granted village status by Manso de Velasco in 1742, under the name of Villa de Logroño de San José. However, the name Melipilla prevailed, an Indian expression meaning «four-sided place», on account of the valley's shape. It is now a bustling town, the urban center for the surrounding villages, hamlets and farms. Its **Feria de Animales** (livestock market) is interesting (see map); it operates on Wednesdays. The **square** is shady and has a central fountain. Unfortunately, its colonial buildings were badly damaged or wiped out by the 1985 earthquake. To return to Santiago, it is best to take the four-lane highway. It offers fine views over the intensely farmed valley.

2 TO MALLARAUCO AND THE BARRIGA RIDGE

★★★ *a 180–km round trip, with 55 km of gravel road. Allow one day; best in a sunny spring day. It is advisable to take food for a picnic.*

The tour shows the contrast between the fertile valleys and the arid Coastal Range, visiting an old non-irrigated farm transformed into a green valley through sheer human effort, and offers superb views of the Santiago valley and the Cordillera of the Andes from the Barriga ridge.

Take Route 78 up to Melipilla (km 67, described above). Take exit 4 in Melipilla map. The road gives fine views and passes the **Santa Ana** farm at km 74, with well-kept gardens and a pretty house; three km later it reaches the village of **San José**, where the namesake farm once owned by Mateo de Toro y Zambrano is located.

At km 81 a gravel road branches off to the fertile

MALLARAUCO VALLEY the name comes from ma-lla, a wild potato, and raghco, clay water. This valley entered Chilean history quite early on, when the natives gathered here to plan their first raid against Santiago, six months after the village had been founded.

A mayorazgo –ie, an entailed estate– had been established here by 1750. The valley lands had no irrigation until after 1873, when the last mayorazgo heir, the visionary Patricio Larraín Gandarillas, had a 40-km canal dug from the Mapocho river, with tunnels of up to about one

kilometer bored through the intervening ridges. The construction took twenty years and transformed this agriculturally poor area into a fertile valley, propelling its farms Mallarauco, Mallarauquito, and Pahuilmo into some of Chile's most prosperous. Now it has rich cropland and dairy fields, renowned for the **creamy cheese** of the Pahuilmo farm. It is an 18-km tour into the valley and back.

Return to the main road at km 99 and continue to **María Pinto** at km 110. It is a small farming town named after the original owner of these lands. At km 124 a paved road branches right to climb the

BARRIGA RIDGE the green cultivated valleys give way to wilder scenery, with a superb view over the Santiago valley and the backdrop of the Andes to the east. Vehicle traffic is very sparse, making this a good area for a picnic or for wandering or hiking. Sometimes you can see some hang-gliders circling up above.

To return to Santiago, climb down the other side of the ridge through Padre Hurtado to Route 78.

3 TO THE PUANGUE CREEK AND CUNCUMEN

★★ *a 184–km round trip from Santiago, with 38 km of gravel road. Allow one day; best in autumn or spring. It is advisable to take food for a picnic.*

An excursion into a scenic, little-known rural area.

Take Route 78 out of Santiago; twelve km beyond Melipilla a bridge spans the **Puangue Creek**, at a spot with lots of trees. Next comes Puangue, not exactly a village but a place on the road, with a church that is an old sanctuary of the Virgen del Carmen. In the past it was the focus of large pilgrimages, but it has been displaced by the sanctuary of Lo Vásquez.

Beyond Puangue the landscape changes and the road climbs small hills closing the valley. On the crest of the hills a road branches left to Cuncumén. Take this as your new km 0. One km into this gravel road heading south you will see the houses of the old **Hacienda de San Diego** (now called Santa Carolina), interesting constructions from the turn of the century. This farm used to be a mayorazgo stretching up to the Maipo river in the 18th century. It was eventually divided into three farms, which you will later see from the road. Each owner painted his houses and accompanying buildings a different color.

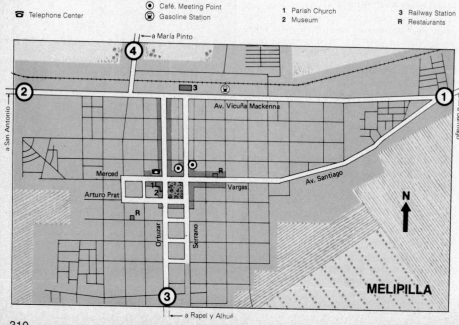

☎ Telephone Center
ⓒ Café, Meeting Point
Ⓖ Gasoline Station
1 Parish Church
2 Museum
3 Railway Station
R Restaurants

MELIPILLA

Next comes a forking of the road; take the left branch, heading for La Floresta. The road approaches the Puangue creek and follows it until its confluence with the Maipo river. From that point there is a superb **view** over the Maipo basin and the large plains unfolding eastward, and the hamlets of Codigua and El Carmen on the far bank. This is a good spot for a picnic. No bridge spans the river here, a fact which accounts for the isolation of the place.

The road continues through wheat fields and passes the modest hamlet of **La Floresta** at km 19; it is nestled at the foot of hills that are very green in springtime. It then climbs a ridge with a thick

plant cover and, at km 24, it reaches

CUNCUMEN an old, small village whose name means «a place that is red». The streets are modest and they follow the slopes of the flat hills the place lies on. In late winter and spring, the hills turn green and lend the village a look reminiscent of a southern rural hamlet.

Take now the road leading to Melipilla and soon you will be climbing the small Cuncumén rise. There is a good view from the top.

At km 31 turn left at the road junction and at km 38 you will reach Route 78, which leads to Santiago.

SECTION J   COSTINO

This Section comprises the rolling lands stretching south of Melipilla and including lake Rapel, up to the villages of La Estrella and Litueche. The name «coastal lands» was coined in the Cachapoal and Tinguiririca valleys to refer to those lands which, although not reaching the coast, are influenced by the sea's moisture.

The Coastal Range tapers down to low hills and rounded shoulders that let the moist winds blow through. The scenery is typical of the non–irrigated lands fed by moisture blown in from the ocean, with shrubs and some taller native trees in the ravines. The rivers and creeks run through deeply incised basins which do not create valleys on the sides. Only near the coast there are some meadows, plains, and salty lagoons where salt from the seawater is extracted.

In the past, a large portion of these lands was part of a Jesuit farm which originally sprawled over 50,000 hectares and had its center –and Novice House– at Bucalemu (between Rocas de Santo Domingo and the mouth of the Rapel river). By 1778 Pedro Fernández de Balmaceda bought this farm and established the Balmaceda mayorazgo, entailing the undivided inheritance of the property to a given line of his descendants. By 1800 it had 24,000 head of cattle and 16,000 head of sheep. Once a year, a great slaughter was carried out to obtain hides, fat and jerked meat that would then be exported to Lima, Peru. The farm remained undivided until early this century.

The great man–made Rapel lake, created a few years ago, slashes the area along the middle. It transformed the scenery and lent it new attractiveness; the place has become a recreation and watersports center. South of the lake there are some old, picturesque towns where isolation has kept alive the Chilean peasant traditions.

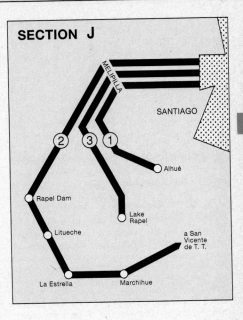

SECTION J

MELIPILLA · SANTIAGO · ② ③ ① · Alhué · Rapel Dam · Lake Rapel · Litueche · a San Vicente de T. T. · La Estrella · Marchihue

5

the entrance is the beautiful house of **Hacienda Alhué**, a 19th–century building housing an interesting private collection of carriages and calashes (ask for permission to visit at the site).

Villa Alhué unfortunately, the village's rich architectonic heritage, which included a beautiful church, an old parish house, picturesque mud–brick houses, kerosene lamps mounted on millstones, etc, was almost entirely wiped out by the 1985 earthquake. Efforts are being made to save some buildings enjoying National Monument status and to restore the village's colonial charm.

TOURS OF THE AREA

1 TO VILLA ALHUE ★★
a 340–km round trip from Santiago, with 80 km of gravel road. Allow one day; any time of the year. It is advisable to take food for a picnic.
A visit to an old, isolated town with a rich tradition in an interesting setting.
Take Route 78 to Melipilla, and then Exit 3 in Melipilla city map. At km 101 is the Las Arañas junction; take the road branching left up to km 122 to follow the signposted gravel road branching east to Villa Alhué, opposite the Santa Inés farm. The road heads towards the Alhué ridges alongside a creek, through a long farmed valley ringed by spurs of the Coastal Range, which here reaches great heights. At km 141 is a forking of the road; the right branch leads to Villa Alhué. At

2 TO CENTRAL RAPEL, LITUECHE, LA ESTRELLA AND MARCHIHUE ★★ *a 247–km round trip, with 95 km of gravel road, ending at San Vicente de Tagua Tagua. You can either stay there overnight or drive directly back to Santiago along the Pan–American highway, an additional stretch of 142 km. Allow one or two days, best in spring. Taking food might be a good idea.*
A circuit to one of Chile's major engineering works, the Rapel Hydroelectric Power Station, travelling on scenic country roads and passing quaint villages at some of the Central Zone's less accessible -and least known places.
Take Route 78 to Melipilla, and there exit 3 on Melipilla map. At km 101, at Las Arañas junction, take the right branch to the impressive

CENTRAL RAPEL at km 128. The power plant is fed by the energy of 700 million cubic meters of

lake Rapel

water accummulated in the 40–km–long Rapel lake, formed by a concrete dam holding back the water of the Cachapoal and the Tinguiririca rivers. The 112–m–high curved dam wall is 350 m long at the top. It contains the power plant, with five turbines and the corresponding generators. The road passes over the complex, which was finished in 1970. The real thrill, though, is to come in the spring, when the water from melting snow swells the lake to the point where the flood gates have to be opened: the water charges down the spill-way and arches upward with a mighty roar, an unforgettable display of raw power.

The road then climbs some hills giving a good view over the **Rapel lake;** at the junction take the signposted gravel road to

Litueche at km 145. It was an Indian settlement in the past, thence its haphazard layout; it lies on some rounded hills. The front verandas of its gaily-painted houses are joined at the ends, creating veritable roofed sidewalks. Flower pots decorate each façade. The village has the typical atmosphere of a sleepy Chilean rural town, with people chatting on the corners and a generally more relaxed rhythm to everything.

Take the road heading south, which runs through soft rolling land and crosses the Las Damas creek and the namesake hamlet. At km 156 take the road branching left, running through colorful cropland to reach, at km 163, the village of

LA ESTRELLA evolved from an Augustine monastery which attracted people to settle in the vicinity and was granted village status on June 30th, 1898. It nestles in the dell between low hills. From the hills at the village's entrance you can see the picturesque clay–tile roofs slanting a many angles. The village is small and has a haphazard layout; its large brick church presides over its green square, the favorite gathering point for the locals.

A stroll through its quaint streets will let you take in the place's old–time atmosphere.

Continue south a further 19 km to a signposted junction to

Marchihue a town at km 188. It is a picturesque place with wide streets and houses with adjoined façades, some with verandas on the street side. Odd–looking horse–drawn carts –typical of this area, with enormous, thin wheels– can be seen rolling along its streets. Handicrafts of reed and straw are made here.

Get back to the junction and continue straight ahead beyond it; the road heads northeast away from the coastal lands towards the Central Valley. Tree clusters and manor houses of old farms are to be seen on the way; among the most attractive

manor houses are those of the **Los Maitenes** and the **La Esperanza** farms. At km 211 is the quaint village of

San José de Marchihue evolved from an old farm and located in a scenic, isolated setting between the Tinguiririca river and the Las Cadenas creek. This zone is renowned for its excellent fishing of fresh–water mackerel (pejerrey), anglers trying their luck from the bridges spanning both streams. It has a pretty school in the old fundo houses and a small church, the latter not well kept.

Leaving the town, at km 230, is **Pichidegua;** beyond the Codao bridge continue straight on the paved road to San Vicente de Tagua Tagua, and thence to Santiago.

3 TO LAKE RAPEL ★★★
a 300–km round trip on a paved road. For one day in spring or summer, or more if you want to stay at the lake. Take food or eat at Punta Verde Club Hotel on the lake.

A tour to the scenic man-made lake Rapel, fed by the Tinguiririca and Cachapoal rivers. It is an expanding tourist zone offering accommodations and excellent facilities for watersports.

Take Route 78 out of Santiago to Melipilla; take there Exit 3 in Melipilla map. At km 96 is Las Arañas junction; take the paved road branching left, skirting the **Longovilo Satellite Tracking Station** at km 101 (no visitors allowed).

At km 115, from the top of the rise, you can see lake Rapel ahead. The road then crosses the

Alhué creek and the El Durazno bridge. At km 127 is

LAKE RAPEL the country's largest man–made lake with 40 km in length, it contains 700 million cubic meters of water and is fed by the Tinguiririca and Cachapoal rivers. The concrete wall holding back the water was concluded in 1968. In 1970 the lake reached its present size. Slowly at first, the lake started to wake up to its tourist potential. Campsites, restaurants and other tourist facilities have been set up, and roads are being built and paved. The lake has two arms, one along the Tinguiririca river and the other along the Cachapoal, forming inlets; farther west the lake is squeezed by hills and meanders for 20 km to the dam. Thus far there are roads only around the lake arms; a large portion of the northern and southern shore are inaccessible (see lake map). There are no bridges spanning the Cachapoal leading south to the Tinguiririca river and the

LAKE RAPEL

southern shore.

The excellent climate, added to scenic beauty and favorable conditions for watersports, have turned lake Rapel into an increasingly attractive tourist spot. During the daytime the main activity is enjoying the lake and its water; at night, it is sitting around bonfires or going to the entertainment spots around the lake. Most recreational activity is concentrated along the southern shore of the Cachapoal arm, where vegetation is somewhat thicker and where the campgrounds, hosterías and private clubs are located.

Puente El Durazno is a good spot for angling; trout and pejerrey fishing is good. Between here and El Manzano, at km 134, there are hosterías and campsites. El Manzano is a picturesque little place with mud-brick houses roofed with clay tiles, a square and a pretty church. From El Manzano a road branches right and runs for eight km close to the shore, sometimes approaching the waterfront. Along the road there are some fine summer

houses, private clubs, campsites, an hostería with a restaurant, cabins, a cafeteria, campsite and a boat ramp. A bit farther along is a signposted road branching right to the lakeshore, at

PUNTA VERDE an area on the northern banks of the peninsula, this area attracts the most visitors because it is sheltered from the wind and offers good campsites and hosterías. Among these the most outstanding is Punta Verde Club Hotel, which includes 30 apartments and all kinds of equipment for nautical sport. Also whithin this area you will find other campgrounds with excellent facilities and boat ramps. On the other arm of the lake is

Llallauquén an excellent, frequented spot for angling. It has a campsite; many landowners rent spots for camping on the lakeshore at convenient prices, but with no amenities.

On the western shore urban development is under way, accessible from the road branching to the dam.

EXCURSIONS

5

EXCURSIONS TO THE MAIPO VINEYARDS

Grapevine was introduced in Chile by the first Spanish conquerors, with the purpose of producing wine for the Eucharist in Catholic masses. Grapevines and small vineyards were always to be found at every farm in the Central Valley. However, it was not until 1851 that the first winery was set up, by Silvestre Ochagavía, who imported French vinestock and brought French wine expert M Benard to organize the operation. His lead was promptly followed by other wealthy farmers and mining entrepreneurs, who made large investments in agriculture. Vineyards were planted throughout the central zone and christened after the owner's name: Errázuriz at Panquehue (Aconcagua Valley), Urmeneta at Limache, Valdés at Cunaco (Tinguiririca Valley). Other preferred a female saint's name, as they thought wine-making was a feminine art due to the delicacy of its production: such is the case of Viña Santa Carolina, taken from the name of the vineyard's founder's wife, Carolina Iñíguez. The largest and most famous vineyards were planted at the Pirque Plains and Maipo, areas which at that time were but starting to be incorporated into productive uses with the construction of a vast irrigation canal network (see description under Section D).

Good Chilean export wines have Valle de Maipo printed on the label, a symbol of the best provenance. Enologists attribute the special quality of these wines to the great amount of lime contained in the Maipo river water, which lends the wine a rich color, heavy consistency and an unmistakable fumée taste. However, these lands do not give high volumetric yields, prompting the large wineries to plant vineyards in other regions, setting aside the Maipo vinestock for their choicest wines.

These vineyards and wineries make for very interesting excursions. Some permit visitors to see their wine vaults, with huge oak casks where the wine matures in darkness. In some cases, their parks and manor houses can also be visited.

Vintage takes place in March, a period of beehive activity of grape harvesting and hauling and pressing, with the sweet smell permeating everything. The vineyards described below (they have salesrooms in case you want to try their products)

are listed by date of foundation:

Viña Ochagavía established in 1851 by Silvestre Ochagavía at his farm located next to the southbound Pan-American highway, at the present-day San Miguel commune of Santiago. The original vineyards and wine vaults are gone; only the manor houses remain, owned by the Municipality.

Viña Subercaseaux founded in 1856 by Ramón Subercaseaux at Pirque, who irrigated the plain and planted vinestock brought from France. When he died, in 1859, the vineyard was divided among his sons and daughters. Emiliana, the wife of Melchor Concha y Toro, contributed with her share of the inheritance to establish the Concha y Toro winery.

Viña Cousiño Macul established in 1871 by Luis Cousiño on the slopes of Macul, it was irrigated by the San Carlos canal. Cousiño was the heir and owner of the Lota coal mine and the period's most powerful businessman. He imported French vinestock and brought French builders, cask makers, vault managers and enologists to set up his winery.

The vineyard's park is among Chile's finest, and has been featured in European publications. It was designed by the renowned French landscape architect Guillaume Renner and remodelled in 1928 by Brydon, and Englishman. Its layout is irregular, as it is centered around a small lake and not the main residence. Waterfowl swim in it and beautiful trees surround it, the different species combined with remarkable harmony. It has been carefully tended for over a century, letting the trees grow without being maimed by human intervention. Thus, old trees still have their first branches, now thick and heavy and spreading out close to the ground, something rather unusual in gardening: high-canopy trees, such as piceas, have their lower branches here creeping on the floor; black oak (Quercux ilex) and Magnolio grandiflora attain unusually large crown diameters; cedars, in three varieties, soar majestically; isolated and monumental blue spruce droop their branches among over a hundred further species. The park is not open to the public; it can only be seen from the road. To see it, take Av Quilín (see Santiago map), which skirts the vineyard's edge; it was the old road to the fundo. The trees end at the great wrought iron gate, sporting the family blazon; it is identical with the one at the Cousiño palace at Dieciocho street in Santiago; both were brought from France in 1876. Taking the road branching right you will skirt the park's perimeter until you reach the bodegas –the wine vaults– and the salesroom (Mon–Fri 08:30–12:00 h & 14:00–17:00 h; Tour by the vine cellar 11:00 h).

Viña Santa Carolina it was founded in 1875 by Julio Pereira in lands of Ñuñoa irrigated by the San Carlos canal. The vineyard was named after the patronymic saint of his wife Carolina Iñíguez. True to the times, he brought French experts to help him set up the winery. The farm had a beautiful residence from the colonial times and farming buildings where the wine vaults were set up, now boasting National Monument status. The vineyard was located behind the present–day National Stadium. The spread of the city forced the owners to move the vineyard to the areas of Molina and San Fernando. The **casa patronal** and the **bodegas** are open to the public, as well as the salesroom, Rodrigo de Araya 1431, behind the National Stadium. The salesroom is open Sat from 09:00 h to 13:00 h, and the house and wine vaults can be visited in groups or tours prior arrangement at phone 238 2855, Santiago.

Viña Santa Rita founded in 1880 by Domingo Fernández Concha at his farm at Alto Jahuel, on the slopes of the hills closing the valley towards Paine, it has excellent soils basking in sunlight from the west. The farm has been in production since colonial times and it is located next to the old southbound road from Puente Alto. Bernardo O'Higgins rested here after the disaster of Rancagua and its vaults hid Manuel Rodríguez after one of his raids. Next to the vineyard fine residences and a church and 22–ha park –designed by Renner– were built in 1883. The complex enjoys the National Monument status but does not allow visitors.

Viña Concha y Toro it was established in 1883 by Melchor Concha y Toro on the Pirque grapevine plantations inherited by his wife, Emiliana Subercaseaux. It was improved with the introduction of imported vinestock and the construction of large vaults. The park and the magnificent country mansion also date from that period; the mansion is depicted in the labels of their Santa Emiliana brand. Concha y Toro is now Chile's largest wine producer, with more than ten large vineyards in the area of Maipo, Rancagua, and San Fernando, including the 305–ha Peumo vineyard, Chile's largest one–piece grapevine plantation (see Section F). At Pirque are the original **vineyard and wine vaults**, producing the choicest wines.

Access is on the road to Puente Alto beyond the Maipo river (see Section D). Salesroom and guided tours through the vaults and the vineyard, Mon–Sat 10:00–13:00 h & 15:00–18:00 h. For large groups, make prior arrangements at phone 850 1407.

Viña Undurraga it was founded in 1885 by Francisco Ramón Undurraga in his property of Santa Ana de Talagante. He planted French and German vinestock –the latter brought from the Rhine area–, hiring prestigious French enologists for the task. He then erected the wine vaults and, true to the times, had a magnificent mansion built, complete with park. The mansion has received illustrious visitors, such as the monarchs of Belgium and Norway, and the Duke of Windsor, among others. At the original site, wine is still being produced and bottled in the distinctive Undurraga bottles.

Located at km 34 of the old road to Melipilla, the **house, wine vaults and park** are open to visitors. And, of course, also the salesroom, Mon–Fri 09:30–12:00 & 14:00–16:00 h. For large groups, arrangements at phone 817 2308.

Viña Cánepa when in 1927 José Cánepa bought farmland in Chile's best wine producing zones, he could not have foreseen the huge success of his company nor its enormous potential. The vineyards, located at the choicest spots of the Maipo Valley, Curicó and Lontué, are ideal for French vinestock (Cabernet–Sauvignon, Sauvignon Blanc, Chardonnay), but also for German ones such as Riesling–Rheinland, and others. It runs South America's most modern winery at Camino Lo Sierra 1500, Maipú (Mon–Fri 10:00–13:00 h & 14:00–18:00 h).

RODEO EXCURSIONS

Origins rodeos (not to be mistaken with the U.S. variety) were born in the colonial days when Chile was a prime cattle–producing country. The haciendas were then large tracts of land with no sort of boundary separating one from the other. This made it possible for herds of up to 30,000 head of cattle to form, forcing the hacienda owners to get together once a year to sort out their animals. The event for this was called a rodeo –literally, a rounding up–, which enabled them to identify and brand their cattle. By the middle of last century the system had evolved; now there was a large stone corral to gather the animals, at whose exit a tight row of mounted cowboys waited for the animals to emerge. When they identified an animal belonging to their farm, they would «escort» it –one cowboy at each side– in a rapid sprint to their respective corrals. This pair of riders, known as **collera**, was to bring the animal to the pen in the shortest time possible and return for the next one. This was accomplished by a cowboy pushing the animal from behind with his horse, while his mate steered it along a fence. This last stage was the one that gave rise to the traditional sport of Chile's countryside.

In 1860 the present «arena» was designed, shaped like a half–circle and known as **medialuna**, ie, crescent. In 1947 a set of rules was officially approved for rodeo, establishing a crescent diameter of between 19 and 25 m, with a 10–m stretch for the **atajadas**, the segment where the animal's gallop must be braked. The **apiñadero** –the corral– must be adjoined to the crescent, and the animals must come one by one through the gate known as **toril.**

The ceremony starts when the young animal emerges and is received by the collera, turning two full rounds in the apiñadero. The gate is then thrown open and animal and riders gallop into the crescent. While one rider pushes the animal from behind, the other one takes position to brake its run, but touching it with the breast of his mount all the way to the braking point; there, he must ram the animal against the wall to stop it, to start the run in the opposite direction. The **puntaje de atajada**, ie the score obtained in this manoeuver, varies according to where he rammed the animal to stop it: head and neck, zero points; shoulders, 2 points; belly, 3 points. The highest score, 4 points, is when the animal is stopped by ramming its hind quarters. There are also difficult–to–avoid negative points.

The show is entertaining and has the full flavor of Chilean countryside traditions, with typical huaso outfits (the apparel has its own set of rules) and thoroughbreds of domestic horse races, all to the tune of tonadas and cuecas, traditional Chil-

5

ean music. To round it up, participants flock after the competition to the adjacent ramada, a make-shift country-style restaurant, to gulp down some chicha –cider– and eat empanadas. The Zone covered by this chapter has a sizable number of medialunas, which usually hold one contest per year; even the smallest villages boast one medialuna. The most famous are that at Rancagua, where the **Champion de Chile** is held in March; Los Andes, where lately the **Champion Chico** has been held.; and San Vicente de Tagua Tagua. The season goes from early September until late May.

The Federación de Rodeos, phone 384639 in Santiago, provides information on the rodeos scheduled for the following fortnight, so that you can make your excursion to Santiago's environs coincide with a rodeo.

EXCURSIONS ON HORSEBACK

Chile is, by European standards, a fairly large country with a small population. Thus, even in this densely–populated district around Santiago, there are many areas that are still wild, where no roads have been built and where adventure can still be lived. Excursions on horse are the best way to get away from the beaten track and into these pris-tine areas, eating around a campfire and camp-ing under the stars.

The excursions –some can be made in one day– go into the mountain valleys, through high–altitude meadows at the foot of tall mountains, to remote lakes swarming with wild geese, or volcanoes capped by eternal snow, or a mighty glacier. These areas are buried under a thick shroud of snow in winter, and the meadows in summer are clad with grass and some scrub, ringed by vast fields of gray–brown stones littering the plains, the slopes and even the hill summits. These sharp-edged slabs, known as lajas, are produced by water seeping into rock fissures in summer and then expanding in winter under subzero tempera-tures, blowing the rocks to pieces. This process is permanently under way, degrading the ground. Only in the summits, where the ice never melts, masses of solid rock can be seen. Wildlife here includes condors, soaring far up above, other carrion birds and smaller birds, and large gree-yellowish lizards soaking up sunshine on slabs of rock, among other fauna. The mountain scenery is grand, silent, bathed in crisp, crystal–clear air.

The season goes from December through March. Excursions are usually from one day or one week-end to an entire week long.

Groups are open tours accepting from 6 to 14 persons.

Gear parka or windbreaker, warm pants, hiking boots, sunglasses, hat, gloves and sunscreen cream.

The service includes horses, guides and food, and sleeping bags and other camping gear for longer excursions.

Your contact Santiago García, ☎ 218 2216, who organizes excursions departing from Villa Paulina, Cajón del Maipo, and Juncal on the Colorado river. The Astorga family at Casacada de las Ani-mas, in San Alfonso, Cajón del Maipo, ☎ 35 1871, the same itinerary is run by Marcos A Liberona, in Valparaiso ☎ 21 3050, starting out from Juncal on the Aconcagua river.

Departures from Baños Colina (Cajón del Maipo)

To Lake El Diamante ★★★ for one week. The trail heads into the mountains, with an overnight stop before reaching Nieves Negras. On the following day you traverse **Nieves Negras**, at 2,400 m altitude,

and start to descend skirting the Salinilla river; the overnight stop is at scenic meadows, after having ridden a long stretch along a **glacier.** On the following day you continue descending along-side the Torrecillas river, Colorado river, El Papal, to reach the great **Lake Diamante**, one of the largest lakes deep in the Cordillera and a para-dise for anglers. The next two days are spent making fishing excursions, with the camp pitched at the foot of the **Maipo volcano**, which can be climbed. The return route follows the Maipo pass, passing the headwaters of the Maipo river, and staying at Río Blanco over-night, after visiting splendid high-temperature **thermal springs**. The last day is a scenic descent to Los Quellehues.

Paso del Azufre ★★ one day. The trail heads into the area around the San José volcano, wading beautiful brooks.

To the Headwaters of the Carreño Creek ★★★ two days. An excursion to two small lakes called Yesillo, which have ice floes drifting on their sur-face. The colors, when the sun shines, are gor-geous.

To the Headwaters of the Carreñito Creek ★★ one day. The excursion reaches the foot of the great Mount Corona, with a beautiful small lake.

To Quebrada de La Engorda ★★ two days. The trail heads into a ravine, with superb mountain scenery.

Departures from Villa Paulina (on the road to Farellones)

To Mount La Paloma ★★★ three days. An excur-sion into the upper Mapocho basin. The first day you ride to **Piedra Carvajal**, in a sheltered grassy valley at 3,200 m altitude and peppered with small **lakes**. The second day you continue to the foot of the **La Paloma** and **El Altar** glaciers, and eat lunch at a deserted mining camp after exploring the area. On the last day, after a hearty breakfast, you return through the **Yerba Loca valley** to Villa Paulina.

To Cerro El Plomo ★★★ three days. A thrilling, varied excursion visiting thermal springs, glaciers, lakes, climbing the Tupungato volcano, camping at the foot of Mount Chimbote, etc.

Departures from Estación Juncal (on the road to Portillo)

To Juncal River ★★★ three days. The trail heads upstream along the Juncal river to the Nacimiento area, where you camp with an extraordinary view to **Mount Juncal**, the enormous **Mount Aconcagua** and the **Los Leones peaks**. On the second day you con-tinue to the **Juncal glacier**, near whose fissured walls you will eat lunch before returning to camp. On the third day you continue to Morro Verde, a place with many glacier tongues, to return in the after-noon to the starting point.

To Tres Lagunas ★★ two days, visiting small mountain lakes.
To Cerro La Cumbre ★★ five days.
To Laguna del Toro ★★ four days.
To to Foot of Mount Aconcagua ★★★ eight days.

RIVER RAFTING

The many rivers in this zone are mostly suitable only for experts: Aconcagua, Mapocho, Maipo, and Cachapoal. They are all very beautiful rising from their headwaters in the mountains up to the Pan-American highway, but very swift, rocky and squeezed into narrow canyons. Beyond the Pan-American highway towards the coast the rivers are gentler, but they lack the thrill: you have to row like mad because the current barely carries you, and scenically they are a write–off.

The best you can do is get in touch with the experts, **Expediciones Altué**, at phones 232 1103 & 233 6675 of Santiago, to raft down the most scenic portion of the Maipo river. The season goes from October through March, using rafts accommodating from 5 to 7 people. Come down on 4 rafts on different schedules. Requirements: you must be at least 12 years old and able to swim. The excursion includes transportation to the departure point, rafting down the river, and lunch at some scenic spot outdoors. The other experts are the Astorgas of San Alfonso (phone 251 7506), one of whose members, Ricardo, is undoubtedly one of the best–known modern explorers of Chile.

Descent of the Maipo River the river is swift and carries a lot of water, with some lengthy rapids and many obstacles. It is surely not suitable for conventional watercraft, but it poses no difficulty for specialized ones. The meeting point is the **Los Héroes** campsite, located one km before you reach San José de Maipo (see Section C); you can leave the car there. The excursion leader, together with giving you some basic instructions, distributes the necessary gear. Then a jeep brings the group to the starting point, **Melocotón**. At the beginning the descent is on white, placid waters which soon give way to the more rapid sort. Half way down, the rafters make a landing on a solitary beach ringed by native vegetation, to have some refreshments and relax for a while. The journey continues now through an area of major rapids through the most scenic part of the entire stretch, until you eventually reach the placid waters on the campsite, where you disembark for a hearty Chilean–style lunch.

NB this is the same organization that offers the rafting expeditions described in Zone 9 and Zone 10.

SKI EXCURSIONS

The segment of the Cordillera of the Andes around Santiago has five winter sports centers, all with good access roads, namely: Portillo, up from the Aconcagua Valley; Farellones–Colorado, La Parva, and Valle Nevado, east of Santiago; and Lagunillas, up from the Cajón del Maipo. Some are internationally renowned, attracting many visitors from the Northern Hemisphere (when it is high summer in their home countries) and Argentina and Brazil. The ski season goes from June –depending on the first snowfalls– through September and even October in the higher–altitude centers.

The resorts are quite crowded in season, particularly on weekends. Some recommendations:
• When driving to these resorts in June and July, bear in mind that the roads are covered by ice and snow: snow chains are mandatory; they can be rented next to the police controls before starting the ascent.
• Start early in the morning, as up–going traffic is permitted only until 1300h. Return traffic from 14:00 h or 15:00 h (check!).
• Park the vehicle in departure position. Take appropriate clothing, sun glasses, and sun–blocking cream.
• Phone 220 9501, Santiago, provides information on traffic schedules, and on road and snow conditions for Farellones and Colorado.

LAGUNILLAS located 67 km from Santiago in the Cajón del Maipo. Beyond San José de Maipo, a 16–km road branches left to the ski resort. The police control at San José de Maipo will demand snow chains if conditions require it. Lagunillas is an old winter center, scenic and now equipped with modern lifts. There are several shelters and installations of international clubs.

Facilities restaurant, refreshments, ski rental and ski school.

Slopes there are three runs: La Lola, with a 1–km tow lift, 27° gradient and 270 m drop. Pancho, tow–lift, 350 m, 28° gradient, 100 m drop in altitude. Novicios, tow–lift, 350 m, 17° gradient, 160 m drop.

Portillo

PORTILLO is located 152 km from Santiago on the highway to Los Andes and Mendoza. In winter traffic is controlled by the police at Los Andes and Río Blanco; snow chains will be demanded if road conditions require them. This is one of South America's most renowned ski resorts, perched at 2,855 m altitude in a highly scenic setting around Laguna del Inca. It has excellent slopes, ranging from easy to challenging. Its most famous run is **Jack's Rock**, where the world speed record was broken. Information at phone 231 3411, Santiago.
Facilities Hotel Portillo, with over 400 beds, heated outdoor swimming pool, solarium, disco, sauna, movie theater and several restaurants, all for the exclusive use of its guests. For daytime visitors, a self–service restaurant and a ski rental shop.
Slopes well–tended, interconnected by a network of 12 lifts, including two chairlifts seating two abreast, with a total length of 5,281 m. Maximum altitude: 3,350 m above sea level.

5

SERVICIES AVILABLE

(H) Hotel

Ski School

Cafeteria

Restaurant

Ski Patrol

Emergency Telephone

Bathrooms

Rental Equipment

(T) Tickets

(E) Car Park

Skating

SKI RUNS
Very Difficult
Difficult
Moderate
Easy

SKI LIFTS

Doble Chairlift

Quadruple Chairlift

Draglift

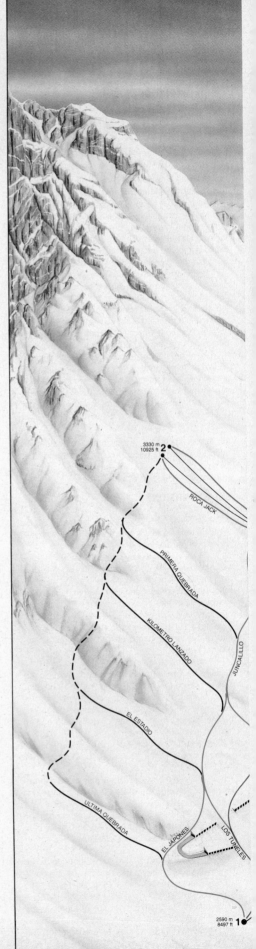

3330 m
10925 ft **2**

ROCA JACK

PRIMERA QUEBRADA

KILOMETRO LANZADO

JUNCALILLO

EL ESTADIO

ULTIMA QUEBRADA

EL JAPONES

LOS TUNELES

2590 m
8497 ft **1**

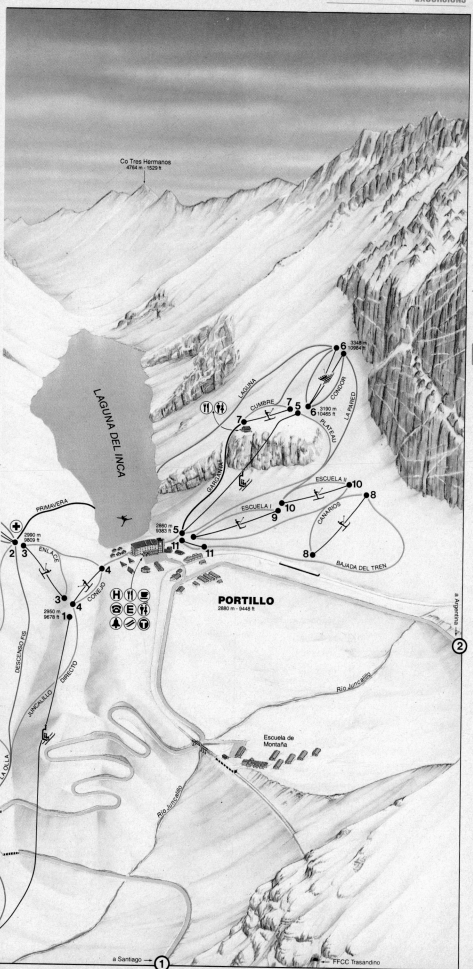

Co Tres Hermanos
4764 m - 1529 ft

LAGUNA DEL INCA

LAGUNA

CUMBRE

6   3348 m
     10984 ft

CONDOR

LA PARED

6   3190 m
     10465 ft

PLATEAU

GARGANTA

ESCUELA II

ESCUELA I

CANARIOS

8

BAJADA DEL TREN

PRIMAVERA

2990 m
9809 ft

ENLACE

CONEJO

2860 m
9383 ft

PORTILLO
2880 m - 9448 ft

a Argentina

2950 m
9678 ft

DESCENSO FIS

JUNCALILLO

DIRECTO

LA OLLA

Río Juncalillo

Escuela de
Montaña

Río Juncalillo

a Santiago — 1

FFCC Trasandino

FARELLONES - COLORADO is made up of two villages, the highest one at 2,500 m altitude, offering good accommodations and excellent slopes. Located 50 km from downtown Santiago upwards of the Mapocho river gorge. Winter traffic is controlled by the police at El Arrayán; if chains are requested, you can rent them from the people offering them next to the control. Mountain–bound traffic until 13:00 h, Santiago–bound traffic from 14:00 h or 15:00 h (check to make sure).

Facilities accommodations, restaurant, café, ski rental, ski repair shop. Group and individual ski lessons. Season from June to September/October. Information at phone 220 9501, Santiago.

Slopes well–kept runs, 16 lifts (T–bar, Poma and four chairlifts seating three and four abreast), with a total length of 15,650 m. Maximum altitude 3,333 m above sea level.

5

SERVICIES AVILABLE

(H) Hotel

(♠) Ski School

(¶¶) Restaurant

(✚) Ski Patrol

(☎) Emergency Telephone

(††) Bathrooms

(∅) Rental Equipment

(T) Tickets

(E) Car Park

SKI RUNS

▬ Very Difficult

▬ Difficult

▬ Moderate

▬ Easy

SKI LIFTS

Double Chairlift

Triple Chairlift

Draglift

Double Draglift

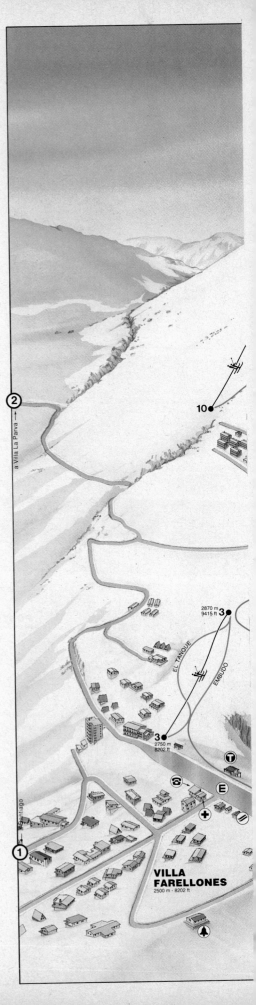

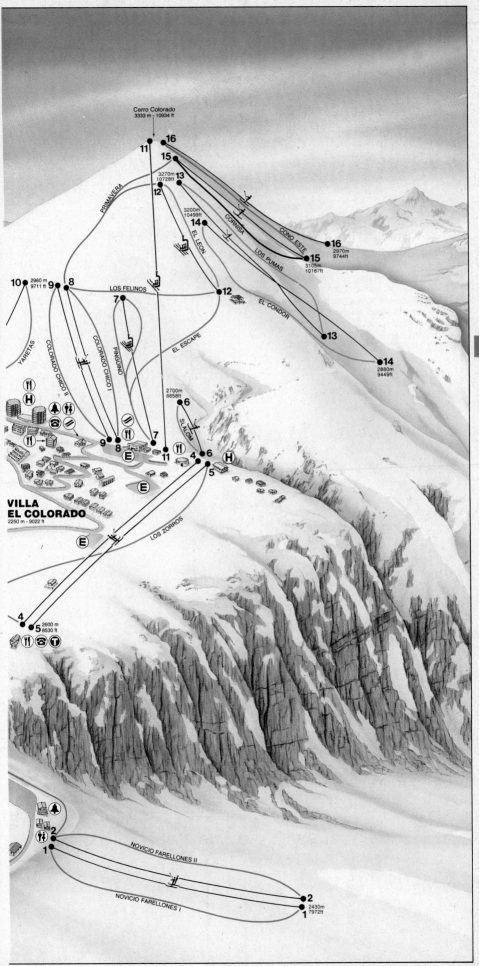

Cerro Colorado
3333 m · 10934 ft

11 16

15

3270m
10728ft 13

12

3200m
10499ft 14

CORNISA

CONO ESTE

16
2970m
9744ft

EL LEON

LOS PUMAS

15
3105m
10187ft

10 2960 m
9711 ft 9 8

LOS FELINOS

12

EL CONDOR

7

13

YARETAS

COLORADO CHICO II

COLORADO CHICO I

PINGUINO

EL ESCAPE

14
2880m
9449ft

2700m
8858ft 6

SLALOM

9 8

7

11

4 6

H

E

5

E

LOS ZORROS

E

4 5 2600 m
8530 ft

VILLA
EL COLORADO
2250 m · 9022 ft

2

1

NOVICIO FARELLONES II

NOVICIO FARELLONES I

2

1 2430m
7972ft

5

La Parva

LA PARVA located at 2,816 m altitude, the village has a good view over the Santiago valley –Santiago's smog permitting.
Facilities Hotel, apartments for rent (phone 231 3411, Santiago), restaurant with a big terrace, food shops, ski rental, and ski patrol school.
Slopes well–kept runs, 12 modern lifts, including two chairlifts seating four abreast, with a total distance of 9,673 m. Maximum altitude 3,630 m.

5

SERVICIES AVILABLE

(H) Hotel

(🔔) Ski School

(🍽) Restaurant

(⛑) Heliski

(✚) Ski Patrol

(☎) Emergency Telephone

(🚻) Bathrooms

(⊘) Rental Equipment

(T) Tickets

(E) Car Park

SKI RUNS
— Very Difficult
— Difficult
— Moderate
— Easy

SKI LIFTS

Double Chairlift

Triple Chairlift

Quadruple Chairlift

Draglift

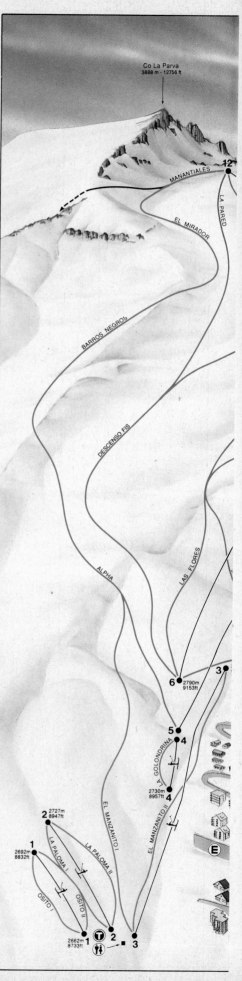

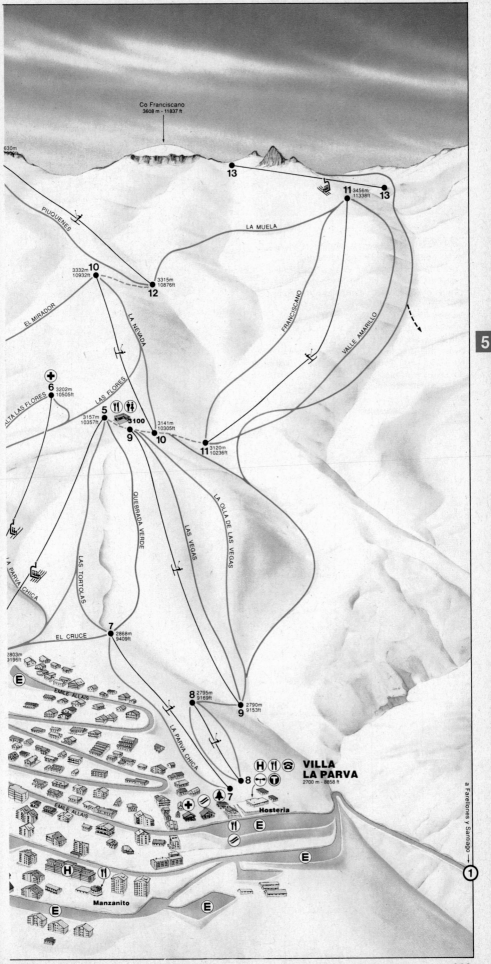

Co Franciscano
3608 m - 11837 ft

5

Valle Nevado

VALLE NEVADO is the most modern of the ski resorts, opened in 1988 and still expanding; it is
Chile's largest. Its 14-km access road branches
east off Curve 40, on the lower reaches of the
village of Farellones. Information at phone 231
3414/5/6, Santiago.

Facilities lLuxurious hotels (pricey), with 800 beds
(and growing); apartments, ski rental, ski school,
children's skiing area.

Slopes well–prepared runs. In the first stage, eight
lifts –including two chairlifts seating 3 and 4
abreast– have been set up, with a total length of
7,000 m and maximum altitude 3,670 m above
sea level.

5

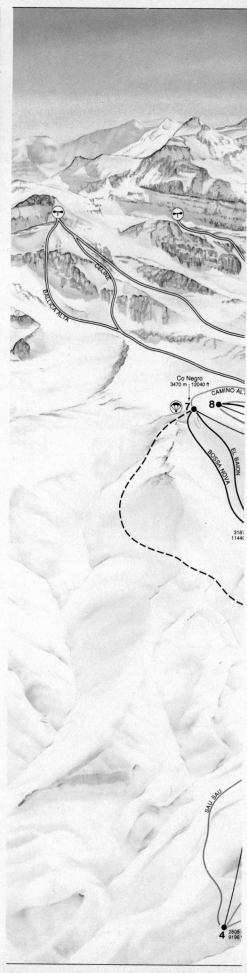

SERVICIES AVILABLE

(H) Hotel

(♠) Ski School

(☕) Cafeteria

(🍴) Restaurant

(🚁) Heliski

(🪂) Parapente

(✚) Ski Patrol

(☎) Emergency Telephone

(🚻) Bathrooms

(⊘) Rental Equipment

(T) Tickets

(E) Car Park

SKI RUNS

▬▬▬ Very Difficult

▬▬▬ Difficult

▬▬▬ Moderate

▬▬▬ Easy

▬▬▬ Free Skiing

SKI LIFTS

Chairlift

Quadruple Chairlift

Draglift

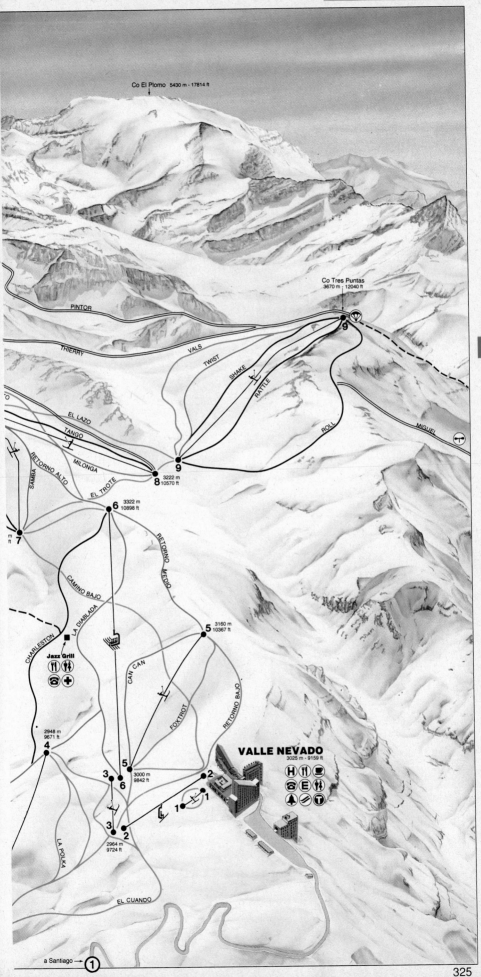

Co El Plomo 5430 m - 17814 ft

Co Tres Puntas
3670 m - 12040 ft

9

PINTOR

THIERRY

VALS

TWIST

SHAKE

RATTLE

ROLL

MIGUEL

EL LAZO

TANGO

MILONGA

9

8 3222 m
10570 ft

SAMBA

RETORNO ALTO

EL TROTE

6 3322 m
10898 ft

7

RETORNO MEDIO

CAMINO BAJO

LA DIABLADA

CHARLESTON

Jazz Grill

5 3160 m
10367 ft

CAN CAN

FOXTROT

RETORNO BAJO

2948 m
9671 ft

4

3 3000 m
9842 ft
6

5

2

1

1

VALLE NEVADO
3025 m - 9159 ft

3

2

2964 m
9724 ft

LA POLKA

EL CUANDO

a Santiago → 1

5

Zone 6
CENTRAL COASTAL STRIP

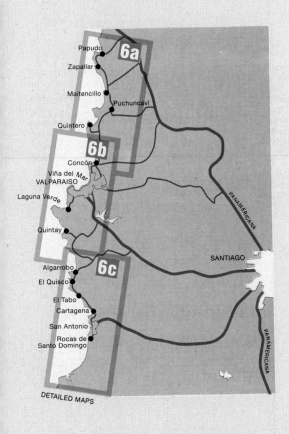

Detailed maps

6a
- Papudo
- Zapallar
- Maitencillo
- Puchuncaví
- Quintero

6b
- Concón
- Viña del Mar
- VALPARAISO
- Laguna Verde
- Quintay

6c
- Algarrobo
- El Quisco
- El Tabo
- Cartagena
- San Antonio
- Rocas de Santo Domingo

PANAMERICANA

SANTIAGO

PANAMERICANA

DETAILED MAPS

- Arica
- Iquique
- Antofagasta
- Copiapó
- Easter Island
- La Serena
- Valparaíso
- SANTIAGO
- Is R Crusoe
- Talca
- Concepción
- Temuco
- Valdivia
- Osorno
- Pto Montt
- Castro
- Chaitén
- Coihaique
- Cochrane
- Puerto Natales
- Punta Arenas
- Puerto Williams
- Is Diego Ramirez

6

90° 60° 53°

CHILEAN
ANTARCTIC
TERRITORY

OVERVIEW

This Zone comprises the coastal area between the Papudo bay to the North and the Santo Domingo seaside resort to the South. It lies entirely within Region V, whose administrative capital is Valparaíso.

Its gentle climate and the proximity of Santiago and its surrounding urban centers, which together account for 55% of the country's population, have made of this Chile's prime summer playground, its seaside resorts by far the most frequented. Viña del Mar is the tourist capital, with over 450,000 visitors during the summer season. The remaining 24 resorts receive nearly one million visitors in season.

We have divided the Central Coastal Strip into the following sections;

Section 1 Zapallar including Papudo and Cachagua.

Section 2 Maitencillo with the resorts of Marbella, Horcón, Ventanas and Quintero.

Section 3 Valparaíso and Viña del mar the heart of the Central Coastal Strip, including Concón, Reñaca, Laguna Verde and Quintay.

Section 4 Algarrobo including El Quisco, El Tabo, Las Cruces, and Isla Negra.

Section 5 San Antonio and the popular neighboring resorts, including Cartagena.

Section 6 Santo Domingo including excursions along the coastal area up to the Rapel river.

REGIONAL DISTANCES

Algarrobo																
157	Cachagua															
30	187	Cartagena														
99	51	129	Concón													
5	162	25	104	El Quisco												
14	171	16	113	8	El Tabo											
127	30	157	28	132	141	Horcón										
188	46	218	89	193	202	57	La Ligua									
21	178	8	120	15	7	148	209	Las Cruces								
143	14	173	37	148	157	16	42	164	Maitencillo							
171	14	201	65	176	185	44	23	192	28	Papudo						
122	42	152	23	127	136	16	70	120	31	56	Quintero					
41	198	11	140	35	27	168	229	19	184	212	163	Rocas de Santo Domingo				
37	194	7	136	31	23	164	225	15	180	208	159	4	San Antonio			
76	81	106	23	81	90	51	112	97	60	98	46	117	113	Valparaíso		
77	73	107	15	82	91	43	104	98	52	80	38	118	114	8	Viña del Mar	
161	7	191	55	166	175	34	33	182	18	10	46	202	198	88	80	Zapallar

6

Zone 6
CENTRAL COASTAL STRIP

DIVISION BY SECTIONS

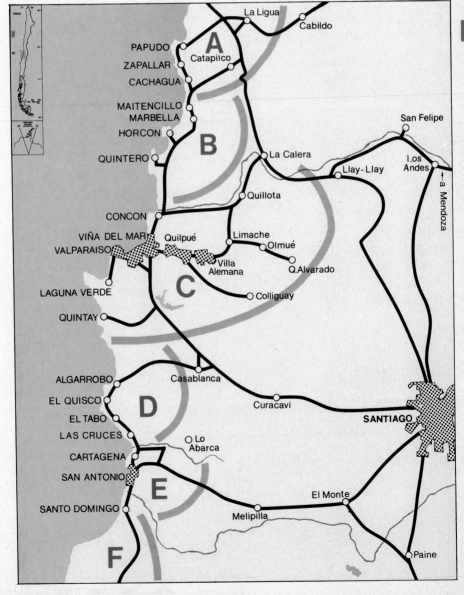

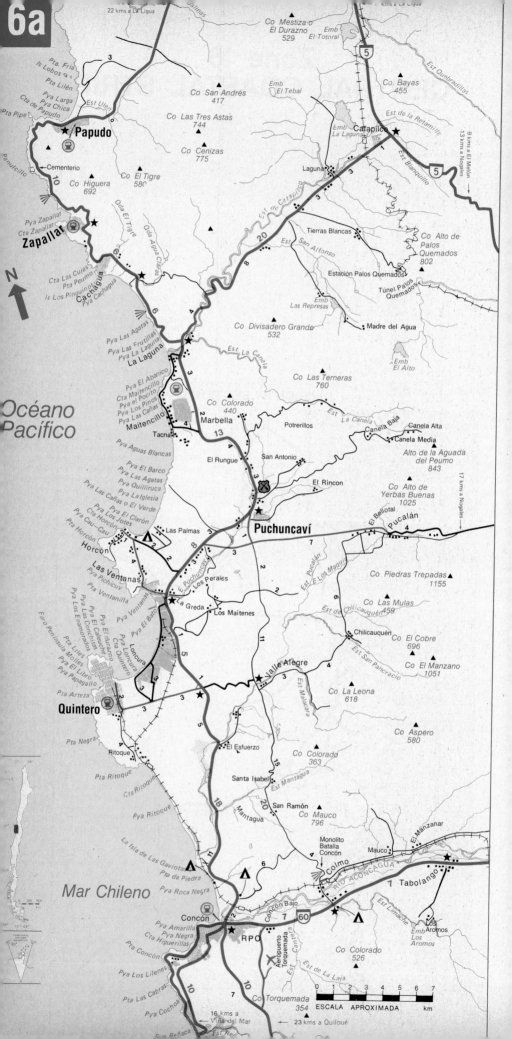

6a

22 kms a La Ligua

Co Mestiza o
El Durazno
529

Emb
El Totoral

5

Pta. Fría
Is Lobos
Pta Lilén
Pya Larga
Pta Chica
Cta de Papudo
Pta Pipe

3

Est Ulen

Co San Andrés
417

Co Las Tres Astas
744

Emb
El Tebal

9 kms a El Melón
113 kms a Nogales

Co Bayas
455

★ **Papudo**

Catapilco ★

Est de la Retamilla

Cementerio

Co Cenizas
775

Co Higuera
692

Co El Tigre
580

Laguna

3

Est Blanquillo

5

Pya Zapallar
Cta Zapallar
Zapallar

20

Tierras Blancas

Co Alto de
Palos
Quemados
802

Cta Las Cujas
Pta Peumo
Is Los Pinguinos
Cachagua
Pya Cachagua

6

8

Est San Alfonso

Estación Palos Quemados

Túnel Palos
Quemados

Pya Las Agatas
Pya Las Frutillas
Pya La Laguna
La Laguna

3

Co Divisadero Grande
532

Emb
Las Represas

Madre del Agua

Pya El Abanico
Cta Maitencillo
Pya el Pocito
Pya Los Pinos
Pya Las Cañas
Maitencillo

3

4

Co Colorado
440

Marbella

13

Potrerillos

Est La Canela

Co Las Terneras
760

Emb
El Alto

Tacna

4

Canela Baja

Canela Alta
Canela Media

**Océano
Pacífico**

Pya Aguas Blancas
Pya El Barco
Pya Las Agatas
Pya Quilliruca
Pya La Iglesia
Pya Las Cañas o El Verde
Pya Los Jotes
Cta Horcón
Pya Cau–Cau
Pta Horcón
Horcón

El Rungue

San Antonio

3

El Rincon

Alto de la Aguada
del Peumo
843

Co Alto de
Yerbas Buenas
1025

17 kms a Nogales

Las Palmas

8

El Bellotal

Puchuncaví

Pucalán
Pucalán

4

Las Ventanas
Pta Pichicuy
Pya Ventanilla

E Puchuncaví

2

3

Los Perales

La Greda
Los Maitenes

Co Piedras Trepadas
1155

Est E Los Maquis

Est Pucalán

6

Est Chilicauquén

Chilicauquén

Co Las Mulas
159

Pya El Calauche
Cta Quintero
Pya El Durazno
Pya Las Conchitas
Faro Península Molles
Pya El Libro
Pya Papagallo
Pta Arteza

Loncura

Pya Ventanas
Pya El Bato

1
5
1

11

Valle Alegre

3

Est Malacara

Co El Cobre
696

Est San Pancracio

Co El Manzano
1051

Co La Leona
618

Quintero

3

El Esfuerzo

Co Colorado
363

Co Aspero
580

Pta Negra

Ritoque

5

15

Santa Isabel

Est Mantagua

San Ramón

Co Mauco
796

El Manzanar

Pta Ritoque
Cta Ritoque
Pya Ritoque

18

20

Mantagua

Mauco

★

Monolito
Batalla
Concón

La Isla de Las Gaviotas
Pta de Piedra
Pya Roca Negra

11

6

Colmo

RÍO ACONCAGUA

1

Tabolango

Est Limache

Mar Chileno

Concón

2

Concón Bajo

7

60

Los
Aromos
Emb
Los
Aromos

RPO

Pya Amarilla
Pya Negra
Cta Higuerillas
Pta Concón

Aeropuerto
Torquemada

Est Cantera

Co Colorado
526

Pya Los Lilenes
Pta Las Cabras
Pya Cochoa

10

10

7

Co Torquemada
354

Est de La Laja

354   **ESCALA   APROXIMADA**   km

16 kms a
Viña del Mar

23 kms a Quilpué

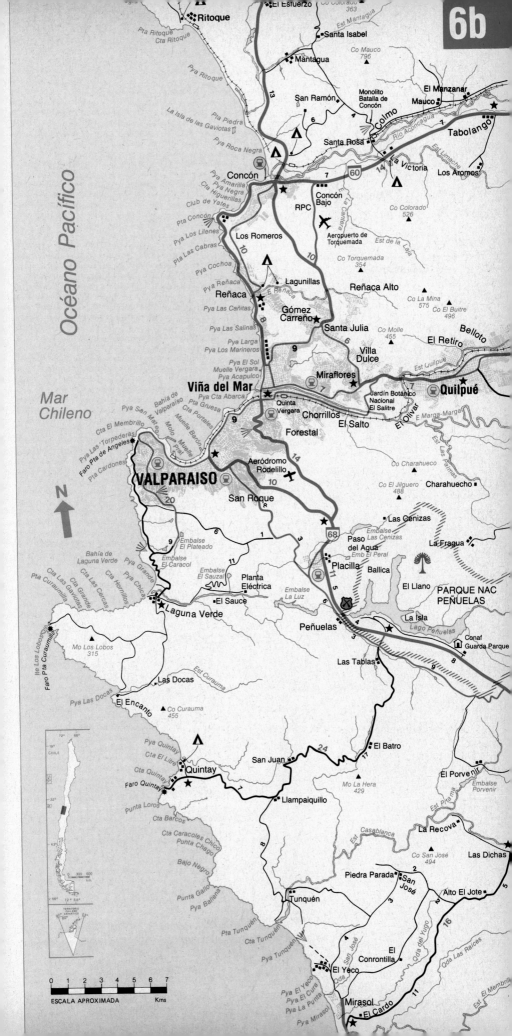

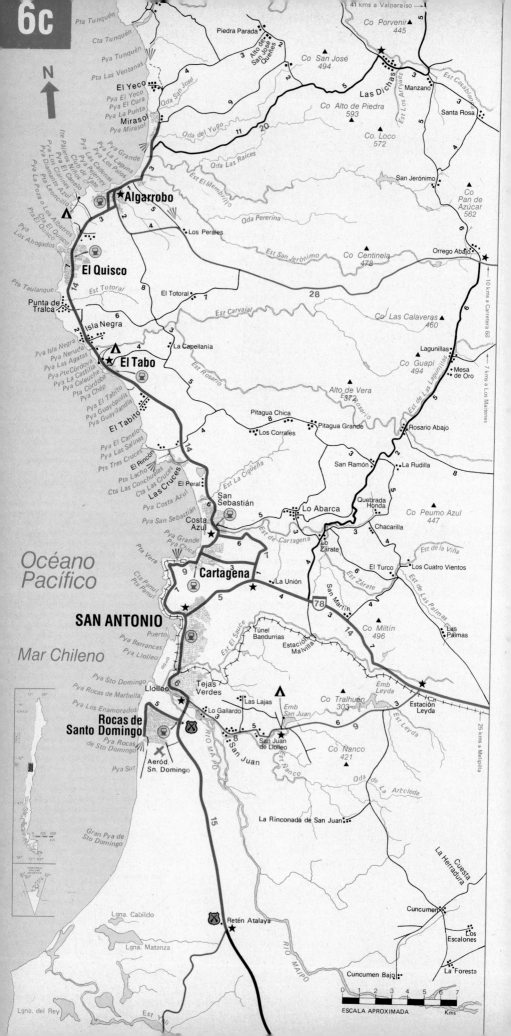

THE LAND, ITS HISTORY, ITS PEOPLE

DESCRIPTION this Zone contains Chile's leading port complex, made up of the general cargo terminals of Valparaíso and San Antonio, the crude oil and bulk mineral ore terminals at Quintero, and the clean–fuels terminal at Las Salinas, in Viña del Mar. Combined, they move the largest tonnage in the country and are major points of entry and shipping for agricultural, industrial, mining and other products to and from Santiago and the surrounding region.

Here is also a significant concentration of specialized industries, such as Chile's largest copper refinery on the shore of the Quintero Bay, the largest oil refinery at Concón, and a number of chemicals industries at Viña del Mar. Valparaíso, in addition, is the country's main naval port, seat of the First Naval Zone, of the Naval Academy and the remaining Special Schools of the Navy.

This area's gentle climate and the proximity of Santiago and surrounding urban centers, which together account for 55% of the country's population, have turned the area's seaside resorts into the most frequented in Chile. Viña del Mar is the foremost summer center, an old resort transformed now into Chile's tourist capital. Together with the remaining 24 resorts along this coastline, this is the country's undisputed number one summer playground.

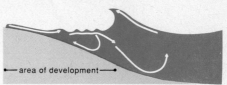
— area of development —

one-wave surf pattern

two-wave surf pattern

three-wave surf pattern

— area of development —

FORMATION OF THE COASTAL STRIP a few eons ago, long before the Andes Mountains rose to their present height, the Coastal Mountain Range emerged gradually as a result of a complex and dynamic pressure process in the earth's crust. Slowly, successive folding of the crust and erosion processes made seawater flood part of the continent. During this process, which lasted millions of years, marine sediment accumulated near the coast. A long period ensued in which crust layers slowly rose to form the Coastal Range and, later, the Cordillera of the Andes. Part of the sea bottom emerged and the ocean water acquired its present boundaries, uncovering seaboard floor which formed terraces rising in steps, visible between Cachagua and Concón, between Algarrobo and Cartagena, and also south of San Antonio up to the Rapel river.

This dynamic process is still under way; a clear proof of it occurred in 1822, when an earthquake triggered the rising of the sea bottom at the Quintero bay. The waves are still reshaping the coastline, eroding and exposing the crust's primary rocks, and slowly carving out the soils formed by marine sediment terraces. This erosion produces the sandstone and shell–sand cliffs visible along this entire coastline at long beaches such as Cachagua, Maitencillo, etc.

CLIMATE Chile's Central Coastal Strip has a privileged climate, known as Western Warm Temperate Climate, found at very few other places in the earth (see map below), such as San Francisco (USA), Gibraltar and Costa Azul in the Mediterranean, Cape Town in South Africa, Perth and Adelaide in Australia, and the northwestern coast of New Zealand. This climate is defined by cold sea currents running along the coastline and by temperature–moderating winds blowing from the sea. As a result, they show very little variation in temperature throughout the year and, usually, they are areas of moderate rainfall in winter and drought in summer.

The cold Humboldt current runs along Chile's Central Coastal Strip. It is akin to an enormous ocean river formed by several superimposed currents, with a width of 600 km at the surface and reaching some 400 m below the surface, flowing at speeds ranging from 40 to 60 meters per hour. Temperature at the surface varies from 10° to 18° C, depending on the season. It flows from the Antarctic coast along Chile's coast up to southern Peru, where it veers into the inner vastness of the Pacific Ocean. The temperature of the Humboldt current gives rise to a climate which, at Valparaíso, has a mean temperature of 20° C at 1300h in summer, and in winter of 15° C. The mean difference between daytime and nighttime temperatures in winter and summer is 5° C. Mean relative air humidity at midday in summer is 65%. Annual

rainfall averages 462 mm, falling between May and October. November through April are considered dry months.

WIND AND WAVES the wind regime on the coast is quite simple: in winter, during low–pressure storms, the wind blows from the NW; from October through April, in turn, the winds from the SW predominate. In both cases the wind blows from the ocean, from high–pressure centers lurking thousands of kilometers away. The wind drives the waves against the coast. There are many windless days; however, the waves continue to reach the coast with great impetus, where they unload the energy accumulated in the enormous vastness of the Pacific Ocean. There are days, very few and usually in November and December, when there is neither wind nor waves and the ocean is, for once, truly pacific. These are glorious days for divers and fishermen who work near the coastal rock outcrops.

The waves travelling on the ocean surface break against the beach when they meet shallow areas. The low water depth makes the height of the wave increase; the water supply to the wave is thus interrupted and the crest cannot complete its cycle, and collapses. A foamy front then crawls towards the shore.

Alert observers will have noticed that there are some beaches, such as Zapallar, where only one wave breaks at a time, sliding towards the beach, retreating and then leaving the stage to the next wave. Other beaches, such as Playa Amarilla at Concón, have two waves running simultaneously: one breaking and the other one foaming its way towards the beach. Lastly, there are beaches such as Cachagua, Ritoque, Maitencillo, etc, with 3 or more waves rolling simultaneously, one breaking and the others running as foam to the beach. We shall label each here as «one–wave surf pattern», «two–wave surf pattern», and so forth.

This depends on the bottom's slope: the greater the slope, the fewer the waves rolling simultaneously. The gentler the slope, the more waves. Thus, one look will tell you where the floor falls abruptly under the water, or whether it is possible to walk farther into the sea. In the latter case, watch out for some trench–like depressions in the sand.

BEACH SAND the sand varies both in hue –from gray to whitish– and in grain size, ranging from coarse sand mixed with crushed shells to very fine sand easily borne away by the wind.

Sand comes from two sources: one is the mechanical action of the waves on the coastal rocks and stones, crushing them, rounding their corners and eroding them until they are small enough to

6

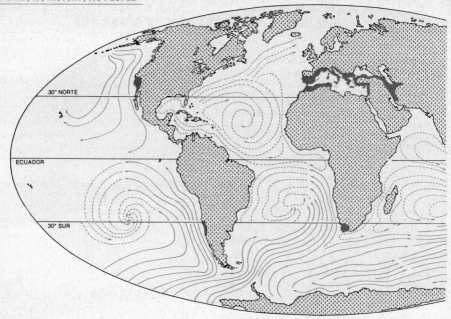

be carried away suspended in mid–water and deposited on the beach. Another source, by far the most important, are the water courses flowing down from the mountains swiftly and with great volume in winter. Along the way they grind stones and carry them to the sea, which dumps the resulting sand on the beach during the high tide. This accounts for the fact that the largest beaches always occur at the mouth of rivers and other streams.

The color of the sand depends on the type of rock it came from. The great rivers flowing from the Andes Range, such as Aconcagua, Maipo and Rapel, crush gray–hued volcanic rock. Thus, the Ritoque beach, spawned by the Aconcagua river; those at Barranca and San Antonio, spawned by the Maipo river; and those at Santo Domingo, spawned by the Rapel river, all have gray–hued sands. By contrast, the streams flowing from the Coastal Range crush an older, more degraded type of rock –known as maicillo– which has a yellow or whitish hue. Therefore, the beaches at the mouth of these streams, such as Papudo, Zapallar, Cachagua, Quintero, Reñaca, Viña del Mar, Algarrobo, etc, have golden or whitish sands.

The size of the sand grain depends mainly on the length of the river or stream bringing the sand to the beach. Long rivers have a greater potential for crushing the mother rock. Thus, long rivers such as the Aconcagua, Maipo and Rapel produce a fine sand. By contrast, short streams such as those at Zapallar, Las Cruces, Algarrobo, etc, produce mid–sized sand grains. Beaches lacking a nearby stream, such as the pools of Maitencillo, have sand produced exclusively by erosion of the immediate rocks and are therefore much coarser. They are characterized as well by having the sand heavily mixed with the remnant of shells of marine animals dwelling in those same rocks.

FISH AND SHELLFISH you will find them displayed at every fishing cove and seafood outlet, an almost compulsory stop for every vacationer worth his salt. These places also usually offer a dish of assorted seafood known as "mariscal", said to bring life back to the deadest of souls. Add a glass of white wine and you will have an unforgettable meal.

The most abundant fishes in this coastline are **merluza** (a sort of hake), **jurel** (a cangaroid fish), **sardine, pejegallo, sierra** (sawfish), **tollo** (spotted dogfish), **reineta**, and **cabrilla**. The more delicious fishes are also the more expensive, such as **congrio** (conger eel), **corvina** (a type of drum fish), **lenguado** (sole or flatfish), and **albacora** (a tunny–like fish). Shellfish are all those aquatic animals with a shell instead of scales, including genera such as crustaceans'

lobster, prawn, shrimp, and crab; and those possessing a shell, such as **loco** (a kind of abalone), **macha** (a bivalve mollusk), **cholga** (ditto), **choro** (ditto), etc. Stretching the definition, shellfish includes as well the odd group of **piure** (a strange–looking rock dweller) and others.

These fishes have various habitats; there are those roaming far off the shore within the Humboldt current and which come near the coast only occasionally, such as jurel, merluza and sardina, and which are caught using trailing nets by fishing vessels or encircling nets by non–industrial fishermen. Albacora, which also lives away from the coast, is fished with a harpoon. Another group of fishes dwelling nearer the coast, and caught only by non–industrial fishermen using fishhooks, are congrio, corvina, lenguado, cabrilla, and others. Shellfish, in turn, have a more stationary habitat and, with the exception of shrimp, which live in deep water far off the coast and are caught using trailing nets, all live near or on rocks and beaches, and are gathered manually by fishermen and divers.

Nowadays Chile has a vast seafood trading network, refrigerated trucks bringing the catch from the fishing coves to the consumption centers. There are fishing terminals at San Antonio and at Caleta Portales, Valparaíso. Auctions start at 3 o'clock in the morning and the catch is distributed among the coastal seafood outlets. Unfrozen seafood must be bought fresh; to recognize the freshness of a fish, its gills must be bright red, not pale red. Shellfish, in turn, must be alive when bought. In the case of bivalve mollusks, this can be ascertained by the valves reacting by closing when touched. In the case of locos (a kind of abalone), its flesh must retract when touched. As for sea urchins, watch the foam around the mouth for movement. In all cases, a sharp nose comes in handy.

Out of the astounding variety of seafood products, we describe below the most common:

1 Congrio (conger eel) as the name suggests, it is not really a fish but an eel, given away by the lack of a caudal fin and of scales. It dwells among the rocks at depths of about 300 m. There are two varieties: Red and Black. Its flesh is tasty, tender and white. Fish bones are easy to remove.

2 Corvina (a type of drum fish) it approaches the coast with the high tide –usually to its deep regret. Of white, firm flesh, its fishbones are easy to remove.

3 Lenguado (a type of flatfish) as its English name suggests, it is flat, wide and thin, with both eyes weirdly placed on the same side. It lies on the sandy bottom near the beaches. Firm, tasty flesh.

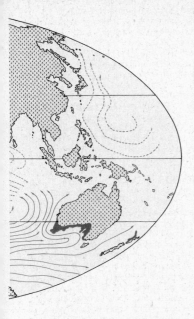

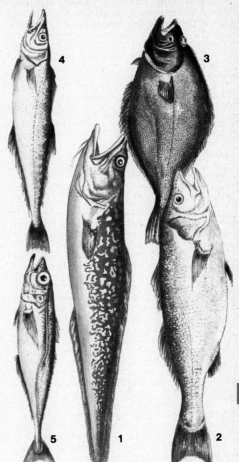

6

4 Merluza (also called Pescada) (a type of hake) a migratory fish living in the Humboldt current, of very hydrodynamic form. It is very abundant; its tasty flesh is served sliced into filets, but removing its fishbones is laborious.

5 Jurel (a cangaroid fish) of similar habitat as merluza, it approaches the coast preying on sardine schools. It is the most abundant; tasty but has lots of fishbones.

6 Loco (a relative of abalone) perhaps the tastiest shellfish, with firm, white, smooth–tasting flesh. Occurring only in Chile and southern Peru, it is now an endangered species and its extraction is forbidden.

7 Erizo (sea urchin) a strange shellfish having a somewhat globular body studded with long, calcareous, moving spines and containing five yellow–orange «tongues» considered a delicacy.

8 Macha (tellina a bivalve mollusk) at lives buried in the sand in shallows of the sea, particularly directly underneath the breakers. Abundant and cheap, it is eaten raw or baked in its shell with a cheese sauce.

9 Almeja (clam) it lives in a habitat similar to that of macha, and it is abundant and tasty. To eat them raw, select mid–sized clams, as they tend to be tastier.

10 Ostión (a variety of oyster) extracted to near extinction, the present output comes from shellfish farms located in Northern Chile. It is delicious.

11 Mytilidae a group of saltwater bivalve mollusks that anchors to rocks, ships and other objects in the water; most of the output comes now from farms in the South. The most common are: **Choro zapato** (giant mussel), the largest one, with yellowish flesh considered a delicacy; **cholga,** somewhat smaller and more abundant, with a smooth taste; and **chorito,** the smaller cousin of choro zapato, with a strong taste and the unavoidable partner of a good "arroz a la valenciana", a rice dish of Spanish roots studded with shellfish, chicken and pork.

12 Oyster a seawater bivalve mollusk now mainly coming from oyster farms in the South. Chilean oysters occur only in these waters, but they are a close relative of the other varieties found around the world. It is really delicious.

OCCUPATION OF THE COAST from quite early on – by 1600– all the lands in Central Chile were allotted to the most prominent Spanish conquerors or their descendants. The main latifundia (large landed estates) along the coast were located, from North to South, at **Pullally** –La Ligua and Longotoma valley– with Papudo on the coast; **Catapilco** valley, with the Maitencillo fishing cove on the coast; the **Puchuncaví** and **Pucalán** valleys with the Quintero fish-

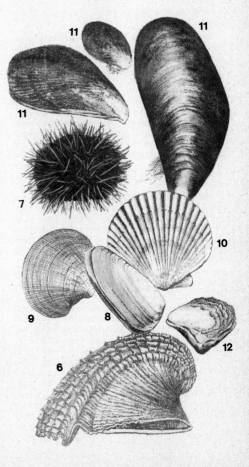

ing cove on the coast; the **Tabolango** and **Colmo** areas and the Concón fishing cove on the coast; the **Viña del Mar** and **Siete Hermanas** haciendas, covering the areas of Viña del Mar, Valparaíso and inland areas; **Lo Orrego,** from Casablanca towards the coast, with the natural harbor of Algarrobo; the **Lo Abarca** and **Leyda** area, with the Cartagena cove, and, south of the Maipo river, the large coastal haciendas of **El Convento,** run by the Order of Saint Dominic, and **Bucalemu,** run by the Jesuits.

During the colonial period, the farming output exceeded by far domestic consumption and the surplus was exported to the Peru Viceroyship. During the first years of the conquest, the incipient trade was free of constraints and the main farm owners built their own ships to transport their output. Small shipyards operated at Concón and Papudo; at the latter, in 1561, García Hurtado de Mendoza confiscated the only ship remaining to return hastily to Peru.

During the 17th and 18th centuries trade was controlled by the Central Administration, which levied a duty on imports and exports. All sea trade took place during the summer months, with ships sailing down from Callao, Peru, bringing consumer goods such as textiles, clothing, weapons, ammunition, etc., and loading here farming produce consisting mainly of wheat, leather and animal fat for the manufacture of candles. The sailing ships were small, the annual traffic to bring wheat to the central zone requiring more than 35 vessels. The port of Valparaíso was the prime point for loading and unloading goods for and from the zone. Gradually the place acquired a stable population and in the early 18th century a fort with a permanent garrison was established at the Castillo de San José.

The coves along the central Coastal Strip were also copper and gold mining centers, the corresponding works located in coastal valleys and ravines. By 1820 there was a small copper refinery and some storage compounds at Concón; later, large gold washing works were set up at the Catapilco creek, with a shipping port at Maitencillo. Starting in the mid-19th century, Zapallar, Quintero, Algarrobo and San Antonio operated during the summer as shipping ports for the output of the coastal farms.

The most significant development was the creation in Valparaíso in 1822 of a sort of «free port». European immigrants settled there and started to run the agricultural product import and export business. Later, in association with copper, silver and then saltpeter miners, they financed the mining development in northern Chile; they also teamed up with the pioneers of Magallanes to finance the establishment of the large livestock-raising farms in the deep South. Valparaíso's businessmen took part in every significant development last century: in the coal mines of Lota, Schwager, Lebu, and Curanilahue; in the large irrigation canal projects in the Aconcagua and Maipo river valleys; in the laying of railways through the North, Center and South of the country, and also of the Trans-Andean Railway. Furthermore, large investments in urban services in Chile's main cities, such as electrification, and construction of gas and telephone networks, were all managed from Valparaíso. Starting in 1912, the initial stages of industrialization were financed from Valparaíso, with the establishment of the first basic industries, such as textile factories, large wheat mills, sugar refineries, etc.

From 1840 onwards, Valparaíso was Chile's leading financial, trading and business center, a role which remained unchanged and unchallenged until early this century. However, as a result of a process then taking place throughout the world, the economic and business might concentrated in the world's large seaports moved to the political capital of the respective country. Such was the case at Liverpool, Le Havre, Bordeaux, Callao, Valparaíso, etc. Thus, in a slow process started by 1920, the main banking, trading, industrial and mining head offices which had had their seat in Valparaíso, as well as the leading businessmen

and entrepreneurs, emigrated to Santiago.

Valparaíso started to take then its present role of great port service center and seat of specialized industries. In the early 1920s the large-sized mechanized port facilities went on stream at Valparaíso and San Antonio and the minor seaports operating in the nearby coast were phased out. During the 1940s a road was built along the Central Coastal Strip, linking the coastal cities and towns. From 1956 to 1967 oil industry facilities were built in the area, with a port at Quintero and a refinery at Concón. The Quintero industrial complex was built during this period, including a copper refinery, thermoelectric power plants and a shipping port for bulk minerals.

SEASIDE RESORTS there are at present 25 seaside resorts in the 130 km of Central Coastal Strip, with intense activity and hefty investments in recreational facilities, a process taking place since the turn of the century. Formerly very few visitors came to the coast, only the friends or relatives of the coastal landowners. A significant change started to take place by 1830, with the creation of a national merchant fleet, in which many small sailing vessels plied the coastal waters. Thus, the coastal farms could ship out their output directly through the nearest cove, for which purpose warehouses were built on the coast at the more sheltered places, usually near the rocks. These **warehouses** were the real origin of coastal tourism.

The manor houses of the coastal landed estates were always located away from the coast, near rivers or creeks. The construction of the warehouses made it possible for relatives and friends of the landowners to come in large groups and spend a few weeks on the coast during the summer, lodged in those warehouses, which were equipped with bunk beds and temporary kitchen facilities.

This bright idea soon found many followers, who camped for the summer in sheds erected next to the warehouses. The warehouse, in turn, performed as a manor house of sorts. By 1865 there were warehouses at Papudo, Zapallar, Maitencillo, Quintero, Concón, Algarrobo, Cartagena, and San Antonio. Every one of them was located at the respective fishing village, on the higher ground, next to the rocks and near a cove of placid waters; they were never built on the open beach or at places with strong surf.

Viña del Mar emerged in 1874 as a residential quarter of Valparaíso and became a seaside resort around 1880, with the construction of a Gran Hotel which received tourists from Santiago. Between 1880 and 1900 a further five seaside resorts came into being: Algarrobo by 1885, Cartagena and Las Cruces by 1890, Zapallar in 1893, and Papudo in 1897. Their origin can be traced to Santiago residents who had taken a liking to seaside holidays while spending some time in Europe, where the new seaside resorts of Biarritz, Deauville, Trouville, Cannes, and others, were in full swing. This influence is evident in every Chilean seaside resort born around this period, which copied from them the street layout, the architecture of the great villas, and even introducing new trees to the scenery, such as palms and araucarias, so popular then in the Mediterranean.

These early resorts, with the exception of Viña del Mar, evolved from the farms' warehouses. Their first houses, like the warehouses themselves, were erected on the rocks; only later they started to be built on the beach. This is evident at Zapallar, with the large houses near the fishing cove; Maitencillo and Concón, where the Gran Hotel is next to the rocks and not on the beach; and also at Algarrobo, Las Cruces, etc. The reason for this was that the early holiday-makers were not really acquainted with the sea, and preferred to bathe in pools among the rocks; here, separate shades and cabins were set up for men and for women. In Zapallar, a round stone cabin on the rocks of the fishing cove indicates the original bathing spot.

The beaches started to be used later, by 1915, when the more daring learned to ride the waves and put up with the undertow; men and women started then to bathe together and sunbathe in a more informal fashion, lying on the sand.

Between 1900 and 1935 further seaside resorts were established along this coast. Llolleo sprung up after the railroad reached the place in 1912. Similarly, shortly after the railway reached Papudo in 1910, a real estate company was formed (1917) which developed the place as a resort. Quintero also acquired a railway link and the resort started to take shape around 1910. Concón and Maitencillo

each got a hotel by 1920; El Quisco, El Tabo and Isla Negra were born out of the division of the land into lots and subsequent sale in the 1930s. The last resorts to appear were Santo Domingo, in 1942, Reñaca in 1947, Cachagua in 1956 and Marbella in 1982. Now the Central Coastal Strip has 25 seaside resorts, each having a complete tourist infrastructure; they are all linked by the coastal road.

ROUTES FROM SANTIAGO TO THE CENTRAL COASTAL STRIP

From Santo Domingo in the south to Papudo in the north it is 140 km as the crow flies. Along this stretch of coastline there are twenty further seaside resorts. Three routes lead from Santiago to this area, namely Route 78 to San Antonio (the most southerly of the three routes); Route 68 to Valparaíso and Viña del Mar, and the northbound Route 5 (the Pan-American highway). Secondary roads branch off these main highways to the various resorts.

1 ROUTE 78 leads to resorts from Santo Domingo to Algarrobo. The distance from Santiago to San Antonio is 109 km, with 65 km of four-lane highway (from Santiago to Melipilla) and 44 km of two-lane highway, narrow and congested. Gas stations in Santiago and its outskirts, at km 20 (Padre Hurtado), and at km 65 (Melipilla). Restaurants and cafés only in Santiago. A toll is paid. See illustration.

Km 0, Plaza de Armas of Santiago. The first 22 km are slow and strenuous, navigating your way through city traffic up to Padre Hurtado. There starts the four-lane highway, the closest thing to a US freeway or a German Autobahn in Chile, expeditious and well laid out. Between km 18 and 24 the following restaurants are located, in this sequence: Hoff Kuchen, Mazapán Santa Ana, Lomitón, Parrillada a la Argentina, Hornitos de Peñaflor.

Km 22, police road control and a road branching right to Valparaíso via the Barriga ridge; see point 2 below.

Km 25, a road branches left to the southbound Pan-American highway, another one branches right to Peñaflor, as well as an old, attractive road to the coast described under Zone 5, Tour 1 of Section H. The freeway traverses a flat farmed valley, with fruit orchards, vineyards and horticulture. At km 45 there is a weighing plaza for trucks, and one km farther along a bridge spanning the Maipo river. Next comes the El Paico Toll Plaza, where only coast-bound vehicles pay. At km 60 a road branches right to Pomaire and at km 64, another road branches left to Melipilla, both described under Zone 5, Tour 1 of Section H.

At km 67, a road branches right to Casablanca via the Ibacache ridge. The freeway ends and the road becomes narrow, congested. Its layout is old, running through cropland and crossing the Puangue creek at km 78; this stream comes from the north, through Curacaví, to join the Maipo river farther down. A short distance further along is the old Puangue chapel.

The road then climbs to cross the Coastal Range. At km 80 a road branches right to Cuncumén, described under Tour 3 of Section H. This curvy stretch ends just beyond the underpass of the Santiago-San Antonio railroad, at km 83. The flat, non-irrigated Leyda valley unfolds ahead, with a picturesque railway station and many stands selling honey and fruit (km 89).

At km 91, a road branches left to Santo Domingo (see point 4 below). The road runs through pine and eucalyptus forests, reaches a junction at km 104 and descends straight ahead to San Antonio, 5 km from the junction.

From the road junction, the right branch is the best alternative for Cartagena (see diagram). Continuing straight ahead, the highway runs into the coastal road leading to seaside resorts lying further north, such as San Sebastián (km 111 from

Santiago), Las Cruces (km 116), El Tabo (km 125), El Quisco (km 130), and Algarrobo (km 135). This stretch of coastline is described in Zone 6, Sections D and E.

2 Secondary Road to Valparaíso and Viña del Mar Via the Barriga Ridge this is the old road to Valparaíso, which runs through a scenic ridge described under Zone 5, Tour 2 of Section H. This detour enables you to bypass the toll plaza when travelling to the coast.

3 Secondary Road to Valparaíso and Viña del Mar Via the Ibacache Ridge it was known as the «Ladies' Route» during the colonial period, as women preferred it because it offered an alternative to the dreaded Lo Prado and Zapata ridges. The stretch from Melipilla to Casablanca is 54 km long, with 18 km paved and the rest graveled.

Taking Melipilla as your km 0, the paved road leads to Bollevar (km 149), in an area described under Zone 5, Tour 2 of Section H. It then traverses a flat farmed valley, passing the large, well-run Hacienda Chorombo, owned by Industrias Carozzi. Several further farms are crossed, and then the road climbs the Ibacache ridge, in a curvy but gentle stretch. At km 43 the road descends into the Casablanca valley to meet Route 68 at km 54.

4 The Branch Road to Santo Domingo is a 17-km paved stretch offering the best alternative to reach Santo Domingo and Llolleo. It crosses the soft rolling country of the Coastal Range, through what used to be the great colonial Hacienda San Juan, of the Balmaceda entailed estate. Taking the Leyda junction as km 0, the San Juan reservoir can be seen from km 9, ringed by country retreats. The road then descends towards the coast, passing the hacienda's housing compound (remains of the park can be seen off to the right). At km 16 is Lo Gallardo, described under Zone 6, Tour 1 of Section F; it used to be owned by poet Vicente Huidobro's family. At km 17 is a bridge spanning the Maipo river and a road branching left to Santo Domingo, right to Llolleo.

7 Route 68 leads from Santiago to Valparaíso (121 km), Viña del Mar (120 km), Reñaca (127 km), Concón (134 km). A road branches off Route 68 to Algarrobo (112 km from Santiago), El Quisco (117 km), El Tabo (126 km), and Quintay (122 km). Gas stations in the outskirts of Santiago and just beyond Curacaví, at km 52. Restaurants and cafés along the way. There is a toll plaza for coast-bound vehicles right before the Lo Prado tunnel, and for Santiago-bound vehicles at Casablanca. Both can be bypassed (see detours 2 & 8).

Km 0 is at Santiago's Plaza de Armas. Take Av Libertador B O'Higgins heading west; it leads directly to Route 68. At km 13 is the intersection with Av Circunvalación Américo Vespucio and the highway to the airport. This is the city limit.

At km 17 there is a bridge over the Mapocho river and a short distance further along, another one over the Lampa creek. Beyond a small rise a valley opens up, with Parque Carén and the Club de Tiro at km 18, Lo Aguirre mine at km 24, and then the toll plaza (only coast-bound vehicles pay). Off to the right is the dome of the Instituto de Investigaciones Nucleares (km 27).

At km 28 is the entrance to the 2,800-m-long Lo Prado tunnel, finished in 1970. From the other end

6

337

there is a superb view over the Mallarauco and Curacaví valley, 200 m lower than the tunnel's mouth. The highway descends with ample curves and reaches the valley's floor at km 37. The road from the Barriga ridge joins Route 68 from the left (see point 2 above).

Route 68 runs along the flat, fertile Curacaví valley, with fruit orchards, vineyards, many stands selling fruit or pastries, and good restaurants, among which Antumapu and Agua de Piedra stand out. At km 47 is the first access to the town of Curacaví, established in the colonial days, head town of its municipality and renowned for its pastries and cider. The highway skirts the town running along the Puangue creek, which flows southward to join the Maipo river. The flat valley ends at km 54. Then the road climbs another Coastal Range spur for 8 km to reach the Zapata tunnel. In this area there are several country-style restaurants, including Hostería Los Hornitos, and the Issa pastry shop.

At km 61 is the mouth of the 1,300-m-long Zapata tunnel, the midpoint between Santiago and the coast. Beyond the tunnel is the Casablanca valley, flat and poor in water resources; the highway crosses it almost in a straight line. At km 66 is the toll plaza, where only Santiago-bound vehicles pay; it can be skirted by taking the road branching right two km before the toll when coming from the coast (see point 8 below). In season, in this area you will see stands selling asparagus, cheese and raspberries.

At km 77 a road branches left to Algarrobo, El Quisco and El Tabo (see point 9 below). At the intersection is the Lomitón restaurant, with playgrounds and other attractions for children. At km 77 the highway starts to skirt Casablanca, a municipality and an old way station on the road to Valparaíso. On the side of the road opposite the town is the Chiletabacos manufacturing plant.

At km 79 the road climbs a gentle rise; at km 84 is Santuario de Lo Vásquez and its great church, site of a major pilgrimage on December 8. On its side is the Major Seminary of the Valparaíso Diocese.

At km 93 is Lake Peñuelas and a Forest Reserve under Conaf administration. The lake is man-made and serves as drinking water reservoir for Valparaíso.

At km 99 a road branches left for Quintay and Tunquén (see point 10 below). At km 101 there is a police road control, and at km 106 a forking of the road. The left branch leads to Valparaíso in 10 km; the right branch to Viña del Mar in 14 km, and continues to Reñaca and Concón along the Coastal Road.

8 Zapata Ridge Detour a 15-km paved stretch with a gentle gradient but very curvy; there are some blind curves. The road offers good views over the valley and is lined by lush native vegetation. It enables Santiago-bound travelers to bypass the toll plaza.

9 Detour to Algarrobo a 33-km stretch from Route 68, it is the shortest route from Santiago to the resorts of Algarrobo, El Quisco, and El Tabo. A well laid-out road, it runs through rolling semi-arid fields.

10 Detour to Quintay and Tunquén a 24-km curvy, undulating gravel road running through tree-filled ravines and slopes, and pine and eucalyptus plantations. At km 17 there is a signposted junction, the right branch leading to Tunquén beach in 8 km (no amenities) and the left branch to Quintay

6

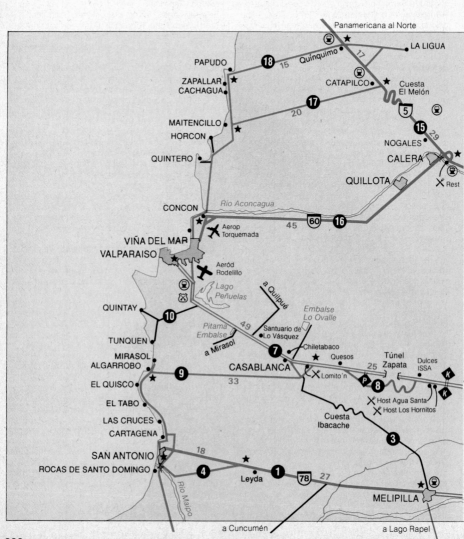

in 7 km. The last three km of the latter branch are a steep descent to the picturesque Caleta Quintay, with restaurants and summer houses. A short distance before the fishing cove a short dirt road branches right to Playa Quintay, a white-sand beach with a few summer houses and a campground.

⑮ Route 5, Pan-American highway its northbound section has three secondary roads branching off towards resorts on the central coastline: Quintero (180 km from Santiago), Maitencillo (148 km), Cachagua (156 km), Zapallar (160 km), and Papudo (170 km). A two-lane highway, it has 33 km of four-lane stretches near Santiago and at portions with inclines slowing down heavier vehicles, in order to facilitate overtaking. Still, it is quite congested in the Santiago-bound direction on Sundays in summer and at the end of long holiday periods. There are gas stations every 20 km on average. The best restaurants are between km 80 and 110 from Santiago.

Km 0 is at Santiago's Plaza de Armas. At km 11 is the intersection with Av. Circunvalación Américo Vespucio (at present with traffic lights, but a new modern intersection is under construction). Then follows an agricultural-industrial area up to km 22, with a road branching left to Lampa and another one branching right to Colina.

At km 27 is a toll plaza, where northbound vehicles must pay. Right beyond it is a weighing plaza for heavy vehicles. The road runs through rolling terrain, now irrigated with water tapped from deep wells. At km 40 a road branches left to Polpaico, with a mine and a large cement factory.

At km 45 the road starts to climb the short La Trampilla escarpment. The next 37 km the Pan-Am traverses a semi-arid rolling plateau. At km 75 is Estación Las Chilcas, and the road starts the de-

scent along the bottom of a highly scenic ravine, with mammoth boulders hanging precariously from the slopes. Ahead is the Llayllay valley. See description under Tour 2, Section B. At km 79 the road reaches the valley floor and runs level for the next 49 km. There are several good restaurants, including Alamo Huacho at km 85, with Chilean food, Hostería Shell at the gas station on the Llayllay junction (km 87), and Mucho Gusto at km 108. At km 90 a highway branches east to Los Andes and Argentina. One km further along is a toll plaza (northbound traffic does not pay, only Santiago-bound vehicles). At km 94 is the short La Calavera tunnel; the road runs alongside the Aconcagua river.

At km 100 there are stands selling flowers on the roadside. Next comes a bridge across the Aconcagua river, with a superb view towards Mount Aconcagua on clear days. Just before the bridge, a gravel road branches left to the highly scenic Palmar de Ocoa at the La Campana National Park. The Pan-Am heads north through the La Calera valley.

At km 109 is the first detour for the coast, leading to Viña del Mar, Quintero and Horcón; see point 16 below. You must take the exit to the right, which veers left to an overpass across the highway.

Continuing on the Pan-Am, Nogales is at km 116 and El Melón at km 119. The latter is a mining town and processes the limestone from the mines off to the right of the highway.

At km 125 starts the climb of the 10–km-wide El Melón ridge, with spectacular sights over the Calera and Catapilco valleys. The southern slopes are heavy with native trees, including canelos. The road zigzag down the northern side to the Catapilco valley.

At km 138 is the second road branching left to

6

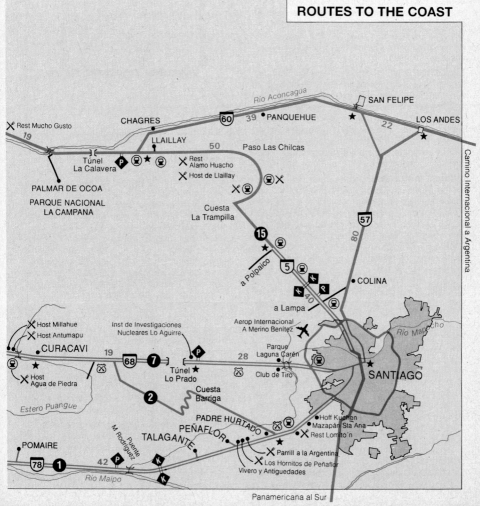

ROUTES TO THE COAST

the coast (see point 17 below), leading to Maitencillo, Cachagua and Zapallar. The Pan–Am continues straight; the first detour to La Ligua branches right at km 147, and the second at km 154.

At km 155 is the Quíquimo junction, with a gas station. The third road towards the coast branches left to Papudo (see point 18 below). Route 5 (the Pan–Am) continues northward all the way to Arica, nearly two thousand kilometers farther along.

16 **Detour to Concón, Route 60** 45 km of paved road, used mostly by traffic to or from the upper Aconcagua valley and Argentina. It is the best alternative for going to Quintero and Horcón (see description under Zone 6, Section C, Tour 2). Route branches west from Route 5 and runs along the Aconcagua river, skirting the towns of La Calera, La Cruz, and Quillota. 4 km before reaching the coast there is a badly signposted forking of the road. The left branch leads to Viña del Mar through the area of Achupallas. The right branch

leads to a traffic circle on Concón's edge. There, a road branches right, crossing the Aconcagua river and heading north along the coast, leading to Quintero in 26 km (180 km from Santiago).

17 **Detour to Maitencillo** a 20–km paved stretch which is the best alternative for Maitencillo (148 km from Santiago), Cachagua (156 km), and Zapallar (160 km). The road runs along the Catapilco valley for 15 km and then follows the meandering course of the Catapilco creek. Note the yellowish hue of the surrounding hills: it is maicillo, the brittle rock typical of Coastal Range hills.

The road leads to the Coastal highway. Straight ahead is Maitencillo, to the right is Cachagua and Zapallar.

18 **Detour to Papudo** 15 km, of paved road lead directly into the seaside resort, 170 km from Santiago, running between dry rolling hills with gentle slopes and curves.

SECTION A   ZAPALLAR

This Section comprises the stretch of coast between the Papudo bay to the North and the mouth of the Catapilco creek at La Laguna to the South. Inland it extends to the valleys of La Ligua and Catapilco. In this district are the renowned resorts of Papudo, Zapallar and Cachagua, in addition to a number of small beaches. Zapallar is the main attraction, as well as one of Chile's most exclusive and beautiful seaside resorts.

In this area the Coastal Range cascades directly onto the sea, leaving a few valleys and narrow beaches here and there; the highest peak in the Central Coastal Strip, mount La Higuera, is located between Papudo and Zapallar. These tall hills shelter the area from the predominating SW wind in summer, giving the resorts prized microclimates and nourishing a lush plant cover in the ravines cleaving their way into the hills, such as El Tigre and Aguas Claras.

The Coastal Route runs for 21 km through this section, always some way up from the shore –thus affording good views over the sea– and with several natural look-out points (see general map). Near the highway new urban developments have sprung up, as well as lots of single summer houses. Between Papudo and Zapallar, the road passes a cemetery gracefully perched atop a cliff overlooking the ocean.

Distances from Zapallar to Santiago, 180 km on the Pan–American highway via Quínquimo, 172 km on the Pan–Am via Catapilco, and 189 km along Route 68 via Viña del Mar. To Viña del Mar, 71 km. To Algarrobo, 148 km on the coastal road and then Route 68 taking the road branching off at Casablanca. To San Antonio, 179 km along the same route. To Santo Domingo, 183 km, same route.

PAPUDO a resort with a long tradition and once quite fashionable, lies on a bay facing North and sheltered from the south wind by steep hills. It has an excellent beach of placid waters, the best for watersports in the area. The Costanera –the waterfront street– is the busiest part of town, day or night, lined with restaurants and cafés, an amusement park, a yacht club and some discos. It offers all kinds of services, from medical through mechanical through legal.

The name of Papudo was due to a local chieftain, owner of these lands, who was called "Carande" or "Cara Grande" and who, on account of having a double chin, was nicknamed papudo by the Spaniards, «papa» being one of the Spanish words for chin. The nickname became popular in time and the entire territory of Chieftain Carande

got to be known as Papudo. In 1599 this bay became part of the large hacienda Pullally –located near La Ligua– and was used as the shipping port for the hacienda's output.

The founder of the summer resort was Fernando J Irarrázabal, owner of the hacienda Pullally, who in 1897 sketched the layout for a small urban development, sold plots of land and built a magnificent chalet. In 1910 a railway branch line reached Papudo and a metal pier was built, transforming Papudo into the most accessible and important resort–seaport in this stretch of coast, along with Viña del Mar. In 1917 a society called «Balneario de Papudo» was formed, which became the driving force behind the development of the modern resort. The present urban layout dates from that period, as well as some of the large houses still to be seen, together with a church built in a classical Spanish style.

A stroll along the Costanera will show you these milestones of the «Golden Twenties», presiding over the bustling present–day resort. Busiest of all, of course, are Sundays in summer.

Where To Eat good seafood and service at La Casona and El Castillo. For quick meals, try the Costanera restaurants. For a picnic, the northern tip of Playa Larga.

SECTION A

La Ligua
Pan-American Highway
to SANTIAGO
Catapilco
ZONE 4
Aguas Claras Ravin
Mt La Higuera Lookout
El Tigre Ravin
(4)
(3)
(2)
(1)
SECTION B
Papudo
ZAPALLAR
Cachagua
Pacific Ocean

ZAPALLAR is a small, sheltered, shell–shaped cove, surrounded by steep hills which harbor a very pleasant microclimate where lush vegetation thrives. That, and its careful urban development, have made it the most select and privileged resort in the entire coast. Zapallar is famous for its large trees, its beautiful summer mansions and its gardens. The place is superbly sheltered from the wind and has a remarkably stable climate throughout the year. The white–sand beach is relatively small, Restaurant César pampering its customers on a terrace on the edge. Zapallar offers a complete range of urban services, such as supplies, telephones, gas station, some pensiones, a hotel, motel and an excellent tennis club.

Zapallar means «squash field», and it was created as a resort on an initiative of Olegario Ovalle, owner of the local hacienda, who decided to give his friends plots of land at the place under the condition that they built their houses within two years. This peculiar origin made the neighbors, from the very beginning, take care not only of their plots of land, but also of the general area: forests were planted, the streets were harmoniously laid out, and the embankments at the edge of the beach were built.

Zapallar has been the victim of two wholesale catastrophes: an earthquake in August 1906, when construction had just started, and another earthquake in 1965. The first one levelled the entire village, except for six large houses which remained standing but were full of cracks. One of these was the Gran Hotel de Zapallar –demolished recently– which was the great social center at the time. In 1916 Zapallar became the head town of its own municipality, evolving to the beautiful resort of today.

What To See take a stroll along the waterfront promenade, known here as **La Rambla**. It starts at Isla Seca and skirts the beach and bay to its other end at the fishing cove, the **caleta de pescadores**.

Papudo

Continue to **Mar Bravo**, the best spot for watching the sunset. Evenings are perfect for strolling along **Av Zapallar** to see the old summer mansions (see locations in map), such as the **Municipalidad,** built in 1922 by architect Josué Smith for the Aldunate family, and the nearby **House Ossandón,** with palms crowning its garden and shading the tennis court. On this street and right above the beach is **House Edwards,** a copy of the famous house of Nuremberg's «Butcher», with slanting roofs and a façade with carved wooden friezes. There are also the splendid **House Aldunate Concha**, in Tudor Style, and Houses **Concha, Vicuña,** and **Wilson.**

Bear in mind that we have used the names of the original owners in naming these mansions; they have other owners now.

Where To Eat good cuisine, atmosphere and view at César on the beach. For quicker meals, cheaper and with children, try Los Troncos or Residencial Las Terrazas in town.

CACHAGUA is a fashionable seaside resort lying on a gentle slope at the northern tip of a long beach. The most notorious feature is the style of its beautiful summer houses, built of logs, with

6

a La Ligua y Santiago

PAPUDO

CLUB DE GOLF

Pya. Larga

N

Cta. de Pescadores
Club de Yates

a Zapallar

☎ Telephone
◉ Café, Meeting Point
⊕ Gasoline Station
A Town Hall
B Buses to Santiago

ACCOMMODATIONS
1 H Moderno
2 M D'Peppino
3 H Turismo
4 H Carande
5 Bh Valencia
6 H La Abeja
7 Bh El Golf
8 H Donde Tito
9 Bh Papudo
10 Bh La Plaza
11 H Mocelli

RESTAURANTS
6 La Abeja
15 La Cabaña
16 El Casino
17 Club de Yates
18 La Casona

Zapallar

thatched roofs and stuccoed with lime, and most of only one floor. The streets lack either a rigorous layout or sidewalks.

Cachagua means «grass field», and came into being when the owners of the Cachagua farm decided to sell off a slice of it. The manor houses can still be seen on the side of the access road.

Its beach is the longest in this district, flat and fine–sanded, very suitable for playing volleyball or beach tennis. It is one of the few areas in the Central Coastline where surf can be practiced. Opposite Isla de los Pingüinos is the small **Playa Las Cujas,** with placid sea and surrounded by beautiful rocks with very good spots for scuba diving or snorkeling.

A ride on horseback (horses for hire directly on the beach) to the southern tip of the beach can be recommended. You can also try your luck at an-

gling (good flatfish and corvina) or digging machas at the breakers, or chasing crab in the evening. Or simply stroll along the beach to the southern tip, known as Playa de Piedras Preciosas (Precious Stone Beach), at the foot of steep cliffs from where hang–gliders jump off. There is a Golf Club which also has tennis courts.

This resort is quite new and offers few services; to satisfy any «major» need you will have to go to Zapallar or Papudo. There are no hotels; however, some private houses offer accommodation for young people. This «family character» makes nightlife a sort of homey affair.

Where To Eat Club de Golf. Another restaurant on the beach, with an excellent view. Hostería at the bus stop is cheaper. Picnic at the farther end of the long beach.

Non–Urban Beaches these are natural beaches lying between Papudo and Cachagua, sharing the features of being less frequented and lacking amenities. From North to South, they are:

Larga the beach stretching northward of Papudo, with one-wave surf pattern and draped with dunes. A quiet place, lonely and sheltered from the wind at the northern tip, a good spot for camping. Access for cars along the road leading to the drinking water plant.

Piedras Preciosas is the stretch of beach at the southern end of Cachagua's long beach. It is small, rocky, flanked by tall hills, beautiful and a good spot for trying your luck at angling; flatfish and corvina are said to be fairly abundant. It is also a good spot for a picnic. Access is laborious:

6

☎ Telephones	**RESTAURANTS**	E M Aguas Claras	5 Aldunate Concha
⊕ Gasoline Station	A César		6 Concha
⇟ Lookout Point	B Morea	**HOUSES OF INTEREST**	7 Wilson
✻ Hospital	C El Bote	1 Errázuriz	8 Vicuña
2 Town Hall		2 Aldunate	9 Pérez
	ACCOMMODATIONS	3 Ossandón	10 Municipal Stadium
	D M César	4 Edwards	

ZAPALLAR

either walk along the waterfront from Cachagua, or slide down the sandy slope from the road above, or walk northward from La Laguna, following a path among the rocks.

Las Frutillas lies north of La Laguna, with fine, light sand with some crushed shells. It has a three–wave surf pattern and is not very frequented. Access is on foot from La Laguna (about 500 m).

TOURS FROM ZAPALLAR

1 TO THE AGUAS CLARAS RAVINE ★★★

seven km from Zapallar. A short excursion, a good spot for a picnic in spring or summer.

Accessible by car or on foot, this is a typical ravine from this coast, with lush vegetation containing some majestic, old oak trees.

Three km south of Cachagua a road branches left: it is easy to miss it, so look carefully. Drive or walk one km into this road, a veritable tunnel under the vegetation; a brook runs on the side, the ground is mulch.

The road fords the brook and then climbs the hills zig–zag fashion, the plant cover thinning out as altitude increases. From the summit there is a sweeping view over the coastline. This road was the old route between Cachagua and Catapilco.

In the late 1870s there was intense gold digging in this area; some tunnels are still to be seen on the slopes. Do not let children wander into them: many have vertical shafts that are nearly invisible in the darkness. This ravine is a Nature Sanctuary, preserving an untouched patch of the forest which in the past used to cover every ravine in this coast.

2 TO EL TIGRE RAVINE ★★★

accessible only on foot, after a three–hour walk.

Cachagua

A visit to a relict forest considered so valuable by geographers, botanists and ecologists, that they rank it as equivalent to the renowned Talinay forest at Ovalle.

Climb from Zapallar behind the manor houses or from Cachagua following the brook (see map). The path is steep and it crests the hills rising behind Cachagua and Zapallar to descend on the other side to Quebrada El Tigre, the ravine. This is an intermediate ravine with a thick plant cover resembling the forests in Southern Chile, and which has been preserved here for thousands of years by a microclimate featuring high moisture condensation. The predominating tree species are belloto (oak), peumo and olivillo, thriving along species of Central Chile's flora, together with ferns, lichens and long lianas hanging from the trees.

3 TO THE HIGUERA LOOK–OUT ★★

only accessible on foot, after a 1¹/₂–hour climb. Access from Zapallar from behind the Club de Tenis and from Papudo from behind the Club de Golf.

This is the path linking both resorts over the hill crests. A

6

a Santiago y Valparaíso

Estero Sta Rosa

Fundo Cachagua

①

CACHAGUA

Cerámica Cachagua

CLUB ECUESTRE

CLUB DE GOLF

N ←

a Quebrada del Tigre

Escuela

KOENENKAMOF

Estadio

Parroquia

AV. CACHAGUA

VICUÑA

EL QUEBRACHO

AV CACHAGUA

AV LOS MOLLES

LAS DOCAS

Playa de Cachagua

Estacionamiento

LOS DADOS

PEUMOS

AV QUEBRADA

LOS PINGUINOS

Playa

AV DEL MAR

bajada Las Cujas

AV LOS EUCALIPTUS

Restaurante

AV DEL MAR

②

a Zapallar y Papudo

bajada El Parque

Las Cujas

Las Cujas

Pozo del Lobo

Isla de Los Pinguinos

Océano Pacífico

beautiful, slow climb up the slope to a pass on the coast's highest hill, with a superb view reaching as far away as Valparaíso in clear days.

4 TO LA LIGUA AND CATAPILCO ★★★

around trip of 81 km from Zapallar on a paved road. Restaurants and services at La Ligua. Allow half a day.

An excursion to the fertile La Ligua river valley, which will give you a foretaste of the so-called Norte Chico –the Little North– and to the town of La Ligua, renowned for its fruit and non-industrial textiles. These were, in addition, Chile's richest gold-bearing grounds.

Take exit labelled 2 in Zapallar map, through Papudo and then head inland on the paved road to Quínquimo, on the Pan-American highway. From there, follow the signposted road to

LA LIGUA   the name means «site of the sooth-sayer». The village evolved from a mining camp established in the mid–18th century and was officially founded on June 21, 1754, by Governor Domingo Ortiz de Rozas. It was laid-out in 1789 and was granted city status on June 3, 1874. The village has a lot of orchards enclosed by mud-brick walls, the fruit trees peering above the walls. Both climate and soil are privileged, nourishing the rich fruit groves; outstanding are its nuts, papayas, avocados, cherimoyas and lucuma. The last two make delicious ice cream.

The place is also renowned for its pastries –**dulces de La Ligua**–, which can be bought almost everywhere, but most of all for its **textiles**, a household industry with products for sale at almost every house. The largest producer is **Baltra**, housed in an old building by itself worth the visit. The shops are open weekdays and only partially on Sunday mornings. The local restaurants offer typical Chilean dishes, such as pastel de choclo (corn pie), empanadas (a sort of meat pie wrapped in a thin wafer of dough), cazuela (a kind of meat stew), and costillar (spicy pork ribs).

To return, drive back to the Pan–Am and follow it southward up to the Catapilco junction and turn right. From the village a farm road leads to **Laguna de Catapilco**, a good place for a picnic with a small lake perfect for windsurf.

Catapilco   the name is Mapuche, catan = to bore; pilco = hole; both words together mean «boxlike valley». Since pre–Conquest times, gold was washed from the creek using the trough system or the Chicken–craw method. The latter consisted of releasing chickens to feed by pecking on the surface sand, then killing them to recover any gold deposited in their craws. The gold–bearing sands are to be found at the banks of the creek flowing along the coast–bound road.

There, in 1877, the Catapilco Mining Co set up a plant and built a canal through solid rock to bring water from some 10 km away to their central installation at the village of La Laguna, near the sea. With steam–driven pumps, they produced powerful water jets which pulverized 10 thousand tons of soft rock every 24 hours. To fire the plant, the area's native forests were all turned into firewood. The mining company was a commercial success and disappeared around the turn of the century.

The road running along the Catapilco creek meets the coastal road at La Laguna, a few kilometers south of Cachagua and Zapallar.

SECTION B   MAITENCILLO TO QUINTERO

This section covers the stretch of coast between the mouth of the Catapilco creek to the North and the Aconcagua river to the South. Inland it stretches to the Coastal Range with mount Mauco as its highest peak. The Coastal Range veers away from the coast, the entire seaboard being raised sea bottom, low and rolling, with soils of degraded sand. This is evident along the coastal road and on the beaches, where every cliff looks sandy and has fossil sea shells among its components.

The coastline between the Aconcagua river and Quintero has been shaped by this short and powerful river, which carries significant volumes of sand into the sea. The sand is gradually deposited on the beaches lying to the north of the river's mouth, pushed by the ocean currents and the prevailing wind. Thus arose the large sand dune fields visible from the road.

Coastal Road   it runs for 44 km through this district, always away from the waterfront and with an occasional peek at the ocean. It passes some inland villages dating from colonial times, such as **Rungue**, a modest one–street hamlet, and **Puchuncaví,** in the past a seat of Peruvian Indians which later became a reservation, then a parish town and officially a village as from 1875. On the approach to Quintero, the road runs behind the region's largest industrial complex, with a great copper refinery boasting South America's tallest smokestack, a crude–oil terminal, and a 2–unit thermo–electrical power station.

Two detours offer you a chance to drive southwards along the beach for a while:

Loncura Detour   about 1 km after you pass the junction for Ventanas and Horcón, the road skirts the power station (with twin smokestacks). Right beyond the power station a road branches right towards the beach (unsigned), which it reaches at a point where a long pier juts into the sea. Turn left to skirt the bay (dirt road), passing the remain-

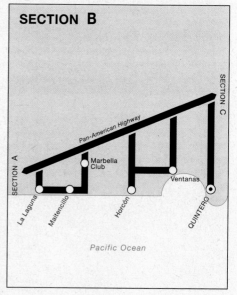

ing industrial facilities, then a smaller dock, a forested stretch and, finally, Loncura, a village on the beach. A road branches left there leading to the paved Concón–Quintero road. Turn left at this road, and you are headed South (towards Concón and Viña del Mar) once more.

Detour through Maitencillo   at La Laguna, the point where the road from Catapilco and the Pan–Am meets the coastal road, a branch road heads for the coast and passes a succession of small and medium–sized beaches along the Maitencillo resort; it rejoins the coastal road 7 km north of Puchuncaví.

NB on Sundays in summer, traffic jams can occur between 16:00 h & 21:00 h on the Quintero-Concón road, starting some 5 km before the bridge spanning the Aconcagua river. You will find gasoline at Maitencillo, the Ventanas junction, and Quintero.

Distances from Quintero to Santiago, 176 km via Concón, Calera and Pan–Am highway. 159 km via Viña del Mar and Route 68. To Papudo, 41 km. To La Ligua, 65 km. To Viña del Mar, 41 km. To Algarrobo, 118 km via Route 68 and Casablanca detour (see map). To Santo Domingo, 145 km.

Maitencillo beach

MAITENCILLO is the longest, narrowest seaside resort in this district, its houses clustered at the foot of a sandy cliff. The coastline is rocky, dotted with small beaches and quiet pools. A waterfront street runs along the entire resort, almost at water level. There are two biggish beaches, one at either end: **Playa Blanca** on the southern tip, **Playa Maitencillo** at the opposite end.

Just north of Maitencillo and on the banks of the Catapilco creek is **La Laguna**, a small summer spot offering horses and boats for hire. The coast here is renowned among scuba divers, who flock to the place even in dead winter. Maitencillo does not offer much in the way of services, forcing visitors to drive to Puchuncaví (12 km to the South) to satisfy any major need. Accommodations at Hotel Las Rojas, Hotel Javiera Carrera, and Cabañas Cerro Colorado.

Where To Eat Maitencillo is famous for its fresh seafood from its own fishing cove. La Caleta and Hotel La Roca are good spots; excellent cuisine at La Caracola and at La Pajera (summer only). Quicker meals at La Pérgola. For a picnic, try the outlying beaches.

MARBELLA CLUB an elegant, vast touristic center (270 ha) with an **urban development area**, summer houses, and condominiums. It has a **recreation and sports area**, with a golf course, tennis and paddle tennis courts, a polo field, and a riding school. It also has a **touristic area** with a modern 46 – room Motel. The Club House and disco are the heart of night life for Zapallar and Cachagua.

HORCON a highly picturesque fishing village with two-story wooden houses clustered at the bottom of wooded cliffs surrounding a small, wind–sheltered cove. A couple of longer beaches lie to either end of the village. Together with the local fishermen, a host of artists and artisans, poets and former hippies have made of this their hideaway. The place is quiet and dreamy most of the year, picking up on weekends; in summer it is a beehive, packed to extremes.

Horcón has a curious renown among the young backpackers making the Great American Circuit down to Tierra del Fuego: their sine–qua-non stops include Cuzco and Machu Picchu in Peru; Arica, Horcón, and Cucao at the Chiloé island. Horcón has, undeniably, a different atmosphere from the run–of–the–mill seaside resorts in Central Chile.

On June 29th every year, or on the first Sunday after that, the locals celebrate the **Festivity of Saint Peter**, the patron saint of fishermen. The entire village decks itself with garlands and other ornaments, the boats are festooned from bow to stern; one of them carries the saint's image around the bay. Gaily–clad confraternities of chinos come from other fishing coves and inland villages to dance their devotion to the saint. It is interesting.

From the western tip of the cove a footpath climbs the cliff to descend on the other side onto the Cau–Cau beach, one of the most beautiful in the area (see local beaches). Here is the first house built by a summer visitor, by 1936, who used to organize memorable parties. His passion were greyhounds, which he raised assiduously; their descendants are still to be seen around, and they are used for hunting hares.

To the east is Playa Larga, a long beach at the foot of a wooded cliff embracing a very placid sea.

Accommodations at one hostería and at several pensiones.

Where To Eat at the hostería and the various restaurants right on the beach, or a bit farther from the beach through narrow alleys. All specialize on seafood (offering the catch of the day).

Ventanas a small fishing village located on the northern tip of the large crescent of the Quintero bay. The beach is vast, with a quiet, shallow sea especially suitable for children. The restaurants are not fancy but they all specialize on seafood at reasonable prices. The name of the village stems from the window–like opening made by sea and wind on a large rock at a point about 1 km from the town. Ventanas is best avoided in summer, when low–budget vacationers invade the place and bury the beach beneath a sea of makeshift tents. Off season, however, the place offers nice walks past the «ventana» (the window–like rock) along a beautiful rocky coastline.

Loncura is another fishing village more or less at the middle of this same bay, and it is also a sort of down-market summer resort. Quiet off season, it has a good, open beach with placid, shallow

6

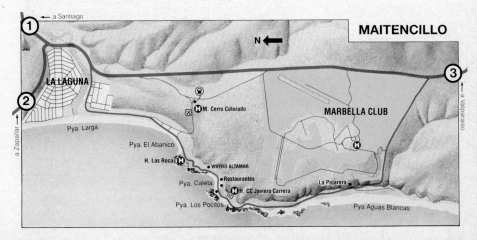

MAITENCILLO

← a Santiago

N ←

① ② ③

LA LAGUNA

a Zapallar

a Valparaíso

Pya. Larga

M. Cerro Colorado

Pya. El Abanico

H. Las Rocas

VIVERO ALTAMAR

Pya. Caleta

Restaurantes

H. CC Javiera Carrera

MARBELLA CLUB

La Pajarera

Pya. Los Pocitos

Pya Aguas Blancas

water. In summer it is good for jogging. There are some good restaurants.

QUINTERO has a string of good beaches which are its main attraction. It is home to the third most important yacht club in the Central Coastal Strip. Among the watersports commonly practiced here are yachting, windsurf, water ski and scuba diving. Diving gear and instructors are available for hire. At the muelle, the dock, there are boats for hire. If you like angling from the shore, try the Loncura or the Ritoque beaches (to the East and to the South, respectively). At the latter you can rent horses for a ride along the beach. For children, there is an amusement park.

Sunsets from **El Papagayo** beach are memorable, as is a walk along the waterfront promenade starting from the dock at **El Durazno** beach. You can also make the 20–min boat cruise to the cape (La Puntilla). Discos, restaurants, nightclubs, the Club de Yates or simply bonfires on the beach fuel night life. Quintero offers all urban services, and its accommodations range from hotels to residenciales.

The bay and the village were named after Alonso Quintero, a pilot working for conqueror Diego de Almagro, who discovered the place in 1536. The bay was visited by English privateer Thomas Cavendish in 1587, but he ran into a party of Spanish soldiers who dispatched 12 of his men before he left the place.

During the colonial period these lands were part of a large hacienda acquired around 1820 by Lord Cochrane, who spent long periods in this area. His house –now gone– was located right next to the harbor, and there he wrote his famous farewell manifest prior to leaving Chile, printing it in a litho press he set up at Quintero (Chile's first of its kind). During the 1822 earthquake, one of the guests in town was Maria Graham, an English lady, who wrote her «Diary of my Residence in Chile», with chilling descriptions of the earthquake and exceptionally readable chronicles of Chile during those years.

The creator of the harbor and resort was the great entrepreneur Luis Cousiño, who laid out the streets and was the driving force behind the construction of the railway, financing it with his own capital and that of other private individuals, paying them with plots of land near the harbor. His wholly unexpected death halted the work for a few years. Now it is a busy resort.

Where To Eat along the waterfront street near the Yachting Club and on the promenade along the beaches you will find a number of restaurants with dining rooms giving excellent views from their terraces over the sea.

Non-Urban Beaches between Maitencillo and the mouth of the Aconcagua river the coastline is mostly abrupt, with cliffs, ravines and occasional streams breaching them and then washing into the ocean. Still, there is a string of small, lonely beaches worth visiting. From Maitencillo southwards you will find the following:

Aguas Blancas located right to the South of Maitencillo, access is on foot. It is long, narrow and lies at the foot of a sandy cliff. It has a three–wave surf pattern, shallow and safe for children. Good fishing, and is good for camping or for a picnic. Lonely off season and quite frequented in summer.

South of Aguas Blancas, walking along the seashore, there are several small beaches tucked away between rocky cliffs. Access is difficult, at times impossible. Some can be reached by climbing down the cliff; climbing back up, however, can be very laborious. They are lonely, white–sanded, with calm water and excellent for bathing, diving, fishing or camping.

Las Agatas is located at the foot of steep cliffs, which provide the only access, beyond the northern end of the Quilliruca beach (see below). Dark–sanded and somewhat stony, it is sheltered from the wind and has a few pools among the rocks. It is a good spot for looking for agates (a semiprecious stone).

Quilliruca is located at the northern end of Horcón's Playa Larga. Accessible through a pri-

☎ Telephone Center	**B** Parish Church	**2** H Isla Capri	
★ Touristic Informations	**C** Yacht Club	**3** H Mónaco	**8** Bh La Moderna
⊕ Gasoline Station	**D** Buses to Santiago	**4** H California	**9** Bh Panamericano
⊙ Café, Meeting Point	**R** Restaurants	**5** H El Refugio	**10** Bh Ave Fénix
✱ Hospital	**ACCOMMODATIONS**	**6** Bh Casa de Piedra	**11** Bh María Alejandra
A Town Hall	**1** H Yachting Club	**7** Bh Ferry Boat	**12** Bh San Victor

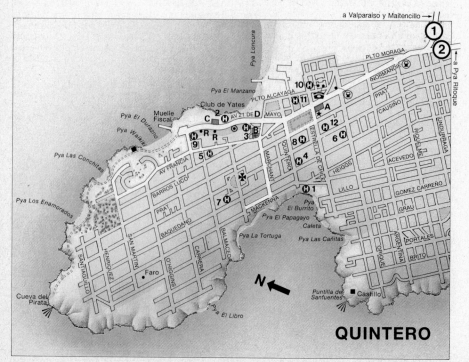

QUINTERO

6

vate road where a passage fee is charged (see main map), or walking four km along the beach from Horcón. It is lined by steep cliffs which shelter it from the SW wind. It is flat, with dark, fine sand containing ground fossil seashells, and has a 2–wave surf pattern. A small brook washes into the ocean. The place is good for diving, bathing, and camping.

Horcón's Playa Larga it stretches North from Horcón. It is long, narrow and curves in a flat crescent. From South to North it is divided into several stretches: Los Jotes, Clarón, Las Cañas or El Verde, and Iglesia. It has dark, compact sand, a one–wave surf pattern and is fairly flat. Frequented in summer, it has some campsites –or rather, spots for camping (a fee is charged).

Cau-Cau is located just west of Horcón, beyond the cape. Access is through a footpath. Mid–sized and sheltered by wooded cliffs, it has fine, light–colored sand, and a one–wave surf pattern with fairly strong undertow at times.

Very peaceful off season, it can get really crowded in summer.

El Tebo located southwest of Horcón, consists of two small beaches separated by a headland jutting into the sea. Access is on foot following footpaths along the coast. Placid, crystal clear sea, it is a very good spot for scuba diving or snorkeling. The two beaches are narrow and rocky, with a narrow strip of white, coarse sand with a seashell component. The place is flanked by wooded slopes suitable for camping. In summer it is frequented.

Ritoque is located just north of the Aconcagua

Horcón fishing cove

river mouth, and is the longest beach in this area, with 11 km. It is steep, open to the SW wind, dune–draped, with fine, dark sand, and a 3 to 5–wave surf pattern. It is excellent for angling and for a picnic. It can be divided into three sections: the northern tip (accessible by gravel road from Quintero), with some summer houses and a good restaurant where surfers gather. The cove is pretty, sheltered and lonely during the off-season, but quite frequented during the summer. Horses can be hired and, when the tide is low, buggies and cars can be driven along the beach.

The southern end near the mouth of the river is very popular in summer; access is through a path along the railway. The central section, in turn, is the longest and loneliest, with a single access trail opposite the rocky islet; it is good for angling and for strolling, particularly on calm days.

6

SECTION C   VALPARAISO AND VIÑA DEL MAR

This Section covers the coastal strip between the mouth of the Aconcagua river to the North and the Quintay bay to the South. Inland it stretches to include the Quillota valley, the Limache valley up to Quebrada Alvarado and, farther South, lake Peñuelas. It is home to about 850.000 people.

Morphologically, this area's main feature is the great height of the Coastal Range, with the tall peaks of La Campana and El Roble rising inland, and the spurs marching to the sea, ending in rocky capes at Valparaíso, Laguna Verde and Quintay. These tall hills afford protection against the SW wind, leaving some sheltered bays and, inland, giving rise to microclimates at Quillota, Limache and Olmué, where high–quality fruit production is abundant. Renowned are its papayas, lucuma, cherimoyas, avocados and vegetables. The coastal sierras also determine the course of rivers and streams, the main ones being the Aconcagua river, flowing from the Andean icecaps; the Marga Marga river, flowing through Viña del Mar and with its mouth right next to the Casino; the Peñuelas creek, which washes into the sea at Laguna Verde, and the Quintay creek, which empties at the namesake fishing village.

This is Chile's foremost tourist area. In summer, it is the busiest in the entire Central Coastal Strip. Concón, Reñaca, Viña del Mar and Valparaíso are a great urban complex with life of its own, offering visitors attractions the year round. Further South, and also included in this section, are Laguna Verde and the beautiful cove of Quintay.

Distances from Viña del Mar to Santiago, 120 km on Route 68; to Quintero, 41 km on the coastal road; Cachagua, 67 km; Zapallar, 71 km; Papudo, 82 km; Quintay, 50 km along Route 68 and a branch road from Lago Peñuelas; Algarrobo, 77 km along Route 68 and a branch road from Casablanca; El Quisco, 75 km; San Antonio, 112 km; Santo Domingo, 104 km, all of these along the

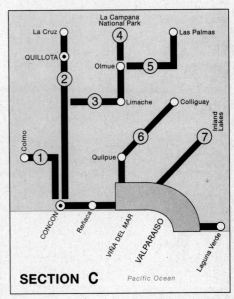

SECTION C   Pacific Ocean

same route; Limache, 33 km on Route 60; Quilllota, 49 km; Los Andes, 133 km; Mendoza, 367 km.

Coastal Road it runs for 30 km from Concón to Las Torpederas beach, at Valparaíso's southern tip. It has three clearcut sections: Concón–Viña del Mar, skirting the coastal rocks and beaches; Viña del Mar–Valparaíso, where it becomes the connecting intercity highway; and Valparaíso–Las Torpederas, once again skirting beaches and rocks. More than a coastal road, this route is here a waterfront avenue, providing access to the string of beaches and their restaurants along this stretch of coast.

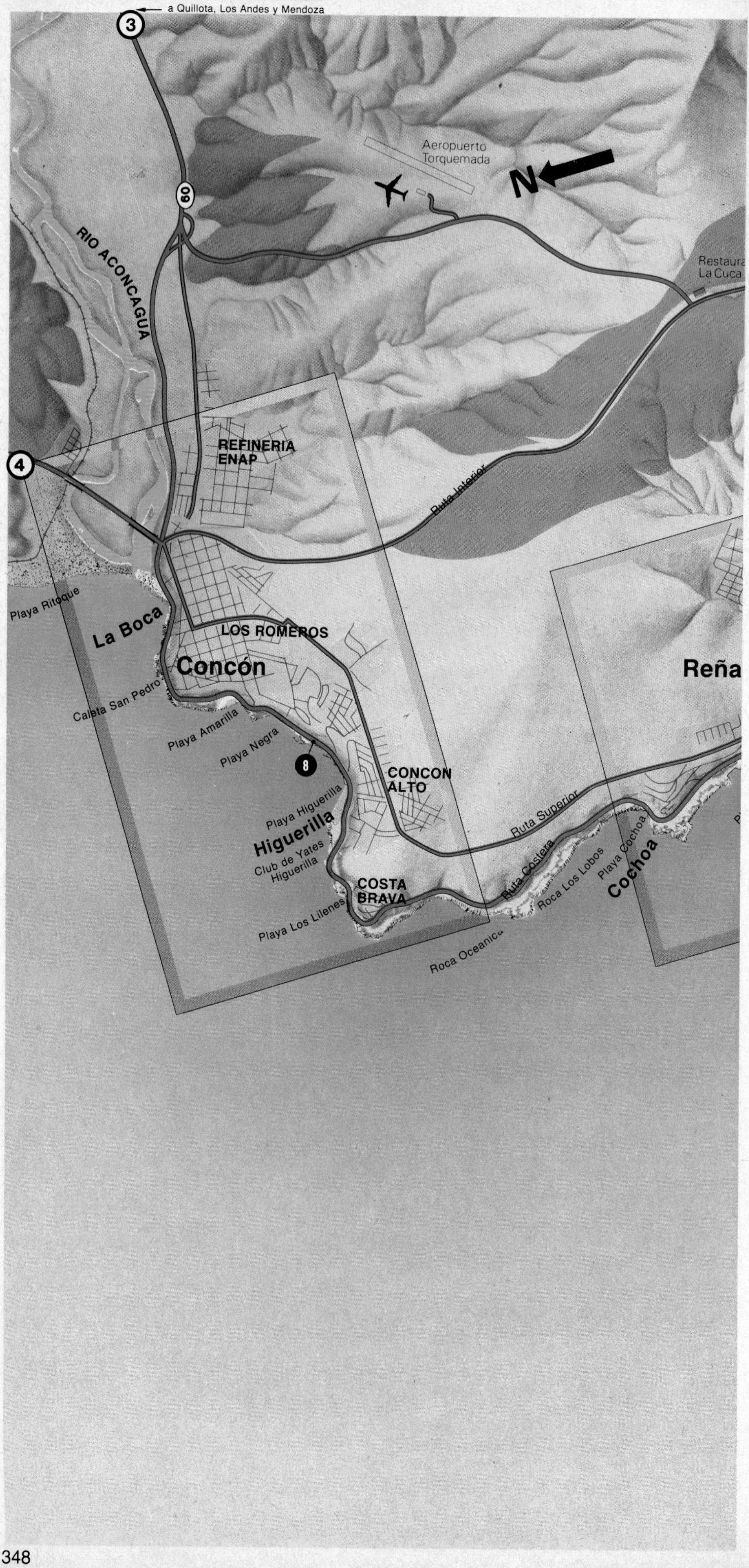

a Quillota, Los Andes y Mendoza

③

⑥⓪

RIO ACONCAGUA

Aeropuerto
Torquemada

N

Restaura
La Cuca

a Quintero y Zapallar →

④

REFINERIA
ENAP

Ruta Interior

6

Playa Ritoque

La Boca

LOS ROMEROS

Concón

Caleta San Pedro

Playa Amarilla

Playa Negra

8

Playa Higuerilla

Higuerilla

Club de Yates
Higuerilla

**CONCON
ALTO**

Reña

Ruta Superior

Ruta Costera

Roca Los Lobos

Playa Cochoa

Cochoa

**COSTA
BRAVA**

Playa Los Lilenes

Roca Oceanica

a Quilpué

(5)

(10)

PARQUE
DEL SALITRE

VILLA
DULCE

CANAL
BEAGLE

EL SALTO

(10)

MIRAFLORES
TO

MIRAFLORES

CHORRILLOS

SPORTING
CLUB

FORESTAL

DEL MAR

6

QUINTA
VERGARA

NUEVA
AURORA

(1)

68

(2)

68

a Acapulco

Playa Estero

Co
CASTILLO

RECREO

Playa Caleta Abarca

Balneario Recreo

Club de Yates
Recreo

ESPERANZA

Terminal
Pesquero

(15)

PLACERES

Camino Los Ingleses

LAS ZORRAS

(14)

Jardín
Pumpin

Von Moltke

O'HIGGINS

Av Washington

(14)

Portales

Caleta Portales

BARON

Muelle Barón

VALPARAISO

a Quebrada verde

Puerto

Molo

(6)

(13)

PUERTAS
NEGRAS

Caleta Membrillo

Membrillo

Escuela
Naval

Av G

Bretaña

Av Quebrada Verde

Mirador
Marina
Mercante

(13)

PLAYA
ANCHA

Estadio

Playa Las Torpederas

Piedra Feliz

NB: if you have already made the Concón–Viña del Mar coastal stretch and want to travel a bit faster between the two, avoiding the bumper–to–bumper traffic particularly acute on weekend afternoons, it is advisable to take either of the two inland roads linking these cities (see map).

CITIES AND RESORTS IN THE AREA

CONCON   a residential town and seaside resort located 18 km North of Viña del Mar. Lying on a hillside adjacent to the mouth of the Aconcagua river, it overlooks a gorgeous bay lined with houses and buildings, condominiums, small forests and gardens.

It has three good beaches and a Yacht Club right alongside the road. Concón's shopping area is at the northern tip, **on the river bank,** with restau-

rants, seafood shops, supermarkets, etc. Another center is **Higuerillas,** at the opposite end of the bay and next to the Yacht Club, with good restaurants having superb views, and seafood outlets.

Concón appeared early in Chilean history. In 1543, on the beach next to the river, a temporary boat–building yard had started the construction of a ship that was promptly destroyed by Chieftain Michimalongo; this was the first skirmish between Spaniards and natives. In 1822 a small copper refinery operated at the place, and the village became the shipping port for the produce of the valley's inland farms.

The seaside resort appeared at the turn of the century with the construction of the Gran Hotel – at the same site as today's version– and whose elegant lounges and parlors were the center of an intense social life. Spacious summer residences were erected on Playa Amarilla and on the sur-

	RESTAURANTS	10 Don Chicho	23 Cp Las Gaviotas
Telephon Center	1 Edelweiss	11 La Picá de Emeterio	24 M Solymar
Gasoline Station	2 Fogón Marino	12 Trocadero	
Cafe, Meeting Point	3 Lilenes	13 El Tirol	**INEXPENSIVE RESTAURANTS**
Lookout Point	4 Vista al Mar		15 Seafood Stalls
Excursion Suggested in Text	5 Albatros	**ACCOMMODATIONS**	16 Las Delicias
	6 Alicia	20 M Las Delicias	
A Parish Church	8 Massa	21 Centro Turístico Mantagua	**DISCOTHEQUE**
D Tennis Court	9 Reinaldo's	22 H Internacional Playa Amarilla	30 César

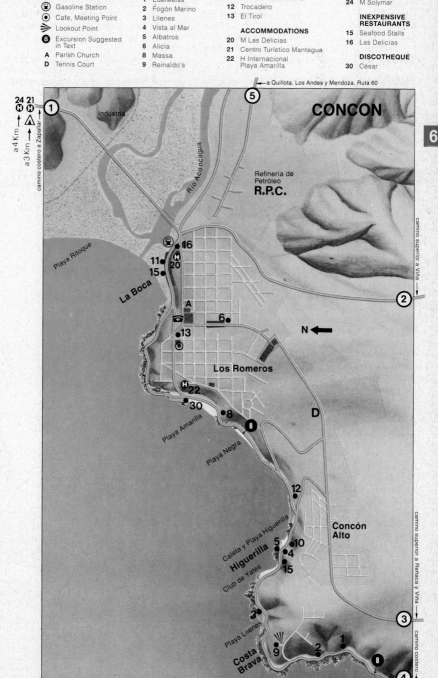

6

351

Viña del Mar, San Martín avenue

rounding rock outcrops. The resort then expanded towards the hills, upon the slopes and into the forests, which are now peppered with summer houses. Concón offers a complete range of tourist services, accommodations ranging from hotels through motels to condominiums, and restaurants for all tastes. The action centers around **Playa Amarilla** and its spacious promenade.

REÑACA six km north of Viña del Mar along the coast is this beautiful beach, about 2 km long, lined by fairly steep cliffs sliced across by the Reñaca brook. The first plots of land of the farm of which Reñaca was part were offered for sale as recently as 1947; soon summer houses started to be built near the beach, as well as casas-quinta, houses set in their own orchard, which Viña del Mar residents set up in the area along the brook.

The pace of development of this part of Viña del Mar has been breathtaking. The great beach, empty of visitors in 1965, was the stage for jeep races and family–party soccer matches. Just one decade ago Reñaca became the foremost tourist hot–spot. Spectacular buildings crawl up the cliff-sides like giant stairs.

At **Las Cañitas** is the largest urban development undertaken in the last few years, turning Reñaca into the most developed area in this Section.

The **beach** is very popular with young people and a magnet for thousands of up–market visitors in summer. Its waterfront promenade –**the costanera**– is the place to be in the evening. There is a number of hotels and motels, and a host of restaurants along the beach.

Several very good discos, cafes and drive–in eateries, grill–bars and a bowling alley keep night-owls busy to their heart's content.

VIÑA DEL MAR (pop 300.000). Chile's chief sea-side resort, lies 120 km from Santiago following Route 68. It has a casino, lots of hotels, motels, residenciales, restaurants and discothèques, in addition to excellent beaches lined with ample promenades. It offers an entire range of services supporting tourist activity **throughout the year.** It has been dubbed garden city on account of its being surrounded by green areas such as the **Quinta Vergara, Sausalito, Sporting Club, Granadilla Golf Club** and **National Botanical Garden,** in addition to the ubiquitous flower beds and gardens and squares. Inner streets are shaded by leafy trees; tall palms march along the lagoon of the Marga–Marga and giant maple–like trees form a veritable tunnel at the southern portion of Av Libertad.

Viña del Mar's residential quarters have chalets set in lush gardens; the seafront avenue is lined with apartment buildings with balconies overlooking the ocean, punctuated by squares and gardens. To the right of the mouth of the Marga-Marga is the **Casino Municipal**, with its gambling

rooms, nightclubs and restaurants open year–round; it is one of the leading entertainment spots in town.

Viña del Mar's history is recent, barely a century old. The place was an hacienda since the colonial days and its name comes from a vineyard growing where the Quinta Vergara is now located. In 1855 it was connected by railroad with Valparaíso and since then porteños –Valparaíso residents– started to visit the Viña del Mar valley, making it a favorite area for outings, horse races and bathing (at Miramar beach, now disappeared). By 1872, some porteños, mainly foreigners, leased plots of land close to the railway line, where they built their houses surrounded by large gardens, one thing the constricted level portion of Valparaíso found impossible to offer. The owner of the hacienda, Viña Dolores P de Alvarez, had her residence and a most beautiful, exotic park in the area of the present–day Quinta Vergara (described under excursions on foot).

In 1874 Viña del Mar was founded as a town; it acquired a municipality five years later, and the parish church and the Sporting Club in 1882. In the meantime, the elegant Gran Hotel had been erected –now gone–, triggering the flow –as yet unceasing– of Santiago residents to this stretch of coast.

The flat plain and the Av Libertad portion were divided into plots and sold in 1892; soon, large summer mansions sprouted together with permanent residences for people who had moved here from Valparaíso. Since then, the resort city has experienced uninterrupted growth.

In the first decade of this century the mansions of Quinta Rioja, Quinta Vergara and House Carrasco at Av Libertad were built, among others. In the fruitful 1930s, the above were followed by the Municipal Theater, Hotel O'Higgins, Palacio Residencial, Municipal Casino, Las Salinas resort, and the coastal road to Concón. Soon afterwards the coastal strip was built up, with Hotel Miramar, the Caleta Abarca resort, Av Marina and Av Perú.

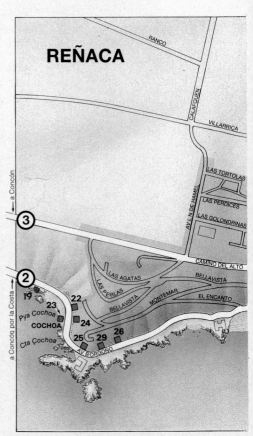

6

☎ Telephone Center
◉ Café, Meeting Point
⇥ Lookout Point
A Parish Church
B Bowling
C Post Office
D Tennis Court

ACCOMMODATIONS
1 H Oceanic
2 Holiday Motel
3 H Presidente
4 M del Pacifico
5 M Nilahue

6 M Amancay
7 M Los Ositos
8 Cb La Muerte
9 M Safari
10 M Iguasú
11 M Manquehue
14 M Natania
12 M Caja de EEPP
13 Cs Reñaca

RESTAURANTS
19 Stella Maris
20 Anastassia
21 Cura Nurin
22 Pacífico

23 Cochoa
24 Toconao
25 Rincón Marino
26 El Poncho
27 Eglantine
28 La Cueva del Oso
29 Pica de Mi Compadre
35 Tabla'o
39 Alster Salón de Té

INEXPENSIVE RESTAURANTS
30 Los Pomairinos
31 Long Beach
32 Mastrantonio

34 Sua Pizza

SITES POPULAR WITH THE YOUNG
B Bowling
31 Long Beach
36 Bruno Tavelli
37 La Mela
38 Pirulas

DISCOTHEQUES
40 Topsi
41 Yo Claudio
42 Casados Club

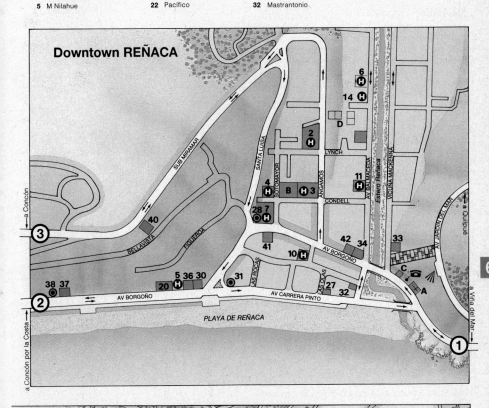

The city has been sort of refurbished in the last few years, and a second generation of buildings has sprung up along the coast on plots where not so long ago there were only single summer residences. The city is a bustling place, the heart of town during the day lying along street Valparaíso, which is the shopping street and the gathering point for young and old. For recreation, the beaches; for night life, the many discos, nightclubs, restaurants and the like along the coast.

VALPARAISO located 115 km from Santiago following Route 68, Chile's main port –and now the seat of Congress– climbs the crescent of hills around it in a maze of alleys, winding streets and connecting stairs and funicular railways. At the foot of the hills lies the narrow belt of flatland, partially reclaimed from the sea, where the business center, with its beautiful architecture, and the port are located.

Valparaíso combines in its urban landscape the giant bulk of ships moored at the wharves with the narrowness of its main streets. Ingenuity has turned an abrupt piece of coastline into one of the world's most picturesque ports, particularly arresting when seen from the sea at dusk: a semi–circle of lit–up hills cascading down to the water.

The Quintil bay was christened Valparaíso in 1536 by Juan de Saavedra –a pilot of the Diego de Almagro expedition– after his native town in Spain. In 1542, Pedro de Valdivia granted the bay the title of seaport «to serve the trade of these lands and of Santiago». In 1599 a chapel was built at the site where now the Iglesia Matriz sits, a cluster of modest dwellings surrounding it.

As is the case with most seaports in the Americas, Valparaíso has no clear date of foundation. During the 17th and 18th centuries, the port only had seasonal activity; ships sailed down from Callao in summer and then the port was very busy, just to lay dormant during the rest of the year. Nevertheless, to support the harbor activities, permanent warehouses, houses and churches were built, together with a fortress with a garrison, called Castillo de San José, at the Cordillera hill, up from present–day Serrano square.

In the early 19th century, after Chile attained independence, the ports of Chile and the Americas were opened to world trade and Valparaíso found itself strategically located along the shipping routes circling Cape Horn from the Atlantic, headed for the Pacific islands and coastline. This gave a tremendous boost to Valparaíso, which became a port of call and resupply after the harsh rounding of Cape Horn. Its warehouses stored goods and merchandise which was to be reexported to other ports in the Pacific and Oceania.

English, German and French immigrants settled at the port and started to run the import trade. They also brought with them foreign capital to finance development of copper and silver mining and, later, of nitrate mining, in addition to the major public works undertaken in the second half of the 19th century.

Valparaíso became the country's leading commercial and financial center, with the establishment of the first banks and a stock exchange. It was, furthermore, a pioneer in every urban development in Chile, such as railways, electricity, trams, telegraph, telephone, gas networks, etc. The beautiful mansions erected in the residential quarters of town and on the Alegre and Concepción hills all date from that period. Many of these buildings have become conventillos, tenements inhabited by low–income families.

Today, Valparaíso is a great bustling city, the capital of Region V, Chile's principal seaport and, since recently, the seat of Congress, which is housed in a purpose–built building. With a popu-

6

☎ Telephone Center
★ Touristic Information
◉ Café, Meeting Point
Ⓦ Gasoline Station
⇗ Lookout Point
❼ Excursion Suggested in Text
A National Congress
C Naval Museum
L Town Hall
M Cathedral
N Bus Terminal
B Cardonal Market
P Feria Persa (flea market)

PLACES OF INTEREST
G Old Customs House
H Matriz Church
S Padres Franceses Church
T Jesuit Church
F Paseo 21 de Mayo
V Paseo Portales
W Polanco Elevator
J Old Government Building
D La Victoria Square
E Italia Square
K O'Higgins Square

RESTAURANTS
11 El Castillo
12 Club Alemán
13 La Trattoria
14 Bogarín
15 El Dragón de Oro
16 La Bussola
17 Proa al Cañaveral
18 Club Español
20 Hamburgo

ACCOMMODATIONS
1 H Lancaster
2 H Prat
3 H Condell

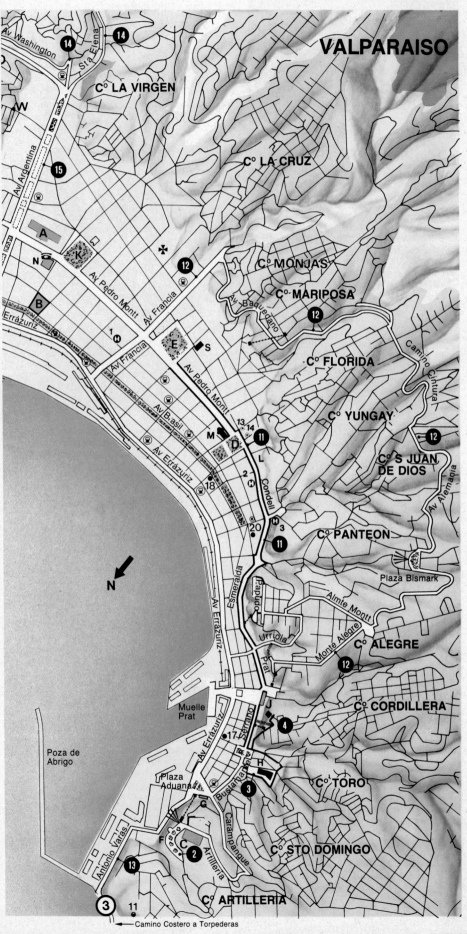

VALPARAISO

Cº LA VIRGEN

Cº LA CRUZ

Cº MONJAS

Cº MARIPOSA

Cº FLORIDA

Cº YUNGAY

Cº S JUAN DE DIOS

Cº PANTEON

Plaza Bismark

Cº ALEGRE

Cº CORDILLERA

Cº TORO

Cº STO DOMINGO

Cº ARTILLERIA

Av Washington

Sta Elena

W

Av Argentina

N

A

K

B

Errázuriz

Av Pedro Montt

Av Francia

E

S

Av Francia

Av Brasil

Av Errázuriz

Av Pedro Montt

Av Baquedano

Camino Cintura

Av Alemania

M

D

L

Condell

Esmeralda

Papudo

Urriola

Prat

Almte Montt

Monte Alegre

N

Muelle Prat

Av Errázuriz

Serrano

J

H

Poza de Abrigo

Plaza Aduana

G

F

C

Antonio Varas

Bustamante

Carampangue

Artillería

Camino Costero a Torpederas

Reñaca beach

lation of over 300.000, it is the commercial and administrative center for a vast region, as well as the place where people from the urban cluster of Viña del Mar, Reñaca and Concón work, in addition to many other people from the inland cities of Quilpué, Villa Alemana and Peñablanca.

Valparaíso is also a major university center, with one of the leading technical universities in Chile – the Santa María, housed in a beautiful cluster of buildings perched atop a bluff– and several others.

Laguna Verde is located 18 km south of Valparaíso, following a gravel road starting from the Playa Ancha quarter in Valparaíso and passing near the Punta Angeles lighthouse, the first lighthouse on the West Coast of the Americas. This is a new coastal road (so far only graveled) running atop some huge rocky cliffs plunging into the ocean. The road itself makes for a spectacular ride.

Laguna Verde is a small village nestled on a vast beach of white sand, in a sheltered harbor flanked by tall, pine–clad hills. The place is picturesque, isolated, and it has a campsite under shady olive groves. Supplies are available and you can buy the catch of the day from the local fishermen. The place's mainstay are forestry and agriculture. There is also a thermoelectric power plant which provides emergency power for the zone.

A dirt road starts from Laguna Verde leading in 10 km, through pine forests to **Las Docas beach.** The bathing beach is scenic, quiet and excellent for sunbathing. In the past, is was a favorite hideout for smugglers.

Quintay is located 104 km from Santiago and 45 km from Viña del Mar. Take the gravel road branching west at Peñuelas (28 km), winding its way through hilly terrain and enormous forest plantations. The sea and the coastal cliffs can be seen from afar. Quintay is divided into two sections: the resort and the fishing cove.

The Resort is located at the northern end of the bay, with a beautiful, fine–sanded beach, and a 2 or 3–wave surf pattern, fairly flat gradient and excellent for bathing. Not too frequented, it is also good for a picnic or for camping. There are hosterías offering rooms and cabins at reasonable prices. At the fishing cove there are some modest restaurants offering very good seafood.

The Fishing Cove is set on a small, sheltered beach. Adjacent to the cove are the remains of an old, Japanese–owned whaling factory long since inoperative. Locals claim that whales are still to be seen in the area. Large whalebones adorn many houses and hosterías in Quintay.

URBAN BEACHES IN THIS AREA

The main beaches from North to South are:

AMARILLA Concón's leading bathing beach, with 400 m in length, fine sand and a placid, one–wave surf pattern. Wind–sheltered, it has a restaurant, a café and facilities (change cabins, showers, children's playground). It is usually full, as it is the favorite beach both for vacationers and Concón residents alike.

Negra is located 500 m south of Concón. It is narrow, dark-sanded and with some rock outcrops. Good bathing for children and adults alike.

Higuerilla lies 100 m north of the namesake fishing cove; access is through the buildings along the seafront. it is small, with very placid waters, suitable for children and ideal for windsurfers. It has a good view towards the yacht harbor.

LOS LILENES located 13 km north of Viña del Mar and 3 km south of Concón, is small, sheltered and with quiet sea, good for swimming. It has a nice restaurant, cabins for changing and a huge dune–draped hill spilling onto the beach, favorite playground for children. It has ample parking space.

COCHOA located 8 km north of Viña del Mar, is a small, wind-sheltered beach, nice surf. It has change cabins, and is surrounded by good restaurants with terraces overlooking the beach, and by seafood shops. Car parking.

REÑACA located 6 km north of Viña del Mar, it has white sand and pounding surf, not really suitable for swimming. Usually windy, its northern end is more sheltered. Parking lot. This is the busiest beach in summer in the entire central Coastal Strip and a hot–spot for the young. Cabins for changing and showers are available on the beach, as well as a range of restaurants and cafés.

LAS SALINAS 3 km north of Viña del Mar, is small, sheltered and the sea is quiet, suitable for swimming. There are restaurants on the beach, cabins for changing, showers and good parking lots in the vicinity. It is the most frequented beach when the sun gets friendlier in early November and December, as it is wind–sheltered. In summer it is packed.

Los Marineros just south of Las Salinas, it stretches for 2.400 m up to the Muelle Vergara, in the city itself. White-sanded, open to the wind. The sea is deep and the surf strong, not suitable for swimming. A mid–density beach, there are no facilities available; it is visited mostly by families looking for a quieter spot and no parking problems.

ACAPULCO is a 200–m–long beach lying between Av Perú and the Muelle Vergara. White–sanded, quiet sea, and sheltered by the tall apartment buildings lining it. Frequented by the locals, who usually just walk over to the beach.

CALETA ABARCA lies at the heart of Viña del Mar, with 300 m in length and white sand; very good for bathing and swimming. Surrounded by beautiful buildings and gardens, it is the city's most developed beach. It has a promenade, a restaurant, cafés, discos, changing cabins and showers. Ideal for sunbathing in November and December. In summer it is packed; good access by public transportation.

PORTALES located between Viña del Mar and Valparaíso, it is accessible from the intercity highway. Quiet waters, one–wave surf pattern, a nice waterfront promenade and a good restaurant adjacent to the busy fishing cove. Popular.

Las Torpederas is picturesque and located at Valparaíso's southern tip. Sheltered and with quiet sea, it is good for children and adults alike. It is quite popular with Valparaíso residents.

GASTRONOMY

Valparaíso, Viña del Mar, Reñaca and Concón have a wide range of restaurants, impossible to describe in extenso. We list below those ranking as outstanding.

· The restaurants are listed first by location: **Valparaíso, Viña del Mar** or **Coastal Road** (Reñaca, Cochoa, Higuerillas and Concón). Second, by their features: the **best cuisine and overlooking the ocean**, or a simpler **waterfront** restaurant, or a **specialty restaurant**, or one offering the **day's menu,** or finally those falling within the **"picada"** category, i.e. good value at a low price.

Based on the above, we have selected the following restaurants:

Viña del Mar, Wulf castle

BEST CUISINE AND OVERLOOKING THE SEA the restaurants in this category fulfill three conditions: they are located on the waterfront, are finely appointed and offer fine service, in addition to having superb cuisine. They are also in the upper price range.

In Valparaíso on the Muelle Prat is the **Bote Salvavidas,** with the best view of the harbor and specialized in seafood prepared according to the international cuisine. Outstanding is its Greek–style fish.

In Viña del Mar at Av Marina, perched atop the rocks, is **Cap Ducal,** specialized in European cuisine and offering its own creations as well.

On the Coastal Road on the rocks beyond Cochoa and the Los Lobos look–out point is **Stella Maris,** nicely decorated and specialized in international cuisine. A bit farther on, between Cochoa and Higuerillas, is **Edelweiss,** with a view towards the ocean and rocky cliffs; fish, shellfish and meat prepared according to French cuisine. Outstanding are its fondues and flambé deserts. **Reinaldo's** is on the way to Costa Brava; spectacular view and international cuisine.

COASTAL RESTAURANTS these are more tourist–oriented, somewhat cheaper than the above and with a simpler architectural style. They are mostly specialized in seafood.

On the Coastal Road renowned is **La Picá de Mi Compadre,** located at the Montemar curve –between Reñaca and Cochoa–, with good Chilean cuisine. Outstanding are its plateada –a beef dish– and the lucuma cake. At Cochoa is **El Pacífico,** specialized in seafood. At Caleta Higuerillas is the misleadingly named **Vista al Mar** (not much of a view over the sea), but with very good fish and shellfish dishes; outstanding is its flatfish on black butter. **Albatros,** also at Higuerillas and built on a rock outcrop, overlooks the yacht harbor; it has both indoor and outdoor dining areas, the latter on a terrace above the sea. **Don Chicho,** at Higuerillas, is picturesque and service is headed by its very owner, who comes from the adjacent fishing cove; it specializes in seafood. At Concón, next to the mouth of the river is **La Picá de Emeterio,** with good fish and shellfish in a modest but pleasant setting.

SPECIALTY RESTAURANTS these are city restaurants, their specialty cuisine ranging from excellent to good, and fine decoration. They range from reasonable to pricey.

In Valparaíso **El Castillo** is traditional, perched atop a cliff over the El Membrillo cove; it has a good view and specializes in international cuisine. **Proa al Cañaveral,** at Av Errázuriz 304, opposite the harbor, is decorated with nets and other sea–related objects and specializes in seafood. **Bar Inglés,** at Cochrane 851 and with access from two streets, is a traditional bar and restaurant, very busy at lunch-

time on weekdays. **Café Turri,** at Paseo Gervasoni, accessible by Turri funicular railway at Prat opposite the Turri Clock (see map) and also by car through Tomás Ramos street; it is a good restaurant housed in an old mansion with a superb view over the harbor. **Galeone D'Oro,** at Independencia 1760, half a block off Victoria square, spotless, with the best Italian cuisine in the region. **La Bussola,** at Independencia on Plaza Italia, is a quaint old mansion with excellent Italian cuisine at reasonable prices.

In Viña del Mar at Av San Martín 597 is the traditional **San Marco,** with Italian and international cuisine with a level of excellence unchanged over several decades. **Mare Nostro,** at 4 Norte between 1 & 2 Poniente, offers the widest variety of seafood prepared according to international cuisine. **Armandita,** at Av San Martín 501, a busy restaurant specialized in Argentine grilled meat. **Gipsy,** at Av San Martín corner of 8 Norte, specializes in French cuisine and renowned pancakes. Picturesque **La Cuisine,** next to the bus terminal, has fine French cuisine at reasonable prices. **Machitún Ruca,** at Av San Martín (see map), has the best typical Chilean and Mapuche cuisine, its sauces ranked as outstanding; the place is well taken care of and pleasant. **Max und Moritz,** Av San Martín 631, on a side street, offers German cuisine and beer in a typically German atmosphere, at reasonable prices. **Cantina Gigi,** opposite the above restaurant, offers Italian food in a family atmosphere. **Mastrantonio,** with two addresses, one at 2 Norte corner of 6 Poniente and the other one in Reñaca, at the edge of the creek and the beach, offers varied Italian dishes in an informal, busy atmosphere; reasonable prices.

DAY–MENU RESTAURANTS these specialize in offering lunch on working days, with one to three different menus; their patrons are mostly office workers from the business and administrative quarter. Reasonable prices and fast service.

In Valparaíso at Plaza Aníbal Pinto is the traditional **Café Riquet. Westfalia,** at Cochrane 847, good, cheap and full. **La Cuisine,** Urriola 342, more exclusive. **La Rotonda,** Prat 701, fast. **Club Valparaíso,** on the top floor of the Cooperativa building on Plaza Aníbal Pinto, spacious and with a spectacular view. **Club Alemán,** Salvador Donoso 1337, pleasant. **Club Español,** Av Brasil 1589, good, overlooking the harbor.

In Viña del Mar the traditional **Samoiedo,** Calle Valparaíso 637, busy and pleasant. **Anayak,** Quinta 156, frequented and luminous. **Club de Viña,** on the square to the side of the railway station, with spacious rooms and more intimacy.

«GOOD–VALUE» RESTAURANTS as in every city, here are some of these establishments whose fame spreads by word of mouth.

6

357

In **Valparaíso** for meat dishes, **El Parrón**, on the hill behind Caleta Portales. For Chinese food, the best is **Dragón de Oro**, directly off Condell, downtown. The **Cocinerías** (food stalls) at Caleta Portales, the only place where you can enjoy a seafood soup at 6 o'clock in the morning, together with the fishermen returning from their night at sea.

In **Viña del Mar** chilean dishes –specialty pork–, at **Las Gaviotas**, San Antonio street; particularly good for groups.

Coastal Road at Playa Cochoa there are **marisquerías** –seafood eateries– where you can enjoy a hearty dish and a glass of wine for a very reasonable price. At Concón, opposite the bridge spanning the Aconcagua, is **Las Deliciosas**, with tasty meat, cheese and shellfish empanadas (fried version), either to eat at the place or to take out.

CAFES usually in Chile they go by the name of Salón de Té, and they have a long tradition in high–quality pastries.

In **Valparaíso** on Plaza Aníbal Pinto is the traditional **Café Riquet**, with fine French-style pastries.

In **Viña del Mar** nice view over the sea from the terraces of **Hotel Miramar**. German pastries at the pleasant **Café Alster**, Valparaíso 227. Very popular and with superb café helado con crema –coffee and icecream and whipped cream– and other specialties is the **Samoiedo**, Valparaíso 637, and the nearby **Anayak**, Quinta 156.

In **Concón** excellent pastries at **El Tirol**, a charming place with a splendid view located near the square (see map). It offers a good chance for a stop on an evening drive along the coast.

ENTERTAINMENT PLACES

There are plenty of opportunities for entertainment for all age groups, including some specialized sports centers.

For Children a circuit by launch around the harbor from the Prat pier (Muelle Prat) in Valparaíso can be recommended; departures at all times. **Amusement park** at plaza Simón Bolívar in Valparaíso; in Viña del Mar there is one at Av Costanera between Viña del Mar and Reñaca, and at plaza Colombia in Av Perú. Another one functions on the riverbed of the Estero de Viña in summer. There is a bicycross course at the Sporting Club.

Dancing Establishments the best is **César**, on the Amarilla beach. The **Topsy** disco is housed in a spectacular building which cascades down the slope, in Reñaca. Also at Reñaca is the **Reñaca Club**. In Viña del Mar, **La Scala**, on Caleta Abarca beach. The last two lean more toward rock music.

Sports Centers for tennis devotees, the best are the courts of **Tenis Sausalito**, adjacent to the namesake small lake in Viña del Mar (tel 976249). The **Bowling** at Reñaca is popular and entertaining. For golfers, the **Granadilla Golf Club** in Viña del Mar (see map). At Viña del Mar's **Sporting Club** (see map) is the Hipódromo racecourse, with races Friday afternoons and Sundays; its main event is the Derby horse race, first sunday in February. Also at the Sporting, football (soccer) fields can be rented.

PERIODICAL EVENTS

New Year on the Bay at midnight on December 31st, the arrival of the new year is celebrated by a firework display on the bay and harbor of Valparaíso, which is watched best from the terraces and look–out points on the surrounding hills and from rock outcrops on the seashore. Arrive at least one hour in advance to even find a parking slot and choose a place with a good view. For large groups, it is best to hire a boat at Muelle

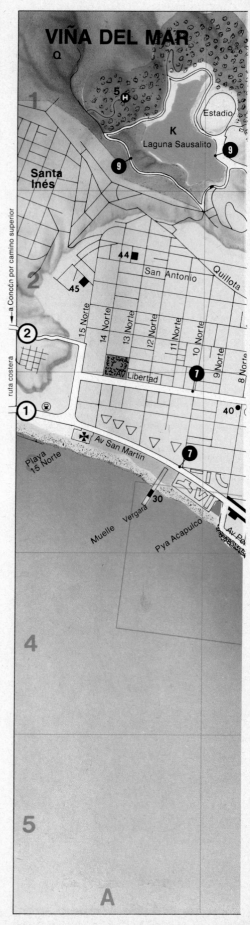

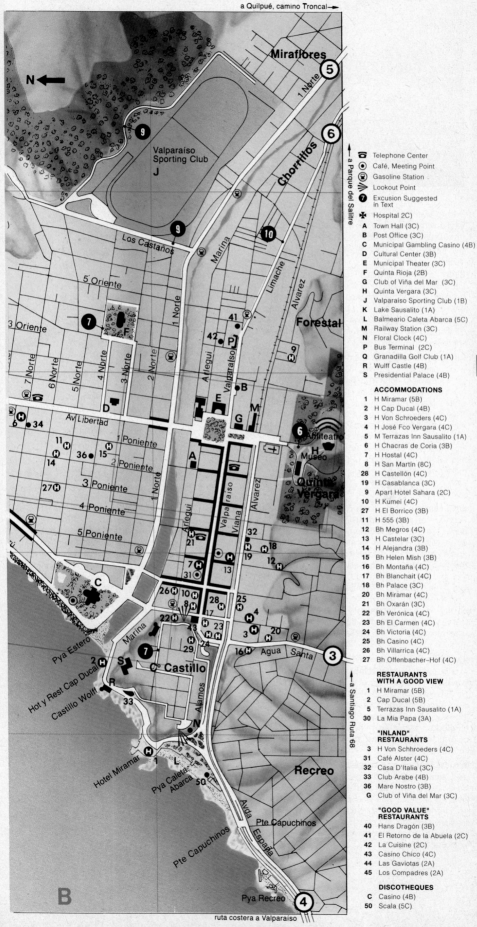

a Quilpué, camino Troncal→

Miraflores

Valparaíso Sporting Club J

Chorrillos

Forestal

Los Castaños

5° Oriente

3 Oriente

7 Norte · 6 Norte · 5 Norte · 4 Norte · 3 Norte · 2 Norte · 1 Norte

Av Libertad

1 Poniente

2 Poniente

3 Poniente

4 Poniente

5 Poniente

Pya Estero

Marina

Hot y Rest Cap Ducal

Castillo Wolff

Hotel Miramar

Pya Caleta Abarca

Pte Capuchinos

Pte Capuchinos

Avda España

Recreo

Pya Recreo

ruta costera a Valparaíso

a Parque del Salitre

a Santiago Ruta 68

Agua Santa

C° Castillo

🕿 Telephone Center
◉ Café, Meeting Point
⊙ Gasoline Station
⚲ Lookout Point
❼ Excusion Suggested in Text
✳ Hospital (2C)
A Town Hall (3C)
B Post Office (3C)
C Municipal Gambling Casino (4B)
D Cultural Center (3B)
E Municipal Theater (3C)
F Quinta Rioja (2B)
G Club of Viña del Mar (3C)
H Quinta Vergara (3C)
J Valparaíso Sporting Club (1B)
K Lake Sausalito (1A)
L Balmeario Caleta Abarca (5C)
M Railway Station (3C)
N Floral Clock (4C)
P Bus Terminal (2C)
Q Granadilla Golf Club (1A)
R Wulff Castle (4B)
S Presidential Palace (4B)

ACCOMMODATIONS

1 H Miramar (5B)
2 H Cap Ducal (4B)
3 H Von Schroeders (4C)
4 H José Fco Vergara (4C)
5 M Terrazas Inn Sausalito (1A)
6 H Chacras de Coria (3B)
7 H Hostal (4C)
8 H San Martín (8C)
28 H Castellón (4C)
19 H Casablanca (3C)
9 Apart Hotel Sahara (2C)
10 H Kumei (4C)
27 H El Borrico (3B)
11 H 555 (3B)
12 Bh Megros (4C)
13 H Castelar (3C)
14 H Alejandra (3B)
15 Bh Helen Mish (3B)
16 Bh Montaña (4C)
17 Bh Blanchait (4C)
18 Bh Palace (3C)
20 Bh Miramar (4C)
21 Bh Oxarán (4C)
22 Bh Verónica (4C)
23 Bh El Carmen (4C)
24 Bh Victoria (4C)
25 Bh Casino (4C)
26 Bh Villarrica (4C)
27 Bh Offenbacher–Hof (4C)

RESTAURANTS WITH A GOOD VIEW

1 H Miramar (5B)
2 Cap Ducal (5B)
5 Terrazas Inn Sausalito (1A)
30 La Mia Papa (3A)

"INLAND" RESTAURANTS

3 H Von Schhroeders (4C)
31 Café Alster (4C)
32 Casa D'Italia (3C)
33 Club Arabe (4B)
36 Mare Nostro (3B)
G Club of Viña del Mar (3C)

"GOOD VALUE" RESTAURANTS

40 Hans Dragón (3B)
41 El Retorno de la Abuela (2C)
42 La Cuisine (2C)
43 Casino Chico (4C)
44 Las Gaviotas (2A)
45 Los Compadres (2A)

DISCOTHEQUES

C Casino (4B)
50 Scala (5C)

Valparaíso, Paseo 21 de Mayo

Prat to watch the show from the water. Arrangements must be made in advance and the party must board the boat prior to 23:00 h, as the harbor will thereafter be closed for the duration of the display.

Derby a horse race held on the first Sunday in February at the Sporting Club racecourse in Viña del Mar. It is a major horse-racing event, as it is one of the three making up the «Triple Crown», together with El Ensayo and Saint Leger. It attracts quite a crowd and has more than a tinge of a social event as well.

Off Valparaíso Regatta held on the first and second weekends (Saturday & Sunday) in February off Valparaíso, Viña del Mar, and Concón. The most traditional of Chilean regattas, it is organized by the Naval Academy for ocean-going yachts of different categories. It is held on the Valparaíso harbor between four buoys located at Punta Angeles –open sea–, San Mateo off Caleta El Membrillo in Valparaíso, off Caleta Abarca in Viña del Mar, and off the rocky shores of Concón. This circuit is made four times on the Saturday and Sunday of two consecutive weeks. Over 40 yachts with colorful sails take part.

Song Festival held on the first or second week in February at the Quinta Vergara's outdoor auditorium (see Urban Excursion 6). It goes on for a week, with two performances, one in the afternoon at the other one in the evening. It ranks as one of the major popular song festivals, with a song contest and shows performed by international artists. The more than 30.000 spectators play a significant role throughout the whole festival, cheering or booing whoever happens to take their fancy; collectively –and deservedly– they have been dubbed «the monster» by the press. It ought not to be missed.

San Pedro Festivity held on the 29th of June when it falls on a Sunday (otherwise on the following Sunday) in the morning, it is the fishermen's traditional festivity. At Caleta Portales, fishermen organize a procession on their festooned boats around the bay. At Caleta Higuerillas, the festivity is celebrated on the shore with the participation of the colorful and gaily-clad dancing confraternities known as chinos.

Musical Performance Contest a high level event held annually during the second or third week in November at Viña del Mar's Municipal Theater; it lasts for a week, with one performance per day. An international contest, it alternates between violin, singing, piano and classical guitar. The entrants are young artists representing the world's best music academies.

URBAN EXCURSIONS

Both Valparaíso and Viña del Mar deserve more than just a visit to their beaches. While the series of pirates, earthquakes, fires and other calamities which have visited the place have not left much in the way of historical relics, there still remains a lot to be seen. Below we suggest some city excursions to discover the loveliest corners, look-out points and parks. Some can be made on foot, some by car or bus. We list them separately.

The Valparaíso-Viña del Mar Intercity Highway in Viña del Mar every street leading to the ocean runs into the waterfront avenue. Follow this southward to Valparaíso and it will automatically bring you to the intercity highway, starting beyond Caleta Abarca and ending at Valparaíso's western tip. There is a succession of curves and straight stretches, where at every forking you must take the right branch. The landmarks along the way are: Caleta Portales, where the road becomes wider; it is the only section with traffic lights; the Nudo Barón, at Valparaíso's entrance and with a bridge over the highway; the following stretch is called Av Errázuriz and runs straight alongside the fences of the railway and the harbor; Sotomayor square, with the monument to Prat and the railway station; and, finally, the Plaza Aduana, with the red building of the Customs House. To return from Valparaíso to Viña del Mar, take Av Errázuriz, following always the right branch at every forking.

EXCURSIONS ON FOOT

Best place for parking in Valparaíso is Av Errázuriz near the railway station. It is also the best place for starting the tours. In Viña, park on the square of the Parroquia (church) and travel to Valparaíso either by commuter train (schedules: tel 680501), a very nice ride skirting the shore and the harbor, or by bus (half an hour).

1 TO THE PRAT PIER (MUELLE PRAT) ★★★

located in Valparaíso, right next to the railway station, it has handicraft shops and offers a fine platform for watching the moored ships and the bustling port activity.

Open launches accommodating 40 to 60 passengers offer tours around the harbor for a reasonable price. It is an interesting cruise, particularly on a sunny day. Do not take pictures of the naval ships or of Navy installations: you will have to show your papers if caught and your film could be confiscated. At the pier there is an excellent restaurant, the Bote Salvavidas, with a terrace overlooking the harbor.

2 THE PASEO 21 DE MAYO ★★★

in Valparaíso, above the Plaza Aduana and overlooking the harbor.

An excursion to the best look-out point in town.

Walk five blocks westward from the railway station along Av Errázuriz. This street is devoted to port services, with some hotels and restaurants on the second floor overlooking the wharves, and access gates to underground storage rooms at ground level, typical of Valparaíso. Along the way you will see port-related shops and one or two antiquarians dealing in naval implements, such as ancient diving helmets, compasses, lanterns, etc. The avenue ends at the **Plaza (or Plazuela) Aduana**, triangular in shape and flanked by the building of the

Customs House (NM) erected in 1854 and still fully active. Inside you can see the vast, bustling rooms. To its side is the

Artillería Funicular Railway («Ascensor»), which climbs the Playa Ancha hill; it was built in 1893 and it used to be powered by a coal engine. The cars have large windows, offering a stupendous

6

view over the harbor and Valparaíso's peculiar architecture. The upper terminal is at the

PASEO 21 DE MAYO located on a vast esplanade atop the cliff's edge. Shaded by large trees, it has banks and a balustrade and a kiosk overlooking the city and the harbor. It is certainly the best angle from which to look at Valparaíso.

Behind the Paseo are the beautiful gardens and building of what, until recently, was the Naval Academy. Now it has been transformed into a splendid **Naval and Maritime Museum** (Tue-Fri 09:30-12:30 h & 14:30-18:00 h; Sat & Sun 10:30-18:00 h). It is worth a visit.

This Paseo, built at the turn of the century, was the center of social life for the residents of the Playa Ancha hill, who used to stroll through here in the evenings. The rails of an old tram which

used to transport passengers between here and the various quarters of the hill are still to be seen.

To go back down, either take the ascensor or walk down one of the typical winding Valparaíso alleys descending on one side of the ascensor and leading to the Plazuela Aduana. On the first curve there is an old house of beautiful architecture, seemingly suspended above the cliff; it was built of imported American oak at the turn of the century.

3 THE PLAZA MATRIZ QUARTER ★★★
a stroll ot about one hour.
A visit to Valparaíso's oldest quarter.

Walk three blocks southward from the railway station (see map) and continue along the narrow alley of La Matriz, full of street vendors, to reach

☎ Telephone Center	**C** Railway Station	**K** Flower Shops	**5** Bar Inglés
★ Touristic Information		**L** Turri Clock	**6** Popeye's Club
◉ Cafe, Meeting Point	**PLACES OF INTEREST**	**M** Handicraft Market	**7** El Candil
⊠ Gasoline Station	**D** Paseo Yugoslavo		**9** Cinzano
⇗ Lookout Point	**E** Paseo Gervasoni	**RESTAURANTS**	**10** Café Riquet
❼ Excursion Suggested in Text	**F** Paseo Atkinson	**1** Bote Salvavidas	**11** Café Turri
A Regional Government Building	**G** Anglican Church	**2** Del Mónico	**12** Westfalia
B Post Office	**H** Lutheran Church	**3** La Rotonda	**13** La Cuisine
	J Baburizza Palace Art Museum	**4** Club Valparaíso	**14** La Nave

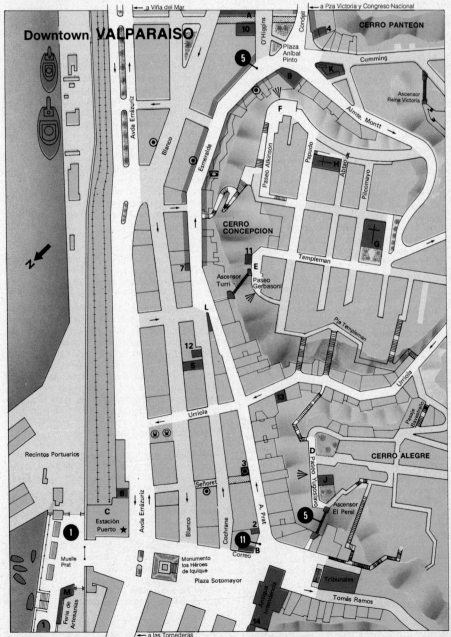

6

361

Valparaíso, Sotomayor square

6

SQUARE OF LA MATRIZ CHURCH (NM) the church was erected in 1873 at the same site where the first chapel was built in 1559, followed by a sequence of churches destroyed by successive earthquakes. The name comes from having been the first temple in town. Until the early 1900s, boats could moor directly alongside the edge of the square. The need for space made it necessary to reclaim land from the sea in the following decades, and now La Matriz stands in the middle of the flat part of town. It is surrounded by streets and by a splendid square lined by balustrades and with steps to follow the terrain's slope. The church, with a massive tower and built in neoclassical style, contains an image of Christ in Agony of the 17th century Sevillan school, donated by the king and queen of Spain.

Continue the tour along **Santo Domingo street** –to the right–hand side of the church–, the city's first inhabited nucleus. At the site where now the police station stands, during the colonial period there was a small residence of the Jesuits, which was later occupied by the Order of Santo Domingo. After the attainment of independence the building was used for theater performances. In 1828 it housed Chile's first bicameral Congress. Continue along **Santiago Severín street,** one of the oldest and where several members of the city's first council had their residences. Then walk down **Clave street,** narrow and lined with shops, to reach the

Echaurren Square surrounded by old buildings, including some of the large, old **emporios** of the past, a sort of forerunner of today's supermarket, with their lovely mahogany–varnished shelves and the show windows with beveled glass. Have a look around the **Market**, a classical iron structure on whose upper floor you will find the cocinerías, or food stalls, which are good places for a cheap lunch. A charming picada restaurant (ie, good value) is on La Matriz street just off the Matriz square.

4 CORDILLERA HILL ★★

a one–hour stroll; it is advisable to make it after Tour 3.

A visit to Valparaíso's first residential hill.

Walk two blocks from the railway station to Plaza Echaurren, the first square in town and where the troops stationed at Castillo San José –up the Cordillera Hill– used to hold their parades; there is no trace left of this Castillo. The Cerro Cordillera started to be settled in 1820 by foreign merchants who had come to live in Valparaíso, transforming it into the first residential quarter in town.

Continue along **Serrano,** at the foot of the hill, Valparaíso's most elegant street until the turn of the century, some large houses with huge porticos and marble steps bearing witness to it. At mid-block is the **ascensor Cordillera**, Valparaíso's first fu-

nicular railway (1855), running along a straight stair climbing one of the steepest slopes in town. Take the ascensor to Plazuela Eleuterio Ramírez; the streets starting there are flanked by houses lined with tin plates, which were once the residences of wealthy Valparaíso families. Turn left of Merlet street; at its end is

Lord Cochrane's House a splendid semi–colonial mansion dating from 1842, which was never inhabited by the illustrious admiral. It lies on an esplanade overlooking the cliff, just above Plaza Sotomayor and with a superb view over the city. Its main tower housed Chile's first astronomical observatory, set up by engineer Mouat. The house has been refurbished and now houses the interesting **Lord Thomas Cochrane Museum**; it is worth a visit (Tu–Sun 10:00-13:00 h and 14:00-18:00 h). To return, get back to the ascensor's landing and walk down Castillo street, the old route leading to the fortress above, to finally reach Plaza Echaurren.

5 VALPARAISO DOWNTOWN ★★★

a two–hour stroll.

A walk along the streets, hills and look-out terraces that have made this town famous.

Almost adjacent to the railway station is **Plaza Sotomayor**, hemmed in by tall buildings. Facing the shore is the former **Intendencia**, built in 1919, now housing the Commanding Headquarters of the First Naval Zone. Opposite is the monument to the **Heroes of Iquique**, unveiled in 1886. Beneath this monument is the beautiful crypt containing the remains of Prat, Serrano, Condell and others fallen heroically during the Battle of Iquique (see Land & History, Zone 1). The crypt is open to the public on the 21st of May every year. An international contest was held for the construction of these statues and one of the entrants was no less than the famous Auguste Rodin; his model was rejected, but it was later cast in bronze and now stands outside Viña del Mar's Cultural Center on Av Libertad. Other buildings worth visiting are the **Courts of Justice** (Tribunales de Justicia), lying to the side of the Intendencia alongside a small square. To the left, looking almost like a door of a building, is the access to the **Ascensor El Peral,** which climbs Cerro Alegre to the

PASEO YUGOSLAVO a lovely terrace crowning the cliff and from where the main streets of **cerro Alegre** radiate. The place is surrounded by charming old houses and gardens from the early decades of this century. Next to the Paseo is

Palacio Baburizza built in 1916 in Art Nouveau style; it was the residence of Pascual Baburizza, a great nitrate tycoon. Now it houses the **Fine Arts Museum**, which contains an interesting collection of paintings by French, Spanish and Chilean artists from the turn of the century (Tue-Sun 10:00–18:00 h).

To continue, walk down the **Pasaje Apolo**, which starts more or less at the midpoint of the Paseo. It is narrow, descending through stairs and gardens, and it provides access to private houses. It leads to Urriola street, which in turn leads to Valparaíso's financial heart at

CALLE PRAT the street is narrow, winding and lined by tall buildings. Most of the buildings –some are beautiful– were erected after the devastating earthquake of 1906.

Among them stands out the building housing the **Bolsa de Comercio**, Valparaíso's Stock Exchange at the corner of Urriola and Prat. It was Chile's first and its pit can be visited at midday. Opposite is the Renaissance–style stone building erected to house the head office of **Banco de A. Edwards y Cía**. Now it houses another bank.

By mid–block is the building erected by the former **Banco de Londres** (now Banco O'Higgins) with bronze, polished stone and marble lining brought directly from England. At the end of the block is the **Turri building**, tapering towards the corner and crowned by a clock tower. The street changes its name to Esmeralda, where the **Optica Hammersley building (NM)** is located, the oldest, narrowest building, made of timber covered with tin plates and with imported, prefabricated ornamentation. Opposite the Turri building is the access to the **Ascensor Cerro Concepción**. Take it to climb to the

| PASEO GERVASONI | a small look-out terrace surrounded by fine, well-kept houses dating from late last century. Continue through a short alley to **Templeman street** and climb two blocks along this street to the **St Paul Anglican church** and its picturesque square known as **14-seat promenade**, in the past the heart of the quarter's social life. The church has an interesting architecture and inside there is a **polychróme organ** donated by Queen Victoria, in addition to two tablets commemorating the Englishmen from the neighborhood who fell in both world wars. Open for visitors.

Retrace your steps down to **Papudo street**, with splendid, elegant houses, some in German style, and elaborate gates with ornaments in shining bronze. At the end of the street rises the slender bell tower of the **Lutheran church**, a beautiful building erected on a sharp corner. Continue along the narrow alley descending to the left to reach the

| PASEO ATKINSON | a flat look-out esplanade from where the streets of Concepción hill radiate. It is perhaps the most beautiful of Valparaíso's paseos, owing to its simplicity and the quaint old houses which lend it an atmosphere from times long past.

To descend, follow the stair leading from Paseo Atkinson to Esmeralda street near the building of the El Mercurio daily. Continuing along Esmeralda you will reach

| PLAZA ANIBAL PINTO | now a crossroads for car and bus traffic, as well as for pedestrians. To one side it is flanked by modern buildings, to the other by constructions dating from nearly one and a half centuries ago, such as those of **Klickman** and **Riquet**. At the center is the **Fuente de Neptuno**, a fountain framed by two large palms.

For Lunch the **Club Valparaíso**, on the 14th floor of the Cooperativa building, offers good food and a sweeping view. For «once», the typically Chilean teatime in mid afternoon, try the traditional **Café Riquet**. Both are located at Plaza Aníbal Pinto.

6 QUINTA VERGARA ★★★

located in Viña del Mar, behind the parish church (see map); parking at the entrance (Mon-Sun 07:30-18:00 h; in summer 07:30-20:00 h).
A nice stroll, particularly in the morning, suitable also for families with children. A must.

One of the most beautiful parks on the coast, with ample avenues, a fine mansion now housing a **Fine Arts Museum** (in winter, Tue-Sun 10:00-14:00 h and 15:00-18:00 h; in summer until 19:00 h) and the outdoor auditorium where the famous **International Song Festival** is held every February. The Quinta, nestled in a natural hollow hemmed in by hills, has a peculiar history. Since the colonial days, here stood the manor house of the Hacienda Siete Hermanas, which stretched across the hilly country from Viña del Mar to Valparaíso. It was owned by the Carrera family, kin of those other Carreras prominent in Chile's history.

By 1840 the hacienda was acquired by a Portuguese named Alvarez, a rich merchant and shipowner, who built his residence at this place. His wife, Dolores Pérez, was a lover of plants and started to give shape to the Quinta, entrusting his son Salvador with exotic plants that she brought from the Far East and Australia. She introduced a number of species into Chile, including Araucaria excelsa and many others still thriving at the Quin-

Viña del Mar, Quinta Vergara

ta, some of which the specialists have been unable to classify.

Salvador's only daughter married José Francisco Vergara, a many-sided public figure and founder of Viña del Mar, who carried on the tradition of looking after the beautiful garden, introducing further species. His daughter, Blanca Vergara de Errázuriz, commissioned in 1908 the construction of the present **Palacio Vergara (NM)**, in Venetian style, projected by architect Héctor Petri. She also redesigned the Quinta's gardens, conserving a subtropical flora which sets it apart from the rest of the parks in Chile.

EXCURSIONS BY CAR

We suggest the following tours to gain an overall picture of Viña del Mar, Valparaíso and the seaside resorts:

7 A CIRCUIT AROUND VIÑA DEL MAR ★★★

allow some two hours for this.
A circuit to take in Viña del Mar's main streets, squares, monuments and beaches in a single tour.
Start on **Calle Valparaíso** heading for the square. This is the city's shopping street, with the fairly relaxed tempo which characterizes Viña del Mar. Along its 6 blocks are large and small stores, offices and a number of cafés, including the **Samoiedo** and **Anayak**, the prime gathering points. Somewhat more intimate is the **Big Ben**, in the Galería de Cristal. **The square** is shaded by large, leafy trees; on one side is the neoclassical building of the **Club de Viña**, built in 1910, the **Municipal Theater**, dating from 1930 and, on the corner, the **Hotel O'Higgins**, opened in 1935. There is also **House Subercaseaux**, now housing the Hotel Español.

Cross now the **Puente Libertad**, the bridge spanning the Marga-Marga creek, and continue along **Av Libertad**, shaded by huge overhanging maple-like trees. This is the flat portion of the Viña valley, of old known as the Población Vergara; it is laid out in a pattern of square blocks and the streets are identified according to a sequence of cardinal points: North, West and East (Norte, Poniente, Oriente).

Three blocks beyond the bridge, to the right, is the **Mansión Carrasco**, built around 1920 for the powerful nitrate magnate Emilio Carrasco; now it is municipal property and houses the Cultural Center (Mon-Fri 10:00-13:00 h and 14:00-20:00 h, Sun 10:00-14:00 h), with the Benjamín Vicuña Mackenna Library and historical archives. In front of its portico is the **Monument to the Heroes**, an original sculpture by **Auguste Rodin** donated by the French government. The mock-up in gypsum was submitted by the artist in 1885 to the contest for the monument to Prat, but it was not selected.

Turn right on 4 Norte; at number 784 is the **Fonck Archeological Museum** (Tue-Fri 10:00-18:00 h; Sat

☎ Telephone Center
★ Café, Meeting Point
◉ Touristic Information
Ⓢ Gasoline Station
A Town Hall (2B)
B Post Office (3C)
C Viña del Mar Parish Church (3B)
D Handicraft Market (3A)
E Municipal Theater (2C)
F Museum of Fine Arts (1B)
G Club de Viña del Mar (3B)

H Art Gallery (2B)
M Railway Station (3B)

ACCOMMODATIONS
1 H O' Higgins (2C)
2 H Alcázar (3B)
3 H Viña del Mar (3B)
4 H Español (2C)
5 H Hispano (4B)
6 Bh Ona Berri (2B)
7 H Rondó (4B)

8 Bh Viana (3B)
9 Bh Magallanes (2A)
10 Bh Edhison (4C)

RESTAURANTS
1 H O'Higgins (2C)
2 H Alcázar (3B)
4 Cabeza de Buey (2C)
15 Samoiedo (2A)
16 Anayak (2A)
20 Centro Español (3A)

21 Chinese Food (2A-2C)
22 El Mezón con Z (3B)
23 Caribian (2B)
M Tasca Caballo de Hierro (3B)

TOURIST SERVICES
U Cars-Rent a Car (3C)
V Alen Rent a Car (3B)
W Automóvil Club (1C)
Y Travel Agencies (1B - 2B)
$ Money Exchange

← a Reñaca y Concón

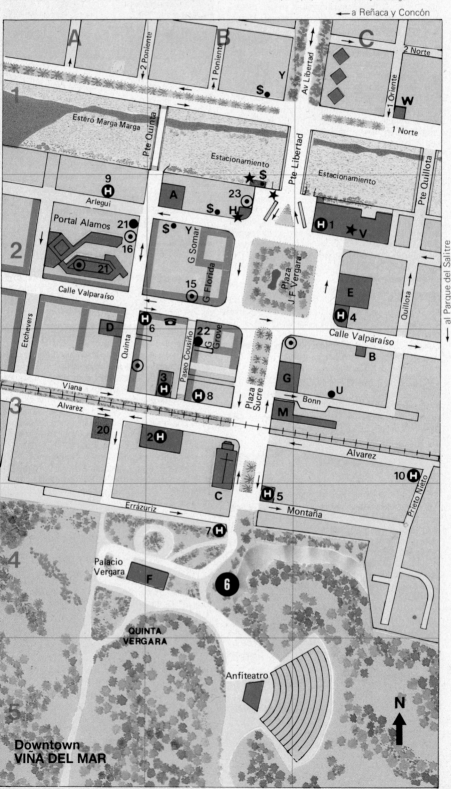

Downtown VIÑA DEL MAR

& Sun 10:00-14:00 h). It contains a significant collection of Easter Island objects and Mapuche silver ornaments. 4 Norte ends at Quillota street. Along the way you can see beautiful mansions and gardens of the city's most exclusive residential quarter. At the end of the street are the palms and tall Araucaria excelsa trees of **Quinta Rioja (NM)** (Tue-Sun 10:00-14:00h & 15:00-18:00 h), a mansion set in a park, built in 1906. It was owned by a high-ranking businessman from Valparaíso and now it is municipal property, housing a **Museum**; it is also used for official receptions. Its gardens deserve a stroll –although they cover now only half the area as in the past–, beautifully laid out in a pattern punctuated by palms. The splendid parlors contain furniture from the turn of the century.

Continue along 3 Norte to get back to Av Libertad, and follow this to the right until its end. Turn left to reach the **coastal road** connecting all the beaches, passing restaurants and offering a constant view to the sea.

The first part runs close to a long beach on the left and fuel storage facilities on the right, followed by the Navy's Escuela de Especialidades. Beyond a rocky point is **Las Salinas beach**, and then the road winds its way among some rock outcrops crowned by beautiful houses to reach **Reñaca**, the heart of summer life. The road now runs between the sea and the hills, the latter covered by buildings cascading in steps down the slopes. Along the Reñaca beach there is a long promenade: it is the place to be at sunset time.

Continue to the rocky point called **Montemar**, where the Marine Biology Center is located; beyond the curve is the small **Cochoa bay,** with a fishing cove, stands selling shellfish, and many restaurants. A further 500 m will bring you to the **Mirador de Los Lobos**, a look-out terrace overlooking a sea–lion colony just off the shore, with the Cochoa bay behind.

This road continues to Concón (described under next tour). For lunch in this area, see the Gastronomy section above.

Retrace the road to Reñaca, which now gives you a nice view to Valparaíso in the distance. The coastal road leads straight to Av San Martín, flanked by tall apartment buildings. The best view of the urban waterfront is from the tip of **Muelle Vergara** (see map), with a promenade and a restaurant; very popular with sunset watchers.

Continuing along San Martín the **Casino Municipal** soon comes into view. It is a large building inaugurated in 1932, with gambling rooms, restaurants, ballrooms and a cabaret, which make it the foremost recreation establishment in Viña del Mar. Turn right beyond the Casino into **Av Perú**, the waterfront street and promenade, one of the best spots for taking a stroll. When the surf is strong, the place is lots of fun.

Turn right at the end of Av Perú to retake Av San Martín. Continue beyond the Casino and across the bridge and then turn right at **Av Marina**, following this until the end. The avenue skirts **Cerro Castillo** in what is the oldest and perhaps the most beautiful stretch of urban waterfront street in Viña del Mar. It is flanked by apartment buildings and a few fine mansions from the turn of the century. In the first part of this stretch you can see the **Brunet castle** up on the hill, built of stone and with towers crowned by battlements. Right on the waterfront is the hotel and restaurant **Cap Ducal**, shaped like a ship. Ahead and on the rocks lies the **Wulf castle** (Sea Museum, Tue-Sat 10:00-13:00 h and 14:30-18:00 h, Sun 10:00-14 00 h) and on the cliffs up above you can see the terraces of the **Presidential Summer Palace**. The avenue turns a curve at the small Miramar beach and then it passes **Hotel Miramar**, the best hotel in town, with a swimming pool and terraces right on the waterfront. Adjacent to the hotel starts the

Caleta Abarca Beach its promenade bustling in

Viña del Mar, Perú avenue

summer. To round up the tour, we suggest you drive up **Cerro Castillo**, whose look–out terraces can give you a sweeping view over the town and its beaches. Take Alamos street, next to the **floral clock** (see city map) and continue skirting the hillside until you reach Vista Hermosa street, a sort of **balcony street** overlooking Valparaíso street and the valley stretching inland. Continue to the **Castillo Brunet** gate and then along Iberia street to Callao street, where the access to the **Presidential Summer Palace** is located. Drive down along this street to turn right at Balmaceda, continuing to its end at **Paseo Lydice**, the end station of this tour and a point offering you a view towards Caleta Abarca, Valparaíso and the sea.

Follow the road shown in map to leave Cerro Castillo.

8 COASTAL ROAD TO CONCON ★★★

a curvy 11 km stretch skirting the waterfront at the foot of rocky cliffs.

A tour through beaches, look-out terraces, seafood stalls and restaurants (see Gastronomy section), quite popular at sunset time.

Take the coastal route to Reñaca. Beyond Cochoa is the Los Lobos look–out point, overlooking a rocky islet where sea lions frolic. Then comes **Roca Oceánica**, with a parking lot. It is a small headland with paths leading to look–out points offering fine views of the Valparaíso bay.

A short distance later is **Los Lilenes beach** –parking available–, with a huge sand dune rising behind, ideal for children. Then comes **Higuerillas** and the yacht harbor, with seafood stalls on the roadside. Farther ahead is **Playa Amarilla** in Concón and, finally, the mouth of the Aconcagua river, with further seafood stalls and restaurants.

NB the large number of cars along this road make this a very slow journey. A faster option to return to Viña is to take either of the two inland roads (see map).

9 SAUSALITO AND THE SPORTING CLUB ★★★

ideal for families with children. Allow about one hour for this tour.

A tour to a green spot in town, offering sports facilities as well.

See map. Take Av 1 Norte heading east to Av Los Castaños; at the end is **Sausalito**. It is a scenic small lake originally built as an irrigation reservoir for the old hacienda and which now lures water–ski devotees. Along the lakeshore there are beaches, a swimming pool (09:30-18:00 h), tennis courts, rowboats and motorboats for water ski. In the same area is the **Municipal Stadium**, sitting 25.000, and behind it is the **Club de Tiro**, a shooting range.

Retrace Av Los Castaños up to the gates of the **Sporting Club**. An entrance fee is charged. This is the town's racecourse and a lovely place for stroll-

6

☎ Public Telephones
ⓖ Gasoline Station
◉ Cafe, Meeting Point
⇛ Lookout Point

ACCOMMODATIONS
1 H San Martin (2C)
2 H Cap Ducal (4B)
3 H Alborada (3B)

4 H Monterilla (4B)
5 H Las Américas (4B)
6 H Balia (5A)
7 Bh Las Condes (3B)
8 Bh San Martín (4B)
9 H El Borrico (3C)

RESTAURANTS
1 Green Pub (2C)
2 Cap Ducal (4A)

10 Casino (4A)
11 Parrilladas Armandita (3B)
12 San Marco (2B)
13 Gigi (2C)
14 Machitún Ruca (3B)
15 Mastrantonio (4B)
16 La Mia Papa (1C)
17 Gipsy (2C)
18 Pollo Stop (4A)

19 Chez Gerald (3B)
20 Diego Pizzas (2C)
21 Gelatería Italiana (2C)
22 El Cabezo (1B)

GOOD VALUE RESTAURANTES
25 Nahuel (2C)
26 Max und Moritz (2C)
27 Seafood stall Rafael (2B)
28 Seafood stall El Delfín (2B)

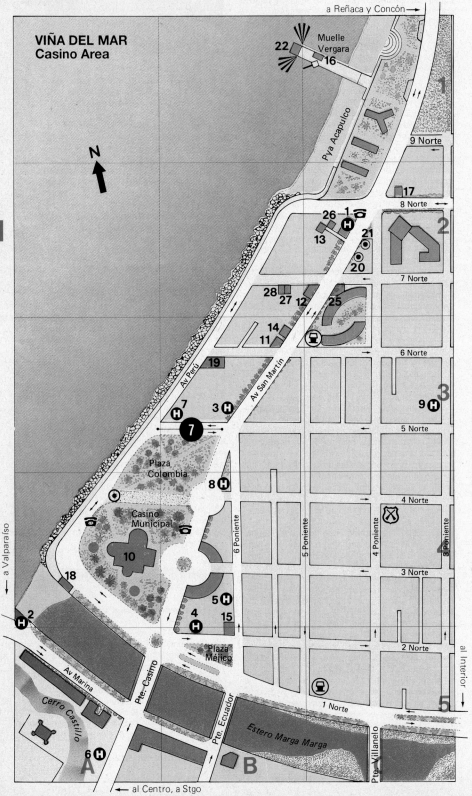

VIÑA DEL MAR
Casino Area

a Reñaca y Concón →

Muelle Vergara

a Valparaíso ←

al Interior

Plaza Colombia

Casino Municipal

Av Perú

Av San Martín

Av Marina

Cerro Castillo

Pte. Casino

Pte. Ecuador

Estero Marga Marga

Pte. Villanelo

Plaza Mélico

9 Norte
8 Norte
7 Norte
6 Norte
5 Norte
4 Norte
3 Norte
2 Norte
1 Norte

6 Poniente
5 Poniente
4 Poniente
3 Poniente

Pya Acapulco

← al Centro, a Stgo

A   B   6

ing. Horse races from the Club Hípico of Santiago are shown on video on Wednesdays, Saturdays and Sundays, and on Mondays and Thursdays live horse races are held here in summer. There are also hockey and rugby fields, equestrian courses as well as two tennis clubs, a track course and a bicycross course.

10 PARQUE DEL SALITRE ★★

located on the outskirts of Viña del Mar, it is ideal for families with children. Allow one morning.
This park is the National Botanical Garden, a fine place for strolling.

Take exit 6 in map of Viña del Mar. Along the way you will cross the **El Salto** quarter of town, with some large trees of old country retreats. The area has now become an industrial quarter. Beyond the El Salto railway station there is a small bridge and to the right a **monolith** commemorating the fact that the following section of road was Chile's first paved road; it was the old route to Limache. One km down the road there is another monolith: this one commemorates famous admiral Gómez Carreño, who died here in an automobile accident. Turn left to cross the bridge across the Marga–Marga and you will reach the entrance to the

PARQUE DEL SALITRE (Tue-Sun and Holidays 09:00-18:30 h, closed on Mon) a vast park and forest planted in the 1930s in a small valley nestled between the hills. You may drive along the road starting from a round esplanade surrounded by beautiful tree species, then continuing along an avenue lined with trees which boast marvelous colors in the autumn. Then comes a stretch of lawn flanked by trees and a palm grove, to then reach a vast pond with a promenade; several paths start from here into the woods. The return leg follows a different section, passing the plant nurseries, and some lawns available for playing or for a picnic.

This park was created for private use by Pascual Baburizza, a nitrate tycoon, who personally planted many of the now very large trees. When he died, the park became property of the Corporación del Salitre, which opened it to the public. Later, when it already was in state hands, it was transformed into the **National Botanical Garden**. It is very well kept and has over 3.000 valuable, beautiful plant species, some of them priceless from the point of view of botany. Such is the case of the **Toromiro shrub** (Sophora toromiro) growing on the access esplanade, a plant that is extinct in its natural range of Easter Island; its very hard, dark wood was used in the past for making the famous Easter Island «speaking tablets» and «toromiros».

Opposite is the **Native Fauna Park**, where you can see species in partial captivity such as vicuñas, guanacos, alpacas, ñandúes, pudúes, etc. Open 10:00-18:00 h, an access fee is charged. Guided tours on horseback are on offer. Check with Conaf, telephones 970108 & 680841.

11 ALONG VALPARAISO'S PLAN ★★★

a three–hour circuit by car through the plan, Valparaíso's narrow band of level ground; best on weekdays.
A tour across the heart of the city ending up at a look-out terrace overlooking the area you have just covered, which includes sights already described under Tours on Foot.

Follow the intercity highway to its end at Plaza Aduana (see map, also Tours on Foot). Turn around the square to take Bustamante street, skirting the foot of the hill; two blocks later you will cross La Matriz, with the church at its end. (see Tour 3). This is the city's oldest section, where the warehouses and the church were located.
Note the structure of the city, with a portion of level ground squeezed between the hills and the sea, known as el "plan" and consisting largely of

Valparaíso, lift

land reclaimed from the sea; and the upper city, with tortuous alleys and houses jumbled on the slopes, hanging precariously above the precipitous cliffs. Now and then, some quebradas –ravines– cleave a short way into the hills and make room for the typical squares of this city, such as Plaza Echaurren.

Rainwater flowing down these quebradas is directed to the sea through **vaulted canals** running under the streets. The name of the hills changes from one **quebrada** to the next. Traffic around the hills takes two forms: through streets descending into a quebrada and then leading to the **squares**, or through streets following the contour of the hills or running along the **crests**, ending at an **ascensor** – funicular railway– which commutes between the upper and lower levels of the city.

The tour continues along the street **skirting the foothill**. Beyond Plaza Echaurren the street's name changes to **Serrano**, and thereafter changes its name after each square. Serrano runs at the foot of the Cordillera hill (there is an ascensor) and is the heart of the popular Barrio del Puerto, the port quarter (see Tour 4). It ends at Plaza Sotomayor, the city's civic center, with the Intendencia –Regional Government–, the post office and, in the middle, the monument to the Heroes of Iquique. Continue along the narrow, canyon–like, bustling **Prat street**, the financial quarter (see Tour 5), lined with interesting buildings. The street changes its name at the so-called **Crucero de Reyes,** with the **Turri building** tapering to a narrow point and crowned by its characteristic clock. The street is now called **Esmeralda** and makes a wide bow around Concepción hill. This is a shopping street, with lots of offices and businesses, cafés, bookstores, and the old **Pümpin** flower shop. This is Valparaíso's narrowest section, the land having been reclaimed from the sea in the past century.

Esmeralda leads to **Plaza Aníbal Pinto**, with a small Neptune fountain and surrounded by the old Klickman and Riquet buildings and by other modern buildings. Continue along the foothill, now following **Condell street**, with large stores. You will pass **Plaza Ecuador**, a major hub for traffic coming from the hills. Two blocks farther on is

Plaza Victoria around the square are the **Cathedral church** and the **Severín Library**. In the square itself there is a **bronze fountain**, sculptures and large trees, among which stands out a gigantic Australian gum tree. This was the outskirts of town around the 1820s; it had a small theater and in the esplanade circuses pitched their tents and even bullfights were held, before they were outlawed. The boom which the city underwent in the mid–19th century brought urban development to the area; by 1880 Plaza Victoria had become the town's most elegant center.

Among the most memorable buildings from that period were Juana Ross de Edwards' neoclassical

6

367

Valparaíso, National Congress

palace, which stood where the Cathedral church now stands; the great Victoria theater; and the Church of the Holy Spirit. In that church the funeral service for the heroes of Iquique was held when their remains were repatriated. The trees date from that period. It was also then that the fountain and the sculptures were set up; they were brought from Lima, Peru.

All the buildings now to be seen date from after 1906: in that year, a devastating earthquake levelled all the previous ones.

Continue now along the wide and long **Av Pedro Montt,** which heads east from the middle of Victoria square across the widest bit of the level part of town, losing importance as it gets farther from the square. Here are the cinemas and commercial stores.

It passes two squares, the first of which is **Parque Italia,** with Chile's oldest ornamental trees, as in the past this used to be a private property which by 1870 served as a country retreat and was a favorite spot for a Sunday outing. It was the stage for major events as well; among others, Chile's first aerostatic balloon soared into the heavens from here. It fell on the sea and only the pilot could be rescued. Behind the square, on Independencia, is the

Padres Franceses Church the metropolitan church of this French religious order which arrived in Chile around 1840. It founded a school and a seminary at Los Perales, in Quilpué. The Valparaíso establishment acted as a support base for the order's foremost undertakings: its missions in the Polynesian islands. The church contains fine woodwork at the altar, sacristy and choir loft.

At the end of Av Pedro Montt is the

NATIONAL CONGRESS an impressive building of 40.000 square meters, housing the Senate, the Chamber of Deputies, the Library of Congress and associated services. Inaugurated in 1990, it is the largest civic complex built in Chile since 1938, when Santiago's Barrio Cívico was built. It epitomizes Chile's effort to decentralize and break with the Spanish tradition of concentrating economic and political power in the capital city. Public visits during legislative sessions on Mon, Thu & Fri 10:00 –17:30 h.

Cross Av Argentina and continue one block straight towards the hill, to have a look at the Jesuit church.

To round up the circuit, follow Av Argentina two blocks towards the sea, to turn right at Quillota street. Climb the Barón hill, with old houses lined with tin plates and more or less gaily painted. Some 300 m into the climb you will reach the

Portales Look–Out Terrace with white balustrades. The place commands a sweeping **view of Valparaíso**, its hills and the harbor –in short, one of the best views of this unique city.

To get back to the intercity highway, follow the same street. Midway down the slope stands the huge bulk of the

Church of San Francisco its tall bell tower helps to orient ships coming to moor in Valparaíso. This has prompted sailors to nickname the city as Pancho, a nickname for Francisco, as a homage to the tower which guides them from afar.

12 ALONG THE HILLS OF VALPARAISO ★★★

a car circuit for about three hours, any season, preferably in the morning and, if possible, not on Sunday.

This is the so-called Camino de Cintura, which offers splendid views of the city and of a good stretch of coastline. On clear days, you can even see the Andes range across the country, with the towering Aconcagua peak, the tallest in the American continent and in the Western Hemisphere.

Take the intercity highway from Viña del Mar to Valparaíso up to Nudo Barón –where the highway passes under a bridge. Take the right branch and after some blocks turn left into **Av Francia** (see Valparaíso map). This avenue heads straight to the hills, crossing Av Brasil, Av Pedro Montt, Victoria, Independencia, and Colón. This last street runs along the foothill. Take **Av Baquedano;** you must look for it, as it is not very conspicuous, but it is the best option for climbing the hills. Not too steep but quite curvy, it skirts the Eduardo de la Barra high school and passes lots of dwellings precariously clinging to the slope. It finally meets the

CAMINO DE CINTURA the only street which runs level along the entire crescent of hills surrounding the Valparaíso bay. Its construction was started in the 1930s, when the hills were already long inhabited. Existing streets were joined with each other by filling up ravines or building bridges. This is why the Camino de Cintura, or **Av Alemania,** does not have a uniform look, but changes from hill to hill. In its length of slightly over 3 km it crosses hundreds of streets, alleys and other roads leading to the lower city. This may be confusing, but remember to take always the widest, most level-looking option; in case of doubt, ask a pedestrian.

Along the way there are numerous natural lookout points offering different perspectives over the city and its bay. The first hill to be traversed is Florida, with the impressive house of poet Pablo Neruda **La Sebastiana** (Tu-Sun 10:30-18:00 h); then you cross to Bellavista, follow by Bellavista, which looms above Plaza Victoria, then San Juan de Dios, then La Loma, to end up at the lovely **Plaza Bismarck** on the Cerro Cárcel. This square, with a large school on its rear side, commands a superb view over the city; farther down you can see the large bulk of the jail (thence the hill's name) and the cemetery, lying on a piece of hill projecting over the heart of the city.

The road continues along a stretch lined with nice old houses, anticipating the nearby Cerro Alegre, which is reached at Plazuela San Luis, a small, sort of rambling place. Three streets lead down from here to the seafront. This is the end of the tour along the Camino de Cintura. But before you drive back, take some time to make a short tour around

CERRO ALEGRE rising right above the harbor. It was a barren hill at the turn of the 19th century, until foreign traders decided to build their residences here by 1840, becoming in time one of the most elegant quarters of town. Some houses from that period still remain, but most of the ones still to be seen date from early this century. Among the lovely streets, buildings and churches, there are three look-out terraces, each at a different point of the hill (described under Tour 5).

NB for those wishing to retrace the road, you can continue beyond the starting point (Av Alemania corner of Baquedano) along a newly built section leading up to Av Santa Elena (see Valparaíso map).

13 PLAYA ANCHA COASTAL ROAD ★★★

a road passing beaches, look–out terraces, seafood stalls and restaurants, to continue along a newly built stretch of gravel road running atop cliffs to Laguna Verde.

A beautiful excursion that car drivers have yet to discover, with beautiful views along the coast.

From the Plaza Aduana of Valparaíso, take **Av Antonio Varas**, which runs along the port's outer fences; at its end is the access to the **sheltering mole**. There is an old, massive gun cast in Quillota in 1865, placed now at the site where in the past a small defensive fort used to stand. Atop the cliff you can see the bulk of the **Silva Palma** naval barracks, from where the nautical salvos are fired.

The street is now called **Av Altamirano** and continues along the coast, passing a shipyard and reaching the **El Membrillo** fishing cove, where you can see the arrival of the fishing boats (bongos) early in the morning, loaded with the catch of the night which they offer directly to the public. There are good seafood stalls and very good restaurants at the site.

Next come the small squares of Carvallo and Rubén Darío and some look–out terraces on the waterfront. A promenade runs along the waterfront, with views over the entire coastline from Concón to Viña del Mar. Atop the cliff you can see the modern buildings of the **Naval Academy**. The coastal road ends at the popular and picturesque **Las Torpederas beach**, a busy spot in summer.

A short detour up the **Playa Ancha hill** can be recommended. It rises above the Costanera, the waterfront road. Take Av Torpedera starting from across the bathing beach to the Alejo Barrio park, and follow the road around this park. You will see a stadium, the bicycle race course, the access to the **Naval Academy** and the campus of the **Universidad de Valparaíso**. Continue along **Av Gran Bretaña** to visit a traditional quarter of town, with some nice chalets built in the 1920s, featuring slender towers overlooking the bay.

Retrace the road to the Torpederas beach and drive back along the waterfront street to the cemetery. Between the cemetery wall and that of the Punta Angeles lighthouse there is an alley. Follow this to reach the **Coastal Road** which, running atop high cliffs, meets the road to **Laguna Verde**. This road is planned to be extended to Algarrobo.

14 VALPARAISO'S COUNTRY VILLAS ★

a drive around the hills behind Valparaíso. Allow two hours; any season. Best in the morning.

A visit to the area where, by 1890, English merchants built country villas and parks to spent their time out of the city.

Following the intercity highway from Viña del Mar to Valparaíso, take the left branch when you reach the **Nudo Barón**, where a bridge crosses over the highway. This branch climbs a bridge and descends to **Av Argentina** (see map). Continue straight to the end of this avenue, where you will find a triple forking: to the right, **Santa Elena**, which leads into a ravine; in the middle, **Washington**, which climbs the hill; and to the left the highway to Santiago (Route 68).

The tour starts with a short visit along Santa Elena, skirting an old building which in the past was a convent, then a seminary and now a school. The road is short and winds its way along the bottom of the ravine, passing the **Chocolates Costa**

Valparaíso, houses on the hill

plant; colorful houses clamber up the slope. It is a rather unexpected spot, a residential quarter with lots of gardens. The idea was originally from the owners of the Costa chocolate company –originally a family company– to provide housing for the firm's owners, employees and workers. The beautiful houses are arranged hierarchically between the hills and in the cités –tenement houses– along the street.

Retrace the road back to Av Argentina and take now the middle branch –**Washington**– which climbs the hill. After the initial curve, it ascends gently along the slope, with a fine view towards the **Molino hill** straight ahead, thickly covered with houses and one of the poorest quarters of town.

Av Washington now follows a long curve and eventually reaches a small square with a gas station. Take there the street branching left **(Von Moltke)**. This is the O'Higgins quarter, with thickly packed houses reaching nearly to the very summit. Av Washington, which continues climbing, used to be the **old road to Santiago**, its myriad curves tormenting drivers from colonial days until 1955, when the new access road was finished. Just into the Von Moltke street, to the left is the gate to the

JARDIN SUIZO (Swiss Garden) (Mon–Sat 08:00-17:00 h; Sun 08:30-12:30 h), a famous plant nursery established in 1891 and, of the three large nurseries of its kind in Chile, the only one still in operation. Along its many years in activity it has introduced a large variety of plants into Chile, which have beautified Viña del Mar's gardens. Established by Benjamin Pümpin, it has passed from fathers to sons, keeping alive a splendid botanic tradition. It is delightful to stroll around the park with its rich variety of trees and shrubs, its shady spots and the greenhouses filled with the most exquisite collection of exotic indoor plants, gathered in over a century of dedicated effort.

Continue along Von Moltke following the traffic signs to the top of the hill, and take there the dirt street called **Camino de los Ingleses**. This is the **Las Zorras** quarter, where, starting in 1891, several English merchant families settled in landed villas («quintas») with large parks covering the hills and the ravines. The road –then private– was named after these families. The merchants rode downhill on horseback to Prat street, where they had their offices. Some large trees remain, a few houses, and the parks, which have been acquired by institutions or clubs.

Turn left to descend following Camino de los Ingleses. At the beginning it skirts the upper boundary of the Jardín Suizo. To the right are the long, decayed walls, and the trees and fences of

Quinta Kennrik now it is a girls' home. You can get permission to visit the park. The place has a large mansion with a beautiful avenue leading to it; this avenue ends at a terrace opposite the houses. Then comes a park descending in steps into the ravine. The main house, perched at the summit, commands a superb view of the distant sea. It was owned by successive English families and it is a beautiful example of the British lifestyle here at the turn of the century.

The road ends on the highway to Santiago (Route 68). Drive two km up this highway to continue among further landed villas, small forests and tall Chilean palms on the hills. The area is starting to be encroached upon by urban developments. On the way is the Quintil park, a municipal plant nursery which can be visited.

To return you have two options: continue a further seven km to the junction with the branch of Route 68 going to Viña, the longest route of the two, but with the best scenery; or drive down along Route 68 to Valparaíso, through Av Argentina to take the intercity highway.

TOURS INTO THE INLAND VALLEYS

There are several nice, sunny spots inland, conveniently away from the coastal fogs, offering you quiet country scenery as an alternative to the beach bustle.

1 COLMO AND THE SURROUNDING AREA ★ ★

a round trip of 40 km. Allow two hours. Best in the afternoon.

An excursion to a nearby country spot with history and good scenery.

From Concón follow the road to Quillota (Route 60), which bypasses the oil refinery. The road is level and runs near the river. Seven km ahead is the small Victoria bridge. To the left, before crossing the bridge, is the **Colmo Plant Nursery**, with interesting plants in its greenhouses.

Just beyond the Victoria bridge a signposted road branches left to Valle Alegre. Follow this road for one km to the **Colmo bridge** spanning the Aconcagua. A nearly disused, robust bridge built in the 1920s, it used to be a vital link in the only costal road running north until the 1950s, when the present coastal road and the Concón bridge were built. Beyond the bridge, to the left, there is a group of trees; they are part of the park of the

HACIENDA SANTA ROSA DE COLMO   now very deteriorated by the combined effects of the earthquakes of 1906, 1965 and 1971. The present owners are refurbishing some of the manor houses, a few farm buildings and the park. Access is permitted to the yard of the old estancia, flanked by old, traditional buildings, the park's large trees and a strange, 2-story farm construction with a gallery girdling it. This farm was purchased around 1850 by Ramón Subercaseaux, a wealthy industrialist, owner of the Arqueros mine at La Serena; he also built railroads and, using new technologies, canalized the water of the Aconcagua river and irrigated these lands. His daughter Victoria inherited the farm; she married Benjamín Vicuña Mackenna, a famous politician and writer, who had the farm houses built, gave a boost to agriculture and spent long seasons in this farm writing his copious literary works, until his death here in 1884. His funeral was a great event. His coffin was brought by horse carriage to Quillota, whence it continued by special train to Santiago. There, his body was carried in a solemn procession along the Alameda to the Cathedral Church.

On the brick structures supporting the iron gate are the original plates with the initials of VSV and BVM, in memory of the old owners.

Continue along the dirt road to Valle Alegre, climbing a hill. Upon this hill the military commanding post was located during the

Concón Battle during the Revolution of 1891, the army of the Congresista party –raised and organ-

ized in Northern Chile– landed at Quintero and marched south along this road to engage the Balmacedista army awaiting it across the Aconcagua. From this hill, the battle was directed on August 21; it ended with the defeat of the Balmacedista forces and their retreat to Valparaíso. The hill gives a sweeping view over the valley, now intensely cultivated. At the summit there used to be a commemorating marble monolith until 1988, when it was removed and placed close to the main road across the river.

2 QUILLOTA AND LA CRUZ ★ ★ ★

a 102-km round trip from Concón; allow half a day. Best in the morning. Restaurant at El Boco.

A visit to a pleasant city lying at the heart of the Chile's best fruit-growing valley.

Follow Route 60 out of Concón, heading east. **Tabolango** –a cluster of houses– is at km 10. In the past, this was a center of Inca administration (Curaca) for the lower valley until the Spaniards arrived. At km 15 the great **Quillota valley** unfolds to the east, intensely cultivated to grow vegetables. There are a few farm houses, some sheltered from view by the trees of their parks. There are many fruit orchards, growing mainly avocado, cherimoyas and lucuma.

Stay on the highway and drive past Quillota to La Cruz. At km 38 the road ascends a bit and offers a wide **view** over the treetops of the fruit orchards carpeting the valley. Next to the hill is the gravel detour to La Cruz (unsigned). It curls right to pass below the highway, passing the railway station and reaching the square of

LA CRUZ   rather than a village, this is a long street lined with fruit orchards enclosed by high mud-brick walls. This is Chile's foremost fruit-growing country, with major plant nurseries and the main Pest Control Station.

Driving along the street towards Quillota you will see scores of signs offering fruit for sale (very convenient prices). At km 43 is the main square of

QUILLOTA   when the Spaniards arrived here, the Quillota valley was populated by natives under the hegemony of the Inca empire; their chieftain was the famous Michimalongo, who had his seat near San Isidro. The natives were promptly subject by the Spaniards into the serfdom system known as encomienda, whereby the Indians were forced to engage in unpaid labor. These lands were greatly coveted by the Spaniards for their good climate and fruitfulness.

By 1609 the Franciscan Order set up a chapel on the lands where now the **Church of San Francisco** stands. The **Village of Quillota** was founded in 1717 round the church. Its administrative territory stretched from the valley of La Ligua to Casablanca and included rich lands owned by the Colony's large feudatories, such as the entailed estates of Irarrázabal at Pullally, Cerda at La Ligua and Azúa at Quillota and Purutún.

Life at Quillota in colonial days centered around administrative and religious activities. The place had five churches: La Matriz (parish church), San Francisco, La Merced, Santo Domingo, and San Agustín. By 1792, Santiago Irarrázabal, owner of the Pullally estate, planted at Quillota's main square the first cherimoya tree, which had been brought from Peru. He then harvested the first fruits and gave his friends in the valley some cuttings for planting. So was the production of this fruit started in Chile.

In 1837, the Army Headquarters was set up here for the expedition to Peru. On June 4th, its commander, colonel Vidaurre, arrested at this place Minister Diego Portales, whom he murdered while bringing him to Valparaíso. The development of the city gained momentum in the second half of the

6

19th century, when financiers and entrepreneurs from Valparaíso acquired land and had large irrigation works undertaken in the valley.

What To See Quillota has the typical look of a Central Valley rural town, low buildings lying side to side lining the streets. The **square** is quaint, shady and graced by palms. A fallen cypress has been laboriously carved into an **allegory to agriculture.** Around the square there are two churches, the **Parroquia** (mass March-Oct, Mon-Fri 12:00-19:00 h; Sun and Holydays 10:00, 12:00, 19:00 h; Nov-Feb, Mon-Fri 12:00 and 20:00 h, Sun and Holidays 10:00, 12:00, 20:00 h) and Santo Domingo (mass Mon-Sat 09:00 h, Sun 08:00 and 11:30 h, no mass on wed; in winter sat and Sun 18:30 h; in summer Sat and Sun 19:00 h). Visit also the old church of **San Francisco** (mass Sun 11:00 h & 12:30 h), located next to a small square with tamarinds, in full bloom in September.

At San Martín 366 is the **Casa Colorada**, the city's oldest house, dating from 1722. Bernardo O'Higgins stayed at that house in 1822, when he granted Quillota city status. Now it is a private residence. For a view over the city and its valley, climb to the **look-out point** on the **Mayaca hill**. You can round the tour with a visit to **Boco**, the orchard section, with the resort of **El Edén** (swimming) and a good restaurant. Colectivo taxis make the run from Quillota.

Pleasure trips to Olmué, La Campana mountain top

offers facilities for travellers, such as the excellent swimming pools at the **Scala de Milán** hotel, **Hotel Copihue** and at the **Balneario Municipal**. There are horses for hire at the main square. In late January, a renowned country music festival is held under the name of Festival del Huaso. Along the road you can buy fresh fruit, fine homemade marmalades, and a famous local chicha, a type of cider that has won several awards, and handicrafts of clay and hemp.

Where To Eat **Rancho Carolina** at the beginning of the road has excellent service and a nice setting. **Parador de Betty** with good cuisine, **Hotel Copihue**; with a swimming pool, under shady trees; its once (late afternoon teatime) is legendary; **Scala de Milán**, with swimming pool; **Los Acacios** and **Llacolén**.

Olmué is a good jumping-off point for some interesting excursions into the surrounding area (see following tours). To return, you may choose between the Camino Troncal through Villa Alemana and Quilpué, or retracing the road you took to get here. The distance is the same.

3 TO LIMACHE AND OLMUE ★★★

a round trip of 68 km from Concón on a paved road; allow half a day, or a whole day if you stop at the swimming pools in the area. Winter is not a good season. There are several restaurants.

A short excursion to a scenic area inland. While inlanders flock to the seaside in summer, the coastal dwellers head inland to this spot.

Leave Concón (km 0) following the highway to Quillota. At km 17 take the signposted road branching right to Limache. At km 23, at San Pedro, you will run into the secondary Quillota-Limache road; turn right to follow this road, which climbs the spur of mountains separating the Quillota and Limache valleys. Below this pass, the railway crosses the mountains through a tunnel. At km 28 is

Limache a sleepy rural town arranged round **Av Urmeneta**, lined with large maple-like trees which metamorphose it into a green tunnel. It has several quintas –landed villas– dating from the turn of the century, with gardens crowned by different kinds of palms. They were built by wealthy residents of Valparaíso and Viña del Mar who wanted to have a country retreat.

Limache developed thanks to José Tomás Urmeneta –he had a mansion across from the railway station–, the wealthiest miner, industrialist and businessman in the late 19th century. He bought these lands around 1860 and had large irrigation works undertaken.

At República St. and Camino Troncal is the **Casa de la Cultura**, an old house now a National Monument.

The opposite end of Av Urmeneta leads to the Camino Troncal, the trunk road linking the inland towns with Viña del Mar and Valparaíso. Taking this road to the left you will reach

OLMUE rather than a town, this is a road in the valley leading in 7 km to a small village clustered around the square. It dates from 1612, when lands were granted to the Indians. The lands were again measured and allotted in 1781. Now it is an active municipality and the land has been divided into small orchards engaged in fruit production. There are many houses set in large gardens and with swimming pools, where families from Viña del Mar spend their holidays. A busy spot in summer, it

4 EXTENSION TO LA CAMPANA NATIONAL PARK

★★ *a 20-km extension from Olmué, with 6 km gravel road. Not advisable in winter. Take food.*

A visit to a mountain village and a scenic natural forest.

Head east into the valley from Olmué's main square. The road climbs and passes a stretch with orchards enclosed behind low stone walls. The slopes are more arid and **mount La Campana** towers straight ahead.

At km 7 the paved road reaches a hamlet called **El Granizo**, with a mountain-village atmosphere. The trees turn golden in the autumn and are shrouded in snow in winter. There are small orchards at either side of the road. Horses are offered for hire, and nearby is an airfield for glider planes. Beyond El Granizo, where the pavement ends, take the gravel road branching right. It winds its way up the hill for three km to the entrance to the

LA CAMPANA NATIONAL PARK run by Conaf, the Chilean Forest Service, a small access fee is charged. It is a lush native forest where the predominant species are boldo, peumo, maitén and lots of lingue and canelo. The park is well kept, with paths winding their way into the woods and open spaces for picnic. A brook gurgles among the rocks. A rough, steep trail climbs mount La Campana to within 200 m from a terrace with a memorial tablet set to commemorate Charles Darwin's climb to this spot in 1836. On clear days, you can see all the way to the coast.

Warning do not attempt to climb La Campana without a guide or if you lack mountain climbing experience.

5 QUEBRADA LAS PALMAS ★★

a 30-km extension of the Limache–Olmué tour, with

6

10 km gravel road. Best in spring and summer. Take food.

An excursion into a scenic mountain valley and an old religious sanctuary.

A paved road heads south from Olmué's main square. It crosses the Pelumpén creek at km 3; turn left beyond the bridge and continue 8 km into the valley on the paved road running alongside the creek. The creek forms several pools, easily accessible from the road and suitable for bathing. The scenery changes into scrub peppered with huge boulders: you are now above the level irrigated by the canals. Soon you will reach the hamlet of **Quebrada Alvarado**, with some very old houses. The village lies at the foot of a stretch of mountain road known as **Cuesta La Dormida**, hemmed in by tall mountains. This was the pass used by Pedro de Valdivia to reach the coast.

Take there the narrow gravel road branching left, running for 5 km along the Las Palmas brook. The valley is squeezed by the hills; vegetation is lush near the road and sparser farther up the slope. Small landowners share the valley with people who have built summer retreats in stone masonry. Fruit orchards have been terraced into the slopes. To the north looms mount La Campana, with some Chilean palms growing among the rocks. At the site where a concrete bus stop stands, take the road branching right. It leads in 1 km to the

| CAPILLA DEL NIÑO JESUS DE LAS PALMAS (MN) | a small

chapel erected halfway up the slope, isolated and framed by a group of Chilean palms planted at the site several centuries ago. The sanctuary dates from the 17th century and was a major pilgrimage point for the Indians during the colonial period. It contains a polychrome–wood image, and the main festivity is at midnight on the 24th of December, the so–called «Misa del Gallo» (midnight mass), with pilgrims streaming in from the surrounding district. The place commands a superb view over the valley. It is worth a visit.

6 COLLIGUAY ★

a 120-km round trip from Viña del Mar, with 96 km gravel road. Allow a whole day. Take picnic and swimming gear. Good any time of the year, except winter.

A circuit around a large district where coastal residents retreat to during the summer months.

Leave Viña del Mar following the Camino Troncal to Quilpué (exit 5 in Viña del Mar map). At km 12, at the farther end of Quilpué, a signposted road branches off to Colliguay and Casablanca. Take the road to the left, which curls under an overpass and crosses the Camino Troncal, heading south.

The road passes cultivated fields, irrigation dams suitable for swimming, and Los Perales, an old manor house which once was the Padres Franceses' seminary. At km 12 is La Retuca, a cluster of dwellings. Take there the road branching left, which leads in 15 km to the foot of the hills closing the valley. It then climbs out of the valley on a very curvy stretch giving splendid views of the surrounding countryside. A further 19 km will bring you to

Colliguay a small village lying on a plateau surrounded by hills. A brook flows through the place, forming several pools which have attracted people to build country retreats here, and some institutions to set up summer centers. The plant cover is typical of semi–arid lands, punctuated by oases along the Puangue creek, which flows southward to Curacaví and thence to the Maipo river.

7 THE INLAND DAMS ★★

a round trip of 52 km from Viña del Mar to lake Peñuelas, 70 km to Pitama and 102 km to Lo Ovalle. Allow half a day. Suitable for any season. It is advisable to take food.

An excursion to nice spots for a picnic on a lake shore, watching the windsurfers.

Lake Peñuelas leave Viña del Mar following the highway to Santiago (Route 68). The Lago Peñuelas National Reserve is beyond the police road control post. To the left, some 5 km beyond the control is the access to the angling area, where a small access fee is charged. Picnics and angling are allowed. Pejerrey, a variety of freshwater mackerel, is abundant. A stroll along the shore can be interesting, watching the many bird species coming to this man–made lake created at the turn of the century as a water reservoir for Valparaíso.

Pitama Dam at km 33 from Viña del Mar, beyond lake Peñuelas, a signposted road branches right to Algarrobo and Las Dichas. Take this road, which skirts the edge of the dam; a passage fee is charged. The lake offers good fishing, and clean shores, with easy access to the water's edge for a good bath. The place is popular with windsurfers.

Lo Ovalle Dam follow Route 68 to Santiago to the first detour to Casablanca at km 42. Continue one further km along the highway to a signposted road branching left to Lo Ovalle. This dirt road leads in 9 km to the dam; an entrance fee is charged. Excellent fishing; there is an esplanade for picnics and serving as a bathing beach. This is another popular spot with windsurfers.

6

SECTION D   ALGARROBO TO LAS CRUCES

This Section covers the coastal area between the Tunquén beach to the North and the Las Cruces seaside resort to the South. Inland it stretches to the Pitama dam, Hacienda Lo Orrego and the village of El Totoral. This is an area of low hills forming terraces at different levels and devoid of high Coastal Range peaks.

It has a string of eight seaside resorts, of which Algarrobo is the main one, renowned for its facilities for watersports.

These resorts have lots of summer houses and a relatively low number of hotels. Furthermore, owing to their proximity to Santiago, they are among Santiago residents' favorite playgrounds. In summer the area is invaded by an avalanche of inlanders; the resorts are packed during weekends.

The most frequented spot is Las Cruces, the number of visitors decreasing gradually northwards to Algarrobo.

The Coastal Road runs in this section for 18 km along the coast, but close to the waterfront only at El Quisco and Isla Negra. There is an extension of this road (a dirt stretch) northwards from Algarrobo to Mirasol and Tunquén, right along the seashore. The shortest way to reach Route 68 heading for Viña del Mar is to take the road starting from Mirasol to Las Dichas and Tranque Pitama, but it is only a dirt road –dusty in summer an impassable in winter.

Warning the Coastal Road has bumper–to–bumper traffic on Sunday afternoons in summer.

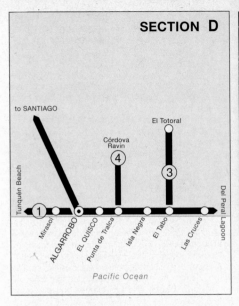

SECTION **D**

to SANTIAGO

El Totoral

Córdova Ravin

④

③

Tunquén Beach

Del Peral Lagoon

①

Mirasol
ALGARROBO
EL QUISCO
Punta de Tralca
Isla Negra
El Tabo
Las Cruces

Pacific Ocean

Algarrobo, El Canelo beach

Distances from Algarrobo to Santiago, 112 km via Casablanca and Route 68, and 135 km along the coastal route via Cartagena; to Viña del Mar, 57 km via Pitama Dam and Route 68; to Quintero, 99 km, same route; to Zapallar, 127 km.

SEASIDE RESORTS IN THIS AREA

Mirasol is the most northerly resort in this Section; as a resort it is quite incipient, with some summer houses and some urban development, but no clear layout of public spaces.

ALGARROBO is the foremost seaside resort in this Section, nestled in a small, sheltered bay, the summer houses lying on the surrounding slopes.

The sea is placid and suitable for all kinds of watersports, which are practiced assiduously here. It is also the «home port» for the leading regattas along the coastline. It has an excellent **Yacht Club**, and a splendid **marina** has been recently built.

The heart of the resort is, of course, the beach, with its **waterfront promenades** and streets. The most popular beach is **San Pedro**, next to the Yatch Club, which concentrates as well watersports activities.

Quieter is the beach of **Los Tubos. Del Pejerrey** and **Cadenas,** in turn, are fashionable and quite fre-

6

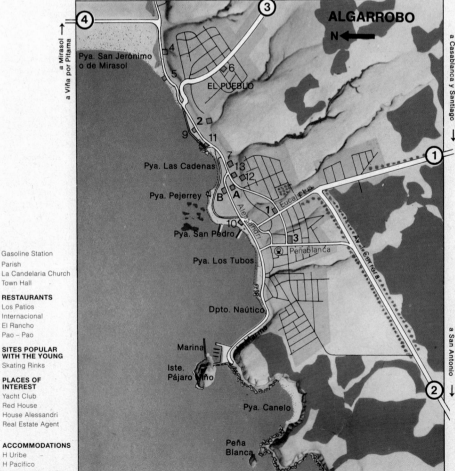

a Casablanca →

③

ALGARROBO

N ◄—

↑ a Mirasol
a Viña por Pitama

④

4

Pya. San Jerónimo o de Mirasol

5

6

EL PUEBLO

2

9

11

Pya. Las Cadenas

7

13

12

Pya. Pejerrey

B A

1

10

Pya. San Pedro

3

Peñablanca

Pya. Los Tubos

a Casablanca y Santiago ↓

①

a San Antonio ↓

Dpto. Naútico

Marina

Iste. Pájaro Niño

Pya. Canelo

②

Peña Blanca

Ⓢ Gasoline Station
1 Parish
2 La Candelaria Church
3 Town Hall

RESTAURANTS
4 Los Patios
5 Internacional
6 El Rancho
7 Pao – Pao

SITES POPULAR WITH THE YOUNG
9 Skating Rinks

PLACES OF INTEREST
10 Yacht Club
11 Red House
12 House Alessandri
13 Real Estate Agent

ACCOMMODATIONS
A H Uribe
B H Pacifico
5 H Internacional

quented. **Canelo** and **Canelillo** are sheltered, and less frequented.

Algarrobo's streets follow the slopes' contours; they are shaded by large trees and lined with beautiful houses, among which **House Alessandri** stands out in the main avenue.

The town evolved from a cove through which the output of Hacienda Lo Orrego was shipped out. In 1845 the cove was upgraded to Coasting Trade Port and some warehouses were built. Soon, summer houses for farm residents started to mushroom at the place. The quarter known as **el pueblo** dates from that period, where some old buildings still survive, such as the **casa roja** (red house) from 1860, with a shrine to the Virgin embedded in the wall, and to its side the building now housing a hotel. Next to the hill is the **La Candelaria** chapel, erected in 1837 by the parish priest of Lo Abarca, Manuel Beltrán; its belfry was made by Pedro Subercaseaux. Inside, it keeps an image of the Virgin of the Rosary, dating from the 17th century, with a swarthy face and black hair.

The seaside resort itself started to take shape after 1873, when an advertisement in a Santiago newspaper offered summer houses in Algarrobo. The houses were built around the «pueblo». The resort's layout was undertaken in the 1920s after the railway reached Cartagena, but the big boost came from the paving of the road to Santiago and the establishment of the Municipality, which actively promoted development.

In the evenings the young get together in the shopping centers or around the skating rinks; the adults stroll towards the **Quebrada de los Doctores**, a short distance inland, or watch the sunset from the Marina or the El Canelo beach.

Where To Eat Los Patitos restaurant offers the best food, together with **Internacional** and **Pao-Pao** restaurants. Cheaper and abundant is **El Rancho.** Quick meals and children-friendly atmosphere at the confitería shown in map.

At **Playa Mirasol** or on the way there you will find good spots for a picnic. In that area is the new Pao-Pao complex, with a restaurant (good view) and a discothèque. Salón de Té **La Bruja**, located at the end of Mirasol beach, offers Austrian pastries.

EL QUISCO located four km south of Algarrobo, is connected to it by the coastal road, which here is lined by a row of eucalyptus. The resort is divided into two sections, North and South, the latter being more active and containing the social and urban center. The beach is good, the sea is placid, it has a splendid Yacht Club, a fishing cove and a waterfront promenade along the entire beach. The shopping area lies along the coastal road, where the town hall, accommodations, and a gas station are to be found.

El Quisco was formed in the 1930s when plots of land from neighboring fundos –large farms– were offered for sale. The municipality was created in 1956. An evening stroll along the **waterfront promenade** or watching the sunset from the look-out point at the **peninsula** can be delightful. **At night**, El Quisco becomes the busiest spot in the district, its discos attracting people from Algarrobo, El Tabo and Las Cruces, in addition to the locals. The best disco is at the Club de Yates.

Where To Eat La Caleta restaurant offers seafood directly from the fishing cove; good and plentiful. **Der Münchner**, located on the roadside opposite the beach, is good.

Punta de Tralca a cape and beach, is renowned not as a resort, but because it belonged to the Seminary of Santiago and for the religious retreats and important meetings of the Catholic hierarchy held at the place. Now a large portion of the peninsula has been divided into plots, with the aim of forming a resort here. Not too frequented in summer, the beach is beautiful, wide, with pounding surf and very strong undertow, not too good for swimming. There is an access road.

Isla Negra is located on a promontory four km

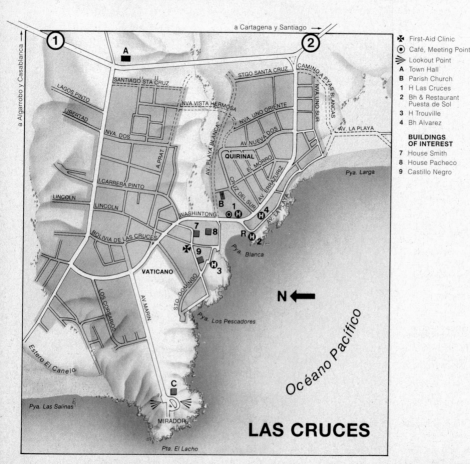

Map legend:
- ✳ First-Aid Clinic
- ◉ Café, Meeting Point
- ⊳ Lookout Point
- A Town Hall
- B Parish Church
- 1 H Las Cruces
- 2 Bh & Restaurant Puesta de Sol
- 3 H Trouville
- 4 Bh Alvarez

BUILDINGS OF INTEREST
- 7 House Smith
- 8 House Pacheco
- 9 Castillo Negro

a Cartagena y Santiago

LAS CRUCES

Océano Pacífico

south of El Quisco. The Córdoba brook runs, emptying into a lagoon next to the beach. It is a quiet resort, more family oriented, its houses and streets are suited to the topography and graced by lush vegetation. The larger houses are located some way up the slope and have thereby a superb view over the ocean.

There are two beaches, one lying on the northern portion and accessible through a footpath, with little sand and lots of rocks, and the other lying on the southern portion, accessible through streets leading downward among the houses; this beach is sandy, has beautiful rock outcrops, but its strong surf makes it unsuitable for bathing. From the beach you can see a house crowned by a stone tower: it is **La Chascona**, the house of **Pablo Neruda**, the Nobel –laureate chilean poet (now a museum, for visits call in advance tel 7778741, Santiago). He built the house himself, and there he kept his exotic collection of shells and nautical objects.

On the southern end of the resort is the Córdoba lagoon. Upstream there is a ravine with lush vegetation, an ideal spot for a picnic. Isla Negra is renowned for its colorful **embroidery in wool**, with marine or peasant motifs done in a naive style, for sale at the CEMA shop in the northern portion of the resort, or directly by the embroiderers themselves.

Where To Eat Hotel Santa Elena, on the highway next to the bridge over the brook; it specializes in frog's legs.

El Tabo is located 2 km south of Isla Negra, lying on a plain sloping gently to the sea. The coastal road crosses the resort as a big avenue and is the center of social and commercial life, with tennis courts, skating rinks, seafood shops, kiosks and lots of traffic, particularly in summer. It has two beaches, **El Caleuche**, to the north, with pools among the rocks, and **Chépica**, the most frequented, wide and shallow. Here is the best hotel in this Section, **Hotel Motel El Tabo**, housed in an old, beautiful building surrounded by large, well-kept gardens. Here is also the Motel Rocas de Córdoba.

Early morning is jogging time for many, while evening attracts others to watch the sunset while strolling along **Playa Larga**, to the south.

Where To Eat best is the restaurant at Hotel El Tabo. Confitería El Bodegón offers quick meals in a children–friendly atmosphere. Cheaper restaurants 4 km south along the coastal route.

LAS CRUCES lies 7 km south of El Tabo and 8 km north of Cartagena. Playa Blanca beach embraces the small bay, which is sheltered by two hills. It had a period of glory at the turn of the century and has now become a busy summer resort. In 1911, a horse–drawn railway made the run between Cartagena and Las Cruces. Large summer houses had been erected on the slopes of both hills. By 1925, the northern and southern parts of town started to be named Vaticano and Quirinal, respectively. At the former there were several chapels. The day started early with a bath at **Los Pescadores** or **Las Salinas** beaches; in the afternoon, outings or visiting were the rule, until rosary time. Then, to bed.

At Quirinal, by contrast, the day started somewhat later, with a bath at **Playa Blanca**. In the afternoon, it was strolling and dancing until supper time. Some buildings from that period are still to be seen, such as the mansion erected by architect Josué Smith (see map), the house of painter Arturo Pacheco Altamirano, with a boat named Angelmó, made of stone. The Castillo Negro was built in English style by architect Héctor Hernández. The parish church rising on the crest of the hill was designed by Friar Pedro Subercaseaux in 1945.

Las Cruces is a popular resort, its beaches Blanca, Grande, Los Pescadores and Las Salinas teeming in summer; at the last named there is a section for picnic and tents. In the evening, the place to be is the **El Lacho point,** reached both by car (Osvaldo Marín street) or foot (path starts at Playa Blanca). The look–out point there commands a view of the coastline stretching from Punta de Tralca to Santo Domingo.

Where To Eat Between El Tabo and Las Cruces is Ché Carlitos, specialized in meat. Good views and food at hotels Bellavista and Las Cruces. Quicker meals at the sites shown in map.

NON-URBAN BEACHES

TUNQUEN is a scenic, 2–km–long beach flanked by tall hills and with a small valley behind, through which the Casablanca creek flows. Its sand is white, its sea excellent for bathing. Tunquén is the only great beach in Chile's Central Coastal Strip that has not yet been turned into a seaside resort. There are two access roads (see map). The shortest road (dirt) starts from Mirasol and leads to the beach's southern end; the car must be left atop the hill, then walk down to the beach. The other access is a detour branching off the Mirasol–Las Dichas road, which crosses some pine forests, climbs slopes and then descends to the rear part of the valley; an access fee is charged. Paths lead from here to the northern end of the beach, where an informal campsite has been set up, and to the southern end, more solitary and beautiful. It is worth it.

La Cruz or El Yeco lies to the north of Mirasol. Access is via the hamlet of El Yeco, where you must leave the car and descend the cliff on foot. Another option is to walk over the rocks from the El Hoyo beach. La Cruz is a very scenic beach draped by tall sandy cliffs. Gold–sanded, its sea is excellent for bathing, with a three–wave surf pattern. Not too frequented, it is good for picnics.

Puente Córdoba and La Castilla located south of Isla Negra, it starts right beyond the namesake brook. Access is through the short road branching towards the sea at the bridge. The beach is steep, with coarse brown sand, 2–3–wave surf pattern, not suitable for bathing but good for sunbathing. Swarming in summer, its easy access from the road makes it popular with low–budget vacationers who come by bus on Sundays, when it is best avoided.

Larga south of El Tabo and stretching all the way to Las Cruces. It receives different names along the way, depending on which vacationing establishment happens to lie close by. Kiosks are set up on this beach in summer, and opposite Chépica there are tennis courts and skating rinks. Easy access; lots of roads branch off the main highway for the beach. The beach is wide, white–sanded and has a two or three–wave surf pattern. Good fishing of corvina and flatfish. It is very crowded in summer.

TOURS OF THE AREA

1 TUNQUEN BEACH ★★★
an outing for one day. See description under Non–Urban Beaches above.
A beauty spot for a picnic.

2 LAGUNA DEL PERAL ★★
a lagoon located one km south of Las Cruces and right next to the coastal road towards the sea. Access to the southern bank of the lagoon.
Shallow, its shore is covered by reeds. It is somewhat of a

6

nature sanctuary, harboring a great variety of waterfowl. There are black-necked swans, five types of duck, taguas and a further 19 bird species.

chapel made of mud brick, now housing a museum of farming objects; open only in summer.

3 EL TOTORAL ★★

eight km from Algarrobo on a dirt road. Access one km south of Punta de Tralca bridge, and from the northern end of El Tabo (see general map). Allow half a day.

An excursion along soft rolling countryside and pine and eucalyptus forests. At the village of El Totoral there is an old

4 QUEBRADA DE CORDOBA ★★

six km from Punta de Tralca on a dirt road. Allow half a day. Take road starting south of the Punta de Tralca bridge (same road as to Totoral); after 6 km, turn 500 m to the right towards the creek.

A scenic ravine for an excursion on foot, with lush native shrubs and a brook carrying water only in summer.

SECTION E   CARTAGENA TO SAN ANTONIO

This Section covers the stretch of coast between Cartagena's long beach and the mouth of the Maipo river. Inland it reaches up to Lo Abarca. Geographically, this section features a spur of the Coastal Range thrusting into the ocean, lending a particular beauty to this coastline.

This entire coastal strip is densely populated. The main centers are Cartagena, a major seaside resort and the second oldest after Viña del Mar, and the neighboring port of San Antonio. Owing to its proximity to Santiago, in summer it becomes the playground for throngs of city dwellers with the resulting traffic jams and crowded beaches. This teeming human mass, with the accompanying vehicles, amusement parks and other paraphernalia produce a striking metamorphosis in the seaside resorts. Perhaps the best time to visit the area is in spring, when the weather is mild and the countryside, after the winter rains, is green and fresh, and the beaches are free to roam. Restaurants are open, but uncrowded.

Coastal Road   it runs from San Sebastián to

Cartagena behind large sand dunes, the ocean shimmering in the distance. It then heads for the shore, skirting the hills of Cartagena, continuing along the waterfront street and the beaches, to round points Vera and Panul running atop the cliffs. This stretch gives a superb view of the resort and its bay. The road then continues to San Antonio and Llolleo, with its wide avenues, to finally reach the bridge spanning the Maipo river.

Warning   on Sundays in summer, particularly after 4 o'clock in the afternoon, expect traffic jams on the highway to Santiago.

Where To Eat   for grilled meat, **Parrillada Argentina**, on the road between San Sebastián and Cartagena. Good views from the balcony and good food at **Hotel Biarritz**, in Cartagena. **D'Bórquez**, at Av Chile in Llolleo, is quite frequented and renowned for its dishes à la carte and for its seafood. For cheap, abundant seafood dishes (mariscales and shellfish), try the restaurants inside the **Estación**, on the costanera (the waterfront street) in San Antonio. Shellfish on the go at the **pescaderías** (seafood

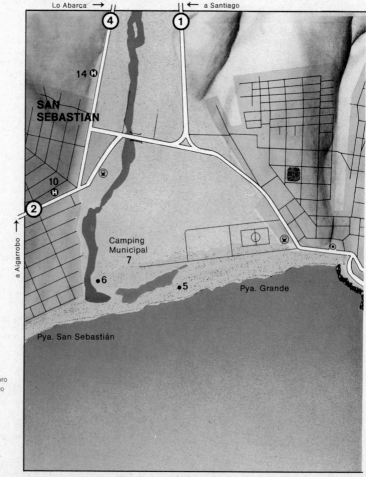

☎ Telephone
◉ Café, Meeting Point
Ⓖ Gasoline Station
A Town Hall
B Post Office
C Railway Station
D Real Estate Agent
E Skating Rinks
5 Paseo a Caballo
6 Paseo en Balsa
7 Municipal Campground

PLACES OF INTEREST
1 House of Vicente Huidobro
2 Tomb of Vicente Huidobro
3 House of the Torreones
4 Foster Castle

ACCOMMODATIONS
10 H Riviera
11 H La Bahía
12 H Biarritz
13 H Playa
14 H Lo Abarca

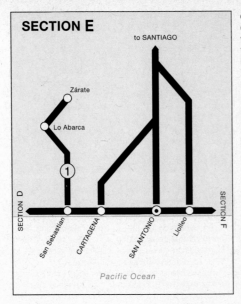

SECTION E

to SANTIAGO

Zárate

Lo Abarca

①

SECTION D

San Sebastián   CARTAGENA   SAN ANTONIO   Llolleo   SECTION F

Pacific Ocean

of summer houses, summer camps and some campsites. This is the heart of institutional vacationland: many organizations, such as industries, clubs and associations have set up summer–holiday establishments here for their members. The beach is long and quite frequented. The busiest part of town is the waterfront street, with shopping areas, restaurants and the like.

CARTAGENA is scenically beautiful, the hills plummeting to the sea leaving a small, sheltered bay embraced by a beach. Large, old houses with no gardens climb the slopes Valparaíso–fashion. In the upper reaches is the **square,** with a parish church and a cinema, marking the center for the permanent residents. The lower section is the summer quarter, with the **Playa Chica** –small beach– and a bustling, wide waterfront street (the costanera) lined with hotels, pensiones and restaurants, painted mostly white. From the costanera a **promenade** heads north, skirting the rocky cliffs covered with picturesque houses. The promenade ends at **Playa Grande**, where another large costanera skirts the beach. An outdoor market is set up here on Sundays offering foodstuffs and other articles, and some amusement installations in summer.

Cartagena is an old town. It was named after Luis de Cartagena, who was granted coastal lands in 1615. From quite early on it was a shipping port for the produce of the Lo Abarca valley inland. In 1770 there already was a small stable population and in 1790 it was granted the status of import and export seaport. The seaside resort started to take form in the late 19th century with the arrival of families from Santiago, invited by the Huidobro family, owners of the neighboring lands. The visitors came by train to Melipilla and from there continued by horse–drawn carriage. Soon a veritable construction frenzy swept the place and in a few years it boasted a sizable number of summer retreats. There was also the high–flown Hotel Zimmer (which burned to the ground in 1929). Enormous prefabricated chalets were brought from France, together with cement and bathroom fixtures from Britain, and American oak for flooring and walls. Thus, Eulogio Berguesio had a church erected for his personal use (on the side of Playa Chica; now only the walls and façade remain); Olegario Serani commissioned the twin–tower mansion on the resort's southern slope, and Foster built his castle on the rocky bluff.

The railway reached Cartagena in 1919, bringing with it an avalanche of visitors. In the summer of 1948, while walking to his house above Playa Chica («A» in map), the famous Chilean poet **Vicente Huidobro** died. As he had wished, he was buried in a lonely slope behind the houses («B» in map); his gravestone has an engraved inscription reading Abrid la tumba, en el fondo se ve el mar («Open the grave, at the bottom the sea can be seen»).

In summer Cartagena becomes a whirlwind of activity, of a very popular kind. Noisy, motley, peppered with awnings and tents, and festooned with loudspeakers and garlands. Springtime, by contrast, is a peaceful time, the most suitable for visiting the place.

Where To Eat the best food is at **La Bahía,** facing the Playa Chica, open year-round.

SAN ANTONIO a port and resort lying on a fairly steep slope and closed to the North by the Panul headland, where the lighthouse stands. A long beach stretches south to the Maipo river. A sizable number of tourists come here in summer, but the town is really fueled by its bustling port, growing mostly at the expense of Valparaíso. San Antonio is the supply center for the coastal strip stretching south of Valparaíso, with active commerce and permanent nightlife in its streets, cafés, restaurants, dancing establishments and other entertainment locales typical of port cities. The busier sections are the square, two shopping streets climbing up the hills, the **costanera,** the harbor, and the railway station. It is a picturesque

stalls) on the costanera in San Antonio. For a quick meal with children, try the confiterías of San Antonio (see map). For a picnic, Cartagena's Playa Grande.

Distances from San Antonio to Santiago, 109 km on Route 78; to Viña del Mar, 110 km on coastal road, via detour to Casablanca and Route 68; to Quintero, 145 km on same route; to Zapallar, 179 km.

SEASIDE RESORTS IN THE AREA

San Sebastián an elongated town lying between the coastal road and the beach. Several streets lead from the highway to the beach. There are lots

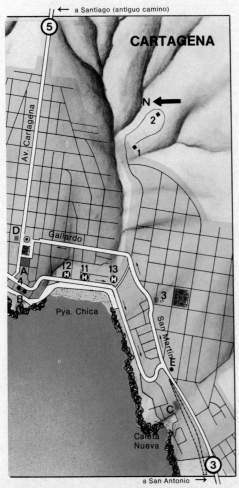

← a Santiago (antiguo camino)

⑤

CARTAGENA

N

②

①

Av. Cartagena

D

Gallardo

A
4

12 11 13

B

3

Pya. Chica

San Martín

C

Caleta Nueva

③

a San Antonio →

6

place, with many restaurants and with a great **seafood market**.

San Antonio is very well sheltered from the North wind and, like the rest of the fishing coves, it was the shipping port for the output of the surrounding farms. In 1853 Vicente Larraín laid out the residential quarter, as well as the areas for the port facilities, the church and the customs house. In 1865, during the war with Spain and the blockade of Valparaíso by Spanish warships, San Antonio became the alternative port with over 30 ships being loaded or unloaded daily.

The great boost came in 1911 with the opening of the railway connecting it to Santiago. The construction of the port facilities was started with blueprints by Brockman Engineers and construction work by Auguste Galtier, of Paris. The port was inaugurated in 1917. Both the city and the port were severely damaged by the 1985 earthquake.

The coastal road continues southward skirting the harbor and passes **Barrancas**, a residential area originated when the port was built. The museum of Science and Archeology is worth a visit.

A Tip for Lunch Juanita restaurant, at Antofagasta 159 in Barrancas, offers abundant seafood dishes at reasonable prices.

LLOLLEO is located 4 km south of San Antonio. It was born as a seaside resort when the railroad reached the site in 1912. Unlike Cartagena, it was planned as a «garden city», with isolated chalets

set in their own garden and with streets lined with palms (Phoenix cannariensis). It is delightful to stroll through its rolling streets, beautiful square and old mansions. For lunch, the best is the **D'Bórquez** restaurant at Av Chile. In summer Llolleo is as bustling a place as the rest of the seaside resorts, with visitors going to its beach crossing a sandy tongue between two small lagoons where **black-necked swans** are often to be seen. The beach is wide and long, with gray, fine sand brought here by the Maipo river.

TOUR OF THE AREA

1 A CIRCUIT AROUND LO ABARCA AND ZARATE

★★★ *a 31-km round trip from Cartagena, with 12 km of gravel road. Allow half a day.*
Take food or eat at the quinta de recreo at Lo Abarca.

An excursion on the old route connecting Santiago to the coast, along which the horse-drawn carriages travelled from Melipilla to Cartagena, to visit an old and picturesque village.

A road branches off the Coastal Road to Lo Abarca, right beyond the bridge over the Cartagena creek. It runs along the ravine for about five km, then climbs out of it, giving goods view towards the sea behind, framed by the ravine walls. In the other direction you can see the bell tower of

LO ABARCA a village preceded by a church

		ACCOMMODATIONS		
☎	Telephone Center			8 Bh Castillo (Llolleo)
◉	Café,Meeting Point	C Railway Station	1 H Casablaca	
⊚	Gasoline Station	D Railway Station	2 H Turismo Hockey Club	**RESTAURANTS**
⏝	Lookout Point	E Seafood Market	3 Cb Undumar	10 Juanita
✱	Hospital	F Waterfront Promenade	5 H Alhambra (Llolleo)	11 Navoli
A	Provincial Government	H Municipal Museum	6 H Oriente (Llolleo)	E Pescaderías
B	Town Hall	J Non-Industrial Shipyards	7 Bh Tropicana (Llolleo)	C Railway Station
		K 21 de Mayo Lookout Point		

6

(mass; in winter Sun, 18:00 h; in summer Sun 18:30 h) and a semi–demolished nave. To the side is the **Museum** (Mon–Fri 13:00–18:00 h, Sat and Sun 09:00–16:00 h; in summer until 18:00 h) and the square, with the typical mud–brick houses clustering around it. During the 18th and 19th centuries it was a major administrative center for a large district, but declined during the present century as a result of having been left outside of the main routes. In 1972 the last two–story mud–brick house was demolished, a piece of historical value disappearing in the process. The place was named after a family called Abarca who lived in this zone since 1797. The school was founded in 1867 and there are still school books from that period.

The museum keeps documents and books from the 18th, 19th and 20th centuries; exhibits include photographs, bones, furniture, pots and other objects. From 1930 to 1935, the Purísima de Lo Vásquez religious festivity was held here; later, the Valparaíso curia ordered the image to be moved to its present location by Route 68.

3 km ahead is Zárate, a farming village, and taking a 4-km detour to the right you will reach Route 78 to San Antonio and Cartagena.

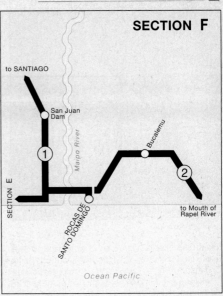

SECTION **F**   ROCAS DE SANTO DOMINGO

This Section covers the coastal area south of the Maipo river mouth where the resort of Rocas de Santo Domingo is located, with the area's longest beach (20 km). Inland it stretches to the road leading to the mouth of the Rapel river. There are no tall hills in the area, as the Coastal Range here peters out into soft rolling country. The shore is flanked by sandy cliffs with some conchuela layers (crushed fossil seashells), illustrating the fact that this is a section of raised sea bottom. Inland, the countryside is typical of non–irrigated coastal farmland.

Coastal Road   it runs for 47 km from the bridge across the Maipo river to the bridge spanning the Rapel. 36 km are paved, the rest gravel. The road runs away from the coast through vast grazing lands and some old farm houses (see Tours of the Area). Gasoline at Santo Domingo.

6

SAN ANTONIO AND LLOLLEO

Santo Domingo beach

Zapallar, 183 km. To the southbound Pan–American highway at Pelequén, 135 km along the newly built –and paved– Fruit Route.

ROCAS DE SANTO DOMINGO lies on a forested knoll rising on the southern bank of the Maipo river mouth, facing a wide stretch of open ocean reaching from San Antonio south to Punta Toro. It is a chic, fashionable, pleasant seaside resort with a modern layout following the terrain's contour. It has large summer residences set in manicured gardens, streets and parks shaded by trees. Unlike the previously described seaside resorts, Santo Domingo is a rather quiet place, activities centering mainly on the beach, the exclusive golf club, indoors in the splendid mansions, strolling along the shady streets and parks, and in the evening on the rocks of the Puntilla, which form terraces over the shore that are perfect for watching the sunset.

The name is derived from the first owners of the place during the colonial period: the Dominican Order. The origin of the seaside resort is recent, and more or less unusual. At a site where only dunes, thistle and hares were to be found, visionary developers Carlos Cariola and Ernesto Bozo formed a real estate company whose avowed aim was to create the best resort on the coast. A national architecture contest was held to design its layout; the winner was Smith Miller of Santiago. Forests and ornamental trees were planted, which were for years watered with water brought by oxcart. Sewage, drinking water and electricity networks were laid, the streets and sidewalks were paved, and there you had it: 1.000 plots of 1.000 square meters each were ready to be offered for sale in 1942. They were promptly snapped and soon they held superb summer residences and gardens.

The owners undertook other large improvements,

Non–Urban beaches the only such beach is **Playa Larga**, stretching for 20 km southward of Santo Domingo to Punta Toro, on the mouth of the Yaly creek. The sand is dark and fine, the surf has a 3–wave pattern, good for angling from the shore. Open to the SW wind and dune–draped, the beach also has marshes and lagoons, in addition to a salt pit in full production. One of the best excursions from Santo Domingo is to walk the length of the beach or ride along it on horseback. Access from the highway is difficult. It is easier reached on foot from Santo Domingo. Lonely, it is suitable for picnics or camping.

Distances from Santo Domingo to Santiago, 115 km on Route 78 via San Antonio and 98 km via San Juan. To Viña del Mar, 120 km via Coastal Road and the detour from Algarrobo to Casablanca, then Route 68. To Quintero, 157 km;

6

← a Bucalemu

②

ROCAS DE SANTO DOMINGO

Correos

①

Municipalidad

Aeródromo

N ←

CLUB DE GOLF

Medialuna

Bencina

El Golf

Av. A. Phillips

Las Rocas

Tenis

Iglesia

Av. El Bosque

Club Hotel

Bellavista

Calle del Pinar

Comercio

Litoral

Litoral

Av. del Parque

Cipreses

Mar Bella

Litoral

a San Antonio y Santiago ↑

Mirador

Av. del Mar

Playa Sto. Domingo

Pya. Los Enamorados

Piedra del Sol

such as the **Golf Club**, and managed to obtain for it its own municipal administration, which from the very beginning has been keen on preserving and enlarging the **green areas** and public spaces. A stroll along the main **avenue**, with beautiful trees and houses and gardens, can be delightful, to walk then down to the beach along the **costanera**.

Where To Eat good service and views at the **Club Hotel Las Rocas**: for a picnic, the Playa Larga stretching southwards beyond the costanera. Supplies at the local supermarkets.

TOURS OF THE AREA

1 TO THE SAN JUAN DAM ★★

a 35–km round trip from Santo Domingo on a paved road. Allow two hours. An entrance fee is charged.

A circuit through an area of orchards and country retreats to visit a dam.

At the northern end of the bridge across the Maipo river a road branches inland to Leyda. It soon passes Lo Gallardo, a one–street village whose mainstay are some local industries. It evolved from an Indian village in the middle of a reservation established in the mid–18th century. The road crosses an industrial area, established here on account of the availability of water from the creek. Near the industries, on a knoll jutting into the valley, there is a park planted in 1915, containing exotic species; here were the manor houses (destroyed by the 1965 earthquake) of the huge Hacienda San Juan, which stretched all the way to Leyda and Melvilla. A short distance ahead, the road skirts the shores of the **San Juan dam**, surrounded by large eucalyptus, with boats for hire and good spots for a picnic and bathing.

2 TO THE MOUTH OF RAPEL RIVER ★★★

a 93–km round trip from Santo Domingo, with 72 km paved; allow half a day. Take food.

An excursion through the coastal countryside, passing old hamlets to finally reach the Rapel river canyon.

Take Exit 2 out of Santo Domingo (see map). At km 14 is the Atalaya police station and a short distance ahead a road branches left: it is the so–called «Fruit Route», which skirts lake Rapel to meet the Pan–American highway at Pelequén. It is used to bring the South's fruit output to the port of San Antonio. Continuing towards Bucalemu, to the right is the access to El Convento, an old hacienda. Ask for permission to pass through; a secondary road will bring you to **Las Salinas**, close to the coast, where salt is extracted from seawater by solar evaporation.

Back on the road and continuing to km 26, on the banks of the Yaly creek, are the manor houses of

| HACIENDA DE BUCALEMU | an enormous ranch of 54.000 ha where the Novice House of the Jesuits was located until 1767. It then became part of the entailed estate established by Pedro Fernández de Balmaceda in 1778. Shortly before Chile attained independence, it had 24.000 head of cattle and 16.000 head of sheep. Once a year a large slaughter was performed (thence the name of the nearby pond) to obtain fat, hides, and meat for salting; the products were then exported to Peru.

The last heir (who had kept his Spanish nationality), afraid that his property could be expropriated during the war with Spain in 1865, decided to sell it to his Chilean brother in law, Claudio Vicuña, the most prosperous and inventive landowner in the late 19th century, in addition to being a politician and presidential candidate. Vicuña had a 36–ha **park** built in 1875, under the direction of French landscape architect Guillaume Renner; to this day, this park remains one of Chile's finest. Over the years, this great hacienda has been progressively subdivided. The house and the park are owned since 1968 by the Chilean Army, which uses it as a relaxation center for its officers. Visitors are not allowed, but the park can be seen from the road.

At km 43 is the tiny village of the **San Enrique** farm, with beautiful houses, a park and farming buildings. Beyond the hills, a short distance ahead, the road descends into the canyon of the Rapel river.

6

MOVING AROUND BY CAR

The coastal strip can be divided into two areas defined by their access routes: **Papudo–Valparaíso** and **Algarrobo–Santo Domingo.**

Papudo–Valparaíso coming from the North, it is best to leave the Pan–American highway at the Quínquimo road junction and take the road heading west to Papudo, to follow then the coastline southwards.

From the South, take Route 68 from Santiago to Valparaíso and then follow the coast northwards. A faster access from the South to Papudo, Zapallar and Cachagua is to take the northbound Pan–American highway up to the Catapilco or the Quínquimo junctions, and follow then the roads branching west (see map below).

Algarrobo–Santo Domingo coming from the **North** on the Pan–Am take road heading west from Calera to Concón, continue to Viña del Mar, then follow a stretch on Route 68 inland to Casablanca to take there the signposted road to Algarrobo, heading back towards the coast (see map below). From the **South,** leave the Pan–Am right before San Bernardo, head west to Calera de Tango and continue on Route 78 towards the coast.

BUS SERVICES

The chart below shows bus service routes and frequencies towards and along the coast. The first batch of buses leaves Santiago between 06:30 and 07:00 h; the last departures are around 21:30 h.

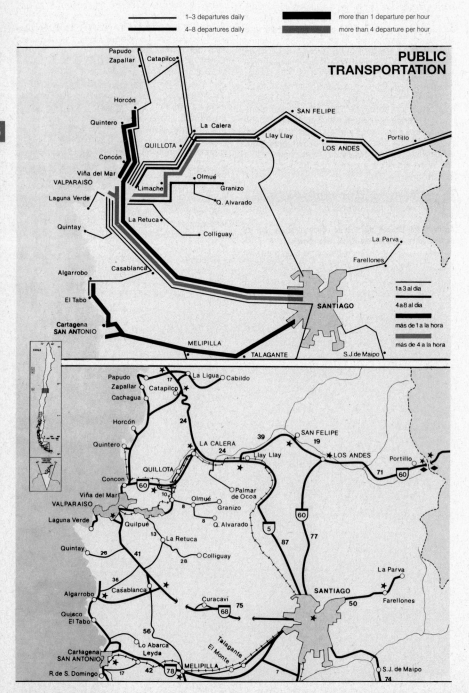

Zone 7
THE PACIFIC ISLANDS

Arica
Iquique
Antofagasta
Copiapó
Easter
Island
La Serena
Valparaíso
SANTIAGO
Is R
Crusoe
7
Talca
Concepción
Temuco
Valdivia
Osorno
Pto Montt
Castro
Chaitén
Coihaique
Cochrane
Puerto Natales
Punta Arenas
Puerto Williams
Is Diego
Ramirez
90° 60° 53°
CHILEAN
ANTARCTIC
TERRITORY

7

Anakena

Hanga-Roa

EASTERN ISLAND
(RAPA NUI)

San Juan
Bautista

ROBINSON CRUSOE ISLAND

DETAILED MAPS

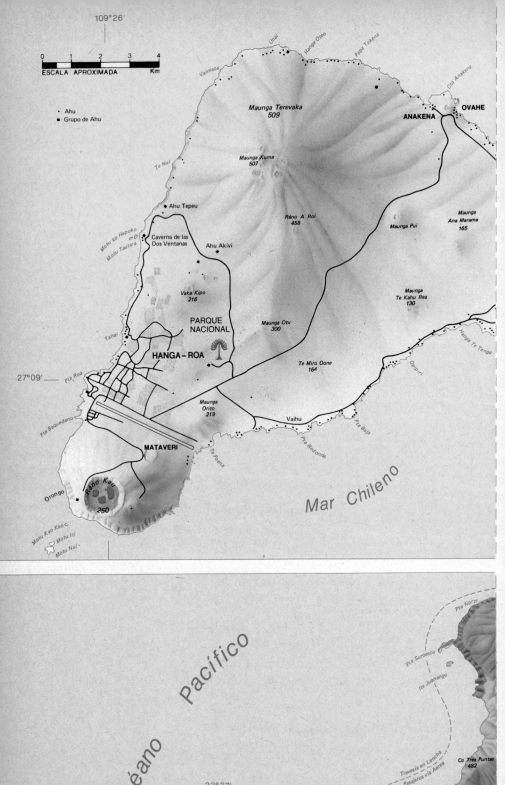

109°26'

ESCALA APROXIMADA

Km

• Ahu
■ Grupo de Ahu

Maunga Terevaka
509

ANAKENA OVAHE

Te Nui

Maunga Kuma
507

• Ahu Tepeu

Ráno A Roi
458

Maunga Pui

*Maunga
Ana Marama*
165

Motu ko Hepoko

Caverna de las
Dos Ventanas

♦ Ahu Akivi

Motu Tautara

Vaka Kipo
216

*Maunga
Te Kahu Rea*
130

**PARQUE
NACIONAL**

Maunga Otu
300

Tanai

HANGA–ROA

27°09' — *Pta. Roa*

Te Miro Oone
164

Opoiri

Hanga Te Tenga

Pta Baquedano

*Maunga
Orito*
219

Te Pama

Vaihu

Pta Baja

MATAVERI

Pta Redonda

Mar Chileno

Orongo

Ráno Kau
250

Motu Kao Kao o.

Motu Iti

Motu Nui

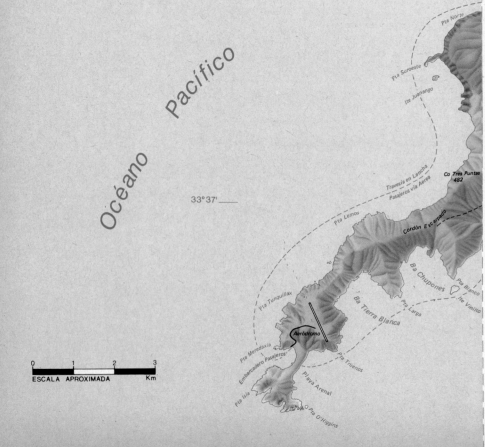

Océano Pacífico

Pta Norte

Pta Suroeste

Ite Juanango

33°37' —

Co Tres Puntas
482

Travesía en Lancha
Pasajeros vía Aérea

Pta Lémos

Cordón Escarpado

Ba Chupones

Pta Blanco

Pta Tunquillas

Ba Tierra Blanca

Pta Larga

Ite Vinilio

Pta Isla

Aeródromo

Embarcadero Pasajeros

Pta Meredaxia

Pta Truenos

Playa Arenal

Pta O'Higgins

ESCALA APROXIMADA

Km

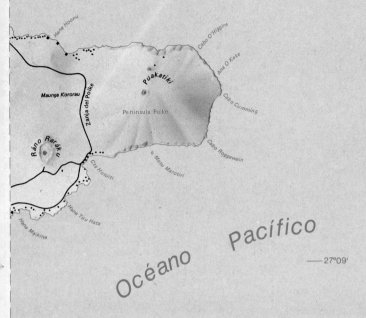

Hana Hoonu
Cabo O'Higgins
Ana O Keke
Puakatíki
Maunga Kororau
Cabo Cumming
Zanja del Poike
Peninsula Poike
Ráno Raráku
Cabo Roggewein
Cra Honuiti
Motu Marotiri
Hana Tuu Hata
Hana Majkina

Océano Pacífico

—27°09'

N

EASTER ISLAND
or RAPA NUI

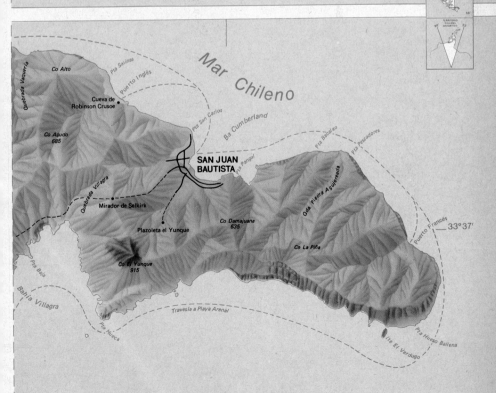

Co Alto
Pta Salinas
Quebrada Vaquería
Puerto Inglés

Mar Chileno

Cueva de
Robinson Crusoe
Pta San Carlos
Ba Cumberland
Co Agudo
685
Pta Bacalao
Pta Pescadores
Quebrada Villagra
SAN JUAN BAUTISTA
Pta Pangal
Mirador de Selkirk
Qda Piedra Agujereada
Plazoleta el Yunque
Co Damajuana
635
Pta Baja
Co La Piña
Puerto Francés
—33°37'
Co El Yunque
915
Bahía Villagra
Pta Huasca
Travesía a Playa Arenal
Pta Huego Ballena
fte El Verdugo

ROBINSON CRUSOE ISLAND
(del Archipiélago Juan Fernández)

78°50'

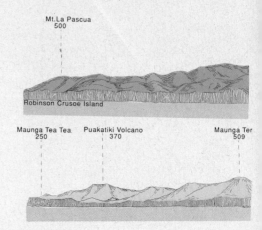

Mt.La Pascua
500

Robinson Crusoe Island

Maunga Tea Tea
250

Puakatiki Volcano
370

Maunga Ter
509

OVERVIEW

Chile's Pacific islands are sporadic, i.e., they occur isolated in the ocean. This Zone reviews Chile's Easter Island and Robinson Crusoe island.

Easter Island (Isla de Pascua, Rapa Nui)   is a scientific enigma. During the island's heyday, the life and deeds of its 15,000 inhabitants were recorded on rongo rongo «speaking» tablets (they were practically the only people native to the New World possessing a written language). When Chile took possession of the island late last century, there were little over one hundred islanders left; none of them was capable of interpreting the ancient writings, nor of relating anything regarding the real culture of his forebears. But the gigantic, gaunt stone statues they left behind still pepper the island, bearing witness to a great culture. There are few parallels elsewhere to Easter island culture. Its ancient inhabitants called it Te Pito o Te Henua

The Navel of the World. It was isolated for over one millennium, the islanders having no human contact other than among themselves. Geographically, it is the world's most isolated spot.

Robinson Crusoe   is a rugged island -part of the Juan Fernández group- covered by rich, singular vegetation and harboring a varied wildlife. Both flora and fauna originated in the mainland, but millennia in isolation made them evolve into autochthonous strains of particular beauty and interest. In 1977 the island was granted the status of World Biosphere Reserve.

Visiting either or both islands is a unique experience. They are outstanding case studies of the effects of isolation: cultural development in Easter Island, natural evolution at Juan Fernández.

7

Zone 7
THE PACIFIC ISLANDS

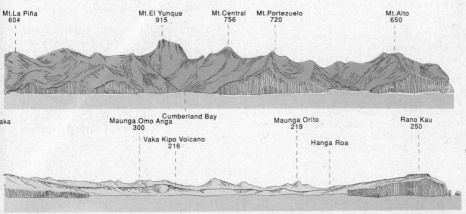

Mt.La Piña 604 Mt.El Yunque 915 Mt.Central 756 Mt.Portezuelo 720 Mt.Alto 650

aka Maunga Omo Anga 300 Cumberland Bay Maunga Orito 219 Rano Kau 250

Vaka Kipo Voicano 216 Hanga Roa

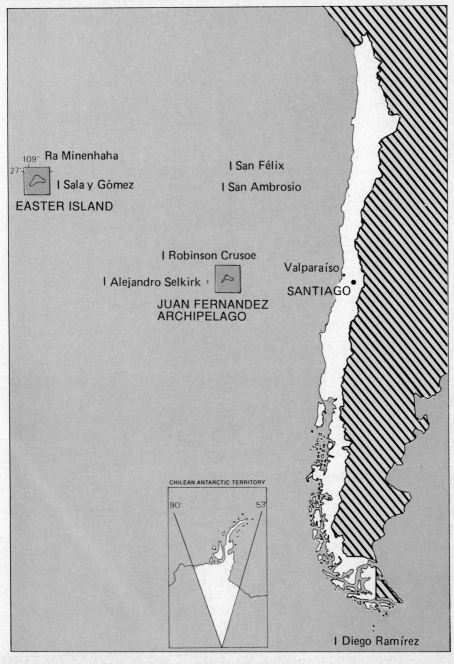

109° Ra Minenhaha
27°
I Sala y Gómez
EASTER ISLAND

I San Félix
I San Ambrosio

I Robinson Crusoe
I Alejandro Selkirk
JUAN FERNANDEZ
ARCHIPELAGO

Valparaíso
SANTIAGO

CHILEAN ANTARCTIC TERRITORY
90° 53

I Diego Ramírez

7

HOW TO GET THERE

Easter Island is accessible only by air, as supply ships run on irregular schedules. Lan Chile has scheduled flights from Santiago (on Sundays, Wednisdays and Fridays, at 12:30 h) (en esta época es a las 13:30 h) overflying Juan Fernández islands and landing at Easter Island's Mataveri airport 5 hours later (1530 h local time; 2 hours behind Chilean mainland time). One hour later the airplane continues the 5½ hour leg to Papeete, Tahiti.

Light clothing is most appropriate any time of the year, with some sort of rain gear for the occasional shower. The climate is subtropical, with a mean annual temperature of 18,5° C. A wide-brimmed hat, sunglasses, sunscreen cream, and bathing apparel are a must, together with shoes suitable for walking on stony ground or for climbing. A flashlight («torch» for the lovers of British English) comes in handy for cave exploration. The telephone is a cheap, convenient way to make contacts beforehand or secure reservations: a call from Santiago to Easter Island is as cheap as a call from Santiago to Valparaíso.

The best season for visiting **Robinson Crusoe Island** is from October through March. Two airline companies fly from Santiago (Cerrillos Airport), operating airplanes with capacity for 5 passengers and a 10-kg luggage allowance per passenger. The plane lands at an airstrip at the western tip of the island, and from there it is 1½ hours by motorboat to the village of San Juan Bautista.

Transportes Chris runs a ship (Charles Darwin) from Valparaíso, 36 to 48-hour passage, returning after a 7-9 day stay at the island.

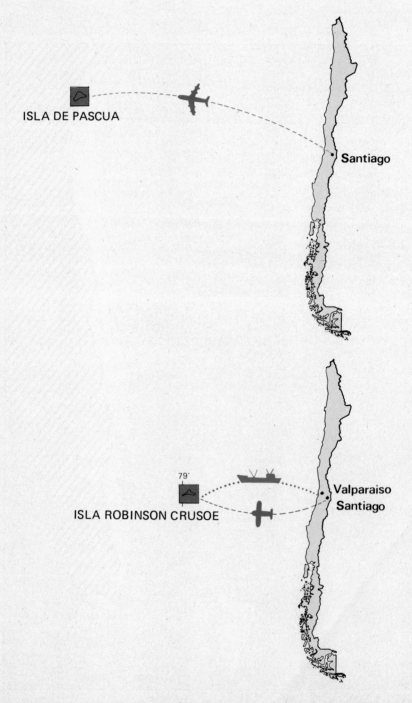

ISLA DE PASCUA

Santiago

7

79°

ISLA ROBINSON CRUSOE

Valparaiso
Santiago

SECTION EASTER ISLAND

THE LAND, ITS PEOPLE, ITS HISTORY

ORIGIN some two-and-a-half million years ago a volcano later to be known as Poike erupted, followed by its siblings Rano Kau and, lastly, Maunga Terevaka. The tips of these three volcanoes formed the vertices of a triangle in the middle of the ocean. Within this triangle, a further 70-plus new craters belched and spewed lava from the earth's depths until spawning a peculiar landscape sprawling over 180 square kilometers. The island's present topography features rolling hills and extinct volcanoes, with a few relatively flat pastures. The coastline is abrupt and rocky, with many cliffs and no sheltered coves. There are only three beaches, sporting white-pink coral sand: Anakena, Ovahe and La Perouse. A short distance offshore some rocky islets jut out, including Motu Marotiri, Motu Iti, Motu Nui and Motu KaoKao.

CLIMATE maritime with subtropical characteristics. The coldest months are July and August, with a mean temperature of 17,8° C, while February is the warmest month, with an average of 23,7 °C. Rainfall occurs throughout the year, with an annual mean of 1,138 mm and May as the rainiest month. Even on cloudy days there is great luminosity.

FLORA evidence has been unearthed of the island being clad, some 3 thousand years ago, with a thick forest containing over 40 different tree species. Both volcanic cataclysms and human intervention -moai used to be transported on wooden rollers- wiped out the forests. Today the island is a rather arid place, covered in part by pastures and speckled with small (introduced-)eucalyptus groves. Thirty-four indigenous species have been preserved, including some brought into the island by the first immigrants, believed to have arrived from Polynesia around AD 300-800. Toromiro, perhaps the best-known woody species on account of its having been used in primitive handicrafts, is one of the species extinct in the island, but in the process of being reintroduced. Under the water surface a variety of algae thrive, along with corals. The latter are not as large anymore as when they used to provide the material for the eyes of certain moai; now they are used in handicrafts.

FAUNA the whole wildlife spectrum of the island suffered as a consequence of the island's overpopulation in times past. Some bird species still return to visit the island now and then, such as tavake, makohe, some fardelas and gulls, and more rarely the most legendary of all, the manutara (Easter Island gull).

Sea fauna is somewhat more varied, including a large-sized lobster called hakarana, edible fish such as nanue, poopó and toremo, among others, and some unusually-shaped fish such as *titeve* (urchin fish), trumpet-fish, box-fish, butterfly-fish, etc. Underwater rocks support various types of mostly small snails, their shells used by craftsmen for making necklaces.

PRIMITIVE INHABITANTS two contending theories seek to explain where the first immigrants came from. Until the first half of this century, they were believed to have come from somewhere in Polynesia. Later, a rival theory proposed South American ancestors. The similarity between constructions in High Peru and Easter Island can be striking.

The most ardent supporter of the South American theory is Thor Heyerdahl, a Norwegian who even sailed in a raft (the Kon Tik*i*, built by craftsmen

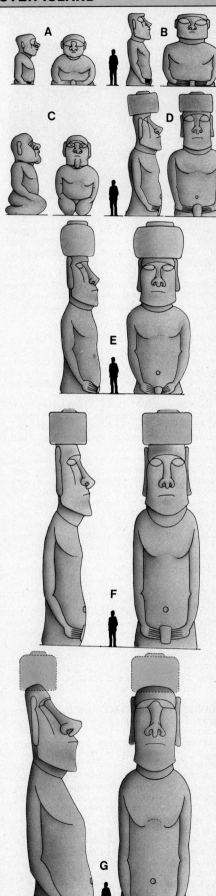

A Moai Escoria Roja (Tahai)
B Moai Ahu Vai (Tahai)
C Moai Tuturi (Rano Raraku)
D Moai Ko Te Riku (Tahai)
E Moai Ahu Tog
E Moai Ahu Tongariki (Hotu Iti)
F Moai Paro (Ahu Te Pito Kura)
G Moai Rano Raraku (Terminal)

7

Moais scattered over the hillaide

from Titicaca lake) across the Pacific to Polynesian islands, in order to demonstrate that it was possible for South Americans to have sailed westwards to colonize the South Pacific islands.

The theory in support of Polynesian ancestors suggests that the first immigrants to Easter Island came from Marquesas Islands. This theory has gained increased acceptance among scientists in recent decades.

POPULATION AND CULTURE Rapa Nui is believed to have been colonized between the fourth and the eighth century AD. Originally few in numbers, the first immigrants multiplied over the centuries and, in utmost **isolation**, developed a surprisingly complex culture.

The highly-stratified Rapa Nui society was made up of a series of groups with a so-called single-line kinship and was headed by a king, believed to descend directly from the gods of creation. Each clan -mata- occupied an inland territory and a strip of coast, where the clan's religious, political and social center was located, together with the ceremonial altar -**ahu**- where deified ancestors were worshiped. These were represented by stone statues, the **moai**. A wide **esplanade** stretched from the ahu away from the coast, where community activities were held. In front of the ahu were groups of houses inhabited by high-ranking persons; there were also fireplaces, paved areas and other cult-related structures.

The coastline is strafed with ahu. The peculiar thing is that all the statues face inland, paying homage to what the natives considered the only inhabited land in the world.

The rest of the population was scattered in inland settlements located next to their croplands. The settlements consisted of a hare paenga -dubbed now «boat-house» on account of its resembling an upturned boat- roofed with plants, usually reeds, surrounded by a number of unu pae, hearths where food was cooked over hot stones. They also had some chicken pens.

EVOLUTION AND DECADENCE over the centuries, Rapa Nui society became increasingly devoted to ancestor worship, with an ever larger share of its population dedicated to erecting huge altars and sculpting giant stone figures, and a consequently dwindling number of people dedicated to food production. These factors, added to the mounting pressure exerted by an ever larger population living in a place of limited resources and a fragile ecological balance, seem to have triggered a crisis in the social system.

The crisis peaked in the 16th and 17th centuries, when successive wars broke out among the clans. The ahu were gradually destroyed (every single moai was pushed over) and the quarries where the statues were sculpted were abandoned. Caves became the preferred dwelling places, as they offered both shelter and a hiding place. A tremendous scarcity of food ensued, with cases where enemies were eaten out of need or rage.

A new religious cult appeared after the crisis, worshiping fertility represented by the egg of Manutara (Easter Island's gull or gaviotín pascuense, a migratory bird nesting at the Motu Nui islet, off the coast at Orongo). This was the birdman cult, with its ceremonial center at the village of Orongo, located at the upper end of Rano Kau's crater. A competition was staged among the heads of the different clans to obtain the first Manutara egg. The winner was granted the title of Tangata Manu (birdman).

OUTSIDE INFLUENCE on April 6, 1722, an Easter Sunday, the island was discovered and christened by the Dutch admiral Jacob Roggeven, who headed a 4-vessel fleet. Nearly half a century went by before Europeans visited the island again; the new visitors included Capt. James Cook (1774) and French Capt. La Perouse (1786). From then on, the island became a usual stopover point on the route to Oceania. Between 1859 and 1862, slaver ships took more than 1,000 islanders to work at the Peruvian guano beds. To make matters worse, pests and diseases introduced by the foreigners decimated the locals until only 111 of them were left.

In 1870 the first Chilean warship -O'Higgins-called at the island, and in 1888, urged by Capt. Policarpo Toro, Chile took Easter Island under its sovereignty.

PRESENT DEVELOPMENT nearly all of the present 2,000 inhabitants -a fourth of them mainlanders-live in the village of Hanga Roa. This results from the fact that during a long time the island was leased out to a private sheep-farming company, which built a wall surrounding Hanga Roa and forbade the inhabitants from venturing into the rest of the island. The company ceased to operate in 1952 and the island was once more made free for the islanders to roam and settle at will.

Not surprisingly, there is a steady archaeological activity at the island, carried out both by Chileans and foreigners. The areas containing archaeological remains have been granted the status of a National Park (covering about one third of the island) and are under Conaf (Chilean Forest Service) administration.

Fishing and farming had been the two traditional sources of sustenance and income for the islanders. But after air service was initiated with the opening of the Mataveri airport in 1967, tourism grew rapidly to become the main cash earner for the island's inhabitants. At present there are around 500 beds available for visitors.

WHAT TO SEE

HANGA ROA is home to almost the entire population, and boasts a post office, telephone office, court of justice, a bank, school, hotels and a couple of discotheques, among other amenities. The fishing cove is a permanently active place, next to which are the remains of an ahu complete with moai, with a little beach at its foot. A bit to the south, almost at the foot of Hotel **Hanga Roa**, is another fishing cove, Hanga Piko. The twice-yearly supply ship is loaded and unloaded at this point. Construction of a port at this site is planned.

Inside the church, the statuary mixes traditional catholic figures with symbols derived from Easter Island's own culture. The Sunday mass offers the chance to hear arresting religious songs sung in Rapa Nui language, with a marked Polynesian rhythm.

At night the music comes from an altogether different sort of gathering place: the island's discotheques, assiduously frequented by locals and visitors alike. The **Mercado Artesanal** and the **Mataveri** airport are the permanent handicrafts exhibition and sale centers, although handicrafts can also be bought directly from the craftsmen themselves. The Museum, although containing mostly reproductions, does provide a certain insight into the old culture.

7

TOURS

1 A VISIT TO TAHAI ★★★

a walking tour for half a day.

Walk to caleta Hanga Roa, where you will see a partly destroyed ahu and a small moai standing on a platform of recent construction. Take the coastal road towards the cemetery and then the coastal path. A short way ahead is

TAHAI with buried and broken moai left as they were found prior to restoration of the site. At Tahai's center, the first group of moai belongs to the temple of **Ahu Vaiuri**. Facing this group is the esplanade, used for ceremonial and religious gatherings. Next to it, clan heads, priests and high-ranking people built their houses. The elliptical foundations of some of these houses -Hare Paenga- are still to be seen.

Adjacent to a stone ramp is the **Ahu Tahai.** Farther north there is another ramp paved with stones sloping into the sea, and then a solitary moai, **Kote Riku**, with its topknot of reddish stone called pijau.

To return, climb the path across from the Ahu Tahai to the flat area on top used as a parking site. There is a modern house which the owner, Gerardo Velascio, designed in the boat-house tradition. Next to this house is a road leading back to Hanga Roa.

2 TO PUNA PAU, AHU AKIVI AND CAVES ★★★

22 km, for half a day by car or motorbike.

Leave Hanga Roa through Av. Policarpo Toro heading south, until reaching the Mataveri runway. Turn east (left), and you can see the **Puna Pau** quarries on the slopes of a volcano. The moai's reddish topknots were quarried and sculpted there. The road eventually turns northeast; at the junction take the road branching off to the left, leading to

AHU AKIVI with 7 moai. Some 700 meters from the backs of the moai are 2 small stone columns: during the summer solstice (Dec 21), the sun seems to be wedged exactly between them, putting in a word for the early islanders' mastery of astronomy.

The rounded pebbles decorating the ahu's sloping **platform** came from a beach; they were the ballast of the Appoliné Emilie, a ship wrecked here last century.

Nearby are some very green banana trees

Ahu de Anakena

growing in a ground depression: it is the entrance to the **Tepahu Caves**, also known as the Banana Caves, among the largest in the island. You can enter here and emerge and the other end, some 150 meters away.

A path leads to the **Ahu Tepeu**, remarkable for the fine masonry work of its platform, rivaling that of the Incas. The moai here are still toppled face-down, as they were left after the crisis described above. Strewn about are the remains of many **Hare Paenga** (boat-houses)

If you are driving a high-clearance vehicle, return through the track running south along the coast. Otherwise, retrace the same road taken to get here. If you do take the coastal track, a guide can show you the entrance to the **Cave of Two Windows** («Cueva de Dos Ventanas»). Some 50 meters into the cave there is a forking leading to two windows on the face of a sheer cliff plummeting to the ocean.

3 TO VINAPU, RANO RARAKU AND ANAKENA ★★★

46 km altogether. For 1 day. Take food.

Leave Hanga Roa following Av. Policarpo Toro until reaching the Mataveri runway. Turn left and drive along the runway to the end. To the left, you can see a small hill -Maunga Orito- containing the island's main obsidian quarry. Obsidian is the shiny black stone of which most of the early tools were made. Continue straight to the coast to a site known as

7

		ACCOMMODATIONS			TIPS	
☎ Telephone	T Church					
⊙ Café, Meeting Point	H Hospital	1 H Hanga Roa	3 H Victoria		A Handicrafts Market	
R Restaurant	D Discotheque	2 H Topa Roa	4 H Hotu Matua		B Rent Boat–Dive	

HANGA ROA

(map)

Anakena beach

diameter and over 200 m deep.

Take the path to an ahu in an advanced state of crumbling, where three orifices bored in the stone indicate the season of the year when projecting the shadow of a stick. At the end, to the right, is Orongo's largest concentration of petroglyphs, with images of **Tangata Manu**, the birdman; **Make Make**, the god that created him; and **Komari**, the fertility symbol. The site commands a view to the three islets where the manutara nested. He who found the first egg laid by manutara was anointed birdman.

A local guide is advisable for all the tours described above.

VINAPU with the ruins of two ahu, one of which bears a striking resemblance to Machu Picchu's stone masonry work. The moai which used to sit atop this structure have been toppled, one of them lying semi-buried and staring to the heavens.

Three km ahead is **Hanga Pau Kura**, where the destructive intentions of those pushing over the moai are in plain evidence: the moai faces were broken against the ground. Less than 2 km beyond is **Vaihú**, also in the same state as it was left during the crisis. Note some red-stone topknots thrown into the sea. Three km farther is **Aka Hanga**, an archaeological center. Take the road branching off to the left, some way ahead. The moai lying face down near the road were abandoned during their transportation to the ahu. This road leads to

RANO RARAKU the volcano containing the quarry where nearly all the moai existing were sculpted. Note a board with drawings illustrating the method believed to have been utilized by the islanders for transporting the moai. Here are over **300 moai** in various stages of completion, including one measuring a jaw-dropping 21 meters in height, equivalent to a 7-story building. Climb to the crater's edge, from where you can see a reed-covered pond and a number of further moai sculpted in quarries on the crater's inside walls. You will also see 8 perfectly-round holes, which remain a total mystery to this day.

Following the road to the coast you will see the remains of **Ahu Tongariki**, once the largest platform, until its colossal statues where washed away by a tidal wave in 1960. Ten ruin-strewn kilometers ahead is

ANAKENA with two restored **ahu** and the island's most beautiful beach. It used to be a residential center of the ancient rulers. A small grove of palm trees has been planted. A short way to the east is **Ovahe**, a lovely pink-sanded beach with a cave.

The shortest way to return to Hanga Roa is along the interior road crossing the island through the Vaitea farm.

4 TO VOLCANO RANO KAU AND ORONGO ★★★

9 km there and back, for a half-day.

Leave Hanga Roa through Av. Policarpo Toro; turn right at the end until reaching the road running along the coast. Turn left and drive on to the small esplanade used as a parking site. Right below this small cliff is **Ana Kai Tangata** cave, not very deep but over 3 meters high. Note the birdman paintings on the ceiling.

If you are driving, the road climbing to volcano **Rano Kau** is straight ahead of the esplanade. If you are walking, take the path, which leads more directly to the top. Both road and path end at the Conaf warden station. Here is the access (entrance fee) to

ORONGO ceremonial village. To the left is the huge **crater** of volcano Rano Kau, with 1,6 km in

5 SPECIAL TOURIST SERVICES ★★★

an attractive way to immerse oneself in the island's beauty and mysteries.

Snorkeling or Diving Excursions at caleta Hanga Roa (the fishing cove) diving gear is available for individuals or groups. Experts will guide you to the more beautiful underwater spots.

Boat Tours Organized at caleta Hanga Roa, taking you to the Motu Nui islet, where would-be birdmen awaited the arrival of the manutara. A cave with paintings of god Make Make can be visited.

Horse Hire horses are the best way to see the island and can be hired next to Hotel Hotu Matua.

Motorbike Hire another excellent option for touring the island. There is no organized motorbike hire, but arrangements can be made directly with motorbike owners on the street.

7

SECTION ROBINSON CRUSOE ISLAND

THE LAND, ITS HISTORY, ITS PEOPLE

ORIGIN several million years ago, one of the Pacific Ocean floor's hot spots known as «chimneys» started spewing magma from the earth's depths until the material erupted breached the water surface. In time it became the island known as **Robinson Crusoe**, spreading over 47.1 square km and located on the Nazca Plate. This latter fact accounts for the island's getting a few centimeters closer to the mainland every year. Later, a new spewing phase of the same chimney gave rise to the smaller **Santa Clara** island (22.3 km²), which emerged less than 1 km from Robinson Crusoe. Over the millennia, both islands continued crawling their way towards the mainland, while the chimney's volcanic activity remained fixed at the same spot. Its next large spewing phase took place several thousand years later, the resulting island -**Alejandro Selkirk** (44.6 km²)- thus emerging 180 km away from the first two. The three islands, plus a handful of islets surrounding them, make up the **Juan Fernández Archipelago.**

FLORA AND FAUNA the islands soon became a privileged habitat for birds and mammals, offering them a safe breeding ground, temperate climate and abundant nourishment. The birds brought with them seeds and insects which promptly colonized the islands and which, after millennia in isolation, evolved into species of unique genetic features. Examples of this are the enormous variety of ferns thriving in forests above 1,400 m altitude (at La Palmilla), Luma and Mayu-monte, with their extraordinarily hard wood, giant Naranjillos and Chonta or Juan Fernández Palm, whose beautiful wood is coveted to an alarming degree by craftsmen. The most important species was undoubtedly Sandal, whose perfumed wood invited indiscriminate felling and subsequent extinction. Among the bird fauna stand out the Red Hummingbird, its colors displayed fully in flight, the Rayadito and the Churrete. The most notorious mammal is the two colored hair seawolf. The entire archipelago was granted the status of **Biosphere Reserve** by UNESCO and is also a National Park under Conaf administration.

HUMAN PRESENCE the archipelago was discovered on Nov 22, 1574, by the Spanish

Selkirk's look-out

seaman Juan Fernández, who had decided to sail away from the mainland coast in order to elude the winds and currents prevailing there. During the 17th and 18th centuries, pirates and privateers visited the place, but it was an unwilling visitor who put the archipelago in the map: Alexander Selkirk, put ashore from HMS Cinque Ports in 1704 and rescued after 4 years of solitary stay on Robinson Crusoe. He inspired the novel Robinson Crusoe, by Daniel Defoe.

In 1750 the village of San Juan Bautista was founded at Cumberland Bay, the most sheltered harbor in Robinson Crusoe island. By 1779 there were already 7 fortresses bristling with guns. The island's isolation offered Spain a splendid place for setting up a penal colony, to which high-ranking Chilean patriots struggling for independence from Spain were deported after their defeat at Rancagua. In 1915, during the First World War, two British ships and one German one, the Dresden, engaged in a sea battle which ended with the scuttling of the German cruiser, still sitting on the bottom of the bay.

THE PRESENT there are currently some 500 people living in the archipelago, all of them in the village of San Juan Bautista and many engaged in fishing for the pincerless lobster, an appreciated delicacy in the mainland. Services include a Post Office, a Wireless Station, a Registry Office, a Polyclinic, a School, a Museum administered by Conaf and a hotel and some residenciales. The rest of the

7

F	Fortress Santa Bárbara			
P	Cave of the Patriots	**R** Restaurant	**ACCOMMODATIONS**	**2** H Green
T	Telegraph	**C** Cemetery	**1** H Cabins Daniel Defoe	**3** H Pangal

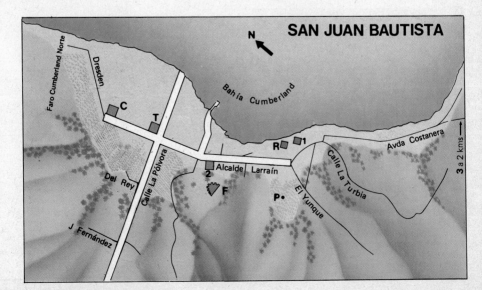

SAN JUAN BAUTISTA

N

Faro Cumberland Norte

Dresden

C

T

Bahía Cumberland

R **1**

Avda Costanera

3 a 2 kms

Del Rey

Calle La Pólvora

2 Alcalde Larraín

F

P•

El Yunque

Calle La Turbia

J. Fernández

Robinson Crusoe airport

island is rugged, with beautiful paths to enjoy the spectacular flora and fauna

TOURS AROUND THE ISLAND

1 TO THE FORTRESS AND PATRIOTS' CAVES

★★★ *for one-and-a-half hours.*

Adjacent to the village is the **Santa Bárbara Fortress**, the most important of the installations erected during the 18th century to safeguard Spanish sovereignty. Near the fort are seven caves known as **Cuevas de los Patriotas** (Patriots' Caves), which offered shelter to the Chilean patriots deported in 1815. One of them preferred to commit suicide rather than put up with the penal colony's appalling conditions.

2 A VISIT TO THE CEMETERY ★

Located near the shore, the cemetery contains the graves of some of the Dresden sailors, as well as the tomb of Baron Alfredo de Rodt, who, following his powerful colonizing drive, settled here and set the foundations for the present population. He lived in the island until his death.

3 TO SELKIRK'S LOOK-OUT ★★★

For 3 hours. Take food.

Alexander Selkirk climbed to a look-out point on a pass halfway up the island's highest peak, the anvil-shaped El Yunque, and there he lit his signal fires and scanned the horizon in the hope of spotting some ship that would rescue him. The path starts on the side of Santa Bárbara fort and winds its way up through forests and among giant ferns. The look-out point is 550 m above the sea, and contains two tablets commemorating Selkirk's ordeal. One of them was set by Brittish naval officers from HMS "Topaze" while the other one was set by Selkirk's descendants.

4 TO PLAZOLETA DEL YUNQUE ★★ *for 2 hours.*

The Plazoleta del Yunque is located at the foot of the namesake mountain, which rises nearly 1,000 meters above the sea. This site was chosen by Hugo Weber, a surviving German seaman from the Dresden, to stay 12 years in isolation from the world and from the village itself. Inevitably, he came to be known as the German Robinson Crusoe. Only scant remains of the foundations of Weber's rustic abode are to be seen.

The 3-km path leading to the Plazoleta is lined with many varieties of fern and shaded by the giant leaves of Nalcas and Pangues, dubbed «Robinson's umbrella».

5 TO ROBINSON'S CAVE ★★★

for 3 hours, with 20 minutes by boat.

The boat heads north, and soon the cave can be seen on a hillside, some 50 meters from the shore. On the soft hill overlooking the bay are the guns of the fort defending the island from British pirates and privateers. Thence the name of **Puerto Inglés** (English Port).

6 TO PUERTO FRANCES ★★

for 3 hours, with one hour by boat.

The boat this time heads south, to the site chosen by French pirates to come ashore. The Spaniards obligingly erected a fort in 1779 up the slope facing Puerto Francés in order to shoo off the pesky visitors.

7 TO PLAYA ARENAL ★★★

for 1 or 2 days, take sleeping bag, food and water.

The only sandy beach to speak of is **Playa Arenal**, located at the southeastern end of the island, ie, quite a distance from the village. The boat takes about two and a half hours to reach the beach, sailing near islets, cliffs and rocky spots swarming with sea wolves and, in short, a scenery different from the rest of the island. Playa Arenal and its clear, warm waters offer a delightful chance to bathe in the Pacific. Some caves nearby can provide shelter for the night.

8 LOBSTER FISHING ★★★

a one-day boat tour.

The local fisherman's daily routine consists of checking by boat his dozens of lobster traps scattered around the island. The crustacean is the islanders' wage-earner, processed and marketed by three larger companies. Visitors can arrange to accompany a fisherman making his rounds. Be sure, say the "connaisseurs", to have him include the preparation on board of a **Perol**, a reportedly unforgettable lobster stew.

Zone 8
SAN FERNANDO
to SAN CARLOS

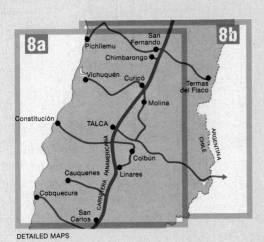

8a **8b**

San Fernando
Pichilemu
Chimbarongo
Vichuquén Curicó
Termas del Flaco
Molina
Constitución
TALCA
Colbún
Cauquenes Linares
Cobquecura
San Carlos
CARRETERA PANAMERICANA
ARGENTINA CHILE

DETAILED MAPS

Arica
Iquique
Antofagasta
Easter Island
Copiapó
La Serena
Is R Crusoe
Valparaíso
SANTIAGO
Talca
Concepción
Temuco
Valdivia
Osorno
Pto Montt
Castro
Chaitén
Coihaique
Cochrane
Puerto Natales
Punta Arenas
Puerto Williams
Is Diego Ramirez

8

90° 60° 53°

CHILEAN
ANTARCTIC
TERRITORY

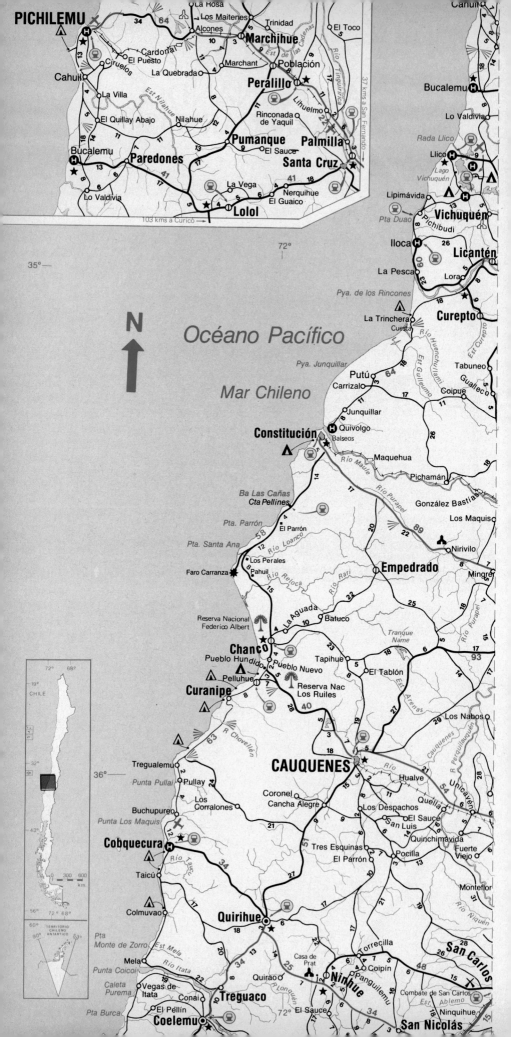

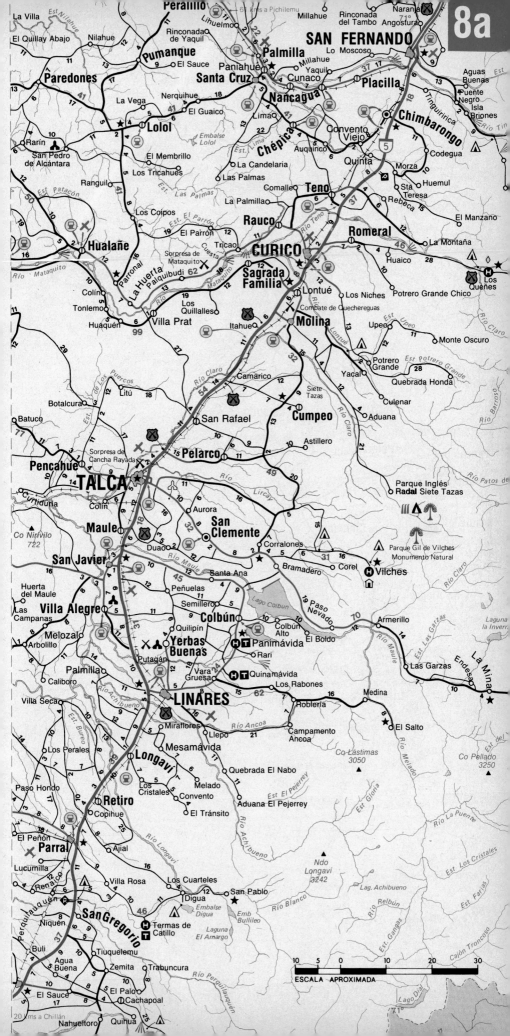

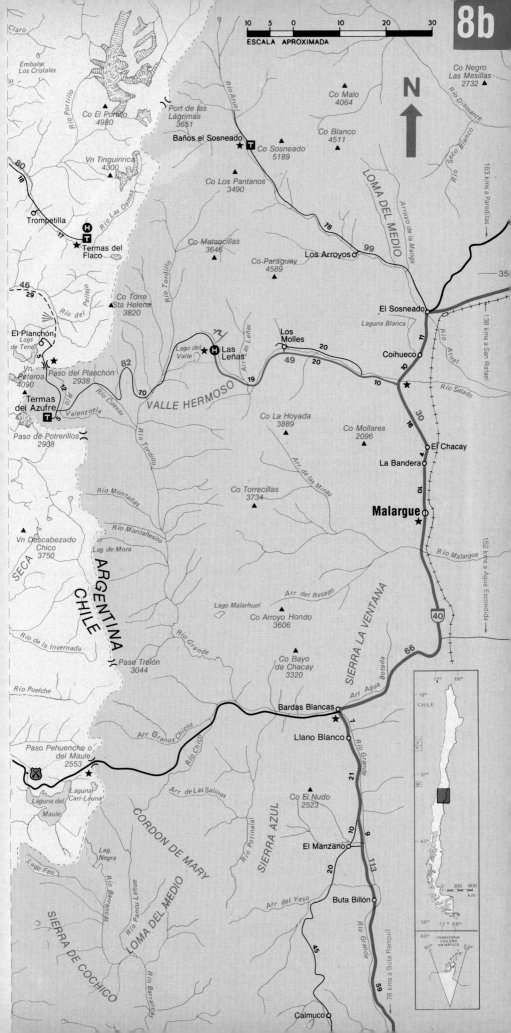

OVERVIEW

This Tourist Zone is a comprised of territories lying in Regions VI and VII, and includes the vast Central Depression –the Chilean heartland, core of Chile's «huaso» (combination farmer and cowboy) traditions and the site of major historical events. Zone 8 can be divided into three distinct geograpical areas:

Andean Area encompassing the towering Andes range, where the headwaters of some large rivers tumbling towards the ocean are located. It contains majestic volcanoes, native forests, thermal springs and lovely dells nestled at foothills.

Central Plain traversed lengthwise by the Pan–American highway and seat of the main urban centers and of scenic countryside. It boasts some bustling industry and is peppered with beautiful colonial towns and landed estates. It has a relatively thick network of rural roads served by buses, enabling travellers to reach every place of interest.

Coastal Area including the Coastal Range, seaboard valleys and the mouth of some large rivers, with vast forests marching down to the seashore. It offers seaside resorts, small villages sitting on the ruins of ancient Indian settlements, and superb beaches.

This zone possesses good tourist infrastructure; accommodations and restaurants are readily available, as well as campgrounds and areas suitable for «wild camping». Plenty of public transportation. The Zone has been divided into four sections:

Section A San Fernando the city and its surroundings, from the Andean foothills to Pichilemu.

Section B Curicó the city and its surroundings, plus the coastal strip.

Section C Talca the city and the vast area enclosed by the Claro and Maule river basins.

Section D Parral a large portion of the coast and the inland area, including Cauquenes, Ninhue and Termas de Catillo.

REGIONAL DISTANCES

Cauquenes														
85	Cobquecura													
106	129	Constitución												
204	295	169	Curicó											
40	63	58	244	Chango										
241	332	206	37	281	Chimbarongo									
146	283	145	136	238	173	Lake Colbún								
321	412	286	117	361	154	253	Lake Vichuquén							
93	230	112	111	185	148	53	228	Linares						
382	473	347	178	422	141	314	295	289	Pichilemu					
259	350	224	55	299	18	191	172	166	123	San Fernando				
296	387	261	92	336	55	228	79	203	86	37	Santa Cruz			
142	279	114	62	234	99	74	179	49	240	117	154	Talca		
80	171	177	176	128	213	115	290	65	354	231	268	114	Termas de Catillo	
117	254	134	125	209	162	29	242	24	303	180	217	63	89	Termas de Panimávida

Zone 8
SAN FERNANDO
to SAN CARLOS

DIVISION BY SECTIONS

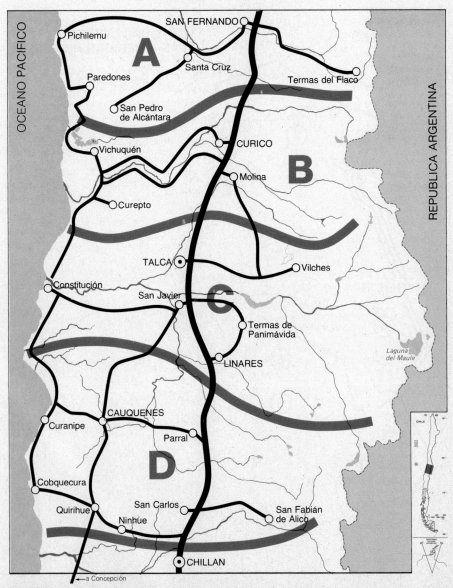

DETOURS OFF THE PAN–AMERICAN HIGHWAY

A detour off the beaten track (ie, the Pan–American highway) can be rewarding. Scenic rural roads cut across the Central Plain to the coast or the Andes, passing through sleepy villages and towns and skirting rivers or beaches.

The following tours will give you a chance to fully appreciate this Zone:

1 Grand Tour of the Coast ★★★ 300 km of coastal strip, visiting busy seaside resorts, lots of tiny villages and beaches. Good ocean fishing. 533 km altogether, on gravel and dirt roads.

2 Rural Town Route ★★★ fruitful, beautiful countryside dotted with farming towns of interesting architecture. 115 km on gravel roads.

3 A Tour through Vichuquén and the Coast ★★★ the contrast between inland countryside and coastal scenery, visiting rural towns with unusual architecture, such as San Pedro de Alcántara and Chanco, and larger urban centers such as Constitución and Cauquenes. 291 km altogether, 79 km of which are paved.

4 A Tour through Vichuquén and Constitución ★★ a shorter alternative for experiencing the inland-coast contrast, travelling along the Maule and the Mataquito rivers. 227 km altogether, 60 of which are paved.

5 Colonial Route ★ old route used during the Conquest and Colonial period, cutting through the Central Plain countryside and offering an alternative route to the Biobío area. 180 km on gravel roads.

6 A Tour through Hot Springs and Villa Alegre ★★★ 127 km of paved roads going through rural towns and farms with large farmhouses, historical sites, the city of Linares, thermal resorts and the large Colbún–Machicura dam.

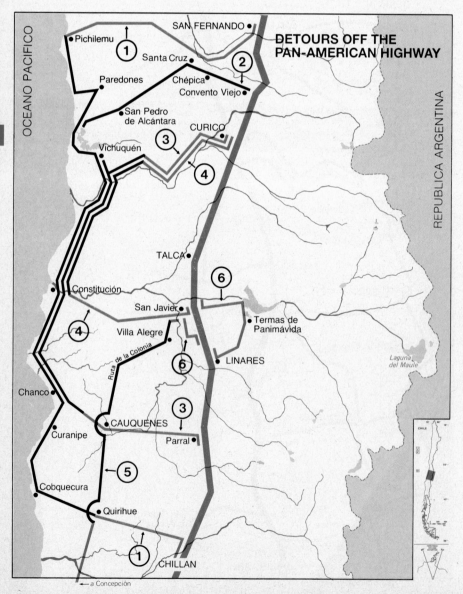

THE LAND, ITS HISTORY, ITS PEOPLE

DESCRIPTION this area stretches from Angostura de Pelequén in the North to the Ñuble–Itata river system in the South. The Andes and the Coastal Range march parallel southwards along the eastern and western edges, respectively.

Large rivers flow from East to West –such as Tinguiririca, Mataquito, Maule, and Itata– draining vast Andean watersheds. Smaller but swollen streams act as tributaries to the larger water bodies or drain Coastal watersheds, providing irrigation water for the coastal strip.

From this zone south, the Andes gradually becomes lower and the foothills can be farmed as they are less steep, forming inland hollows and valleys with microclimates which favour the native forests.

In contrast, the Coastal Range is low, averaging less than 500 m in height, having no outstanding peaks and formed mostly of rolling hills which fall towards the coast forming vast plains.

EARLY INHABITANTS tribes of hunters roamed the area during the last Glacial period, stalking large animals such as mastodons, American horses, swamp deer and other species adapted to the cold climate.

As the climate became milder, larger and more organized hunting tribes appeared, following the seasonal movements of their prey from the Andes to the coast and back to the Andes. During the summer months they trekked to the mountain valleys looking for animals grazing in mountain meadows; in winter, they descended to the coastal valleys to hunt animals grazing in coastal pastures.

As these tribes improved their animal taming and farming skills, they began to settle along the rivers and on coastal valleys, becoming in time the Indian tribal–nation known as Mapuches. In this area, the Mapuches called themselves Picunches.

Recent research has concluded that Mapuches were an ethnic and linguistic entity scattered from the Choapa river in the North to Chiloé in the South. This 1,400–km–long territory contained markedly different areas in terms of climate, flora and fauna, thus giving rise to differing dialects and customs among its human inhabitants.

By 1470 the Inca empire had spread through Chile down to the Maule river, imposing military, economic and cultural domination. This manifested itself in new ceramics styles, types of crops and irrigation techniques. Later, as a result of an internecine dispute affecting the Inca heartland, part of the Inca settlers and warriors retreated back to the North.

When the Spaniards arrived, native population in this area was sparse, well below the numbers found south of the Biobío and north of the Tinguiririca rivers. Most natives lived in scattered settlements not qualifying as villages or towns. The inhabited areas on the coast were Vichuquén, Cahuil, Huenchillami, Loanco, Buchupureo, Cobquecura and a number of other sites. Native Indians were promptly forced into a serfdom system by the Spaniards, many of them being relocated to the far North as mining hands.

The native economy was geared to securing sustenance; in order to irrigate their crops, the Mapuches settled near rivers and streams. The lands in the Central Plain, nowadays rated as first class, were then virgin and uninhabited. They were not turned into productive uses until the 18th century, with a boom in livestock farming, and the 19th century, with the completion of large irrigation works. Llama (a camelid) rearing under the Mapuches did not go beyond meeting household needs; llamas were tended by herdsmen or placed in pens.

ORIGINAL LANDSCAPE no more than 2% of the 1,4 million hectares of flatland in this zone are thought to have been cultivated, with an additional 15% altered somewhat as a result of wildfire, firewood collection and browsing by livestock. Thus, over 80% of the total flatland area, in addition to the Andean foothills, remained thoroughly untouched.

The Central Plain tree plant cover included thick woods growing on stream and river banks and in ravines, including such native species as boldos, peumos, arrayanes, canelos and maquis. Vegetation was somewhat sparser in open areas, where shrubby espinos (a type of acacia) and algarrobos (a Prosopis species) tended to predominate.

Ravines and Mountain Valleys usually enjoyed rainy microclimates nourishing splendid forests containing oak, cinnamon trees, arrayán and coigüe. Many of these forests have survived to this day.

The coastal hills and plains receive more rainfall than the central plain; in addition, air humidity is higher at the coastal strip and fog is common. This enables farmers to grow crops in fields not served by irrigation, and to take their livestock out to graze in spring and summer. This accounts for Indian tribes settling mostly here, a practice imitated by the first Spanish conquistadors.

Landscape transformation the introduction and proliferation of livestock of European origin pasturing semi–wild in the central plain– and the felling of trees to obtain timber both for urban and hacienda constructions depleted native forests on river banks. Subsequent drainage of swampy grounds and construction of irrigation canals wiped out most shrubbery. Inadequate tilling techniques applied at the coastal hills and plains –an area subject to heavy seasonal downpours– brought about rapid soil erosion and impoverishment, prompting farmers to migrate inland to the central plain, early in the 18th century.

LAND OWNERSHIP during the 16th century, the economy of this zone was based mainly on subsistence farming and gold mining. The emergence of the Peruvian market, along with the need of providing supplies to the frontier army (seeking to subdue the fiercer Mapuche tribes farther south), gave rise in time to the first defined farming properties. Small plots of land were allocated in coastal valleys from Vichuquén to Cobquecura, the laborers being native Indians. These plots lacked clearcut boundaries and were not very much in demand, as most Spaniards moved farther south to Arauco, beyond the Biobío river.

In 1600 a great Mapuche uprising forced the Spaniards to vacate their towns in the south and flee to central Chile (this area included). The newcomers needed access to land ownership to secure their livelihood. Thus, by the mid 1700s, all the land in this area had been allotted to both Spaniards and natives. Thereafter land ownership was acquired solely through inheritance or purchase.

THE HACIENDA the sustained demand from Perú for farming produce from this area made it necessary to introduce a much larger productive unit: enter the hacienda or fundo. The original size of the hacienda was increased through the acquisition of smaller plots and neighboring farms. The religious orders operating in the area ended up being the largest landowners.

8

The sheer size of these haciendas and their economic weight attracted the larger part of the population –mostly mestizos, ie, persons of mixed parentage– to them. Haciendas life on the estates was one of semi-isolated development. Were largely self-sufficient, at any rate for the needs of the 17th– and 18th-century rural dwellers. They produced their own food, textiles and clothing, leather goods and candles and fruit, and had their own smithies and wine cellars and beef jerked producers. So came into being the Chilean rural society.

The haciendas were a place of refuge for the large creole population, who settled as peons, or farm hands performing different duties. But soon a new kind of farm worker appeared: the inquilino or tenant, paying rent for a small plot of land on the fringes of the hacienda and serving the purpose of protecting the owner's interests. This settled farm worker provided the raw material for the «huaso chileno» –the Chilean peasant– and his idiosyncrasy.

The buildings at the hacienda were large enough to hierarchically house owners, laborers, workshops and warehouses; adjacent to them were the animal pens. No significant examples of these building complexes remain from the 17th and 18th centuries, but there are some good ones from the 19th century, such as haciendas San José del Carmen de Huilque and Huilquilemu, east of Talca.

URBANIZATION

URBANIZATION during the first two centuries of Spanish domination (16th and 17th centuries) there were no cities or other urban centers in this area. Most urbanizing efforts were concentrated at the then ends of Central Chile, namely La Serena and Concepción. Inhabitants in this zone tended to cluster around small rural settlements and haciendas, located near the coastal strip.

Traffic took place along a coastal trail –known as the Coastal or Maule road– lying basically on the old pre-Columbian paths linking fishing villages and Indian settlements located more or less at regular intervals. The Central Plain route, followed originally by the Spanish conquistadors, did not see much traffic, as the lands it traversed were still largely uninhabited and wild.

Among the prime objectives of colonization during the 18th century were religious indoctrination, education, introduction of the rule of law and, most paramount, bringing the growing mestizo population into the embrace of Spanish traditions. The scattered nature of the population in this area, and the dense settlements of communities on private estates. For this reason and by precise instruction from the Crown, however, made the fulfilling of these objectives exceedingly difficult. Therefore, the Crown issued specific orders to the governors of Chile to undertake the foundation of towns and villages, both for Spaniards and natives. Governor Manso de Velasco founded then San Fernando (1742), Curicó (1743), Talca (1742), Linares (1755), and Cauquenes (1742).

These new urban centers, straddling at regular intervals the Central Plain road, pulled traffic towards the central valley. New roads linked then the central valley to the coastal plains and the coastal road, providing a network which made nearly all locations accessible. Urban centers were laid in accordance with the Statutes of Laws for the Indies, stemming from a Renaissance concept which dictated that the placement, orientation and size of the new town had to be chosen carefully, the layout being in square blocks arranged hierarchically from the Plaza de Armas –the main square–, which in turn was flanked by the buildings of the main civil, military and religious institutions.

Parallel to this founding of new towns, urban status was granted to Indian settlements and villages located at the site of ancient tribal seats, keeping their original names and haphazard lay-

out; such is the case of Vichuquén, Lora, Bucalemu, Buchupureo, etc.

All other towns and villages in this zone were founded after Chile attained independence.

RURAL ARCHITECTURE

RURAL ARCHITECTURE depending on their function and the requirements of each period, the layout of rural homesteads evolved. Little is known about the large haciendas of the 17th and 18th centuries, but it is likely that they followed a pattern similar to that of large convents, organized on the basis of multiple courtyards, such as at the houses of Hacienda San José del Carmen de Huique, built early last century. Rural dwellings in the 17th and 18th centuries had an eminently defensive character; square in layout and facing an inner court, they had but one or two openings to the outside. Such is the case of San Agustín de Puñual, where the Chilean hero Arturo Prat was born. The «arquerías» appear to date from a later period; they are 2-story rectangular buildings with storage rooms on the ground floor and living quarters upstairs.

The 19th century brought new approaches in rural architecture, resulting from more widespread urbanization and greater security in rural areas. Large, single-story houses with a U-shaped layout appeared, with large verandas facing the roads. In smaller towns and villages, houses also acquired a roofed veranda where a substantial part of social family life was played out.

The veranda first appeared around the house's courtyard; later, it was laid along the outer walls, facing the large parks of hacienda houses, or the street in village houses. The roofed veranda acted also as a sort of sunlight attenuating device, filtering the light flowing into the rooms. Verandas usually had floors of carefully laid brick patterns and carved wooden pillars set on individual stone bases. These verandas are the main and most attractive feature in this Zone's rural architecture.

HANDICRAFTS

HANDICRAFTS indigenous techniques originally applied to the production of household utensils evolved into a highly perfected style used now by communities with a significant handicraft output.

Pottery was not made using a turntable, but from moist, well-kneaded clay rolls molded with specially-shaped wooden pieces. The various objects (jars, bowls, plates, figures) feature an even black finish, obtained by baking them in special fires made with cattle dung and smoked with dry leaves. The most outstanding handicrafts communities are at Ciruelos, Pilén and Chanco.

Loom-woven goods the loom used has its origins in pre-Conquest Indian techniques, spinning with a spindle and twisting the yarn by hand. Dyes were obtained from various plants: yellow from michay and quila roots; gray from chilco and quintral; black from colliguay and quintral, mixed with a type of mud called robo; brown from hualo, boldo, dry quintral and radal; red from relbún roots, and orange from sorrel roots. White is the wool's natural color. These woven goods (ponchos, blankets, rugs, bedspreads, etc) are renowned for their varied designs and color patterns, and for the tightness of their weft which makes them watertight. Major production centers are at Pencahue, Curepto and Quinamávida.

Wickerwork the largest wickerwork center is at the area of Chimbarongo. Wicker is obtained through a lengthy process involving twig submersion in water to detach the bark, slicing the twig lengthwise with cross-shaped knives and then slicing the resulting strips successively until the strip used for wickerwork attains the desired width. The wicker goods produced are furniture, baskets, rugs, trunks, panniers and ornaments, a significant proportion of them destined for export.

Horsehair weaving a delicate sort of weaving using horsetail or oxtail hairs as «yarn», dyed in vivid colors to produce miniature butterflies, ladies with parasols, huasos on horseback, tiny baskets, hats or flowers. This unusual handicraft –unique in the Americas– emerged some 200 years ago, and has been passed from generation to generation at the small village of Rari, inland from Linares.

Huaso implements the various farming activities performed by huasos require a number of special items for their garments and horse–riding outfit, traditionally produced using local materials and styles. The saddle, for instance, differs from its counterparts anywhere else; it includes unsheared sheepskin saddle pads and large, carved wooden stirrups closed around the toes. Other items are reins, lasso, hats, short ponchos and large round metal spurs. Major production centers are at Linares, Maule, Santa Cruz, Ninhue and Coihueco. At all these sites work in progress by these highly-skilled artisans can be watched by visitors.

PRESENT LANDSCAPE irrigation has brought vineyards, vegetable plantations and other crops into this zone. Tree–lined irrigation canals divide the land into octagonai plots, and thick tree stands are usually part of the park surrounding farmhouses. Trees, important elements in the Central Zone's landscape, are not natural occurrences in the central plain, but rather the expression of social tastes of a given period. They are all exotic to this zone –poplars, Babylonian willows, eucalyptus, Radiata or Monterey pine, and cypress– introduced during the second half of last century. This fondness for planting trees changed the appearance of the countryside, populated squares and lined main streets and avenues at San Fernando, Curicó, Talca, Linares and Parral.

During the past decade, new agroindustrial activities have changed radically the face of this Zone:

Fruit production thousands of hectares of fruit–tree orchards, particularly apples, and the endless columns of fruit–laden trucks clogging the streets in March, headed for packing installations or the shipping ports, constitute now one of the prominent features of this area. Next to the Pan–American highway are large agroindustrial facilities easily recognized by the enormous amount of bins piled up high on their landings.

Forestry this is the second-largest zone afforested with Radiata pine in Chile. Formerly denuded, eroded coastal hills and some Andean foothills are now green-clad with vast pine forests, not visible from the Pan-American highway. Chile is one of the two most important forest countries in the Southern Hemisphere, together with New Zealand. This forest resource feeds hundreds of recently established sawmills, as well as a huge pulp mill in Constitución.

PRESENT DEVELOPMENT the importance of agriculture in this Zone is evidenced by over 45% of its population living either in the country or in towns smaller than 2,000 inhabitants. Nearly 2 million hectares –half a million of which are irrigated– are devoted to agriculture, forestry and livestock farming.

The area's main agricultural products are wine and table grapes –this region has 50% of the total area given over to vineyards in Chile–, fruit (almost 40,000 hectares, 90% for export and agroindustrial utilization), forest products, grains (mainly rice, wheat, and corn) and sugar beets.

Agroindustry, as mentioned above, also plays an important role. There are large rice mills, oil and sugar–beet processing plants, wineries providing 55% of the country's wine, fruit packing houses, dairies and Chile's largest match factory.

PAN–AMERICAN HIGHWAY

For those travelling straight through to more southerly destinations, we offer below a description of the most interesting sights along the Pan-American highway.

PAN–AMERICAN HIGHWAY FROM SANTIAGO TO CHILLAN ★★★ *407 km, 5–6 hours. Dual carriageway until San Fernando (km 137), thereafter it is a 2-lane highway. Two tolls and a profusion of service stations along the way.*
First leg of the so-called Panamericana Sur or Longitudinal Sur, the only thoroughfare to the South.

Twenty–six km after leaving Santiago (km 0), the southbound Pan–American highway bypasses **San Bernardo** and the landscape takes on a more rural aspect, with small, intensely cultivated plots, flower and tree nurseries, livestock farms, etc. Many producers sell their wares directly to the consumer through shops placed right alongside the highway. There are also many restaurants, some of them pretty good.

At km 37, the Pan–American highway crosses the **Maipo river**, which carries little water in summer between its stony banks. Shops continue lining the highway, various crossroads and traffic circles leading to Buín, Linderos and **Paine** on the river bank, at km 51, making this stretch the most dangerous in the entire Pan-Am highway, particularly at night, due to vehicles stopping on the roadside or pedestrian and bicycle-riders on the road itself.

At km 63 is Angostura de Paine, where the road is squeezed between two hills and a stream. Not only the road is squeezed; the whole Central Plain goes through a bottleneck formed by an Andean counterfort stretching west to meet the Coastal Range. Hence the name: «Angostura» means «narrow gap». Beyond Angostura is a toll; only those headed South pay.

The road continues through somewhat larger fields, and the first fruit production complexes start to appear. At km 92 is

RANCAGUA the highway skirts the eastern fringes of the city. Rancagua and its surrounding towns are described in the Central Chile volume.

A short way beyond Rancagua the road crosses the Cachapoal river; at the southern end of the bridge is a police road control. The valley is intensely cultivated. The Pan–Am highway runs near a number of small towns, such as **Malloa**, a major tomato–producing center. On the roadside are modest shops selling fruit and country–style brooms.

At km 123 is **Pelequén**, a small town to the left of the road. Another road branching off to the right leads to Peumo and Lake Rapel. Here starts the so-called «fruit route», a new road providing an expeditious route to the shipping port of San Antonio.

Next is another narrow gap between the mountains, called **Angostura de Pelequén**. To the right is a quarry producing the pink stone used in many monuments and buildings in Santiago. At km 137 is

SAN FERNANDO (described under Section A). Here ends the dual carriageway. From now on, overtaking the trucks clogging the road will become a laborious –and at times risky–3 undertaking.

At km 145 is **Chimbarongo,** a major wickerwork center. The roadside shops return in force, particularly right before and right beyond the road junction leading to the town. Wickerwork artisans are busily producing on the spot.

Farther on you slice through the heart of apple country. Large apple orchards are followed by large apple packing houses and these by further large apple orchards, and so on. Sizable vineyards pop up now and then at either side of the road, this is the heart of the apple growing district.

At km 191 the road bypasses

CURICO (good restaurant by the highway), described under Section B.

At km 217 the highway crosses the **Claro river,** flowing along the bottom of its deep gorge. To the right is a railroad bridge, and a campground on the river bank.

At km 253 you start to skirt the eastern edge of

TALCA described under Section C.

At km 274, three metal bridges, running almost side by side, span the **Maule** river. Two of them are for road traffic and the other one for the railway. This river marked the southern boundary of Inca expansion in Chile, which happened a hundred years before the Spanish invasion.

Beyond the river is the junction for **San Javier** and **Villa Alegre,** worth a detour described under Section C, Tour 2.

At km 306 is the access to Linares. There is a good motel near the road. Some packing houses of interesting design can be seen near the highway.

Farther ahead the highway crosses many rivers and streams; some restaurants offer frog legs in their menus.

At km 400 is a large sugar beet processing plant, and 3 km later, a bridge spanning the Ñuble river. At km 407 is

CHILLAN described in the next Tourist Zone.

Where to Eat on the Road Curicó: Da Orestino, at the Esso gasoline station, and Aguas Negras at the Copec gasoline station. Linares: restaurant Málaga on the roadside. Parral: Esso service station. Chillán: several restaurants; see city map.

Lodgings Along the Road only campground at the Río Claro bridge, beyond Curicó. The best motel is Málaga, at the Linares road junction. Hotels and motels in Chillán (see city map; described in Zone 9).

SECTION A   SAN FERNANDO

It comprises the valley of the Tinguiririca river, running westward from the Andes to the coast, and from Angostura de Pelequén in the North to Convento Viejo in the South. It is an eminently rural area, with significant agricultural and agroindustrial production, and large vineyards and fruit–tree plantations. Some tourist resorts are located at the foot of the mountains and on the coast.

The center of this area is the city of

SAN FERNANDO (pop 15,400). A provincial capital, it was founded in 1742 under the name of Villa de San Fernando de Tinguiririca, to honor the Prince of Asturias. It was the first city founded in the central valley during the 18th–century city-founding drive. It has kept its character of service town for the vast agricultural valley surrounding it; many farm–machinery repair shops attest to this role. Both in the town and surrounding area you will find significant examples of colonial architecture and some notable churches.

What to See from afar it is possible to see the Byzantine **dome** of a church towering above the town's flat skyline.

Driving into town on Av O'Higgins you go through busy bus terminals; turning right on Manuel Rodríguez, you will see on the left a church of curious architecture (closed after the 1985 earthquake). At the end of the street is an old U-shaped farmhouse, surrounded by enormous trees and housing workshops and warehouses still in full swing.

Taking Carampangue and then Manso de Velasco, you can visit the ancient **House of Nincunlauta (NM)** formerly owned by Juan Jiménez de León who donated the 450 cuadras (a cuadra is a square piece of land of a city-block length to a side) of land on which to found this city. The house, dating from the 18th century, is undergoing restoration and contains a small museum of farm machinery and paintings. The

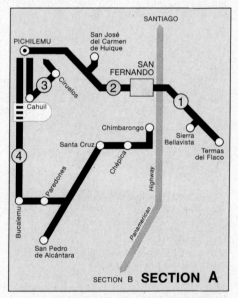

SECTION B **SECTION A**

caretaker is a craftsman specialized in leather; apart from showing you around the house, he can display and explain his leather–working skills. Half a block away from here is the Capilla del Hospital (Hospital's Chapel), a National Monument built in finely–laid brickwork with delicate filigree–like carvings on upper edges and cornices.

Some other examples of 18th–century rural architecture can be found at the **Houses of Pedehue**. Take the road to Termas del Flaco and turn right 2 km beyond the Pan–Am highway underpass. After a row of small country dwellings you will see 2 U–shaped houses with verandas running the length of their inner facade.

Fifteen km north of San Fernando and 5 km towards the Andes (signposted) is the fabulous

Hacienda Los Lingues, with a beautiful colonial–style house, a chapel, a significant collection of furniture and other valuable objects, and a thoroughbred horse farm. Now it is a hotel and restaurant affiliated with the exclusive world chain Relais & Châteaux (372 hotels and restaurants in 37 countries); only 4 are in South America. It is worth a visit; check beforehand with tels 235–2458 or 225–0838 in Santiago.

hacienda Los Lingues

TOURS FROM SAN FERNANDO

1 TO TERMAS DEL FLACO AND SIERRA BELLAVISTA ★★★ *188 km round-trip, with 20 km paved but in poor condition; the rest is a gravel road. The road is narrow and winding, with traffic directed toward the Termas Mon–Sat 14:00-20:00 h, Sun & holidays, 05:00–12:00 h. Back from the Termas, Mon–Sat 06:00–14:00 h, Sun & holidays 14:00–24:00 h. Gasoline at San Fernando. It takes one day; take food or eat at restaurant on the road.*

A tour to a mountain resort in the Andean foothills and to thermal springs in the High Andes.

The road leaves San Fernando (km 0) towards the East, running through cultivated fields. It is lined with poplars for some stretches.

At km 17 is the village of **Puente Negro,** set on the bank of a stream shaded by large willows and boasting a restaurant specializing in cazuelas and roast chicken. The road starts to climb and runs along the Tinguiririca river, which tumbles along the bottom of a deep eroded gorge.

At km 29 is the turn–off for **Sierra Bellavista,** a beautiful place 15 km from the road junction, with mountain–style holiday houses nestled in pine–clad hills overlooking a private artificial lake. You return to the original road at km 59.

From this point the gravel road climbs more steeply, winding its way up the mountains. At km 109 is **Termas del Flaco** featuring mineral hot springs and a lodging in a nice setting. 500 m to the northeast, at a place called **El Dino,** tracks of a dinosaur–like animal and its young covered with lava. This animal lived in our continent and disappeared 120 million years ago.

You go back by the same road; 79 kms to San Fernando

2 TO PICHILEMU ★★★
120 km from San Fernando; 86 km are paved,

8

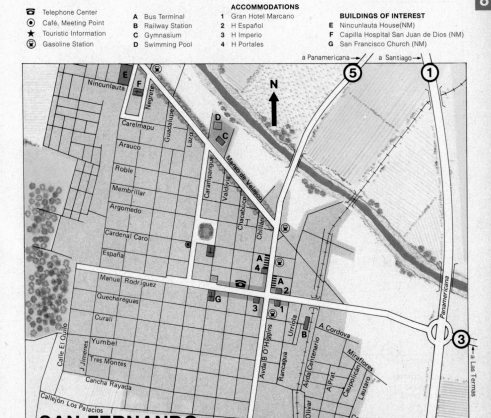

☎	Telephone Center
◉	Café, Meeting Point
★	Touristic Information
⊞	Gasoline Station

A	Bus Terminal
B	Railway Station
C	Gymnasium
D	Swimming Pool

ACCOMMODATIONS

1	Gran Hotel Marcano
2	H Español
3	H Imperio
4	H Portales

BUILDINGS OF INTEREST

E	Nincunlauta House(NM)
F	Capilla Hospital San Juan de Dios (NM)
G	San Francisco Church (NM)

SAN FERNANDO

the rest gravel. Gas stations on the road.

A tour to a seaside resort, driving along an irrigated valley and through arid coastal lands, with some interesting old manor houses on the way.

After leaving San Fernando (km 0), the road crosses the Tinguiririca river. To the left is a railway metal bridge built in 1867; with a length of 122 m, it was then the longest bridge in Chile. The road cuts through vineyards.

At km 17 is a detour to the village of **Placilla**. At the end of its main (and only) street is Viña Macaya, where visitors are offered the chance to taste their wines.

At km 24 is the village of **Nancagua**, with an **old manor house** now housing the town hall and set in a large park of conifers and palm trees. On one side is a large church with an imposing nave. It is worth making this small detour.

The thick tree stands seen from the road usually indicate the site of manor houses. At km 28, next to the railway station, are the **Houses of Cunaco,** from what was the largest hacienda in this valley by the mid–19th century. The houses and their park date from around 1880. The inner courtyards date from the 18th–century. From the road, a wide avenue lined with Chilean palms can be seen, leading to the park. At the far end is the manor house.

At km 37 a detour to the left for Santa Cruz, described in the next tour below. At km 40 is the village of Palmilla, with a gas station.

At km 55 watch for a metal bus stop and a signpost reading «A Talhuén». Turn there to the right about 1 km, then left and a short way ahead, across from a telephone booth, turn right once more. Go straight and beyond a stream you will

see the imposing complex of

SAN JOSE DEL CARMEN DEL HUIQUE on land remaining from a 30,000–hectare farm established in 1756. In 1828, the owner erected the houses and buildings making up this complex. In 1852 he built the chapel. His daughter, Gertrudis Echeñique, married a Chilean president Federico Errázuriz Echaurren.

The access drive ends at a vast **esplanade** running parallel to the facade of the manor houses. The main building –U–shaped and lined with verandas– surrounds a **courtyard** with a beautiful garden crowned by palm trees, opening up to the esplanade. On the southern edge is the **chapel**, with a 23–m–tall bell tower.

Around this core lie the 15 secondary courtyards –of different sizes and arranged in a complex structure– and buildings where the various hacienda chores used to be performed. It is the largest farm housing complex remaining in the country, and since 1976 it belongs to the Chilean Army, which does a very good job of preserving it. No visitors are admitted. It can only be observed from the outside.

Returning to the main road, the paving ends at Marchihue, at km 73, and goes on as far as the village of Alcones at the foot of the Coastal Range-km 86. Crossing this range by a road surrounded by pine forests, you reach km 120 and

PICHILEMU (small forest) which is the capital of the province of Cardenal Caro- 4,300 inhabitants. It is a famous seaside resort full of bustling summer holiday makers enjoying all kinds of sports,

8

PICHILEMU

Legend:
- ☎ Telephone Center
- ◉ Café, Meeting Point
- ★ Touristic Information
- Gasoline Station
- Lookout Point
- ✳ Hospital
- Bus Terminal
- A Church
- B Town Hall
- C Post Office
- D Ex Railway Station
- F Horse hire
- G Gymnasium
- P Parish Church

fun fairs, a variety of restaurants, night life and ancient homesteads, hotels, casino, and a hundred year old park surrounded by balustrades which reach down as far as the main beach, bearing witness to a glorious and magnificent past.

What to See walk or drive down the Costanera, running along the seafront of both the main beach (**Playa Principal o Terrazas**) and Playa Infiernillo. There area several look-out points along the way. Colorful balustrades enclose the old trees and palms of Parque Ross, formerly owned by one of the founding families.

Return on Av La Marina, climbing among pines shaped into geometric forms, leading into the park and to the century-old **Hotel Ross** and the old building of **Hotel Casino**, where the first gambling casino in Chile opened in 1908. After a walk through the park, go on towards the center of town where you find street vendors peddling their wares: sweets, games and handicraft; there are also restaurants, bitros (cafes) and club houses. The look-out point at the summit of Cerro La Cruz offers a good view of the town and surrounding area.

In late afternoon, the young people head en masse for the Costanera and the look-out at **Infiernillo** to watch the sunset. At dusk they walk slowly back to their favorite hangouts, such as El Rincón, across from Playa Principal, or along street Ortúzar.

South of Playa Infiernillo the coastline is abrupt, plummeting to the surf below. Among the cliffs, however, are some lonely beaches worth visiting. The least lonely is **Punta de Lobos**, where the **National Surf Championship** is held every year. It is located 6 km south of Pichilemu on a dirt road. It has a restaurant specializing in seafood; there are some strange rock formations on its southern end. Its main attraction are the top-quality waves for practicing surf. Some claim they rank among the best in the world for this sport, and rent lodgings in Pichilemu during the summer to hone their skills here.

Where to Eat on the main beach, Hostería Paldoa,

La Gloria, Los Colchagüinos and Rex serve international food, are specialized in seafood. Many good, inexpensive restaurants at Av La Marina and Ortúzar.

3 THE COASTAL LANDSCAPE ★★★

a short tour from Pichilemu; 47 km on a poorly-surfaced dirt road.

An area of pre-Conquest roots, visiting salt works and nice beaches.

Leave Pichilemu on the road to Cahuil, which runs for 13 km next to numerous beaches.

Cahuil is a fishing and salt-producing village, originally a seat of the Promauca Indians. A salt pan is located in an adjacent lagoon formed by the Nilahue stream, worked since pre-Hispanic times. Salt water from the sea gets trapped in square ponds of 10 meters to a side; in three to four months, the water evaporates, leaving behind a thick crust of what here is known as «coast salt». In late January, small white cones of salt can be seen on some ponds, the first «harvest» of the season. In the lagoon are man-made beds of large-sized mussels known as «choros zapato»

★ Touristic Information   **B** Grotto
A S P de Alcántara Church (NM)   🗏 Interesting Façades

SAN PEDRO DE ALCANTARA

☎ Telephone Center
⦿ Café, Meeting Point
★ Touristic Information
⊛ Gasoline Station
A Hotel Plaza
B Restaurant Club Social
C Bus Terminal

D Covered Market
E Municipal Stadium
F Indoor Gymnasium

OF INTEREST
G Carillón, Plaza de Armas
H Talabartería Colchagua

SANTA CRUZ

(suggesting a size like that of a shoe), and oysters, available for sale or consumption at many restaurants in the village.

Five km ahead on the road skirting the lagoon is the tiny village of **Barrancas**, where craftsmen manufacture chairs with seats of interwoven straw. Six km farther is **El Copao**, where townsfolk offer low–priced clay pottery. A further 8 km brings you to **Ciruelos**, with a century–old **church** containing statuary of European origin and an old holy–water font where Chile's first cardinal José María Caro was baptized. Before reaching your point of departure you go through picturesque groups of old houses such as Las Comillas, Buenos Aires, lastly Pueblo de Viudas, only 3 kms from the resort town.

4 THE COUNTRYSIDE ★★★
176 km on gravel and dirt roads from Pichilemu

to Chimbarongo, at the Pan–Am highway. Gasoline at Santa Cruz. Take food.

A tour along the coast, through the lagoon at Cahuil to Bucalemu, and then inland through rural villages back to the Central Plain at Chimbarongo.

From Pichilemu, Km 0 , go down the coast as far as Cahuil on Km 13. From there you cross the lake by ferry (room for 2 cars, 07:00–20:00 h, in summer) takes you across the lagoon. Keep then to the right, drive to the top of the hills and then take the road south. It is a scenic road running through cultivated fields cut against the sea, forests or the mountain backdrop. There are several look–out points commanding a view of the entire width of the land. At km 36 you reach **Bucalemu** (to the right across the bridge), a modest fishing hamlet at the end of a long beach with good ocean fishing.

Turn inland here to drive through the countryside. At km 49 you arrive at Paredones, with a nice church, houses with long verandas lining the streets, and a peculiar sidewalk a bit raised above the street level. Leave Paredones on the dirt road to Lolol, running through forested hills to arrive at km 71 at a road junction. Turn right and, 11 km later, you reach

San Pedro de Alcántara a village formed in the 18th century around a Franciscan convent. Houses have their access doors at the corners, lending their facades a peculiar octagonal look. Most have an inner courtyard with lots of trees and plants. The **convent** is now a National Monument, with a gallery around an inner court and a chapel placed before an esplanade with two long rows of Chilean palms. Religious festivities are held here.

A road leads from here to Llico, at lake Vichuquén, in 18 km.

To complete the tour, return to the original road and drive on to **Lolol**, at km 99. Where the streets are bordered by picturesque tile-roofed verandas and continue until reaching km 132 to

SANTA CRUZ a town of 11,500 on the southern bank of the Tinguiririca river. It is the hub of a busy agricultural area. At the **main square**, a **carillon** chimes the time every fifteen minutes.

Continue towards Chépica, the road lined now by towering eucalyptus and with some large country houses set in their own parks. At some of them the owners grant permission to walk through their parks.

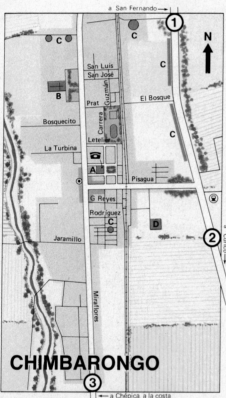

☎ Telephone Center	**B** Parish Church
◉ Meeting Point	**PLACES OF INTEREST**
Ⓖ Gasoline Station	**D** Workshops
A Town Hall	**C** Santa Elisa Winery

CHIMBARONGO

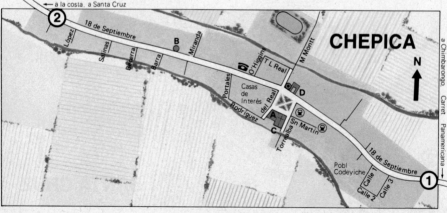

	PLACES OF INTEREST
☎ Telephone	**A** Chépica Parish House
◉ Meeting Point	**B** Handicrafts Worhshop
Ⓖ Gasoline Station	**C** Bus Terminal
	D Town Hall

CHEPICA

At km 151 you arrive at

Chépica a one–street village with houses sporting long galleries joined one with the next, from where the townsfolk watch the world go by in the evenings. At the shady main square the view opens up to and the great façade of the Parochial Church comes into view. A beautiful spot and well worth visiting.

At km 176 you reach

Chimbarongo of renowned wickerwork craftsmanship. The village lies parallel to the Pan–Am highway. You can see wicker–weaving in progress at the many workshops lining the main street, Miraflores where you will hear a detailed explanation of their techniques and can admire their skill. The village **parish** has domes made entirely of brickwork.

SECTION B   CURICO

· This section comprises the area of the Mataquito river basin, along with its tributaries Teno and Lontué, and the coastal area from Bucalemu to Constitución. It includes a Protected Nature Area in a very beautiful mountain setting, and the renowned lake resort of Vichuquén.

The main feature of this coastline is that the mountains recede inland, leaving behind a wide, softly rolling seaboard. Vineyards and fruit for export production are the main wage-earners in the central plain, and wheat and timber at the coastal area. The main urban center of this district is

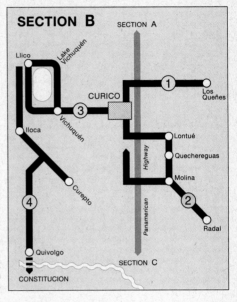

CURICO a provincial capital of 60,500 people founded in 1743 by Manso de Velasco under the name of San José de Buena Vista de Curicó. It was moved to its present location in 1747 due to the extremely humid ground at the original site. It is the communications, trade and supply hub for a large number of agroindustrial installations in the vicinity.

This is also an attractive city with excellent hotels, and interesting trips can be taken from here as you will see farther on. Well worth stopping over.

What to See drive along **Av Manso de Velasco**, wide and with a park-like central strip shaded by large trees similar to sycamore maple. You can also climb the 65–m–tall **Cerro Condell**, a knoll swelling in the middle of the town, to gain a view of the whole area; on clear days, you can see the Andes in the background.

After this breathtaking view, carry on into town by Camilo Henríquez, passing through an exhibition of huge agricultural machinery, and turn down Yungay street until you reach

The Plaza de Armas one of Chile's best, is surrounded by 60 Phoenix canariensis palms and has a wrought–iron pavillion forged in the New-Orleans fashion of the late 18th century. Built in 1904, it has been granted National Monument status.

The square also contains many century–old trees of exotic provenances –each with an identifying label– and sculptures made by Chilean artists. In one of the fountains swim black–necked swans. After a walk through the shopping center, take your car and drive on up Yungay street as far as Av San Martín; there you turn left and reach the

Iglesia del Carmen a vast structure of three naves. To end this tour, return to the plaza and drive up Carrera Street to the right, crossing the wide avenue, to arrive at the small square of **San Francisco** and namesake **church**, with a convent which, in the old times, was located at a site known as Convento Viejo, some 30 km northward. It was moved to this location when Manso de Velasco founded the city. Inside is the **Virgen de la Velilla**, the only copy of a statue of the Virgin existing at Santuario de Mata de Monte Agudo, in Spain. It was brought from there in 1734.

Where To Eat el Fogón Chileno offers good grilled meat; very good service at Club La Unión. Other restaurants shown on city map. At the Pan-Am highway, Da Orestino, with Italian cuisine, and Aguas Negras. Curicó is famous for its marzipan cakes.

TOURS FROM CURICO

1 TO LOS QUEÑES ★★

102 km round trip, with 32 km paved and the rest bumpy gravel. For one day; take food or eat at Los Queñes.

An excursion to a mountain summer resort.

Leave Curicó (km 0) on the Pan–Am highway towards the North. At km 3 take paved road to the right, leading eastward through the tiny hamlet of **Romeral** (km 9, famous for its vino añejo, a port–like wine) as you further, you will see lovely samples of colonial homesteads. At km 24 is a large 2–story manor house with a glass gallery, surrounded by luxuriant trees.

The road approaches the Teno river and starts to run parallel to it. As it climbs upstream, the valley becomes narrower and the landscape changes: native vegetation covers the slopes, tilled fields and pastures stretch in the flatland, their boundaries lined with poplars.

At km 35, after climbing the Los Maquis hill and after winding your way up a curvy stretch of road, the landscape changes again: the Teno river tumbles swiftly through a series of deep canyons, with the towering Andes providing a suitable backdrop. The road then climbs two more curvy stretches, crosses streams cutting through lush vegetation and several good spots for wild camping, until at km 51 it arrives at

Los Queñes set at the confluence of the Teno

8

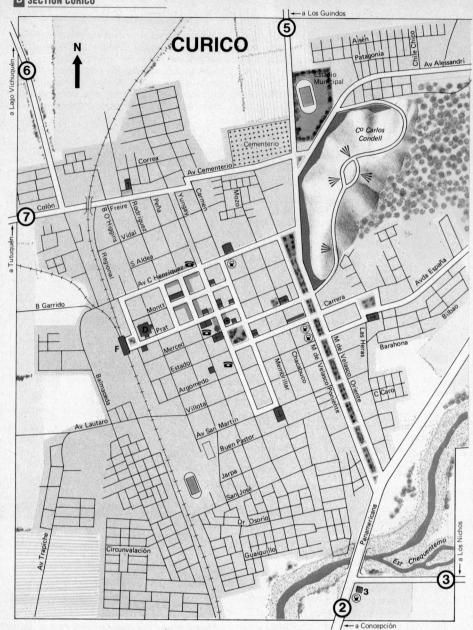

CURICO

and Claro rivers at an altitude of 590 m. Along-side the typical rural dwellings is a group of mountain summer cottages built in stone and facing the rivers, where fishing is very good. There is also a good **campground** and a hostel. It is a good spot for starting on trekking expeditions into the high Andes.

2 TO RADAL AND LARGE VINEYARDS ★★★
148 km round trip, with 48 km paved and the rest gravel. A winding mountain road. Takes one day; take food.
A tour visiting large wineries, historical sites and a beautiful Protected Nature Area.

Leave Curicó (km 0) on the Pan–Am highway heading South. A short way ahead, to the right of the road, is **Bodega Miguel Torres** (signposted), maker of quality wine. Their facilities can be visited during working hours, taking the chance to taste or buy wines.

At km 13 a road branches off to the left leading to Lontué. Beyond the railway underpass is **Viña San Pedro**, another large–sized winery. Its roots date back to 1701, when Cayetano Correa acquired these lands and planted grapevine of the «País» strain, a hardy plant. By 1850 fine vinestock was introduced from France; the present winery was established in 1865. The wine vaults with their giant casks can be visited (Apr–Nov, Tu–Th 10:00–11:30 h and 15:30–16:30 h; Dec–Mar, Tu-Fri 10:30–11:00 h and 15:30–16:30 h); wine is on offer for tasting and buying.

Drive through Lontué and take the road to Mo-lina, which bends to the right. It runs through vineyards and is lined by poplars. At km 19 is **Hacienda Quechereguas**, where a surprise engage-ment between Chilean and royalist troops took place in 1814, during the war for independence. Ask for permission to visit the colonial–style house, the storage buildings, and the inner court, situated at the end of a long poplar–lined avenue.

At km 26 you arrive at

Molina (pop 12,600), founded in 1834 and lo-cated in the very heart of Chile's wine country. It is worth stopping to walk through the plaza and visit the old church.

A gravel road starts at the southwestern cor-ner of the square, leading in 50 km to

Radal 7 Tazas is administrated by Conaf and is 50 km inland towards the mountains. It is located

☎	Telephone Center	
⊙	Café, Meeting Point	
⊞	Gasoline Station	
⫸	Lookout Point	
A	Post Office	
B	Market	
* F	Railway Station	
H	Old Façades	
J	Del Carmen Church	
K	San Francisco Church	
M	Town Hall	

	2	Comercio
	3	Hostería Shell
*	4	Mazapán
	5	Centro Español
	6	Fogón Chileno
*	7	Aguas Negras
*	12	Da Orestino

ACCOMMODATIONS
8   H Luis Cruz Martinez
9   H Comercio
11 R Rahue

RESTAURANTS
1   Club La Unión

TOURISTIC SERVICE
C   Bus Terminal
* D   Rural Bus Station
* E   Buses to the Coast
L   Automovil Club Car Rental

TIPS
G   Pizzería

*   See general map of Curicó

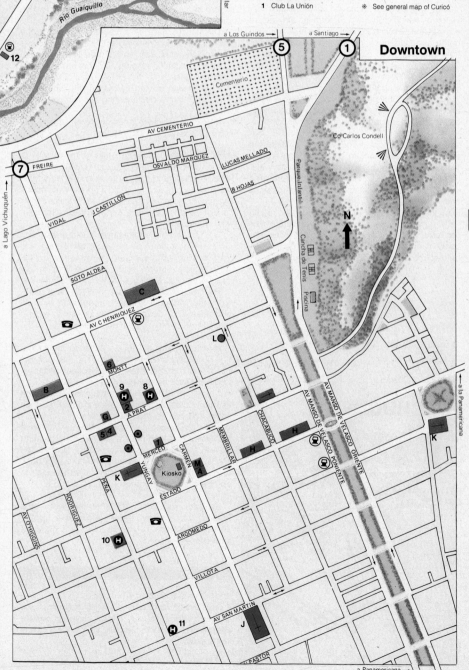

Downtown

Radal; Siete Tazas

on the river bed of the Claro river amid beautiful scenery and is noted for its waterfalls, the most famous of which are: the **Velo de Novia** (Bride's Vail) which is 50 m high , and **Las Siete Tazas** (the Seven Cups), a geological formation in the Claro river valley of seven pools which form at the foot of each of the seven waterfalls, and where you can bathe surrounded by dense indigenous vegetation, raulí, coigue, ciprés de montaña, mañío, laurel, olivillo, avellano and copihues, a bright red, bell-shaped flower which is Chile's national flower. There is a campground and a picnic area.

9 km farther into the mountains is **Parque Inglés**, another beautiful mountain spot with a picnic area, bathing area, good fishing and hiking possibilities.

Returning towards Molina, at km 126 take the road to the Pan-American highway. Right before the railway crossing, right next to the train station, is an outdoor **exhibit** of old agricultural and winery machinery, with ancient tractors, ploughs and locomotives.

At the Pan-Am highway, 400 m to the South (left), turn right to visit the old wine cellars of **Viña San Pedro**, built underground in vaulted brick masonry over 100 years ago. Ask for permission beforehand at the head office in Curicó.

8

★ Touristic Information
  Town Hall
A Museums

B Ancient Wheat Barn
C Picnic Area
▤ Façades, Houses of Interest

The tour ends at Curicó (km 148).

3 TO LAKE VICHUQUEN ★★★

117 km from Curicó, 84 km are paved. The rest is gravel in good condition. Takes 2-3 hours one way. Gasoline at Hualañé.

A visit to a renowned, beautiful lake resort set among mountains near the coast, alive with watersports and offering hotels and campgrounds. It is a good point from which to set out on tours along the coast.

Leave Curicó (km 0) on a road that runs its entire length along the northern bank of the Mataquito river. At km 85 is the village of **Hualañé**.

Two km beyond Hualañé, take the road to the right leading to the lake; 5 km after this junction take the signposted road to the left leading to Vichuquén, where you arrive at km 110.

Vichuquén dates from before the arrival of the Incas. It was originally a settlement of coastal Indian tribes. In their tongue, the place was calle huichu–que–n, meaning «isolated place». The Incas established here a mitimae (colony) and mixed in with the locals. Vichuquén still conserves its one–street layout, descending in steps towards a ford and containing many houses from the 18th century.

The houses have long covered porches in the front, each one connected with the next. There is an ancient **wheat barn** and a **museum** across the chapel, containing religious objects saved from a fire that destroyed the old church, silver work, pottery, stones worked by the original inhabitants and other items documenting the history of the place.

Continuing another 7 km along a stream, the road brings you at km 117 to

LAKE VICHUQUEN a scenic lake with 40 km^2 of warm, deep–blue water, surrounded by pine forests. A road runs along the lakeside leading to different resorts and residential areas. Watersports –windsurf, water ski, sailing– are practiced profusely; at times the lake surface seems forested with sail masts.

The first village is **Aquelarre,** a lake resort with Swiss–style summer houses, a small beach and wide availability of supplies. A nice view at Hostería Aquelarre; they rent rooms only to family groups that have made reservations in advance.

The lake offers all tourist facilities (see map). Camping Vichuquén is a campground with all amenities in a gorgeous setting. A tour around the lake is a must, best done clockwise in the afternoon.

At estero Llico, the lake's outlet to the sea at the El Rodeo crossroads, stop at the look–out points and admire the black–necked swans at **Laguna de Torca National Reserve,** which also boasts the category of Nature Sanctuary on account of its rich wildlife. Nearby is an airstrip that receives some 100 private planes in season.

If you like seafood, stop at Residencial Miramar in **Caleta Llico.** A long beach, flanked by large sand dunes, stretches towards the north. Next to the fishing hamlet is the metallic structure of a dock built around 1890, part of a failed project to open a canal to the lake and turn it into a navy base.

Go back passing in front of the aerodrome (airport) which at the peak season is a hive of activity, and cross the bridge to end the circuit of the lake.

4 A TOUR ALONG THE COAST ★★★

127 km on an unsurfaced dirt road; not suitable after rain. Gasoline at Curepto.

A circuit through beach resorts, a variety of handicraft and excellent cuisine of seafood. You can choose to continue along the Great Coastal tour, crossing the Maule river by ferry from Quivolgo.

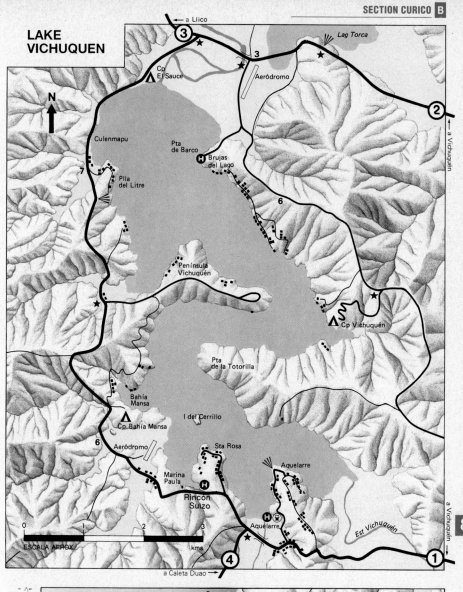

LAKE VICHUQUEN

N

a Llico →

3

Cp El Sauce

3

Lag Torca

Aeródromo

2

→ a Vichuquén

Culenmapu

Pta de Barco

Brujas del Lago

7

Plla del Litre

6

Península Vichuquén

Cp Vichuquén

Pta de la Totorilla

Bahía Mansa

I del Cerrillo

Cp Bahía Mansa

6

Aeródromo

Sta Rosa

Marina Paula

Rincón Suizo

Aquelarre

Aquelarre

Est Vichuquén

→ a Vichuquén

8

0   1   2   3

ESCALA APROX.   kms

4

← a Caleta Duao →

1

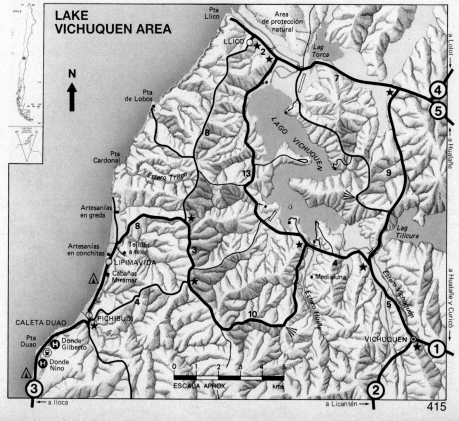

LAKE VICHUQUEN AREA

CHILE

N

Pta Llico

Area de protección natural

LLICO

2

Lag Torca

→ a Lolol

Pta de Lobos

7

4

5

8

→ a Hualañé

Pta Cardonal

LAGO VICHUQUEN

Estero Trilico

13

9

Artesanías en greda

8

Lag Tilicura

Artesanías en conchitas

Tejidos a telar

LIPIMAVIDA

3

Medialuna

4

a Hualañé y Curicó →

Cabañas Miramar

Estero Huñe

Estero Vichuquén

4

CALETA DUAO

PICHIBUDI

10

5

Pta Duao

Donde Gilberto

VICHUQUEN

1

Donde Nino

3

0   1   2   3   4   5

ESCALA APROX.   kms

← a Iloca

2

→ a Licantén →

lake Vichuquén

Start at the El Rodeo road junction (km 0), at the northern end of Lake Vichuquén. At km 2 take road to the left, running along the crest of several hills covered by pine forests. At km 16 you can see the sea below and a plain peppered with houses on a beachfront.

At km 23 is **Lipimávida**, a hamlet by the beach. Its artisans offer loom–woven blankets and rugs, and pottery. The road continues on an earthen ledge above the beach. To the left, the hills are clad with pine forests or wheat fields. Wheat thrashing is still done the old way, and the grain is hauled in huge ox–drawn carts.

At km 29 is **Caleta Duao**, a small fishing hamlet with a restaurant specializing in seafood. Horses can be hired for riding along its long beach. Next to the beach is a long earthen platform used as a landing strip but in summer and spring also for country–style horse races.

At km 35 is

Iloca one of the most popular beach resorts in the area, with several hotels (eg, Hotel Curepto) and restaurants (eg, Hostería La Puntilla). Sin Envidia is quite inexpensive. Good fishing at the spot known as La Pesca, at the mouth of **Mataquito river.**

The road comes to the mouth of the Mataquito river and then runs for a short stretch along its bank. It soon comes to a junction (here is Fundo Lora, where you can buy outstanding homemade butter and cheese). Take the detour to cross the river over the new bridge Lautaro, at km 52. Beyond the bridge, turn left and then take the road branching off (9 km) for

Curepto is a very old town with a lovely church on the plaza and huge colonial houses with verandas. It is famous for its woven goods and well worth a visit.

Return to the junction at the bridge (km 70) and take the road for Quivolgo, which heads back to the coast and goes through Trinchera (short detour to the beach) at km 88, crosses the Huenchullami stream at km 91, with wheat fields flanked by pine forests, and turns away from the coast, and at km 107 is **Putú**.

The road now leaves the coast and runs between low coastal hills and agricultural adobe and tile building, next to the typical farm labourers houses. Junquillar, a small hamlet with houses built of stone slabs using a clay–and–hay mix for mortar.

At km 127 is Quivolgo. On the top of a knoll to the left is the ancient **House of Quivolgo**, with a large gallery encased in glass windows. It was once the most important coastal hacienda with major shipping facilities.

A detour turns to the right, starting across from the house brings you, after 3 very poorly-surfaced kilometers, to the large colonial buildings used as **wheat storage** facilities, and where the famous maulinos barges were loaded. From here you can see the mouth of the Maule river and, on the far bank, the city of Constitución.

Drive back to the House of Quivolgo and go on 1 km on the main road towards the river.

To the side is **Moteles Quivolgo** (very good), then the landing to the ferry (a fee is paid; 08:00–20:00 h in summer) bringing you across the river to Constitución.

Continuation of the coastal tour is described under Section C.

SECTION C   TALCA

This section comprises the area from the Claro river basin in the North to Achibueno river in the South, and from the coast around Constitución to Laguna del Maule, high up in the Andes with the imposing volcanoes of Descabezado Grande and Chico. The axis of this farming, industrial and wine–producing area is the Maule river and its center is

TALCA capital city of Region VII; 128,500 inhabitants. Its foundation failed in 1692, and succeeded in 1742, under the name of Villa de San Agustín de Talca. «Talca» is derived from an Araucanian term meaning «Site of Thunder». Talca soon attained a more urban appearance than the other cities founded in that period, namely Curicó and San Fernando, thanks to the richest landowners deciding to build their residences here. They also financed the construction of the main square, town hall, church and other public buildings. A quarter of a century later Talca concentrated a very active export–oriented mill industry.

It is now a thriving regional manufacturing and trading center.

What To See we suggest that you first visit the centre of town and then view the city from above. The entrance to Talca is complicated and the best

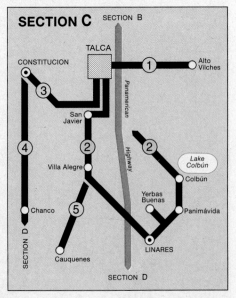

☎ Telephone Center
◉ Café, Meeting Point
★ Touristic Information
⛽ Gasoline Station
≫ Lookout Point
✳ Hospital
A Cathedral Church (3A)
B Entel Chile (3B)
C Post Office (3A)
D Railway Station (2C)

E Town Hall (3A)
F Bus Terminal
G O'Higginian Museum (3A)
H Regional Government (3A)

ACCOMMODATIONS
1 H San Marcos Gamero (3A)
2 H Plaza (3A)
3 H Claris Anexo (3A)
4 H Napoli (3B)
5 H Casagrande (3A)

6 H Amalfi (3B)
7 H Claris (3A)
8 H Cordillera (3B)

RESTAURANTS
10 Rancho Folklórico
12 Centro Español (3A)
13 Club Talca (3A)
14 Cabaña El Bosque
15 Shangay (3A)
16 El Alero de Gastón (2A)

INEXPENSIVE RESTAURANTS
20 El Fogón del Maule
21 El Solar del Campito
22 Círculo de Sub Oficiales
23 Angelmó (2B)

DISCOTHEQUES
20 El Fogón del Maule
25 Las Terrazas
26 Uni's Discotheque (2B)
See General Map of Talca

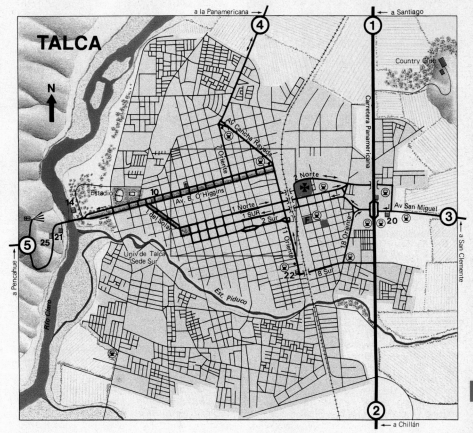

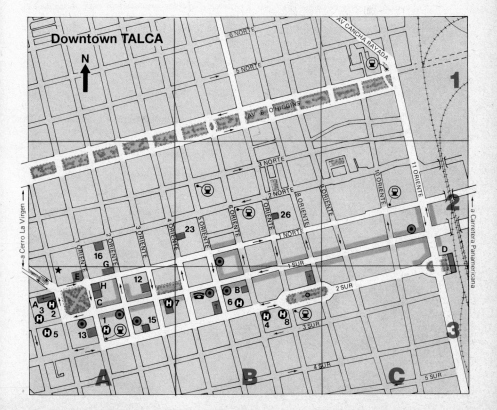

Talca, square

way in is by the central crossroads to the **Plaza de Armas**, shaded by such exotic species as jacarandas, cedars, palms, magnolias and various conifers. Around the square are the main public buildings; the commercial street is 1 Sur. At the market you can find handicrafts and inexpensive food stalls offering the regional specialties. Facing the square is also the

O'Higgins Museum at the corner of 1 Norte and 2 Oriente (Mon–Thu 09:00–12:45 h and 14:30–18:45 h; Fri 09:30–12:45 h and 15:00–18:45 h). An old colonial–style house (National Monument) built in 1762 and where Bernardo O'Higgins, Chile's founding father, lived when he was 9 years old. Several historical events took place at this house, such as the only encounter between Bernardo O'Higgins and his father, Ambrosio; the seat (1813–1814) of Chile's first governing body –the Junta de Gobierno– after Chile's declaration of independence; and the signing by O'Higgins, for the second time, of Chile's **Independence Act**, on February 2, 1818. A well–preserved house with two inner courtyards housing a valuable collection of paintings by national and foreign artists, in addition to an archaeological collection including pre–Columbian utensils, bored–through stones, spearheads, etc, and sculptures and coin collections. And, of course, the **O'Higgins Room**, decorated in the style of the 1800s and containing portraits of historical personages and a vast collection of

★ Touristic Information
Town Hall
A Façades of Interest

B Villa Alegre Church (NM)
Abbe Molina Tomb
R Restaurant Criollo, tipical food

VILLA ALEGRE

valuable historical documents and manuscripts. It is well worth a visit.

One block from the museum (1 Norte and 3 Oriente) is **Casa de Cuadrado,** bearing witness to colonial architecture with a fine access hall and a flowery inner court.

To end your visit, take your car and leave by the pretty diagonal street of Isidoro del Solar until you reach Alameda Bernardo O'Higgins a wide avenue with a shady, wooded middle strip containing century–old trees similar to sycamore maples. At its eastern end there is a sports area with a municipal swimming pool and, to a side, the grounds where the yearly regional fair, FITAL, is held.

The Alameda ends at the **Río Claro resort**, on the river bank, with a small beach, picnic areas, restaurants and boat hire. Ideal place to relax.

Cross the bridge and climb the **cerro La Virgen** to the esplanade at the summit, containing a simple chapel, picnic tables and commanding a panoramic **view** of the city, the surrounding countryside and the volcanoes in the far-away Andean range.

Where To Eat   Talca, as a relatively large town, offers numerous restaurants. If you are looking for the rather unusual cuisine, try La Guañaca, with its pork-roll soup, a dressing for meat called chancho en piedra, fried pejerrey (a type of fresh-water mackerel) and fried frog.

For fine cuisine, the traditional Club de Talca. Other specialties at city restaurants and at the Río Claro resort; for further frog delicacies, Hostería Pabellón, 5 km down the Pan–American highway to the South. Inexpensive food at the market food stalls.

TOURS FROM TALCA

1   TO VILCHES ★★★

132 km round trip, with 44 km paved and the rest gravel road, not exactly in the best of shape. For one day; take food. If planning to camp, get supplies in Talca. Best from Sept. to March. Alternative transportation by bus twice daily from Talca, at 13:00 h and early evening, back at 07:00 h and 17:30 h.

A beautiful, traditional excursion from Talca, visiting the interesting Villa Huilquilemu and a scenic mountain resort.

Leave Talca (km 0) on the road to San Clemente. To the left you can see the stone buildings of the Universidad Católica campus, with its poplar–lined perimeter.

km 4 is the **Feria de Agricultores**, a livestock trade fair housed at a modern–looking roofed amphitheater where you can view the exhibition corrals and "passarelas". It is worth staying a short while to watch the performance of buying and selling animals. The scenery becomes rural, with apple and peach orchards and rows of tall poplars casting some shade on the road. At km 8 is

VILLA HUILQUILEMU   (Tue–Fri 15:00-18:00 h, Sat 16:00-18:30 h; Sun and Holidays 11:00–14:00 h). Now in the hands of the Universidad Católica, the 4.7-hectares plot of land contains a sprawling house –built in 1850– about one hectare in area, including the courtyards. It is a fine, very well preserved example of the period's architecture, with long galleries supported by grooved pillars surrounding the various courtyards. It houses a **Museum of Religious Art**, with a valuable collection of furniture, statuary and paintings; a **Museum of Handicrafts** with exhibits from 25 handicrafts centers; a **Machinery Yard** (Corralón de las Máquinas), with old machines and implements for farm work and wine production; and a wine deposit and sampling center. At the end of a long covered walk is a lovely park with century–old sequoias, cedars, araucarias, palms, oaks and magnolias. In the middle of the park is the **Patio de América,** with an exhibition of contemporary sculptures.

Back on the road, at km 17 you can see the odd architecture of the manor house **Flor del Llano,** with a single 100–m–long body lined with a full–length gallery facing the Andes.

At km 20 is the village of **San Clemente,** with a Cema shop selling handicrafts. By km 30, after the road ducks under the power lines descending from the mighty Colbún–Machicura hydroelectric complex, the scenery becomes more rugged and the road starts to climb.

At km 35, the road forks, take the left branch to Vilches. The right branch leads to Laguna del Maule, a wonderful tour through fantastic mountain scenery were it not for the abysmally poor condition of the road. The road to Vilches climbs through slopes covered by thick native vegetation and a few sunflower and corn fields, then goes through La YOC, at km 40, a good place for picnicking.

At about km 60 is **Alto Vilches,** nestled in a large pine forest and with many summer log cabins scattered along the road. There is a picnic area and a campground. Drive on to km 66, to the

Area de Protección Vilches a Protected Nature Area under Conaf administration, covering 16,884 hectares and located at 1,200 m altitude. It has its own rainy microclimate nourishing a thick native forest of hualo, coigüe, lenga, ñirre, raulí, quillay, peumo, lingue, radal and avellano, and lots of mammal and bird wildlife. To the right of the entrance is Conaf's Environmental Information Center (Centro de Información Ambiental), with exhibits on the local flora and fauna.

Stroll down to **Quebrada de los Coigües,** a place where the only sound to be heared is the chirping of birds. From here, following the park warden's directions, you can hike along the more than

Villa Huilquilemu Museo

20 km of beautiful trails: down to the Lircay river to fish or bathe in any of its many volcanic flagstone pools, or to Laguna de los Patos (a pond), Mirador del Valle (a look-out point), Laguna El Alto (another pond), or Piedra Las Tacitas, a stone construction presumably made by aboriginal inhabitants. You can also climb to volcano Descabezado (3,830 m).

2 **RURAL TOWN CIRCUIT, THROUGH LINARES AND HOT SPRINGS ★★★** *206 km round trip, with 160 km on an excellent paved highway and 40 km on a gravel road. Rushing, you can take in all the sights in one day; staying overnight at Linares or the thermal baths you can take it easier. Year round. Gasoline at Linares and Colbún.* **A lovely circuit through little-known places set in a nice countryside, ending in a thermal bath.**

Leave Talca (km 0) on the Pan–American high-

8

ACCOMMODATIONS	RESTAURANTS

☎ Telephone Center
◉ Meeting Point
🅖 Gasoline Station
A Market

B Linares Museum
C Cathedral Church
D Bus Terminal
E Railway Station

6 H Curapalihue
3 H Turismo
4 H Londres
5 Hs Málaga

1 Centro Español
2 Club de La Unión
5 Hs Málaga

way heading South. The road runs through cultivated fields, crossing at km 15 the **railway-road bridge** spannig the Maule river, opened in 1885. It is one of Chile's most interesting steel structures, weighing 1,111 tons and consisting of two continuous, 442-m-long, 5-m-tall beans.

Deseigned by the engineers Domingo Santa María and Benjamin Vivanco, it is one of the most important and most beautiful metallic structures in the country.

At km 19 take detour to the right for **San Javier**, a busy trading center. Go through Avenida de las Palmeras towards Villa Alegre. The **next 13 km** contain numerous farmhouses set amidst shady parks. This trip should be taken slowly in order to appreciate the subtle details in these houses which belong to the past century. Some of them produce their own wine, which they offer in stands along at the roadside. At km 34 is

Villa Alegre with a church granted the National Monument status, built in 1890 of mud bricks on stone foundations. One of the houses in the main street has a peculiar zig-zagging gallery facing the street, which is lined with **orange trees**. In spring and summer, these trees lend a sweet scent to the whole village. Local handicrafts at the Cema Chile shop, on one side of the square.

Then continue your journey taking the road which leads to the Panamerican Highway, a road which runs between vineyards and reaches the highway at km 39, then turn south until you reach km. 56 on the crossroads to

LINARES a provincial capital of 46,500. An active manufacturing center well known for its sugar manufacturing plant -from sugar beets- and a busy center of business activity, with a good hotel and a motel at the road junction, it was founded in 1794 by a decree from Ambrosio O'Higgins under the name of Villa de San Ambrosio de Linares.

What To See the highway brings you directly to the **Plaza de Armas.** On one side is the **Cathedral**, built in Romanesque–Byzantine style. The pulpits, presbytery and the altar are made of Carrara

marble. It contains also one of the largest mosaics in South America, created by Giulio di Girólamo. In the basement is Capilla de los Recuerdos, with wall paintings made by Pedro Subercaseaux. At Avenida Valentín Letelier, with large maple–like trees, is the **Museo de Linares** (Tue– Sat 10:00–17:30 h; Sun 10:00–13:00 h). Housed in an old colonial–style house, it contains a vast collection of handicrafts from neighboring centers, and a collection of Chilean paintings from different periods, in addition to a historical room with weapons, uniforms and valuable documents.

Where To Eat the specialties here are spicy pork ribs (costillar de chancho) and sausages (longanizas). Club de la Unión with international food, and Centro Español are recommendable, with the quaint atmosphere of inner courts in old houses.

The circuit continues with a short, 12–km detour (see city map) on a paved road to

Yerbas Buenas a village which stepped into the history books with the so–called «Yerbas Buenas Surprise» of 1813, the first armed engagement in Chile's struggle for independence. The houses can be as long as a whole block, with long covered verandas and shady courtyards. **Parroquia Santa Cruz** contains an image of the Virgin brought from Spain in 1585. **Casa de Pareja**, the lovely old colonial homestead where royalist general José Antonio Pareja used to live, is now the Library and Historical Museum, with historical manuscripts and other relics, in addition to handicraft exhibits. It is well worth taking this short side trip.

Return to Linares on the same road, to arrive at the city at km 83. Take now the road for Colbún and the thermal baths (see city map). At km 96 is the village of **Vara Gruesa**, with craftsmen specialized in carving the white wood of pear trees into beautiful stirrups, lamp bases and other articles. It is interesting to watch them while at work.

At km 98, take the 3–km detour to **Quinamávida** («place of five hills»), which features a thermal bath in a scenic setting, a hotel located in a 380-hectare country estate, a swimming pool and baths where the water emerges at between 18 and 27°C, mud baths and, on weekends,

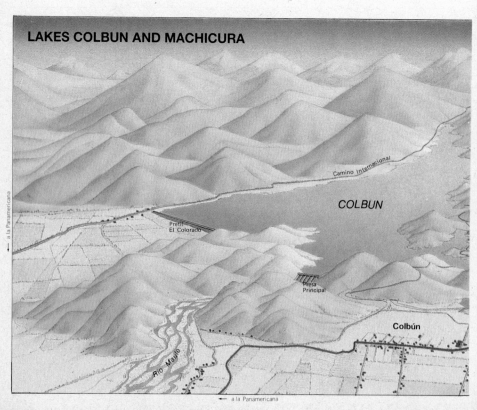

LAKES COLBUN AND MACHICURA

COLBUN

Camino Internacional

a la Panamericana

Pretil El Colorado

Presa Principal

Río Maule

Colbún

← a la Panamericana

barbecues and Chilean folk music. Back on the main road, 5 km beyond the junction (km 110) is

PANIMAVIDA («Place of Lions»), with a lovely square shaded by large trees, many shops and stalls selling local crafts, a church with a slender bell tower, and, on one of the sides, **Hotel y Termas de Panimávida**, a traditional spa with reputed medicinal waters and a vast, manicured park ornamented with statues and water fountains. It has excellent accommodations, a large restaurant, a thermal pool, thermal and mud–bath cabins, mini–golf course, a playground for children and a cinema. The best place to stay is at this hotel.

From here, a short visit to the hamlet of **Rari** is a must, 1.5 km away, with horsetail and ox-tail hair weaving, a unique craft in the Americas. At every house -each with a gallery, leafy courtyards and grape arbors you can see weaving in progress. In the outskirts of the village, on the banks of the stream, there are many spots for picnicking with a view to the superb mountain backdrop.

The circuit continues to the north on a paved road leading to Colbún at km 119. A short way ahead, at an electric power substation, take the gravel road to the right leading in 20 km to **Lake Colbún**. The road crosses the modern canal bringing the water to the Machicura dam and then climbs a small incline commanding a view of the huge man–made lake. The road then skirts the southern edge of the lake, approaching the shore at times. At several spots on km 139 are accesses to the lakeshore from where watersports can be practiced.

The lake is of quite recent origin, its full -and considerable tourist potential yet to be realized. There are some summer cottages, a hotel-restaurant and a campground.

The 40–km–long lake was formed by damming the Maule river to feed the huge Colbún–Machicura hydroelectric complex, the largest in the country. Unfortunately the gigantic dam with

its mighty floodgates is neither visible from the road nor open to the public.

The circuit ends by returning to the village of Colbún at km 159 and from there, on the paved road, back to the Pan–Am at km 191 and Talca at km 206.

3 TO CONSTITUCION ★★

110 from Talca on paved roads. Hotels, gasoline and restaurants at Constitución.
A tour to this section's main seaside resort, which is in turn the starting point for other excursions.

Driva from Talca (km 0) to **San Javier** at km 21. Take the road for Villa Alegre and at km 26 turn right along the coast road. The road leads you among crops that have no irrigation and down gentle slopes towards the coast.

At km 28 the road crosses the placid **Loncomilla** river –with banks covered by a thick vegetation and with a restaurant offering roast duck and fried frogs– and then descends gently through soft, rolling cultivated fields. Then come the arid slopes of the Coastal Range to arrive at km 61 at

Nirivilo a colonial village with a Parrochial Church, a National Monument built in 1834. This is a modest though beautiful chapel having wide lime painted adobe walls, and where relatives of don Bernardo O'Higgins are buried.

The barren slopes soon give way to pine-forested slopes and large sawmills, and the road zigzags its way down a steep mountain side to reach, at km 110,

CONSTITUCION founded by Ambrosio O'Higgins in 1794 under the name of Nueva Bilbao, it had the aim of becoming the main shipping port for the grain producers of the Talca area and coastal haciendas. It did achieve this status, complete with a railway leading to its port. The seaside resort dates from the early 1900s, when Talca's high society started using its superb beaches as a summer playground. Gradually it received complete tourist infrastructure. It is home now to 20,800 people and a major manufacturing center based mainly on forest industries, fisheries and the large Celco pulp mill.

What to See the access road brings you directly to Mac Iver street, near the front of the Celco pulp mill. To the left is the 4–km–long **beach area**,

8

MACHICURA

A Casa de Pareja (Museum)
B Parish Church

D Square
⊟ Houses with Varandas

YERBAS BUENAS

Constitución; La Iglesia stone

they also cross the river to Quivolgo.

At the end of O'Higgins street is the access to **Cerro Mutrún**, with good views of the mouth of the river, the town and its beaches, and the surrounding scenery. In the woods on the western side of the hill are picnic areas.

Constitución is a good starting point for tours along the coast, such as:

4 TO CHANCO ALONG THE COAST ★★

58 km to Chanco on a gravel road. Take food and watch your gasoline: the next point for topping up is at Cauquenes, 38 km away.
A one-day outing from Constitución, or, alternatively, the first leg of a longer coastal tour to Cobquecura.

Leave Constitución, km 0, on the paved road to San Javier. At km 6 take the road branching off to the right for Chanco. It runs through the hills and approaches the coast amidst orderly Radiata **pine plantations**. Soon, at km 19, lonely, lovely beaches with black sand can be seen below.

At km 35, before arriving at bridge Loanco, is a wooden gate; it is the access to Faro Carranza, a good place for fishing. The road then turns inland towards the south, through huge sand dunes which surround the long beach. This takes you to Pahuil 43 km farther on, a small village where beans and potatoes grow. At km 58 is

Chanco a village of colonial-style houses sitting on the ruins of an ancient Indian fishing settlement. The atmosphere is like a half-century jump to the past, with basket-like ox-drawn carts creaking under wheat, charcoal or firewood loads along streets lined with old veranda-fronted houses were you can see the wheat storehouses, the plaza, the San Ambrosio Church with its lovely interior paintings of the saints, and a placid rhythm to everything. Home workshops are busily producing a simple kind of pottery. Chanco lent its name to a very tasty kind of cheese first pro-

lined with restaurants and surrounded by unusual rock formations, such as Arco de los Enamorados («Lover's Arch»), Las Termópilas («Thermopylae»), and Piedra de la Iglesia («Church Stone»). The beaches have fine black sand. At the end of the road is an old dock.

On your return trip, go through the Plaza de Armas where you will see old public buildings, meeting places and the ancient church built in 1860. From the square go to the river bank to visit the **Astilleros del Maule**, shipyards where a traditional kind of vessel is built, the falucho maulino, large barges using a type of locally-grown oak. These ships usually are about 21 m long and some 5 m from keel to deck. Formerly, sail-driven faluchos used to ply this coast with grain cargo to Central Chile and even as far as Perú.

Go back to the center of town and turn down calle Cruz úntil you reach the banks of the river and can walk down the public pier from where tourist **launches** take pleasure trips up the Maule river as far as Orrego island or Rancho Astillero;

8

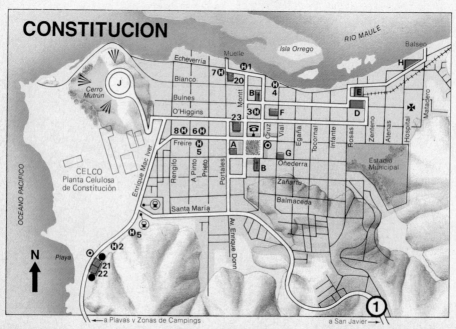

ACCOMMODATIONS		

☎ Telephone Center	**B** Church	**1** H Constitución
◉ Café, Meeting Point	**C** Post Office	**2** H Blanco Encalada
★ Touristic Information	**D** Bus Terminal	**3** H Pradenas
◉ Gasoline Station	**E** Railway Station	**4** H Santa Ana
⋙ Lookout Point	**F** Cultural Center	**5** H SNA Maule
✕ Hospital	**G** Private Market	**6** Bh Ramírez
A Town Hall	**H** Maule Shipyards	**7** H Colonial
	J Lookout Point, Picnic Area	**8** Bh Chepita

RESTAURANTS	
7 H Colonial	
20 La Caleta	
21 Blue Moon	
22 Villa Mar	
23 Club La Unión	
G Private Market	
● Inexpensive Restaurants	

duced here. Unfortunately, it is not produced here anymore.

At the northern end of the town is the **Federico Albert National Reserve**, with 145 hectares covering an area of eucalyptus, cypress and pine woods and encroaching sand. Part of the raison d'être of the reserve is to stop the advance of these dunes; in fact, the woods were planted early this century to protect the village from the sand. There is a visitor's center with exhibits on the local flora and fauna, and models and photographs explaining the methods employed to check sand dune encroachment. There are also paths leading to an ample beach, Laguna del Toro and other sites, as well as a picnic area and a children's playground.

Here you have the choice of returning on the same road or continuing towards the south along the coast, or driving to Cauquenes. The corresponding descriptions are under Section D, Tour 3.

5 TO CAUQUENES ON THE OLD FRONTIER

ROUTE ★ *109 km one way, with 76 km on a poorly-surfaced gravel road. Gasoline at Cauquenes.*

A circuit on what used to be the route to the frontier (the boundary between conquered territory and the land of the Mapuches country) during the Conquest period, used by Pedro de Valdivia and again around 1700 during the foundation of cities in the Central Plain. Construction of a highway to Concepción along this route is planned.

Leave Talca (km 0) on the Pan–American highway to the South, to take the turn–off for San Javier at km 21. From there take the road to **Villa Alegre**. At km 25 take the road to the right, leading to the coast, and at km 28, just beyond the bridge over the Loncomilla river, is the road junction for Cauquenes, where the gravel stretch starts. The road runs towards the southwest through wheat and sugar–beet fields and across many streams and canals irrigating the whole area. After km 45 the road starts to climb the shoulders of the Coastal Range and the scenery turns arid. At km 71 you intersect a road coming from the north; turn left. At km 104 you meet the paved highway from Parral. Turn right and at km 106 is **Cauquenes**. The city and the tours from there are described under Section D, Tour 3.

SECTION D   PARRAL

It comprises the area from the Longaví river in the north to the Itata–Ñuble river basin in the south, and from the Andes to the coast. There are many coastal villages with good seafood. The Coastal Range shrinks down to low, round hills covered with pine forests and crops. Lovely mountain valleys harbor thermal baths set amidst lush vegetation fed by swift rivers the most outstanding of which is the Nevado de Longaví which is 3,242 m high. The main urban centers are Parral, Cauquenes and San Carlos, concentrating the area's agroindustrial activity. Due to its location, the natural point from which to start tours of this district is

Parral a city of 21,300 with major agroindustrial companies, among which the rice industry stands out. The Cema handicrafts shop (next to the Municipalidad) has attractive loom–woven goods. Founded in 1795 by Ambrosio O'Higgins under the name of Reina Luisa de Parral, to honor Charles IV's wife, this city shares with its counterparts farther south the lack of historical buildings: they have all been levelled by violent earthquakes during the 19th century and the years 1939 and 1960 of this century. Its claim to a place in history is as the birthplace of Chilean Nobel Prize–laureate poet Pablo Neruda.

TOURS FROM PARRAL

1 TO TERMAS DE CATILLO AND THE DAMS OF
DIGUA AND BULLILEO ★★★ *92 km round trip on a gravel road. Take food. Accommodations at Termas de Catillo or campsites at the dams.*
A short, nice tour to the foot of the Andes; bathing possibilities at the thermal springs or at the dams. Good fishing.

Leave Parral, km 0, on the Pan–Am highway to the south, and 200 m ahead is the signposted turn–off for Termas de Catillo. The road runs past fields lined with poplars and after 26 km –beyond the village of Catillo– reaches

Termas de Catillo (open in high season and the months right before and right after), nestled 320 m above the sea in a scenic setting, it includes a hotel with thermal baths, fitness room, children's playgrounds and vast green areas with manicured flower beds. Paths leading to nearby streams meander through the surrounding forest.

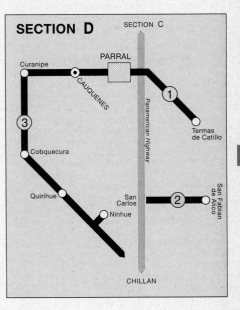

To continue the tour, go back to the village of Catillo and take the road to the left leading in 11 km (km 37 of the tour) to **Embalse Digua**, a dam in a rugged mountain setting. A good place for watersports, bathing, fishing rainbow trout and "pejerreyes", camping or have a picnic at many spots along the shore.

Back on the road, drive a further 12 km towards the east, climbing some mountainsides and descending to run along the Longaví river, amidst lush vegetation. At km 49 of the tour is the hamlet of San Pablo, whence a road leads in 4 km to **Embalse Bullileo**, a quiet, placid dam flanked by high mountains and lush forests. A very good spot for fishing and camping.

2 TO SAN FABIAN DE ALICO ★★★
94 km round trip from the Pan–American highway at San Carlos; 20 km paved and the rest gravel. See map of next Zone, Concepción and south of Biobío.

A visit to an unusually beautiful site; you can make it in one day or camp there to explore the surrounding area.

Leave the Pan–Am highway at San Carlos (km 0), taking the road running east. At km 10 is the small settlement of **El Sauce,** with a few scattered rural houses near the road. At km 17 is a police control point where you have to check in. At km 22, beyond the hamlet of Cachapoal, the road starts to climb small cultivated hills, with large trees in the ravines and mud-brick houses surrounded by vegetable gardens and grapevines. Beyond the hills, after km 32, the road skirts the **Ñuble river** valley, flanked by mountains covered by native forests. Now and again the rushing river forms some quiet pools along its stony bed, offering ideal spots for salmon fishing and camping.

At km 47 is

San Fabián de Alico a village founded in 1865 on a wide embankment above the river. The access road to the village is a veritable tunnel under towering sycamores. Turn on calle 18 de Septiembre towards the **Plaza de Armas;** is equally shady, flanked on three sides by public buildings and on the fourth by a corn field. Several excursions can be made from here: by ferry on the Ñuble river, 2 kms up the cañon, Laguna de la Plata, 30 km into the mountains, accessible only by horse (can be hired in the village) or by jeep. Wild camping is possible at many spots on the river banks, and a more established kind of camping at the campgrounds of Alico, 500 m from the village, and El Valiente, 4 km away.

3 **TO CAUQUENES AND THE COAST** ★★★

a total of 259 km, with 131 km paved and the rest dirt and gravel roads. Minimum two days, accommodations and gasoline at Cobquecura, Pelluhue and Cauquenes.

A lovely trip through the old sites of the Colonial Route to the frontier towards a most spectacular stretch with marvellous beaches.

Start from Parral's main square (km 0) along Av Aníbal Pinto to the train station, on the western part of town. Take the signposted paved road to Cauquenes, running past the livestock market and then past wide cultivated fields, with the Coastal Range straight ahead. At km 27 the road crosses the pleasant Perquilauquén river and runs alongside the railway track. At km 56 a gravel road coming from the north intersects the highway; it is the Colonial Route described in Section C above.

A short way ahead, at km 61, is

Cauquenes (pop 23,800), a provincial capital founded by Manso de Velasco in 1742 under the name of Las Mercedes de Manso de Tutuvén, on land given over by the indian chief Asencio Galdámez. This was the only village named after the distinguished Governor and its founding was registered in the plan for the new road to Concepción through the central valley, going through the recently founded cities of San Fernando, Curicó, Talca and Cauquenes.

What To See in the distance you can see the twin bell towers of the church, perched atop a hillock on the town's western side. Reach the Plaza de Armas, the mainstream of the city which is surrounded by imposing buildings which form the civic centre; in the middle of the plaza there are green areas and hundred-year-old trees. Half a block from the Plaza de Armas is the **Mercado Municipal,** a covered market, selling handicrafts – particularly black pottery from Pilén, a village 15 km away.

To continue the circuit, leave the square towards the north on Calle Urrutia, turning left on O'Higgins and heading for the coast. Large ox-drawn carts resembling huge wheeled wicker baskets can be seen on the road, hauling wheat, charcoal and firewood. The road runs through hills covered by scanty vegetation to arrive at km 72 at the Tutuvén dam, with a 20-sq km lake good for watersports and fishing, and for picnicking.

Ahead is a thick pine forest straddling the road and turning it into a sort of shady gallery. At km 90 is

Los Ruiles National Reserve covering 43 hectares and under Conaf management. It protects a stretch of surviving native forest containing such indigenous species as ruil, coigüe, gualo, canelo, avellano and raulí, and flowers such as copihue (Chile's national flower), caique and chilque. A path winds through the forest; there is a picnic area.

At km 94 is the 7–km detour to the left for **Pelluhue,** a fishing hamlet (flatfish –sole– is common) with fine beaches of black sand, restaurants, a campground and a gasoline station. Continuing 14 km on the road running along the coast, through wheat fields and small pine stands, you reach

Curanipe a seaside resort with fine beaches flanked by rock outcrops jutting into the sea. The crescent–shaped main beach is excellent for bathing, sheltered by a pine–clad promontory. Go down the mainstreet and shopping area with its neat buildings and continuous facades. It is a pleasant summer resort, with orderly houses sporting hydrangea flower beds.

The road continues through pine forests marching to the seashore. After crossing the Chovellén river, at km 130 is **Tregualemu,** with a couple of old farm houses from hacienda Tregualemu and a wide beach open to the southwesterly winds. The road then swerves inland and climbs a small incline covered by pine forests, with wheat fields and pastures at the summit. The area becomes more rugged, the road winding its way up and down hillsides.

At km 148 are the scattered houses of **Buchupureo** and at km 153, on the beach, is a large rock formation known as **Iglesia de Piedra** (Stone Church), with a large cave resembling a church nave.

At km 159 is

COBQUECURA another town sitting on the ruins of ancient Indian settlements. During last century it was an important grain producing area, using Buchupureo as its shipping port. The walls of its houses are made of stone slabs placed flat on top of each other, using clay as mortar. Boundary walls follow the same fashion and are capped with a shingled roof. The town offers good accommodations and beaches, and restaurants specialized in seafood. You can also continue 8 and 16 km, respectively, to visit the beaches of **Taicú** and **Colmuvao.**

The circuit leaves the coast here and turns inland, climbing a steep stretch among pine forests and large sawmills, to reach **Quirihue** (pop 5,600) at km 196, a farming village situated astride the old Colonial Route. Here you can choose whether to go on to Concepción on the paved road to Coelemu (see map of Concepción Zone) or to return to the Pan-American highway.

Assuming you choose the latter option, leave Quirihue on the paved road to Coelemu and 3 km later turn left on the highway to Chillán. At km 217 take the signposted 2-km detour to

San Agustín de Puñual (Tue–Sun 10:00–18:00 h), the house where Chile's naval hero Arturo Prat was born. A fine example of rural colonial architecture, the house has no openings to the outside and faces a large courtyard in its middle. You may visit the rooms furnished in the style of the

8

1800s and containing implements dating from that period. There is also a museum dedicated mainly to the Iquique Naval Battle and including personal objects which belonged to Prat. The place is very well preserved by the Chilean Navy.

Back on the road, a short detour to the left can be recommended at km 219, to visit **Ninhue**, a picturesque colonial village with a beautiful Chapel and outstanding loom-woven goods.

The tour ends at Cocharcas, on the Pan-Am highway, next to a large IANSA sugar mill. 10 km ahead is Chillán.

8

RURAL TRANSPORTATION

Rural buses offer a convenient way for travellers to tour the many towns and villages in this area, setting off from the main cities at the Pan-American highway. The rural bus network is vast and covers practically the entire zone, including places not easily reached by car.

The chart below shows routes and frequencies for weekdays, each line a route and its thickness indicating the number of daily departures in one direction. The rule of thumb is that on Saturdays frequencies drop to a half, while on Sunday low-frequency routes (one to three departures daily) are not covered at all. In season, however (ie, in summer), weekend frequencies from San Fernando, Curicó, Talca and Linares to the main seaside resorts and beaches increase considerably.

Frequency low-frequency routes are the lion's share of the rural network, and usually correspond to the pattern of early morning departure from rural towns to the main cities, returning the same evening. If the distance is short, there might be two departures daily. In cases with three departures daily, there is always an early morning bus leaving the city for the village.

Departure times the first batch of buses depart, in any route, between 07:30 and 08:30 h; the second at 10:30-11:00 h, and the third at 16:30-18:00 h, at which time low-frequency buses return from the cities to the villages. There are no departures over lunchtime, with the exception of high-frequency routes; departures later than 20:00 h are rare. The time when you most certainly will find transportation out of a city is at 16:30-18:00 h, and out of a village or town, early in the morning.

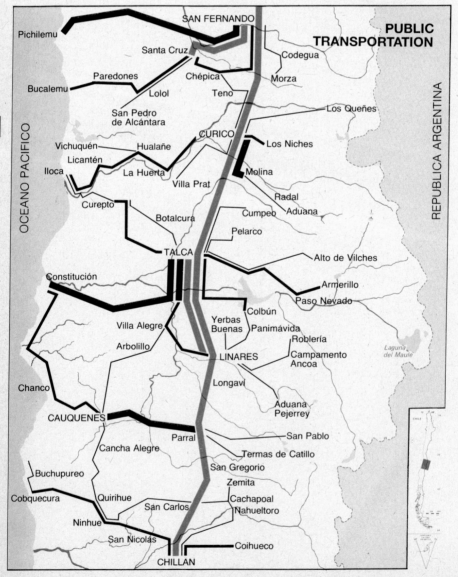

Zone 9
CONCEPCION and
SOUTH OF THE BIOBIO

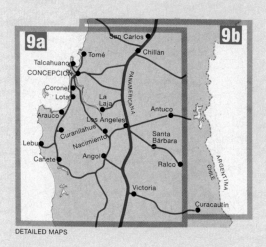

9a

San Carlos
Chillán
Tomé
Talcahuano
CONCEPCION
PANAMERICANA
Coronel
Lota
La Laja
Antuco
Arauco
Los Angeles
Curanilahue
Santa Bárbara
Lebu
Nacimiento
Cañete
Angol
Ralco
Victoria
Curacautín

9b

ARGENTINA
CHILE

DETAILED MAPS

Arica
Iquique
Antofagasta
Copiapó
Easter Island
La Serena
Valparaíso
SANTIAGO
Is R Crusoe
Talca
Concepción
Temuco
Valdivia
Osorno
Pto Montt
Castro
Chaitén
Coihaique
Cochrane

9

Puerto Natales
Punta Arenas
Puerto Williams

Is Diego Ramirez

90°   60°   53°

CHILEAN ANTARCTIC TERRITORY

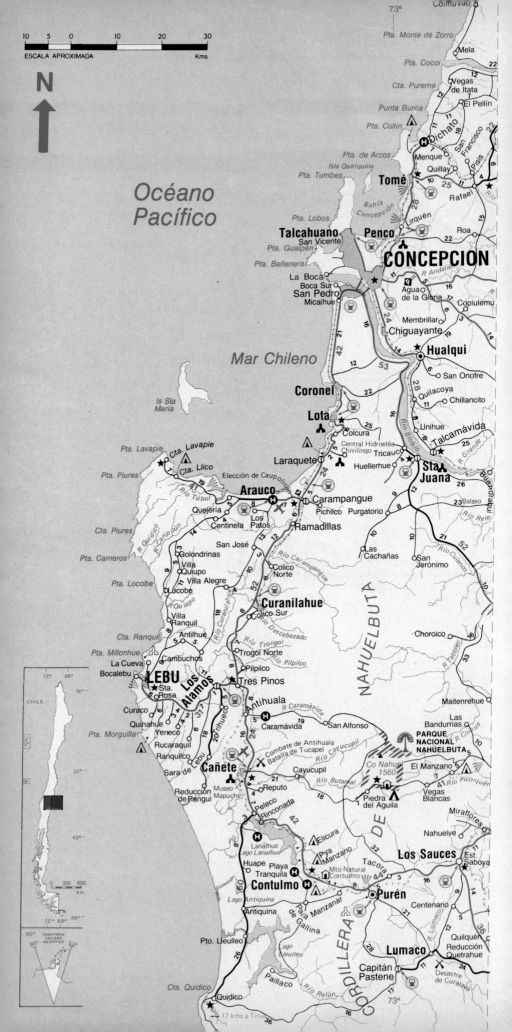

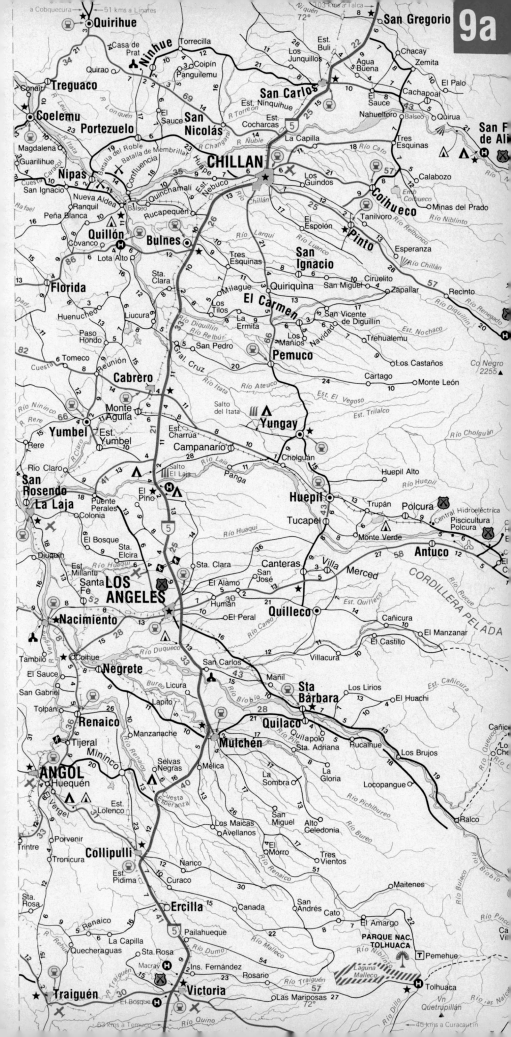

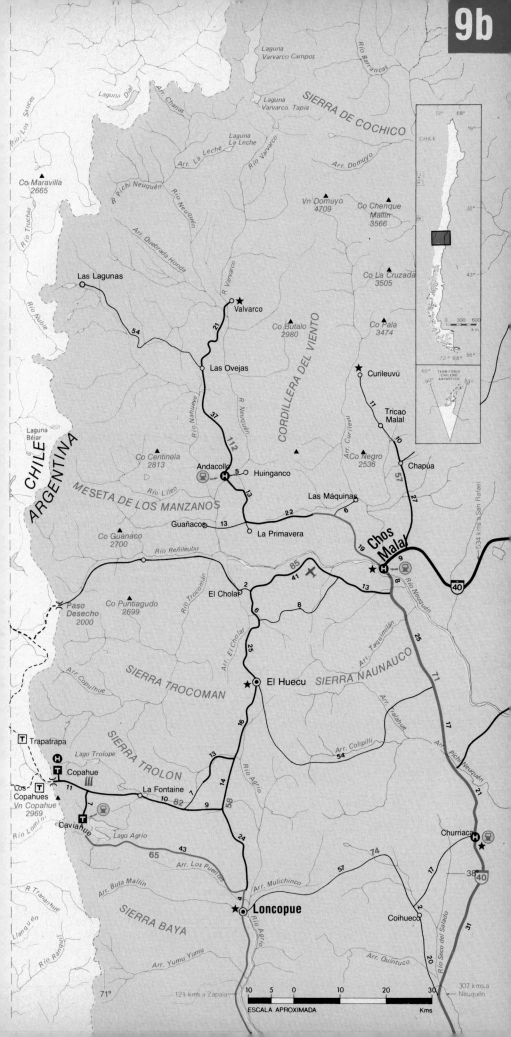

9b

OVERVIEW

This Tourist Zone comprises nearly all of the territory of Region VIII, Biobío, plus the Malleco province of Region IX, Araucanía. The reason for this arrangement is that the area's roads make it possible to explore it as a single tourist unit.

The Central Plain here undergoes a transition from the irrigated farmland of its northern portion to the higher–rainfall, thickly wooded areas in the south. The coastal landscape throughout this territory is typically southern in its luminosity and the predominantly evergreen forests. The Andean foothills start to show the first high–altitude cypress and araucaria forests.

This Zone's main attractions are of an urban and historical nature, with a large number of towns and villages boasting important relics from the 280 years during which this was La Frontera (The Boundary). Greater Concepción, Chillán, Los Angeles and Angol are attractive cities.

The Zone has been divided into four sections:

Section A   Chillán and Los Angeles it comprises the Central Valley between both cities and the area stretching both to the Andes and the coast.

Section B   Concepción with the largest urban and industrial concentration, and a smattering of fine beaches on the coast north of the Biobío river.

Section C   Arauco covering the western portion of the Nahuelbuta Range with attractive beaches, interesting coal mines and historical sites.

Section D   South of the Biobío with the lowlands of Angol and Traiguén and the highlands of Victoria, Curacautín and Lonquimay.

REGIONAL DISTANCES

Angol																
195	Arauco															
112	83	Cañete														
192	73	142	Concepción													
77	118	35	177	Contulmo												
219	38	107	35	142	Coronel											
169	185	254	112	289	147	Chillán										
187	111	180	38	215	73	104	Dichato									
157	345	269	221	234	256	198	259	Lake Laja								
167	90	55	149	90	114	261	187	324	Lebu							
64	252	176	128	141	163	105	166	93	231	Los Angeles						
212	31	100	42	135	7	154	80	263	107	170	Lota					
44	138	156	164	121	100	141	143	129	211	36	107	Nacimiento				
206	87	156	14	191	49	126	28	235	163	142	56	178	Penco			
251	267	336	194	371	229	82	186	280	343	187	236	223	208	Termas de Chillán		
177	101	170	28	205	63	94	10	249	177	156	70	133	20	176	Tomé	
72	228	145	242	110	252	219	280	207	200	114	245	116	256	301	270	Victoria

9

Zone 9
CONCEPCION and
SOUTH of the BIOBIO

DIVISION BY SECTIONS

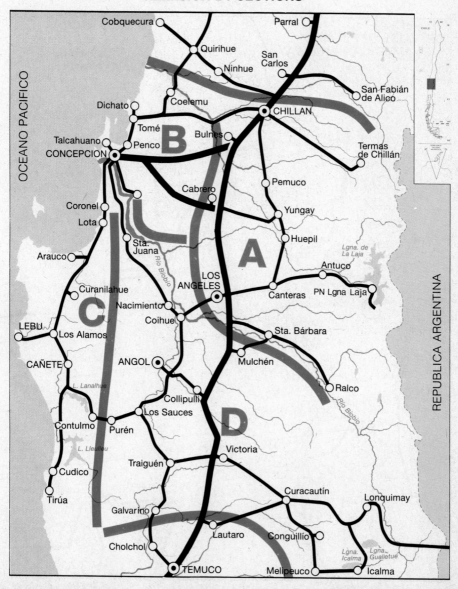

DETOURS OFF THE PAN–AMERICAN HIGHWAY

This is the only zone in Chile with three main high-ways running lengthwise in addition to the Pan–American highway: the 175–km paved coastal road; the paved Lowlands road, through Los Angeles, Angol and Traiguén; and the partly paved piedmont road from Chillán through Yungay to Antuco. They offer a refreshing alternative to the rather monotonous Pan–American highway.

1 A Visit to Concepción ★★ the most expeditious route to visit Concepción and return again to the Pan–American highway. Described under Access Roads to Concepción.

2 Colonial Route ★★ from Talca through Cauquenes to Concepción, described in Zone 8.

3 The Mill Route ★★★ a beautiful alternative along the old route to Chillán used to bring out the wheat from Ñuble to the mills and seaport of Tomé. It reaches Concepción following a scenic stretch of coast. See Sections A and B.

4 Conquerors' Route ★★★ a route through the scenic, historical lands of Arauco, with forts and other relics of Chile's conquest. The Pedro de Valdivia Route continues south to the city of Imperial passing through Lumaco and Chonchol. See Section C.

5 A Detour off the Conquerors' Route ★★★ same as the above, but with a detour to Angol and Pan–American highway. See Section D.

6 Along the Biobío ★★★ visiting the frontier forts of Santa Juana and Nacimiento to continue through the Angol lowlands to Traiguén and return to the Pan–Am. See Section D.

7 Through the Lowlands ★★ the shortest detour to see the Angol-Traiguén area and return to the Pan–Am. See Sections A and D.

8 An Excursion into the Andean Foothills ★★★ through farmland and wooded mountain scenery to lake Laja and the Itata waterfall. See Section A.

9 International Route ★★★ a splendid journey to the headwaters of the Cautín river, crossing the Andes through Chile's longest tunnel to the upper Biobío river area. See Section D.

③ Identifying number of the above detours

▬▬ Pan-American highway

▬▬ Paved roads

▬▬ Graveled roads

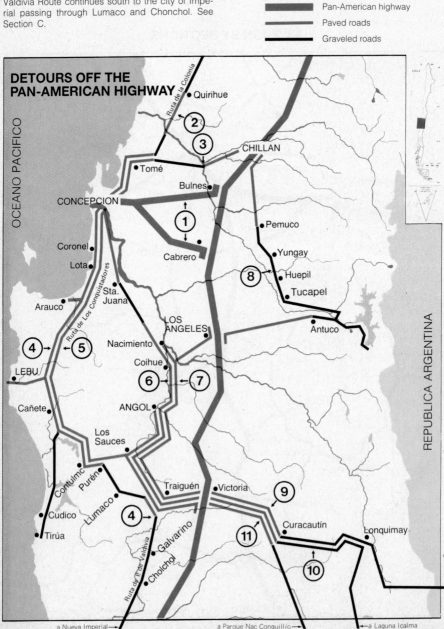

DETOURS OFF THE PAN-AMERICAN HIGHWAY

THE LAND, ITS HISTORY, ITS PEOPLE

DESCRIPTION this Tourist Zone stretches from the Itata & Ñuble rivers in the North to the cities of Traiguén, Victoria, Curacautín and Lonquimay in the south. It includes nearly the whole of Region VIII, Biobío, and the Malleco province in Region IX, Araucanía. The Biobío river divides the zone into two distinct portions:

North of the Biobío with the classical Central Chile division: a towering **Cordillera de los Andes** with its snow-capped peaks and volcanoes, such as the Chillán, Antuco and Sierra Velluda; the wide **Central Valley**; and the **Coastal Range**, uninterrupted, wide and low, rather a succession of hills interspersed with valleys and some villages.

South of the Biobío where the **Cordillera de los Andes** is cleft into two parallel arms by the Biobío river, which flows from south to north. The eastern arm, running along the border with Argentina, is lower than the western arm, which contains the towering volcanoes of Tolhuaca, Lonquimay and Llaima. The **Central Valley** is wide and drops markedly towards the foot of the **Coastal Range**; the many rivers flowing westward are prevented from following a direct route to the coast by the lack of passes in the Coastal Range, being deflected north to the Biobío river or south to the Imperial river. The Coastal Range is known here as **the Nahuelbuta Range** and is an abrupt, massive, high chain stretching without any break from the Biobío to the Imperial river. The **Seaboard** is wide, and came into being when a section of the continental shelf emerged here.

EARLY INHABITANTS the natives inhabiting this area were called Araucanos by the Spaniards, but they referred to themselves as **Mapuches** (people of the earth). Their territory stretched from the Itata river in the north to the Toltén river in the south. The tribes farther north were called **Picunches** (people of the north), while those from Valdivia to Chiloé were called **Huilliches** (people of the south). From an ethnic and linguistic standpoint, the Indian tribes from Illapel to Chiloé were a single people, with natural differences in dialect and customs derived from their different environments. A clear demonstration of this occurred in 1557, when chieftain Lautaro, setting out from central Araucanía, attempted to march to Santiago heading a Mapuche–Huilliche army; he was stopped by the Spaniards on the banks of the Mataquito river (Battle of Peteroa, April 4, 1557).

This Zone's Mapuche tribes were in turn divided into three groups, according to the area where they dwelled:

Coastal Dwellers nomadic tribes living of the sea, trading in fish and kelp with the tribes dwelling in the heartland.

Lafunches were those dwelling in the Central Valley. They were semi-sedentary tribes engaged in incipient agriculture and livestock farming, and grouped into family clans, without forming towns or villages. Their dwelling, called ruca (hut), lasted about six years, after which time it would be moved to a neighboring location where the land was not yet degraded.

Pehuenches were nomadic tribes of hunters and gatherers living on the eastern and western Andean foothills. They went to the highlands in summer to collect pehuén, the cones of the araucaria (a valuable conifer which looks like an umbrella when adult, native to Chile and Argentina and granted protection in Chile under a Natural Monument status; it is known in English as monkey puzzle). Pehuén was a major item in their diet as well as a trading item, together with animal skins, in the barter taking place with the Central Valley tribes and with other tribes living in the pampas beyond the Andes. With the introduction of horses by the Spaniards, the Pehuenches acquired great mobility, roaming deep into Argentine territory.

The official charts of the times labelled **Costinos** (Coastal Dwellers) those Mapuches living on the western side of the Nahuelbuta range; **Abajinos** (Lowland Dwellers) those living east of the Nahuelbuta, in the area now containing Angol, Traiguén, and Lumaco; and **Arribanos** (Highland Dwellers) those living from the present–day Pan–American highway toward the Andes. This last group was the Pehuenches, the most belligerent – and most feared.

THE FRONTIER ZONE Concepción was the first outpost established in the South, in 1550. Less than a decade later, a further seven cities had been founded farther south, attracting a large portion of the conquerors, as native labor was here abundant and the climate suitable for farming.

The Colonial Period with the rout of the Spaniards at Curalaba (1599) and the subsequent wholesale Mapuche uprising, the new colonial frontier had to be rolled back as far north as the Biobío and all the settlements farther south relinquished. Concepción then became the head frontier town and seat of a so–called Permanent Army –unique in America– which was to defend this fragile outpost for the next two hundred years. There were actually two borders to defend: the river and the Andes. Through the latter the Pehuenches used to raid into Spanish country and harass the frontier outposts. Over those two long centuries, both military and missionary parties attempted uncounted times to move into Mapuche territory, setting up forts and missions which, inevitably, were very short-lived.

Not less than 35 attempts were made to establish forts and villages on the southern bank of the Biobío; 17 on the Arauco coast; 8 inland from Angol and Purén; 10 east of Concepción and 8 in the Andean foothill area. Furthermore, during that period of incessant war 18 parleys were conducted with the Mapuches. They led to some trade between the warring parties, but not to peace.

At the end of the colonial period, the outposts of Arauco on the coast, and Nacimiento, Santa Juana and Santa Bárbara, on the southern bank of the Biobío, had become safely established, as were Chillán and Los Angeles nearer the Andes, and the villages of Yumbel, Rere and Coelemu in the vicinity of Concepción.

The Republic during the first fifty years of independence (ie, until ca. 1860), the frontier remained stationary at the Biobío. By 1843, however, Chile had taken possession of the Strait of Magellan, in 1850 the first German settlers arrived in the Valdivia area, and in 1853 Puerto Montt had been founded. Thus the Mapuche territory became an island within a country which was gradually starting to take shape.

A curious event triggered the demise of this island. In 1860–61, an eccentric Frenchman talked the Mapuches (on the Chilean and Argentinian side of the border) into proclaiming him their king, promising them to champion their rights and help them to establish their own country. With the title of Orelie Antoine I, Emperor of Araucanía and Patagonia, he handed the Chilean government a declaration of independence for his kingdom. The Chileans were not exactly thrilled; they promptly arrested him and decided to occupy the territory militarily. Orelie Antoine I eventually left for France, living thenceforth as Emperor in Exile, hanging a coat of arms above the door of his mansion outside Paris, having suitable stationary printed, and rubbing elbows with the European high and mighty. His grandson still carries the title and paid a visit to his «territories» in the Araucanía a couple of years ago. He was much better received by the amused Chileans than his forefather –particularly by the press, which had a field day.

The occupation of Araucanía started when colonel Cornelio Saavedra pushed the border south to the Malleco river in 1862, setting up eight forts, four km apart from each other, between Angol and Collipulli. The campaign was suspended for five

9

435

years and renewed in 1867, with the occupation of the Arauco coast and the establishment of a string of fortified outposts on the eastern slopes of the Nahuelbuta range, pushing the border now to the Toltén river (see Land & History Zone 10).

One last portion remained, which was tackled a decade later. In 1881, colonel Leopoldo Urrutia thrust out from Angol, which had already been connected by railroad to Santiago, into the central portion of Mapuche territory. He set up forts at Ercilla, Victoria, Lautaro and founded Temuco, to continue in the following summer all the way to Villarrica, pacifying the Araucanía definitely.

THE FORTS the tours suggested will offer you the chance of visiting several of the forts –or what remains of them– built during the colonial period and during the Araucanía pacification campaign. These fortified outposts are classified as follows.

Castle with a perimeter wall made of stone or brick masonry and surrounded by a dry moat or a natural cliff, it was a permanent defensive post set up at highly strategic locations.

Fort the perimeter wall was made of logs set vertically on the ground, tied with leather straps or lianas, and surrounded on the outside by a dry moat. Against the inner side of the wall earthen ramps or terraces were built to allow defenders to peer over the wall. These forts were erected swiftly to secure bridgeheads, and were also used during the pacification campaign. Only the moats and earthen ramps survive.

Stronghold this concept was developed in the 18th century. Strongholds had the purpose of defending a settlement or village established around it. In case of danger, the village dwellers took shelter within the fort. A unique case in the Americas is the castle and stronghold of Nacimiento, with the civilian population distributed among three streets which converged at the castle, the whole complex being protected by a surrounding wall.

When visiting the forts or the cities originating around the strongholds, one cannot help but be amazed at their smallness and isolation within a vast hostile territory. Their objectives were to be a visible symbol of sovereignty, to gather and forward news, and to protect trade. But they were swiftly evacuated if the situation took a nasty turn; then, they would be promptly razed by the Mapuches. Rarely could they withstand a protracted siege; whenever possible, they would be evacuated through a river or the sea.

The forts were also major trading posts. During the peaceful periods, merchants would settle next to them to trade with the Mapuches, giving them alcohol, silver coins, metals and weapons in exchange for textiles (ponchos, tunics and blankets) to meet urban and rural demand for these articles in the rest of the country. Many attempts were made to stamp out this trade, as it strengthened the Mapuche capacity for war, but the Mapuches were almost the sole suppliers of textiles during the colonial period. The main trading posts were the strongholds of Arauco, Nacimiento and Los Angeles.

THE COLONIZATION the territory covered by the Araucanía exceeded 3.5 million hectares. Once pacified, it was promptly measured and declared fiscal land open for settlement. Half a million hectares were allocated for Mapuche reservations. A further 1.12 million hectares were sold through public tenders between 1881 and 1900, and 60,000 hectares were set aside for foreign settlers brought by the government.

The total number of foreign settlers arrived in the peak period of 1883-1887 was 3,762, from 13 different European countries, mostly Swiss (1,756), German (788), French Basque (283) and Spanish (214). They settled in the area of Los Sauces, Traiguén, Victoria, and Ercilla, and nearly a third of them eventually emigrated to the rest of the country. Those who did remain gave a tremendous farming and industrial boost to the Araucanía, which is plainly visible to this day. The last part of foreign settlers was a group of Italians who settled at the area of Capitán Pastene in the early part of this century.

POLES OF ACTIVITY this zone became a major wheat producer quite early on, as well as the main producer of wine until around 1870 when the wine industry took off in Chile's central valley. Other activities have become predominant since then:

Coal coal mining was started at Lota by Matías Cousiño in 1852 and soon followed by many other industrialists, such as Schwager in Coronel and Maximiliano Errázuriz in Lebu. Coal extraction grew explosively, fed by the demand for coal for steamships, railroads, and, most importantly, for the copper refineries on the coast of La Serena.

Lota was –and still is– Chile's largest coal mine, and was run by four generations of the Cousiño family. They made this into the period's largest energy source and they started the industrialization of the zone, with the first factory producing refractory ceramics for furnace lining. They also started the first afforestation projects in the country, built the first hydroelectric station, a porcelain and glass factory and many other auxiliary industries. Lota was the largest industrial complex in Chile until foreign investment in the large copper mines started pouring in.

Wheat Farming the province of Malleco was dubbed Chile's Granary from 1881 to 1930. With the auctioning of lands in the Araucanía, powerful farmers from the frontier area moved to these lands and undertook a colossal clear-cutting of the native forests, clearing the land for wheat crops which fed a mighty milling industry.

The most outstanding pioneer was José Bunster, who started as a frontier merchant in Nacimiento. In 1862 he moved to the newly established fort at Angol, quickly realizing the great agricultural potential of the recently conquered lands. He bought land, clear–cut the forests, raised wheat crops and built his first mill at Angol. With the pacification of the Araucanía, he extended his holdings to Traiguén, where he acquired 6,000 hectares and produced more than 8,000 tons of wheat in 1886. He built mills at Nueva Imperial, Traiguén, Collipulli and Angol, and he introduced mechanized harvesters and automatic wheat mills. Bunster was a great industrialist and benefactor of the Malleco area, dominating the wheat market until he died in London in 1903.

The indiscriminate clear-cutting of the native forests and the raising of crops on hillsides gave rise, inevitably, to land erosion and degradation, which in turn decreased its productive capability and, eventually, brought about the disappearance of the milling industry. Today, vast reforestation projects with radiata pine are aimed at reclaiming these lands for productive use.

Industrial Boom the Huachipato Steel Mill went on stream in 1950, together with the first stage of the Laja Hydroelectric Complex, triggering an enormous industrial expansion which catapulted Concepción to Chile's second largest industrial center. At present there are fourteen basic industry complexes, plus a much larger number of secondary industries. There is also a new seaport terminal at San Vicente.

AFFORESTATION systematic afforestation trials with exotic species were started in Chile by Compañía Minera Lota in 1881, with the establishment of large man–made plantations in the Arauco province, carrying out trials with eucalyptus, cypress, a kind of Australian myrrh, and radiata pine.

By 1945 the Compañía Manufacturera de Papeles y Cartones, CMPC, had already planted large extensions of radiata pine south of Concepción, at Pinares, to feed its pulp and paper mills. Soon, other companies afforested large tracts from Salto del Laja (the waterfall that can be seen from the Pan–Am) to Mulchén. A Decree Law issued in 1974 subsidizing 75% of the afforestation costs led to a skyrocketing expansion of the area afforested in Chile, with over one million hectares –mostly of radiata pine– among Regions VII, VIII and IX. Over 65% of such plantations are located in this Zone.

This massive afforestation effort has transformed the landscape and brought about the construction of new roads, railways and seaport facilities. There are five large pulp & paper industries: at Arauco, Concepción, two in Nacimiento, and one in Laja. Logging yards and sawmills dot the landscape,

9

Forestry is one of the largest industries in this Zone, and Chile's third largest cash earner, after copper and agribusiness.

Radiata pine (Pinus radiata) arrived by accident from California, where it is known as Monterey pine: its seeds were thought to be Oregon pine seeds. Once planted in Chile, radiata pine amazed everybody with its exceptionally rapid development, by far surpassing that achieved in its native land: it reached maturity as early as 18–20 years. It is now the mainstay of Chile's forest industry, covering close to a million hectares. The other major radiata pine grower, where it has shown the same astounding adaptation, is New Zealand. It is reportedly the world's most planted tree, with extensive plantations in 15 countries.

Radiata pine's annual growth depends on the amount of days, during its vegetative growth period, with a certain air and soil temperature and humidity. This Zone –particularly the Arauco area– seems to offer ideal conditions, with radiata pine achieving here record-setting growth rates.

Laja waterfall

AFFORESTATION it is a drastic, some say even brutal, process in which the plot to be afforested is first clear-cut, burning the slash and whatever undergrowth remains. Then, radiata pine seedlings fresh from the nursery are planted in orderly rows. From then on, the tree stand will be subject to several management measures, such as pruning, thinning, opening of fire-breaks and logging roads, until the trees reach maturity (10–15 years for woodpulp, 18–25 years for sawnwood). Logging is performed on the entire even-aged stand.

The land is then used for raising wheat crops: wheat seeds are cast among the remaining stumps and roots, and harvesting is performed with a sickle. After about three seasons, the land is too degraded for wheat crops, and reforestation is then carried out.

Contrary to early beliefs, it has been found that native trees growing in the vicinity of radiata pine plantations tend to regenerate on the clear-cut radiata pine stands.

POPULATION AND DEVELOPMENT this Zone has over 2 million inhabitants, accounting for about 17.7% of the country's total population and making up Chile's second most populous area. Discounting the population of the Metropolitan Region (Santiago), the people who resides in this zone expresses the 30% of the inhabitants of the remaining regions of the country.

The main cities are Concepción, Talcahuano, Chillán, Los Angeles and Angol, with a combined population exceeding 700,000. The cities of Lota, Coronel, Penco and Tomé contribute with a further 170,000. There are 12 other cities with more than 10.000 inhabitants each

The former statistical calculations show a high concentration of population produced by the vigorous industrial and agricultural development. Here is the second industrial pole and the first forest resource of the country with 65% of the total production of pine forest in addition to 5 celulose factories and 2 ports for lumber industry.

This zone is the greatest producer of coal in the country with a mass of mines extending from Coronel to Lebu. The main coal mine of the group is Lota.

The electric power is produced by 3 Centrals of the Hidroelectric Power Station Complex of Laja in addition to the Thermoelectric Power Station of Bocamina in Lota generating as a whole 950 MW.

The fishing production has flourished in the last decade attaining an explosive development and transforming deeply the landscape and seaports.

As mentioned above, this Zone is Chile's second most industrialized region, its largest coal producer, with plentiful hydroelectric power, and has the largest forest area. Fishing has also experienced spectacular growth in the past few years.

9

PAN–AMERICAN HIGHWAY

For those wishing to travel straight through to more southerly destinations, we list here the main attractions visible from the Pan-Am.

PAN–AMERICAN HIGHWAY FROM CHILLAN TO TEMUCO
★★★ *a stretch of 277 km, paved and good, with gasoline stations at intervals of about 40 km.*
The scenery now includes, when coming from the north, the first patches of native forests, with a backdrop of perfect cone-shaped, snow-capped volcanoes.

At km 26 from Chillán, the northern access road to Concepción (86 km) branches right. The Pan-Am crosses the Diguillín, Relbún and Itata rivers, to reach the south access to Concepción at km 59, used by heavy trucks (85 km). The Pan-Am now runs among large radiata pine plantations. The ground is a grayish sand, similar to that found at beaches. A likely geological explanation for this rather unusual soil is that this once was a sound, similar to the Reloncaví sound located farther south, receiving the sands borne by the Biobío and Laja rivers over millennia. At km 80 is the

LAJA WATERFALL with a splendid view from the highway bridge. The waters of the Laja river plunge mightily into a rocky canyon. Access to the waterfall is along the northern bank, walking through a campground, and through the **Salto del Laja Hotel and Restaurant,** with its swimming pool and park, on the southern bank.

The eyesore here is the invasion of commerce around the bridge, marring what could be a beautiful, relaxed contemplation of nature.

The area offers accommodations in hotels and campsites, taking advantage of its location halfway between Santiago and Puerto Montt (see Services & Prices).

The highway continues among pine forests and sawmills, to reach at km 103 the northern access and at km 107 the main access to

LOS ANGELES (see description under Section A). It is a good jumping-off point for excursions into the mountains and the Central Valley. There is a good restaurant and motel on the Pan-Am opposite the main access to the town.

At km 123 is the village of San Carlos. Enter the village turning left and advance one block, then turn right and advance two blocks to the south, to visit the

San Carlos de Purén Fort founded by Governor Gabriel Cano in 1723 on the northern bank of the Biobío river basin, overlooking the area where now the road bridges are located. Reconstructed in 1970, it is in a poor state of conservation.

Back on the Pan-Am, the road starts to descend into the Biobío, crossing it over two consecutive bridges, beyond which the road ascends again to the central plain. There is a **panoramic view** to the southwest, with the **Nahuelbuta range** presiding above the lowlands where **Angol** is located.

Chillán, square and Cathedral

At km 130 the road descends into the Bureo river basin and reaches the access road to Mulchén. There are two huge sawdust mounds from sawmills operating here since two decades ago.

For the next 35 km, the road is flanked by rows of trees, first aromatic myrrh (aromo) and then ra-diata pine plantations, with vast logging yards. The road crosses three deep gorges, through which flow the Renaico, Mininco and Malleco rivers.

There is a campsite and a small beach close to the bridge over the **Renaico river** (km 149). The road climbs a pine–clad slope to descend beyond it into the **Mininco river** basin, at km 152, with a gigantic log-yard. Beyond the bridge the road climbs another forested slope, to run through a plain towards the **Malleco river**, at km 165. There is a road junction for Collipulli, a ceramics shop, service stations and a restaurant. The deep gorge of the Malleco river is spanned by the

MALLECO VIADUCTS a couple of impressive bridges. The best look-out is at the southern end of the road bridge.

The Railroad Bridge inaugurated on October 26, 1890 by President JM Balmaceda, is the most striking sample of steel engineering structure in Chile, with 407.5 m in length and 97.6 m high. Supported by five tall towers, it was designed by Victoriano Aurelio Lastarria and prefabricated by Schneider et Cie, at Creusot, France, and shipped to the site packed in crates. Assembly took three years, in an incredible system which used no scaffolding. The main girder was assembled on firm ground and then slid over the tower heads balanced by counterweights. There was only one fatal accident, in which a worker slipped and fell into one of the cylinders capping the towers. The diagonal reinforcements between towers and girders were added later to provide better support for the weight of modern locomotives.

The Road Bridge was built between 1968 and 1973 out of concrete and steel, and has a length of 310 m and a height of 85 m. Thin concrete pillars support a large reinforced concrete girder which rests upon a metal mesh. One of the metal tighteners snapped in 1976 –now repaired– leaving a visible drop on the road bed. Walk along this road bridge nearby the railway. It is an unforgettable spectacle.

The Pan–American highway becomes now somewhat more interesting, with some stands of southern forests crowning hillocks surrounded by well–farmed fields. Native oak trees rise lonely in the fields, while the volcanoes are now closer to the road. The **Sierra Velluda** («Hairy Range») is opposite Los Angeles, its peaks seeming to be separated by hairs. Farther south is the perfect cone of the **Lonquimay volcano**, followed by the **Llaima**. The Lonquimay began erupting through a new crater –christened Navidad– on Christmas day 1988, laying waste to the surrounding area. The eruption, while not violent, lasted nearly two years and thrilled legions of tourists with its nightly fireworks.

At km 206 is the junction with the Victoria and Traiguén road. Here ends this Zone. There is a restaurant and a hotel at this junction. The scenery now will be dominated by native forests, the highway running through rolling fields to pass the junction for Lautaro at km 247 and reach, at km 277,

TEMUCO Chile's newest large city, described under Zone 10. The Pan–American highway runs through the city, thereby offering you a good chance to stop for a meal or some sightseeing.

Where To Eat best is the Casino Familiar of the Colonia Dignidad (of German stock), with very good cuisine, fast service and a nice setting. To arrive there, follow the road from Bulnes to Concepción out of the Pan–Am for 10 km; then, follow the sign pointing left, through a short gravel stretch (good). The Hotel Salto del Laja also offers good food and a nice view to the waterfall. Simpler, faster meals at the service station on the central access to Los Angeles. At Victoria, the Hostería El Bosque on the Pan–Am junction is good. For Temuco, see Zone 10.

Accommodations best is Hotel Salto del Laja, with cabins. Motel Montserrat on the central access to Los Angeles, and Hostería El Bosque, with cabins, on the junction with the access to Victoria, are also good. At Colonia Dignidad's Casino Familiar there is a campsite on the river bank. Further campgrounds at the Laja waterfall, Huaqui river, and Mininco river.

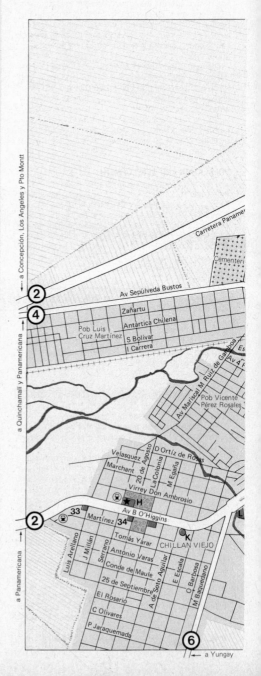

9

SECTION A   CHILLAN AND LOS ANGELES

This Section covers the Central Plain and the Andes mountains from the Ñuble river and the city of Chillán in the north, to Los Angeles and the Biobío river in the south, an area falling entirely within Region VIII, Biobío. During the colonial period, this was frontier country, under permanent threat of Mapuche attacks from several fronts: from the south came the fierce «lowland dwellers», and from the east the bellicose Pehuenche nomads, who staged raids through the natural passes at the upper Ñuble river and lake Laja.

The main urban centers are Chillán and Los Angeles, both evolved from strongholds located on the route followed by these natural passes.

CHILLAN (pop 120,000) is the capital of the Ñuble province, nestled on a vast, fruitful plain from where the Coastal Range cannot be seen. The Andean peaks also seem very distant. It is a major agroindustrial center and service town, with a number of good hotels and restaurants and very active commerce. It has a regular layout, with wide streets shaded by large trees. Adjacent to it, on

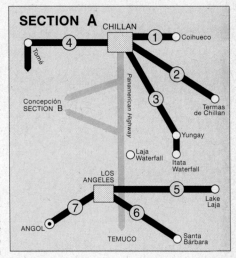

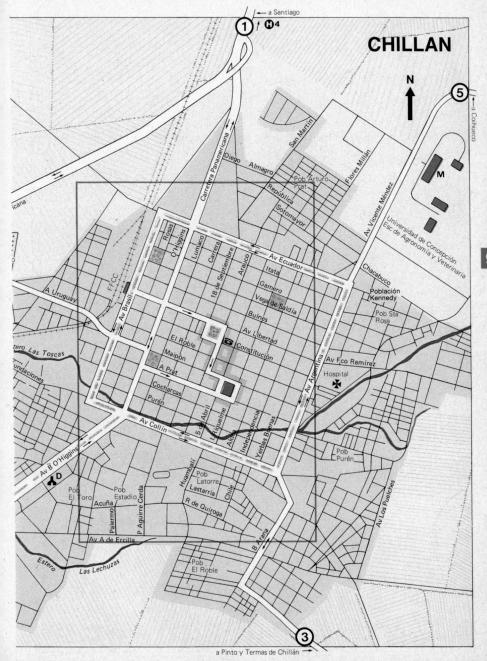

☎ Telephone Center
◉ Café, Meeting Point
★ Touristic Information
Ⓐ Gasoline Station
✳ ✚ Hospital
P Town Hall (2B)
A Bus Terminal (3B)
B Rural Bus Terminal (2A)
R Railway Station (2A)
C Cathedral Church (3B)
✳ **D** San Juan de Dios Chapel (NM)

PLACES OF INTEREST

E Chillán Market (3C)
F Mural by Siqueiros (Escuela México) (2B)
G Handicrafts Shop (Taller de Tejidos) (3B)
✳ **H** O'Higgins Park Handicrafts Gallery
N Franciscano Museum (2C)
J Arturo Prat Museum (4B)

✳ **K** Basketry
✳ **L** Ficher Tannery
✳ **M** U. de Concepción Park
S Chillán Open-Air Market (4B)

ACCOMMODATIONS

1 H Isabel Riquelme (3B)
2 H Rucamanqui (3B)
3 H Cordillera (3B)
✳ **4** Hs Las Encinas
5 H Quinchamalí (3B)
6 H La Floresta (2B)
7 H Martín de Gamboa (2B)
8 H Claris (2B)
9 H Libertador (2A)
10 H Real (2B)
11 H Americano (3B)
12 H Santiago (2B)
13 H Los Cardenales (2A)
14 H Regional (2B)

RESTAURANTS

1 H Isabel Riquelme (3B)
30 Centero Arabe (2C)
31 El Valdiviano (2B)
32 Jai Chang (Chinese Food) (2B)
✳ **33** La Tranquera (Peña)
✳ **34** Los Adobes
35 Quick Lunch (3B)
36 Ñuble Club (2B)
37 Taipe (Chinese food) (2B)
E Market Food Stalls (3C)

TOURIST SERVICES

20 Hertz (2B)
21 Hispano Tur (3C)
22 Turisclass (3B)
23 Automovil Club Rent a Car (3A)
24 Centrotur (3B)
✳ See location in general map of Chillán

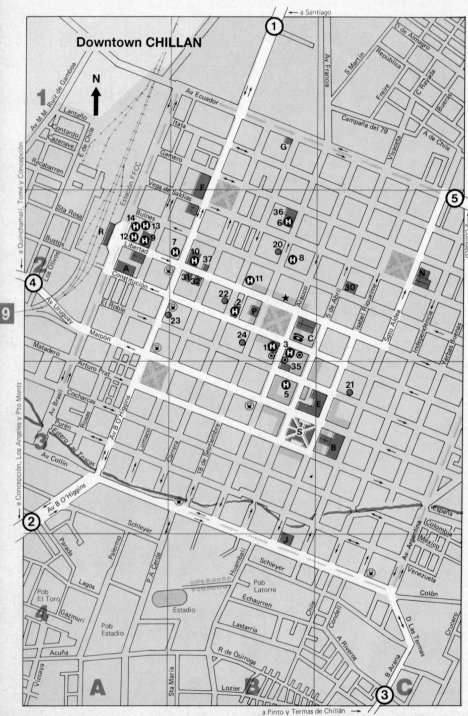

Downtown CHILLAN

the southern side, is Chillán Viejo, the original town. It has changed location and been more than once levelled by earthquakes and other calamities. In 1565, Rodrigo de Quiroga established the fort of San Ildefonso, as a defense against Mapuche raids from the Andes. In 1580, Martín Ruiz de Gamboa founded the village of San Bartolomé de Chillán on the river bank. It was attacked, razed and re-built on several occasions until 1751, when Ortiz de Rozas ordered its reconstruction at the site of present-day Chillán Viejo. An earthquake in 1835 forced President Joaquín Prieto to found the present Chillán and ordered the inhabitants of the old town to move. Not everyone complied. The poorer citizens remained at Chillán Viejo, and both towns grew simultaneously.

Another violent earthquake shook the cities in 1939, killing 15,000 and levelling 90% of the buildings. It was rebuilt using earthquake–proof techniques, which proved their worth when a new earthquake rocked the place in 1960. There are very few buildings that are more than 50 years old.

What To See (see maps) start at the main square, the **Plaza de Armas**, with shady trees. On one side is the **Cathedral**, with nine parabolic arches and the inside bathed in soft, indirect light. It was built between 1941 and 1961. Next to it is a 35 m high cross as a memorial to those killed by the earthquake. We recommend to take a walk along Arauco and Isabel Riquelme streets full of active commerce to arrive to

FERIA DE CHILLAN supplies the farms around the city and is Chile's most well-stocked handicrafts market, with ceramics, textiles, basketry, wood carvings, straw hats, horse riding gear, spurs and the like. Its orderly alleys, lined with small stands overflowing with merchandise, make an interesting, colorful walk. Most handicrafts have a useful purpose, and are bought by the local peasants. The Féria is well worth a visit.

Take the car and drive along Sargento Aldea street up to

Museo Franciscano (open during parish hours, except Sundays) is a convent from 1835, with a cloister and a church from 1906. It used to be located at Chillán Viejo. It contains an interesting collection of sacred and historical objects, mostly from the San Alfonso Convent and School, founded here in 1585 to preach the Gospel among Mapuches. It was the headquarters of the Franciscan missions operating farther south and here the sons of illustrious chieftains were educated. It ran 15 mission churches from the Bueno river to Chillán, and from here the Franciscan convent at Angol was founded in 1862, the first in the recently reconquered Araucanía. The church's dome offers the best panoramic view of the city and the surrounding countryside.

Continue by car up to Av Ecuador and to the right to Av Vicente Méndez where is the **park of the Agronomy School**, shaded by conifers and maple trees not found in Central Chile. On Av Bernardo O'Higgins (between Gamero and Vega de Saldías) is Escuela México, with the

Mural Paintings by Siqueiros and Guerrero on the library and corridor walls (open during school hours). The school was donated by the Mexican people after the 1939 earthquake. The murals were painted between 1941 and 1942 by the world–renowned muralists David Alfaro Siqueiros and Xavier Guerrero, and depict allegories of Chilean and Mexican history.

Follow Av O'Higgins to **Chillán Viejo**. Beyond the bridge, the avenue widens out and is shaded by four rows of evergreen oaks; to the left is the **San Juan de Dios Chapel**, now a National Monument, built of mud–brick and poorly preserved. It dates from 1791 and was part of a large hospital now disappeared. Ahead is the

Bernardo O'Higgins Park (Apr–Nov, Mon–Fri 09:00–13:00 h and 15:00–19:00 h; Dec–Mar, Mon–Fri 09:00–13:00 h and 14:30–19:30 h, Sat 09:00–13:00

h). Two wooded hectares behind a large esplanade and a 60–m–long stone mural depicting the life and deeds of Chile's founding father. It is erected on the site where O'Higgins was born on August 20, 1778. It contains a Cultural Historical Center and the park where his native house was located; the stone pavement from that time has been preserved.

Where To Eat best cuisine and fine service at Hotel Isabel Riquelme, and at Hotel Las Encinas, with a good swimming pool, three km north of town on the Pan–Am. Restaurants La Tranquera and Los Adobes, in Chillán Viejo, offer good traditional dishes (ask for the price list before ordering!). Cheaper dishes at the market place food stalls and shellfish shops (with children), with typical dishes such as corn pie (pastel de choclo). Fast food at the get–together sites shown in map.

TOURS FROM CHILLAN

1 TO COIHUECO AND DAM ★★

a round trip of 62 km, paved and with, only 8 km graveled. Take food.
A visit to a wood–carving center and a dam suitable for swimming.

Follow the road shown in Chillán map, heading east through farmland. At km 27 is

Coihueco a quaint village renowned for its carved-wood handicrafts, including tables, lamp stands and decorative figures. You can see the artisans at work. There is a crafts shop on the access street. Four km ahead, on a gravel road, is the

Coihueco Dam nestled in a wooded mountain setting. Windsurfing, water ski and sailing are the main watersports. It is a good spot for bathing and a picnic.

2 TO TERMAS DE CHILLAN ★★★

eighty km from Chillán, 52 km paved and the rest gravel, good but at the end steep. Allow one day for this, gasoline and meat for a barbecue at Pinto, restaurants on the road, as well as a very good spot for a picnic.
A beautiful excursion into the mountains, through splendid native forests, gorges and a river, to end up at an excellent hotel and ski resort.

Leave Chillán (km 0) following the road shown in map, which runs through wheat fields and along the Chillán river. At km 20 and again at km 23 there are good campgrounds on the river bank, shaded by willow trees and poplars. At km 25 is the village of Pinto, on the Andean foothills, renowned for its butcher shops offering excellent meat for grilling or barbecue.

At km 30 the road starts to ascend and soon the massive **Chillán peaks** loom ahead. The Chillán river tumbles noisily on the side and the land is increasingly covered by beautiful native forests. At km 45 a road branches right to Diguillín, a popular spot for picnicking and bathing on the Chillán river.

At km 53 is **Recinto**, a small village nestled at the foot of a slope, with a hotel, a restaurant and many weekend and summer houses. The road climbs flanked by native forests, and at km 56 passes the **Los Lleuques** resort, by the Renegado river amidst the lush vegetation and in a scenic mountain setting. Pavement gives way to gravel, and the road becomes somewhat narrower and winding -and steeper. The scenery now includes rocky hills, with steep cliffs crowned by old–growth native forests. At km 63 is an area with weekend plots next to the river, called here **Piedras Comadre**, the name of a spectacular rock face rising to the right of the road. At km 66, park and walk a short distance to the

Pincheira Cave an enormous natural cave in the cliff where a royalist guerrilla group headed by the Pincheira brothers used to hide; they ransacked Chillán in 1819.

For the next 10 km, the road runs amidst beautiful mountain scenery with splendid old–growth native forests and some spots suitable for a picnic. At km 73 is **Las Trancas**, an esplanade with ferns

9

and copihues, Chile's national flower. Here is a police checkpoint and a restaurant (Parador Jamón, Pan y Vino), offering accommodation in cabins, snow–chain hire for the climb in winter, and interesting horse riding expeditions into the mountains.

The road climbs on wide curves; stop at km 78 to visit the scenic Los Pangues cave, signposted. At km 80 the forest ends and you are at

TERMAS DE CHILLAN (1,800 m altitude), lying on the slopes of the Chillán volcano. Its main attractions are its thermal baths and fine ski slopes in a beautiful setting. The modern Hotel Pirigallo has three outdoor thermal pools, with different types of mineral water. In the winter season, it offers ski rental and ski instructors. It has several lifts, including South America's longest chair lift, with 2,500 m.

A campground is open in summer in a forest next to the hotel, the main attraction being hiking excursions to the areas with fumarolic activity and mud baths, and to ride in the chairlift to enjoy the scenery. Interesting horseback excursions are organized from here to the volcano and farther into the deep mountain valleys, the most striking being the hike to the **Aguas Calientes valley** (three days by horse), exploring little–known areas. Tents and other camping gear, and guides, are provided by the hotel.

3 TO YUNGAY AND THE ITATA WATERFAL ★★★

a 182–km round trip from Chillán, with 50 km paved but in poor condition, and the rest graveled. Allow one day, take food. Gasoline at Pemuco and Yungay.
An excursion through farmland to the Itata waterfall. You can continue from there to Los Angeles, visiting lake Laja on the way (see Tour 6).

Follow the road shown on Chillán map. Old mud–brick houses merge the city with the countryside, which has wheat fields, rows of poplars and small, old villages. At km 35, on the right, is an interesting example of countryside architecture: long stables supported by pillars with an enormous clay–tiled roof under which fodder is stored. A long bridge spans the Diguillín river and at km 38 is the Molinera Ñuble agroindustrial plant. On its side is the Santa Patricia forest and plant nursery.

The ground becomes more rolling, with the Andes in the background, to reach at km 44 a willow–lined river and the village of **Pemuco**, with mud-brick houses roofed with heavy clay tiles and tree–shaded streets. At km 69, after crossing wheat fields and several streams, is

Yungay with a square shaded by old mañíos, a beautiful native tree, and quaint streets. There is an hostería with accommodations, restaurant, campsite, gasoline and a telephone. Following Tacna street 500 m north from the square is the El Alamo campground. Leave the village following Esmeralda street to the west (not the road to Cholguán).

At km 73 the road starts to cross a vast plateau covered by radiata pine plantations, property of Industrias Cholguán. At km 79 is the bridge over the **Itata river**; continue straight ahead. At km 87, signposted, is a 1.6–km detour to the right to the **Saltillo del Itata**, a small waterfall (1.5 m) with a pool suitable for swimming in a scenic setting and nestled amidst willows and poplars. There is a campground and a picnic site. Retake the original road, to reach in 2.5 km a forking with a sign reading «Peso máx. 10 ton». Take the right–hand branch, which winds its way for 4 km through private lands to reach, at km 91, the

ITATA WATERFALL a splendid 75–m plunge, the water arching out of the lip to crash noisily into a deep canyon below. It is worth a visit.

If you wish to continue the excursion, go back to Yungay and drive on to Cholguán, Huepil, Tucapel and Canteras (39 km on a gravel road), to continue to lake Laja (see Tour 6).

4 TO TOME AND CONCEPCION ★★★

93 km to Tomé, 56 of which are paved and 37 gravel. To Concepción, 119 km, only 7 km more than via Bulnes or Florida. Gasoline at Tomé.
A different, attractive way to come to Concepción, stopping to see the famous Quinchamalí ceramics craftsmen, coastal villages and a nice stretch of coast with busy seaside resorts.

Leave Chillán on the road shown in map, which runs on a flat plain, heading for the distant Coastal Range. At km 31, follow the narrow road to the left for 200 m to visit

Quinchamalí a village sprawling on a long street parallel to the road, with craftsmen specializing in black ceramics; there are many shops selling their creations. You can see the craftsmen at work, modelling their figures without a turntable and baking them in homemade furnaces, fired with cow dung. They also produce other types of handicrafts, such as baskets, textiles, guitars and paintings. It is worth a detour.

At km 33 the pavement ends and **The Nueva Aldea Ferry** brings you across the Itata river (08:00–13:00 h and 14:00–18:00 h). Outside of this period, tip the ferry operator living on this side of the river. The alternative is to drive along the road through Confluencia to Ñipas. Across the river are the first foothills of the Coastal range. At km 44 we suggest a 2–km detour to the right to

Ñipas (pop 1,400), seat of Town Hall Ranquil. A picturesque and neat village overlooking the beautiful and placid Itata river, surrounded of willows. There is a road bridge with the best view of the town. The Chilean sculptor Virginio Arias was born in 1855 in this place.

Get back to this road (km 48), continuing through rolling fields and newly afforested land. The pine forests are slowly replacing the vineyards which made these lands famous since colonial days. The vines creep over the ground and at times spread alongside the road like bramble. They are from a sweet but thick–skinned strain brought by the Spaniards.

At km 53 is **San Ignacio**, a one–street village smack in the middle of vineyard country, with houses surrounded by verandas and, of course, vines.

Vineyards continue until km 55, where a short, 3–km climb flanked by native forest starts. The rolling plateau which follows is covered by pine plantations.

At km 71 the «Colonial Route» meets this road from the right, coming from Talca, Cauquenes and Coelemu. A short way ahead is a narrow bridge from 1923 and an old hacienda with **house of Urrejola**, a large courtyard with a huge oak surrounded by houses lined with roofed verandas. The horse stables are across the road.

Then comes the village of **Rafael**, in a sea of radiata pine plantations and sawmills.

The road continues through wooded hills to reach Tomé at km 95. This road saw its heyday between 1850 and 1920, when carts hauled wheat from the Chillán area to the mills and shipping port at Tomé. Description of Tomé and the stretch of coast to Concepción under Section B.

TOURS FROM LOS ANGELES

LOS ANGELES (pop 72,000) is the busy capital of the Biobío province, lying in the middle of what during the colonial days was known as Laja Island, surrounded by the swift Biobío and Laja rivers. It is the city with Chile's fastest population growth in the past decade, spurred by its powerful agroindustries, the increase in the afforested areas and the woodpulp plants within its jurisdiction.

It was founded as a fort under the name of Santa María de los Angeles by Manso de Velasco in 1739, and was granted village status in 1748. Destroyed and reconstructed several times, it was the summer quarters of the Frontier Army during the colonial period, moved from Concepción to defend the border on the Biobío. In 1860, Orelie

Antoine I, the self–proclaimed emperor of the Araucanía, was arrested south of here and brought to the jail on the square. Two years later, colonel Cornelio Saavedra set out from here to found the forts on the new frontier along the Malleco river.

What To See follow the central access from the Pan-American highway (good motel at the road junction), leading directly to the **plaza**. The **Museo Histórico** is on the square (09:00–13:00 h & 15:00–19:00 h), devoted to Bernardo O'Higgins. There is a busy feria –open air market– and the **Iglesia del Perpetuo Socorro**, on **calle Colón**. The church has three naves and a colonial cloister, with patio of the Carmelites. Turn back along Valdivia street up to the pretty **Av Ricardo Vicuña**.

Go through it and continue along Valdivia street up to Lynch street where lies the **Iglesia Padres Alemanes**. At last, turn back to the square and go along Lautaro street to the left up to the **park**. with a shady pond, good for a pause.

Where To Eat good cuisine at Centro Español, and upstairs at Los Primos; downstairs for quicker meals. Chilean–style barbecues (parrilladas) and other traditional dishes at Rancho de Julio, El Arriero, and, on the Pan–American highway, Javiera Carrera. The cheapest meals are at the restaurants near the bus terminal.

5 TO LAKE LAJA ★★★

ninety km from Los Angeles, with 76 km paved and the rest good gravel. Allow 1¹/2 hours one way. Take food. Accommodations and camping at the lake. Gasoline only at Los Angeles.

An interesting, easy excursion into the volcanic Andes and to an emerald–green lake in a national park.

Take the road heading east from the Pan–American highway (km 0), running straight through a farmed plain. At km 27 is a signposted road junction for

Hacienda Canteras take road to the left for 200 m (do not get confused with a memorial monolith next to a gate one km before) to a great esplanade with a **chestnut tree**. At this site used to be the houses of the hacienda received as land grant by Ambrosio O'Higgins, a member of the Frontier Army. From these lands set out more than 5,000 head of cattle to Osorno in 1792 to re–found that city. The hacienda was inherited by Bernardo O'Higgins, who organized here a battalion of peasants who took part in the liberation of Chile. The chestnut tree was planted by B O'Higgins.

The road climbs gently amid pine plantations. The hills come nearer, the valley becomes narrower and weird rock formations are to be seen here and there: they are **lava tongues** solidified into

☎ Telephone Center
◉ Café, Meeting Point
Ⓖ Gasoline Station
A Capuchinos Church
B Padres Alemanes Church
C Town Hall

D Bus Terminal
E Market
F Los Angeles Historical Museum

TOURIST SERVICES
10 Agencia Interurbana

RESTAURANTS
1 Rancho de Julio
2 El Arriero
3 H Müso
5 H Mazzola
8 Los Primos

ACCOMMODATIONS
3 H Müso
4 H Mariscal Alcázar
5 H Mazzola
6 H Turismo Monserrat
7 H Turismo Mallorca

strange shapes. The scenery becomes more arid, stony and scrubby, but decorated with the first patches of **Andean cypress** (ciprés de la cordillera). At km 59 is **Antuco** (pop 1,600), a picturesque mountain village with a small hostería. It was founded in 1874 to guard the mountain pass. At km 62, on the left and signposted, is the

Fort of Ballenar destroyed, only the platform remains. It was founded in 1788 by Ambrosio O'Higgins on a strategic point to defend the mountain pass.

In the distance, a group of converging pipelines can be seen; they belong to a large hydroelectric station which, in turn, is part of the **Laja Hydroelectric Complex**, made up of El Abanico unit, which taps the river water; El Toro, entirely underground and with the water intake at the bottom of the lake, and Antuco, also underground, which receives the waters from El Abanico and El Toro. This complex supplies the powerful industries of Region VIII. No public visits are permitted, but you can drive near the place as described in the return trip.

Pavement ends at km 76, at El Abanico, a service village. The road runs close to the Laja river, with some hydraulic works, native forests and man-made plantations of high-altitude species, to reach at km 84 the entrance to the

| LAGUNA DEL LAJA NATIONAL PARK | covering 11,600 hectares and under Conaf management. It has a campground, picnic areas and an excellent staff of park rangers who also act as guides for excursions. There are also good ski slopes, run under concession by the Los Angeles Ski Club.

There is a superb view from the entrance. A short, narrow valley closed at the far end by a 200–m–high saddle, through which the road runs. That is the volcanic plug which dammed the river and formed the lake. To the left are high hills with the **Los Chilcos waterfall**; to the right, the arid, flattish **Antuco volcano**, the cone of which blew off many millennia ago. The lake drains underground into the beautiful **Ojos del Laja** («Laja Eyes»), a 30–min walk from here.

The road continues 4 km further to climb the moraine plug and reach the

Ski Center with several houses, private shelters, clubs and two Poma lifts with a combined capacity of 800 persons/hour. The Los Angeles Ski Club offers accommodation and a restaurant the year round. A poorly surfaced road branches left to **Puerto Endesa,** with a concrete boat ramp. One km father, on a very bad road, is the Universidad de Concepción ski club, and then

| LAKE LAJA | with emerald–green water and stark, rocky barren shores of volcanic material and lots of peninsulas and headlands. The far shores are covered by Andean cypress. The road is now somewhat better and skirts the lakeshore to Los Barros (10 km), a place with more vegetation. A trail runs level to the pass and the border; the road on the Argentinian side also runs on level ground. This is why the Pehuenches favored this pass. Many fishing fans camp on its shores in summer, when there is no snow and night temperatures do not fall below 10°C.

For those wishing to explore the area further, we suggest driving down from the Park entrance 10 km to the Abanico junction and then continue downward on the paved road 5 km further to another junction (unsigned), whence a gravel road branches right to Pichichén (km 15). You will reach a police control in 5 km. Ask for permission to go to the piscicultura de Polcura, a fish farm; this road is controlled by Endesa, a power company. The road crosses the Laja river; turn left. A paved road to the El Toro power station starts there, but is not open to the public.

The gravel road (very good) continues for 11 km along the northern bank of the river to reach another police control at km 31, where you can see a high–voltage yard and the tunnel outlet from the Polcura underground power station. The Laja river, which had been swallowed upstream by the hy-

droelectric complex, reappears here.

The road continues, now winding, near the high–voltage power lines jumping over the pine–clad mountains.

At km 40 is the village and **fish farm of Polcura**. You may visit the fish farm and buy trout. The road now becomes more curvy and surfaced. At km 50 is **Trupán**, an irrigation dam, with trees and a restaurant. An old railroad branch line passes through here which used to come from the Monte Aguila station in the trunk line running south from Santiago. Then comes the village of Trupán, with streets shaded by acacias. Follow now the signposted road to Huepil. At km 63 is the access to the farming village of **Huepil**, with a gasoline station. For those wishing to visit the Itata Waterfall, 30 km from here, see description under Tour 3.

To continue to Los Angeles, take the road heading south. At km 69 is the small village of **Tucapel**. The Tucapel Nuevo Castle was founded here in 1723 to protect the area against Pehuenche raids. It was granted National Monument status, although nothing remains of it. Continuing to Canteras, at km 71 is a modern bridge spanning the Laja, next to the intakes for the Laja Sur and Laja Norte canals. The road continues straight through pine forests.

At km 86 is the Canteras junction, where O'Higgins' hacienda was located, described at the beginning of this tour. Los Angeles is at km 113.

6 | **TO SANTA BARBARA AND THE UPPER BIOBIO**

★★★ *it is 90 km from Los Angeles to Ralco. Only 16 kilometers are paved. Gasoline at Santa Bárbara. Allow one day. You can camp at the site.*
An excursion into the Upper Biobío, where the swift river is squeezed by a narrow canyon.

Leave Los Angeles following the Pan-American highway heading south until San Carlos, km 16. Take there the gravel road branching left. At km 31 is a junction and then the road runs near the Biobío river, which here runs wide, in a flat valley. At km 41 is

Santa Bárbara (pop 4,600), a village of wood-frame houses, head of Town Hall of the northern riverside. Its origin was a stronghold founded in 1756 by Manso de Velasco, and so christened in honor of María Bárbara de Braganza, Fernando VII's wife. It became an important center but was deserted in 1819, to be repopulated in 1833. A short walk from here, over the bridge across the river, climb the hill at Quilaco up to the irrigation canal for a sweeping view over the district.

For the next 20 km the road runs through a wide valley, away from the river and through wheat farm-land; forested hills rise in the distance. The valley becomes progressively narrow and at km 61 the road starts to wind its way up on rocky cliffs that plunge to the roaring river below. Rafting buffs may pause here to dedicate one minute to their improbable forerunners: in the past, logs from logging operations further up in the mountains used to be bundled together into a kind of raft and sent downstream –with a man steering the raft with a long pole through the rapids.

The road continues to Ralco, crossing some tributaries. In some areas the land opens up a bit to permit access to the river shore for camping or fishing. Ralco is at km 90.

7 | **TO ANGOL VIA RENAICO** ★★

a 64-km paved road from Los Angeles.
An excursion into the heart of the Malleco province.

Follow the road indicated in the Los Angeles map, which crosses the Biobío river at km 27. Beyond the bridge is a round–about with roads leading to Nacimiento and Negrete. Continue straight; after a strange curve you cross the railroad and reach the Coihue railway station, with lots of railroad cars bringing timber from Nacimiento. Here is the

9

House Díaz Garcés the only mansion surviving from the golden years of wheat farming. Wooden, two–storied and 60 m long, it has a windowed gallery on the upper floor and over forty rooms. Two large araucarias, Chilean palms and camellias populate the front yard, while on the side are the remains of a large mill.

At km 40 is a bridge and the access to **Renaico**

(pop 4,500), with an atmosphere straight from the old days of wheat farming. At km 56 is another bridge across the Malleco, the river which acted as border from Angol to Collipulli in 1862. At km 60 is the Huequén round-about; the road to the right leads to Angol, at km 64. City description under Section D.

SECTION B   CONCEPCION

To facilitate description, this sector covers the narrow strip of land between the Coastal Range and the sea, from the Itata river in the north to the Biobío river in the south. This is the heart of Region VIII, with busy seaports, the country's second–largest industrial hub and a sizable financial and services center. Over 600,000 urban inhabitants live in this area, with its midpoint in the so–called Metropolitan Concepción, which includes the cities of Concepción and Talcahuano.

ACCESS ROUTES TO CONCEPCION

There are two «conventional» access routes from the Pan–American highway, and a number of others such as the Colonial Route from the north, through Talca, Cauquenes and Coelemu, described in Zone 8; the route from Chillán via Tomé and Penco (described under Section A); the route from the south via Nacimiento (described under Section D); and the most spectacular one, along the Conquerors' Route described under Section C.

The access routes from the Pan–Am are:

1 North Access via Bulnes, Quillón and Florida, a winding 86–km route through the Coastal Range. It brings you also to an excellent restaurant of the German settlement of Colonia Dignidad (Casino Familiar), 10 km into the road from Bulnes, and then two km to the left (signposted).

2 South Access via Cabrero, with 76 km to Concepción on a modern highway. This route is preferred for heavy truck traffic.We recommend paved detour of 11 km. to Yumbel to know the church and image of San Sebastián, worshipped with great popular religious festival on January the 20th.

CONCEPCION (pop 270,000), a busy, pleasant city, capital of Region VIII. A diagonal avenue connects downtown with its university, of high standing, while a modern highway links it to Talcahuano, Penco and San Pedro, making this into a single large urban center known as Metropolitan Concepción.

It was founded by Pedro de Valdivia at Penco in 1550 (that's why the people from Concepción are called penquistas), and from 1565 to 1573 it was the seat of the Real Audiencia –the main governing body– and Chile's political, military and administrative capital. When the southern cities were relinquished in 1600, the Bishop from La Imperial moved to Concepción, which also became the seat of the Frontier Army and the main bastion during the Arauco war.

A violent earthquake and tidal wave levelled the city at Penco in 1751, and in 1764 a decree ordered its reestablishment at the present location. The new city was laid out by the then land surveyor Ambrosio O'Higgins.

A number of citizens of this region played significant roles in Chile's struggle for independence, such as Bernardo O'Higgins, Juan Martínez de Rozas, Ramón Freire, Joaquín Prieto and Manuel Bulnes. O'Higgins signed Chile's

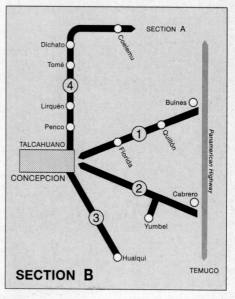

SECTION B

Independence Act at the Los Perales military camp, near Talcahuano, and it was first proclaimed at Concepción's main square, the Plaza de Armas, on January 1, 1818.

Fast–paced industrialization and population growth, together with the effects of earthquakes in 1939 and 1960, have left very few relics of its past.

Where To Eat in Concepción itself, the best cuisine and attention is at Le Chateau. With children, it is best at Millaray with typical Chilean food and international cuisine, on the southern bank right beyond the bridge. The Rincón Campesino has also a zoo, and is located at Nonquén valley, behind the University of Biobío. Quick dishes at the «get–together» sites shown in map. Cheaper meals at the market food stalls. Picnic at **Parque Ecuador**.

Outside of the city and with a view onto the sea, good restaurants at Bentotecas (Sea food restaurants) in Talcahuano, and restaurant Oriente in Penco. There are three good restaurants on the river bank at km 3 of the road to Santa Juana and Nacimiento.

A WALK THROUGH THE TOWN allow at least 2 ½ hrs. Note that the north–south streets have names of personages associated with the formation of the republic, while those running east–west have names of Mapuche chieftains.Park the car nearby to the

Plaza de la Independencia the main square, has large, shady trees and a central fountain made of pink stone with a bronze column representing Ceres, the goddess of agriculture (1865). Chile's independence was proclaimed here. **Pedestrian streets** Barros Arana and Pinto start from the square. We suggest to taste the traditional ice-creams and walk one block off the square westward up to the typical **Market**, colorful and popu-

9

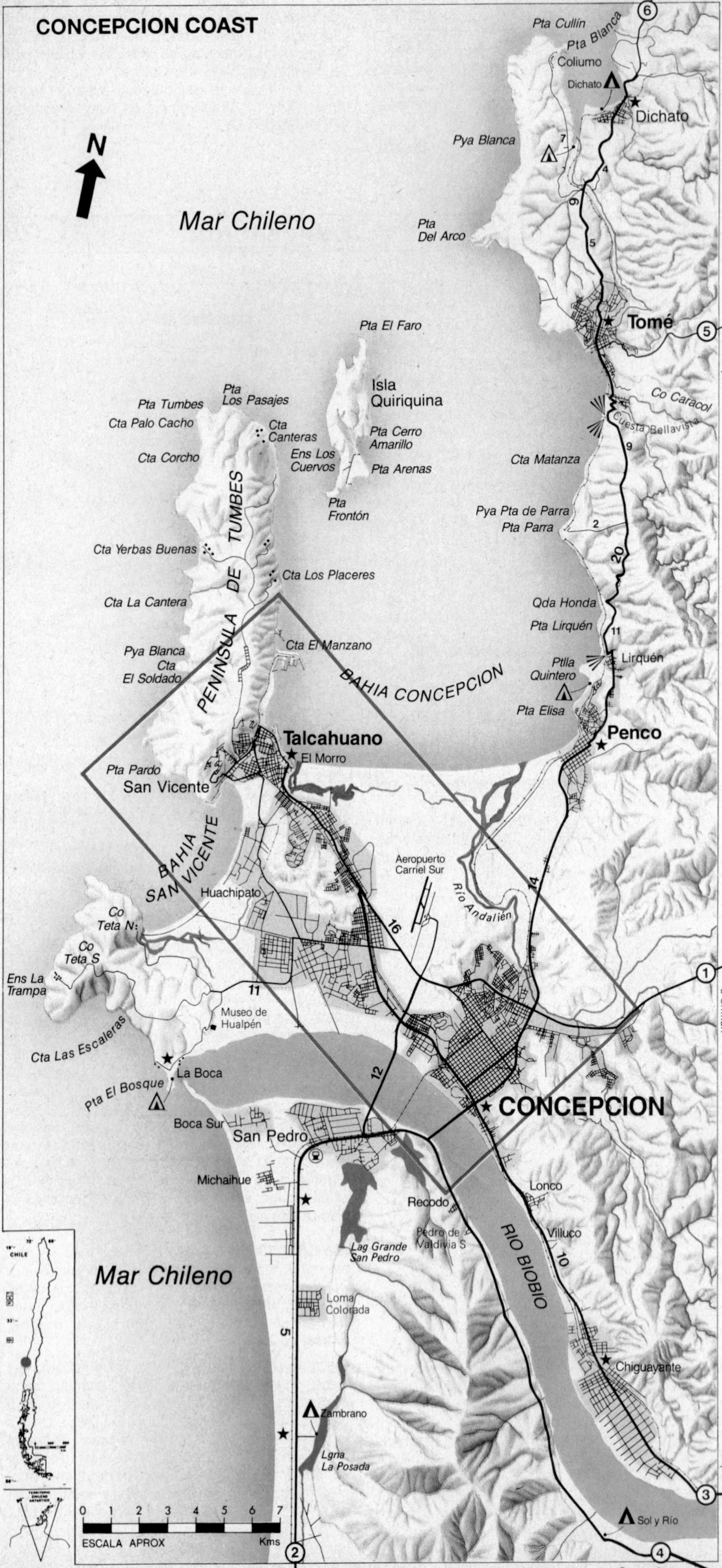

CONCEPCION COAST

N

Mar Chileno

a Coelemu

Pta Cullín

Pta Blanca

Pta Blanca

Coliumo

Dichato

Dichato

Pya Blanca

Pta
Del Arco

Tomé

a Nipas

Pta El Faro

Co Caracol

Isla
Quiriquina

Cuesta Bellavista

Pta Tumbes

Pta
Los Pasajes

Cta Palo Cacho

Cta
Canteras

Pta Cerro
Amarillo

Cta Corcho

Ens Los
Cuervos

Cta Matanza

Pta Arenas

Pya Pta de Parra
Pta Parra

Pta
Frontón

Cta Yerbas Buenas

Qda Honda

Pta Lirquén

Cta Los Placeres

Cta La Cantera

Ptlla
Quintero

Lirquén

Pya Blanca
Cta
El Soldado

Cta El Manzano

Pta Elisa

BAHIA CONCEPCION

Talcahuano

El Morro

Penco

Pta Pardo

San Vicente

**BAHIA
SAN VICENTE**

Huachipato

Aeropuerto
Carriel Sur

Co
Teta N

Co
Teta S

Río Andalién

a Chillán

Ens La
Trampa

Museo de
Hualpén

Cta Las Escaleras

La Boca

CONCEPCION

Pta El Bosque

Boca Sur

San Pedro

Michaihue

Lonco

Recodo

Villuco

Pedro de
Valdivia S

RIO BIOBIO

Mar Chileno

Lag Grande
San Pedro

Loma
Colorada

Chiguayante

a Hualqui

Zambrano

Lgna
La Posada

Sol y Río

CHILE

0 1 2 3 4 5 6 7

ESCALA APROX   Kms

a Coronel y Lota

a Santa Juana

9

lar with handicrafts and food stalls, particularly those specializing in seafood. Take the car and drive along Lincoyán street eastward up to the beautiful **Parque Ecuador**, to visit the

Galería de la Historia (summer: Tue–Fri 09:00–13:00 h and 16:00–20:00 h; Sat, Sun and Holidays 10:00–13:0 0h and 15:00–18:00 h) An entrance fee is charged. Provides a complete insight into the region's history through dioramas, with carved figures in three–dimensional settings. Continue on street Lamas to the north, to Larenas, to visit the

PINACOTECA DE CONCEPCION (Mon–Sun 09:00–19:00 h; closed on holidays). It houses the country's most complete collection of Chilean paintings from all periods, in large rooms and well displayed. At the entrance is a mural –Latin American Presence– by Mexican artist Jorge

Concepción, University Town

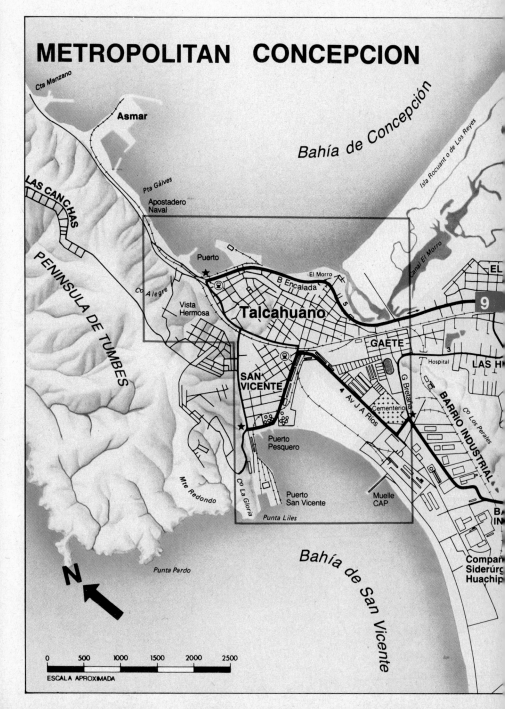

METROPOLITAN CONCEPCION

447

González Camarena.

Two blocks down Chacabuco street is the | UNIVERSIDAD DE CONCEPCION CAMPUS | there is a great **amphitheater** at the entrance, with a **metal sculpture** depicting Enrique Molina Garmendia, the university's founder (1919) and first rector. The buildings are located on the perimeter of the great campus, leaving a large **central esplanade** with perspective to the different buildings preceded by the tall **Clocktower**. Continue by car skirting the perimeter to visit the **Stadium** opposite to the curved building, building of classrooms and afterwards turn back along Larenas street up to Chacabuco.

The Diagonal Aguirre Cerda, starting from the campus entrance, has a lot of student cafes. The **railway station** has a mural by Gregorio de la Fuente depicting the History of Concepción. Across the **Puente Viejo** (Old Bridge) to San Pedro there is a good view of the city.

A TOUR AROUND METROPOLITAN CONCEPCION allow half a day. It is advisable to make this tour before lunch, taking food or lunching in Talcahuano. See maps of Concepción coast, Metropolitan Concepción, and those of the cities of Concepción and Talcahuano.

Follow Av Pedro de Valdivia along the river towards Chiguayante, through pleasant residential areas, old sprawling houses and lots of ox-drawn carts hauling charcoal, firewood or fruit from the country to the city.

From the **square of Chiguayante**, a residential

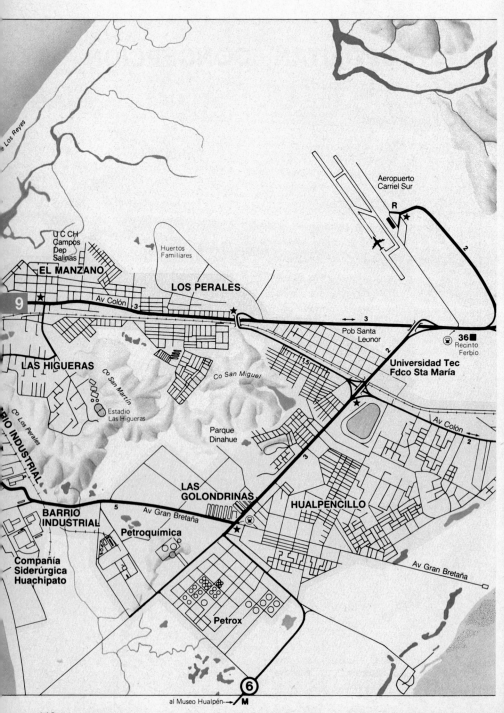

quarter with an old textile industry, return to Concepción to follow streets Víctor Lamas and then Roosevelt to the round–about (see map of Metropolitan Concepción) to take the highway to Talcahuano, which goes through several round–abouts and passes the Ferbio fair grounds to reach

TALCAHUANO (pop 210,000), with two ports, one on Concepción bay and the other at San Vicente, a Navy base, shipyards, a fishing center and a large industrial area, including the Huachipato steel mill, petrochemical industries, an oil refinery and many others.

The sheltered harbor has been used as a port since 1774, and boasted a defensive stronghold at the present Apostadero Naval (the Navy base).

The port started to boom by 1872 with the arrival of the railway, becoming the South's main seaport, and then it picked up momentum when the Huachipato steel mill went on stream in 1950.

Drive into Talcahuano along the coast (see Talcahuano city map) to reach the Paseo **Ventana al Mar**, with the best view of Concepción bay and Quiriquina island. Behind is the strange **La Tortuga** building.

Continue through Blanco Encalada to the harbor to visit the busy **fish market**; to the side, the **Bentotecas** (seafood restaurants), overlooking the harbor and the Yacht Club.

Continue along the coast to **Puerta Los Leones**, the access to the Apostadero Naval (the Navy base) and the Asmar shipyard. Paying an entrance fee you can visit the

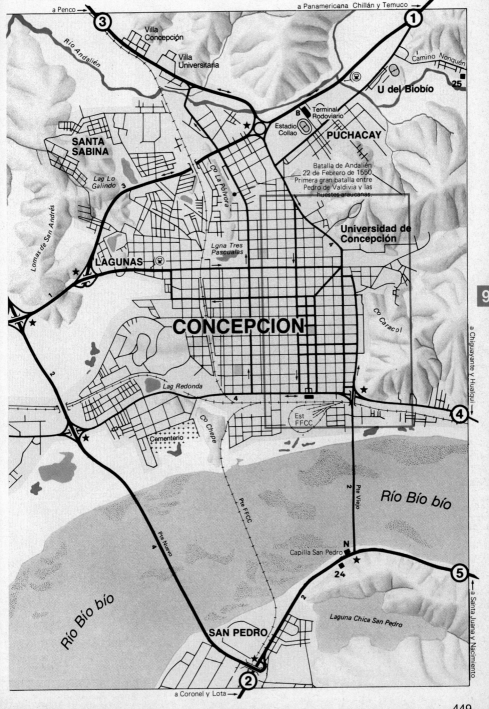

9

449

☎ Telephone Center
★ Touristic Information
◉ Café, Meeting Point
◎ Gasoline Station
⟫ Lookout Point
✠ Hospital (1B)
A Railway Station (4B)
✳ B Bus Terminal
C Regional Government (3B)
D Cathedral Church (3B)
E Town Hall (3B)
F Market (3A)
G Picture Gallery (2B)
H History Museum (3C)

J U de Concepción (2B)
K Palace of Justice (2B)
✳ M Hualpén Museum
✳ N San Pedro Chapel
P Post Office (3B)
✳ R Carriel Sur Airport

ACCOMMODATIONS
1 H Araucano (3A)
2 H Alborada (3A)
3 H Alonso de Ercilla (2B)
4 H El Dorado (3B)
5 H Tabancura (3B)
6 H Ritz (3A)
7 H Cruz Del Sur (2A)

8 Apart Hotel Concepción (4A)
9 H Cecil (4A)
10 Bh de Turismo (3B)
11 Bh San Sebastían (3A)
✳✳ Campsite

RESTAURANTS
1 H Araucano (3A)
20 Club de Concepción (3B)
21 Chateau (2B)
22 Chungua (3B)
23 Parque (3C)
F Market Food Stalls (3A)
✳ 24 Millaray
✳ 25 Rincón Campesino

26 Rest Argentino (3A)

TOURIST SERVICES
6 Ritz (Tourist Agency) (3A)
✳ R Rentautos
30 Automóvil Club (3B)
31 Hertz (2B)
32 Western Car Rental
33 Larma (3B)

DISCOTHEQUES
✳ 21 Recinto Ferbio

✳ See Metropolitan Concepción Map
✳✳ and Concepción Coast Map

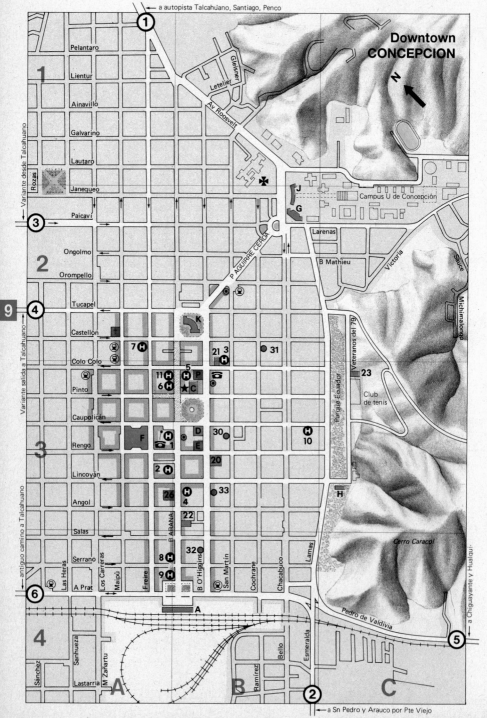

IRONCLAD HUASCAR (Tue–Sun 09:30–12:00 h & 14:00–17:00 h in winter; in summer until 18:00 h). It is the world's second oldest ironclad afloat (a scant four years younger than the Warrior, at Portsmouth, whose first commander was Lord Cochrane's son) and a relic from the Iquique sea battle (see Land & History, Zone 1). Very well preserved, you can visit the cabins, engine room, the magazine and the formidable prow gun. The life and deeds of the ship are related through loudspeakers during the visit.

The Ironclad Huascar is sounded in front of Plaza Prat and of a nice building (1903) called **Vaticano,** the seat of the Command of Naval Station. The access to the ironclad is by raft.

Continue the tour along **Colón street** the commercial core of the city and reach the square with a beautiful **church** and municipal buildings. Up the steep San Martín street, following Castellón to the end to finally turn right at Martínez de Rozas, you reach the Mirador, a look-out point with a sweeping view of the city and the bay of Concepción. At the end is the cape where the naval shipyard and the lighthouse are located.

To go back down, follow San Martín for one block and then turn left on Castellón up to Valdivia, which runs alongside a railroad track through a cut in the hill. Continue heading south to take Latorre, skirting the hill to the end.

Follow now the paved street climbing the La Gloria hill to the look–out commanding a superb view of the San Vicente bay, the Tetas del Biobío hills, the timber and the fishing port, the industrial quarter and Concepción in the distance (see map of Metropolitan Concepción).

Once you drive down from the hill, you can visit the **Fishing Port.** Follow La Marina street, then Malaquías Concha street up to the railway and there turn right, following J A Ríos to the north gate of the Huachipato steel mill and then turn left into Gran Bretaña; four blocks heading north you reach a rocky point.

This is **Los Perales** hill, where Bernardo O'Higgins camped before attacking the defeated Spanish forces waiting to board their ships at the port. Here O'Higgins signed the Chile's Independence Act on December 31, 1817, which was proclaimed on the following day at Concepción's square.

Continue on Av Gran Bretaña (see map of Metropolitan Concepción) to visit the **Industrial Quarter,** with its huge coal heaps, blast furnaces and other facilities of the steel mill and lamination process of the **Huachipato smelter.** Opposite is a string of basic industries. Ahead, forest–products and petrochemical industries and an oil refinery.

Turn right at Av Golondrinas and then left to make a detour behind the steel mill to Hualpén (signposted, see Concepción Coast map). It is a 7-km gravel road through rolling country with eucalyptus forests and some native forests, to visit the

HUALPEN MUSEUM AND PARK (summer Tue–Sun 09:00–12:00 h & 14:00–19:00 h; winter until 18:00 h). Free pedestrian access; only cars pay. This is an old hacienda, with a house, a park and a private collection which Pedro del Río Zañartu (1840–1918) donated to the city of Concepción for its preservation and to protect its ecology. The house and the park are open to the public, but the hacienda has been given the National Monument status to preserve native coastal species.

Pedro del Río was a great businessman, farmer, whaler, nitrate miner and writer. He undertook three trips around the world between 1880 and 1900, gathering objects to add to his collection.

The house (ca 1885) is large, solemn, square, with a tiled roof, a central court and a windowed gallery running the length of the façade. The mansion's drawing rooms and bedrooms retain the original furniture, while the rest of the rooms house an extraordinary collection of eastern cabinetwork, weapons, coins, smoking pipes, religious iconography, Egyptian art, Mapuche and Indian silver objects, precious stones and much more. The variety and quality of the items –some highly valued– making up the collection is impressive.

The park dates from the same period as the house, surrounds a hillock overlooking the river and includes sculptures, mazes, fountains, look-out points, plant–lined paths and ancient eucalyptus, palms and native trees. It is well worth a visit.

Continue 4 km further to the **Mouth of the Biobío,** a popular river and sea beach. It is a good spot for a picnic.

Retrace the road to the junction of Av Golondrinas and Gran Bretaña and continue on Av Las Golondrinas until Av Colón, the old road connecting Concepción and Talcahuano. Turn right on Av Colón, driving through residential areas, schools and university campuses, taking the overpass leading to the

New Bridge spanning the Biobío. With 2,450 m in length, it is Chile's longest road bridge. To the side is the railway bridge, its length in meters equal to the year it was built, 1884. The New Bridge ends at a curve of the Lota road. Turn left for about 400 m to reach the access to the scenic

Lake San Pedro elongated and hemmed in by wooded hills. It is a good place for bathing and practicing watersports, including rowing. It has several boating clubs; adjacent is the small lake Llacolén.

Back on the road, continue east to visit, opposite Hostería Millaray, the

San Pedro Chapel a modern church with a terrace overlooking the city; in the evening the city lights are reflected on the placid river. This is a sanctuary of the Virgin of the Candelaria, with a statue donated by Governor Alonso de Ribera to the Fort of San Pedro in 1603, and having its own festivity.

Return to Concepción across the **Old Bridge,** Chile's second longest, with 1.7 km.

TOURS FROM CONCEPCION

Concepción is traditionally a jumping–off point for excursions south of the Biobío, to Lota and Arauco (see Section C), and Biobío upstream to Santa Juana and Nacimiento (see Section D). As these areas are covered in their own sections, we shall review here only those areas lying north of the Biobío.

3 TO THE COUNTRYSIDE AT HUALQUI ★★★

a round trip of 48 km on a paved road; allow two hours.
A visit to an old farming village, driving along the northern bank of the Biobío.

Leave Concepción following Av Pedro de Valdivia to Chiguayante. **Chiguayante** is a residential quarter 10 km from Concepción, with villas and tree–shaded streets. Here is the Caupolicán Chiguayante textile factory (salesroom open Mon–Fri 09:30–13:30 h and 15:00–19:30 h, Sat 9:30–13:30 h).

Continue upstream through new quarters and nice scenery, particularly at a curve of the river framed by the pine-clad Nahuelbuta mountains. The river is placid and has some nice beaches.

You will meet lots of ox–drawn carts, with huge metal wheels and basket–like tops, bringing farm produce to the Concepción markets or selling it door to door, announcing themselves with a horn.

At km 24 is a great curve of the river, with a secluded valley watered by the Hualqui river. Here is

9

Hualqui (pop 8,000), a farming village with vegetable and fruit orchards. Two attempts were made to establish an outpost here to defend the border: one in 1577, when Rodrigo de Quiroga erected a fort which did not prosper, and the present village, founded in 1757 by De Amat y Junyent.

You can continue a 28 km further on a gravel road along the river bank to **Talcamávida**, founded also by De Amat in 1757, opposite the strong-

hold of Santa Juana de Guadalcazar (1666), to defend the river pass.

A further 40 km will bring you to **Rere**, with a colonial church and one–m–diameter bells which are national monuments. Return to Concepción through the paved road from Yumbel.

4 ALONG THE COAST TO PENCO AND THE ITATA
RIVER ★★★ *from Concepción to Penco, 14 km;*

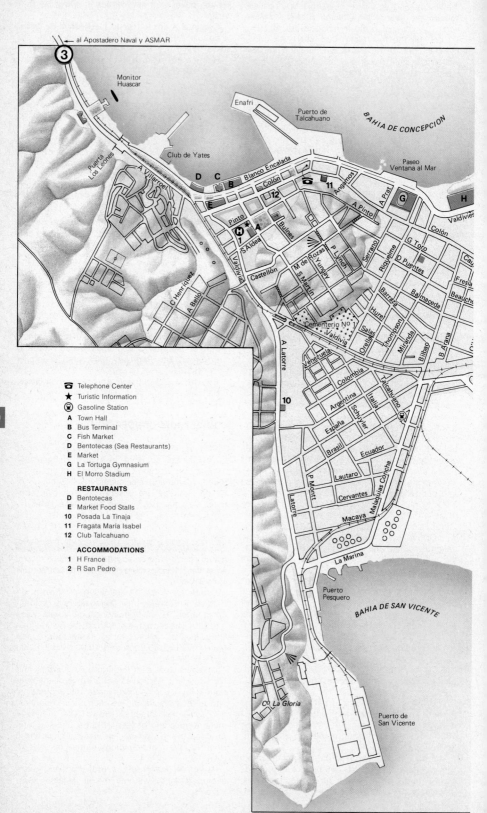

☎ Telephone Center
★ Turistic Information
Ⓢ Gasoline Station
A Town Hall
B Bus Terminal
C Fish Market
D Bentotecas (Sea Restaurants)
E Market
G La Tortuga Gymnasium
H El Morro Stadium

RESTAURANTS
D Bentotecas
E Market Food Stalls
10 Posada La Tinaja
11 Fragata María Isabel
12 Club Talcahuano

ACCOMMODATIONS
1 H France
2 R San Pedro

17 km to Lirquén and 28 km to Tomé on a paved road. From there, an 8–km paved road to Dichato and then 23 km on a dirt road to the mouth of the Itata. Altogether 66 km, of which 34 km are paved. Gasoline at Penco, Lirquén and Tomé. Allow a whole day for this, with beaches and restaurants on the way. If you leave early, you can continue to Chillán the same day via Tomé (described under Section A).

A scenic tour visiting this Zone's best beaches, with interesting cities. The beaches near the mouth of the Itata are excellent for sea fishing.

See maps of Concepción Coast and Metropoli-

tan Concepción: follow the road to Penco, labelled 3 in the latter map. At km 14 are

PENCO AND LIRQUEN (pop 31,000). Despite the two names, it is a single city divided by a hill which also gives rise to two bays, beaches and

☎ Telephone Center
Ⓖ Gasoline Station
⤸ Lookout Point
A Spanish Fort
B Town Hall
C Parish Church

RESTAURANTS
1 Casinorientes
2 Moso
3 Chinatown Seafood Eateries

OF INTEREST
4 Venta Loza Penco
5 San Juan Ceramics

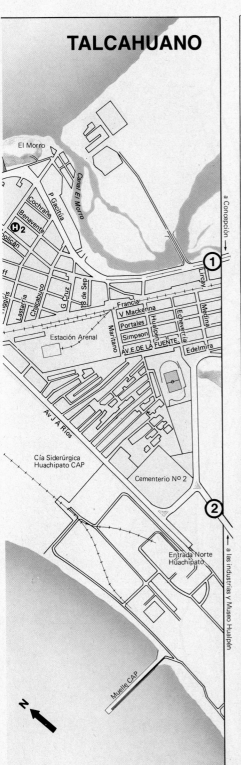

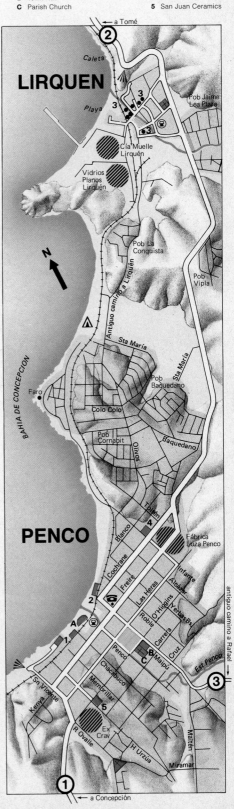

9

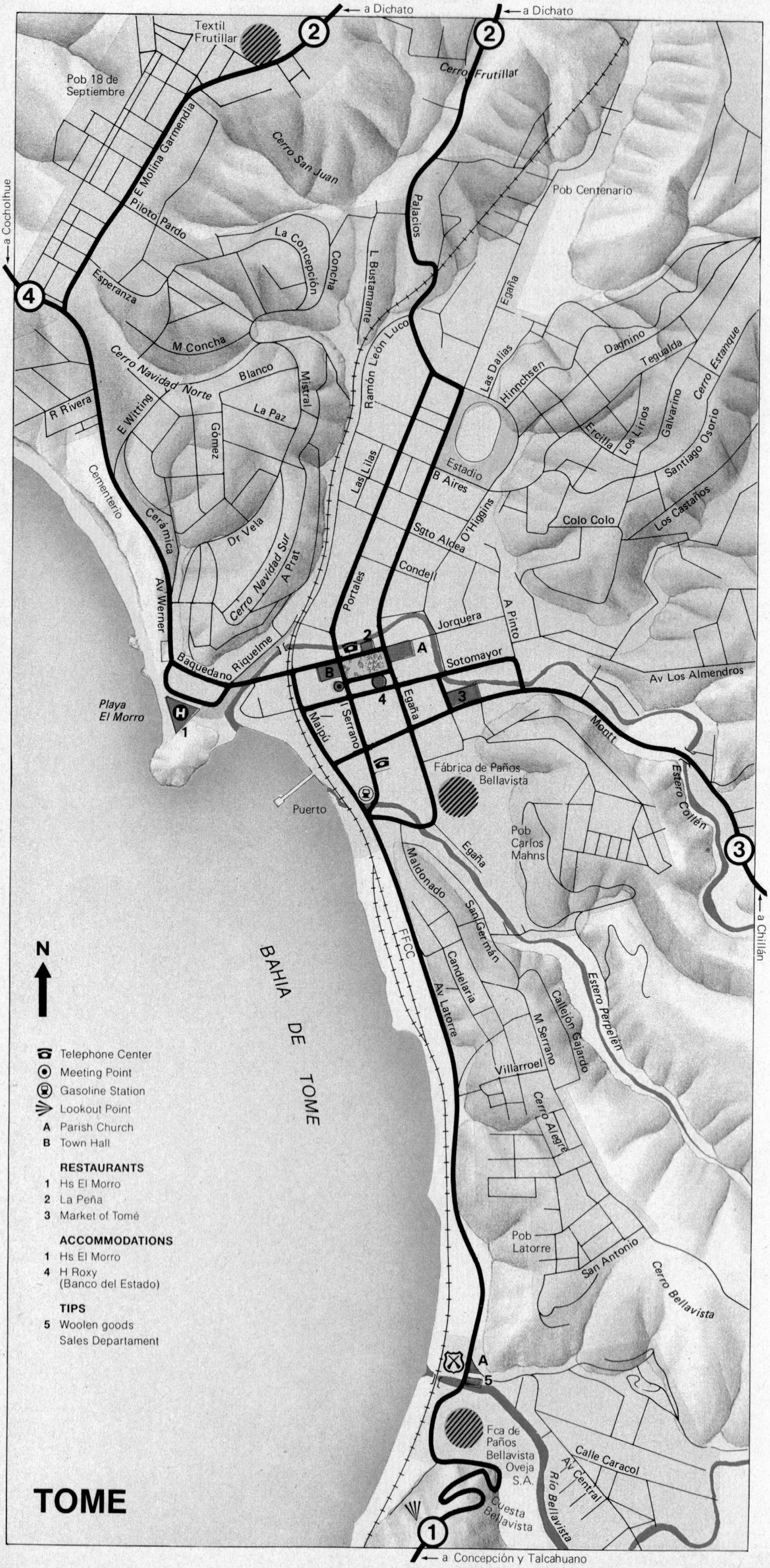

→ a Dichato

→ a Dichato

Textil
Frutillar

Pob 18 de
Septiembre

Cerro Frutillar

Cerro San Juan

Pob Centenario

a Cocholhue →

E Molina Carmendia

Piloto Pardo

Palacios

Egaña

Esperanza

La Concepción

Concha

L Bustamante

Ramón León Luco

M Concha

Cerro Navidad Norte

Blanco

Las Dalias

Himchsen

Dadnino

Tequalda

Cerro Estanque

R Rivera

E Wirting

Gomez

La Paz

Ercilla

Los Lirios

Galvarino

Santiago Osorio

Los Castaños

Cementerio

Cerámica

Ceránica

Dr Vela

Cerro Navidad Sur

Las Lilas

Estadio
B Aires

O'Higgins

Colo Colo

A Prat

Sgto Aldea

Av Werner

Baquedano

Riquelme

Portales

Condell

Jorquera

A Pinto

Sotomayor

Av Los Almendros

Playa
El Morro

H
1

2
📷
B
A
Serrano
4
Egaña
3

Maipú

Montt

Estero Cortén

Puerto

📷

⛽

Fábrica de Paños
Bellavista

Pob
Carlos
Mahns

a Chillán →

Egaña

Maldonado

FFCC

San Germán

Candelaria

Av Latorre

Villarroel

M Serrano

Callejón Galardo

Estero Perpelén

Cerro Alegre

N

BAHIA

DE

TOME

📞 Telephone Center
⊙ Meeting Point
⛽ Gasoline Station
⇘ Lookout Point
A Parish Church
B Town Hall

RESTAURANTS
1 Hs El Morro
2 La Peña
3 Market of Tomé

ACCOMMODATIONS
1 Hs El Morro
4 H Roxy
(Banco del Estado)

TIPS
5 Woolen goods
Sales Departament

Pob
Latorre

San Antonio

Cerro Bellavista

☓ **A**
5

Fca de
Paños
Bellavista
Oveja
S.A.

Calle Caracol

Av Central

Río Bellavista

Cuesta
Bellavista

TOME

① → a Concepción y Talcahuano

9

seaports, each with its own attractiveness. Penco was the first settlement established in the South, in 1550, under the name of Concepción del Nuevo Extremo, by Pedro de Valdivia. Rebuilt by García Hurtado de Mendoza in 1557, it gave rise to the city of Concepción, which was moved to its present location in 1764 after the original village had been wiped out by an earthquake and a tidal wave.

Penco became a major industrial town early this century, with the establishment of a sugar refinery (now closed) and a crockery factory.

Lirquén started out as a fishing cove, a character which it preserves to this day. In 1913 the coastal railroad reached it and soon a glass factory and a privately-owned shipping port were established. It is now one of the main shipping ports for forest products.

What To See (See map) on the access to Penco you will see the sugar refinery on the right-hand side, with a pretty church. On Urzúa is **Cerámica San Juan**, a ceramics factory (May–Oct, Mon–Fri 09:30–13:00 h and 14:30–19:00 h, Sat and Sun 09:30–19:00 h; Nov–Apr, Mon–Sun 09:30–20:00 h). You can see the manufacturing process.

The square is flanked on one side by the Penco brook, spanned by narrow bridges at every street.

Following Maipú street is the white-sanded beach, very popular in summer. Here is the

La Planchada Fort (NM) built of stone by Governor José de Garró in 1687, with 64 m in length and a battlement sporting the León de Castilla coat of arms. The walls facing the sea are still to be seen. It was attacked by pirates in 1694 and 1720, and during the War of Independence it was used as a prison for patriots. On one side is now **Restaurant Oriente**, frequented by people coming from Concepción.

Continue to Lirquén. On the street leading out of Penco you will see the crockery factory with external channels covered of caolín, a fine white clay used in pottery and crockery making. **Salesroom:** Mon–Sat 09:00–12:30 h and 14:00–18:00 h. An impressive place covered completely with the traditional production of Loza Penco. Good prices. Lirquén is 3 km ahead. On the access road you will pass the glass factory. Visit the so-called **Barrio Chino** (Chinatown), a maze of alleys with seafood stalls and small **seafood eateries**, authentical gastronomic centers with the best seafood of the coast. Very famous are the Cholguasos, the steamed cholgas (aulacomya ater) and the machas (mesodesmadonacium) with matico (piper angustifolium).

On the beach is a picturesque fishing cove adjacent to the Lirquén Port Complex, with yards overflowing with export logs and sawnwood, and a loading wharf.

Leave Lirquén heading north, climbing a pine-clad promontory. By the curve on the top there is a look-out point commanding a **view** of the Concepción bay, Quiriquina island and Talcahuano. The road continues above the sea for a while, to turn later into forested hills.

At km 25 there is a 2-km road branching left to the **Punta de Parra** beach; it is private (access fee). It is beautiful, white-sanded and touristed.

The road continues through forested hills, climbs the Cuesta Bellavista and then descends (**good views**) to reach at km 34

TOME (pop 35,000), an industrious, busy seaport, textile and forest center, and holiday resort. Its houses are squeezed between the hills and the beach, with little flat area. Old wooden houses, some gaily painted, cling to the slopes behind. They are relics from the times when Tomé was an exclusive seaside resort.

By mid last century, large investors (Cousiño and Urmeneta, among others) established mills and a port to ship the Ñuble wheat output to markets in California and Australia. In 1865 the

Paños Bellavista textile factory was founded, taking advantage of the good water supply. In 1913 the Chillán–Concepción railway reached Tomé. Two new textile factories, Oveja Tomé and Fiap Tomé, went on stream in 1913 and 1932, respectively.

What To See at the bottom of the road climbing down the Cuesta Bellavista, right before the bridge, is the Bellavista Tomé textile factory (est 1923), with vast concrete buildings, a church in romantic byzantine style and the workers' residential areas in the valley upstream. **Salesroom** open Mon–Fri 09:00–13:00 h & 15:00–19:00 h; Sat & Sun 11:00–18:00 h; good prices for textiles.

The harbor is a secluded bay, flanked on one side by a rocky promontory. Beyond the promontory is the

El Morro beach white-sanded, with a placid sea, a waterfront avenue and the Hostería El Morro, property of the Banco del Estado. This is the seaside-resort part of town.

Leave Tomé (km 34) following street Baquedano to the north, then Av Werner and finally Molina Garmendia heading for Dichato.

At km 35 starts a 4-km detour to the left, recommended, bringing you at km 39 to

Cocholhue Beach and Fishing Cove a quaint group of summer houses, restaurants, a fishing cove and a beach with rocky outcrops. Good for bathing and camping.

Get back to the highway at km 49 and continue northwards. At km 47 is a 7-km detour to the left leading to

Coliumo Beach a lovely peninsula closing the bay where Dichato is located. It has summer houses and three nearby sites: Coliumo, Caleta and Tres Morros. Excellent beaches, placid sea and camping spots in a nice setting. At km 51 is

9

☎ Telephone Center
M Sea Museum

RESTAURANTS
1 Chichi
2 Costanera
3 El Kalifa
4 Sta Elena

5 Tío Agustín
6 El Candil

ACCOMMODATIONS
1 H Chichi
2 Costanera
3 El Kalifa

455

DICHATO a picturesque, scattered, popular resort with a crescent-shaped, white-sanded beach at the end of the Coliumo bay. It has many bourding houses, motels and hotels. Very good for bathing.

The dirt road leading to the mouth of the Itata river is not passable after rain, as the roadbed is clayish and there are some steep gradients.

Leave Dichato (km 0) following a short climb flanked by pine forests until a 2-km detour leading to the beautiful

Pingueral Beach small and flanked by pine forest, with golden sand and calm waters. It is very popular in summer. Back on the road, you continue among forests turning away from the coast.

At km 8 is a descent to the **Puda beach** and brook. Long, golden-sanded and beautiful, it has pounding surf and a crystalline, algae-rich sea. It is a good fishing spot. The road continues above the rocky coast. At km 12, a new descent to the brook and beach of **Merquiche**, small and solitary and with thundering surf. At km 14 is **Burca beach**, accessible through a short detour,

with strong surf; good for fishing. The road climbs and runs for a while through hills overlooking the ocean among pine forests alternating with wheat fields.

At km 20 is yet another short detour descending to the brook and beach of **Purema**, with a few houses lying on a large open bay, with strong surf washing the dark sand. Good for fishing.

At km 26 is the **Vegas de Itata** village, overlooking the mouth of the Itata and the sea. A road lined with old eucalyptus leads to the river bank, where boats are available for the crossing.

For those wishing to continue from here to Chillán, there is a good road running 25 km along the river to **Coelemu** and from there a further 20 km to **San Ignacio**, to take from there the road to Chillán described under Section 1. Total distance from the mouth of the Itata to Chillán is 95 km.

Motocross fans can have the motorbike crossed by boat to the other bank of the Itata for a superb ride along coastal forest roads to **Colmuvao** and from there to **Pichilemu**.

SECTION C   ARAUCO

This section covers the area lying between the Nahuelbuta range and the sea, which falls within two provinces, Concepción and Arauco. In the past it was a transit route to the South known as the «Conquerors' Route». It became Chile's coal supplier from the mid 19th century onwards. However, this brought some development only on the coast, as the traffic routes were by sea, and by railway from Concepción to Curanilahue and from Lebu to Angol. There were no real roads until 1963, when the present highway finally put an end to the isolation of this sector.

The Nahuelbuta («Place of Tigers») Range is a high, long massif running uninterruptedly from the Biobío river to the Imperial river. No river crosses it and has only two natural passes, at Contulmo and, farther south, at Tirúa, both used by the conquerors.

Afforestation with radiata pine has brought about a tremendous change in the landscape, the ecology and the economy; at present, radiata pine is the area's main resource.

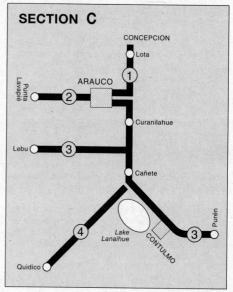

TOURS OF THE AREA

1 TO LOTA AND ARAUCO ★★★ *a stretch of 75 paved kilometers from Concepción. Allow one day. Beaches at Laraquete.*
A chance to visit some historical sites, the coal mining town of Lota with its superb park, and the beaches of Arauco. This is the first leg of the Conquerors' Route.

Leave Concepción (km 0) heading south across the Biobío. The road runs straight, with the Nahuelbuta Range far to the left.

At km 20 the road crosses a brook flowing from a lake not visible from the road. Here took place the **Battle of Lagunillas** on Nov 18, 1557, between the Spaniards and the Mapuches, the latter headed by the famous chieftain Caupolicán. The Mapuches were defeated and chieftain Galvarino was taken prisoner; the Spaniards amputated both his hands. At km 30 is

Coronel (pop 67,000), a city which grew around the Schwager coal mining company. Now it is a busy fishing industry center; the fishing vessels can be seen in the sheltered harbor. There is a monument to those fallen during the Coronel Sea Battle between a British and a German fleet (Nov 1914); the British were defeated, two of their ships sunk.

Next comes **Playa Blanca**, a popular beach with a campground, many restaurants and other eateries. The best here is Las Rocas; Pinares

and Las Brisas are cheaper. At km 37 is

LOTA (pop 48,000), a coal mining town with the houses clinging to hill slopes. It is crisscrossed by railroads with seven tunnels within the town (see map). Lota is divided into two sections:

Lota Alto (Upper Lota) on the hill. It was founded by Matías Cousiño in 1849 when work started at the coal mine (see Land & History). It is the residential quarter for most of the mine's personnel; here are the mines, industries and their management. It used to be private property. Now it forms one unit with

Lota Bajo (Lower Lota), the original settlement evolving from a fishing cove (1841). It has spread onto the hills as a large service town for the mine and its related industries.

The Mines of Lota include Chile's main coal mine, owned by Enacar. Located near the sea shore, its core is at Pique Carlos, with a vertical drop of 495 m and stretching 1,300 m horizontally towards Laraquete. Pique Alberto has a vertical drop of 504 m and extends 900 m under the ocean's surface.

9

A visit to Pique Alberto (Mon–Fri departures at 11:00 and 15:00 h) Duration 2 ¹/₂ to 3 h, appropiate gear is provided. Each person pays, expensive. Contact Cousiño St pho 249039).

Visiting an underground mine in operation, wearing the miners gear, is a fascinating experience you will be able to see the underground to the surface. Worth a visit.

What To See at a square on Carrera street, Lota Bajo, you can see the curious **handicrafts made of carved coal stones**. The church on the main square contains a 130-cm statue of the Virgin carved in coal. The **Market**, next to the old train station, is a busy place of narrow alleys.

On Carlos Cousiño street of Lota Alto is the **Church of San Matías** (1928), a fine construction in romanesque style. Inside, on a simple crypt on the left-hand side, are the remains of the «coal industry's father», Matías Cousiño (1810–1863), identified only by his initials on the access gate. Opposite the church are **old pabellones** -lodgings– for mining families, with long corridors and a shared washing trough. It is an interesting example of an industrial population of the beginning of the century.

On the main square there is a monument to Matías Cousiño.

LOTA PARK (May–Aug, Mon–Sat 08:00–18:00 h, Sun and holidays 10:00–18:00 h; Sep–Apr, Mon–Sat, 08:00–20:00 h; Sun and holidays, 10:00–21:00 h access fee) is a 14-ha park perched atop the peninsula, designed from 1862 to 1872 by an English landscape architect called Bartelet and continued by G. O'Reilly. The driving force behind the park was undoubtedly Cousiño's wife, Isidora Goyenechea, who watched over its development and ornamentation until her death in 1899. She brought from Europe such ornaments as fountains, pavilions, statues, lanterns, banks, fences, jars, and had several buildings erected, the main one being a palace which was destroyed by the 1960 earthquake. The great frontispiece of the fireplace, made of carved wood, has been preserved at the Club de Concepción.

The palace, started in 1885 once Cousiño finished his impressive residence in Santiago known as Palacio Cousiño, was never used. His heirs preferred a small, pretty house on top of the cliff, also wiped out by the 1960 earthquake (see map). The descendants of the Cousiño family preserved and extended the park. It is now splendidly maintained by the Enacar coal company.

What To See walk along the paths shown in the map to the **lighthouse**, commanding superb views. Note the careful **distribution of trees**, with tasteful contrasts in color and texture; there are never more than three of the same kind together. The **benches** have a reclining back to enable a relaxed observation of the foliage. There is a wrought-iron **Chinese pavilion** with a family monogram –the same of Vinos Cousiño Macul–, a collection of jars and 24 allegorical statues, including one of **Venus** bathing, on the central fountain, by Allégrain, and one of Mapuche chieftain **Caupolicán**, by Nicanor Plaza, on the central esplanade. Peacocks and pheasants roam freely.

In a depression is the tomb of Carlos Cousiño (1859–1931) facing his great achievement, the **Pique Carlos**, one of the coal mines, of which two towers can be seen: the reinforced concrete one is used for ventilation and extraction of waste material, while the metal one –known as the cage– is used for lowering or lifting personnel and hauling coal up.

Where To Eat best restaurant is El Delfín; Las Rocas at Playa Blanca is also good. Cheaper meals at the market food stalls.

Leave Lota (km 37) following Schneider street south, climbing the hill and crossing the wooded peninsula. Two km ahead (signposted) take detour to the right leading in 900 m to the **Lota Fort**. Located on an esplanade overlooking the bays

THE COAL DISTRICT

a Concepción

Pta Coronel

Yobilo

Villa Mora

Schwager

Coronel

Pta Puchoco

Pya Negra

Océano Pacífico

BAHIA DE CORONEL

Est Manca

Pya Blanca

Cta Lotilla

Mar Chileno

Lota

Pta Pique
Parque de Lota

BAHIA DE LOTA

Río Colcura

Empresa Forestal Colcura

Fuerte de Lota

Pya Colcura

Batalla de Marihueño
26 de Febrero de 1554
Francisco de Villagra, en
viaje hacia Tucapel (Cañete)
para vengar muerte de
Pedro de Valdivia, es
derrotado por Lautaro.

Co. Villagran

Planta Hidroeléctrica Chivilingo

Cta Chivilingo

Río Chivilingo

Pya Chivilingo

Pta Andalién

Pya Laraquete

Río Las Cruces

CHILE

Laraquete

Río Lía

El Llano

a Arauco

N

0   1   2   3
ESCALA APROXIMADA   Kms

9

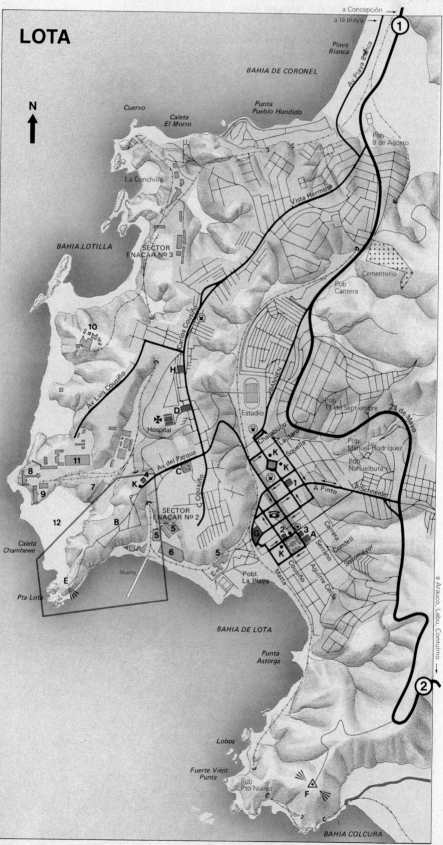

☎ Telephone Center
◉ Café, Meeting Point
Ⓖ Gasoline Station
⟫ Lookout Ponit
✳ Hospital
A Town Hall
B Lota Park
C Matías Cousiño Square

D San Martín Parish
E Lighthouse
F Lota Fort
G Market
H Coal Museum

OF INTEREST
K Handicraft on Coal

RESTAURANTS
1 El Delfín
2 Cámara de Comercio
3 Socorros Mutuos
4 Jacaranda
G Market Eateries

INDUSTRIAL AREA
5 Refactorios Lota Green

6 Fábrica ladrillos
7 Maestranza
8 Pique Carlos
9 Pique Alberto
10 Pique Grande
11 Planta de lavado
12 Escoria de la mina

LOTA

of Lota and Colcura, it was a Spanish strong-hold (1661) upgraded in 1865 to a fortress protecting the habour.

The road descends into the **Colcura** valley. Here is the Colcura forest company, Chile's oldest, founded in 1881 by the Cousiño family. It engaged in afforestation with eucalyptus, Australian myrrh and some pine species, mostly hardwoods for use in the coal mine. Its forests extended all the way to Curanilahue.

The road now skirts Mount Villagrán, where chieftain Lautaro defeated the Spaniards commanded by Francisco de Villagra. At the end of this stretch of mountain road is the

Chivilingo Hydroelectric Power Station (open only in summer, Mon–Fri 10:00–18:00 h, Sat, Sun and holidays from 10:00–20:00 h, entrance fee).

Take a 2-km road branching left, skirting the river bank. It was Chile's first hydroelectric power station, and the second in South America, designed by Thomas Alva Edison for the Lota mine. It was commissioned by Carlos Cousiño and went on stream in 1897. Earlier, on an initiative of Isidora Goyenechea, Chile's first fish farm had been set up at this place using French technology and introducing salmonoid species. The power station is now an interesting industrial museum where all its original machinery has been conserved. It is worth a visit.

Back on the highway (km 53), the road runs close to the **Chivilingo beach**, popular (too popular) and full of tents in summer. The road then climbs among forests to descend now at km 57 to

Laraquete Beach near the bridge before the village

a dirt road branches left to the Las Cruces river. Here you can look for the famous **cross stones**, a rarity: they are round stones which, when cracked and polished, show a dark cross dividing them into four lengthwise sections. Laraquete is a village at the northern end of the large beach on the Gulf of Arauco. It is a quiet place with a fishing cove, many restaurants specializing in crab and some in frog legs. The best are Rapa Nui and JM.

Lota park

The road crosses a plain covered by pine forests and dotted with large mounds of sawdust, and soon passes (km 63) the facilities of **Celulosa Arauco**, a large pulp & paper mill. Five km later is the village of Carampangue. Take there the road branching left to Arauco.

This road runs for 7 km through cultivated fields and crosses three bridges. The hill jutting towards the road is the place where Caupolicán is traditionally believed to have been elected Toqui (highest chieftain) of the Mapuches in 1556. At km 73 is a small and interesting ceramics workshop producing refined pieces. It is worth a stop. At km 75 is

ARAUCO (pop 8,600) is a placid town flanked by hills and lying next to a long white-sanded beach. It was founded in 1555 by Pedro de Valdivia and moved to its present location at the foot of the Colo Colo hill in 1590. Levelled and

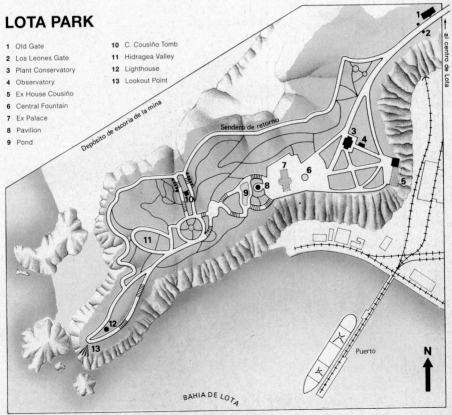

LOTA PARK

1 Old Gate
2 Los Leones Gate
3 Plant Conservatory
4 Observatory
5 Ex House Cousiño
6 Central Fountain
7 Ex Palace
8 Pavilion
9 Pond

10 C. Cousiño Tomb
11 Hidragea Valley
12 Lighthouse
13 Lookout Point

al centro de Lota

Depósito de escoria de la mina

Sendero de retorno

Puerto

N

BAHIA DE LOTA

rebuilt on innumerable occasions, it was long a military outpost of Concepción. In 1845 it was visited by Ignacio Domeyko, who found remains of the fort and a large stone blazon of the Lion of Castilla. In 1886 it received a boost by the arrival of French Basque settlers. Its present development is fuelled by the pulp & paper mill.

The church, on the square, has the bell tower and columns of the previous church, which was destroyed by an earthquake in 1960. There is excellent accommodation at the Hostería Arauco and Hotel Plaza. Restaurants at the Club Social and the Hostería. Picnic on the beach or at the Colo Colo hill. The best place for camping is on

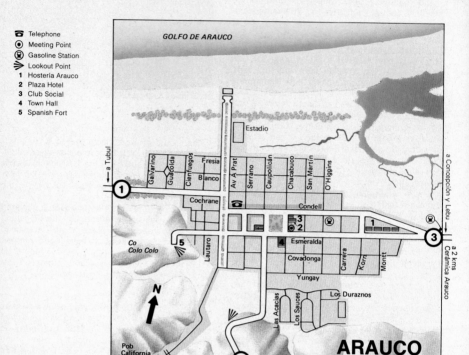

Telephone
Meeting Point
Gasoline Station
Lookout Point
1 Hostería Arauco
2 Plaza Hotel
3 Club Social
4 Town Hall
5 Spanish Fort

Telephone
Gasoline Station
Meeting Point
A Town Hall

B Post Office
C Handicrafts Shop
RESTAURANTS
1 Hanga-Roa

2 Lebu

ACCOMMODATIONS
3 Gran Hotel
4 Hotel Central

PLACES OF INTEREST
5 House Ebensperger
6 Landsberger Tannery

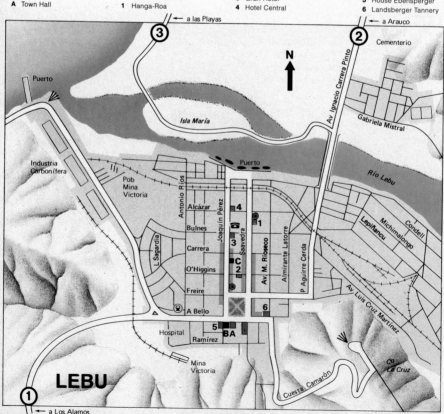

9

the river banks near the bridge on the access road to Arauco.

2 TO PUNTA LAVAPIE ★★★

a round trip of 86 km from Arauco on gravel and dirt roads. Allow no less than four hours. Take food. Restaurant at Lavapié.

An excursion to the tip of the Gulf of Arauco, with nice beaches, cliffs and good scenery.

Leave Arauco (km 0) heading west, the road skirting hills lying close to the coast, to reach, at km 11,

Tubul a fishing cove next to the Raquil river. Its inhabitants are engaged in harvesting and farming an algae known locally as pelillo (raw material for agar–agar) using an interesting nursery technique. Boats are offered for hire to visit the rocky cliffs on the estuary, with many cavities used as nests by marine birds. At km 32 is

Llico a sheltered, white–sanded beach with a fishing cove and summer houses. It is the best and most beautiful beach on the Gulf. The road runs now on top of high cliffs with a sweeping view over the open sea, to reach **Punta Lavapié** at km 43. It is a fishing cove and a beach tucked against a high cliff and near a lighthouse. The restaurant at the fishing cove specializes in shellfish.

3 TO LEBU AND LAKE LANALHUE ★★★

188 km to Contulmo, with 153 km paved and the rest gravel. A further 20–km brings you across the Nahuelbuta range to Purén, and thence (paved) to Victoria on the Pan–American highway to continue south. Gasoline at Lebu and Cañete.

A circuit continuing along the Conquerors' Route, with major mining centers and the lovely lake Lanalhue, to cross the wooded Nahuelbuta range at Contulmo.

Leave Arauco (km 0) heading for Carampangue at km 7. Take there the paved highway running south (right) through a rolling plain covered with pine plantations. Roads branch left to the Colico Norte and Colico Sur coal mines. At km 28 is

Curanilahue (pop 24,000), taking a four–km paved road forking right. It is a busy coal mining center (there are coal mines in the town itself), its houses huddled tightly on the hillsides.

Back on the main road (km 36), you will soon see the yards of a large forest company and vast pine forests. Several roads branch east: to Colico at km 38; Trogol at km 50, and Pilpilco at km 57. These are all coal mines exploiting the coal layer running south parallel to the road. At km 60 is a road junction; take the paved road to the right, leading in 30 km to Lebu. Most of the roads branching left from this highway lead to Mapuche reservations near the coast. At km 90 is

LEBU (pop 17,000), the capital of Arauco province. The descent to the town is spectacular, with views over the valley rolling to the sea, the Lebu river and the river port. On the far bank are several sawmills. The town is hemmed in by hills.

Its livelihood comes from coal mining, which was started here by Matías Rioseco in 1852, and later expanded by Maximiliano Errázuriz and JT Urmeneta. The coal mine is now property of Enacar.

What To See there are a couple of 3–m–long **bronze guns** on the square, cast in Lima in 1778. They are called **El Rayo** (Lightning) and **Marte** (Mars) (other guns just like them are at La Moneda in Santiago, the government palace.) The guns are set on an exceedingly light carriage; it is not clear how they ended up at such an out–of–the–way location. The three–storied house on one of the corners on the square was built in 1914 for the local Ebensperger family; it is now an old people's home. Towards **Bocalebu**

on the beach you will see a coal washing industry, with sooty buildings surrounded by mounds of coal and water gushing out everywhere. Beyond the **shipping dock**, at the mouth of the Lebu river, you will see people **harvesting the coal** carried by the river from natural coal mines upstream.

A short excursion can be recommended to **Millaneco beach**: Take the exit labelled 3 in Lebu map and follow the road for 4 km. The beach is beautiful and sheltered, with large caves; one is natural, the rest were made early this century.

Back in Lebu, the **Landsberger tannery** makes an interesting visit. The Cerro La Cruz behind the town (see map) will give you a sweeping view of the area.

Accommodations and Food lunch at Hanga Roa and Millaneco beach. Cheap meals at the market. The hotels are modest. Best spot for camping is the beach at the beautiful Isla Morhuilla 9 km south (see general map).

Leave Lebu (km 98) retracing the road back to the junction (km 128). Turn right towards Cañete. At km 140 is the village of Antihuala, where Caupolicán fell prisoner to the Spaniards (Nov 5, 1558). From the village, a road heads east (left) to Hostería Caramávida (4 km), nice and clean, with a native plant garden and frequented by fishing fans. That road climbs to the Nahuelbuta National Park to reach Angol. Only suitable for 4WD vehicles, it is a fantastic shortcut across the mountain range.

Back on the main road, at km 152 is the last filling station, on the access to

Cañete (pop 13,000), a farming and forestry center with a rich history. A few km north of here, Pedro de Valdivia set up Fort Tucapel in 1552; in the proximity of the fort, he was attacked by surprise and killed, along with fifty of his men, by chieftain Lautaro on December 25, 1553. García Hurtado de Mendoza founded the village of Cañete five years later; he christened the place in honor of his father, the Marquis of

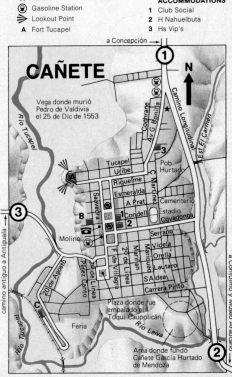

☎ Telephone Center	**B**	Town Hall
◉ Meeting Point	**C**	Railway Station
★ Turistic Information		**ACCOMMODATIONS**
Ⓖ Gasoline Station	**1**	Club Social
⤢ Lookout Point	**2**	H Nahuelbuta
A Fort Tucapel	**3**	Hs Vip's

a Concepción →

CAÑETE N

Vega donde murió Pedro de Valdivia el 25 de Dic de 1553

Río Tucapel

Cochrane
Av G Bonilla
Camino Longitudinal
Est El Carmen

Tucapel
Uribe
Riquelme
Esmeralda
A Prat
Condell
Pob Hurtado

Saavedra
Martínez

Cementerio
Estadio Covadonga

Molino

Serrano
Videla
Orella
Lautaro
S Aldea
Carrera Pinto

F de Villagra
20 de Abril
20 de Línea
Pérez Canto
F del Canto
Maripan
Marquez

camino antiguo a Antiguala

Plaza donde fue empalado el Toqui Caupolicán

Río Leiva

Feria

Área donde fundó Cañete García Hurtado de Mendoza

a Contulmo y Museo Araucano

9

Cañete. It was deserted in 1602 and founded anew by Cornelio Saavedra in 1868.

What To See follow street Uribe until the original location of **Fort Tucapel**; the remains now to be seen correspond to the stronghold set up here later by Cornelio Saavedra. It occured here the **death of the chilean conqueror Pedro de Valdivia** who was surprised by the chieftain (cacique) Lautaro in the valley in front of the fort and defeated on December the 25th of 1553.

Leave Cañete (km 153) heading south; the road is graveled. A short distance ahead is the

MAPUCHE MUSEUM (summer, Tue–Sun 10:00–12:30 and 14:00–18:00 h; entrance fee). It lies in the countryside, at the site where President Juan Antonio Ríos was born in 1888; it was built in his honor. The museum provides an insight into Mapuche culture and history through excellent displays (including war and household implements) charts and documents. It has a very good collection of Mapuche garments, silver objects and ceramics displayed in large rooms open to a garden containing native plants. Outside is an authentic **mapuche ruca** (dwelling), offering a chance to see the building technique: bent branches, tied with interwoven boqui (a creeping plant) and lined with coirón, a type of bunch–grass. The museum is well worth a visit.

Back on the road, at km 157 is a junction for Peleco. At a fork next to large sawmills, take the east (left) branch to the highly scenic

LAKE LANALHUE (see map), nestled among hills and flanked by pine forests. This and neighboring Lake Lleulleu are the only lakes in the Coastal Range. Best accommodation at Hostería Lanalhue (at the forking take west branch instead of east, and then the road branching left leading to the southern shore of the lake; see map). Also Posada Campesina Alemana, access from Contulmo, and Hotel Central at Contulmo, no private bath but very good homey meals. For camping, Playa Laguer (access fee).

The main road skirts the northwestern shore of the lake for 30 km to Contulmo, with nice views of the lake through the pine forests; there are many summer houses. On the far shore you can see the Hostería Lanalhue, built decades ago by the state railroad (along with the large Pucón, Puerto Varas and Portillo hotels, now privately–owned). Access to the Hostería Lanalhue used to be by boat from the train station of a branch line running along the lake in the past. There are public beaches at Playa Blanca, nice but popular in summer, with many people camping in tents, and Playa Laguer (access fee).

At km 187 is

Contulmo (pop 1,400), a picturesque little town at the southeastern end of the lake. It was founded as a fort in 1868 by Cornelio Saavedra on his way to Purén. In 1884 a group of Prussian German settlers arrived in what was then a very remote corner. There are many unmistak-

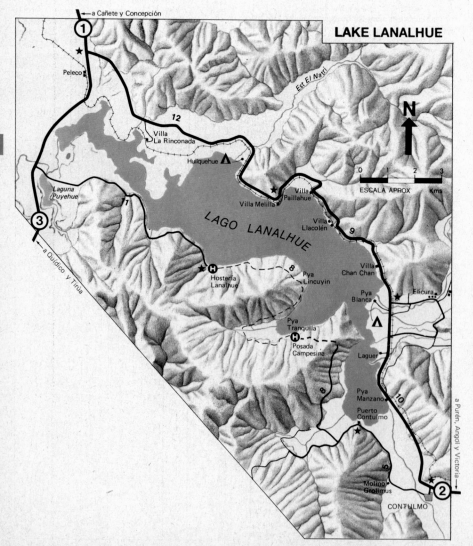

LAKE LANALHUE

able signs of their presence. Communications then were by ox–drawn cart to Angol. In 1910, a railroad connected Lebu to Peleco; in 1938 this railroad reached Angol across the mountain range.

What To See the German hand can still be seen in many houses. The square is shaded by large linden trees, there is a curious fountain shaped like Chile's coat of arms, the water spurting from the star. On one side is the municipal building. The Schulmeyer general store (1912) is a veritable frontier trading post, with the wares hanging from the ceiling and an atmosphere of times long gone. There are other houses from the early days. The Hotel Central, friendly, has a good restaurant and a busy bar in the evening, when farm owners from far and wide drop in for a chat. Hotel Contulmo is also very good, hospitable owners. A short walk up the slope to the cemetery will give you a view over the village, the valley and the tip of the lake.

Tips excellent homemade cherry and raspberry marmalade: ask around. Also the delicious homemade butter and cheese of the Thiele family at the station.

A 15–km excursion from Contulmo along the southern shore of the lake can be recommended, to visit the **Grollmus Mill and House** (14:00–18:00 h; voluntary donation) In km 3, a large wooden house with Brazilian araucarias in front, dating from ca. 1923. Next to it, a mill established in 1928 and a private hydroelectric power plant which used to supply the village with electricity. The mill with its wooden gears (everything made locally) can be visited. The owner boasts a fantastic collection of flowering plants in a lush garden, including 23 varieties of copihue (Chile's national flower) ranging from pure white through striped white and pink, to a seldom–found vivid red.

Puerto Contulmo is at km 5, a little cape from where agricultural produce used to be shipped to Peleco, whence it would be forwarded to Lebu overland. There is a beach.

Crossing the beach and skirting the promontory you reach

Playa Tranquila a beautiful beach, at km 14. Here is Posada Campesina, a hotel in a German–style house, renowned for its "once" (the traditional late afternoon tea and cake, sandwiches or biscuits) with home–made sausages, and set in a well–kept park. There are boats for hire. A curiosity: fish flock to the shore to wait for food thrown by the onlookers. Farther ahead is Lincuyín beach, frequented by windsurfers.

To cross the Nahuelbuta range to reach Purén, drive two km from Contulmo (km 189) into the valley to start the 5–km winding climb up the range, among thick pine forests. The crest is at km 196. Here is also the

Contulmo Natural Monument (88 ha), with a park warden house, paths into the forest and a picnic area. Under Conaf administration, it is a very beautiful patch of old–growth native forest with luxuriant ferns, a sort of relic of the plant cover that used to extend throughout the region.

The road is now paved and hemmed in by mountains, running along a winding stream. After cresting the ridge there is no descent, but a horizontal stretch along this natural pass. This is the same route followed both by the Mapuches and the Spanish conquerors. At km 209 is **Purén**, described under Section D. If you wish to follow the **Pedro de Valdivia Route**, as it was called during the colonial period, continue to Lumaco, Traiguén, Galvarino, Cholchol, Nueva Imperial and, finally, Carahue, where Ciudad Imperial was located, Chile's most important city until its destruction in 1599.

4 TO LAKE LLEULLEU AND TIRUA ★★

a round trip of 120 km from the Peleco road junction, on a gravel road. No gasoline on the way. Take

food, or eat at the restaurant at Quidico.

A circuit along a little–touristed coastal area which, during the 18th and 19th centuries, was the only pass authorized by the Mapuche chieftains to cross their territory to the south; the Spaniards called it Frontier Route and connected Concepción to Valdivia.

Take the Peleco road junction as your km 0. The road descends gently away from the Nahuelbuta range. At km 3 is the turn–off for **Hostería Lanalhue**, on the lake's western shore.

The road crosses several Mapuche reservations; at km 15 is the hamlet of Huentelolén, a modest group of houses with a **Centro Artesanal** offering pretty basketry and Mapuche handicrafts at good prices.

At km 23 the road is joined from the left by a dirt road –suitable only for 4WD vehicles– coming from Contulmo. Lake Lleulleu can be seen in the distance. At km 29 you cross the bridge over the outlet of

LAKE LLEULLEU lonely and more beautiful than lake Lanalhue. Beyond the bridge a road branches left for **Puerto Lleulleu**, which consists of two houses, a dock, a boat ramp and a diesel–powered boat plying the lake's waters in winter and in summer chartered to visitors. The lake is spectacular, with three arms, the most beautiful being the south one. It meanders among hills, cliffs and lonely beaches flanked by native forest. There are beautiful spots for camping. On the eastern arm is the village of Hullinco, with a beach, a school and a rural clinic.

The road approaches the sea to reach, at km 46

Quidico a fishing cove with a nice beach open to the wind. Frequented in summer, it has several residenciales (boarding houses) and restaurants specializing in seafood. At the turn of the century, it was a busy shipping port for lingue bark.

ACCOMMODATIONS
1 Hotel Central
2 Hotel Contulmo

OF INTEREST
3 Schulmeyer General Store

☎ Telephone
⌇ Lookout Point
A Town Hall
B Post Office

CONTULMO

N

← a Cañete
① ②
→ a Purén
③
→ antiguo camino a Purén

Gral Bonilla
al Puerto y Playa Tranquila
Camino Vecinal
Los Canelos
Los Notros
Los Tilos
Lleu-Lleu
Lanalhue
B A
Nahuelbuta
1
2
3
Millaray
Fresia

9

A stretch of 17 km, first atop a cliff over the sea and then away from the coast, brings you at km 60 to

Tirúa (pop 650), a picturesque hamlet located on the banks of the Tirúa river and away from the sea. Here is the end of the road. Ahead the Coastal Range juts into the sea. In the past, important Mapuche chieftains lived here, exacting a toll from travelers journeying upstream to cross the pass of Los Pinares (so named for its araucaria forests) to continue through Carahue or Trovolhue and then along the coast to Queule and Valdivia. It is a fantastic trek, described in Zone 10. Following this route in the Mapuche

times was not without hazards. In 1778, the Bishop of Concepción was captured by a party of mounted Mapuches at the pass of Los Pinares and his fate was decided by the outcome of a chueca game, similar to hockey. Luckily for him, his protector, Chieftain Curamilla from Tirúa, won the game and the bishop got away only with the scare. In 1795, over 5,000 head of cattle were herded through here from Hacienda Canteras (Los Angeles) to Osorno, to found the city as commanded by Ambrosio O'Higgins.

This district was described by Ignacio Domeyko in 1845, under a commission of the Chilean government.

SECTION D   SOUTH OF THE BIOBIO

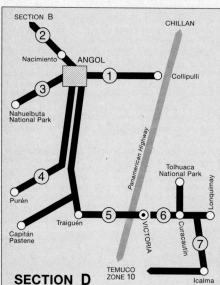

on the new frontier along the Malleco, in December 1862.

It was granted city status in 1871, and five years later it was connected by rail with Santiago. The place was now called Angol, and from here set out in 1881 the expeditionary force that wrested definitely the Araucanía from the Mapuches and which ended with the foundation of Temuco. Angol was a major economic and administrative center, and the jumping-off point for the Chilean and foreign settlers who occupied these lands.

Angol was also the birthplace of an unusually high proportion of Chilean writers. Now it is a pleasant farming and forestry village, with two small hotels.

This Section covers the area from the Biobío river in the north to the Quino river –just beyond Victoria– in the south. On the east, it borders on the Biobío river, which there runs south–north, and on the west with the Nahuelbuta Range.

No river in this sector reaches the ocean directly. The Nahuelbuta Range diverts all streams either north to the Biobío or south to the Imperial.

This was the heart of the Mapuche territory, and here Orelie Antoine I attempted to establish his kingdom. The area was wrested from the Mapuches between 1865 and 1880, and open to settlement by foreigners from 1883 to 1888.

This area soon became Chile's granary, with hundreds of mills, mechanized farms and thousands of ox–drawn carts hauling grain to mills at Angol, Traiguén, Collipulli, etc. Thousand of hectares of woodland were clear–cut to turn them into wheat farmland. The great pioneer here was José Bunster (see Land & History). However, bad farming techniques and erosion prompted degradation of the topsoil and a consequent end to profitable farming. Hopes are now focused on afforestation with radiata pine.

The center of this Section is

ANGOL (pop 31,000), nestled at the foot of the Nahuelbuta Range and on the bank of the Vergara river. This river is navigable by small vessels, which sail down to the Biobío confluence and on to Concepción. This strategic location prompted the Spaniards to found here the village of Los Confines in 1553, and re–found it on seven subsequent locations after being razed as many times by the Mapuches. The outpost could not be made secure until the establishment here of the main fort

☎ Telephone Center		**M** D. Bullock Museum
◉ Meeting Point		**RESTAURANTS**
★ Touristic Information		1 Las Torres
ⓖ Gasoline Station		2 Club Social
⇘ Lookout Point		3 Hs Las Araucarias
✷ Hospital		4 Sparlatto
A Bus Terminal		**ACCOMMODATIONS**
B Railway Station		10 H Olimpia
C Rural Bus Terminal		11 H Millaray
D Town Hall		12 R Olimpia
E San Francisco Convent		
F Post Office		**PLACE OF INTEREST**
G Discotheque		15 Serra Ceramics
Club Aéreo		16 Lablee Ceramics

9

What To See the <u>Bunster square</u> is perhaps one of Chile's finest, a double row of linden trees enclosing an open space with a fountain containing **four marble sculptures (NM)** by Virginio Arias. Around the fountain are some elms and four large trees, one at each corner: a magnolia, a blue cedar, a blue fir, and a Cryptomeria elegans.

Cerámica Serra (Apr–Sep, Mon–Sun, 09:00–19:00 h; Oct–Mar, Mon–Sun, 08:00–21:00 h, see map), a ceramics shop, is worth a visit. The **Church and Convent of San Buenaventura** (services Sat 19:30 h, Sun 08:30, 12:00 & 19:30 h) was the first church built in the Araucanía (1863) and headed the missionary work in the region. Walk up Colima street (see map) for a view the town and the surrounding countryside.

Take the road to Huequén (3 km) and beyond the junction, on the left is

El Vergel de Angol (park, Mon–Sun 09:00–20:00 h; museum, Mon–Sun 09:00–13:00 h & 15:00–19:00 h). Founded by José Bunster by 1880, the park contains a large plant and tree nursery. Bunster brought Japanese garden designers to make the park. In 1919 the park was acquired by the Methodist community, which established an Agricultural Institute, still in operation. The institute preserved the park under a new design and introduced more plants, and its first director, Dr D Bullock, founded an anthropological museum.

The **park** has old trees, including sequoias, oaks and cypresses, and lawns.

The **Dillman Bullock museum** has interesting exhibits of pre–Mapuche and Mapuche artifacts. **Sale of Plants**: the best collection of the country with azaleas, rhododendrons, camellias in addition of 19 varieties of copihue (lapageria rosae).

Where To Eat best is the Club Social. With children, best is the get-together place shown in map.

TOURS AROUND THE AREA

1 **FROM COLLIPULLI TO ANGOL ★★**

a 32-km paved stretch from the Pan–American highway.

The most expeditious access to Angol from the Pan–Am, running along the Malleco river.

The Pan–Am reaches Collipulli (pop 11,000), founded in 1867 as the next-to-last of the ten forts set up by Cornelio Saavedra on the Malleco frontier. There is an old mill on the top of the cliff over the Malleco river. At the foot are the **Malleco Viaducts** described under the «Pan-American highway» on this Zone.

The road to Angol crosses Collipulli (km 0), descending gently through rolling land towards the Nahuelbuta Range. At km 16 it approaches the Malleco river, which here runs wide, and runs along its bank. It soon crosses over to the southern bank, to run through wheat farmland and orchards.

At km 26 is **El Vergel**, described above. The road crosses a bridge and the farming village of Huequén. At km 28 is a roundabout and the junction with the Los Angeles–Traiguén road. Angol is at km 32.

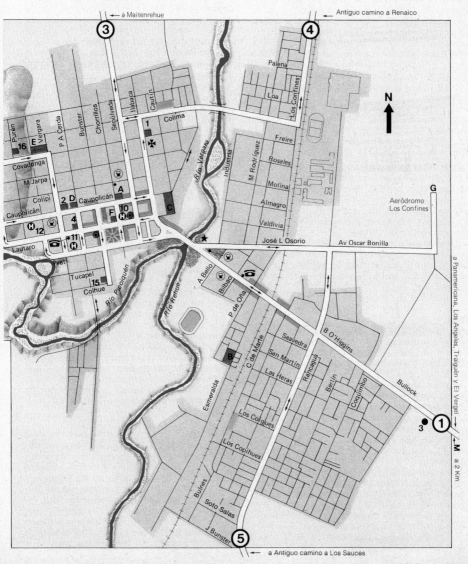

2 TO CONCEPCION VIA NACIMIENTO ★★★

148 km, with 86 km paved and the rest gravel. Gasoline at Nacimiento.
A circuit along the Biobío river, visiting the old forts of Nacimiento and Santa Juana.

Leave Angol (km 0) heading towards the road junction at km 4; turn north to Coihue, a stretch described under Tour 6 of Section A. Just beyond the Coihue railway station turn left, the road now running through a pine–clad plain. Beyond the Vergara river, at km 42, is

NACIMIENTO (pop 12,000), a village lying on a hillock of the Nahuelbuta Range overlooking the plain unfolding to the east, on the banks of the navigable Vergara river. It is expanding rapidly, spurred by the nearby Inforsa and Sudamérica pulp and paper mills, and by several large saw-mills.

Nacimiento was the most important military out-post on the defensive line established along the Biobío, as well as a major trading center with the Mapuches.

Founded as a fort in 1603, it was destroyed and rebuilt three times until 1749, when it was turned into a «Stronghold with Castle», as the labellings went at that time. The houses were protected by a fortified wall and spread along three streets «in the manner of an unequal quadrilateral in the form of a swallow's tail», as the official description read.

When the frontier was pushed farther south in the nineteenth century, Nacimiento lost strategic importance, but started to develop wineries, ceramics and brick industries. Now it is a major forest center.

What To See any of the three original streets - Freire, San Martín and O'Higgins– brings you to the Castle (National Monument), made of brick and looming above the river. The superb view from the castle shows you, to the north, the confluence of the Biobío and Vergara rivers, among wide fields and old Mapuche lands; towards the south, extensive pine forests covering the valley, the buildings of the pulp and paper mills towering above the greenery.

The road continues for 52 km through the rolling, pine–clad foothills of the Nahuelbuta Range, with vine fields farther up. The road finally reaches the small village of **Santa Juana**, at which exit, at km 94, is the

Santa Juana de Guadalcazar Fort founded in 1626 and razed on several occasions until attaining its present form, in 1666. This is another of the defensive outposts along the Biobío, strategically located above the river and protected by a wall and a moat with a bridge at the entrance. The fort is being restored.

The road now runs through farm and forest land, always along the Biobío, which now flows wide, placid and dotted by sand banks. This was the frontier for 200 years. There is a modest campsite on the river bars.

At km 148 is Concepción.

3 TO THE NAHUELBUTA NATIONAL PARK ★★★

an 80–km round trip from Angol on a part gravel, part dirt hill road, not suitable after rain. Gasoline at Angol. Take food. There is a campground at the park. A bus goes to the park on Sundays in summer. Allow 1 ¹/₂ hours for the climb up to the park.
An excursion to one of the most beautiful national parks, with an impressive forest of araucarias and lichens.

Leave Angol following the route shown in map. At km 19 is **Balneario El Manzano**, on the banks of the Picoiquén river, next to a ravine with large rocks among pools suitable for bathing. Very popular in summer.

The gravel road now runs among pine forests and cultivated fields. Vegas Blancas is at km 30, beyond which the dirt road climbs abruptly to the park entrance at km 35. Continue to km 40, the Visitors' Information Center, with a small museum dealing with the local flora and fauna (open from Dec to Mar all days, from 08:00 to 22:00 h. An entrance fee is charged).

Nahuelbuta National Park

NAHUELBUTA NATIONAL PARK (6,832 hectáreas, administered by Conaf (an entrance fee is charged) and located on the crest of the Nahuelbuta Range and Turberas (restricted access), in the wet valley called tembladera (bog), because it moves when walking; surrounded by beautiful bushes and small plants and native orchids, at altitudes ranging from 1,100 m to 1,450 m above the sea. This is one of the last relicts of the majestic araucaria forests on the Coastal Range. The place is absolutely beautiful, in any weather. Clear days bring the added bonus of superb views over the surrounding district. There is a campground and a picnic area, and paths and trails to various special spots.
Piedra del Aguila («Eagle's Stone») is a rocky outcrop accessible through a short climbing path, offering a natural look-out point perched smack atop the crest of the ridge (1,450 m altitude), with a view to both the Pacific ocean on the west, and the snowy volcanoes of the Andes on the East, clear across the country.
Araucarias (monkey puzzle) is the predominant tree in the park. It occurs in association with coihue and lenga and, higher up, isolated, with its roots clinging firmly the rocky ground. Araucaria bark, as it grows older, forms strange polygonal plates with rounded edges, giving rise to mosaic–like patterns. The oldest araucarias in the park are over 2,000 years old and are decorated by «white–beard» lichens hanging from their branches and trunks.

4 TO CONCEPCION VIA PUREN AND ARAUCO ★★★

fifty–eight km (paved) to Purén, and thence 250 km to Concepción, with a 35–km stretch of gravel road; the rest is paved. It is advisable to make this route from the starting points described under Section C.
An alternative route north to Concepción through lake Lanalhue and the coal district.

Leave Angol heading for the Huequén road junction at km 4. Take there the road heading south, which runs through soft rolling country where not a tree or bush is in sight. To achieve this, the pioneers razed the native flora. This, in turn, brought about heavy erosion in many areas, degrading the land dramatically. The saving crop here has been radiata pine, plantations of which have become really ubiquitous.

At km 33 is the **Los Sauces** road junction; take the road heading right, towards the Nahuelbuta range. At km 58 is

PUREN (pop 5,500), lying on the exit of the pass through the Nahuelbuta range, a strategic location in the old days of struggling against the Mapuches. Founded as a fort by Pedro de Valdivia himself in 1553, it was obligingly razed by the Mapuches, almost at once. The present village evolved from a re–foundation of the settlement in 1869, by Cornelio Saavedra. Some of its houses still bear the influence of the German settlers who occupied these lands during last century. The **fort** (1869) squats on a hillock overlooking the valley.

9

5 SOUTH VIA TRAIGUEN AND VICTORIA ★★

it is 99 km (paved) from Angol to Victoria. Add a further 72 km of gravel road (round trip) if you want to visit Lumaco and Capitán Pastene. Gasoline at Traiguén, Victoria and Capitán Pastene.

An alternative route to the south, offering the chance to visit Traiguén, Lumaco and the Italian settlement of Capitán Pastene.

Leave Angol heading for the Huequén road junction at km 4. Take there the road heading south, passing Los Sauces at km 33. The countryside has better tended fields and softer hills, as the distance from the Nahuelbuta Range increases.

At km 64 is a signposted gravel road branching right to Lumaco. Follow this road, which winds its way up among hills.

At km 78, on the right, is the privately-owned **Bellavista forest**, a thick, old forest containing 76 varieties of conifers, including sequoias, picea, cedars, larix, chamanceaparis and pines. The trees are entangled, making it difficult to tell trees apart by foliage alone. Identification is made possible by studying the trunks and bark, and the myriad cones strewn on the ground. If you are a tree buff, ask for permission to visit the forest.

At km 89 the Lumaco valley appears, with a river running north. The Pedro de Valdivia Route used to pass through here from Purén, continuing south to the Imperial river (description under Section C).

On this plain the Spaniards were routed by the Mapuches in 1599, the Chieftain Pelantaro slaying in the process Governor Martín Oñez de Loyola. This victory triggered a widespread uprising of the Mapuches which forced the conquerors to relinquish their seven towns located south of the Biobío.

At km 90 is a bridge and beyond it **Lumaco**, a small village evolved from a fort set up by Cornelio Saavedra in 1869. This territory is located within a Mapuche reservation and is the site of the colorful **Fiesta de Piedra Santa**, a festivity held on January 20. It includes chueca games, dances, traditional garments, rituals and the sacrifice of animals.

The road climbs then out of a narrow valley among pine forests, where the roadbed of the old railway running to the Saboya station can still be made out. At km 100 is

Capitán Pastene (pop 1,600), a village founded in 1904 by Italian immigrants. It has an orderly layout, with wide streets bearing –naturally– Italian names such as Garibaldi, Verdi, Dante, and houses much neater looking than the run–of–the– mill Chilean rural village, rose and palm gardens and all. Nestled on the foothills of the Nahuelbuta range, it lies on sloping ground, with large pine forests behind and a sawmill in the village. There is a gasoline station.

Retrace the road back to the paved highway at km 136. Turn right (south) to reach, at km 141,

TRAIGUEN (pop 13,000) a town evolved from a fort set up in 1878. Six years later, it received a party of multinational settlers, mostly Swiss, who made these rich lands flourish. In 1889 the railway reached it and turned it into the center for settling and wheat farming in the frontier area, elbowing Angol out of this position. José Bunster had his main mills here, the settlers built factories, distilleries and workshops. Traiguén lives now somewhat in the shadow of its more powerful neighbor, Temuco.

What To See the large building of **Muebles Traiguén**, on the square, houses a firm founded in 1888 by a Swiss immigrant, and still running. There is a **small electric locomotive** from 1901 at the railway station, the first of its kind to run in Chile, used to move railway cars around in Bunster's mills.

Visit the beautiful and solemn **cemetery** accessible through a long avenue of evergreen oaks up to a hill with orderly distribution of tombs of the relatives of remarkable settlers who pioneered these lands.

Continue the tour of 30 km up to Victoria along the road running eastward and straight through a fertile farmland, passing nearby an «island hill» («cerro isla») that divides the plain arriving at last to the Pan-American highway at km 171.

☎ Telephone Center
◉ Meeting Point
⊞ Gasoline Station

≫ Lookout Point
A Spanish Fort
B Town Hall
C Parish Church

RESTAURANTS
1 American Bar
2 Central

OF INTEREST
3 Ceramics Shop
4 Boarding Houses

NACIMIENTO

VICTORIA (pop 20,000), the main city of a great valley stretching east to the Andes and the starting point of the road to Curacautín. It evolved from a fort set up in 1881, during the last thrust of the Araucanía campaign, in which the troops moved along the central plain founding, in addition to Victoria, Ercilla, Lautaro and, finally, Temuco. The name of the city is due to its having been founded at the same time as Lima was conquered by Chilean troops during the War of the Pacific. This military leaning can be also seen in the choice of street names: those running north–south have been named after famous battles, while those running east–west bear the name of generals. Av Suiza was christened to honor the first settlers, arrived from Switzerland in 1884.

What To See the **square** is pleasant, surrounded by busy commercial streets. Next to the train station is a **market**. The **Mondión tannery** is worth a visit for those interested in leather processing.

6 TO CURACAUTIN, THERMAL BATHS AND LONQUIMAY ★★★ to Curacautín, 56 km, paved. To Lonquimay, a further 60 km, graveled. Gasoline at Curacautín and Lonquimay.

A beautiful excursion to a high–altitude valley behind the Andes, visiting thermal baths and, as an extension, the mountain lakes of Galletué, Icalma and the Conguillío National Park. See Sections A & B of Zone 10.

Follow exit 4 in map of Victoria (km 0). The road runs through rich farmland stretching well beyond Curacautín. The rivers are swift and flanked by beautiful native forests. At km 56 is

Curacautín (pop 12,100) located on the banks of the Cautín river, it is the head town of a valley hemmed in by the towering Tolhuaca, Lonquimay and Llaima volcanoes, which can be seen from the town. Mapuche tribes living on both sides of the Andes used to halt here during their summer

journey into the mountains to collect araucaria cones, a major item in their diet.

In 1882, a fort was set up at what was then known as Ultra Cautín, and then used as jumping–off point to explore this unknown territory. Trails were hacked through the thick temperate rain–forest covering the land. The village was laid out in 1894 and the lands were sold through public tender in Santiago, being acquired by Chilean settlers.

Curacautín has a hotel and a campground at Trahuilco.

What To See opposite the train station is Chile's oldest plywood factory (1938), processing araucaria from the area. On its side is a French–style house and a park. From the **Cautín river**, 3 km from the town, there is a good view to the Llaima volcano.

Curacautín is an excellent jumping–off point for excursions into the Andes, among which the most breathtaking is the one to the Conguillío National Park, described under Zone 10. Other excursions are to the Tolhuaca Thermal Baths, towards the north, and Manzanar thermal waters and Lonquimay to the east.

Tolhuaca Thermal Baths a beautiful excursion 33 km from Curacautín on a gravel road running along the Dillo river. At the hot springs there is a hotel, restaurant, campground and a group of natural thermal baths and pools on the river. The thermal waters gush inside a cave at 93°C, an ideal natural –and large– place for steam baths. The hot springs were discovered in 1893 by a Russian named Bitikoff, commissioned by the Chilean government to open up trails to carry out measurements of the state lands. The thermal baths are open in summer. Eight km beyond the thermal baths is the

Tolhuaca National Park run by Conaf, with camp-

☎ Telephone Center
◉ Meeting Point
⌖ Gasoline Station
A Railway Station

B Newspaper "Las Noticias de Victoria"

ACCOMMODATIONS
1 H El Bosque

2 Hs y M El Bosque
3 Hs Mackray
4 H Royal

PLACES OF INTEREST
10 Railway Bridge
11 Mondión Tannery

VICTORIA

sites and interesting hikes to the **Malleco waterfall**, where the river plunges 50 meters over the rocks, and **lake Malleco**, beautiful and with good fishing. From here is an alternative route back to the Pan-American highway through Inspector Fernández. Check beforehand about road conditions; usually winter degrades the road badly.

To continue to Lonquimay, leave Curacautín, km 0, following the paved international road heading east, running parallel to the railway and crossing Andean foothills and streams to finally meet the Cautín river. It then follows the river upstream. At km 16 is the spectacular **Salto del Indio**, a 60–m-high plunge, following a 500–m detour to the right; it is worth it. At km 18 is Hostería Abarzúa (accommodations) and, a short way beyond it, the

Manzanar Thermal Baths with a good hotel, a garden, cabins with thermal waters and a large thermal pool on the bank of the Cautín river. Open year round, it is very frequented in summer. In winter, excursions are staged from here to the Lonquimay Volcano Ski Center.

At km 22 is the **Salto de la Princesa** waterfall, with a drop of 50 m in a beautiful setting. The valley becomes squeezed by the mountains as it nears the Cautín headwaters. At km 25 and again at km 29 are two large volcanic stones, **Piedra Cortada** and **Piedra Santa**. The Mapuches passing through here stopped at this place, which for them had a sacred value.

At km 30 is the picturesque village of Malalcahuello, where the access and administration of the **Malalcahuello–Nalcas National Reserve** are located. The reserve, run by Conaf, has a rich flora and fauna –and the best spot for camping, beautiful and quiet. A ski center is being established on the slopes of the Lonquimay volcano, with lifts and a restaurant. Here ends the pavement.

Three km ahead on the international road is a fork, offering two alternatives to reach the village of Lonquimay, **Las Raíces tunnel** or the **mountain road,** each 26 km long. The **tunnel** is a railroad tunnel, but adapted for cars. It is South America's longest tunnel, with 4,528 m, located 1,010 m above sea level and wholly lined with reinforced concrete. In winter, stalactites hang from the ceiling. The tunnel was built in 1930 with the aim of joining the Pacific and Atlantic oceans with a railroad. This aim is yet to be attained.

The **mountain road** climbs amidst splendid native forests with gorgeous views over the Biobío basin and beyond the border into Argentina. **Note** the most frequented of the two alternatives is the tunnel, open 06:00–24:00 h. Three km beyond the tunnel's exit is the Retén Sierra Nevada police station, and 4 km further is the turn–off for the Galletué and Icalma lakes, described in the following tour.

At km 59 from Curacautín is

Lonquimay (pop 2,700), a small village on the bank of the Lonquimay river, a tributary of the Biobío. It has a small hotel, a restaurant, a gasoline station. It was founded as a fort in 1882 and attained village status in 1897, being christened Village Portales. The name was later changed into Lonquimay. The place is located east of the great volcanoes and the higher Andean peaks. The border runs on an arid, lower range on the eastern edge of an enormous valley gashed by the deep canyon of the Biobío river. This territory, although lying east of the Andes, was claimed by Chile on account of its being the upper basin of the Biobío and containing its headwaters.

There are still some Mapuche tribes living in this valley, the tribes known as Pehuenches. It was famous for its gold-bearing sands and, later, for the huge herds of cattle passing through here in the times of open frontiers. Now it is the main route for exporting this zone's products.

The area offers interesting excursions, such as continuing 14 km on the international road to **Lolén**, along the swift Biobío river. Further ahead is Liucura, the border customs, SAG, and police outpost. The most spectacular way to return from Lonquimay is via the **Galletué** and **Icalma lakes**, described below.

7 TO CUNCO VIA LAKES GALLETUE AND ICALMA

★★★ *124 km to Melipeuco and 156 km to Cunco from Lonquimay, on a gravel road. Gasoline at Lonquimay, Melipeuco and Cunco. Camping at the lakes.*

A beautiful excursion through the high valley behind the Andes, amidst ancient araucaria forests and some Mapuche communities. From Melipeuco, you have the option of rounding up the journey through the stunning Conguillío National Park.

Take Lonquimay as your km 0 and follow the road to Curacautín until the junction at km 13. Take the signposted road branching left to Icalma via Fusta, which soon starts to climb a mountain slope -Fusta amid native forests to reach the high ground where araucaria grows.

At km 35 is a scenic river, good for a dip. At km 38 a great valley opens up, with flattish hills and not much vegetation. At km 42 is

Lake Galletué small and lying on a vast pampa. There are several campsites and boats for hire.

At km 49, on the right, there is a string of flat-topped hills. The road continues among araucarias and at km 63 is the **Ruca Nuca bridge**, with a streamlet flowing eastward. This is the mighty Biobío, whose headwaters are at

LAKE ICALMA small and lined with forests, surrounded by Mapuche reservations. The road skirts the southern shore, with several campgrounds and areas for camping in the wild.

At km 70 is the village of Icalma, with a customs outpost, a police station and a state-run store. The border runs three km east of here; the road into Argentina is used mostly by timber trucks.

At km 80 the road leaves the lake shores and soon dives into a fantastic, enormous araucaria forest. At km 90 the road crosses a ridge and then starts a long, winding descent along deep glacial valleys, some with their forests burnt out. As Icalma lies on a high-plateau, it is best to visit it following the route here described, in order to avoid this very long climb.

At km 112 the road reaches a valley bottom with grazing lands. Another road joins it from the left, coming from some Andean villages. Soon the landscape is littered with volcanic debris.

At km 130, a road branches right towards the Conguillío National Park and Curacautín, completing this circuit. If you would rather continue to the Pan–American highway, drive a further 2 km to Melipeuco, a quaint village with a hotel, several restaurants, gasoline station and shops.

Thirty–two km down the valley is Cunco. This route is described under Section A of Zone 10.

9

RURAL TRANSPORTATION

Rural buses offer a convenient way for travellers to tour the many towns and villages in this area, setting off from the Zone's main cities. The rural bus network is vast and covers practically the entire zone, including places not easily reached by car.

Services the chart below shows routes and frequencies for weekdays, each line a route and its thickness indicating the number of daily departures in one direction. The rule of thumb is that on Saturdays frequencies drop by half, while on Sunday low–frequency routes (one to three departures daily) are not covered at all. In season, however (ie, in summer), weekend frequencies from the main inland cities to the main seaside resorts and beaches increase considerably.

Frequency low–frequency routes are the lion's share of the rural network, and usually correspond to the pattern of early morning departure from rural towns to the main cities, returning the same evening. If the distance is short, there might be two departures daily. In cases with three departures daily, there is always an early morning bus leaving the city for the village.

Departure times the first batch of buses depart, in any route, between 07:30 and 08:30 h; the second at 10:30–11:00 h, and the third at 16:30–18:00 h, at which time low–frequency buses return from the cities to the villages. There are no departures over lunchtime, with the exception of high–frequency routes; departures later than 20:00 h are rare. The time when you most certainly will find transportation out of a city is at 16:30–18:00 h, and out of a village or town, early in the morning.

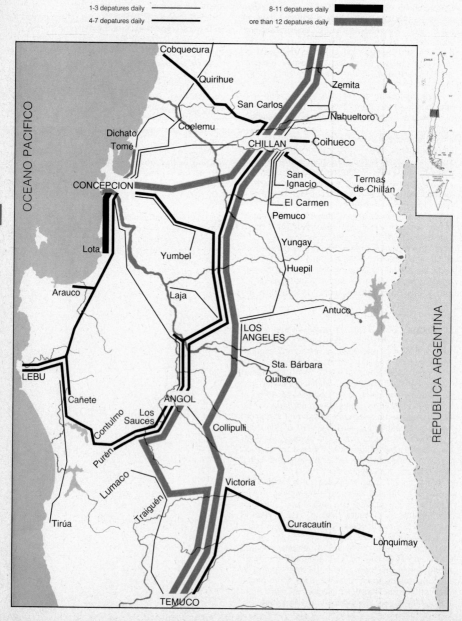

Zone 10
TEMUCO to VALDIVIA

10a

Victoria
Curacautin
Puerto
Saavedra
TEMUCO
Melipeuco
Gorbea
Villarrica
Pucón
PAN-AMERICANA
Panguipulli
VALDIVIA
Corral
Los Lagos
Futrono
La Unión

10b
Lonquimay
ARGENTINA
CHILE

DETAILED MAPS

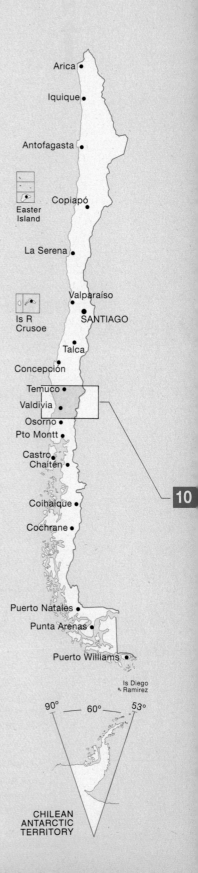

Arica
Iquique
Antofagasta
Easter
Island
Copiapó
La Serena
Valparaíso
Is R
Crusoe
SANTIAGO
Talca
Concepción
Temuco
Valdivia
Osorno
Pto Montt
Castro
Chaitén
Coihaique
Cochrane

10

Puerto Natales
Punta Arenas
Puerto Williams
Is Diego
Ramirez
90°   60°   53°
CHILEAN
ANTARCTIC
TERRITORY

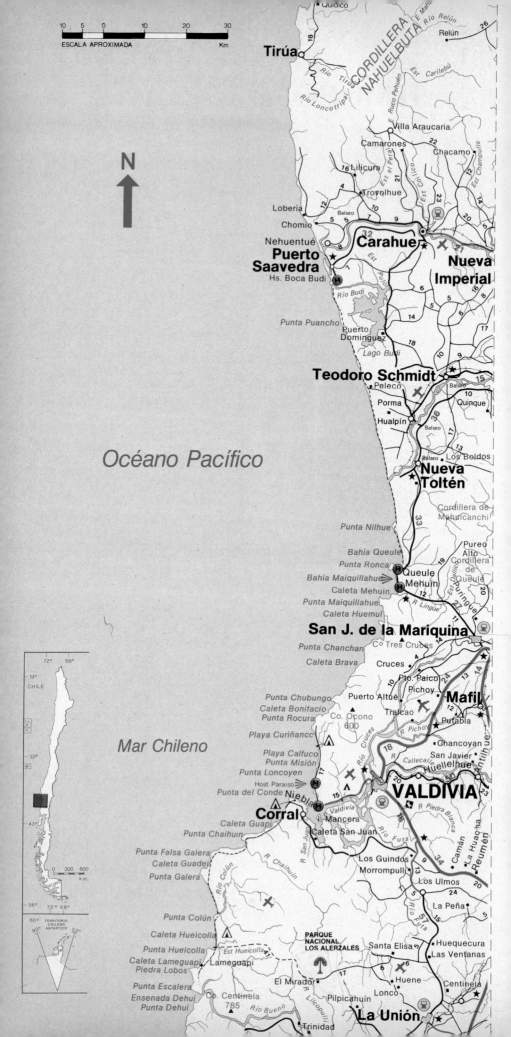

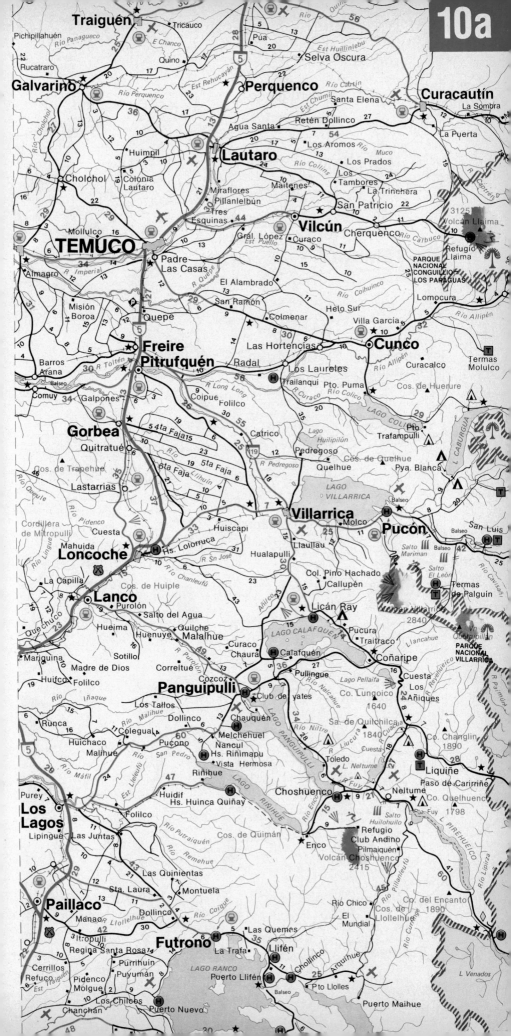

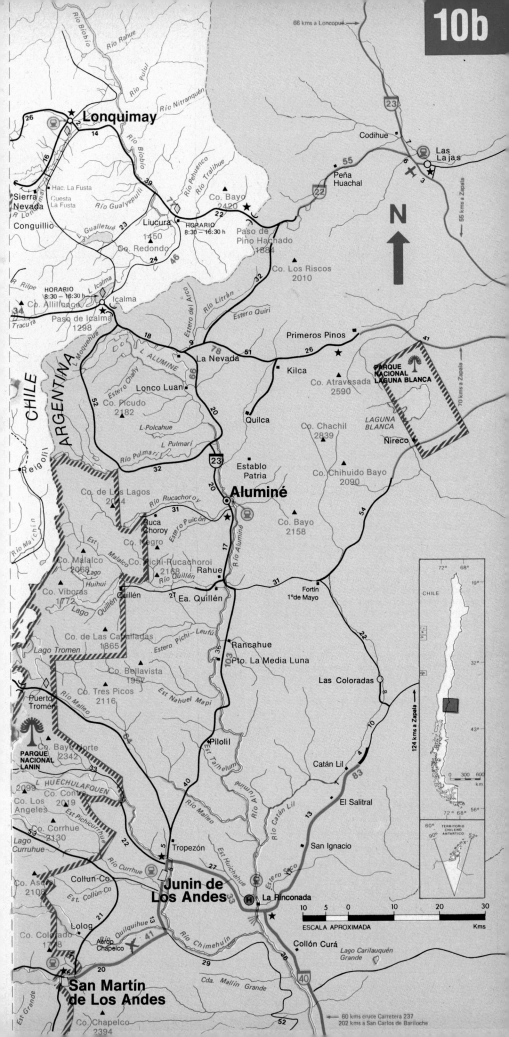

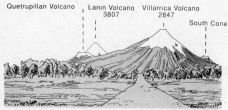

view from Freire

View from the Look-out at Lastarria Range

OVERVIEW

This Tourist Zone covers territories lying within Regions IX and X, and is the northern portion of Chile's Lake District, one of the world's most beautiful lake countries.

The typically southern landscape of native forests and snowy volcanoes starts to predominate just north of Victoria, some 70 km from Temuco. Lonely leafy trees preside over farmed fields, the most notable of these trees being pellín oak, its silvery trunk standing in stark contrast with the dark soil it rises from.

The Pan–American highway runs through softly rolling country. The soaring volcanoes are now much nearer; as each one slides past, new ones appear into view. Rainfall is somewhat higher than farther north; the best season for travelling is Dec–Mar. Volcanoes, native forests, lakes and superb fishing are the main features of this area.

Between Temuco and Valdivia are ten highly scenic lakes of varying sizes and altitudes, connected by a web of roads. The most touristed is lake Villarrica, Chile's second most important holiday center.

Tourist infrastructure is exhaustive, with accommodations ranging from hotels to campgrounds and lots of restaurants. The area is linked by road to Argentina, making it possible to visit neighboring San Martín the Los Andes in the Argentine lake district.

The Zone has been divided into five sections, namely:

Section A   Temuco the city and the surrounding area from the Llaima volcano on the east to the coastline on the west.

Section B   Lake Villarrica including the higher–altitude lakes of Caburgua and Colico.

Section C   Seven Lakes with the string of lakes draining through the Calle Calle river into the Pacific.

Section D   Valdivia covering the city, its rivers and its picturesque coastal villages.

Section E   Routes to Argentina covers the international passes to San Martin de los Andes in Argentina.

REGIONAL DISTANCES

Carahue														
104	Cunco													
172	122	Licán Ray												
196		155	Mehuín											
236	203	202	91	Niebla										
21	83	151	175	215	Nueva Imperial									
198	192	66	99	136	177	Panguipulli								
32		204	228	268	53	230	Puerto Saavedra							
167	161	55	130	160	168	109	199	Pucón						
189	183	172	7	98	168	106	221	137	Queule					
294	288	162	158	105	273	96	326	225	167	Riñihue				
133		195	222	259	112	221	165	200	229	406	Volcán Llaima			
55	49	177	141	181	34	143	87	112	134	239	78	Temuco		
217	191	146	72	19	196	117	249	141	79	86	240	162	Valdivia	
171	71	30	105	142	105	84	203	25	112	208	156	87	123	Villarrica

Zone 10
TEMUCO to VALDIVIA

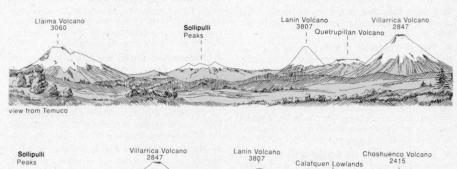

Llaima Volcano 3060 · **Sollipulli** Peaks · Lanin Volcano 3807 · Quetrupillan Volcano · Villarrica Volcano 2847

view from Temuco

Sollipulli Peaks · Villarrica Volcano 2847 · Lanin Volcano 3807 · Calafquen Lowlands · Choshuenco Volcano 2415

DIVISION BY SECTIONS

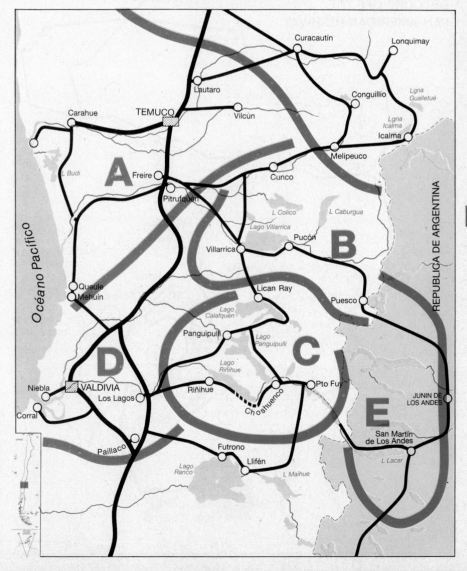

477

DETOURS OFF THE PAN-AMERICAN HIGHWAY

This is one of the areas where leaving the Pan-American highway is most rewarding. We suggest the following detours:

1 A Circuit Along the Pacific Coast ★★★ a circuit through a little-touristed area along the coastline. It is only 40 km longer than along the Pan-Am to Mariquina, albeit graveled. See Section A, Tour 6.

1a Visiting Lake Budi ★★★ an extension of the above detour, traversing Mapuche territory to visit Chile's only salt lake.

2 Through Conguillío ★★★ it is not a proper detour, but a visit to the fantastic Conguillío National Park, behind the Llaima Volcano. See Section A, Tour 2.

3 A Visit to Villarrica ★★ fine scenery and the gorgeous Villarrica volcano and National Park will reward those choosing this detour, on a paved road fifty km longer than straight through the Pan-Am from Freire to Loncoche.

4 A Detour Through the Glacial Moraine ★★ a nearly entirely paved detour of 201 km through the moraines that gave rise to various lakes, visiting the main town of three major lakes, Villarrica, Calafquén and Panguipulli. It is only 40 km longer than along the Pan-Am from Freire to Los Lagos.

5 A Peek at Lake Panguipulli ★★ a detour of 136 km, 20 km of which are graveled, and only 44 km longer than along the Pan-Am from Lanco to Los Lagos.

6 A Different Access Route to Valdivia ★★★ particularly suitable for those making detours 4 or 5 above, it follows the Calle Calle river downstream to Valdivia. The road is graveled.

7 The Inter-Lake Circuit ★★★ a fantastic circuit deep into lake country, among volcanoes, native forests and breathtaking scenery. Check beforehand about the conditions of the Riñihue–Enco stretch, as it is the most easily degraded in winter.

8 Transvolcanic Circuit ★★★ a circuit through some of the Zone's finest scenery, with a taste of adventure traversing the country behind the volcanoes and visiting a string of six lakes draining into the Calle Calle river, plus lakes Maihue and Ranco. Note: The area between Puerto Fuy and Llifén is now private property and its owners do not authorize passage.

9 The Grand Circuit ★★★ a combination of Detours 2 & 8 is much more than just a trip: it is a whole vacation. Throw in lakes Caburgua and Colico by the north shore through Cunco and you get an unforgettable tour.

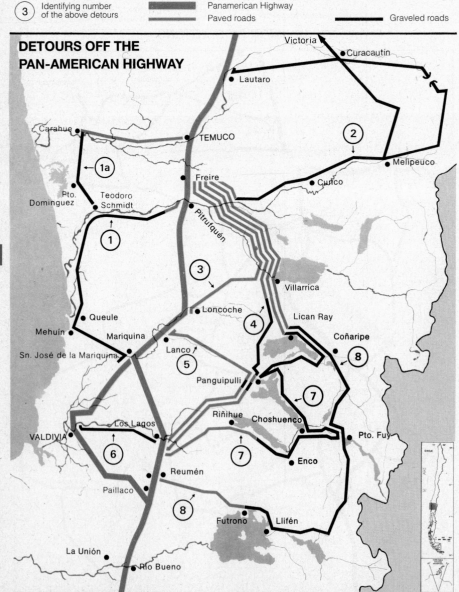

DETOURS OFF THE PAN-AMERICAN HIGHWAY

THE LAND, ITS HISTORY, ITS PEOPLE

MORPHOLOGY

Formation of the Valleys   unlike the **Torrential Valleys** of Chile's Central Zone, created by torrents of rainwater and at the bottom of whose V–shaped basin a stream or brook flows, the Andean valleys in this Zone have a U–shaped profile. They were formed by the slow creeping of voluminous glaciers from the mountain tops to the lowlands, crushing and grinding whole mountains and carving the valley walls and bottom in the process. Usually the walls of these **glacial valleys** are sheer rock faces.

The road to the border runs straight into the Andes, with no dramatic climbs as the case would be farther north in Chile. The Central Plain is rolling, not yet filled up by sedimentation brought about by rain–induced erosion. The heavy, frequent rains support luxuriant native forests and make agriculture possible without irrigation.

Lake Formation   this area contains the first lakes in the Central Plain, their origins dating back some 10 thousand years, when glaciers started to retreat. Careful observation of the lake's outlet, usually on its western end, will show you a dam–like formation which trapped the waters to form the lake. These are **glacial moraines**, an accumulation of debris from when the glaciers melted in the past. Most lakes in the south feature a moraine dam, best seen from the opposite end of the lake; in lake Villarrica, for instance, it is best seen from Pucón looking west. Some roads climb these moraines; note the rounded boulders joined by a sandy mortar–like soil: it is glacial sediment. **Lake Caburgua** (in the mountains up from Pucón) is a different case. Volcanic in origin, it was dammed by a porous plug of volcanic slag and ash, which permits water to seep through under the ground and emerge farther down at the Ojos del Caburgua ponds. **Lake Pirehueico** (south of Panguipulli) was spawned by an eruption of the Choshuenco volcano, which filled up the Fuy valley with slag (at the area of Neltume), creating a lake behind. This volcanic plug has scarcely been eroded over the centuries, as it consists of a crystallized lava vein of very hard basalt, giving rise to the superb **Huilo Huilo waterfall**, among Chile's grandest and most beautiful.

The Seven Lakes are Calafquén, Pellaifa, Neltume, Pirehueico, Lacar (across the border in Argentina), Panguipulli and Riñihue, and they are anomalous in two ways. One is that these lakes form a string, each draining into the next and finally, through the San Pedro river, the Calle Calle's main tributary, into the sea. This results from the fact that the moraine damming lakes Calafquén and Panguipulli was so high, that the accumulated water flowed eastwards to drain through the lowest lake in the string, lake Riñihue.

The second anomaly is that between a couple of these lakes runs the first Argentine river washing into the Pacific, a situation encountered again several times farther south. The reason for this is that the glaciers flowed down both sides of the Andes, creating lakes in both areas. The moraine forming the Argentine lake Lacar turned out to be so high, that water was «pushed» backwards towards the Chilean side through the Huahún river, carving the lowest pass across the Andes, with only 600 m above sea level.

The Volcanoes the Cordillera of the Andes is part of the so–called «Pacific Fire Rim». This section of cordillera alone has the active volcanoes Llaima, Villarrica, Quetrupillán, Lanín and Mocho-Choshuenco, and several extinct ones in the area of lake Caburgua. Chile's most consistently active volcanoes are **Villarrica** and **Llaima**, with ten eruptions each this century alone. An eruption in one of them can easily trigger a chain reaction. It is known that in 1640, 1750 and 1765, all the above volcanoes erupted simultaneously.

Mapuche lore still recalls these cataclysms which forced them to abandon their lands. The native forests in the valleys between Freire and the Andes are not older than 250 years, confirming the reports. Their snow caps make Chile's volcanoes doubly dangerous. When one of them erupts, the lava melts the ice and snow and provokes savage flash floods carrying mud, lava, ash and logs down the slopes and destroying whatever happens to be on their way. Lava tends to flow more slowly and less abundantly, but burns everything it comes in contact with. The last time lava reached the shores of lake Villarrica was in 1968. In 1971, the Villarrica erupted and the flood wiped out the old village of Coñaripe; only memorial crosses remain.

TORRENTIAL VALLEY

10

GLACIAL VALLEY

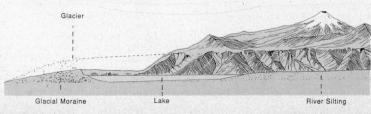

Glacier

Glacial Moraine   Lake   River Silting

LAKE FORMATION

HISTORY

The Temuco–Valdivia Zone includes adjacent territories which were incorporated into Chile 250 years apart: Valdivia up to the Cruces river valley, incorporated in 1645, and the so–called Frontier Region, pacified a scant century ago.

The Mapuche Indians the inhabitants of this zone were called Araucanos by the Spaniards, but they preferred to refer to themselves as Mapu-che («men of the earth»); they called their tongue Mapu–dungun («tongue of the earth»). The Mapuches occupied the territory from the Illapel valley to the North to the Chiloé island to the South. Ethnically and linguistically they were a single people, but the sheer length of their territory gave rise to minor differences in dialect and customs. Those in Chiloé were sedentary, monogamous, fishermen and farmers, while those in this area were polygamous, fishermen, farmers, nomadic herdsmen, and gatherers of araucaria pine cones in the Cordillera.

The number of Mapuches in the area from the Biobío river to the Reloncaví sound was estimated at half a million by 1600. They did not form towns or villages, but lived grouped into family clans. Their numbers are now much smaller, and few are pure–blooded (perhaps some 20,000).

Mapuches had a keen sense of property over family and household utensils, but not over land and animals; these goods were for the common benefit of the clan. The animals were shared out among the children and the land was abandoned when it became degraded. This accounts for the ease with which they moved to other locations when their lands were occupied.

The Mapuche Landscape the relatively high number of Mapuches in the old days and their agricultural technique of cultivating the land intensively until soil degradation set in, coupled with browsing by livestock, account for the landscape described by the early chroniclers, of open lands with softly rolling hills crowned by Mapuche rucas –dwellings– and dotted with forest stands.

When the population decreased, the scenery changed radically as the forests advanced. Depopulation was caused by wars and smallpox epidemics, in addition to the extremely violent volcanic activity of the 17th and 18th centuries, which forced Mapuches to desert the Andean valleys and the areas near the lakes.

Spanish Influence the most significant changes brought about in Mapuche life by the presence of Spaniards on their borders were a semi–permanent state of war and the abduction or "malón" as a means of obtaining goods; in agriculture, the introduction of wheat and barley, and apple trees, which spread quite fast. In livestock farming, the introduction of beef and dairy cattle, sheep, and horses. Horses expanded the innate sense of mobility of the Mapuches, helping them to roam deeply into the Argentine pampas, where they imposed their language upon the local tribes and intermingled strongly with them.

Spanish Conquest and Colonization during the first half–century of the Spanish conquest, the driving force was to explore and settle the entire territory granted to the conquerors by the King of Spain. Pedro de Valdivia, after nine years spent consolidating his dominion over the country's central zone, surveyed the area to the south by land to the Reloncaví sound. Eight cities were founded south of the Biobío; Valdivia, Osorno and La Imperial (present–day Carahue) were Chile's most prosperous, and indeed America's. But in 1598 a great general Mapuche uprising forced the Spaniards to relinquish the cities, industries and farms south of the Biobío. The only city surviving was Castro, tucked away in the island of Chiloé.

The Biobío Frontier in the 1640s, a Parley of Quillén brought the legal establishment of the Biobío river as the border between the Spanish and the Mapuche territories. This situation lasted until 1892.

Second Foundation of Valdivia the Pacific coast,

with the discovery of the pass through Cape Horn, lay wide open for raids by the fleets of Spain's European enemies. The Peru Viceroyship, to which Chile was subordinate, decided then to fortify Valdivia and its coast in order to defend the South Pacific. The city was founded anew and in 1645 the forts of Corral and Niebla were set up at either side of the estuary, while another fortress sat in midstream at isle Mancera; Fort Cruces was set up some distance upstream of the settlement to protect its eastern approaches. For nearly one century, this stronghold and naval bastion –the only Spanish enclave in this area– was directly subordinate to Lima.

From 1740 until the Foundation of the Republic in 1740, the city of Valdivia came to be subordinate to the Capitanía General de Chile, and a policy of strong territorial expansion started to be carried out. Private individuals were authorized to hold farmland, religious missions were established, Los Llanos (present–day La Unión) was rediscovered, the road to Chiloé was reopened and in 1796 Osorno was founded. By the end of the century, large tracts of land in the Valdivia and Osorno area were privately owned.

Chile's first Constitution in 1822 established the country's southern border at Cape Horn. However, the only settlements south of the Biobío river were Valdivia, Osorno and Castro (Chiloé). The rest of the country had not been incorporated into the republic.

The Bulnes Decade (1840-1850) several actions were undertaken to incorporate these territories: in 1843 the Straits of Magellan becomes parts of Chile; in 1846 Ignacio Domeyko proposed to assimilate Mapuches culturally and religiously; between 1842 and 1845, Bernardo Philippi, gathering Chilean flora and fauna for the Museum of Berlin, was commissioned by the Chilean government to survey the inland lakes in the Osorno and Llanquihue areas; in 1845, legislation was passed which turned all vacant lands into state property; in 1848, Philippi was appointed Settlement Agent in Germany to entice immigrants to settle southern Chile; and in 1850 Vicente Pérez Rosales was appointed Settlement Agent in Valdivia to allot lands to the immigrants sent by Philippi from Germany.

German Immigration in the Valdivia area there were no free state–owned lands to homestead. German immigration was therefore directed towards the Llanquihue area. But Valdivia itself received a hefty German influx. The immigrants, with their own means, established industries and farms which, by the turn of the century, transformed Valdivia into Chile's leading industrial city.

Incorporation of the Araucanía until 1881 the Mapuche territory was an island in the country. In 1862, the frontier was pushed from the Biobío river south to the Malleco river, and Angol was founded. In 1865 the border was set at the Toltén river, delimiting the area of expansion for the city of Valdivia.

Fifteen years later, almost at the end of the War of the Pacific and when the railway had reached Angol, the government decided to unify the country. The army pushed forward to the Cautín river, on whose banks the city of Temuco was founded in 1881. The following year the frontier was pushed south to Nueva Imperial and Carahue, to continue to Freire and Villarrica along the Toltén river, where the village was founded anew at the same location as the previous Spanish village.

The Mapuche territory, once pacified, was incorporated with astounding speed. In a scant dozen years the railway reached Temuco and the journey from Santiago took only 36 hours. Between 1885 and 1896, over 8,000 settlers from nine different countries arrived to homestead lands between Angol and the Cautín river. By the turn of the century, few state–owned lands were left to allot. It is worth remembering that the pacification of the Araucanía, as pioneering as it may sound, was carried out when in Santiago the Municipal Theater, the landscaping of the Santa Lucía hill, the Cousiño Palace and the Central Station had all been completed.

10

Allotment of the Araucanía Lands the Mapuche population between the Biobío and Toltén rivers was estimated at somewhat over 60,000 in 1876. The large size of this territory left huge tracts unoccupied, which were then brought under State ownership. They were apportioned firstly among settlers (40 hectares each), and the rest auctioned –starting in 1896– in larger tracts (400 ha and above). By 1912 the process of «reducing» the Mapuche territory was concluded, by apportioning delimited lands to each family clan; the total area distributed among them was about 300,000 hectares.

Finally, from 1906 onwards, the state–owned lands in the Andean valleys started to be slowly settled, by farmers of Chile's Central Zone, giving rise to a system of small holdings preserved to this day.

Present Development this Zone accounts for 3.4% of the country's population, with nearly 400,000 inhabitants. Temuco is the capital city of Region IX, Araucanía, and Valdivia the capital of Region X, Valdivia. The main traditional activity is farming, with major wheat and barley crops. During the past decade, agriculture has undergone a strong process of industrialization, introducing crops such as sugar beet and raps, and large forestry and dairy farming operations which have made of this a burgeoning Zone.

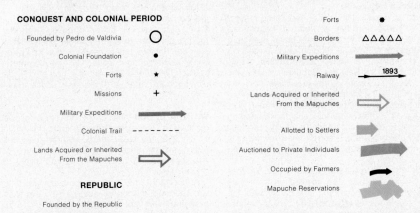

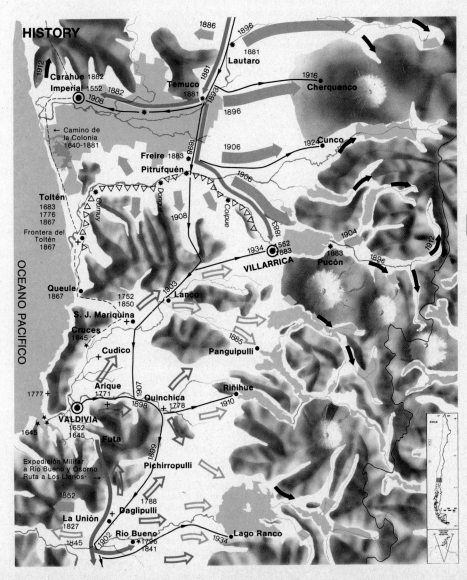

PAN–AMERICAN HIGHWAY

For those wishing to travel straight through to more southerly destinations, we list below the main attractions visible from the Pan–Am.

PAN - AMERICAN HIGHWAY FROM TEMUCO TO

PAILLACO ★★★ *the paved highway offers two alternatives: via Los Lagos, with 191 km, and via Valdivia, with 211 km.*

The Pan-Am starts to run through a thoroughly southern landscape, with native forests, large rivers and towering, perfect-coned volcanoes.

South of Temuco (km 0; city description in Section A), the Pan-Am has a stretch of double-carriage highway and crosses the Cautín river, running through soft-rolling reddish land. On the left is a picturesque religious construction in a style introduced by the Bavarian Capuchin monks who preached the Gospel in the Araucanía.

At km 12 is the Metrenco Sanctuary with a restaurant and campground across the street.

At km 14 is the Quepe toll –only those heading north must pay– and then an open, carefully farmed plain. There is a superb view towards the Villarrica volcano (see illustration at the beginning of this Zone).

This area was an impenetrable jungle. When a 50-m wide strip was opened through it in 1898 to lay the railway, according to a chronicle of the time, «the trees were axed until only a slender section of wood kept them standing; when a stretch of them had been thus prepared, they would all be felled simultaneously, knocking over the adjacent rows of trees and clearing a whole strip of jungle in one stroke, with a deafening din and cracking...». At km 27 is

Freire¹ with a square containing an impressive array of conifers. A paved branch road to Villarrica and Pucón starts here. Four km ahead is the **Toltén river**, with a railway bridge supported by giant steel tubes –a revolutionary technique for the time–, built by Gustave Verniory in 1898. At km 31 is **Pitrufquén**, with the best plant nurseries for azaleas, camellias and rhododendrons. Worth a visit during the blossoming season Set to Nov. See Tips.

At km 43 is **Gorbea**, the last town in this area with a nice square. It is well known for her cherries, chestnuts, good chicha from March to April, and her excellent sausages (See Tips). The Pan-Am runs here on the valley, avoiding the laborious but beautiful crossing of the Lastarria range.

At km 78 is a road junction for Villarrica (paved), and three km later the Pan-Am bypasses **Loncoche**. A short way ahead is Hostería Lolorruca on the right-hand side, offering good accommodation and food.

The Pan-Am now runs on the Cruces river

valley –it crosses the river several times–, bypassing **Lanco** on km 96, with a branch road for Panguipulli (paved). At km 119 is a forking offering two options to continue south: via Los Lagos or via Valdivia.

LOS LAGOS OPTION this is a newly built section of Pan-American highway, running through soft-rolling country dotted with native forests, bypassing Máfil at km 133. At km 162 the road crosses the swift **San Pedro river** and reaches the forest town of **Los Lagos**, a scattered place on a hill overlooking the river. A paved branch road to lake Riñihue starts here, as well as an unpaved secondary road to Valdivia, described under Section D.

At km 181 is a paved road junction for Futrono on lake Ranco (see Zone 11); ten km later is Paillaco, where the Pan-Am is joined by the road coming from Valdivia. There is a police checkpoint.

VALDIVIA OPTION this is the old route followed by the Pan–American highway. From the forking at km 119, the road heads towards the coast, bypassing San José de la Mariquina at km 121 and then running on a plain with relatively degraded land.

At km 132 is the Pichoy Airport, serving Valdivia. The land is soon crisscrossed by rivers and peppered with ponds; the road seems to run above water. These are the Pichoy marshes, created when the ground sank during an earthquake in 1960 and became waterlogged by the Pichoy river. It is a beautiful area teeming with birds.

The road makes ample curves through pine forests and reaches Valdivia and the Calle Calle river at km 161. City description under Section D.

The Pan–Am continues southeast alongside a small river with large reed-lined ponds and lots of black–necked swans. This is another water-logged area brought about by the 1960 earthquake.

At km 177 is a road junction for Los Ulmos and the seaport of Corral. The Pan-Am now crosses the Coastal Range, with hills of a coarse yellowish sand known as maicillo. By the road are low, round trees with longish leaves: they are Long-Leaved Mañíos, one of the few conifers native to Chile.

At km 211 is the Paillaco junction with a police road control. This alternative is only 20 km longer than through Los Lagos.

Food and Accommodation Temuco and Valdivia offer the widest range of both. Lolorruca is a good alternative on the road, 4 km south of Loncoche. There is a modest campground next to the first bridge across the Cisnes river, just beyond Lanco, and a campsite near the San Pedro bridge opposite Los Lagos.

SECTION A   TEMUCO

This section covers the area from the Llaima volcano and the Conguillío National Park in the Andes, to the vast stretch of coast from the Imperial to the Toltén river. The center is the city of

TEMUCO (pop 160,000) capital of Region IX, Araucanía. Chile's youngest large city, it was founded barely over a century ago (1881), on the banks of the Cautín river and as the head town on the new frontier. It burgeoned quickly, spurred by multinational immigration –particularly Spaniards, Frenchmen and Germans. It is now a thriving city and among the most developed in Chile. It preserves valuable relics from its past. It also has the best and most extensive collections of the mapuche culture.

What To See shopping hours Mon–Fri 09:00–13:00 h and 15:00–19:00 h; Sat 08:30–13:00 and 15:30–18:00 h). Visit the **galería Artesanal** (see map), on Av Caupolicán, offering Mapuche handicrafts. Here you can order "ponchos" and rugs made to your specifications.

The Market is the traditional outlet for Mapuche handicrafts. Unfortunately, a recent remodelling deprived it of most of its architectural attractiveness. It contains silver objects, knitwear and woollen goods, and even valuable antiques for the connoisseurs. There are several restaurants offering typical dishes.

Continue along calle **M Rodríguez** for four more blocks; on this street you will find the main stores that supply the farming regions, large shops, hardware stores and dealers in leather goods. At the end of this street is the **Feria** (open market) and the **Railway Station**. Mapuche craftsmen come directly from their reservations to offer their creations at this market (Mon–Sat 09:00–14:00 h). Bargaining is part of the selling process for a Mapuche; still, keep in mind that each item is the result of a whole winter of work by the Mapuche woman back at the reservation.

Return to the centre of town, along calle Portales to start your journey by car. The old bridge across the Cautín river (follow Vicuña Mackenna) lies alongside the **Railway Bridge** (1898). Following the paved right branch at the forking beyond the river, you reach the village of **Padre Las Casas** and the Pan–Am. Turn right once more and come Temuco by the southern industrial district, crossing the new bridge turn left into **Av Alemania**, in Temuco itself, is shaded by large trees and has nice sprawling houses. This street epitomizes Temuco's thriving nature. Here is the

Museo Regional de la Araucanía (in summer,
Mon–Sat 09:00–19:00 h; Sun 10:00–13:00 h; in winter Tue–Sat 09:00–18:00 h; Sun 10:00–13:00 h) providing an insight into Mapuche history and culture.

Following Av Alemania to turn south on Hochstetter you come to the

Municipal Swimming Pool (Piscina Municipal),
with modern swimming pools of crystalline water in a beautiful park.

Cerro Ñielol (see map) you get there through Prat
Street, 10 blockes from Plaza de Armas. This place –which is a National Park– will give you a sweeping view of the city from the look–out at the summit.

Where To Eat the cafeteria at the Piscina Municipal and the restaurant at the Cerro Ñielol look–out are children-friendly and offer fine views. Nueva Estancia specializes in beef. Fine cuisine and excellent service at Club Alemán. Chilean dishes and seafood at the Market food stalls and restaurants. Quick meals at the site indicated with an asterisk in map. Picnic at the Cerro Ñielol park (tables). Takeout food at the Rapa Nui Restaurant.

On your return trip, you can rest at Isla Verde Center, 9 km north of Temuco.

TOURS FROM TEMUCO

1 TO THE LLAIMA VOLCANO ★★★
a round trip of 162 km. Take food and gasoline.
A visit to the Los Paraguas section of the gorgeous Conguillío National Park, with a fine view over the Central Valley.

Follow the Pan–Am 9 km to the north, to a place called Cajón, and take there the asphalt road branching right. It runs level up to **Vilcún**, after which (graveled) it starts to climb gently up to **Cherquenco**. In the last stretch, the road is narrow and climbs steeply among forests. Look for lake **Quepe** on the left (unsigned, cross a fence), small and emerald–green, untrampled and with a beautiful spot for free–lance camping. The road becomes little more than a trail, lined with majestic **araucarias** and other patches of native forests; the scenery is wonderful, with views of snowy peaks and the great valley below.

The road ends at a shelter on the volcano. Here start several paths leading to the permanent snows farther up.

9 km north of Temuco, at the Pan–Am, is Isla Verde Center, a good option to stop on the road, especially if you are travelling with children.

2 TO THE CONGUILLIO NATIONAL PARK ★★★
a circuit of 251 km, allow at least one day. Cabins and campground at Conguillío. Take food. Gasoline at Melipeuco and Curacautín. This tour can also be combined with the circuit through

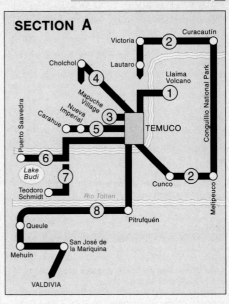

SECTION A

Lonquimay and lake Icalma described under Section D of Zone 9.
A visit to a wonderful National Park, among the best equipped in Chile.

There are several alternative routes leading to the park. We suggest to start from Temuco (km 0) through **Las Hortensias** and then **Cunco** (km 59); the town is described under Tour 11, Section B. Continue towards **Melipeuco** (km 91), to climb behind the Llaima volcano to the

CONGUILLIO NATIONAL PARK 60.850 hectares (open all day in summer, a fee is asked). It has cabins, boats for hire and park rangers providing information and guiding hikers (motor boats are not allowed). The park consists of a high–altitude Andean valley with four small lakes created by volcanic slag plugging the water outlets. The largest is **lake Conguillío**. The other three –**Verde, Arco Iris** and **Captrén**- are more recent, not older than 30-50 years: dead forests can still be seen under the water. The scenery is untouched, with 1,200–year-old araucaria forests, and oaks, cypresses, coihues and raulíes growing among waterfalls and stark, craggy lava fields from the latest eruptions. It is well worth a visit.

To return, we suggest to drive to Curacautín, whence a paved road brings you to the Pan–American highway at Victoria. On the way south from Temuco to Victoria is

Lautaro a town evolved from one of the forts set up by the expeditionary force marching to the Cautín river in 1881; it lies on its banks. Its **Parque Isabel Riquelme** is worth a visit, next to the fish farm which spread salmonoid species in Chile's southern streams. You can combine this trip with the Lonquimay and lake Icalma circuit described under Zone 9, Section D.

3 TO MAPUCHE COUNTRY ★★★
a 35-km circuit with 21 km of dirt road, not recommendable after rain. Take exit 4 in map.
A chance to visit a Mapuche community in their ancestral lands.

4 km from Temuco the cultivated fields suddenly give way to rolling, sandy ground, the grass barely growing. This is a Mapuche reservation, the land property of the community. The holdings are small and separated –if at all– by some shrubs known as **pica-pica** surrounding wheat fields. Some cows and sheep can be seen, always tended by a herdsman dubbed **live fence:** this is the traditional occupation of Mapuche men in the family structure.

10

Also to be seen are groups of rucas (see below), cemeteries and many degraded and eroded fields affected by overcultivation.

THE RUCA is the traditional Mapuche dwelling. The wealthier Mapuches have up to three of them, using them to sleep, cook and as a storage room, respectively. Other families have only one ruca for all three purposes. Now it is common to see, next to the rucas, some simple wooden sheds with roofs of corrugated zinc where products and animals are kept. There is always a pen made of twigs intertwined in basket fashion. Bear in mind that Mapuches do not like to have their picture taken.

The road continues to Mollulco, with a church. Turn left to follow a road leading to Estación Labranza, where you reach the paved highway to return to Temuco.

4 TO A MAPUCHE VILLAGE ★★

a circuit of 84 km, with 50 km paved. Take gasoline.

A tour through Mapuche reservations seen from the road, and to a relatively pure Mapuche village.

Leave Temuco towards Cholchol, traversing a scenery similar to the one of Tour 3 above, to continue to Nueva Imperial and then return to Temuco. **Cholchol** is a picturesque village in a relatively pure Mapuche cultural environment, lying on the bank of a slow-moving river with several spots suitable for bathing. Return through the road to Nueva Imperial, described in Tour 5 below.

An alternative for those travelling north is to continue from Cholchol to Galvarino and Traiguén, following the old Conquest Road described under Zone 9.

5 TO NUEVA IMPERIAL AND CARAHUE ★★★

a round trip of 82 km from Temuco on paved roads. Gasoline and restaurant at Carahue.

A visit to the river and setting of the most prosperous city during the Spanish Conquest.

Take exit 3 out of Temuco. At km 34 is

Nueva Imperial a village with gaily-painted houses, in a curious form of urban expression carefully kept alive by its inhabitants. A 21 km Paved road will bring you further to

CARAHUE sitting atop a hillock facing the south. This is the site where Pedro de Valdivia founded the famed city of La Imperial. It was a bishopric with a cathedral church, and had mills, granaries and a sizable population. The town was deserted in 1599 as a result of the Mapuche uprising which rid the entire Araucanía of Spanish presence.

Founded anew in 1882, it became a river port through which the zone's wheat output was shipped, taking to advantage the fact that the Imperial river is navigable up to here; a railway brought the cargo from the heartland.

Carahue's atmosphere harks back to those days, with its wharves, old storage buildings, trading houses and streets climbing to the square above.

For those wishing to continue to **Trovolhue,** follow the unpaved road along the river for 12 km heading for the coast, to take the road branching right at that point. The road crosses some hills to reach the Trovolhue river valley, a total distance of 22 km from Carahue. This is a very scantily-touristed area, with a secluded valley receiving the streams flowing from the Nahuelbuta Range. It is a very good jumping-off point for hikes along the coast to see the lively **sea-lion colonies.**

6 TO PUERTO SAAVEDRA ★★

a round trip of 174 km from Temuco; it is a 64-km extension of the above tour.

An excursion to the Pacific coast and the mouth of the river draining lake Budi.

Follow the route to Carahue described above. From there, cross the Imperial river, following the road running close to the river for 34 km to reach the coast. At the curve on the river, you can see **Doña Inés island,** the site where a wealthy public figure chose to build his house and park in 1895. It is reputedly the first summer residence built in southern Chile. At km 87 is **Puerto Saavedra,** founded in 1895 as a service village for the pilots steering the ships up the river. It grew to respectable proportions over the years, but it was razed by a tidal wave in 1960. Reestablished now behind the sand dunes, it is a supply town for the coastal farmers. Continue three km towards the south to

Boca Budi the mouth of the stream draining lake

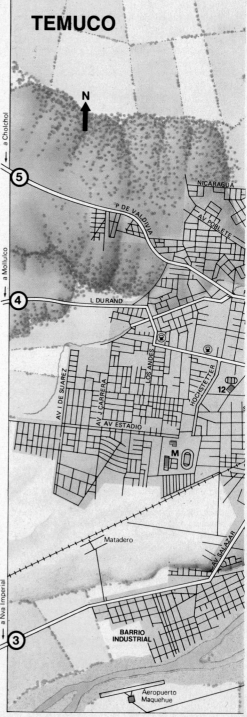

TEMUCO

Budi. There is a hotel–restaurant. The coastal scenery is flat; to the south the Queule promontory can be seen. The beach is seemingly unending, wind–swept and with sand dunes on the back. A trail used to run along this beach, the only passage allowed by the Mapuches for the Spaniards to travel between Concepción and Valdivia.

7 TO PUERTO DOMÍNGUEZ AND LAKE BUDI

★★★ *it is 82 km from Temuco to Puerto Domínguez and a 18 km further to Teodoro Schmidt. Take gasoline.*

An excursion through Mapuche country to the picturesque lake Budi, with a possible extension to Queule and Mehuín, on the coast.

Follow the 55–km paved road from Temuco to Carahue. Cross the bridge across the Imperial river and take the signposted gravel road to Puerto Domínguez. At km 82 is

PUERTO DOMÍNGUEZ AND LAKE BUDI the village is small and with an orderly layout along the lake's shore. It has a port, boats for hire and a ferry plying the routes along the shore. Excellent fishing. This is Chile's only salt-water lake, home to an enormous number of waterfowl, the most striking being black–necked swans. The lake is flanked by hills clad in lush native vegetation. **Isla Huapi** is an interesting spot for visiting (ferry, 45 minutes), with a friendly Mapuche community.

A 18 km further on a gravel road will bring you to **Teodoro Schmidt**, a village christened in honor of a German surveyor commissioned by the Chilean government to explore these lands in 1881.

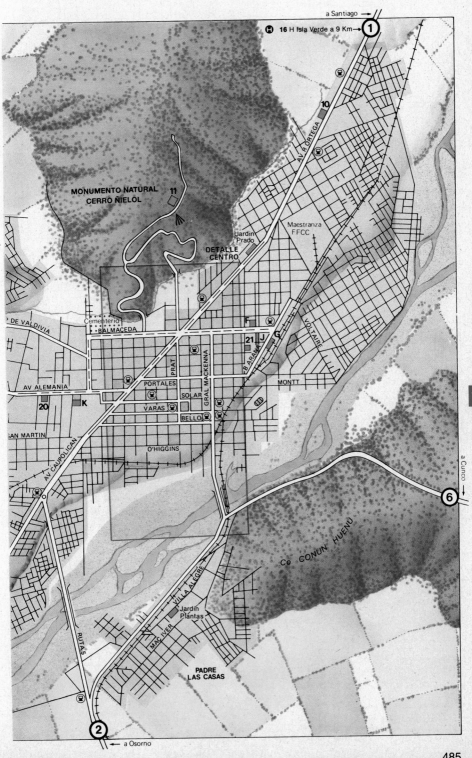

10

485

Downtown TEMUCO

a Mirador C Ñielol

Co. Ñielol

Cementerio

Piscina

LOS CONDORES

a Santiago

JANEQUEO

PATAKE

BILBAO

LAS ACACIAS

PRAT

L

AV BALMACEDA

MIRAFLORES

LAUTARO

RODRIGUEZ

PORTALES

MONT

C SOLAR

VARAS

BELLO

SAN MARTIN

O'HIGGINS

LEON GALLO

IMPERIAL

IMPERIAL

AV CAUPOLICAN

D

E

D

C

A

E B

D

D

B

PRAT

BULNES

ALDUNATE

G MACKENNA

CRUZ

ZENTENO

V MACKENNA

LINCH

LAGOS

LAS HERAS

CARRERA

BLANCO

a Osorno

a Av Alemania

L GALLO

Rio Cautín

a Las Hortensias

a Padre Las Casas

N

10

486

Legend

- ☎ Telephone Center
- ★ Touristic Information
- ⊙ Café, Meeting Point
- ⊛ Gasoline Station
- ⇒ Lookout Point
- ✴ Hospital (3A)
- A Regional Government (4B)
- B Town Hall (4B)
- C Post Office (3B)
- D Bus Terminal (4B)
- E Buses to Argentina
- ✴ F Rural Bus Terminal
- ✴ G Railway Station
- H Municipal Market (3C)
- J Outdoor Market
- ✴ K Araucania Museum
- L Galeria Cema (2B)
- ✴ M Municipal Swimming Pool

ACCOMMODATIONS
1 H Nuevo de la Frontera (4B)
2 H La Frontera (4C)
3 H Nicola's (3C)
4 H Bayern (2B)
5 H Aitue (3C)
6 H Turismo (4B)
7 H Continental (4B)
8 H Emperador (4B)
9 H Espelette (4A)
✴ 16 H Isla Verde

RESTAURANTS
1 H Nuevo de La Frontera (4B)
✴ 10 La Nueva Estancia
✴ 11 La Cumbre del Co Ñielol
✴ 12 Club Alemán
✴ 16 H Isla Verde
13 Grill Piscina Municipal (3C)
14 Centro Español (3B)
15 El Mesón de Sancho (3C)
H Puestos Mercados (3C)

TIPS
✴ 20 Mapuche Jewelry
✴ 21 Mapuche Bookstore

22 Leather Shop (3C)
✴ L Galería Cema (2B)
J Feria

TOURIST SERVICES
30 Car Rental (4C)
31 Internacional Tour (3B)
32 Turismo Araucanía (4C)
33 Lan Chile (4C)
34 Ladeco (3B)
✴ See Map of Temuco

To continue the tour, take the ferry to the other side of the river. It is free Mon–Fri 08:00–13:00 h and 14:00–18:30 h; Sat 08:00–12:00 h and 14:00–18:00 h (give a tip); outside these hours, the ferry operator lives right next to the landing and he can cross you for a modest tip any time, any day. A road runs along the southern shore to Queule on the Pacific coast, described in Tour 8 below.

Another option –quicker– is to continue directly from Puerto Domínguez to Hualpín on the Toltén river and take the free ferry there (in summer Mon–Sat 07:30–13:00 h and 14:00–19:00 h).

Captrén lake

8 A DETOUR ALONG THE PACIFIC COAST ★★★

152 km from Temuco to San José de la Mariquina, of which 121 km are graveled.

This is one of the alternatives to the Pan–Am for travelling south. It is 40 km longer than following the Pan–Am directly, and offers you a different, untrampled scenery.

Follow the Pan–American highway south of Temuco up to **Pitrufquén**. Take there the branch road running west to the coast, along the Toltén river. This road follows the string of forts erected in 1867 when this river became the new frontier between the Mapuche territory and the rest of Chile. **Nueva Toltén** is the village founded to replace the old town razed by a tidal wave in 1960. Toltén was a fishing village which, from colonial times, served as an outpost of Valdivia for contacts with the Mapuches south of the river.

The road turns away from the Toltén river and heads for Puerto Boldos in the **Queule river** valley. The Queule river runs placidly for 20 km to reach the sea. From prehistoric times it was a busy fishing center: The scenery is picturesque. At its mouth is the fishing cove of

QUEULE a cluster of houses clinging to a hillside. The waterfront street has boat ramps, lots of small docks, several boat–building yards, large barges out of commission and a few fishing vessels. There is also a hotel and a beach on the river. Motorboats can be hired to sail to the sea-lion colony on the impressive cliffs closing the bay. The boat tour lasts about 90 min, and if you

are lucky might have chance of tasting the delicious clams (choros) which are typical of this area.

The road to Mehuín climbs a short but steep gradient and then runs above the cliff. The scenery is beautiful. **To the north**, you can see the Queule bay and the river, with a headland beyond which hides the mouth of the Toltén river from view. A long beach extends to the north up to a point where the Nahuelbuta Range juts out to sea. Ignacio Domeyko surveyed this area in 1845, writing afterwards that these hills were covered with impenetrable forest, where cattle straying from the path would never be found again. **To the south**, green cliffs above the open Pacific Ocean march south as far as the Valdivia estuary. This is a little–travelled area, as this Zone's visitors tend to concentrate more in the lake district farther inland.

Seven km along the top of the cliffs, you pass near the beach of **Cheuque**, wind–sheltered and pleasant, good for camping; **Pichicullín**, more open to the wind; **Universitaria**, white–sanded and nice

CONGUILLIO NATIONAL PARK

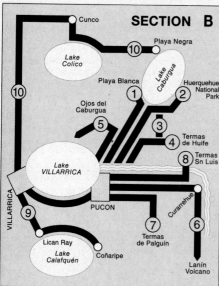
Machi Mapuche

frequented beach in the place, particularly during weekends. Hostería Millalafquén offers a great variety of seafood.

The road to Mariquina runs 27 km along the **Lingue river**. Two km before Mariquina, a road branches right to the **San Luis de Alba Fortress** (22 km), built by the Spaniards in 1647on the bank of the Cruces river to protect navigation and the farming and missionary activities in the area. It was reconstructed by the Universidad Austral. At km 27 from Mehuín is

SAN JOSE DE LA MARIQUINA a village with sprawling old houses, parks and gardens, clustered along the Cruces river. It was the seat of the Bishopric of Araucanía –now in Villarrica– and the buildings of the Seminary, the School and the Sanatorium are still to be seen.

surf, to end up at Playa Grande, the most frequented, at

Mehuín a fishing cove and seaside resort on the mouth of the Lingue river. Windy and with several lodging houses and restaurants, this is the most

SECTION B   LAKE VILLARRICA

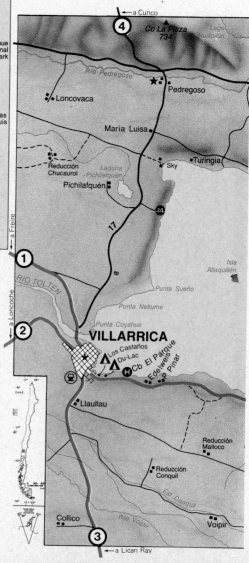

This Section covers the area of the upper Toltén basin, from the Pan–American highway to the Andes. This includes the valleys and upper tributaries of the Toltén river, such as the Allipén, Trancura and Liucura river valleys, in addition to the great lakes Villarrica, Colico, Caburgua and Huilipilún.

These lakes are the most northerly of the long string stretching towards the south. The district is privileged both in scenery and climate, the latter temperate on account of the warm Puelche winds blowing from the Argentine pampas. Its center is

LAKE VILLARRICA huge and beautifully set at the foot of the perfect, snow–capped cone of the active Villarrica volcano (2,700 m above the lake). A paved, highly–scenic 24–km road connects the town of Villarrica, on the western end, with Pucón, on the eastern end.

The southern shore of the lake is Chile's second leading tourist center, with over 70,000 visitors in season and a growing number of winter

10

tourists coming to enjoy the ski slopes on the Villarrica volcano. The towns of Villarrica and Pucón offer first–class accommodations. The 24–km stretch between both towns has few public accesses to the water's edge: the entire area is full of condominiums, over 15 hotels and campgrounds, and some of Chile's most luxurious summer retreats, tucked away behind their manicured parks.

VILLARRICA founded by Gerónimo de Alderete in 1552, had the purpose of exploiting the gold–bearing sands in the neighborhood and protecting the route across the Andes to the pampas and the Atlantic coast, which then were part of the Capitanía General de Chile. Beleaguered by the Mapuches after their uprising in 1598, the last inhabitants of Villarrica, cut off from any help, were killed by 1602. Nearly three centuries later, on January 1882, a military party headed by Leopoldo Urrutia reached the lake and held the Parley of Voipir, where the Mapuches accepted final submission to the State of Chile. Urrutia founded Villarrica on the ruins of the old village.

It commands a splendid view to the volcano and attracted tourists from quite early on. During the 1940s, hotels were built to offer accommodation to fishermen coming to the Toltén river. Now, in addition to a tourist center, it is the seat of the Araucanía Bishopric.

During the second week in February the famous **Mapuche Cultural Week** is held, with music, singing, dancing and handicrafts. During the third week

the **4–Wheel Drive Lake Zone Raid** is held, through beautiful and little known roads.

PUCON evolved from a military outpost set up in 1883, east of the present beach. The village grew very slowly. In 1904, a group of German immigrants settled on the northern bank of the Trancura river. The principal merchants were Holzapfel and Ansorena who dealt in lumber and cattle which were loaded and sent across the lake from the port of La Poza.

Pucón was long Chile's sport fishing center. A boat was specially designed here to row down the rivers (see illustration under Excursions Section) and from 1930 the Hotel Gudenschwager was catering to fishermen. The great boost occurred in 1934, when the Gran Hotel Pucón, built by the State Railway, was inaugurated. At the same time, the Loncoche–Villarrica branch line started to operate. The terminal was at the wharf on the lake. Passengers would disembark from the train into a boat that would bring them across the lake to a landing on the beach of the Gran Hotel.

In the 1940s the road along the lake's coast was finished. Small hotels and residenciales, some run by German families, were frequented by artists, fishermen and intellectuals from Santiago, who gave a distinct flavor to the nascent lake resort.

The coastal road was paved in 1969, triggering an explosive establishment of hotels, condominiums, residenciales, campgrounds and private homes along the 24–km stretch. Both Villarrica

LAKE VILLARRICA

10

☎	Telephone Center	
★	Touristic Information	
◉	Café, Meeting Point	
⊛	Gasoline Station	
A	Church (2C)	
B	Post Office (2B)	
C	Bus Terminal (3C)	
D	JAC Bus Terminal (3C)	
E	Town Hall (3C)	
F	Museum, Library (2B) (3C)	
G	Railway Station (4G)	
H	Dani Anders Plant Nursery (3A)	

ACCOMMODATIONS

1 H Yachting Club (3C)

2	H El Ciervo (3C)
3	Hs Kiel (3C)
4	H Villarrica (3C)
5	H G de Aderete (3B)
6	Cb Gudeschage (3B)
7	Hs Rayhuen (3B)
8	M Lautaro (3C)
9	H Yandaly (3C)
10	Cb Millaruca (5C)
11	Cb Traitraico (2B)
12	Hs Bilbao (2C)
13	Cb Trigal (3C)
14	M Melilafquen (3C)
15	M Los Ositos (3C)
16	Hs Huelquimey (3C)

17	H Balneario (4C)
18	H Fuentes (3B)
19	Hs La Colina (6A)
20	H Puchy (3B)
21	Cs Los Castaños (5D)
22	Cs Du-Lac (5D)

RESTAURANTS

1	Yachting Club (3C)
3	Kiel 36 (3C)
4	Villarrica (3C)
31	El Rey Del Marisco (3C)
32	El Saxo (3C)
33	El Paso (4B)
33	Conga Salsa (4B)
34	2001 (3C)

35	Rivoli (3C)
36	La Tranquera (4C)
37	Club Social Treffpunkt (3B)
38	Campo Lindo (3B)
39	Baimaran (3C)
40	El Paisa (3C)

TIPS

50	Tornería Suiza (2C)
51	Artesanía en Madera (2B)
52	Fábrica de Muebles y Quitasoles (4C)
53	Feria Artesanal (4C)
54	Boteros Bajada de Río Toltén (2B)
55	Sindicato de Boteros (2C)

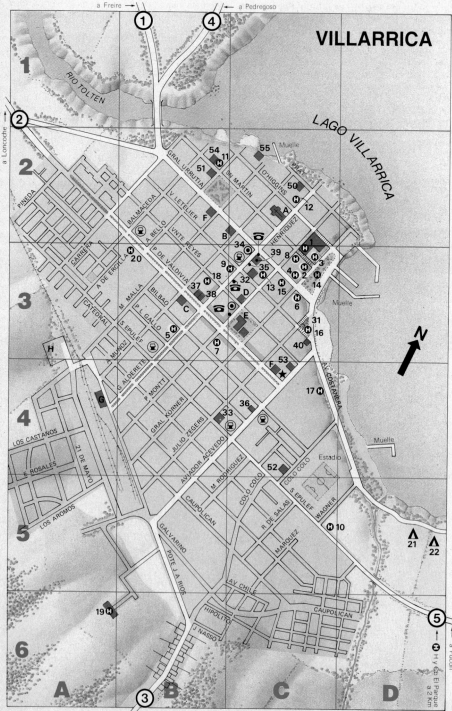

VILLARRICA

and Pucón have excellent restaurants, dancing establishments, busy commerce and all kinds of tourist services, from car rentals to package tours and adventure tourism.

A modern Ski Center was opened on the slopes of the Villarrica volcano in 1988, within the Villarrica National Park, giving a boost to winter tourism in the area.

What To See Villarrica and Pucón can be easily explored in a single visit. The Costanera in Villarrica has good beaches and a superb view to the volcano. There are boats for hire. The **coastal road** is highly scenic, with views over the lake – and the Llaima volcano in the distance– and excellent campgrounds, hotels, restaurants and other facilities on the way.

In Pucón, the shady **square** opposite the Gran Hotel has large elms and native trees. A beautiful raulí tree across the hotel entrance was mutilated recently to offer a better view to the hotel.

The **Playa Grande**, with dark volcanic sand, is very popular for swimming and watersports. Walk along the waterfront to the mouth of the Pucón river. **La Poza** is also a good beach, and has a yacht club.

Pucón, Playa Grande

☎ Telephone Center	**ACCOMMODATIONS**	11 H La Posada (2B)
◉ Café, Meeting Point	1 Gran Hotel Pucón (2B)	12 H El Principito (3B)
★ Touristic Information	2 H Antumalal	13 Hs Nillarahue (3B)
ⓖ Gasoline Station	3 M Interlaken (3A)	14 Hs Don Pepe (3C)
A Customs (3B)	4 H Araucarías (2B)	24 Cb La Palmera (2B)
B Town Hall (3B)	5 H Gudenschwager (2B)	25 H Casablanca (2B)
C Post Office (2B)	6 Hs Suiza (3B)	26 Hs Los Tilos (2C)
D Church (2B)	7 M Mapulay (3C)	
1 Municipal Casino (2B)	8 Cb El Dorado	**RESTAURANTS**
E Boatmen Union (1B)	9 M Lemantú (2B)	12 La Marmita
T Bus Terminal (3C)	10 Hs Salzburg (3B)	de Pericles (3B)
		15 Cagliostro (3C)

16 El Fogón (3B)	19 Suiza Pastries (3B)
17 Las Terrazas (3B)	20 Lingerie (4B)
18 El Rinconcito (3B)	21 Wood-veneer Flower (3B)
27 El Conquistador (3B)	22 Holzapfel Báckerei (2C)
TIPS	23 Empanadas (3B)

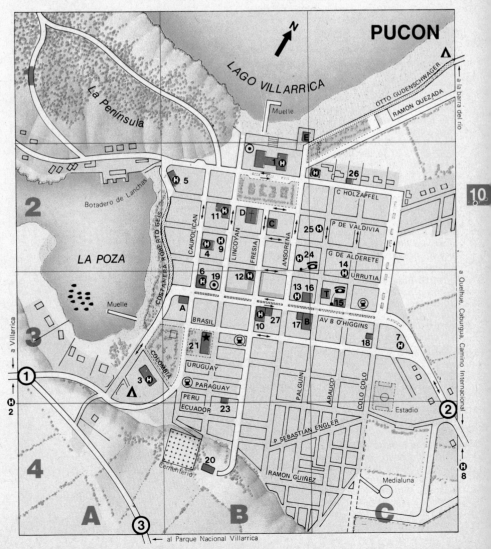

Where To Eat good cuisine and views at the Gran Hotel, Hotel Antumalal (beautiful park, 2 km into the road to Villarrica), and Hotel Interlaken. In Villarrica, the Yachting Club, Hostería Kiel, and Rey del Marisco (seafood). The get–together points shown in map are good for families with children. Picnic is only advisable along the Playa Grande, as close to the mouth of the river as possible, or within the National Park (9 km).

Municipal Casino at The Grand Hotel from Mon–Sun –casual wear– open from 18:00–21:00 h and more formal from 22:00–03:00 AM.

SHORT EXCURSIONS

Owing to the peculiar geography of Pucón and it's surroundings there are many short excursions of 2 to 3 h to be made in the morning or in the afternoon.

A Las Costaneras the best in the afternoon, still and pleasant. You may take a walk along the **costanera Otto Gudenschwager** up to it's end, surrounded by beaches and houses with beautiful gardens. On returning continue along Holzapfel street up to
La Poza going over the waterfront street at sunset's time and visit the port of launches (boats) watching the lights of Villarrica reflected in the lake.

B To the Villarrica Volcano traditional ascent with clear and cloudless weather for fantastic view to the lakes Villarrica and Huilipilún. Café on ski center. From Pucón (Km 0) go up along gravel road which in the first stretch is circled by lots, particular houses and handicraft shops.

At Km 9 the game warden place of Parque Nacional Villarrica (Villarrica National Park). An entrance fee is charged. Access from 08:30 to 18:00 h (time of ascent) the schedule is flexible. Farther on, the road divides in two:
Visit to the Park follow singposted gravel road branching left from the Villarrica–Pucón highway, running among coihue forest the view to the lake is beautiful.

At Km 14 is a singposted path leading in 800 m to a **volcanic cave**, deep and jagged, it's mouth moss– lined. To the side is the «rivebed' along which lava flows when the volcano chooses to erupt. Continue to the end of the road on the volcano slope to the old shelter.
To the Ski Center take the wide, winding road branching right running among coihue forest at the edge of the road. Look at the different strata of volcanic ash and debris along the road.

The forest becomes smaller and lastly disappears. At km 13 from Pucón you may find the cafeteria of the ski center. There you may use the chairlift whisking you in summer to the heights. It is spectacular.

C Coastal Road Villarrica this traditional tour is becoming harder because the particular properties obstruct the view to the lake.
The best hour is sunset time when you may observe the last evolutions in the lake's waters of the sailing vessels, windsurfs and skiers.

D Gathering of Hazelnuts ideal to go with children on cloudy days. Hazelnuts are red–coloured on February and very easy to gather. They can be toasted in the oven at home. If you go out 3 km from Pucón along the international route and in the junction to Quelhue, branch left and continue 4 km up to Toltén river, then right there is the best place for gathering of hazelnuts.

E A Hike to Reducción Quelhue it is advisable to go in the morning or in the afternoon (if it is uncloudy). There is an impressive view to the snow–capped Villarrica, Quetrupillán and Lanín volcanoes and circled field with a Rehue where rogations are performed. The reduction is placed in the valley to the north of Trancura river. Depart

from Pucón along the international route up to the ending paved road just there turn left advancing 2 km along straight leading to a **hanging bridge** (maximum 2500 kg) spanning Trancura river. Cross the bridge and at 300 m you find the road coming from Ojos del Caburgua (see Tour 5); turn left along straight road and at 1 Km there are stores.

Continue along the main road at 500 m from the forking with the stores is placed the Rehue.

Following diagonally to the right up to the hills, you may cross a «baden»(road depression) along a dry estuary and follow by car the lake through the road skirting the hills. Farther on there is a house of game– warden of CONAF (Conaf Ranger house) from where the lake is seen. In this place a great area of the forest was burnt, but now the place has been reforested planting pino oregón (oregon pine) 2 km further is the nice beach of the lake –6 Km from the bridge– with view of Pucón.

F To the Marimán Waterfall it is advisable for warm afternoons to bathe in the cold waters of Trancura river. Take picnic and swimming gear. A 33 km round trip from Pucón

From Pucón (km 0) take the road to Caburgua up to bridge Metreñehue on km 11 (see Tour). Advancing 4 Blocks, detour off to the right along 3 km up to **Salto Marimán** (Marimán Waterfall) (open from Dec 8th to Mar 1st). Signposted. This is private property–expensive entrance fee is

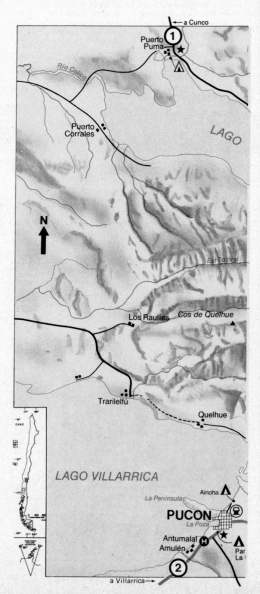

charged with descending paths passing through waterfalls of Trancura river with deafening din of the water cascading on the rocks.

This place is a wonderful ecological reservation with wild native forest. There are look-out points, sites for picnic, resting and fishing. Bonfires are forbidden.

Continue along the same road and cross the ancient german colonia (settlement) of Llafenco, settled in 1904. Now there are remnants of a few houses and nostalgic orchards with apple trees.

Along the road you will find a beautiful, shaded lake beach suitable for bathing and picnic.

Continue along the road up to the Llafenco pond (balseo)we recommend to cross it by raft and to come back to Pucón along the international route. Schedule of attention of the rafting service: Mon to Sat 08:00–13:00 h and 14:00–18:30 h.

Tip the boatman who will carry you any time.

G To Liucura River for cloudy days with children. You may cross by boat and visit an interesting mill Good place for strilling and fishing. A 30 Km roundtrip. From Pucón (Km) along the road to Caburgua up to bridge Metreñehue at Km 11 (see Tour 1).

Advancing 2 block along the way, enter to the left and advance again 1 km up to the forking, right there turn right and 1.5 km further, at a new forking turn right again up to the shore of the **Liucura river** at km 15 from Pucón. Nice place to takes a walk. Do honk and wait for the boats coming from the houses of **familia Muñoz** (Muñoz family) at the other side (a little fee is charged).

Mr Muñoz was the first settler who came to this place and developed many engineering works to produce electric energy.

ORGANIZED EXCURSIONS

Professional teams (Altué, Anden Sport Tours and others), offer entertaining and exciting **rafting expeditions down the rapids** of Trancura (3 hours).

Suitable for any one over 10 years of age; the rafting is filmed and exhibited to excursionists.

These operators also offer **guide climbs to the Villarrica volcano** (4 h), supplying all the necessary gear. There you be walking on snow , so you must wear good boots, sun block and sunglasses. If you do not have sunglasses with you, you can rent them at El Pollo in Pucón, together with crampons and ice ax. Do not attempt the climb alone; a guide is highly recommended. Sulphur at the top can be hazardous. The volcano rumbles constantly, making this a thrilling, once in a lifetime experience.

For fans of **mountain bikes**, they organized a ride to the Ojos del Caburgua ponds (4 h). **The tour of**

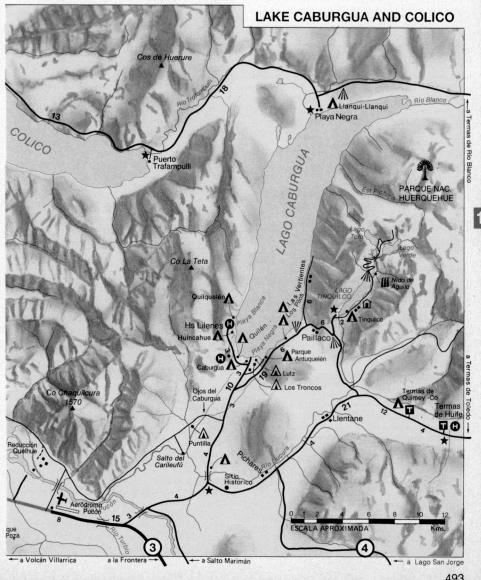

LAKE CABURGUA AND COLICO

10

Chinay in vehicle is entertaining, climbing through Palquín Thermal baths to Villarrica National Park with its spectacular Araucarias.

TOURS OF THIS SECTION

1 TO LAKE CABURGUA ★★★

25 km to the lake and 28 km to Playa Blanca, with campgrounds and an Hostería.

An excursion to a beautiful lake of volcanic origin and white-sanded beaches, unusual in an area of black volcanic sand.

Take the road to Argentina out of Pucón (km 0). At km 8 is a bridge over the **Turbio river**, a large stony riverbed through which the floods rush down when the volcano erupts. Soon there is a forking; the road to Argentina veers right, take the left branch.

At km 11 is the **Metreñehue bridge** over the Trancura river. A short distance beyond the bridge, a road branches right to Colonia Llafenco and the Marimán waterfall (Tour 3). The road continues through forests and, at km 15, a road branches right to Termas de Huife (Tour 4). Then, the **Liucura bridge** over a swift river loved by rafting fans.

At km 19 a trail branches left to Ojos del Caburgua (Tour 5). At km 22 another road branches right to Paillaco and the Huerquehue National Park (Tour 2). At km 25 is

LAKE CABURGUA (also called Caburga), elongated and set among wooded mountains. It originated from a volcanic explosion whose lava and ash plugged the outlet. It drains underground to the Ojos del Caburgua. The hills around the lake have intrusions of crystalline rocks –known as «fly wing»– typical of Coastal Range hills. These give rise to the only white–sanded beaches in the southern lakes.

The road reaches **Playa Negra**, on the southern shore and very popular in summer, with telephone, supermarket, many campgrounds and boat hire. The isolated hill to the west and another one farther south are small volcanoes, their craters turned into lakes; they are to be thanked for the ash and lava plug that gave rise to Caburgua.

A short distance before Playa Negra, –you will find on your way **Hostería Playa Blanca**–, a road branches left leading in 3 km to the lake's western shore, to

Playa Blanca (White Beach) actually there are 2 campings lying on slopes between the public road and the beach. Access fee for parking the car on the slopes. Free entrance for pedestrians in the last camping entering 50 m along horizontal road and farther on a straight to the beach.

It is a very beautiful beach with whitesand and crystal–clear water, peppered and shaded by old arrayanes –with reddish and thin barks– and by pitras, a kind of tree similar to the boldo, both with white flowers on February and with their roots clawing the ground near the water's edge. It is a nice and pleasant place to spend a journey.

You may take food or eat in the hosteria. Boats and water bicycles for hire.

2 TO THE HUERQUEHUE NATIONAL PARK

★★★ *a round trip of 72 km from Pucón. Allow one day, including a hike for all ages up on the mountains. Camping possible. The road (dirt) is not suitable after rain.*

A delightful excursion to a fine lake. The real beauty is in the higher reaches, at the end of a path climbing the surrounding hills to a string of small lakes set like gems in fairy-tale forests.

Follow the road to lake Caburgua described in Tour 1 above. At km 22, turn right on the signposted road to Paillaco. The road runs above the Caburgua's southeastern shore, with grand views to the lake and the Llaima volcano in the

distance. Campgrounds (Camping of family Gramer, km 25, is highly rec) and cabins are on offer: follow the signs.

At km 28 a 6-km road branches north along the lake's eastern shore, with summer cottages and beaches.

At km 29 is the tiny village of Paillaco. Here ends the graveled road; the rest is dirt, hugely dusty when dry and slippery when wet, we recommend to drive with lights on due to the large amounts of dust. The road winds its way up a treeless slope with fine views to the wooded Liucura river valley and a string of volcanoes for a backdrop.

At km 34 is

LAKE TINQUILCO small and nestled in what seems to be a volcanic crater. The settlers sell kuchen –cakes– and offer boats for hire. Here is the gate and guardhouse of the **Huerquehue National Park** from 12,500 há (entrance fee).

There is a campsite on the waterfront. The road continues 1.5 km further to the house of a settler. Here starts a well–marked trail, almost entirely uphill but not too steep, through a gorgeous forest of huge trees and palm–like ferns, past the **Nido de Aguila** waterfall and rocky cliffs, leading to a breathtakingly beautiful group of small lakes surrounded by untouched forests. Araucarias crown the mountaintops.

The first lake coming into view is **Laguna Chica**; the path skirts the shore to a forking with a descriptive map of the place. Fifty m to the right is **Laguna El Toro** and 500 m to the left is **Laguna Verde**. Both are lovely and have beaches suitable for swimming and camping.

3 FROM LAKE CABURGUA TO TERMAS DE

LIUCURA ★★ *a stretch of 6 km from Paillaco to the road leading to Termas de Huife. It is a dirt road, not suitable after rain.*

The shortest road from Caburgua to the thermal baths, and an alternative route to return to Pucón from Huerquehue National Park.

Paillaco (km 0) is at the junction for the Huerquehue National Park. There is a general store. A dirt road branches south, and just beyond the junction there is a forking; take the left branch. It is a narrow road, climbing and dipping through the countryside and with a few blind curves. Drive carefully.

At km 5 is a forking. The left branch is short, and leads to the **Tinquilco Waterfall**, located in private land; an entrance fee is paid. The waterfall is actually three waterfalls, a path leading to the two upper ones; the road ends at the lowest of the three. Lake Tinquilco drains underground into this river.

Back at the forking, continue and cross the Liucura river over a wooden bridge, to reach the main road at km 6. Opposite is a small chapel.

Turning right at the junction, you will reach Pucón in 26 km. Turning left, termas de Quimey-Co is 4 km away, and Termas de Huife a 5 km further.

4 TO TERMAS DE LIUCURA ★★★

thirty–six km from Pucón, a good excursion for a rainy day. There are thermal baths and a café.

A chance to combine a hot bath with a dip in the cool waters of the Liucura river.

Take the road from Pucón (km 0) to Caburgua up to the forking at km 15. Follow the right branch until km 18, where a short detour to the left brings you to an

Archaeological Site with the ruins of a mud–brick house which belonged to a Spanish encomendero (holder of an estate granted by the Spanish King during the colonial times, with the local natives forced into unpaid labor under a serfdom system). He exploited the gold–bearing sands of the Liu-

10

cura river. It is Chile's oldest Spanish ruin, pre-dating even the destruction of Villarrica in 1602.

At km 19 is **Pichares**, a cluster of houses established in 1972. The road then crosses the Coilaco river and, at km 20.5, a road branches right to Laguna San Jorge.

Continuing to the termas, the road passes near the houses of settlers who sell cheese, honey and vegetables.

At km 27 is the Huepi junction with its small chapel. The road to lake Caburgua described under Tour 2a branches left here; 700 m into this road is the wooden bridge spanning the Liucura river.

The road heads east through woodland, with views over the Liucura river valley. At km 31 are the

Quimey–Co Thermal Waters

it is a private place: a fee is paid. Park the car and walk down the path through the forest to the river. Hemmed in between a cliff and the river is a small hostería and a large pool made of stones next to the river, where very hot water gushes from the ground. There is also a campsite.

Continuing the tour, at km 36 is

TERMAS DE HUIFE (public access 09:00–20:00 h, upmarket, everyone above 8 years of age pays and it is not cheap). It is the best–equipped thermal bath in the zone and the most modern in Chile. It has a building housing individual baths and a large hotel with apartments and a restaurant. There is a café on a terrace overlooking two pools of thermal waters. Open the year round, information can be obtained from tel 441222.

The pools were built at the same level as the river water, so as to make it possible to alternate between the very hot thermal waters and the cool river water.

If the access gate is closed, it is because the pools have reached their maximum capacity to accommodate people. It is good during cloudy or rainy days, and also when you arrive around 19:00 h, before the access is closed, to take an evening bath.

Continuing the road from Huife, at the first house on the left ask about the «wild» (naturales) thermal baths on the river. Pay a small fee and walk the long path to the hot water pools at the edge of the river.

The road continues to the village of Huife and then it crosses forested lands with gates.

4a TO LAGUNA SAN JORGE ★★

29 km from Pucón, at least half a day, you can take food or camp there. A graveled stretch of 17 km, of which the last 3 km are badly surfaced. Not recommendable after rain. The trip takes 1,5 h. In summer, the laguna is in shade after 19:00 h.

A visit to a little known place with a small laguna. Good fishing and boats for rent. It was settled by old pioneers.

From Pucón (km 0) take the road to the Liucura–Huife Termal Baths (see description in Tour 4). At km 10 a road branches to the left leading to lake Caburgua. Go straightforward and at km 14 you will reach the village of Pichares.

From **Pichares** (km 0) take the road to Huife and cross the bridge over the Cohilaco stream. At km 1 the signposted road at your right to Cohilaco Alto. At km 3 you will cross the Cohilaco stream and 500 m ahead is a road junction, with a school and a general store.

The road then runs through a narrow canyon; at km 4 you will cross the northern shore of the stream. The valley now gets broader, there are houses and large exotic trees, such as conifers and chestnuts, showing how old the human settlement here is. Part of the road is very curvy and surrounded by dense forests. It is convenient to honk when you come to the curves.

At km 11,5 the road comes to a T–junction.

Termas de Huife; hotel

Take your right. This stretch begins with a hard and zigzagging slope. A short distance ahead is a sawmill; from now on take always your right at every turn of the road. A short distance ahead you will cross an access gate.

At km 15 is

Laguna San Jorge

it measures 1,200 m from east to west and 500 m from north to south. It was originated by a small volcano at the mouth of the laguna. The northern part of the laguna is surrounded by low hills covered with jungle, whereas the southern shore has taller hills with some araucarias on their summits.

At the southern shore there is a vast lawn esplanade with a beach. It is the only access to the laguna. An excellent place to picnic or to camp at. A modest fee is paid. They also rent boats.

The road continues 2 km inland, but there is no other access to the laguna. We recommend a walk to the mouth and the nearby forest with plenty of red coicopihue flowers in February.

5 TO THE OJOS DEL CABURGUA ★★

twenty–one km from Pucón; there is a good café in the vicinity. Allow one afternoon, or a whole day (take food).

A visit to the headwaters of a river fed from underground by the Caburgua lake, with nice scenery and suitable for bathing.

Leave Pucón (km 0) following the road to lake Caburgua. At km 19 is a junction with a large cross ("El Cristo") right next to the road. Take there the road branching left; two km ahead is a gate and a kiosk offering drinks. A fee is paid to visit the

Ojos del Caburgua

beautiful pools surrounded by lush forest, fed from underground by the Caburgua lake and by some brooks. Bathing and picnic permitted.

A 500 m further along the road and a short distance to the left is **La Puntilla**, a pretty spot at the point where two rivers come together. The water is placid and there are some islets. Boats can be hired to row to or around the islets. It is a good spot for bathing and for a picnic. Continuing another 500 m on the same road you cross the Carileufú river. Right beyond the bridge is a signposted road branching left to the

Carileufú Waterfall

a small waterfall with a large, modern country house with a café specialized in German pastries baked in a wooden oven. the place is frequented by people from Pucón, particularly during rainy or cloudy days. There are some paths to walk along the river, and a boat for hire to row under tunnels made by the arching roots of trees. The main road runs up to the Villarrica lake and the Mapuche Reservation of Quelhue from where you may turn back to Pucón along the new hanging bridge of Trancura. It is a 12 km stretch.

This hard and rocky road is crossed by many depressions and stony irregularities. At last the rough descent to Quelhue along which you must

10

drive very carefully. We recommend to do the tour following all indications given to avoid the dangers of the ascents. From Carileufú Waterfall (km 0) the road runs crossing through lots and houses of settlers, with a beautiful view.

At km 3, at the edge of Liucura river, the **Casa Muñoz** (Muñoz House). House whose owner, Mr Muñoz was an ingenious settler who created and installed a waterfall to generate electric power to activate a sawmill, a mill and domestic electricity. He was the first settler in the place. Very interesting. It is worth a visit. The road continues skirting the Liucura river and at km 4 ascends surrounded by pretty forest with a spectacular **view** to the junction of Liucura and Trancura rivers.

At km 6 the road descends along a rocky and rough path up to the Quelhue valley. The road which ends in the plain continues running straight and gently up to the km 8, turning there to the left up to the **hanging bridge** (inaugurated in 1991 with max capacity of weight: 2,500 kg) spanning the Trancura river. From there 1 km southward up to the paved international highway and 3 km further up to Pucón.

This way continues up to the western shore of Villarrica lake. Strech described in Short Excursions, E A Hike to Reducción Quelhue.

6 TO PUESCO ALONG THE TRANCURA VALLEY

★★★ *Puesco is 60 km from Pucón, and the international border a 16 km further down the road. Take gasoline and food. Campsite and hostería at Puesco.*
An excursion along the glacial Trancura valley and to a remote corner of the Villarrica National Park.

Leave Pucón (km 0) following the road to Argentina. At km 8, beyond the bridge over the Turbio river, take the right branch at the fork. You can see a deep gash on the side of the Villarrica crater, along which lava flows towards the Turbio river.

At km 16 is the Llafenco ferry crossing and at km 18, next to a small chapel, the turn–off for the Palguín Thermal Baths. The road traverses the length of the glacial valley to the mountains on the border with Argentina. A glacier crept through here in times past grinding the countryside into a flat valley with cliffs of exposed rock on the sides.

At km 25 is the village of Catripulli. The road becomes more curvy. At km 36 is a signposted road branching left to a municipal campground on the river bank, and two modest thermal baths.

At km 37 is

Curarrehue a service village for the valleys deep into the mountains, established in 1912. It has a mountain–village look, as the place gets snowed in winter. It has a church built by the Capuchin mission. A road –only suitable for 4WD vehicles– heads from here to Reigolil and the northern shore of lake Caburgua.

Beyond Curarrehue, both the road and the river veer sharply left, running along the hills on the border. These are crowned by rocky peaks known as Las Muelas («molar teeth») and by some solitary araucarias. The scenery is beautiful. At km 60 is the **Puesco Border Control** (08:00–19:30 h in summer), set in a fine native forest, next to an hostería and a Conaf ranger house with a campground. To go up to the park and the Lanín volcano, you must leave your passport here and return the same day; no camping is permitted higher up.

Continue along the road to Argentina, which climbs a curvy but not steep stretch through lingue forests.

At km 68 is

Lake Quillelhue surrounded by forests and with a large abandoned house. This used to be a shelter and inn whence a ferry set off to cross the lake, before the road was built skirting its shore.

At the far end is a police outpost. The first araucarias near the road can be seen. At km 70 the road crosses the Lanín river. There is a fantastic view to the

LANIN VOLCANO with its 3,747 m above sea level, it is the highest volcano in the south. Its summit is snow–capped even in high summer; a magnificent pure araucaria forest covers its slopes. An interesting hike can be made from here to **lake El Toro** (ask for information at the Conaf office in Puesco).

The border is at km 76, surrounded by ancient araucarias. This road leads to Junín de Los Andes, in Argentina.

7 PALGUIN THERMAL BATHS, WATERFALLS AND QUETRUPILLAN SECTION OF VILLARRICA NATIONAL PARK

★★★ *thirty km to the Palguín thermal baths and a 7 km further to the entrance to the Quetrupillán section of the Villarrica National Park (check with Conaf at Pucón about the conditions of this last stretch of road). Restaurant and café at Palguín, a more modest version thereof at Salto del León.*
An excursion to the most beautiful waterfalls in the region, stopping at a thermal bath and visiting a pure–araucaria forest.

Leave Pucón (km 0) following the road to Argentina up to km 20, taking there the signposted road branching right to Palguín. At the junction is a Capuchino-style chapel and Ovalle's Ranch, with an area for barbecues and camping.

The road is narrow and flanked by dense forest, and soon traverses the **Huenuñanco** Mapuche reservation; the Mapuches offer woollen goods on the roadside.

At km 27 is the

Palguín Waterfall (the road sign indicating this has an uncanny tendency to disappear). The waterfall can be seen from a look–out point on the side of the road. The entire mass of water arches from a rocky lip to crash noisily into a deep rocky canyon, clouds of spray billowing all around. The look–out platform lies atop a dangerous cliff: be careful with the children.

Over the next 3 km of road there are three further waterfalls, accessible after paying an entrance fee.

Salto de la China («Jump of the Chinawoman»), a detour of 1,300 m to the left, with a small hostería and a campsite (no amenities). A fee is paid to continue to the waterfall following a 200–m path along the river bank.

A narrow stream plunges 73 m to a pond, forming a rocky amphitheater lined with giant–leaved nalcas, ferns and red fuchsias. It is worth a visit.

Salto del León back on the road, a short way ahead is another detour of 1,000 m to the left; a fee is paid at the entrance. At the end of the car road a 300–m path starts winding through a forest of enormous native trees. The waterfall is not as high as the previous one, but carries more water and falls in two steps, each giving rise to a pond encased in lush vegetation and bathed in mist. A path leads almost to the foot of the first waterfall.

A short distance ahead on the road is the **Salto de las Turbinas**, with a detour for the car and a footpath leading to it. At km 30 are the

PALGUIN THERMAL BATHS located within a beautiful nature park, with individual thermal cabins, a pool next to the river and a traditional hotel with a modern annex with rooms with private bathrooms and hostería offering hearty meals (owner speaks German). A fee is paid to use the baths and the pool.

Continue a 8 km further through native forests to reach, at km 37, the entry to the

10

QUETRUPILLAN SECTION of the Villarrica National Park, the most beautiful part of the park. The name comes from a volcano located to the south. The park is here 6 km wide; there is a guard-house, a free campsite and a spectacular forest which starts with giant coihues, continues with raulí –with its heart-shaped leaves– and ends with araucaria. Farther up the forest thins out and mañío replaces the pure araucaria forest.

A 22-km road descends from here to Coñaripe. Winter degrades this road significantly. Check with Conaf Pucón (Lincoyán 372) about road conditions.

8 TO MENETUE AND SAN LUIS THERMAL

BATHS ★★ *a 57-km round trip from Pucón. There is a modest hotel at Termas de San Luis.*
Picturesque thermal baths and pretty lagoons.

Leave Pucón (km 0) following the road to Argentina. At km 23 –after crossing bridges Palguín, Pitrahue and Capedaña– is the turn-off for the Menetué ferry. Follow this road (left) to the ferry (Mon–Fri, 08:00–13:00 h and 14:00-18:30 h; Sat 08:00–12:00 h and 14:00–18:00 h). The boatman lives right across and will bring you anytime to the other side for a tip. The road continues 1 km to a junction; follow the signposted road branching right to reach, at km 26, the

Menetué Thermal Baths a placid, pretty and clean place, next to a brook with grassy banks. It includes 8 thermal cabins, single and double, some with a tub. In the brook there is a pool of cool water. There are two cabins offering accommodation, but no meal service.

Retrace the road from Menetué (km 26) to 100 m before the ferry (km 28); turn left to continue along the northern bank of the Trancura river, which cannot be seen from the road. At km 30 is a T-junction. Take the road to the left; the road-bed is sandy up the slope. From the top you can see

Lake Catripulli with reedy shores and a few houses. The settler in one of the houses offers boats for hire (fishing is said to be good). Windsurfers use this lake to practice, as it is swept by a constant wind.

Back to the T-junction, continue to the San Luis bridge across the Trancura (km 31.5). Take there road branching left, leading in 2 km to

San Luis Thermal Baths modest but frequented the year round. There is a hotel with homey meals. The thermal baths are located inside a large hall at the bottom of a ravine; people wait in line outside for their turn. It also has an area suitable for a picnic or camping.

An easy excursion from here is to retrace the road 1 km to take the road heading east, skirting two swampy ponds teeming with birds, until the end of the road. Continue on foot climbing among boulders (about half an hour) to **laguna del León**, a small, elongated lake hemmed in by wooded mountains. Good fishing.

Following a path along the left-hand shore you come to the house of a settler who has a boat for hire and sells very good cheese. Here you can camp or enjoy a picnic.

To return, drive back to the San Luis bridge; beyond it is the international road. Turning right on this road you reach Pucón in 27 km.

9 TO LAKE CALAFQUEN ★★★

a 90-km round trip from Villarrica to Coñaripe. Food at Lican Ray and Coñaripe. Allow half a day.
A visit to the area's second most important tourist center.

Leave Villarrica (km 0) following the 31-km paved road to Lican Ray (see map). See town description under Section C.

Continue along the lake's northern shore passing lovely beaches and huge lava rivers which transformed the landscape in 1971. On the slopes are Mapuche reservations. Coñaripe is not very pretty, but it does have a nice view, particularly at sunset. There is a small hotel.

10 TO LAKE COLICO ★★★

it is 61 km or 83 from Villarrica by the 2 routes described in this tour and which lead to the northern bank of the lake. Windy gravel road, low speed limit. 1 day minimum with facilities for camping an possible visits to the northern bank of the lake Caburgua. Provisions and gasoline only in Cunco. As a point of support we recommend hotel Trailanqui with camping and restaurant equidistant from the 2 different proposed routes.
A trip to the beautiful but little known lake and access to lake Caburgua by the northern bank, the most beautiful and solitary.

From Villarrica (km 0) go to the bridge over Toltén river and immediately after crossing it, take the gravel road on the right which is signposted to Los Laureles. The road is virtually straight and separated from the lake which you see in the distance.

At km 7, entrance on the right of the Motel **Los Boldos** and on km 12 the **little village** and **bridge Pedregoso**. Next to old tree lined avenues of an estate. There a road appears on the right which leads to the northern bank of the lake with access only to private property with no view.

Crossing the Pedregoso bridge the road slopes gently up offering views over the lake and continues amongst hills. At km 15 you can see to your right the **lake Huilipilún**. There is no access to it.

Further on you will come across very bumpy land built up with houses and working fields. At km 23 you can cross the bridge Huilipilún and at km 31 there is a junction which offers two routes:

Route through Los Laureles convenient for those heading to Cunco and continuing to Melipeuco, Icalma or National Park Conguillío. Continue straight along the road northbound and 3 km along on the right is the pleasant hotel, restaurant and camping **Trailanqui** with good cuisine and beautiful surroundings.

1 km further on the road crosses the **Allipén bridge**, over the river which comes from the mountains (cordillera) and on the right hand side it joins with the small Curaco river which empties into lake Colico.

At km 39 you arrive to **Los Laureles**, former railway station and town on trunk road between Freire and Cunco. Following this to the right on km 59 is **Las Hortensias** -the old railway station- and from where the paved road to Temuco begins. Carry straight on to arrive at km 71 to

Cunco main municipality of the area with commercial activity, a pretty plaza (square) and interesting missionary church of the Capuchin order. Here you can stock up with supplies and gasoline. From here the road runs to the mountains (cordillera) which leads to Melipeuco and Icalma Lagoon.

In Cunco take the road to the south between cultivated hills and forests, the road crosses the Allipén river by way of a beautiful bridge and at km 83 you will arrive to **Lake Colico** (Description on next route).

Route along the San Pedro road after the junction at km 31 turn right to the lake Colico throught the basin of the river but with the river out of sight. At km 43 you must follow the road to the left. The road continues towards the south bank of the river -10 km- but this can hardly be seen since the road runs behind splendid and landscaped summer houses.

Following the road to the left at km 1 you cross

10

the **Pitrunco bridge** across the river which empties into Colico. At km 48 a right angle, a chapel and a country house. At km 51 you cross a bridge and at km 55 it leads into the road which joins Cunco with Colico.

Turn right and continue before crossing the hanging bridge at km 60 and arrive at km 61 to

LAKE COLICO on its bank is situated **Puerto Puma**, an old timber port and today it is a popular beach with simple camping facilities. This lake was the last of the great lakes to be discovered -it appeared on maps in 1903- due to the fact it has relatively small basin and the river which drains it did not reveal this great and beautiful looking glass of water. It is oval shaped, surrounded by steep hills on the northern bank with large beaches on the southern bank in addition to large and luxurious summer houses that have been built. Almost all these houses can only be reached by motor lighter from Puerto Puma.

Continue journey towards the east by (cornice road) across the northern bank of the lake with full views that in 13 km arrives at the **Trafampulli bridge** (km 74), which crosses the river leading into the lake at the other end. Here a short road branches off to the south, leading up to private property.

From Trafampulli the road enters the rivers valley with surprisingly well cultivated and beautiful fields and old colonial houses. A spectacular forest of tepas and laurels which leads to km 88, that is to **Playa Negra** (**Black beach**) on the northern bank of

lake Caburgua. It is a stoney beach with space for camping; also colonial houses which offer food and drink. The view across the lake is most beautiful.

From here a road -now open- runs along the northern bank of the Caburgua with a spectacular **view** across the lake which can be seen completely and even to the end where the Villarrica volcano is.

At km 8 of the road, surrounded by much zarzamora (blackberry), you arrive at the end of lake Caburgua where you will find **río Blanco** which leads into it, its extensive beach, the enchanting **Laguna Chica** which breeds salmons for sports fishing and opposite at the other side of the river a spectacular house and fields watered automatically as are golf courses; it is the house of the Englishman James Sharp, built in 1987, where race horses are bred. The road -a bad one- continues up river and you can visit the beautiful **Thermal baths of the Río Blanco**, described in Excursions in 4WD at the end of this section.

TOURS TO OTHER SECTIONS

For those staying for a longer period around lake Villarrica, take note that the distances to other places of interest described in this Zone are such that you can visit most of them on day trips. Temuco is 87 km away, Valdivia 115 km, Termas de Liquiñe 71 km and the circuit to Queule and Mehuín, on the Pacific coast is 276 km long.

SECTION C   SEVEN LAKES

This is a group of relatively less well-known lakes, whose abrupt topography has made it difficult to build roads: the road around lake Panguipulli was finished as late as 1983, together with the one skirting the shores of lake Riñihue. The latter deteriorates markedly in winter, and its maintenance is poor. Lake Pirehueico has only one ferry crossing it, with no fixed schedule. This is, nevertheless, no real impediment to carrying out interesting excursions in this area.

While some attempts to move into this zone were made during the colonial period, efforts to this end were given up by 1780. The first settler who came here to stay was Manuel Ovalle in 1883; the first at present-day Panguipulli was Guillermo Angermaier, who arrived in 1885. In 1903 a Capuchino mission was set up at Panguipulli –a splendid church remains– and, later, at Coñaripe and Liquiñe. In 1910 the first railway branch line reached Riñihue and steamers started to ply these lakes to trade with the areas inland, setting off from the head towns of Calafquén, Panguipulli and Riñihue. A road reached Panguipulli in 1935 and, in 1954, the village boasted its own railway branch line.

Tourist Infrastructure off Panguipulli, enchanting servicetown, Calafquén, a beautiful and newly discovered holiday-makers resort and Lican Ray, undoubtedly the centre of tourism in this area; in the rest of this region there are some very good hotels surrounded by splendid scenery, but these are found in isolated spots, not having supportive tourist services from nearby towns or cities.

LICAN RAY a young village and the heart of this section. It has a strange history: In 1958 it was a village of settlers connected only by boat with the rest of the world. That year it was expropriated and dismantled by the government, as it was going to be flooded when the Pullinque dam started to accumulate water. However, the terrible earthquake of 1960 made the authorities have some second thoughts. A decision was made not to let the water reach such a high level, and in 1965 the state, owner of those lands, laid out a

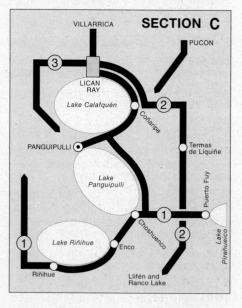

tourist village and gave away or sold the plots under the condition that the new owners had to build houses and finish urbanizing the place. Now it is one of the few towns in the South where most houses are summer houses.

It has a complete tourist infrastructure and is crowded and lively in season.

TOURS FROM LICAN RAY

1 INTER-LAKE CIRCUIT ★★★

181 km from Lican Ray to the town of Riñihue, and a 122 km further to return directly to Lican Ray. Allow one day. Hosterías on the way offer accommodation and food. Gasoline at Panguipulli.

A circuit around five beautiful lakes.

Leave Lican Ray (km 0) following the road skirting the lake's northern shore towards the east. You will see solidified lava rivers from the 1971 eruption on the way. At km 21 is

Coñaripe a village engaged in forestry with an hostería and a park on the lake shore, where in the past the port and a state–railway station were located. The state company bought railway sleepers here.

Take there the road skirting the lake's southern shore, which is steep and leaves little room for beaches, but has a splendid view towards the Villarrica volcano.

At km 48 a road branches left for Choshuenco and, 2 km later, another road branches right to the lake resort of Calafquén, small and beautiful, with a fantastic view of the volcano across the lake.

Back on the road, continue straight to reach, at km 57,

Panguipulli; Capuchina church

PANGUIPULLI in the old times, wood–fired steamers towed barges creaking under the weight of timber from lakes Calafquén and Panguipulli, unloading their cargo here onto the railway cars of the branch line running west. Beautifully set, the town has roses planted in most streets. There is a **church** built by the Capuchino mission, and restaurants, hotels and gasoline stations. The lake has excellent fishing.

Retrace the road 8 km to the Choshuenco road junction (km 65). Take the road heading south, which soon crosses the Pullinque river –draining lake Calafquén and passes the tiny village of Coihueco. The road then approaches the shores of **lake Panguipulli** and skirts the length of its coast, rugged and with sandy beaches.

At km 76 is a sandy beach; another one, **Malalhuaca**, at km 81, and yet another one, **Puñir**, at km 88. All are sheltered by native forests. At km 95 is **Toledo**, the old core of a forest farm. At km 97 a road branches right to **Payahuinte beach**, the most beautiful of the lot and with a spot for camping.

At km 100 is a bridge spanning the Fuy river followed by a road junction. Take road heading

left to reach, at km 119,

LAKE PIREHUEICO the road ends at a nondescript village of **Puerto Fuy**, with a good concrete ramp serving as landing for the ferry crossing the lake and connecting with a road to Argentina through the Huahúm Pass. The lake worms its way for many kilometers into a fantastic mountain scenery. At the far end is a huge abandoned building, resulting from an ambitious project for a hotel many years ago. There are no trails or paths along the shore, which is abrupt and covered by thick forests.

Retrace the road and at km 126 –police control outpost– is the village of **Neltume**, with a large plywood factory established in 1943. One km farther and to the left, is the

HUILO HUILO WATERFALL one of Chile's highest and most spectacular (be careful with the children: the paths to the look–out points are slippery and steep). You can climb all the way down to the river. The river is squeezed into a 10–m–wide canal and plunges into a deep gorge lined with lush jungle and ferns. The din is deafening. The

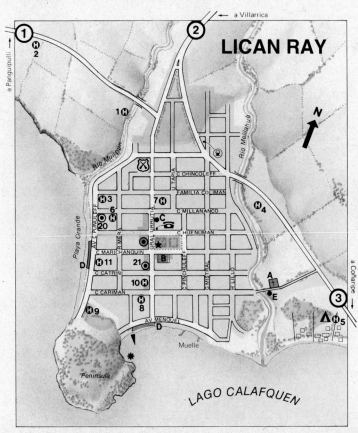

← a Villarrica

LICAN RAY

10

a Panguipulli →

Rio Meillanue
Rio Mulipuri
Playa Grande
Playa

C CHINCOLEFF
FAMILIA COLIMAN
C MILLANANCO
C HUENUMAN
C MARICHANQUIN
C CATRIN
C CARIMAN
AV. MENQUEF
U TAPIA
GRAL URRUTIA
C PINGUILEF
G MISTRAL
H LILLO
C PUNULEFF

a Coñaripe →

Muelle
Peninsula

LAGO CALAFQUEN

N

☎ Telephone Center
◉ Café, Meeting Point
★ Touristic Information
Ⓖ Gasoline Station
✳ Boat harbor
◄ Boat Ramp
A Parish Church
B Meeting Point
C Bus Stop
D Boat Hire
E Horse Hire

ACCOMMODATIONS
1 Cb El Conquistador
2 Cb Quimelafquén
3 H Refugio
4 Cb Köhler
5 Cb y Cs Foresta
6 Cb Duhatao
7 Cb Ruca Rayen
8 Cb Rucamac
9 Hs Victor's - Playa
10 Cb Lican Ray
11 H Rucalafquen

RESTAURANTS
3 El Refugio
9 Victor's - Playa
20 Café Las Velitas
21 Ñaños

waterfall is condemned: the dam for a new hydro-electric power complex will flood the entire area.

Continue on this same road and at km 133 take the signposted detour to the right to see **lake Neltume**, small and with a lovely beach for bathing and camping.

At km 142 is

Choshuenco a small village on the shores of lake Panguipulli. It used to be a shipping port. There is a good hostería and three boats. Frequented in summer. The road you followed to get here was just a trail through impenetrable forest as recently as 1947. Now it is lined with cultivated fields and grazing lands.

Continue from Choshuenco (km 142) to Enco, skirting the southern shore of lake Panguipulli and then the scenic **Enco river**, which drains the lake. Panguipulli, in turn, receives the waters from lakes

Calafquén, Pellaifa, Lacar, Pirehueico and Neltume. Near Choshuenco there was a famous fishing lodge with a beautiful park built by an Englishman in the 1940s. The original mansion burned down. See Fishing Excursions.

You may climb the Choshuenco volcano, with three private shelters and a stunning view. At km 157 is

LAKE RIÑIHUE with a small port at **Enco**. A road starts here, skirting the lake's southern shore; beautiful views. At the beginning is a stretch of steep road which can become deteriorated in winter. Check beforehand.

At km 187 is the picturesque village of **Riñihue**, formerly a railhead and the lake's main port. It has accommodation in pensiones and a campground by the lake. Three km before the

SEVEN LAKES

village is the splendid Hostería Huinca Quiñay.

To return to Lican Ray, follow the paved road leading in 40 km to Los Lagos; take there the road to Panguipulli –there is a short graveled stretch– and, from Panguipulli, follow the road to Lican Ray, skirting lake Calafquén's western shore.

2 A CIRCUIT BEHIND THE VOLCANOES ★★★

151 km of gravel road from Lican Ray to Llifén. The last stretch, however, from Puerto Fuy to Llifén, crosses lands now privately owned, and the owners do not authorize passage.

A little–trampled circuit through beautiful scenery, which can be combined with the Inter–Lake tour. If you start from Pucón, take the road behind the Villarrica volcano via Termas de Palguín. Check with Conaf–Pucón about the condition of this route.

Huilo Huilo waterfall

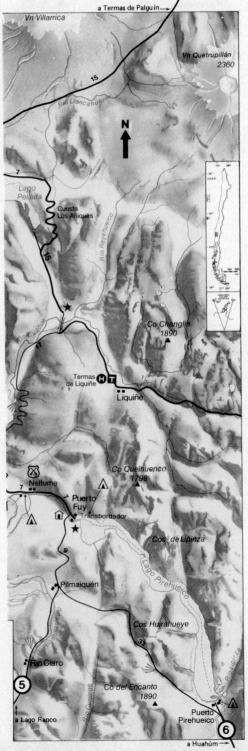

Leave Lican Ray (km 0) towards Coñaripe (km 21). Farther into the valley, the road climbs a steep, rough stretch called **Los Añiques**; from the crest there is a gorgeous view over lake Pellaifa, accessible through a short detour at the bottom of the descent. From the valley, grand views of Villarrica and Choshuenco volcanoes, closing the valley. At km 43 is

Liquiñe a Mapuche village on the bank of a river, with an abrupt hill with a waterfall and a missionary Capuchino church. There is an hostería with natural **thermal springs** set amid the native jungle.

Retrace the road 7 km from Liquiñe up to a junction (km 50) with a road heading south. This road soon crosses the **Cuacúa river**, a placid, convoluted stream. The scenery is beautiful, with native forests and views of lake Neltume. The road reaches a beach at the point where the lake drains into a river.

At km 67 this road meets the Choshuenco–Puerto Fuy highway (see Tour 1). Follow this road to the left to reach **Neltume** at km 74. Continue to Puerto Fuy, at km 81, on the shores of lake Pirehueico. From there the road continues south over a bridge crossing the Fuy river where there is a police check point.

3 A TOUR AROUND LAKE CALAFQUEN ★★★

a 27–km gravel road to Calafquén.

A circuit through a scenic route to a pretty little lake resort.

Leave Lican Ray (km 0) towards the west, skirting the lake shore, with several beaches and campgrounds. The road climbs gradually and at km 17 it meets the Villarrica–Panguipulli road. Follow this road to the left, which runs away from the lake, and take the signposted road branching right at km 25, leading in 2 km to

CALAFQUEN a pretty lake resort with nice houses, but no tourist infrastructure.

For those wishing to make a complete circuit around the lake, Coñaripe is 36 km away (scenic road, good views), and Lican Ray 55 km away.

10

501

SECTION D   VALDIVIA

This section covers the rivers Calle Calle, Cruces, Tornagaleones and Futa, and a beautiful stretch of little-known coast.

The heart of this Section is the city of

VALDIVIA (pop 115,000) a provincial capital, river port and one of Chile's most pleasant cities. Founded in 1552, it was deserted by 1598 and occupied by Dutch pirate Sebastian de Cordes in 1600. Founded anew in 1645, it was fortified late in the 18th century. A significant influx of German immigrants gave the town a tremendous boost, catapulting it to become Chile's leading industrial city, with breweries, mills, shipyards, machinery factories and the country's first blast furnace, in 1913. The German imprint has been preserved to this day. Valdivia was levelled by the 1960 earthquake and completely rebuilt since.

What To See the wharves on the river and the riverside promenade –the Costanera–, with the city's main market, are worth a visit. Fishes and other seafood, and farm produce, are on offer (Mon–Sun 08:00–14:30 h; Main days Wed & Sat). All the constructions and installations on the river shore sank over two meters with the 1960 earthquake and stayed below the water level. What you now see has all been rebuilt since.

The Pedro de Valdivia **bridge** to Isla Teja –an island bounded by rivers Calle Calle, Cau Cau and Cruces flies over the parks of some turn-of-the-century mansions, built on the German style then prevailing.

To the left is the

Valdivia History Museum (summer Mon–Sun 10:00–13:00 h & 15:00–19:00 h; winter, Tue–Sun, until 18:00 h) which contains a valuable collection of items from the colonial days and from the German immigration. The building housing the Museum was the residence of Karl Anwandter, a spokesman for and member of the first group of German immigrants in Valdivia. Behind the museum and on the park of the German School is the private cemetery of the Anwandter family, containing the tombs of some of the first settlers.

The same street leads to the **Universidad Austral,** a «university town» with a very beautiful botanical garden and arboretum with species from all over the world. Farther ahead is Parque Saval, with interesting flora.

On the second block of Picarte –the access street turning right beyond the bridge over the Calle Calle– is a **Spanish Fortified Tower** (1774), guarding a former gate located at the end of the city's eastern defensive wall. At the beginning of street General Lagos is the twin tower, also dating from 1774, at the other end of the wall. In the neighborhood are several **buildings** dating from 1870 onwards, some housing institutions and others turned into hotels. At the end of General Lagos (No 2026) is the manorhouse and park of the Huachocopihue farm, followed by the shipyard and the Miraflores campus of the Universidad Austral.

To end this trip we suggest you go down **Arturo Prat Riverside** and return to the pier, continuing along the huge avenue under the brigde, bordering the residential area, up to the end. As a result of the violent earthquake in 1960, the whole city sank over 2 meters; thus all that was on the banks of the river remained under water and had to be rebuilt as we see it today.

Shopping hours in Valdivia are Mon–Fri 09:30–13:00 h & 15:00–19:30 h; Sat 09:00-13:00 h).

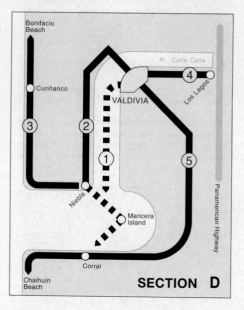

SECTION D

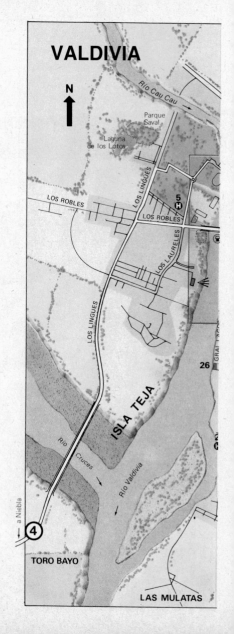

VALDIVIA

10

Where To Eat the floating restaurant Camino de Luna, on the Costanera, offers good meals with a nice view. For families with children, the places indicated with an asterisk in map.

VALDIVIAN WEEK during 2nd and 3rd week in Feb, in different points in the city. On the Calle–Calle shove ferias artesanales set up and there is an exhibit of the international painting contest «Valdivia and its River». In Parque Saval, there are race tracks. The great show is on the last night by the river, with ships, beauty pageant and fire norks. A very popular event, take hotel reservations in advance.

RIVER EXCURSIONS Valdivia has several beaches and villages on the estuary of the Valdivia river (also known as Valdivia bay), such as Corral (a port), Amargos (a fishing cove), Niebla and Mancera (beach resorts), etc.

Over ten passenger boats –ranging from motorized boats to yachts– ply the waterways from Valdivia to the above locations, making an interesting excursion. Boats are available for hire for groups of 5-25 people. Informations at the Sernatur tourist office at the wharf. Scheduled boat services are as follows:

To Mancera and Corral a guided tour sailing down the Valdivia river to Isle Mancera, visiting Castillo

Valdivia

San Pedro de Alcántara, a fortress built by the Spaniards, to continue to Corral and visit Castillo San Sebastián de la Cruz, another Spanish fortress. It sails then into the open sea before returning to Valdivia. Departure is at 13:30 h, and the tour lasts about 5 $\frac{1}{2}$ hours. Lunch and tea service aboard optional.

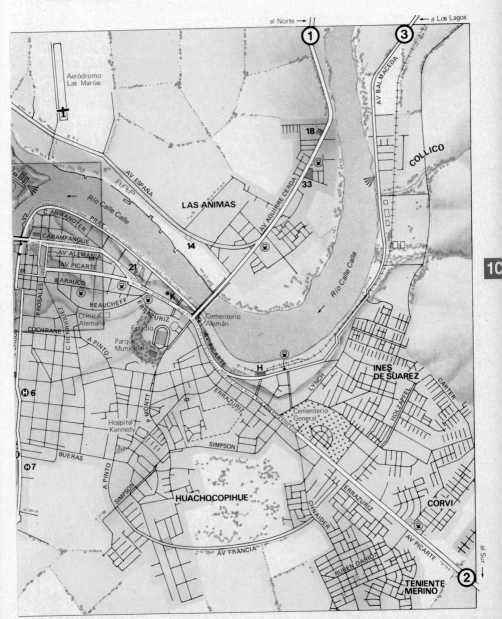

Night Cruise departure 21:30 h, it lasts one hour and includes a cocktail on board. It sails the entire length of Valdivia upstream to Collico.

Passenger Boats to Corral cheaper than the tourist boats, departure every ca 1 ½ hours; the journey to Corral takes about 1 ½ hours. Brief stops at Niebla and Mancera, you can buy tickets for the various legs, stopping over and then continuing on the next boat. Last boat departs from Corral ca 20:00 h in summer.

Tourist Boats on Río Cruces the organized tours

visit the Spanish fortress of Castillo San Luis de Alba at Amargos.

TOURS FROM VALDIVIA

2 **TO NIEBLA, CORRAL AND THE SPANISH FORTS** ★★★ *visiting these locations on your own, either by bus, car or passenger boat.*
The tour starts at Niebla, which can be reached by road and river. From Valdivia (km 0), the road (paved) crosses Isla Teja

---

☎	Telephone Center	※ **H**	Railway Station	**RESTAURANTS**
★	Touristic Information	**J**	Museo Austral (3A)	10 Café Palace (3B)
◉	Café, Meeting Point	※ **K**	Colonial Fortified Towers	11 Dino´s (3B)
Ⓩ	Gasoline Station	**L**	Prochelle Park (2A)	12 Café Haussmann (3B)
☞	Lookout Point			13 La Protectora (3B)
※ ✚	Hospital		**ACCOMMODATIONS**	※ 14 El Fogón Palestino (3B)
A	Town Hall (3B)	**1**	H Pedro de Valdivia (2B)	15 Delicias y
B	Cathedral Church (3B)	※ **2**	H Naguilán	Shopperías München (3B)
C	Post Office (3B)	**3**	H Villa del Río (1C)	16 Centro Español (3B)
D	Market (3A)	**4**	H Melillanca (3C)	17 Camino de Luna (2A)
E	Boat Dock and	※ **5**	H Isla Teja	※ 18 El Rancho
	Boat Hire (2B)	※ **6**	H Raitué	1 Don Pedro (2B)
F	Riverside Market (3A)	※ **7**	Cb Pumantú	※ **3** Villa del Rio
G	River Port (3A)	**8**	H Palace (3B)	19 Café Paula (3B)
		9	Hostal Villa Paulina (4B)	20 Gelatería Entrelagos (4B)

TIPS	**TOURIST SERVICES**
30 Mazapanes Sur (3B)	※ 21 Bus Terminal
31 Mazapanes Entrelagos (4B)	22 Ladeco (3B)
32 Chocolates	※ 23 Hertz (3C)
Camino de la Luna (3C)	24 Automovil Club (3B)
※ 33 Licores Fehremberg (3B)	25 Turismo Conosur (3B)
	※ 26 Turismo Mendez
	※ See General Map of Valdivia

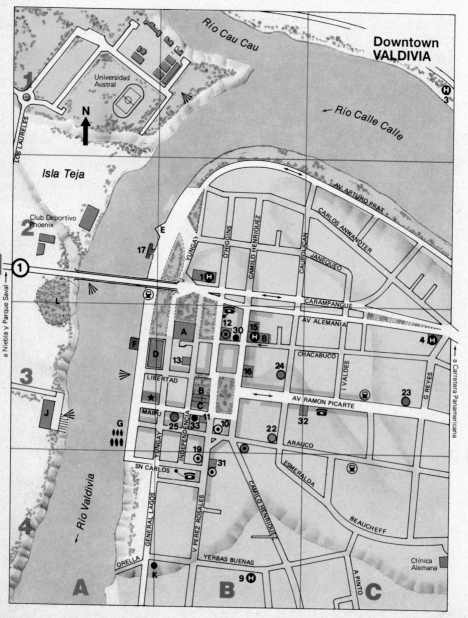

and then heads south, crossing the Cruces river over a bridge finished in 1987 (455 m long and 21 m high). At km 9 is a good campsite. At km 18 is

Corral fort

NIEBLA a beach resort with restaurants, hosterías and residenciales. On a promontory is the fortress of **Castillo de la Pura y Limpia Concepción de Monfort de Lemus (NM)**, erected in 1671 and christened in honor of the Viceroy of Peru, Count of Lemus. In 1767 the engineer Juan Garland improved the layout, built the powder magazine and a furnace to heat up the cannonballs, and lined the walls with cancahua stone, making it inaccessible from the sea. The fort has a battery of 18 guns which, in combination with the guns at Mancera and Corral, covered the width of the estuary. To continue the tour, a hired or a passenger boat can bring you across to

MANCERA a small, picturesque island, now a summer resort with old houses and pretty gardens. Here is the fortress **Castillo de San Pedro de Alcántara (NM),** whose construction started in

SPANISH FORTS

1✳ Morro Gonzalo Gun Battery (Destroyed)	5✳ Chorocamayo Gun Battery (Destroyed)	9✳ Piojo Gun Battery (Destroyed)
2✳ San Carlos Gun Battery (Destroyed)	6✳ Fortress San Sebastian de La Cruz	10✳ Fortress Monfort de Lemus
3✳ Del Barro Gun Battery	7✳ Fortress San Pedro de Alcántara	11✳ Del Molino Gun Battery
4✳ Amargos Fort	8✳ Carboneros Gun Battery (Bajo Agua)	12✳ Fortress San Luis De Alba

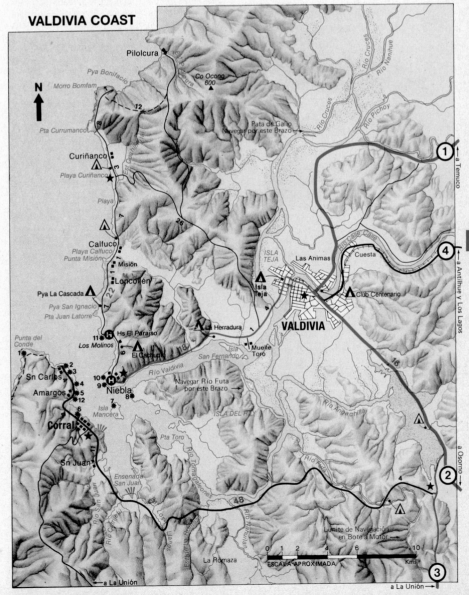

VALDIVIA COAST

10

505

1648. It was improved in 1680 and 1762 when the Military Government of Valdivia set up its headquarters here. It has a superb view, and the small church and convent of San Francisco. It had a battery of 10 large–diameter guns.

Take the next passenger boat for

CORRAL Valdivia's main seaport. Cargo is unloaded from merchant ships onto smaller river boats which then bring it to Valdivia. Here landed the first German immigrants in 1850. Corral boomed with the **Corral Blast Furnace,** the first in Chile, fed with firewood; it brought about the depletion of all the native forest in the area. The 1960 tidal wave wiped out all industrial installations along with the lower part of the village. Here is the fort **Castillo de San Sebastián (NM).** Its construction was started in 1647; the cancahua–stone masonry dates from 1678, and it was remodelled by Juan Garland in 1764 using stone and brick masonry. It had a 24–gun battery, and was the mightiest in the estuary. A tunnel on its base was dug to permit the passage of the railway from the Blast Furnace to the port. A nice, 2–hour walk along the beach will bring you to the busy beach and fishing cove of

Amargos here is the fortress **Castillo de San Luis de Amargos (NM),** erected between 1655 and 1660, and improved by Juan Garland in 1764. It had a battery of seven guns.

A road continues along the coast to **San Carlos,** where the San Carlos Battery was located. Camping on the beach. The road continues through the gun emplacement of **Batería del Inglés** to end at Morro Gonzalo, a promontory.

On February 2, 1820, the Chilean fleet commanded by Lord Cochrane attacked the Batería del Inglés emplacement and disembarked a party of 310 men headed by Beauchef and Miller. During the night, they overran the San Carlos emplacement and the forts of Amargos and Corral. The next morning, Niebla and Corral surrendered. That was the end of the great Spanish stronghold.

NB Corral can also be reached overland. See Tour 5 below.

3 **TO THE OCEAN BEACHES ★★★**
a round trip of 86 km from Valdivia. Take food and swimming gear. There is a campground.
A visit to the Pacific coast, with beautiful beaches at the foot of lush cliffs.

Leave Valdivia (km 0) following the paved road

to Niebla at km 18. Continue on the road to the Pacific coast, running above sheer cliffs.

At km 22 is **Los Molinos beach,** with Hostería El Paraíso a short distance ahead. Then comes **San Ignacio beach** at km 26. Loncollén is at km 30 and Calfuco at km 33. A long stretch above cliffs follows, with superb views, to reach **Curiñanco** at km 43, a village and a beach.

The road beyond this point is badly surfaced, and reaches in 10 km **Bonifacio beach.** Camping possible at San Ignacio and Curiñanco (modest campsite at the latter).

4 **A DIFFERENT ROUTE TO/FROM VALDIVIA ★★**
fifty km of gravel road from Los Lagos to Valdivia.
A little–trampled route connecting Valdivia and the Pan–American highway.

From Valdivia (km 0), take the road to Antilhue starting from Collico (exit 3 in map of Valdivia, and 4 in map of Valdivia Coast). The scenic road runs through traditional farmland, along the deep and navigable **Calle Calle river.** Los Lagos (km 50) straddles the Pan–American highway.

5 **OVERLAND TO CORRAL ★★★**
It is 65 km to Corral. Take gasoline. There are restaurants and campgrounds.
Another option to reach Corral and visit the old Spanish forts.

Leave Valdivia (km 0) following the Pan–American highway way heading South. The road runs past large marshes teeming with waterfowl, particularly black–neck swans. At km 14, turn right on signposted road to Los Ulmos, with one lane paved.

At km 16 turn right on the signposted road to Corral. At km 20 this road crosses the Futa river, navigable and of old the waterway followed by the settlers heading for the plains of La Unión. There is a good spot for camping.

The road continues along the river, with picturesque forests. At km 35 it crosses the Naguilán river to run later alongside the Tornagaleones river, with a superb view over the Corral bay. At km 54 is the San Juan fishing cove, with a long white–sanded beach called Los Morritos, with a campground, some modest restaurants and vegetable gardens. The road runs along the coast, with Isle Mancera across, past the ruins of the blast furnace destroyed by the 1960 tidal wave.

At km 65 is the access to Corral, described under Tour 2. A road climbs the hill and runs south along the crest of the hills to **Chaihuín beach,** a beautiful place.

SECTION E   ROUTES TO ARGENTINA

A lake and an important border resort. It is visited by many tourists who frequently go to Lake Villarrica.

This section covers the international passes to San Martín de los Andes in Argentina.

A **TO SAN MARTIN DE LOS ANDES THROUGH**
PUCON-PUESCO ★★★ *180 km from Pucón to San Martín de los Andes and 120 km from the Puesco Border Control. It takes 4 hours. Take food. First gasoline station at Junín de los Andes after 140 km. The leg Pucón-Puesco is described in Section B, Tour 6.*
A nice opportunity to visit the Argentinian plain (pampa) and the important lake resort of San Martín de los Andes.

Puesco Border Control 60 km from Pucón, 16 km from the border, and 120 km from San Martín de los Andes. It has a Police Post, International Police, Customs, and a Sag Control Post. There

is a hostería and a Conaf ranger house with a campground.
Schedule in summer 08:30-20:00 h to get in; exit until 19:30 h. Personnel´s lunch time 13:30-14:30 h.
Documentation adults are required to show an official ID. Children with their parents: an official ID and birth certificate or familly registration document. Children alone: an official ID and a notarized permission signed by both parents, and a visa extended by an Argentinian consul. Cars: registration documents or a notarized permission from the owner of the car.
Fees no fees on weekdays; Sat and Sun approximately US$ 0,75 per person. The Puesco stretch (km 0) is described in Section B, Tour 6. At km 62 are the Villarrica National Park on the Chilean side, and the Lanín National Park on the Argentinian side. Both parks have magnificent pure araucaria forests around the great Lanín Volcano.

10

Araucarias grow in stony volcanic soil; the older ones have nuts («piñones») like balls with fleshy edible seeds. The older trees can also be distinguished by polygonal bark formations on their trunks.

At km 19 is the **Tromen Border Control** with Customs, Police Station and Rangers.

Schedule 08:30-20:00 h entrance; exit 08:00-19:00 h (Argentinian time). Fees weekdays approximately US$ 0,35 in australes or pesos; Sat and Sun approximately US$ 1,00 per person.

Follow the road to the left of the Border Control to visit **Lake Tromen**. Hikers can get information to climb the Lanín Volcano (2 days). There is a shelter high up.

The road descends gently through the broad valley of the Mamuil Malal river and the forests give way to a landscape of pastures and bushes characteristic of the patagonic steppe. Behind, as a dramatic background, is the Lanín Volcano.

At km 28 the Lanín National Park ends in a patch of araucarias. The road goes straight forward through a huge steppe. At km 35 there is a bridge over the Mamuil Malal river and the Lanín Volcano is not seen anymore. There is an estancia house with poplar windbreaks.

At km 46 is the last araucaria patch called Primeros Pinos. Ahead is the Hostería San Humberto with a garden and a river beach; it is a good place to stop and freshen up.

At km 52 is the Puesto de Paja village. The road leaves behind the Mamuil Malal valley and runs southward through lava-capped hills of beautiful tints. At km 66 you see from above the great valley where Junín de los Andes is. Not too far away is the Carretera Nacional 23 which to the left takes you to Aluminé (104 km). Follow to the right.

At km 75 there is a road junction; take the paved road and go to your right and cross the river over the Chimehuín river. This river flows into the nice **Lake Huechulafquén**. After 22 km by a graveled road, at km 80, is

Junín de los Andes, a small farming village located on the valley, with a regiment in the outskirts. There is a good hotel and the Alejandro I Restaurant at the entrance of the town.

The paved road runs southward through the valley to km 91 and after crossing Quilquihue river turns to the west to approach to Lake Lacar. After the Chapelco Airport you cross the glacial moraine which gave way to the lake. At km 116 a road branches to the right leading to lake Pirehueico in Chile. At km 120 is San Martín de los Andes.

B **TO SAN MARTIN DE LOS ANDES THROUGH**

PASO CARIRRIÑE ★★★ *205 km from Villarrica to San Martín through Lican Ray, Coñaripe, Los Añiques hill and Liñique thermal baths. Gasoline only at Villarrica, Lican Ray and San Martín. Campgrounds and restaurants in the Argentinian side at Loglog lake, Curruhué, and a modest one at the Lahuen Co termal baths.*

A nice excursion both to the Chilean and the Argentinian side.

Soon after leaving the Liñique thermal baths (km 0) you will cross **Liñique**, a town with a nice missionary church surrounded by hills and forests. Ahead is the **Customs Complex** (09:00-19:00 h) and the road runs uphill alongside the river canyon (cajón del río), a curvy road with dense forests.

At km 21 is the border and you arrive to the Lanín National Park. The gravel road goes downhill through a deep valley surrounded by mountains, with many watersheds around. At your right are the

Lahuen Co Thermal Baths with modest facilities and mineral water springs ranging from 49° and 70° C. It makes a nice stop. Follow the road, at km 29 you will see

Lake Epulafquén with fishing wharfs. It is the

western extremity of the lake that later on continues into lake Huechulafquén. A nice spot with abrupt mountains and the same type of forest as Valdivia.

Further on you will pass the southern shore of **lake Verde**, partially surrounded by the slag coming from the gorgeous Hualquihue volcano.

As you advance the trees begin to disappear and give way to the characteristic bushes of the plain. Then lake **Curruhué Grande** emerges. The road runs through its southern shore; little vegetation and the last patch of araucarias.

At km 70 is lake **Curruhué Chico**. You will cross some hills -there are many parrots at the end of the summer season- until you get to the Collón Cura bridge at km 90. A road leaves to the left leading to Junín de los Andes. Go on southbound until at km 95 you arrive to

Lake Loglog at its eastern extremity, with no trees. There is a restaurant; it is a good fishing and hunting zone. At km 111 you will get to San Martín de los Andes.

C **TO SAN MARTIN DE LOS ANDES THROUGH**

LAKE PIREHUEICO ★★★ *54 km from Puerto Pirehueico to San Martín de los Andes. Gravel road in good condition. Gasoline only at San Martín. Hostería at Huahum. The road to Puerto Fuy goes by the western shore of Lake Pirehueico, description in Section C, Tour 1.*

A different way to get to San Martín de los Andes, crossing the gorgeous lake Pirehueico and skirting lake Lacar.

Puerto Fuy at the shore of lake Pirehueico is a modest village with a big beach where you can camp. There is a concrete ramp to board the

Mariela ferry an old and slow metalic ferry for 16 cars. You remain either in your own car or sit on the rails. Schedule in summer: Tu., Th., Sat. and Sun. departures from Puerto Fuy at 09:00 h to arrive at Puerto Pirehueico at 11:15 h. It returns at 17:00 h and arrives at Puerto Fuy at 19:15 h; in winter: Tue, Thu and Sat. departures at 08:00 h and returns at 13:15 h. When the Portillo and the Puyehue passes are closed, it works every day to the above mentioned schedule (see Services and Prices).

LAKE PIREHUEICO 36 km long, narrow and curvy. You never see the whole lake; however, due to the fact that is surrounded by untouched forests, it is perhaps the most spectacular lake of the zone. There are few beaches and sometimes you can see puma traces on them. The lingue tree abounds giving a green tonality to the landscape. It is hard to understand why it is not a national park.

The ferry trip takes 2:15 h. On the other side you get to

Puerto Pirehueico with a small general store and a boarding house. Nearby, northbound, there are three nice lagoons with good fishing spots and campgrounds (boats for rent). At the southern shore is the short-lived **Hostería Pirehueico**, a stately building constructed by the Government. It was inaugurated in february 1947 by President Gabriel González Videla, who almost drowned while fishing at river Huahúm.

Customs Post at the port. Same schedule and conditions as the Puesco Customs (see the previous tour); however, since there is no International Police services, you should get the pass given by them at any city or at Villarrica.

The road goes to the border (km 11) alongside river Huahúm. At km 7 there is a village supplying the country estates (fundos) that export timber to Argentina. The road continues through a canyon surrounded by forests until at km 11 you get to

Paso Huahúm at 659 m above the sea level it is the lowest border pass (only at Patagonia there are lower ones). It is always open, snowless. It is an

10

closed. On such occasions trucks and tourism buses use it. There is a project to build an international road by the lake Pirehueico shore.

After the border, the road skirts the river Huahúm that receives the waters of lake Lacar from Argentina.

At km 13 is the **Huahúm** village at the lake Lacar shore with Argentinian **Customs** and an hostería with selfservice.

LAKE LACAR   belongs to the Argentinian Lanín National Park; very similar to lake Pirehueico, with forests and few beaches. The vegetation changes here, for the «ciprés de la cordillera» (Libocedro chilensis) emerges displacing thus the Valdivian forest; toward San Martín de los Andes the forest ends and the pampa begins. This characteristic is found over and over again along the Argentinian mountains up to lake Puelo.

Lake Lacar flows into the Pacific Ocean through Chile. In a north-south sense this is the first time that this occurs, and it helps one to understand why this border pass is so low.

This can be understood because a geological fault made a gash in the range, so that during the glacial period a huge snow veil covered the mountains, flowing simultaneously to Panguipulli in Chile and to San Martín de los Andes in Argentina.

When the ice melted down, the moraine on the Argentinian side (you can see it on the road from San Martín to Junín) was higher because it was closed between mountains and thus the waters were forced to flow into Chile. The road continues to Huahúm among curves and forests, behind the hills with occasional views to the lake, for arrive at km 54 to San Martín de Los Andes.

EXCURSIONS

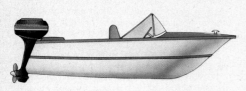

BOAT EXCURSIONS

In an area so full of water bodies –from lakes through placid and swift rivers to the open sea– and superb fishing, towing a boat or renting one is highly rewarding. We have explored some of the possible excursions in this district. «Clean», in the descriptions below, means a water course without rock outcrops or the like (the water itself is very clean in the usual sense).

Queule River ★★

a clean, deep river sailed by small cargo vessels. Lighter craft can be launched either at Puerto Boldos –a difficult ramp– or at Queule, whence you can sail upstream. With the assistance of a local estuary pilot, sail into the sea to visit the nearby sea–lion colony. It is advisable to travel from Pitrufquén, as the route from Mehuín has a short but steep gradient, difficult to negotiate with a heavy trailer.

Cautin River from Carahue ★★

another deep, clean river, of old navigated by large ships. The scenery of rolling fields and Mapuche settlements is gorgeous. A round trip of 70 km, it offers good fishing of corvina and robalo at the confluence with the Nahuelte river. Earthen boat ramp at Quillén, 1 km from Carahue; the whole stretch of river is very good for water skiing. It is advisable to sail down on the left–hand side of Inés island: at Puerto Saavedra there is a dock.

Valdivia Watershed ★★★

this is one of Chile's most attractive areas for boat excursions. Valdivia offers excellent boat ramps, gasoline service directly to the boats, and several boat harbors. Furthermore, there are two hotels with their own boat ramp and harbor.

You can program short excursions to return to Valdivia in the evening, or a grand tour of four days staying the night at anchor in some sheltered cove (get the track of the Valdivia river at the Gobernación Marítima).

A Circuit Along the Tornagaleones River a deep, clean,

placid river, ideal for water–skiing. Sail down the Valdivia river to Del Rey island, to round the Mancera island from behind to reach Corral, and thence back to Valdivia through the Tornagaleones river. It is a beautiful cruise, with mountain scenery and beautiful beaches. It is worthwhile going in and visit the bays where you can see the ruins of the Corral Foundry and the old Spanish forts; the round trip covers 60 Kms.

Sailing the Cruces River Upstream clean and deep. Sail the Cau Cau river upstream up to the confluence with the Cruces river, and farther upstream through the Wetland Nature Sanctuary upstream of Valdivia. Gorgeous forests on the river banks, lots of waterfowl and lots of boats plying the waterways. You can visit the Spanish fort San Luis de Alba on the way. It is a 65-km round trip: allow one day.

Sailing the Futa River Upstream narrow, deep and clean, slow to medium. Sail down the Valdivia river to Fernando island and into the Futa river on the side of Del Rey island. The Futa is flanked by the tall, wooded hills of the Coastal Range. There are some cleared areas with farmhouses, and some boat traffic bringing farm produce to the Valdivia market. In November and December you will find here the best cherries in the area.

This was the route to the South in the past, travellers having to row upstream up to the road to La Unión.

The total circuit is 60 km long; allow one day.

Sailing the Calle Calle River Upstream wide, placid, clean and deep, it is the area's best river for water–skiing. The scenery here is different from the above rivers, flanked by high hills but permitting wide visibility; the railway runs along one of the banks. In the past, large boats sailed up to Huellehue, the end station for the logs sent tied into rafts down the river from logging operations around the lakes far inland. The total circuit is 40 km long.

FISHING EXCURSIONS

Origins sport fishing in the South was introduced by the first European settlers. At times they would collect –using baskets– the numerous fishes trapped in ponds on the river banks. These fishes were small and did not offer a challenging battle, thereby not satisfying the Europeans, more used to the fighting salmon of the Old World. In 1893, Isidora Goyenechea set up Chile's first fish farm, at the **Chivilingo** river, south of Lota, using French technology and introducing the salmonoid species.

In 1905, the state set up a **fish farm complex** at the **Blanco river**, a tributary of the Aconcagua river in Central Chile, introducing several salmonoid

10

species, such as Salmo salar, S. trutta, S. fario, and S. irridens. The fishes were let loose in various rivers farther south up to Maullín. In 1910, the first «Chilean» salmon was caught in lake Villarrica, successfully crowning the salmon project started years earlier. In 1914, the state had further fish farms set up at Lautaro and Maullín, in order to «populate» the South's fresh water bodies. In 1930, species of Alaskan salmon were introduced, including Oncorchynchus tacharyscha, nesca, kisutch, etc.

This is the base of our present sport fishing, fostered by the state for over 80 years. It now has attained international renown. There used to be salmons of up to ten kilos, but now they have become scarcer as a result of the termination of state–subsidized fish farms and unauthorized commercial fishing.

Fishing Infrastructure the rapid growth of sport fishing led to the appearance of the first hotels in the vicinity of the mouths of rivers. In 1930, the Hotel Gudenschwager of Pucón used as its telegraph code the word «salmones». By then there were fishing shelters on lakes Villarrica and Panguipulli, and soon at Choshuenco, Llifén, and Puerto Nuevo, to crown the effort with the opening of the state–built Gran Hotel Pucón in 1934.

Simultaneously, a **boat** was designed and perfected for the rivers of Chile's South (see illustration), until it attained its present dimensions: 3.5 m in length, oarlocks located midway between prow and stern, bottom smooth and curved, with an aft–looking seat in the rear for the fisherman. Made of wood, its sides consist of a single 55–cm–wide plank, the bottom of 3 or 4 planks, and the stern is made of a single board.

It is superbly designed for fast turns in strong currents, and is sturdy, has a shallow draft and a very robust bottom enabling it to withstand bumps against submerged rocks and to be dragged into or out of the water over rough surfaces.

In 1936 there appeared the first advertisements offering to row down the Pucón, Villarrica and Llifén rivers. Originally, the stretches to be rowed were short and were of a rather exploratory nature, to see which rivers were more suitable for the activity. The early attempts were not exempt of accidents. At the Huahúm river in the summer of 1947, for instance, when the state–built Hotel Pirehueico was being inaugurated, President González Videla's boat capsized with nearly tragic consequences.

In the late 1950s, private individuals built shelters and four **fishing lodges** open to the international fishing fraternity. The lodges were comfortable houses located at strategic locations, set in beautiful parks and having excellent boat houses. One of the lodges was located at lake Todos los Santos, another at **Cancahuasi**, at the far end of lake Panguipulli between the Fuy and Enco rivers, and two on the Toltén river, **Catrico** and **Coipue**. The ruins of the last of these lodges can still be seen.

The Pucón airfield and the Hotel Antumalal – formerly catering to fishermen only– date from that period.

Fishing Safaris the spontaneous influx of foreign fishermen became in time a constant, scheduled traffic of fishermen from all over the world lured by the particular attractions of sport fishing in the world's southernmost country.

An Austrian, Alfred Heusser, was one of the pioneers. He organized fishing safaris for which participants –men and women– would fly directly to southern Chile without stopping in Santiago. They were also a daring bunch, rafting down the Liucura, Toltén, Allipén, Quepe, Enco, Fuy and other rivers. For foreigners, the Chilean type of fishing was quite a novelty. They were used to fishing from the shore or standing in the current at particular spots wearing long fishing boots. In southern Chile, by contrast, rivers are accessible only by boat under the guidance of an expert boatman. This special communication between fisherman and boatman, together with the thrill of

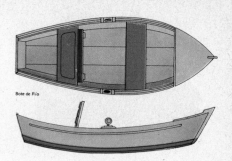

Bote de Río

rapids and the size of the fish, gave Chile a position of renown in the international fishing community.

This activity has decreased somewhat, oriented mainly to lake Rupanco and rivers in the deep south, in the area of Aysén. Still, rivers are rowed down with fishing in the morning among rapids, jungle and some quite pools where the boatman halts the boat. Then lunch at a place and at a time chosen by the boatman, who also is the cook: part of the salmon catch will be roasted or otherwise prepared for the fishing party. Usually there follows a short nap on the river bank, to continue fishing until late afternoon. The best organized fishing expeditions are to be found at Pucón and Villarrica at the Sindicato de Boteros (Boatmen Union); the boatmen also provide all the necessary gear.

HIKING

To Valdivia From the Bueno River ★★★

the journey starts by sailing down the Bueno river to its mouth. Then, on foot for 95 km skirting the coastline up to the Corral Forts, whence a boat brings you back upstream to Valdivia. Allow 4 to 5 days for this. The hike can also be made in the other direction. To arrive at **Trumao**, the point of departure on the Bueno river, it is advisable to come by train if travelling southwards, or by bus if coming from Osorno. A steamer sails from Trumao Saturday morning for the mouth of the river and returns Sunday at midday. Bring your own food.

The river journey starts with an expansive scenery which soon becomes hemmed in by the Coastal Range all the way to the river mouth. For five hours, the steamer meanders along the river shores, sometimes stopping at settlers' houses or sawmills. Some fishing boats and motorized boats can be seen sailing to the mouth of the river, where some summer houses are located.

The mouth of the river is crossed by boat and the trek starts on a trail climbing up and down to **Hueicolla** (17 km), a summer village with only 20 houses, a small general store and a very badly-surfaced road heading inland. Nearby is the picturesque fishing cove of **Lameguapi**, the only one in the area. The path continues along the 8–km Huaicolla beach, with softly-lapping surf and macha –an edible mollusk– banks, to Punta Colún. Punta Colún is crossed through a jungle-lined path which descend on the other side to the Colún river, where a settler lives. A boat can be hired to bring you across the river to start the long hike along the **Colún beach** (12 km), flanked by a green–clad cliff graced by waterfalls issuing here and there until Punta Galera.

The path climbs straight to cross Punta Galera and then reaches two small, beautiful secluded beaches, with pools where fishes get trapped when the tide recedes. The trail continues along the crest of a cliff for 17 km to Chaihuín beach, crossing **Falsa Galera** and **Huinio** points. The path gradually becomes a cart trail with some settlers and cultivated fields.

Chaihuín Beach is perhaps one of the South's

10

most beautiful beaches. A navigable, meandering river washes here into the ocean. Access from above is difficult. Its sand is white and is sheltered by a crescent of hills. At its northern end is Chaihuín fishing cove, where an alerce industry operated around the turn of the century; it issued its own currency for shopping at its stores. There remain only some roadbeds for the railway which brought the material to the shipping port.

A coastal road leads from Chaihuín to Corral; the local fishermen usually sail along the coast to Corral. Continuing by land to Morro Gonzalo (at the southern end of the Valdivia Bay) the road runs along the coast for 20 km, skirting small beaches, rocky stretches and forests. Between Morro Gonzalo and Corral (8 km) are the **Spanish forts** and **gun emplacements**, which in a single night –running through what then was thick jungle– were seized by Lord Cochrane's forces during the struggle for independence.

The journey ends sailing from Corral upstream to Valdivia.

Along the Colonial Route ★★

a hike along a portion of the only path authorized by the Mapuches for Spaniards –and later Chileans– to travel overland between Concepción and Valdivia. It is 75 km along sandy coast between Puerto Saavedra and Toltén and Queule farther south; allow three to four days for the journey. **Puerto Saavedra** is reached by bus from Temuco; you can continue to **Boca Budi**. The path then continues along the beach for several kilometers until the sand gives way to coarse gravel, and the cliffs force you to climb and walk along their crest. Farther ahead you climb down to the waterfront once more. This is Mapuche country; you will see some of them on the way, their rucas and a settlement, Peleco. Beyond the **Toltén river** you cross the **Ñilque** headland, with the **Queule** hills ahead as your goal.

To Pucón Through the Andean Valleys ★★★

this hike starts from the northern side of **lake Caburgua** along the Blanco river valley to the Maichín river valley, to reach Curarrehue and from there hike down to Pucón. It is an 80 km hike, allow between 4 and 5 days; take food. Start from Temuco by bus to the northern section of lake Caburgua via Cunco and lake Colico. The hike begins from lake Caburgua to the mouth of the **Blanco river;** follow from there the logging road running between the cliff and the jungle. There are wild hot springs in the area. The valley climbs towards the Maichín river, which runs southwards. This is frontier territory, the last zone with native forest being exploited in the old forest reserve occupied by settlers, in 1912. Here is **Reigolil,** a cluster of houses on the river bank. A cart trail leads from here to **Curarrehue,** in the Trancura valley, where you can take a bus to return to Pucón.

Climbing the Villarrica Volcano ★★★

there is no other public transportation to the Villarrica National Park than taxis. Either hitchhike or walk. Allow 8 to 9 hours for the climb up and down from the shelter (refugio) at the end of the road, well within the park and on the volcano's slope. Climbing gear (crampons and ice ax),

sunblock, sunglasses, and good boots are essential, and a guide is highly recommended. The crater has sheer, 100 m deep cliffs on its inner face plummeting to the three blowholes, which belch smoke and sulfur fumes uninterruptedly amid a gut-wrenching underground rumble. A piece of cloth moistened with lemon juice is a good protection against sulfur fumes. Rent climbing gear and sunglasses at El Pollo (Palguín street, Pucón); for further info (guides and so on) ask at the tourist office.

While decending, beware of slipping on the ice: the fall can be pretty long. Should fog creep in, descend immediately.

You will find that climbing an active volcano is a thrilling, unforgettable experience; the scenery, in addition, is fantastic.

FOUR-WHEEL-DRIVE EXCURSIONS

FROM PUCON TO THE NORTHERN SHORES OF LAKE CABURGUA

a 244–km circuit through the northern portion of lake Caburgua, lake Colico, Villarrica and back to Pucón. Allow about 12 hours for driving and some stops (there are thermal baths on the way). Take food and gasoline. There are 100 km where 4WD is essential. Wait a couple of days after heavy rain before attempting this circuit. Leave Pucón (km 0) following the road to Argentina up to Curarrehue at km 43. Turn left at the crossroads just beyond the bridge over the Trancura river. The road runs along the Maichín river valley, with fine scenery and a backdrop of volcanoes. At km 47 a bridge spans the Maichín river, running through a deep canyon. The road then heads north along the western bank of the river. **Maite** is at km 54, with a suspension footbridge used by local settlers.

Between km 58 & 64 the river is hemmed in by sheer, green–clad hills crowned by hexagonal rock formations. A waterfall thunders into a pool nearby. The road runs now along the border passing the village of **Quiñenahuin** at km 66, with a school, a small chapel and a footbridge spanning the river. There is a daily bus service to this village from Pucón. The dirt road from here on is sandy in stretches and much more difficult. At km 72 is a large state school and another footbridge. At km 77 is **Campo Grande**, a wide esplanade with a house and round huts with a central totem where the Mapuche community gathers for prayers and festivities. The road now runs through a sandy area; the first araucarias are to be seen. At km 81 is

Reigolil a village with a school, a chapel, a store, a sawmill, and a police frontier outpost. It is located 6 km from the border. There are two small lakes nearby, frequented by fishermen. A large valley unfolds northwards to lake Icalma.

The road is very poorly–surfaced and turns away from the river to run along a tributary flowing from the west. For the next 30 km there are no settlers. At km 88 is the Sollipulli river; the bridge has been washed away, so you must ford the river (ca. 50–cm depth). Do not attempt it after a strong rain. These are old logging roads, now abandoned. Some pumice layers can be seen on the roadside, evidencing the volcanic origin of this soil.

The road climbs to a **T–junction** at km 89, with beautiful araucarias right next to the road. Turn left towards the river, which you ford at km 90 (this bridge has also been washed away). Then comes another climb to reach a look–out point commanding a view to the **Sollipulli peaks** to the North. The road is lonely and you must open and close several gates barring it. At km 92 is a deserted sawmill and at km 96 you crest a pass. Now the rivers flow towards lake Caburgua.

The road is flanked by a fairy–tale forest of large coihues, followed by a vast tract of burnt forest, with gray trunks protruding above the scrub. On the hill crests are some araucarias. A brook is forded and a curvy, steep descent be-

10

gins; at the bottom is a forking (km 103). Take the left branch.

The road climbs a very rough gradient, with superb scenery of high mountains with rocky faces and a myriad brooks and streams flowing towards the Caburgua. You are now running along the Blanco river valley. At km 105 are the first houses of settlers. Beyond the bridge, at km 107.5, is a house. Here are the

<u>**Río Blanco Hot Springs**</u> adjacent to the house are camping spots, shady and with hearths on the river bank. A footbridge brings you to the north bank, where, in a sunny clearing, a powerful hot spring gushes forth, the water collecting in a large natural rock pool next to the river. Alternating hot and cold baths is a real treat. The owners charge a small fee and can provide some basic food. The local settlers (altogether 15 families in this narrow, isolated valley) frequent the place.

Retrace the road from the hot springs (km 107) to the forking at km 112. The road descends and a 60-m **waterfall** plunges from a rocky cliff to the Blanco river. The road now runs level with the river, crosses a couple of bridges over a tributary and then runs on a ledge carved in the rock face above **lake Chica**; opposite is the **Morro,** a hill on the lakeshore, tended like a golf course, watered by sprinklers and with a large house. In the lake there are salmon farming installations for sport fishing. The place is owned by an Englishman called James Sharp, who travels every year from England and raises thoroughbreds.

The road continues on a narrow ledge and reaches **lake Caburgua** at km 119. The view is spectacular: a white-sand beach ahead, lake Caburgua stretching south, hemmed in by tall mountains and, straight ahead, the **Villarrica volcano.** At km 125 is a crossroads; turn left towards **Playa Negra,** a stony, tree-lined beach with picnic tables.

The gravel road now is considerably better, running level through cultivated fields to reach the Trafampulli bridge and **lake Colico** at km 139. It then runs on a narrow ledge along the northern shore of the lake. On the far shore some summer houses can be seen, accessible only by boat. **Puerto Puma** is at km 155, with a beach and spots for camping. The road heads North to Cunco; at km 161, take the signposted road to Villarrica. At km 173 is Pitrunco bridge, spanning the river through which lake Colico drains.

One km later is a T-junction; turn right and continue to km 186, where you take the signposted road branching left, which reaches Villarrica at km 217 and Pucón at km 244.

If you want to visit the Río Blanco hot springs in a normal car, make this circuit in the opposite direction. It is 137 km from Pucón to the hot springs.

10

RURAL TRANSPORTATION

Rural buses offer a convenient way for travellers to tour the many towns and villages in this area, setting off from the Zone's main cities. The rural bus network is vast and covers practically the entire zone, including places not easily reached by car.

The chart below shows routes and frequencies for weekdays, each line a route and its thickness indicating the number of daily departures in one direction. The rule of thumb is that on Saturdays frequencies drop by half, while on Sunday low-frequency routes (one to three departures daily) are not covered at all. In season, however (ie, in summer), weekend frequencies from Temuco and Valdivia to the main seaside and lake resorts and beaches increase considerably.

Frequency low-frequency routes are the lion's share of the rural network, and usually correspond to the pattern of early morning departure from rural towns to the main cities, returning the same evening. If the distance is short, there might be two departures daily. In cases with three departures daily, there is always an early morning bus leaving the city for the village.

Departure times the first batch of buses depart, in any route, between 07:30 and 08:30 h; the second at 10:30–11:00 h, and the third at 16:30–18:00 h, at which time low-frequency buses return from the cities to the villages. There are no departures over lunchtime, with the exception of high-frequency routes; departures later than 2000h are rare. The time when you most certainly will find transportation out of a city is at 16:30–18:00 h, and out of a village or town, early in the morning.

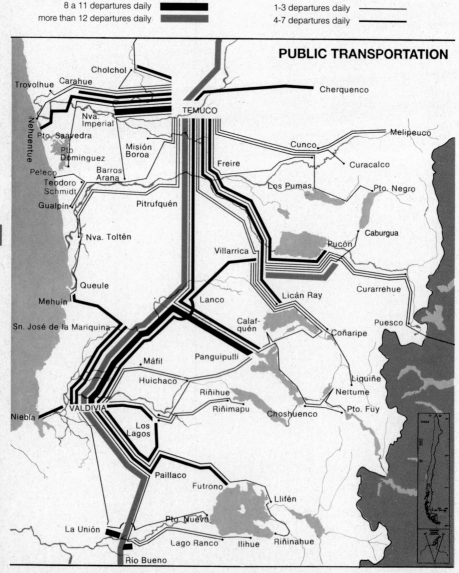

TIPS

In this section we list some places of outstanding quality for shopping or eating.

Temuco the best Mapuche handicrafts are to be found at the **Mercado,** the **Feria** and **Galería Artesanal.** In summer, a Mapuche silver jewelry and textile shop is open to the public at the **Escuela Artesanal** of the Pontificia Universidad Católica at Av Alemania 0422 (Mon–Fri 09:00–18:00 h). Nice begonias at **Escuela Capuchina** in Padre Las Casas, accross from the river (Mar–Sep, Mon–Sat 08:00–12:00 h and 14:00–18:00 h; Oct– Feb, Mon–Sat 09:00–13:00 h and 15:00–19:00 h). The **Nueva Estancia** restaurant deserves a visit: it has the best grilled meat in the South (see location in town map). **Shell–Norte** has a café, sauna, telex, telephone and is open round the clock. Shopping hours in Temuco are Mon–Fri 09:00–12:30 & 14:30–17:00 h; Sat 09:00–13:00 h.

Gorbea Cecinas **Tabbat** offers excellent sausages, ranked as the best in the South together with Moeddinger in Llanquihue. The factory can be visited Mon–Fri 08:00–12:30 h & 14:00–18:30 h.

Pitrufquén a fabulous plant nursery –**Jardín Las Encinas**– in full bloom between September and November, at the corner of Sargento Aldea and Casanova. There are five further plant nurseries in town. **Jardín Los Molinos,** 2 blocks before the latter, with Smaller and more economic plants, open all day.

Villarrica wooden furniture, ornaments and other objects of excellent quality at **El Rehue** (Summer, Mon–Sat, 09:30–20:00 h, Sun 11:00–14:00 h; winter. Mon–Fri 09:00–12:00 h and 14:00–19:00 h: Sat 10:00–17:00 h) and at **Tornería Suiza.** Excellent **marmalade** 8 km into the road to Lonchoche; specialty is raspberry and chestnut marmalade.

Pucón **wood–veneer flowers,** colored, and **carved wooden trays** are among the renowned local handicrafts. French pastries at **café Suiza,** excellent German pastries at **Holzapfel Bäckerei.** Chilean traditional dishes at the sites indicated in town map. At the Ojos del Caburgua is the **Cafetería Salto del Carileufu,** specializing in kuchen, strudel and pizzas.

Loncoche Mapuche scenes carved in a single piece of wood at Taller de Filemón, renowned also abroad (Andrés Bello 0236, always open).

Valdivia delicious marzipan at **Confitería Entrelagos** and **Confitería Sur.** Sweet alcoholic beverages at **Licores Fehrenberg.** Shopping hours in Valdivia: Mon–Sat 09:30–13:00 h & 15:00–19:00 h). See locations in town map.

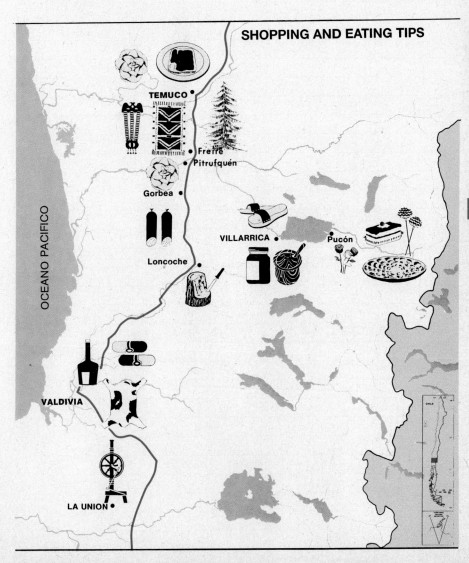

SHOPPING AND EATING TIPS

OCEANO PACIFICO

TEMUCO

Freire
Pitrufquén

Gorbea

Loncoche

VILLARRICA

Pucón

VALDIVIA

LA UNION

10

Notes of This Zone

10

Zone 11
OSORNO to
PUERTO MONTT

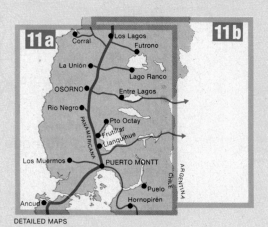

11a
Corral
Los Lagos
Futrono
La Unión
Lago Ranco
OSORNO
Entre Lagos
Rio Negro
Pto Octay
Frutillar
Llanquihue
PANAMERICANA
Los Muermos
PUERTO MONTT
Ancud
Puelo
Hornopirén

11b

CHILE
ARGENTINA

DETAILED MAPS

Arica
Iquique
Antofagasta
Easter
Island
Copiapó
La Serena
Valparaíso
Is R
Crusoe
SANTIAGO
Talca
Concepción
Temuco
Valdivia
Osorno
Pto Montt
Castro
Chaitén
Coihaique
Cochrane

11

Puerto Natales
Punta Arenas
Puerto Williams
Is Diego
Ramirez

90° — 60° — 53°

CHILEAN
ANTARCTIC
TERRITORY

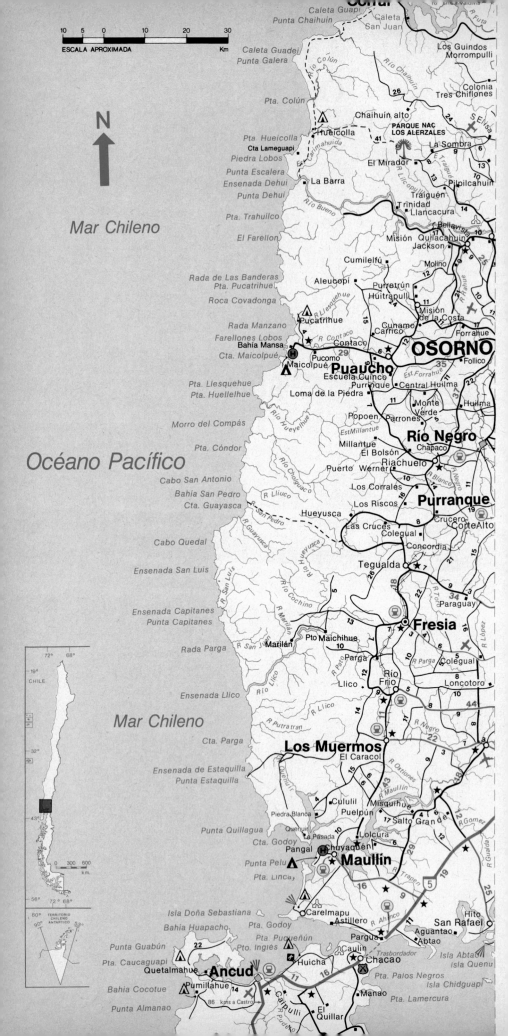

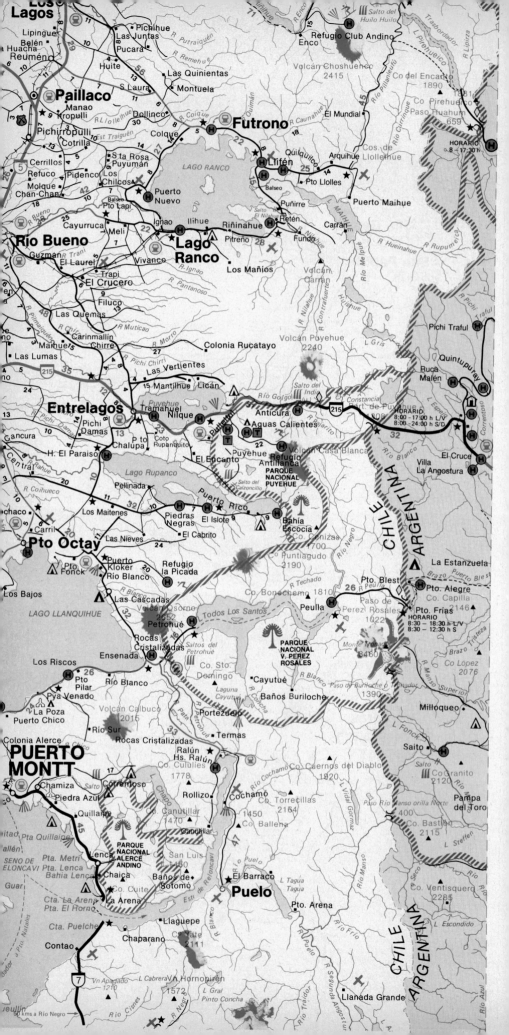

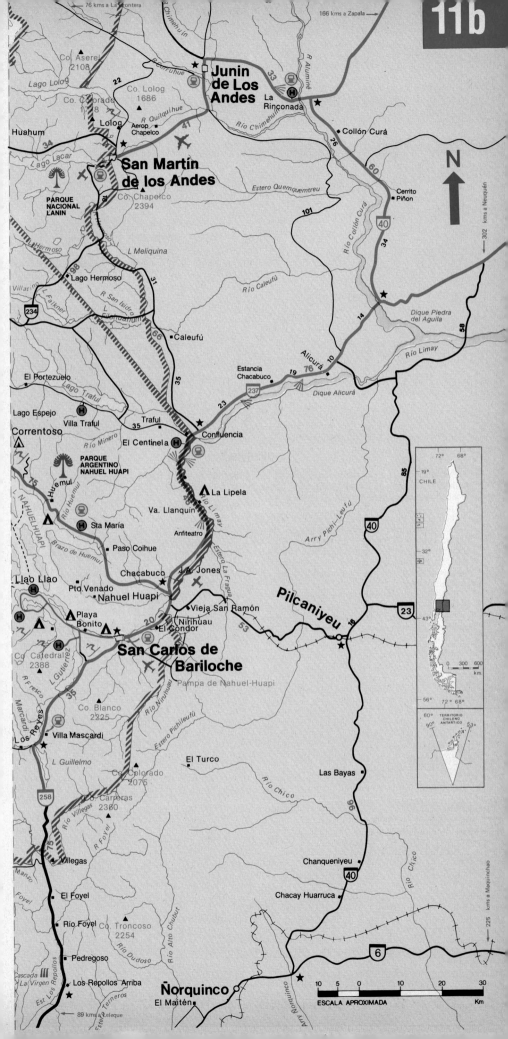

Puyehue Volcano
2240

Yate Hill
2111

OVERVIEW

This delightful park-like zone has soft rolling farmland, as well as hilltops and river banks, cloaked with native tree species. A string of fascinating volcanoes lines the eastern horizon.

The Pan-American highway runs almost straight, going up and down through the landscape. Here, natural landmarks include the Río Bueno, Chile's second largest river, Lago Llanquihue, the only lake that can be seen from the Pan-Am, and Seno de Reloncaví, a vast sea inlet headed by the city of Puerto Montt.

There is complete tourist infrastructure not only around lake Llanquihue and Puerto Montt, but also at lake Ranco and, particularly, lake Puyehue, paradoxically, the two least known lakes. This Zone has been into four Sections:

Section A   Lake Ranco as well as lake Maihue and its surrounding area.

Section B   Osorno with the city of Osorno as the center of a vast, beautiful district stretching between the cities of La Unión and Río Bueno to the North, lovely beaches on the Pacific coast, and lakes Puyehue and Rupanco near the Andes.

Section C   Lake Llanquihue and its surrounding area, as well as lake Todos los Santos and the villages of Ralún and Cochamó in the Reloncaví Estuary.

Section D   Puerto Montt and the area lying on both sides of the Reloncaví Sound.

Section E   Routes to Argentina with a description of roads from Chile to lake Nahuel Huapi as far as San Carlos de Bariloche.

11

REGIONAL DISTANCES

Ancud														
86	Calbuco													
127	101	Frutillar												
282	256	163	Futrono											
304	278	185	22	Llifén										
184	147	70	99	121	Osorno									
202	176	141	170	192	77	Puyehue								
166	140	96	254	273	153	174	Petrohué							
83	57	50	208	227	107	128	89	Pto Montt						
240	204	114	189	211	96	94	202	151	Pto Rico					
100	74	30	188	210	87	108	66	23	131	Pto Varas				
67	69	117	272	294	179	200	159	76	299	93	Maullín			
190	154	110	265	287	172	188	46	103	214	80	173	Ralún		
297	261	171	91	113	107	178	259	210	197	193	280	273	Valdivia	
248	213	114	143	165	50	27	202	159	65	136	223	216	151	Entre Lagos

Zone 11
OSORNO to
PUERTO MONTT

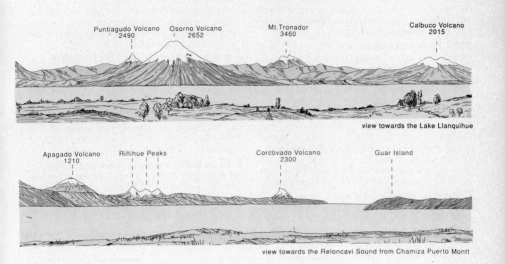

Puntiagudo Volcano
2490

Osorno Volcano
2652

Mt.Tronador
3460

Calbuco Volcano
2015

view towards the Lake Llanquihue

Apagado Volcano
1210

Riñihue Peaks

Corcovado Volcano
2300

Guar Island

view towards the Reloncavi Sound from Chamiza Puerto Montt

DIVISION BY SECTIONS

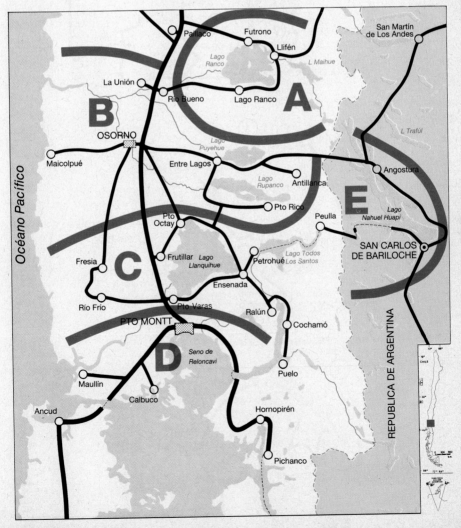

DETOURS OFF THE PAN-AMERICAN HIGHWAY

As in the previous Zone (Temuco to Valdivia), it is well worth leaving the beaten track to take a closer look at the beauty of the land. We suggest the following routes:

1 A Peek at Lake Ranco ★★ a route skirting the western shore of the lake from Futrono to the village of Lago Ranco. The total drive is 168 km: 117 km of gravel road; the rest is paved. It is 140 km longer than by taking the Pan-American highway from Paillaco directly to Río Bueno.

2 Old Route to La Unión ★★ this route, used during the colonial period, crosses the Coastal Range and passes through the town of La Unión. The total distance is 57 km, of which 23 km is paved. It is 10 km shorter to La Unión than by taking the Pan-Am.

3 Along the Old Route to Chiloé ★★★ a journey from Osorno, through Huilma, Riachuelo, Colegual, Fresia, and Río Frío to reach Puerto Varas, skirting the foothills of the Coastal range. The total distance is 142 km, with 30 km paved and the rest graveled, and 66 km longer than along the Pan-Am from Osorno to Puerto Varas.

4 Glacial Moraine Circuit ★★★ a circuit skirting three lakes, passing through their principal towns: Entre Lagos; Puerto Octay; Frutillar; and Llanqui-

hue. The total distance is 152 km, with 47 km paved. This route is 72 km longer than by driving directly from Osorno to Llanquihue on the Pan-Am.

5 Inter-Lake Route ★★★ a trip to see lake Puyehue, the southern part of lake Rupanco and the eastern and southern portions of lake Llanquihue. Total circuit: 171 km with 97 km paved. It is 100 km longer than by taking the Pan-Am from Osorno to Puerto Varas, and one of the most scenic routes in the area.

6 A Drive Half-Way Around Lake Llanquihue ★★ take the road branching east at Corte Alto, skirt the shores of lake Llanquihue and join the Pan-Am again at Puerto Varas. Total distance:130 km, with 50 km paved.

7 El Seno de Reloncaví ★★★ this circuit shows you the world of islands and straits of the Reloncaví Sound. The entire 90-km stretch is graveled.

8 To the Southern Highway ★★★ Puerto Montt is the starting (or ending) point of the newly opened Southern Highway, which crosses one thousand kilometers of virtually untouched territory, re-nowned for its beauty. The entire highway is described in Zone 13.

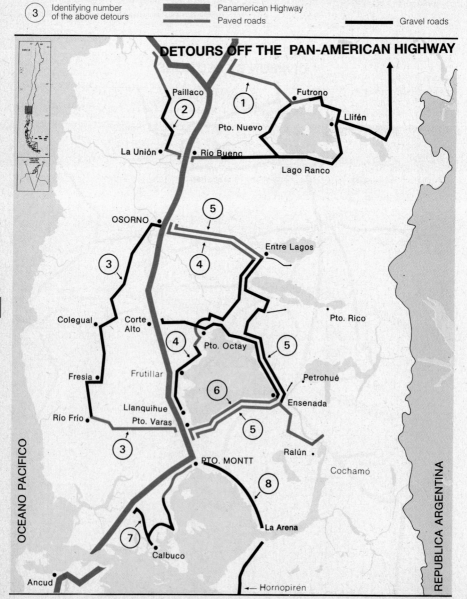

11

THE LAND, ITS HISTORY, ITS PEOPLE

MORPHOLOGY OF THE LAND

Lake Formation as described in Zone 10, Temuco to Valdivia, the presence of lakes in this area is due to glaciers carving the Cordillera of the Andes and plugging the water outlets with **moraines.** **Osorno volcano** rose after the glaciers were gone (its slopes have not been eroded by glaciers) deflecting the Petrohué river, toward Ralún; the Petrohué used to flow into lake Llanquihue. The lava from the Osorno volcano dammed the area now containing lake Todos Los Santos.

At **Salto del Petrohué** the river cascades over large masses of very hard lava which have eroded very little over the centuries. The lava is black and is made up of a large number of smaller rocks welded together by a glassy substance. This crystallized lava cracked upon cooling and later was re-welded by a new lava layer.

The **Reloncaví sound** was originally a glacial lake, but either erosion or ground sinkage made it part of the ocean.

The active volcanoes in this Zone Carrán, Riñinahue, Puyehue, Osorno and Calbuco, as well as extinct ones, such as Casablanca, or Antillana, and Puntiagudo, are part of the Andes range, which constitutes an important segment of the Pacific Ocean's **"Ring of Fire."** Puntiagudo- whose name means "sharp-pointed"- is very old. Rain-induced erosion has eliminated all but its crystallized lava chimney. It is extraordinarily beautiful.

The most active in the last decades have been Riñinahue and Carrán volcanoes. The former emerged in 1922 on Puyehue's northern slope in an eruption that sent ash as far as Buenos Aires. A major earthquake in 1960 reactivated it. The Carrán volcano, a small outcrop of mud and ash, emerged at the Nilahue river valley in 1955, erupted again in 1979 and is still in the process of being formed. It has substantially changed the surrounding landscape. Chile's volcanoes are doubly dangerous due to their snow caps. When one erupts, the lava melts the ice and snow and provokes flash floods carrying mud, lava, ash and logs down the slopes and destroying whatever happens to be on their way. Lava, in turn, tends to flow more slowly and less abundantly, but burns everything it touches.

Low-activity volcanoes are Puyehue, which has not erupted since 1921, and Osorno, dormant since 1850. The Calbuco volcano has not erupted since 1960; in 1893, a mighty explosion shattered its cone. A strong eruption can trigger a chain reaction along string of volcanoes. Old chronicles tell of a period of intense volcanic activity between 1735 and 1780, when Llaima, Villarrica, Puyehue and Osorno volcanoes erupted. Osorno had intense activity in 1790, and then again in 1834 and 1835. Its lower slopes are now covered with forests, but the drawings made by naturalist R A Philippi in 1852 show a wide strip of lava flowing down toward Ensenada. Another of his drawings, with a view from Petrohué, depicts the volcano and its slopes totally covered with slag and ash. Today, Petrohué is again covered by young forests fed by the abundant rain.

The Great River is the popular name of the Bueno river, the only one in this area flowing directly from the Andes into the Pacific Ocean. It carries the outflow from four large lakes: Maihue, Ranco, Puyehue and Rupanco. Its basin is enormous and the heavy and frequent rains in the area make the Bueno river the Aysen Region's second largest, surpassed by the Baker river.

HISTORY

The Native People between Illapel to the North and Chiloé to the South were the **Mapuches**, linguistically and ethnically a single nation with only minor differences in tribal dialects and customs. By 1600, an estimated half a million between the Biobío river and the Reloncaví sound, with the greatest concentration in the Temuco area and on the plains of La Unión and Osorno. The tribes inhabiting these plains were called **Huilliches.**

Original Landscape the relatively high number of Mapuches in the old days and their agricultural technique of cultivating the land intensively until soil degradation set in, coupled with ranging livestock, account for the landscape described by the early chroniclers of «open lands with softly rolling hills crowned by Mapuche rucas -dwellings- broken by occasional groves.

When the population decreased, the forests advanced, causing a radical change in the scenery. Depopulation was caused by wars and small-pox epidemics, in addition to the extremely violent volcanic activity of the 17th and 18th centuries, which forced Mapuches to desert the Andean valleys and the areas near the lakes. The shores of Lake Llanquihue eventually were invaded by rain forest and the lake was forgotten. When the plains of La Unión and the foothills near Osorno were re-occupied in the 19th century, they were still in this sort of primeval state.

Spanish Conquest during the first half-century of the Spanish conquest, the conquerors placed strong emphasis on exploring and settling the entire territory granted them by the King of Spain. Pedro de Valdivia, after nine years spent consolidating his dominion over the country's central zone, surveyed the land stretching south to the Reloncaví sound. Eight cities were founded south of the Biobío, including **Osorno** in this Zone and **Castro** in Chiloé. Osorno was a major farming town with a church, a nun's convent, and mills, and was renowned for the quality of its textiles. But in 1598 a major Mapuche uprising forced the Spaniards to relinquish the cities, industries and farms south of the Biobío. The only city surviving was Castro, tucked away on the island of Chiloé. The inhabitants of Osorno were evacuated through the southern colonial road, founding Carelmapu and Calbuco in 1602.

Reconquest in 1645 **Valdivia** was founded anew, but this time as a stronghold guarding the southern Pacific coast and not really concerned with the heartland. It was directly subordinate to the Peru Viceroyship. In 1740, the city of Valdivia came under the jurisdiction of the government of Chile and a policy of strong territorial expansion was imitated. Private individuals were authorized to hold farmland; religious missions were established; Los Llanos (present-day La Unión) was rediscovered; the road to Chiloé was reopened; and in 1796, **Osorno** was founded. By the end of the century, large tracts of land in the Valdivia and Osorno area were privately owned.

The Bulnes Decade (1840-1850) several actions were undertaken to incorporate the Bulnes territory: in 1843, Ignacio Domeyko proposed the cultural and religious assimilation of the Mapuches; between 1842 and 1845, **Bernardo Philippi**, gatherer of Chilean flora and fauna for the Museum of Berlin, was commissioned by the Chilean government to survey the inland lakes in the Osorno and Llanquihue areas; in 1845, legislation was passed which turned all vacant lands into state property; in 1848, Philippi was appointed Settlement Agent in Germany to entice immigrants to settle southern Chile; and in 1850 **Vicente Pérez Rosales** was appointed Settlement Agent in Valdivia to allot lands to the immigrants sent by Philippi from Germany.

Incorporation of Llanquihue the great agents behind the settlement of the South, B E Philippi and Vicente Pérez Rosales, explored the entire

11

523

region in search of vacant -and therefore State-owned lands suitable for homesteads; ideally, these lands had to lie near the coast to facilitate communication. Land in the Llanquihue area between the Reloncaví sound to the South and the Rahue river to the North, and between the Andes to the East and the old road to Osorno to the west fully met these requirements. While exploring this land they discovered Lake Llanquihue, surrounded by thick rainforest and located near the ocean. Several other expeditions surveyed the Reloncaví Sound in search of a suitable port, and finally chose a harbor protected by the Tenglo island.

With this information, Pérez Rosales devised a plan for occupation of the territory along a north-south axis, with a terminal port on the Reloncaví sound, a road connecting it to the lake, ports on the northern and southern ends of the lake and a road to Osorno, thus joining this entire new territory to the axis running lengthwise through the country. Within a year from the arrival of the first settlers, **Puerto Montt, Puerto Varas** and **Puerto Octay** had been founded and the trails had been opened to link Lake Llanquihue with Osorno.

German Settlement in late November 1852, the first 212 German settlers arrived at present-day Puerto Montt. They promptly occupied the lake shores until 1880, when the State ceased to grant tracts for homesteading. Each German settler obtained a piece of land and a number of goods from the State, payable over a very long period under extremely favorable terms: 75 «blocks» of land (one block was ca. 125 m to a side, ie, somewhat more than a hectare) plus 12 «blocks» per child, free lodging at the port until the land could be received, a pair of oxen, one cow with a calf, 500 boards, 100 pounds of nails and a monthly allowance for one year, free medical assistance and medicine, certificate of ownership

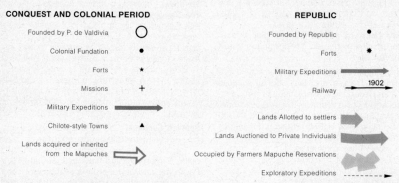

CONQUEST AND COLONIAL PERIOD

Founded by P. de Valdivia	○
Colonial Fundation	●
Forts	★
Missions	+
Military Expeditions	➡
Chilote-style Towns	▲
Lands acquired or inherited from the Mapuches	⇨

REPUBLIC

Founded by Republic	●
Forts	✳
Military Expeditions	➡
Railway	1902
Lands Allotted to settlers	➡
Lands Auctioned to Private Individuals	➡
Occupied by Farmers Mapuche Reservations	
Exploratory Expeditions	----➤

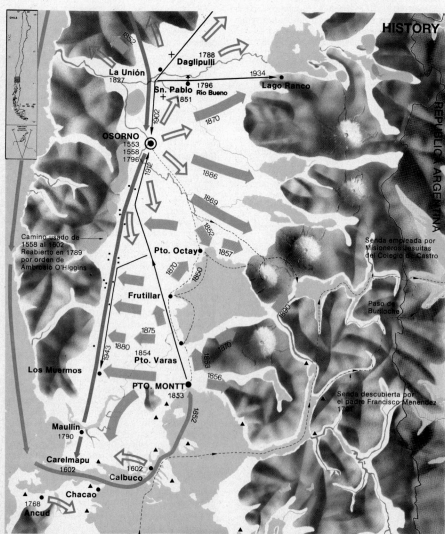

11

524

under the condition that a house be built and two «blocks» fenced off, and Chilean citizenship to those who requested it.

Clearing the temperate rainforest and transforming the land into the rich countryside of today was an undertaking of almost epic proportions. The jungle was so thick, that two young settlers lost their way while opening the trail to Puerto Varas and were never seen again. Within ten years, a vast area had been cleared of forests, industries had been set up and regular shipping services across the lake, as well as oxcart services between Puerto Varas and Puerto Montt, had been established.

Allocation of Land the areas around Osorno, La Unión, Calbuco, Carelmapu and Maullín (all towns or villages of Spanish origin) were obtained by those living in the respective towns through direct purchase from Mapuches or by inheritance from them after a long period of racial intermingling. The lands kept by the Mapuches under the status of «reservations» were located in the area of the old colonial route and on the slopes of the Coastal Range, plus an area at the far end of Lake Ranco.

The remaining lands in Llanquihue and around Lakes Rupanco and Puyehue were considered State property. The district of Llanquihue was cleared for settlement and by 1880 a belt of orchards surrounded the lake and a 7-km stretch had been cleared toward **Nueva Braunau.** The influx of immigrants ceased in 1880, and the State auctioned the lands still vacant in larger tracts, of up to 800 hectares. These tracts were acquired mostly by German immigrants and by residents of Osorno, La Unión and Valdivia. By the turn of the century, all the land in this Zone had been allotted or sold.

National Integration the true integration of this zone into the rest of the country occured when the state-owned, Santiago-based Osorno, in 1902. Construction of a railway line from Puerto Montt to the North started in 1906 and reached Osorno and the main trunk line in 1912. This opened new markets for regional products and brought considerable prosperity both to the cities and to the countryside. The large houses now to be seen in the region's cities and countryside date from that period.

Tourism also arrived: the first summer retreat in the area was set up by a well-known Santiago resident at the Centinela peninsula of Puerto Octay. The great promoter of tourism in this Zone was the State-owned railway, which built the Gran Hotel Puerto Varas in 1935 and ran tourist shipping services from Puerto Montt to the islands.

Present Development this is Chile's fourth largest industrial center, fueled mainly by agroindustries, the main employer for the half million inhabitants of this Zone (4.4% of Chile's total). Grains, potatoes, sugar beets, fodder, and livestock and dairy products (65% of the national total) are among the main products. Osorno runs Chile's leading livestock market.

During the 1980s a veritable revolution took place in the agroindustrial sector, with the appearance of high-yield berries, especially raspberries and asparagus, as well as other new crops and industries. Most remarkable is the explosive development of the fishing industry, with new canneries, oyster farms, seaweed cultivation and salmon farms.

PAN–AMERICAN HIGHWAY

The main sights between Paillico and the tip of the Pan-American highway on the mainland at Pargua, on the Chacao strait, are described below.

PAN - AMERICAN HIGHWAY FROM PAILLACO TO PUERTO MONTT AND THE CHACAO STRAIT ★★★

it is 155 km to Puerto Montt and 211 to Chacao. Gasoline available at the La Unión road junction, 3 km before Osorno and on the southern access to Puerto Varas.
A beautiful stretch of the Pan-Am, running through rolling countryside and, for 25 km, along the shore of Lake Llanquihue.

From the Paillaco junction (km 0), the Pan-Am runs near the Coastal Range to reach, at km 26, the road leading from La Unión to Río Bueno, two attractive cities described under Section A. At the junction is an hostería and a gasoline station. A short distance ahead, the road crosses the

BUENO RIVER   placid, but nevertheless carrying a lot of water. It is navigable up to the city of Río Bueno and drains lakes Ranco and Maihue.

At km 37, the Pan-Am bypasses San Pablo and then reaches, at km 56, the access to

OSORNO   (city description under Section B). Besides being a very pleasant city, it is an ideal jumping-off point for a number of excursions within the Zone. At the crossroads leading to the city, a road branches east to Argentina through lake Puyehue and another road leads to Puerto Octay on lake Llanquihue. There is a municipal campground right next to the junction.

The next leg, 67 km to **Frutillar Alto**, is a straight line broken only once by the depression of the Negro river. This is rather unusual, for Chile's geography does not easily allow the construction of straight roads.

At km 81 is the junction for **Río Negro.** At km 94 a road branches off to **Purranque** and at km 123 the Pan-Am bypasses **Frutillar Alto**, which has a train station and a road leading down to **Frutillar** on the lakeside.

At km 139 is a long descent offering a breathtaking view of

LAKE LLANQUIHUE   its great sheet of water reflecting the perfect cone of Osorno volcano. On the near shore is the town of **Llanquihue.** The highway descends to cross the Maullín river, which drains the lake. This is the only occasion the Pan-Am skirts a lake.

The road leaves the lake and runs through damp, open land with a regrowth from a native forest that burned long ago. This is the area where two young settlers, while opening a trail north of Puerto Montt, lost their way in the thick jungle and were never seen again.

At km 149 is the central access to **Puerto Varas** and, at km 153, the city's south access, with a gasoline station. The road then heads straight south to reach, at km 166,

PUERTO MONTT   from afar you can see the city and the great Reloncaví sound spreading beyond. City description in Section D. The road descends straight into the city.

The Pan-American highway veers right before the descent to head for the Chacao strait. At km 192 a road branches left to **Calbuco** (Tour 7) and at km 211 another one branches right to **Maullín** (Tour 6). The mainland portion of the Pan-American Highway South ends at Pargua (km 222) on the

CHACAO STRAIT   Pargua has a few houses and a landing for the ferry plying the route to the island of Chiloé, whose cliffs can be seen across the water. The ferry docks across the strait at Chacao.

11

village of Lago Ranco

Ferries two companies cover the route between the mainland and Chiloé. First departure from Chacao Mon–Sat 06:00 h, last departure from Pargua at 22:15 h. Sundays and holidays first departure from Chacao 07:10 h. Passage takes 30 min.

Food & Lodging along the Pan-Am given the proximity of cities such as Osorno, Frutillar, Puerto Varas and Puerto Montt, there are few services offered directly on the Pan-American highway. For lunch, Hostería Cuca at the La Unión junction, Hostería Tramahuel at the San Pablo junction, and Socaví, at the Río Negro junction; Lodging only at Hostería Cuca, with cabins.

SECTION A   LAKE RANCO

This Section comprises the upper basin of the Bueno river, where lakes Ranco and Maihue are located. East of these lakes are the vast valleys of Nilahue and Rupameica, with Mapuche reservations, and the great Blanco river valley, which runs North-South behind the volcanoes. It is an especially beautiful area.

LAKE RANCO is speckled with islands and has a road that runs along its entire shore. It has very good tourist infrastructure and excellent fishing, and a few areas with summer houses.

How To Get There the lake is accessible from the **North** from Reumén to Futrono (43 km from Reumén, paved); from the **West** from the La Unión junction at the Pan-Am to Puerto Nuevo (40 km, gravel); from the **South** from Río Bueno to Lago Ranco (50 km, of which 28 km are paved), in this leg we recommed a short sidestrip (signposted) to the river to see the Cachillahue petroglyph, thought to be of Cunco Indian origin, whose meaning remains a mystery; and from the **Northeast** from lake Pirehueico via the road from lake Maihue and Llifén (65 km, gravel). This latter road has been reported closed to the public, however. Check beforehand.

LAKE MAIHUE is long, its southern shore lined with steep forest-hills hills rising directly from the water. The northern shore has steep portions and some flat areas rolling smoothly to the water's edge. A road runs along its northern shore. Inland from it is the Rupameica valley, with a large Mapuche reservation renowned for having preserved many early indigenous customs.

TOURS OF THE AREA

1 **A CIRCUIT AROUND LAKE RANCO ★★★**
a 120-km gravel road, with two ferry crossings (08:00-19:00 h) at Calcurrupe and Puerto Lapi. Restaurants and accommodations along the way.
This is one of the three lakes -together with Llanquihue and Calafquén which has a road running along its entire shore. A beautiful tour.

We shall describe the route clockwise starting from Futrono.

Futrono is a busy service town nestled on the lake's northern shore and enjoying a sweeping view of the lake and its many islands. The largest is Isla Guapi, a Mapuche reservation. Futrono offers all urban services, and has a harbor, a boat ramp and a modern hostería near the water's edge.

FUTRONO TO LLIFÉN (22 km) the road descends a short gradient and skirts a large bay embracing

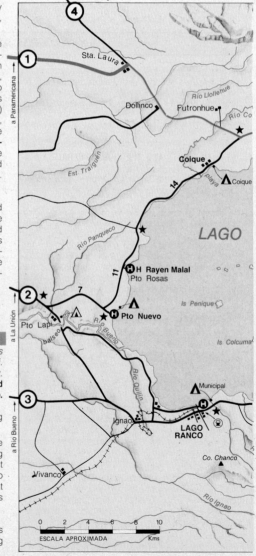

11

Isla Illeifa, a privately-owned, beautifully landscaped island. Then it crosses the swift Quiman
river. The road loses sight of the lakeshore while
crossing a headland, to rejoin it thereafter while
running along Golfo Azul to the **Cunahue river.** A
road branches left here heading into the river
valley, beautifully hemmed in by rock cliffs and
surrounded by rain forest. It is a very good spot
for a picnic. The road to Llifén continues beneath
steep hills and along the shore to

LLIFEN a lovely village nestled in a plain next to
the mouth of the Calcurrupe river. It evolved from
a small hotel catering to fishermen. Around 1950,
three English fishermen built their houses here
and gave a special flavor to the place. Now it is
the lake's indisputable tourist center. It has several excellent hosterías, and its best beach is
Bonita, with fine sand shaded by century-old
boldos. To reach the beach, hire a boat at Puerto
Llifén and row to the other side of the mouth of
the river. Another unforgettable excursion is a
fishing boat trip down the **Calcurrupe** river, which
can be arranged with boatmen at Puerto Llifén or
in the various hosterías. Llifén is also a good
jumping-off point for excursions into the Maihue
valley and the namesake lake stretching southeast.

Where To Eat **Hostería Huequecura** has good food
and a beautiful view of a private beach and the
lake. **Villa La Cascada** and **Hostería Chollinco** offer a
view of river scenery; the latter has a swimming
pool surrounded by large, naturally occuring
rocks.

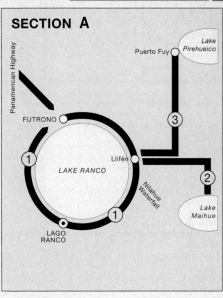

SECTION A

Area accommodations include the above
hosterías and four campsites nearby.

FROM LLIFÉN TO LAGO RANCO (47 km) a ferry
brings you across the Calcurrupe river (08:00–

LAKES RANCO AND MAIHUE

11

12:00 h & 14:00–17:00 h). Outside the normal hours, the boatman -who lives next to the landing will carry you across you for a small tip. The road then runs over a short plain to climb a rough gradient; at the bottom, on the other side, near the bridge is the

Nilahue Waterfall noisily plunging in two steps; you can walk down to the bottom. There is a modest campsite in the vicinity. Next to the southern end of the bridge a private road branches east to logging tracts and to recently formed **Carrán volcano.**

The road (badly surfaced) continues to Riñinahue. The scenery is volcanic, with toppled trees and ash spewed by the Carrán volcano when it first appeared in 1954 and then during its second eruption, in 1979. The bottom of the Riñinahue river valley, however, is covered by temperate rainforest.

Next to the bridge a road branches right to the old **Hostería Riñinahue,** which has a beach, a pier, and boats for renting. Fishing and general excursions are organized to visit Laguna Pichi El Encanto and the active Mirador volcano.

The road (still badly surfaced) continues along the lake's most striking stretch of shore, on a ledge carved out of the steep rocky cliffs; of forest-crowned hills. It passes **Pitreño** and then **Ilihue**. Lots of summer houses are under construction here. A short distance ahead is the village of

Lago Ranco a railhead town and an old logging port. It has some small hotels, residenciales and houses for rent during the summer. The beach is good, with a boat ramp and a secluded harbor. There are two campsites nearby and you can visit the Arturo Möller Sandrock Museum with permanent exhibits of Mapuche culture.

FROM LAGO RANCO TO PUERTO NUEVO (23 km) three km out of Lago Ranco, take the road running along the shore to the ferry which crosses the Bueno river. The road runs on the glacial moraine, among rolling hills with stands of native trees and crop land, and it passes through a fabulous forest of large oaks devoid of undergrowth. The ferry is at Puerto Lapi. Take the next road branching right, heading for Puerto Nuevo, the oldest fishing center on the lake, with the

modern and excellent Hostería Puerto Nuevo and a campground. There are rowboats, windsurf boards and laser boats for hire. Fishing boat excursions down the Bueno river are organized.

FROM PUERTO NUEVO TO FUTRONO (28 km) the road runs along the lakeshore, past the picturesque **Hostería Rayén Malal** (a converted old manor house) and past **Coique,** a long, open beach, that is very popular in summer. Nearby is a campsite.

2 ⬛ **FROM LLIFEN TO LAKE MAIHUE** ★★★
a round trip of 64 km from Llifén.
A visit to a beautiful lake, and a possible visit to a Mapuche reservation.

Follow the road heading into the Calcurrupe river valley. At km 3 is **Hostería Chollinco,** and at km 11 a fork: the right branch goes to **Puerto Llolles,** with a beautiful beach next to the point where the lake drains into the Calcurrupe. It is a good spot for picknicking and camping (there are camping facilities). Here is also the exclusive **Cumillahue Lodge,** catering to foreign fishermen.

The main road heading to the Blanco river, soon follows the Cumilahue river valley, which becomes progressively constricted by the surrounding mountains until km 19, where the manor house of estancia **Arquilhue** is located. It is private property, and the road is usually barred.

The road continues to Baños de Chichui Thermal Baths, with four cabins, a short distance from the Curringa river. Ask for permission to continue to the Blanco river, at km 25.

Across the bridge, the road heads south towards the lake, running along the Blanco river to its mouth, with a lonely, beautiful **beach** overlooking the valley, the **Rupameica** Mapuche reservation and the Puyehue volcano.

3 ⬛ **TO LAKE PIREHUEICO** ★★★
perhaps the most spectacular scenery in this Section, with a good road running behind the Mocho and Choshuenco volcanoes along the Pillanleufú river valley. Unfortunately, the new private owners do not permit public passage. Check with the tourist office to find out if this road has been opened.

SECTION B   OSORNO

This Section covers the large district around the city of Osorno. It stretches between the cities of La Unión and Río Bueno to the North, and Río Negro and Purranque to the South, and from the Pacific coast to the Andes. It is a rich agricultural district.

Curiously, these cities and lakes and this stretch of coast tend to be overlooked by travellers visiting this zone, lured by the areas farther south or farther north. But they are well worth visiting and have a complete tourist infrastructure.

LA UNION (pop 17,000), near the Bueno river, lies on the banks of the Llollelhue, which meanders through the town. It was founded during the early days of the Republic as an urban support center for the local farmers.

The settlement became highly industrialized under the influence of German immigrants who arrived around the mid 19th century. It had famous breweries, tanneries, linen mills and flour mills. Some of these industries are still active. The architectural imprint left by the German settlers can still be appreciated.

What To See the square, with a **parish church** built in 1904. Across the river is the **Molino Augusto Grob** flour mill (see map), with industrial buildings

← a Trumao y Hueicolla

③

Telephone Center
Café, Meeting Point
Gasoline Station
Lookout Point
M1 Railway Station
M2 Bus Terminal

OF INTEREST
A Parish Church
B Industrial Quarter
C Grob Turbine

ACCOMMODATIONS
1 H. Consistorial

TIPS
D1 Linos La Union

LA UNION

11

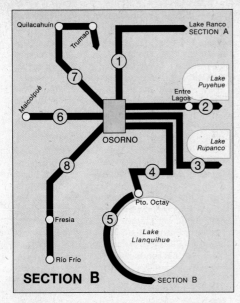

Quilacahuín

Trumao

Lake Ranco
SECTION A

①

⑦

Lake
Puyehue

Entre
Lagos

②

Maicolpué

⑥

OSORNO

Lake
Rupanco

⑧

④

③

Fresia

⑤

Pto. Octay

Lake
Llanquihue

Río Frío

SECTION B

SECTION B

Río Bueno is a thriving town of 15,000, evolved from a fort built by the Spaniards on the bank of the river.

What To See across the river perched on a cliff is the fortress of **San José de Alcudia (NM)** (1777), well preserved and commanding a view over the river and the valley. On the attractive square is the **Furniel mansion**, featuring a turn-of-the-century German architecture. It has a tragic past which earned it the nickname of Palace of Tears.

There is a beach on the river; restaurant Mesón Quimey, in addition to food, offers fishing excursions down the river from Puerto Lápiz (45 km). There is a campsite next to a beach at Curaco (parcela 38), four km down the road to lake Ranco. Accomodations at Residencial Richmond and Hospedaje Roma.

OSORNO (pop 95,215), founded twice at the same site (1558 and 1796), in a wind-sheltered depression near a bend in the Rahue river. The city is midway between the plains and the lakes to the East, and farmland next to the Coastal Range. This makes it an excellent jumping-off point for touring this Zone. It offers excellent accommodations and restaurants, and is a lively, thriving city bearing the imprint of its German immigrants. Shopping hours are Mon–Fri 09:00–13:00 h & 15:00–19:00 h; Sat 09:00–13:00 h).

What To See across the river, at the end of Av República, is the **Mirador de Rahue**, a look-out point offering you a panoramic view of the city and the surrounding countryside, with a string of volcanoes in the East.

The township of Rahue remained independent from Osorno until 1928, and was a service town for the Mapuche communities near the Coastal Range. It still conserves some of this character. Its **roofed Mercado** (Mon–Sat 08:00–13:00 h; best days Thu & Sat) offers produce from small farms. At 14:00 h, the same building is occupied by rural buses which one or two hours later set out for the coast.

The **Fort Reina María Luisa** (see map) was built in 1793 by order of Ambrosio O'Higgins, and served as his residence during the repopulation of Osorno (1796). Not much remains, but what does has been restored.

The **residential quarter** (streets O'Higgins, Matta and Cochrane) has fine old residences, mostly made of wood. In this quarter is the **Museo Municipal** (see map) (Mon–Fri 10:00–13:00 h & 16:00–18:00 h and also open on sundays during sum-

brought from Germany. On its side is the **Linen Textile Mill.**

TO OSORNO VIA TRUMAO ★★★

forty-two km of gravel road and a ferry crossing (a small fee is paid; any time).
A stretch of the old Colonial Route, visiting an interesting church along the way.

Take the exit labelled 3 in map of La Unión. At km 11 begins the descent to the ferry crossing. Continue 1 km and on the left is the Franciscan church of the **Trumao Mission**, dating from the mid 19th century. Built of wood, it has a commanding view of the entire river valley.

Continue to the ferry, which takes you across the Bueno river; there are earthen loading ramps suitable for all kinds of trailers. Cargo **steamers** plying the route to the mouth of the river (known as La Barra) are to be seen (see Excursions). On the south bank is the railway station. Eleven km ahead on the road to Osorno is the Quilacahuín junction.

A couple of km down this secondary road is a curious **round building** (that was constructed long ago) used for drying and thrashing wheat, and storing machinery. Such old buildings are known as **campanarios.**

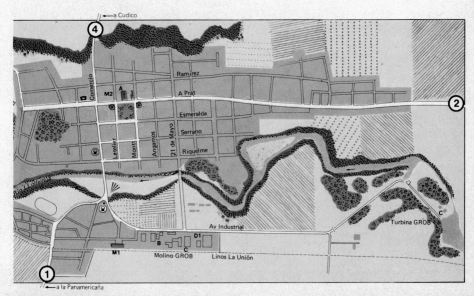

a Cudico

④

Ramírez

Comercio

M2

A Prat

Esmeralda

Serrano

Riquelme

Letelier

Montt

Angamos

21 de Mayo

Río Lollehue

②

Turbina GROB

Av Industrial

D1

B

C

Molino GROB

Linos La Unión

M1

①

a la Panamericana

Osorno, square and Cathedral

auctions. Opposite the market is the most modern **butcher shop** in the South, (open to the public).

Where To Eat best German cuisine at **Peter's Kneipe** and in the traditional **Club Alemán**. For quick lunches for the whole family, stop in at **Café Dino's** or **Casa del Altillo**. A gastronomic festival is held in Osorno every year, with the participation of some 20 establishments from around the province. Specialties include smoked salmon, duck, wild boar and deer. And, of course, there are German pastries. Check at the Tourist Office to find out which establishments received awards this season.

Public Transportation Osorno has four bus terminals: **Interprovincial** (J in general map), with buses North to Concepción and Santiago, and South to Puerto Montt (and destinations in between), and to lake Ranco and Maicolpué; **Mercado** (P in general map), with service to lakes Puyehue and Rupanco; **Estación Vieja** (L in map) to lakes Llanquihue and Rupanco; **Mercado Rahue** (G in general map) with service to the coast.

mer, 15:30–18:00 h), containing a good collection of archaeological artifacts and providing an insight into the Region's history.

Along **Mackenna street** are more fine old wooden mansions from the early days. The **Osorno-Livestock Market** (Feria Ganadera de Osorno) Chile's largest, is interesting to see. It operates in the morning and from the galleries you can watch the

TOURS FROM OSORNO

1 TO LAKE RANCO ★★★
eighty km to the village of Lago Ranco via Río Bueno, with 62 km paved. From the village you

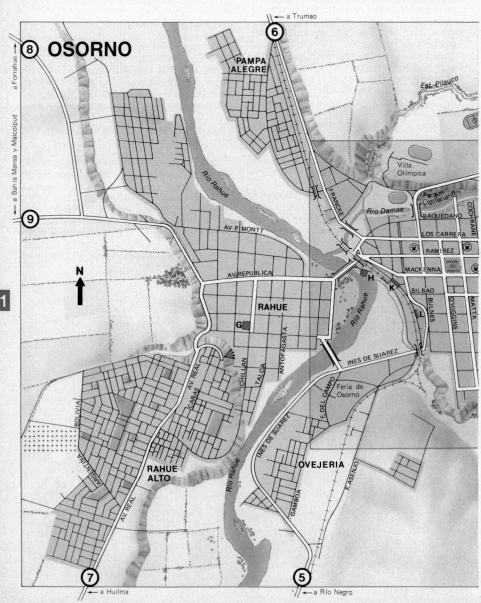

11

can make the tour described under Section A above.

2 | TO LAKE PUYEHUE ★★★

it is 93 km by paved road to the Los Pajaritos Customs Complex located on the Argentine border; 46 km to Entre Lagos; 75 km to Termas de Puyehue; and 97 km to the Antillanca hotel and ski resort in the Puyehue National Park. Allow at least one day. Gasoline at Ñilque.

The road to Argentina runs along the shore of lake Puyehue, a scant 10 km away from lake Rupanco. Curiously enough, these two lakes are not very well known in Chile. There are no large tourist complexes like those of Pucón, Lican Ray, Llifén or Frutillar, but both lakes do offer excellent accommodations. Here are some of the South's best equipped hotels and thermal baths (Ñilque and Termas de Puyehue), and the Puyehue National Park, one of the best organized and equipped in Chile, with a thermal bath at Aguas Calientes and the excellent Antillanca hotel and ski resort on the slopes of the extinct Antillanca volcano surrounded by magnificent scenery.

One-and-a-half km out of Osorno is the **University.** At km 3.6 is the **Golf Club,** set in a natural park. Some enormous, luxurious residences can be seen on the countryside to the right. The farm-

land is intensely cultivated, with occasional patches of thick native forest. Ahead, a string of five volcanoes grace the Andes.

At km 34, a road branches left to the Pilmaiquén Hydroelectric Power Station (3 km), which diverted and swallowed the water feeding the scenic **Pilmaiquén waterfall,** condemning it to oblivion.

At km 46 is the lake and

Entre Lagos an old lake port receiving timber and other products from the Puyehue and Rupanco area. A branch rail line used to reach it. Today, it is fast becoming a tourist center.

Near the road junction is the restaurant Pub de Campo, with good grilled meat and steaks, and fairly stiff prices. More modest is the Jardín del Turista. A gravel road branches south, described in the next Tour.

The highway continues to Argentina running along Lake Puyehue's shores, passing beautiful beaches and crossing hills and headlands. At km 50, a road branches right to **Puerto Chalupa** (8 km), a picturesque cluster of houses and a port on the northern shore of lake Rupanco, with a good beach and good fishing. Branching off of this road is a signposted road to

COTO RUPANQUITO the renowned deer hunting

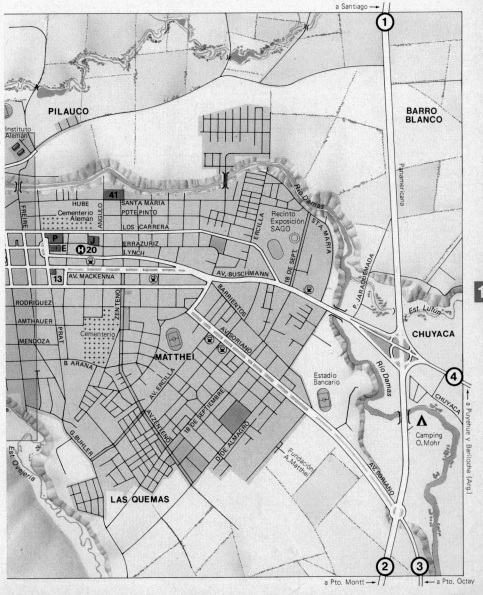

11

☎ Telephone Center
★ Touristic Information
⊙ Café, Meeting Point
⛽ Gasoline Station
⇗ Lookout Point
✳✚ Hospital
A Town Hall (3C)
B Provincial Government (3C)
C Post Office (3B)
D Cathedral Church (2C)
✳**E** San Francisco Church
F Municipal Museum (3C)
✳**G** Rahue Market
H Fort María Luisa (3C)
✳**J** Bus Terminal
K Railway Station (3B)

L Old Railway Station (3B)
M Osorno Livestock Market (4A)
N Centenario Park (1B)
✳ **P** Market

ACCOMMODATIONS
1 H García Hurtado de Mendoza (3C)
2 H Del Prado (4C)
3 H Waeger (3C)
4 H Interlagos (2C)
5 Gran Hotel Osorno (2B)
✳20 H Rayantu
6 Bh Riga (4C)
✳ 7 H Villa Eduviges
8 H Tirol (3B)
9 Bh Schulz

10 Bh Hein (3C)
✳▲ Mohr Campsite

RESTAURANTS
11 Dicker's (2C)
12 Don Quijote (3B)
✳ 13 Sancho Panza
14 Club Alemán (2B)
15 Peter's Kneipe (3C)
16 Dino's (3B)
17 Club Osorno (3C)

TOURITS SERVICES
20 Lan Chile (3C)
21 Ladeco (3C)
22 Turismo Globus (3C)
23 Turismo Ñiltur (2C)
24 Turismo Pilmaiquén (3C)

25 Turismo Hueney (3C)
26 Turismo Lagos Austral (2C)
27 Turismo Oasis (2C)
28 Automivil Club Rent a Car (3C)
29 Salfa Sur Rent a Car (3C)
30 Hertz Rent a Car (3C)
23 Ñilcar Rent a Car (3C)

TIPS
40 Fishing Gear (2C)
✳ 41 Begonias and Conifers
42 Handicrafts (3C)
43 Confitería Flor (2C)
44 Confitería Real (2C)
45 Butcher (4A)

✳ See General Map of Osorno

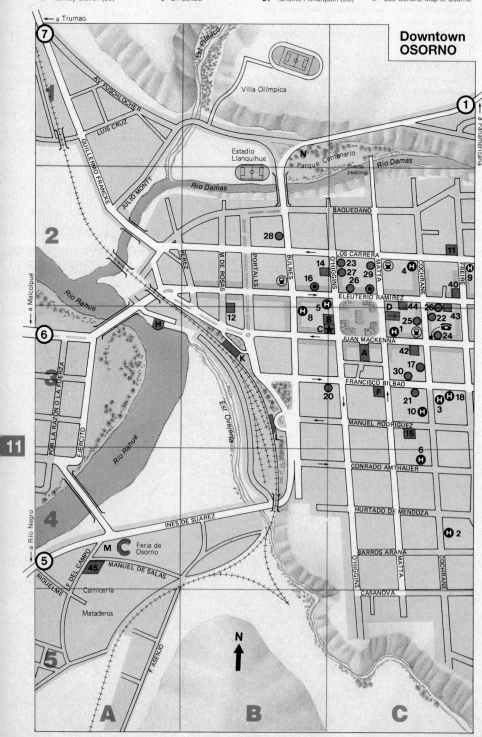

Downtown OSORNO

11

grounds frequented by foreign big game lovers. Here, hunting is aimed only at the ecologic control of adult animals. Those not keen on shooting the graceful animals with a gun can do it with a camera: photo safaris are on offer. Small groups (no children) are accepted. Contact fax 064/232741, Osorno.

The highway to Argentina continues along the lakeshore. At km 53 is **Hostería Chalet Suizo**, located in a nice setting. Between km 56 and 59 are the best-equipped campgrounds in the area. At km 63, a road branches right to **El Encanto**, a beautiful bay and beach on the northern shore of lake Rupanco. By following this gravel road you reach at km 6 the village of El Encanto, with a gorgeous **view** of lake Rupanco and the sharp-pointed Puntiagudo volcano in the background. Continue to the lakeshore and turn right to reach the El Encanto bay and beach. It is a lovely, lonely place suitable for camping and bathing.

Back on the highway cross the **Ñilque headland,** with nice summer houses. At km 67, on a small bay, is the excellent **Ñilque hotel,** with its own beach, boat harbor and offering a complete range of services.

At the end of the lake, facing the slopes of some steep hills, the road offers a superb view of the Puyehue volcano, the Golgol river valley and the islands.

At km 71 is a road that goes to the mouth of the Golgol river, with a good beach and a campsite in the midst of a lush rain forest.

At km 76, the road forks; one branch goes to Anticura and Argentina; the other to Antillanca. Here are the hot springs of **Termas de Puyehue,** with a large, excellent hotel and thermal baths and a hotspring-fed indoor pool.

The road to Argentina runs along the Golgol river valley, crossing the river twice (excellent fishing) and passing through some beautiful native forests.

At km 93 is Anticura, featuring cabins, a campsite and a parking area - all of which belong to the Puyehue National Park. A signposted path across a stretch of lush temperate rainforest takes you in 20 minutes to the

Salto del Indio where the Golgol river plunges into a pool overgrown by with vegetation.

At km 97 is the **Los Pajaritos Customs Complex**. The gravel road to the border (at km 120) is smooth and in good condition, and runs through extraordinarily beautiful mountains and woodlands, with a couple of small lakes nearby and not a soul in sight. The road leads to Bariloche, in the Argentine lake district.

PEYEHUE NATIONAL PARK stretches from the Golgol river to the eastern shore of lake Rupanco. The park contains 107 thousand hectares of exuberant vegetation, and includes part of Puyehue volcano. The park's visitor center, which has an exhibit presenting local flora and fauna, is at

Aguas Calientes next to the Chanleufú river. A thermal bath center, Aguas Calientes offers indoor and outdoor thermal pools, individual and family thermal cabins (open until 19:00 h only), a hostel (hostería), and a motel. The campground, run by Conaf, unfortunately charges a pretty stiff price for each site. Campgrounds on the lakeshore are cheaper and better. The entire area is full on weekends.

There are several routes into the forest, but for striking scenery, take the road climbing from Aguas Calientes to the Antillanca ski resort (18 km), which passes through gorgeous, old-growth native forests and by small jewel-like lakes, such as Espejo (with waterlilies), El Encanto and El

lake Rupanco and Puntiagudo volcano

Toro. During the summer, access is unrestricted. In winter (July-September), from 08:00 h to 10:00 h and again 12:00-16:00 h, only traffic uphill is permitted; the rest of the time only traffic headed downhill is allowed.

At the tree line is

Hotel Antillanca a winter sports center with 4 ski lifts and slopes for all tastes, located in the heart of Puyehue National Park. The hotel is excellent and has a cafeteria, a restaurant, sauna and indoor pool. Open year round, it offers attractive, organized excursions in summer, such as a climb to the crater of Antillanca via a 4-km road suitable for cars. The views are wonderful, with Osorno, Puyehue and Puntiagudo volcanoes thrusting their snow-capped cones up from the lakes and forests. This is a very good place to stay overnight on the way to or from Bariloche, Argentina.

3   TO LAKE RUPANCO ★★★

around trip of 224 km from Osorno, with exactly half of the distance paved. Allow one day. Restaurant at El Islote. Take sufficient gasoline.
An excursion to a beautiful lake nestled in the mountains.

Leave Osorno following the road to Argentina. At Entre Lagos (km 49), take the road branching right (South) to lake Rupanco (km 62); long and flanked by mountains. The road passes Marina del Rupanco, a new tourist resort, and Hostería El Paraíso, with its own beach and boat ramp. On the bridge spanning the river drains the lake, boats are offered for hire, both for fishing excursions and for sailing down the river.

The road continues straight to meet the south access to the lake at km 73; turn left (East) toward the mountains. At km 84 a road branches left for **Pellinada** (8 km), a lovely native forest reaching to the lakeshore. Good fishing.

At km 86, the road skirts the forest-enclosed **Laguna Bonita,** a small lake, and then descends to Lake Rupanco's at the Piedras Negras bay. To the left is El Islote peninsula which has a. At **Piedras Negras** (km 96) there is an hostería and other services (a daily bus comes from Osorno at 16:45 h, one hour earlier on Sat). This is where the most beautiful part of the lake begins, the mountains drop down to the lake shore and forests with large trees can be found.

At km 102 is Hostería **El Islote**, with a beach, a boat ramp, a boat harbor, and a campsite. Deer are raised on the island a short distance off this shore. The road continues another 16 km through gorgeous scenery to **Bahía Escocia**, a hotel run by a charming Scottish couple. They organize «fishing safaris», boating and walks. No visitors, only passengers allowed.

11

To return, it is best to continue straight to the west until you meet the paved Osorno-Puerto Octay highway.

4 GLACIAL MORAINE CIRCUIT ★★★

a total distance of 152 km from Osorno to Puerto Varas, 100 km on gravel roads.

An interesting excursion along the glacial moraines of lakes Puyehue, Rupanco and Llanquihue.

Follow the route (described in Tour 3 above) through Rupanco until meeting the road labelled 4 in the map of lakes Puyehue and Rupanco. Follow road 4, crossing the great hacienda Ñuble Rupanco and passing through its central installations at **Central Rupanco**, which are organized like those of the large estancias in Magallanes. At the paved Osorno-Puerto Octay highway turn left to **Puerto Octay** on lake Llanquihue. Follow the lakeshore to Puerto Varas via a beautiful road described under Section C.

5 THE INTER-LAKE CIRCUIT ★★★

a stretch of 171 km from Osorno to Puerto Varas, with 78 km of gravel roads.

A beautiful circuit past lakes Puyehue and Rupanco, to continue along the eastern shore of lake Llanquihue.

Follow the same route as Tours 3 & 4 above until you reach the road labelled 5 in the map of lakes Puyehue and Rupanco. Follow this road up to Puerto Klocker on lake Llanquihue and continue along the lakeshore until Ensenada and finally Puerto Varas. The shore of lake Llanquihue is described under Section C.

6 A TOUR TO THE COAST ★★★

a 136-km round trip from Osorno, gravel roads.

Allow one day. Take food or eat at Hostería Miller at Maicolpué; accommodations available. Take enough gasoline.

Cross the Coastal Range to the Pacific coast, with cliffs and white-sand beaches.

Leave Osorno following the road shown in the Osorno map until **Puaucho**, at km 35, straddling a crossroads and founded to provide services to the scattered Huilliche population. Continue West along the scenic Tarahuin river, where unusual **handicrafts** made of tree roots are offered.

At km 60 a road branches off to Pucatrihue. Continue straight to **Bahía Mansa**, an old port on a rugged, rocky, beautiful bay reached after a curvy descent. Today, it is a busy fishing cove. Continuing along the coast until you reach, at km 64,

Maicolpué a popular bathing resort with a white-sand beach and steep hills rising behind, clad in virgin native forests reaching all the way to to the water's edge. There is an hostería, restaurants and a campground.

Retrace the road to the fork at km 60 and continue to the North, on a road running along the bank of a placid river surrounded by dense forests with gigantic ferns. At km 68 is Pucatrihue, a seaside resort with a seemingly unending white-sand beach open to the wind. There are some summer houses, lots of sand dunes, rocks and cliffs. Popular in summer. There is daily bus service to both places.

7 MISSION ROUTE ★★★

a 107-km round trip from Osorno. Allow one day; take food.

An excursion to the religious missions that were established in the late 18th century in Mapuche territory.

Leave Osorno taking the road to Maicolpué. At

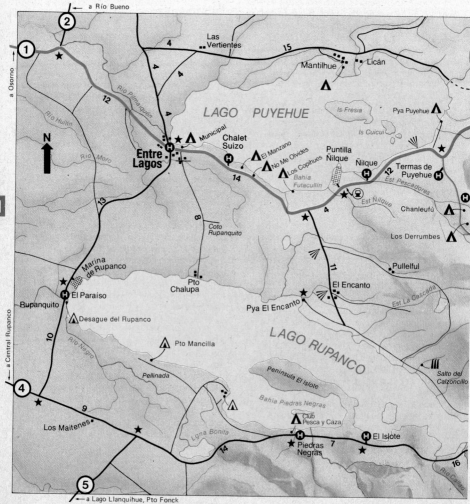

km 3, take the road branching right to Forrahue (km 14). At Forrahue turn North (right), following the Rahue river. At the San Juan de la Costa road junction follow the branch road for 16 km to a mission set up in the midst of the Huilliche Mapuche territory.

Back on the main road, continue North to reach the river near a large island, where you will see a small **wheat mill**. Worth a visit. Nine km later, the road crosses to the other bank of the scenic Rahue river, where the village of **Quilacahuin** is located. This was another large mission in the area. The road then continues along the Bueno river for 10 km to **Trumao**. On the northern bank settlement is the church of another mission. These were the three missionary centers set up by the Franciscan monks to serve the Huilliche population.

From Trumao, return to Osorno following the route described under City of La Unión.

Puerto Varas

8 ALONG THE OLD ROUTE TO CHILOE ★★★

total distance of 131 km to Puerto Varas, with 31 km paved. Allow one day; take food. Gasoline at Fresia and Río Frío.

This is the route the Spaniards used during the colonial period to reach Maullín and Chiloé, crossing one of the more densely populated Mapuche territories.

Leave Osorno following the road to Huilma (km 22). Continue to the old and busy village of Riachuelo at km 37 and then to **Crucero**, at km 51. At the fork, take the branch heading for the coast up to **Colegual,** at km 59. There, turn South and drive to **Tegualda** at km 76, a servicetown with a railway station on the old branch line connecting Corte Alto to Los Muermos.

The road continues to **Fresia,** at km 94. The entire forest production of the **Llico river valley** on

the coast passes through here (see Excursions).

Continue to **Río Frío** at km 128 and from there to Puerto Varas. The road through the area settled by German immigrants is paved, and is described under Section C (below).

This route was used by the Spaniards until the Mapuches staged their uprising. It was then forgotten, taken over by rain forest and reopened as a trail in 1789.

LAKES PUYEHUE AND RUPANCO

11

SECTION C   LAKE LLANQUIHUE

The third largest natural lake in South America is the center of this highly scenic section, with the perfect cone of the Osorno volcano presiding over the district, in the company of the extinct Puntiagudo volcano and Mount Tronador. The main tourist centers are Puerto Varas, Frutillar and Puerto Octay, all on lake Llanquihue. Lake Todos los Santos, perhaps the most beautiful of all, has no real tourist centers, only small hotels at Petrohué and Peulla.

This section also covers the farmland stretching West to the coast and the shores of the great lake lands cleared of dense forests and made productive by hard-working immigrants, most of whom came from Germany.

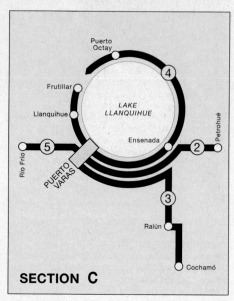

SECTION C

PUERTO VARAS was founded in 1854 as a lake port and outlet for the district's products to Puerto Montt. It is a thriving, beautiful, well-kept city with **roses** on the streets and a privileged view across lake Llanquihue toward Osorno volcano. The first push for a tourist-oriented future was given in 1934, with the construction of the Gran Hotel Puerto Varas (now a casino) and later by the opening of the road along the southern shore to Ensenada. More hotels followed, the layout of the city was improved, and the waterfront avenue **Costanera del Lago** was finished, propelling the town to its present position as undisputed «capital» of the lake. It offers an entire range of commercial and banking services, restaurants and accommodations, and other tourist services. Its proximity to Puerto Montt, coupled with the explosive growth of this latter city, has turned it into a satelite city for Puerto Montt.

What To See here a simple walk through its rosebush lined streets is rewarding. The **parish church** was built by German immigrants in 1917. The **Gran Hotel and Casino** has a lovely garden. A climb up to the look-out and park on **Cerro Philippi** will give you a superb view of the city, the lake, the volcano and everything else. A walk along the **Costanera** to **Puerto Chico** will reward you with the sight of charming houses built around the turn of the century. Beautiful excursions can be made from Puerto Varas along the shore of lake Llanquihue to Ensenada, Petrohué and lake Todos los Santos.

Where To Eat Club Alemán in the city; **Ibis**, on the Puerto Varas Costanera near Puerto Chico; **Hotel Puerto Pilar** on the road to Ensenada (lake view); and **Hostería Ensenada.** The **market** is a good place to eat seafood at a reasonable price.

Casino at the Gran Hotel (Winter, Mon–Sun, 20:00–02:00 h; Summer, Mon–Sun 20:00–02:00 h).

The best beaches are **Niklitscheck** and **Hermosa**, 10 km out of Puerto Varas on the road to Ensenada (an access fee is paid), and in **Petrohué** next to the hostería.

Organized Tours Eco travel on Av Costanera offers excursions to the Alerce Andino National Park, access to the Osorno volcano and rafting on the Petrohué and Maullín river.

LLANQUIHUE the first settlers came here in 1852 and built a port on the beach for boat travel to Puerto Varas. Its geographic location is due to the lake's drainage through the Maullin river (originally called "Drainage") which starts here. It has been a municipality since 1968 and an important agricultural and industrial center, with firms such as Lechera del Sur, Nestlé, Cecinas Llanquihue, Molino Porvenir and Garage Kaufmann-Mercedes Benz.

What To See from the road enter via the south access (ave. Pérez Rosales). You will pass by Garage Kaufmann and Cecinas Llanquihue. Then you will cross river Maullín. Follow the road to the

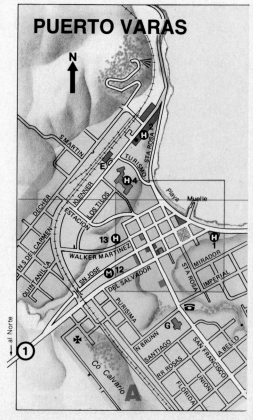

PUERTO VARAS

Downtown

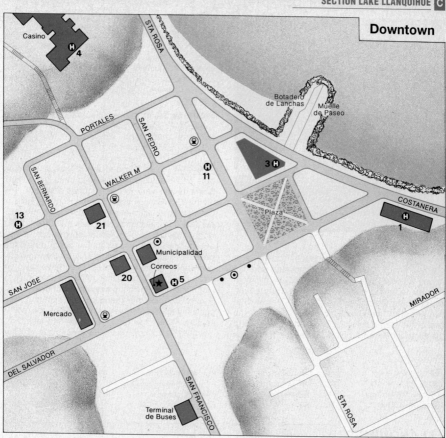

Casino
H 4

STA ROSA

Botadero
de Lanchas
Muelle
de Paseo

PORTALES

SAN PEDRO

WALKER M

SAN BERNARDO

H 3 H

11 H

13
H

21

Plaza

COSTANERA

1 H

Municipalidad
Correos

20

★ H 5

SAN JOSE

Mercado

MIRADOR

DEL SALVADOR

SAN FRANCISCO

Terminal
de Buses

STA ROSA

TOURIST SERVICES
- ☎ Telephone Center
- ⊙ Café, Meeting Point
- ★ Touristic Information
- ⋙ Lookout Point
- ⛽ Gasoline Station
- ✳ Hospital (2A)
- E Raiway Station (1A)
- G Parish Church (2A)

TOURIST SERVICES
- ● Tourist Offices & Car Rental
- A Eco Travel (2B)

ACCOMMODATIONS
- ✳ 1 H Nuevo Bellavista
- 2 M Cabañas del Lago (1A)
- ✳ 3 H Licarayén
- 4 Gran Hotel Puerto Varas
- ✳ 5 H Asturias

- 6 M Altué (1C)
- 7 M Ayentemo (2C)
- 8 Cab Colegual (2C)
- 9 Cab El Trauco (2B)
- 10 Hs Loreley (2B)
- ✳ 11 Hs La Sirena
- 12 M Sacho (2A)
- ✳ 13 H Candilejas
- 14 M Alerce (2C)

RESTAURANTS
- ✳ 4 Casino
- ✳ 1 Nuevo Bellavista
- 2 Cab del Lago (1A)
- ✳ 20 Club Alemán
- ✳ 21 Asturias
- 22 Ibis (2C)

- ✳ See Map Puerto Varas
  Downtown

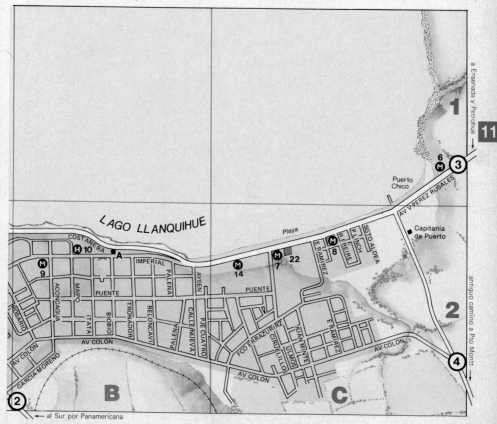

a Ensenada y Petrohué →

11

1

6 M 3

Puerto
Chico

AV V PEREZ ROSALES

Capitanía
de Puerto

LAGO LLANQUIHUE

Playa

COSTANERA

H 10
A

IMPERIAL

M 9

ACONCAGUA

MAIPO

ITATA

BIOBIO

TRONADOR

RELONCAVI

PALENA

AYSEN

CALLE NUEVA

PJE CUATRO

PUENTE

PUENTE

M 14

M 7 22

P. FLEIRE

P. INCH

E. RAMIREZ

SOTO ALDEA

8

2

FCO ERRAZURIZ

CIRUELILLOS

ULMOS

JUAN MINTE

E. RAMIREZ

AV COLON

AV COLON

AV COLON

ROSARIO

GARCIA MORENO

AV COLON

2

antiguo camino a Pto Montt

4 →

B

C

2

← al Sur por Panamericana

537

Frutillar

downtown section to visit the plaza. You can also visit the beach with a long wooden pier, and two large artificial black-necked swans on the sea.

From downtown head north on Baquedano street where the railway station, the Firemen Station and the Club Gimnástico Alemán are. At the end of the paved road, go left to visit Totoral and the **Ancestors' Memorial.** Follow to Frutillar Bajo. This

leg is described in Tour 4.

Food and accommodations Café Pattu's is nice. There are several boarding houses, which serve delicious German breakfasts, such as **Edelweis** on the way to Totoral, **Werner** on the way to Loncotoro, and **Cabañas El Cisne, Posada Alemana** and **La Casona** in town. **Playa Werner** is suitable for camping.

Events **Bierfest,** or the Beer Festival, during the first week of February (Sat and Sun) with German desserts, music and, as you'd expect, a beer drinking competition.

FRUTILLAR was founded in 1856 as a shipping port for the settlers living next to Lake Llanquihue. Beautiful and very well-kept, it has a superb view of the Osorno volcano. The houses are built in German style, with lovely gardens. Here, the **Chilean palm** can be found. No other palm tree in the world grows naturally this far south. Frutillar has experienced a significant tourist boom during the past two decades, fueled mainly by the ingenuity and efforts of his inhabitants. They have restored and refurbished traditional buildings and built a magnificent waterfront **promenade** with flower beds. Frutillar is a summer resort of high standing, with good hotels, residenciales and houses for rent in season. It has the best beach on the lake.

Frutillar also organizes the prestigious Frutillar

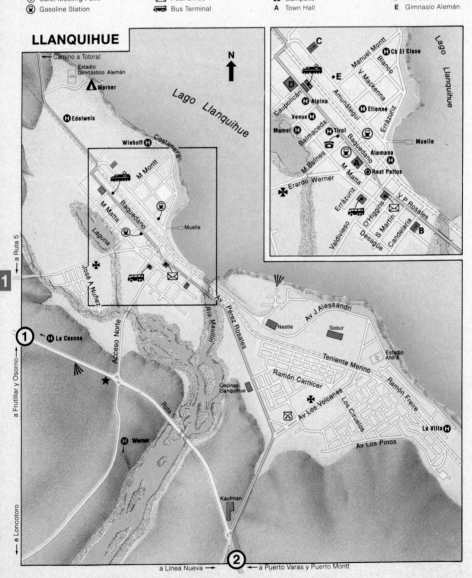

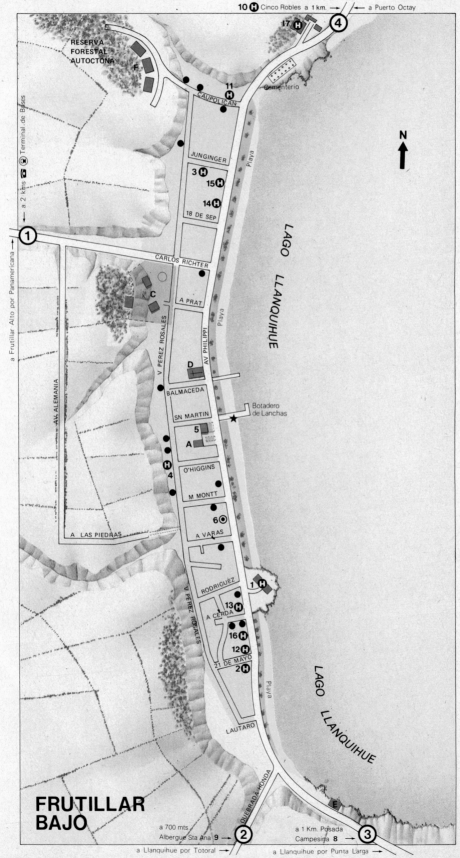

☎ Telephone Center
◉ Café, Meeting Point
★ Touristic Information
≫ Lookout Point
A Town Hall
C Museo de la Colonizacion Alemana
D Church
E Yacht Club
F University Center

ACCOMMODATIONS
1 H Frutillar
11 Casona del 32
12 Hs Vista Hermosa
2 Hs Trayén
13 Hosp Winkler
3 M Piscis
4 M Meli Ruca
10 H Cinco Robles
17 H Salzburg

14 M Monserrat
15 Cb El Bosque
16 Hosp Las Rocas
● Boarding Houses & Houses

RESTAURANTS
1 H Frutillar
2 Hs Trayén
5 Club Alemán
6 Salon de Té Futilar
10 H Cinco Robles a 1 km.

TIPS
7 Honey

COMIDA ALEMANA Y KUCHEN
1 H Frutillar
5 Club Alemán
8 Posada Campesina
9 Albergue Sta. Ana
10 Marmalade Cinco Robles

→ a Puerto Octay

FRUTILLAR BAJO

a 700 mts. Albergue Sta Ana **9**
a Llanquihue por Totoral →
a 1 Km. Posada Campesina **8**
a Llanquihue por Punta Larga →

11

539

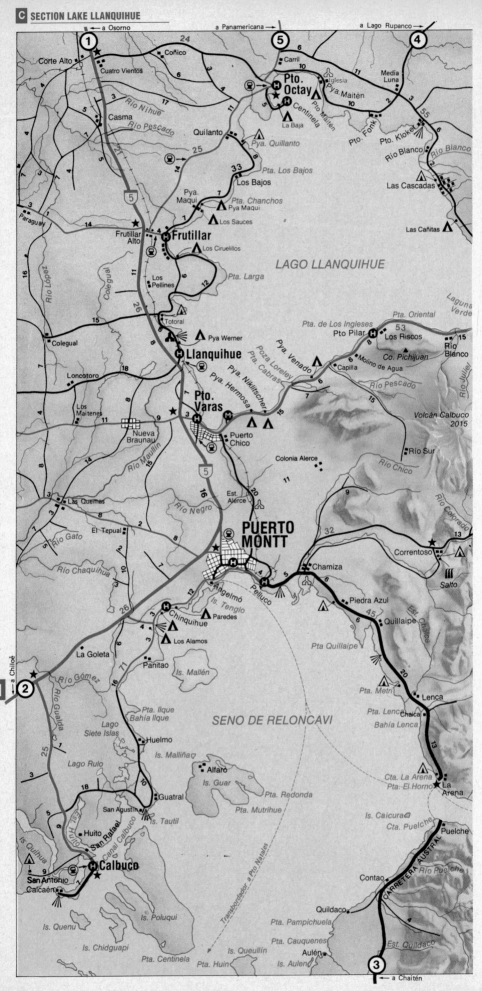

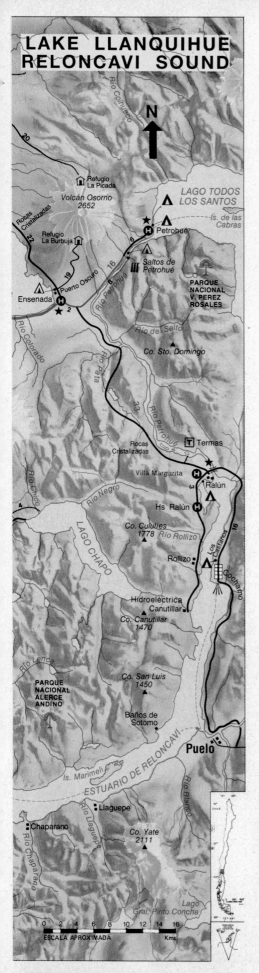

LAKE LLANQUIHUE
RELONCAVI SOUND

N

Refugio
La Picada

Volcán Osorno
2652

LAGO TODOS
LOS SANTOS

Rocas
Cristalizadas

Refugio
La Burbuja

Petrohué

Is. de las
Cabras

Puerto Oscuro

Saltos de
Petrohué

Ensenada

PARQUE
NACIONAL
V. PEREZ
ROSALES

Rio del Salto

Co. Sto. Domingo

Rocas
Cristalizadas

Termas

Villa Margarita

Ralún

Hs Ralún

Co. Cululíes
1778   Rio Rollizo

Rollizo

LAGO CHAPO

Hidroeléctrica
Canutillar

Co. Canutillar
1470

PARQUE
NACIONAL
ALERCE
ANDINO

Co. San Luis
1450

Baños de
Sotomó

Puelo

Is. Marimeli

ESTUARIO DE RELONCAVI

Llaguepe

Chaparano

Co. Yate
2111

Gral. Pinto Concha

0 2 4 6 8 10 12 14 16
ESCALA APROXIMADA   Kms.

Musical Week (see Frutillar Musical Week below).

What To See the Frutillar we have just described is really Frutillar Bajo, 1.5 km from the Pan-American highway and from its sister town Frutillar Alto. At the northern end of the Costanera is a **Forest Reserve.** The beautifully kept **cemetery** is also interesting and offers a very good view of the bay.

Museo de la Colonización Alemana (summer, Mon–Sun 10:00–13:00 h & 15:00–20:00 h; closed on Mondays during winter). Its buildings, furniture and machinery provide an excellent insight into the life of the second generation of German settlers, after they had pushed back the native forests, cleared land for farming and successfully introduced their products into the Chilean market. The buildings were moved from their original locations to the museum. It is well worth a visit.

Accommodations and Food nearly all accommodations in Frutillar Alto and Bajo are very good to excellent, ranging from hotels to private houses. See map and ask at the Tourist Information kiosk. **Hotel Frutillar** and **Posada Campesina** offer you meals and rooms with a lake view. Good German cuisine, in addition to the above, at **Club Alemán.** **Albergue Santa Ana** (on the road to the South) is also good; Cinco Robles (500 m into the road North) offers homey meals.

Frutillar Musical Week (10 days starting during the 1st week in Feb, every evening at 20:00 h) the concerts are held at the Municipal gymnasium with 1,000 seats; the Symphony Orchestra of Chile, the Chilean Airforce Symphony Band, chamber groups, national and international soloists, and the Chilean National Ballet group participate.

TOURS FROM PUERTO VARAS

2 **TO ENSENADA AND PETROHUE** ★★★

a 132-km round trip from Puerto Varas, with 120 km paved. Restaurants at Ensenada and Petrohué.
An excursion along the southern shore of lake Llanquihue to the spectacular Todos los Santos lake and to the Vicente Pérez Rosales National Park, Chile's oldest, established in 1926.

At km 9 and 10 from Puerto Varas are the beaches of **Niklitschek** and **Hermosa.** At km 15 is **Poza Loreley,** a strange overgrown pond accessible by boat. At km 19 is the Venado beach and a campsite. At km 21 is a bridge over the Pescado river, with excellent fishing and a beautiful **chapel,** one of the loveliest among the many found around the lake.

At km 24 is an old **watermill,** aptly named Die Wassermühle, which can be visited. It is being transformed into a museum and restaurant under the sponsorship of the Club Alemán of Puerto Varas.

Eight km ahead is the **Puerto Pilar** hotel and cabins and restaurant (nice view). At km 35 is **Los Riscos,** where the cliffs come close to the shore. Here rises Mount Pichi Juan, so christened to honor the Mapuche who guided expeditions to the lake.

At km 50 is

Ensenada the easternmost port on the lake, where tourist boats arrived with passengers from Puerto Varas before the coastal road was finished. There is an hostería and a nearby campsite. The road continues East along the Petrohué river valley, flanked by thick forests and old lava fields looking like a gash in the greenery. At km 58 is the

Salto del Petrohué where the river plunges over very hard volcanic rocks. In the background is the beautiful Puntiagudo volcano.

At km 66 is

LAKE TODOS LOS SANTOS the road ends at the port of **Petrohué,** with a Visitors' Center for the National Park, park rangers, picnic areas and a camp-

11

Ralún, hotel gardens

ground, there is also a fine beach and a very good hostería. There are interesting hikes; ask at the Conaf office. Day trips by boat to **Peulla** (departure 10:45 h) and a half-day boat excursion to Margarita island, with its crater lake, are offered.

Trips to Bariloche, Argentina, via Peulla are organized in Puerto Varas and Puerto Montt (Andina del Sud): Enjoy extraordinarily beautiful scenery, crossing the Cordillera and boating across the three most beautiful lakes in Chile and Argentina.

3 TO RALUN AND COCHAMO ★★★

a round trip of 194 km from Puerto Varas, with 160 km paved. Allow one day. Take food or eat lunch at the luxurious Hostería Ralún or Hostería Villa Margarita, in Ralún Village.
An excursion to the tip of the Reloncaví Estuary.

Follow the road to Ensenada (km 50). There, take the paved road to Ralún, which runs through a glacial valley flanked by steep mountains covered with virgin forests.

At km 75 is a **hot spring**. On the hills opposite the thermal springs are some strange hexagonal

rock formations known as **viguerías.** At km 78 is **Ralún**, an old Chilote-style (Chilote means from Chiloé) village in Chilote style on the shores of the estuary. Three km from the village is Hostería Ralún which is being rebuilt after a fire destroyed the original building late 1991.

The road continues along the shore of the estuary to the **Canutillar Hydroelectric Power Station,** powered by the water from lake Chapo (tapped underground and carried through a tunnel) up in the hills.

To continue to Cochamó, cross the bridge spanning the Petrohué river in the village of Ralún. The road, now gravel, runs on a ledge above the shore, with a beautiful view of **Yates volcano** straight ahead.

At km 94 is picturesque

Cochamó the main village in the area, with a **church** dating from 1909 and steep streets. There are pensiones, a restaurant, and a campsite and thermal baths in the neighboring beach. The road continues along the shore to the Puelo river. When the weather is good you can drive to the village of **Puelo.**

4 A DRIVE HALF-WAY AROUND LAKE LLANQUIHUE ★★★ *a total distance of 156 km, of which 83 km is paved. Allow a whole day; take food.*
A beautiful circuit giving you an insight into the history of the lake's settlement. In the past Llanquihue was flanked by impenetrable jungle. The settlers established villages only at Puerto Varas and Puerto Octay. Otherwise, they only had «centers», with a dock for shipping out their products, a chapel and a cemetery.

Follow the road from Puerto Varas to Ensenada (km 50). There take there the gravel road running North along the lakeside. One km from Ensenada is **Laguna Verde**, a small lake. The road crosses a lava field, which reached the lake in 1835 and is now being colonized by vegetation.

At km 52 a road branches right to the new ski

✚ Hospital	**C** Parish	**2** Wulf
⊠ Police	**D** Town Hall	**3** Hausdort
Ⓖ Gasoline Station	**E** Museum El Colono	**4** Ignacio Wulf
★ Touristic Information	**10** H Haase	**5** Yagade
A Rural Education Institute		**6** Vargas
B Parish House	**INTERESTING HOUSES**	**7** Grauss
	1 Bastidas	**8** Hausdorf

9 B Schmidt	
11 Werner	
12 Peñasco	
13 Barrientos	
14 Puschel	
15 Soto	

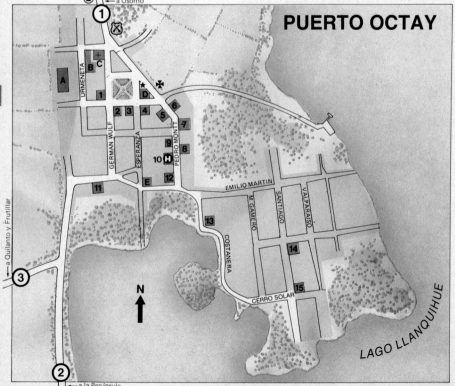

PUERTO OCTAY

11

center **La Burbuja**, on the slopes of volcano, with ski lifts, a café and a shelter. The 19-km road is more or less in poor condition.

At km 57 you can see strange hexagonal rock formations known as **viguerías** by the roadside. They were formed from cooling lava.

At km 72 is

Las Cascadas
with a group of over 70 summer houses, a beach, a campsite and daily bus service from Osorno. Lican Ray on lake Calafquén, and Las Cascadas are the only places exclusively devoted to summer tourism in the South. At km 74 is the lonely **Río Blanco** chapel, with a cemetery. The eastern shore of the lake and Osorno volcano are part of the Vicente Pérez Rosales National Park.

Next comes the bay of Puerto Klocker, with a road branching right to the ski shelter of **La Picada**, on the slope of the volcano. At km 83 is a fork in the road: the right branch goes to lake Rupanco, the one straight ahead to Puerto Octay, and the left one to **Puerto Fonck.** Following the left branch, at km 85 you encounter a chapel, an interesting cemetery and a beautiful beach with the only surviving old dock on the lake.

Continuing along the lakeshore you reach **Maitén beach** at km 95, frequented on weekends, and a **chapel** that has a tablet commemorating the 100 year anniversary of the arrival of the first German settlers.

PUERTO OCTAY a picturesque village on a quiet bay enclosed by the Centinela Peninsula. It was founded in 1854 as a port on the northern tip of the lake. It was linked to Osorno by a trail (today a paved highway) which was used by the first German settlers who cleared the area around the lake. The advent of the railroad deprived the village of its important role as shipping port on the lake.

A 5-km road leads to the **Centinela** peninsula, where the first summer house built on the lake (now a hotel) is located. It was built in 1912 by the then incumbent Interior minister.

This road, now paved, continues to Quillanto (km 116) and then runs along the bay where Pérez Rosales' boat capsized, nearly killing him, during his first survey of the lake. There is a spectacular **view** of three volcanoes, islands, the lake and the Puerto Octay peninsula. At km 124 is **Los Bajos,** with the ruins of docks, a pretty cemetery, some old houses and a splendid manor house. The road continues past a string of small, attractive beaches including **Maqui beach** at km 131, which has a campground, finally reaching **Frutillar** at km 138.

There are two options if you wish to circle the lake:

Around Punta Larga, a 12 km stretch skirting the peninsula until you get to the next option.

Cutting across Punta Larga this is a road climbing from Frutillar that cuts across the peninsula. At 6 km it meets the road mentioned in the previous option. A short distance ahead is Puerto Domeyko. For the next 2.5 km, the road passes through rolling hills until reaching Bahía and Playa Totoral.

At 600 m from the beach, take the road at your right to visit the **Lutheran church** and **the cemetery** -the first settlers are buried here. A short climb takes you to the

Ancestors' Memorial
(Unsern Ahnen) built in 1937 to commemorate the area's first settlers. It is a large stone wall with 80 names inscribed on bronze plaques. From here you get a splendid view of the lake.

6 km ahead is the city of Llanquihue. Take the Pan-Am road from here to get to Puerto Varas and you will have closed a 156 km circle.

5 TOUR HEARTLAND ★★

a round trip of 84 km on a paved road.

A visit to the area which the settlers transformed from impenetrable forest and swamps into what is today still rich farmland.

Leave Puerto Varas heading for Nueva Braunau at km 7, with a large dairy plant. The area was settled by Austrian immigrants in 1875. Following the gravel road to the right you can see the houses of the first settlers.

Continue on the paved road to the coast, running through softly rolling land dotted with beautiful country houses.

At km 42 is

Río Frío an orderly village with a church built in 1909 by German settlers.

SECTION D   PUERTO MONTT

This Section covers the entire area around the Reloncaví sound, including the Estuary of Reloncaví, the mainland coast stretching West with the towns and villages of Calbuco, Pargua and Carelmapu, up to the Maillín river. Its center is the city of

PUERTO MONTT (pop 84,195), the capital of Region X, Los Lagos, which includes the provinces of Valdivia, Osorno, Llanquihue, Chiloé and Palena. Located on the northern tip of the vast Reloncaví sound and with its harbor protected by the Tenglo island, the city spreads along a narrow seaboard and climbs the slopes enclosing it to the north. It was founded in 1853 by Vicente Pérez Rosales with German immigrants who had come to settle the lake Llanquihue area. In the early days it was a service town providing support for the colonization effort. In 1912, the railroad from Santiago reached it (a distance of a little over one thousand kilometers) and it became the main port for the route to Chiloé, Aysén and Magallanes.

Since 1985, the city has experienced considerable growth and development, fueled by more than 30 salmon farms, in addition to forestry and fishing industries and service companies. New

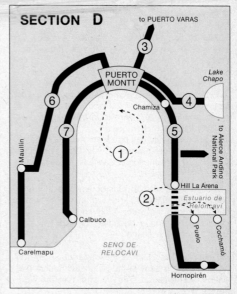

SECTION D

to PUERTO VARAS

PUERTO MONTT

Lake Chapo

Chamiza

to Alerce Andino National Park

Maullín

Hill La Arena

Estuario de Reloncaví

Calbuco

Pueblo

Cochamó

Carelmapu

SENO DE RELOCAVI

Hornopirén

11

Puerto Montt

hotels, restaurants, cafés and shops have opened. The growing need for housing has transformed Puerto Varas into a satelite community.

What To See shopping hours are Mon–Fri 09:00–13:00 h & 15:00–19:30 h; Sat 09:00–13:00 h. Follow the waterfront street **-Costanera-** 3 km to the East to

Pelluco Puerto Montt's bathing beach, with black sand, hotels and restaurants in a small bay (water not too pure). At the other end of the Costanera is Angelmó, with Tenglo island less than 100 meters away. On the Costanera you will see two monuments: the **first locomotive** used on the railroad from Santiago, and a **Chilote launch**, today seldom seen.

ANGELMO is a fishing port and **terminal port** for **ferries** sailing South, the **main port** for the **vessels** plying the routes to the islands, **a seafood** market with lots of good seafood restaurants, and home to the largest **handicrafts market** in the Region. (The busiest days are Mon & Fri mornings. Seafood restaurants Mon–Sun 10:00–20:00 h. Handicrafts market same days 09:0–19:00 h.)

Drive up to the Intendencia (see downtown map) for a panoramic **view** of the city and the Reloncaví sound.

The Cathedral Church and the Iglesia Matriz both date from the turn of the century and were refurbished in 1963, with interesting woodwork. The **Museo Regional** has Chile's most complete collection of artifacts from the southern archipelagos, in addition to a good selection of regional historical pictures and objects.

Where To Eat fine cuisine and a good view at Hotel Pérez Rosales and at Club de Yates. Kiel and La Casona restaurants at km 8 on road to Chinquihue; Posada Top at km 10. Seafood at the Angelmó restaurants. Restaurant Pazos (ph 252552) in Pelluco specializes in curantos. For fast, economic meals for the whole family see the places marked with asterisks in the map. Picnic at the beaches of Chinquilla.

Lodging the city has abundant accomodations, from expensive places to modest boarding houses. See description in Services section at the end of this guide.

A scenic paved road runs southwest along the coast to **Chinquihue** (10 km), with beaches, house on stilts above the water, busy shipyards, oyster farms, yachts and a backdrop of snowy volcanoes beyond the sound.

Shipping Puerto Montt is the departure point for cruises to the islands in the Reloncaví Sound, the Chiloé archipiélago, Aisén, and Laguna San Rafael.

Reloncaví Sound many passenger launches arrive in the morning at Angelmó and return to the islands in the evening. Personally contact the captains. Information at the capitanía de puerto. There you can also obtain information about transportation to some of the islands around Chiloé. **Aisén and Laguna San Rafael** there are several, shorter and longer (2-3 days) tourist excursions. Ships have a limited capacity. Their departure times are flexible; always make reservations and confirm.

Complete information about ships in the services section at the end of this guide.

To Puerto Chacabuco in Aysén Ro Ro Evangelista has two weekly departures; passage takes 22 hours, for 420 passengers and cars (Navimag, ph 254480, Puerto Montt, and pho 6963211/2/3/4 in Santiago). Río Cisnes has one departure weekly with passengers and cars, accommodations in cabins for a 6-day circuit touring the Aysén channels and travelling on the Carretera Austral. Contact Empremar (see ph numbers above).

To Puerto Natales in Magallanes the Ro Ro Tierra del Fuego roll-on-roll-off car-and-truck ferry has three departures monthly; passage takes 72 hours; 160 passengers in cabins and reclining seats. Check with Navimag (see Services and Prices).

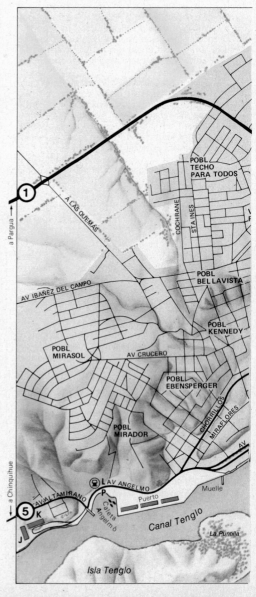

TOURS FROM PUERTO MONTT

1 BOAT CRUISE ★★★

for 2 hours, sailing along the coast from Angelmó.
Interesting, but the boatman waits until the boat
is full before leaving.

2 BOAT TRIP UP THE ESTUARY ★★★

a cruise taking most of the day, organized by
tourist agencies in Puerto Montt.
A scenic cruise in a fjord that penetrates deep into the
Cordillera of the Andes.

The journey starts early morning by bus, which
takes the Carretera Austral to La Arena. The
launch is boarded there and sails into the
Reloncaví estuary, passing near sea-lion colonies
and stopping at the houses of some of the early
settlers. The scenery is spectacular, with **Yates**
volcano towering behind. The volcano was christened by an English seal hunter who lived in
Chiloé and assisted in the Fitzroy expedition. The
launch stops at **Puelo** and then continues to

<u>**Cochamó**</u> the main village on the estuary. The
boat tour ends with lunch at the beautiful Hotel
Ralún.

Puerto Montt, Angelmó

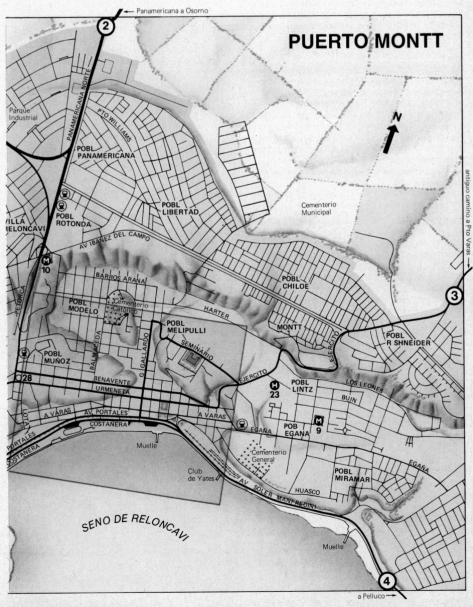

The return leg is by bus, which takes a paved highway back to Puerto Montt.

3 TO PUERTO VARAS ALONG THE OLD ROUTE
★★ *twenty km on a gravel road.*
An alternative to the Pan-Am, with the flavor of the old days.

Take exit 3 in the Puerto Montt map. The road approaches the railway line at the Alerce station. Stop to have a look at the **President's Chair**, a gigantic alerce (a valuable native conifer) stump, the largest known in Chile. President Pedro Montt and his whole entourage sat here once while on a trip to inspect the construction of a railroad. A huge alerce forest used to grow here.

After driving past farms you reach the lake at Puerto Chico, near Puerto Varas.

4 TO LAKE CHAPO ★★
a round trip of 94 km on a gravel road. Allow half a day. Take food.
An excursion to a lake perched high up in the mountains, skirting the Calbuco volcano from behind.

Take the road to Pelluco and continue up to Chamiza, at km 9. Before the bridge, take the left branch at the fork, heading for **Correntoso**, at km 32, where you can take a 2 km detour to a small waterfall with a river beach (good for camping). You are now within the Alerce Andino National Park. Continue to

Lake Chapo flanked by tall mountains and dense forests. A tunnel drains water from this lake to the Canutillar Hydroelectric Power Station, on the shores of the Reloncaví Estuary.

5 THE FIRST LEG OF THE CARRETERA AUSTRAL
★★★ *forty-five km from Puerto Montt to La Arena, and another 61 km to Hornopirén (Río Negro), with a ferry crossing from La Arena to Puelche. See shipping services in services sections. (5 crossings daily, reservations at Transmarchilay, ph. Puerto Montt 254654, Puerto Montt). Allow one day. Gravel road. Gasoline and accommodations at Hornopirén.*
An excursion along the first leg of the famed Carretera Austral, opened in 1988.

Leave Puerto Montt (km 0) towards Pelluco. At km 9 take the road to the left to visit

Chamiza a village with a **Lutheran church** flanked by two large araucarias. This used to be a settement of German immigrants. Near the beach are the remains of a port of hydroplanes that traveled from Puerto Montt to Punta Arenas and back. The adventurous pilots stopped at **Puerto Edén**, on Channel Messier, for refueling.

The road runs along the coast until km 21. **Piedra Azul** offers handicrafts.

At km 32 is **Lenca**, which has a large forestry industry. Opposite Lenca is **Chaica**, with a lovely church at the base of a headland.

ROUTE TO ALERCE ANDINO NATIONAL PARK from Lenca (km 0) a dirt road enters the range on the left side of the Chaicas river, which has several attractive waterfalls. At km 7 is the Park entrance and the Ranger's house. For the next 5 km the road is rough and steep, passable only by durable vehicles. The reward is a forest with millenary alerces and Laguna Chaiquenes. It is worth a visit because it is the only place where you will see an alerce forest.

The road now runs on a ledge directly above the sea up to **La Arena**, at km 47, where the ferry docks. Camping is allowed near the ramps.

The ferry takes you across the estuary in a 30-min crossing to **Caleta Puelche,** your new km 0. At km 13 is Contao, a logging port with telephone link and a pensión. The road dives into a thick

jungle until km 25, where a road branches off to **Huailahué**, a picturesque fishing cove with a **residencial.** The road climbs a small range and on the other side is a hot spring. At km 61, at the foot of the small, perfect cone of Hornopirén volcano, is

HORNOPIREN also known by the less intriguing name of Río Negro. It has hotels, campgrounds and a gasoline station, and a modern fish farm.

Llancahué Termal Baths located on small forest-covered Llancahué island, which is populated by a few setters who salt fish for a living.

The thermal baths and modest hosteria are owned and managed by a nice German couple. Boaters anchor here to see the twilight from the hosteria with the small Llanchid archipelago in the

11

background... **it is one of the most beautiful scenes in all of the southern Chilean zone.**

There are two different types of thermal baths here: the typical bathtub-kind in a room and the thermal spring-type found on the beach where you can have a warm sea bath even on cold, rainy days.

How to Get There make reservations in advance. In Santiago call pho 6711507 or 6713228. The hosteria owns a boat that can pick up passengers at Pichi Colo bay (a 45 mins cruise), Hornopirén (60 mins), and Cholgo (30 mins). Send a radio message to the hostería from Radio Reloncaví at Puerto Montt (calle Illapel 60), confirming day and time of arrival at the embarkment bay. You can also rent launches at Hornopirén and Cholgo.

The continuation of the Carretera Austral is described in Zone 13.

6 **TO MAULLIN AND CARELMAPU ★★★**

a round trip of 178 km with 34 km of gravel roads. Allow one day. Gasoline at Maullín.
An excursion to the Pacific coast.

Take the Pan-American highway toward Pargua. At km 45 take the signposted road branching right to **Maullín**, (km 71) a port on the estuary with constant boat traffic. It has an hostería.

Five km ahead is **Pangal**, a long beach with a campground and an hostería amid the pine forests and sand dunes. Retrace the road up to the signposted junction for Carelmapu. Follow this road

ACCOMMODATIONS					
1	H Vicente Pérez Rosales (3C)	13	H Miramar (3A)	26	H Raysan (2C)
2	H Colina (3C)	14	Apart Hotel Millahue (2A)		**RESTAURANTS**
3	H Burg (3C)	15	H Gamboa (2C)	1	H Vicente Pérez Rosales (3C)
4	H Millahue (3E)	16	H Viento Sur (2E)	3	Amsel (3C)
5	H Montt (3D)	17	Bh Sur (3D)	5	H Montt (3D)
6	H Le Mirage (2D)	18	Bh Benavente (2A)	7	H Royal (3D)
7	H Royal (3D)	19	Bh Urmeneta (3D)	12	Hostal Panorama (2E)
8	H Central (2C)	20	H Reloncaví (2C)	※ 10	M Bologna
※ 9	Melipulli	21	Bh Familiar Polz (3A)	30	Dino's (3C)
※ 10	M Bologna	22	Bh Familiar Téllez (3A)	31	Club Alemán (3D)
11	M Punta Arenas (3E)	23	Bh Calipso (3E)	※ 32	Yachting Club (4E)
12	Hostal Panorama (2E)	※ 24	Bh Touristen Heim	R	Rodoviario (4A)
		25	H O'Grinn (2C)		

TOURIST SERVICES	
40	Viajes Angelmó (3C)
41	Denny's Rent a Car (2D)
42	Sport Rent a Car (2D)
43	Automóvil Club (3C)
44	Budget Rent a Car (2D)
45	Ladeco (2D)
46	Aéreo Regional (3E)
47	Lan Chile (2D)
48	Hertz Rent a Car (2D)
49	Transmachilay (3E)
※	See Location in General Map of Puerto Montt

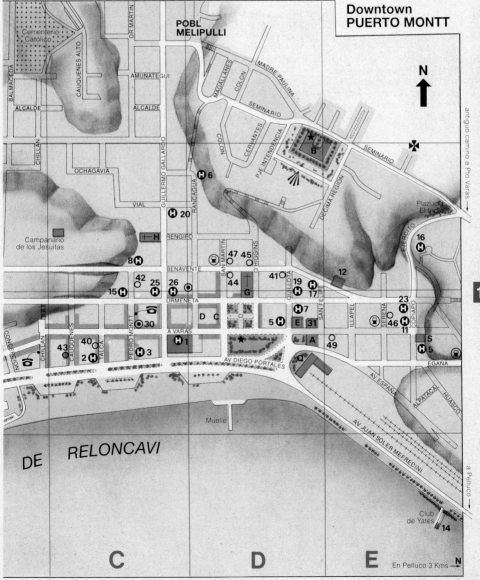

Downtown **PUERTO MONTT**

(graveled). At km 89 is

Carelmapu a fishing village founded in 1602 by the Spaniards fleeing the destruction of Osorno. Bad luck seems to have followed them: the place was soon ransacked by Dutch pirates. This was the mainland terminal of the old Colonial Route from Valdivia to Chiloé. You can see Ancud right across the Chacao strait. On Feb 2, the locals celebrate the **Fiesta de la Candelaria**, a religious festivity, when gaily decorated vessels come from all over Chiloé.

The circuit ends 3 km up the road at **Playa Brava**, vast and lonely beach wedged between cliffs and thundering surf with a grand view of the Coronado gulf. Legend has it that the variety of wild strawberries found here -Fragaria chiloensis is the granddaddy of all the strawberries found today around the world.

7 TO CALBUCO ALONG THE COASTAL ROAD

★★★ *a 122-km round trip from Puerto Montt, with 69 km paved. Allow one day. Hostería and gasoline at Calbuco.*

A road providing a foretaste of Chiloé, with palafitos (houses on stilts above the water), small shipyards, beaches smelling of seaweed, and lots of boat traffic near the coast.

Follow the road to Chinquihue (labelled 5 in Puerto Montt map). At km 11 the pavement ends, and a couple of km ahead is a hillock offering a splendid view of Calbuco, Osorno, Puntiagudo, Yates and Tronador volcanoes, and other snowy peaks further South.

At km 15 take the south branch at the fork, heading for **Huelmo** (km 34). The village has a nice beach and fish farms. From here continue on the road heading south along the coast. You will see traditional Chilote-style (Chilote means from Chiloé) with intertwined twigs.

At km 44 is **San Agustín.** The road heads inland until km 62, where it meets a paved road which runs along the coast of a deep, beautiful estuary. At km 65 is a church and a footbridge.

At km 71 is

CALBUCO strategically perched atop a hill overlooking the sea, with a harbor on each side. It is linked to the mainland by an embankment which has a road. It was founded in 1604 as a village and fortress by the Spaniards who had fled from Osorno after that city was razed by the Mapuches. It is 250 years older than Puerto Montt and was the only permanently inhabited non-Mapuche settlement in the area until the arrival of the German settlers in 1853. The friendlier Indians of the islands were promptly subjected by the Spaniards to the serfdom system known as encomienda, whereby the natives were forced to provide free labor. By 1843, the entire area inland from here to Osorno had once again become impenetrable jungle.

It was a pretty quiet place until 1700, when alerce and cypress logging took off. By 1900, after the arrival of the German settlers, it had some canneries and the large industrial complex of the Oelckers Bros, with shipyards, a smelter, and a fleet of service ships plying the routes to the south. The depletion of area shellfish has prompted some canneries to move farther South.

What To See the mounds of shells outside the canneries. The **square**, perched on the upper side of town, offers a panoramic view of the neighboring island and the strait. The wooden church on the square has an image of **St Miguel** brought by the founders in 1604. Those wishing to hire a boat contact Mario Villarroel at ph 481 (office hours), or hire one directly at the harbor.

Retrace the road 4 km to San Rafael, and take the gravel road heading west, which crosses a channel (5 km) on a raised bed of rock. You are now on **Quihua island.** Another 4 km takes you to San Antonio, with a small beach of fine sand, the best in the area. A footbridge leads to other beaches suitable for camping.

To return to Puerto Montt, take the paved road to the Pan-Am and from there you reach the city in about 25 km.

11

SECTION E ROUTES TO ARGENTINA

Close to the border is Bariloche, the second most important touristic city of Argentina after Mar del Plata. Due to its attractions and the existence of two border passes, Bariloche has become part of the tour to the Chilean Southern zone.

In this section the international passes to Bariloche are described.

1 TO BARILOCHE THROUGH PUYEHUE ★★★

248 km from Osorno and 151 km from Los Pajaritos Customs Complex. 198 km paved road and 151 km gravel road. Gasoline at Ñilque (Chile) and Angostura (Argentina). There are restaurants and hotels in the eastern zone of lake Puyehue (Ñilque, Puyehue Termal Baths, and the beautiful Antillanca); campgrounds at both places. Exchange for US and Chilean currency at Bariloche. The tour between Osorno and Los Pajaritos is described in Section B, Tour 2.

A road crossing the beautiful Puyehue National Park in Chile and the Nahuel Huapi National Park in Argentina. The road skirts lake Espejo and Nahuel Huapi.

Los Pajaritos Customs Complex in the middle of a native forest, with Customs, cafeteria and goodies. 97 km from Osorno on a paved road.

Schedules, documentation, fees similar to those of Puesco Pass (see Zone 10, Section E, Tour A).

From the Customs House (km 0) the road climbs gently a forest with occasional zigzags. At km 12 the paved road ends and a compact road of volcanic sand begins. You can see the «barbas» or parasites hanging from the «lenga» trees. You can visit two ponds at the left side. At km 23 is the

Puyehue Pass at 1,308 m above sea level. The border is signaled by a modest Virgen de la Paz and several signposts. The road descends gently through a dense lenga forest and crosses several rivers. At km 35 there is a huge monolitic rock.

At km 40 is the

Puyehue Border Pass (08:00–19:00 h, Argentinian time); the Customs procedures do not take long.

There is a short valley ahead where **lake Piré** is; apt for camping.

At km 51 the road runs by a hillside with little lateral visibility. At km 55 you can see

Lake Espejo it is seen from the above as from a balcony, surrounded by forests and steep slopes. At its extremity, just below the balcony, there is a bathing resort with a good hotel, beach and boats.

A short distance ahead is the Ultima Esperanza branch of lake Nahuel Huapi There are some nice cabins (Cabinas Aruco).

At km 62 is

Lake Correntoso it is seen from a very tall concrete bridge spanning a short river that links the Correntoso with lake Nahuel Huapi. It is a nice place with a view to both lakes. At one side is the good Hostería Correntoso.

A paved road beginning here skirts the branch to km 63 where the modern Hotel La Posada is at the shore. The road continues to Hotel Lomas de Correntoso and at km 66 is

VILLA ANGOSTURA a small lake resort at the lake Nahuel Huapi shore, located on a straight of the Quetrihue peninsula. 3 km from the road is **El Messidor**, a summer residence for the Neuquén Government. There are two lake ports with ships to cruise **Los Arrayanes Park** and Bariloche. There are restaurants, cafes, hotels, and gasoline stations.

When you leave Angostura, a 9 km long road branches to the left for **Cerro Bayo**, a ski center with an impressive view to lake Nahuel Huapi.

LAKE NAHUEL HUAPI the largest lake of the area, 570 km2 with cooler and windier waters than the Chilean lakes. It has a glaciar origin as its many shores, bays, islands, and branches show. You will see the moraine plug on your way to Bariloche.

It was discovered in 1670 by jesuit missionaries who came from their Residence at Castro, Chiloé, and founded a mission in the Huemul peninsula to evangelize the pampa natives. The mission was abandoned in 1718 due to the martyrdom of five of its priests. Its history is depicted

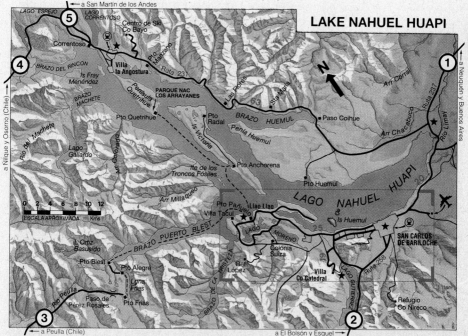

LAKE NAHUEL HUAPI

on the Bariloche Cathedral frescoes. Explorer Francisco Moreno went up river Limay and rediscovered the lakes shores on January 22, 1876.

As you continue your trip (km 66), the modern, paved road skirts the lake for 34 km. You never see the whole lake; at the beginning of it the long Quetrihué peninsula is across, then Victoria island, and finally the long Huemul branch closed by the Huemul point.

Of particular interest are Puerto Manzano (km 74) with nice houses. There is a modest hostería (Las Flores, km 87) with a sand beach apt for camping. Later on, the «Ciprés de la Cordillera» disappears to give way to a bush called coigüe. Now you are skirting the Huemul branch in order to cross to Hostería Santa María (km 98) with a good beach for camping.

The branch ends at km 107 and the road goes inland. The emerging bushes announce the steppe.

At km 117 the road skirts from some distance the northern shore; you get an impressive **view** of the lake and Bariloche with its striking **Cerro Catedral** crowned with granitic rocks. At the right-hand of the city is the Melipal neighborhood with Cerro Otto and its funicular.

At km 130 you meet at your left a road coming from Neuquén and San Martín de los Andes (description in Zone 10, Section E, Tour B). Take the road at your right to go to the moraine plug that closes the lake. A short distance ahead there is a look-out with a good view and a plaque commemorating the Francisco Moreno's discovery of 1876.

The road skirts now the southern shore and crosses the bridge spanning river Limay (km 133), the place where the river waters flow into. Then the road gets into the outskirts of the city; at km 151 is the downtown section of San Carlos de Bariloche.

2 TO BARILOCHE THROUGH LAKE TODOS LOS SANTOS ★★★ *11 ¹/₂ km from Puerto Montt to Bariloche, lunches and stops included. Several ship transfers and 4 legs on bus. This tour is operated by the Andina del Sud Co., reservations at different travel agencies of Puerto Montt, Puerto Varas, and Santiago.*

A two-day trip *from Apr 1–Aug 30, departures from Puerto Montt Mon to Fri 10:30 h, arriving to Bariloche next day at 16:30 h, lunch at Petrohué and lodging at Peulla. Also, from Nov. 15-Feb. 28, departures from Puerto Montt Mon-Sat 14:45 h, arriving to Bariloche next day at 17:45 h, lodging at Peulla, lunch at Puerto Blest, and a visit to the Los Cántaros waterfall.*

A one-day trip *from Sep 1–Mar 31, departures from Puerto Montt (Monday to Saturday) at 08:30 h, and arriving to Bariloche at 21:00 h. Lunch at Peulla.*

Note *arrivals to Bariloche are given in Argentinian time (+1 Chilean hour). The leg Puerto Montt-Petrohué is scheduled for 2 h, including a visit to the Petrohué waterfall. You can also board on Puerto Varas or Petrohué. Cars can be left at some hostería, arrangements should be made personally with the manager. There are cafes and restaurants at Petrohué, Peulla, and Puerto Blest. Only those ships cruising lakes Todos los Santos and Nahuel Huapi have a cafeteria. During winter the trip takes 2 days.*

Approximate fees *ticket US$ 45,00; lodging at Peulla with breakfast and one meal US$ 30,00 for two persons; lunch US$ 9,00.*
A chance to cross the mountain range and sail through the 3 most beautiful lakes of Chile and Argentina.

Leg 1 2 h. Departures 08:30 h from Puerto Montt on a tourism bus; it stops at Puerto Varas to pick up passengers. It skirts lake Llanquihue to Ensenada; it stops for 15 minutes at the Petro-

hué waterfall, arriving at Petrohué at 10:30 h.

Leg 2 2 h on ship. Departures 11:00 h to cross lake Todos los Santos in National Park Pérez Rosales, with green waters and steep hillsides covered with forests. There are views to the Osorno, Puntiagudo, and Tronador volcanoes. The ship passes by Margarita island. Now and then they send mail to some solitary colonists of the region; the mail is put into inflated bags and they blow the whistle while the addressee rows speedily to get his mail. After 2 h Peulla is reached at 13:00 h.

Leg 3 disembark at Peulla accross from the old hotel where lunch is served. There is a small village of 800 inhabitants; it has a school, Customs, International Police and a SAG post. Procedures and documentation are similar to those described in Zone 10, Section E, Tour A. The bus trip takes 2 h, 23 km to the border, and 4 more km to Puerto Frías; departure at 14:30 h. Peulla is approximatedly at 200 m above sea level; the road gently rises into woods, skirting river Peulla. 5 km after crossing it is Casa Pangue with a Police Station.

There is an impressive view to the river canyon and to

Cerro Tronador an extinguished volcano at 3,460 m above sea level, with impressive glaciers and periodical rock and ice landslides. The road goes up a steep and curvy slope until it gets to the Pérez Rosales Pass (km 23) at 990 m above sea level.

A short distance before the pass there is a look-out with a striking view. During winter this leg is made on modern snowcats or caterpillar buses. The road goes down a hill for 4 km to get to Puerto Frías (700 m above sea level) at 17:30 h (Argentinian time).

Leg 4 at Puerto Frías there is a dock and an Argentinian Customs post where you go through the necessary procedures. At 17:45 h you board a catamaran to sail in 20 minutes the small and beautiful lake Frías. Arrival to Puerto Alegre at 18:05 h.

Leg 5 bus boarding at 18:30 h for a short 6 km trip (15') on a marshy area with thick forests. Arrival at Puerto Blest on the lake Nahuel Huapi shore at 18:45 h.

Leg 6 Puerto Blest is at the end of the long Blest branch. It has a dock (muelle) and a hostería. At 19:00 h you board a modern catamaran for 3 or 8 passengers. This wanderful cruise through lake Nahuel Huapi takes 1,5 h. The ship sails by Centinela island where the tomb of Francisco Moreno is; it skirts the Llao Llao peninsula to arrive to Puerto Pañuelo at 20:30 h.

Leg 7 at Puerto Pañuelo tourism ships can be seen as well as the good Hotel Llao Llao. Here you take the bus for a 25 km trip alongside the Costanera to downtown Bariloche, arriving at 21:00 h.

A Short History of this Touristic Circuit the Pérez Rosales pass was discovered and used by jesuit missionaries; later on it was used by the settlers of lake Nahuel Huapi for trade. The first touristic trip was organized by Ricardo Roth Schütz, a young man who brought a group of French tourists from Buenos Aires to Bariloche and from there to Puerto Montt via the Pérez Rosales pass.

Mr Roth's parents were Swiss and German. He was born in Buenos Aires and was educated in Switzerland. His father was the director of the Museum of La Plata. Ricardo came to Peulla in 1901 and he began purchasing estates in lake Todos los Santos and the bordering zone. In 1913 he founded the Andina del Sud Transportation Co. and helped the zone development with ships in lake Todos los Santos, Frías and Nahuel Huapi, besides building hosterias in Ensenada, Petrohué, Peulla and Puerto Blest.

The first tour was made through estates, roads, paths, and shelters of his own, as well as using ships he owned. That first attempt was so successful that from then on three generations of his descendants have supported and controlled this touristic circuit.

EXCURSIONS

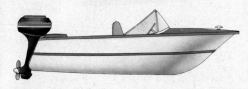

BOAT EXCURSIONS

A motorboat is handy to have in this Zone. Some of the possible boat excursions are described below.

To the Mouth of the Bueno River the Bueno is a slow, deep, meandering river devoid of rocky outcropings, and therefore excellent for water-skiing. The departure point, Trumao, accessible from Osorno or La Unión, has earthen boat ramps suitable for all kinds of trailers.

When you encounter the first island, take the left branch. Then comes the Rahue river. A road runs next to the river until well into the Coastal Range. There are lots of forest farms in the area, accounting for the sawmills you will see, and launches chugging with their cargos of timber. The river becomes narrows at times to a width of approximately 30 m, and sometimes it runs a little bit faster meandering through jungle-clad mountains. The forests accompany the river to its mouth at the sea. Several streams flow into the Bueno, the largest of which is Molino de Oro. Few settlers live near the river banks, but fishing and leisure boats are to be seen heading for the mouth of the river (La Barra), where a dock and a few summer houses are located. Access is only through the river, by private boat or one scheduled launch. The round trip is 130 km. Allow.one day and take food and fuel.

To the Mouth of the Llico River a wide and placid coastal river, affected by tides (it is dangerous to come too near the sand bar at the mouth when the tide is receding). Access is through the Totoral gravel road branching off the Pan-American highway to Fresia, and from there to Puerto Maichihue. It has a concrete boat ramp and a Fish & Game house where you can leave the car. Traffic includes boats, motorboats and launches bringing farm produce and forest products out to Maichihue. The meandering course to the mouth takes about 3 hours, and is squeezed by the hills of the **Cordillera de Sarao.** The northern bank is virgin, while the southern is cultivated and has a few settlers. The sawmills along the way are open to the public. Salmon fishing is good up to the Marilán river; thereafter robalo fishing is better. On the sand bar is a Fish & Game Lodge with an hostería and some private summer houses. Cross the sand bar on foot to reach a white-sanded beach on the sea (it is dangerous to go near the mouth when the tide recedes). The round trip is about 70 km long. Allow one day.

The Maullín River a wide, deep river which grows progressively narrower upstream and is affected by tides throughout its length. At Maullín there is an excellent concrete boat ramp, a good hostería and fuel supply in summer. Begin the excursion by cruising upstream for 22 km; beautiful thick forests overhanging both banks. Check with the locals on how far you can go, as the river is rapidly filling with silt. Head back downstream along the northern bank, visiting several ports, among them Lepihue, a station on the old road to Osorno, and turn North into the estuary of the Quenuil river, where the forests give way to sandy banks on the sea coast. Here is the country's largest natural field of choros zapato, a large edible mussel-like mollusk typically found in Southern Chile. There are several fish farms as well. It is dangerous to attempt to sail out to sea through the sand bar when the tide recedes, as the current is too strong. The round trip is 70 km; allow one day.

The Reloncaví Estuary a cruise along a saltwater fjord, sheltered, but with some wind and waves at midday. There is a good concrete boat ramp at Ralún and an excellent hotel with its own port. The road to Ralún is paved. Proceed to Cochamó or head to where the estuary meets Reloncaví sound. The scenery in this area is especially beautiful.

To Lake Todos Los Santos a cruise on the open lake, with wind and waves. There is an earthen boat ramp at Petrohué; no fuel supply, but good accommodations at Peulla, at the far end of the Cayetué arm, and in Petrohué. For safety, it is advisable to hug the coast. Head into the Cayetué arm of the lake, overhung with vegetation, and visit the Vuriloche thermal baths, then continue to Peulla. To return, motor along the northern shore, close to the slopes of Puntiagudo volcano. It is a very beautiful trip, with fantastic views of volcanoes and virtually no signs of human habitation. Together with lake Pirehueico, this lake has no roads around it. The entire cruise is about 125 km long.

HIKING

Hiking is particularly rewarding in this area with so many spots not accessible by boat or road. Some possible routes are presented below:

Along the Puelo River Valley a nike in an area with some settlers but no roads, only paths. **Puelo** is accessible by Cochamó or from Puerto Montt by passenger boat (passage 7 hours). The first leg of the hike takes about three hours, to **Los Gualos** on the Puelo river. A boat brings you in 10 minutes upstream to **El Barraco** (there is a charge for all boat rides; agree on the fare beforhand). You are now at the tip of the **Tagua Tagua** lake. You can row to the other side in about two hours. The next leg proceeds along the eastern bank of the river toward the mouth of the **Manso river** (1 1/2 hours), which is crossed by boat. A 10-hour hike follows to **Llanada Grande,** a village with a police station that has radio communication. From here, continue to the breathtaking lakes lying near the Argentine border, Azul, Blanco, Totoral, Las Rocas

11

and Inferior, all with good fishing. The first is reached after a 4-hour hike. After passing this series of lakes you come to **Segundo Corral,** another village with a police station.

You can return by airplane, as both villages are served by regular flights. It is more interesting, though, to continue to the border (Customs outpost) and cross into Argentina.

Take a trail skirting **lake Puelo** (2 hours) to the far end, where there is a dock, a few houses and public transportation to

EL BOLSON (15 km), a small town but a major tourist center with a sizable hippie population from far and wide. From here there are several daily bus services to Bariloche, enabling you to return to Chile through the Puyehue pass. The entire tour is fascinating, but you be sure to take lots of food with you.

Note Aero Reinarz has flights to Llanada Grande and Segundo Corral, See Services section.

Patagonia Adventures Co (Calle P Hube 418, pho 541944) 92513) offers riding tours and cruises to lake Puelo, the valley and a visit to a glacier. You can contact them to return to Argentina.

From Ralún to Lake Todos Los Santos take the bus to Ralún from Puerto Montt or Puerto Varas. This trail was used by the Jesuit missionaries around 1670 to travel from Castro to the mission they had established at Nahuel Huapi, Argentina. The hike starts by crossing the Petrohué river and following the 14-km path ascending to the pass of **Cabeza de Vaca** (500 m altitude).

From the crest you can see the snowy top of the Yates volcano at the end of the estuary to the South, and Cayutué fjord with Puntiagudo volcano for a backdrop. The path descending to the edge of the lake is 12 km long and skirts pretty **lake Cayutué**, with good fishing and overhung with jungle. A cart trail leads from there to the lake below

(6 km). There are few houses. To reach Petrohué, walk to the mouth of the Cayutué inlet and arrange with a local to take you in his boat to the path of the ships sailing to Peulla at 1100h and returning from there around 1630h. Take enough food; here you will only find honey and cheese. The total stretch is 25 km; allow at least two days.

To the Cerro Tronador Glacier the trail starts from Casa Pangue, 5 km out of Peulla on the road to Argentina. There is daily bus service from Peulla passing by the glacier; you can also rent horses at Hostería Peulla. From **Casa Pangue**, it is a 13-km round trip to the **glacier,** following the Peulla river valley.

This is one of the most beautiful hikes in the lake Todos Los Santos area. The mountain, visible along the entire path, has three snow-capped peaks resting on a platform which ends on a cliff; below is a slope where the glaciers start. The mountain is called **Tronador** («Thunderer») because its upper reaches are constantly -and noisily shedding chunks of rocks and ice, particularly right before a change in the weather. Do not attempt to walk on the glacier's ice: the cracks and crevices are dangerous.

11

Zone 12
INSULAR CHILOE

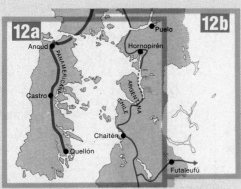

12a

Puelo

Ancud

Hornopirén

PANAMERICANA

Castro

ARGENTINA

CHILE

Chaitén

Quellón

Futaleufú

12b

DETAILED MAPS

Arica

Iquique

Antofagasta

Copiapó

Easter
Island

La Serena

Valparaíso

SANTIAGO

Is R
Crusoe

Talca

Concepción

Temuco

Valdivia

Osorno

Pto Montt

Castro
Chaitén

Coihaique

Cochrane

12

Puerto Natales

Punta Arenas

Puerto Williams

Is Diego
Ramirez

90°   60°   53°

CHILEAN
ANTARCTIC
TERRITORY

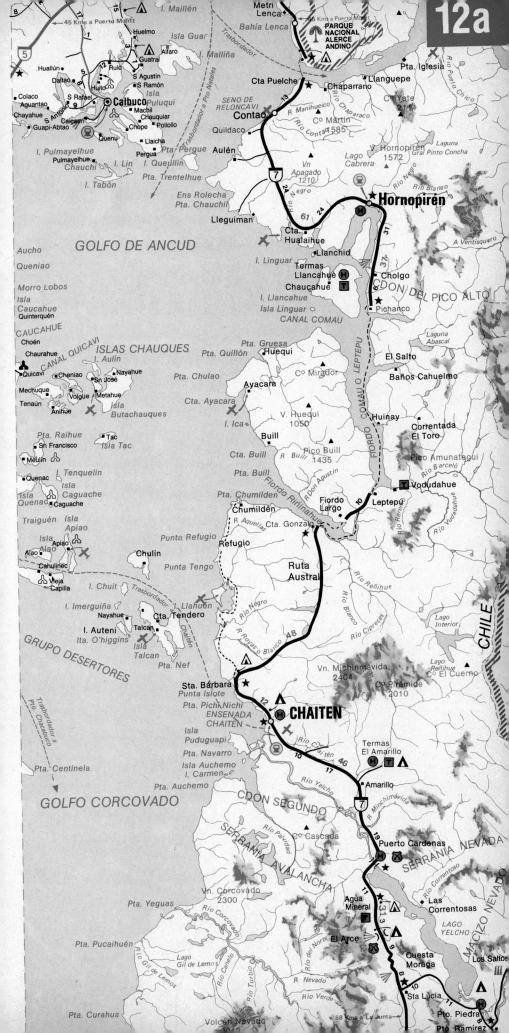

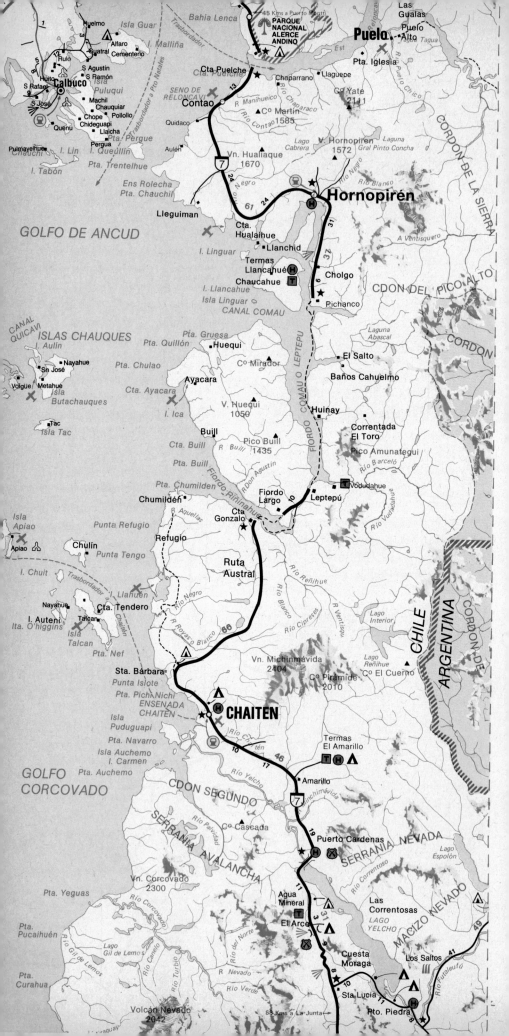

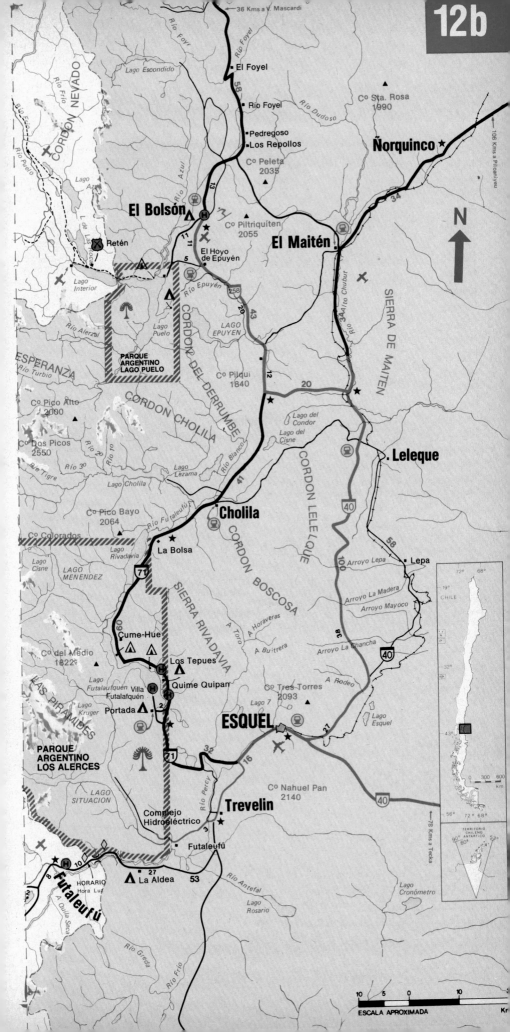

← 36 Kms a V. Mascardi

CORDON NEVADO

Río Frío

Río Foyf

Río Foyel

Lago Escondido

■ El Foyel

58

■ Río Foyel

Río Foyel

Río Dudoso

Cº Sta. Rosa
1990 ▲

● Pedregoso
● Los Repollos

Cº Peleta
2035 ▲

Ñorquinco ★

106 Kms a Pilcaniyeu →

Lago
Azul

13

Río Azul

El Bolsón △ Ⓗ

Cº Piltriquitén
2055 ▲

El Maitén

34

N

✕ Retén

11

11

El Hoyo
de Epuyén

5

△

258

Río Epuyén

20

43

34 Alto Chubut

Río Alto Chubut

SIERRA DE MAITÉN

Lago
Interior

Lago
Puelo

**PARQUE
ARGENTINO
LAGO PUELO**

CORDON DEL DERRUMBE

Río Alerzal

LAGO
EPUYEN

12

20

★

★

Lago del
Condor

ESPERANZA

Río Turbio

CORDON CHOLILA

Cº Pilqui
1840

Lago del
Cisne

Cº Pico Alto
2000 ▲

Río 1º

Cº Dos Picos
2550

Río 2º

Río 3º

Río Tigre

Lago
Lezama

Río Blanco

41

Lago
Cholila

Lago Cholila

CORDON LELELQUE

Leleque

40

58

Cº Pico Bayo
2064 ▲

Río Futaleufú

Cholila

CORDON BOSCOSA

100

Arroyo Lepa

Cº Colorados

Lago
Rivadavia

★ La Bolsa

● Lepa

Lago
Cisne

LAGO
MENENDEZ

71

SIERRA RIVADAVIA

Arroyo La Madera

Arroyo Mayoco

A Horaveras

A Toro

A Horaveras

38

40

660

Cume-Hue △△△

Los Tepues △

A Bu trera

Arroyo La Chancha

Cº del Medio
1822 ▲

Ⓗ

△

Lago
Futalaufquén

Villa
Futalafquén

Quime Quipan

A Rodeo

Cº Tres Torres
2093 ▲

LAS PIRAMIDES

Ⓗ

2

Lago 7

ESQUEL

Lago Kruger

Portada △

27

**PARQUE
ARGENTINO
LOS ALERCES**

71

32

16

Lago
Esquel

LAGO
SITUACION

Río Percy

Cº Nahuel Pan
2140

40

← 78 Kms a Tecka

Complejo
Hidroeléctrico

Trevelin

3

★

■ Futaleufú

Ⓗ 10

★

27

Futaleufú

8

HORARIO
Hora Luz

△ La Aldea

53

Río Antefal

Lago
Cronómetro

A Quila Seca

Río Greda

Río Frío

Lago
Rosario

CHILE
72° 68°

19°

32°

43°

300 600
km

56° 72° 68°

TERRITORIO
CHILENO
ANTARTICO

90° 0°

60°

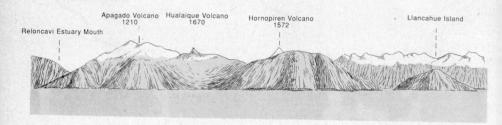

Andes Mountains, as seen from the islands

Reloncavi Estuary Mouth

Apagado Volcano
1210

Hualaique Volcano
1670

Hornopiren Volcano
1572

Llancahue Island

OVERVIEW

This zone includes the island of Chiloé, the archipelago lying east of it and the mainland coast from the Comau to the Reñihue fjords.

Topographically, this area is quite different from the Chilean mainland north of Puerto Montt, which is characterized by the Andes and the Coastal ranges marching parallel north to south and the Central Valley running lengthwise between the two. Here, the Central Valley is flooded by the sea, the tops of the submerged Coastal Range becoming a maze of islands, while the Andes sink their feet in the ocean.

Chiloé was conquered by the Spaniards in 1567 and remained an isolated outpost until 1853, when Puerto Montt was founded. During these three centuries, a distinctive culture developed on the basis of racial mingling (Spanish–Mapuche) and an all–pervading influence of sea and religion.

We have divided this zone into four sections, namely:

Section A Ancud the northern portion of the island, where influence from the mainland has been strongest.

Section B Castro the historical heart of the island, with abundant testimonies of its past.

Section C Quellón the southern portion of the island, with areas only recently colonized.

Section D The Archipelago covering the inner islands and the mainland coast.

12 REGIONAL DISTANCE

Achao													
99	Ancud												
45	88	Castro											
103	146	58	Cucao										
126	27	115	173	Chacao									
92	37	81	139	64	Chepu								
25	74	20	78	101	67	Dalcahue							
109	37	125	183	25	74	84	Linao						
75	118	30	46	145	111	50	155	Puqueldon					
111	154	66	80	181	147	86	191	56	Queilén				
144	187	99	109	214	180	119	224	89	121	Quellón			
85	68	74	132	52	61	60	27	104	140	173	Quemchi		
52	103	27	85	130	96	27	111	57	93	126	87	Rilán	
65	99	60	118	83	92	40	58	90	126	159	31	67	Tenaún

Zone 12
CHILOE

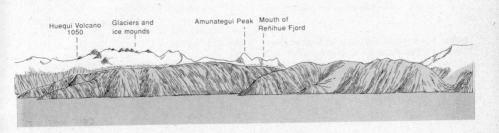

Huequi Volcano 1050 · Glaciers and ice mounds · Amunategui Peak · Mouth of Reñihue Fjord

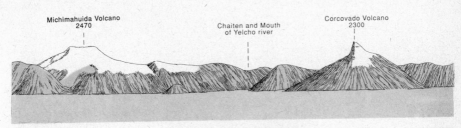

Michimahuida Volcano 2470 · Chaiten and Mouth of Yelcho river · Corcovado Volcano 2300

DIVISION BY SECTIONS

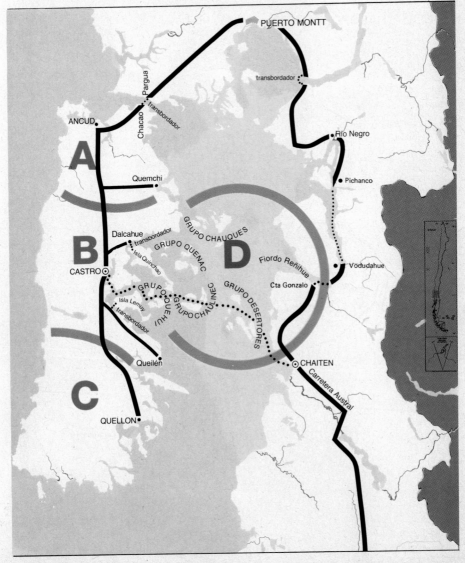

MOVING AROUND IN CHILOE

Access is by car ferry from Pargua to Chacao, or from Chaitén to Chonchi. Many roads branch off the Pan–American highway, most heading east –ie, to the inland sea– and only three to the Pacific coast: Cucao, Chepu and Guabún. The Pan–American highway is mostly paved, but watch out for treacherous bumps and hollows. The rest is gravel –usually loose: **take curves and gradients carefully.**

Ferries run between Pargua and Chacao every 20 minutes. There are ferries also from Dalcahue to Quinchao island and from the vicinity of Chonchi to Lemuy island. Ferries to the mainland, departures from different ports, see description in shipping services in the Services section.

Bus Services link Santiago and Castro, and there are several daily departures to/from Puerto Montt. Rural bus services are abundant, linking Ancud and Castro with every town and village. The earliest batch of departures occurs between 07:30 h and 08:00 h; the second, 10:30–11:00 h; third, 16:30–18:00 h. Departures after 19:00 h are rare.

Passenger Boats ply the waters from Tenaún to the Butachauques island group; from Achao to the Quenac, Apiao and Chaulinec groups; from Castro to Chelín and Quehui, and from Quellón to the adjacent islands.

Cargo Boats have Castro as their main port; sometimes they take passengers. They cover the route to the Desertores islands, and to the mainland (Río Negro –Hornopirén–, Caleta Buill, and Chaitén).

BUS DEPARTURE FRECUENCY

More than 8 departures daily

5-8 departures daily

3-4 departures daily

1-2 departures daily

SHIPPING SERVICES

----D---- departures daily

----S---- 2-3 weekly departures

AIRPLANES

Charter Services

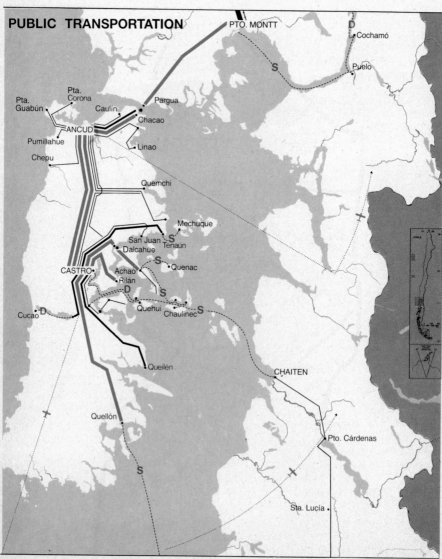

PUBLIC TRANSPORTATION

THE LAND, ITS HISTORY, ITS PEOPLE

MORPHOLOGY this zone has been shaped by two great phenomena, namely tectonic movements and the last Ice Age. The collision between the Nazca and the South American plates, apart from building the mountain ranges, has given rise to large faults gashing the mainland at 45° angles from the meridian, producing the Reloncaví, Comau and Reñihue fjords, and the lake Yelcho valley. The pressure building up at the plate collision front has given rise to strings of volcanoes, such as the Hornopirén, Huequi, Michimahuida, and Corcovado, all lying along a nearly straight line. The other factor was the ice age. The pressure exerted by the giant ice-caps as they crept along the faults provoked a colossal erosion of the central valley, which eventually became flooded by sea water; it also broke the continuity of the Coastal Range. Thus, the submerged Coastal Range became the **Chiloé archipelago**, the Central Valley an **inland sea**, and the **Cordillera de los Andes** a fiord-gashed range tumbling directly to the sea.

DESCRIPTION the main island in the archipelago is the Isla Grande de Chiloé, South America's second largest after Tierra del Fuego, with some 180 km in length and covering almost 10,000 square kilometers. The Coastal range marches along its entire length, but is traversed crosswise by a sort of fissure where lakes Huillinco and Cucao are located. The northern mountains are known as Pichué and the southern ones as Pirulil. This range has no peaks exceeding 1,000 m, and consists mostly of rounded mountains. Nevertheless, it does block the moist winds blowing in from the Pacific, thus helping to create a microclimate in the island's eastern coast.

The inland sea islands are relatively flat, arranged in groups and separated from one another by beautiful channels. The groups are Chauques, Quenac, Quehui, Chaulinec and Desertores.

CLIMATE the island presents two distinct climates: the **Pacific coast** climate, with humid winds blowing permanently and very high rainfall; vegetation, consequently, is lush. The **inland sea**, sheltered by the Coastal Range, has a microclimate with less rainfall than Valdivia, but frequent overcasts.

TIDES the difference in tide levels varies greatly in this area, even along the same latitude. At Cucao, on the Pacific, the difference between high and low tide is 2.5 m, while at Quemchi, on the inland sea, it is 7 m. This is due to the fact that the water flows into the inland sea through the Corcovado gulf and the Chacao channel, having to cover long distances over shallow areas, thus increasing the water level difference. This also gives rise to considerable water disturbances in the areas where the two currents meet, making them hazardous for small boats.

Twice a day, the low tide leaves vast stretches of uncovered tideland behind, trapping fishes and other sea animals. This has had a certain influence on Chiloé's cultural development since the earliest times.

ORIGINAL INHABITANTS the Spanish conquerors found native Indians living on Chiloé's eastern coast area and on the Chacao channel shores. Chiloé's southern coast and the mainland portion of this zone were uninhabited. The natives were a mixture of **Mapuches** pushing down from the north, and **Chonos**, the original inhabitants who were elbowed out by the Mapuches, eventually moving to the Aysén archipelago. Communication was on foot through the beaches during low tide, or sailing by canoe or **dalca** (see below). Topographic features and sailing difficulties kept the coastal dwellers

separated into five groups: 1. Calbuco archipelago; 2. Chacao channel from the Pacific to cape Tres Cruces, where huge maelstroms and strong currents prevented communication by boat; 3. Cape Tres Cruces to cape Tenaún; 4. Tenaún to Chonchi, including the Castro archipelago; and 5. the land of the Payos, from Chonchi to the Chaihuao shallows, south of Queilén, an area feared by both Spanish and aboriginal seamen. Further south there was no human presence.

The natives dwelled in straw huts near the beaches or forests, without forming villages. Their family clans –**caví** or **cabí**– were ruled by a chieftain and included up to 400 people. Seven or eight **cavis** made up a **levo** or tribe, which acted as a political unit. The main difference with the Mapuches dwelling at the Biobío zone was that the Chiloé ones were monogamous and sedentary. They cultivated potatoes –an indigenous plant–, maize and quínoa (a type of goosefoot). They were great craftsmen with llama wool, spinning it into yarn and producing knitted garments.

Their farming tools were all made of wood, and they fenced their crops with cane or branches intertwined in basketwork fashion. They also fished and gathered shellfish. Skillful seamen, they sailed in **dalcas**, a boat made of boiled wooden planks denoting a refined technique. Dalcas are thought to be a cultural contribution from the Chono people.

Population the first estimate of Chiloé's native population was made by the Jesuits in 1609, with between 10 thousand and 12 thousand people. However, this census was taken after the terrible smallpox and measles epidemics which had swept Chile in 1561 and 1580, respectively. In 1633 the native population was once more decimated, one third being wiped out by a typhoid fever epidemic. In 1657 and 1696, two smallpox epidemics nearly finished off the natives. Censuses taken by the religious missions found, from 1734 to 1788, a native population fluctuating between 9,400 and 11,600 inhabitants. Charles Darwin, in 1838, mentioned 11,000 people bearing Mapuche names. In 1935, a regional historian stated that in Chiloé there was no Mapuche-speaking population. The Spanish population, by contrast, had climbed from 200 in 1600 to 10,627 in 1774 (including mestizos, ie, those of mixed parentage); to 31,000 in 1832, and to 91,000 by 1900.

The Mapuche people, by mingling their genes with those of the Spanish conquerors, gave birth to the Chilotes, ie, the people of Chiloé.

Chonos are now extinct. They dwelled in the area from the Guaitecas archipelago to the Ofqui isthmus, pushed south by the invading Mapuches. The Jesuit missionaries moved in 1700 up to 300 Chono families from Aisén to the Guar island, north of Calbuco, and eight years later they moved them again to the uninhabited islands of Chaulinec and Apiao, from where they used to sail around the archipelago to trade with the natives living there. The chonos, thanks to their remarkable skills as navigators, became indispensable guides for the Spanish expeditions to the southern islands.

Caucahues like the Chonos, spoke a different language from that of the Mapuches. They dwelled on the mainland coast south of the Golfo de Penas and were discovered by Jesuit missionaries in the 1620 southern expedition. In 1743 they moved some of them to the Cailín island, of the Chiloé group, where the missionaries set up a reservation dubbed «the world's remotest corner of Christianity». In 1752 the natives numbered 200, but by the turn of the following century the mission was abandoned and the Caucahues were brought to

12

Chaulinec, where they intermingled with the locals.

SPANISH COLONIZATION Chiloé was first sighted in 1540 by navigator Alfonso de Camargo, and properly discovered in 1553 by Francisco de Ulloa. Five years later, a Spanish party –which included poet Alonso de Ercilla– crossed the Chacao channel. In 1567 Martín Ruiz de Gamboa took possession of the islands, christening them Nueva Galicia, and founded **Santiago de Castro** on February 12. The occupation of Chiloé was a natural step in the policy of expanding south started by Pedro de Valdivia.

The Early Years the conquerors, who numbered some 200 by 1600, divided among themselves all the inhabited lands and subjected the adult natives to a serfdom system known as encomienda. It consisted of unpaid labor which the natives performed as a «tribute» to the king of Spain. This enabled the Spaniards to exploit the gold-bearing sands of Cucao, produce woollen goods and log the alerce forests, exporting their output to Lima. The success of the Chiloé encomienda resulted from the natives' meekness and submissiveness, expressly acclaimed by chroniclers from the very beginning. This auspicious start soon soured, however, with the 1598 uprising of the mainland Mapuches –started with a decisive victory at Curalaba–, which eventually led to the destruction and deserting of the seven Spanish towns between the Biobío river and Chacao. This area was not to be regained by the Spaniards until two and a half centuries later. This development left the Chiloé settlements totally cut off from the rest of Spanish Chile and from the trading routes.

The survivors of the destruction of Osorno fled to Chiloé and settled in 1602 at **Carelmapu** and **Calbuco**. In 1600 and 1643, the island was visited by Dutch pirates; the first one, Baltazar de Cordes, occupied Castro for two months, while his colleague Henriek Brower burned Castro and Carelmapu.

A ship from Lima called once a year, but periods of three or more years could go by without any contact with the outside world. Some barter was performed when the ship called, the outgoing products being blankets, woven and knitted goods, timber, ham, fat, and carved wooden trunks; these were acquired at dirt-low prices, while the prices for the products imported by Chiloé were outrageously high.

Poverty was extreme, prompting many Spaniards to emigrate. In 1646, after a violent earthquake shook the island, the Spanish inhabitants requested official permission to desert the island. They were turned down, as Chiloé was then a major supplier of fat and timber for Lima.

Chiloé lay totally outside the economic and social developments taking place in Central Chile during the 17th and 18th centuries.

Internal Development during the 17th and 18th centuries, the chilotes became socially and racially consolidated. The Spanish population settled in the countryside and the islands, with intensive racial intermingling with the native Mapuches. Everyone wore the same type of garments, and everyone owned patches of land farmed for subsistence. It was a pretty stable, egalitarian society.

The political center was Castro, although it was nearly deserted most of the time, people coming only for religious festivities. The military authority had its seat at Chacao, where the ship from Lima called once a year, turning the place then into a lively market town. Calbuco and Carelmapu were defensive outposts which livened up only in summer, during the alerce felling season.

The Jesuit Order played a preponderant role in the religious and cultural spheres, preaching the Gospel among the natives, setting up schools and teaching them how to build churches and mills, and introducing land cultivation techniques used to this day. The feeling of being the world's most southerly human settlement pervaded life at the island, and provided a justification for the colossal missionary efforts of the Jesuits: for them, the Cailín mission embodied the southernmost Christian outpost in the world. For the Spanish Crown, Chiloé served to protect its possessions in South America's southern tip. For this reason, every year small military and religious expeditions would set out from Castro through the pampas towards the Atlantic, and south to the Strait of Magellan.

Chiloé played this strategic role well into Chile's independence from Spain: the expedition to take possession of the Strait of Magellan for Chile was organized and set out from Ancud in 1843.

The Reincorporation british expansionism threatened the southern Pacific possessions by the mid-18th century. Spain reacted by strengthening its fortress at Valdivia and building a fort at Ancud. In 1767 Chiloé became directly subordinated to the Viceroy of Peru. The population at Chacao was moved to the new stronghold at Ancud, which became the island's political and military capital. A road was opened through the jungle from **Ancud** to Castro in 1781, in order to give territorial continuity to this outpost. It was followed seven years later by another road from Valdivia to Carelmapu. Ancud became also a port of call for the merchant ships coming from Europe through the Strait of Magellan.

INDEPENDENCE curiously enough, despite long years of neglect by the Crown, Chiloé was the only part of Chile that remained loyal to the Spanish king. In fact, the first Chilean attempt at independence was defeated by a royalist expedition organized in and launched from Chiloé by admiral Pareja, with one fifth of Chiloé's male population taking part in it. Few places in the Americas did so much to protect the King's possessions during the struggle for independence. In 1817 the Spanish general Antonio Quintanilla took command of the archipelago and organized its defense, repelling the attack of Lord Cochrane's forces in 1820, and of Freire's in 1824. Only in 1826 (eight years after Chile's independence) the island was wrestled free from Spain. Freire defeated the Spanish forces, and the last Spanish flag flying in South America was finally struck in Ancud.

Trade opening to the trade routes after Independence brought considerable benefits to the archipelago, which became the main supply center for the whalers plying the southern Pacific waters. From the mid-18th century to the turn of the 19th century, Chiloé was the prime supplier of sleepers for railway lines being built throughout the continent, Ancud being the main shipping port. This spurred the establishment of the present villages – Quellón, Dalcahue, Chonchi and Quemchi, among others– at sites where previously only a chapel was to be seen. The new settlements were engaged in logging, food production, livestock farming, and shipping.

Inland Settlements up until the end of the colonial period, only the coastal areas were settled. The boom in livestock farming late last century finally prompted the clearing of areas inland from Chonchi and Dalcahue. This process was encouraged also by the granting of tracts of land to German, British, French and Spanish immigrants in 1895, inland from Chacao and Quetaimahue. With the construction of the Ancud–Castro railway (1912), inland areas also became available for colonization.

The entire territory south of the Cucao lake was granted under concession in 1905 to a company engaged in alcohol production, based at Quellón. Those lands now belong to two large private farms. The only state lands in the Isla Grande de Chiloé are those within the Chiloé National Park.

12

The mainland coastal area, in turn, was wholly state–owned at the turn of the century. The first people coming there were engaged in alerce logging, with facilities on the coast and even modern steam–powered sawmills at Caleta Buill and Refugio. Later, livestock farmers from Chiloé brought cattle to the Chaitén and Yelcho valleys. Stable settlements evolved naturally from these first outposts.

Population and Emigration the islanders had traditionally boasted a high birth rate. However, the last censuses have shown nil population growth, or even a decrease. This results from emigration spurred by poverty in the countryside, stemming in turn from lack of markets for their main product, potatoes. Emigration has historically been high, Chiloé natives being found from the saltpeter mines in the north, to the Argentine and Magellanic pampa sheep farms in the south, as sailors, laborers in the colonization of Llanquihue and the Araucanía, and lastly as settlers in mainland Chiloé.

The Chiloé laborer is hard working, austere and devout. Chiloé emigrants are estimated to double the number of people still living in the islands. However, they keep strong ties to their home villages.

Religion and Education the chilotes are profoundly religious. Community organizations are actively engaged in keeping the faith alive and maintaining the island's numerous churches. Education used to be imparted at schools administered by community organizations. This effort by the islanders to preserve their religion and culture in absence of state support led to the more than 150 churches existing today, and the much larger number of schools, to be found even at the remotest corners. As a result, this archipelago was and still is the area with the lowest illiteracy rate in Chile. In the island's society, priesthood and teaching have always been held in greatest esteem; hundreds of islanders have become teachers and priests, most of them working in the rest of Chile.

RELIGIOUS MISSIONS uring the early years, missionary work in Chiloé was performed by members of the Merced Order and by Franciscans. In 1608 the first Jesuits arrived, and four years later they set up a Residency in Castro to preach the Gospel to the natives. They were so successful in the following 160 years, that religiousness is now one of the most deeply ingrained traits of the Chiloé culture. (In 1767 the Jesuits were expelled from the entire continent; at the time, there were 12 of them at Chiloé, their southernmost outpost in the world.)

The few missionaries from Chiloé set out to preach the Gospel north as far as Osorno, east to the Argentine pampas, and south to the tribes near the Strait of Magellan. This impressive deployment was carried out by foot or on fragile canoes sailing through stormy seas. Proudly, they would one day write: «Sparing was Nature in Chiloé, but liberal in bestowing grace... In its natural paucity, it achieved the excellence of being a Garden of the Church».

Missionary Method Employed in Chiloé to cope with their apostolic mission in a place of difficult geography and scattered population, the Jesuits took a three–pronged approach: they trained natives as catechists -known as **fiscales**-; they built chapels at every cabí; and, lastly, they performed annual visits to each chapel on a cycle known as **circulating mission**.

The fiscales were authorized as an institution in 1621. The natives so appointed were relieved from the serfdom of the encomiendas and could not be moved away from their place of residence. The fiscal had to teach the doctrine, pray for the rest of his community and see to it that the prayers and songs were not forgotten. The fiscales had a

Dalcahue

Chonchi

Curaco de Vélez

Chonchi

Chonchi

Curaco de Vélez

12

Curaco de Vélez

hierarchy based on seniority, and each fiscal was assigned a group of fifty people. The institution received official recognition in 1763 and was given rules and regulations in 1862 by the bishop of Ancud. Today, every community has a fiscal, who traditionally keeps the keys to the chapel.

The Chapels the Jesuits prompted the provincial government to issue orders for the encomenderos to build chapels for the natives. In 1717, there were 69 communities having a chapel; by 1767, they were 79. Now they are over 150 in this area; some of the chapels now existing date from the earliest

period.

The Circulating Mission was a circuit by sea visiting every single community in Chiloé once a year, rigorously following a preset itinerary. Every 17 of September, two missionaries sailed from Castro, carrying with them their sacred vestments and three portable altars, the latter acting as well as luggage boxes: they contained a statue of Christ, to be born during the processions by the chieftains; a Holy Heart to be carried by children; a statue of St John to be born by unmarried men and one of St Isidro to be born by those married; a statue of «Our

SOME OF CHILOE'S CHURCHES AND CHAPELS

Drawn to same scale   ✷ National Monument

✷ Quinchao   Quehui   ✷ Quilquico

✷ Chonchi   ✷ Dalcahue   Aldachildo

Huyar   Apiao   Detif

12

Lady of Pains» to be born by unmarried women, and one of St Notburga to be carried by married women. All of this was loaded on two canoes which set out to call at each coastal community, and would return to Castro by early winter.

At each stop, the same ritual was performed. From the beach, the missionaries and the locals would walk in a singing procession to the church, where they would set up the three altars. Then, they read the registry book, with the life and deeds of the parishioners, to round up the day with a sermon and a rosary. The following day started with edifying readings, weddings, baptisms, and more sermons. The main act of the day was confession and penitence. On the third day, a penitential procession was performed, and then a mass and communion, to board the canoes coming to pick the missionaries up from the next port of call.

At each chapel they stayed three days, but every five or six stops, they would stay longer, 4 to 5 days, to stage large penitential processions with attendance from all the neighboring chapel communities.

Missions, Residences, Reservations the mission-

* Villipulli

* Achao

* Rilán

Chelin

* Nercon

* Tenaún

12

Quetalco

Quicaví

Dibujo a igual escala

Llau Llao

* Indica Monumento Nacional

ary area of the Chiloé Jesuits stretched from Osorno in the north to the Atlantic in the east, and to the Strait of Magellan in the south. They once ventured inland from Osorno, but were repelled by the Mapuches. Then they set out to carry their mission at the Argentine pampas, from 1670 to 1718; they discontinued this effort after several missionaries had been tortured and killed. Permanent visits were made to the islands lying towards the Strait of Magellan.

Their main **residence** was in Castro. Later, they established residences in Chequián (1717), south of the Quinchao island, and at Queilén (1743). These two were replaced by the residences of Achao and Chonchi, in 1743 and 1754, respectively, with churches surviving to this day. The Chono and Caucahue natives, in turn, were moved to **reservations**. The Chono reservation was at Guar island, north of Calbuco, but was later moved to Apiao and Chaulinec. The Caucahues, in turn, were moved to the Cailín island, south of Quellón.

Franciscan Missionary Work after the expulsion of Jesuits from the American continent in 1767, the native population of Chiloé was deprived of religious guidance. The void was filled by the Franciscan Order in 1771, with 15 priests from the Colegio de Ocopa, Peru. They settled at various points throughout the archipelago, and carried on the work started 160 years before. Many churches bear witness to their efforts, which continue to this day.

RELIGIOUS ARCHITECTURE nine of the 150 churches have been granted a National Monument status, namely those of **Achao, Chonchi, Quilquico, Quinchao,** and **Villipulli,** built in the second half of the 18th century; **Dalcahue** and **Nercón,** in the early 19th century; **Rilán,** built in the late 19th century; and **San Francisco de Castro,** erected at the turn of this century. Built totally of wood –the earliest ones used wooden pegs instead of nails–, they share a place in the history of church architecture with all-wood churches in the US, Germany and Scandinavia dating from the 18th century. Apart from their individual attractiveness, their abundance is striking: they are rarely more than ten km apart from one another. The missionaries, rather than being content with mere religious architecture, strove for the creation of **religious urbanism,** to transform the

archipelago into what they called the «Garden of the Church». They first set out to urbanize the areas near the coast on the inland sea, the main medium for transportation and one of the axis around which life rotated at the archipelago. These churches are not topography–related in the manner of a castle or a lighthouse, which tower above the surrounding terrain and dominate the landscape. They are located almost at water level and do not make for a «skyline». They are rather an ornament in this «Garden of the Church».

Church Archetype a formal archetype was abided by over several centuries, but now it is disappearing; the new churches have few or none of the early elements. The two main features of the archetype were an esplanade and the church itself. By the mid–19th century the cemetery became a third element, although without a well defined position with respect to the other two. Another addition was the casemita, a house for the travelling missionary which is still to be seen in some chapels.

The Esplanade was a long open space somewhat wider than the church, where the penitential processions were held, as well as other ceremonies related to the visit of the circulating mission. This esplanade became the main square of villages and towns growing around the church.

The Church is a rectangle made up of two sections joined together: a vertical volume including the portico, the choir loft above it, and the bell tower; and the horizontal volume, containing the nave.

The Portico stretched across the whole width of the church, and faced the esplanade; from there, the missionary addressed the parishioners. Three doors led to the nave. The choir loft was above the portico, overlooking the main nave; choir music played a vital part in the liturgy. Above the choir started the bell tower, usually a square box crowned by an octagonal cylinder tapering into a cross.

The Nave is divided into three spaces separated by rows of pillars. The lateral naves had a flat ceiling, while the central one was vaulted. In some churches, the roof continues outside beyond the wall edge to the ground, providing shelter for overnight stays of the parishioners during the missionary visits.

Architectural Styles the oldest church is the one

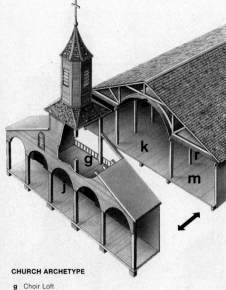

CHURCH ARCHETYPE

- **g** Choir Loft
- **j** Atrium
- **k** Central Nave
- **m** Lateral Nave
- **r** Flat Ceiling
- **s** Vaulted Ceiling

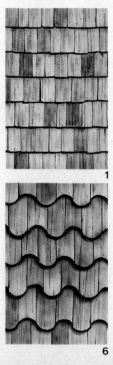

1

6

12

at Achao, contemporary of the one at Quilquico. The earlier churches show a strong influence of German religious buildings; at the time, the missionary work in Chiloé was being carried out by Bavarian Jesuits, among them fathers Fried, Hubert, Strasse, and Mayer.

The 18th century's neoclassical style, which in many cases was implanted on old churches, such as at Chonchi, introduced several new elements, among them a triangular design on the façade and a flattening of the arcades, such as at Tenaún.

CIVILIAN ARCHITECTURE the chroniclers of the time (ca 1770) described civilian construction thus: «The houses of Castro and Chacao, and those in the countryside, are all of wood and, save for a few having wooden roofs, all have thatched roofs». Thatched roofs, providing excellent insulation and protection against rain, are deeply embedded in Mapuche tradition; some interesting samples can be seen in the islands of Quinchao and Lemuy.

The buildings we show on these pages date all from the turn of this century. Built on the seaport villages most engaged in trading, they reflect the international architectural tastes of the time, with a strong Northern European influence.

The **palafitos**, houses built on stilts over the water, are not an architectural style created in Chiloé. They were adopted at Ancud, Quemchi, Castro, Chonchi and some other ports to make a fuller use of the seafront area, during the period of intense trading activity last century. Today only a few samples survive in Castro.

Among the features that are more particularly chilote is a tendency to break the façade volume with balconies or other protruding elements. The most typical of all, however, are the shingled outer surfaces. Shingles –known here as tejuelas– are arranged into almost filigree patterns, and are inspired upon the ancestral textile weaving craftsmanship of the chilotes.

SHINGLES or tejuelas deserve a special mention. Rarely used during the colonial period, they were later introduced by German settlers in the area of Llanquihue and Puerto Montt, who used them profusely in their buildings. The tejuela is a thin, long, narrow piece of alerce wood laid with others in a series of overlapping rows as a covering for roofs and walls. Alerce, in turn, is an extremely durable

wood, impermeable even without any kind of coating or impregnation. The visible part of the tejuela is about one third of its total length, and the different shapes into which the visible end is cut give rise to patterns once they are laid into rows. Formerly, they used to be 90 cm long, 15 cm wide and 1 cm thick. Now they are smaller, ca 50 x 12 x 1 cm. The most common patterns are (see illustration above):

1 Straight Cut this is the most elemental cut, used in modest constructions or on secondary walls of important buildings.

2 Polygonal Cut a classical cut used at Puerto Montt and Pelluco.

3 Round Cut very common, used on the Dalcahue church.

4 Convex Cut a round cut leaving a small straight portion at the tip; used at the Dalcahue parish house.

5 & 6 Concave–Convex Cut a single cut provides the two ends; a beautiful pattern is created by alternating the shingles. The best samples are at Curaco de Vélez.

7 & 8 Alternated Cut combining straight and polygonal or round cuts, very frequent in present–day constructions. Found at Castro and Ancud.

9 Bevelled Cut the most difficult cut, as it entails using a plane to bevel the edge. Found exclusively at the Quinchao island.

10 Triangular Cut used on the coast from Quetalco to Tenaún.

HANDICRAFTS Chiloé handicrafts are very good value both in price and craftsmanship. Many goods in daily usage are still made by hand: textiles and wicker baskets, for example, are woven by thousands of anonymous hands in the countryside. Tejuelas are also hand–made, as well as the wooden boat frames. Many utensils are still made of stone. The handicrafts on offer at the markets are acquired equally by islanders and tourists. The largest such market is at **Angelmó**, in Puerto Montt, but the Sunday–morning market at **Dalcahue** includes mostly the producers offering their wares directly to the public. The **markets** at Ancud, Castro, and Achao have a large variety of items at good prices.

Textiles a traditional home industry since colonial times, its main products are woollen blankets and

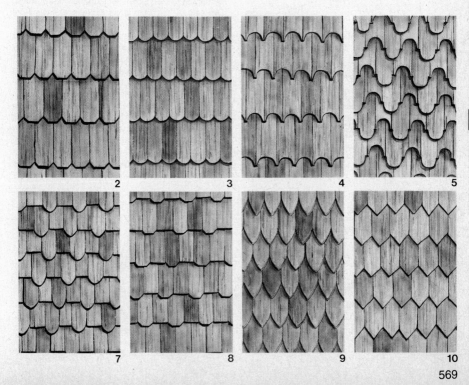

2   3   4   5

12

7   8   9   10

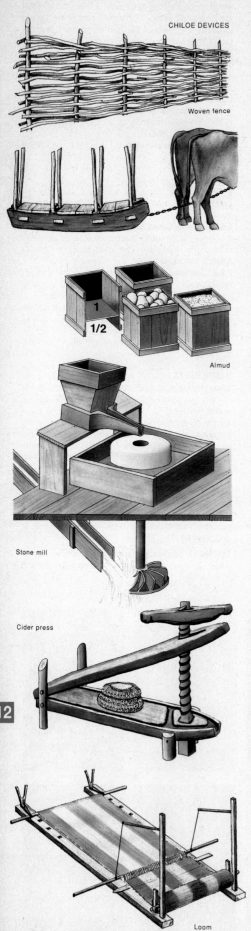

CHILOE DEVICES

Woven fence

Almud

Stone mill

Cider press

Loom

socks, and knitted cardigans, coats and caps, using hand–spun sheep wool, not too twisted to permit it to be highly flexible. The patterns consist mostly of ocher and gray stripes, using natural dyes, in addition to other stripes made with aniline–dyes. The main producing area is known as the «wool belt», stretching from Castro through Dalcahue, and to the far end of Quinchao island. Best bargains are when you buy directly from the producer.

Basketry baskets are woven using a variety of vegetal fibers. The range of products is large, including baskets, shopping bags («meshes»), ornaments and utensils. The main producing center is the island of Lingua, opposite Achao. The main fibers used are:

Quilineja a vine with a thin, strong, reddish stem, widely used in the past for weaving the most delicate baskets. Difficult to master, this fiber is not used anymore. Fine samples of it can be seen in museums.

Boqui a climber with a strong fiber, used for heavy–duty baskets and ropes.

Ñocha a plant growing at the edge of ponds, up to one meter tall, with a thin, flexible stalk. Twisted into braids, it can be used to weave meshes formed into sacks –for potatoes or shellfish, for example– and bags, including the ubiquitous pirgua, the housewife shopping bag.

Quiscal the most widely used fiber nowadays, obtained from a plant with wide, long leaves whose fruit is known as chupón. The whitish fiber is wrapped around long, thin ñocha cords, which are then rolled in a spiral to form the basket.

Cancahua is a type of sandstone found only at Ahuí, a peninsula opposite Ancud, which is carved into fireplaces, ovens and braziers used throughout Chiloé.

CHILOE CONTRIVANCES the almost total absence of metals and the abundance of natural forests were the two driving forces behind some very ingenious Chiloé tools or devices. The Museo Chilote in Puerto Montt has very interesting exhibits of these contrivances, including a wooden door lock and a wooden sacho anchor (see below). The devices we show in this page are all still widely used.

Woven Fences using rods of arrayán, a common shrub of flexible wood and thin bark, twisted among poles of luma, an extremely hard wood. Devised by the Mapuches to keep animals from walking into cultivated fields.

Birloche is a wooden sled pulled by oxen, used for hauling all kinds of bulk cargo on mud, sand or stones. Still widely used in the islands.

Almud is a small wooden crate or box used in all Chilote markets as a container and display device for grains, potatoes, carrots, onions, shellfish, etc. It is also a measure of volume, the oddity being that on one side it holds one almud –some eight liters– and on the opposite side (turning it upside down) exactly half that volume. It is not wholly Chilote, though: it is original of Spain.

Stone Mill was made entirely of wood, save for the two millstones. Introduced by the Jesuits, some

12

Sacho Anchor

samples can still be seen (see tour from Castro to Dalcahue below). Simple and robust, it consists of a funnel where wheat was poured, falling directly into the center of the millstones, a box where the flour accumulates, and a water–propelled axis providing the necessary rotary motion.

Cider (Chicha) Presses were also made entirely of wood, in order not to alter the color or the taste of the resulting cider. The apples are first beaten with a wooden mallet called dornajo, placed into flexible ñocha baskets and then pressed with the cider press. They can be seen in action in February.

Chilote Loom different from the one used by Mapuches farther north. It is horizontal, anchored on the room's floor, where the weaver works kneeling.

Sachos are boat anchors consisting of a round stone imprisoned by wooden staves, the latter with one end embedded into curving pieces of wood joined into a cross. At the other end, the staves are tied together with a boqui rope. The rope fastening the sacho to the boat was called beta.

SECTION A   ANCUD

This section covers the northern portion of the Isla Grande de Chiloé, from the Chacao channel to Quemchi. Its center is the city of Ancud, where the contrast between Chilote and European culture –the latter brought by immigrants late last century– is still to be seen.

How to Get There the Pan–American highway leads in 87 km (paved) from Puerto Montt to Pargua, where the ferry docks. Ferry departures every 20 minutes, passage time 30 min.

Chacao is a small farming village and port of entry to Chiloé. Founded in 1895 by foreign settlers, it has an interesting church with two bell towers. Chacao Viejo, a major port and fort during the colonial period, was located farther east.

The 33-km paved road to Ancud runs on rolling hills, with good views over the Chacao channel and the **Pudeto estuary,** with its long road bridge.

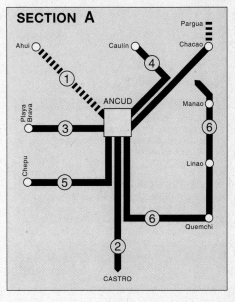

SECTION A

ANCUD (pop 10,000) is the city with the best infrastructure in Chiloé. It was an international seaport until the turn of the century, with narrow streets lined with commercial houses and a classical chilote architecture with abundant shingled roofs and walls. It was founded in 1767 as a port and fort to protect the trading routes to Cape Horn. Defended by the San Antonio and Ahuí forts, on the peninsula opposite the town, and several gun batteries emplaced at different points, this was one of the most formidable strongpoints in the South Pacific. Being the best placed town on the island, it became its political and military capital.

From then on, Ancud also acted as the jumping–off point for the expansion into Chile's southern reaches. The expedition to settle the Strait of Magellan sailed from here in 1843. It was also a port of call for merchant ships plying the Pacific routes and for the whaling vessels prowling the Antarctic waters. The boom in timber trade late last century coincided with the establishment of European settlers in this area.

When the railway reached Puerto Montt in 1912, Puerto Montt became a terminal port which quickly overtook Ancud in such role. The town started a gradual decline which, in 1982, lead to its replacement as capital of Chiloé by the city of Castro.

What to See shopping hours are Mon-Fri 09:00–13:00 h & 15:00–19:30 h, Sat 09:00–13:00 h. The **Costanera** has good views over the **Quetalmahue gulf** and the cliffs crowned by old houses. Taking the Costanera to its northern end and then continuing on **Baquedano**, with its nice old houses, to turn left at San Antonio, you can visit the

SAN ANTONIO FORT erected in 1770 on an esplanade protected by guns guarding the access to the port, it was South America's last point where the Spanish flag flew; it capitulated on January 19, 1826. Following Bellavista to the north, is the fort's restored **powder magazine** (polvorín). Straight ahead is the **Arena Gruesa beach**, very popular in summer.

Opposite the powder magazine, the street Antonio Burr climbs up the

Huaihuén Hill to a Look–out at the summit, with a panoramic view over the city and the **Chacao channel**, the Cochinos islet and, on the far shores, the mainland, with the cliffs around **Carelmapu**. Towards the north, you can see the Maullín coast, with the rock outcrops and islets of Doña Sebastiana, Horcones and others in the **Coronados gulf.** To the left are the **Ahuí** and **Corona** capes, with ruins of forts and gun emplacements. Continuing to the east is the **Pudeto estuary**, with a long road bridge and a fishing port and marina.

The downtown streets of Ancud are the place's main attraction, narrow and lined with tall wooden houses sporting tejuela–lined façades.

REGIONAL MUSEUM (Mon–Sat 10:00–20:00 h, Sun 11:00–19:00 h in summer), on the main square, has interesting historical exhibits, including mythological figures and handicrafts from the islands, displayed in rooms or courts. There is also a life–size replica of the Ancud schooner, which sailed from here to take possession of the Strait of Magellan in 1843. It also has a room dedicated to the Chilean poet, Nobel prize winner, Gabriela Mistral. It is well worth a visit.

The **Mercado** is nearby, a picturesque market offering sea products, handicrafts and **cancahua stone fireplaces.** The **Cathedral** and **San Antonio** churches have interesting architectural styles.

Where To Eat Hostería Ancud, good cuisine and views. Cheap meals and good parking at El Sacho (at the marketplace), cheap meals at Café Lydia. For families with children, the places indicated with

12

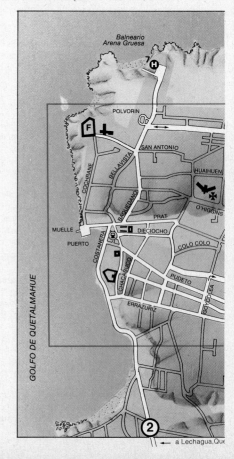

Ancud

asterisk (✳) in the map; seafood at the market-place.

TOURS FROM ANCUD

1 TO AHUI AND PUNTA CORONA BY BOAT ★★

three daily departures from the Ancud pier, by passenger boat. Cruise lasts about three hours.
A visit to fort Ahuí on the far shore and to the quarries where the soft cancahue stone is extracted.

2 PAN–AMERICAN HIGHWAY TO CASTRO ★★★

round trip 178 km. The road is paved throughout, but watch out for treacherous humps and hollows.
The section of road leading to Castro, one of the island's highlights.

Leave Ancud (km 0) skirting the Pudeto estuary and over the bridge. The road runs through rolling woodland. In late February, the ulmo trees (similar to elms) are in full bloom.

Some of the main roads branching off the Pan–American highway are at km 22 to the right, to Chepu (Tour 5), and at km 41 to the left for Quemchi, opened through the jungle in 1960 by the Servicio Militar del Trabajo, a working outfit for people making their military service.

The road soon crosses the Puntra and Butalcura rivers, the island's longest. At km 66 the road to Dalcahue branches east. On the hilltop, the mono-lith is a memorial to a battle in 1824, where the Chilean troops under the command of Ramón Freire, landed at Dalcahue and attempting to at-tack Ancud from the rear, were defeated by the royalist forces.

At km 88 is Castro, described in Section B.

3 TO QUETALMAHUE AND MAR BRAVA ★★★

forty–eight km round trip on a gravel road. Allow three hours. Take food.
A circuit skirting the Quetalmahue gulf to the stormy Pacific coast, where strange rock formations can be seen.

Take road 2 out of Ancud (km 0) (see map). At km 7 is the **Lechagua beach**, the most popular in town. At km 14 take road forking left for Pumilahue and continue to the junction at km 16, turning right to reach **Playa Brava** (rough road) at km 21. A unsigned road runs north to attractive rock forma-tions and a good spot for swimming.

Continue on the same road taken to get here, which at km 27 runs into the main road to Ancud. From this junction you can continue 6 km to the north to **Guabún beach**, a sheltered cove with a white-sand beach very good for bathing or picnicking. Following the same road is the **Corona lighthouse** (km 16), skirting the gulf on a very badly surfaced road, but with interesting bird fauna.

To return to Ancud, go back to the junction. This road skirts the gulf and passes **Quetalmahue**, with a

small port and pelillo works, a sea algae exported to Japan to make agar-agar.

4 TO THE CAULIN OYSTER FARM ★★

sixty km round trip, 12 km of which are gravel. Allow two hours.
A visit to an oyster and mussel farm, offering the chance to get acquainted with the techniques employed. The farm is located in a nice setting and run by its owner. Needless to say, you can gorge yourself on first-quality oysters at a very convenient price.

Leave Ancud (km 0) on the road to Chacao. Take the graveled road for Caulín branching left at km 24, to reach the shore at km 30. Follow the short road along the shore (sometimes it is neces-sary to wait for the low tide).

5 TO CHEPU ★★

round trip of 75 km, with 35 km graveled. Allow half a day. Take food and fishing gear.
An excursion across the Coastal Range to the Pacific Ocean at the

☎ Telephone Center	4 H Polo Sur
★ Touristic Information	5 Hostal Monserrat
◉ Café, Meeting Point	6 Hs Ahüí
⊛ Gasoline Center	✳ 7 Cb Las Golondrinas
⤜ Lookout Point	✳ 8 M Huahuén
✚ Hospital	9 Bh Wechsler
A Town Hall	10 Hosp Bellavista
B Bus Terminal	11 Hosp Montenegro
C Post Office	12 Bh Turismo
D Cathedral Church	13 Hosp Lucuy
E San Francisco Church	
F San Antonio Fort	**RESTAURANTS**
G Regional Museum	1 Hs Ancud
✳ J Gymnasium	2 H Lidia
M Marketplace	4 H Polo Sur
	20 Sacho
ACCOMMODATIONS	21 Austral
1 Hs Ancud	M Market Foodstalls
2 H Lidia	
3 H Quintanilla	✳ See General Map of Ancud

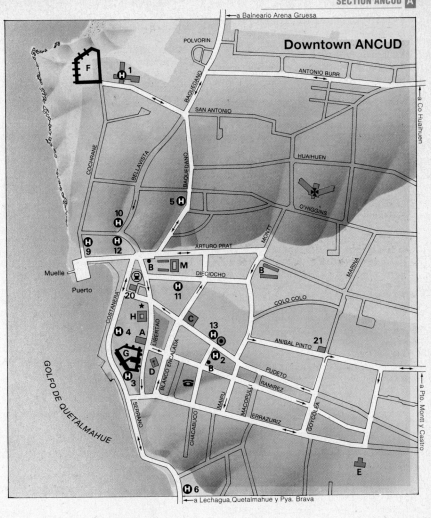

Downtown ANCUD

← a Balneario Arena Gruesa

POLVORIN

ANTONIO BURR

→ a Co Huaihuen

BAQUEDANO

SAN ANTONIO

F

1

HUAIHUEN

O'HIGGINS

COCHRANE

BELLAVISTA

BAQUEDANO

MONTT

MARINA

5

10

9

12

ARTURO PRAT

DIECIOCHO

B

M

B

Muelle

Puerto

COSTANERA

20

11

COLO COLO

ANIBAL PINTO

21

H

A

LIBERTAD

C

13

GOLFO DE QUETALMAHUE

4

G

D

2

B

PUDETO

3

BLANCO ENCALADA

IRAMIREZ

MAIPU

MACOPULLI

ERRAZURIZ

GOYCOLEA

SERRANO

CHACABUCO

E

6

← a Lechagua, Quetalmahue y Pya. Brava

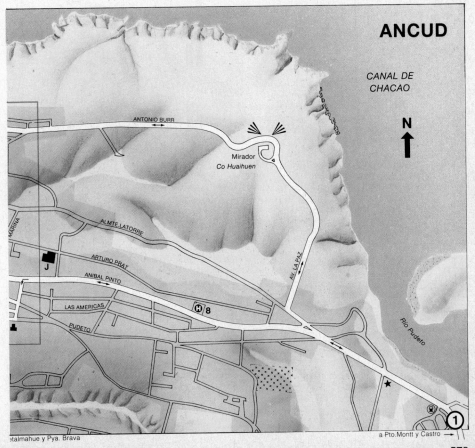

ANCUD

CANAL DE CHACAO

ANTONIO BURR

N

Mirador
Co Huaihuen

MARINA

ALMTE.LATORRE

J

ARTURO PRAT

ANIBAL PINTO

AV. LA PAZ

LAS AMERICAS

8

PUDETO

Río Pudeto

12

1

← etalmahue y Pya. Brava

a Pto.Montt y Castro →

mouth of the Butalcura river, the island's longest. At the bottom of the river valley you will see large patches of dead trees protruding above the water: it is the ground that sunk during the earthquake in 1960. The excursion ends at Anguay, on the edge of the Chiloé National Park; from here, you can walk three km close to the shore, with views to the Metalqui island and its large sea lion colony.

Take the Pan–American highway to Castro. At km 14 take road branching right, which reaches the Chepu and Anguay estuary at km 32; here is a fishing lodge (see Fishing Excursions).

To return, take the road branching right at km 40, through Coipomó, the shortest route to the paved Pan–American highway. From here you can either continue to Castro or return to Ancud.

6 TO QUEMCHI AND RETURN THROUGH LINAO AND MANAO ★★ *round trip of 150 km, with 61 km gravel road. Allow one day, food at Quemchi, gasoline at Ancud.*

A tour along the coast of the inland sea, with splendid views to islands and the Andes mountains in the mainland. In the past one of the most isolated parts of the island, it started to change when, late last century, the Cía. Maderera Valparaíso set up large sawmills and founded Quemchi. In 1895, over 200 Scottish, German, French, Belgian and Spanish families settled at the districts of Huillinco, Pumanzano and Linao, opening the first roads. The impenetrable forests of the past are gone, the landscape now typical of cattle and dairy farms.

Leave Ancud on the Pan–American highway to Castro. At km 40 take road to the left for Quemchi, opened in 1960. Four km before Quemchi, take road branching right to

AUCAR ISLAND at km 65. Visit the island crossing the 500–m–long footbridge. The chapel and its cemetery sit amid green lawns. On the water near the shore lots of black–necked swans can be seen. At km 71 is

Quemchi (pop 247), a village with picturesque streets, a municipal textile factory and lovely miniature ships made by local craftsman Mr Triviño.

Continuing to the north, you reach the Tubildad stream at km 76, with a mussel farm. The road then runs through forests and cattle and dairy farms, to reach Lluico at km 89. It is one of an elongated village lying along a fine–sanded beach with superb views to the volcanoes Osorno, Calbuco, Yates and Hornopirén, in the mainland. The chapel next to the beach is worth a visit.

Linao is reached at km 99. A wide bay with a sheltered harbor, it was a busy port in the past. Now only a few houses remain. At km 102 is a crossroads; straight ahead are Pumanzano, Huillinco and San Juan, the lands colonized by Europeans. Drive on along the coast to reach

Manao at km 117. Lying on a peninsula jutting out between the Hueihué gulf and the Manao bay (both with oyster farms open to the public on weekdays), Manao has a very good beach with fine sand, good for bathing.

Continue skirting the bay to the north, to reach the Pan–American highway at km 123 and Ancud at km 150.

SECTION B   CASTRO

This section comprises the central portion of the Isla Grande de Chiloé. It stretches north to Quicaví and south to Queilén; it also includes the islands of Quinchao and Lemuy, both accessible by road form the main island. The section's center is

CASTRO (pop 16,000). Lying on the shores of a fjord, the town was founded on February 12, 1567, by Capt. Martín Ruiz de Gamboa; it is one of the three oldest cities in Chile (together with Santiago and La Serena) still existing. However, the many setbacks during its long history have left no relics from the earlier times. In 1600, the town was occupied for two months by Dutch pirate Baltazar de Cordes; its liberation was achieved by a woman, the heroine Inés de Bazán. Forty years later, it was again razed, this time by Dutch pirate Henriek Brower.

Castro was the political capital of the Spanish province until 1788, when it was replaced by Ancud. The city revived late last century with the boom in the timber industry, and after 1912, when the railway to Ancud was finished. Gradually it regained its role as geographical center of the archipelago, until being again made into the capital in 1982.

SECTION B

What To See shopping hours are Mon–Fri 09:00–13:00 h and 14:30–19:00 h, Sat 09:00–13:00 h. On the northern access to the city and by the bridge over the Gamboa river you can see the palafitos, wooden houses –some quite large– built on stilts above the water. The Feria (open air market) and the Mercado de Artesanía on the waterfront offer good handicraft purchases, including woollen caps, sweaters and other articles. The

COSTANERA DEL PUERTO (the waterfront street) is busy with passenger boats running scheduled services to and from the islands, and sloops coming from the islands to sell their wares here. The

busiest days are Wed & Sat mornings. There are also palafitos cocinería, ie, eateries on stilts, with seafood and vegetables carefully displayed. One block to the south is a shipyard building chilote–style vessels made of ciprés de las Guaitecas wood, a fine–smelling timber of the cypress family. (During the colonial period, Chiloé was renowned for its carved cypress trunks which perfumed the garments stored in them.)

For a good view over the city and the surrounding area, drive or walk to the **Mirador** (look–out point) next to the statue of the Virgin. The adjacent cemetery is well worth a visit: the tombs all have a little house on top, where the relatives of

Telephone Center
Café, Meeting Point
Gasoline Station
Lookout Point
✚ Hospital
A Town Hall
B Bus Terminal
C Handicrafts Market
D Farm Produce Market

E Museum
F San Francisco Church
G Gymnasium
H Post Office

ACCOMMODATIONS
1 Hs Castro
2 H Unicornio Azul
3 H Gran Alerce
4 M Auquilda

5 H Plaza
6 H y Cb Niklitschek
✳ **7** Centro Turístico Nercón
✳ **8** Cb Pudú
9 Hospedería O'Higgins
10 Bh Mirasol
11 H Costa Azul
12 H La Bomba
13 Bh Lidia

14 Bh Rosa Alvarez

RESTAURANTS
1 Hs de Castro
2 H Unicornio Azul
20 Don Octavio
21 Sacho
R Foodstalls

✳ See Castro Coast Map

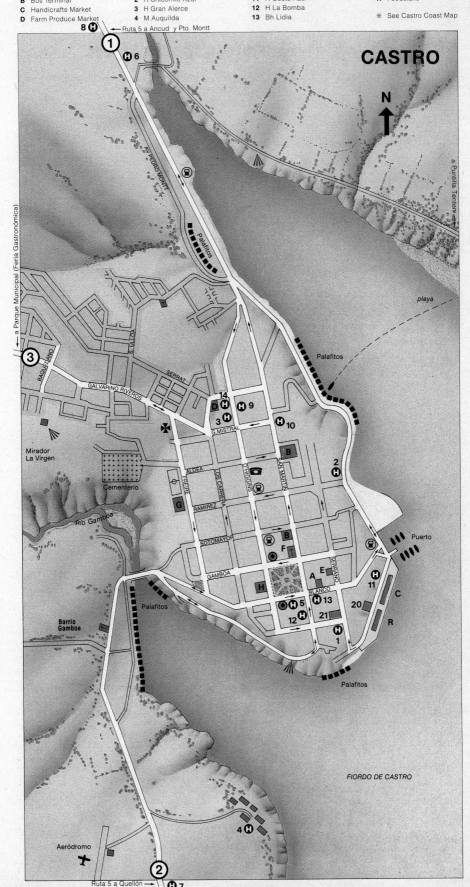

CASTRO

N

575

Houses on stilts at Castro

the departed ones can engage in communication with them.

The small **Municipal Museum** (in summer, Mon-Fri 09:00–13:00 h & 14:30–19:00 h, Sat 09:00–13:00 h; in winter, Mon–Fri 09:00–12:00 h & 14:30–17:00 h) holds interesting exhibits on Chiloé's history, mythology and handicrafts.

CHURCH OF SAN FRANCISCO (NM) (services March-Oct, Mon–Sun 19:00 h; from the second Sun of Oct–March, Tue–Sun 20:00 h, Sun and holidays 09:00 h, 11:00 h), on the square, was built in 1906. Interestingly, it was projected for masonry construction by Italian architect Eduardo Provasoli and interpreted in local timber by local craftsmen. Large–sized (1,300 m²), it has a fine interior, with excellent wooden cornices, arches, altars and choir. Outside it is lined with zinc–iron plates, sporting rather unusual colors for a church.

A FOLKLORE FESTIVAL is held in the third week of February, with music and customs of Chiloé. It is held on Sat & Sun at the Parque Municipal, with communal groups cooking the most typical Chiloé dishes: curanto, yoco, milcao, chochoca, tapados, mellas, mistelas, golden liquor, etc. A veritable **gastronomic marathon** with very friendly public and lively folklore.

Where To Eat good cuisine and a fine view at Hostería de Castro and Hotel Unicornio Azul; both are specialized in choros zapato, a large–sized mussel. Good views also at Motel Auquilda. Quick, cheaper dishes for families with children at the place indicated with asterisk (*) in map. Cheaper still at the food stalls at the Costanera. For seafood, Don Octavio, Costanera. Picnic at beach Ten Ten, to the north of the city.

Accommodations there are four good hotels and motels, plus five other simpler hotels. For accommodation at private houses, ask at the tourist office on the square (open only in summer).

Tour Services H Unicornio Azul runs a bus tour on Sunday to Dalcahue and Tenaún, then by boat to Chauques islands. The tour lasts one day, everything included. Similar tours can be arranged with taxi drivers on the square. Arrange the price beforehand. At the harbor there are tourist boats making cruises around the Castro fjord.

TOURS FROM CASTRO

1 TO DALCAHUE, ACHAO AND QUINCHAO ISLAND ★★★

134 km round trip, almost entirely on gravel roads. Allow one day. Restaurants at Dalcahue and Achao. Best on Sunday morning. Ferry to Quinchao every half hour, 07:30–21:00 h.
The most interesting tour in Chiloé, running along the «wool belt», the traditional woolen–article center, and an area rich in history.

Leave Castro on road 1 on map. At km 4 turn right to

LLAULLAU a hamlet with quaint tejuela–houses and a beautiful chapel in a nice setting. On Jan. 24 there is a religious festivity.

At km 9 is the Putemún chapel and one km ahead, the Quinta de Putemún, a picturesque restaurant where you can see an indigenous **cider press** (see Land & History). In February you can drink the freshly-pressed apple juice.

At km 15, beyond the Puacura bridge, turn 200 m to the right to see a **wooden watermill**. At km 16, before the Hueñocoihue bridge, a road to the left leads to another watermill, on a ravine. Both mills have old machinery still in operation, and both are privately–owned (ask for permission to visit).

At km 20 is

DALCAHUE a picturesque village lying at the point where, in 1824, Chilean general Ramón Freire landed with his patriot troops to fall onto the Spanish stronghold of Ancud from behind. He was defeated on the plains of Mocopulli. The present village emerged with the cattle farming and timber industry booms of late last century.

We recommend make a visit to the following places of interest:

IGLESIA PARROQUIAL (MN) one of the largest and oldest in the island. It is estimated to have been erected between 1750 and 1790, with a portal with nine arches and a slender tower presiding over the channel. The interior has three naves, with an interesting altar and wooden, dressed statuary. To visit it, ask for the keys at the parish house.

COSTANERA Y FERIA ARTESANAL is the lively heart of the village. Here is also the Municipal Complex, with a small **Museum** and the **Sailor's Lodge** (Casa del Navegante) (Nov–March, 09:00–19:00 h), a palafito building used as home–away–from–home for travelling seamen. The handicrafts fair (April–Oct, Sun 07:00-12:00 h; Nov-March, Sat 14:00–20:00 h, Sun 06:00–20:00 h) and, loyal to a long tradition, craftsmen from the islands come to offer their wares directly to tourists and shop-owners. This is the only **Handicrafts Market** in Chiloé where you can find truly high quality textiles.

At the entrance of the village is the **boat yard**, where boats and sloops are built. Much of the work is still done by hand. The frames are sawn directly from a suitably shaped branch, and held in place by copper nails; the boats are caulked using alerce bark.

Food and Accommodations best is restaurant Dalca. On market days there are food stalls offering typical dishes. There are only four pensiones, packed in summer. Lodging at private houses is possible. Ask at the tourist office.

Continue to Quinchao island, taking the ferry (km 0), following the road to Achao. The island is hilly, with rich land and one of the most densely populated in Chiloé. Nice scenery and the most famous churches in the archipelago. The road eventually tops a rise from which there is a panoramic view of Curaco de Vélez and its harbor, reached at km 12.

CURACO DE VELEZ is a very old village which boomed sometime around the mid–19th century, when cattle farmers and whalers settled here. Some nice houses remain from that period of prosperity. Its carpenters were famous, specializing in boats and ships, and houses. The streets **Las Animas** and **Galvarino Riveros** (a Navy admiral born here) boast an enormous variety of tejuelas on their houses.

Back on the road to Achao, to the left of the bridge immediately after the junction is a small

Dalcahue

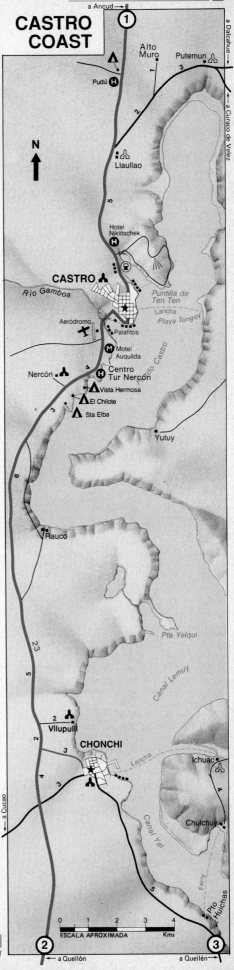

CASTRO COAST

water mill that can be visited. A rise at km 20 affords a grand view over the islands of Lemuy and Chelín, and to Point Rilán. At km 25, another superb **view** over the islands of Quenac, Llingua, Linlín, and Point Tenaún. The road descends one km to

ACHAO it evolved from a Jesuit residence set up in 1743 as a mission covering the islands. Native population started to settle around it, until it became a village. Now it is the head town for the 23 islands of the archipelago. Its port is busy with sloops and boats from all the major islands. There are several restaurants and residenciales. There is a **Museum** on the square, with a collection of chilote artifacts and utensils; also handicrafts shops, and crochet-work at Delicias 066. On the square is the

SANTA MARIA CHURCH (NM) the oldest in Chiloé, started in 1735 and finished after 1767. Built entirely of cypress and alerce wood, using luma–wood pegs instead of nails, it used to have wide eaves affording shelter from the rain. The ceiling inside is painted indigo blue with golden stars; the altar, statuary, balustrades and ornaments are in a rich baroque style. The church was carefully restored after the 1960 earthquake. It also has a museum in the plaza (Dec-Feb, Mon-Sun, 10:00–13.00 h and 15:30–19:00 h, Sun and holidays, 11:00–13:00 h and 15:00–18:00 h) with its Chilote objects and instruments collection.

A road starts from Achao to the south, leading in 35 km to **Quinchao**, taking a short detour to the right. Quinchao is a quaint hamlet on a beach, with a few houses and the large

CHURCH OF QUINCHAO (NM) built in the 1700s and refurbished in a neoclassical style late last century. One of the largest colonial churches in Chiloé (1,020 m²), it still has the outsized eaves to provide shelter to the hundreds of pilgrims visiting it on December 8. Inside it is very simple, the floor covered with large, axe–made wooden planks. The fence–encircled cross on the esplanade outside is a memorial of an earlier missionary visit.

Retake the road south, skirting a large estuary which practically dries out during the low tide, and where the locals search for shellfish. In the rural landscape some typically chilote devices, including woven fences, are still to be seen.

Take road branching right at km 41 to **Matao**, a beach with a tiny, old village with a chapel.

Return to the junction, turn right to **Chequián**, with the area's best beach for bathing and picnicking. The beach is beautiful, and has a good view to the islands. A Jesuit mission was located here in the old times, before being moved to Achao. Dalcahue is 43 km from here; Castro, 63 km.

2 **TO CHONCHI AND LEMUY ISLAND ★★★**
round trip of 107 km, 60 km of which are gravel

12

road. Restaurant at Chonchi. Ferry to Lemuy 08:00–20:00 h. Rushing, you can do the complete circuit in one day.

A tour along the coast, with interesting churches, the seaport town of Chonchi and the beautifully cultivated Lemuy island.

Leave Castro on the road south up to Nercón (km 4); 50 m to the right is the

CHURCH OF NERCON (NM)   very old, it was refurbished in neoclassical style late last century. The statuary and the altar are interesting, as well as the wall stucco imitating marble, a technique found only in one other case in Chiloé, at the chapel of Chelín island.

Back on the main road, you can see the village of Rauco on the left, with oil storage tanks. At the junction at km 18, take road to the left for Villipulli to reach the coast at km 20.

CHURCH OF VILUPULLI (NM)   built in the 1700s, it was visited by Charles Darwin in 1853. With a portal of five arches, it is crowned by a very slender tower. The ceiling is flat, and it has a statue of a seating Virgin. Ask the fiscal for the keys at the adjacent house. The area surrounding the church has not been urbanized, in keeping with old Chiloé traditions.

Back on the main road at km 22, the turn-off for Chonchi is at km 24.

CHONCHI   is dubbed the «three–story town», as its houses are arranged in steps on the hillside. It evolved from a Jesuit missionary residence set up here in 1754. Construction of the church was immediately started. The official foundation of the village occurred by decree in 1764, and it was slow to prosper. It finally received a boost late last century, with a boom in cattle farming and as a shipping port for forest products. Its beautiful houses and streets date from that period, and they are preserved now as a historical group.

The **main street** with its large, colorful wooden houses, and the **costanera** with its shops are worth a visit. Try the **licor de oro**, the **enguindados** or guindados (both are alcoholic beverages) and the sweet **roscas chonchinas** (a sort of doughnut).

For lunch, restaurant Remi's and the Antiguo Chalet, a fine house on the harbor which is also a very good hotel. Cheap meals at the market's food stalls. To pitch a tent, only the private lands on the exit to Queilén.

CHURCH OF SAN CARLOS (NM)   started by the Jesuits in 1754, it was left unfinished; in 1859 it was refurbished in a neoclassical style. A large church (750 m²), it has a portal with five arches and a heavy tower in three stages. Inside, the most attractive feature is the quality of the woodwork on pillars and altar.

Opposite the church (km 27) starts the road to Queilén, skirting the Yal channel to Puerto Huicha at km 32. Here is the ferry for Puerto Chulchuy at Lemuy island (every 2 hours, 08:00–20:00 h in summer, 08:00–18:00 h in winter, passage 20 min.)

On Lemuy, the road runs through rolling, carefully cultivated fields, to reach Ichuac at km 36. This used to be the old ferry docking point from Chonchi.

Church of Ichuac another old church refurbished in neoclassical style late last century, but very badly preserved and in desperate need of maintenance.

Some **straw houses** –walls of wooden planks and thatched roofs– can be seen in the fields near the road. They are used as storage rooms or pens. Now there are few of them, and they are very similar to the house architecture in

Chiloé during the colonial period. At km 41 is the **Puqueldón estuary** and the small village of the same name. From its square, take the road to Puchilco and, at km 45, take the detour to the left, leading in 5 km to

Aldachildo   one of the oldest villages in the island, its houses lined along the waterfront. Its church is also very old, with a tall, slender tower.

Back on the main road, at the junction (km 55) take road to the left to San Agustín (km 57). Take short detour to the left, leading to **Puchilco** through forests and small lakes with coihues (a tree) swarming with parrots in summer. At km 61 is a rise commanding a **superb view** of the islands of Quehui and Chelín, the Chaulinec group farther out, and the towering **Michimahuida volcano** in the mainland.

The road descends to a lovely, lonely beach called **Marico,** good for bathing and picnicking. To return directly to Castro, retrace the road (46 km).

For those wishing to tour the island further, take the road south from San Agustín (km 0) to **Lincura** (km 4), a small village with the lonely **Huiñay beach.** Continue to the end of the island, at **Detif** (km 12), a hamlet with a church and **Apahuén** beach, very good for camping.

3   TO QUEILEN AND SURROUNDING AREA ★★

round trip of 163 km, of which 117 km are gravel. Allow one day. Take food.

A circuit on a road recently opened through the forest, running near cliffs with good views of the inland sea, and visiting old villages previously isolated.

Drive south from Castro to the access to Chonchi (km 23). The road to Queilén starts opposite the Chonchi church. At km 31 a road branches left to **Teupa,** a nice bay with a mussel farm. Dolphins can frequently be seen here. It is a good spot for a picnic. The chapel at Teupa has an interesting cemetery, with **mausoleums** resembling small houses lined with tejuelas (shingles).

Back on the main road (km 39), a significant change can be seen in the scenery farther south. The traditional fences disappear and are replaced by recently cleared lands under cultivation. At km 47, take road branching left for **Terao** (2 km), a small village with a row of houses and an old chapel facing the sea. Get back to the main road (km 52) and continue to the south through a thick jungle. At km 54 is **lake Tarahuin** with plenty salmon for fishing, and 9 km later the Santa María valley, with a few houses and fields surrounded by a dark forest.

At km 65 there is another junction (4 km to the left is **Ahoni,** 20 old houses, a jetty, a beach). At km 78, still another junction (3 km to lake Pío Pío, enclosed by the jungle and with a very rich bird life; good fishing). At km 83 is **Aituy,** a hamlet with an orderly tree–lined street leading to the church. The road then climbs some cliffs offering a splendid **view** of the Andes mountains in the mainland, with the **Michimahuida** and **Corcovado** volcanoes. At km 91 is

QUEILEN   (pop 2,000), a picturesque seaport village sitting on a long, narrow, sandy peninsula, with two main streets running across leading to beaches at either end. This is the only village in the region having one beach at each flank. The **large beach** is good for camping and bathing. The Jesuits set up a residence here in the 18th century, but the village emerged only late last century. In 1900 a small party of British and Spanish fishermen settled here, but they did not prosper. Later, a timber plant started to operate here. Now the main activities are cattle farming, fishing and timber extraction. There is a simple and clean hotel on the square.

4 TO QUILQUICO AND RILAN ★★

round trip of 64 km, with 52 km gravel road. Allow half a day. Take food.
A visit to an interesting church.

Leave Castro following the Pan-American highway to the north. At km 6 take road branching right to Dalcahue. At km 10, turn right for Rilán, which is at km 29. A small village nestled in a dell, with the enormous

CHURCH OF RILAN (NM) built by Franciscan missionaries in the mid-18th century, it has an enormous, 25–m–high tower in three stages, presiding over the village and the surrounding area. The portal has 5 arches in neoclassical style. Its fine woodwork was a forerunner for the great Franciscan church at Castro. Religious festivity held on February 11.

5 TO CUCAO ON THE PACIFIC COAST ★★

round trip of 116 km, with 78 km on a gravel road. Not advisable after rain. Allow one day. Accommodation at Huillinco.

Leave Castro following the road south; at km 24 take road branching west to Huillinco, climbing gently among cultivated fields and old farmhouses. At km 33 is lake Huillinco and the village of Huillinco established by 1935 as a lake port for new settlers on the coast in a lovely setting, with a beach, hotel and a youth hostel. The opening of the road to Cucao deprived it of its «way station» role as a lake port.

The road, finished in 1983, skirts both lakes and crosses peculiar bridges made using forked poles, a typical chilote technique. At km 58 is the beach of

CUCAO in 1834, Darwin travelled especially from Ancud to visit this place. It has a certain charm, although it lacks architectural highlights. The oldest constructions here were washed away in 1960 by a giant tidal wave. It is a 20–km–long white–sand beach, with thundering surf and a string of thickly forested mountains behind. It used to be inhabited by Mapuche tribes, and was visited by Jesuit missionaries as the first stop in their annual «circulating missions» (see History). Gold was found –and promptly extracted– at the northern end of the beach. Cattle farmers settled here in 1935. Now there is a chapel, a school, a shop and a few houses of friendly settlers. Some offer accommodation and horses for hire. Ask around.

CHILOE NATIONAL PARK the park starts on the northern bank of the river. Access is through the suspension footbridge and along signposted paths to the reception area and the flora and fauna museum. Farther ahead is a campground (no car access; free–lance camping in camper vans on the beach before the bridge). About one km beyond the campground starts the **tepual**, a spectacular forest where one walks on the tepa roots. Nearby is a settler who produces apple cider with the peculiar chilote cider press. Horses can be rented at Cucao for rides along the beach to the gold mines, or to **lake Huelde** (4 km), surrounded by a beautiful, thick jungle.

6 BACK NORTH THROUGH QUEMCHI AND TE-

NAUN ★★★ *130 km to Chacao, 184 km with the suggested detours. Graveled road throughout. Allow one day. Restaurant at Quemchi. Best after rain, to avoid dust.*
A recently opened road running along the coast, offering an alternative route for the return journey.

Drive from Castro to Dalcahue (km 23). There take road to Mocopulli and, two km later, take road

branching right to Quemchi and Tenaún. The road runs through fields only lately opened for cultivation, although the nearby coastal strip has been inhabited for the last 400 years. At km 33 a detour to the right leads to Quiquel, an ancient village on a nice bay.

At km 37 a road branches east to descend in three km to

QUETALCO squeezed between a cliff and the seashore, this was once the main missionary center in the area. The large three–story building was in the past a major store. The chapel dates from last century, and is lined with pointed shingles. In 1760, the Spaniard running the local encomienda (land granted by the Spanish king with a number of Indians at the disposal of the assignee under a serfdom system) and Jesuit father Francisco Menéndez set out from here to explore the lake Nahuel Huapi (Argentina) and the Bariloche pass to Argentina.

Get back to the main road at km 43. At km 51 is the San Juan stream, nice scenery with large coihues (a native tree), ferns and giant nalca leaves, good spot for a picnic. At km 59 a road branches right; taking this road, at km 63 is a forking. Take the right–hand branch. A very steep stretch follows –better to walk it down if the road is not in suitable condition– and at the bottom is

SAN JUAN a small hamlet on the shores of a large inlet. Renowned for its boat builders –you can see them at work–, it has a small, nice beach and a large chapel dating from last century. A cemetery was located right behind it, but it sunk in the sea with the 1960 earthquake; the new one was set up farther up the hill. At the tip of the inlet are the remains of a fish pen, built to trap fishes when the tide recedes. There is also a natural sanctuary of sea birds and numerous black–necked swans swimming near the shore.

Return to the road fork (km 71); turn right to reach in 3 km the beach of

Calén an old farming settlement with a chapel reconstructed in 1890, shingled and with a curious triple cross. Superb **view** to the islands and the mainland volcanoes.

Get back to the main road (km 79). Continuing to the east, at km 82 is the village of Tocoihue and the junction with the Tenaún–Quemchi road. A bit over one km beyond the village is the island's only waterfall, cascading in a single 45–m drop. Turn right to reach, at km 89,

PUEBLO E IGLESIA DE TENAUN an old sheltered port where small vessels wait out the storms before daring the Tenaún cape and shallows, it has been a traditional meeting place for navigators. In 1786, the great explorer father Francisco Menéndez, freshly returned from the Argentinian pampas, and the great cartographer of Chiloé, Capt José de Moraleda, got together here to chat about their respective journeys. The village boomed late last century with the trade in alerce wood brought from the Chauque islands and from the mainland.

It is now a pretty village with a **Church** (NM) three–stage central tower, 25 m tall; structure from the mid–18th century, refurbished in neoclassical style; at the turn of the century it was lined with zinc plates and two towers were added at the portico, the only such case in Chiloé. The parish house sports an impressive collection of gladiolus plants.

Get back to the main road at Tocoihue (km 96) and continue northward to a junction at km 101. The right branch leads in 8 km to

QUICAVI a very old, small village nestled between a cliff and the shores of a narrow inlet. In the Chiloé mythology, Quicaví is the place where «the

12

Tenaún

cave» is located, where the great lodge of Sorcerers of Chiloé meets. The locals claim that they often see the sorcerers wearing their «macuñ» -a flying jacket floating as lights between the cliff and the sea.

The **chapel** is worth a visit. It was refurbished at the turn of the century; opposite the chapel, on a slope, is the **cemetery**. **Footbridges** enable pedestrian movement along the shore at high tide.

Retake the main road to the north at km 155. Ahead is the village of **Montemar**, and then recently logged forests. Soon the road passes the beautiful, jungle-lined lake Popetán. At km 125 the road peeks over the Caucahue channel and **Aucar island**. The rest of the road is described under Section A, Tour 6.

SECTION C   QUELLON

This section covers the portion of Chiloé lying south of lakes Huillinco and Cucao, and of river Compu. This area was not settled during the colonial period, its occupation starting only this century. During the colonial period, Jesuit missionaries visited the coastal area, with chapels at Pailad, Tranqui island, Chadmo, Compu and Huildad. In 1743, the Jesuits brought Caucahue Indians from the southern reaches of the Corcovado gulf to the uninhabited island of Cailín, dubbing it thereafter «the world's most southerly Christian enclave». At the turn of the 20th century, a colonization plan was put into effect, establishing settlements of European fishermen at islands Coldita and Laitec, and on the Inio river. The southern portion of the island was leased to the Cía Nacional de Alcoholes, which founded Quellón.

The Pan-American highway reaches Quellón in the early 1970s. The surrounding land has only recently been put to productive use, and offers a different scenery from the rest of the island.

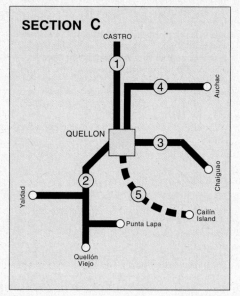

SECTION C

1   THROUGH THE PAN-AMERICAN HIGHWAY TO

QUELLON ★★★ *round trip of 196 km from Castro, 112 km of which are gravel road. Allow one day. Accommodation, food and gasoline at Quellón.*
A tour to the southernmost town of Chiloé.

At km 34 south of Castro is **lake Tarahuim**, with accommodation and very good fishing. At km 47 is **lake Natri**, surrounded by softly rolling woodland. A road branches off from the Pan-American highway to the shore (good camping spot). At km 57 is an inlet called **Moluco**, with black-necked swans.

The road now runs close to the coast, and at km 82 it passes **Compu**, with its isolated chapel on the beach. It then turns inland again to run through the Chadmo Central and Chadmo Bajo plains, at km 72 and 79. At the nearby **Chadmo bay** the original Mapuche language is still spoken, and the Mapuche customs preserved. This is the place chosen by the most prestigious chieftains to set up their residence.

The road then runs across fields and houses of recent settlers, most of which have come from outside Chiloé. At km 88 is the farming village of Coinco; a road branches east to **Estero Huildad**, formerly the southernmost settled spot on this coast. At km 98 is

QUELLON the end-point for the Pan-American highway on the island and the port of entry for the Aysén fishing companies. It is the home port for a hefty fishing fleet and has a booming seafood canning industry. The ferries to Aisén, however,

have sort of moth-balled Quellón as terminal port until the Pan-American highway to Castro is finally paved. Quellón was founded in 1906 by the firm Destilatorio Quellón SA, which pioneered the production of acetone, methylic alcohol and charcoal in this island, having a lease to 150,000 hectares. It built the port. Forest logging and the introduction of cattle farming transformed the landscape.

What To See   the **Municipal Museum** (Mon–Fri, 08:15–13:00 h and 14:15–18:00 h). The **Costanera** has handicrafts workshops (best days are Mon–Fri mornings, the market days). At the police station you can see an authentic **bongo**, the canoe used in the old times in Chiloé.

Where To Eat   at Hostería Quellón and Fogón las Quilas ask for the fabled Quellón king crab (centolla). Cheaper meals, good for families with children, at the hotels at the Costanera and the seafood stalls adjacent to the wharf. Picnic at the Quellón Viejo beach.

Ferries To Aysén   as mentioned above, departures from here are temporarily suspended. The ferries have moved to Chonchi.

TOURS FROM QUELLON

2 TO QUELLON VIEJO AND YALDAD ★★★

thirty km round trip on a gravel road; allow two hours. Take food.

A tour to the southern tip of Chiloé's road network.

Take the road heading west out of Quellón, skirting the bay for 2 km to a crossroads. Turn left and, one km later, turn right at the junction, to reach **Quellón Viejo** at km 4. A long, lonely beach with the Laitec and Coldita islands ahead, in 1881 a minor port and coal deposit was set up here for the Chilean Navy, linked by messenger pigeons with Castro. Only the chapel on the beach survives.

Retrace the same road and, at km 5, take the road branching right for **Punta Lapa** (km 7), at the tip of the Quellón Viejo beach. Nice view of the Corcovado gulf and the Cailín island, good spot for a picnic. There is also a restaurant and cabins for rent.

Return to the junction (km 10) and turn left for Yaldad. The road climbs a rise (good **views** of the town and the bay) and then runs through a canelo forest. At km 19 is

Yaldad a very small village with a good beach, boat slip, mussel farm, few houses and a **church**. Here are, reportedly, the only active **bongos** in Chiloé, the traditional canoe made of a fire–hollowed tree trunk. Across the bay is **Puerto Carmen**, the seat of the estancia stretching over the entire southeastern portion of the island.

3 TO CHAIGUAO BEACH ★★

twelve km on a badly surfaced road. Take food.

A visit to the area's best beach.

Leave Quellón toward Castro and turn right at the first junction (on the edge of town). The road passes by the Pesquera Quellón and skirts the inlet; the Corcovado volcano looms straight ahead in the mainland. At km 4 is the Oqueldán stream. The road climbs a rise; on the other side is a bridge and then the modest hamlet of Chaiguao. At the far end, a short sandy stretch of road across fenced fields leads to

Chaiguao Beach long, with fine sand and lots of wild strawberries in February. Across the water is Cailín island and, on the mainland, the towering Andes mountains. Good for bathing and camping.

4 TO AUCHAC ★★

twelve km from Coinco and 22 km from Quellón. It is best to make it on the return leg to Castro.

A small fishing village in an unusually (for Chiloé) rugged setting.

Take the Pan–American highway out of Quellón to Castro. At km 10 is Coinco. Take road branching east (right). At km 12 is the Huildad river; follow the road skirting the northern bank. (Soon there is a signpost to the right for **Curahue**, a small village straddling the road to a stony beach.) At the next junction, turn right; the road climbs to a small plateau and then descends until km 22, to reach

Auchac a small fishing village squeezed between a 30–m–high cliff and the beach. Good view to the Corcovado gulf and the string of volcanoes in the mainland. Ahead is the island of Chaulín.

5 TO THE ISLANDS BY BOAT ★★★

an excursion of about 3–4 hours.

Boats can be hired at the Quellón harbor. Sail along the Chaiguao channel to Chailín island, a former Caucahue Indian reservation established by the Jesuits, to land at the **Huellonquén** cove. Walk across the island –ca 500 m– for a good view from the top of the rise.

Another excursion is to Pirata Ñancupel's cave.

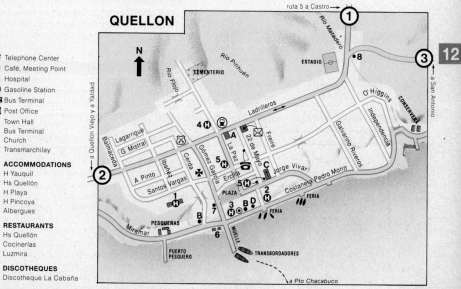

QUELLON

☎ Telephone Center
◉ Café, Meeting Point
✚ Hospital
⛽ Gasoline Station
🚌 Bus Terminal
✉ Post Office
A Town Hall
B Bus Terminal
C Church
D Transmarchilay

ACCOMMODATIONS
1 H Yauquil
2 Hs Quellón
3 H Playa
4 H Pincoya
5 Albergues

RESTAURANTS
2 Hs Quellón
6 Cocinerías
7 Luzmira

DISCOTHEQUES
8 Discotheque La Cabaña

12

SECTION D   THE ARCHIPELAGO

This sector includes the islands lying east of Chiloé, with the exception of Lemuy and Quinchao (these two can be reached by car), and the mainland coast from the Reñihue fjord to the Pumalín bay.

The islands are clustered into five groups: **Quehui**, with 2 islands; **Chaulinec**, with 3; **Desertores**, with 6; **Quenac**, with 6; and **Chauques**, with 16. The islands are mostly flat, their maximum altitude ranging from 30 to 80 m. The shores, however, are often abrupt, the fishing or farming villages nestled on the few beaches. All except those at the Desertores group have reached their maximum population capacity, and are consequently thoroughly farmed.

How To Get There   there are regular boat services as follows:

From **Castro** to Chelín and Quehui islands, departures Mon–Sat 13:30 h and return at 07:00 h on the next day. To Chaulinec and Apiao Tue & Thu at 10:30 h. To the Desertores group there are only unscheduled cargo boats.

From **Dalcahue** to Mechuque, departures Tue & Thu at 14:00 h, return on Mon & Fri at 07:00 h.

From **Achao** to Chaulinec and Quechui, dep. Mon & Fri 15:00 h, return Mon & Fri 07:00 h.

From **Tenaún** to Chauques group (Mechuque), Mon & Fri, coordinated with bus from Castro to Tenaún.

Boat Hire   the best way to rove around the archipelago is to hire a boat. See Excursions.

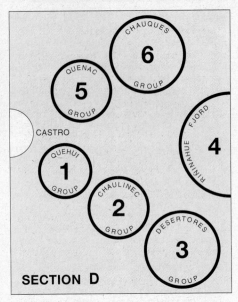

SECTION **D**

THE ARCHIPELAGO

1   QUEHUI GROUP ★★★

consisting of the Quehui and Chelín islands, the archipelago's richest and most urbanized. Daily scheduled boats from/to Castro.

QUEHUI ISLAND   is one of the few with a good, sheltered harbor, with a splendid port and a village with a general store and an oyster farm. It was one of the stops in the annual circuit of the 18th–century circulating missions. Opposite is the village and church of

CHELIN ISLAND   with a few houses and a general store clustered around the church, its tower presiding above the village. Inside, the church is stuccoed white in imitation of marble –as in Nercón–, with dressed statuary in the altar. Behind the church, up the hill slope, there is a grotto and a look–out with a superb view over the channel.

2   CHAULINEC GROUP ★★★

three islands, the main giving the name to the group. Three hundred Chono families were brought here during the colonial period by Jesuit missionaries. The islands boomed at the turn of this century, as a result of their strategic location in the traffic routes from Puerto Montt to Aysén and Magallanes. They became a port of call and resupply port for the ships plying that route. All the islands in the group are now thoroughly farmed.

CHAULINEC ISLAND   is the largest and highest of the three, with two villages, **Chaulinec** and **Capilla Vieja**. Basic services –general store, post office, police– are found at the former, making it a good spot for resupplying during a boat tour around the archipelago.

APIAO ISLAND   is strangely shaped, with an inlet almost slashing it into two pieces. At the far end is Chiloé's largest oyster farm. With rolling shores

and no villages, it only has a **chapel** and a **missionary house**. These are optimally placed for their purposes during the missionary visit, almost level with the water on a sandy tongue accessible both from the inner lagoon and the Alao strait.

Alao island has a small village with a modest chapel and a port open to the south wind.

3   DESERTORES GROUP ★★

these six islands clustered near the mainland were not settled until early this century. The name is a variation of «Islas Desertas» (Uninhabited Islands), as Beagle Capt Fitzroy named them in his survey of the area in 1840. They have a scant 780 inhabitants and large tracts are still virgin land. Navigation routes here are wind-dependent: with south wind, they pass between Chulín and Talcán islands; with north wind, between Nayahué and Nalcán islands to the mainland.

CHULIN ISLAND   (pop 260) is the most populated of the group, life centered around the chapel. There is also a fishing cove on the southern shore.

Talcán island is the largest, but also the poorest in resources. There are two fishing coves: Talcán, on the strait separating this island from neighboring Nayahué, and Tendedor, on the namesake bay. On the southern shore is a sheltered river mouth which offers a haven in case of storm.

4   MAINLAND COAST FROM REÑIHUE TO MORRO

VILCUN ★★★ an area of steep, heavily wooded mountains plummeting directly to the sea, with a few coves and plains suitable for farming. By 1760, this zone received a seasonal influx of people engaged in alerce logging. In 1910, some settlers from Chiloé decided to stay in the mainland, opening fields and clearing the jungle along the coast.

This is one of Chile's most beautiful areas for sailing. Although mostly open sea, it does have some fjords and inlets well worth a visit. **Bahía Pumalín** is a secluded, sheltered bay, with beautiful shores and a few settlers; **Poza de Chumildén**, located at the mouth of the Reñihue fiord, has a few houses and a chapel. Three beautiful, jungly islets lend it a tropical look. A navigation chart (or an experienced guide) is an absolute must: there is only one safe access channel.

REÑIHUE FJORD spectacular, with rocky islets, sheer walls and calm waters, sheltered from the south wind. Near the far end is the smaller **Largo fjord**, with a ramp for one of the ferries serving the Carretera Austral, and still farther in there is yet one more fjord –**Blanco**– branching off the main one, with a salmon farm at the end.

5 QUENAC GROUP ★★★

these six islands, as a result of their proximity to the main island and to Achao, were settled quite early on, and they still preserve the Spanish–Mapuche traditions.

CAGUACHE ISLAND at the center of the archipelago, has a single settlement located at its southern tip, a few houses clustered around a large church. Chiloé's largest religious festivity – **Jesús Nazareno de Caguache**– is held here on August 30, with pilgrims arriving from throughout Chiloé and the archipelago. Near the village is a look–out on the summit of a hill, with superb views over the surrounding islands.

QUENAC ISLAND is the group's largest, with a village offering all basic services. It is the best place for resupplying during a tour around the archipelago. At the turn of the century, this was home to prosperous timber companies and farmers, and also to an old, huge church which burned down in 1959 and with it the entire village. The village was then reconstructed in the chilote style.

Meulín island has two villages. **Meulín** sits opposite Quenac, 15 houses and a church on a stony beach, flanked on one side by a high headland; **San Francisco**, on the other side of the island, a sheltered cove with a good view of the mainland from the hillock where the chapel sits. **Linlín island** is renowned for its **woollen handicrafts**, particularly blankets. There are two villages, Linlín and Curaco de Linlín, each with a church.

Llingua island is the **basketry center**, with fine wicker baskets made mostly during the winter months.

6 CHAUQUES GROUP ★★★

perhaps the most beautiful group, consisting of 16 hills connected by sandy shallows which the high tide floods, turning the hills into islands separated

Islands of the Archipelago

by a maze of beautiful channels. The group is separated into two clusters of islands, Butachauques, lying to the east, and Mechuque, to the west. During the colonial period, the population of these islands was exclusively Indian, and considered Chiloé's most pure–blooded. The circulating Jesuit mission called at the Cheniao, Anihue and San José chapels. At the turn of this century, large-scale alerce logging started to gather momentum. Later, a cannery was set up at Mechuque.

THE MECHUQUE CLUSTER OF ISLANDS has as its main village tiny **Mechuque**, with a carefully maintained square surrounded by neat houses and some palafitos, ie, houses on stilts. **Anihue** island has no villages but it does have a chapel. **Voigüe** (excellent beach) and **Cheniao** are villages lying on sandy «tongues», just a few houses and, of course, a chapel.

THE BUTACHAUQUES CLUSTER OF ISLANDS several islands with tall hills among which a channel worms its way. The village of **San José** is surrounded by forests and cultivated fields; **Matahue**, at the far end of the channel, has an oyster farm, as does **Nayahué**, located on the shores of a large lagoon, next to a 4–m–high sand bar from which there is a good view to the gulf of Ancud, with the Calbuco and Osorno volcanoes in the mainland.

12

EXCURSIONS

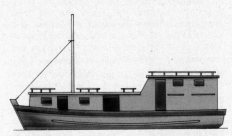

Lanchón de Paseo

BY BOAT

One of the best ways to capture the Chiloé feeling is to sail around the archipelago by boat. However, the few boats available for hire are neither comfortable nor cheap. Still, unless you are towing your own boat, they are the only possibility for visiting those islands not served by scheduled boats.

The boats range from motorized sailing vessels to passenger launches with seats arranged as in a bus. All have some sort of cooking facilities and some a toilet as well.

Warm clothing and rain gear are advisable, as well as the necessary safety equipment, like life vests. A sleeping bag and other camping gear are also helpful.

The best time for crossing open waters is at dawn or at dusk, when the wind is calm. Usually, sailing time is 6–9 hours a day, with landings at different villages and shore excursions; nights are spent at anchor in some sheltered harbor.

There is no established boat hire service. You must contact the boat captains directly. Payment is per day spent sailing (one third of the price per day lost weathering a storm).

In Castro check at the two main hotels. The captain of the Albatros can be contacted at Tel 2452. You may also ask directly at the wharf.

In Dalcahue ask at the Capitanía de Puerto (Port Authority) for the captain of the boat running the service to Mechuque. Departures Mon & Thu in the afternoon. Night is spent on board off Mechuque. The cruise lasts two days and visits the Chauques and Quenac island groups.

In Achao contact (through the Capitanía de Puerto) the captain of the boat making the run to Chaulinec. This cruise lasts two days, after a night spent on board off Chaulinec, visiting the Chaulinec and Quehui island groups.

12

BY AIRPLANE

This is the best way to obtain an overall view of this intricate geography, with its many islands, fjords, lakes and volcanoes, and to reach places –particularly in the mainland– only accessible by plane. Just call the local Club Aéreo (Ancud T 2410 & 2612, Castro 2264) and in about 20 min you will have your plane ready –provided the weather is adequate.

Over the Archipelago, Chaitén and Lake Yelcho
★★★ departure from Castro, the excursion lasts two hours. A very good opportunity to see all the islands, overflying Desertores, Chaitén and lake Yelcho, skirting the walls of volcano Michimahuida towards the Reñihue fjord, and back over the Chauques group and Achao.

Over the Archipelago ★★★
a one–hour tour taking off from Castro, overflying Lemuy island, the Quehui, Chaulinec, and Quenac groups; the return flight follows the coastline, over Achao and Rilán back to Castro.

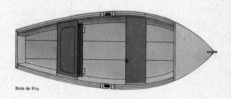

Bote de Río

FISHING EXCURSIONS

Both sea and river fishing are good here. For the former, the best are the bays of Ancud and Quellón, with night fishing of jurel –a type of jack fish–, corvina –a type of drum fish–, robalo and sawfish. For river fishing:

Chepu River near its mouth, in a nice setting of calm waters and a backdrop of large trees (described under Section A). Accessible by car, bus or airplane. There is a lodge of the Club de Pesca y Caza (fishing & hunting club), a boat ramp, boat hire, a campground and accommodations. Contact Mr Mario Gutiérrez, T 2612, Ancud. Take sleeping bag and food.

Pudeto River (Ancud) and its tributaries San Antonio, Huicha, Mechaico and Negro. Trout is abundant in authorized season, salmon in winter. Boats can be hired from Mr Mario Gutiérrez, T 2612, Ancud.

HIKING

There are some interesting –and challenging– hikes through untouched areas of Chiloé. Rain gear is essential, as well as plenty of food.

Through the Chiloé National Park ★★★
starting from river Chepu –described under Section A– towards the south, walking some 6 hours along the coast. The National Park has a totally untouched, impenetrable jungle –including old alerces and tepas–, mountains and thundering Pacific surf. Pudus (one of the world's tiniest deer) and mink can be seen in the wild.

The bus arrives at the Chepu river; from here, it is a 3–km walk to the mouth of the river, which you have to cross by boat to continue south. You skirt some sand dunes up to Punta Pulga; a path leads then across cape Ahuenco to the large **Tongoy beach**, with a wall of jungle in the back and a rock outcrop at the south end. This outcrop can be skirted when the tide is low to reach the Lar river. A short way beyond is a **Conaf guardhouse**; the warden has a wireless and provides information on further hikes from here.

Another hike is from the park's southern edge (accessible by car and «Arroyo» bus from Castro; forget about hitchhiking), at Cucao. Some ten or 15 km north of here is the Cole Cole river. Great views.

To reach the Pacific coast from Piruquina ★★★
a possibility to cross the park from east to west. A few km north of Castro. A road leads west for 12 km, to the Puchagán river. If you are hitchhiking, Sunday will be your best bet, as the road will have some traffic. Then it is a 12–hour walk to reach the coast. The first five hours are spent climbing the Coastal Range, amid native forests of alerce and a local variety of cypress. The summit, however, is covered by coirón grass and cypresses burned by a great fire in 1942. The path –opened in 1946 by settler José Hammelmann– climbs down through more forests, to reach in 2 hours the **Alto de la Ventana** («window rise»), from where the sea can be seen in the distance. The beach is a further 4 hours down the path. The beach has white sand, excellent fishing and mollusks ready for the taking. There is also a lovely valley, ideal for camping. Lots of wild myrtle berries and strawberries on the beach. Take salt if you want to salt some fish.

12

SHOPPING TIPS

Puerto Montt the best and most varied Chiloé handicrafts are to be found at the **Feria Artesanal of Angelmó**, open daily 09:00–20:00 h. In the morning, you can also find craftsmen arrived from the islands to offer their products directly.

Ancud the **Mercado** offers a large variety of seafood and the hand–carved cancahua–**stone fireplaces**. Cheap, abundant dishes at the neighboring foodstalls.

Dalcahue hosts the largest **producers' market** in Chiloé. Craftsmen stream from the islands to Dalcahue on Sunday morning. Basketry, woolen articles with hand–spun wool and large carpets and blankets are among their best.

Castro the crafts shops at the Costanera offer a wide variety of the archipelago's handicrafts.

Chonchi the Costanera shops offer the typical **rosca**, a sort of doughnut, and **Licor de Oro** («Golden Liquor»), a local, homemade alcoholic beverage.

Quellón the local **Poncho** is renowned for its quality, grey with an exclusive pattern of black and white fret

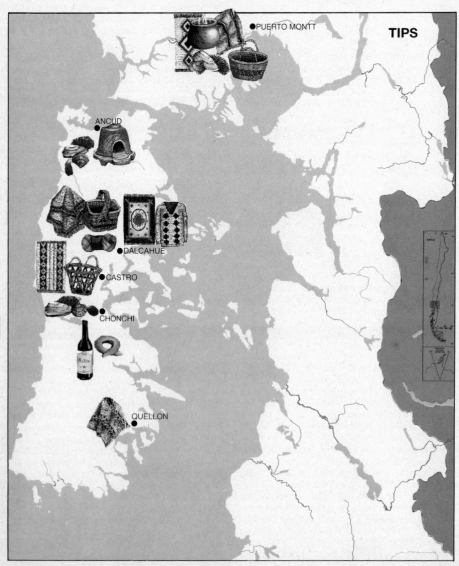

12

Zone 13
THE SOUTHERN HIGHWAY

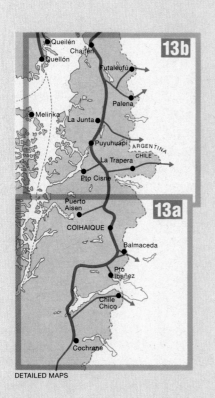

13b

Queilén
Chaitén
Quellón
Futaleufú
Palena
Melinka
La Junta
Puyuhuapi
ARGENTINA
CHILE
La Trapera
Pto Cisne

13a

Puerto Aisen
COIHAIQUE
Balmaceda
Pto Ibañez
Chile Chico
Cochrane

DETAILED MAPS

Arica

Iquique

Antofagasta

Copiapó

Easter
Island

La Serena

Valparaíso

Is R
Crusoe

SANTIAGO

Talca

Concepción

Temuco

Valdivia

Osorno

Pto Montt

Castro
Chaitén

Coihaique

Cochrane

Puerto Natales

Punta Arenas

Puerto Williams

13

Is Diego
Ramírez

90° 60° 53°

CHILEAN
ANTARCTIC
TERRITORY

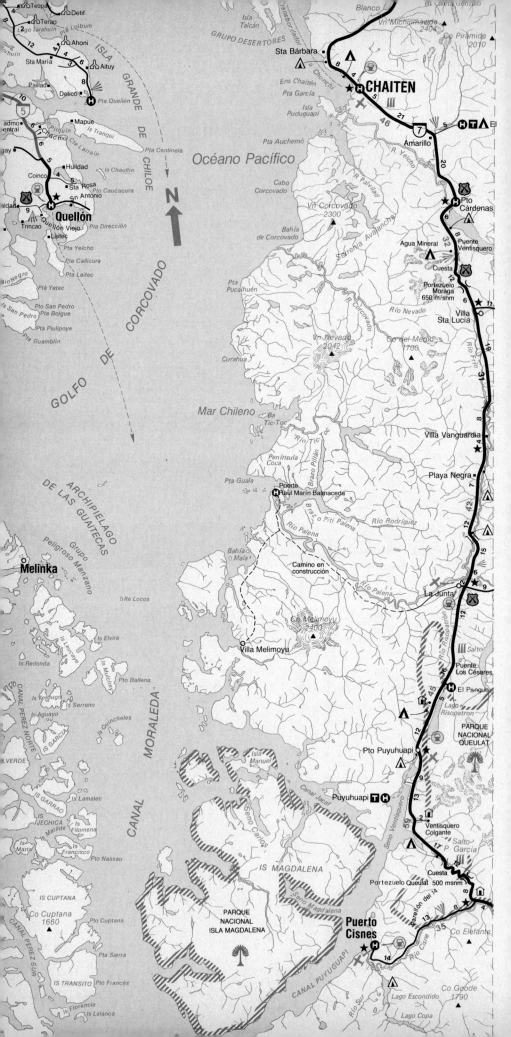

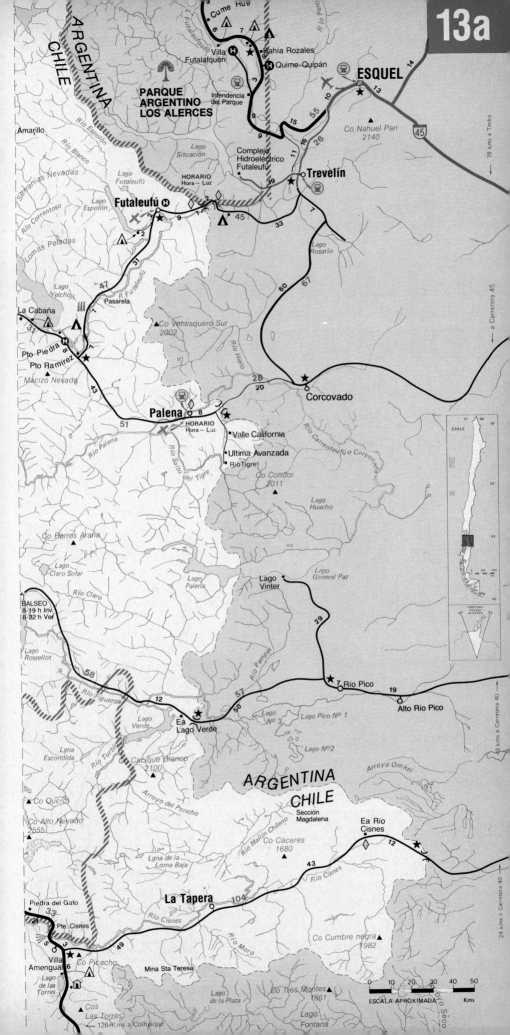

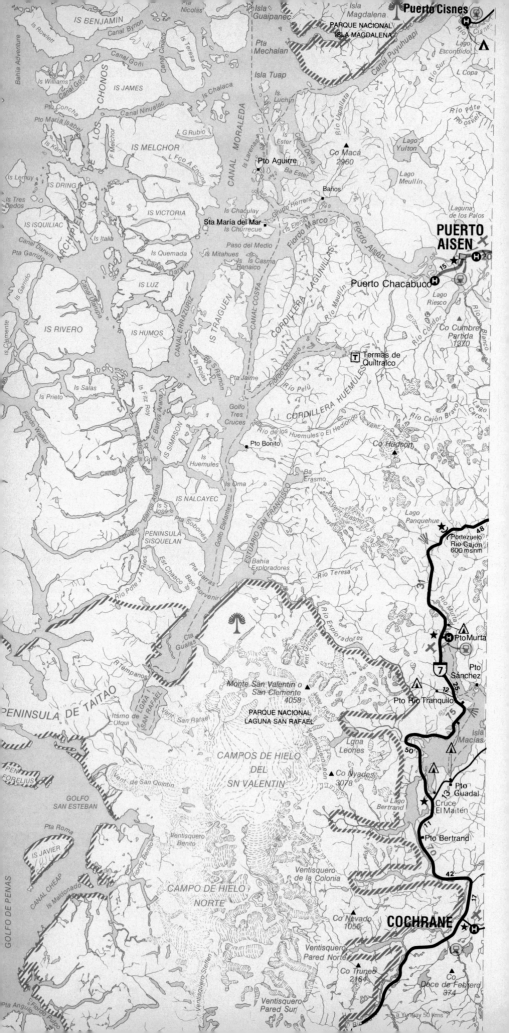

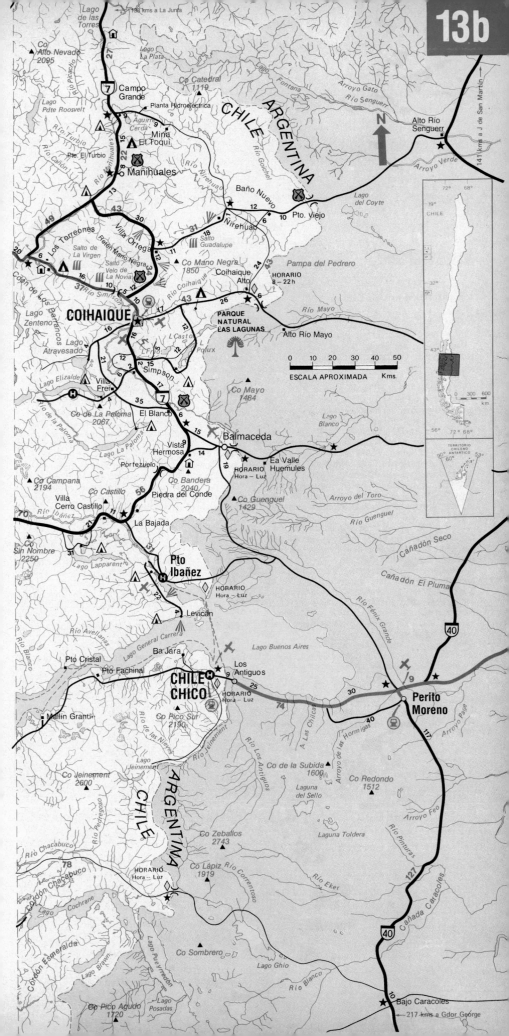

Lago de las Torres
Lago La Plata
Co Alto Nevado 2095
198 kms a La Junta
Co Catedral 1119
Río Fontana
Arroyo Gato
Río Senguerr
141 kms a J de San Martín

CHILE
ARGENTINA
N

Campo Grande
Planta Hidroeléctrica
Aguirre Cerda
Mina El Toqui
Río Ñirehuao
Baño Nuevo
Lago del Coyte
Alto Río Senguerr

Río Turbio
Pte. El Turbio
Río Mañihuales
Río Mañihuales
Mañihuales
Baño Nuevo
Pto. Viejo

Los Torreones
Villa Ortega
Retén Mano Negra
Ñirehuao
Salto Guadalupe
Pampa del Pedrero

Salto de La Virgen
Salto Velo de La Novia
Río Simpson
Co Mano Negra 1850
Coihaique Alto
HORARIO 8 – 22 h

Colón de Los Barrancos
Río Simpson
Río Coihaique
Río Mayo

Lago Zenteno
COIHAIQUE
PARQUE NATURAL LAS LAGUNAS
Alto Río Mayo

Lago Atravesado
L Castor
L Pollux

Lago Elizalde
Simpson
Co Mayo 1484
Lago Blanco

Río de la Paloma
Villa Frei
El Blanco
Balmaceda

Co de La Paloma 2067
Vista Hermosa
HORARIO Hora – Luz
Ea Valle Huemules

Lago La Paloma
Portezuelo
Co Bandera 2040
Co Guenguel 1429

Co Campana 2194
Co Castillo
Piedra del Conde
Arroyo del Toro
Río Guenguel

Villa Cerro Castillo
La Bajada
Cañadón Seco

Co Sin Nombre 2250
Río Ibáñez
Lago Lapparent
Cañadón El Pluma

Pto Ibáñez
Río Fénix Grande
40

Levicán
Lago Buenos Aires

Río Avellanas
Río Blanco
Ba Jara
Lago General Carrera

Pto Cristal
Pto Fachinal
CHILE CHICO
Los Antiguos
30
Perito Moreno
9
117

Mallín Grande
HORARIO Hora – Luz
74
A Las Chicas
40
Arroyo Paje

Co Pico Sur 2190
Río de las Nieves
Co de la Subida 1600
Arroyo de las Hormigas
127

Co Jeinement 2600
Lago Jeinement
Río Jeinement
Laguna del Sello
Co Redondo 1512
Arroyo Feo
Río Pinturas

Río Chacabuco
Co Zeballos 2743
Arroyo Feo

Río Pedregoso
CHILE
ARGENTINA
Río Correntoso
Laguna Toldera
Río Eker

Cordón Chacabuco
78
HORARIO Hora – Luz
Co Lápiz 1919
Cañada Caracoles
40

Cochrane
Lago Brown
Lago Pueyrredón
Río Blanco
Bajo Caracoles
10
217 kms a Gdor George

Co Pico Agudo 1720
Lago Posadas
Co Sombrero
Lago Ghio

ESCALA APROXIMADA Kms.
0 10 20 30 40 50

CHILE
TERRITORIO CHILENO ANTARTICO

MEAN ANNUAL RAINFALL

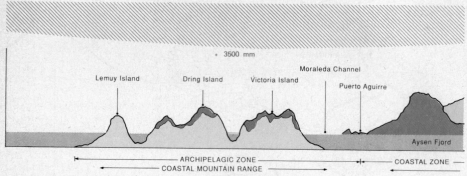

+ 3500 mm

Lemuy Island   Dring Island   Victoria Island   Moraleda Channel   Puerto Aguirre

Aysen Fjord

|← ARCHIPELAGIC ZONE →|← COASTAL ZONE →|
|← COASTAL MOUNTAIN RANGE →|

TOPOGRAPHIC AND RAINFALL DIAGRAM

OVERVIEW

This zone covers the section of mainland Chile stretching from the Comau fjord in the north to lake General Carrera in the south, the area traversed by the recently opened Carretera Austral (Southern Highway). Chaitén, Futaleufú and Palena are located in the Palena province, which lies in Region X. The remaining area falls within the boundaries of Region XI (Aisén). The total population of this zone is 81,632 inhabitants.

The **Carretera Austral Presidente Pinochet** is a great undertaking started in 1976 under an initiative of the then President of Chile. The main portion of the road was opened for public use in 1983, running from Coyhaique to Chaitén. The section north from Chaitén to Puerto Montt was finished in 1988, together with the extension to Cochrane from Coyhaique. The total length of the Carretera –so far– is over 1,000 km. Work is still under way on a further extension up to the mouth of river Baker in the south, and in opening further roads branching east and west off the Carretera.

The Carretera Austral follows the best possible route through the area, based on aerial cartographic surveys. All collateral works –such as rainwater ditches and ducts– are definitive, as well as the concrete bridges. Although it is graveled all the way and it is pretty narrow at times, blind corners and all, driving the length of the Carretera is no adventure in itself. In fact, it is better surfaced than some other, long–established roads in the rest of Chile. However, its supporting infrastructure is still quite spartan, being the road so recent and running through one of Chile's most sparsely populated areas. It is advisable to keep a reserve canister of gasoline, although this is by no means an absolute must. This is Chile's best area for free-lance camping, and special care has been taken to indicate every place of interest for camping fans. Hitchhikers must bear in mind that rainfall here is abundant and that traffic can be quite sparse at times.

The real treat is to make detours off the main road, exploring the untouched cold jungles, glaciers, calm lakes, and hidden waterfalls in the surrounding area, and being constantly rewarded by sightings of a wildlife that does not -yet- see man as an enemy. The history of the area is so recent, that it is still possible to meet the first settler who opened a given area.

This Zone has been divided into four sections:

Section A Chaitén from the Comau fjord in the north to the Palena river in the south.

Section B Central Area from the Palena river to the Cisnes river. It is the most spectacular section.

Section C Coyhaique the first area settled in Aysén.

Section D Lake General Carrera remote and mysterious, and beautiful.

REGIONAL DISTANCES

Balmaceda

533	Caleta Gonzalo														
320	830	Cochrane													
57	476	354	Coihaique												
436	56	774	420	Chaitén											
434	208	772	418	152	Futaleufú										
380	269	677	323	213	211	Lake Verde									
322	211	619	265	155	153	58	La Junta								
175	685	145	209	629	627	585	474	Murta							
122	468	414	60	376	374	315	257	269	Ñireguao						
472	205	759	415	149	89	208	150	624	407	Palena					
124	454	421	67	361	359	264	206	276	109	356	Puerto Aisén				
256	338	558	204	282	280	185	127	413	196	277	181	Puerto Cisnes			
95	605	287	129	508	506	411	353	189	194	503	196	328	Puerto Ingeniero Ibáñez		
238	254	576	222	198	196	101	43	431	214	193	163	84	301	Puyuhuapi	
359	133	697	343	77	75	136	78	552	335	72	284	205	431	121	Santa Lucía

13

Zone 13
SOUTHERN HIGHWAY

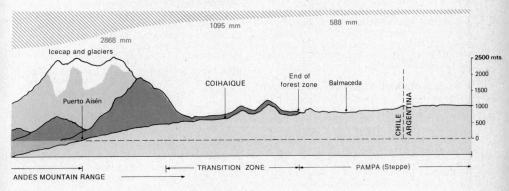

2868 mm

1095 mm

588 mm

Icecap and glaciers

2500 mts.
2000
1500
1000
500
0

Puerto Aisén

COIHAIQUE

End of forest zone

Balmaceda

CHILE

ARGENTINA

ANDES MOUNTAIN RANGE

TRANSITION ZONE

PAMPA (Steppe)

DIVISION BY SECTIONS

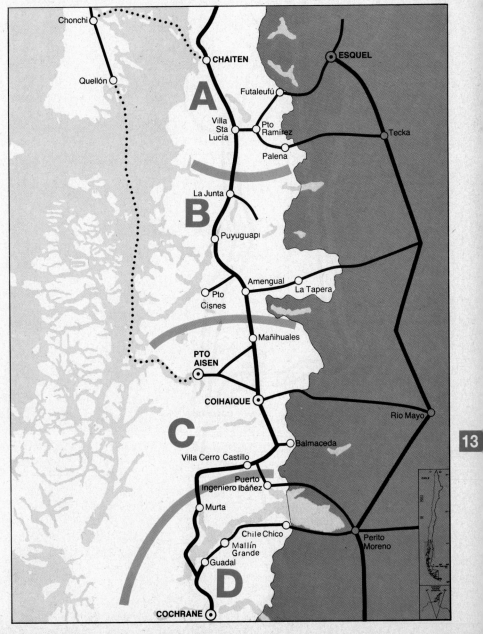

HOW TO COVER THE ZONE

There are three possible circuits covering the entire zone, all going and returning through different routes -thus constantly providing something fresh for the eye.

1 Carretera Austral–Chiloé starts from Puerto Montt southward over land, with ferry crossings to reach Chaitén, then on to Coihaique and Cochrane, to return by sea from Puerto Chacabuco via the island of Chiloé.

2 Puerto Montt–Puerto Chacabuco–Chaitén sailing on the Evangelistas of Navimag from Puerto Montt, through the channels and calling at several island ports along the way, to disembark at Puerto Chacabuco. Thence, by land to Coihaique, then south to Cochrane and, lastly, north to Chaitén, to board there the ferry for Chiloé. If you are not driving, there is an excellent option to Puerto Chacabuco in the modern and fast catamarán Patagonia express; see Services Section.

3 Puyehue–Argentine National Parks–Carretera Austral crossing into Argentina from Osorno, driving through the beautiful and well–equipped Argentinian national parks of Nahuelhuapi, Puelo, and Los Alerces, to return into Chile through Futaleufú. From there to Chaitén and to the south. The return trip entails retracing part of the Carretera up to Chaitén, with some parts on ferry, to continue overland back to Puerto Montt.

Note check with Transmarchilay (see addresses/telephone numbers under Services section) whether it is necessary to make reservations for the ferry crossings between Puerto Montt and Chaitén. (See Shipping services in the Service Section).

By Air Lan and Ladeco have regular flights from Santiago to Coihaique. These flights stop and carry passengers to and from Puerto Montt. Charter flights administered by companies in Puerto Montt to Chantén, Palena y Futaleufú. See Services Section.

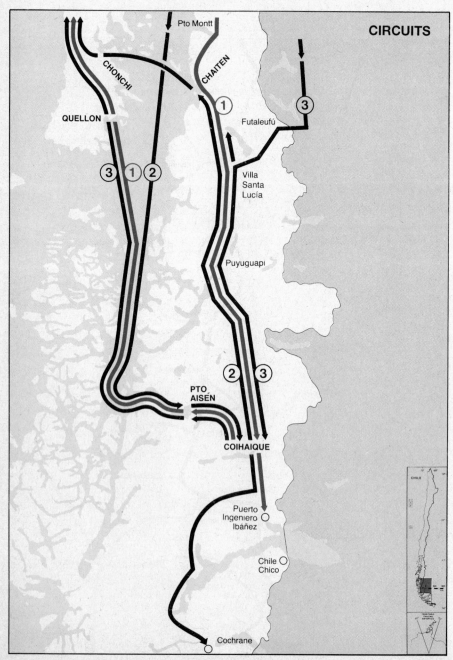

THE LAND, ITS HISTORY, ITS PEOPLE

ORIGINS this zone, same as Chiloé, has been largely shaped by tectonic movements and by the last Ice Age. Large faults gash the mainland at 45° angles, creating the Puyuhuapi fjord and other such inlets. The retreating glaciers, at the end of the last Ice Age, eroded the valley bottoms to such a degree that sea water eventually flooded them and gave rise to the present–day channels and fjords.

CLIMATE AND TOPOGRAPHY unlike the rest of Chile, here the Andes fall directly into the sea, and the tops of the submerged Coastal Range give rise to the archipelagos and their tortuous channels to the west. An additional oddity is that part of the Chilean territory here lies at times east of the Andes. Three distinct climatic zones can be made out: the **coastal and insular** area (Aisén), with over 3,000 mm of rainfall annually; the **transition area** (Coihaique), with around 950–mm rainfall; and the **bunch–grass pampa** or steppe (Balmaceda), with 500–mm rainfall annually.

RIVERS the major rivers in this zone are the **Futaleufú** (Yelcho), **Palena, Cisnes, Simpson** (Aisén), and **Baker**. Only the Cisnes and Simpson rivers have their basins entirely within Chilean territory. A significant portion of the other basins lies beyond the border.

EARLY INHABITANTS the aboriginal island people were the **Chonos,** experts in sailing these waters by canoe. They became extinct by 1870. A few of them were assimilated in Chiloé, to where they had been brought by Jesuit missionaries in the 18th century. South of the Ofqui isthmus, at the mouth of the Baker river, were the **Caucahues,** some of whom were also brought to Chiloé by the Jesuits. The highland steppes were roamed by the **Tehuelches,** a nomadic people who left rock paintings surviving to this day. The thickly–forested Andes proved an impassable barrier for the highland and island tribes, preventing them from making contact with one another.

CONTACT WITH EUROPEANS this zone's intricate waterways were discovered and explored by Spanish navigators during the early stages of the Conquest. They called the area Trepananda. The great explorer and geographer Moraleda (1794) was of the opinion that Spain would never settle these coasts, because they lacked good access by sea and land (the forests were impenetrable). Charles Darwin described this area (1828) as a «green desert».

CHILEAN OCCUPATION influenced by the above opinions, the State long regarded these lands as marginal; the official gaze was focused upon Chiloé and Magallanes, leaving this **in–between** area unattended; it was the last portion of mainland Chile to be settled. There were only some half–hearted official attempts at exploration and settlement, the most significant being the three expeditions led by Capt E Simpson, who reached the edges of the Coihaique valley in 1871, and a settlement set up at the Los Leones lake (at the mouth of the Palena river) in 1884; it was soon deserted.

The first explorer of the frontier land was the Englishman G C Munsters (1869), who spent a year travelling with the Tehuelches and came into Chile at Alto Palena. Soon thereafter, official Argentine expeditions explored the frontier area. Francisco Moreno surveyed the Patagonia and discovered lake O'Higgins (1876–1877); Carlos Moyano discovered lake General Carrera (1880); J L Fontana found the headwaters of the Cisnes river (1882). A group of Welsh settlers established at Trelew, on the Atlantic coast, occupied the 16 de Octubre valley, on the upper Futaleufú river. J Richard (1896) found the Ñireguao valley.

Chile lacked information on these lands. Therefore, the government commissioned Dr Hans Steffen, a German teaching History and Geography at the Instituto Pedagógico of Santiago, to explore the area. He took his commission quite seriously: in a monumental effort, he surveyed the entire zone, walking up from the mouth to the headwaters of rivers Palena

(1894); Puelo and Manso (1895); Aisén and Mañihuales (1896); Cisnes (1898); and Baker and Cochrane (1899). An outstanding border dispute with Argentina on this area was submitted for arbitration to the King of England in 1899. The present boundaries resulted from his verdict in 1902.

The fertile upper valleys of rivers Manso, Puelo and Futaleufú were settled by Welsh immigrants arrived from Trelew. In a referendum held at Trevelín in 1901, they opted for Argentinian nationality.

COLONIZATION BY FARMING COMPANIES the Chilean government decided to apply here a colonization policy similar to that applied in Magallanes. The one difference was that this area had no service towns whatsoever. The best lands of the transition and pampa areas were given under concession to three livestock farming companies, under the condition that they ship their products out through Chilean territory and that they bring settlers into the area. **Sociedad Industrial de Aisén** (SIA) started to operate in 1903, with 826,900 hectares. **Sociedad Exploradora del Baker** followed in 1908, officially running 80,000 hectares but actually controlling a great deal more. Last, **Sociedad Ganadera Cisnes** came into being in 1924, with 150,000 hectares. The main shareholders were estancia owners from Magallanes, and the only company which complied with the conditions of the contract was SIA, which built trails and brought its products out through Puerto Aisén. The other two companies depended totally on Argentina, where its stockholders owned further tracts along the border. The concessions had been granted for a limited amount of time, and the government reduced gradually the size of the areas allocated until, in 1969, all contracts were terminated. Now there are four large privately–owned estancias in the area, covering some 50,000 hectares on average.

COLONIZATION BY PRIVATE INDIVIDUALS this type of colonization was tacitly accepted, but regularized only by 1937. Chilean farmers from the central zone were the first settlers. Driving their herds, they moved south along Argentinian Patagonia. When the arbitration verdict established the international boundary, they crossed into Chilean territory, settling Balmaceda (1901), Puerto Ibáñez (1908), Chile Chico (1909), Valle Simpson (1912) and Lago Verde (1914).

A violent Argentine police repression against Chileans living on the Argentinian frontier lands (1920) pushed the Chileans across the border into the lands lying along the edges of the large livestock farming concessions, and also into Futaleufú and Palena.

It was also private individuals who settled the coast, originally quite on their own and, much later, with some state support. They came from Chiloé and were mostly engaged in logging the cypress forests. F A Westhoff, a Lithuanian emigrant, settled down at the Guaitecas islands in 1859 and founded Melinka (after his wife's name). He owned over 200 ships engaged in the timber business. Ciriaco Alvarez (1880) set up warehouses, a house and a sawmill in the vicinity of Puerto Aisén, and eventually came to be known as the cypress king; hundreds of lumberjacks from Chiloé worked for him on the islands.

INSTITUTIONAL DEVELOPMENT for nearly two decades there was no public or urban infrastructure to speak of. The first village was founded by private individuals (Balmaceda, in 1917). The large livestock farming companies did not establish any settlement, only camps for their workers. A police station was set up in 1920 next to the casco -the administrative, workshop and housing compound- of the SIA estancia in Coihaique. Puerto Aisén started to take form around 1924.

In 1928, the Territory of Aisén came officially into its own, with Regional Government (Intendencia) and Municipal Administration (Municipio) at Puerto Aisén. Coihaique and Cochrane were founded in the following two years, and the settlements in Palena, Chile Chico and Puerto Ibáñez were granted town status. A road from Puerto Aisén reached Coihaique in 1936. Trails were also opened to the heartland, enabling

13

COLONIZATION

Sheep Farming Companies

Firts Concessions

Present Livestock Farming Companies

Individual Settlers

Firts Settlers

1901 to 1920

1921 to 1930

1931 to 1940

1941 to 1950

1951 to 1960

1961 to 1985

EXPLORATIONS

→ George Charles Muster

━ Capt. Enrique Simpson

→ Dr. Hans Steffen

← Argentine Explorers

← Chilean Settlers

SETTLEMENTS

Fundation or Official Status
Granted to Existing Settlements

Firts Settlements

From 1929 to 1930

+ From 1932 to 1959

● From 1968 to 1970

■ After 1982

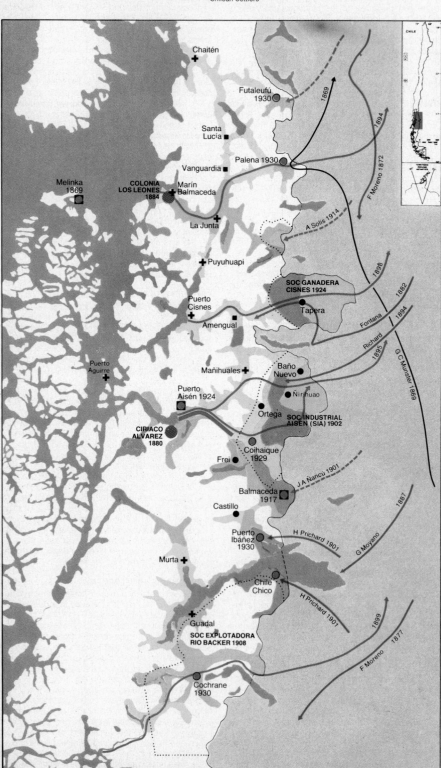

Chaitén

Futaleufú 1930

Santa Lucía

Vanguardia

Palena 1930

Melinka 1869

COLONIA LOS LEONES

Marín Balmaceda

La Junta

Puyuhuapi

SOC GANADERA CISNES 1924

Puerto Cisnes

Tapera

Amengual

Puerto Aguirre

Mañihuales

Baño Nuevo

Ñirihuao

Puerto Aisén 1924

Ortega

SOC INDUSTRIAL AISEN (SIA) 1902

CIRIACO ALVAREZ 1880

Coihaique 1929

Frei

J A Ñancu 1901

Balmaceda 1917

Castillo

Puerto Ibáñez 1930

Murta

Chile Chico

H Prichard 1901

G Moyano

Guadal

SOC EXPLOTADORA RIO BACKER 1908

F Moreno 1877

Cochrane 1930

1869

1894

F Moreno 1872

A Solís 1914

1898

1882

Fontana

1894

Richard

1895

G C Munster 1869

H Prichard 1901

1887

1899

CHILE

13

settlers to move from Coihaique to Mañihuales and Campo Grande; from Puerto Cisnes to the border, and from Chaitén to lake Yelcho and Palena.

THE GREAT FIRES when the area granted under concession to the large farming corporations started to be reduced in size, the land becoming available was offered to individual settlers. These lands were located in the densely-wooded intermediate sector, the settlers having to clear the forest gradually to open land for livestock farming. The system they used was controlled fires. In 1937, however, a colonization law came into effect which was to unleash a colossal ecological disaster: it set as a condition for granting ownership of the land to the settler that the forests be clear–cut, making the land apt for farming. Fire was once more the tool employed. By 1940, a long cycle of gigantic fires started to sweep the land, their smoke reaching all the way to the Atlantic coast. The beautiful, ancient forests never regenerated. Now thousands of dead logs lie upon the hillsides for kilometers on end, particularly at Alto Palena and Mañihuales.

PRESENT DEVELOPMENT the area received a significant boost with the construction of a road linking Coihaique and Puerto Ibáñez, Valle Simpson, and Mañihuales, and another road from Chaitén to lake Yelcho and Palena. Small airfields were built at each settlement. In 1962, a hydroelectric plant went on

Ferry

stream at Puerto Aisén and by 1969 seven villages had been founded at the freshly–expropriated livestock farms. The task of integrating and developing this area has received a strong boost in the last ten years with the opening of the Carretera Austral road network, the establishment of ferry services by Transmarchilay, the opening of new areas for colonization, and the creation of Region IX, with its capital at Coihaique.

SECTION A   CHAITEN

This section comprises the mainland portion stretching from the Reñihue and Comau fjords in the north, to the Frío river valley in the south. It includes the Palena province and the northern reaches of Region XI (Aisén). The Frío river runs southward and is joined half way down by its main tributary, the Palena river, to which it then loses its name.
Note the stretch Puerto Montt–Hornopirén (Río Negro) is described in Zone 11, Sector D, under Tour 5.

1 CARRETERA AUSTRAL FROM RIO NEGRO (HORNOPIREN) TO CHAITEN ★★★ *a 97–km stretch of gravel road, plus about 5 sailing hours –plus waiting times for the ferries. Allow one day. Accommodation, supplies and gasoline at Río Negro and Chaitén. Ferry reservations in advance, see Shipping services in the Service Section.*
The northern portion of the Carretera Austral, the last to be opened for public use (1988).
The Ferry service changes its itinerary anually. Here we will explain the 2 different routes used by these.
2 Ferries route departutve by car from río Negro–Hornopirén (Km 0) on the coastal road running next to a placid channel. The thickly–wooded **Isla de Los Ciervos** sits across the water; it owes its name to the red deer and pudús (a sort of mini–deer) dwelling in its forests, together with some beavers. The forest contains some millenary alerce trees, a conifer similar to larch. The island is accessible through a fishing cove on its southern coast. Guided tours to various ponds in the island are on offer.
The rugged Llancahué island comes next into view, with its fabulous thermal waters and hiking trails amid lovely scenery. The road runs above a cliff and crosses the swift Blanco river at km 9. Then, at km 21, it becomes curvy, at times steep, offering good views of the cliffs and the fjord. At km 30 is the old settlement of **Cholgo**, where a modern salmon farm has recently been established, with very good facilities. A boat can be hired here to **Termas de Llancahué**, with a small, un-assuming hotel (good food). There is a hot spring at the hotel, and cabins to take thermal baths. Another hot spring surges underwater at the beach below the hotel. A warm evening bath in the placid sea, with the sun setting on the small Llanchid archipelago straight ahead, is trance–inducing. Glorious.
The road climbs again to become just a narrow ledge carved on a rocky cliff, at times up to 100 m above the waters. Drive carefully; there are some blind corners. At km 37 is **Pichanco**, with a solitary ramp to board ferry Mailel (4–5 times daily)

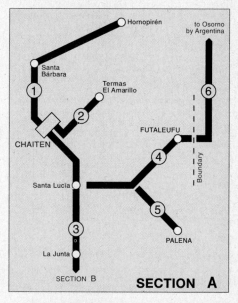

Hornopirén

to Osorno by Argentina

Santa Bárbara

(1)

Termas El Amarillo

(2)

(6)

FUTALEUFU

CHAITEN

(4)

Boundary

Santa Lucía

(5)

(3)

PALENA

La Junta

SECTION B

SECTION A

for the 2¹/₂ hour crossing the length of the Comau (also known as Leptepu) fjord. It is best to board the ferry in reverse: the dock is rather steep at the other end. The ferry sails along the

Comau Fjord with steep walls and snowy peaks at the far end. Soon after setting out, the ferry passes the steep, narrow **Quintupeu** fjord to the left. In 1915, the German battleship Dresden hid here from the pursuing British fleet. The crew was protected by the Llanquihue German colony. The names of some Dresden sailors are still to be seen carved on the fjord's rocky walls.
A second fjord comes soon into view, branching off to the east; here are the Cahuelmó thermal baths. Some scattered houses of settlers can be seen on the steep coast of the Comau fjord. The ferry docks at

Leptepu a solitary place at the mouth of the Vodudahue river. Nearby are very old alerces, some around 4,200 years old, among the world's oldest living trees. Two km from the ramp, only accessible by boat, are the spectacular **Porcelain Hot Springs,** next to the river among whitish stones and with pools of steaming water at 60° C, amid jungle and ferns. To visit these springs, broadcast a message on Radio Reloncaví in Puerto Montt

13

Chaitén and Corcovado volcano

(between 12:00 and 14:00 h) asking to be picked up at the ferry landing; the settler will come for you in an open boat. He charges a very modest fee and has meat, bread and vegetables on offer. Take a tent if you want to camp there.

The climb out of the Leptepu dock is quite steep at the beginning, then levels out. A coarse–gravel stretch crosses the wooded peninsula. At the Pillán bridge a short road branching left leads to **Blanco fjord,** off the tip of Reñihue fjord, where a modern fish farm started operations recently. The main road ends at **fiordo Largo,** where the next ferry docks. The ramp is steep, and you either board in reverse or turn the vehicle around once aboard. This ferry has only half the capacity of the previous one. For those pulling a boat trailer, see Zone 12, Section D, Tour 4, about possible boat excursions along this fjord.

The crossing of the **Reñihue fjord** takes about 30 min; the ferry hugs the coast and docks at **Caleta Gonzalo,** another solitary place with a spot suitable for camping.

Single ferry route departure from Hornopirén and 5 sailing hours, skirting the coast between the islands **Los Ciervos** y **Llancahué.** The ferry sails through channel Comau into the open sea –this is the rougher part– and after skirting the peninsula gets into the **Reñihue fiord** to disembarck at **Gonzalo Cove.**

From Caleta Gonzalo (km 0), the road climbs through virgin forest at the foot of volcano Michinmávida (2,404 m). At km 10, ramrod alerces can be seen, some living and some burned, their trunks measuring up to 2.7 m in diameter. Nearby is **lake Negro,** difficult of access and hemmed in by

sheer mountains plummeting to its shores. Ahead, the road climbs for a short stretch to **lake Blanco,** with beautiful scenery and excellent fishing.

At km 27 a river is crossed, carrying volcanic slag from the Michinmávida, and then the road descends gently toward the coast, to reach, at km 44,

Santa Bárbara take short detour to the right. The bridge is out of order, but the stream can be forded to visit the area's best beach, with black sand and good for bathing. There is a fishing cove at the south end. A long beach stretches north-ward, with a virgin jungle at its rear, ending at the **Morro Vilcún** promontory. The beach is a very good place for camping away from it all.

The road continues along the coast. At km 52 is the Los Arrayanes Municipal Campground, with facilities and located next to a beach. A few kilometers ahead are port facilities and the dock for the ferry from Chiloé, and at km 56 is

CHAITEN (pop 3,200), the capital of Palena province since 1981. Of recent establishment, it only had two or three houses in 1933. The small ferry Tenglo of state–owned Ferronave started to call monthly in 1938. In 1946 a wireless station was set up, and the Servicio Militar del Trabajo, a working outfit for people making their military service, started construction of the road to lake Yelcho. The settlement had only one street then, christened Juan Tudesco after the place's first parish priest. Chaitén was the supply post for the Yelcho, Palena, and Futaleufú settlers. The supplies used to be transported by boat, eight rowers struggling upstream up to Puerto Cárdenas and then through the lake to Puerto Ramírez. Then, by horse on the trail to Palena.

Now Chaitén offers all the services, including hotels, such as Mi Casa, with a good view, and Schilling, in addition to several residenciales and campsites. It has good communications, including an airfield with paved runway, and port facilities for the ferry linking it to Chonchi, Chiloé, and Pargua. The town is well laid, with wide streets. From the **Costanera** there is a view to **volcano Corcovado.**

How To Get There **by Sea** the ferries communicating Chaitén with the island of Chiloé and/or Puerto Montt change their ports of call annually. (see present itinerary in Shipping services in the Services Section). **By Air** there are companies with departures from Puerto Montt; see air services in Services Section.

TOURS FROM CHAITEN

2 TO TERMAS DEL AMARILLO ★★★
round trip of 62 km. Follow the Carretera 26 km to

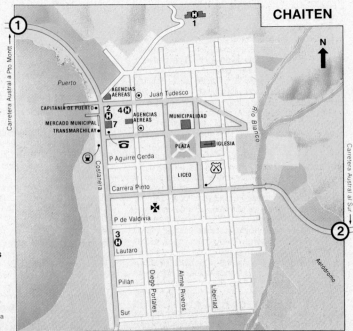

CHAITEN

Telephone
Café, Meeting Point
Touristic Information
Gasoline Station
Hospital

ACCOMMODATIONS
1 H Mi Casa
2 Hs Shilling
4 H Continental
3 Bh Futaleufú

RESTAURANTS
7 Café Rest Sta Barbara
Cocinerías Mercado

Carretera Austral a Pto Montt
Carretera Austral al Sur
Puerto
AGENCIAS AEREAS Juan Tudesco
CAPITANIA DE PUERTO
MERCADO MUNICIPAL TRANSMARCHILAY
AGENCIAS AEREAS
MUNICIPALIDAD
PLAZA IGLESIA
P Aguirre Cerda
Costanera
Rio Blanco
LICEO
Carrera Pinto
P de Valdivia
Lautaro
Pillán
Diego Portales
Aime Riveros
Libertad
Sur
Aerodromo
N

13

the south, in the direction of lake Yelcho. At the village there take branch to the left leading in 5 km to the Termas.

A lovely, densely–wooded mountain dell with thermal waters. Two wooden sheds with a concrete pool inside, very hot water running continuously. Also an outdoor thermal pool, cabins sleeping four, telephone, a sauna, and a campsite with no facilities but where a meal service can be arranged at the basic restaurant at the site. Accommodation is being improved.

A failed attempt to build a road from here to Futaleufú in 1956 provides an interesting challenge to devotees of trekking who don't mind wet feet (this is a rainy area). The trail follows the river Michimahuida and skirts the namesake volcano, to reach lake Espolón in 4 to 7 days. From there it is not far to Futaleufú.

3 CARRETERA AUSTRAL TO LA JUNTA ★★★

it is 46 km to Puerto Cárdenas, 78 km to Santa Lucía, 151 km to La Junta. Take food.

The road runs through vast, old–growth forests, and glaciers, with the Cordillera de los Andes marching on both sides.

Leave Chaitén (km 0) following the Carretera to the south. At km 5 a waterfall tumbles down the face of a rocky cliff. At km 26 is a bridge and the village of **Amarillo**. A valley marches into the mountains, its green slopes in stark contrast with the icecap of volcano Michimahuida, towering close by.

The road reaches Puerto Cárdenas at km 46. This section of the road was finished in the 1960s. **Puerto Cárdenas** is a hamlet on the shores of lake Yelcho. It has an airfield, public telephone, accommodation at Hostería Yelcho (frequented by devotees of fishing), and a large boat ramp. The village dates from the 1940s, but the opening of roads has eroded its former role as a trading post. However, it may have a bright future in the tourist business as the main port of

LAKE YELCHO one of Chile's most beautiful lakes, its emerald–green waters hemmed in by tall, steep mountains capped by icebergs and with slopes heavy with forest. There are very few open beaches.

A boat cruise through the lake is recommended, lasting from 1 to 6 days and visiting coves, islands and lakeshore settlements, and enjoying superb rainbow trout fishing (other varieties include Brook trout and sea trout). The luxurious boat Puma sleeps 6 passengers, plus 5 crew members, and can be hired for one day or up to a week. The owner of the small steamer Cristina, with more modest accommodations, can be contacted on the side of the port. See section Services and Prices.

The road section from Puerto Cárdenas to the south was opened for public use in February 1982. A new bridge –the largest in the Carretera– spans the **river Yelcho** at the northern tip of the lake. The road then follows the lakeshore; at km 52 is a beach suitable for camping.

At km 53, the road turns away from the lakeshore. One km ahead is the **Cavi** tourist complex, with a restaurant, an inn, cabins and a campground. At km 57 there is a sign reading **Agua Mineral**; walk 60 m into the jungle to pools of cool, bubbling mineral water.

At km 60 is

Ventisquero Bridge (signposted). A privately–owned campground is on the river bank, amid the native forest. It includes roofed fireplaces. There are two paths, one on each side of the river, to the hanging **Yelcho glacier** which can be seen from the bridge (2 hours). Note the huge leaves of the nalcas lining the paths: they offer unbeatable protection in case of an unexpected rain shower. The paths reach the foot of the glacier itself, whence numerous waterfalls cascade down the slope.

Ahead the Carretera starts to climb gently. It is the stretch known as **Cuesta Moraga**. Assistance in case of emergency can be found at km 63, at the Moraga police station, or at the road building camp at km 66. The summit is reached at km 72 (650 m above sea level). There is a good **view** over the lake Yelcho basin and the glaciers to the north, and to the south towards the long valley of the Frío river. The descent, called Moraga Sur, is also gentle and runs above the Frío river over a ledge

view from the Southern Highway

cut on the hill side. Some beautiful cascades can be seen. At km 78 is

Santa Lucía a village established in 1982 at the point where the road to Futaleufú and Palena, and thence to Argentina, branches east. Here is also a military cavalry camp, surrounded by a curious stockade and main gate conveying a sort of Far West look. The streets have already been laid out, but there is only a handful of houses.

The Carretera continues southward close to the Frío river, through fields opened by settlers arrived in the 1940s. They came down from Palena on the frontier along the river, and from lake Yelcho on trails they hacked through the jungle.

From km 90 onwards, the road runs on a ledge above the wide, milky, meandering Frío river. Its color results from the many glaciers feeding it. At km 97 the road crosses to the right–hand side of the river and reaches, at km 105, **Villa Vanguardia**, with eight good houses, drinking water and electricity supplies. The village was built by the state to provide services for the Carretera. Check in Chaitén whether the houses are available for rent by tourists. The first house on the right, before the gate, offers supplies, bread, and good, cheap homemade meals (and a telephone).

At km 109 is the boundary between Regions X and XI (signposted), and the point where rivers

FRIO AND PALENA MEET the Palena river comes from Argentina and runs into the Frío river on a wide curve with sandy banks. The river will now be called Palena, although it runs on the same course followed by the Frío river to this point. Some paths lead to the river banks.

The history of the name Palena is interesting. At the turn of the 18th century, an Italian Jesuit priest, father Mascardi, based at Castro on Chiloé, obsessed with the idea of finding an easy passageway to the Argentine pampas and carrying out his missionary work among the Tehuelche tribes there, set out by canoe to explore the area south of the Corcovado gulf. He discovered the mouth of this river, and rowed possibly up to La Junta. He christened it Palena after his native town near Pescara, on the Adriatic sea. The name was preserved thanks to geographers of the Chilean Navy's Hydrography Institute, who have sought to pay homage to the early explorers of these regions.

The road now runs away from the river, to reach, at km 116, a place called **Playa Negra**. Here lives the settler Raúl Gallardo, the first to arrive here in 1951, rowing upstream from the mouth of the river. During the 1950s, the area from the river confluence to the sea started to be colonized. The settlers opened a trail to the town of Palena to bring supplies.

At km 120 the land is clear of trees, with pastures in the plain and burnt forests on the slopes. At km 128 is the Palena bridge inaugurated in 1991. It is a narrow gap in the river, with a rocky cliff. A space in the forest has been made suitable for camping, with a small beach.

The road runs a further 15 km southward along the same valley. At km 143 the land opens to the east, announcing a large river –the Rossellot– flowing down from the Cordillera, and a valley opens to the west,

13

where the Palena river veers right and flows towards the ocean. This is the La Junta valley. At km 149 is the **Rossellot bridge** It was built in 1991 over the river Rossellot that originates in the mountain lakes. Before the bridge at your right hand is the Hostería Entre Ríos and 2 km ahead you get to La Junta. Both the hostería and the town are described at the beginning of this section.

4   A DETOUR TO FUTALEUFU ★★★

seventy–nine km from Santa Lucía or 155 km from Chaitén. A single–track gravel road passable in any normal car. Supplies but no gasoline at Futaleufú. Gasoline at Esquel (Argentina).

Fine scenery, travelling the length of the Futaleufú river along secluded valleys hemmed in by sheer mountains, and a challenging river for expert kayakers: the rapids are thrilling, to put it lightly.

From Santa Lucía (km 0), the road descends gently amidst forests to the northern end of lake Yelcho. At km 11 is **La Cabaña**, close to the lake, with lush conifers planted by young settlers arrived from Osorno in the 1940s. Now it is a comfortable hostería.

The road creeps for five km along a spectacular ledge carved on the face of a rocky cliff above the lake. At km 25 is a short detour to the left for **Puerto Piedra**, set on the banks of the Futaleufú river. It used to be the port where the ferry from Puerto Cárdenas, at the other end of lake Yelcho, docked. Now it has no more activity than that at the unassuming Hostería Alexis, and a very good municipal campground on the river bank. Boats for hire.

At km 31 the road forks; the right branch leads to Palena, the left one to Futaleufú. There is also a short detour to **Puerto Ramírez**, on the river bank. In the old times, the settlers disembarked here, after having rowed upstream all the way from the sea, to continue by horse to Palena. The road runs right up against sharp–cut rock walls to reach, at km 38, the

Futaleufú Bridge   a modern structure resting on the rocks constricting the roaring rapids below.

The road continues close to the river, through untouched lands. The river runs fast but smoothly, except for some occasional, hair–rising (for kayakers) rapids. The rapids start at km 45, where a suspension footbridge spans the river. Two km ahead there is a white–sand beach with pools of crystal–clear water, a good spot for picnicking and bathing.

At km 55 the road leaves the river banks and traverses cultivated lands, skirting **lake Lonconao** at km 71 and reaching, at km 76, the road branching off to the left for

LAKE ESPOLON   a long lake with good beaches and superb fishing. Several colonists line here, they rent motor and rowing boats. There are also cabins, campgrounds and hostería La Casa de Campo. It is worth a visit. Return to the main road, cross the Espolón river and a couple of km ahead is

FUTALEUFU   (pop 893). A well–laid frontier town, with wide, well-lit streets, it offers all the basic services. It has a good, small hostería and an airfield. The first settlers arrived here in the 1920's through Argentina, clearing the jungle. (The house of the first settler is shown in the town map.) By 1930 a horse trail was opened to the coast and soon thereafter a police outpost was set up, together with a post office and a registry office, to give a whiff of Chilean presence to a place entirely dependent on Argentina. In 1940 a large fire wiped out the jungle.

Effective contact with the rest of Chile started to take form as late as the 1960s, with the establishment of airline connections. It can be reached by road since 1982, when it became part of the Carretera Austral road network. Entrepreneurs have responded well to the place's attractiveness as a «way station» between Argentina and Chile, its superb.fishing and the fine scenery surrounding it. Good hotels have been set up, such as Hostería Posada Campesina La Gringa, in the town itself – along with the basic but recommended Hotel Continental–, and cabins and campgrounds on lake Espolón. In addition, there is an exclusive fishing lodge, Chilean Fly Angling, 8 km towards the border (see Services Section).

What To See   the log house of the first settler. At laguna Espejo, on the side of the hill, there is a stairway climbing to a look–out point with a view over the town and the valley. At bridge Jelvez –2.5 km on the road to the border– there is a short detour to the right to a suspension footbridge above breathtaking rapids.

To continue to Esquel, Argentina, drive 10 km on to the customs outpost (to speed up the formalities, it is advisable to request the permit from Policía Internacional at the city of departure and hand it to the officers at the control outpost). Two km ahead is the Argentine immigration outpost and, right beyond, a modern bridge spanning the Futaleufú river. From here, it is 33 km on a gravel road to **Trevelin**, a village founded by Welshmen last century, who in 1901 decided in a referendum that this should be Argentinian territory (see Land & History). A further 26 km on a paved road bring you to **Esquel** a city with complete tourist infrastructure.

5   TO PALENA AND THE CALIFORNIA VALLEY

★★★ *from the forking at Puerto Ramírez it is 51 km, one way, on a gravel road. Accommodation, food and gasoline at Palena.*

A tour through lands long since colonized, including the California valley and the Encuentro river, one of the two cases in Chile in which a river acts as the international boundary.

The road heads from Puerto Ramírez (km 0) towards rocky mountains, which it reaches at km 29. It then enters the wide valley of the Palena river. The extensive zone which burned in 1940

13

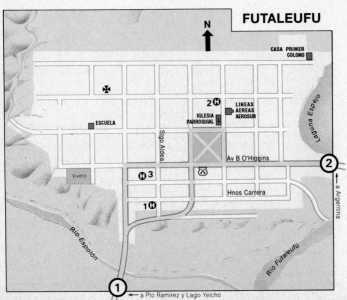

FUTALEUFU

N

CASA PRIMER COLONO

ESCUELA

IGLESIA PARROQUIAL

LINEAS AEREAS AEROSUR

Laguna Espejo

Av B O'Higgins

Hnos Carrera

Vivero

3

2

1

Sigo Aldea

a Argentina

Rio Espolón

Rio Futaleufú

1   a Pto Ramirez y Lago Yelcho

✠ Hospital
1 Hs Campesina La Gringa
2 Continental Hotel
3 Carahue Hotel

still bears the trunks of standing, dead trees. At km 43, the road reaches

PALENA (pop 919). Lying on a small plateau nestled between the river and the hill, the town has an irregular layout, as it grew around a farm road. It is a fairly prosperous town with all the basic services, and the most densely populated frontier outpost. It originated more or less at the same time as Futaleufú, and under similar circumstances. In 1929 it was granted village status and a trail linking it to Puerto Ramírez was made. In 1962 it found itself sitting smack in the middle of a very serious border dispute between Chile and Argentina, which ended with arbitration by the Queen of England; her verdict set the boundary at the **Encuentro** river and gave Chile the green, fertile **California Valley** then in dispute.

6 TO OSORNO VIA ARGENTINA ★★★
817 km from Palena; from Futaleufú, 666 km. Part of the road is paved, the rest gravel.
A beautiful circuit through the Argentine national parks of Los Alerces, Puelo, and Nahuelhuapi, with gorgeous lakes and outstanding tourist infrastructure, visiting Bariloche and returning into Chile through the Puyehue pass and one of Chile's finest national parks.

SECTION B   CENTRAL AREA

This section stretches from the town of La Junta in the north to lake Las Torres in the south, where Chile is squeezed by the Argentinian lake Fontana. The Carretera Austral in this section peeks over the ocean to turn once more into the inland valleys. Almost this entire area had no roads prior to the Carretera, only trails or paths. The Queulat National Park, until the Carretera reached it, had never been crossed by man.

This is the area with the greatest farming potential.

La Junta a busy –albeit still somewhat drab– little village with a good future, was founded as recently as 1983. It has telephones, supplies and gasoline, and accommodations at Hostería y Cabañas Espacio Tiempo (comfortable cabins with a fireplace and hot water; excellent food at the hostería). It sits at the confluence of rivers Rossellot, Palena and Risopatrón, and it will become a crossroads: a road is being built eastwards to Lago Verde on the border, and westwards to Puerto Marín Balmaceda, on the ocean; thence another road is to head south to Puerto Melimoyu. There are large tourist projects under way, including eco–hotels at the mouth of the Palena river.

The first settlers arrived at this valley from the sea, rowing the Palena river upstream.

SECTION **B**

TOURS

1 NAVIGATION TO LAS TONINAS ★★★
the first thing to be done to make this tour is to contract a touristic set or packet of tours for seven days and round trip with Complejo Las Toninas (Las Toninas Complex). Starting point in Entre Ríos hotel next to Rossellot bridge.
Visit to a modern ecological-touristic center placed at the mouth of Palena river, in the middle of the most wild archipelago and untouched jungle.

The wharf of the Entre Ríos Hotel is at the edge of Rossellot river. The tour is downstream by covered Zodiac boat during 4 hours up to Las Toninas.

Just at the beginning of the navigation, there appears the intersection with the Palena river. The river flows widely surrounded by lots of lands of the settlers of the place. Farther on there begins the untouched jungle. Past 1 1/2 hours of navegation we can find

Termas Puerto Bonito (Puerto Bonito Thermal Baths) place surrounded of jungle and uninhabited.

Entering a few meters along a pathway, a great natural thermal pond is found with waters reaching 45°C and coloured like cognac because of the high concentration of tannin coming from trees. Be careful when bathing. Near at hand there is another spring of cold water with pond full of wild flowers swimming on its surface. It is a very nice place. Allow at least 45 min.

Navigation continues winding downstream, encircled by forest, with a sweeping view to the imposing and beautiful Melimoyu volcano (2.400 m Lastly the current of the river flows northward up to the mouth at Golfo de Corcovado (Gulf of Corcovado). Shortly before this mouth we desembark to the left at

LAS TONINAS BEACH & WILDERNESS RESORT which is an ecological and touristic project whose stockholders have commited themselves to keep this place pure and in natural condition. There are facilities for owners and visitors. It has an extension of 1.025 hectares and a large peninsula looking to the sea and to the river.

It is on its initial stage and there are many «yurts», that is a kind of round-shaped cabins, with all commodities for 8 persons. Opposite to the sea there is the beautiful beach Las Toninas of 3 1/2 km. and surrounded by forest. On the other side there lies the smaller Cerro Colorado beach at the feet of an impressive rocky huge mass.

Activities of fishing, riding on horseback, visits to glaciers, explorations, trekking through untouchable jungle and navigation to the island where «toninas» (a kind of dolphin) can be seen; are available here in this place.

There are two options for round trip: to travel direct to Puerto Montt by Patagonia Express catamaran stopping here or to get back upstream navigating up to La Junta.

2 A VISIT TO LAKE ROSSELLOT ★★
one km north of La Junta, take road branching east, leading to lake Rossellot (9 km).
A visit to a lake surrounded by untouched cold jungle.

The road runs on a ledge above the meandering river, with a view over farmland. At km 9 a ferry crosses the river, 500 m from lake Rossellot. Long and with heavily wooded shores, the lake has beautiful beaches and superb fishing. A path leads from the ferry to the lake. Those towing their

13

Highway next to Puyuhuapi Channel

own boat can launch it by the ferry. The stretch of road to lake Verde is still under construction.

3 CARRETERA AUSTRAL TO LAKE LAS TORRES
★★★ *from La Junta, 43 km to Puyuhuapi, 137 km to Puerto Cisnes, 143 km to lake Las Torres, and 269 km to Coihaique. Gasoline at Puyuhuapi and Puerto Cisnes. It is advisable to stay overnight at Puyuhuapi or Puerto Cisnes.*
A stretch with some of the finest scenery in the Carretera.

The road heads south from La Junta (km 0) through grazing lands, approaching soon a mountain range looming on the left., The scenery takes on a wilder look, with more jungle. At km 12, next to a rock wall, a beautiful waterfall plunges down the slope. Three bridges later, at km 28, is the northern tip of

Lake Risopatrón elongated, with a «waistline» in the middle, and forested slopes plummeting directly into the dark waters, leaving no beaches. At the point where the lake drains there is a beautiful area with cabins for rent (Cabañas El Pangue), frequented by fishing devotees.

This is also the boundary of the northern arm of the spectacular Queulat National Park; at km 33 is one of the guardhouses. The Carretera skirts the lakeshore for 12 km; at km 44, there is a good **view** over the Puyuhuapi fjord, known as Canal Puyuhuapi. One km ahead is

Puyuhuapi a seaport village offering basic services, gasoline (until 21:00 h), a general store, telephone, good accommodation at Hostería Puyuhuapi –at the house of one of the early settlers– and friendly German atmosphere at Hostería Alemana and Hostería Ludwig, both very good., There are several other residenciales. The one striking feature that catches the eye are three huge, European–style wooden houses, seemingly out of place here. They bear witness to the place's

singular history.

Four young German settlers arrived here in 1935, to what was then a thick jungle, influenced by the writings of the great explorer Hans Steffen (see Land & History). They were supposed to be the forerunners of a large group of German families living in the Sudetenland –then still under Czech control. However, the outbreak of WW2 in 1939 put an end to these plans. The four lonely pioneers with their respective families developed a prosperous farm and agroindustry here. Unfortunately, in 1971 their lands were expropriated and divided into plots. Most of the descendants of the original settlers have since emigrated. Noteworthy is the fact that the settlers, with the assistance of heavy machinery provided by German societies, built the road to Los Césares, in the late 1960s. This prompted the Public Works ministry to build the Carretera Austral through here, and not through Lago Verde, once the most favored option.

Another striking feature in Puyuhuapi is its famous

CARPET FACTORY it was established in 1950 by settler Walter Hopperdietzel, a textile engineer, to provide work for his father, a textile technician freshly arrived from war–devastated Germany. The factory turns out very high–quality carpets. You can see the whole manufacturing process, from wool dyeing to the complex designs weaved knot by knot. The amazing thing is that this level of quality was being churned out at this remote corner thirty years before the Carretera Austral reached the place.

TERMAS DE PUYUHUAPI another surprise. Fourteen km by sea, tucked away on the channel and with a backdrop of untouched jungle, there is a good hotel with thermal waters, offering cabins and an outdoor thermal pool surrounded by giant ferns. Access: Ten km south of Puyuhuapi, next to the airfield, is a signposted access to the hotel's office and a boat to take visitors to the thermal baths. The thermal baths are reached from Puerto Montt by the excellent (atamaran Patagonia Express. The catamaran continues to lake San Rafael.

From Puyuhuapi (km 45) are the 15 km of the one and only occasion when the road runs right next to the Pacific Ocean, on a one–track ledge carved into the rocky cliff. At km 60 the Carretera turns away from the sea, and heads for the valley of Ventisquero Grande river. Two km beyond the bridge at km 65, a road branches off to the left for

VESTISQUERO COLGANTE (Hanging Glacier). Two km from the Carretera, past a **Queulat National Park** guardhouse, is a small plateau with a superb view to an awesome icecap, perched atop the mountains, with massive glaciers branching down from it and hanging over the cliffs, spewing mighty cascades. Picnic is possible (latrines and abundant firewood). There are trails leading to the

☎ Telephone Center	B Church	E Cheap Food	2 Hs Ludwig
ⓢ Gasoline Station	C Carpet Factory	**ACCOMMODATIONS**	3 Bh Alemana
A Telex Chile	D General Store	1 H Hotelsa	● Boarding Houses
	//← a Chaitén		

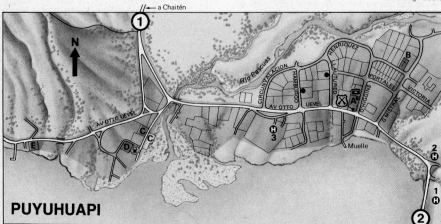

PUYUHUAPI

a Coihaique →

602

waterfalls: gorgeous.

The Carretera continues not far from the sea, with the **Magdalena island** in the background. At km 75 you reach the end channel Puyuhuapi and to get into the fjord and river Queulat, at its mouth these is a Learch, campgrounds; another good spot is at km 84, next to the bridge spanning the Queulat river. All around is untouched cold jungle; the area is quite wild: in the territory making up the **Queulat National Park** there had never been any paths or settlers.

Queulat Cabins in the middle of the National Park Queulat by a fjord with fishing boats, sea fauna and birds. It is the best place to stop and explore the arca. At least 3 days (for contacts see the Service Section)

At km 84 there is a river for camping. At km 87 the road Starts chimbing the fabulous.

| **CUESTA QUEULAT NORTE** | a zigzagging stretch winding its way to the Queulat pass, flanked by virgin forests, and by towering peaks crowned by ice-caps and overhung with glaciers. At the beginning of the climb is the roaring **Padre García waterfall.** On the left–hand side of the look–out point is a path climbing down. Here you will see a complete collection of **native ferns and lichens.** Don't take them as a souvenir: they do not survive outside their habitat.

At km 96 is the pass (500 m above sea level). The descent beyond is gentle, crossing three times the Chucao stream. Some way ahead is **lake Los Quetros** and Conaf guardhouses. The rangers can provide information. The valley becomes narrower, with tall, ice–capped mountains to the west and beautiful waterfalls, such as the **Salto del Cóndor** at km 102. Soon after that, the road comes to the edge of the National Park and to a forking (km 104); the right–hand branch leads to Puerto Cisnes, the left–hand branch to Coihaique. A visit to Puerto Cisnes can be recommended.

4 DETOUR TO PUERTO CISNES ★★★

seventy kilometers round trip (from and back to the main road).

A quaint village at the mouth of a fjord, with singular stories of the pioneering times.

Soon after the fork (km 0), the road starts to run alongside the **Cisnes river** (good for rafting, modest rapids, except for the hair–rising drop at Piedra del Gato). At km 6 the valley and the river are squeezed, with towering, sheer rock faces: you are crossing the highest section of the Andes, which in Aisén run near the coast. At km 8 you can see, to the left, the massive icecap perched atop the Andes. At km 21 a great rock face, called **Cerros del 14,** rises above the forest.

At km 27 there is a good camping spot on the green meadow by the river. At km 33, the road reaches a beach created by the mouth of the **Cisnes river,** and then turns north, running between a cliff and the sea shore, to reach, at km 35,

| **PUERTO CISNES** | (pop 1,700). All services, telephone, gasoline until 21:00 h. Accommodation at Hostal Michay, Posada Gaucho and other pensiones or residenciales; there is also a youth hostel and a campsite. Restaurants York and La Tranquera. The Costanera runs along the beach, and the village climbs gently behind to San Luis hill. The public buildings are interesting. Visit the **taller artesanal** (handicrafts workshop).

Explorer Hans Steffen surveyed the Cisnes river in 1896 from its mouth to its headwaters. By 1929 a sawmill operated here, next to the mouth of the river. Four years later, a trail was built reaching 10 km upstream. In 1952 the first permanent settlers arrived.

Five years later, a person arrived who would play a crucial role in shaping the village. Eugenia Pircio–Biroli, a brilliant, hard–working, cultivated Italian devoted her life and energy to making this village grow. In 1959, together with father Calvi of the Dom Guanella foundation, obtained state lands and built an Agricultural boarding school for orphans from Central Chile, to form future settlers. She eventually became the town's mayor, pro-

moted the construction of all facilities and even influenced the place's architecture.

BACK ON THE CARRETERA AUSTRAL the road fork was at km 104. Three km beyond the Steffen bridge spanning the Treinta y Dos river, the road reaches the **Cisnes river,** running below a massive rock wall called **Piedra del Gato,** into which the road was laboriously carved. This is the only section of the Carretera where fatal accidents occurred, while carving the rock. Ropes and spikes can still be seen on the rock face. The river drops through rocks strangely carved by the water.

The road then turns west, away from the Cisnes river. At km 30 the view opens up towards ice-capped mountains on the west, while the peaks of **Mount Picacho** loom straight ahead. To the east is the Río Grande valley, with lands settled in the 1950s. At km 129 a **bridge** spans the Cisnes river and, to the side, the **footbridge** is still to be seen, part of the old trail to the coast.

The road then climbs a short, winding stretch to a pass, and at km 134 is

Villa Amengual a small settlement flanked by tall mountains, founded in 1983 to provide services to the settlers in the area. Most houses are deserted in summer, as the people are working out in the fields. The settlers arrived from the border with Argentina in the 1940s.

At km 137 the road to La Tapera and the border (May–Aug 08:00–21:00 h; Sep–Apr, 07:00–23:00 h), branches east, and six km ahead is

Lake Las Torres a small, beautiful lake protected under a National Reserve status and administered by Conaf. Good fishing, a free campsite and a backdrop of stately **peaks** separating it from lake Fontana, in Argentina.

We have reached the southern limit of this section.

☏ Telephone Center
⛽ Gasoline Station
✚ Hospital
B Public Library
C Town Hall

D Parish Church
E School
H Rest La Tranquera
1 Villa Las Hortensias

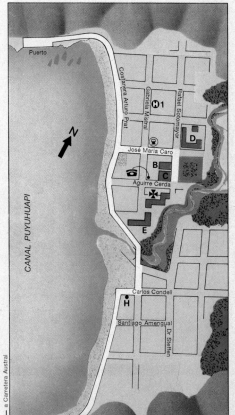

PTO CISNES

13

5 A DETOUR TO LA TAPERA AND ESTANCIA CISNES ★★ *forty–nine km round trip from the Carretera to La Tapera, 77 km to Estancia Cisnes, and 81 km to the border. Take food and enough gasoline.*

A road opened in 1985, running across great native forests which thin out as the road climbs, to finally disappear by La Tapera. Here the pampa starts to unfold, with its bunch–grass cover and large sheep farms.

La Tapera was one of the sections into which the large Estancia Cisnes was divided. The estancia was expropriated in 1970, and La Tapera became a small village, with basic infrastructure.

Estancia Río Cisnes is a village evolved from the casco of the formerly gigantic Cisnes sheep farm, established in 1924. It used to bring its products out through Argentina, until this road was built. The main compound was built after the pattern of the Magellanic sheep farms, with large shearing–sheds, wool–washing sheds, and the houses arranged under a strict hierarchy. The vegetable gardens and tree orchards are sheltered behind windbreaks.

The customs and immigration outpost is open 08:00–20:00 h in winter, 07:00–21:00 h in summer.

SECTION C   COIHAIQUE

This section stretches from lake Las Torres in the north, to Puerto Ibáñez in the south, covering the Aisén river basin and reaching down to the large lake General Carrera. It is the most densely populated area in Region IX, with Coihaique as capital city and Puerto Chacabuco as its seaport.

The road runs close to the pampa, to the east of the Andes, through lands cleared by settlers long ago.

TOURS

1 CARRETERA AUSTRAL TO COIHAIQUE ★★★
from lake Las Torres to Mañihuales, 50 km; to Coihaique, 126 km, and to Aisén, 112 km. No gasoline or accommodation on the way. Provisions at Mañihuales. Allow a bit more than half a day.
The scenery becomes less wild as the road approaches the capital city.

From lake Las Torres (km 0), it is 6 km to **lake Zaranda**. The road runs along a plain covered by untouched forests, with the wonderful **mount Las Torres** and glacier–capped cliffs in the background. Soon this gives way to cleared, worked fields, on a rolling plain. Beyond km 20 is a broad plain at the foot of the sharp–peaked **mount Toqui** is **Campo Grande**. At km 27 a road branches east to the El Toqui mine. From this road junction the construction of the Carretera Austral started towards the north in 1976, reaching Chaitén in February 1983. The stretch of road from here to Coihaique is older, but some corrections were

made in the route it follows and definitive bridges were built.

A DETOUR TO THE TOQUI MINE AND VALLEY ★★
twenty km to the mine on a good gravel road.
For those interested in mining.

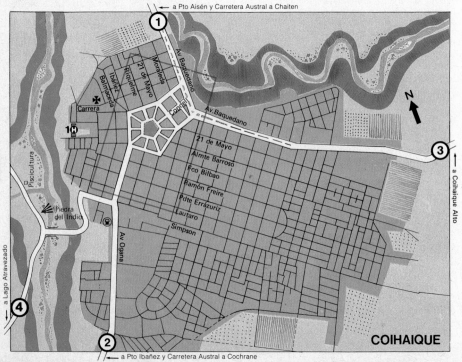

COIHAIQUE

The valley was opened by settlers by 1940, who burned the great native forest. Only scant remains of it can be seen near the snow line. **Mount Cathedral** towers in the background. The mine can be visited prior permission of Soc Contractual Minera Toqui, phone 698 4295 in Santiago, or 211487 in Coihaique. The mine has modern facilities –including a hydroelectric plant– and produces zinc, lead, and tin.

From the junction for the mine, the Carretera continues to the end of the Campo Grande valley, with **lake Pedro Aguirre Cerda** at km 29. If you want to camp, look for a house by a forest on the lake shore. It offers a wind–sheltered camping spot, and a small beach (no facilities). The road then climbs to a low pass, and descends into the broad valley of **Mañihuales river.**

At km 42 there is a small suspension bridge to the right (5 ton max); there are no good roads on the other side.

At km 49 is

Mañihuales (pop 970), providing basic services, telephone, general stores, a Conaf campsite and a small inn. The village was founded spontaneously by settlers who hacked their way through the forest in 1935. The Mañihuales river was christened by Hans Steffen, after the ubiquitous mañíos –a valuable native tree– growing on its banks. In 1962 the place received village status. Nearby is the Mañihuales National Reserve, under Conaf administration (park ranger, campsite, picnic area).

At km 62 the road forks: the left–hand branch leads to Coihaique (63 km) and the right one to Puerto Aisén (49 km). The latter branch was built in the 1970s. Take the left branch for Coihaique, running along the

Emperador Guillermo valley

EMPERADOR GUILLERMO RIVER VALLEY the valley was christened by Hans Steffen, who discovered it on January 27, 1896, on the birthday anniversary of Kaiser Wilhelm (Emperador Guillermo). It was then an impenetrable jungle, later (1940) burned to the ground by settlers. The ground is now covered by coirón –a type of bunch–grass– and fallen, dead trees. Both the lack of seed trees and the voracity of introduced hares have conspired to thwart the forest from regenerating itself. This sad scenery will be rather commonplace as one progresses south.

The road crosses the bridge over the Emperador river at km 80, to climb to a pass and then descend to another valley.

At km 92 is

Villa Ortega a modest hamlet established in 1967 during the agrarian reform heyday, with the associated allocation of state lands. The place was named after the first settler in the area, one Gumercindo Ortega; the area, in turn, was named **Mano Negra** after a nearby mountain with several snow–shrouded pinnacles. The road to Ñiriguao branches off from here.

The road climbs up and down the Alvarado range, and reaches the Mano Negra police station at km 113, in an area sheltered by **poplar windbreaks.**

At km 116 the roads runs into the paved Coihaique–Puerto Aisén highway. From the upper part there is a splendid view over the Simpson valley marching towards the ocean. Ten km to the left is

COIHAIQUE (pop 37,217). It was founded in 1929 by the provincial government to provide urban services to private settlers, and to the giant estancia of Soc Industrial de Aisén (SIA), which since 1906 had its headquarters at the site of present–day Escuela Agrícola, up the river from Coihaique. In 1948 the town achieved municipal status and, in 1974, its degree of development and its central location made it the natural choice as the capital of Region XI. The town is laid around a pentagonal square, which never fails to disorient newcomers.

What To See the small **Museo Regional de la Patagonia** is well worth a visit, with photos of early settlers, historical documents, records of the early explorers, and other exhibits. It is located at the school on the square. Taking the road to Aisén, one km from the bridge over the Coihaique river, turn off to the right on a dirt road leading to the **Coihaique National Reserve**, under Conaf administration, with fine scenery and superb **views** over the city, the entire valley and the surrounding mountains.

Taking the road to the airport, look right from the **bridge** over the Simpson river for the **Piedra del Indio,** a rock outcrop on the river bank which looks like an Indian face in profile.

13

☎ Telephone Center	2 H Cordillera
◉ Cafe, Meeting Point	3 H Los Ñires
★ Touristic Information	**TOURIST SERVICES**
Ⓖ Gasoline Station	20 Transmarchilay
⌐ Lookout Point	21 Lan Chile
✳✠ Hospital	22 Ladeco
A Regional Government	23 Mar del Sur
B Cathedral Church	**RESTAURANTS**
C Post Office	10 La Bomba
M Wharf	11 Kalu
	12 La Parrilla
ACCOMMODATIONS	✳ See General Map
✳ 1 Hs Coihaique	of Coihaique

Downtown

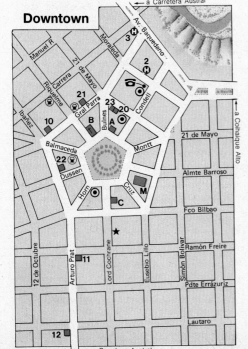

Coihaique

Accommodations best are Hostería Hotelsa, Hotel Cordillera, Hotel Chible, Hotel Los Ñirres and La Pasarela Cabins. Numerous other residenciales and pensiones, and lodging in private houses is also possible (look for signs on windows).

Food the hostería and Cordillera, also El Colono and Calu. Café Oriente is very popular. Cheap meals at La Parrilla and at Casino de Bomberos (at the fire station). Supplies at Supermercado Brautigam.

TOURS FROM COIHAIQUE

2 TO LAKE ELIZALDE AND 6 LAGUNAS ★★★
nearly 100 km on gravel road, allow at least half a day. Take food. Accommodation and food at Hotel Lago Elizalde.
A circuit around Simpson valley, with views over the eastern slopes of the Andes.
Take the Carretera Austral to the south, to Balmaceda and Puerto Ibáñez. At km 6 is the **Foltzick cliff**; at km 16 the road branching left for lakes Castor and Pollux (see Tour 4), and a short way beyond the **El Salto** waterfall, which freezes in winter.
At km 18 take signposted road to the right leading to **Villa Simpson** at km 20, a village established more or less spontaneously around 1936, the busiest in the valley. Go on straight, crossing the Simpson river at km 26 and reaching another crossroads at km 28, at **Villa Frei**. This village was founded in 1969 by the then President, but has not prospered. One of the roads leads to lake La Paloma (7 km), another to lake Elizalde. Take the latter, reaching at km 32

LAKE ELIZALDE narrow and with forested shores, it is part of a string of five lakes draining west towards Puerto Aisén. Superb fishing. Drive along the lakeshore to reach a small port with boats for hire. A short way ahead, at km 36, is Hostería Lago Elizalde, in a lovely setting. A further –and careful– 4 km will bring you to a pond suitable for camping.
Return to Villa Frei (km 59), and take road to the left for **Seis Lagunas (Six Ponds),** odd ponds with no apparent outlet among cultivated rolling land.
At km 80 the road crosses a stream and reaches a hill; to the left it leads to lake Atravesado (see next tour). To the right, it leads to Coihaique. You can buy honey from the settlers by the road. At km 92 is Coihaique's Teniente Vidal Airport.

3 TO LAKE ATRAVESADO AND VALLE LAGUNAS
★★ *seventy km round trip on a rough gravel road (last stretch suitable only for 4WD vehicles). Allow half a day. Take food.*

A visit to the tip of Valle Lagunas, with a 60-m waterfall plunging in two stages, right by the roadside.
Leave Coihaique (km 0) on the road to the Teniente Vidal airport; at km 4 take road to the left to reach the junction for Seis Lagunas and lake Elizalde at km 16. Go on straight, reaching a pond at km 20 and **lake Atravesado** at km 24. Good fishing.
Continuing on the same road, at km 31 is the waterfall. The road ends at km 35, at the tip of **Valle Lagunas.**

4 TO LAKES FRIO, CASTOR AND POLLUX ★★
seventy km round trip, gravel road; allow half a day, take food.
An excursion to the highlands on the border, where trees are somewhat stunted, mostly lovely ñirres and lenga, with three beautiful, reed–encircled lakes with good fishing.
Leave Coihaique (km 0) on the road south described at Tour 2. At km 16 take road to the left, reaching **Lago Frío** at km 24, the smallest of the three (good fishing).
At km 31 is **lake Pollux** and three km farther, **lake Castor**, the largest one, reaching the Argentine border with its northern tip. The road linking both lakes is appalling. Lake Castor is better reached through a good 10–km detour from the road to Coihaique Alto.

5 TO ÑIREGUAO THROUGH COIHAIQUE ALTO
★★★ *the complete circuit is 150 km long, allow no less than five hours, only for 4WD or high–clearance vehicles. If you are driving a normal vehicle, drive back on the Carretera Austral to Villa Ortega, and take road to Ñireguao starting there (126 km round trip). Take food.*
A circuit through the Coironales pampa, an area colonized by the large sheep farms, to the lunar landscape of Ñireguao.
Leave Coihaique (km 0) on the road to Coihaique Alto on the border, running along the Coihaique river. At km 4 is the **Escuela Agrícola**, formerly the headquarters of the SIA sheep farming company, the main house of which was built in 1919. At km 17 is the turn off to the right for lakes Castor and Pollux, described above.
At km 21 is

Dos Lagunas a Natural Monument with a guardhouse, picnic areas and paths to different corners of lakes **Toro** and **Escondida**. It is worth a stop.
The trees become smaller, the rocks rounded, as the landscape turns slowly into pampa. Here are many sheep farming estancias, easy to spot because of their pens and shearing sheds. At km 36 the forest ends and the seemingly unending pampa unfolds. Flamingoes can be seen in the scattered ponds.
At km 43 is **Coihaique Alto**, a frontier settlement and immigration and customs outpost (07:00–23:00 h in summer; 08:00–21:00 h in winter).
Turn off before the control outpost, following a bumpy trail to the left (north). At km 54, at the ford in the stream, there are **Tehuelche rock paintings** under a rocky overhang. Unfortunately, visitors have all but wiped them out, after we reported their location in the 1985 edition. This has forced us to withhold the location of other interesting archaeological sites.
A bit farther ahead, at a wooded point at km 59, there is a grand **view** over the

ÑIREGUAO PAMPA over 80,000 hectares of nearly flat plains, covered with coirón –a type of bunch grass– stretching away to Argentina. Here are the headwaters of the Ñirihuao river, flowing to the Pacific. This used to be a great lake; to the west, the glacial moraine damming it up can still be seen. The eye–catching feature here is a series of strange, flat–topped rock outcrops somehow resembling a lunar landscape, to which the place owes its name of **Valle de la Luna**. Go on to the Ñireguao river at km 68, crossing it over a wooden bridge, to reach, at km 74,

Baño Nuevo formerly one of the sections of the SIA estancia. It still has the shearing sheds, washing shed, sheep folds and workers' houses, sheltered from the wind by rows of trees. On one side is the small village established when the estancia was expropriated in 1969. The cooperative which then ran the place went bankrupt and in 1985 the 44,000 hectares of the property were acquired by a new owner. The road continues to Argentina (border crossing open 08:00–19:00 h).

To return, take the nearly straight road heading west, descending gently through the **Valle de la Luna** to reach, at km 86,

Estancia de Ñireguao the casco –central compound– of the large estancia owned by SIA and operating here from 1906. It epitomizes the cascos of sheep farms, with a large administration house, surrounded by splendid, wind-sheltered gardens and orchards. Ask for permission to visit. It is now a small, privately-owned sheep farm.

At km 88, beyond a road junction, is **Villa Ñireguao**, also created after the expropriation. There is a telephone and a general store. Continue on the road to Villa Ortega. From the crest of the rise there is a good **view** of the **Ñireguao** valley, this time from its western edge.

At km 102 is the **Mano Negra Forest Reserve** and, two km later, the **Salto de Guadalupe** waterfall, the headwaters of the Emperador Guillermo river. At km 116 is Villa Ortega and the Carretera Austral. The leg to Coihaique (km 150) is described under Tour 1.

6 TO BALMACEDA AND PUERTO IBAÑEZ ★★★

round trip to Balmaceda, 118 km, allow half a day. To Puerto Ibáñez, a 324-km round trip, including the suggested detours. It is advisable to stay overnight at Puerto Ibáñez. Take enough gasoline.
A beautiful circuit to lake General Carrera and the first leg of the final stretch of the Carretera Austral, described in Tour 7.

Leave Coihaique (km 0), on the Carretera to the south, already described until km 20. The Huemules bridge is at km 36, at the confluence of Blanco river and another river flowing down from Balmaceda. Here is the village of **El Blanco**.

At km 43 is the

DETOUR TO BALMACEDA ★★

sixteen km on a straight road. Turn off here and return through Vista Hermosa to the south.
A 32-km detour for those who have not had a chance to see the pampa.

BALMACEDA was the first village established in the Aisén region, on January 1, 1917, under an initiative of the settlers established here since 1901. The main promoter was José Antolín Silva, who convinced the scattered settlers in the arid pampa to settle as a group, in order to enjoy the benefits of a village. The nearest settlement then was on the Atlantic coast, through which they brought their products out by cart.

They staked out 1,000 lots and made a Spanish-style central square. They sold plots and built a school. In 1920, the **Hotel Español** was built –recently disappeared in a fire– and the government granted it village status in 1928. In 1945 the Chilean Air Force set up a base here, and in 1950 the road to Coihaique was opened to public use. This latter development undermined Balmaceda's leading role. It operates now the largest regional airport (it can accommodate jet airplanes). The border crossing is open May–Aug, 08:00–20:00 h; Sep–Apr, 07:00–23:00 h.

Take now the road to Vista Hermosa, on the old road to the capital. Vista Hermosa (52 km direct from Coihaique) is now a camp of the Road Works Department (Vialidad), on the old road to the border. There is a grand **view** over the Argentinian pampas.

At km 61 starts the vast **Cerro Castillo Forest Reserve**, with superb scenery and afforestation programs under way. At km 63 is **lake Chinay** and the guardhouse. The road thereafter crosses five times the same stream, with forests and good camping spots.

At km 78 is **Piedra del Conde,** a triangular stone resembling a human face in profile next to the road.

At km 83 is the Portezuelo pass (1,120 m), flanked by naked hills and **rock outcrops** protruding like statues, with green, gray and pink streaks. At km 85 the road climbs down the

CUESTA DEL DIABLO a 5–km-long stretch of zigzagging road with a grand view over the **Ibáñez river** valley, running east-to-west. It starts at the **Hudson volcano**, which erupted mightily in August 1991, looming on the west. The ashes it spewed reaches all the way to the Falkland (Malvinas) islands, over 500 km of the Atlantic coast to the east.

To the right is the colossal **Cerro Castillo**, crowned by slender pinnacles soaring above the snow and resembling a castle.

In km 91, the leg from here to Cochrane is described under Sector D.

The landscape south of the road junction at km 91 is of rolling hills, topped with naked rock outcrops. This land was swept by glaciers in times past, and anticipates the scenery at lake general Carrera. There are many settlers. The forest soon gives way to shrubs. At km 105 are three ponds. At km 117 there is a grand view over lake General Carrera, and three km ahead is

Puerto Ibañez (pop 1,337), a well-laid village offering basic services, general stores but no gasoline. Best accommodation at Residencial Ibáñez. The first settlers arrived in 1908 and the settlement achieved village status in 1931. The **Taller Artesanal** (handicrafts shop) offers leather-covered ceramics, unique in Chile, and boleadoras, known in English as bolas, a thong with heavy balls at the ends used for throwing at and entangling cattle. This is an agricultural village with poplar-lined orchards and the main port on the lake. It was also affected by the Hudson eruption. Shipping from here is described under Section D. For those not wishing to sail through the lake, the following tour can be recommended, as Puerto Ibáñez does not offer the best view of the lake.

A DETOUR TO LEVICAN ★★★

sixty–six km round trip on a gravel road. Take food.
A good view over South America's second largest lake.

Leave Puerto Ibáñez (km 0) following the signposted road to the left. At km 2, next to a cliff on the right–hand side and under a rocky overhang –cross the fences– you can see **Tehuelche rock paintings.**

At km 6, is the

RIO IBAÑEZ WATERFALL mighty, spectacular, loud, plunging in three steps. Perhaps one of Chile's finest, and spanned by modern bridges. At km 8, taking a short detour down to the left, a small forest on the river bank offers a very good spot for camping and fishing.

The road skirts the Ibáñez bay, with a good **view** of its emerald–green waters from km 26 (the color stems from the glacier–spawned streams emptying here). The rest of the lake is deep blue. On the far shore is Chile Chico.

At km 29 the road descends to

13

Levicán a nice group of agricultural plots watered by a network of irrigation canals, also fallen victim to the Hudson volcano. There is a long, windy beach with a view to Ibáñez bay. The road ends abruptly at km 33, on a small, uninhabited inlet with a concrete ramp for ferries used during a period of border disputes. It is a good camping spot. To return, retrace the road.

7 TO AYSEN AND PUERTO CHACABUCO ★★★

sixty–eight km to Puerto Aisén and 82 km to Puerto Chacabuco, paved throughout. This is the last tour for those wishing to return by sea through Chiloé.

The main access route to Coihaique, running along the Simpson river valley. It was the first road in this region, with a trail opened from Puerto Aisén in 1901 and broadened by SIA in 1904, to become a road in 1930 up to the cliff (now tunnel); it reached Coihaique in 1936.

Leave Coihaique (km 0) on the paved road to Puerto Aisén. At km 15 is the tunnel through the cliff, built in 1985. Here starts the **Río Simpson National Park**, lying along the river, squeezed by sheer cliffs graced by numerous waterfalls.

At km 28, to the right, is the vaporous Salto **Velo de la Novia** waterfall; a path leads to its edge. On the cliffs across the river is a black–and–white rocky face known as Las Pizarras, with several thin waterfalls.

At km 33 there is a basic campground set up by Conaf, next to the river, with roofed fireplaces, and latrines.

At km 36 is the **La Virgen** waterfall and one km ahead the

Río Simpson National Park Information Center with a small museum displaying exhibits of local fauna and flora, and a **thick tree trunk**: its growth rings have been counted and dated from 1576 to 1980; ie, Chile's history in a piece of lenga tree. Across from here is an isolated rocky outcrop known as Queque Inglés (English Cake).

At km 41 is the old village of **Los Torreones**, and at km 48 a **bridge** spans the Mañihuales river. At km 50 is the junction with the road coming from the north. The valley becomes broader; the river, after its confluence with the Mañihuales, changes its name to **río Aisén**. These lands have been worked since the earliest times, and trails are being opened from here to new areas to settle.

At km 62 is Villa Pangal, next to the airfield. Five km ahead is Conaf's **El Mallín Forest Nursery**, with excellent production of native flora and of introduced conifers.

At km 68 is Puerto Aisén, and 14 km ahead, across the large suspension bridge, is

Puerto Chacabuco a busy little port which overtook Puerto Aisén as the main shipping port and ferry terminal back in the 1960s. There are several hotels and residenciales.

PUERTO AISEN (pop 13,050) offers all services and has good hotels, gasoline, a main square with old trees. It used to be the capital. Initially a shipping and storage port set up for and by SIA livestock company in 1914, it became a village in 1920 and a municipal head town in 1928. The port became eventually choked with silt and was moved to Puerto Chacabuco. Nevertheless, it

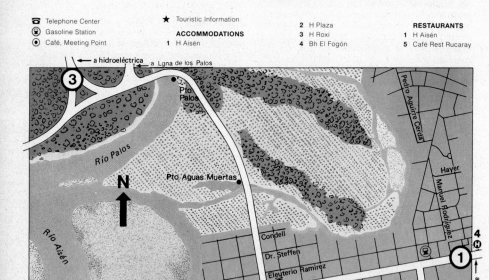

☎ Telephone Center
Ⓖ Gasoline Station
◉ Café, Meeting Point

★ Touristic Information
ACCOMMODATIONS
1 H Aisén

2 H Plaza
3 H Roxi
4 Bh El Fogón

RESTAURANTS
1 H Aisén
5 Café Rest Rucaray

PTO. AISEN

13

retains its character of head town for the entire insular area.

A visit to **lake Riesco**, 50 km round trip, is recommended.

SEA TRIPS FROM PUERTO CHACABUCO

8 TO LAGUNA SAN RAFAEL ★★★

2 to 7 sailing days in different types of boats. Different routes to the laguna for a prolonged stay.
A fabulous trip through the channels and islands of Western Patagonia, to reach the San Valentín glacier on the sea, the nearest to the Equator in the world.

From Puerto Chacabuco there are several ships sailing to Laguna San Rafael, some of them with luxury facilities and different passenger classes. They have regular services in high season on fixed routes.

There are also boats for what could be called **adventure tourism**, with a smaller passenger capacity –6 to 12– and an irregular departure schedule. They either wait for full capacity with different tourist groups, or are hired as a whole for charters. Theirs is a longer journey –5 to 7 days– sailing through the fascinating channels and islands of the Aisén archipiélago. In general, they have excellent facilities and good cuisine. They sail during the day, staying overnight at small bays so that they can program hikes and visits to geysers. Another option are **schooners**, representing more casual and more economic tourism. You can talk directly with their captains at Puerto Palos and Puerto Aguas Muertas in the city of Puerto Aisén. A nice option for an exploration trip.

The two main attractions of this tour are:
The Laguna- itself with its floating icebergs, the stunning San Valentín glacier shedding small glaciers continuosly, and the walk by the rocky shore to see the gradual glacier's retreat.
Channels, islands, and geysers are the other great attractions of this tour. The leg between Puerto Chacabuco and the laguna goes through narrow channels, surrounded by large hills, and numerous bays, fjords, and estuaries. The make an unforgettable scene. On the continental shore there are innumerable geysers.

Due to the nature of the itinerary, some ships sail only by night, which does not enable you see a great part of the route; however, in summer dark begins at 22:00 h and it dawn breaks before 06:00 h.

Other boats do not sail by night. Some of them depart from Puerto Chacabuco at twilight, sailing through the Sisén fjord. They stop a some bay along the route and continue the cruise at dawn.

While choosing transportation, you should consider the following:
The ticket cost is high because operating the ships is expensive; besides, it is a 400 km round trip with food and lodging on board. Some ships carry passengers on different decks at different fees.

A larger group of tourists might easily charter a schooner for adventure tourism for as many days as they wish. Estimate the value per person and compare it to other options.

If you sail by day throught the channels you will see all the options described in this tour. If you sail only by night, you will see just the magnificent laguna San Rafael.

SHIPPING

The ships' descriptions, capacity, route addresses and telephones, are indicated at the end of this guide.

San Rafael lagoon

Motonave Skorpios I and II from Puerto Montt to The laguna and intermediate points in 7 days. It dies non stop at Puerto Chacabuco.

Catamarán Patagonia Express from Puerto Chacabuco to the laguna; 2 weekly departures, 2 days and 2 nights sailing by night, 1 weekly departure.

Odisea, and Visun Motorized sailing vessels from Puerto Chacabuco to the laguna and intermediate points, 6 days salining by day. 1 weekly departure.

Lancha Patagonia from Puerto Chacabuco to the laguna and intermediate points, 5 days sailing by day, 1 weekly departure.

Lanchas Ventisquero and San Quintín from Puerto Chacabuco to the laguna and intermediate points; they have to be chartered.

NB Lancha Patagonia and the Odisea and Visun motorized vessels can be chartered anytime during the year.

8a TO TERMAS DEL CHICONAL ★★★

one hour sailing with the Nalcayec motorboat, daily departures. Allow one day, take food; you may also camp at the place. (See Services & Prices.)
A short cruise to a nice thermal spring on the coast.

The boat sails from Puerto Chacabuco. The thermal springs have five ponds made with stones, in a natural setting with lush vegetation. There is a cafeteria with rest-rooms.

9 DUE NORTH ★★★

a cruise that lets you go either to Chiloé and Puerto Montt or directly to Puerto montt. For ship´s descriptions, see the Services section.
A chance to return north through the unforgettable channels.

There are 3 ships on this route. Empremar may add a new one.
Catamaran Patagonia Express from Puerto Chacabuco to Puyuhuapi thermal baths (overnight) continuing to Puerto Chacabuco to Puyuhuapi thermal baths (overnight) continuing to Puerto Montt. It sails only by day, only for passengers, once a week.
El Colono from Puerto Chacabuco to Chonchi, Chiloé, and to Puerto Montt. 26 h saling day and night; it carries cars and passengers, twice a week.
RR Evangelista from Puerto Chacabuco to Puerto Montt in 22 h saling day and night. It carries cars and passengers, twice a week.

13

SECTION D LAKE GENERAL CARRERA

This section covers from the Ibáñez river in the north to the Baker river basin in the south, and is centered around lake General Carrera, Chile's largest and the second largest in South America, after lake Titicaca in Peru/Bolivia.

The section of the Carretera Austral running behind the lake, to reach it at Puerto Tranquilo, was opened in 1988. In 1991 a leg by me southern shore, between el Maitén and Chile Chico, was inaugurated.

The Carretera Austral has already reached Cochrane, and the section to Puerto Yungay, on the Pacific and 124 km from Cochrane, is under construction.

LAKE GENERAL CARRERA the eastern portion lies in Argentina and is called lake Buenos Aires. Discovered in 1880 by Argentine geographer Carlos Moyano, its shores at present-day Puerto Ibáñez and Chile Chico were explored in 1901 by H Prichard, an anthropologist with the US's Cornell University, who was looking for Tehuelche remains. Chilean settlers came into the valley from Argentina at the turn of the century. The largest urban center here is Chile Chico, but the main port on the lake is Puerto Ibáñez since 1925, when the road from Coihaique reached it. Guadal was established as a port of access to the Baker valley, reached now by the Carretera Austral, and Murta is the head town for the valley. There are large forests; several sawmills operate there.

There are other settlements on the lake shores, without access by road but served by ferries, such as Puerto Cristal and Puerto Sánchez on the northern shore. Both started out as mining settlements, producing zinc, lead and copper, which they initially shipped out through Argentina; later, through Puerto Ibáñez to the Pacific. On the southern shore are Fachinal and El Mallín, both now served by the Carretera. To the east, on the Argentinian side, the lake shores are flat, lying on the pampas unfolding towards the Atlantic. On the Chilean side, near Puerto Ibáñez and Chile Chico, the scenery is more Alpine, with huge, rocky mountains devoid of vegetation, eroded to round shapes by retreat-

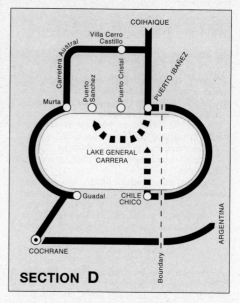

SECTION D

ing glaciers. These giant rocks are so sheer at times –such as at the southern shore–, that road-building becomes a laborious undertaking.

The deep blue color of lake General Carrera's water contrasts with the emerald–green hue in some of the bays, where the mouths of glacier rivers are located. The lake drains into the Pacific through the Baker river, with the most abundant water of any Chilean river.

SHIPPING AT LAKE GENERAL CARRERA

The **car ferry Pilchero** of Transmarchilay offers the only regular public shipping service on the lake, running on fixed schedules. For cars, passengers, cattle and cargo, the ferry calls at all ports on the lake. For schedules and reservations, see shipping services in Services section.

Puerto Ibáñez the main port on the lake, described in Section C. The Pilchero leaves on Saturday at 11:00 h to Chile Chico ($2^1/_2$ hours); arrives back at Puerto Ibáñez on Sunday, at 16:30 h. During week days, the ferry calls at the other ports on the lake.

CHILE CHICO a small town of 3,536 inhabitants with a splendid sunny microclimate, enabling it to boast a sizable number of lush fruit orchards. However, the eruption of the Hudson volcano nearby in August 1991 buried the entire area under a thick layer of ash and sand. It is not clear when –and whether– it will recover its lush appearance.

Gasoline available. Border crossing open 07:00–23:00 h in summer.

Chile Chico dates from 1909, when Chilean settlers arrived from Argentina. In 1917, a conflict known as the **Chile Chico War** took place here: the settlers expelled sheep farmers and police forces attempting to drive them out of these lands, because a concession to the lands had been granted in Santiago. The village was organized and received official recognition in 1931. It depended on Argentina until 1952, when the road to Puerto Ibáñez was finished.

How To Get There if you are driving, cross on Friday into Argentina (pass open in winter from 08:00–20:00 h; summer from 07:00–23:00 h), skirting the lake on the Argentinian side to cross back into Chile Chico. To return, take the ferry on Sunday to Puerto Ibáñez. Make reservations. If you

☎ Telephone Center
◉ Café, Meeting Point
Ⓖ Gasoline Station
✚ Hospital
A Custom

ACCOMMODATIONS
4 Hs de La Patagonia
1 Bh Nacional
2 Bh Agua Azules
3 Bh La Frontera

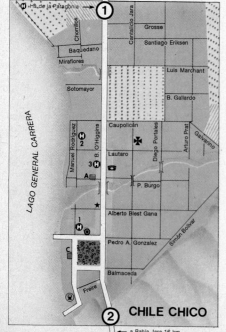

② **CHILE CHICO**
← a Bahía Jara 16 km.

13

are not driving, cross on the ferry on Saturday to Chile Chico, to return on Sunday.

TOURS FROM CHILE CHICO

TO LAKE JEINIMENI NATIONAL RESERVE ★★★
an interesting circuit of 102 km (round trip) along the Jeinimeni valley, where the river acts as boundary with Argentina, to reach the namesake valley. It is located on a highland, many black–necked swans to be seen. Camping sites available.

TO BAHIA JARA AND FACHINAL ★★★
a circuit on the lake shore to the west, 112 km round trip. At km 12 is **Bahía Jara**, with a very good beach and a campsite. Farther ahead is a small lake inevitably named Laguna Verde, after the green color of its (mineral) water, to end up at Fachinal, with orchards, trees and beaches at the lake's narrowest point. Fine scenery.The road, opened in 1991, continues 70 km ahead to meet the Austral highway; in El Maitén junction, for description see southern highway.

CARRETERA AUSTRAL

CARRETERA AUSTRAL FROM VILLA CASTILLO JUNCTION TO COCHRANE ★★★ *from the junction to Cochrane, 252 km; from Coihaique to Cochrane, 341 km. Accommodation in Cochrane. Gasoline at Coihaique and Cochrane. Take food. Camping gear advisable.*
One of the most spectacular stretches of the Carretera Austral.
The Carretera from Coihaique to Puerto Ibáñez is described under Section C, Tour 6. At km 89 from Coihaique, at the foot of the awesome Cerro Castillo, the Carretera Austral branches off to the right. Take this junction as your new km 0. The road runs along the Ibáñez river valley, among forests and cultivated fields, and at km 8 it reaches

Villa Castillo a small village founded in 1966. It lies on a narrow rocky ravine, with a superb view to the fantastic range of **Mount Castillo.**
At km 10, a short, narrow bridge spans the **Ibáñez river**, roaring far below through a narrow canyon. Beyond the bridge a secondary road continues straight ahead –only for 4WD vehicles– climbing to a plateau and skirting the small lakes of **Verde Alto** and **Lapparent**, in a spectacular ride through forests and remote lakes, to retake the Carretera 35 km later.
From the bridge over the Ibáñez river (km 10), the Carretera bends west running along the valley; at km 26 it passes near **Laguna Verde**, nice scenery. Access to the point where the lake drains in three km ahead, taking a detour. From the heights there are good views over the Ibáñez basin, with the **Hudson volcano** in the west (the one that erupted), where the headwaters of the Ibáñez river are located.
At km 48 the road climbs out of the Ibáñez valley into magnificent forests, through the Cofré pass at km 68 (600 m above sea level).
From km 75 there is a view over the wooded **Murta river** valley.
The road descends to this valley and follows its course to km 108; here is the 4–km detour to
Puerto Murta (pop 586), a small port on an arm of lake General Carrera. Founded in the 1930s, it has been moved several times as the port became silted. Its main activity is logging, with several active sawmills; it exports its output through Chile Chico to Argentina.
The road runs close to the shores of this arm, the scenery showing a transition from forest country to Patagonian pampa.
At km 132 it reaches **Puerto Tranquilo**, a quaint hamlet on the banks of the Tranquilo river, with a ferry jetty. Transport can be arranged here to **Puerto**

lake General Carrera

Sánchez (accommodation) and to the
Marble Cathedral it is a marble headland carved and bored by the water into fantastic shapes. It has several smooth caves you can traverse by boat. At Tranquilo a boat can be hired from Mr Evaristo Vargas (one hour, rowing). Several tourist agencies arrange this tour at Coihaique as well.
From Puerto Tranquilo there is a 12 km road to lake Tranquilo, nice **scenery** and good for camping.
The Carretera continues on a ledge above the lake for 11 km. At km 146, by the bridge, there is an access to lake Tapial, good for camping. At km 161, from the bridge over the Leones river, there is a fantastic view of the glaciers spawning the river. Horses can be hired from the local dwellers, to ride to lakes **Fierro, Leones** and **Sur**, with the glaciers hanging directly above them. Allow one day for this.
At km 179 there is a signposted detour to the left, the best place for camping on the lake. A short way ahead is a suspension footbridge over the stream draining the lake General Carrera into the adjacent lake Bertrand.
At km 188 is the El Maitén road junction, on the Negra pond, a good spot for camping. From here, it is 13 km to Puerto Guadal and 69 km to Cochrane.

The branch to the left skirts the lake shore, passes **Puerto Guadal**, a small village with a very good microclimate and a lovely beach called **Perla del Lago**. The road from here to Cochrane was opened several decades ago, and made this port the outlet for the valley's products.
The road continues 36 km behond Puerto Guadal, to **Mallín Grande**, with orchards and pastures. From here it continues 31 km on a ledge skirting the lake to **Puerto Fachinal**, and 50 km ahead is **Chile Chico.** A total 130 km from the road junction in el Maitén.
From El Maitén (km 188), the Carretera Austral continues south to reach, at km 205, **Puerto Bertrand** (road branching right), a small village on the Bertrand lake, with a jetty and boats for hire. Good fishing. The village is at the headwaters of the **Baker river**, the one carrying most water in Chile. It empties into the ocean 200 km to the west. Puerto Bertrand used to receive the output of Cochrane valley, brought by boats rowing upstream, and forwarded it to Guadal by ox–driven carts, whence it would be shipped across the great lake.
At km 217 the road climbs the Cuesta del Diablo, descending on the other side to the confluence of rivers **Baker** and **Neff**, the latter milky as it is fed by a glacier.
At km 225, a road branches right to balsa Neff (ferry), with a beach and good spots for fishing and camping.
At km 237, a bridge spans the **Chacabuco river**, running along one of the best cattle farming val-

13

611

Chile Chico

brought sheep from their estancias on the Argentinian side of the border. The Estancia Valle Chacabuco is still operating, covering 62,000 hectares.

The village of Cochrane was founded in 1930 by the Chilean government, but it consisted of only a school and a general store until 1954, when the public offices were set up. Now it is a thriving village.

TOURS FROM COCHRANE

TO LAKE COCHRANE ★★

five kilometers from Cochrane, the lake has no sandy beaches, but good fishing and camping spots.

TO LAKE ESMERALDA ★★

ten km from Cochrane, taking the road numbered «3» in the map. The lake lies on a semi-steppe, with shrubby vegetation and rocky shores.

leys in this region. A road branches off from here to the border (passable only in summer) and into Argentina through the **Roballos pass.**

At km 257 (341 km from Coihaique) is

COCHRANE (pop 1,500), a provincial capital providing all the basic services, including accommodation, telephone, and gasoline. Here ends the Carretera Austral –for the moment. It is being extended to other points further south.

Cochrane has also a busy airfield serving inland lakes and the coastal areas not yet reached by the road network.

This valley was discovered in 1899 by explorer Hans Steffen, who surveyed the Baker river from its mouth to its headwaters. In 1908, these lands were leased to the Sociedad Exploradora del Baker, formed by Magellanic sheep farmers who

TO ARGENTINA THROUGH ROBALLOS PASS ★★★

ninety-five km to the border, on the only road prior to the Carretera. The road is poorly surfaced, badly in need of maintenance; it fords several streams of varying depth. Only recommendable for 4WD, high-clearance vehicles. It runs through a valley with good pastures for livestock farming. It offers a chance to return north through a different route.

TO CALETA TORTEL RAFTING ON THE BAKER RIVER

★★★ an increasingly popular excursion, using Zodiac-type boats and under the guidance of experts. Sice Travel offers this tour, phone 251 2881 in Santiago, phone 233466 in Coihaique.

☎ Telephone Center	**A** Town Hall
◉ Café, Meeting Point	**B** Post Office
⊞ Gasoline Station	**C** Government Building
✚ Hospital	**D** General Store

E Endesa	**ACCOMMODATIONS**
F Conaf	1 H Wellman
G Playground	2 Hs Pensión La Tranquera
H Lookout Point	3 R Sur Austral

13

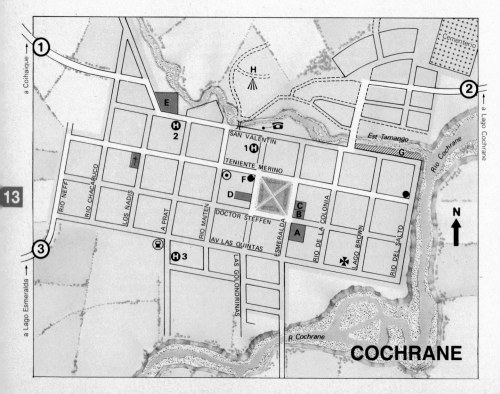

COCHRANE

EXCURSIONS

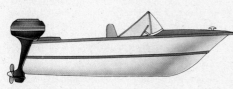

BY BOAT

Towing your own boat when making the Carretera Austral will be thoroughly rewarding. Not only there are uncounted lakes along the way, most with boat slips or ramps, but also many places on the far shores with no road access, affording you that coveted bit of total privacy.

Lake Yelcho concrete boat slips at Puerto Cárdenas and Puerto Piedra. From the latter, you can sail through the Futaleufú river and the lake. Warning: The lake is dangerous with strong north wind.

Lake Espolón easy to sail, beautiful, all across to the far shore.

Lake Rossellot there is no boat slip, but at the ferry landing it is easy to lower the boat onto the water. The lake is stunning, and the fishing superb. Good beaches.

Puyuhuapi sailing through the fjord to the thermal baths (Hotel Termas de Puyuhuapi) will give you nice views over the surrounding glaciers.

Lake Elizalde a graveled, steep boat ramp, but gorgeous scenery from the water.

Lake General Carrera boat slips at Puerto Ibáñez and Levicán. Only for cruises close to the shore, as the waves on the open lake can be tricky.

From Puerto Tranquilo you can sail to the Marble Cathedral (see description above).

13

PUBLIC TRANSPORTATION

Bus Services the main «hubs» are Chaitén and Coyhaique. From Coihaique there are fairly frequent services (several per week) to Puerto Cisnes and Mañihuales in the north; to Puerto Aisén and Puerto Chacabuco on the coast; and to Balmaceda and Cochrane in the south. Less frequent services to Chaitén, to inland villages and to Osorno through Argentina, via Bariloche.

From Chaitén, services run to Puerto Montt along the Carretera and to the inland towns of Futaleufú and Palena, to Puerto Cisnes, and to Coihaique.

Air Services twice daily from Santiago and Puerto Montt to Coihaique. Light aircraft fly to remote destinations in the areas of Chile Chico, lake Verde and lake O'Higgins.

Shipping Transmarchilay ferries serve Chaitén and Puerto Chacabuco from Chonchi, Pargua and Quellón. Double-check ports of departure and schedules as they change relatively often. Navimag has two weekly departures from Puerto Montt to Puerto Chacabuco (vehicle and cargo ferry), and one weekly departure for passengers, sailing along the coast and islands to Puerto Chacabuco.

To Laguna San Rafael there are several weekly departures (different companies) from Puerto Montt and Puerto Chacabuco. Also fast Catamarán Patagonia Express carries ont trips from Pto Montt, Chacabuco, Laguna San Rafael. See description in Services Section at the end of this guide.

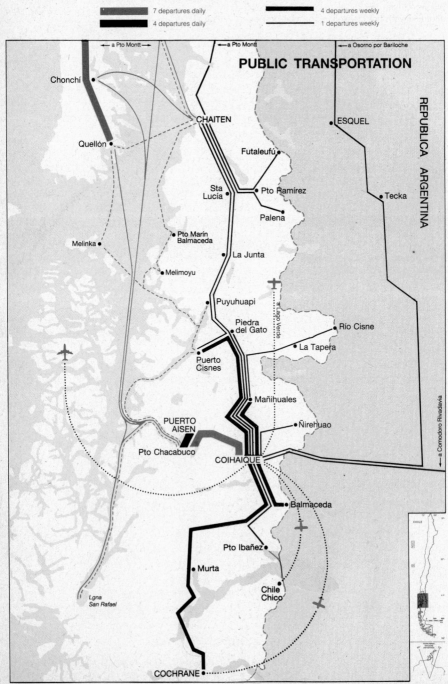

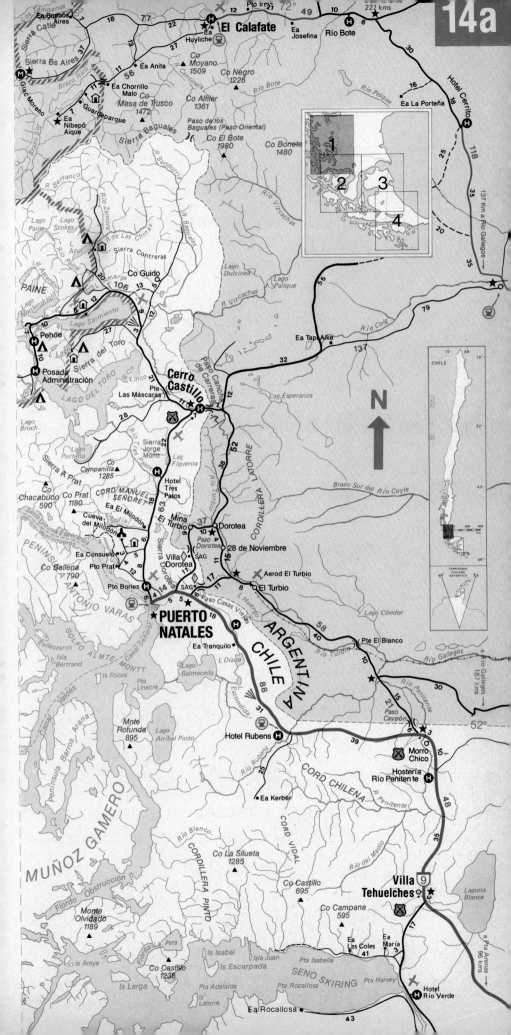

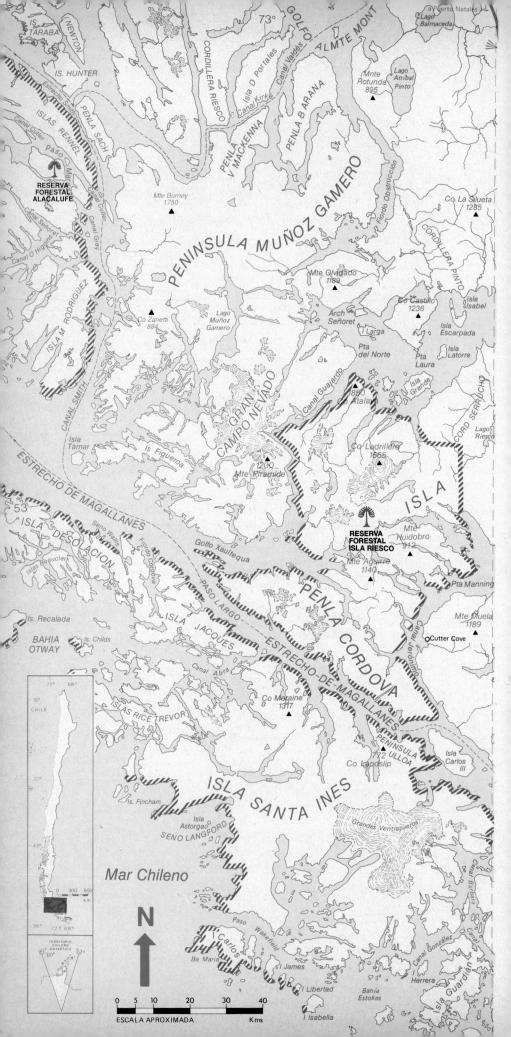

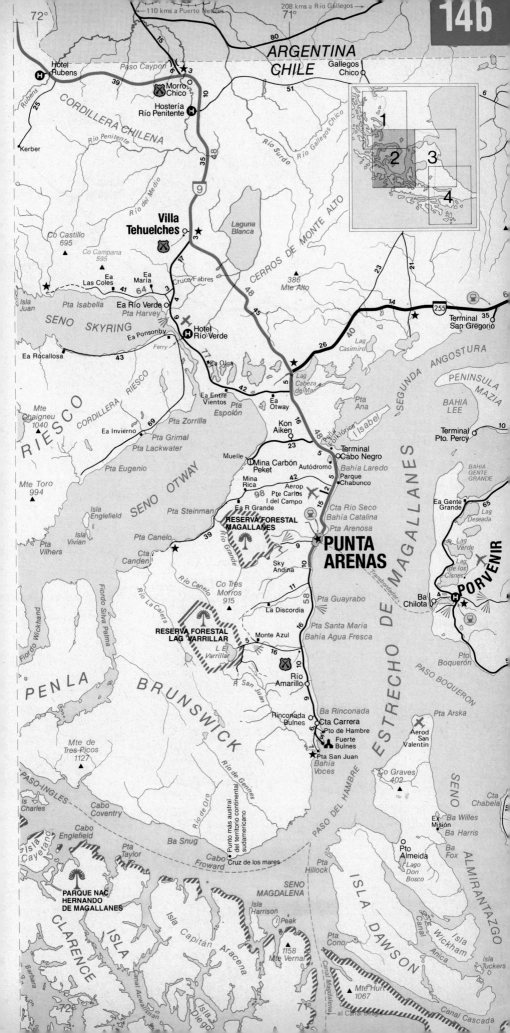

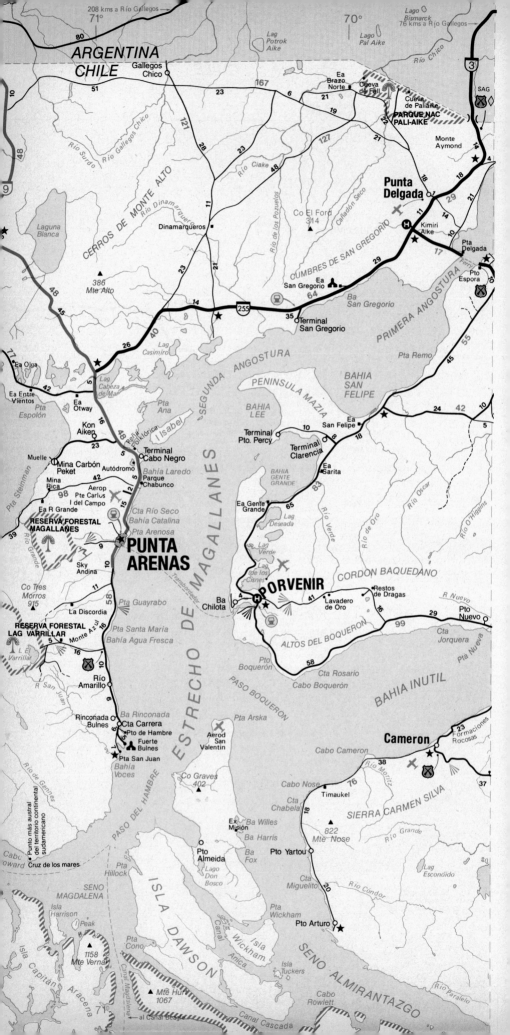

68°

52°

0 5 10 20 30 40
ESCALA APROXIMADA   Kms

N

Chorrillo de los Frailes
El Fraile
El Cóndor
Lag Grande
Paso Integración Austral
Pta Tandy
43
106
Posesión
45
Cabo Posesión
Pta Daniel
Pta Wreck
Cabo Virgenes
Pta Dungenes

ESTRECHO DE MAGALLANES

Cabo Orange
Mar Chileno
Pta Catalina
Cta Norte
BAHIA LOMAS
Pta Camacho
43
Cabo Espíritu Santo
Calafate
44
60
23
Cerro Sombrero
28
16
Batería Lynch
Cullen
Cabo Nombre
Yacimiento Chillán
35
50
15
Río Cullen
Ea Tres Lagos
Cruce San Filaret
SERRANIAS DE SAN
SEBASTIAN
Pta de Arenas
Ea China Creek
Batería Flamengo
18
8
24
BAHIA SAN SEBASTIAN
Lago Bello
Lag Vergara
13
Pte Cisne
Las Gaviotas
San Sebastián
Cabo San Sebastián
Onaisin
33 43
SAG
San Sebastián
Paso San Sebastián
18
8
Cementerio Inglés
Río San Martín
19
Ea Sara
Lag Ema
Ea Las Largas
94
Rio C Silva Chico
3
Ea La Florida
Río Chico
Ea 3 A
41
Lag Amalia
Lag Almirante O'Connor
SIERRA CARMEN SILVA
Ea El Estero
Ea Río Chico
Lag de la Suerte
Lag Grande
Cabo Domingo
Puesto El Medio
Río Evans
Ea Las Flores
Ea El Salvador
50
Misión Salesiana
Draga
Est Wilson
Lag Mercedes
Río Grande
Río Grande
Aserradero Sección Rusffin
Aerod Rusffin
Cruce Moneta
Sección Río Grande
Ea Menéndez
Lago Lynch
Río Riveros
Ea Onamonte
Lago Blanco
Guanacos
Lago Chico
Valle Castor
Ea Vicuña
Ea San Justo
CHILE
ARGENTINA
Río Herminita
Río Grande
Lag Cabo Peñas
Lag San Luis
Río del Fuego
241 kms a Ushuaia

Río Grande

Océano Atlántico

CHILE
72° 68°
19°
32°
43°
300 600
km
56° 72° 68°

TERRITORIO CHILENO ANTARTICO
90° 53°
60°

1
2
3
4

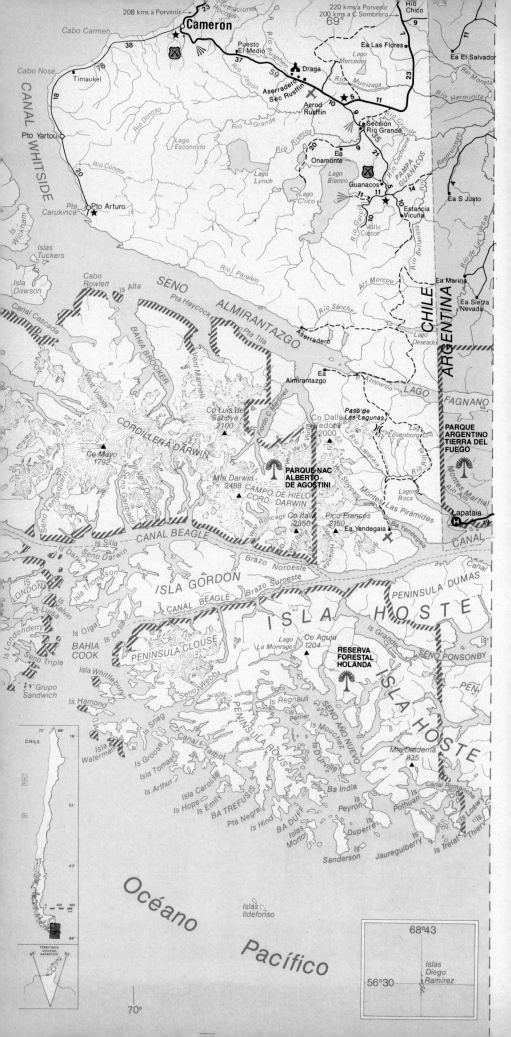

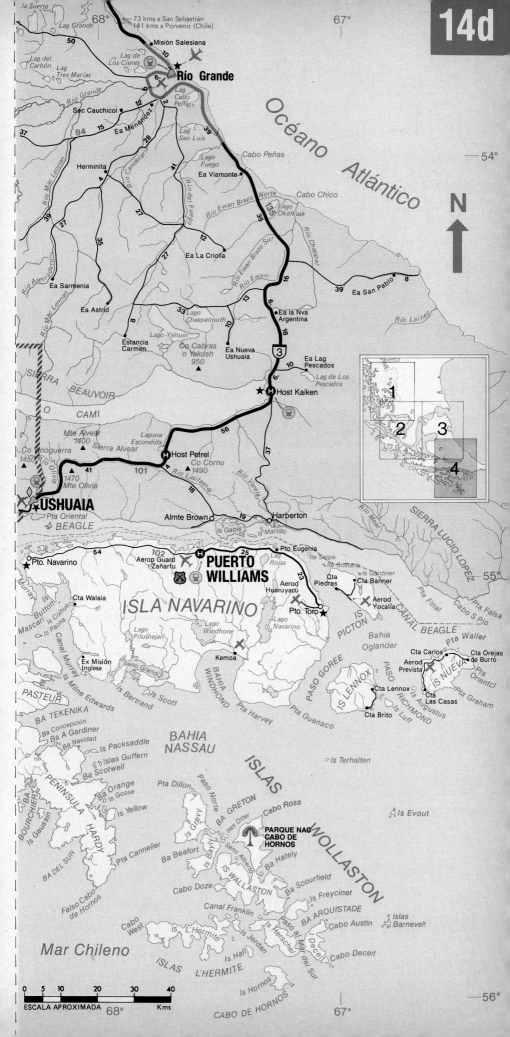

OVERVIEW

This Zone can be divided into two distinct geographic areas: the Western Patagonia archipelago, lying west of the Andes and consisting of a maze of islands, channels, and fjords; and Eastern Patagonia, lying east of the Andes, comprising forest–clad Andean foothills and vast steppes stretching to the Atlantic.

Of this large region, only the area accessible by road –located in Eastern Patagonia– shall be described, together with the Beagle Channel/Isla Navarino sector in Western Patagonia, as it is accessible by road through Argentina and by air from Punta Arenas.

The four sections into which we have divided this Zone have been arranged for the convenience of travellers coming by car from the North via the highway from Río Gallegos, Argentina. Puerto Natales is left for last, since it includes several alternate routes north.

Section A Punta Arenas includes the pampa and Andean foothills located to the north of the Strait of Magellan, with its center at Punta Arenas.

Section B Tierra del Fuego pampa and foothill areas of Tierra del Fuego's main island, Isla Grande, located south of the Strait of Magellan.

Section C Puerto Williams includes the Beagle Channel and Puerto Williams, the main town in the Chilean side, on Isla Navarino. It is a jumping–off point for spectacular sailing trips through glacier–draped channels to Cape Horn.

Section D Puerto Natales comprises the Ultima Esperanza territory, an especially scenic part of Magallanes, the highlight of which is Torres del Paine National Park. This can be the starting point for the return journey north.

MEAN ANNUAL RAINFALL

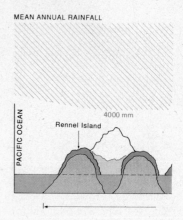

TOPOGRAPHIC AND RAINFALL DIAGRAM

MEAN ANNUAL RAINFALL

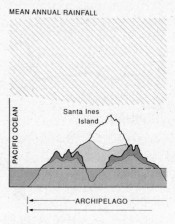

TOPOGRAPHIC AND RAINFALL DIAGRAM

REGIONAL DISTANCES

★ Ferry Punta Delgada
★ Transbordador Punta Arenas

Aduana Monte Aymond															
304★	Cameron														
408	458★	Cerro Castillo													
106★	198	428★	Cerro Sombrero												
251	205★	365	269★	Fuerte Bulnes											
357★	105	569★	251	344★	Lago Blanco										
189	199★	305	209★	106	310★	Mina Peket									
243	290★	165	263★	200	401★	140	Morro Chico								
257★	47	411★	151	158★	158	152★	243★	Onaisín							
486	536★	78	506★	443	675★	383	243	489★	Pehoe						
198★	149	309★	125	56★	260	50★	141★	102	387★	Porvenir					
345	395★	63	365★	302	534★	242	102	348★	141	246★	Puerto Natales				
195	149★	309	215★	56	260★	50	144	102★	387	307★	246	Punta Arenas			
32	272★	377	75★	218	326★	160	212	226★	455	167★	314	164	Punta Delgada		
194	237★	240	220★	150	348★	81	72	190★	88	88★	174	88	166	Río Verde	
211★	93	451★	105	198	146	192★	283★	46	529★	142	388★	142★	180★	233★	San Sebastián

Zone 14
MAGALLANES

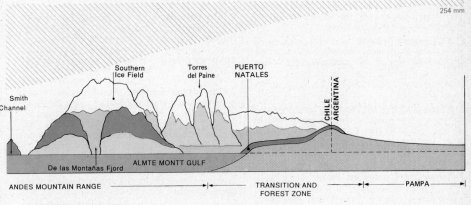

254 mm

Smith Channel · Southern Ice Field · Torres del Paine · **PUERTO NATALES** · CHILE ARGENTINA

De las Montañas Fjord · ALMTE MONTT GULF

ANDES MOUNTAIN RANGE ⟶ | TRANSITION AND FOREST ZONE ⟶ | PAMPA ⟶

PUERTO NATALES AREA

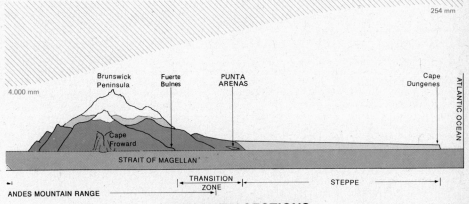

254 mm

4.000 mm

Brunswick Peninsula · Fuerte Bulnes · **PUNTA ARENAS** · Cape Dungenes · ATLANTIC OCEAN

Cape Froward

STRAIT OF MAGELLAN

ANDES MOUNTAIN RANGE ⟶ | TRANSITION ZONE ⟶ | STEPPE ⟶

DIVISION BY SECTIONS

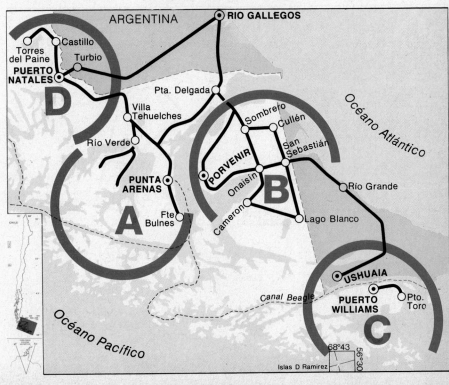

ARGENTINA · RIO GALLEGOS

Torres del Paine · Castillo · Turbio · **PUERTO NATALES**

D

Pta. Delgada

Villa Tehuelches · Sombrero · Cullén

Río Verde · **PORVENIR** · San Sebastián

PUNTA ARENAS · Onaisin · B · Río Grande

A · Fte Bulnes · Cameron · Lago Blanco

Océano Atlántico

USHUAIA

Canal Beagle · **PUERTO WILLIAMS** · Pto. Toro

C

Océano Pacífico

68°43 · 56°30

Islas D Ramirez

CIRCUIT DESCRIPTION

The various tours described in this Zone's four sections are grouped as follows:

1 Route of the Early Colonists in the southern reaches of this region are the ruins of the first attempts at colonizing it: Puerto de Hambre (1584) and Fuerte Bulnes (1843). Territorial occupation spread northward along the shores of the Strait of Magellan, bringing about the founding of Punta Arenas (1848) and, later, the establishment of the San Gregorio sheep farm. The circuit is described in Section A, under Tours 1 and 2.

2 A Geographic Overview a circuit providing an overview of Magallanes' geographical features: sedimentary steppes, the Andes Mountains and other ranges, islands, isthmuses, channels, lakes, sounds and gulfs. Described in Section A, under Tours 5 and 6.

3 A Taste of History and Prehistory a short circuit visiting the first livestock farming settlements at Natales, and the Milodón Cave, where the remains of a legendary prehistoric animal –a type of ground–dwelling sloth– were found. Described in Section D, Tour 1.

4 Torres and Cuernos del Paine a visit to a strikingly beautiful massif of bizarrely–shaped peaks surrounded by glaciers and captivating lakes; an area teeming with wildlife. Described in Section D, Tour 3.

5 The Oil Route oil exploration and drilling are carried out in the coastal waters of the Strait of Magellan and also on Tierra del Fuego. Derricks, pipelines, refineries, off–shore platforms, and the camps housing the workers are to be seen. Described in Section B, under Tours 4 and 5.

6 The Gold Route in the Cordón Baquedano range, commanding the best view to the Strait of Magellan, free–lance gold miners are still trying their luck,, and the remains of gold mining equipment used during the last century's gold rush can be seen. See Section B, Tour 2.

7 The Fuegian Estancias Patagonian estancias, or large sheep ranches feature administrative, residential and workshop compounds known as cascos. This circuit includes the first estancias. The cascos, now villages, still contain their fine, original buildings. See Section B, Tours 3 and 4.

8 Lakes and Mountains deep within the southern forests is spectacular Lago Blanco, with excellent fishing, herds of guanaco and busy beavers. See Section B, Tour 3.

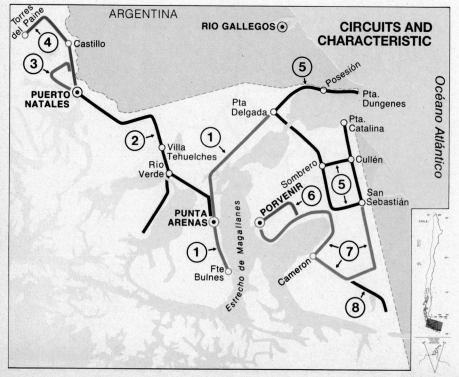

THE LAND, ITS HISTORY, ITS PEOPLE

MORPHOLOGY this Zone stretches from the Cordillera del Paine in the north to Cape Horn in the south, and from the eastern foothills of the Andes to the Pacific Ocean in the west. The westernmost section, with its fabulous channels, islands, fjords and glaciers, is not accessible by road, and there are no regular shipping or air services for the area.

The Andes range lies in the region's western portion. After the last Ice Age, its glaciers retreated and ocean water flooded the river valleys, creating deep penetrating fjords. Some veritable inland seas were also formed in this way, such as the Almirante Montt gulf and the Otway and Skyring sounds. Farther south, retreating ice masses and a geological fault gave rise to the Strait of Magellan and the Magdalena channel – the passageway leading to the Beagle channel and Navarino island. The southward–running Cordillera de los Andes begins bending east, until achieving a due east course by the time it reaches the Beagle Channel. Torres del Paine, to end up running due east at the Beagle channel.

In contrast to the rest of Chile, this zone has no Coastal Mountain Range, as it petered out at the Taitao peninsula farther north. Here, the Andes plummet directly to the sea, their exposed tops giving rise to the maze of islands and channels described above.

To the east is a vast, nearly flat plain created millions of years ago by glaciers which, in their retreat, deposited sediment and levelled the land all the way to the Atlantic.

STRAIT OF MAGELLAN shaped like an S, its southernmost point lies at Cape Froward (Brunswick Peninsula), where a large cross was erected recently, paying homage to Pope John Paul II and marking the end of the South American continent.

Cape Froward is situated at the meeting point of two differently formed sections of the Strait of Magellan. The section from here to the Pacific runs along a geological fault cutting a swath across the Andes. The section toward the Atlantic, in turn, runs along a valley once interrupted by moraines deposited by retreating glaciers which, in time, produced a string of separate lakes. The moraines eventually gave way, allowing the lakes to join and created the Strait's Primera and Segunda Angostura (First and Second Narrows).

The lakes existed until the end of the last Ice Age, some 10 thousand years ago. Before the isthmuses were washed away, Indian tribes used them to cross over into Tierra del Fuego to become the now extinct Ona people.

CLIMATE the zone's climate is due largely to three factors: its latitude, stretching from 51° S to 56° S; a strong marine influence, moderating the temperatures; and violent winds blowing from the Pacific.

The Pacific winds collide with the Andes Mountains, where they unload all of their moisture, and continue cold and dry across the pampas. At Puerto Edén, situated on a Pacific island, there is practically no dry season to speak of: more than 4,000 mm of rain pour down in a year. By contrast, at Cape Dungenes, located at the eastern mouth of the Strait of Magellan, a scant 254 mm is the entire annual rainfall supply. Not surprisingly, the western portion of the Andes is covered by lush forests, while the eastern plains are a near–desert speckled with bunch grass.

Temperatures in the coastal areas do not fluctuate much, due to the moderating influence of the ocean, but the high latitude makes them relatively cold. The annual mean high at Puerto Edén is 10° C (14° C in January and 5° C in July), while the mean low is 5.4° C (7,8° C in January and 0,7° C in July). At Punta Dungenes the mean high and low are 10,2° C and 4° C, respectively, while at Puerto Williams both mean values are a bit lower.

During the winter, the snow line drops almost to sea level. As a result, the inland pampas including, those on Tierra del Fuego, and near Puerto

Natales, Cerro Castillo and Torres del Paine, are cloaked in white, making estancia chores difficult and causing some areas to become inaccessible.

ORIGINAL INHABITANTS this Zone's peculiar topography and its rich terrestrial and marine wildlife facilitated occupation by four aboriginal peoples, each speaking a different language and occupying a different geographical area.

The **Aonikenk (Tehuelches)** were tall nomadic hunters. Due to the size of their footprints, so the story goes, the area was named Patagonia, meaning "Land of the Big Feet".

They roamed the eastern foothills of the Andes as far north as Bariloche, going from mountain meadow to mountain meadow, following small and large game. In the 18th century they succeeded in domesticating wild horses living in the pampas, enabling them to extend their range following the river valleys all the way down to the Atlantic coast.

Guanacos, huemules (a large deer now almost extinct) and rheas provided them with everything from meat to shelter. The skins and feathers were traded with the first settlers colonizing the coastal lands. The first westerner to live among them for one year was explorer George Charles Musters, who set out from Punta Arenas in 1869 and accompanied different tribes and chieftains until reaching the area of Bariloche, in Argentina. The vast livestock farming operations that sprang up in the Argentinian pampa under government concessions in 1900 blocked the Tehuelches' freedom of movement and eventually brought them to near extinction.

The **Shelknam (Onas)** were nomadic hunters occupying the pampean areas of Tierra del Fuego. They journeyed to the island at the end of the last ice age, some 10 thousand years ago, when it was still connected to the mainland by moraine dams. Their customs were similar to those of the Tehuelches, but they were highly adapted to the rigorous Fuegian climate. They traded with the Yahgan tribes living in the Beagle channel area, walking across mountain passes located near present–day Ushuaia. The Onas were tragically and violently exterminated (see Tierra del Fuego Section).

The **Yamanas (Yaghans, Yaganes)** were nomadic coastal dwellers living in the area around Beagle channel, where they had occasional contacts with the Alacalufes. An Anglican mission, originally set up in Ushuaia in 1876 but later moved to Chilean territory on Navarino island, strove for 70 years to preserve these aboriginal people and preach them the Gospel; the Yahgans were nonetheless all but wiped out by disease and alcoholism introduced by seal hunters and whalers, and later by the 1893 gold rush.

The **Kaweshkar (Alacalufes)** also were nomadic coastal dwellers, sailing along the channels and among the islands from Golfo de Penas to the Strait of Magellan. They hunted seals and sea lions, fished and gathered shellfish. They thrived in an area with the extremely harsh weather, to which they were astoundingly well adapted, rainfall exceeds 4,000 mm a year, piercing, biting winds blow year round and the seawater is chilled by the ever–present glaciers.

A small Alacalufe community still survives in Puerto Edén, from where they still set sail among the islands. Their near extinction was due to disease and alcoholism introduced by seal hunters and whalers, who operated in the area until the middle of this century.

14

DISCOVERY AND ATTEMPTS AT COLONIZATION

Chile was discovered on October 21, 1520, by **Fernão Magalhães (Hernando de Magallanes, Magellan)**, a Portuguese captain then in the service of the Spanish Crown, during an exploratory journey seeking a seaway that would allow passage around or through the American continent to reach the Spice Islands in the west. He sailed along the uncharted South American Atlantic coast until he

Punta Arenas and Straits of Magellan

found the mouth of the strait, on November 1, 1520. Struggling against unrelenting headwinds and tides, he sailed along the strait until he finally emerged into the comparatively calm waters of the ocean at the other end, which he promptly christened the Pacific Ocean.

The Strait of Magellan opened a route from Europe to the American continent's Pacific coast. It was soon traversed by Spanish naval and merchant fleets, but also by pirates and privateers seeking to plunder the colonies. **Francis Drake** was one of them, paying his visit in 1578. King Felipe II decided then to strengthen the Strait against attacks by building forts. The commission was given to **Pedro Sarmiento de Gamboa**, who sailed from Spain with 15 ships and 4,000 men toward the Strait. Gales ravaged the fleet and only 3 ships with some 300 settlers and priests completed the journey. Sarmiento founded two villages, each with a town hall and a church, in 1584: **Nombre de Jesús**, at Cape Dungenes, and **Rey Felipe**, at San Blas bay. A violent gale caused the only remaining ship, with Sarmiento on board, to break free from its moorings and blew it out into the open sea. After several unsuccessful attempts to sail back into the Strait, Sarmiento returned to Rio de Janeiro, Brazil, to organize the rescue of the abandoned settlers.

Two successive rescue expeditions ended up in misfortune; one in shipwreck, the other in a mutiny. Sarmiento was finally captured by an English pirate and sent to prison in England, where he was released through intervention by Queen Isabel of Spain. He set out by land to return to Spain, but was again made a prisoner while crossing France. Until his death, he wrote repeatedly to King Felipe begging him to send help to the Strait settlements.

In 1587, the pirate Thomas Cavendish sailed along the Strait and sighted some survivors on the shores of Munición bay, near the First Narrows. He rescued only one of them, who gave an account of both settlements' tragic end ravaged by starvation.

Other privateers and corsairs sailed these waters: R Hawkins in 1594; B Cordes and O Noort in 1600; and G Spilbergen in 1615. The following year Dutch seamen Jacob Le Maire and Cornelius van Schouten discovered a route through the Cape Horn archipelago, indefensible from land and more suitable for sailing ships.

CHILEAN SOVEREIGNTY the nascent republic inherited its boundaries from those delimiting the colonial territory. Chile's first Constitution defined the nation's southern boundary as lying at the tip of Cape Horn, but more pressing matters turned attention away from these lands. Four subsequent developments again focused the government's attention on Magallanes; the hydrographic surveys carried out in the southern channels by the officers of the English ship Beagle from 1826 to 1832; the occupation of the Malvinas Islands by England in 1833; the inauguration in 1840 of a steamer service to the Pacific through the Strait of Magellan, the best passageway for this type of ship; and France's apparent intention of setting up an enclave in this region.

Secretly, Chile's President Bulnes ordered that a colonizing expedition be organized. A ship was built in Ancud, Chiloé, which sailed on May 23, 1843, with 21 sailors and soldiers, tools, provisions, a few chickens, 3 dogs, 2 pigs and a pregnant goat.

This meager party, after 5 months at sea, arrived at the Strait of Magellan and erected **Fuerte Bulnes**, a fort that was Chile's first settlement on the Strait. The site that was chosen, on a rocky promontory surrounded by a thick forest, proved unsuitable to serve as the core for a larger settlement. Thus, in 1848, the fort's governor, José de los Santos Mardones, moved the population farther north along the Strait of Magellan shore and founded Punta Arenas on December 18 of that year, at the place where the Magellanic forest meets the steppes, unfolding to the east. The small settlement grew slowly and received some men in uniform banished into internal exile, as well as some repeat criminals, who would later be behind such bloody episodes as the Cambiazo mutiny of 1851. The pampas, in turn, had been made unsafe by Tehuelche raids. The Tehuelches killed governor B E Phillipi in 1852 in the vicinity of lagoon Cabeza de Mar, as retaliation for the outrages perpetrated by Cambiazo against them.

Punta Arena's penal town character remained until 1867, when President JJ Pérez issued a decree facilitating colonization by foreigners and granting Punta Arenas the status of a duty-free minor seaport. The village started to grow, fueled by trade and as a supply port for the growing steamer traffic through the Strait, as well as for the numerous sealer and whaling ships plying the region's archipelagos. Foreign settlers, mostly Yugoslavs and Britons, set up business establishments, trading houses, hotels, butcher shops, bars and stores.

COLONIZATION OF THE HEARTLAND in 1852, Governor BE Phillipi brought some sheep from Chiloé; one year later the animals numbered 34 and, by 1864, they were 240. In 1877 Governor Dublé Almeyda, under government authority and in a Chilean Navy ship, sailed to the Falkland islands (Islas Malvinas) and purchased 300 sheep, which he then sold to British businessman **E Reynard**; the latter, in turn, let them loose on Isabel island in the Strait of Magellan. The following year, other entrepreneurs acquired sheep, brought them in a vessel belonging to one **José Nogueira** and let them loose on the Marta and Magdalena islands, also in the Strait. These sheep farmers chose the islands as they offered a natural «fence» affording protection against Tehuelche raids. An additional 500 sheep were brought from the Falklands (Malvinas) and acquired by Marius Andrieu, who placed them at **San Gregorio bay**, the first sheep farming concession in the mainland, on the Strait's northern shore. It required fences and defenses against the Tehuelches.

It was a risky, costly business. Each sheep placed at Punta Arenas cost £1–1,5 due to the high losses (30%–50%) incurred during the passage from the Falklands –many died of trichinosis and lack of food and water– and the kilometers of fences and production facilities necessary for operation. Most of these pioneer sheep farmers failed, but the high world price of wool –one of the only three textile fibers existing at the time, together with cotton and linen– prompted **José Menéndez** to acquire the rights to San Gregorio in 1882. In time, he was to become the so-called «King of Patagonia.»

Outstanding border disputes with Argentina were settled through a treaty signed in 1881. The Chilean government, aware of the need to allocate lands in this frontier region, offered to lease 570,000 hectares in 1884, divided into 90 plots located north of the Strait in the vicinity of Punta Arenas. As a result, José Menéndez added an additional 30,000 hectares to his name at San Gregorio, and **Sara** and **Mauricio Braun** –brother and sister– acquired the adjacent plot, forming the estancia Pecket Harbour. **José Montes** acquired a plot in the Laguna Blanca area and **José Nogueira**, the same Nogueira whose ship had brought the first flocks of sheep, acquired another one in the vicinity of the Otway and the Skyring sounds. Smaller plots were leased to other local entrepreneurs. The major ranch-owners continued to enlarge their holdings. Menéndez ended up controlling some 90,000 hectares at San Gregorio; the Brauns and Montes, similarly-sized farms.

Nogueira married into the Braun group, taking Sara as his wife, thus pooling their holdings.

Proper sheep farming required ignificant start-up capital, which was raised in Valparaíso through the establishment of sheep ranching companies. The necessary technology was imported from the Falklands (Malvinas) and Great Britain, brought mostly by knowledgeable Scottish managers, foremen and carpenters.

Subsequent exploration revealed that Tierra del Fuego was also remarkably suitable for sheep ranching. The Chilean government promptly offered leases to the lands adjacent to the Gente Grande bay taken by the namesake company and, in 1889-90, another 1,310,000 hectares, acquired by José Nogueira. The Punta Arenas sheep ranchers, drawing on the experience gained, formed companies which they then floated through £-denominated shares of stock in the Valparaíso, Buenos Aires and London stock exchanges, exercising control from Punta Arenas.

Nogueira formed 4 estancias in the Tierra del Fuego lands under his control; Bahía Felipe, adjacent to the Strait; and Caleta Josefina, San Sebastián, and Cameron, further inland. The last three became in time the Sociedad Explotadora de Tierra del Fuego (SETF), a company managed after Nogueira's death in 1893 by his widow Sara Braun, with the assistance of her brother Mauricio.

The vigorous expansion experienced by SETF caused it in 1910 to become Chile's largest-ever farming operation, with over 3,000,000 hectares under its ownership, or under lease or tenancy arrangements, and wielding power and influence beyond mere commercial circles.

In 1899, in Punta Arenas, the so-called «Strait Embrace» was established by Chilean President F Errázuriz and his Argentine colleague JA Roca. The latter offered Chilean estancieros all kinds of state support if they would undertake to populate and bring into production the barren lands of Argentine Patagonia. The following year, José Menéndez established the estancias 1º and 2º Argentina, which were to become the origin of the city of **Río Grande**, in the Argentinian portion of Tierra del Fuego

When the vast pampas of Ultima Esperanza were offered for lease in 1905, the Soc Explotadora de Tierra del Fuego acquired control of all the lands lying along the border, as well as control of the adjacent lands on the Argentinian side. It established Magallanes' largest sheep processing plant at Bories, serving both countries. In 1908, José Menéndez and Braun & Blanchard founded the Sociedad Anónima Importadora y Exportadora de la Patagonia, incorporated simultaneously in Chile and Argentina, with trading, shipping, farming and financial interests. It opened branch offices in

Argentina's main Patagonian ports, where it acquired control of additional vast ranch farming lands. Intermarriage eventually brought the holdings of the Menéndez and Braun families under the roof of a single controlling unit.

The sheep ranching industry made a gigantic contribution to the Region in terms of capital and production technology, as well as in the preparation of artificial pastures. However, this vast region remained largely unpopulated; the big ranching companies did not permit people to settle the land; everyone was merely an employee. Beginning in 1938, when the leases to state lands started to expire, the successive governments maintained a policy of subdividing part of the land into plots, subsequently allocated to individual settlers. Thus, the large estancias diminished gradually in size until, in the 1960s, they were finally expropriated and broken into smaller plots or exploited through cooperative schemes. Villages and municipalities were established at the estancias' former administration and housing compounds, known as cascos. The 1982 census showed this Region's rural population to be among the lowest in Chile, with 7,5% of the total.

OIL flowed here for the first time on December 29, 1945, at the Manantiales N° 1 well located on Tierra del Fuego. This is Chile's sole oil-producing zone, meeting up to 50% of the country's oil needs and 100% of its liquefied gas requirements. The producing areas are located in the northern portion of Tierra del Fuego (10%), the Cape Dungenes

A	Administration Headquarters
M	Derrick and Barge Maintenance and Repair Yards
B	Warehouses and Maintenance Depots
⊙	Residential Compound

GAS

	Gas Refinery
	Gas Scrubbing Plant
G	Gas Storage Complex
▲▲	Petrochemical Industry
●	Gas Shipping Port

OIL

▉▉	Incoming Oil Manifold
	Oil Refinery
P	Oil Storage Complex
■	Oil Shipping Port
----	Oil, Gas and Combined Pipelines
✳	Offshore Platforms
●	Onshore Oil Wells

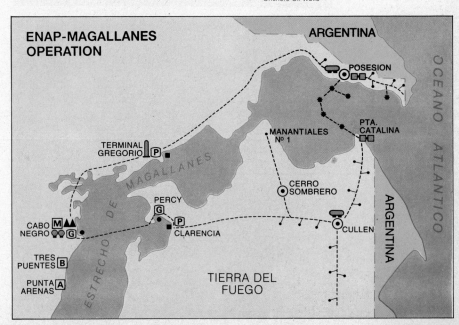

629

14

Onshore Derrick and Drilling Equipment the derrick is a 47-m-tall metallic structure consisting mainly of the hollow **master shaft**, with a boring bit at the tip. The shaft, driven by a **turntable**, rotates in order to produce a drilling motion; as the shaft sinks deeper, new sections are added to it until reaching depths of some 3,000 m. A special kind of **mud** is injected into the shaft for cooling and lubricating purposes, as well as to line the well's walls with an impermeable coating and push upwards the material removed by the boring bit. If the well taps an oil reserve and starts producing, it will be lined with tubing and a «Christmas-tree» **valve** (wellhead valve) will be installed at its mouth to control outflow.

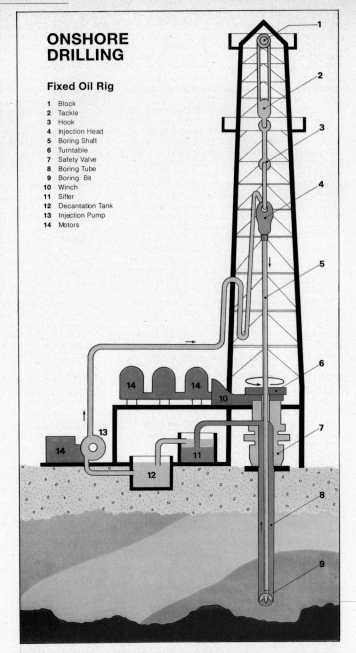

ONSHORE DRILLING

Fixed Oil Rig

1 Block
2 Tackle
3 Hook
4 Injection Head
5 Boring Shaft
6 Turntable
7 Safety Valve
8 Boring Tube
9 Boring Bit
10 Winch
11 Sifter
12 Decantation Tank
13 Injection Pump
14 Motors

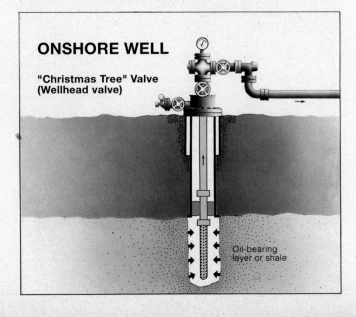

ONSHORE WELL

"Christmas Tree" Valve (Wellhead valve)

Oil-bearing layer or shale

14

OFFSHORE DRILLING PLATFORM

Movable Platform

1 Drilling Derrick
2 Heliport
3 Platform
4 Supporting Pillars
5 Steered Drilling

127 mts
Máximo

Offshore Drilling Platforms are significantly more complex structures, as they must be able to perform four functions: sail on the ocean, settle themselves on the sea floor, operate a drilling rig and house the operating equipment and personnel. It includes a large **platform** with several decks, containing the **drilling rig**, living quarters accommodating 45 people, a warehouse, a control center, 2 cranes and a heliport. The platform is equipped with three **telescoping pillars** which rest on the ocean floor and rise up to 127 m above it, permitting operation in water depths of up to 92 m, so that the platform remains above the waves. To move from one location to another, the platform is towed with the pillars providing the necessary buoyancy. It also has its own means of propulsion to fine-tune its position on the desired spot. Drilling is similar to that described for onshore oil rigs. Producing wells offshore require other structures known as

Fixed Platforms two towers are erected above the producing wells. The ones in operation at the Strait of Magellan weigh a combined 1,500 tons and are as tall as a 25-story building. The platforms' outer pillars, 98 cm in diameter have a tube running down their length which is driven into the ocean floor by a pile driver. The platforms contain different decks. The **left platform** houses the wellhead valves and accommodates production rigs in the lower deck. The upper deck contains the living quarters, drinking water tanks, control center and power generators. A raised top deck acts as a heliport. The **right-hand tower**, joined to the other by a bridge, has a single deck containing the heaters and an arm stretching away with a flareblazing permanently at its tip to burn out potentially hazardous gases. A pipeline starts from this platform to the incoming manifolds on the shore.

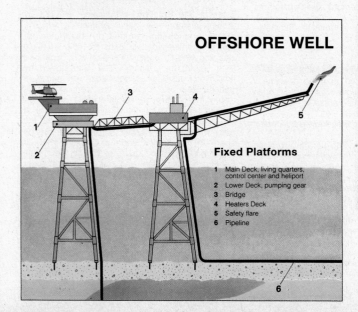

OFFSHORE WELL

Fixed Platforms

1 Main Deck, living quarters, control center and heliport
2 Lower Deck, pumping gear
3 Bridge
4 Heaters Deck
5 Safety flare
6 Pipeline

14

and Posesión sector on the Strait's northern shore (16%), and the offshore fields in the Strait itself (74%). The offshore drilling platforms went on stream in 1979.

In addition, around one third of the country's natural gas wells are located here. Their enormous actual and potential output provides the basis for a future petrochemical complex at Cabo Negro, the first stage of which was the construction of a methanol plant, described below.

The company in charge of prospecting and development is Enap-Magallanes, the region's heavyweight, with three residential compounds, 6 storage and processing centers, and 5 production areas, all interconnected through overland pipelines, road networks, seaports, airports and heliports. A schematic representation of Enap's operations is shown below.

The prospecting and drilling effort carried out in the past four decades is mind-boggling. Over 2,400 wells have been drilled, each reaching from 1,700 to 3,000 m below the surface, and stretching over 5,300 km if all were places end to end. Derricks and offshore platforms are the most visi-

ble bits of this activity.

MAGALLANES TODAY the Zone's population grew by 48% from 1970 to 1982, bearing witness to the rapid pace of its economic development. Oil accounts for the largest share (30%) in the gross regional product, followed by the traditional livestock industry, with over 2,6 million head of sheep (over 50% of Chile's total) and 130,000 head of select cattle. Industrial output has also risen considerably, fueled by new or expanded machinery repair and maintenance plants, shipyards, packing houses, fish and shellfish canneries and cold storage plants.

Two recent developments augur well for the future; the opening in 1987 of Chile's most modern coal mine at Otway Sound, and the start up in 1988 of the world's largest and most advanced methanol plant at Cabo Negro (both in the vicinity of Punta Arenas). The methanol plant, with an output of 800 thousand tons per year, is fed by a 1,5-m-diameter natural gas pipeline that begins in Posesión.

SECTION A   PUNTA ARENAS

The Magallanes province stretches from the boundary with Argentina in the north, which runs along parallel 52° S Latitude, to the Strait of Magellan, in the south. Here the Andes mountains run diagonally to the Brunswick peninsula, where rugged Cape Froward marks the southernmost point of the South American mainland. South of the Strait, there is a scattering of islands.

The population centers and the large livestock estancias are located to the east of the Andes. Punta Arenas, is the only city in Chile where the sun sets on the Cordillera.

Access by Land all access roads run through Argentine territory. From Santiago, the shortest paved route is through Mendoza (km 0), taking the highway that leads to Buenos Aires up to Mercedes (km 359). At the junction take the road leading to Justo Durac up to Vicuña Mackenna (km 462); this road intersects a large highway heading south. Follow this highway, which passes Santa Rosa at km 748, reaches the coast at San Antonio at km 1,228, and then runs along the coast through Rawson, Comodoro Rivadavia (km 1,832), and Santa Cruz (km 2,235), finally reaching Río Gallegos at km 2,545.

A more scenic option is to start from Osorno (km 0) in Chile, head through Paso Puyehue to Bariloche (km 245) –fine scenery all the way–, and then continue south through Parques Nacionales Argentinos to Esquel, where a highway runs diagonally through the pampas heading for the Atlantic coast at Comodoro Rivadavia (km 1,203). Continuing along the coast to the south, Río Gallegos is reached at km 1,916.

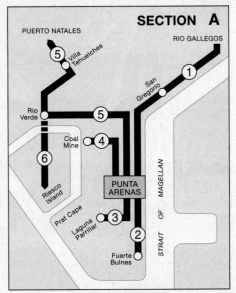

SECTION A

1 **FROM RIO GALLEGOS TO PUNTA ARENAS ★★★**
total distance 264 km, with 60 km paved. Gasoline at Río Gallegos and San Gregorio. The border is open from 08:00 - 22:00 h. Enquire about the necessary papers for the car («tríptico»).
Overland access to Punta Arenas offering fine views of the Strait of Magellan.

Leave Río Gallegos following the road to Paso Integración Austral. At km 13 there is a police checkpoint. The road runs through rolling pampas until km 69, where the Argentine customs outpost is located, 1 km before the border.

The Chilean Immigration and Customs checkpoint is located at km 71, at **Monte Aymond.** At km 84 a road branches off to the left to Cape Dungenes (Punta Dungenes, described under Section B). The road approaches the Strait and oil drilling installations can be seen. At km 102, to the right, is the access to **Punta Delgada,** a village set up at the former casco (administration and housing compound) of a once large sheep ranch. At km 113, a road branches off to the ferry crossing at

Primera Angostura (the Strait's First Narrows). The road now runs along the Strait's shores to reach, at km 142,

Estancia San Gregorio established in 1878 by pioneer entrepreneur Marius Andrieu; it was one of the first sheep ranches on the mainland, operating on leased state lands. In 1882, the lease was acquired by José Menéndez, who expanded it to 90,000 hectares by 1894. Surrounded by employee houses, shearing sheds, warehouses, a general store and a chapel, this complex reflects turn-of-the-century architectural style and is an excellent example of the classic casco (core) of an estancia. From the estancia's entrance, the rusty wreckage of **steamer Amadeo CNM** can be seen on the Strait's shores. Built by 1880, it became in 1892 the flagship of the Cía. Menéndez Behety merchant fleet and was the first steamer bearing Punta Arenas registration. After 50 years plying these waters, the company's board decided to run it aground, in front of the first estancia owned by Menéndez.

At the end of wide San Gregorio bay (km 151) is the **Oil Terminal,** where there is also a gasoline station. The road leaves the Strait and at km 217 intersects the paved highway, linking Punta Arenas and Puerto Natales. Turning left, at km 264 you reach

PUNTA ARENAS with around 97,137 inhabitants, the

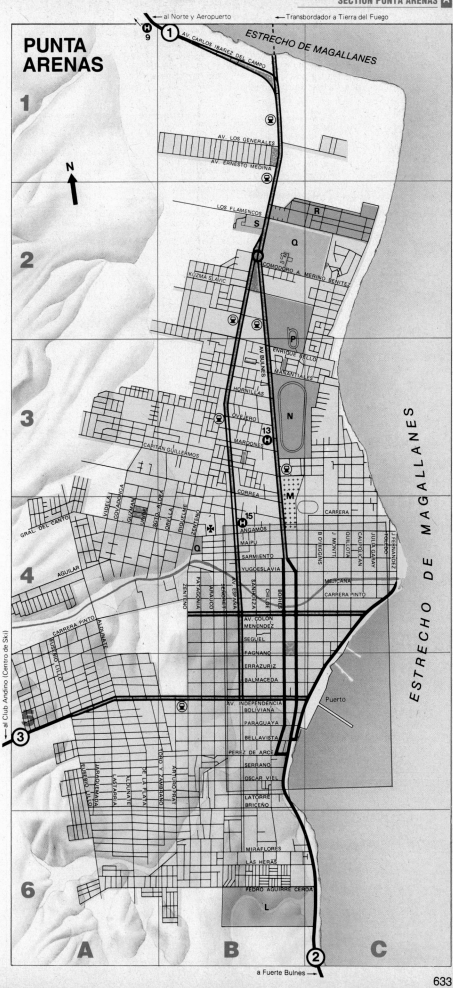

PUNTA ARENAS

al Norte y Aeropuerto →   ← Transbordador a Tierra del Fuego

ESTRECHO DE MAGALLANES

1

N

2

AV. CARLOS IBAÑEZ DEL CAMPO

AV. LOS GENERALES

AV. ERNESTO MEDINA

LOS FLAMENCOS

R

S

Q

COMODORO A. MERINO BENITEZ

KUZMA SLAVIC

3

AV. BULNES

ENRIQUE BELLO

MANANTIALES

HORNILLAS

OVEJERO

13

MARDONES

N

CAPITAN GUILLERMOS

CORREA

M

CARRERA

GRAL. DEL CANTO

VIDELA

COLVADONGA

GUZMAN

JUSTEL

SGTO. ALDEA

OBELLA

RIQUELME

ZENTENO

15

ANGAMOS

MAIPU

B. O'HIGGINS

J. MONTT

QUILLOTA

CAUPOLICAN

JULIA GARAY

TOLEDO

J. FERNANDEZ

4

AGUILAR

Q

SARMIENTO

YUGOESLAVIA

MEJICANA

CARRERA PINTO

PATAGONIA

ZENTENO

ARAUCO

SEÑORET

AV. ESPAÑA

SANHUEZA

CHILOE

BORIES

AV. COLON

MENENDEZ

SEGUEL

FAGNANO

ERRAZURIZ

BALMACEDA

CARRERA PINTO

ALDUNATE

EUSEBIO LILLO

AV. INDEPENDENCIA

BOLIVIANA

Puerto

al Club Andino (Centro de Ski) →

PARAGUAYA

BELLAVISTA

3

PEREZ DE ARCE

SERRANO

OSCAR VIEL

LATORRE

BRICEÑO

TORO Y ZAMBRANO

DE LA PLATA

ARTURO PRAT

JARAQUEMADA

ALDUNATE

LASTARRIA

EUSEBIO LILLO

6

MIRAFLORES

LAS HERAS

PEDRO AGUIRRE CERDA

L

ESTRECHO DE MAGALLANES

14

A   **B**   **C**

2

a Fuerte Bulnes →

capital of Region XII (Magallanes y Antártida Chilena) is the world's southernmost city. The city's economy is fueled by providing services for the region's oil production and coal mining concerns, petrochemical industries, sheep industry and a booming, recently established fishing industry. It is also a major supply port for the Strait's growing ship traffic, and the main jumping-off point for Antarctic expeditions –scientific, as well as tourism-oriented, by ship or by plane.

The city still bears the mark of the early entrepreneurs' philosophy, namely that isolation and loneliness are bearable only when one lives splendidly and in contact with the great outdoors.

☎ Telephone Center
★ Touristic Information
◉ Café, Meeting Point
🅖 Gasoline Station
⇛ Lookout Point
✚ Hospital (4B)
A Town Hall (3B)
B Regional Government (2B)
C Cathedral Church (2A)
D Enap Headquarters (3B)
E Sara Baraun Palace (2B)
F Braun Menéndez Museum (2B)
G Regional Museum (1B)
H Post Office (2B)
J Immigration (3B)
K Cerro La Cruz Lookout (2A)

✳ **L** María Behety Municipal Park (6B)
✳ **M** Cemetery (4B)
✳ **N** Hippodrome (3B)
✳ **P** Stadium (3B)
✳ **Q** University (2B)
✳ **R** Duty-free Zone (2C)
✳ **S** Instituto de La Patagonia (2B)

ACCOMMODATIONS
1 H Cabo de Hornos (2B)
2 H Los Navegantes (2A)
3 H Colonizadores (4B)
4 H Plaza (3B)
5 H Condor de Plata (2A)
6 H Mercurio (3A)
7 H Savoy (2B)

8 Hos de la Patagonia (1B)
✳ 9 Centro Turístico Pta Arenosa (1A)
10 Hos Del Estrecho (2B)
11 H Montecarlo (2A)
12 R Roca (2B)
✳ 13 R Bulnes (3B)
14 H Ritz (2C)
✳ 15 R Centenario (4B)
16 R Paris (3A)
17 R Bustamante (2C)

RESTAURANTS
1 Cabo de Hornos (2B)
E Club de la Unión (2B)
30 Sotito's Bar (3B)
31 El Quijote (2B)
◉ Garogha (2B)

32 Vegalafonte (2B)
33 Mónaco (2B)
34 Acapulco (1A)
35 Asturias (2B)
36 Torre Vieja Mar (1A)
37 Dinos Pizza (1B)
38 Roca Pizza (2A)

TOURIST SERVICES
20 Lan Chile (2B)
21 Ladeco (2B)
22 Aerovia DAP (2B)
23 Agencias de Viajes (2A)
24 Automovil Club Chile (2B)
25 Hertz Rent a Car (2B)
✳ See General Map of Punta Arenas

Downtown PUNTA ARENAS

Newer buildings, such as that of the Gran Hotel Cabo de Hornos, public institutions and the headquarters of local firms, have sought to conserve this approach. The oldest residences, the main square, the cemetery, the museum and the main shopping street are all well worth a visit.

The city was founded in 1848 when the settlers, previously established at Fuerte Bulnes, were moved to this site –named Sandy Point (Punta Arenosa) in the navigation charts of the time–, as Fuerte Bulnes had proved unsuitable to serve as the core of an expanding, permanent settlement. Punta Arenas' present location was selected on account of its abundant supply of firewood, the availability of water, a harbor, and more area for future expansion, as well as its more sheltered situation, allowing better protection against the rigorous Patagonian climate.

Punta Arenas lies at the foot of the Andes mountains and at the edge of the steppes unfolding to the east. Its development as a colonial outpost was slowed up initially by the decision to use it as a penal town for insurgent military and common criminals. In 1851, an officer named MJ Cambiazo headed a bloody uprising, murdering the town's authorities and ransacking the village.

The M Montt administration, bent on keeping this important outpost, granted the Magallanes region the status of colonization area, thus officially removing Punta Arena's character of penal colony. The first governor appointed thereafter was José Schytha, who kept climatological records and carried out agricultural trials. The settlement, however, largely remained as a penal colony until 1877. Its main sources of income were the supply of water and coal, the irregular shipping traffic along the Strait, and its role as a supply port for a growing fleet of sealer and whaling ships plying the Western Patagonia archipelagos.

The decade from 1875 to 1885 saw the consolidation of the town. The new governor, Diego Dublé Almeyda, travelled to the Falkland (Malvinas) islands in 1876 to import a flock of 300 sheep, setting in motion what was eventually to become a huge, influential sheep farming industry (see Land & History).

In 1881, 172 steamers and 36 sailing vessels called at Punta Arenas. By then, the town's future tycoons were already living in Punta Arenas: José Menéndez; José Nogueira; José Montes; and Tomás Saunders. Sara and Mauricio Braun, still young, would inherit and expand Nogueira's empire.

Before the turn of the century, over 570,000 hectares of livestock land had been allocated under leasing agreements in this area. Punta Arenas boasted an opera theater, the large mansions of sheep tycoons and a beautiful cemetery. The 1910 gold rush lured a new wave of immigrants, repeated later with the outbreak of World War I. The giant sheep ranching corporations had their headquarters, slaughterhouses and cold-storage compounds in Punta Arenas. There were also two shipping companies, and insurance and merchant companies operating throughout Patagonia.

Oil was discovered in the 1940's and on Dec 29, 1945, the first well, Manantiales 1, in Tierra del Fuego, went on stream, changing the face of both the city and the Region. Punta Arenas is the administrative center for Enap's regional operations, as well as the residential center for its personnel engaged in oil development. In the 1970's, the fishing industry made its appearance, and in 1987 the extensive coal reserves in the vicinity of Punta Arenas –ranked among the world's largest– started to be exploited. At Cabo Negro, a large methanol plant went on stream in 1988, the first unit of a planned vast petrochemicals complex.

What To See the shopping area, the docks and the southern portion of the city are best seen in the morning, while the light is better for views over the Strait of Magellan in the afternoon, from the northern part of town.

`DOWTOWN` walk up calle Fagnano to the look-out on Cerro La Cruz for a view of the city.

The **Main Square** is lined with cedars. In its center,

Punta Arenas; Square and Hotel in winter

a bronze statue on a high pedestal –with an inscription reading «José Menéndez a Hernando de Magallanes» («To Hernando de Magallanes from José Menéndez») depicts the Portuguese navigator; the base has reclining Fuegian natives... Tradition has it that those who kiss the Ona Indian's big toe will return to the city.

Around the square are the Cathedral, the Government building, Enap, Hotel Cabo de Hornos and the beautiful

Palacio Sara Braun now enjoying National Monument status.The palace was built in 1895 by French architect Nurma Meyer; all materials and furnishings imported from Europe. It was the residence of Sara Braun, the widow of José Nogueira, the founder of the Soc Explotadora Tierra del Fuego. Now it houses the Club de la Unión.

On Hernando de Magallanes, half a block off the square, is the

Palacio Mauricio Braun-Menéndez (NM) now housing a museum of regional history (Apr-Sep, Tue - Sun, 11:00-13:00 h; Oct-Mar, Tue, Sun, 11:00 -16:00 h). The mansion was built by the Braun Menéndez family and all of its original furniture and decorations have been preserved. Other rooms contain very good exhibits of the region's history. It is well worth a visit.

It used to be the residence of Mauricio Braun (Sara Braun's brother), who married Josefina Menéndez Behety, a daughter of the great entrepreneur and tycoon José Menéndez. It was designed and built in 1906 by French architect Antoine Beaulier, who also designed other mansions and public buildings in the city.

Pedro Montt and **J A Roca** are the main shopping streets. At the **harbor** you can see the hulls of old moored ships, now used as floating storerooms.

A short way south along the **Costanera** brings you to **María Behety** park, with picnic sites. Drive up to Cerro Mirador (9 km west of town; follow Av Independencia through town and up the hill), a **ski resort** with a superb **view** of the city, the Strait of Magellan and Tierra del Fuego.

Afternoons are the best time for visiting the northern part of town. At the beginning of Av Bulnes is

Museo Regional Salesiano «Mayorino Borgatello» (in summer, mon, 10:00-13:00 h and Tue-Sun, 09:00-13:00 h and 15:00-18:00 h; in winter, Tue - Sun, 10:00-12:00 h and 15:00-18:00 h), with excellent exhibits presenting the habitat and history of Patagonia's aboriginal peoples, as well as the region's natural history. Other rooms provide an insight into the historical evolution of the Magallanes region, with very good photographs and charts. The artifacts on display were all collected by Salesian missionaries and scientists. Continuing on **Av Bulnes** many monuments are to be seen on the street's central platform, one of the most outstanding being a group depicting a shepherd, his horse and a flock of sheep. Do not miss the

Cemetery · one of the most interesting in Chile, with manicured flower beds and avenues lined by tall cypresses. It contains splendid mausoleums of the

14

pioneer families, including that of José Menéndez, who died in Buenos Aires and was buried in the city he helped to build. A solemn tombstone indicates the place where the last Onas, a now-extinct Tierra del Fuego Indian people, are buried. It is also well worth visiting.

Continuing on Av Bulnes, to the right is the **hippodrome**, followed by a **stadium** and then by the modern **campus of Universidad de Magallanes**. At the end, to the left, is

Instituto de la Patagonia (Mon-Fri 08:30-12:30 h and 14:30-18:30 h; Sat 08:30-12:30 h. library and bookstore only Mon-Fri; open-air museum Mon-Fri; on Sat. and Sun. only through prior arrangement with the administration). A center engaged in research on Magallanes' history and resources, it runs an **open-air museum** in one of the gardens, containing machinery and dwellings from the colonization period. The library and bookstore are excellent.

Duty-Free Zone (Zona Franca) (Mon-Sat 10:00-12:00 h and 15:00-20:00 h). A short distance from Instituto de la Patagonia is the duty-free compound, a mall-like building containing shops in two levels and a roofed, heated central court.

Farther north, at **Tres Puentes**, is the wharf for the ferry to Tierra del Fuego. Continue to the north on Av Carlos Ibañez, which runs along the shore, to **Parque Chabunco** with a nice forest extending to the edge of the water.

Return to Punta Arenas along Av España, which has some historically and architecturally interesting houses.

Where To Eat the best cuisine is at Hotel Cabo de Hornos and Hotel Los Navegantes, the most elegant at Club de la Unión. Sotito's is very good. Several fast-food restaurants are marked on the map. Cheap meals at Mónaco (Mon-Sun 08:30-22:30 h) and the market, in Galeria Acapulco. Picnic sites at parks María Behety and Chabuco.

TOURS FROM PUNTA ARENAS

2 TO FUERTE BULNES ★★★
128 km there and back on a graveled road. For 1 day. Take food.
A traditional excursion from Punta Arenas to the area where the first settlements were established, with beaches on the Strait.

Leave Punta Arenas, km 0, along the Costanera to the south. The road runs near the shore and past fishing coves (fish and shellfish offered) and cultivated fields. At km 26 is a bridge and the **Agua Fresca police station**. A road branches off to the right for Lake Varillar (Tour 3).

At km 45 starts **Bahía Aguas Claras**; at its southern end is **Rinconada Bulnes**, with some weekend houses. At km 49 is Punta Carrera, with a **cemetery** dating from the colonization period (1885). At km 51 is a triple fork and a milestone indicating **Chile's Geographical Midpoint**, a point equidistant from Arica and the South Pole. Take road to the left leading in 2 km to

Puerto de Hambre, a fishing cove flanked by rocky, forested headlands. Here, Pedro Sarmiento de Gamboa founded the village of Rey Felipe, on March 25, 1584, building houses and a church for 100 settlers and missionaries. Cut off from the outside world by a gale that blew out to sea the only remaining ship, and left to face the region's harsh winters without any chance of receiving supplies, the settlement met a tragic end. The English pirate Thomas Cavendish made a landfall here in 1587 and found a body hanging from the gallows at the square, and the corpses of some settlers lying in their houses, fully dressed. He named the place Port Famine. Some foundations can still be seen.

Return to the triple fork and take the middle road, leading in 5 km to

FUERTE BULNES the first Chilean settlement in these southern reaches; it was founded in October 1843 on the rocky promontory of Santa Ana, commanding a view of the Strait of Magellan. The colonizing party had sailed from Chiloé five months before, under the command of Capt. Juan Williams,

and included B E Phillipi (a naturalist later to become Punta Arenas' governor), 11 sailors, 8 soldiers and 2 wives. They all stayed at Fuerte Bulnes. The settlement was moved to Punta Arenas in 1848.

Fuerte Bulnes has been reconstructed, including each of its various sections, the outer perimeter wall and the main gate, all built in logs.
There is a picnic site in the adjacent forest.
Return to the triple fork and take now the road to the right leading in 6 km to

Río San Juan here is the grave of Pringles Stokes, captain of the Beagle, who died here while the famous English ship, which charted Chile's southern coasts between 1826 and 1832, and in which Charles Darwin later made his equally famous journey,was being repaired. Stokes was replaced by Capt. Fitzroy.

The San Juan river is well-stocked with fish. To return to Punta Arenas, retrace the same route.

3 TO LAGUNA PARRILLAR ★★
94 km round trip on a gravel road. For 1 day, take food. Alternative return via a road only suitable for high-clearance, 4WD vehicles.
The nearest native forest Punta Arenas, with a small lake and fine scenery.

Leave Punta Arenas (km 0) following Costanera south toward in the direction of Fuerte Bulnes. At km 26, beyond the Agua Fresca bridge, turn right into a lovely valley flanked by soft rolling hills. The road gradually climbs to the altitude where a dense natural forest begins. The Strait spreads below; the Tierra del Fuego coastline shimmers in the distance.

At km 47 is the entrance to **Laguna Parrillar National Reserve**, a beautiful area under the supervision of a Conaf warden station. Check with the warden about hikes to the lake, the paths through the forest or the location of the picnic areas (these are equipped with a fireplace and shelters against wind and rain; water is available).

To return, either retrace the same route or, if you are driving a high-clearance off-road vehicle and have an adventurous disposition, drive 7 km down to take the road branching off to the left at Aserradero Monte Azul (a sawmill). The trail crosses the Agua Fresca river and cuts through the forest to Estancia La Discordia, where an 11-km road climbs down to the Strait.

4 TO THE NEW COAL MINE ★★
96 km round trip, 54 km of which are paved and the rest gravel. For half a day.
A visit to Otway sound, with a magnificent view of the mountain range at Brunswick peninsula, and to a new coal mine.

Leave Punta Arenas (km 0) following Av. Bulnes and continue northward on the highway to Puerto Natales. At km 27 is a Carabineros station; take the gravel road to the left branching off there. The road runs across the Brunswick peninsula over a rolling steppe separating the Strait of Magellan from Otway sound.

At km 36 is the casco (administrative and housing compound) of the old Kon Aike estancia; at km 40 the road reaches the eastern shore of the vast **Otway sound**, flanked on the west by enormous Riesco island. Eight km ahead along the coast is

Pecket Mine opened in 1987, it is the first open-pit mine tapping the gigantic coal strata stretching all the way to Riesco island, ranked among the world's largest coal reserves. It makes use of modern extraction techniques; the coal is loaded via a long mechanized dock onto ships which sail into the Strait of Magellan through the Jerónimo channel. Check with the administration about the possibility of visiting the installations.

To round out the tour, drive a bit farther along the coast to the penguin breeding colonies. In the past, thousands of penguins nested in the caves. Now only a handful remain, visible only when it is not too windy

5 TO PUERTO NATALES THROUGH RIO VERDE
★★★ *the direct route to Puerto Natales runs along a*

230-km paved road. The route through Río Verde is 34 km longer, and 71 km are over gravel. A trip for 1 day, with gasoline stations at Puerto Natales.

A circuit to a scenically different part of Magallanes. The route through Río Verde offers a chance to have a look at the area's two great sounds.

Leave Punta Arenas (km 0) following Av Bulnes to the north. At km 22, Enap's Cabo Negro facilities can be seen, consisting of a large maintenance and repair shop, a gas scrubbing plant and storage tanks, and the tall stack of the methanol plant towering nearby. At km 43, by the seawater lagoons known as **Cabeza de Mar**, take the gravel road to the left. At km 50 is the casco of **Estancia Otway**, one of the region's oldest.

The road runs across the steppe of an isthmus which, to the south, rises into a broad cordillera to become the Brunswick peninsula. At km 58 the road reaches the shores of the **Otway sound** and runs along the coast. Abundant bird fauna is to be seen, including black-necked swans and rheas. The road continues along the **Fitz Roy channel**, which connects the Otway and Skyring sounds and separates the mainland from Riesco island. The names of the channel and of both sounds are those of the captain and officers, respectively, of the English ship Beagle, which first charted these intricate waters (1826-1829). Most of the geographical features here were christened by Fitzroy and his lieutenants. At km 85 is **Hostería Río Verde** open only in high season, a pleasant inn frequented by residents of Punta Arenas. A ferry crosses from here to Riesco island, described under Tour 6. The road soon crosses **point Harvey**, with a spectacular **view** of **Skyring sound**. At km 91, to the left, is

Río Verde a village which mushroomed around the casco of an old estancia, with very well preserved houses and sheds, all in a beautiful setting

overlooking the sound.

At km 94, a road branching off to the left runs another 41 km along the northern shores of Skyring sound to **Río Pérez,** an excellent fishing spot. The road to the right –difficult during the rainy season– leads to the paved highway (route 9) linking Punta Arenas and Puerto Natales (km 114). Three km beyond the intersection is

Villa Tehuelches a small village next to the highway, founded in 1966 after the large estancias were expropriated. Originally heralded as a prototype for Magellanic rural «core settlements», it has experienced scant growth in two decades. It has a restaurant, a car repair shop and a tourist information office. The vast expanses of the steppes surrounding **Laguna Blanca** roll away opposite the village. These were the lands of the now extinct Laguna Blanca sheep ranch company.

The road heads toward the peaks of **Cordillera Chilena**, running through forests that contrast sharply with the meager vegetation of the pampas. At km 138 is the access to Hostería Río Penitentes, a good stop-over point. A short distance ahead, a road branches right for **Gallegos Chico**, running eastward along the Argentine border to Punta Delgada. This road leads to the **Pali Aike National Park**, containing Fell's cave and archaeological remains.

At km 150 is the hamlet of **Morro Chico**, named for a peculiar rock outcropping. Here is the Caypón Pass to Argentina (now closed).

The highway runs westward close to the border, with a view of the Argentine pampas rolling away to the north; to the south is the **Cordillera Chilena** range.

Hotel Río Rubens, at km 183, offers accommodation, a restaurant, and horseback tours to fishing spots. The road turns north, following a bend in the border, and crosses the Rubens river, a tributary of Penitentes river (flows through Morro Chico), which empties into the Atlantic.

At the top of the **Cordón Auco** range (km 200), there is a fine view over the **Diana plain**, which falls away gently to the west to the shores of the **Gulf of Almirante Montt**. Across the horizon march the snow-capped Andean peaks.

This plain is not a grassy steppe, but bush land with some patches of forest (much forest has been clearcut to open the land for sheep farming). The richer vegetation results from higher rainfall owing to the Pacific Ocean's proximity.

At km 210 the road starts to skirt **lake Diana**, and at km 215 is the highly recommended **Motel Llanuras de Diana**, with a restaurant (hidden from the road). At km 230 is the **Casas Viejas** border control (daily 8:00-24:00 h), for a road leading to the Casas Viejas pass (5 km) and to the **El Turbio** coal mine and village in Argentina. This is the best alternative for those wishing to return north via Río Gallegos (Argentina).

The highway then skirts the foothills of **Sierra Dorotea**, where another road branches off to the border and into Argentina through the Dorotea pass, to El Turbio. Puerto Natales is at km 246 (city description in Section D).

☎ Teléfono Público
A Municipalidad
B Iglesia Parroquial
A Correos
C Casa Huéspedes
D Carabineros de Chile
E Posta

F Garage
G Gimnacio
H Comedores
J Casa Esquiadores
K Junta de Vecinos
M Centro Comunitarios
N Escuela

VILLA TEHUELCHES

a Pto Natales →

②

N ↑

F
E
M
B
A
F
N
D
C
J
K
G
H

RUTA INTERPROVINCIAL N°9

①

6 A VISIT TO RIESCO ISLAND ★★★

140 km round trip from ferry at Hostería Río Verde; 310 km round trip from Punta Arenas. Take enough gasoline and food. If planning a day-trip, leave early.

A popular fishing and camping spot in a beautiful setting overlooking the Otway sound.

Leave Punta Arenas (km 0) taking the highway to Puerto Natales. At km 43 take the gravel road branching off to the left, leading in 85 km to Hostería Río Verde (described under Tour 5), where the ferry for Riesco island sets out (08:00-11:45 h and 13:00-18:45 h). Should the ferry be at the Riesco dock, call for it with a honk.

At **Isla Riesco**, roads run along the shores of both sounds. Take the road to the left, winding along the rugged Otway sound coastline for 70 km, with superb views of islands and the snow-capped peaks and fjords of the Brunswick peninsula. At the end of the road is **Río Grande**, a river well stocked with fish. There are some basic camping facilities.

14

7 **CRUISE TO GLACIERS AND PUERTO WILLIAMS**
★★★ *in the Terra Australis, a first-class ship; the biggest tourism investment made in Chile in 1991. Seven-day journey, departures Weds from Sept - March. See services section.*

The country's most spectacular cruise. Great possibility to get to know the Patagonian archipielago in all its splendor.
See itinerary description in Section C, Puerto Williams.

SECTION B   TIERRA DEL FUEGO

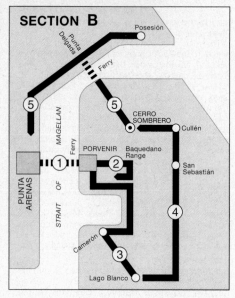

This section covers the large island off the extreme south of South America, bound by the Strait of Magellan on the north, the Atlantic Ocean on the east, the Beagle channel on the south and an assortment of channels on the west. It was christened in 1520 by Hernando de Magallanes. It owes its name to the fires lit on the shores by Ona indians. The island remained largely unexplored until 1879, when an expedition led by Navy lieutenant Ramón Serrano traversed it from Gente Grande bay to San Sebastián bay, on the Atlantic coast.

Over 4,000 Ona natives inhabited the island's steppes, stretching from the mouth of the Strait to the Darwinian foothills in the south, where the steppes are replaced by bush and Magellanic forests. The Onas were burly, tall, nomadic hunters, skilled in the use of slings and arrows with which they hunted guanacos and birds. They jealously guarded their territory. The Gente Grande («Large People») bay was so named by the first explorers to honor the Onas. For almost half a century they thwarted all attempts by the fragile colonial outpost of Punta Arenas to penetrate inland.

The boundaries between Chile and Argentina in these southern lands were laid in 1881, the north-south border dividing Tierra del Fuego being drawn from Cape Dungenes southward. But maps covering Tierra del Fuego were as yet nonexistent. The border was later found to run over Atlantic waters at San Sebastián bay, and, as a result, had to be shifted to the west, to its present location.

Sarmiento's surveys showed these lands to be exceptionally well suited for sheep raising. The following expedition, led by Jorge Porter in 1880, discovered the Porvenir bay and found gold at the Boquerón range. In less than 20 years, the entire steppe portion of the island was given over to sheep raising and mining works.

Hundreds of miners from the United States and Europe streamed to the Boquerón range from 1882 onward to prospect for gold or work at the existing gold mines. The gold mines were mechanized by the turn of the century. Powered dredges remained in operation until the depletion of the gold deposits in 1909.

Meanwhile, the state had offered 20-year leases to those lands suitable for raising sheep. In 1883, the **Sociedad Ganadera Gente Grande** began developing the pampas stretching north of Cordón Baquedano. José Nogueira was granted a concession for 310,000 hectares at the Bahía Felipe area and, in 1890, obtained a lease for an additional million hectares to form the Sociedad Explotadora de Tierra del Fuego. These lands lay around Bahía Inútil.

In 1899, Chilean President Federico Errázuriz and his Argentine colleague Julio A Roca met in Punta Arenas, in what was to be called the «Strait Embrace». Roca urged Menéndez and other estancieros to set up operations in the Argentine portion of Patagonia, until then uninhabited. The following year, the Menéndez group established the estancias Argentina 1 and Argentina 2, covering the entire steppe area of Argentine Tierra del Fuego. The cores of these estancias became in time the town of Río Grande. The Bridges brothers, sons of the Anglican pastor who founded Ushuaia, settled farther south, at Viamonte. They were the first settlers born in Tierra del Fuego.

The settling, farming and mining of Tierra del Fuego prompted the demise of the Ona indians, who found it much easier to hunt sheep than the hard-to-catch guanacos. The Onas were cruelly hunted down by organized parties put together by gold mining entrepreneurs and by professional gunmen; these were paid in head of sheep. José

Fagnano, a Salesian missionary who arrived at Punta Arenas in 1886, obtained a concession for Dawson island, where he set up a reserve which received about 1,000 Onas sent by estancia owners. In 1893, he set up a further reserve in the vicinity of Río Grande, Argentina, harboring a number of natives. For a nomadic people, though, freedom of movement is an absolute necessity. Many Onas died of disease or by sheer inability to adapt to the new circumstances. The mission at Isla Dawson was shut down in 1912. The renowned anthropologist M. Gusinde tallied only 276 surviving Onas in 1920, most under the protection of the Bridges brothers in their estancia Viamonte. A beautiful tombstone dedicated to the Unknown Ona stands as a memorial to these remarkable Indians in the Punta Arenas cemetery.

When the leasing contracts expired in 1938, the state progressively subdivided the large estancias until 1965, when agrarian reform legislation terminated all leasing arrangements and put an end to the vast sheep farming companies.

Nowadays, there are many medium and small-sized estancias in Tierra del Fuego, some operating as cooperatives. The cascos (administrative and living compounds) of the old estancias have evolved into villages or towns, such as Onaisin (formerly Josefina) and Cameron. The main products are wool and frozen meat, mostly for export.

In the 1940's, prospectors struck oil in the northern reaches of the island; the first well in operation was Manantiales, which started pumping in 1945. The oil industry brought incessant change: new roads and refineries, and oil and gas pipelines. Oil derricks and residential compounds sprouted along the coast, along with storage tanks and processing plants. Offshore platforms started drilling and pumping by the mid-1970's in the Strait itself (see Land & History.)

1 **FERRY FROM PUNTA ARENAS TO PORVENIR-**
★★★ *2.5-hour passage, for passengers and cars. The ferry leaves from Tres Puentes, Punta Arenas (See schedules and reservations in Shipping services of Services section). This schedule makes it possible to visit Porvenir and return on the same day. Reservations at Punta Arenas, phone 227020.*

Arrive at Tres Puentes well before boarding time when travelling by car. Buses and colectivo taxi services to and from the ferry. Obviously, a clear day will give you better views of the city and the Strait's coastline.

The unrelenting wind will provide a taste of the difficulties encountered by the sailors plying these waters in sailing vessels. The ferry docks at **Chilote bay**. Four km to the south (bus service) is

PORVENIR (pop 6,386. a municipality and provincial capital, Porvenir evolved from a police outpost set up in 1883 during the gold rush. It was granted city status in 1894 as a supply and service center for the new sheep ranches.

What to See there is a Museo Provincial (Mon-Fri, 08:30-12:45 h & 14:30-18:00 h) established in 1980. It contains a valuable collection of archaeological artifacts and natural history exhibits, charts and photographs providing an insight into the gold rush and the large-scale sheep farming industries operating until 1910. In addition, there are exhibits of the pioneers of cinematography in Chile, Radonic Scarpa and José Bohr, who filmed Porvenir before 1910.

The Costanera is frequented by flamingoes and black-necked swans. Some old houses recall the glory of the old days. Following the Costanera to the south, right through town and up the hill, is a **look-out** point

Accommodation and Food there are good hotels, residenciales and pensiones. At the old Club

Estancia Ovejera

Yugoslavo you can dine overlooking the harbor.

TOURS FROM PORVENIR

2 **A VISIT TO THE BAQUEDANO RANGE** ★★★

for one day; 115-km round trip climbing the range and returning through Bahía Inútil. The road along Bahía Inútil is passable only from Dec. through March. The «short version», retracing the road to return to Porvenir, is an 82-km round trip, passable year-round. **The best panoramic views of the Strait and Tierra del Fuego, visiting former gold mines.**

Leave Porvenir (km 0) following the route marked «4» in the town map. The road climbs the

		ACCOMMODATIONS	RESTAURANTS
☎ Telephone Center	✠ Hospital	1 Hs Los Flamencos	1 Hs Los Flamencos
★ Touristic Information	A Local Government	2 H Rosas	2 H Rosas
◉ Café, Meeting Point	B Town Hall	3 Bh Colón	10 Club Yugoslavo
▲ Tickets for Punta Arenas Ferry	C Parish Church	4 H Central	11 Casino Bombero
Ⓖ Gasoline Station	D Post Office	5 Posada Los Cisnes	12 Rest Pto Montt
⋙ Lookout Point	E Regional Museum	6 H Tierra del Fuego	
	F Dock		

Estancia Vicuña; Tierra del Fuego

Baquedano range, reaching the highest point at km 20; there is a good **panoramic view**. It then runs across a softly rolling plateau crisscrossed by rivers and streams where independent miners (pirquineros) still pan for gold. Stone terraces and dams have been built to separate gold from gravel, as the soil crumbles into the water from the small cliffs lining the stream. Note the odd rain shelters made from grass tufts.

At km 40, a bridge spans the **Río del Oro**. Two-hundred meters ahead, walk left through a field to see a **gold dredge** operating until the turn of the century.

During the rainy season, return to Porvenir retracing the same road. Otherwise, continue along this road, descending to the lowlands to reach Bahía Inútil at km 57. Turn right at the junction. The road runs along the coast and reaches Porvenir at km 115.

3 **A VISIT TO CAMERON AND LAGO BLANCO** ★★★
265 km to Lago Blanco (8 hours). Take gasoline, food and camping gear.
A tour to the remotest areas of Tierra del Fuego, with fine scenery along the way. It is worth the effort.

Leave Porvenir (km 0) at the crack of dawn following the road running along enormous **Bahía Inútil**. The coastal lands are flat, with scattered hamlets and fishing coves, making it a rather uneventful 100 km, until reaching the first major intersection. (The route straight ahead from the intersection, leading to Río Grande and Ushuaia, is described under Section C). Take the road to the right, leading in 3 km to

Onaisin a village that grew up around the casco of the old estancia Caleta Josefina, the first sheep ranch established in 1893 by the Soc. Explotadora Tierra del Fuego, on a vast expanse of leased lands stretching from the 33rd to the 34th parallel. Some of the original buildings still stand. A short way ahead is the **British Cemetery**, with the graves of foreign personnel –mostly Scottish livestock farmers– who used to run the estancias for the large sheep farming companies.

At km 117, at the southern end of Bahía Inútil, the **Marazzi** river empties into the ocean. Archaeological remains dating from 7,600 BC have been found here. The road then runs along the southern shore of the bay. After km 125 the land becomes uneven for a while, to continue, after a short stretch, as flat as before, but now peppered with isolated stones left by retreating glaciers.

At km 140, so-called **sea pens** can be seen, stone-enclosed spaces, a few meters offshore, which get flooded when the tide is high, trapping fishes when the tide recedes. At km 150 is

Cameron another village established around the casco of a former estancia founded in 1904 by Soc. Explotadora de Tierra del Fuego; given the name of the company's well-known manager. Original buildings still remain, showing the classical lines of the architectural style introduced by the English managers. The houses were lined on the outside with metal plates stamped with intricate moldings. The village is set at the bottom of a shallow canyon, sheltering it from the wind.

The original estancias used to stretch over 300,000 hectares and more. The head manager lived at the casco, which had central administration offices, maintenance and repair shops, shearing sheds, and a number of selected rams for breeding. The estancia was subdivided into sections, each run by a manager and equipped with smaller-scale infrastructure. The sections, in turn, were divided into posts, where a solitary shepherd lived with his horses and trained dogs, in charge of a sizable flock of sheep.

A road that starts at Cameron runs along the coast for 80 km to sawmills at **Puerto Yartou**, established in 1930, and to the **Condor** river, (a short distance further), a famous fishing spot. There are plenty of spots for camping.

From Cameron (km 0), take the road leading to Lago Blanco, which heads inland and runs through several **posts** of the former estancia.

At km 37 take a 200-m-long detour to the left to see a **gold dredge** granted National Monument status. It is the best preserved of its sort. Brought from England in 1904, it operated until around 1910. A short way ahead are the installations of **the Ruffin Section**, part of the former estancia.

A Town Hall	**C** School	**E** Guest House
B Police Station	**D** Library	**G** Shearing Shed

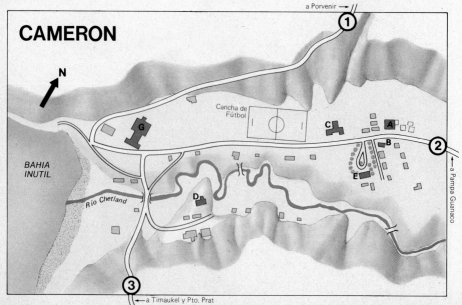

CAMERON

N

a Porvenir → ①

Cancha de Fútbol

G

C

A

B

②

→ a Pampa Guanaco

BAHIA INUTIL

E

Río Chetland

D

③

← a Timaukel y Pto. Prat

14

Beyond Ruffin, the pampean landscape is interspersed with the first patches of Magellanic forests. At km 68 is **Sección Río Grande**, with some facilities of the former estancia and a large metal bridge built to bring cattle to the other side.

At km 69 is a detour to the right leading to estancia Onamonte. Here you can ask for permission to walk to the lovely **lake Chico**, which has excellent fishing.

At km 90 is the **Pampa Guanacos** police outpost and a fork in the road. The left branch cuts through a forest and in 10 km reaches the **estancia Vicuña** (est 1915), with a magnificent administration building. The right branch runs through Magellanic forests along the foot of the Fueguina range. At km 16 of this road is a **sawmill**, and also a road branching off for the lake. Ten km ahead is stunning

Beaver Valley (Valle de los Castores) with fascinating forests and wildlife, including guanacos, birds and, of course, **beavers** and their dams. Beavers were introduced from Canada, propagating from Ushuaia throughout the island.

Back at the sawmill, the road branching off to the right, a narrow track suitable only for 4,wheel,drive, high-clearance vehicles– runs through forests to the rim of

LAKE BLANCO surroundedby trees, and having the snow-capped Cordillera Fueguina for a backdrop. This is by far Magallanes` most beautiful lake, teeming with waterfowl and offering excellent camping sites on the beaches; abundant firewood near al hand. Lago Blanco is one of Tierra del Fuego`s best lakes for fishing.

4 FROM LAGO BLANCO TO CERRO SOMBRERO

★★★ *234 km from the Pampa Guanaco police station; 257 km from the lake. Gasoline at Cullen and Cerro Sombrero.*
A circuit running for over 150 km alongside the border with Argentina, pasing by numerous picturesque estancias.

From Retén Pampa Guanaco (Pampa Guanaco

police station) (km 0), retrace the road followed to get here. At km 21 from Pampa Guanaco is the Río Grande Section. At the intersection (km 30), take unsigned road to the right. At km 38, the road passes near **Cerro Ona (Ona Hill)**, a ancient place where Onas used to stop and where archaeological remains dating back 10 thousand years have been found.

At km 41 the road bends north to run parallel with the border and crosses many streams and brooks flowing toward the Atlantic. Soon it starts to traverse the **Carmen Silva sierra**, with a string of estancias, each boasting different architecture and settings. The road climbs up to high points in the sierra, offering fine **views** of the Atlantic coast, and at km 119, it meets the road from Porvenir to San Sebastián, w hich runs across the plain connecting the Inútil and San Sebastián bays. Turn right. At km 129 is the **San Sebastián** border control outpost. The road straight ahead leads to the border, and to Río Grande and Ushuaia, Argentina (described under Section C).

Take the road heading north, to Cullen, running through soft rolling pampas speckled with small lakes swarming with bird fauna. This is also oil country. Pipelines run alongside the road. Oil heating units, derricks, headwell valves and other associated paraphernalia can be seen (see Land & History). At km 182, the road reaches

Cullen an oil processing complex established in 1962. Its main function is to recover propane, butane and gasoline contained in natural gas, and to inject the residual gas back into the oil wells. There are large storage tanks and multiple pipelines bringing the resulting products to the shipping ports of Percy and Clarencia. Gasoline and basic supplies are available.
The road turns west to reach, at km 234,

CERRO SOMBRERO (pop 687). Nestled atop an isolated hillock to which it owes its name, the village was established in 1958 as a residential and servzices complex to support Enap's operations in Tierra del Fuego. It includes over 150

a Punta Espora y Bahía Azul

① ③ ②

CERRO SOMBRERO

N

a Porvenir

a Cullén y San Sebastián

Ⓖ Gasoline Station
1 Boarding House
2 Car Mechanic
3 Police Station
A Parish Church
B Gymnasium
C Indoor Botanical Garden
D Indoor Swimming Pool

E Cinema
F School
G Hospital
H Supermarket
J Restaurants
K ENAP Office
M Warehouse, Maintenance Shop

houses, and community facilities, such as a gymnasium, a heated indoor swimming pool, an indoor botanical garden, cinema, church, hospital and airport, as well as maintenance shops and warehouses.

It is now a municipality and administrative town for the northern portion of the island. Gasoline is available, and there is a well-stocked supermarket and a restaurant. The only accommodation is an unpretentious, but friendly, residential used by truck drivers transporting cargo to and from the Argentine mainland. To stay at Enap's guest house, permission must be obtained beforehand at Enap's central offices in Punta Arenas. Another option is to drive on to Punta Espora, board the ferry before 22:30h, and stay at the Hostería Tehuelches in Punta Delgada.

An excursion from Cerro Sombrero to **Punta Catalina** (152 km round trip) will allow you to see the offshore drilling and extraction platforms in the Strait of Magellan.

An alternative route to return to Porvenir (125 km) is the road running along the Strait and skirting the San Felipe and Gente Grande bays, passing near the oil terminals and three lakes right before Porvenir.

5 RETURN THROUGH PUNTA DELGADA ★★★
forty-three km from Cerro Sombrero to Bahía Azul. There is no need for reservations for the ferry; see schedule in Shipping services in Services section. Of the 223 km from Cerro Sombrero to Punta Arenas, 50 km are paved. If a visit to Posesión is included, the total distance is 370 km. Gasoline at San Gregorio.

Leave Cerro Sombrero (km 0) following the road numbered 1 in the Cerro Sombrero map. It is chilean Tierra del Fuego's busiest road, as it is the main access to the island and the obligatory route to the Argentine side. A short distance outside Cerro Moreno is the airfield, with regular Enap air traffic to Punta Arenas. In the vicinity is the **Manantiales 1** monument, Tierra del Fuego's first sucessful oil well. It is now dry.

The road runs across a plain, reaching **Bahía Azul** at km 43, at the **Strait's First Narrows** (Primera Angostura). The Strait here is a scant 5 km across, the coast low and sandy. Straight ahead is Punta

Delgada. At both points, the ferry docks at a simple concrete ramp. This is the speediest way across the Strait, albeit dependent on the prevailing conditions: here, there is a difference of up to eleven meters high and low tides 11 m, producing strong currents. In addition, the fierce winds blowing from the pampas pose a further difficulty. Small wonder that neither Hernando de Magallanes nor Sarmiento de Gamboa succeeded in sailing back into the Strait after a sudden gale had blown them into the open sea.

The passage takes about 30 minutes. From **Punta Delgada** a road climbs 16 km to meet the highway to Punta Arenas (km 59). A detour to the right is recommended for visiting Enap's off-shore project.

Drive north from the road junction (km 0) and, at km 29, take the road branching off to the right; it runs the length of the very narrow strip of land lying sandwiched between the Argentine border and the Strait's shore, ending up at Cape Dungenes, at the Strait's mouth on the Atlantic. At km 76 is

Posesión an oil and gas processing facility and personnel compound established by Enap in 1971. There are 52 houses for permanent residents, and accommodations for receiving more than three hundred oil operation workers between their platform and other shifts, in addition to basic services and an airfield. The plant scrubs natural gas, extracting propane, butane and gasoline, and injects the residual gas into the oil wells. An 8-inch pipeline brings part of the output to the Cabo Negro plant; and a 1.5-m gas pipeline feeds the methanol plant, also located at Cabo Negro.

A busy heliport serves rotary-wing aircraft ferrying supplies and personnel to the numerous offshore drilling and extraction platforms peppering the Strait's waters (see description in Land & History). The platforms are joined by an underwater pipeline, which brings their output to Posesión and Punta Catalina. The various oil fields have been given peculiar names such as Spiteful, Ostión, Pejerrey, etc.

To return to Punta Arenas (235 km), retrace the road up to the junction with the Punta Arenas-Monte Aymond highway. Follow this road to Punta Arenas (segment described under Section A, Tour 1).

SECTION C   PUERTO WILLIAMS

This is the remotest part of the extensive Magallanes territory. Being an island, access is expensive, but not difficult. It comprises the southernmost bits of South America, made up of islands and channels, the Cape Horn group and the Diego Ramírez islands.

This section stretches south of the Andes mountains, known here as **Cordillera de Darwin,** which runs from west to east. The administrative center of this area is **Puerto Williams**, the world's southernmost town with a permanent population, located on Isla Navarino next to the **Beagle channel**.

This used to be the name of the Yahgan's (Yagáns) country. The Yahgans were a nomadic people living off the sea, sailing among the Beagle channel islands. During the winter period, they gathered in the area of Murray channel (between Hoste and Navarino islands). They were discovered in 1830 by capt. Robert Fitzroy and his crew, aboard the English ship Beagle. (Many of the names of geographical or topographical features stemmed from his expeditions.) Cape Horn had been discovered in 1616, but no one had ventured into these intricate waterways.

Fitzroy took four young Yahgans to England to educate them there for two years. In London, they were brought before King William IV. Two years later, in 1832, they were brought back to their ancestral lands by the Beagle and put ashore at Wulaia cove. They soon reverted to their original ways and 22 years later, in 1851, Jimmy Button – as Beagle crew members had christened one of the young Indians taken to England– led a group of natives which beleaguered and finally killed

seven Anglican missionaries, headed by Allen Gardiner, who had settled down at Banner cove, Picton island. That was the tragic end of the first attempt at colonization of the area. Again, in 1859, Jimmy Button was the instigator of the murder of four Anglican missionaries who had settled at Wulaia cove, Navarino island.

The Anglican mission center was located on the Falkland (Malvinas) islands. After 18 years of heroic efforts and sacrifice, the missionaries succeeded in setting up a mission in Ushuaia in 1869. It was soon encircled by the huts of Yahgan families who were taught the art of cultivating the soil.

In 1871, at the age of 28, Anglican pastor Thomas Bridges arrived in Ushuaia, accompanied by his wife, a small daughter and three other missionaries. They gave a new boost to the settlement. Bridges had travelled from England to the Falkland (Malvinas) mission when he was nine years old, where he acquired his religious formation. He also learned the Yahgan language from Indians brought to the mission to receive an education. He spent the rest of his life on the Beagle channel coast, where his other five children were born (the first Tierra del Fuego natives of European stock) and where he wrote the world's only Yahgan dictionary. He struggled unceasingly for a better standard of living for the Yahgan natives, until his death in 1898.

His son Lucas Bridges, born in Ushuaia in 1875, lived among Yahgans and Onas, was fluent in their languages and publicly defended the natives, even against the interests of the powerful English estancieros of Tierra del Fuego. He wrote **El Ultimo Confín de la Tierra (The World's Last Corner),** a touching, endearing account of the tragic clash between cultures. In 1918 he took charge of managing an estancia by the Baker river, in the Aysén region, for a Magallanes livestock farming company. He built a small road alongside the river, and a small ship to bring out his products by way of the river and lake General Carrera. Later he acquired the estancia, the largest in Aisén. (The Carretera Austral –see Zone 13– is now trying to reach this area.) He was what you could rightly call a full-blooded pioneer.

From 1882 to 1883, the French Navy ship Romanche stayed at the southern bay of Hoste island's Hardy peninsula, with the Mission Scientifique du Cap Horn. It included astronomers, naturalists and students who had come to watch the passage of Venus across the face of the Sun. A short time earlier (1881), the boundary between Chile and Argentina on Tierra del Fuego had been agreed upon. In 1884 an Argentinian ship called at Ushuaia, the Argentine flag being then raised for the first time at the mission. All this territory depended on Punta Arenas for its supplies and communications until well into the present century. Ushuaia became the administrative center for the Argentine portion of Tierra del Fuego. It was, also, a penal colony for repeat criminals.

The gold rush struck in 1890-91. Over 800 gold miners streamed in from the Americas and Europe to Nueva, Lennox and Picton islands, and to Puerto Toro on Navarino; many of them were Dalmatians (now called Yugoslavs). They seaeched for and mined gold for several years. By the turn of the century, when the government started to offer state lands for sale or lease, the sheep ramching rush took off, luring over a hundred settlers. These two immigration waves created the population base which brougth into existence the settlement of

PUERTO WILLIAMS (pop 1,050). Named after Juan Williams, The founder of Fuerte Bulnes, the town has naval base and is the area's main urban center. There is an excellent hotel, a telephone office, post office and airport. The Museo Martín Gusinde is excellent (Tue-Fri 10:00-13:00 h and 15:00-18:00 h: Sat & Sun 15:00-18:00 h), providing an insight into the history of the Yagan people, and presenting exhibits on the local resources, the most noteworthy voyages, such as those of the Beagle (Darwin and Fitzroy), and the local wil dife. Gusin was a world-renowned anthropologist and priest of the Verbo Divino order, who worked with the Yahgans and Onas from 1918 to 1923.

How and When to Get There accesible by air, land and sea, each means of travelling having its own rewards. The best time is way is overland in

The steamer Terra Australis in the Beagle channel

summer. From Sept on, by air or sea, observing the snowy peaks in the chain flanking the Beagle channel: an unforgettable view.

By Air a 75-min flight from Punta Arenas, weather permitting. Superb views of the Strait of Magellan, Almirantazgo sound and the snow-covered Cordillera Darwin, featuring tide water glaciers. Aerovías DAP operates twin-engine aircraft seating 16 (Tue & Sat, return the same day). There is also a Chilean Navy airplane (one or two flights weekly) which takes passengers, if space is available. Check in person with the Comandancia en Jefe de la Armada in Punta Arenas.

By Sea the most spectacular option There are no scheduled trips to Puerto Williams. However, Empremar and Chilean Navy vessels sail frequently to the naval base there, and they take passengers if space is available. Check with Empremar in Punta Arenas and with the Comandancia en Jefe de la Armada. 7 - day round-trip aboard the Terra Australis, a luxury cruise ship. Route and description of the vessel in the Services section, at the end of this publication.

The Terra Australis leaves from Punta Arenas sailing along the Strait of Magellan, Past Dawson island, and later through Magdalena Channel, flanked by snow-crowned Mount Sarmiento to visit Agostini glacier. The voyage continues through glacier-lined the Beagle Channel to Puerto Williams and afterward to Ushuaia, Argentina. On the return leg, the ship enters Garibaldi sound to visit a gigantic tide water glacier.

By Land it is 475 km from Porvenir to Ushuaia, with gasoline and accommodation available on the way. The stretch from Porvenir to the border is described under Section B. On the Argentinian side, the road runs close to the coast, through **Río Grande** at km 239, a small town with hotels, restaurants and gasoline stations, and again along the coast for a while. It then turns inland, where there is more vegetation, past beautiful **lake Fagnano** and a village with good accommodations and a gasoline station. It is advisable to stay here overnight. The next leg, 101 km long, crosses the densely wooded Cordillera Darwin, with spectacular views of the Beagle channel and the islands stretching south to Cape Horn. At km 475 is

USHUAIA a small city with good infrastructure and much tourist traffic in summer. The passage to Puerto Williams is filled with scenic wonders and takes about three hours. Immigration formalities dealt with on board. Contact by phone the Capitanía de Puerto of Puerto Williams.

TOURS FROM PUERTO WILLIAMS

Visit to Ushuaia in high season an Argentinian ship makes the cruise daily. It is an interesting touristic city.

Flight to Cape Horn only in charter flights by Dap

14

SECTION D   PUERTO NATALES

This section covers the northern portion of the Magallanes Region, with the large inland sea of Almirante Montt gulf, the Ultima Esperanza sound and the Obstrucción fjord. It is bound on the north by the Cordillera de Paine and the Baguales range; on the east, by the Argentine border; on the west, by the Andes Mountains, with the Sarmiento and Riesco mountain chains. The Almirante Montt gulf is linked to the ocean by the narrow Kirke passage.

This section has been left for last since it includes a convenient jumping-off point for a return journey month following a different route from the one used to reach Punta Arenas.

The Almirante Montt gulf was discovered in 1557 by mariner Juan Ladrilleros and rediscovered in 1579 by Sarmiento de Gamboa, while looking for the Strait of Magellan's eastern mouth. The area, however, remained uncharted until 1830, when the Adelaide, an English schooner under the command of officers Skyring and Kirke, carried out the first thorough reconnaissance of the gulf.

Despite its close proximity to Punta Arenas, this area was the last to be settled. In 1879, when the first sheep ranches were being established around Punta Arenas, the 50-km trip to the Cabeza de Mar lagoons was considered perilous due to the frequent raids staged by the nomadic Tehuelche tribes. In 1881, when the borderline between Chile and Argentina was finally agreed upon. The boundary in this area was drawn initially along the high Andean peaks. However, two expeditions organized by the Chilean Navy (in 1879 under the leadership of Lt Juan Tomás Rogers, and in 1889 led Capt Ramón Serrano) discovered that the streams here flow westwards to the Pacific Ocean. (The Chile-Argentina border was to lie along the water divide, ie, the territories where streams flow westward were to be Chilean, the ones where streams flow eastwards, Argentinian). Consequently, the border was redrawn along its present course in 1902.

In 1892 and 1897, two geographic surveys mapped the area and ascertained its potential for livestock farming. The first expedition was led by Capt. Eberhard, while the second, a Swedish one, was led by Otto Nordenskjöld. Eberhard discovered the Milodón Cave and was one of the first settlers in the area. A German-born emigré in transit along the Strait of Magellan, he disembarked in Punta Arenas and decided to stay there. His brother continued to California, their original destination, where he later founded the renowned Eberhard Faber pencil making company.

The area was open to settlement in 1893, and the lands lying along the coast were promptly occupied by European settlers (mostly from Germany and England) who had previously come to Punta Arenas. Access was by sea, the main port being Puerto Prat.

In 1905 the Chilean government offered leases to the huge plains lying along the border. Soon, four large estancias were established in the area: Tranquilo, in the Diana plains; Cerro Castillo; Cerro Guido; and Torres del Paine. The first three belonged to the Soc. Explotadora de Tierra del Fuego, which proceeded to set up a large slaughterhouse, cold-storage facilities, tanneries and wool-washing installations at Puerto Bories. The area is now linked to Punta Arenas by a paved highway.

PUERTO NATALES (pop 14,250). The capital of the Ultima Esperanza province, Puerto Natales was founded in 1911 and soon overtook Puerto Prat as the residential center and shipping port for the area's products.

Lying on a gently-sloping point facing the **Kirke**

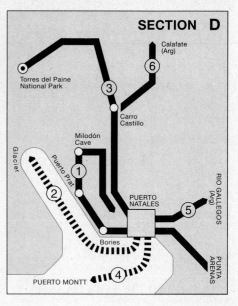

passage, the town has a nice view of the **Riesco range** to the west. It provides services for the area's intense livestock activity. Many of its inhabitants work at the coal mines in Río Turbio, Argentina, and come to town over the weekend. It has good infrastructure for accommodating the growing number of tourists using the town as a jumping-off point for visiting the spectacular Torres del Paine and Balmaceda national parks, and the nearby fjords.

What To See the municipal administration is located in a building dating from the estancia heydays. A walk up **Av Mejicana** offers the best **panoramic view** of the town, the gulf and the surrounding mountain ranges. Follow the Costanera 4 km to

Bories (also Puerto Bories), a large industrial complex established in 1913 by the Soc. Explotadora Tierra del Fuego to process the output of its three estancias in the area, and of the other *estancias* it operated on the Argentinian side of the border. Now only the cold storage facility and the slaughterhouse are in operation. The former installations included deep-freeze plants, tanneries, meat preservation facilities, and wool-washing plants. Two fires destroyed a large part of the original installations. The administration building and the houses for high-ranking employees bear an unmistakably English architectural touch.

Accommodation and Food hostería Cisne de Cuello Negro, right next to Bories. In Puerto Natales proper, Hotel Capitán Eberhard is best. Quick meals at Midas and at Don Alvarito à la carte.

TOURS FROM PUERTO NATALES

1 **A VISIT TO PUERTO PRAT AND THE MILODON CAVE** ★★★ *for half-day, 48-km round trip, gravel road.*

A visit to the first settlement in the area, on the Ultima Esperanza sound, and to a cave where the remains of a prehistoric animal were found.

Take the Costanera north out of Puerto Natales (km 0). At km 6 is the intersection with the highway from Punta Arenas. At km 8 is another intersection; to the right is the airport. Take the road to the left, leading in 20 km to

☎	Telephone Center	**D** Post Office	**7** Bh Temuco		
◉	Café, Meeting Point	**E** Telex	**8** Bh Dickson		
★	Touristic Information	**F** Vegetable Market	**9** Bh Grey		
Ⓖ	Gasoline Station	**ACCOMMODATIONS**			

TOURIST SERVICE

Ⓧ Police Station	**1** H Juan Ladrilleros
✚ Hospital	**2** H Capitán Eberhard
A Municipal & Provincial Government	**3** H Palace
	4 H Natalino
B Sea Traffic Authority	**5** Bh Bulnes
C Parish Church	**6** H Austral

RESTAURANTS

- **1** Juan Ladrilleros
- **20** Midas
- **21** Costanera
- **22** La Bahía
- **23** Ultima Esperanza
- **24** Don Alvarito

- **10** Lan Chile
- **11** Ladeco
- **12** Buses Sur
- **13** Buses Fernández
- **14** Buses to Río Turbio (Arg)
- **15** Ferry to Pto Montt
- **16** Buses Victoria Sur
- **17** Buses Coopra
- **18** Cutter Tour to Glaciers

a Bories y Torres del Paine →

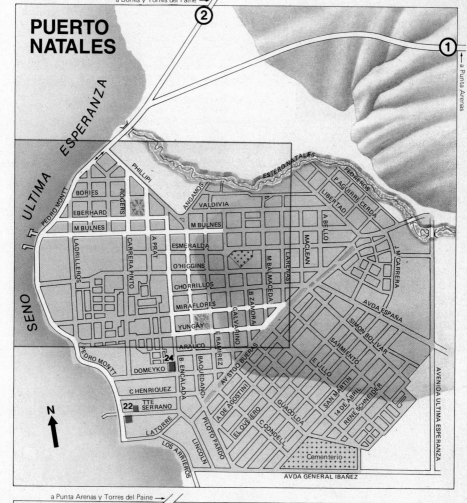

PUERTO NATALES

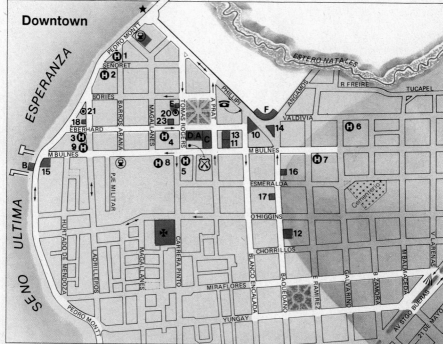

Downtown

14

Torres del Paine

station provides information on this monument. There is a strange rock formation known as the **Silla del Diablo** (Devil's Seat). The road ends at a look-out point with superb **views** over the Eberhard fjord and the Ultima Esperanza sound. A short path leads to a **cave,** 30-m high and 200-m long, where in 1895 Capt Eberhard found the nearly intact remains (skin included) of a prehistoric animal called a milodón (mylodont), a type of ground sloth. The finding caused such a stir, that Wellington Furlog, a scientist at Cornell University in the United States, set out in 1907 to comb Patagonia in search of living specimens of this species.

Near this cave are several smaller ones, where remains of human settlements dating back 5,000 years have been found.

To return, drive back to the junction and take the branch to the left. It leads in 5 km to the road linking Torres del Paine and Puerto Natales. The latter is 21 km to the right.

Puerto Prat lying on the Eberhard fjord off the Ultima Esperanza sound. The settlement was established in 1897 and granted seaport status the following year. In 1904 it was connected by telegraph to Punta Arenas and became the main port and settlement in the area. The establishment of Puerto Natales and the port and industrial complex at Bories undermined its role, leading to its eventual demise as a maritime shipping point to. Only a few houses and a cemetery on a small island remain.

A road runs from here along the coast to **Estancia Consuelo,** the first one established in Ultima Esperanza and still owned by the Eberhard family.

Right beyond Puerto Prat is a road junction. Take the branch to the right and, 4 km later, the road branching to the left. It leads in 2 km to the Conaf warden station for the

Milodón Cave National Monument the warden

2 SAILING TO THE GLACIERS ★★★

a 6-hour trip by motor boat or a whole day by cutter with regular departures from Puerto Natales in season. Take clothing affording protection against the wind and food in some cases. The motor boat "21 de Mayo" and the cutter "compass Rose" sail to Ultima Esperanza Sound. The cutter "Trinidad" sails to Kirke Pass and Las Montañas Channel. See Services Section for complete information.

An interesting trip through the Ultima Esperanza sound to the large Balmaceda and Serrano glaciers branching off from the Patagonian icecap, at Balmaceda National Park.

Departure at 08:30 h in summer. The boat hugs the forested coast, flanked by rugged mountains. Sea lions and cormorants can be seen on the rocks. After some 4 hours, the boat reaches the foot of Balmaceda mountain (2,035 m), draped with glaciers branching off the huge Patagonian icecap to the sea. The boat skirts the **Balmaceda glacier** and then stops at the **Serrano glacier** where

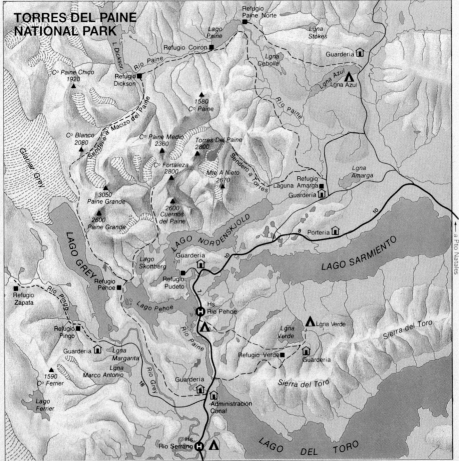

TORRES DEL PAINE NATIONAL PARK

14

passengers can go ashore and walk through the forest to the glacier's edge. Ice floes drift nearby. Truley impressive. The rugged scenery around Ultima Esperanza sound forms a superb backdrop. The return trip hugs the opposite coast of the sound.

3 TO TORRES DEL PAINE NATIONAL PARK

★★★ *two-day stay constitutes a bare minimum; ten days adequateto see the park properly. The park's entrance is 118 km from Puerto Natales. Gasoline and other supplies, accommodations and camping at Cerro Castillo and in the park.*
A visit to Chile's most captivating national park.

Leave Puerto Natales (km 0) following the Costanera to the north. At km 8 is the turn-off for Puerto Prat; at km 16, the road to the Milodón Cave branches off to the left. At km 22, another road branches west to Estancia Milodón (6 km beyond the farm is **lake Sofía,** with nice beaches suitable for camping).

The road approaches the **Señoret range;** at km 43 is **Hotel Tres Pasos,** an old building with a bust of Gabriela Mistral, Chile's Nobel-prize winning poetess. She used to spend the summers here when she was the director of the Punta Arenas girls' school. The road winds along the foot of the peaks of Montt sierra and then runs across a vast rolling pampa. At km 62 is

<u>Cerro Castillo</u>   a village evolved from the casco of the large namesake estancia established by Soc. Explotadora de Tierra del Fuego in 1906. It is arranged according to the classical layout of these sheep ranches: a large shearing shed, pens and wool-cleaning shed, all located downwind from the personnel compound, administrative offices and warehouses. Some distance away, the orderly-arranged houses for foremen and higher-ranking employees. Lastly, the head manager's house, with a garden and an orchard enclosed by windbreaks. The estancia complex grew to be a village, with the addition of new buildings. The former administrator's residence now houses a good hostería.

A few meters beyond runs the Argentine, border with the Cancha de Carrera customs station, open from December through March. The road leads to Calafate, Argentina (described under Tour 6 below).

Across the border, the Soc Explotadora de Tierra del Fuego had huge estancias forming a single unit with those on the Chilean side. Their products were shipped out at Bories. The estancias had to be sold in the 1950's, as the Argentine authorities forbade foreigners to own land along the border.

Continuing from Cerro Castillo, at km 73 a road branches off to the right leading to **lake Porteño** (33 km), a good spot for camping.

At km 76 a bridge spans Las Chinas the river. The road climbs for a while, reaching an intersection at km 97. To the right is the Cerro Guido section; to the left, the national park.

From the intersection there is a good panoramic view of the complex assortment of lakes draining into the Ultima Esperanza sound. To the north, the sharp, black peaks of **sierra Baguales** soar above the flat plain. To the west, the awesome Paine massif. The road to the left skirts **lake Sarmiento** and reaches, at km 118, the

TORRES DEL PAINE NATIONAL PARK   established in 1959 and granted the status of Biosphere Reserve by UNESCO in 1978. Under the administration of Conaf, it has 3 entrances: Porterio Sarmiento, Laguna Amarga y Laguna Azul.

There are two hotels: Hostería Pehoé, by the lake; and Posada Río Serrano. There are also three compsites equipped with fire places, tables and benches, and latrines in Río serrano, Pehoé and Laguna Azul. There are shelters along the hiking trails.

The administrative and information center has displays, maps and photographic material on the different hikes, as well as the Park's characteristics. Next to this center you can rent horses for the day. There are also 50 km of vehicle roads within the park, leading to the various lakes, ponds, rivers

Lake Pehoe; Cuernos del Paine and hostel

and waterfalls. The trails are suitable for hikes lasting from one day to the 10 day Granddaddy hike, past spectacular Grey glacier and ground the back of the **Paine massif,** which includes the majestic **Cuernos** as well as the **Torres del Paine** peaks.

It is highly advisable to register with the park rangers (guardaparques) before setting out on any hike. Registration is reguired for all major hikes

HIKING THROUGH THE TORRES DEL PAINE NATIONAL PARK   there are some 250 km of well-marked trails throughout the park, leading to iceberg-strewn lakes, glaciers, thick Magellanic forests, the foot of the mighty massif and waterfalls. All areas have rich and varied wildlife.

Torres del Paine attracts Each year, a significant number of local and foreign **trekking** aficionados, (South Africas increasingly popular word for hiking), who consider this area sine qua non for any full-blooded trekker. Guides and gear can be hired from the organizations listed in the Services and Prices section. Arrange for a hiking package wich can include tents, backpacks, sleeping bags, horses, food and, of course, a guide. No previous trekking experience is reguined.

Recommended Gear   strong footwear, neither too hard nor too soft, sunglasses, rain- and windproof clothing, a hat, thick socks and a woollen sweater. If trekking on your own, bring a tent, a cooking stove and cooking gear, sleeping bag, canteen, a good backpack, a first-aid kit, plenty of food and a good map, and be sure to get some hiking advice from the Conaf wardens.
The most popular hikes are:

To Torres del Paine   leading to a small lake at the foot of the Torres del Paine peaks; it can be made in one day, but it is more sensible to shoulder camping gear and spend the night. From the Laguna Amarga guardhouse and campsite (and shelter), it is 1 1/2 hours to an estancia (camping also possible here). Cross the Asencio river , either by the footbridge or via a ford 100 m downstream. From here, it is about 4 hours to the lake at the foot of the Torres. If night should smeak up on you, there is a very basic shelter in the forest before the climb up the moraine to the lake.

To Glacier and Valley del Francés   (Note that in Spanish the words ventisquero and glaciar are used interchangeably for glacier) a beautiful valley with a glacier that spawns a river. You need 2 days. Access from the Pehoé guardhouse is no longer possible, as the bridge spanning the Paine river has been washed away. You must start from the Administration Center; the path runs the length of a flat expanse created by the retreat of Grey glacier in times long past, and then runs along the Grey river (the color of the water is due. It is some 3 hours at a brisk pace to the **shelter** (refugio) at the northern end of **lake Pehoé.** It can accommodate some 20 people, but it is perhaps better to pitch a tent. The surrounding area has been stripped clean of firewood: collect some on the way. From the shelter to the Ventisquero Francés it is about

14

three hours. The path continues beyond the river at the tip of the glacier; crossing can be somewhat hazardous.

A Circuit Around the Back of the Paine Massif
this is the longest (and toughest) hike, making a complete circuit around the awesome massif. You need no less than 6 days; and a guide. The path can be difficult to find.

You can start either from the Administration center or from the Laguna Amarga guardhouse, depending on whether you want to make your circuit clockwise or counterclockwise.

From Refugio Laguna Amarga to **lake Paine** it is at least 8 hours, through vast plains skirting the eastern foothills and with the Paine river to the right. At the lake there is a small shelter (Refugio Coirón). From there, it is 3 hours to **lake Dickson**, with another shelter. The path continues alongside the **Los Perros** river, through a beautiful forest, reaching a glacier some 6 km ahead. There are sheltered sites for pitching a tent.

The next leg is to **El Paso**, not advisable to tackle without a guide or after a storm: the path might be covered with snow and you would not be able find it. You need a minimum of 10 hours. Most of the way you go through a dense forest flanked by towering mountains. At the end of the forest is the stunning **Grey Glacier**, hanging over **lake Grey** and shedding large chunks of ice that are pushed by the wind to the other end of the lake. The shelter here was destroyed by a fire. From this point it is about 5 hours to the refugio at **lake Pehoé** and a mother 3-6 hours to the Administration compound.

RETURN TO THE NORTH FROM PUERTO NATALES

4 **TO PUERTO MONTT BY SEA ★★★**

today the only existing boat is the "Coral Gable" which .(links Pto Natales with Pto Montt in 4 days. It carries cars but ...not passengers. However, It is a good chance to send your car, and return by air.

5 **TO RIO GALLEGOS, ARGENTINA ★★★**

it is 302 km to Río Gallegos, gravel road, through the Dorotea pass (Mon.Sun, open round-the-clock; fee paid only outside the normal working hours: 08:00 to 17:20 h). Gasoline and restaurants at El Turbio and Río Gallegos.

The first leg for those returning north through Argentina. Some estancias on the pampa and a coal mine.

Leave puerto Natales (km 0) following the paved highway to Punta Arenas. At km 9 take signposted

road branching off to the left, to Paso Dorotea. Police and customs are at km 20. Beyond the border, the landscape changes from arid pampa to Magellanic forest. Some coal mines can be seen. At km 24, Argentine customs. The road descends and the forest becomes thinner. At km 29 is

Río Turbio   a well-equipped mining town, wearing a black shroud (compliment of the nearby coal mine). The mine's output is shipped by railroad to Río Gallegos, where it is loaded onto ships.
The road continues alongside the rail line and the river Turbio. At km 176, the El Blanco bridge spans the river, which now changes its name to Río Gallegos. Some estancias and a few railway stations break the pampa's monotony. At km 275 is the paved highway running from north to south, the main road in Argentinian Patagonia. Taking this road to the right, at km 302 you reach

RIO GALLEGOS   with excellent hotels and restaurants, this is Argentina's most important city in Patagonia.

6 **TO RETURN JOURNEY TRHOUGH CALAFATE**

★★★   atown on the Argentinian side, 286 km north of Cerro Castillo and 348 km from Puerto Natales. Gasoline and accommodations at Cerro Castillo, Esperanza and Calafate. The best option is to hop over the border at Cerro Castillo when returning from Torres del Paine.
Calafate is an important tourist destination in Argentina, nestled on the shore of its most beautiful lake and offering attractive excursions to the nearby glaciers.

Puerto Natales-Cerro Castillo leg described under Tour 3. Beyond **Cancha de Carrera pass** (km 0) a road runs to Esperanza, through arid pampa and past estancia Tapi Aike, at km 45. **Esperanza** ,a service village on the banks of river Coyle, is at km 120.

Here begins a road heading northeast; at km 187 is Hotel Cerrillos, and at km 236 there is an intersection. Take paved road to the left; at km 286 is

CALAFATE   a village on the edge of lake Argentino, a major tourist center with good hotels, restaurants and a museum. Roads lead to Los Témpanos channel, and there are boat services for exploring the extraordinarily beautiful scenery of **Parque Argentino Los Glaciares.** A road heads east from Calafate to reach, at km 230, the paved road running north along the Atlantic coast, which you can use to get back to Chile.

14

PUBLIC TRANSPORTATION SERVICES

Bus Services. six daily departures between Punta Arenas and Puerto Natales. To Santiago vía Bariloche, 7 departures weekly. To Río Gallegos, daily departures from Pta. Aenas and from Pto. Natales, 2 departures weekly. Also transportation 4 times a week to Río Grande in Tierra del Fuego, 2 from Pta Arenas and 2 from Porvenir.

There are daily departures except on Mon, from Pto Natales to the Torres del Paine National Park (only in high season)

Air Services in Services Section.

Shipping Services ferry to Porvenir, with several departures weekly. To Pto Montt in a multiuse ship with 3 or 4 departures monthly. For schedules and addresses, see shipping services in Services Section, at the end of the guide.

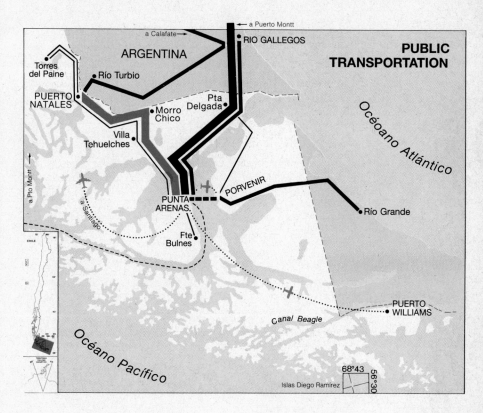

Zone 15
CHILEAN ANTARCTIC
TERRITORY

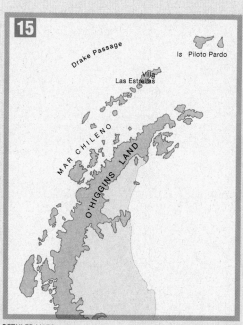

15

Drake Passage

Is Piloto Pardo

Villa
Las Estrellas

MAR CHILENO

O'HIGGINS LAND

DETAILED MAPS

Arica

Iquique

Antofagasta

Easter
Island

Copiapó

La Serena

Valparaíso

SANTIAGO

Is R
Crusoe

Talca

Concepción

Temuco

Valdivia

Osorno

Pto Montt

Castro
Chaitén

Coihaique

Cochrane

Puerto Natales

Punta Arenas

Puerto Williams

Is Diego
Ramirez

90° — 60° 53°

15

CHILEAN
ANTARCTIC
TERRITORY

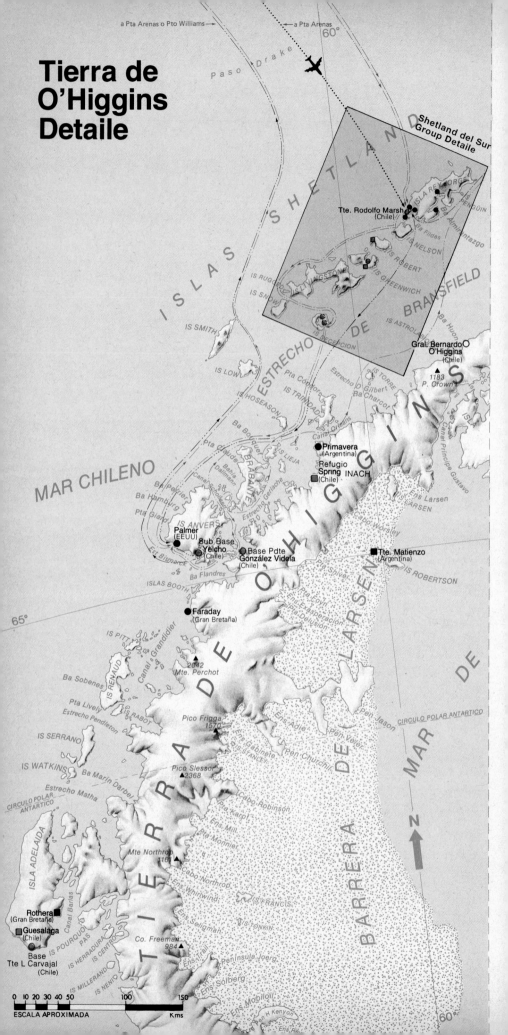

Tierra de O'Higgins Detaile

a Pta Arenas o Pto Williams →

a Pta Arenas

60°

Paso Drake

Shetland del Sur Group Detaile

ISLAS SHETLAND DEL SUR

Tte. Rodolfo Marsh (Chile)

ISLA REY JORGE

B. Pingüino

Ba Amirantazgo

B. Fildes

IS NELSON

IS ROBERT

Ba Nelson

IS GREENWICH

IS RUGGED

IS LIVINGSTONE

IS SNOW

IS ROBERT

ESTRECHO DE BRANSFIELD

IS SMITH

IS LOW

Pta Condor

IS HOSEASON

IS TRINIDAD

IS DECEPCION

IS ASTROLABIO

IS TORRE

Estrecho D Gilbert

Ba Charcot

Gral. Bernardo O'Higgins (Chile)

1183 P. Otown

Canal Príncipe Gustavo

MAR CHILENO

Ba Botella

Canal Orleans

Pta Claude

Canal Schollaert

Estrecho Lieja

BRABANTE

Bahía Dallmann

Estrecho Gerlache

Primavera (Argentina)

Refugio Spring (Chile)

INACH

Cabo Worsley

Ens. Larsen

LARSEN

Ba Pelirer

Ba Hamburg

Pta Giard

IS ANVERS

Palmer (EEUU)

Sub Base Yelcho (Chile)

Base Pdte González Videla (Chile)

Est Bismarck

Ba Flandres

ISLAS BOOTH

Tte. Matienzo (Argentina)

Pta Shiver

IS ROBERTSON

65°

Faraday (Gran Bretaña)

IS PITT

Canal o Grandidier

2042 Mte. Perchot

Pta Fonn

Ens Erasperacion

Pta Erasperacion

Pta Delusion

TIERRA DE O'HIGGINS

BARRERA DE LARSEN

MAR DE

IS RENAUD

IS RABOT

Ba Sobenes

Pta Lively

Estrecho Pendleton

Pico Frigga 1570

Ens Adie

Pen Jason

Pen Veier

CIRCULO POLAR ANTARTICO

IS SERRANO

Ba Marin Darbel

Pico Slessor 2368

Ens Gabinete

Pta Stanley

Pen Churchill

IS WATKINS

Estrecho Matha

Cabo Robinson

CIRCULO POLAR ANTARTICO

Pta Karpf

Ens Mill

ISLA ADELAIDA

Canal Barias

Mte Northrop 1161

Cabo Northrop

Ens Whirlwind

Pta Monnier

Rothera (Gran Bretaña)

Guesalaga (Chile)

Base Tte L Carvajal (Chile)

Canal Pourquoi

PAS

IS HERRADURA

IS POURQUOI

IS CENTRO

Co. Freeman 984

Ens Trail

Pen Insula Joerg

S FRANCIS

S TONKIN

Ens Seligman

Ens Solberg

IS MILLERAND

IS NENIO

N

0 10 20 30 40 50   100   150

ESCALA APROXIMADA   Kms

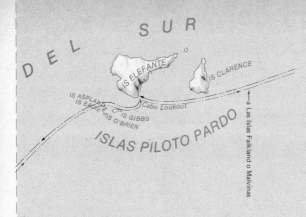

DEL SUR

IS ELEFANTE

IS CLARENCE

IS ASPLAND
IS EADIE
IS GIBBS
IS O'BRIEN

Cabo Lookout

ISLAS PILOTO PARDO

→ a Las Islas Falkland o Malvinas

IS D'URVILLE

IS BRANSFIELD
(Argentina)
Esperanza

IS JOINVILLE

Pta Moody

Hope Bay
(Gran Bretaña)

Paso Antártico

Petrel
(Argentina)

IS DUNDEE

IS ANDERSSON

IS AGUILA

IS VEGA

MAR CHILENO

Pta Falsa Isla

ROSS

Vicecomodoro Marambio
(Argentina)

IS SEYMOUR

IS SNOW HILL

65°

WEDDELL

● ● Bases
■ ■ Refuge

OCEANO PACIFICO

60°

ISLAS DIEGO RAMIREZ

Paso Drake

Tierra de O'Higgins Detalle

53°

60°

CHILEAN ANTARCTIC TERRITORY

IS SHETLAND DEL SUR

Mar Chileno

MAR CHILENO

90°

60°

MAR DE WEDDELL

70°

CIRCULO POLAR ANTARTICO

MAR DE BELLINGHAUSEN

IS O'HIGGINS

TIERRA DE O'HIGGINS

80°

POLO SUR

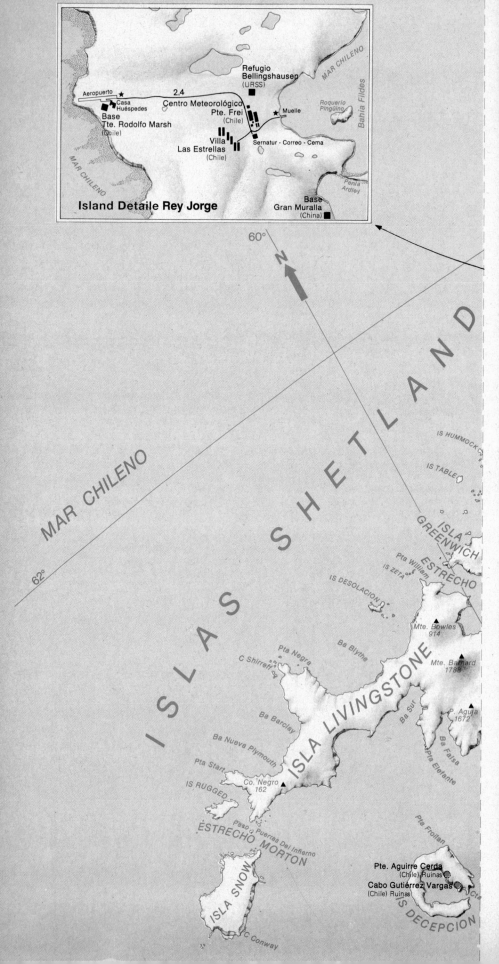

Shetland del Sur
Group Detaile

Island Detaile Rey Jorge

Aeropuerto

Casa
Huéspedes

Base
Tte. Rodolfo Marsh
(Chile)

2,4

Centro Meteorológico
Pte. Frei
(Chile)

Refugio
Bellingshausen
(URSS)

Muelle

Roquerío
Pingüino

Bahía Fildes

MAR CHILENO

Villa
Las Estrellas
(Chile)

Sernatur - Correo - Cema

Peña
Ardley

Base
Gran Muralla
(China)

MAR CHILENO

60°

N

62°

MAR CHILENO

ISLAS SHETLAND

IS HUMMOCK

IS TABLE

ISLA
GREENWICH

ESTRECHO

Pta William

IS ZETA

IS DESOLACION

Mte. Bowles
914

Ba Blythe

Pta Negra

C Shirreff

Mte. Barnard
1738

P. Aguja
1672

Ba Barclay

ISLA LIVINGSTONE

Ba Sur

Ba Nueva Plymouth

Pta Falsa

Pta Elefante

Pta Start

Co. Negro
162

IS RUGGED

Paso Puertas Del Infierno

ESTRECHO MORTON

Pta Froilan

ISLA SNOW

Pte. Aguirre Cerda
(Chile) Ruinas

Cabo Gutiérrez Vargas
(Chile) Ruinas

IS DECEPCION

C Conway

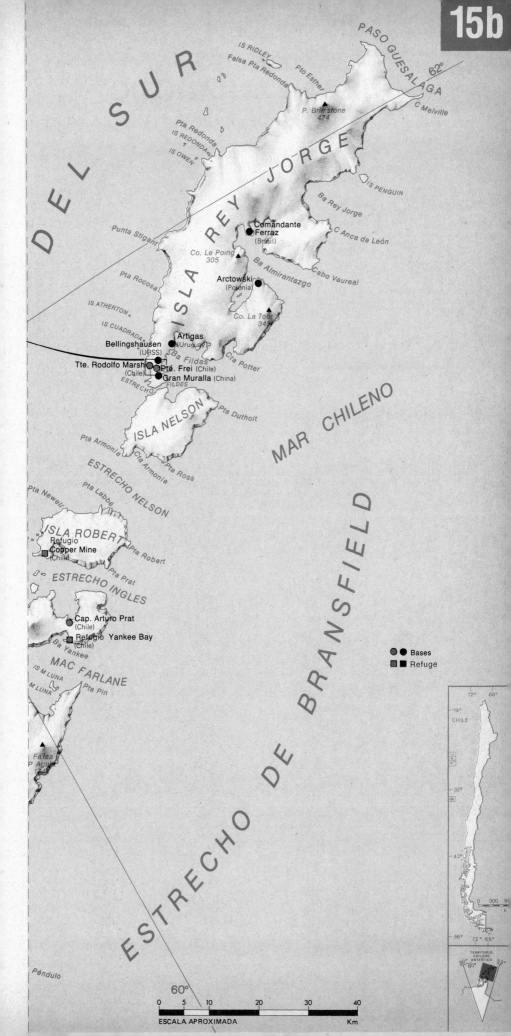

DEL SUR

PASO GUESALAGA

62°

C. Melville

IS RIDLEY

Falsa Pta Redonda

Pto Esther

P. Brimstone
474

Pta Redonda

IS REDONDAS

IS OWEN

ISLA REY JORGE

IS PENGUIN

Ba Rey Jorge

Punta Stigant

Comandante
Ferraz
(Brasil)

C Anca de León

Co. Le Poing
305

Ba Almirantazgo

Cabo Vaureal

Pta Rocosa

Arctowski
(Polonia)

IS ATHERTON

IS CUADRADA

Co. La Tour
345

IS ROBERT

Cta Potter

Artigas
(Uruguay)

Bellingshausen
(URSS)

Ba Fildes

Tte. Rodolfo Marsh
(Chile)

Pte. Frei (Chile)

Gran Muralla (China)

ESTRECHO

FILDES

Pta Duthoit

MAR CHILENO

ISLA NELSON

Pta Armonia

Cta Armonía

Pta Ross

ESTRECHO NELSON

Pta Newell

Pta Labbé

ISLA ROBERT

Refugio
Copper Mine
(Chile)

Pta Robert

ESTRECHO INGLES

Pta Prat

ESTRECHO DE BRANSFIELD

Cap. Arturo Prat
(Chile)

Refugio Yankee Bay
(Chile)

Ba Yankee

MAC FARLANE

IS M LUNA

M LUNA

Pta Pin

● ● Bases
■ ■ Refuge

Falsa
P Agu

Péndulo

60°

CHILE

19°

32°

43°

56°

72° 68°

300

TERRITORIO CHILENO
ANTARTICO

90°

60°

53°

0   5   10   20   30   40

ESCALA APROXIMADA   Km

Zone   15
CHILEAN ANTARCTIC
TERRITORY

DIVISION BY SECTIONS

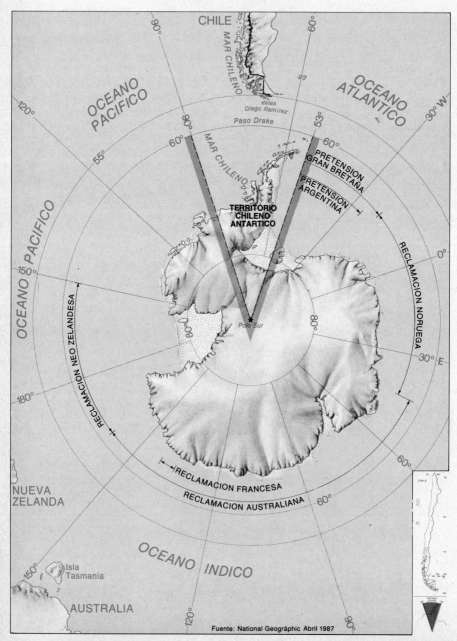

Fuente: National Geográphic Abril 1987

THE LAND, ITS HISTORY, ITS PEOPLE

FORMATION OF THE CONTINENT the Antarctic, according to the continent-drift theory, was once part of the supercontinent known as Gondwana and made up of the present land masses of South America, Africa, Madagascar, India, Australia and Antarctica.

Gondwana eventually split into separate pieces which drifted over the eons to their present locations. This accounts for the geographic, mineralogical, botanical and zoological similarities encountered among these land masses.

During its drifting phase, Antarctica was subject to several climatic regimes, a fact which accounts for the occurrence of coal strata, fossil trees and remains of prehistorical mammals found under the present ice layers.

GEOGRAPHIC LOCATION the geographical South Pole is located at the heart of the Antarctic. The entire continent, with the exception of the uppermost tip of Tierra de O'Higgins and the South Shetland islands, is located within the **Antarctic Circle**. Therefore, sunbeams hit the antarctic area, at best, in a very slanted fashion, bringing no warmth with them. Additionally, during the winter months all the territory within the Antarctic Circle receives no sunlight whatsoever, being immersed in a long, continuous night. To compensate, during the summer months the sun never sets, skimming the horizon and then rising again.

CLIMATE the above features set the stage for a remarkably inhospitable climate, with the world's lowest temperature (-88,3° C) recorded at the Soviet Vostok research station on August 24, 1960. This frosty climate gives rise to a thick ice sheet overlying the entire polar continent. The ice cap, in turn, cools the air masses and produces roaring winds.

The northern tip of Tierra de O'Higgins and the South Shetland islands, thanks to being situated outside the Antarctic Circle, enjoy a more friendly climate, with a mean annual temperature of - 2,1° C.

Katabatic Winds are a typical antarctic phenomenon, whipped to a frenzy by the cooling of the air masses upon contact with the ice layer. With gusts of up to 150 km/h, they can blow for days on end, rendering all outdoor activities impossible.

GLACIOLOGY the thick antarctic ice sheet accounts for 91% of the world's fresh water reserves. Should all this ice melt, the water level of the earth's oceans would rise by 30-60 m.

The ice layer's thickness averages some 2,000 m, making of this the world's highest continent in terms of mean altitude. The thickest layer measured so far is 4,267 m.

The ice layer is not static. It flows slowly towards lower altitude areas and to the coast, where it adopts different patterns.

Ice Shelves stretch along a significant portion of the antarctic coastline. The largest ones occur at the Weddell Sea and at the Ross Sea. They are vast flat ice sheets which, having a foothold on land, spread out over the ocean surface. When the wind or tides break bits of them up, flat-topped icebergs go sailing away.

Glaciers are ice rivers of great thickness running down along the bed of mountain basins towards the lowlands or the ocean. They can be up to 100 km wide, and jut into the ocean without melting for hundreds of kilometers.

Ice walls occur at sites where the coast plunges too abruptly into the sea to permit the ice to flow naturally into the water. They are veritable ice cliffs, many tens of meters tall, which regularly shed off chunks which become icebergs of beautifully jagged lines.

Pack Ice occurs by freezing of sea water during the winter period. It is particularly dangerous, as it can form over a stunningly short time, trapping and subsequently crushing ships by sheer pressure. During the winter, the frozen ocean surface amounts to approximately 20 million square kilometers; in summer it shrinks to some 3 million square km.

The antarctic coastline is estimated to be made up of 45% ice shelves, 10% glaciers, 40% ice walls and a meager 5% of rocks and open beaches.

ANTARCTIC WILDLIFE

Despite the inhospitable weather, the antarctic coastal areas harbor a rich and varied wildlife: the surrounding ocean ranks among the world's most productive. The key element in the food web is krill, a tiny shrimplike crustacean which feeds on plankton and is itself eaten by virtually all Antarctica's marine life.

The blue whale the largest animal that has ever existed on the earth, with up to 32 m in length and weighing 150 tons, migrates during the summer to southern seas to gorge itself on krill. Blue whales used to abound in the vicinity of the South Shetland coasts.

Killer whales are the largest and fiercest predators in antarctic seas. They prey on seals, tunnies, dolphins, and, in groups, they attack even the largest whales. They are up to 9 m long and are easy to recognize for their black loins and white belly, and their prominent triangular dorsal fin.

When they show up, sea animals and birds flee to safety. Killer whales are very intelligent, swift and strong: they can outswim all other sea creatures. Paradoxically, they are also very docile and cooperative in captivity, stealing the show in the few aquaria featuring them.

Sea elephants are the largest of all pinnipeds (seals), males reaching as much as 8 m in length. They stake out territories and establish harems of up to 12 females. Their main feature is a trunk-like appendage for a nose, with which they emit trumpetlike sounds.

They can be found at the South Shetland islands and the subantarctic territories, romping in large groups on stony beaches or ice shelves.

Weddell seals are easily recognized by their rounded body, small head and benevolent air. They live farther south than any other mammal and they have an amazing diving capacity: they can plunge up to 800 m below the water surface and stay for over one hour without resurfacing for air.

The Antarctic fur seal was intensely hunted for its fine fur during last century. Today it enjoys a protected-species status and its numbers are rebounding. It has a pointed nose and walks on its front fins. Of a gregarious nature, it gathers in large groups on rocky beaches.

Penguins are seabirds found only in the Southern Hemisphere. Their wings evolved into paddlelike flippers, penguins are charming in their clumsy walking on ice or rocks. Their orderly gregarious nature enables them to gather in tightly-packed communities of up to 1 million individuals in a scant 2-sq-km area.

Among the best known antarctic species are the **Adélie** penguins, with a black head and white «goggles»; they build their nests using pebbles and lay 2 eggs, incubated both by the male and female parent. **Papua** penguins are the third largest, reaching up to 80 cm in height; they sport white triangles over the eyes, set up small colonies and are the most docile and shiest.

They can dive to depths of as much as 100 m **Antarctic** penguins(Barbiquejo), with a white head and the neck slashed by a black stripe, are the most numerous, with colonies of up to 14 million individuals tucked away in rugged, almost inaccessible sites.

Other Birds there is a number of other species of flying seafowl, such as the stately albatross, the swift skua, giant petrel, blue-eyed cormorant, antarctic dove, and many others found in smaller numbers.

15

Penguins

HISTORY

Antarctica lacks a native human population. Its history boils down to reconnaissance of its coastline, followed by the laborious efforts to traverse the continental mass to the south pole, and, lastly, by the establishment of permanently-manned stations engaged in scientific research or of downright civilian settlements, such at the Chilean Villa Las Estrellas.

RECONNAISSANCE OF THE COASTLINE Antarctica was discovered by a Spanish expedition headed by Gabriel de Castilla, who sailed from Valparaíso in his ship Buena Nueva and sighted the South Shetland islands in 1603.

One century and a half later (1772), English captain James Cook circumnavigated the Antarctic, making in the process a reliable chart which later proved very helpful for seal hunters and whalers to find new grounds for engaging in their gory trade.

In 1819, English captain William Smith, blown off course by gales, discovered and named the Shetland islands and was the first to set foot on King George island. He sighted over 40 whaling ships in the area.

US seal hunter Nathaniel Palmer was the first to set foot on the Antarctic mainland, in 1821, at Tierra de O'Higgins. That same year, a Russian expedition under the command of Bellinghausen circumnavigated the polar continent.

Important exploration of the coastal waters and lands was carried out between 1823 and 1843 by James Weddell, who sailed into the sea now bearing his name and penetrated the ice shelf there, and by capt C Ross who, with his ships Erebus and Terror, discovered the ice shelf now bearing his name and volcano Erebus.

The introduction of steam-powered ships into Antarctic expeditions in 1874 spurred reconnoitering of the antarctic heartland.

THE DRIVE INLAND between 1899 and 1901, three scientific expeditions -an English one headed by Scott, a Swedish one headed by Nordenskjöld and a German one headed by Deygalski- struck inland from different points of the continent, assessing the feasibility of undertaking the great jump to the South Pole.

Three great explorers -Shackleton, Amundsen and Scott- engaged in a virtual race to be the first to reach the pole. In 1909 the Irishman Shackleton came to within 180 km from the pole, but harsh blizzards thwarted his reaching the coveted goal. In 1911 Scott and Amundsen set out for the pole simultaneously from opposing ends of the Ross Sea Norwegian Amundsen arrived first, on Dec. 14 1911, and Englishman Scott 35 days later, on Jan 12 1912, pulling behind him his provision-laden sleds. He and his 5 companions died during the tragic return journey.

Sir Ernest Shackleton attempted in 1914 another colossal adventure; to cross the polar continent from coast to coast. He sailed into the Weddell

Sea, where his ship Endurance was trapped and crushed by pack ice. The wreckage and the crew, stranded atop a giant iceberg, drifted over 2,000 km until running ashore at Elephant island of the South Shetland group.

From there, Shackleton and five other men sailed in a 6-m boat across the treacherous Drake Sea to Georgias islands to seek for help to rescue the remaining 22 crew members stranded on Elephant island. Three ships failed successively to reach the island, until the Chilean Navy cutter Yelcho, under the command of capt Luis Pardo, sailed from Punta Arenas and succeeded in breaching the ice barrier and rescuing the stranded sailors.

In 1929 Richard E Byrd flew over the South Pole and started the era of airplane utilization in Antarctic reconnaissance and exploration; aircraft have contributed greatly to enlarging our body of knowledge on the polar continent.

ESTABLISHMENT OF SCIENTIFIC RESEARCH STATIONS the first human group to winter in the Antarctic was the Belgian expedition headed by Adrian de Gerlache, whose ship was engulfed and trapped by ice in March 1898. This happened in Chilean territory, to the west of Tierra de O'Higgins at parallel 71° S.

In 1907 a Chilean whaling factory operated at Isla Decepción on a seasonal basis.

Since 1940 the need for deeper scientific and geographic knowledge prompted the establishment of permanently manned research stations, the largest of which are the US 's **Mac Murdo** station at the Ross Sea, the **Amundsen-Scott** station, also of the US, located at the South Pole, and the USSR's **Vostok** station at the geomagnetic south pole.

The largest population center within Chilean territory is at King George island (isla Rey Jorge) and includes **Tte Rodolfo Marsh** station (est. 1980), with a large air field; **Centro Meteorológico Pdte Frei** (est 1969), one of the three main meteorological and navigation stations in Antarctica; and **Villa Las Estrellas**, a civilian settlement including a hotel, a nursery, a school, scientific research facilities, a small hospital, post office and a bank. Established by Chile in recent years, this village is the main logistics support center for the remaining 8 countries operating scientific research stations at King George island.

CHILEAN SOVEREIGNTY

After the discovery of America (1492), Spain and Portugal agreed to split the New World between themselves. Spain was to get all lands lying west of longitude 23° 31' W, drawn from pole to pole and known as «Line of Tordesillas». The agreement was legalized by a papal bull issued by Alexander VI (1493) and by the Treaty of Tordesillas (1494).

The above provided the legal basis for Emperor Charles V to grant governorship of all lands located south of the Straits of Magellan (Magallanes) to Pedro Sancho de la Hoz in 1539 and, later, to Jerónimo de Alderete in 1544. In 1555 Jerónimo de Alderete was appointed Governor of Chile and was ordered to take possession of all lands lying to the south of the Straits of Magellan belonging to the Crown of Castilla. Antarctic territories were thus definitively incorporated to the Capitanía General de Chile. Upon attainment of independence, the South American republics inherited the territories originally under their jurisdiction under the principle of Uti possidetis, upon which the drawing of international boundaries of the nascent republics was based.

Chile was fully aware of its sovereignty over southern territories, expressed with the occupation of the Straits of Magellan in 1843 and later through the granting of antarctic concessions.

ANTARCTIC CONCESSIONS the world's first fishing concession for Antarctica was granted by the Chilean government on Dec 31 1902, to Pedro Pablo Benavides. Simultaneously, it leased out to the same person the islands of Diego Ramírez and

San Ildefonso. In 1906, Chile granted a concession to Fabry Toro Herrera to fish and occupy lands at Diego Ramírez, the South Shetland islands and other lands lying to the south. In 1907, Soc. Ballenera de Magallanes, a whaling operation based at Punta Arenas, was authorized by the Chilean government to establish facilities at Decepción island, where it set up a whaling factory and a coal depot. Later, the Norwegian Bugge Hektor Whaling Co. also established an operation at Decepción island, this time with authority granted by the Governor of Falkland Islands, belonging to the British Crown.

TERRITORIAL CLAIMS Chile had continuously exercised de facto sovereignty and utilization of Antarctic territories, so it was surprised when in 1917 England claimed rights internationally to the Antarctic territories lying within longitudes 20° W and 80° W, to which it referred as «Falkland Islands Dependencies.»

In September 1939, Chilean President Pedro Aguirre Cerda commissioned the specialist in international law Julio Escudero Guzmán to examine the Chilean titles to the Antarctic. On Nov 6 1940, the boundaries of the Chilean Antarctic Territory were established definitively by supreme decree as lying along longitudes 53° W and 90° W. In addition to historical and juridical grounds, scientific grounds were also brought up, such as the geographical continuity and contiguity and the geophysical and glaciological similarity between Magellanic and Antarctic territories.

In 1942 Argentina also raised territorial claims to the Antarctic, setting the boundaries of its claim at longitudes 25° W and 74° W. Thus, two other nations have territorial claims coinciding in part with the Chilean Antarctic Territory. A further four countries have claims to different chunks of the polar continent. The United States and the Soviet Union, assiduous explorers and researchers of Antarctica, have neither formulated nor recognized any territorial claims.

ANTARCTIC TREATY the difficulties in international access of the territorial claims drove twelve interested countries -Chile, Argentina, Australia, Belgium, USA, France, Great Britain, Japan, Norway, New Zealand, South Africa and the USSR- to sign the Antarctic Treaty on Dec 1, 1959.

The treaty sets forth that all territories and seas lying south of latitude 60° South shall be utilized solely for peaceful purposes, banning all tests involving conventional or nuclear weapons, as well as the establishment of radioactive waste dumps. It also stipulates the exchange of scientific information

Antarctic   a trip trough the channels

and personnel among the research stations operating in Antarctica.

As regards territorial claims, the treaty dictates that all claims shall be frozen as a statu quo of sorts during the time the treaty remains in effect. Although the treaty's validity is unlimited, any of the participating countries can call for a review of it after it completes three decades in force (1991). A meeting held in Madrid in May 1991 introduced no changes in this respect, but imposed a moratorium on all mining activities in the polar continent for 50 years.

PRESENT SITUATION after the definition of the Chilean Antarctic Territory's boundaries in 1940, a period of sovereignty exercised through yearly reconnaissance and research expeditions started. The first Chilean research station -Capt Arturo Prat- was established in 1947 at Greenwich island. In 1948 the Bernardo O'Higgins station was inaugurated with the attendance of Chilean President Gabriel González Videla, the world's first head of state to set foot on the polar continent. In Antarctica are both permanently and seasonally manned research stations. Within Chilean territory are permanent and seasonal stations belonging to 9 nations: Argentina (3 permanent and 2 seasonal stations); United Kingdom (2 permanent and 1 seasonal stations); USA, Brazil, Poland, Uruguay, USSR, and China, each with 1 station; South Korea and Spain (1 seasonal station each).
Chile operates 3 permanent stations, 1 meteorological station and one village inhabited by civilians. In addition, it possesses 4 seasonal research stations operating during the summer.

TOURISM IN ANTARCTIC

Unique scenery and marine wildlife are the two main attractions of Antarctic tourism. This is one of the world's few nearly pristine environments and little is known about its ecological balance.
Tourism in Antarctica is strictly regulated by the 1959 Antarctic Treaty, which permits access to sites of particular scientific interest solely for research purposes.
Tour operators and tourists alike are obliged to abide by the treaty's provisions regarding non-interference in scientific activities, non-disturbance of animal or plant habitats, no dumping of waste or littering and no introduction of new animal or plant species into the continent.
The stunning landscape of jagged icebergs and icepacks and unusually shaped rock formations never fails to awe visitors. The rich marine wildlife adds its own spectacular touch, with rock outcrops swarming with penguins or seals in stark contrast with the stillness of the areas surrounding them. This wildlife does not see man as an enemy, visitors thus being able to wander freely near or among animal colonies.
The number one country from which to visit Antarctica as a tourist is Chile. In addition to being

the world's southernmost country and hence the one nearest Antarctica, Chile operates an international airport at Punta Arenas and supply seaports at Punta Arenas and Puerto Williams.
Two tourist programs operate on a regular basis from these two locations.

NATIONAL PROGRAM

Travel agency Cabo de Hornos supported by the Chilean air force. It works from November to March. It takes 5 days and 4 nights. It is the only program that lets you stay overnight on the Antarctic Continent. AEROVIAS DAP (DAP airlines) offers charter flights with optional overnignt stays.

Description the tour starts from Punta Arenas in a Lockheed C-130 Hercules four-engine aircraft, overflying the Cape Horn islands and the Drake Passage to land after 2¹/₂ hours at the **Tte Rodolfo Marsh** station, located at the King George island of the South Shetland archipelago. Next to the airstrip is a modern hotel catering to scientists and tourists, with comfortable double rooms (shared

15

bathroom), sitting and entertainment lounges and an informal dining room, all in a cozy atmosphere.

At night, Chilean scientists offer video-supported lectures on the realities and mysteries of Antarctica.

One-and-a-half km away are the **Centro Meteorológico Pdte Frei** weather research station and **Villa Las Estrellas**, a civilian village founded in 1984 and inhabited by Chilean families. It boasts a post office, a bank and a handicrafts shop, among other amenities. Nearby are the Soviet and Chinese scientific research stations.

For those keen on the Been-There-Done-That tradition, at the end of the stay each visitor receives a diploma certifying his sojourn in the Antarctic continent.

Programmed Excursions are, naturally, weather dependent. At any rate, weather conditions are usually most favorable during the period when these tours are carried out.

1 Helicopter Tour reconnaissance flight of island King George, the largest of Shetland del Sur archipielago with 38 km in length and 18 km at its widest. Rugged and mostly overlaid with glaciers, its shores are sheer cliffs pluning to the icy sea, studded with rock outcrops teeming with marine wildlife. It is a spectacular ride.

2 Twin Otter Flights these airplanes are equipped with ski landing gear, thus being able to land on remote ice plateaux inaccessible over land.

3 Amphibian Boat Cruises sailing off from Fildes bay, the boat runs along the coast near rock outcrops and ice islands to Ardley island and its impressing colony of over 10,000 penguins of three species.

4 Walking Excursions short guided excursions to the large sea elephant colony along a path starting at Base Marsh, and to the jaw-dropping cliffs at the end of the airstrip, or to the Chinese or Soviet scientific research stations, where you can chat with the scientists and hear about their research and findings.

Adequate Clothing during the tourist season, the weather is similar to that found at any ski center. Thence, the most appropriate attire is a good ski suit, sunglasses, fur-lined gloves, après-ski boots («moonboots») and woollen socks. And, of course, sunscreen cream with a high protection factor.

Tourists visiting the area are mostly foreigners, mainly from the US and Europe. Many are members of the 100 Club, made up of persons who have stayed overnight in over 100 different countries and who arrive at Antarctica seeking to add one more name to their list.

Unusual visitors include philatelists eager to get a postmark from Antarctica's only post office, and mountaineers and nature-watchers, the latter gorging their eyes in the landscape's grandeur and exuberant wildlife.

SOCIETY EXPEDITIONS PROGRAM

Society Expeditions is a US company running two ships, Society Explorer and World Discovery. During November through January each year, they travel 10 or 11 times to Antarctica, operating from Punta Arenas or Puerto Williams, for cruises lasting around 10 days.

Description both ships are luxury cruise ships with capacity for some 120 passengers in a sole class. Cabins have a private bathroom and are distributed among five decks. In addition, there are entertainment lounges and observation and sunbathing decks.

They boast all amenities common to such cruise ships: heated swimming pool, sauna, fitness room, hair dresser, shops, library, reading and game rooms, cinema, ball room and restaurant offering international cuisine. Cabin size and price depend on the deck they are located in.

Passengers are provided all necessary garments and gear for land excursions.

The circuits offered fall within the categories of normal and extended.

Normal Circuits 6 to 7 in a season, start from bases in Magallanes and last for 10 days. Two days are spent sailing along the Straits of Magellan and

Beagle Channel, hugging some of the world's most beautiful fjords and glaciers. A further 4 days are spent in the to and fro legs across Cape Horn and the Drake Passage, and the remaining 4 days are dedicated to sailing around the Shetland archipelago and the Tierra de O'Higgins coastline, calling at several islands, scientific research stations, glaciers and wildlife spots. Each circuit is so organized as to have the 4 days sailing around the Antarctic Peninsula over a different route - always stressing the wildlife aspect-, so that a traveller can repeat his Antarctic expedition without it being a re-run of the previous one. The rough itinerary is sketched with a dotted line in the main map.

Extended Circuits are 4 in a season, normally at its beginning and end. They are particularly interesting for Chilean nationals and offer two different programs: **Atlantic Route**, boarding the ship in Montevideo and including a visit to the Falkland (Malvinas) islands, Antarctica and return through Punta Arenas; and **Pacific Route,** boarding the ship in Puerto Montt and visiting the stunning Laguna San Rafael, the spectacular Patagonian channels, the Beagle channel, Antarctica and Punta Arenas.

COMPARATIVE ANALYSIS

Both programs offer 4 days at Antarctica. The daily cost per person is 6% higher in the cheapest cabin of the US program.

The Chilean program offers an overview of different human, wildlife and geographical aspects of Antarctic life, overflying the area at intermediate altitudes.A close-up views are provided by the occasional landings and by walking or boat excursions in the vicinity of Base Tte Marsh. The US program, in turn, reconnoiters a significant portion of the Antarctic Peninsula coastline, offering close-up views of the area.

The fact that both programs take a different approach to getting acquainted with Antarctica makes them complementary to each other.

Travellers must bear in mind that climate always plays a significant -and unpredictable- role in Antarctic expeditions, even in summertime. This gives ship cruises a certain advantage, as the ship can still sail under bad weather, while airplanes cannot take off with low visibility and stormy weather.

Tourist Services Section

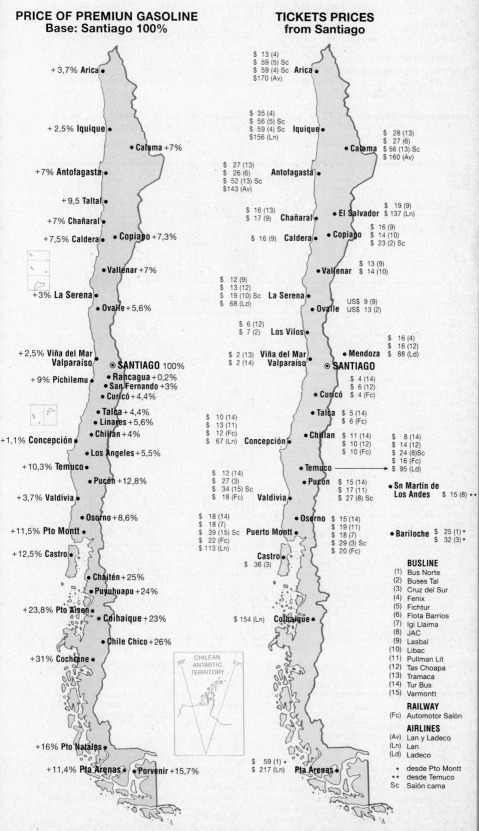

PRICE OF PREMIUN GASOLINE
Base: Santiago 100%

+3,7% Arica
+2,5% Iquique
• Calama +7%
+7% Antofagasta
+9,5 Taltal
+7% Chañaral
+7,5% Caldera • Copiapo +7,3%
• Vallenar +7%
+3% La Serena
• Ovalle +5,6%
+2,5% Viña del Mar
Valparaíso
⊙ SANTIAGO 100%
+9% Pichilemu • Rancagua +0,2%
• San Fernando +3%
• Curicó +4,4%
• Talca +4,4%
• Linares +5,6%
+1,1% Concepción • Chillán +4%
• Los Angeles +5,5%
+10,3% Temuco
• Pucón +12,8%
+3,7% Valdivia
• Osorno +8,6%
+11,5% Pto Montt
+12,5% Castro
• Chaitén +25%
• Puyuhuapu +24%
+23,8% Pto Aisén
• Coihaique +23%
• Chile Chico +26%
+31% Cochrane
+16% Pto Natales
+11,4% Pta Arenas • Porvenir +15,7%

TICKETS PRICES
from Santiago

$ 13 (4)
$ 59 (5) Sc
$ 59 (4) Sc Arica
$170 (Av)

$ 35 (4)
$ 56 (5) Sc
$ 59 (4) Sc Iquique
$156 (Ln)

$ 28 (13)
$ 27 (6)
• Calama $ 56 (13) Sc
$ 160 (Av)

$ 27 (13)
$ 26 (6)   Antofagasta
$ 52 (13) Sc
$143 (Av)

$ 16 (13)   • El Salvador $ 19 (9)
$ 17 (9) Chañaral $ 137 (Ln)

$ 16 (9)   • Copiapo $ 16 (9)
$ 16 (9) Caldera $ 14 (10)
                              $ 23 (2) Sc

• Vallenar $ 13 (9)
          $ 14 (10)

$ 12 (9)
$ 13 (12)
$ 19 (10) Sc La Serena
$ 68 (Ld)

• Ovalle US$ 9 (9)
         US$ 13 (2)

$ 6 (12)
$ 7 (2) Los Vilos

$ 2 (13) Viña del Mar • Mendoza $ 16 (4)
$ 2 (14) Valparaíso $ 16 (12)
                              $ 88 (Ld)

⊙ SANTIAGO

• Curicó $ 4 (14)
        $ 6 (12)
        $ 4 (Fc)

• Talca $ 5 (14)
       $ 6 (Fc)

$ 10 (14)   • Chillán $ 11 (14) $ 8 (14)
$ 13 (11) $ 10 (12) $ 14 (12)
$ 12 (Fc) $ 10 (Fc) $ 24 (8)Sc
$ 67 (Ln) Concepción $ 16 (5)
                                        $ 95 (Ld)
• Temuco →

$ 12 (14)   • Pucón $ 15 (14)
$ 27 (3) $ 17 (11)   • Sn Martín de
$ 34 (15) Sc $ 27 (8) Sc   Los Andes $ 15 (8) **
$ 18 (Fc) Valdivia

$ 18 (14)   • Osorno $ 15 (14)
$ 18 (7) $ 19 (11)
$ 39 (15) Sc Puerto Montt $ 18 (7)   • Bariloche $ 25 (1) *
$ 22 (Fc) $ 29 (3) Sc $ 32 (3) *
$ 113 (Ln) $ 20 (Fc)

Castro
$ 36 (3)

$ 154 (Ln) Coihaique

$ 59 (1) *
$ 217 (Ln) Pta Arenas

BUSLINE
(1) Bus Norte
(2) Buses Tal
(3) Cruz del Sur
(4) Fenix
(5) Fichtur
(6) Flota Barrios
(7) Igi Llaima
(8) JAC
(9) Lasbal
(10) Libac
(11) Pullman Lit
(12) Tas Choapa
(13) Tramaca
(14) Tur Bus
(15) Varmontt

RAILWAY
(Fc) Automotor Salón

AIRLINES
(Av) Lan y Ladeco
(Ln) Lan
(Ld) Ladeco

* desde Pto Montt
** desde Temuco
Sc Salón cama

CHILEAN ANTARCTIC TERRITORY
90° 53°

Prices (US Dollars), January 1992

661

ACCOMMODATIONS
CAR RENTALS
TOURIST SERVICES

SIMBOLS USED

Accommodations

Order of Listings the establishments classified by Sernatur (National Service of Touring), appear first, other establishments appear in alphabetical order.

Type of Accommodation the different types of lodging are: **H**=Hotel, **Hs**=Hosteria (Hostel, Inn), **M**=Motel, **Bh**=Boarding House, **Cg**=Campground, **Cb**=Cabin.

Season the different periods of availability are: **TT**=Year-round, **Tam**=September through March, **TA**=High Season (December 15 through March), **TP**=Fishing Season (November 15-April 15), **TI**=Ski and Snow Season.

Car Rental

Vehicles availables : 🚗 Car, 🛻 Pick-Up Truck, 🚙 4WD, 🚐 Van, 🚕 Limousine, 🏍 Motorcycle.

Tourist Services

Schedule of Services available: ● Usual timetable, ○ Requested timetable

Mode of Transport: 🚗 Car, 🚐 Van, 🚙 4WD, 🚚 Truck, 🐎 Horse, 🚢 Steamer, 🚤 Motorboat, 🚣 Fishing boat, 🛶 Inflatable raft, ✈ Airplane.

Abbreviations Used in this Section **Res**=Reservations, **Fx**=Fax, **Tx**=Telex, **of**=office, **Messenger**=Telephone with messenger service, **s/n**=street addresses without house number, **DDD**=Direct-Dialing Long Distance, Telephone Code, **LD**=Long Distance, **Fl**=Floor.

1 ARICA TO IQUIQUE

Tourist Services offered from
ARICA IQUIQUE

TOURS

TOURS	Vehicle	Season	Duration	Huasquitur Arica,Sotomayor 470 (058)223875 Tx321036	Payachatas Arica,Prat 404 (058)251518 Fx251514	Jurasi Tour Arica,Bolognesi 360 A (058)251696	Iquitour Iquique,Tarapacá 465 B (057)422009	Turismo Lirima Iquique,Av Baquedano 823 (057)422049
City Tour Arica	🚐	TT	3 h	○	●	●		
A Shopping City Tour to Iquique	🚗🚐	TT	4 h 1 day		○		●	●
A Shoping City Tour to Tacna(Perú)	🚗🚐	TT	8 h		●	○		
Museum and Geoglyphs in Azapa, San Lorenzo Pukará, Lluta Geoglyphs	🚗🚐	TT	4 h	●	○	○		
Lluta Geoglyphs, Copaquilla Pucará, Zapahuira, Socoroma Putre, Parinacota, Lake Chungara	🚗🚐	TT	1 h		○	○		
Chiza and Unitas hill Geoglyphs, Of Humberstone, Matilla Pica, Mamiña, hot Springs	🚐	TT	2 day	○		○		
Lluta Geoglyphs, Putre, Parinacota, Lauca National Park	🚐	TT	1d,2d		Week End ●	●	○	○
"Salitreras", La Tirana, Matilla, Pica	🚐	TT	1 day		○		Week End ●	●
"Salitreras", Pintados and Unitas hill Geoglyphs	🚗🚐	TT	8 h				○	○
"Salitreras", Unitas hill Geoglyphs, Tarapacá, Chusmiza hot Springs	🚐	TT	1 day					○
"Salitreras", Mamiña hot Springs	🚐	TT	1 day					○

ARICA (DDD 058)
Accommodations
Hs Arica 4★, TT, Av Comandante San Martín 599, ☎ 231201/ 302, Res Santiago ☎ 6713165. H San Marcos 3★, TT, Sotomayor 367, ☎ 232970/ 232149. H Aragon, TT, Maipú 344, ☎ 252088. H Azapa Inn, TT, Guillermo Sánchez 660, ☎ 222612/ 613, Res Santiago ☎ 335244. H Central, TT, 21 de Mayo 425, ☎ 252575/ 231116, Res Santiago ☎ 6965728. H Diego de Almagro, TT, Sotomayor 490, ☎ 224444. H El Paso, TT, Gral Velásquez 1109, ☎ 231965, Res Santiago ☎ 2324200. H King, TT, Colón 376, ☎ 232094/ 95. H Los Hibiscos, TT, Capitán Avalos 2041, ☎ 222289/ 241179. H Lynch, TT, Patricio Lynch 589, ☎ 231581/ 251959. H Saint Gregory, TT, Diego Portales 3221, ☎ 221914. M Saucache, TT, Guillermo Sánchez 27, ☎ 241458. H Tacora, TT, Sotomayor 540, ☎ 251240/ 229234. Bh Arica, TT, Colón 678, ☎ 251336. Bh Blanquita, TT, Maipú 472, ☎ 232064. Bh Canton, TT, Maipú 608, ☎ 231379. Bh Chillán, TT, Gral Velazquez 719/721, Bh Chungara, TT, Patricio Lynch 675, ☎ 231677. Bh El Hostal, TT, 18 de Septiembre 524, ☎ 251727. Bh Ibañez, TT, Sotomayor 578, ☎ 232346. Bh Leiva, TT, Colón 347, ☎ 232008. Bh Madrid, TT, Baquedano 685, ☎ 231479. Bh Sotomayor, TT, Sotomayor 442/446, ☎ 252336. Bh Velazquez, TT, Gral Velásquez 669, ☎ 231989. Bh Venecia, TT, Baquedano 739, ☎ 252877.

Car Rental
American (🚕) Gral Lagos 559, ☎ 252234. Viva (🚗 🛻 🚙), 21 de Mayo 821, ☎ 251121. Hertz (🚗 🛻 🚙), Gral Velázquez 1109, ☎ 231487.

CAMIÑA
Cg Municipal (basic facilities), TT, 500 m off the square.

CHUZMIZA
Hs Termas de Chuzmiza, TT, Chuzmiza Ravine s/n, Res Iquique ☎ 429573.

CODPA
Hs de Codpa, TT, Codpa s/n, Res Santiago ☎ 339130.

ENQUELGA
Cg Conaf (basic facilities) TA check with Conaf in Iquique.

IQUIQUE (DDD 057)
Accommodations
H Arturo Prat 4★, TT, Aníbal Pinto 695, ☎ 421414/ 423309, Res Santiago ☎ 330906. H Atenas 4★, TT, Los Rieles 738, ☎ 424349. H Barros Arana 3★, TT, Barros Arana 1330, ☎ 424420/ 426709. H Inti-Llanka 2★, TT, Obispo Labbé 825, ☎ 426383/ 422393. H Belen, TT, Vivar 803, ☎ 427237. H Camino del Mar, TT, Orella 340, ☎ 420465. Hs Cavancha, TT, Los Rieles 250, ☎ 421158/ 421897, Res Santiago ☎ 2298745. H Chucumata, TT, Balmaceda 850, ☎ 423655, Res Santiago ☎ 6952196/ 6723987. H de La Plaza, TT, Plaza Prat 302, ☎ 428394. H Durana, TT, San Martín 294, ☎ 428085. H Eben Ezer, TT, Hernán Fuenzalida 981, ☎ 429111/ 423706. H Icaisa, TT, Orella 434,.☎ 420150. H Major's, TT, Bulnes 157, ☎ 422997. H Phoenix, TT, Aníbal Pinto 451, ☎ 421315. H Playa Brava, TT, Av Playa Brava 3115, ☎ 422705/ 426765, Res Santiago ☎ 2742509. H Primeras Piedras, TT, Primeras Piedras s/n, ☎ 421358. H San Martín, TT, San Martín 823, ☎ 423977. H Tamarugal, TT, Tarapacá 369, ☎ 424365/ 426747. Bh Bolivar, TT, Bolivar 478, Bh Catedral, TT, Obispo Labbé 253, ☎ 423395. Bh Colonial, TT, Juan Martínez 1020, ☎ 426097. Bh Danny, TT, Vivar 1266, ☎ 427655. Bh Li-Ming, TT, Barros Arana 705, ☎ 421912. Bh Nan King, TT, Thompson 752, ☎ 423311. Bh Sta Ana, TT, Bolivar 741, ☎ 425375. Bh Vivar, TT, Vivar 1770, ☎ 427224. Bh Wilson, TT, Wilson 422, ☎ 423789.

Car Rental
Hertz (🚗 🚙),Cnel Souper 650, ☎ 426316, Tx 323084. Rents Procar (🚗 🚙), Serrano 796, ☎ 424607. Automóvil Club (🚗 🚙), Serrano 154, ☎ 422422, Fx 427333

LAGO CHUNGARA
Cg Conaf (basic facilities) TA opposite the guardhouse.

MAMIÑA (DDD 057)
H Refugio del Salitre, TT, El Tambo 01, ☎ 751203, Res Iquique ☎ 420330. H La Niña de Mis Ojos, TT, Ipla s/n. H Tamarugal, TT, Ipla s/n, Res Iquique ☎ 424365/ 426747. H La Coruña, TT, Sta Rosa 687, Res Iquique ☎ 422009. Hs El Tambo, TT, Av El Tambo 07.

PARINACOTA
Ref Conaf, TT, in the village s/n; ask at Conaf office in Putre.

PICA (DDD 057)
H San Andrés, TT, Balmaceda 197, ☎ 741319. Hs O'Higgins, TT, Balmaceda 6, ☎ 741322. M Pica, TT, Av Gral Ibañez 57, ☎ 741316. Bh El Tambo, TT, Gral Ibañez 68.

PINTADOS
Cg Conaf (basic facilities) TT, Pampa del Tamarugal National Reserve (Pan–American Highway).

PUTRE
Hs Las Vicuñas, TT, San Martín s/n. Hs San Martín de Putre, TT, Arturo Prat 399.

---

2 ANTOFAGASTA

ANTOFAGASTA CALAMA SAN PEDRO DE ATACAMA Tourist Services

TOURS	Vehicle	Season	Duration	Corza Turismo Antofagasta,S Martin 2769 ☎(055)251190 Tx325119	North Gate Tour Antofagasta,Baquedano 498 ☎(055)251586 Tx225292	Tatío Travels Sevice Antofagasta,Latorre 2579 ☎(055)223532 Fx223192	Cooper Tour Calama,Sotomayor 2016 ☎(056)212414 Fx210107	Talikuna Calama, Gral Velásquez 1948 ☎(056)212595	Takha Takha San Pedro de Atacama Calle Tocopilla s/n	Turismo Ochoa San Pedro de Atacama Toconao s/n ☎22
City Tour Antofagasta	🚐	TT	3 h	●	○	○				
City Tour Calama	🚐	TT	3 h				○	Week End		
Calama, Chiu Chiu, Lasana, San Pedro de Atacama, Moon Valley, Quitor, Atacama Salf Flat	🚙🚐	TT	4 day	○	○	○				
Chui Chiu, Lasana, San Pedro de Atacama, Moon Valley, Quitor, Tatío Geyser	🚙🚐	TT	4 day	○			○			
Tatío Geyser, Caspana, Chiu Chiu, Lasana	🚙🚐	TT	1/2d, 1 day	Week End ●	○	●	●	●		
San Pedro Atacama, Toconao, Atacama Salt Flat, Moon Valley	🚙🚐	TT	6 h 9 h				○	○	○	○
San Pedro de Atacama, Moon Valley, Pukara of Quitor	🚙	TT	4 h 6 h			●	●	○	●	●
La Portada, Hornito, Gático (Ruins), Tocopilla	🚙🚐	TA	1 day	○						

ANTOFAGASTA (DDD 055)
Accommodations
H Antofagasta 4★, TT, Balmaceda 2575, ☎ 224710, Res Santiago ☎ 2324200. H Diego de Almagro 4★, TT, Condell 2624, ☎222840/ 251721. H Plaza 4★, TT, Baquedano 461, ☎ 222058, Res Santiago ☎ 2742509. H Hostal del Sol 2★, TT, Latorre 3162, ☎ 228302. H San Martín 2★, TT, San Martín 2781, ☎ 263503. H America, TT, Copiapó1208, ☎ 263703. H Atenas, TT, Matta 2321, ☎ 263323. H Pieper, TT, Sucre 509, ☎ 263603. H Rawaye, TT, Sucre 762, ☎ 225399. H San Antonio, TT, Condell 2235, ☎ 225086. H San Marcos, TT, Latorre 2946, ☎ 251763, Res Santiago ☎ 6725599. H Tatío, TT, Av Grecia 1000, ☎ 247561. Hs 7 Cabañas, TT, El Huascar Beach. Bh Paola, TT, Prat 766, ☎ 222208. Bh Riojanita, TT, Baquedano 464, ☎ 226313. Cg Las Garumas, TT, El Huáscar Beach.

Car Rental
American's (🚗), Condell 2707, ☎ 226732. Avis (🚗 🚙 🚐), San Martín 2769, ☎ 251190. Hertz (🚗 🚙 🚐), Balmaceda 2566 ☎ 223549. Budget (🚗 🚙 🚐), Prat 206 Shop 5, ☎ 251745-Tx 325027.

CALAMA (DDD 082)
Accommodations
H Olimpo 2★, TT, Santa María 1673, ☎ 212367. H Alfa, TT, Sotomayor 2016, ☎212496. H Atenas, TT, E Ramirez 1961, ☎ 212666. Hs Calama, TT, Latorre 1521, ☎ 211511/ 2817. H Casablanca, TT, Sotomayor 2160, ☎ 211722. H Hostal El Sol, TT, Sotomayor 2064, ☎ 211235. H Lican Antai, TT, Ramirez 1937, ☎ 212970, Res Santiago ☎ 6952196. H Quitor, TT, E Ramirez 2116, ☎ 211716. H Topotel,TT, Camino Aeropuerto 1392, ☎ 212208, Res Santiago ☎ 2744324. Bh EL Tatio, TT, Pedro Leon Gallo 1987, ☎ 212284. Bh Internacional, TT, Gral Velazquez 1976, ☎ 211553. Bh John Keny, TT, Av Ecuador 1991, ☎ 211430. Bh Splendid, TT, Ramirez 1960.

Car Rental
American's (🚗), Granaderos 2625, ☎ 212989. Budget

(🚐 🚙 🚗), Abarca corner of Latorre Copec Gasoline Station, ☎ 211076. **Hertz** (🚐 🚗), Latorre 1510, ☎ 211380.

JUAN LOPEZ (Antofagasta LD)
H Centro Turístico La Rinconada, TT, fishing cove La Rinconada, Res Antofagasta ☎ 222907. **Hs Sandokan**, TT, Fernando Bull s/n, ☎ 942 LD.

MEJILLONES (055)
Hs Luz de Luna, Almte Goñi 99, ☎ 621582.

SAN PEDRO DE ATACAMA
Accommodations
Hs San Pedro de Atacama TT, Camino a Solca s/n, ☎ 11. **Hostal Takha Takha**, TT, Tocopilla s/n.**Bh Chiloe**, TT, Dmgo de Atienza corner of Antofagasta, ☎ 17. **Bh La Florida**, TT,

Tocopilla s/n. **Bh Porvenir**, TT, Pedro de Valdivia corner of B O'Higgins, ☎ 8. **Bh Pukara**, TT, Tocopilla 28. **Cg Pozo Tres**, TT, 3 km from S P de Atacama.

TALTAL
Hs Taltal, TT, Esmeralda 671, ☎ 173. **H Verdy**,TT, Ramirez 345, ☎ 105.

TOCONAO
P Particular, TT, O'Higgins s/n. **P Particular**, TT, Huatiquina s/n.

TOCOPILLA (DDD 055)
H Vucina, TT, 21 de Mayo 2069, ☎ 813088. **H Casablanca**, TT, 21 de Mayo 2054, ☎ 813222/ 813187. **H Chungará**, TT, 21 de Mayo 1440, ☎ 811036.

---

3 COPIAPO AND VALLENAR

COPIAPO CALDERA
BAHIA INGLESA
Tourist Services

TOURS	Vehicle	Season	Duration	Turismo Atacama Copiapo,Los Carrera 716 ☎(052)212712 Fx327003	Turismo Cristobal Copiapo,O'Higgins 656 ☎(052)212075 Fx327003	Portal del Inca Caldera,Carvallo 945 ☎(052)315252 Fx327025	Sernatur Copiapo,Los Carrera 691 ☎(052)212838	Exploradores del Desierto El Salvador, ☎ 472311	Julio Palma Chañaral,Comercio 116 ☎(052)80062
City Tour Copiapo	🚗🚐	TT	3 h	○	Week End ●				
City Tour (Historic) Caldera	🚙	TT	3 h			○			
Copiapo Valley, Paipote, Tierra Amarilla, Vineyars, Amolanas Acueduct	🚗🚐	TT	1 day	○	Week End ●				
Tours to the Coast, Playa Blanca, Bahía Inglesa	🚐	TT	1 day	○					
Pan de Azucar National Park	🚙🚐	TT	1 day						
Desert Blooms between Vallenar, Copiapo and the Coast	🚙🚐	Sept. Oct.	1d,2d						
Lonely Beaches and Sand Dunes	🚙	TT	1/2d, 1 day				○		
Costal Raid betweeen Copiapo, Caldera and Southern Beaches	🚙 Proper	Jan	3 day					Raid Feb ●	
Maricunda and Pedernales Salt Flat, High Plateau, Ojos del Salado	🚙🚚	Dec to Feb	1d,3d					Raid Dic ● ○	○

BAHIA INGLESA (DDD 052)
Accommodations
M Umbral de Bahía Inglesa 3★, Road to a Bahía Inglesa s/n, ☎ 315000. **Cb y Cg Bahía Inglesa**, TT, ☎ 1, Res Santiago ☎ 380521 annex 2312. **Cb Los Jardínes de Bahía Inglesa**, Calle Copiapó 100, Res Santiago ☎ 6967608/ 696622.

CALDERA (DDD 052)
Accommodations
H M Portal del Inca 4★, TT, Carvallo 945, ☎ 315252, Res Santiago ☎ 2742509. **Hs Puerta del Sol** 3★, TT, Wheelwight 750, ☎ 315205, Res Santiago ☎ 6983341. **H Costanera**, TT, Wheelwight 543.
Car Rental
H Portal del Inca (🚐 🚗), Carvallo 945, ☎ 315252.

COPIAPO (DDD 052)
Accommodations
H Diego de Almeyda 4★, TT, O'Higgins 656, ☎ 212075/ 212076, Res Santiago ☎ 330906. **H Derby**, TT, Yerbas Buenas 396, ☎ 212447. **Hs Las Pircas**, TT, Av Kennedy s/ n, ☎ 213220, Res Santiago ☎ 6952196. **H Montecatini**, Infante 766, ☎ 211363. **H Palace**, TT, Atacama 741, ☎ 2112852. **Hs Pan de Azúcar**, TT, Av Ramón Freire 430, ☎ 212755, Res Santiago ☎ 2742509.
Car Rental
Hertz (🚐 🚗), Av Copayapu 173, ☎ 213522/ 211333. **Sial** (🚐),Los Carrera 755, ☎ 213180. **Avis** (🚐 🚗 🚙), Av Lib Bdo O'Higgins 480, ☎ 212827. **Galerías** (🚐 🚗), Southern Pan–American Highway 260, ☎ 212147/ 216981. **Rodaggio** (🚐 🚗), Vallejos 152, ☎ 212153.

CHAÑARAL (DDD 052)
Accommodations
Hs Chañaral, TT, Miller 268, ☎ 480055, Res Santiago ☎ 2742509. **H Mini**, TT, San Martín 528, ☎ 480070. **H Jimenez**, TT, Merino Jarpa 551. **H La Marina**, TT, Merino Jarpa 562. **Cg Pan de Azúcar**, TT, National Park.
Car Rental
Julio Palma Vergara (🚐 🚚 🚗), Comercio 116, ☎ 480062. **Hs de Chañaral** (🚐 🚗 🚙), Miller 268, ☎ 480050

DIEGO DE ALMAGRO (DDD 052)
H Crillon, TT, Juan Martinez corner of J Antonio Ríos, ☎ 41011/ 023.

EL SALVADOR (DDD 052)
Accommodations
H Camino del Inca 3★, TT, Av El Tofo 330, ☎ 472314/ 472311, Res Santiago 713112. **Hs El Salvador**, TT, Av Potrerillos Norte 003, ☎ 472492.
Car Rental
Corser (🚐 🚗 🚙), Av El Tofo 002, ☎ 472731.

HUASCO
Hosteria Huasco, TT, Ignacio Carrera Pinto 110, ☎ 531026.

VALLENAR (DDD 054)
Accommodations
Hs de Vallenar 3★, TT, Alonso de Ercilla 848, ☎ 614195, Res Santiago ☎ 6952196. **H Real de Turismo** 2★, TT, Arturo Prat 881, ☎ 613963. **H Cecil**, TT, Arturo Prat 1059, ☎ 614071. **M Cen-tro Galo**, TT, Highway to Huasco area Media Luna, ☎ 611646/ 613989. **H Ro-Del**, TT, Prat 1190-A, ☎ 614297.

LA SERENA · COQUIMBO · OVALLE
Tourist Services

TOURS	Vehicle	Season	Duration	Giratour La Serena,Balmaceda 327 Of.4 ☎(051)211127 Fx214573	Turismo Videomundo La Serena,Balmaceda 856 ☎(051)212769 Annex 2	Turistica Cristobal La Serena,Cordovez 210 ☎(051)222991 fx320003	Tololo Observatory La Serena ☎(051)213352	INGSERVTUR Coquimbo,Los Lirios 300 ☎(051)312943	Turistica Olitur Ovalle,Mackenna with Aguirre ☎(053)622463	Servicio de Taxis Ovalle,Benavente 702-706 ☎(053)620352-620999
City Tour La Serena, Coquimbo and La Herradura	🚐	TT	6 h	●	○	●		Monday ●		
Fray Jorge National Park, Valle del Encanto, Termas de Socos	🚐	TT	1day	Week End ●	○	○		Friday ●	○	○
Vicuña, Elqui river Valley, Capel Pisco Distillery, Rivadavia and Monte Grande	🚐	TT	1day	Tu and Th ●	○	○		Tuesday ○	○	
Limarí Valley, Valle del Encanto, Ovalle, El Palqui, La Paloma Dam, Monte Patria and Sotaquí	🚐	TT	1day	Friday ●						
Andacollo, Recoleta Dam and Pichasca Natural Monument	🚐	TT	1day					Wednesday ●		
Ovalle, Sotaquí (Vineyards), Monte Patria, La Paloma Dam	🚐	TT	9 h					Thursday ●	○	○
Recoleta Dam, Pichasca Natutal Monument	🚐	TT	6 h						○	○
Visit to Tololo Observatory	🚐	TT	6 h	Week End ●			Week End ●			

COMBARBALA
M La Piscina, TT, Juan Flores 334, ☎ 24.

COQUIMBO (DDD 051)
Accommodations
H Lig, TT, Aldunate 1577, ☎ 311171. H Prat, TT, Aldunate corner of Bilbao, ☎ 311845. H Vegamar, TT, Las Heras 403, ☎ 311773. H Iberia, TT, Lastra 400, ☎ 312141. H Punta del Este, TT, Av Videla 170, ☎ 312768.

CHINCOLCO
H Restaurante Rincon Criollo, TT, Pedro Montt s/n, ☎ 781005 públic phone.

ELQUI (LD 108)
Hs Don Juan, TT, Arturo Prat s/n, ☎ 1x 2 messenger.

ILLAPEL (DDD 053)
Accommodations
H Domingo Ortiz de Rozas, TT, Av Ignacio Silva 241, ☎ 522127. H Alemán, TT, Av Ignacio Silva 45, ☎ 522511. Hs Illapel, TT, Buin 452. H Alameda, TT, Av Ignacio Silva 20, ☎ 522355. H Londres, TT, Vicuña Mackenna 21, ☎ 522668.

LA HERRADURA (DDD 051)
Accommodations
M Brisas del Mar 3★, TT, Los Pastores 90, ☎ 312641. Cb Antares, TT, Lib Bdo O'Higgins s/n, ☎ 312998, Res Santiago 6721050. H Complejo Turístico Mistral, TT, Costanera 1284, ☎ 313538, Res Santiago ☎ 6967820/ 193. H Cristobal Inn, TT, Av Costanera s/n, ☎ 312231, Res Santiago ☎ 333001. H La Herradura, TT, Av Costanera 200, ☎ 311410. M Cg La Herradura, TT, Calle Antigua corner of Escuela s/n, ☎ 312084. M Las Gaviotas, TT, Av Costanera 1755, ☎ 315506. H San Juan, TT, Capri Sur 101, ☎ 311110. Traveller's M, TT, Pan–American Highway, Km 460, ☎ 312045

LA LIGUA (DDD 051)
H Chile, TT, Polanco 7

LA SERENA (DDD 051)
Accommodations
H Francisco de Aguirre 4★, TT, Cordovez 210, ☎ 222991, Res Santiago ☎ 330895. H Alameda, TT, Av Francisco de Aguirre 452, ☎ 213052. H Berlín, TT, Cordovez 535, ☎ 223583. H Casablanca 3★, TT, Vicuña 414, ☎ 225573. H El Escorial, TT, Colón 617, ☎ 224793, Res Santiago ☎ 2742509. Gran H La Serena, TT, Cordovez 610, ☎ 222975. H Londres, TT, Cordovez 566, ☎ 211906. H Los Balcones de Alcalá, TT, Av Francisco de Aguirre781, ☎ 225999. H Mediterráneo, TT, Cienfuegos 509, ☎ 225837. H Pacífico, TT, Edo de La Barra 252, ☎ 225674. H Pucará, TT, Balmaceda 319, ☎ 211966. Cb Quicalán, TT, Balmaceda 2271, ☎ 225668. Bh Brasilia, TT, Brasil 555, ☎ 225248, Res Santiago ☎ 2269438.

Car Rental
Budget (🚐 🚗), Matta 389, ☎ 225312. Dollar (🚐 🚐) Av Fco de Aguirre 337, ☎ 224726. El Faro (🚐), Av Fco de Aguirre 0660, ☎ 222459/ 225745. Hertz (🚐 🚐 🚗), Av Fco de Aguirre 0225, ☎ 213955/ 212639.

LA SERENA WATERFRONT STREET (DDD 051)
Accommodations
M Hs del Mar 3★, TT, Cuatro Esquinas 0690, ☎ 225816, Res Santiago ☎ 2202430. M Canto del Agua, TT, Av del Mar s/n, ☎ 225163, Res Santiago ☎ 2254947. M Capilla del Mar, TT, Pan–American Highway s/n, ☎ 313822, Res Santiago ☎ 2254947. Hs Casa de Piedra, TT, Pan–American Highway km 466 Peñuels, ☎ 311944. Cb de Peñuelas, TT, Av del Mar s/n, ☎ 313860, Res Santiago ☎ 2312128. Cb El Frutillar, TT, Av Miramar s/n, ☎ 312369. M Hipocampo, TT, Av del Mar s/n, ☎ 214276. M Jardín del Mar, TT, Av Costanera s/n, ☎ 225816. Cb Añañucas, TT, Av del Mar Parcela 56 B s/n, ☎ 215881. Cb Maroal, TT, Pan–American Highway with Peñuelas street s/n, ☎ 314078. M Niko´s, TT, Pan–American Highway s/n, ☎ 314028. M Villa Los Plátanos 3★, TT, P.O. Box 403, ☎ 213494.

LOS MOLLES
Cb Lourdes, TT, Vicente Huidobro s/n, Res Santiago ☎ 5589072.

LOS VILOS
Accommodations
M El Pelusa, TT, Caupolicán 411, ☎ 541041. M American, TT, Pan–American Highway km 224, ☎ 541020. M Choapa, TT, Southern road access to Los Vilos s/n, ☎ 541009. M Hardis, TT, Av 1 Norte 248, ☎ 541098. Hs Lord Willow, TT, Hosteria 1444, ☎ 541037. M Hs El Arrayan, TT, Av Caupolicán 1, ☎ 541005. M Santa Emilia, TT, Caupolicán 1877, ☎ 541036. H Bellavista, TT, Rengo 020, ☎ 541073. M New Pacific, TT, Tres Oriente 1447.

MORRILLOS (DDD 051)
M Morrillos, TT, Balmaceda 999, Res Serena ☎ 211170, ☎ 224305.

OVALLE (DDD 053)
Accommodations
H Roxy 1★, TT, Libertad 155, ☎ 620080. H American, TT, Vicuña Mackenna 169, ☎ 620722. H Buenos Aires, TT, Libertad 136 2° Fl. H de France, TT, Libertad 231, ☎ 620828. H El Quisco, TT, Maestranza 161, ☎ 620351. Gran H Ovalle, TT, Av Vicuña Mackenna 210-Fl 2°. H Turismo Ovalle, TT, Victoria 295, ☎ 620159. H Venecia, TT, Libertad 261, ☎ 620968.

PETORCA
H Valsof, TT, Silva 248, ☎ 781007 public.

PICHIDANGUI
Accommodations
M Pichidangui, TT, Francis Drake s/n, ☎ 1, Res Santiago ☎ 461005. Cg y Cb Bahía Marina, TT, Camino Vecinal s/n, Res Santiago ☎ 334708/ 973291. M Antulauquen, TT, Av Costanera s/n, Res Santiago ☎ 6989379/ 2294376. Cb Del Bosque, TT, El Bosque s/n, ☎ 3, Res Santiago ☎ 396372. Cb Del Sol, TT, Santa Inés street, ☎ 3, Res Santiago ☎ 2127762. Hs Puquen, TT, Dos Poniente s/n, ☎ 3.

SALAMANCA
Hs Galvez, TT, Perez 540, ☎ 551017. H Bogarin, TT, Julio Echeverría 440, ☎ 551016.

TERMAS DE SOCOS
H Termas de Socos, TT, Pan–American Highway 368, ☎ 621373 de Ovalle, Res Santiago ☎ 6816692.

TONGOY (DDD 051)
Accommodations
Hs La Villa 3★, TT, Fundición Sur s/n, ☎ 391204/ 956, Res Santiago ☎ 2744677. Hs Alamar, TA, Urmeneta Sur 99, ☎ 391183, Res Santiago ☎ 372154. H Arrocet, TT, Fundición Sur 160, ☎ 391969. H La Bahía, TT, Urmeneta 95, ☎ 391244. H Las Pasmanias, TT, José Tomás Urmeneta 94, ☎ 391205. H Talinay, TA, Av Costanera Sur 76, ☎ 391122/ 391253, Res Ovalle ☎ 622805. H Panorámico, TT, Av Mirador 455, ☎ 391944. H Tambo, TT, Urmeneta Sur 55, ☎ 391132. H Plaza, TT, Fundición Norte 29, ☎ 391184. Cb Tongoy, TA, José Tomás Urmeneta Norte s/n, ☎ 391902, Res Santiago ☎ 2748436. Hs Tongoy, TT, Costanera 10, ☎ 391203/900. H Yachting Club, TT, ☎ 391154, Res Santiago ☎ 2313417/ 2086049.

VICUÑA (DDD 051)
Accommodations
Hs de Vicuña, TT, Sargento Aldea 101, ☎ 411301, Res Santiago ☎ 395334/ 2742509. M Américo, TT, Gabriela Mistral 745. H Yasna, TT, Gabriela Mistral 542.

5 SANTIAGO AND THE SURROUNDING DISTRICT

SANTIAGO Tourist Services

TOURS	Duration	The Gray Line Agustinas 1173 ☎(02)6960518 Tx 441228	Tour Services Teatinos 333 ☎(02)6960415 / 727166	Chilean Ravel Services Agustinas 1291, Fl. 5 Of. F ☎(02)6967820 / 6967193	Festival Tours Alameda 949, Of. 603 ☎(02)6964924 Tx 340986
City Tour Santiago	3 h	O	O	O	O
City Tour Stgo. by night	4 h	O	O	O	O
Exc. to Viña Concha y Toro vineyards	4 h	O	O	O	O
Exc to Pomaire - Undurrraga vineyards	4 h	O	O	O	O
Exc to Hac. Los Lingues	1 day	O	O	O	O
A day in the country in Monaco's	1 day	O	O	O	O
Santiago Viña del Mar	1 day	O	O	O	O
Excursion to the Snow	1 day	O	O	O	O

COLORADO (DDD 02)
Apart H El Colorado, TI, ☎ 2460660. Apartment Monte Blanco, TI, Res Santiago ☎ 393908.

FARELLONES (DDD 02)
Posada de Farellones, TT, Res Santiago ☎ 2460660. H Farellones, TT, ☎221493, Res Santiago ☎721887. H Tupungato, TT, Cancha El Embudo, Res Santiago ☎ 2182216.

LAGO RAPEL
Accommodations
H Punta Verde, TT, Res Santiago ☎ 2086045. M Marina Rapel, TT, ☎ 571956 El Estero, P.O. Box 69 Las Cabras.

LAGUNILLAS
H Refugio del Club Andino de Chile de Lagunillas, TI, P.O. Box 1823 Santiago, Res Santiago ☎ 2238788. H Soc Deportiva Stade Francais, TI, Res Santiago ☎ 2337608.

LA LEONERA
H La Leonera, TT, Res Santiago ☎ 6958209.

LA PARVA (DDD 02)
Condominio Nueva Parva, TI, Nueva Parva 77, ☎ 2121363, Res Santiago ☎ 2332476.

LAS VERTIENTES - EL CANELO (DDD 02)
H Refugio del Club Andino de Chile de Lagunillas, TI, P.O. Box 1823 Santiago. Hs San José, TT, Vista Hermosa s/n, ☎ 8502842.

LOS ANDES (DDD 034)
H Continental, TT, Esmeralda 211, ☎421510/ 1013. H Plaza, TT, Rodríguez 368, ☎ 421929.

LOS LINGUES
H Hacienda Los Lingues, TT, ☎ 882987 Res Santiago ☎ 2233518/ 2250838.

LO VALDES
H Refugio Alemán Lo Valdés, TT, Res Santiago ☎ 8501773.

MELOCOTON
Cb La Paz, TT, Road El Volcán 29618, ☎ 79, P.O. Box 124 San José de Maipo. H Balneario Millahue, TT, ☎ 2, P.O. Box 5 San José de Maipo.

PORTILLO
Hs Cristo Redentor, TT, Res Santiago ☎ 383810. H Portillo, TT, 3007 to 12, Res Santiago ☎ 2313411

RANCAGUA (DDD 072)
H Aguila Real, TT, Av Brasil 1045, ☎ 222047/ 687/ 6753. H Camino del Rey, TT, Estado 275, ☎ 232314/ 227280. H España, TT, San Martín 367, ☎ 223963. H Rancagua, TT, San Martín 85, ☎ 232663. H Turismo Santiago, TT, Brasil 1036, ☎ 221509/ 5060.

RIO COLORADO
Hs Luna, TT, Riecillo, P.O. Box 181, Los Andes. H Novile, TT, Río Colorado s/n. H Refugio Río Colorado, TT, Res Santiago ☎ 490093. Hs Restaurante Donde El Guatón, Riecillo, Res Sarmiento 240, Los Andes.

SAN ALFONSO
Cb Cascada de Las Animas, TT, Res Santiago ☎ 351871/ 7779239. Hs Los Ciervos, TT, Res Santiago ☎ 2276156.

SAN FELIPE (DDD 034)
Hs San Felipe, TT, Merced 204, ☎ 510508.

SAN GABRIEL
Casa Pensión Los Rodados, TT, Road Los Rodados s/n.

SANTIAGO Downtown (DDD 02)
Accommodations
Apart H Agustinas, TT, Agustinas 1990, ☎6951271/6726739 H Carrera, TT, Teatinos 180, ☎ 6982011. H Apart Carlton House, TT, Máximo Humbser 574, ☎ 383130. H Cervantes, TT, Morandé 631, ☎ 6967966/ 6965318. H City, TT, Compañía 1063, ☎695426. H Cristóbal Inn, TT, Sto Domingo 444, ☎ 333001/ 2/ 3. H Crowne Plaza, TT, Av Lib Bdo O'Higgins 136, ☎ 381042. Apart H de Turismo Moneda, TT, Av Brasil 102, ☎6961948/6710477. Hostal del Parque, TT, Merced 294, ☎ 392694/ 2712. H Don Tito, TT, Huérfanos 578, ☎ 391987/ 381024. H El Conquistador, TT, Miguel Cruchaga 920, ☎ 6965599. H España, TT, Morandé 510, ☎ 6985245/ 66066. H Foresta, TT, Victoria Subercaseaux 353, ☎ 396261. H Galerías, TT, San Antonio 65, ☎ 384011. H Gran Palace, TT, Huérfanos 1178 Fl 10, ☎ 6712551. H Imperio, TT, Av Lib Bdo O'Higgins 2876, ☎ 6897774. H Libertador, TT, Av Lib Bdo O'Higgins 853, ☎ 394211/ 12/ 13/ 14. H Metrópoli, TT, Doctor Sótero del Río 465, ☎ 6952196/ 6723987. H Nuevo Valparaíso, TT, Morandé 791, ☎6715698. H Panamericano, TT, Teatinos 320, ☎6723060. H Plaza San Francisco, TT, Av Lib Bdo O'Higgins ☎ 382215. Bh Santo Domingo, TT, Santo Domingo 735, ☎ 396733. H Ritz, TT,Estado 248, ☎ 393401. H Riviera, TT, Miraflores 106, ☎ 331176. H Sao Paulo, TT, San Antonio 357, ☎ 398031/ 2/ 3. H Sta Lucía, TT, Huérfanos 779, ☎ 398201. H Turismo Montecarlo, TT, Victoria Subercaseaux 209, ☎392945. H Tupahue, TT, San Antonio 477, ☎383810/ 393861. R Astoria, TT, S Sanfuentes 2509, ☎ 6892589. R Familiar Tabita, TT,

Príncipe de Gales 81, ☎ 6715700. **R Familiar Eliana**, TT, Grajales 2013, ☎ 726100. **R Gloria**, TT, Almte Latorre 449, ☎ 6988315. **R Mery**, TT, Sidestreet República 36 & 42, ☎ 6968883/ 94982. **R Miraflores**, TT, Riquelme 555, ☎ 6963961. Accommodation **La Española**, TA, Alonso Ovalle 751 & 753, ☎ 338741

SANTIAGO Providencia (DDD 02)
Accommodations
H Presidente, TT, Eleodoro Yáñez 867, ☎ 2255019. **H Lyon**, TT, Av R Lyon1525, ☎ 2741777/ 2257732. **H Los Españoles**, TT, Los Españoles 2539, ☎ 2321824/ 5/ 6. **H Orly**, TT, Av Pedro de Valdivia 027, ☎ 2318947. **H Posada del Salvador**, TT, Av Eleodoro Yáñez 893, ☎ 492072. **H Reina Sofía**, TT, Luis Thayer Ojeda 1250, ☎ 2514349. **H Santa María**, TT, Av Sta María 2050, ☎ 2326614. **H Sheraton San Cristóbal**, TT, Av Sta María 1742, ☎ 2335000. **Tempo Rent**, Furnished Apartments, TT, Nueva Lyon 97, ☎ 2320013.

SANTIAGO Las Condes (DDD 02)
Accommodations
H Acacias de Vitacura, TT, El Manantial 1781, ☎ 2290575. **H Irazú**, TT, Noruega 6340, ☎ 2205941/ 2124359.**H Manquehue**, TT, Estéban Del'Orto 6615, ☎ 2207055. **H Río Bidasoa**, TT, Vitacura 4873, ☎ 2421525.

SANTIAGO (DDD 02)
Car Rental
Aeroin (🚗), Silvina Hurtado 1691, ☎ 2514185/ 2257334. **American** (🚗), Las Condes 9225, ☎ 2119307. **Arka** (🚗), Rancagua 514, ☎ 495745. **Auto Giro** (🚗), Almte Reyes 062, ☎ 2228330. **Automóvil Club** (🚗), Marchant Pereira 122, ☎ 2746261. **Avis** (🚗), La Concepción 334, ☎ 493821. **Bert** (🚗), Bilbao 2032, ☎ 43736/ 2516477. **Bond** (🚗), Vitacura 2737, ☎ 2310867. **Bremen** (🚗), La Concepción 110, ☎ 2749215. **Budget** (🚗), Apoquindo 4900, ☎ 2460888. **Cars** (🚗), Av Apoquindo 4266, ☎ 2287161. **Classic** (🚗), Huérfanos 635 Of.22-A, ☎ 383035. **Cobra** (🚗), Moneda 625, ☎ 384764/ 3614. **Comercial** (🚗), LasCondes 13451, ☎ 2171086. **Coz** (🚗), Vitacura 6848, ☎ 2129497/ 2129342. **Chilean Renta a Car** (🚗), Bellavista 0150, ☎ 376902/ 9650. **Dollar** (🚗), Av Vitacura 5454, ☎ 2083305. **Eliseo** (🚗), Av Seminario 115, ☎ 2047700. **Eurorentacar** (🚗), Av F Bilbao 2245, ☎ 43853/ 462358. **Fargo** (🚗), Holanda 2291, ☎ 462347. **Federal** (🚗), Vitacura 3391. **First** (🚗), Av Andrés Bello 1429, ☎ 499019. **Galerías** (🚗), Padre Mariano 430, ☎ 2746325/ 497630. **Hertz** (🚗), Av Andrés Bello 1469, ☎ 2259328. **Juncal** (🚗), International Airport, ☎ 6019828. **L y S** (🚗), Agustinas 535, ☎ 337600. **Las Palmas** (🚗), Providencia 2653 Shop 9, ☎ 2327614/ 4132. **Lider** (🚗), Vitacura 2941, ☎ 2465030 / 5070. **National** (🚗), La Concepción 212 , ☎ 2517552. **Neder** (🚗), Bustamante 370, ☎ 2225680. **New Rent** (🚗), Av Ossa 2123, ☎ 2272378. **Quality** (🚗), Bilbao 2447, ☎ 092215062/40134. **Ren-tall** (🚗), La Castellana Sur 64, ☎ 2288037/ 3578. **Ski Total** (🚗), Apoquindo 4900 Of 32 32-33, ☎ 2460660/ 6881. **Tatersall** (🚗), Bilbao 1439, ☎ 2231079. **Transporte Los Cobres**

Tourist Services offered from SANTIAGO

TOURS

	Aku Aku — Agustinas 1022, Of. 227, ☎(02)69604 Tx 240184	Chilean Ravel — Agustinas 1291, Of. F, ☎(02)696283Tx 440084	Dicka Operadora — San Antonio 220, Of. 709, ☎(02)33040 Tx 340750	Festivalours — Alameda 949, Of. 603, ☎(02)69 Tx 3340966	Operadores Chile — gustinas 715, apart. 304, ☎(02) 3366557 Tx 645308	Viajes Koala — Agustinas 1182, Of. 702, ☎(02)73781 Tx 340664	Agencia Ragin — Moneda 1137, ☎(02)698704 Tx 340260	South Pacific Ex. — San Antonio 486, Of. 154, ☎(02)33913 Tx 280042	Turismo Cocha — Agustinas 1173, ☎(02)68334 Tx 441228	Las Tuninas Beach & W Resert — Luz 2926, ☎2327558/2327555
Arica, Lluta, Tacna, Chungara	●	●		TT ●			TT ●			
Iquique, Pica, Salitreras, Mamiña				○			○			
Antofagasta, Calama, San Pedro de Atacama		●		●	●	●	●		●	
Tatío Geyser				○						
Elqui Valley								Apr to Dec ●		
Easter Island	TT ●		●	●	●	●	●	TT ●		
Robinson Crusoe Island									TT ●	
Concepción					●					
The Southern Lakes		Nov to Mar ●	TT ●	○	○		○		TT ●	
The Southern Lakes, Valdivia, Puerto Montt, Ralún		Nov to Mar ●	TT ●		○	○	○		TT ●	
Cross Todos Los Santos lake, Peulla, Bariloche		Nov to Mar ●	TT ●	TT ●		TT ●			TT ●	
Puerto Montt, Chiloé	○		Mar to Dec ●	○		○	○		TT ●	
Southern Highway	Dec to Mar ●	Jan to Feb ●	Summer ●		●		○		Jan to Mar ●	○
Laguna San Rafael	Sep to Apr ●	Sep to Abr ●		Sep to Apr ●			Sep to Apr ●		Sep to Apr ●	
Punta Arenas, Torres del Paine		○			○		TT ●	Apr to Dec ●	○	
Hunting and Fishing in Patagonia	○					○	○		○	
Antártica							Oct to Mar ●			

(🚗 🚐 🚙), Vitacura 6848, ☎ 2241297. **Value** (🚗 🚐 🚙 🚌), Apoquindo 3118,☎ 2313176/ 2322476. **Western** (🚗 🚐 🚙 🚌 🚐), International Airport, ☎ 6019730.

SAN VICENTE DE TAGUA TAGUA (DDD 072)
Hs San Vicente , TT, Diego Portales 222, ☎ 571336, Res Santiago ☎ 339130/ 395334.

TERMAS DE CAUQUENES (DDD 072)
H Termas de Cauquenes, TT, ☎ 297226, Res Santiago ☎ 381610.

TERMAS DE JAHUEL (DDD 02)
H Termas de Jahuel, TT, Jahuel s/n, ☎ 511240, Res Santiago ☎ 383810, anexo 216.

TERMAS DEL CORAZON (DDD 034)
H Balneario Termal El Corazón, TT, ☎ 421371/ 422852, Res Santiago ☎ 2234010/ 39020.

VALLE NEVADO (DDD 02)
H Puerta del Sol, TS, ☎ 6980103. H Valle Nevado, TS, ☎ 6980103, Res Santiago ☎ (56-2)206007. Condominio Mirador del Inca, TS, ☎ 6980103.

6   CENTRAL COASTAL STRIP

Tourist Services offered from VIÑA DEL MAR
TOURS

	Hotel Tesidencia 555 Viña del Mar, 5 Norte 555 (032)663596	Ovalle Viajes Viña del Mar Hotel O'higgins (032)882095 Fx 883537	Trans. de Pasajeros Viña del Mar Diego Portales 325 (032)664459	Turiscoval Viña del Mar Arlegui 547, Of 207 (032)661101
City Tour Viña del Mar, Valparaíso	O	O	O	O
Viña del Mar, Algarrobo, Sto. Domingo		O		O
Viña del Mar, Zapallar Papudo		O	O	O
Portillo		O		

ALGARROBO (DDD 035)
H Del Pacífico, TT, Carlos Alessandri 1930, ☎ 481649 Res Santiago 2334037. H Internacional, TT, Carlos Alessandri 1038, ☎ 481145. H Uribe, TT, Pasaje El Teatro D, ☎ 481035, Res Santiago ☎ 2257728. BH Vera, TT, Carlos Alessandri 1521, ☎ 481131. BH Colonial, TT, Carlos Alessandri 1468.

CARTAGENA (DDD 035)
H La Bahía, TT, Av Playa Chica 190, ☎ 211246, Res Santiago ☎ 394434. Hs Lo Abarca, TT, Road to Lo Abarca s/n, Res San Antonio, ☎ 212028. H Playa, TT, Av Playa Chica 98, ☎ 213101. H Bellavista, TT, Ricardo Santa Cruz 216, ☎ 212873. H Reina del Mar, TT, Playa Chica 360. H Victoria, TT, Los Suspiros 281.

EL QUISCO (DDD 035)
Gran H Italia, TT, Av I Dubornais 413, ☎ 481161, Res Santiago ☎ 339192. H Chelita, TT, Av Italia 115, ☎ 481015. M Barlovento, TT, El Quisco 0520, ☎ 481030 M Costanera, TT, Costanera Sur 278. Cb Pozo Azul, TT, Capricornio 234. H La Playa, TT, Av I Dubornais 102. H Las Gaviotas, TT, Santa Juana 154. Hs Santa Elena, TAM, Av I Dubornais s/n, ☎ 233495. Cb Familiares, TT, Av I Dubornais 1044. Bh Oriental, TT, San Pedro 110. Bh La Marina, TT, José Narciso Aguirre 035. Bh Aurora, TT, Calle Del Mediodía 790.

EL TABO (DDD 035)
H El Tabo, TT, José Francisco 037, ☎ 212719. Hs Motel Montemar, TT, Carlos Monckeberg 406, ☎ 213204. H La Posada, TT, Av Errázuriz 719, ☎ 233520. H Bilbao, TT, San Marco 802, ☎ 213204. Cb Rocas de Córdova, TT, Road to Isla Negra Main highway, Res Santiago ☎ 5213612. Bh El Mar, TT, Av del Mar 1111.

HORCON
Habitaciones Arancibia, TT, Av Playa s/n, P O Box 282 of Valparaíso.

LA CALERA (DDD 033)
H Los Leones, TT, Prat 703 Fl 2° & 3°, ☎ 221927. H 21 de Mayo, TT, M Rodríguez 271, ☎ 222443.

LA CRUZ (DDD 033)
H Villa Capri, TT, 21 de Mayo 3799, ☎ 310624.

LAS CRUCES (DDD 035)
H Las Cruces, TT, Errázuriz 783, ☎ 212898. H Puesta de Sol, TT, Av La Playa 855, Res El Tabo ☎ 233520.

LIMACHE (DDD 033)
H Mónaco, TT, Ramón de la Cerda 14, ☎ 411441.

LLOLLEO (DDD 035)
H Alhambra, TT, Providencia 095, ☎ 31935. H Oriente, TT, Inmaculada Concepción 50, ☎ 232188.

MAITENCILLO
Motel Cerro Colorado, TT, Camino Antiguo s/n (Copec), Res Santiago ☎ 2257291. H Las Rocas, TA, Av Del Mar 1685, ☎ 930802.

OLMUE (DDD 033)
Hs El Copihue, TT, Portales 2203, ☎ 441544. H Los Acacios, TT, Av Eastman 2784, ☎ 441652. Hs Llacolén, TT, Diego Portales 1879, ☎ 441978. H y Cb Las Montañas de Olmué, TA, Granizo Alto, Bus Stop 43, ☎ 441253, Res Santiago ☎ 2250923. H Scala de Milán, TT, Prat 5058, ☎ 441414. Hs Las Hamacas, TT, Av Granizo, Bus Stop 34, ☎ 441515.

PAPUDO (DDD 033)
H Moderno, TT, Fernández Concha 150, ☎ 711496. M D'Peppino, TT, Fernández Concha 609, ☎ 711482. H Carande, TT, Chorrillos 89, ☎ 711380. H Restaurante La Abeja, TT, Chorrillos 36, ☎ 711450. H Residencial El Golf, TT, Fernández Concha 415. H Mocelli, TT, Chorrillos 10. BH Valencia, TA, Chorrillos 107 y 149, P.O. Box 19. BH El Golf, TT, Fernández Concha 415. Bh Donde Tito, TT, Fernández Concha 530. Bh Papudo, TT, Fernández Concha 512, ☎ 711482. Bh La Plaza, TT, Chorrillos 119. Bh Bogarin, TT, Cochrane 184.

QUINTERO (DDD 032)
H Yachting Club, TT, Luis Acevedo 1736, ☎ 930061. H and Restaurante Isla de Capri, TT, 21 de Mayo 1299, ☎ 930117. H Mónaco, TT, 21 de Mayo 1530, ☎ 930939. H California, TT, Alonso de Quintero 463, ☎ 930176. H El Refugio, TT, Av Francia 1130, ☎ 930146. Bh Casa de Piedra, TT, Luis Cousiño 2076, ☎ 930196. Bh La Moderna, TT, Luis Cousiño 1781, ☎ 930110. Bh Panamericano, TT, 21 de Mayo 1020, ☎ 930261. Bh Ferry Boat, TA, Av Plaza 1264, ☎ 930305. Bh Sta Elena, TT, Federico Albert 89, ☎ 930170. Bh María Alejandra, TT, Lord Cochrane 157, ☎ 930266. Bh San Víctor, TT, Luis Cousiño 1929.

ROCAS DE SANTO DOMINGO (DDD 035)
Motel Piedras del Sol, TT, Pacífico 010, ☎ 233011, Res Santiago ☎ 2324826. Club H Las Rocas, TT, La Ronda 130, ☎ 231348.

SAN ANTONIO (DDD 035)
H Casablanca, TT, Leoncio Tagle 58, ☎ 212434, Res Santiago ☎ 2238460. H Jockey Club, TT, Av 21 de Mayo 204, ☎ 211777. Cb Undumar, TT, 21 de Mayo 550, ☎ 211908, Res Santiago ☎ 2084835. H América, TT, Av Centenario 330, ☎ 211676.

SAN SEBASTIAN (DDD 035)
H Riviera, TT, Av El Peral 294, ☎ 212443. H Villa San Sebastián, TT, 1ra Oriente Playa 390, ☎ 233748.

VALPARAISO (DDD 032)
H Prat, TT, Condell 1443, ☎ 253081. H Condell, TT, Pirámide 557, ☎ 212788. H Lancaster, TT, Chacabuco 2362, ☎ 217391.

VILLA ALEMANA (DDD 032)
H Central, TT, Av Valparaíso 791, ☎ 952251. H Fersen, TT, Latorre 192, ☎ 952064.

VALPARAISO - LAGUNA VERDE (DDD 032)
Hs El Tilo, TT, Domingo Otaegui s/n. Hs Los Monjes, TT, Parcela N° 4. M Las Docas Fundo El Chaparral, TT, Laguna Verde s/n, Res Santiago ☎ 2461981/71.

VENTANAS
H Los Leones, TT, Pedro Aldunate s/n.

VIÑA DEL MAR Downtown (DDD 032)
Accommodations
H Miramar, TT, Caleta Abarca s/n, ☎ 626677, Res Santiago ☎ 6966826. H O'Higgins, TT, Plaza Vergara s/n, ☎ 882016,Res Santiago ☎ 6966826. H Alcázar, TT, Alvarez 646, ☎ 685112, Res Santiago ☎ 2517350. H San Martín, TT, Av San Martín Corner of 8 Norte, ☎ 689191. H Restaurante Cap Ducal, TT, Av Marina 51, ☎ 626655, Res Santiago ☎ 380975. H Von Schroeders, TT, Von Schroeders 392, ☎ 626022. H de Viña, TT, Viana 619, ☎ 685546. H José Francisco Vergara, TT, Von Schroeders 367, ☎ 626023. H Español, TT, Plaza Vergara 191, ☎ 685145. M Terrazas Inn Sausalito, TT, Granadilla s/n, ☎ 971920. H Hostal Chacras de Coria, TT, 7 Norte 669, ☎ 901419. H Hispano, TT, Plaza Parroquia 391, ☎ 685860. H Hostal, TT, Av Valparaíso 299, ☎ 882124. H Alborada del Mar, TT, San Martín 419, ☎ 975274. H Castellón, TT, Viana 135, ☎ 977019. H Casablanca, TT, Alvarez 282, ☎ 663243. H San Marino, TT, Av Valparaíso 107, ☎ 976771. Apart H Valladolid, TT, 2 Norte 135, ☎ 973887. Apart H Sahara, TT, Alberto Blest Gana 397, ☎ 685161. H Kumei, TT, Av Valparaíso 121, ☎ 901413. Hostal El Borrico, TT, 3 Poniente 579, ☎ 970617/ 978936. H Castelar, TT, Traslaviña 279, ☎ 684368. H Monterilla, TT, 2 Norte 65, ☎ 976950. H Alejandra, TT, 2 Poniente 440, ☎ 974404. H Rondó, TT, Errázuriz 690, ☎ 685073. H Viana, TT, Viana 645, ☎ 684877. H Europa, TT, Alvarez 282, ☎ 663243. Bh Las Condes, TT, 5 Norte 39, ☎ 975562. Bh Montaña, TT, Agua Santa 153. Bh Blanchait, TT, Valparaíso 82-A, ☎ 974949. Bh Palace, TT, Paseo Valle 387, ☎ 663134. Bh San Martín, TT, Av San Martín 304, ☎ 975440. Bh Miramar, TT, Agua Santa 80, ☎ 625608. Bh Patricia, TT, Agua Santa 48, ☎ 663825. Bh Magallanes, TT, Arlegui 555, ☎ 685101. Bh Oxaran, TT, Villanelo 136, ☎ 882360. Bh Verónica, TT, Von Schroeders 104, ☎ 976580. BH El Carmen, TT, Valparaíso 28, ☎ 977310. Bh Victoria, TT, Valparaíso 40, ☎ 977370. Bh Edhison, TT, Montaña 890, ☎ 680756. Bh Caribe, TT, Von Schroeders 46, ☎ 976191. Bh Villarrica, TT, Arlegui 172.

Car Rental
Aste (🚗), Av Libertad 1323 y en Av Francia 340, ☎ 972035. Bert (🚗 🏍), Av Alvarez 762, ☎ 685515. Cars (🚗 🚐), Bohn 837, ☎ 684994. Cartoni (🚗), 1 Norte 741, ☎ 689239. Euro (🚗 🚐 🚚), ☎ 626677. Kovacs (🚗 🚐), Av Jorge Montt 2300, ☎ 971580. Mach Viña (🚗), San Antonio 1065, ☎ 978230.

Cars with Chauffeur
(coastal pleasure trip North and South of Valparaíso). Taxi Turismo, Notro 3689, ☎ 882016.

VIÑA DEL MAR Reñaca (DDD 032)
Accommodations
H Oceanic, TT, Av Borgoño 12925, ☎ 830006/ 830390. Holiday Motels, TT, Angamos 367, ☎ 832822/ 902535, Res Santiago ☎ 2517350. M del Pacífico, TT, Angamos 207, ☎ 833334. M Nilahue, TT, Av Borgoño 14920, ☎ 831677. M Amancay, TT, Balmaceda 455, ☎ 902643. M Los Ositos, TT, Av Borgoño 14650, ☎ 831549. M Presidente, TT, Sotomayor corner of Condell s/n, ☎ 832958/ 902327. Cb La Muerte, TT, Santa Luisa 1371, ☎ 902619, Res Santiago ☎ 2311175. M Safari, TT, B Arana 154, ☎ 833462. M Iguazú, TT, Calle Central corner of Segunda, ☎ 833086. M Brisas de Reñaca, TT, Las Brisas 50, ☎ 902651.

VIÑA DEL MAR Con-Con (DDD 032)
Accommodations
H Playa Amarilla, TT, Av Labarca 6, ☎ 903891/ 811915. Cb Do Brasil, TT, Los Quillayes 1155 Bathing resort Los Romeros, ☎ 811631. M Las Gaviotas, TA, Av Marotto 1409, ☎ 812274.

ZAPALLAR (DDD 033)
H César, TT Olegario Ovalle 345, ☎ 711313. Motel Aguas Claras, TT, Av Zapallar 125, Res Santiago ☎ 6960491/ 6966136.

---

7 THE PACIFIC ISLAND

EASTER ISLAND (LD 108)
Hs Hanga Roa, TT, Av Pont s/n, ☎ 299, Res Stgo ☎ 395334. H Hotu Matu'a, TT, Av Pont s/n, ☎ 242, Res Lan Chile Offices. H Victoria, Av Polikarpo Toro s/n, ☎ 272. H Iorana, TT, Ana Mangaro s/n, ☎ 312, Res Stgo ☎ 332650. H Otaí, TT, Pito Te Henua, ☎ 250. H Chez Joseph, TT, Anareipúa s/n,

JUAN FERNANDEZ ISLAND
Hs El Pangal, TT, El Pangal Area, Res Stgo ☎ 2734354/ 309. H Aldea Daniel Defoe, TT, Daniel Defoe 449. Hs Villa Green, Larraín Alcalde 246 (Cumberland Bay), Res Santiago ☎ 5313772.

---

8 SAN FERNANDO TO SAN CARLOS

TALCA
Tourist Services

TOURS	Vehicle	Season	Duration	Ikarus Talca,1 Poniente 1141 ☎ (071)226150	Taxis Azules Talca,1 Poniente 1060. Of. 53 ☎ (071)221100
City Tour Talca	🚐	TT	6 h	O	O
Constitución and Beaches	🚐	TT	1day	O	O
Gil de Vilches Park (Natural Monument)	🐎	TA	3day	O	
Parque Inglés Radal Siete Tazas	🚐	TA	1day	O	

BUCALEMU
H Rocha, TT, Av Celedonio Pastenes s/n, ☎ 821942 messenger Res San Fernando ☎ 712023.

CAUQUENES (DDD 073)
H Maule, TT, Antonio Varas 545, ☎ 511637.

CONSTITUCION (DDD 071)
Accommodations
H B Encalada, TT, Av Enrique Mac Iver s/n, ☎ 671222. Hs Constitución, TT, Etcheverría 460, ☎ 671480/ 450. Bh Chepita, TT, Freire 160. Bh Ramírez, TT, Freire 292, ☎ 671233.

COASTLINE FROM PELLUHUE TO COBQUECURA
Hs y M Caleta Blanca, TA, Pelluhue, fish market Caleta Blanca, ☎ 591902 messenger. BH Embrujo del Mar, TT, Curanipe, Comercio 420, ☎ 591903 messenger. Cb Rucamar, TA, Cobquecura, Chacabuco 960, ☎ 492230 menssenger.

CURICO (DDD 075)
H Comercio, 3★, TT, Yungay 730, ☎ 310014/ 311516. H LC Martínez, TT, Prat corner of Cármen, ☎ 310552. H Prat, TT, Peña 427, ☎ 311069.

HUALAÑE (LD 108)
Hs Hualañe, TT, Arturo Prat 421, ☎ 481001.

ILOCA
H Iloca 2★, TA, Iloca, Agustín Besoain 221. H Curicó, TA, Iloca, Agustín Besoain 264.

DUAO
Hs Donde Gilberto, TT, Duao, Av Principal s/n. Hs Donde Nino, TT, Duao, Av Principal s/n.

LAGO COLBUN
H Casas El Colorado, TA, Res Talca ☎ 227977. M La Marina del Lago, TT, coast of Lake Colbún.

LAGO VICHUQUEN (DDD 075)
Accommodations
Hs Brujas del Lago, TM, Llico, Punta del Barco, Res Santiago ☎ 2318054. Hs Llico, TT, Llico, Ignacio Carrera Pinto s/n. M Rincón Suizo, TA, Paula Area, ☎ 400012, Res Curicó ☎ 310070.

LINARES (DDD 073)
H Turismo Linares, TT, Manuel Rodriguez 522, ☎ 210636/ 210637.

LOS QUEÑES
Hs Los Queñes, TT, Los Queñes, ☎ 967.

PAN-AMERICAN HIGHWAY (DDD 073)
M y Hs Málaga 4★, TT, Pan-American Highway in the Linares junction, ☎ 211129. Hs and H Alondra, TT, Pan-American Highway near the Villa Alegre junction, Res Linares ☎ 211118. M Sol de Alicante, TT, Pan-American highway 5 kms south of Talca, ☎ 631033 Maule. Res Santiago ☎ 2318989. Chillán 214503.

PANIMAVIDA (LD 108)
H Termas de Panimávida, TT, Res Linares ☎ 211743, Res Santiago ☎ 393911.

PARQUE INGLES
Hs Flor de la Canela, TA, Parque Inglés (Radal), Res Molina ☎ 491613.

PARRAL (DDD 073)
H Brescia, TT, Igualdad 195, ☎ 461675.

PICHILEMU (DDD 074)
H Asthur, TT, Av Ortúzar 540, ☎ Fax 681072, Res Santiago 6722727/ 6983295. H Bar Rex, TT, Av Ortúzar 34, ☎ 681003.M Complejo Turístico Las Terrazas, TT, Av La Marina 201, ☎ 681049. H España, TA, Av Ortúzar 38, Rancagua ☎ 224806. Gran H Ross, TT, Agustín Ross 136, ☎ 681038. M Las Cabañas, TT, San Antonio 48, ☎ 681068. H O'Higgins, TT, Ortúzar 210, ☎ 681099. Bh Antumalal, TT, Joaquín Aguirre 64, ☎ 681004. BH Comercio, TT, Arturo Prat 33. Bh Diego Portales, TA, Dionisio Acevedo 188, ☎ 681089, Res Santiago ☎ 2263190. Bh Galaz, TA, Carrera 125, ☎ 681025. Bh Gonzalez, TT, Aníbal Pinto 48, ☎ 681087. BH Mi Rancho, TA, Los Carrera 177. Bh Montecarlo, TM / TA, Aníbal Pinto 110, ☎ 681027. Bh Oróstica, TT, Dionisio

Acevedo 520. Bh San Luis, TT, Angel Gaete 27, ☎ 681040. Bh Victoria, TT, Joa-quín Aguirre 139, P O Box 24.

QUINAMAVIDA
H Termas de Quinamávida, TM, P O Box 60 of Linares.

SAN FERNANDO (DDD 074)
H Español, TT, Manuel Rodriguez 959, ☎ 711098. H Imperio, TT, Manuel Rodriguez 770, ☎ 714595. H Marcano, TT, Manuel Rodriguez 968, ☎ 714759.

SANTA CRUZ (DDD 074)
H Plaza, TT, Plaza de Armas 286, ☎ 821545.

TALCA (DDD 071)
Accommodations
H Marcos Gamero 4★, TT, 1 Oriente 1070, ☎ 223388/ 223100. H Plaza 4★, TT, 1 Poniente 1141, ☎ 226150. H Napoli 3★, TT, Av 2 Sur 1314, ☎ 227373/ 226010. H Amalfi 2★, TT, Dos Sur 1265, ☎ 225703/ 233389. H Casagrande, TT, Uno Sur 642, ☎ 221977/ 72.

Car Rental
American (🚗 🚙 🚐),2 Sur 917, ☎ 221425. Comercial Lago Colbún (🚗 🚙 🚙), 1 Norte 1518.

TERMAS DE CATILLO
H Termas de Catillo, TM, ☎ 461420, Res Concepción ☎ 225510.

TERMAS DEL FLACO (DDD 074)
Hs El Rancho, TA, Termas del Flaco, ☎ 711832, Res Santiago ☎ 382257. H Cb Las Vegas, TA, Termas del Flaco s/n.

---

9   CONCEPCION AND SOUTH OF THE BIOBIO

CONCEPCION

Tourist Services Turismo Ritz Concepción,Barros Arana 721 ☎ (041)237637	Vehicle	Season	Duration
City Tour Concepción	🚗🚐	TT	4 h
City Tour Talcahuano and Visit to "Monitor Huáscar"	🚗🚐	TT	6 h
Penco, Tomé, Lirquén, Dichato	🚗🚐	TT	1 day
San Pedro Lagoon,Coronel, Lota, Lota Park	🚗🚐	TT	1 day

ANGOL (DDD 045)
H Millaray, TT, Arturo Prat 420, ☎ 711570. H Olympia, TT, Lautaro 194, ☎ 711517.

ANTUCO (LD 108)
Cb Aitué, TT, near the town, ☎ 10.

ARAUCO (DDD 046)
H Plaza, TT, Chacabuco 347, ☎ 551265.

CAÑETE (DDD 046)
H Alonso de Ercilla 4★, TT, Villagrán 641, ☎ 611974. H Comercio, TT, Séptimo de Línea 817, ☎ 611218. Club Social, TT, Condell 283, ☎ 611244. H Derby, TT, Mariñán corner of Condell, ☎ 611960. H Nahuelbuta, TT, Villagrán 644, ☎ 611073. H Vips, TT, General Bonilla s/n, ☎ 611012.

COLLIPULLI
H Savoy, TT, General Cruz 35, ☎ 38.

CONCEPCION (DDD 041)
Accommodations
H Alborada 4★, TT, Barros Arana 457, ☎ 240844, FL O Box 176. H Alonso de Ercilla 3★, TT, Colo Colo 334, ☎ 227984. H El Dorado 3★, TT, Barros Arana 348, ☎ 229400. H Ritz 2★, TT, Barros Arana 721, ☎ 226696. H El Araucano, TT, Caupolicán 521, ☎ 230606, Res Santiago ☎ 6965599. Cecil H, TT, Barros Arana 9, ☎ 230677/ 226603. H Concepción, TT, Los Carrera 1535, ☎ 233271. H Cruz del Sur, TT, Freire 889, ☎ 230944/ 235655. H Tabancura, TT, Barros Arana 786, ☎ 238348/ 49/ 50. Bh de Turismo BR Ltda, TT, Maipú 1587. Bh San Sebastián, TT, Barros Arana 741 Dpto 34/ 35.

Car Rental
Larma (🚗), Av L B O'Higgins 320,☎ 223031. First (🚗 🚙 🚙) Cochrane 862, ☎ 223121 Western

(🚗 🚙 🚐), Av L B O'Higgins 115, ☎ 238474. Renta Anta (🚗 🚙 🚐), Barros Arana 137.

CONTULMO (LD 108)
H Central, TT, Millaray 131, ☎ 611903 messenger. Nuevo H Contulmo, TT, Millaray 116, ☎ 611903 messenger.

CURACAUTIN
M Turismo, TT, Tarapacá 14, ☎ 116. H Plaza, TT, Yungay 157, ☎ 56. Pos Real, TT, Calama 240, ☎ 164.

CHILLAN (DDD 042)
Accommodations
H Claris, TT, 18 de Septiembre 357, ☎ 221980. H Cordillera, TT, Arauco 619, ☎ 215211. H El Americano, TT, Carrera 481, ☎ 221175. H Floresta, TT, 18 de Septiembre 278, ☎ 222253. Gran H Isabel Riquelme, TT, Constitución 576, ☎ 213663, Res Santiago ☎ 2515776. Hs Las Encinas, TT, northern approach Chillán, ☎ 222075. H Libertador, TT, Av Libertad 85, ☎ 223255. H Los Cardenales, TT, Bulnes 34, ☎ 224251. H Martín Ruiz de Gamboa, TT, Av Lib B O'Higgins 497, ☎ 221013. H Quinchamalí, TT, El Roble 634, ☎ 223381. H Real, TT, Av Libertad 219, ☎ 221827. H Regional, TT, Av Brasil 451, ☎ 222414. H Rucamanqui, TT, Herminda Martín 590, ☎ 222927/ 704. H Santiago, TT, Av Libertad 61, ☎ 222068 .

Car Rental
Firt (🚗), 18 de Septiembre 380, ☎ 221218.

DICHATO (DDD 041)
Cb Asturias, TT, Pedro Aguirre Cerda 734, ☎ 681000. H Costanera, TT, Pedro Aguirre Cerda 710, ☎ 681000. H Chiki, TA, Pedro León Ugalde 410, ☎ 681004. M El Kalifa, TT, Daniel Vera 815, ☎ 681027. H Montecarlo, TT, Pedro Aguirre Cerda 655. H Schamaruk, TT, Av Daniel Vera 912, ☎ 681022

LAGO LANALHUE
Hs Lanalhue, TA, west shore, Res Concepción ☎ 234981, Res Chillán ☎ 213663, Res Santiago ☎ 2512685. H Posada Campesina Alemana, TA, south shore, ☎ 611903 messenger Contulmo, Res Contulmo Comercio 135.

LAGUNA DEL LAJA
Cb and Cg Lagunillas, TT, Res Los Angeles ☎ 323606. Refugio Digeder, TT, Res Talca ☎ 226700, en Concepción ☎ 229054.

LARAQUETE (LD 108)
Hs La Quinta, TT, Gabriela Mistral s/n, ☎ 571951 messenger. H Laraquete, TT, Gabriela Mistral s/n, ☎ 571951 messenger. Hs Piedra Cruz, TT, Gabriela Mistral 555. H Sol y Sombra, TT, Costanera Area, Res Concepción ☎ 371901.

LEBU (DDD 046)
H Central, TT, Pérez 183, ☎ 511904. Gran H, TT, Pérez 309, ☎ 511939.

LOS ALAMOS
Hs Caramávida, TT, P O Box 140 Cañete.

LOS ANGELES (DDD 043)
Accommodations
Gran H Müso 3★, TT, Valdivia 222, ☎ 323163. H Mariscal Alcázar 3★, TT, Lautaro 385, ☎ 321275. H Mazzola 1 ★, TT, Lautaro 579, ☎ 311725. M Mayorca, TT, Pan-American highway, northern approach, ☎ 322340. M Monserrat, TT, on Pan-American highway, crossroads to central access, ☎ 311972.
Car Rental
First (🚙 🚗 🚐 🚚 🚙),Caupolicán 350, ☎ 313812.

LOS LLEUQUES - LAS TRANCAS
Cb Pacha Pulay, TT, Las Trancas, Res Viña del Mar ☎ 884310. Motel Villa Laja, TT, Los Lleuques, Javier Jarpa Sotomayor s/n, ☎ 492143 messenger.

PENCO (DDD 041)
H La Terraza, TT, Penco 20, ☎ 451422.

PUREN
Tur H, TT, Dr Garriga 912, ☎ 22.

QUILLON
Apart H Península de Quillón, TT, Libertad 279 at Chillán, ☎ 221078, Res Santiago ☎ 2317200, at Concepción ☎ 229087. Cg Cb La Playa, TAM, Res Concepción ☎ 225753.

RECINTO (LD 108)
H El Nevado, TT, Los Olmos s/n, ☎ 492183 messenger. Hs Turismo Cordillera y La Posada, TT, Res Chillán ☎ 221306.

SALTO DEL LAJA (LD 108)
Hs M Curanadu, TT, 4 km south of the waterfall ☎ 312686.

Hs and M EL Pinar, TT, 2 km south of the waterfall, ☎ 2. M Los Manantiales del Laja, TT, Res Los Angeles ☎ 323606. H Parque Salto del Laja, TT, P O Box 513 Los Angeles. H and Hs Salto del Laja, TT, ☎. 321706.

TALCAHUANO (DDD 041)
H France, TT, Aníbal Pinto 44, ☎ 542230.

TERMAS DE CHILLAN
H Parador Jamón, Pan y Vino, TAS, a 9 km of the hot sprins, Res Chillán ☎ 222682. H Termas de Chillán, TT, Res Chillán ☎ 223887, at Santiago ☎ 2515776.

TERMAS DE MANZANAR (LD 108)
Hs Abarzúa, FL O Box 70 Curacautín, ☎ 1x2 messenger Manzanar. H Termas de Manzanar 1★, TT, P O Box 38 Curacautín, ☎ 1x3 Manzanar.

TERMAS DE TOLHUACA (LD 108)
H Termas de Tolhuaca, TMA, ☎ 164 Curacautín, P O Box 48 Curacautín.

TOME (DDD 041)
H Linares, TT, Ignacio Serrano 875, ☎ 651284. Hs Villa Marina, TA, Sotomayor 669, ☎ 650807. Bh La Casona, TT, El Morro Beach, Baquedano 475.

TRAIGUEN (DDD 045)
H Traiguén, TT, Saavedra 467, ☎ 861412.

VICTORIA (DDD 045)
H EL Bosque, TT, Pan-American Highway junction, ☎ 841960. Hs y M El Bosque, TT, Pan-American Highway junction, ☎ 841960. Hs y M Mackray, TT, Pan-American Highway junction, ☎ 841565 Victoria.

VOLCAN LONQUIMAY
Hs Refugio Volcán Lonquimay, TT.

---

10   TEMUCO TO VALDIVIA

VALDIVIA Y SIETE LAGOS
Tourist Services

TOURS BY LAND AND BY RIVER	Vehicle	Season	Duration	Turismo Cono Sur Valdivia, Maipu 129 ☎(063)212757	Motonave Calle Calle Valdivia, Av Prat s/n ☎(063)215889/ 213235	Motonave Neptuno Valdivia, Av Prat s/n ☎(063)215889	Rio Tour Valdivia, Gral Bueras 1180 ☎(063)216037	Lancha Ainlebu Valdivia, Av Prat s/n ☎(063)215889	Aventuras Lonquimay Lican Ray, Gral Urrutia 301	Excursiones Tio Pedro Lican Ray, Gral Urrutia 450
City Tour Valdivia	🚗🚐	TT	4 h	●						
River Excursions Teja del Rey, Mancera Islans	🚤	TT	6 h	○			●	●		
Tour by Calle Calle River and return to Tesa Island	🚤	TT	4 h				●	●		
River Excursions to Teja, del Rey, Mancera Islans, Corral Ports and Niebla	🚤	TT	1 day		●	●	●			
Lake Ranco, Futrono, Llifén	🚗🚐	TT	1 day	○						
Lake Panguipulli, Lake Riñihue, Choshuenco Volcano	🐎🚗	Oct to Mar	2 day	○						
Liquiñe Hot Springs	🚗	TAM	1 day, 2 day	○						○
Horse Excursions to Quetrupillán Volcano	🐎🚗	TAM	2 day	○					○	○

CUNCO
Hs Camino Real, TT, Cunco, Sta María 753.

LAGO PANGUIPULLI (DDD 0633)
Hs Pulmahue, TA, Choshuenco, Res P O Box 545 Panguipulli. Hs Quetropillán, TT, Panguipulli, Etchegaray 381, ☎ 348.

LAGO RIÑIHUE (DDD 0633)
M Centro Turístico Huinca Quiñay 4★, TT, Res Los Lagos ☎ 337/ 228 , Res Santiago ☎ 6983341. H Riñi mapu, TA, ☎ 388, Res Santiago ☎ 6990559. M Vista Hermosa 3★, TA,

P O Box 565 de Panguipulli, Res Panguipulli ☎ 216.

LAGO VILLARRICA (shore) (DDD 045)
M Curiñanco, TT,☎411205, Res Santiago ☎ 2287417. H El Parque-M Lonquen, TT, ☎ 411120, Res Temuco ☎ 212999/ 3119. M y Cg Lorena, TT, ☎ 411940, Res Temuco ☎214957. M Los Boldos 4★, TT, ☎ 411656. H Marina Tatalafquen, TA, Res Santiago ☎ 2321787, en Temuco ☎ 212638. Cb Misimalí, TT, Pucón ☎ 441959. M Tunquelen, TT, ☎ 411955, Res Santiago ☎ 2125073. Cb Suyay, TMA, P O Box 47 Villarrica, ☎ 411956.

LAGO PIREHUEICO
Barcaza Mariela, Res Panguipulli ☎ (0633) 348.

LAGUNA CONGUILLIO
Cb Parque Nacional Conguillio, TA.

LICAN RAY (LD 108)
Accommodations
Cb Duhatao, TA, Millañanco 8, Res Temuco ☎ 212358. M El Canelo, TA, Machi Cañicul 30. Cb El Conquistador, TA, Loteo Trapel s/n, Res Santiago ☎ 331542. Cb Foresta, TT, P O Box 1014, Res Temuco ☎ 211954. Cb Köhler, TA, P O Box 609, Res Santiago ☎ 2229876. Cb Licanray, TA, Gral Urrutia 135, Res Valdivia ☎ 212288. Cb Quimelafquen, TT, Res Santiago ☎ 2243135. H Refugio, TT, Punulef 510, ☎ 1 messenger. Cb Rucamac, TT, Las Araucarias 025, Res Santiago ☎ 2733950. H Rucalafquen, TA, Cacique Punulef 240. Hs Victor's Playa, TA, Cacique Punulef 120, Res Temuco ☎ 247335.

LONCOCHE (DDD 045)
Motel Lolorruca, TT, Pan-American highway 4 km south of Loncoche, P O Box 56, ☎ 471065/ 26/13. Cb Loncoche, TT, Pan-American highway in the Loncoche junction, P O Box 88.

LOS LAURELES (DDD 045)
HM Trailanqui, TT, ☎ 578218, Res Temuco ☎ 214915.

MEHUIN-QUEULE (DDD 06345)
H Mehuín, TT, Acharan Arce s/n. Hs Pichicuyin Beach, TA, Pichicuyin beach, Post Office Mehuín. Hs Millalafquen, TT, Mehuín, ☎ 279, P O Box 1. Hs Nuria, TT, Queule, Jerónimo Martinez s/n. H Playa Mehuín, TT, Carlos Acharan Arce s/n, ☎ 254.

MELIPEUCO
Hs y Cb Hue-Telen 3★, TT, Melipeuco, Pedro Aguirre Cerda 1, ☎ 1x2 (messenger).

NIEBLA
Hs El Paraíso, TT, Bathing resort Los Molinos. Hs Rucantu, TT, Antonio Duce 798. Hs Villa Sta Clara, TT, Res Valdivia ☎ 212213. .

PUCON (DDD 045)
Accommodations
Cb El Dorado 4★, TT, Av. Bdo O'Higgins 1640, ☎ 441122,

Res Temuco, ☎ 213699/ 2718. H Araucarias 3★ , TM, Caupolicán 243, ☎ 441286, Res Santiago ☎ 2517350. H Antumalal, TT, P O Box 84, ☎ 441011. Hs Don Pepe, TT, Gral Urrutia 592, ☎ 441081. Hs El Principito, TT, Gral Urrutia 291, ☎ 441200. Gran H Pucón, TT, Clemente Holtzapfel 190, ☎ 441001/ 2/ 3, Res Santiago ☎ 2326008. H Gudenschwager, TAS, Pedro de Valdivia 12, ☎ 441156. H Interlaken, TM, Caupolicán s/n, ☎ 441276, Res Santiago ☎ 6963634. H La Posada, TAS, Pedro de Valdivia 191, ☎ 441088, Res Santiago ☎ 5518141. Cabinas Lenumantu, TT, Lincoyán 235, ☎ 441106. Cb Mapulay, TT, B O'Higgins 755, ☎ 441948, Res Santiago ☎ 2084394. Hs Milla-Rahue, TT, B O'Higgins 460, ☎ 441904. Hs Salzburg, TA, Av L Bdo O'Higgins 311, ☎ 441907. Hs Suiza, TA, Caupolicán 355, ☎ 441945, Res Santiago ☎ 2517350.
Car Rental
Hertz (🚗 🚙 🚐 🚚), Fresia 224, ☎ 441052, at Temuco Res ☎ 235385.

PUERTO SAAVEDRA
Hs Maule, TT, Res Temuco ☎ 244650.

SAN JOSE DE LA MARIQUINA
Casa de Reposo, TT, Av Gustavos Exss 102, ☎ 214.

TEMUCO (DDD 045)
Accommodations
H Bayern 3★, TT, Prat 146, ☎ 213915. H Nicolas 3★, TT, Gral Mackenna 420, ☎ 210020, Res Santiago ☎ 2517350. H Aitue 1★, TT, A. Varas 1048, ☎ 211917/ 948. H Turismo 1 ★, TT, Claro Solar 636, ☎ 210583. H Continental, TT, Antonio Varas 708, ☎ 238973/ 211395. Complejo Isla Verde, TT, Pan-American highway 9 km from Temuco, ☎ 371008, P O Box 854 Temuco. H de La Frontera, M Bulnes 733, ☎ 212638, Res Santiago ☎ 2326008/ 21787. H Emperador, TT, Bulnes 853, ☎ 213409. H Espelette, TT, Claro Solar 492, ☎ 211923. Nuevo H de La Frontera, TT, M Bulnes, 726, ☎ 212638.
Car Rental
Automóvil Club (🚗 🚙 🚐 🚚) MB Bulnes 763, ☎210098. Avis (🚗 🚙 🚐), A Prat corner of Andres Bello . Dollar (🚗 🚙 🚐), FL. Lynch/ Portales and Rodriguez. Firt(🚗 🚙 🚐), Bulnes 750, ☎233890. Hertz (🚗 🚙 🚐), Bulnes 750, ☎ 235385. Lagos del Sur (🚗 🚙 🚐), Gral Mackenna 430. Puig (🚗 🚙 🚐)

TEMUCO, VILLARRICA, PUCON — Tourist Services

TOURS	Vehicle	Season	Duration	International Tours (Temuco, Prat 427, ☎(055)212745 Tx367007)	Peskitour (Villarrica, V Letelier 650, ☎(045)411385 / 411940)	Transp. Turísticos (Villarrica, Pedro Montt 365, ☎(045)411078)	Turismo Sol y Nieve (Pucón O'Higgins with Lincoyán, Gran Hotel Pucón)	Servitour (Pucón, Palguín 361, ☎(045)441296)	Turismo Grado Diez (Pucón, Av B O'Higgins 371, ☎(045) 441113)	Altué Expediciones (Pucón, Av B O'Higgins 371, ☎(045)441113)
City Tour Temuco	🚐	TT	3 h	●						
City Tour Pucón and Villarrica	🚐	TT	8 h	●						
Conguillio National Park	🚐	TT	1 day	Mon & Fri ●						
Pucón, Lake Villarrica and Villarrica Volcano	🚐	TT	2 day	Wed & Sat ●						
Lake Caburgua, Ojos del Caburgua and Herquehue National Park	🚐	Sep to Mar	1 day			●	○			
Lake Caburgua and Ojos del Caburgua	🚐	TT	1/2d, 1 day	○			●	●	○	
Termas de Huife Termas de Palguín	🚐	TT	1 day	●	●		●	●	●	
Climbing the Villarrica Volcano	🚐	Dec to Feb	1 day		○	○	●	○	●	●
Around Villarica Volcano and tours into the Mountain Range	🐎🚐	Sep to Mar	1 day				○		●	○
Rafting down Liucura and Trancura rivers	🚣🚐	Sep to Mar	8 h	○						
Mouth Budi, Lake Budi	🚐	Dec to Feb	1 day					○	○	●
Fishing Excursion on Rivers and Lakes	🚣🚐	Nov to Apr	4 h		○	○				

D.Por tales corner of Vicuña Mackenna, ☎ 211513. **Western**, (🚗 🚗 🚙), M Montt 407, ☎ 210728.

TERMAS DE HUIFE (DDD 045)
H Termas de Huife, TT, P O Box 18 of Pucón, ☎ 441222, Res Pucón 441962.

TERMAS DE LIQUIÑE
H Termas de Liquiñe, TT, P O Box 202 Liquiñe.

TERMAS DE MENETUE
Cb de Menetué, Res Viña del Mar ☎ 973322.

TERMAS DE PALGUIN
H Termas de Palguín 1★, TT, P O Box 1-D of Pucón, Res Temuco ☎ 233021.

TERMAS DE SAN LUIS
H Termas de San Luis, P O Box 80 Pucón.

VALDIVIA (DDD 063)
Accommodations
H Pedro de Valdivia, 4★ TT, Carampagne 190, ☎ 212931/ 212933, Res Santiago ☎ 6981432. **H Villa de Río** 4★, TT, Av Ramón 1025, ☎ 216293, Res Santiago ☎ 2517350. **H Naguilan** 3★, TT, Gral Lagos 1927, ☎ 212851/ 52. **H Raitue** 3★, TT, Gral Lagos 1382, ☎ 212503. **H Isla Teja** 2★, TT, Las Encinas 220, ☎ 215014. **H Palace** 2★, TT, Chacabuco 308,

☎ 213319. **Host. Chalet Alemán**, TT, Av. Ramón Picarte 1134 Int, ☎ 218810. **H Melillanca**, TT, Av Alemania 675, ☎ 212509 **H Monserrat**, TT, Picarte 849, ☎ 212032. **Cb Pumantu Raitue**, TT, Gral Lagos 1382, ☎ 212503. **Cb Pumantu**, TA, Gral Lagos 1946, ☎ 213036. **Hostal Villa Paulina**, TT, Yerbas Buenas 389, ☎ 212445/ 6372. **BH Anilebu**, TT, Av Picarte 875, ☎ 212186. **Res Germania**, TT, Picarte 873, ☎ 212405.

Car Rental
First (🚗 🚗 🚙), Pérez Rosales 674, ☎ 215973. **Turismo Méndez** (🚗 🚗 🚙 🚐), Gral Lagos 1335, ☎ 215966. **Sal-fa Sur** (🚗 🚗 🚙), Picarte 624, ☎ 215252. **Hertz** (🚗 🚗 🚙), Pedro Aguirre Cerda 1154, ☎ 218316.

VILLARRICA (DDD 045)
Accommodations
H El Ciervo 4★, TT, Gral Koerner 241, ☎ 411215. **Gran H Gerónimo de Alderete** 1★, Gerónimo de Alderete 709, ☎ 411370. **Hs Bilbao**, TT, Camilo Henriquez 43, ☎ 411186. **H De La Colina**, TT, Pdte Ríos 1177, ☎ 411503. **Hs Kiel**, TT, Gral Koerner 153, ☎ 411631. **M Lautaro**, TA, Pedro Montt 218, ☎ 411568. **Cb Millaruca**, TA, Saturnino Epulef 1504, ☎ 411448. **Hs Rayhuen**, TT, Pedro Montt 668, ☎ 411571. **Cb Río Tolten**, TT, Gral Korner 153, ☎ 411631. **Cb Traitraico**, TA, San Martín 380, ☎ 411064. **H Villarrica**, TT, Gral Korner 255, ☎ 411641, Res Santiago ☎ 380521. **H Yachting Club**, TT, San Martín 802, ☎ 411191, Res Santiago ☎ 2326008. **H Yandaly**, TT, Camilo Henriquez 401, ☎ 411452.

OSORNO TO PTO MONTT

CARRETERA AUSTRAL (Southern Highway)
In Contao **Res Mary**, TT, P O Box 233 Puerto Montt, ☎ 256480, Res Puerto Montt ☎ 252401. **At Hualaihué, Res Johana**, TT, to 82 km of Puerto Montt. **At Hornopirén - Río Negro, H Holiday Country**, TT, ☎ 256777 messenger. **H Hornopirén**, TT, P O Box 650 Puerto Montt.

ENSENADA
Centro Las Cascadas, TT, on the road from Ensenada to Puerto Fonk. **H Ensenada**, TT, at Ensenada, P O Box 659 Puerto Montt, ☎ 2888, Res Puerto Montt ☎ 252363. **Refugio Andino**, TT, at Osorno volcano, Res Ensenada, ☎ Crell 8278 annex 316.

ESTUARIO DE RELONCAVI
H Ralún 5★, TT, Ralún, Res Puerto Montt ☎ 252100, in Santiago ☎ 392345. **H Cochamó**, TA, Cochamó, Juan Jesús Molina 19. **Hs Cb Lodge**, TP, Cochamó, Res Puerto Montt, ☎ 253659.

FRUTILLAR (DDD 06542)
Accommodations
H Casona, del 32 Gastehaus, TT, Caupolicán 28, ☎ 369. **H El Bosque**, TA, Caupolicán 117, ☎ 317. **H Frutillar**, TT, Av Phillipi 1000, ☎ 277, Res Santiago ☎ 394422. **Hospedaje Lilian Epple**, TA, Av Phillipi 1441 Apartment 10. **Hs Los Maitenes**, TT, P O Box 175, ☎ Crell 9130. **Hospedaje Los Tilos**, TA, ☎ Crell 9140. **M Meli Ruca**, TA, O'Higgins 90, ☎ 244, Res Osorno ☎ 234846. **M Monserrat**, TA, Av Phillipi 175. **Cb Piscis**, TA, Santiago Yuninge 95, ☎ 250. **Hs Trayen**, TT, Av Phillipi 1285, ☎ 205. **Hs Vista Hermosa**, TT, Av Phillipi 1259, ☎ 209. **H Winkler**, TT, Av Phillipi 1155, ☎ 388. **Bh Adelita**, TA, Caupolicán 117, ☎ 229. **Bh Costa Azul**, TT, Av Phillipi 1175, ☎ 388. **Bh Las Rocas**, TA, Av Phillipi 1235, ☎ 397. **Hospedaje**, TT, Av Phillipi 883, ☎ 394. **H Panorama**, TT, ☎ Crell 9129. **Hs Posada Campesina**, 1 km on the road to Pta Larga, ☎ Crell 9123.

FRUTILLAR ALREDEDORES (in the vicinity of Frutillar) (DDD 06542)
On Maqui Beach, **Hs Playa Maqui**, TT, P O Box 114 Frutillar, ☎ Crell 9139. On Playa Larga, **Villa Anita**, TA, P O Box 169 Frutillar, Res Quilpué ☎ 911769. **On the Road to Totoral, Bh Fundo Santa Ana**, TT, P O Box 115 Frutillar, ☎ Crell 9106. On Pta Larga. **Cb El Cerro**, TA, P O Box 169, ☎ 372. **Hs Posada Campesina**, TT, P O Box 57, ☎ Crell 9123. On Pan-American Highway and Frutillar Alto, **Bh Rayhuén**, TT, P O Box 40 Frutillar Alto, Res Puerto Varas ☎ 2249.

LAGO PUYEHUE
Hs Isla Fresia 1★, TT, Isla Fresia, P O Box 49 Entrelagos, ☎ 236951. **Cb Aguas Calientes**, TT, Res Osorno ☎ 236988. **Cb Anticura**, TT, P O Box 967 Osorno, Res Osorno ☎ 234393. **H Antillanca**, TT, P O Box 765 Osorno, ☎ 235114 Osorno. **Hs Chalet Suizo**, TT, south shore, ☎ 7208. **Hs Entre Lagos**, TT, Entrelagos, Ramirez 65, ☎ 225. **M Ñilque**, TT, P O Box 1090 Osorno, ☎ 218 Entrelagos, at Santiago ☎ 2321130, at Osorno ☎ 234960. **H Termas de Puyehue**, TT, P O Box 27–0 Puyehue, ☎ 232157, Res Santiago ☎ 2313417/ 2086049.

Cb-Hs Villa Venetto, TT, Entrelagos, General Lagos 601, ☎ 203.

LAGO RANCO (DDD 06353)
On Lake Ranco, **Hs Casona Italiana**, TT, Viña del Mar 145, ☎ 225. **Hs Phoenix**, TT, Viña del Mar 41, ☎ 226. **At Riñinahue, Hs El Arenal del Nilahue**, TP, Res Río Bueno ☎ 507. **Hs Riñinahue**, TT, Res Lago Ranco P O Box 126, en Curicó ☎ 310657. **At Puerto Nuevo, H Puerto Nuevo**, TP, P O Box 289 La Unión, ☎ 06 Los Chilcos, Res Santiago ☎ 2128723. **At Puerto Yáñez, Hs Rayenmalal**, TP, Res La Unión ☎ 2417. **At Futrono** (DDD 0638), **H Puerto Futrono**, TT, Cordero Futrono, ☎ 283. **Hs Rincón Arabe**, TT, Manuel Montt conrner of Valentín Monsalve, ☎ 262. **At Llifén** (DDD 0638), **Hs Cumilahue Fishing Lodge**, TP, road to lago Maihue, ☎ 290 messenger. **Hs Chollinco**, TP, road to lago Maihue, ☎ 202 Futrono. **Hs Huequecura**, TP, ☎ 290 messenger, P O Box 4 Llifén. **Hs Lican**, TP, ☎ 290 messenger, Res Valdivia ☎ 215757. **Hs Villa La Cascada**, TA, ☎ 290 messenger.

LAGO RUPANCO
H Bahía Escocia, TP, P O Box 1099 Osorno, ☎ Entrelagos 254, Res Santiago ☎ 6983058. **Hs.Club de Pesca y Caza El Islote**, TP, placed 53 km away from Entrelagos. **Hs y Cb El Paraíso**, TP, P O Box 10 Entrelagos, Res Osorno ☎ 236239.

LAGO TODOS LOS SANTOS
H Petrohué, TT, Petrohué, P O Box 487 Puerto Montt, Res Puerto Montt ☎ 257797. **H Peulla**, TT, Peulla, P O Box 487 Puerto Montt, Res Santiago ☎ 6971010, en Puerto Montt ☎ 257797.

LA UNION (DDD 0643)
H Turismo, TT, Arturo Prat 630, ☎ 322384/ 322385.

LLANQUIHUE (DDD 06523)
Hs Llanquihue, TA, Calle Mackenna corner of Errázuriz, ☎ 2630. **Hospedaje**, TA, Valdivieso 517. **Hs Wiehoff**, TT, Errázuriz 007.

MAULLIN (DDD 0658)
Complejo Turístico Pangal, TT, located 5 km towards the coast. P O Box 100 Maullín, ☎ 244. **Bh Toledo**, TT, Calle 21 de Mayo 147, ☎ 246.

MAICOLPUE
Hs Miller, TT, water front street of bathing resort, Res Osorno ☎ 233087, P O Box 147 Osorno.

OSORNO (DDD 064)
Accommodations
H Del Prado, TT, Cochrane 1162, ☎ 235020, Res Santiago ☎ 6954553. **H García Hurtado de Mendoza**, TT, Mackenna 1040, ☎ 237111. **Gran H**, TT, B O'Higgins 615, ☎ 232171/ 72. **H Inter Lagos**, TT, Lord Cochrane 515, ☎ 234695/ 2581. **H Tirol**, TT, Bulnes 630, ☎ 233593. **H Villa Eduviges**, TT, Eduviges 856, ☎ 235023. **H Waeger**, TT, Cochran 816, ☎ 233721/ 22, Res Santiago ☎ 6954553. **Bh Hein**, TT, Cochrane 843, ☎ 234116. **Bh Riga**, TT, Amthauer 1058, ☎ 232945. **Bh Schulz**, TT, Freire 530, ☎ 237211.

Car Rental

First (🚐 🚐 🚐), Mackenna corner of Freire, ☎ 233861.
Ñiltur Rent a Car (🚐 🚐 🚐), Los Carrera 951 ☎ 238772.

Servicios Turísticos from OSORNO

Turismo Luna Azul Mackenna 971 Of. 108, ☎ (064)233636. City Tour, Valdivia, Puerto Montt-Puerto Varas and Frutillar, Anticura-Parque Nac.Puyehue-Antillanca, Osorno Volcán Ascencion, Petrohué-Ralún, Ancud, Castro.

PUERTO MONTT (DDD 065)
Accommodations

H Burg 3★, TT, Pedro Montt 56, ☎ 253813/ 253942. **H Colina** 3★, TT, Talca 81, ☎ 253501/ 2. **H Le Mirage** 3★, TT, Rancagua 350, ☎ 255125. **H Miramar** 1★ , TT Andres Bello972, ☎ 254618. **Hs Familiar Polz**, TT, Juan J Mira 1002, ☎ 252851. **Hs Familiar Tellez**, TT, J José Mira 979, ☎ 253838. **H Gamboa**, TT, Pedro Montt 157. **Cb Melipulli**, TAM, Libertad 10, ☎ 252363/ 253325. **H Millahue**, TT, Copiapó 64, ☎ 253829. **H Montt**, TT, Antonio Varas 301, ☎ 253651/ 52. **Apart H Millahue**, TT, Benavente 959, ☎ 254592. **Hs Panorama**, TT, San Felipe 192, ☎ 254094. **H Punta Arenas**, TT, Copiapó 119, ☎ 253080. **H Reloncaví**, TT, Guillermo Gallardo 228. **Hs Touristen Heim**, TMA, Buin 356, ☎ 255671. **H Turismo Bologna**, TT, Pan-American Highway northern approach, P O Box 696, ☎ 253191/ 4858. **H Vicente Pérez Rosales**, TT, Antonio Varas 447, ☎ 252571. **H Viento Sur**, TT, Ejército 200, ☎ 258701/02

Arriendo de Autos

Ansa Internacional (🚐 🚐 🚐) Cauquenes 75, ☎ 252968. **Avis** (🚐 🚐 🚐), Copiapó 43 ☎ 253307. **Budget** (🚐 🚐 🚐), San Martín 200, ☎ 254888. **Colina** (🚐 🚐 🚐), Cardonal 34, ☎ 257279. **Dollar** (🚐 🚐 🚐), Antonio Varas 447, ☎ 252571. **Economy** (🚐 🚐 🚐), Sta María 620, ☎ 255400 / 254125. **First** (🚐 🚐 🚐), Antonio Varas 447, ☎ 252036. **Hertz** (🚐), Urmeneta 1036. **Le Mirage** (🚐 🚐), Rancagua 350, ☎ 26301. **Passport** (🚐), Av Diego Portales 514, Shop 9, ☎ 253811. **Sports** (🚐 🚐), Benavente 309, ☎ 255433. **Western** (🚐 🚐 🚐), Quillota 177, ☎ 254437/ 3794.

PUERTO MONTT - PELLUCO
Cb Los Abedules, TT, Puerto Montt 55, ☎ 254231. **M Rucaray**

3★, TT, Juan Soler M s/n, P O Box 843, ☎ 252395, Res Santiago ☎ 6717766.

PUERTO OCTAY (DDD 0649)
Accommodations

H and Cb Centinela, TT, P O Box 12, ☎ 22, Res Santiago ☎ 2325376. **Hs La Baja**, TT, P O Box 116. **H Haase**, TT, Pedro Montt 344, ☎ 213.

PUERTO VARAS (DDD 6523)
Accommodations

H Asturias 3★, TT, Del Salvador 322, ☎ 232446/ 232375. **M Ayentemo**, TT, V Pérez Rosales 1297, ☎ 232270. **H Candilejas** 1★, TT, Walter Martínez 584, ☎ 232867, Res Santiago ☎ 378532. **Cb Colegual**, TA, V Pérez Rosales 01567 Puerto Chico, ☎ 232922. **Cb del Lago** 4★, TT, Klenner 195, ☎ 232291/ 232707. **Gran H Puerto Varas**, TT, Klenner 351, ☎ 232544. **Hs Loreley** 1★, TT, Maipo 911, ☎ 232226. **Hs La Sirena**, TT, Santa Rosa 710 inner, ☎ 232897. **H Licarayen**, TT, San José 114, ☎ 232305/ 232955. **H Nuevo Bellavista**, TT, Av Vicente Pérez Rosales 060, ☎ 232011. **M Sacho**, TA, San José 581, ☎ 232227. **Cb Trauco**, TT, Imperial 433, ☎ 232462, Res Santiago ☎ 381042 annex 4240.

Car Rental
Turismo Llancahué (🚐), Del Salvador 316, ☎ 232214.

PUERTO VARAS (on the road to Ensenada)

Cb Bellavista, TT, P O Box 41 Puerto Varas, ☎ Crell 8278 annex 323. **Cb Brisas del Lago** 3★, TT, P O Box 24 Puerto Varas, ☎ Crell 8278 annex 316. **Hs y M Dónde Juanita**, TT, 11 km on the road to Ensenada, ☎ Crell 8278. **H Fogón Pucará**, TT, P O Box 132 Puerto Varas, ☎ Crell 8278. **Hs Ruedas Viejas**, TT, Km 11, Res Puerto Varas, ☎ Crell 8278. **H Puerto Pilar**, TT, P O Box 14 Puerto Varas, ☎ Crell 8292, Res Santiago ☎ 336645.

RIO BUENO

Hs and M Puente Río Bueno, TT, on the Pan-American Highway junction, ☎ 574. **H Richmond**, TT, Comercio 755, ☎ 363.

Tourist Services offered from PUERTO MONTT, PUERTO VARAS, FRUTILLAR
TOURS

TOURS	Vehicle	Season	Duration	Andina del Sud Puerto Montt, Varas 473 ☎(065)254692 Tx270035	Buses Bolhe Puerto Montt, (065)254528 Puerto Varas, Del Salvador s/n (06523)/2000	Montravel Puerto Montt, Varas 447 ☎(065)253468 Tx 270157	Turismo Auto Club Puerto Montt Cauquenes 75 ☎(065)254776 Tx 270077	Turismo Rosse Puerto Montt, A Varas 445 ☎(065)257040 Tx 370181	Varastur Puerto Montt, A Varas 437 ☎(065)252203 P Varas San Fco. 242 (06523)2103	H. Frutillar Frutillar, Phillippi 1000 ☎(0654)277
City Tours Puerto Montt	🚐	Jan to Mar	1½ h			●				
Excursion to Frutillar	🚐	Dec to Mar / 8 h		●				Nov to Mar ●		
Excursion to Centinela and Puerto Octay	🚗 🚐	10 h	Dec to Mar ●					T T	T T ○
Excursion to Osorno Volcano	🚗 🚐	TT	7 h					T T ●	T T ●	T T
Excursion to Petrohué	🚗 🚐		7 h		Nov to Mar ●			Dec to Mar ●	T T ●	T T
Excursion to Ralún	🚗 🚐			Dec to Mar ●						T T ○
Excursion to Ralún and Reloncaví Estuary	⛴ 🚐	Nov to Mar	1 day					Nov to Mar ●	Nov to Mar ●	
Excursion to Peulla	⛴ 🚐	TT	10 h	●						
Excursion to Puyehue	🚗 🚐		11 h	Dec to Mar ●				Nov to Mar ●	T T ●	T T ○
Excursion to Antillanca	🚗 🚐		2 day			Winter ●				T T ○
Ancud	⛴ 🚐		11 h	Dec to Mar ●				Nov to Mar ●	T T ●	T T ○
Puerto Montt, Chaitén, Coihiaque and San Rafael	⛴ 🚐	Jan to Feb	9 - 15 day			●	●			
to Bariloche trough the lakes	⛴ 🚐			Dec to Mar ●		T T ○ 2 day	Dec to Mar ○ 3 day			

12 INSULAR CHILOE

ACHAO (DDD 06556)
Bh La Nave, TT, Prat s/n, ☎ 219. **Bh Sao Paulo**, TT, Serrano 052, ☎ 245. **R Delicias**, TA, Serrano 018.

ANCUD (DDD 0656)
Accommodations
Hs Ancud, TT, San Antonio 30, ☎ 2340/ 50, Res Stgo ☎ 6965599. **Hs Ahui**, TT, Costanera 906, ☎ 2415. **M Huaihuen**, TT, Aníbal Pinto 1070, ☎ 2554. **H Lydia**, TT, Chacabuco 630, ☎ 2990. **Hs Monserrat**, TT, Baquedano 417, ☎ 2957. **H Polo Sur**, TT, Costanera 630, ☎ 2200. **H Quintanilla**, TA, Libertad 751, Res Puerto Montt ☎ 252363. **Bh Wechsler y Cia**, TT, Lord Cochrane 480, ☎ 2318.
Car Rental
Alarcón (🚐 🚙), Errazuriz 360, ☎ 3085.

CASTRO (DDD 0657)
Accommodations
M Auquilda 3★, TT, in front of Club Aéreo Castro, ☎ 2458. **M Centro Turístico Nercón**, TT, ☎ 2242. **Cb Llicaldad**, TT, at Costanera 5 km south of Castro, ☎ 5080. **Hs de Castro**, TT, Chacabuco 202, ☎ 2301/2302. **H Gran Alerce**, TT, O'Higgins 808, ☎ 2267. **H and Cb Niklistcheck**, TT, Pan-American Highway 2 km north of Castro, ☎ 5364, Res Castro ☎ 2331.

Hs O'Higgins, TT, O'Higgins 831, ☎ 2016. **H Plaza**, TT, Blanco 382, ☎ 5109. **Cg and Cb Pudú**, TMA, ☎ 5109. **H Unicornio Azul**, TT, Av Pedro Montt 228, ☎ 2359. **Bh Mirasol**, TT, San Martín 815. **H Costa** *Azul*, Lillo 67, ☎ 2440.

CHONCHI (DDD 06553)
H El Antiguo Chalet, TT, Irarrazaval s/n, ☎ 221. **H Chonchi**, TT, O'Higgins 379, ☎ 288, Res Stgo ☎ 2290354.

DALCAHUE (DDD 06555)
Bh Dalcahue, TT, Pedro Aguirre Cerda 003, ☎ 217. **Bh La Feria**, TT, Manuel Rodriguez 017. **Bh Montaña**, TT, Manuel Rodríguez 009. **Bh San Martín**, TT, San Martín 001, ☎ 207.

QUELLON (DDD 06504)
H El Colono, TT, Ladrilleros corner of La Paz s/n, ☎ 254. **H La Pincoya**, TT, La Paz 064, ☎ 285. **H Leo Man**, TT, Pedro Aguirre Cerda s/n, ☎ 298, Res Castro ☎ 5178. **Hs Quellón**, TT, Pedro Montt 297, ☎ 250. **Cb Turislapa**, TT, ☎ 298, on Pta Lapa. **Bh El Coral**, TT, Pedro Montt 177.

QUEMCHI (DDD 0657)
Bh La Tranquera, TT, Yungay 40, ☎ 250.

Tourist Services offered from ANCUD Y CASTRO

TOURS	Vehicle	Season	Duration	Turismo Ancud Ancud, Pudeto 219 2° floor ☎ (0656)2235/3019 Tx297700	Turismo Pehuén Ancud, Lillo 119 (0657)5254 Tx297805 Fx(0657)2432	Chiloé Tour San Martín, Of 5689 ☎(0657)2155 Castro
City Tours Ancud	🚐	Dec to Mar	1¹/² h	◯		
Ancud, Quinchao Island, Castro, Cucao	🚐	Dec to Mar	12 h	◯		
Castro, Cucao	🚐	TT	10 h			●
Castro, Quinchao Island	🚐	TT	6 to 10 h			●
Castro, Chonchi, Lemuy Island	🚐	TT	10 h			●
Castro, Tenaún, Butachauques Island	🚐	TT	10 h			
Ancud, Manao, Quemchi, Tenaún	🚐	Dec to Mar	1¹/² h	◯		
Castro, Ancud	🚐	TT	4 h			●
Castro, Ancud, Playa Brava (Beach)	🚐	TT	12 h			●
Ancud, Corona Lighthouse, Ahuí Fort	🚐	Dec to Mar	4 h	◯		
Mechuque Island, Nahuildad, Queilén	✈	Dec to Mar				◯

13 THE SOUTHEN HIGHWAY

COCHRANE (LD 108)
H La Tranquera, TT, San Valentín 663, Res Coihaique ☎ 231643. **Hs Wellman**, TT, Las Golondrinas 36, ☎ 171. **Bh Sur Austral**, TT, Arturo Prat s/n, ☎ 150, Res Coihaique ☎ 231981. **Bh Rubio**, TT, Tte Merino 4, ☎ 173.

COIHAIQUE (DDD 067)
Accommodations
Hs Coihaique 4★, TT, Magallanes 131, ☎ 231137/ 231737/ 233274, Res Santiago ☎ 2326825. **Gran H Chible**, TT, Moraleda 448, ☎ 231643. **Cb La Pasarela**, TT, Fco Bilbao 326, ☎ 231560, Res Santiago 2315294. **H Los Ñires**, TT, Baquedano 315, ☎ 232261. **Cb Río Simpson**, TT, Res Coihaique ☎ 232183. **Bh Austral**, TT, Colón 203, ☎ 232522. **Bh Coihaique**, TT, Arturo Prat 653, ☎ 231239. **Bh El Reloj**, TT, Baquedano 444, ☎ 231108. **Bh Navidad**, TT, Baquedano

198, ☎ 231159. **Bh Puerto Varas**, TT, Ignacio Serrano 168, ☎ 231212. **Bh San Sebastián**, TT, Baquedano 496, ☎ 233427. **Bh Serrano**, TT, Ignacio Serrano 91, ☎ 211522.
Car Rental
Automundo (🚗 🚐 🚙), Fco Bilbao 509, ☎ 231621. **Automóvil Club** (🚗 🚐 🚙), Fco Bilbao 583, ☎ 231649. **Automotora Fórmula Uno Berrios y Berrios** (🚐), 21 de Mayo 339, ☎ 233363. **Rucaray** (🚐), Teniente Merino 848, ☎ 332862 Puerto Aysén. **Turismo Prado** (🚗 🚐 🚙), 21 Mayo 417, ☎ 231271 / 231329. **Sibb** (🚗), Baquedano 457, ☎ 23126 / 233442. **Hertz** (🚗 🚐), Moraleda 420, ☎ 233456 / 232 999.
Cars with Chauffeur
(itinerary upon request) **Taxis Nieves de Aysen** , Parra conrner of 12 Octubre, ☎ 232804. **Taxis B & B**, Freire 274, ☎ 233072.

675

CHAITEN (DDD 06503)
H Cordillera TA, Juan Todesco 18, ☎ 312. H Mi Casa, TT, Av Norte s/n, ☎ 285, Res Santiago ☎ 363181. H Schilling, TT, Av B O'Higgins 230, ☎ 295. Bh Astoria, TT, Av B O'Higgins 442, ☎ 263.

CHILE CHICO (DDD 067)
Hs de La Patagonia, TT, Camino Internacional , ☎ 411337. Bh Aguas Azules, TT, Manuel Rodriguez 252, ☎ 411320. Bh Nacional, TT, Freire 24, ☎ 411265.

Car Rental
Yolanda Munson (🚗), Manuel Rodríguez 252, ☎ 411320.

FIORDO QUEULAT
Cb Queulat, TAM, ☎ and Fx 067-233302, P O Box 5, Coihaique.

FUTALEUFU (LD 108)
H Continental, TA, Balmaceda 597, P O Box 15. H Posada La Gringa, TA, ☎ Entel 1 messenger, Res Santiago ☎ 2747964.

GUADAL
Hs Huemules, TT, Las Magnolias 360/ 382.

LAGO ELIZALDE (LD 108)
Hs Del Lago Elizalde, TA, Magallanes .131, ☎ 231137/ 231737, Res Santiago ☎ 2326825.

LAGO ESPOLON
Cb Lago Espolón, TA, Post Office Futaleufú. Hs La Casa de Campo, TT, ☎ 224 de Futaleufú, Res Post Office of Futaleufú.

LAGO RISOPATRON
Hs Cb El Pangue, TT, Res Santiago ☎ 2241114.

LAGO YELCHO
Hs Alexis, TT, at Puerto Piedra, Res at Chaitén Libertad 1076. Bh Gesell, TP at Puerto Cárdenas, Res P O Box 42 of Chaitén y ☎ Public phone Puerto Cárdenas. Hs Verónica TT, Post Office Alto Palena. Bh Yelcho, TP, at Puerto Cárdenas, P O Box 52, Chaitén.

LA JUNTA
Hs Espacio y Tiempo, TT, Carretera Austral s/n, Res to Telex Chile. Hs Valdera, TT, A Varas s/n. Bh Copihue, TT, Antonio Varas 611.

MAÑIHUALES
H Continental, TT, Post Office Mañihuales. Bh Bienvenido, TT, Post Office Mañihuales.

MURTA
Bh Lago Gral Carrera, TT, 5 de Abril s/n. Bh Patagonia, TT, Pasaje España s/n.

PALENA
Bh La Chilenita, TT, Pudeto 681.

PUERTO AYSEN (DDD 332)
Cb El Fogón, TT, Sargento Aldea 355. H Gastronomía Carrera, TT, Cochrane 465, ☎ 332551. Gran H Aysén, TT, Chacabuco 130, ☎ 332672. H Plaza, TT, O'Higgins 237, ☎ 332784. H Roxy, TT, Sargento 972, ☎ 332704. Bh El Fogón, TT, Sargento Aldea 355, ☎ 332790. Bh Lo De Nene, TT, Serrano Montaner 57, ☎ 332964.

Car Rental
Viajes Rucaray (🚗 🚙), Teniente Merino 848, ☎ 332862.

PUERTO CISNES
Hs Michay, TT, Gabriela Mistral. Bh Villa Las Hortensias, TA, Gabriela Mistral 112.

PUERTO CHACABUCO (067)
H Moraleda, TT, O'Higgins s/n, ☎ 351155. Cb Parque Loberías de Aysén, TT, Carrera 50, ☎ 351115/ 351112.

PUERTO IBAÑEZ (LD 108)
Bh Ibañez, TT, Beltran Dickson 01, ☎ 227. Bh Mónica, TT, Beltran Dickson 29, ☎ 226, Res Coihaique ☎ 212518. Bh El Chilote, TT, Carlos Sosa 259, ☎ 236.

PUERTO SANCHEZ
Hs Puerto Sánchez, TMA, P O Box 636 Coihaique, Res Coihaique ☎ 231441.

PUERTO RIO TRANQUILO
Bh Carretera Austral, TT, Calle 1 Sur 223. Bh Los Pinos, TT, 2 Oriente 41 street. Bh Darka, TT, 1 Sur 071.

PUYUHUAPI
Hs Ludwing, TA. Hs Puyuhuapi, TMA, Res Santiago ☎ 2326825/ 2315456, en Coihaique 231737. Hs Termas de Puyuhuapi, TMA, P O Box 555 de Coihaique, Res Coihaique ☎ 231441. Bh Alemana, TT, Av Otto Lebel 450.

VILLA CASTILLO
Hs Doña Amalia, TT, Res Coihaique ☎ 231643.

VILLA VANGUARDIA
M Villa Vanguardia, TA, Res Chaitén ☎ 252671, P O Box 59 of Chaitén.

Tourist Services offered from COIHAIQUE

TOURS	Vehicle	Season	Duration	Rio Baker Ravels Coihaique, Condell 149 Of.4 ☎(067)223470	Turismo Quelar Coihaique, Dusen 340 Of. 3 ☎(067)221441	Tirismo Prado Coihaique, 21 de mayo 417 ☎(067)221271	Expo. Coihaique Coihaique, Simón Bolívar 94 ☎(067)222300	Turismo Cordillera Coihaique, René Schneider 80 ☎(067)221718	South Pacific Exped. Coihaique, Condell 149 Of.4 ☎(067)223470
Coihaique, Six Lakes, Lake Elizalde, Simpson Valley	🚐		5 h	● Dec to Mar	○ Dec to Mar	○ TT			
Coihaique, Puyuhuapi, Lake Risopatrón, Chaiko	🚐		2 day	○ Dec to Mar				● Dec to Mar	
Coihaique, San Rafael, Puyuhuapi, Chaitén	✈🚐	Nov to Mar	10 day						○
Coihaique, Cochrane, Baker River	🚐🐎	Dec to Mar	8 day		○				
Coihaique, Puerto Tranquilo, Bertrand, Cochrane	🚗🚐	TT	3 day			○			
Rafting on the Cisne River	🚐🛶	Jan to Mar	7 day		●				
Rafting on the Baker River	🚗🛶	Jan to Mar	8 to 9 day		●		●		
Fishing Excursions on Rivers and Lakes	🚐🛶	Dec to Mar	9 day		○				
Coihaique, Puerto Aisén, Puerto Chacabuco	🚐	TT	8 h			○			

MAGALLANES

Tourist Services offered from PUNTA ARENAS

TOURS	Vehicle	Season	Duration	Paralelo 53 Chiloe 930 ☎(061)22313 Tx 380061	Ventistur José Menéndez 647 ☎(061)223795 Tx 280034 Fx 227545	Turismo Ventur José Noguera 1235 ☎(061)224926 Tx 280383	T. Cabo de Hornos Pza.Manuel Guerrero 1039 ☎(061)222599 Tx 380135	Turismo Comapa Magallanes 970 ☎(061)225505 Tx 380047 Fx956)061)227514	Turismo Pehoé 21 de Mayo 1464 ☎(061)224223 Tx 280001
City Tours Punta Arenas	🚐	TT	2 h	○			○	○	○
Punta Arenas, Puerto del Hambre, Fuerte Bulnes	🚐	Nov to Mar	4 h	●	○		○	○	○
Punta Arenas, Pecket Mine, Penguin Colonies	🚐	Nov to Mar	4 h	●			○		
Punta Arenas Porvenir, Lake Los Cisnes	✈🚐	TT	15 h				○	○	○
Punta Arenas, Laguna Blanca, Porvenir	✈🚐		3 day				Nov to Mar ○	Sep to May ○	
Fishing Excursions	✈🚐		5 - 10 day				Nov to Mar ○	Oct to May ○	
Punta Arenas, Puerto Natales, Milodón cave, Torres del Paine, Grey Glacier	🚗🚐	TT	3 day	TT ●	○	○	Oct to Apr ○	TT ○	●
Punta Arenas, Torres del Paine, Serrano and Balmaceda Glaciers	🚗🚐	Apr to Mar	3 day		○			Sep to Apr ○	
Punta Arenas, Pinguin Colonies, Puerto Natales, Torres del Paine, Porvenir, Lago Blanco, Punta Arenas, City Tour	✈🚐	Nov to Mar	9 day				○		
Rafting on the Serrano River, Return by Cutter	🐎🚐	Nov to Mar	6 day				○	○	
Hiking Throung the Torres del Paine National Park	🚗🚐		6 day				Nov to Mar ○	Oct to Apr ○	

CERRO CASTILLO (LD 108)
Hs **El Pionero**, TAP, Rodolfo Studenrou s/n, ☎ 1 Torres del Paine, Res Puerto Natales ☎ 411594.

PORVENIR (DDD 061)
H **Central**, TT, Bernardo Phillipi 298, ☎ 580077. **Hs Los Flamencos**, TT, Tte Merino s/n, ☎ 580049. **H Rosas**, TT, Bernardo Phillipi 296, ☎ 580088. **Hs Tierra del Fuego**, TT, Carlos Wood 489, ☎ 580015. **Bh Colón**, TT, Damián Riobó 198, ☎ 580108. **H Posada Los Cisnes**, TT, Soto Salas 702.

PUERTO NATALES (DDD 061)
Accommodations
H **Austral**, TT, Valdivia 955, ☎ 411593. **H Capitán Eberhard**, TT, Pedro Montt corner of Señoret, ☎411208/9, Res Punta Arenas ☎ 222313. **H Cisne de Cuello Negro**, TAM, en Puerto Bories, ☎ 411498, Res Punta Arenas ☎ 224223, en Santiago ☎ 6988287. **H Juan Ladrilleros**, TT, Pedro Montt 161, ☎ 411652, Res Punta Arenas ☎ 224926. **H Natalino**, TT, Eberhard 371, ☎ 411968. **H Palace**, TT, Ladrilleros 209, ☎ 411134, Res Santiago ☎ 6983058.

PUERTO NATALES to TORRES DEL PAINE (road)
H **Tres Pasos**, TT, Km 38 of Puerto Natales, Res Punta Arenas ☎ 228113.

PUERTO WILLIAMS
Hs **Patagonia**, TT, Res Santiago ☎ 2288081.

PUNTA ARENAS (DDD 061)
Accommodations
H **Cabo de Hornos** 5★, TT, Plaza Muñoz Gamero 1025, ☎ 222134, Res Santiago 339119. **H Los Navegantes** 4★, TT, José Menéndez 647, ☎ 224677. **H Mercurio** 3★, TT, Fagnano 595, ☎ 223430. **Hs de la Patagonia** 2★, TT, Libertador B. O'Higgins 478, ☎ 223521. **H Colonizadores**, TT, 21 de Mayo 1690, ☎228144. **H Cóndor de Plata**, TT, Av Colón 556, ☎ 227987/ 4301. **Hs del Estrecho**, TT, José Menéndez 1048, ☎ 226011. **H Montecarlo**, TT, Av Colón 605, ☎ 223448. **H Plaza**, TT, J Nogueira 1116, ☎ 221300. **H Ritz**, TA, Pedro Montt 1102, ☎ 224422. **H Savoy**, TT, José Menéndez 1073, ☎225851/7979. **Hs Yaganes**, TT, Northern road Km 7 1/2 Rural, P O Box 650, ☎ 224223/ 506, Res Santiago ☎ 6988287.

Car Rental
Hertz (🚗), E Navarro 1064, ☎ 222013. **Budget** (🚗🚐🚙), O'Higgins 964, ☎ 225696.

PUNTA ARENAS to PUERTO NATALES (road)
H **Llanuras de Diana**, TM/ TAM, P O Box 84, Puerto Natales, Res Punta Arenas ☎ 221247. **Hs Patagonia Inn**, TA, Dos Lagunas Km 26, Res Punta Arenas ☎ 222134, en Santiago ☎ 338480. **Hs Río Penitente**, TM/ TA, ☎ 331694, Res Punta Arenas ☎ 223572/ 224926. **H Río Rubens**, TT, P O Box 84, Puerto Natales, Res Punta Arenas ☎ 226916.

RIO VERDE (LD 108)
Hs **Río Verde Ltda**, TT, P O Box 591 Punta Arenas, ☎ 15x3 Cabeza del Mar.

TORRES DEL PAINE (National Park) (LD 108)
Hs **Pehoé**, TAM, Res Punta Arenas, ☎ 224223/ 506, en Santiago ☎ 6988287. **Hs Río Serrano**, TAM, ☎ 1.

15

CHILEAN ANTARCTIC TERRITORY

ANTARTICA
Hs **Estrella Polar**, october through march, on Rey Jorge island, Res Santiago ☎ 338480.

AIR AND SEA TRASPORTATION
CHILOE AND AISEN

SHIPPING

① **Skorpios I & II** 1 Sep-April. Santiago, Mac Iver 484, Of. 5, ☎ 393105/336187; Puerto Montt, Angelmó 1660, ☎ 252619/996. Luxury ships accommodating 74 and 170 passengers in cabins, respectively. **Itinerary**: Puerto Montt-Corcovado Gulf-Laguna San Rafael-Melinka-Castro-Puerto Montt. Cruise lasts 7 days. Departures Sat. at 1100h.

② **Patagonia Express** 1 Santiago, Fidel Oteíza 1950, floor 13, ☎ 2740119/7975. A swift, luxurious catamaran accommodating 58 passengers. **Itinerary**: Puerto Montt-Termas de Puyuhuapi (overnight stay)-Puerto Chacabuco-Laguna San Rafael-and back.

③ **Odisea and Visón** 2 Dec-March Santiago, Alameda B. O'Higgins 108, local 120, ☎ 330883; Aysén, Sargento Aldea 679, ☎ 332908. Luxury motorized sailing ships accom-modating 6 and 10 passengers, respectively. **Itinerary**: Puerto Chacabuco-Laguna San Rafael- sailing along different channels. Departures Mon. Cruise last 6 days.

④ **Patagonia** 2 Nov-Mar Santiago, Providencia 2088, Of.33, ☎ 251 2881/2882; Coyhaique, 21 de Mayo 461, ☎ 233466, Tourist motorboat with cabins accommodating 12 passengers. **Itinerary**: Puerto Chacabuco-Puerto Gato-Sisquelén-Laguna San Rafael-Elefantes Estuary-Termas de Chiconal-Puerto Chacabuco. Cruise lasts 5 days. Departures once weekly.

⑤ **Ventisqueros and San Quintín** 2 High season. Coyhaique, Presidente Ibáñez 202, ☎ 232234. Motorboats fitted out to accommodate 12 and 10 passengers, respectively. **Itinerary**: charters along the Aysén coastline and to Laguna San Rafael.

⑥ **Lancha Nalcayec** 2 Jan-Mar Same address as Lancha Patagonia. Fourteen passengers. **Itinerary**: Puerto Chacabuco-Termas de Chiconal (hot springs) in the Aysén estuary. Cruise lasts one hour, with a stop at the hot springs.

⑦ **RR Evangelista** 1 3 Santiago, Miraflores 178, floor 12, ☎ 6963211/3212; Puerto Montt, Angelmó 2187, ☎ 25374/253218; Coyhaique, Dussen 340, ☎ 223306. A multi-purpose ship with cabins for passengers. **Itinerary**: January and February, Puerto Chacabuco-Laguna San Rafael and back. Cruise lasts 2 days. Departures once weekly. Regular service, year-round, Puerto Montt-Puerto Chacabuco, journey takes 22 hours, departures twice weekly.

⑧ **T Ro Ro Colono** 1 3 of Transmarchilay. Santiago, ☎ 335959/399984 (info & ticket sales); Puerto Montt, ☎ 254654; Ancud, ☎ 2317/2279; Chaitén, 272; Coyhaique, ☎ 231971; Puerto Chacabuco, ☎ 144. A multi-purpose ship for 200 passengers and 75 cars. Accommodations include four cabins, luxury seats and two classes of reclining seats. Reservations are mandatory. **Itinerary**: Puerto Montt-Chacabuco route: departures Tue & Fri; cruise lakes 26 hours, return Wed & Sat. Puerto Chacabuco-Laguna San Rafael route: Jan-Mar only passengers; departures once weekly, on Sat. at 21.00 h, return Mon. morning; cruise lasts 2 days; a further four departures in winter.

⑨ **T Tehuelche** 1 3 of Transmarchilay; see Tel numbers under Ro Ro Colono. A ferry for 83 passengers and 20 cars. **Itinerary**: La Arena to Caleta Puelche and back; reservations necessary. Jan & Feb, five departures daily; Mar-Dec, 3 departures daily; crossing takes 30 min.

⑩ **B Pincoya** 3 of Transmarchilay, (see Tel. numbers under Ro Ro Colono). For 100 passengers and 30 cars. **Itinerary**: Quellón-Chaitén route, only in January and February, reservations necessary; crossing takes 6 hours, two departures weekly. Pargua-Chaitén route only Mar through December; crossing takes 9 hours, two departures weekly. Quellón-Puerto Chacabuco only Jan & Feb, reservations necessary; crossing takes 20 hours; one departure weekly.

⑪ **B Mailen** 3 of Transmarchilay (see Tel. Nos under Ro Ro Colono). For 83 passengers and 23 cars. **Itinerary**: Ro Negro (Hornopirn) -Caleta Gonzalo only Jan & Feb, crossing takes 5 hours; reservations necessary, one departure daily.

⑫ **T Cau Cau & T Trauco** 3 of Transmarchilay (see Tel. numbers under Ro Ro Colono above), each accom-modating 80 passengers and 18 cars. **Itinerary**: Pargua-Chacao (on Chilo island) and back; throughout the year; crossing takes 30 minutes; uninterrupted service from 0600h to 0300h.

⑬ **T Cruz del Sur & Gobernador Figueroa** 3 Ancud, Chaca-buco 672, ☎ 6562506. **Itinerary**: Pargua - Chacao (on Chilo island); crossing takes 45 min. One hourly departure from 0600h to 0100h.

⑭ **T Pilchero** 3 Tel numbers under Ro Ro Colono above. A ferry for passengers and cargo. **Itinerary**: Puerto Ibáñez-Chile Chico across lake General Carrera; crossing takes 2 hours; one departure on Tue, Wed, Sat and Sun.

TYPES OF TRANSPORT

1 Scheduled passenger-only ships and airplanes.

2 Scheduled or non-scheduled ships or airplanes for passengers only (adventure tourism). Small capacity (up to 12 passengers). Available for charters or until the group is completed.

3 Multi-purpose ships with scheduled departures and Itinerary, carrying passengers, vehicles, and cargo.

AIRPLANES

Ⓐ **LAN** 1 year-round Santiago, Agustinas 1197, ☎ 6723523/699 0505; Puerto Montt, San Martn 200 L 2, ☎ 253141; Coyhaique, Gral . Parra 215, ☎ 231188. **Itinerary**: Santiago-Puerto Montt-Coyhaique. Flight lasts 3 hours; six flights weekly.

Ⓑ **Ladeco** 1 year-round Santiago, Hurfanos 1157, ☎ 6982233. Puerto Montt, Benavente 350, ☎ 253002. **Itinerary**: Santiago-Temuco-Puerto Montt-Balmaceda. Flight lasts 3 1/2 hours; four departures weekly.

Ⓒ **Aero Reinarz** 1 Oct-Mar Puerto Montt, Libertad 621, ☎ 253659. Piper Azteca and Cessna 182 airplanes. **Itinerary**: Puerto Montt-Llanada Grande-Segundo Corral. Flight takes 35 min, leaves on Fri. and returns on Sun. The company runs a fishing lodge, minimum stay three days.

Ⓓ **Aero Osorno** 2 year-round. Puerto Montt, Benavente 761-B, ☎ 253100. Cessna 185 Skywagon. **Itinerary**: Puerto Montt-Llanada Grande-Segundo Corral. No regular schedule.

Ⓔ **Aero Don Carlos** 1 year-round. Coyhaique, Subteniente Cruz 63, ☎ 231981. Cessna 401/402/310, Piper Azteca. **Itinerary**: Coyhaique-Chile Chico-Cochrane. Weekly departures.

Ⓕ **Aero Hein** 1 year-round. Coyhaique, Francisco Bilbao 968, ☎ 232772. Cessna 180, Piper Cherokee, **Itinerary**: Cochrane-Villa O'Higgins-Caleta Tortel; weekly departures.

Ⓖ **Aero Palena** 2 year-round. Puerto Montt, Benavente 292, ☎ 252760. Cessna 182. **Itinerary**: Puerto Montt-Futaleuf-Palena. No regular schedule.

Ⓗ **Aero San Rafael** 2 year-round. Coyhaique, 18 de Sep-tiembre 469, ☎ 233408. Piper Navajo, Piper Seneca, Piper Azteca, Cessna 206, Baron Beechcraft. **Itinerary**: charters to Puerto Montt, Argentinian Patagonia, and South to Villa O'Higgins, Tortel, and Laguna San Rafael.

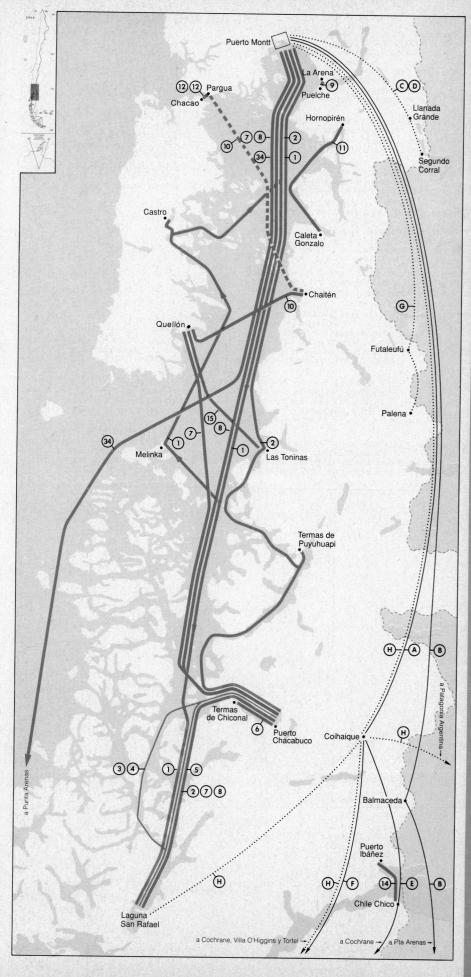

CHILE

Puerto Montt

La Arena
⑨
Puelche
Ⓒ Ⓓ
Llanada
Grande

⑫ ⑫ Pargua
Chacao

Hornopirén

Segundo
Corral

⑦ ⑧
⑩
②
⑪

㉞
①

Castro

Caleta
Gonzalo

Ⓖ

Quellón

Chaitén
⑩

Futaleufú

Palena

⑮
⑧

①⑦
㉞
①
①
②

Melinka

Las Toninas

Termas de
Puyuhuapi

Ⓗ Ⓐ Ⓑ

a Patagonia Argentina

Termas
de Chiconal

Ⓗ

⑥
Puerto
Chacabuco

Coihaique

③④
①⑤
②⑦⑧

Balmaceda

Puerto
Ibáñez

Ⓗ
Ⓗ Ⓕ
⑭ Ⓔ Ⓑ

a Punta Arenas

Ⓗ

Chile Chico

Laguna
San Rafael

a Cochrane, Villa O'Higgins y Tortel →   a Cochrane →   a Pta Arenas →

679

SHIPPING

(30) **Terra Australis** 1 Sept-Mar Santiago, Miraflores 178, 12th floor, ☎ 696 3211/3212. Punta Arenas, Independencia 640, ☎ 22593/226600. A luxury ship with cabins, accommodating 112 passengers in four decks, **Itinerary**: Punta Arenas-Strait of Magellan-Magdalena Channel-Agostini glacier-Beagle Channel-Puerto Williams-Ushuasia in Argentina-Garibaldi glacier-Strait of Magellan-Punta Arenas. Duration: 7 days; weekly departures on Wednesday.

(31) **21 de Mayo Cutter** 1 Jan-Mar Puerto Natales, Ladrilleros 171, ☎ 411176. A passenger boat. **Itinerary**: Puerto Natales-Ultima Esperanza Sound-Balmaceda and Serrano glaciers-Puerto Natales. Duration: 8 hours, departures Wed, Fri & Sat.

(32) **Compass Rose** 2 Jan-Mar Punta Arenas, Roca 886, local 7, ☎ 226370. A motorized sailing ship. **Itinerary**: Same as 21 de Mayo Cutter above. No specific departure schedule.

(33) **Trinidad** 2 Jan-Mar Punta Arenas, Roca 886, local 7, ☎ 226370. A luxury motorized sailing ship accommodating 9 passengers. **Itinerary**: Puerto Natales-Angostura Kirk(narrows)-Las Montaas channel-Santa Mara channel-Roca peninsula-Puerto Natales. Duration: 3 days; no specific departure schedule.

(34) **Coral Gable** 4 Year-round. Puerto Montt, uble 230, ☎ 259217. Ships carries only cargo and cars. **Itinerary**: Puerto Montt-Puerto Natales. Duration: 4 days. Frequency:3 departures montly.

(35) **Melinka Ferry** 3 Punta Arenas, Quillota 766, ☎ 225757/228204. A multi-purpose ship for passengers and 20 cars. Reservations necessary. **Itinerary**: Tres Puentes (Punta Arenas) to/from Porvenir. The crossing takes 2 1/2 hours. Departures from Tres Palos Wed, Fri & Sat at 09:00 h. in the morning, return at 14:00h. Sundays, departure at 10:00 h, return at 17:00 h.

(36) **Bahía Azul** 3 Ferry Punta Arenas, same address as the Melinka Ferry. A multi-purpose ship for passengers and 50 cars. **Itinerary**: Punta Delgada to Baha Azul; the crossing takes 20 minutes, hourly departures. Firt departure from Punta Delgada at 0830h. last departure from Baha Azul at 23:00 h.

(37) **Velero Ksar** 2 Ushuaia, Argentina, Gobernador Paz 460, Dep. 12-9410, ☎ 54901218/6. A sailing ship accommodating eight passengers. **Itinerary**: Charter to Cape Horn, Staten Island, Patagonian channels, South Georgia, and Antarctica, for a minimun of seven days.

AIR AND SEA TRASPORTATION
MAGALLANES

TYPES OF TRANSPORT

1 Scheduled passenger-only ships and airplanes.

2 Scheduled or non-scheduled ships or airplanes for passengers only (adventure tourism). Small capacity (up to 12 passenger). Available for charters or until the group is completed.

3 Multi-purpose, ships with scheduled departures and Itinerary, and carrying passengers, vehicles, and cargo.

4 Multi-purpose, ships with scheduled departures and Itinerary,carrying only vehicles and cargo.

AIRPLANES

(L) **LAN** 1 year-round. Santiago, Agustinas 1197, ☎ 6723523/699 0505. Punta Arenas, Lautaro Navarro corner of Puerto Montt, 213211. **Itinerary**: Santiago-Puerto Montt-Punta Arenas. Duration of flight: 4 h. Five departures weekly.

(M) **Ladeco** 1 year-round. Santiago, Hurfanos 1157, ☎ 6982233. Punta Arenas, Roca 924, ☎ 226100. **Itinerary**: Santiago-Puerto Montt-Punta Arenas. Duration of flight: 4 h. Five departures weekly.

(N) **Aerovías DAP** 1 2 year-round. Punta Arenas, Ignacio Carrera Pinto 1022, ☎ 223956, DHC Twin Otter twin turbo-props; two Cessna 402's. **Itinerary**: Punta Arenas-Porvenir, 12 minutes, twice daily; Punta Arenas-Puerto Williams, 90 minutes once weekly. Charter flights Punta Arenas-Cape Horn-Torres del Paine-Punta Arenas (3 hours).

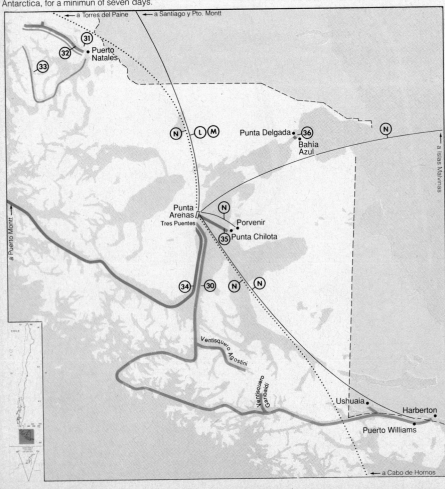

Index of
Cities, Towns
Villages, Places

U

V

W

Y

Z

ROAD MAP OF CHILE

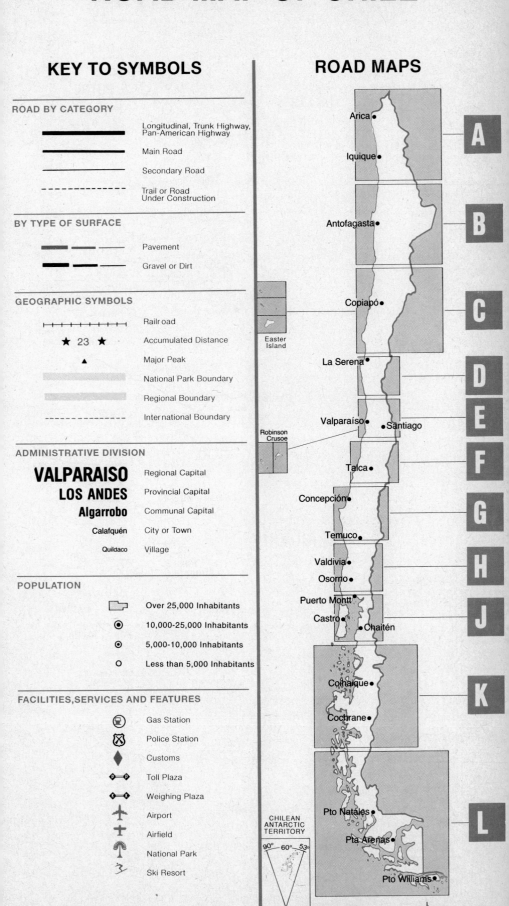

KEY TO SYMBOLS

ROAD BY CATEGORY

Longitudinal, Trunk Highway, Pan-American Highway

Main Road

Secondary Road

Trail or Road Under Construction

BY TYPE OF SURFACE

Pavement

Gravel or Dirt

GEOGRAPHIC SYMBOLS

Railroad

★ 23 ★   Accumulated Distance

▲   Major Peak

National Park Boundary

Regional Boundary

International Boundary

ADMINISTRATIVE DIVISION

VALPARAISO   Regional Capital

LOS ANDES   Provincial Capital

Algarrobo   Communal Capital

Calafquén   City or Town

Quildaco   Village

POPULATION

Over 25,000 Inhabitants

⊙   10,000-25,000 Inhabitants

⊙   5,000-10,000 Inhabitants

○   Less than 5,000 Inhabitants

FACILITIES, SERVICES AND FEATURES

Gas Station

Police Station

Customs

Toll Plaza

Weighing Plaza

Airport

Airfield

National Park

Ski Resort

ROAD MAPS

Arica

Iquique

A

Antofagasta

B

Copiapó

C

Easter Island

La Serena

D

Valparaíso   Santiago

E

Robinson Crusoe

Talca

F

Concepción

G

Temuco

Valdivia

Osorno

H

Puerto Montt

Castro   Chaitén

J

Coihaique

Cochrane

K

CHILEAN ANTARCTIC TERRITORY

90°   60°   53°

Pto Natales

Pta Arenas

L

Pto Williams

I. Diego Ramírez

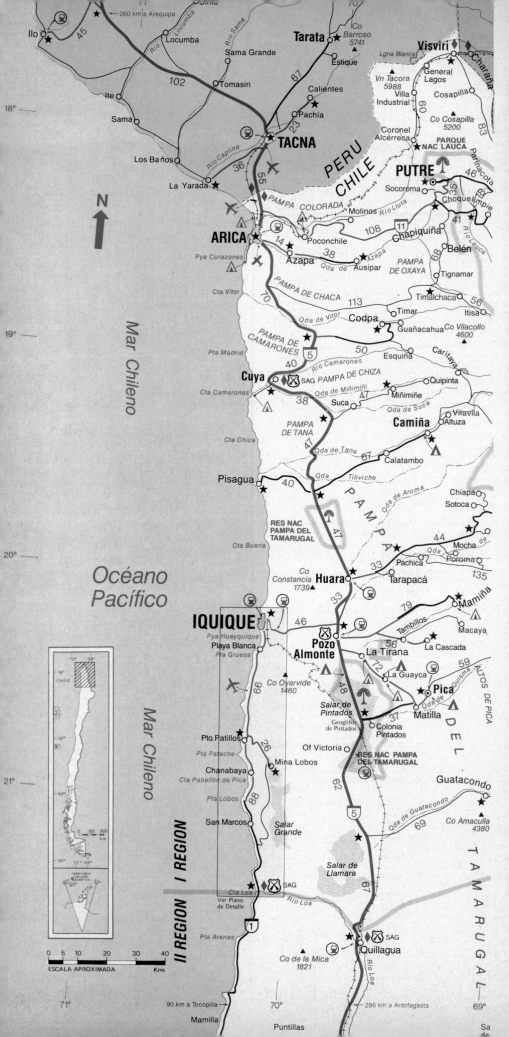

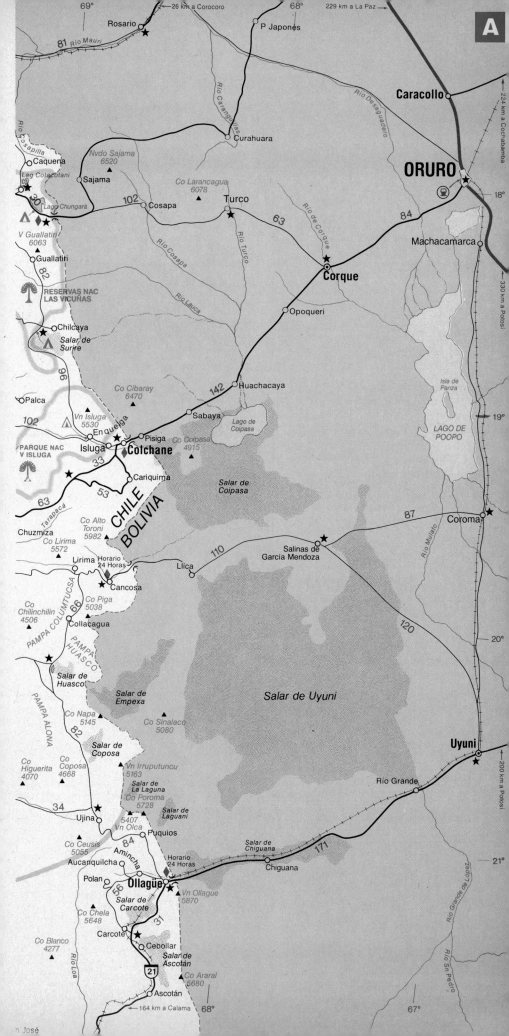

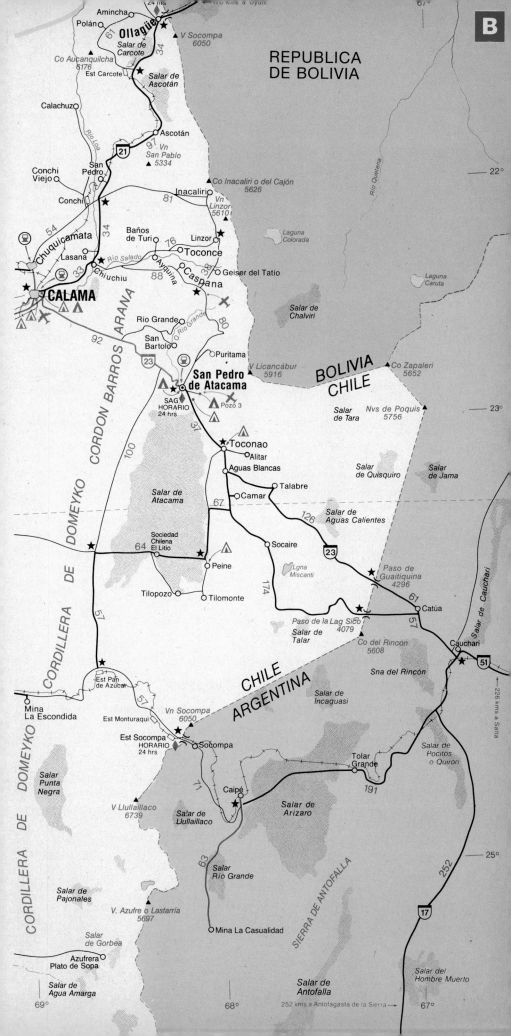

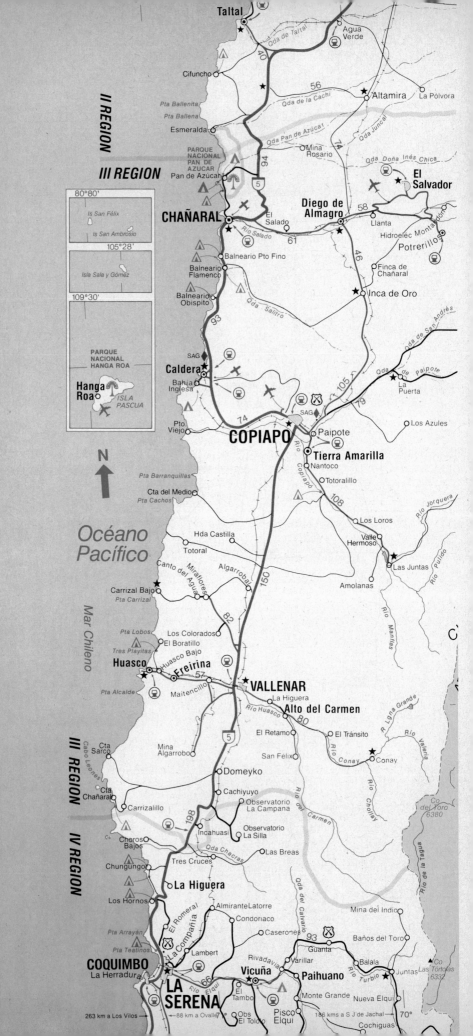

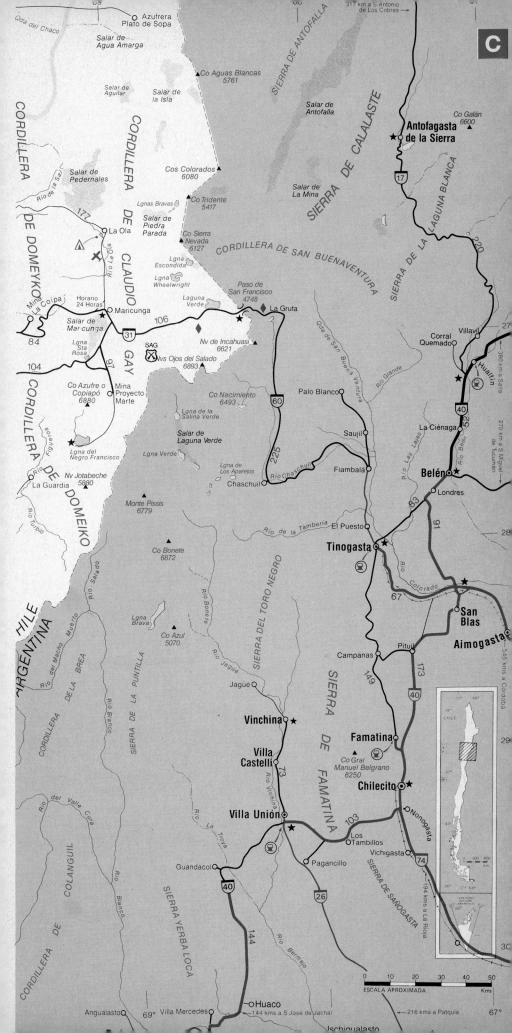

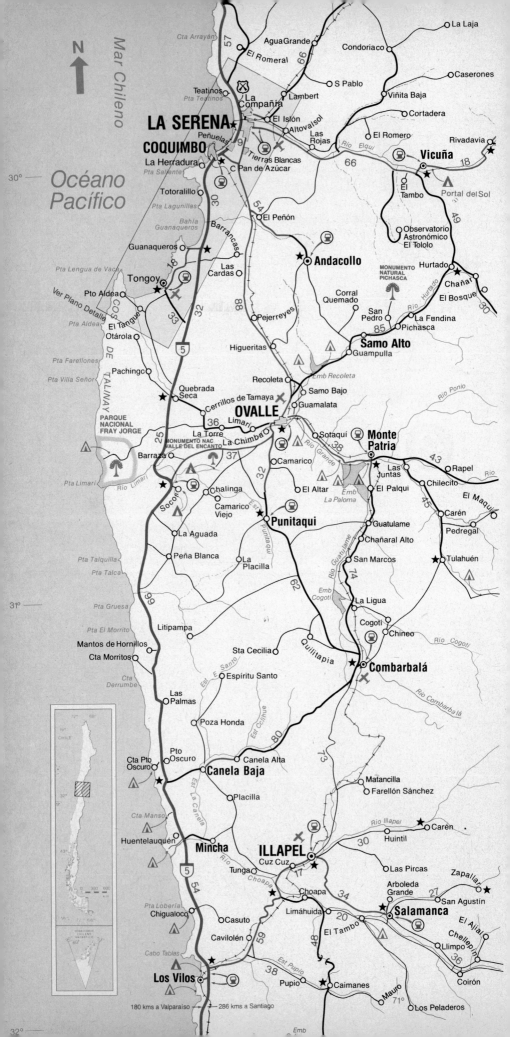

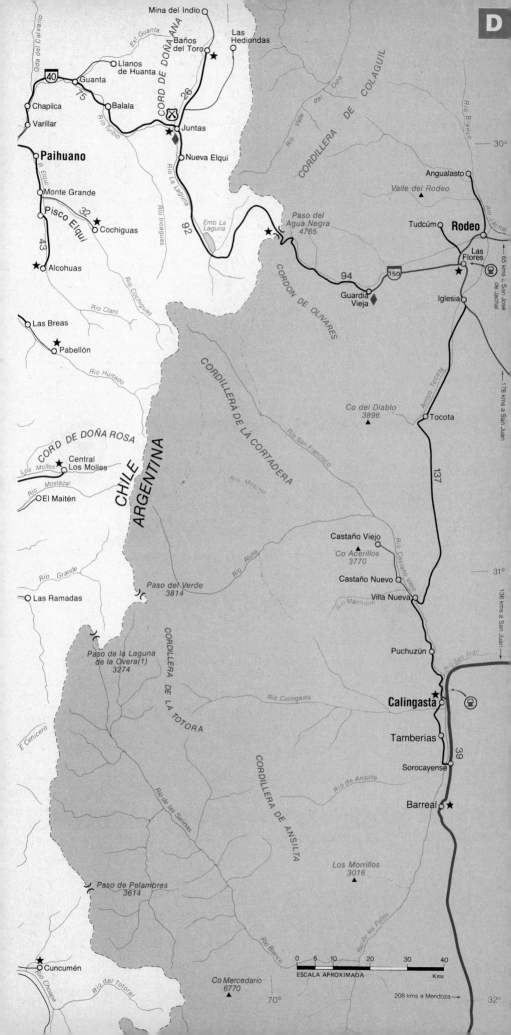

D

Mina del Indio

Baños del Toro
Las Hediondas

Llanos de Huanta
Guanta

Chapilca
Balala

Varillar

40
75

Juntas

Paihuano

Nueva Elqui

Monte Grande

Pisco Elqui 32
Cochiguas

43
Alcohuas

Emb La Laguna

92

Las Breas

Pabellón

Río Hurtado

CORD DE DOÑA ROSA

Central Los Molles

Los Molles

El Maitén
Río Mostazal

CHILE

ARGENTINA

Río Grande

Las Ramadas

CORD DE DOÑA ANA

26

Río Turbio

Río La Laguna

Río Incaguas

Río Cochiguas

Río Claro

Paso del Agua Negra 4765

CORDILLERA DE COLAGUIL

Río Blanco

Valle del Cura

Angualasto

Valle del Rodeo

Tudcúm

Rodeo

Las Flores

94
150

Guardia Vieja

Iglesia

— 30°

65 kms a S.án José de Jáchal

178 kms a San Juan

CORDON DE OLIVARES

CORDILLERA DE LA CORTADERA

Río San Francisco

Co del Diablo 3896

Tocota

137

Arroyo Tocota

Río Melchor

Paso del Verde 3814

Río Atuna

Castaño Viejo

Co Acerillos 3770

Castaño Nuevo

Villa Nueva

Río Castaño Viejo

— 31°

136 kms a San Juan

Paso de la Laguna de la Overa(1) 3274

CORDILLERA DE LA TOTORA

Río Calingasta

Río Manrique

Puchuzún

Río San Juan

Calingasta

Tamberías

Sorocayense

39

Río de Ansilta

CORDILLERA DE ANSILTA

Barreal

E Cenicero

Río de las Salinas

Los Morrillos 3016

Paso de Pelambres 3614

Río Blanco

Río de los Patos

Cuncumén

Río Choapa

Río del Totoral

Co Mercedario 6770

70°

0 5 10   20   30   40
ESCALA APROXIMADA   Kms

208 kms a Mendoza →

32°

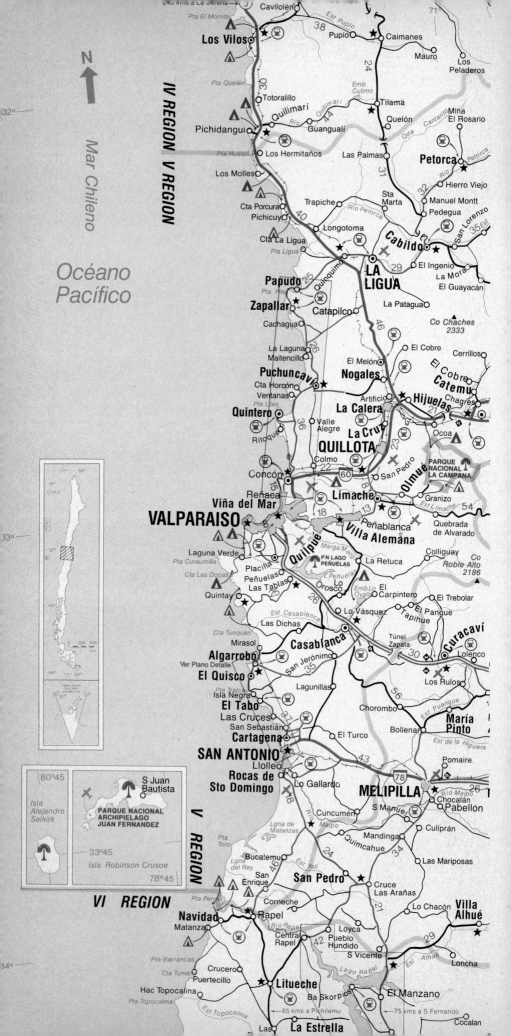

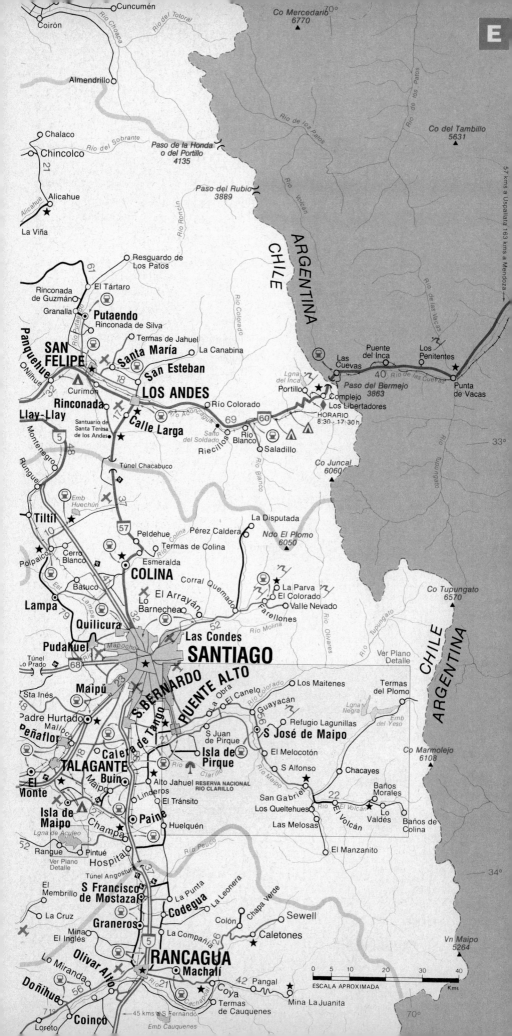

E

Cucumén
Coirón
Co Mercedario
6770
Almendrillo
Chalaco
Chincolco
Río del Sobrante
Paso de la Honda
o del Portillo
4135
Co del Tambillo
5631
Alicahue
Paso del Rubio
3889
La Viña
Río Rocín
Resguardo de
Los Patos
Rinconada
de Guzmán
El Tártaro
CHILE
ARGENTINA
57 kms a Uspallata 163 a Mendoza →
Granalla
Putaendo
Rinconada de Silva
Río Colorado
SAN
FELIPE
Termas de Jahuel
Santa María
La Canabina
Las Cuevas
Puente
del Inca
Los
Penitentes
San Esteban
Complejo
LOS ANDES
Portillo
Los Libertadores
Paso del Bermejo
3863
Punta
de Vacas
40
Río de las Cuevas
Curimón
Rinconada
Río Colorado
69
60
Llay-Llay
Calle Larga
HORARIO
8:30 - 17:30 h
33°
Santuario de
Santa Teresa
de los Andes
Paño
del Soldado
Río
Blanco
Riecillos
Saladillo
Túnel Chacabuco
Co Juncal
6060
Emb
Huechún
Tiltil
57
Peldehue
Pérez Caldera
Ndo El Plomo
6050
La Disputada
Termas de Colina
Cerro
Blanco
Esmeralda
Polpaico
COLINA
Corral Quemado
La Parva
Co Tupungato
6570
Batuco
El Arrayán
El Colorado
Lampa
Lo
Barnechea
Valle Nevado
Quilicura
52
Farellones
CHILE
ARGENTINA
Pudahuel
Las Condes
Túnel
Lo Prado
68
SANTIAGO
Ver Plano
Detalle
Maipú
Los Maitenes
Termas
del Plomo
Sta Inés
La Obra
El Canelo
Guayacán
Padre Hurtado
Refugio Lagunillas
Peñaflor
S Juan
de Pirque
S José de Maipo
TALAGANTE
Isla de
Pirque
El Melocotón
Buin
S Alfonso
Chacayes
El Monte
Alto Jahuel
RESERVA NACIONAL
RIO CLARILLO
Baños
Morales
Linderos
El Tránsito
San Gabriel
Isla de
Maipo
Lo
Valdés
Lgna de Aculeo
Champa
Paine
Huelquén
Los Queltehues
El Volcán
Baños
de Colina
Las Melosas
Rangue
Pintué
Ver Plano
Detalle
Hospital
El Manzanito
34°
Túnel Angostura
El
Membrillo
S Francisco
de Mostazal
La Punta
La Cruz
Codegua
La Leonera
Chapa Verde
Sewell
Graneros
Colón
Caletones
Mina
El Inglés
La Compañía
Vn Maipo
5264
Lo Miranda
Olivar Alto
RANCAGUA
Doñihue
Machalí
Pangal
42
0 5 10 20 30 40
Coya
Mina La Juanita
Termas
de Cauquenes
45 kms a S Fernando
Emb Cauquenes
ESCALA APROXIMADA
Kms
70°
Coinco
Loreto

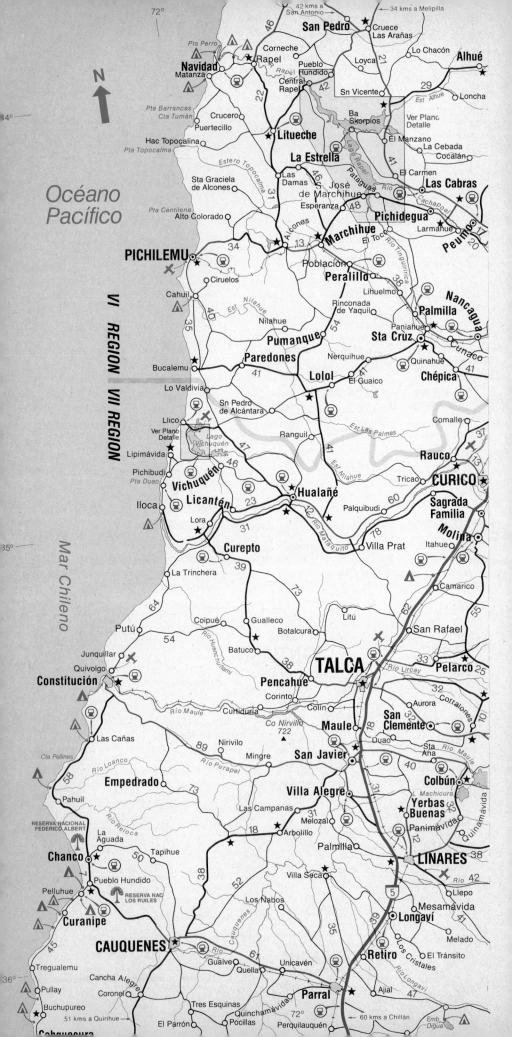

71°
72°

Túnel
Angostura · 87 kms a Santiago
El
Membrillo
San Francisco
de Mostazal
La Punta
Codegua
La Leonera
La Cruz
Colón · Sewell
Graneros · La Compañía
Caletones
Mina El Inglés
Co Paredones
4907
Vn. Maipo
5264
RANCAGUA
Olivar Alto
Machalí
Lo Miranda
Coya
Pangal
Doñihue
Olivar Bajo
21
Río Pangal
Mina La Juanita
Purén
Coinco
Termas
de Cauquenes
Embalse
Cauquenes
Co Yeso
4008
Coltauco
Requínoa
Rosario
Pimpinela
Qta Tilcoco
Cerrillos
Paso de Molina
3830
Lgna
Los Pejerreyes
Malloa
Rengo
Popete
Río Los Cipreses
San
Vicente de
Tagua Tagua
Pelequén
Las Nieves
Co El Palomo
4850
Requegua
Angostura
Los
Maquis
Río Claro
Hac Los Lingues
Roma
Co Sosneado
5189
SAN FERNANDO
El Sosneado
Placilla
Aguas Buenas
Port de las
Lágrimas
3651
Puente Negro
Río Cirilllo
Vn Tinguiririca
4300
Tinguiririca
Chimbarongo
Río
Tinguiririca
75
La Rufina
Convento
Viejo
Codegua
Río Claro
Quinta
Bellavista
Termas
del Flaco
Teno
Huemul
Trompetilla
Las Leñas
Rebeca
Río Teno
Río Las Damas
Los Molles
La Montaña
HORARIO
8:30-18:30 h
Co Cayetano
2886
Cerro Torre
de Sta Elena
3820
Romeral
46
Río Teno
46
Paso del
Planchón
2938
Los
Queñes
El Planchón
Potrero Grande Chico
Lagunas
del Teno
Lontué
Los Niches
Upeo
Monte Oscuro
Vn Peteroa
4090
37
Potrero
Grande
Qda Honda
Baños de
Azufre
Yacal
Río Patos de San Pedro
Paso de Potrerillos
2908
Cumpeo
Aduana
Culenar
Río Colorado
Astillero
Vn Descabezado Chico
3750
CHILE
Radal
RESERVA FORESTAL
PARQUE INGLES
Vn Descabezado
Grande
3830
ARGENTINA
33
PARQUE GIL DE VILCHES
MONUMENTO NATURAL
Corel
Vilches
Río Claro
Río de la Invernada
Paso Nevado
Armerillo
Lgna
La Invernada
Paso Trolon
3044
Lago Colbún
76
Las Garzas
Endesa
Río Puelche
Medina
La
Mina
Río Maule
Los Rabones
24
Tünel
Canal
Melado
El Salto
64
Paso Pehuenche
o del Maule
2553
Roblería
Co Péllado
3250
Ancoa
Campamento
Ancoa
Río Melado
HORARIO
8:30 - 13:00 h
14:30 - 18:48 h
Lgna del Maule
Co Lástimas
3050
Río La Puente
Lgna Negra
Aduana Pejerrey
Nvdo Longaví
3242
Río Achibueno
Lago Feo
0   5   10   20   30   40
San Pablo
ESCALA APROXIMADA
Kms

35

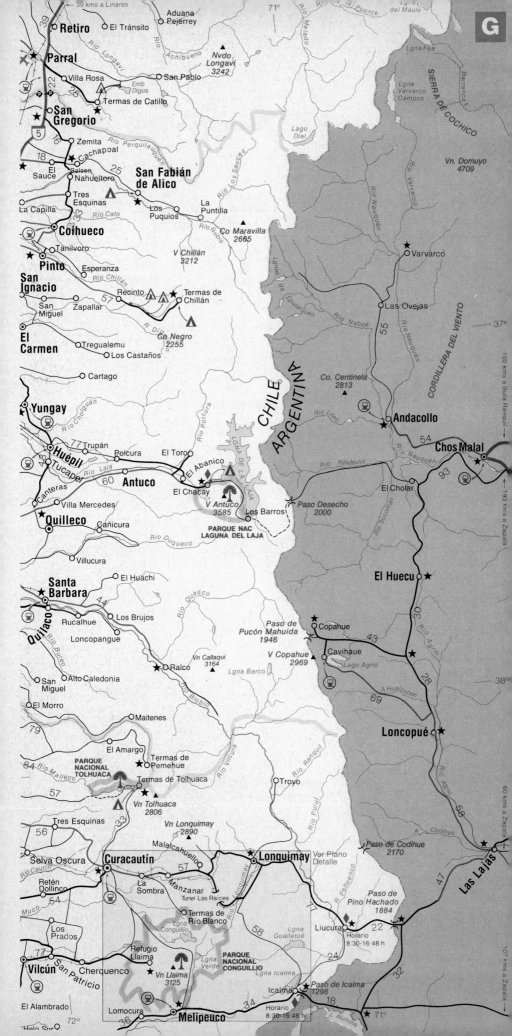

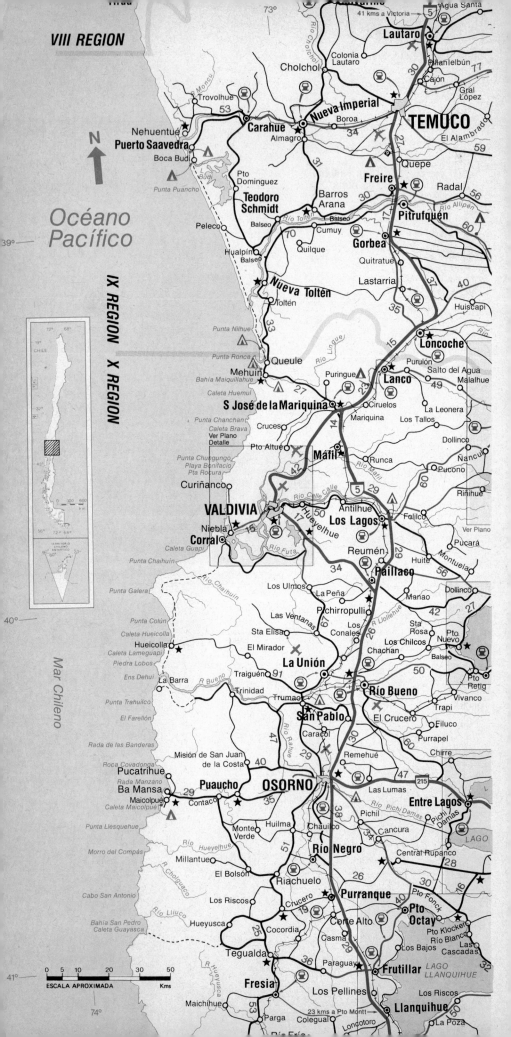

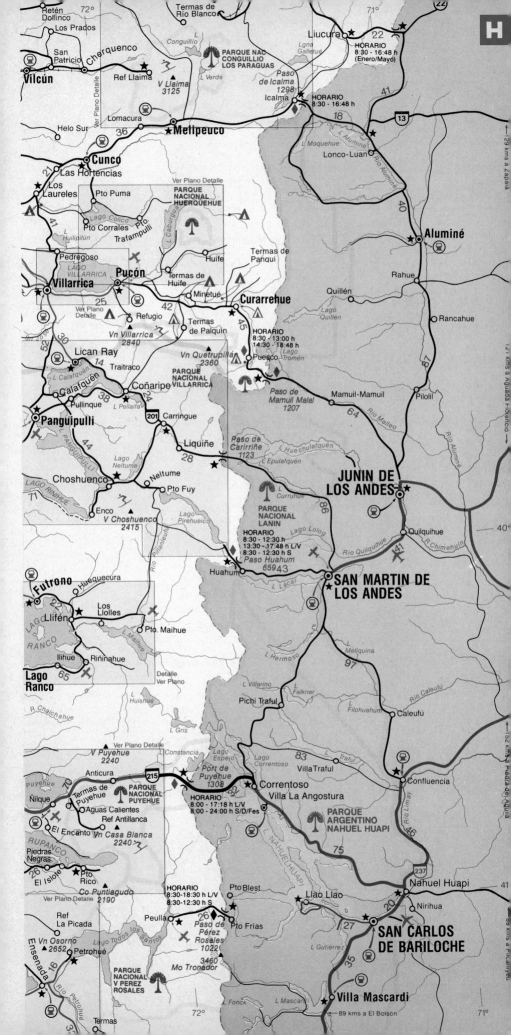

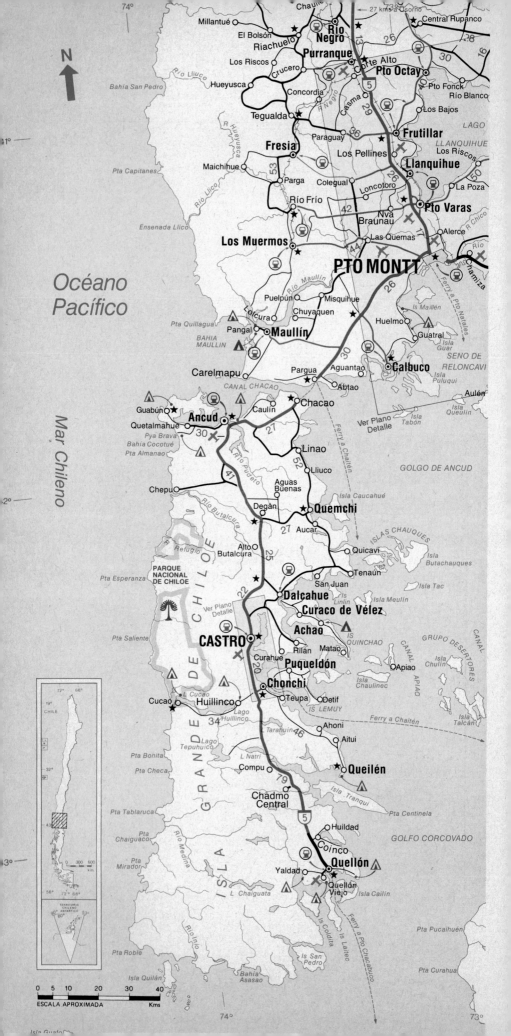

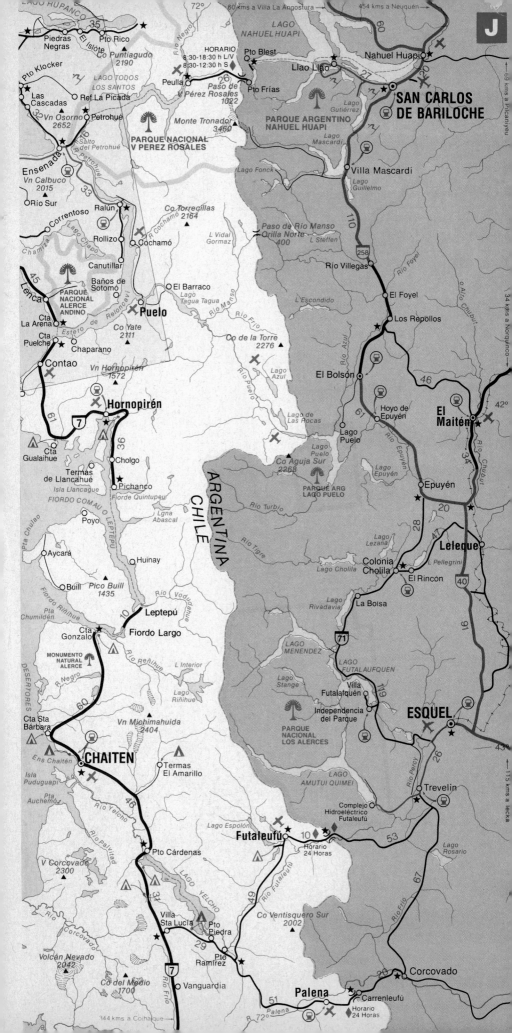

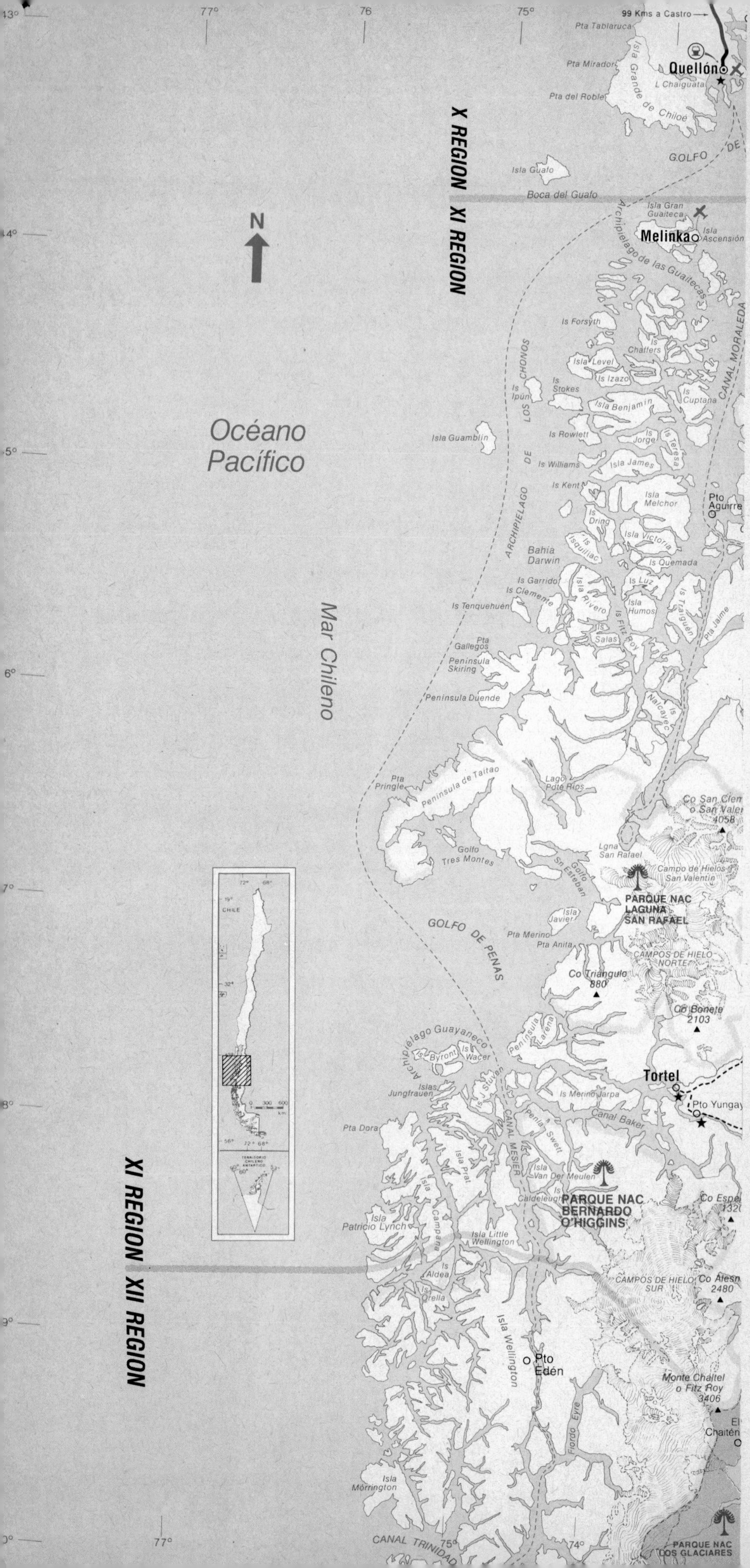

Océano
Pacífico

Mar Chileno

N

X REGION
XI REGION

XI REGION
XII REGION

Pta Tablaruca
Pta Mirador
Quellón
L Chaiguata
Pta del Roble
G.OLFO DE
Isla Grande de Chiloe

Isla Gualo

Boca del Guafo

Archipiélago de las Guaitecas
Isla Gran Guaiteca
Melinka
Isla Ascensión

Is Forsyth
Chatters
Isla Level
Is Izazo
Is Cuptana
Is Ipun
Is Stokes
Isla Benjamin
Is Rowlett
Is Jorge
Is Teresa
Isla Guamblin
Is Williams
Isla James
Is Kent
Isla Melchor
Pto Aguirre
Is Dring
Isla Victoria
Bahía Darwin
Isquiliac
Isla Quemada
Is Garrido
Isla Rivero
Isla Luz
Is Clemente
Isla Humos
Is Tenquehuén
Isla Fitz Roy
Is Traiguén
Pta Gallegos
Salas
Península Skiring
Pta Jaime
Península Duende

Narcayco

Pta Pringle
Península de Taitao
Lago Pdte Rios
Co San Clem o San Valen 4058

Golfo Tres Montes
Lgna San Rafael
Campo de Hielos San Valentin
PARQUE NAC LAGUNA SAN RAFAEL

CAMPOS DE HIELO NORTE

GOLFO DE PENAS
Isla Javier
Pta Merino
Pta Anita
Co Triangulo 880

Co Bonete 2103

Archipiélago Guayaneco
Is Byront
Is Wager
Islas Jungfrauen
Is Stosh
Is Merino Jarpa
Tortel
Pto Yungay

Pta Dora
Isla Prat
Canal Baker

Isla Van Der Meulen
PARQUE NAC BERNARDO O'HIGGINS
Co Espel 320

Isla Caldcleugh
Isla Camana
Isla Patricio Lynch
Isla Little Wellington

Is Aldea
CAMPOS DE HIELO SUR
Co Alesn 2480

grella
Isla Wellington
Pto Edén
Monte Chaltel o Fitz Roy 3406
El Chaitén

Isla Morrington

CANAL TRINIDAD

PARQUE NAC LOS GLACIARES

CHILE
300 600
KM
TERRITORIO CHILENO ANTARTICO

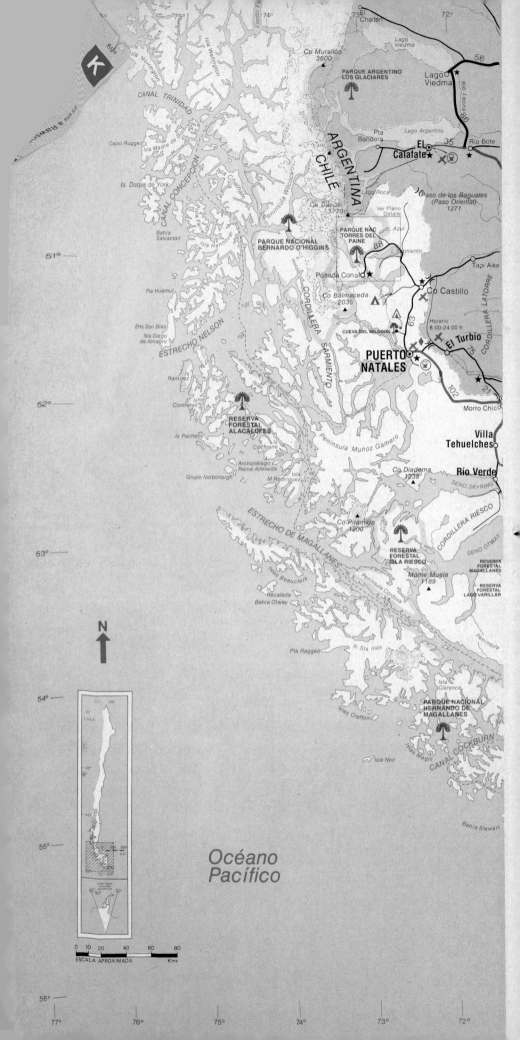